VOLUME I: TO 1800

WORLD HISTORY

3RD EDITION

WILLIAM J. DUIKER
THE PENNSYLVANIA STATE UNIVERSITY

JACKSON J. SPIELVOGEL
THE PENNSYLVANIA STATE UNIVERSITY

Wadsworth
Thomson Learning™

Australia • Canada • Mexico • Singapore • Spain • United Kingdom • United States

History Publisher: Clark Baxter
Senior Development Editor: Sharon Adams Poore
Assistant Editor: Cherie Hackelberg
Editorial Assistant: Jennifer Ellis
Marketing Manager: Diane McOscar
Marketing Assistant: Kristin Anderson
Print Buyer: Barbara Britton
Permissions Editor: Bob Kauser
Production Service: Dovetail Publishing Services
Text Designer: Diane Beasley

Photo Researcher: Image Quest
Copy Editors: Pat Lewis and Brian Jones
Maps: Mapquest.com
Compositor: New England Typographic Service
Cover Designer: Diane Beasley
Cover Image: The Battle of Badr, from volume IV of the
    Siyar-e-Nabi, (The Life of the Prophet.)
Cover Printer: Von Hoffmann Press
Printer: Von Hoffmann Press
Photo credits begin on page 601

For permission to use material from this text, contact us by
Web: http://www.thomsonrights.com
Fax: 1-800-730-2215
Phone: 1-800-730-2214

Wadsworth/Thomson Learning
10 Davis Drive
Belmont, CA 94002-3098
USA

For more information about our products, contact us:
Thomson Learning Academic Resource Center
1-800-423-0563
http://www.wadsworth.com

International Headquarters
Thomson Learning
International Division
290 Harbor Drive, 2nd Floor
Stamford, CT 06902-7477
USA

UK/Europe/Middle East/South Africa
Thomson Learning
Berkshire House
168-173 High Holborn
London WC1V 7AA
United Kingdom

Asia
Thomson Learning
60 Albert Street, #15-01
Albert Complex
Singapore 189969

Canada
Nelson Thomson Learning
1120 Birchmount Road
Toronto, Ontario M1K 5G4
Canada

ISBN 0-534-57169-7

ABOUT THE AUTHORS

WILLIAM J.DUIKER is liberal arts professor emeritus of East Asian studies at The Pennsylvania State University. A former U.S. diplomat with service in Taiwan, South Vietnam, and Washington, D.C., he received his doctorate in Far Eastern history from Georgetown University in 1968, where his dissertation dealt with the Chinese educator and reformer Cai Yuanpei. At Penn State, he has written widely on the history of Vietnam and modern China, including the widely acclaimed *The Communist Road to Power in Vietnam* (revised edition, Westview Press, 1996), which was selected for a Choice Outstanding Academic Book Award in 1982–1983 and 1996–1997. Other recent books are *China and Vietnam: The Roots of Conflict* (Berkeley, 1987) and *Sacred War: Nationalism and Revolution in a Divided Vietnam* (McGraw-Hill, 1995). His biography of the revolutionary Ho Chi Minh will be published by Hyperion Press in the fall of 2000. While his research specialization is in the field of nationalism and Asian revolutions, his intellectual interests are considerably more diverse. He has traveled widely and has taught courses on the History of Communism and non-Western civilizations at Penn State, where he was awarded a Faculty Scholar Medal for Outstanding Achievement in the spring of 1996.

JACKSON J. SPIELVOGEL is associate professor emeritus of history at The Pennsylvania State University. He received his Ph.D. from The Ohio State University, where he specialized in Reformation history under Harold J. Grimm. His articles and reviews have appeared in such journals as *Moreana, Journal of General Education, Catholic Historical Review, Archiv für Reformationsgeschichte*, and *American Historical Review*. He has also contributed chapters or articles to *The Social History of the Reformation, The Holy Roman Empire: A Dictionary Handbook, Simon Wiesenthal Center Annual of Holocaust Studies*, and *Utopian Studies*. His work has been supported by fellowships from the Fullbright Foundation and the Foundation for Reformation Research. At Penn State, he helped inaugurate the Western civilization courses as well as a popular course on Nazi Germany. His book *Hitler and Nazi Germany* was published in 1987 (fourth edition, 2001). He is the author of *Western Civilization*, published in 1991 (fourth edition, 2000). Professor Spielvogel has won five major university-wide teaching awards. During the year 1988–1989, he held the Penn State Teaching Fellowship, the university's most prestigious teaching award. In 1996, he won the Dean Arthur Ray Warnock Award for Outstanding Faculty Member, and in 1997, he became the first recipient of the Schreyer Institute's Student Choice Award for innovative and inspiring teaching.

To Yvonne,
for adding sparkle to this book,
and to my life
W.J.D.

To Diane,
whose love and support made it all possible
J.J.S.

BRIEF CONTENTS

DETAILED CONTENTS

PART 1 THE FIRST CIVILIZATIONS AND THE RISE OF EMPIRES (PREHISTORY TO 500 C.E.) 1

PART 11   NEW PATTERNS OF CIVILIZATION   166

CHRONOLOGIES

MAPS

DOCUMENT CREDITS

PREFACE

For several million years after primates first appeared on the surface of the earth, human beings lived in small communities, seeking to survive by hunting, fishing, and foraging in a frequently hostile environment. Then suddenly, in the space of a few thousand years, there was an abrupt change of direction as human beings in a few widely scattered areas of the globe began to master the art of cultivating food crops. As food production increased, the population in those areas rose correspondingly, and people began to congregate in larger communities. Governments were formed to provide protection and other needed services to the local population. Cities appeared and became the focal point of cultural and religious development. Historians refer to this process as the beginnings of civilization.

For generations, historians in Europe and the United States have pointed to the rise of such civilizations as marking the origins of the modern world. Courses on Western civilization conventionally begin with a chapter or two on the emergence of advanced societies in Egypt and Mesopotamia and then proceed to ancient Greece and the Roman Empire. From Greece and Rome, the road leads directly to the rise of modern civilization in the West.

There is nothing inherently wrong with this approach. Important aspects of our world today can indeed be traced back to these early civilizations, and all human beings the world over owe a considerable debt to their achievements. But all too often this interpretation has been used to imply that the course of civilization has been linear in nature, leading directly from the emergence of agricultural societies in ancient Mesopotamia to the rise of advanced industrial societies in Europe and North America. Until recently, most courses on world history taught in the United States routinely focused almost exclusively on the rise of the West, with only a passing glance at other parts of the world, such as Africa, India, and East Asia. The contributions made by those societies to the culture and technology of our own time were often passed over in silence.

Several reasons have been advanced to justify this approach. Some have argued that students simply are not interested in what is unfamiliar to them. Others have said that it is more important that young minds understand the roots of their own heritage than that of peoples elsewhere in the world. In many cases, however, the motivation for this Eurocentric approach has been the belief that since the time of Socrates and Aristotle Western civilization has been the sole driving force in the evolution of human society.

Such an interpretation, however, represents a serious distortion of the process. During most of the course of human history, the most advanced civilizations have been not in the West, but in East Asia or the Middle East. A relatively brief period of European dominance culminated with the era of imperialism in the late nineteenth century, when the political, military, and economic power of the advanced nations of the West spanned the globe. During recent generations, however, that dominance has gradually eroded, partly as the result of changes taking place within Western societies and partly because new centers of development are emerging elsewhere on the globe—notably in East Asia, where the growing economic strength of Japan and many of its neighbors has led to the now familiar prediction that the twenty-first century will be known as the Pacific Century.

World history, then, is not simply a chronicle of the rise of the West to global dominance, nor is it a celebration of the superiority of the civilization of Europe and the United States over other parts of the world. The history of the world has been a complex process in which many branches of the human community have taken an active part, and the dominance of any one area of the world has been a temporary rather than a permanent phenomenon. It will be our purpose in this book to present a balanced picture of this story, with all respect for the richness and diversity of the tapestry of the human experience. Due attention must be paid to the rise of the West, of course, since that has been the most dominant aspect of world history in recent centuries. But the contributions made by other peoples must be given adequate consideration as well, not only in the period prior to 1500 when the major centers of civilization were located in Asia, but also in our own day, where a multipolar picture of development is clearly beginning to emerge.

Anyone who wishes to teach or write about world history must decide whether to present the topic as an integrated whole or as a collection of different cultures. The world that we live in today, of course, is in many respects an interdependent one in terms of economics as well as culture and communications, a reality that is often expressed by the phrase "global village." The convergence of peoples across the surface of the earth into an integrated world system began in early times and intensified after the rise of capitalism in the early modern era. In growing recognition of this trend, historians trained in global history, as well as instructors in the growing number of world history courses, have now begun to speak and write of a "global approach" that turns attention away from the study of individual civilizations and focuses instead on the "big picture" or, as the world historian Fernand Braudel termed it, interpreting world history as a river with no banks.

On the whole, this development is to be welcomed as a means of bringing the common elements of the evolution of human society to our attention. But there is a risk involved in this approach. For the vast majority of their time on earth, human beings have lived in partial or virtually total isolation from each other. Differences in climate, location, and geographical features have created human societies very different from each other in culture and historical experience. Only in relatively recent times—the commonly accepted date has long been the beginning of the age of European exploration at the end of the fifteenth century, but some would now push it back to the era of the Mongol empire or even further—have cultural interchanges begun to create a common "world system," in which events taking place in one part of the world are rapidly transmitted throughout the globe, often with momentous consequences. In recent generations, of course, the process of global interdependence has been proceeding even more rapidly. Nevertheless, even now the process is by no means complete, as ethnic and regional differences continue to exist and to shape the course of world history. The tenacity of these differences and sensitivities is reflected not only in the rise of internecine conflicts in such divergent areas as Africa, India, and Eastern Europe, but also in the emergence in recent years of such regional organizations as the Organization of African Unity, the Association for the Southeast Asian Nations, and the European Economic Community. Political leaders in various parts of the world speak routinely of "Arab unity," the "African road to socialism," and the "Confucian path to economic development."

The second problem is a practical one. College students today are all too often not well informed about the distinctive character of civilizations such as China and India and, without sufficient exposure to the historical evolution of such societies, will assume all too readily that the peoples in these countries have had historical experiences similar to ours and will respond to various stimuli in a similar fashion to those living in Western Europe or the United States. If it is a mistake to ignore those forces that link us together, it is equally a mistake to underestimate those factors that continue to divide us and to differentiate us into a world of diverse peoples.

Our response to this challenge has been to adopt a global approach to world history while at the same time attempting to do justice to the distinctive character and development of individual civilizations and regions of the world. The presentation of individual cultures will be especially important in Parts I and II, which cover a time when it is generally agreed that the process of global integration was not yet far advanced. Later chapters will begin to adopt a more comparative and thematic approach, in deference to the greater number of connections that have been established among the world's peoples since the fifteenth and sixteenth centuries. Part V will consist of a series of chapters that will center on individual regions of the world while at the same time focusing on common problems related to the Cold War and the rise of global problems such as overproduction and environmental pollution. Moreover, sections entitled "Reflection" at the close of the five major parts of the book will attempt to link events together in a broad comparative and global framework.

We have sought balance in another way as well. Many textbooks tend to simplify the content of history courses by emphasizing an intellectual or political perspective or, most recently, a social perspective, often at the expense of sufficient details in a chronological framework. This approach is confusing to students whose high school social studies programs have often neglected a systematic study of world history. We have attempted to write a well-balanced work in which political, economic, social, religious, intellectual, cultural, and military history have been integrated into a chronologically ordered synthesis.

To enliven the past and let readers see for themselves the materials that historians use to create their pictures of the past, we have included primary sources (boxed documents) in each chapter that are keyed to the discussion in the text. The documents include examples of the religious, artistic, intellectual, social, economic, and political aspects of life in different societies and reveal in a vivid fashion what civilization meant to the individual men and women who shaped it by their actions.

Each chapter has a lengthy introduction and conclusion to help maintain the continuity of the narrative and to provide a synthesis of important themes. Time lines at the end of each chapter enable students to see the major developments of an era at a glance, while the more detailed chronologies reinforce the events discussed in the text. An annotated bibliography at the end of each chapter reviews the most recent literature on each period and also gives references to some of the older, "classic" works in each field. Extensive maps and illustrations serve to deepen the reader's understanding of the text. To facilitate comprehension of cultural movements, illustrations of artistic works discussed in the text are placed next to the discussions. New to the third edition are chapter outlines and focus questions at the beginning of each chapter, which will help students with an overview and guide them to the main subjects of each chapter. Also new to the third edition are a glossary of important terms and a pronunciation guide.

After reexamining the entire book and analyzing the comments and reviews of many colleagues who have found the book to be a useful instrument for introducing their students to world history, we have also made a number of other changes for the third edition. In the first place, it is now noticeably shorter than its predecessors. Textbooks on world history have a natural tendency to increase in length as a result of updates and the incorporation of new historical evidence from the world of scholarship. In this third edition, we have tried to delete excess words while retaining all essential material as well as the narrative thrust of previous editions. We hope that our readers will agree that the result is a more manageable and yet superior product.

Second, we have sought to strengthen the global framework of the book, but not at the expense of reducing the attention assigned to individual regions of the world. The essays entitled "Reflection" that appear at the end of each of the five parts have been lengthened slightly in order to provide us with more opportunity to draw comparisons and contrasts across geographical, cultural, and chronological lines. Each Reflection section now contains two boxed essays, each highlighted with an illustration, to single out issues of particular importance to that period of history. Moreover, additional comparative material has also been added to each chapter to help students be aware of similar developments globally. We hope that these techniques will assist instructors who wish to encourage their students to adopt a comparative approach to their understanding of the human experience.

Third, this new edition contains additional information on the role of women in world history. In conformity with our own convictions, as well as what we believe to be recent practice in the field, we have tried where possible to introduce such material at the appropriate point in the text, rather than to set aside separate sections devoted exclusively to women's issues. New material on women include: women in ancient India, women in ancient China, Aristotle's view of women, women in the work of Homer, women in early Christianity, women in pre-Columbian societies, women in Muslim society, women in Indian history during the Gupta era, women in the Ming era, women in Germanic society, women in the Renaissance, women in early socialism, the movement for women's rights, Soviet women, and women in the postwar Western world. Coverage of notable women in history, including Marie Curie, Berthe Morisot, Margaret Thatcher and Betty Friedan has been added. Several new boxed documents have also been added to introduce more women's voices to the historical record.

Finally, almost all of the chapters in the book have been updated to take account of new scholarship, as well as to bring our treatment of contemporary events up to the present, as we begin to enter a new millennium. A number of new illustrations, boxed documents, and maps have been added, and the bibliographies have been revised to take account of newly published material. The chronologies and maps have been fine-tuned, as well, to help the reader locate in time and space the multitude of individuals and place names that appear in the book.

Changes to the New Edition by Chapter

Chapter 1   New material on early humans; new material on Hatshepsut in New Kingdom Egypt; thorough revision of material on ancient Israel based on the most recent research.

Chapter 2   Minor changes have been made to the section on Harappan civilizations to conform to recent evidence appearing in scholarly literature. Specifically, it is now believed that, unlike other ancient civilizations in the Middle East, the political system on Harappa was decentralized and lacked a theoretical base. The section on the *Arthasastra* has been shortened, while continuing to present the essentials of Kautilya's famous work. New material has been introduced on the role of women in ancient India.

Chapter 3   New material on the role of women in ancient China, in addition to new illustrations.

Chapter 4   New material on women in the work of Homer; new material on Aristotle's view of women; new material on Sparta; revision of material on philosophy in the Hellenistic Era.

Chapter 5   Revision of material on Roman conquest of Italy, decline and fall of the Roman Republic, the Age of Augustus, and Roman law; revision and reorganization of material of Christianity and the Late Roman Empire; new material on women in early Christianity.

Chapter 6   New evidence raises serious questions about the date of arrival of the first human beings in the Americas, as well as suggesting the possibility that some early settlers may have come from Africa. Additional material on the role of women in pre-Columbian societies in the Americas is introduced. There is a brief reference to the recent controversy over the possibility of cannibalistic practices among the Anasazi peoples in North America.

Chapter 7   A new boxed document containing an excerpt from the Koran illustrates the traditional attitude toward the role of women in Muslim society. New material on women's role in rug-weaving is introduced.

Chapter 8   The chapter has been reorganized to focus on the importance of Islam in changing social patterns in early African history.

Chapter 9   New material is introduced to illustrate the role of women in Indian history during the Gupta era.

Chapter 10   Material on the early Ming dynasty (1369–1644) has been moved to a later chapter. The Ming era is now covered primarily in chapter 17. New material on marriage practices and the tradition of footbinding has been added.

Chapter 12   New material on the Vikings and on women in Germanic society; revision of material on fiefholding and manorialism.

Chapter 13 New material on the Black Death, the Hundred Years' War, Machiavelli, Catherine of Siena, Christine de Pizan, and women in the Renaissance; revision of material on education in the Renaissance.

Chapter 14 The psychological impact of early colonial expansion on Europeans is introduced. The section on political systems in Southeast Asia has been shortened, while the essential points continue to be stressed.

Chapter 15 Revision of material on the Protestant Reformation; new material on the Catholic Reformation; England in the seventeenth century, the Thirty Years' War and the military revolution, and Artemisia Gentileschi.

Chapter 17 Material on the early Ming dynasty, previously contained in chapter 10, is now covered here.

Chapter 18 Revision of material on the Scientific Revolution in medicine; revision on the path to Enlightenment.

Chapter 19 New map on the Columbian Exchange; revision of material on the wars of the eighteenth century, the American Revolution, and Enlightened Absolutism; new material on Napoleon.

Chapter 20 New material on European efforts to limit the spread of industrialization to the nonindustrialized world; new material on women in early socialism; revision of material on nationalistic revolts in Latin America, nation building in Latin America, and the national state in Europe.

Chapter 21 Revision of material on the Social Structure of Mass Society; new material on the movement for women's rights, the New Woman at the end of the nineteenth century, the United States as a world power, Marie Curie, and Berthe Morisot.

Chapter 22 The section on colonial philosophy and policy has been streamlined. Material related to the first stages of resistance to colonialism—previously in chapter 25 is now covered here.

Chapter 24 Revision of material on peace treaties at the end of World War I; new material on the social repercussions of the Great Depression and social changes in the Russian Revolution; both new and revised material on the cultural and intellectual trends between World War I and World War II, including a new box on the work of Hermann Hesse.

Chapter 25 Material on the first stages of nationalism has been moved to chapter 22. A reference to recent criticism of Kemal Ataturk's role in the modernization of Turkey is introduced.

Chapter 26 New material on Soviet women, the rise of militarism in Japan, the New Order in Asia, and the home front in Japan.

Chapter 28 Updated to take into account changes in Russia and Eastern Europe in the last three years.

Chapter 29 Updated to include new material on developments in the Western European states, Latin America, Canada, and the United States; revision of material on Great Britain, including a new document on Margaret Thatcher; reorganization and revision of material on Society and Culture in the Western world; new material on women in the postwar Western world; Betty Friedan; new section on Transformation in Women's Lives.

Chapter 30 Updated to include references to recent elections in Nigeria, as well as the evolving political situation in South Africa. Several new illustrations illustrate social conditions in sub-Saharan Africa.

Chapter 31 References to the rise of Vajpayee to the prime ministership, and to the overthrow of Sharif in Pakistan, have been added. The section on Indonesia has been reorganized, and there is a brief discussion of the results of the financial crisis of 1997.

Chapter 32 Updated to include references to the new Obuchi administration in Japan.

Because courses in world history at American and Canadian colleges and universities follow different chronological divisions, a one-volume comprehensive edition and a two-volume edition of this text are being made available to fit the needs of instructors. Teaching and learning ancillaries include:

Instructor's Manual with Testbank   Prepared by Charles F. Ames, Jr., Salem State College. Contains Chapter Outlines, Class Lecture/Discussion Topics, Thought/Discussion Questions for Primary Sources (Boxed Documents), Possible Student Projects, and Examination Questions (Essay, Identification, and Multiple Choice).

ExamView®   Create, deliver, and customize tests and study guides (both print and online) in minutes with this easy-to-use assessment and tutorial system. *ExamView®* offers both a Quick Test Wizard and an Online Test Wizard that guide you step-by-step through the process of creating tests, while its unique "WYSIWYG" capability allows you to see the test you are creating on the screen exactly as it will print or display online. You can build tests of up to 250 questions using up to 12 question types. Using *ExamView®*'s complete word processing capabilities, you can enter an unlimited number of new questions or edit existing questions.

Map Acetates and Commentary for World History, 2001 Edition   Includes more than 100 four-color map images from the text and other sources. Map commentary for each map is prepared by James Harrison, Siena College. Three-hole punched and shrinkwrapped.

History Video Library Includes Film For Humanities (these are available to qualified adoptions), CNN videos, and Grade Improvement: Taking Charge of Your Learning.

2001 World HistoryLink–Available on a multi-platform CD-ROM. With its easy-to-use interface, you can use our existing presentations (which consist of map images from the text and other sources) or customize your own presentation by importing your lecture or other material you choose.

Sights and Sounds of History Short, focused video clips, photos, artwork, animations, music, and dramatic readings are used to bring life to historical topics and events which are most difficult for students to appreciate from a textbook alone. For example, students will experience the grandeur of Versailles and the defeat felt by a German soldier at Stalingrad. The video segments, each averaging 4 minutes long, make excellent lecture launchers. Available on Laserdisk or VHS video.

Study Guide Prepared by Dianna Rhyan Kardulias, Columbus State Community College. Contains Chapter Outlines, Terms and Persons to Know, Mapwork, Datework, Primary Sourcework, Artwork, Identifying Important Concepts Behind the Conclusion, and new Multiple Choice questions and Web Resources. Available in two volumes.

Map Exercise Workbook Prepared by Cynthia Kosso, Northern Arizona University. Has been thoroughly revised and improved. Contains over 20 maps and exercises, which ask students to identify important cities and countries. Also includes critical thinking questions for each unit. Available in two volumes.

World History MapTutor This new mapping CD-ROM allows students to learn by manipulating maps through "locate and label" exercises, animations, and critical thinking exercises.

Migrations in Modern World History 1500–2000 CD-ROM An interactive multimedia curriculum on CD-ROM by Patrick Manning and the World History Center. Includes over 400 primary source documents; analytical questions to help the student develop his/her own interpretations of history; timelines; and additional suggested resources, including books, films, and web sites.

Document Exercise Workbooks Prepared by Donna Van Raaphorst, Cuyahoga Community College. Contains a collection of exercises based around primary source documents pertaining to world history.

Journey of Civilizations CD ROM for Windows This CD takes students on 18 interactive journeys through history. Enhanced with QuickTime movies, animations, sound clips, maps, and more, the journeys allow students engage in history as active participants rather than as readers of past events.

Magellan World History Atlas
Available to bundle with any history text; contains 44 historical four-color maps.

Internet Guide for History, Third Edition Prepared by John Soares. Provides newly revised and up-to-date Internet exercises by topic. Available at

http://history.wadsworth.com.

Kishlansky, Sources in World History, Second Edition
This reader is a collection of documents designed to supplement any world history text. Available in two volumes.

Web Tutor™ There are two volumes to correspond with Volumes I and II of the main text. This content-rich, Web-based teaching and learning tool helps students succeed by taking the course beyond classroom boundaries to an anywhere, anytime environment. *Web Tutor*™ offers real-time access to a full array of study tools, including flashcards (with audio), practice quizzes, online tutorials, and Web links. Available in two volumes.

InfoTrac® *College Edition* An online university that lets students explore and use full-length articles from more than 900 periodicals for four months. When students log on with their personal ID, they will immediately see how easy it is to search. Students can print out the articles, which date back as far as four years.

Historic Times: The Wadsworth History Resource Center

http://history.wadsworth.com/

Features a career section, forum, and links to museums, historical documents, and other fascinating sites. From the Resource Center you can access the book-specific web site, which contains the following: chapter by chapter tutorial quizzing, *InfoTrac*® activities, Internet activities, and hyperlinks for the student, and an online instructor's manual and downloadable PowerPoint files for the Instructor.

ACKNOWLEDGMENTS

Both authors gratefully acknowledge that without the generosity of many others, this project could not have been completed. William Duiker would like to thank Kumkum Chatterjee and On-cho Ng for their helpful comments about unfamiliar issues related to the history of India and premodern China. His longtime colleague Cyril Griffith, now deceased, was a cherished friend and a constant source of information about modern Africa. Art Goldschmidt has been of invaluable assistance in reading several chapters of the manuscript, as well as in unraveling many of the mysteries of Middle Eastern civilization. Finally, he remains profoundly grateful to his wife, Yvonne V. Duiker, Ph.D. She has not only given her usual measure of love and support when this appeared to be an insuperable task, but she has also contributed her own time and expertise to enrich the sections on art and literature, thereby adding life and sparkle to this, as well as the earlier editions of the book. To her, and to his daughters Laura and Claire, he will be forever thankful for bringing joy to his life.

Jackson Spielvogel would like to thank Art Goldschmidt, David Redles, and Christine Colin for their time and ideas and, above all, his family for their support. The gifts of love, laughter, and patience from his daughters, Jennifer and Kathryn, his sons, Eric and Christian, and his daughter-in-law, Liz, were invaluable. Diane, his wife and best friend, provided him with editorial assistance, wise counsel, and the loving support that made a project of this magnitude possible.

Thanks to Wadsworth's comprehensive review process, many historians were asked to evaluate our manuscript. We are grateful to the following for the innumerable suggestions that have greatly improved our work:

Charles F. Ames, Jr.
Salem State College
Nancy Anderson
Loyola University
Gloria M. Aronson
Normandale College
Charlotte Beahan
Murray State University
Doris Bergen
University of Vermont
Martin Berger
Youngstown State University
Deborah Biffton
University of Wisconsin-LaCrosse
Charmarie Blaisdell
Northeastern University
Patricia J. Bradley
Auburn University at Montgomery
Dewey Browder
Austin Peay State University
Antonio Calabria
University of Texas at San Antonio
Alice-Catherine Carls
University of Tennessee-Martin
Yuan Ling Chao
Middle Tennessee State University
Mark W. Chavalas
University of Wisconsin
Hugh Clark
Ursinus College

Joan Coffey
Sam Houston State University
John Davis
Radford University
Ross Dunn
San Diego State University
Lane Earn
University of Wisconsin-Oshkosh
Edward L. Farmer
University of Minnesota
William W. Farris
University of Tennessee
Ronald Fritze
Lamar University
Joe Fuhrmann
Murray State University
Robert Gerlich
Loyola University
Marc J. Gilbert
North Georgia College
William J. Gilmore-Lehne
Richard Stockton College of New Jersey
Richard M. Golden
University of North Texas
Joseph M. Gowaskie
Rider College
Jonathan Grant
Florida State University
Don Gustafson
Augsburg College

Deanna Haney
Lansing Community College
Ed Haynes
Winthrop College
Linda Kerr
University of Alberta at Edmonton
Zoltan Kramar
Central Washington University
Craig A. Lockard
University of Wisconsin-Green Bay
George Longenecker
Norwich University
Robert Luczak
Vincennes University
Patrick Manning
Northeastern University
Dolores Nason McBroome
Humboldt State University
John McDonald
Northern Essex Community College
Andrea McElderry
University of Louisville
Jeff McEwen
Chattanooga State Technical Community College
John A. Mears
Southern Methodist University
Marc A. Meyer
Berry College

Stephen S. Michot
  *Mississippi County Community
  College*
John Ashby Morton
  Benedict College
William H. Mulligan
  Murray State University
Henry A. Myers
  James Madison University
Marian P. Nelson
  University of Nebraska at Omaha
Sandy Norman
  Florida Atlantic University
Patrick M. O'Neill
  Broome Community College
Norman G. Raiford
  Greenville Technical College
Jane Rausch
  *University of Massachusetts-
  Amherst*
Dianna K. Rhyan
  *Columbus State Community
  College*
Merle Rife
  *Indiana University of
  Pennsylvania*

Patrice C. Ross
  *Columbus State Community
  College*
John Rossi
  LaSalle University
Eric C. Rust
  Baylor University
Keith Sandiford
  University of Manitoba
Elizabeth Sarkinnen
  Mt. Hood Community College
Bill Schell
  Murray State University
Robert M. Seltzer
  Hunter College
David Shriver
  Cuyahoga Community College
Amos E. Simpson
  *University of Southwestern
  Louisiana*
Wendy Singer
  Kenyon College
Marvin Slind
  Washington State University
Paul Smith
  Washington State University

John Snetsinger
  *California Polytechnic State
  University*
George Stow
  LaSalle University
Patrick Tabor
  Chemeketa Community College
Tom Taylor
  Seattle University
John G. Tuthill
  University of Guam
Joanne Van Horn
  Fairmont State College
Pat Weber
  University of Texas-El Paso
Douglas L. Wheeler
  University of New Hampshire
David L. White
  Appalachian State University
Elmira B. Wicker
  Southern University-Baton Rouge
Glee Wilson
  Kent State University
Harry Zee
  Cumberland County College

The authors are truly grateful to the people who have helped us to produce this book. We especially want to thank Clark Baxter, whose faith in our ability to do this project was inspiring, and Sharon Adams Poore for her development work. Hal Humphrey, Production Services Coordinator at Wadsworth, was both patient and thoughtful as he guided us through the process of revision for the third edition of our book. Cherie Hackelberg thoughtfully guided the preparation of outstanding teaching and learning ancillaries. Pat Lewis and Brian Jones were outstanding copy editors. Sarah Evertson provided valuable assistance in obtaining permissions for the illustrations. We are grateful to the staff of New England Typographic Service for providing their array of typesetting and page layout abilities. Jon Peck, of Dovetail Publishing Services, was as cooperative and cheerful as he was competent in matters of production management.

A Note to Students About Languages and the Dating of Time

One of the most difficult challenges in studying world history is coming to grips with the multitude of names, words, and phrases in unfamiliar languages. Unfortunately, this problem has no easy solution. We have tried to alleviate the difficulty, where possible, by providing an English-language translation of foreign words or phrases, a glossary, and a pronunciation guide. The issue is especially complicated in the case of Chinese, since two separate systems are commonly used to transliterate the spoken Chinese language into the Roman alphabet. The Wade-Giles system, invented in the nineteenth century, was the most frequently used until recent years, when the pinyin system was adopted by the People's Republic of China as its own official form of transliteration. We have opted to use the latter, since it appears to be gaining acceptance in the United States, but the initial use of a Chinese word is accompanied by its Wade-Giles equivalent in parentheses for the benefit of those who may encounter the term in their outside reading.

In our examination of world history, we need also to be aware of the dating of time. In recording the past, historians try to determine the exact time when events occurred. World War II in Europe, for example, began on September 1, 1939, when Adolf Hitler sent German troops into Poland, and ended on May 7, 1945, when Germany surrendered. By using dates, historians can place events in order and try to determine the development of patterns over periods of time.

If someone asked you when you were born, you would reply with a number, such as 1981. In the United States, we would all accept that number without question, because it is part of the dating system followed in the Western world (Europe and the Western Hemisphere). In this system, events are dated by counting backward or forward from the birth of Christ (assumed to be the year 1). An event that took place 400 years before the birth of Christ would most commonly be dated 400 B.C. (before Christ). Dates after the birth of Christ are labeled as A.D. These letters stand for the Latin words *anno domini*, which mean "in the year of the Lord" (or the year of the birth of Christ). Thus an event that took place 250 years

after the birth of Christ is written A.D. 250, or in the year of the Lord 250. It can also be written as 250, just as you would not give your birth year as A.D.1981, but simply 1981.

Some historians now prefer to use the abbreviations B.C.E. ("before the common era") and C.E. ("common era") instead of B.C. and A.D. This is especially true of world historians who prefer to use symbols that are not so Western or Christian oriented. The dates, of course, remain the same. Thus, 1950 B.C.E. and 1950 B.C. would be the same year, as would A.D. 40 and 40 C.E. In keeping with the current usage by many world historians, this book will use the terms B.C.E. and C.E.

Historians also make use of other terms to refer to time. A decade is 10 years; a century is 100 years; and a millennium is 1,000 years. The phrase fourth century B.C.E. refers to the fourth period of 100 years counting backward from 1, the assumed date of the birth of Christ. Since the first century B.C.E. would be the years 100 B.C.E. to 1 B.C.E., the fourth century B.C.E. would be the years 400 B.C.E. to 301 B.C.E. We could say, then, that an event in 350 B.C.E. took place in the fourth century B.C.E.

The phrase fourth century C.E. refers to the fourth period of 100 years after the birth of Christ. Since the first period of 100 years would be the years 1 to 100, the fourth period or fourth century would be the years 301 to 400. We could say, then, for example, that an event in 350 took place in the fourth century. Likewise, the first millennium B.C.E. refers to the years 1000 B.C.E. to 1 B.C.E.; the second millennium C.E. refers to the years 1001 to 2000.

The dating of events can also vary from people to people. Most people in the Western world use the Western calendar, also known as the Gregorian calendar after Pope Gregory XIII who refined it in 1582. The Hebrew calendar, on the other hand, uses a different system in which the year one is the equivalent of the Western year 3760 B.C.E., considered by Jews to be the date of the creation of the world. Thus, the Western year 2000 will be the year 5760 on the Jewish calendar. The Islamic calendar begins year 1 on the day Muhammad fled Mecca, which is the year 622 on the Western calendar.

THEMES FOR UNDERSTANDING WORLD HISTORY

In examining the past, historians often organize their material on the basis of themes that enable them to ask and try to answer basic questions about the past. The following ten themes are especially important.

1. *Political systems*. The study of politics seeks to answer certain basic questions that historians have about the structure of a society: How were people governed? What was the relationship between the ruler and the ruled? What people or groups of people (the political elites) held political power? What actions did people take to change their form of government? Historians also examine the causes and results of wars in order to understand the impact of war on human development.

2. *The role of ideas*. Ideas have great power to move people to action. For example, in the twentieth century, the idea of nationalism, which is based on a belief in loyalty to one's nation, helped produce two great conflicts—World War I and World War II. Together these wars cost the lives of more than fifty million people. The spread of ideas from one society to another has also played an important role in world history. From the earliest times, trade has especially served to bring different civilizations into contact with one another, and the transmission of religious and cultural ideas soon followed.

3. *Economics and history*. A society depends for its existence on certain basic needs. How did it grow its food? How did it make its goods? How did it provide the services people needed? How did individual people and governments use their limited resources? Did they spend more money on hospitals or military forces? By answering these questions, historians examine the different economic systems that have played a role in history.

4. *Social life and gender issues*. From a study of social life, we learn about the different social classes that make up a society. But we also examine how people dressed and found shelter, how and what they ate, and what they did for fun. The nature of family life and how knowledge was passed from one generation to another through education are also part of the social life of a society. So, too, are gender issues: What different roles did men and women play in their societies? How and why were those roles different?

5. *The importance of culture*. We cannot understand a society without looking at its culture, or the common ideas, beliefs, and patterns of behavior that are passed on from one generation to another. Culture includes both high culture and popular culture. High culture consists of the writings of a society's thinkers and the works of its artists. A society's popular culture is the world of ideas and experiences of ordinary people. Today the media have embraced the term *popular culture* to describe the most current trends and fashionable styles.

6. *Religion in history*. Throughout history, people have sought to find a deeper meaning to human life. How have the world's great religions, such as Hinduism, Buddhism, Judaism, Christianity, and Islam, influenced people's lives? How have these religions spread to create new patterns of culture?

7. *The role of individuals*. In discussing the role of politics, ideas, economics, social life, cultural developments, and religion, we have dealt with groups of people and forces that often seem beyond the control of any one person. But mentioning the names of Cleopatra, Queen Elizabeth I, Napoleon, and Hitler reminds us of the role of individuals in history. Decisive actions by powerful individuals have indeed played a crucial role in the course of history.

8. *The impact of science and technology*. For thousands of years, people around the world have made scientific discoveries and technological innovations that have changed our world. From the creation of stone tools that made farming easier to the advanced computers that guide our airplanes, science and technology have altered how humans have related to their world.

9. *The environment and history*. Throughout history, peoples and societies have been affected by the physical world in which they live. Climatic changes alone have been an important factor in human history. Peoples and societies, in turn, have also made an impact on their world. Human activities have affected the physical environment and even endangered the very existence of entire societies and species.

10. *The migration of peoples*. One characteristic of world history is an almost constant migration of peoples. Vast numbers of peoples abandoned their homelands and sought to live elsewhere. Sometimes the migration was peaceful. More often than not, however, the migration meant invasion and violent conflict.

For hundreds of thousands of years, human beings lived in small communities, seeking to survive by hunting, fishing, and foraging in an often hostile environment. Then, in the space of a few thousand years, there was an abrupt change of direction, as human beings in a few widely scattered areas of the globe began to master the art of cultivating food crops. As food production increased, the population in such areas grew, and people began to congregate in larger communities. Cities appeared and became centers of cultural and religious development. Historians refer to these changes as the beginnings of civilization.

The first civilizations that emerged in Mesopotamia, Egypt, India, and China all shared a number of basic characteristics. Each developed in a river valley that was able to provide the agricultural resources needed to maintain a large population. In each civilization a part of the population lived in cities, which became the focal points for political, economic, social, cultural, and religious development. All of these early civilizations established some kind of government bureaucracy to meet the administrative demands of the growing population and organized armies for protection and to gain land and power. A new social structure based on economic power arose. While kings and an upper class of priests, political leaders, and warriors dominated, there also existed a large group of free people (farmers, artisans, craftspeople) and, at the very bottom stratum, a class of slaves. Abundant agricultural yields in these regions created opportunities for economic specialization as a surplus of goods enabled artisans and craftspeople to create new products.

The new urban civilizations were also characterized by significant religious and cultural developments. The gods were often deemed critical to a community's success, and professional priestly classes regulated relations with the gods. Rulers, priests, merchants, and artisans used writing to keep records and even create new kinds of literary expression. New forms of artistic activity, including monumental architectural structures, occupied a prominent place in the new urban environments.

By and large the early river valley civilizations developed independently, with each grounded in local developments ultimately related to new agricultural practices. Still, contacts between them were already under way and in some cases were affected by new ideas and technology. This trade was often carried out by nomadic peoples from beyond the frontiers of settled states. Though not as organized, these nomadic peoples also began to play a major role in the human experience.

From the beginnings of the first civilizations around 3000 B.C.E., there was an ongoing movement toward the creation of larger territorial states with more sophisticated systems of control. This process reached a high point in the first millennium B.C.E. Between 1000 and 500 B.C.E., the Assyrians and Persians amassed empires that encompassed either large areas or all of the ancient Middle East. The conquests of Alexander the Great in the fourth century B.C.E. created an even larger, if short-lived, empire that soon divided into four kingdoms. Later, the western portion of these kingdoms as well as the Mediterranean world and much of western Europe fell subject to the mighty empire of the Romans. At the same time, much of India became part of the Mauryan empire. Finally, in the last few centuries B.C.E., the Qin and Han dynasties of China created a unified Chinese state.

CHAPTER

I

THE FIRST CIVILIZATIONS: THE PEOPLES OF WESTERN ASIA AND EGYPT

CHAPTER OUTLINE

- THE FIRST HUMANS
- THE EMERGENCE OF CIVILIZATION
- CIVILIZATION IN MESOPOTAMIA
- EGYPTIAN CIVILIZATION: "THE GIFT OF THE NILE"
- NEW CENTERS OF CIVILIZATION
- THE RISE OF NEW EMPIRES
- CONCLUSION

FOCUS QUESTIONS

- In what areas of the world did systematic agriculture develop during the Neolithic Age, and how did this development affect the lives of men and women?
- What are the characteristics of civilization, and what are some explanations for why early civilizations emerged?
- What effects did geography have on the civilizations that arose in Mesopotamia and Egypt?
- What role did religion play in the early civilizations of western Asia and Egypt, and how did Judaism and Zoroastrianism differ from the other religions of the region?
- What methods and institutions did the Assyrians and Persians use to amass and maintain their respective empires?

In 1849, a daring young Englishman made a hazardous journey into the deserts and swamps of southern Iraq. Braving high winds and temperatures that reached 120 degrees Fahrenheit, William Loftus led a small expedition southward along the banks of the Euphrates River in search of the roots of civilization. As he said, "From our childhood we have been led to regard this place as the cradle of the human race."

Guided by native Arabs into the southernmost reaches of Iraq, Loftus and his small band of explorers were soon overwhelmed by what they saw. He wrote, "I know of nothing more exciting or impressive than the first sight of one of these great piles, looming in solitary grandeur from the surrounding plains and marshes." One of these piles, known to the natives as the mound of Warka, contained the ruins of Uruk, one of the first cities in the world and part of the world's first civilization.

Southern Iraq, known to ancient peoples as Mesopotamia, was one of the four areas in the world where civilization began. In the fertile valleys of the Tigris and Euphrates, the Nile, the Indus, and the Yellow rivers, in Mesopotamia, Egypt, India, and China, respectively, intensive agriculture became capable of supporting large groups of people. In these regions civilization was born. The first civilizations emerged in western Asia (now known as the Middle East) and Egypt, where people developed organized societies and created the ideas and institutions that we associate with civilization.

Before considering the early civilizations of western Asia and Egypt, however, we must briefly examine humankind's prehistory and observe how human beings made the shift from hunting and gathering to agricultural communities and, ultimately, to cities and civilization. ❂

❂ THE FIRST HUMANS

Historians rely mostly on documents to create their pictures of the past, but no written records exist for the prehistory of humankind. In their absence, the story of early humanity depends on archaeological and, more recently, biological information, which anthropologists and archaeologists use to formulate theories about our early past.

Although science has given us more precise methods for examining prehistory, much of our understanding of early humans still relies on considerable conjecture. Given the rate of new discoveries, the following account of the current theory of early human life might well be changed in a few years. As the great British archaeologist Louis Leakey reminded us years ago, "Theories on prehistory and early man constantly change as new evidence comes to light."

The earliest humanlike creatures—known as hominids—lived in Africa some three to four million years ago. Known as Australopithecines, they flourished in eastern and southern Africa and were the first hominids to make simple stone tools. The oldest known stone tool—a knife blade that is probably 2.6 million years old—was found in Africa.

A second stage in early human development occurred around 1.5 million years ago with the emergence of *Homo erectus* ("upright human being"). *Homo erectus* made use of larger and more varied tools and was the first hominid to leave Africa and move into both Europe and Asia.

Around 250,000 years ago, a third—and crucial—stage in human development began with the emergence of *Homo sapiens* ("wise human being"). By 100,000 B.C.E., two groups of *Homo sapiens* had developed. One type was the Neanderthal, whose remains were first found in the Neander valley in Germany. Neanderthal remains have since been found in both Europe and the Middle East and have been dated to between 100,000 and 30,000 B.C.E. Neanderthals relied on a variety of stone tools and were the first early people to bury their dead. (Some scientists maintain that burial of the dead indicates a belief in an afterlife.) Neanderthals in Europe made clothes from the skins of animals that they had killed for food.

The first anatomically modern humans, known as *Homo sapiens sapiens* ("wise, wise human being"), appeared in Africa between 200,000 and 150,000 years ago. Recent evidence indicates that they began to spread outside Africa around 100,000 years ago. Map 1.1 on p. 4 shows probable dates for different movements, although many of these dates are still controversial. By 30,000 B.C.E., *Homo sapiens sapiens* had replaced the Neanderthals, who had largely become extinct.

The movement of the first modern humans was rarely deliberate. Groups of people advanced beyond their old hunting grounds at a rate of only two to three miles per generation. This was enough, however, to populate the world in some tens of thousands of years. Some scholars have suggested that such advanced human creatures may have emerged independently in different parts of the world, rather than in Africa alone, but the latest genetic evidence strongly supports the out-of-Africa theory as the most likely explanation of human origin. In any case, by 10,000 B.C.E., members of the *Homo sapiens sapiens* species could be found throughout the world. By that time, it was the only human species left. All humans today, be they Europeans, Australian Aborigines, or Africans, belong to the same subspecies of human being.

The Hunter-Gatherers of the Old Stone Age

One of the basic distinguishing features of the human species is the ability to make tools. The earliest tools were made of stone, and the term *Paleolithic* (Greek for "old stone") *Age* is used to designate this early period of human history (c. 2,500,000–10,000 B.C.E.).

For hundreds of thousands of years, humans relied on hunting and gathering for their daily food. Paleolithic peoples had a close relationship with the world around them, and over a period of time, they came to know which animals to hunt and which plants to eat. They did not know how to grow crops or raise animals, however. They

CHRONOLOGY

THE FIRST HUMANS

Australopithecines	flourished c. 2–4 million years ago
Homo erectus	flourished c. 100,000–1.5 million years ago
Homo sapiens:	
Neanderthals	flourished c. 100,000–30,000 B.C.E.
Homo sapiens sapiens	emerged c. 200,000 B.C.E.

tools became more refined and more useful. The invention of the spear, and later the bow and arrow, made hunting considerably easier. Harpoons and fishhooks made of bone increased the catch of fish.

Both men and women were responsible for finding food—the chief work of Paleolithic people. Since women bore and raised the children, they generally stayed close to the camps, but they played an important role in acquiring food by gathering berries, nuts, and grains. Men hunted for wild animals, an activity that took them far from camp. Because both men and women played important roles in providing for the band's survival, scientists have argued that a rough equality existed between men and women. Indeed, some speculate that both men and women made the decisions that governed the activities of the Paleolithic band.

These groups of Paleolithic peoples, especially those who lived in cold climates, found shelter in caves. Over time, they created new types of shelter as well. Perhaps the most common was a simple structure of wood poles or sticks covered with animal hides. Where wood was scarce, Paleolithic hunter-gatherers might use the bones of mammoths for the framework and cover it with animal hides. The systematic use of fire, which archaeologists believe began around 500,000 years ago, made it possible for the caves and human-made structures to have a source of light and heat. Fire also enabled early humans to cook their food, making it better tasting, longer lasting, and, in the case of some plants, such as wild grain, easier to chew and digest.

gathered wild nuts, berries, fruits, and a variety of wild grains and green plants. Around the world, they hunted and consumed various animals, including buffalo, horses, bison, wild goats, and reindeer. In coastal areas, fish provided a rich source of food.

The hunting of animals and the gathering of wild plants no doubt led to certain patterns of living. Archaeologists and anthropologists have speculated that Paleolithic people lived in small bands of twenty or thirty people. They were nomadic (they moved from place to place) since they had no choice but to follow animal migrations and vegetation cycles. Hunting depended on careful observation of animal behavior patterns and required a group effort to have any real degree of success. Over the years,

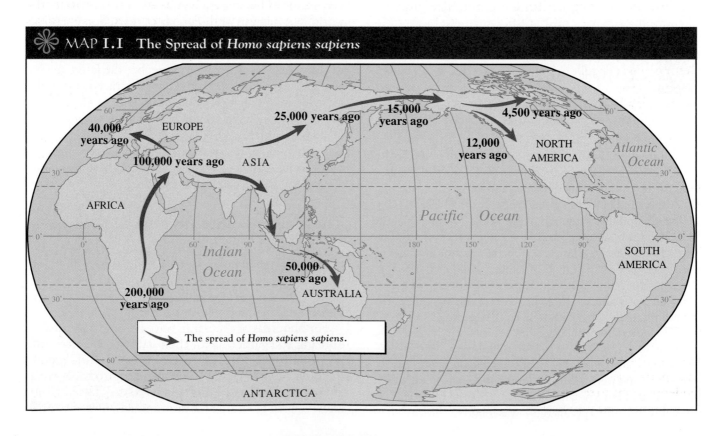

MAP I.I The Spread of *Homo sapiens sapiens*

The map labels: 40,000 years ago (Europe), 100,000 years ago, 25,000 years ago, 15,000 years ago, 4,500 years ago, 12,000 years ago, 50,000 years ago, 200,000 years ago.

The spread of *Homo sapiens sapiens*.

The making of tools and the use of fire—two important technological innovations of Paleolithic peoples—remind us how crucial the ability to adapt was to human survival. Changing physical conditions during periodic ice ages posed a considerable threat to human existence. Paleolithic peoples used their technological innovations—such as the ability to make tools and use fire—to change their physical environment. By working together, they found a way to survive. And by passing on their common practices, skills, and material products to their children, they ensured that later generations, too, could survive in a harsh environment.

But Paleolithic peoples did more than just survive. The cave paintings of large animals found in southwestern France and northern Spain bear witness to the cultural activity of Paleolithic peoples. A cave discovered in southern France in 1994 contains more than three hundred paintings of lions, oxen, owls, panthers, and other animals. Most of these are animals that Paleolithic people did not hunt, which suggests that the paintings were created for religious or even decorative purposes.

The Agricultural Revolution, c. 10,000–4000 B.C.E.

The end of the last ice age around 10,000 B.C.E. was followed by what is called the Neolithic Revolution; that is, the revolution that occurred in the New Stone Age (the word *Neolithic* is Greek for "new stone"). The name New Stone Age is misleading, however. Although Neolithic peoples made a new type of polished stone axes, this was not the major change that occurred after 10,000 B.C.E.

The real change was the shift from hunting animals and gathering plants for sustenance to producing food by systematic agriculture. The planting of grains and vegetables provided a regular supply of food while the taming of animals, such as sheep, goats, cattle, and pigs, added a steady source of meat, milk, and fibers such as wool for clothing. Larger animals could also be used as beasts of burden. The growing of crops and the taming of food-producing animals created a new relationship between humans and nature. Historians like to speak of this as an agricultural revolution. Revolutionary change is dramatic and requires great effort, but the ability to acquire food on a regular basis gave humans greater control over their environment. It also enabled them to give up their nomadic ways of life and begin to live in settled communities.

The shift to food producing from hunting and gathering was not as sudden as was once believed, however. The Mesolithic period ("Middle Stone Age," c. 10,000–7000 B.C.E.) saw a gradual transition from a food-gathering and hunting economy to a food-producing one and witnessed a gradual domestication of animals as well. Likewise, the movement toward the use of plants and their seeds as an important source of nourishment was also not sudden. Evidence seems to support the possibility that the Paleolithic hunters and gatherers had already grown crops to supplement their traditional sources of food. Moreover, throughout the Neolithic period, hunting and gathering as well as nomadic herding remained ways of life for many people around the world.

Systematic agriculture developed independently in different areas of the world between 8000 and 5000 B.C.E. Inhabitants of the Middle East began cultivating wheat and barley and domesticating pigs, cattle, goats, and sheep by 8000 B.C.E. From the Middle East, farming spread into the Balkans region of Europe by 6500 B.C.E. By 4000 B.C.E., it was well established in the south of France, central Europe, and the coastal regions of the Mediterranean. The cultivation of wheat and barley also spread from western Asia into the Nile valley of Egypt by 6000 B.C.E. and soon spread up the Nile to other areas of Africa, especially the Sudan and Ethiopia. In the woodlands and tropical forests of central Africa, a separate agricultural system emerged based on the cultivation of tubers or root crops such as yams and tree crops such as bananas. The cultivation of wheat and barley also eventually moved eastward into the highlands of northwestern and central India, between 7000 and 5000 B.C.E. By 5000 B.C.E., rice was being cultivated in southeastern Asia, from where it spread into southern China. In northern China, the cultivation of millet and the domestication of pigs and dogs seem well established by 6000 B.C.E. In the Western Hemisphere, Mesoamericans (inhabitants of present-day Mexico and Central America) domesticated beans, squash, and maize (or corn) as well as dogs and fowl between 7000 and 5000 B.C.E.

The growing of crops on a regular basis made possible the support of larger populations and gave rise to more-permanent settlements, which historians refer to as Neolithic farming villages or towns. Although Neolithic villages appeared in Europe, India, Egypt, China, and Mesoamerica,

PALEOLITHIC CAVE PAINTING. Cave paintings of large animals provide good examples of the cultural creativity of Paleolithic peoples. This scene is part of a large underground chamber found accidentally in 1940 at Lascaux, France, by some boys looking for their dog. This work is dated around 14,000 B.C.E.

the oldest and most extensive ones were located in the Middle East. Jericho, in Palestine near the Dead Sea, was in existence by 8000 B.C.E. and covered several acres by 7000 B.C.E. It had a wall several feet thick that enclosed houses made of sun-dried mud bricks. Çatal Hüyük, located in modern Turkey, was an even larger community. Its walls enclosed thirty-two acres, and its population probably reached six thousand inhabitants during its high point from 6700 to 5700 B.C.E. People lived in simple mudbrick houses that were built so close to one another that there were few streets. To get to their homes, people had to walk along the rooftops and then enter the house through a hole in the roof.

Archaeologists have discovered twelve cultivated products in Çatal Hüyük, including fruits, nuts, and three kinds of wheat. People grew their own food and stored it in storerooms in their homes. Domesticated animals, especially cattle, yielded meat, milk, and hides. Hunting scenes on the walls would indicate that the people of Çatal Hüyük hunted as well, but unlike earlier hunter-gatherers, they no longer relied on hunting to survive. Food surpluses also made it possible for people to do things other than farming. Some people became artisans and made weapons and jewelry that were traded with neighboring peoples, thus connecting the inhabitants of Çatal Hüyük to the wider world around them.

Religious shrines housing figures of gods and goddesses have been found at Çatal Hüyük, as have a number of female statuettes. Molded with noticeably large breasts and buttocks, these "earth mothers" perhaps symbolically represented the fertility of both "our mother" earth and human mothers. Both the shrines and the statues point to the growing role of religion in the lives of these Neolithic peoples.

The Neolithic agricultural revolution had far-reaching consequences. Once people settled in villages or towns, they built houses for protection and other structures for the storage of goods. As organized communities stored food and accumulated material goods, they began to engage in trade. In the Middle East, for example, the new communities exchanged such objects as shells, flint, and semiprecious stones. People also began to specialize in certain crafts, and a division of labor developed. Pottery was made from clay and baked in fire to make it hard. The pots were used for cooking and to store grains. Woven baskets were also used for storage. Stone tools became refined as flint blades were used to make sickles and hoes for use in the fields. In the course of the Neolithic Age, many of the food plants still in use today came to be cultivated. Moreover, vegetable fibers from such plants as flax and cotton were used to make thread that was woven into cloth.

The change to systematic agriculture in the Neolithic Age also had consequences for the relationship between men and women. Men assumed the primary responsibility for working in the fields and herding animals, jobs that kept them away from the home. Women remained behind, caring for the children and weaving cloth, making cheese from milk, and performing other tasks that required considerable labor in one place. In time, as work outside the

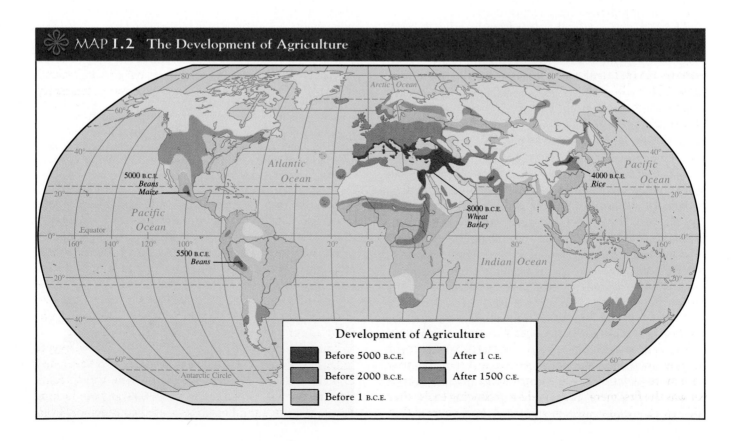

MAP I.2   The Development of Agriculture

STATUES FROM AIN GHAZAL.   These life-size statues made of plaster and bitumen date from 6500 B.C.E. and were discovered in 1984 in Ain Ghazal, an archaeological site near Amman, Jordan. They are among the oldest statues ever found of the human figure. Archaeologists are studying the statues to try to understand their purpose and meaning.

home was increasingly perceived as more important than work done in the home, men came to play the more dominant role in human society, a basic pattern that would persist until our own times.

Other patterns set in the Neolithic Age also proved to be enduring elements of human history. Fixed dwellings, domesticated animals, regular farming, a division of labor, men holding power—all of these are part of the human story. For all of our scientific and technological progress, human survival still depends on the growing and storing of food, an accomplishment of people in the Neolithic Age. The Neolithic Revolution was truly a turning point in human history.

Between 4000 and 3000 B.C.E., significant technical developments began to transform the Neolithic towns. The invention of writing enabled records to be kept, while the use of metals marked a new level of human control over the environment and its resources. Already before 4000 B.C.E., artisans had discovered that metal-bearing rocks could be heated to liquefy the metal, which could then be cast in molds to produce tools and weapons that were more useful than stone instruments. Although copper was the first metal to be used for producing tools, after 4000 B.C.E., metalworkers in western Asia discovered that

a combination of copper and tin created bronze, a harder and more durable metal than copper. Its widespread use has led historians to speak of a Bronze Age from around 3000 to 1200 B.C.E., after which bronze was increasingly replaced by iron.

THE EMERGENCE OF CIVILIZATION

At first, Neolithic settlements were hardly more than villages, but as their inhabitants mastered the art of farming, the villages gradually began to give rise to more sophisticated and complex human societies. As wealth increased, these societies began to develop armies and to build walled cities. By the beginning of the Bronze Age, the concentration of larger numbers of people in river valleys was leading to a whole new pattern for human life—the more complex form of existence that we call civilization.

The first civilizations emerged in Mesopotamia, Egypt, India, and China; in each case, the civilization developed in a river valley that was able to provide the agricultural resources needed to maintain a large population. Although agricultural practices varied considerably from civilization to civilization, each one exhibited certain basic characteristics:

1. *An urban revolution.* Cities became the focal points for political, economic, social, cultural, and religious development. The cities that emerged were much larger than the Neolithic towns that preceded them, and the new configurations in turn gave rise to significant changes in political, military, social, and economic structures.

2. *New political and military structures.* An organized bureaucracy arose to meet the administrative needs of the growing population, and armies were created to provide protection and gain land and power.

3. *A new social structure based on economic power.* Kings and an upper class of priests, political leaders, and warriors dominated, but a large group of free common people (farmers, artisans, and craftspeople) also existed, as did a class of slaves, who were socially at the very bottom.

4. *The development of more complexity in a material sense.* Abundant agricultural yields created opportunities for economic specialization as a surplus of goods enabled some people to work in occupations other than farming. The demand of ruling elites for luxury items encouraged artisans and craftspeople to create new products. As urban populations exported finished goods in exchange for raw materials from neighboring populations, organized trade grew substantially.

5. *A distinct religious structure.* The gods were deemed crucial to the community's success, and professional priestly classes, as stewards of the gods' property, regulated relations with the gods.

6. *The development of writing.* Kings, priests, merchants, and artisans used writing to keep records and even to create new kinds of literary expression.

7. *New forms of significant artistic and intellectual activity.* Monumental architectural structures, usually religious, occupied a prominent place in the urban environments, and smaller examples of individual creativity also proliferated.

Why early civilizations developed remains difficult to explain. Since civilizations developed independently in India, China, Mesopotamia, and Egypt, can general causes be identified that would explain why all of these civilizations emerged? A number of possible explanations of the beginning of civilization have been suggested. A theory of challenge and response maintains that challenges forced human beings to make efforts that resulted in the rise of civilization. Some scholars have adhered to a material explanation. Material forces, such as the growth of food surpluses, made possible the specialization of labor and development of large communities with bureaucratic organization. But some areas were not naturally conducive to agriculture. Abundant food could only be produced with a massive human effort to carefully manage the water, an

effort that created the need for organization and bureaucratic control and led to civilized cities. Some historians have argued that nonmaterial forces, primarily religious, provided the sense of unity and purpose that made such organized activities possible. Finally, some scholars doubt that we are capable of ever discovering the actual causes of early civilization.

CIVILIZATION IN MESOPOTAMIA

The Greeks spoke of the valley between the Tigris and Euphrates rivers as Mesopotamia, the land "between the rivers." The region receives little rain, but the soil of the plain of southern Mesopotamia was enlarged and enriched over the years by layers of silt deposited by the two rivers. In late spring, the Tigris and Euphrates overflow their banks and deposit their fertile silt, but since this flooding depends on the melting of snows in the upland mountains where the rivers begin, it is irregular and sometimes catastrophic. In such circumstances, farming could be accomplished only with human intervention in the form of irrigation and drainage ditches. A complex system was required to control the flow of the rivers and produce the crops. Large-scale irrigation made possible the expansion of agriculture in this region, and the abundant food provided the material base for the emergence of civilization in Mesopotamia.

The City-States of Ancient Mesopotamia

The creators of the first Mesopotamian civilization were the Sumerians, a people whose origins remain unclear. By 3000 B.C.E., they had established a number of independent cities in southern Mesopotamia, including Eridu, Ur, Uruk, Umma, and Lagash. As the cities expanded in size, they came to exercise political and economic control over the surrounding countryside, forming city-states. These city-states were the basic units of Sumerian civilization.

Sumerian cities were surrounded by walls. Uruk, for example, occupied an area of approximately a thousand acres encircled by a wall six miles long with defense towers located every thirty to thirty-five feet along the wall. City dwellings, built of sun-dried bricks, included both the small flats of peasants and the larger dwellings of the civic and priestly officials. Although Mesopotamia had little stone or wood for building purposes, it did have plenty of mud. Mudbricks, easily shaped by hand, were left to bake in the hot sun until they were hard enough to use for building. People in Mesopotamia were remarkably inventive with mudbricks, inventing the arch and the dome and constructing some of the largest brick buildings in the world. Mudbricks are still used in rural areas of the Middle East today.

The most prominent building in a Sumerian city was the temple, which was dedicated to the chief god or goddess of the city and often built atop a massive stepped tower called a ziggurat. The Sumerians believed that gods and goddesses owned the cities, and much wealth was used to build temples as well as elaborate houses for the priests and priestesses who served the gods. Priests and priestesses, who supervised the temples and their property, had much power. The temples owned much of the city land and livestock and served not only as the physical center of the city, but also as its economic and political center.

In fact, historians believe that in the early stages of the city-states, priests and priestesses played an important role in ruling. The Sumerians believed that the gods ruled the cities, making the state a theocracy (government by a divine authority). Eventually, however, ruling power passed into the hands of worldly figures known as kings.

Sumerians viewed kingship as divine in origin—kings, they believed, derived their power from the gods and were the agents of the gods. As one person said in a petition to his king: "You in your judgement, you are the son of Anu [god of the sky]; Your commands, like the word of a god, cannot be reversed, Your words, like rain pouring down from heaven, are without number."[1] Regardless of their origins, kings had power—they led armies, initiated legislation, supervised the building of public works, provided courts, and organized workers for the irrigation projects upon which Mesopotamian agriculture depended. The army, the government bureaucracy, and the priests and priestesses all aided the kings in their rule. Befitting their power, Sumerian kings lived in large palaces with their wives and children.

The economy of the Sumerian city-states was primarily agricultural, but commerce and industry became important as well. The people of Mesopotamia produced woolen textiles, pottery, and the metalwork for which they were especially well known. Foreign trade, which was primarily a royal monopoly, could be extensive. Royal officials imported luxury items, such as copper and tin, aromatic woods, and fruit trees, in exchange for dried fish, wool, barley, wheat, and the metal goods produced by Mesopotamian metalworkers. Traders traveled by land to the eastern Mediterranean in the west and by sea to India in the east.

MAP 1.3 Ancient Mesopotamia

THE "ROYAL STANDARD" OF UR. This series of panels is from the "Royal Standard" of Ur, a box dating from c. 2700 B.C.E. and discovered in a stone tomb from the royal cemetery of the Sumerian city-state of Ur. These scenes from the box depict the activities of the king and his court after a military victory. In the top panel, the king and his court drink wine while at the right a musician plays a bull-headed harp. The middle panel shows bulls, rams, and fish being brought to the banquet hall. The bottom panel shows booty from the king's victory.

The invention of the wheel around 3000 B.C.E. led to carts with wheels that made the transport of goods easier.

Sumerian city-states contained three major social groups: nobles, commoners, and slaves. Nobles included royal and priestly officials and their families. Commoners included the nobles' subjects who worked for the palace and temple estates and other free citizens who worked as farmers, merchants, fishers, scribes, and craftspeople. Probably 90 percent or more of the population were farmers. They could exchange their crops for the goods of the artisans in free town markets. Slaves belonged to palace officials, who used them mostly in building projects; temple officials, who used mostly female slaves to weave cloth and grind grain; and rich landowners, who used them for farming and domestic work.

Empires in Ancient Mesopotamia

As the number of Sumerian city-states grew and the states expanded, new conflicts arose as city-state fought city-state for control of land and water. The fortunes of various city-states rose and fell over the centuries. The constant wars, with their burning and sacking of cities, left many Sumerians in deep despair, as is evident in the words of this Sumerian poem from the city of Ur: "Ur is destroyed, bitter is its lament. The country's blood now fills its holes like hot bronze in a mold. Bodies dissolve like fat in the sun. Our temple is destroyed, the gods have abandoned us, like migrating birds. Smoke lies on our city like a shroud."

Located in the flat land of Mesopotamia, the Sumerian city-states were also open to invasion. To the north of the Sumerian city-states were the Akkadians. We call them a Semitic people because of the type of language they spoke (see Table 1.1). Around 2340 B.C.E., Sargon, leader of the Akkadians, overran the Sumerian city-states and established an empire that included most of Mesopotamia as well as lands westward to the Mediterranean. But the Akkadian empire eventually disintegrated, and its end by 2100 B.C.E. brought a return to the system of warring city-states until Ur-Nammu of Ur succeeded in reunifying most of Mesopotamia. But this final flowering of Sumerian culture collapsed with the coming of the Amorites. Under Hammurabi, the Amorites or Old Babylonians, a large group of Semitic-speaking seminomads, created a new empire.

Hammurabi (1792–1750 B.C.E.) employed a well-disciplined army of foot soldiers who carried axes, spears, and copper or bronze daggers. He learned to divide his opponents and subdue them one by one. Using such methods, he gained control of Sumer and Akkad and reunified Mesopotamia almost to the old borders established by Sargon of Akkad. After his conquests, he called himself "the sun of Babylon, the king who has made the four quarters of the world subservient," and established a new capital at Babylon, north of Akkad.

Hammurabi, the man of war, was also a man of peace. He followed in the footsteps of previous conquerors by assimilating Mesopotamian culture with the result that Sumerian ways continued to exist despite the end of the Sumerians as a political entity. A collection of his letters, found by archaeologists, reveals that he took a strong interest in state affairs. He built temples, defensive walls, and irrigation canals; encouraged trade; and brought an economic revival. After his death, however, a series of weak kings were unable to keep Hammurabi's empire united, and it finally fell to new invaders.

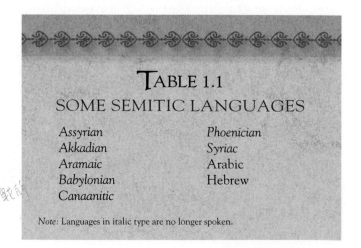

TABLE 1.1
SOME SEMITIC LANGUAGES

Assyrian	Phoenician
Akkadian	Syriac
Aramaic	Arabic
Babylonian	Hebrew
Canaanitic	

Note: Languages in italic type are no longer spoken.

CHRONOLOGY

CHIEF EVENTS IN MESOPOTAMIAN HISTORY

Early development of Sumerian city-states	c. 3000–2350 B.C.E.
The Akkadian empire	c. 2340–2100 B.C.E.
The dynasty of Ur-Nammu	c. 2113–2000 B.C.E.
Hammurabi's reign	c. 1792–1750 B.C.E.

✿ **STELE OF HAMMURABI (CODE OF HAMMURABI, KING OF BABYLONIA).** Although the Sumerians compiled earlier law codes, Hammurabi's code was the most famous in early Mesopotamian history. The code recognized three social classes in Babylonia (nobles, free commoners, and slaves) and included laws dealing with marriage and divorce, job performance, punishments for crimes, and even sexual relations. The upper section of the stele depicts Hammurabi standing in front of the seated sun god Shamash (who was also the god of justice), who orders the king to record the law. The lower section contains the actual code.

THE CODE OF HAMMURABI

Hammurabi is best remembered for his law code, a collection of 282 laws (see the box on p. 12). For centuries, laws had regulated people's relationships with one another in the lands of Mesopotamia, but only fragments of these earlier codes survive. Hammurabi's collection provides considerable insight into almost every aspect of everyday life there and provides us a priceless glimpse of the values of this early society.

The Code of Hammurabi reveals a society with a system of strict justice. Penalties for criminal offenses were severe and varied according to the social class of the victim. A crime against a member of the upper class (a noble) by a member of the lower class (a commoner) was punished more severely than the same offense against a member of the lower class. Moreover, the principle of retaliation ("an eye for an eye, a tooth for a tooth") was fundamental to this system of justice. It was applied in cases where members of the upper class committed crimes against their social equals. For crimes against members of the lower classes, a money payment was made instead.

Hammurabi's code took seriously the responsibilities of public officials. The governor of an area and city officials were expected to catch burglars. If they failed to do so, officials in the district where the crime was committed had to replace the lost property. If murderers were not found, the officials had to pay a fine to the relatives of the victim. Soldiers were likewise expected to fulfill their duties and responsibilities for the order and maintenance of the state.

If a soldier hired a substitute to fight for him, he was put to death, and the substitute was given control of his estate.

The law code also furthered the proper performance of work with what virtually amounted to consumer protection laws. Builders were held responsible for the buildings they constructed. If a house collapsed and caused the death of the owner, the builder was put to death. If the collapse caused the death of the son of the owner, the son of the builder was put to death. If goods were destroyed by the collapse, they had to be replaced and the house itself reconstructed at the builder's expense.

The number of laws in Hammurabi's code dedicated to land tenure and commerce reveals the importance of agriculture and trade in the Mesopotamian economy. Numerous laws dealt with questions of landholding, such as the establishment of conditions for renting farmland and the division of produce between tenants and their landlords. Laws concerning land use and irrigation were especially strict, an indication of the danger of declining crop yields if the lands were used incompetently. Commercial activity was also carefully regulated. Rates of interest on loans were watched closely. If the lender raised his rate of interest after a loan was made, he lost the entire amount of the loan. The Code of Hammurabi even specified the precise wages of laborers and artisans, such as brick makers and jewelers.

The largest category of laws in the Code of Hammurabi focused on marriage and the family. Parents arranged marriages for their children. After marriage, the parties involved signed a marriage contract; without it, no one

THE CODE OF HAMMURABI

*A*lthough there were earlier Mesopotamian law codes, Hammurabi's is the most complete. The law code emphasizes the principle of retribution ("an eye for an eye") and punishments that vary according to social status. Punishments could be severe. Marriage and family affairs also play a large role in the code. The following examples illustrate these concerns.

25. If fire broke out in a free man's house and a free man, who went to extinguish it, cast his eye on the goods of the owner of the house and has appropriated the goods of the owner of the house, that free man shall be thrown into that fire.

129. If the wife of a free man has been caught while lying with another man, they shall bind them and throw them into the water. If the husband of the woman wishes to spare his wife, then the king in turn may spare his subject.

131. If a free man's wife was accused by her husband, but she was not caught while lying with another man, she shall make affirmation by god and return to her house.

196. If a free man has destroyed the eye of a member of the aristocracy, they shall destroy his eye.

198. If he has destroyed the eye of a commoner or broken the bone of a commoner, he shall pay one mina of silver.

199. If he has destroyed the eye of a free man's slave or broken the bone of a free man's slave, he shall pay one-half his value.

209. If a free man struck another free man's daughter and has caused her to have a miscarriage, he shall pay ten shekels of silver for her fetus.

210. If that woman has died, they shall put his daughter to death.

211. If by a blow he has caused a commoner's daughter to have a miscarriage, he shall pay five shekels of silver.

212. If that woman has died, he shall pay one-half mina of silver.

213. If he struck a free man's female slave and has caused her to have a miscarriage, he shall pay two shekels of silver.

214. If that female slave has died, he shall pay one-third mina of silver.

was considered legally married. While the husband provided a bridal payment, the woman's parents were responsible for a dowry to the new husband.

As in many patriarchal societies, women possessed far fewer privileges and rights in the married relationship than men. A woman's place was in the home, and failure to fulfill her expected duties was grounds for divorce. If she was not able to bear children, her husband could divorce her, but he did have to return the dowry to her family. If a wife tried to leave home to engage in business, thus neglecting her house, her husband could divorce her and did not have to repay the dowry. Furthermore, a wife who was a "gad-about, … neglecting her house [and] humiliating her husband" could be drowned. We do know that in practice not all women remained at home. Some worked in business and were especially prominent in the running of taverns.

Women were guaranteed some rights, however. If a woman was divorced without good reason, she received the dowry back. A woman could seek divorce and get her dowry back if her husband was unable to show that she had done anything wrong. In theory, a wife was guaranteed use of her husband's legal property in the event of his death. The mother could also decide which of her sons would receive an inheritance.

Sexual relations were strictly regulated as well. Husbands, but not wives, were permitted sexual activity outside marriage. A wife caught committing adultery was pitched into the river, although her husband could ask the king to pardon her. Incest was strictly forbidden. If a father had incestuous relations with his daughter, he would be banished. Incest between a son and mother resulted in both being burned.

Fathers ruled their children as well as their wives. Obedience was duly expected: "If a son has struck his father, they shall cut off his hand." If a son committed a serious enough offense, his father could disinherit him, although fathers were not permitted to disinherit their sons arbitrarily.

The Culture of Mesopotamia

A spiritual worldview was of fundamental importance to Mesopotamian culture. To the peoples of Mesopotamia, the gods were living realities who affected all aspects of life. It was crucial, therefore, that the correct hierarchies be observed. Leaders could prepare armies for war, but success really depended on a favorable relationship with the gods. This helps to explain the importance of the priestly class and is the reason why even the kings took great care to dedicate offerings and monuments to the gods.

THE IMPORTANCE OF RELIGION

The Mesopotamians viewed their city-states as earthly copies of a divine model and order. Each city-state was sacred because it was linked to a god or goddess. Hence, Nippur, the earliest center of Sumerian religion, was dedicated to Enlil, the god of wind. Moreover, located at the heart of each city-state was a temple complex. Occupying several acres, this sacred area consisted of a ziggurat with a temple at the top dedicated to the god or goddess who owned the city.

The temple complex was the true center of the community. The main god or goddess dwelt there symbolically in the form of a statue, and the ceremony of dedication included a ritual that linked the statue to the god or goddess and thus supposedly harnessed the power of the deity for the city's benefit. Considerable wealth was poured into the construction of temples as well as other buildings used for the residences of the priests and priestesses who served the gods. Although the gods literally owned the city, the temple complex used only part of the land and rented out the remainder. Essentially, the temples dominated individual and commercial life, an indication of the close relationship between Mesopotamian religion and culture.

The physical environment had an obvious impact on the Mesopotamian view of the universe. Ferocious floods, heavy downpours, scorching winds, and oppressive humidity were all part of the Mesopotamian climate. These conditions and the resulting famines easily convinced Mesopotamians that this world was controlled by supernatural forces and that the days of human beings "are numbered; whatever he may do, he is but wind," as *The Epic of Gilgamesh* put it. In the presence of nature, Mesopotamians could easily feel helpless, as this poem relates:

> *The rampant flood which no man can oppose,*
> *Which shakes the heavens and causes earth to tremble,*
> *In an appalling blanket folds mother and child,*
> *Beats down the canebrake's full luxuriant greenery,*
> *And drowns the harvest in its time of ripeness.*[2]

The Mesopotamians discerned cosmic rhythms in the universe and accepted its order, but perceived that it was not completely safe because of the presence of willful, powerful cosmic powers that they identified with gods and goddesses.

With its numerous gods and goddesses animating all aspects of the universe, Mesopotamian religion was polytheistic in nature. The four most important deities were An, god of the sky and hence the most important force in the universe; Enlil, god of wind; Enki, god of the earth, rivers, wells, and canals as well as inventions and crafts; and Ninhursaga, a goddess associated with soil, mountains, and vegetation, who came to be worshiped as a mother goddess, a "mother of all children," who manifested her power by giving birth to kings and conferring the royal insignia upon them.

Human beings' relationship with the gods was based on subservience since, according to Sumerian myth, human beings were created to do the manual labor the gods were unwilling to do for themselves. Moreover, humans were insecure because they could never be sure of the gods' actions. But humans did attempt to relieve their anxiety by discovering the intentions of the gods through divination.

Divination took a variety of forms. A common form, at least for kings and priests who could afford it, involved killing animals, such as sheep or goats, and examining their livers or other organs. Supposedly, features seen in the organs of the sacrificed animals foretold events to come. Thus, one handbook states that if the animal organ has shape x, then the outcome of the military campaign will be y. Private individuals relied on cheaper divinatory techniques. These included interpreting patterns of smoke from burning incense or the pattern formed when oil was poured into water. The Mesopotamian arts of divination arose out of the desire to discover the purposes of the gods. If people could decipher the signs that foretold events, the events would be predictable and humans could act wisely.

THE CULTIVATION OF NEW ARTS AND SCIENCES

The realization of writing's great potential was another aspect of Mesopotamian culture. The oldest Mesopotamian texts date to around 3000 B.C.E. and were written by the Sumerians, who used a cuneiform ("wedge-shaped") system of writing. Using a reed stylus, they made wedge-shaped impressions on clay tablets, which were then baked or dried in the sun. Once dried, these tablets were virtually indestructible, and the several hundred thousand that have been found so far have provided a valuable source of information for modern scholars. Sumerian writing evolved from pictures of concrete objects to simplified and stylized signs, leading eventually to a phonetic system that made possible the written expression of abstract ideas.

Mesopotamian peoples used writing primarily for record keeping, but another category of cuneiform inscriptions includes the large body of basic texts produced for teaching purposes. Schools for scribes were in operation by 2500 B.C.E. Such schools were necessary because considerable time was needed to master the cuneiform system of writing. The primary goal of scribal education was to produce professionally trained scribes for careers in the temples and palaces, the military, and government service. Pupils were male and primarily from wealthy families. Gradually, the schools became important centers for culture because Mesopotamian literature was used for instructional purposes.

Writing was important because it enabled a society to keep records and maintain knowledge of previous practices and events. Writing also made it possible for people to communicate ideas in new ways, which is especially evident in Mesopotamian literary works. The most famous piece of Mesopotamian literature is *The Epic of Gilgamesh*, an epic poem that records the exploits of a legendary king of Uruk. Gilgamesh, wise, strong, and perfect in body, part man and part god, befriends a hairy beast named Enkidu.

Pictographic sign c. 3100 B.C.E.	✳	◡	≈	🌾		◡			
Interpretation	star	?sun over horizon	?stream	ear of barley	bull's head	bowl	head + bowl	lower leg	?shrouded body
Cuneiform sign c. 2400 B.C.E.									
Phonetic value*	dingir, an	u_4, ud	a	še	gu_4	nig_2, ninda	ku_2	du, gin, gub	lu_2
Meaning	god, sky	day, sun	water, seed, son	barley	ox	food, bread	to eat	to walk, to stand	man

*Some signs have more than one phonetic value, and some sounds are represented by more than one sign. U_4 means the fourth sign with the phonetic value u.

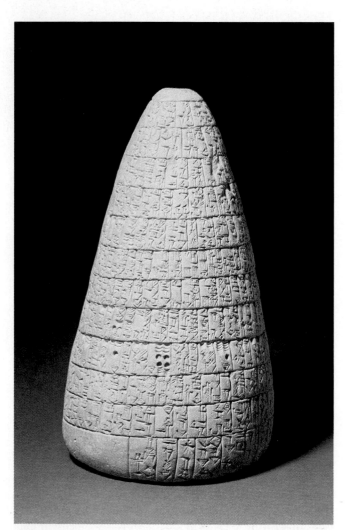

THE DEVELOPMENT OF CUNEIFORM. Pictured here is the cone of Uruinimgina, an example of early cuneiform script from an early Sumerian dynasty. The inscription announces reductions in taxes. The table above shows the development of writing from pictographic signs to the evolution of cuneiform script.

Together they set off in pursuit of heroic deeds. When Enkidu dies, Gilgamesh experiences the pain of mortality and begins a search for the secret of immortality. But his efforts fail (see the box on p. 15). Gilgamesh remains mortal. The desire for immortality, one of humankind's great searches, ends in complete frustration. "Everlasting life," as this Mesopotamian epic makes clear, is only for the gods.

Peoples in Mesopotamia also made outstanding achievements in mathematics and astronomy. In math, the Sumerians devised a number system based on 60, using combinations of 6 and 10 for practical solutions. Geometry was used to measure fields and erect buildings. In astronomy, the Sumerians made use of units of 60 and charted the heavenly constellations. Their calendar was based on twelve lunar months and was brought into harmony with the solar year by adding an extra month from time to time.

EGYPTIAN CIVILIZATION: "THE GIFT OF THE NILE"

Although contemporaneous with Mesopotamia, civilization in Egypt evolved along somewhat different lines. Of central importance to the development of Egyptian civilization was the Nile River. That the Egyptian people recognized its significance is apparent in this Hymn to the Nile (also see the box on p. 16): "The bringer of food, rich in provisions, creator of all good, lord of majesty, sweet of fragrance. . . . He who . . . fills the magazines, makes the granaries wide, and gives things to the poor. He who makes every beloved tree to grow. . . ."[3] Egypt, like Mesopotamia, India, and China, was a river valley civilization.

The Nile is a unique river, beginning in the heart of Africa and coursing northward for thousands of miles. It is the longest river in the world. The Nile was responsible for creating an area several miles wide on both banks of

THE GREAT FLOOD

The great epic poem of Mesopotamian literature, The Epic of Gilgamesh, includes an account by Utnapishtim (a Mesopotamian version of the later biblical Noah), who had built a ship and survived the flood unleashed by the gods to destroy humankind. In this selection, Utnapishtim recounts his story to Gilgamesh, telling how the god Ea advised him to build a boat and how he came to land the boat at the end of the flood.

THE EPIC OF GILGAMESH

In those days the world teemed, the people multiplied, the world bellowed like a wild bull, and the great god was aroused by the clamor. Enlil heard the clamor and he said to the gods in council, "The uproar of mankind is intolerable and sleep is no longer possible by reason of the babel." So the gods agreed to exterminate mankind. Enlil did this, but Ea [Sumerian Enki, god of the waters] because of his oath warned me in a dream.... "tear down your house and build a boat, abandon possessions and look for life, despise worldly goods and save your soul alive. Tear down your house, I say, and build a boat.... then take up into the boat the seed of all living creatures...." [Utnapishtim did as he was told and then the destruction came.]

For six days and six nights the winds blew, torrent and tempest and flood overwhelmed the world, tempest and flood raged together like warring hosts. When the seventh day dawned the storm from the south subsided, the sea grew calm, the flood was stilled; I looked at the face of the world and there was silence, all mankind was turned to clay. The surface of the sea stretched as flat as a rooftop; I opened a hatch and the light fell on my face. Then I bowed low, I sat down and I wept, the tears streamed down my face, for on every side was the waste of water. I looked for land in vain, but fourteen leagues distant there appeared a mountain, and there the boat grounded; on the mountain of Nisir the boat held fast, she held fast and did not budge.... When the seventh day dawned I loosed a dove and let her go. She flew away, but finding no resting place she returned. Then I loosed a swallow, and she flew away but finding no resting place she returned. I loosed a raven, she saw that the waters had retreated, she ate, she flew around, she cawed, and she did not come back. Then I threw everything open to the four winds, I made a sacrifice and poured out a libation on the mountaintop.

---

the river that was fertile and capable of producing abundant harvests. The "miracle" of the Nile was its annual flooding. The river rose in the summer from rains in central Africa, crested in Egypt in September and October, and left a deposit of silt that created an area of rich soil. The Egyptians called this fertile land the "Black Land," because it was dark in color from the silt and the lush crops that grew on it. Beyond these narrow strips of fertile fields lay the deserts (the "Red Land").

Unlike the floods of Mesopotamia's rivers, the flooding of the Nile was gradual and usually predictable, and the river itself was seen as life enhancing, not life threatening. Although a system of organized irrigation was still necessary, the small villages along the Nile could create such systems without the massive state intervention that was required in Mesopotamia. Egyptian civilization, consequently, tended to remain more rural, with many small population centers congregated along a narrow band on both sides of the Nile. About one hundred miles before it empties into the Mediterranean, the river splits into two major branches, forming the delta, a triangular-shaped territory called Lower Egypt to distinguish it from Upper Egypt, the land upstream to the south. Egypt's important cities developed at the tip of the delta. Even today, most of Egypt's people are crowded along the banks of the Nile River.

The surpluses of food that Egyptian farmers grew in the fertile Nile valley made Egypt prosperous. But the Nile also served as a unifying factor in Egyptian history. In ancient times, the Nile was the fastest way to travel through the land, making both transportation and communication easier. Winds from the north pushed sailboats south, and the current of the Nile carried them north. Often when they headed downstream (or north), people used long poles or paddles to propel their boats forward.

Unlike Mesopotamia, which was subject to constant invasion, Egypt was blessed by natural barriers that fostered isolation, protected it from invasion, and gave it a sense of security. These barriers included the deserts to the west and east, the cataracts (rapids) on the southern part of the Nile, which made defense relatively easy, and the Mediterranean Sea to the north. These barriers, however, did not prevent the development of trade. Indeed, there is evidence of very early trade between Egypt and Mesopotamia itself.

In essence, Egyptian geography and topography played important roles in the early history of the country. The regularity of the Nile floods and the relative isolation of the Egyptians created a sense of security that was accompanied by a feeling of changelessness. Egyptian civilization was characterized by a remarkable degree of continuity over thousands of years. It was certainly no accident that Egyptians believed in cyclical rather than linear progress. Just as the sun passed through its daily cycle and the Nile its annual overflow, Egyptian kings reaffirmed the basic, unchanging principles of justice at the beginning of each new cycle of rule.

THE SIGNIFICANCE OF THE NILE RIVER AND THE PHARAOH

Two of the most important sources of life for the ancient Egyptians were the Nile River and the pharaoh. Egyptians perceived that the Nile River made possible the abundant food that was a major source of their well-being. This Hymn to the Nile, probably from the nineteenth and twentieth dynasties in the New Kingdom, expresses the gratitude Egyptians felt for the Nile.

HYMN TO THE NILE

Hail to you, O Nile, that issues from the earth and comes to keep Egypt alive! . . .

He that waters the meadows which Re created, in order to keep every kid alive.

He that makes to drink the desert and the place distant from water: that is his dew coming down from heaven. . . .

The lord of fishes, he who makes the marsh-birds to go upstream. . . .

He who makes barley and brings emmer into being, that he may make the temples festive.

If he is sluggish, then nostrils are stopped up, and everybody is poor. . . .

When he rises, then the land is in jubilation, then every belly is in joy, every backbone takes on laughter, and every tooth is exposed.

The bringer of good, rich in provisions, creator of all good, lord of majesty, sweet of fragrance. . . .

He who makes every beloved tree to grow, without lack of them.

The Egyptian king, or pharaoh, was viewed as a god and the absolute ruler of Egypt. His significance and the gratitude of the Egyptian people for his existence are evident in this hymn from the reign of Sesotris III (c. 1880–1840 B.C.E.).

HYMN TO THE PHARAOH

He has come unto us that he may carry away Upper Egypt; the double diadem [crown of Upper and Lower Egypt] has rested on his head.

He has come unto us and has united the Two Lands; he has mingled the reed with the bee [symbols of Lower and Upper Egypt].

He has come unto us and has brought the Black Land under his sway; he has apportioned to himself the Red Land.

He has come unto us and has taken the Two Lands under his protection; he has given peace to the Two Riverbanks.

He has come unto us and has made Egypt to live; he has banished its suffering.

He has come unto us and has made the people to live; he has caused the throat of the subjects to breathe. . . .

He has come unto us and has done battle for his boundaries; he has delivered them that were robbed.

The Old and Middle Kingdoms

The basic framework for the study of Egyptian history was provided by Manetho, an Egyptian priest and historian who lived in the early third century B.C.E. He divided Egyptian history into thirty-one dynasties of kings. Based on Manetho and other king lists, modern historians have divided Egyptian history into three major periods, known as the Old Kingdom, the Middle Kingdom, and the New Kingdom. These were periods of long-term stability characterized by strong monarchical authority, competent bureaucracy, freedom from invasion, much construction of temples and pyramids, and considerable intellectual and cultural activity. But between the periods of stability were times of political chaos known as the Intermediate periods, which were characterized by weak political structures and rivalry for leadership, invasions, a decline in building activity, and a restructuring of society.

According to the Egyptians' own tradition, their land consisted initially of numerous populated areas ruled by tribal chieftains. Around 3100 B.C.E., the first Egyptian royal dynasty, under a king called Menes, united both Upper and Lower Egypt into a single kingdom. Henceforth, the king would be called "King of Upper and King of Lower Egypt," and the royal crown would be a double diadem, signifying the unification of all Egypt. Just as the Nile served to unite Upper and Lower Egypt physically, kingship served to unite the two areas politically.

The Old Kingdom encompassed the third through sixth dynasties of Egyptian kings, lasting from around 2700 to 2200 B.C.E. It was an age of prosperity and splendor, made visible in the construction of the greatest and largest pyramids in Egypt's history. The capital of the Old Kingdom was located at Memphis, south of the delta.

Kingship was a divine institution in ancient Egypt and formed part of a universal cosmic scheme (see the box above): "What is the king of Upper and Lower Egypt? He is a god by whose dealings one lives, the father and mother of all men, alone by himself, without an equal."[4] In obeying their king, subjects helped to maintain the cosmic order. A breakdown in royal power could only mean that citizens were offending divinity and weakening the universal structure. Among the various titles of Egyptian kings, that of pharaoh (originally meaning "great house" or "palace") eventually came to be the most common.

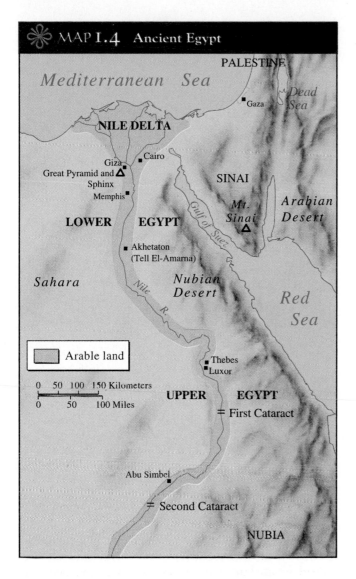

MAP I.4 Ancient Egypt

Arable land

0   50 100 150 Kilometers
0   50   100 Miles

A careful assessment of land and tenants was undertaken to provide the tax base. For administrative purposes, Egypt was divided into provinces or nomes, as they were later called by the Greeks—twenty-two in Upper and twenty in Lower Egypt. A governor, called by the Greeks a nomarch, was head of each nome and was responsible to the king and vizier. Nomarchs, however, tended to build up large holdings of land and power within their nomes, creating a potential rivalry with the pharaohs.

Despite the theory of divine order, the Old Kingdom eventually collapsed, ushering in a period of chaos. Finally, a new royal dynasty managed to pacify all Egypt and inaugurated the Middle Kingdom, a new period of stability lasting from c. 2050 to 1652 B.C.E. Egyptians later portrayed the Middle Kingdom as a golden age, a clear indication of its stability. Several factors contributed to its vitality. The nome structure was reorganized. The boundaries of each nome were now settled precisely, and the obligations of the nomes to the state were clearly delineated. Nomarchs were confirmed as hereditary officeholders but with the understanding that their duties must be performed faithfully. These included the collection of taxes for the state and the recruitment of labor forces for royal projects, such as stone quarrying.

The Middle Kingdom was characterized by a new concern of the pharaohs for the people. In the Old Kingdom, the pharaoh had been viewed as an inaccessible god-king. Now he was portrayed as the shepherd of his people with the responsibility to build public works and provide for the public welfare. As one pharaoh expressed it: "He [a particular god] created me as one who should do that which he had done, and to carry out that which he commanded should be done. He appointed me herdsman of this land, for he knew who would keep it in order for him."[5]

Society and Economy in Ancient Egypt

Egyptian society had a simple structure in the Old and Middle Kingdoms; basically, it was organized along hierarchical lines with the god-king at the top. The king was surrounded by an upper class of nobles and priests who participated in the elaborate rituals of life that surrounded the pharaoh. This ruling class ran the government and managed its own landed estates, which provided much of its wealth.

Below the upper classes were merchants and artisans. Within Egypt, merchants engaged in an active trade up and down the Nile as well as in town and village markets. Some merchants also engaged in international trade; they were sent by the king to Crete and Syria, where they obtained wood and other products. Expeditions traveled into Nubia for ivory and down the Red Sea to Punt for incense and spices. Egyptian artisans exhibited unusually high standards of artisanship and physical beauty while producing an incredible variety of goods: stone dishes; beautifully painted boxes made of clay; wooden furniture; gold, silver, and copper tools and containers; paper and rope made of papyrus; and linen clothes.

Although they possessed absolute power, Egyptian kings were not supposed to rule arbitrarily, but according to set principles. The chief principle was called Ma'at, a spiritual precept that conveyed the ideas of truth and justice but especially right order and harmony. To ancient Egyptians, this fundamental order and harmony had existed throughout the universe since the beginning of time. Pharaohs were the divine instruments who maintained it and were themselves subject to it.

Although theoretically absolute in their power, in practice Egyptian kings did not rule alone. Initially, members of the king's family performed administrative tasks, but by the fourth dynasty a bureaucracy with regular procedures had developed. Especially important was the office of vizier, "steward of the whole land." Directly responsible to the king, the vizier was in charge of the bureaucracy with its numerous departments, such as police, justice, river transport, and public works. Agriculture and the treasury were the two most important departments. Agriculture was, of course, the backbone of Egyptian prosperity, and the treasury collected the taxes that were paid in kind.

CHRONOLOGY

THE EGYPTIANS

Early Dynastic Period (Dynasties 1–2)	c. 3100–2700 B.C.E.
Old Kingdom (Dynasties 3–6)	c. 2700–2200 B.C.E.
First Intermediate Period (Dynasties 7–10)	c. 2200–2050 B.C.E.
Middle Kingdom (Dynasties 11–12)	c. 2050–1652 B.C.E.
Second Intermediate Period (Dynasties 13–17)	c. 1652–1567 B.C.E.
New Kingdom (Dynasties 18–20)	c. 1567–1085 B.C.E.
Post-Empire (Dynasties 21–31)	c. 1085–30 B.C.E.

❧ **PAIR STATUE OF KING MENKAURE AND HIS QUEEN.** The period designated as the Old Kingdom began approximately four centuries after Egypt's unification (c. 3100 B.C.E.) and lasted until approximately 2200 B.C.E. The kings of Egypt (eventually called "pharaohs") were regarded as gods, divine instruments who maintained the fundamental order and harmony of the universe and wielded absolute power. This statue depicts King Menkaure and his queen (fourth dynasty).

By far the largest number of people in Egypt simply worked the land. In theory, the king owned all the land but granted out portions of it to his subjects. Large sections were in the possession of nobles and the temple complexes. Moreover, although free farmers who owned their own land had once existed, by the end of the Old Kingdom, this group had disappeared. Most of the lower classes were serfs, or common people bound to the land, who cultivated the estates. They paid taxes in the form of crops to the king, nobles, and priests, lived in small villages or towns, and provided military service and forced labor for building projects.

The Culture of Egypt

Egypt produced a culture that dazzled and awed its later conquerors. The Egyptians' technical achievements, especially visible in the construction of the pyramids, demonstrated a measure of skill unequaled in the world at that time. To the Egyptians, all of these achievements were part of a cosmic order suffused with the presence of the divine.

SPIRITUAL LIFE IN EGYPTIAN SOCIETY

The Egyptians had no word for religion, because it was an inseparable element of the entire world order to which Egyptian society belonged. The Egyptians possessed a remarkable number of gods associated with heavenly bodies and natural forces. Two groups, sun gods and land gods, came to have special prominence, hardly unusual in view of the importance of the sun, the river, and the fertile land along its banks to Egypt's well-being. The sun was the source of life and hence worthy of worship. A sun cult developed, and the sun god took on different forms and names, depending on his specific function. He was worshiped as Atum in human form and as Re, who had a human body but the head of a falcon. The pharaoh took the title of "Son of Re," since he was regarded as the earthly embodiment of Re. Eventually, Re became associated with Amon, an air god of Thebes, as Amon-Re.

River and land deities included Osiris and Isis with their child Horus, who was related to the Nile and to the sun as well. Osiris became especially important as a symbol of resurrection or rebirth. A famous Egyptian myth told of the struggle between Osiris, who brought civilization to Egypt, and his evil brother Seth, who killed him, cut his body into fourteen parts, and tossed them into the Nile River. Osiris's faithful wife Isis found the pieces and, with help from other gods, restored Osiris to life. As a symbol of resurrection and judge of the dead, Osiris took on an important role for the Egyptians. By identifying with Osiris, one could hope to gain new life just as Osiris had done. The dead, embalmed and mummified, were placed in tombs (in the case of kings, in pyramidal tombs), given the name of Osiris, and, by a process of magical identification, became Osiris. Like Osiris, they could then be reborn. The flood of the Nile and the new life it brought to Egypt were symbolized by Isis gathering all of Osiris's parts together and were celebrated each spring in the festival of the new land.

Later Egyptian spiritual practice began to emphasize morality by stressing Osiris's role as judge of the dead. The dead were asked to give an account of their earthly deeds to show whether they deserved a reward. Other means were also employed to gain immortality. Magical incantations, preserved in the *Book of the Dead,* were used to ensure a favorable journey to a happy afterlife. Specific instructions explained what to do when confronted by the judge of the dead. These instructions had two aspects. The negative confession gave a detailed list of what one had not done:

What is said on reaching the Broad-Hall of the Two Justices [the place of the next-world judgment], absolving X [the name and title of the deceased] of every sin which he had committed. . . .

> I have not committed evil against men.
> I have not mistreated cattle.
> I have not blasphemed a god.
> I have not done violence to a poor man.
> I have not done that which the gods abominate.
> I have not defamed a slave to his superior.
> I have not made anyone sick.
> I have not made anyone weep.
> I have not killed. . . .
> I have not caused anyone suffering. . . .
> I have not had sexual relations with a boy.
> I have not defiled myself. . . .[6]

Later the suppliant made a speech listing his good actions: "I have done that which men said and that with which gods are content. . . . I have given bread to the hungry, water to the thirsty, clothing to the naked, and a ferry-boat to him who was marooned. I have provided divine offerings for the gods and mortuary offerings for the dead."[7]

At first the Osiris cult was reserved for the very wealthy, who could afford to take expensive measures to preserve the body after death. During the Middle Kingdom, however, the cult became "democratized"—extended to all Egyptians who aspired to an afterlife.

THE PYRAMIDS

One of the great achievements of Egyptian civilization, the building of pyramids, occurred in the time of the Old Kingdom. Pyramids were not built in isolation but as part of a larger complex dedicated to the dead—in effect, a city of the dead. The area included a large pyramid for the king's burial, smaller pyramids for his family, and mastabas, rectangular structures with flat roofs, as tombs for the pharaoh's noble officials. The tombs were well prepared for their residents. The rooms were furnished and stocked with numerous supplies, including chairs, boats, chests, weapons, games, dishes, and a variety of foods. The Egyptians believed that human beings had two bodies, a physical one and a spiritual one, which they called the *ka.* If the physical body was properly preserved (hence mummification) and the tomb furnished with all the various objects of regular life, the *ka* could return and continue its life despite the death of the physical body. A pyramid was not only the king's tomb; it was also an important symbol of royal power. It could be seen for miles away as a visible reminder of the glory and might of the ruler who was a living god on earth.

The largest and most magnificent of all the pyramids was built under King Khufu. Constructed at Giza around 2540 B.C.E., this famous Great Pyramid covers thirteen

THE PYRAMIDS AT GIZA. The three pyramids at Giza, across the Nile River from Cairo, are the most famous in Egypt. Pyramids served as tombs for both the king and his immediate family. At the rear is the largest of the three pyramids— the Great Pyramid of Khufu. In the foreground is the smaller pyramid of Menkaure, standing behind the even smaller pyramids for the pharaoh's wives.

...res, measures 756 feet at each side of its base, and stands 481 feet high. Its four sides are almost precisely oriented to the four points of the compass. The interior included a grand gallery to the burial chamber, which was built of granite with a lidless sarcophagus for the pharaoh's body. The Great Pyramid still stands as a visible symbol of the power of Egyptian kings and the spiritual conviction that underlay Egyptian society. No pyramid built later ever matched its size or splendor.

ART AND WRITING

Commissioned by kings or nobles for use in temples and tombs, Egyptian art was largely functional. Wall paintings and statues of gods and kings in temples served a strictly spiritual purpose. They were an integral part of the performance of ritual, which was thought necessary to preserve the cosmic order and hence the well-being of Egypt. Likewise, the mural scenes and sculptured figures found in the tombs had a specific function: they were supposed to assist the journey of the deceased into the afterworld.

Egyptian art was also formulaic. Artists and sculptors were expected to observe a strict canon of proportions that determined both form and presentation. This canon gave Egyptian art a distinctive appearance for thousands of years. Especially characteristic was the convention of combining the profile, semiprofile, and frontal views of the human body in relief work and painting in order to represent each part of the body accurately. The result was an art that was highly stylized yet still allowed distinctive features to be displayed.

Writing emerged in Egypt during the first two dynasties. The Greeks later labeled Egyptian writing hieroglyphics, meaning "priest-carvings" or "sacred writings." Hieroglyphs were sacred characters used as picture signs that depicted objects and had a sacred value at the same time. Although hieroglyphs were later simplified into two scripts for writing purposes, they never developed into an alphabet. Egyptian hieroglyphs were initially carved in stone, but later the two simplified scripts were written on papyrus, a paper made from the papyrus reed that grew along the Nile. Most of the ancient Egyptian literature that has come down to us was written on papyrus rolls and wooden tablets.

Chaos and a New Order: The New Kingdom

The Middle Kingdom came to an end in the midst of another period of instability. An incursion into the delta region by a people known as the Hyksos initiated this second age of chaos. The Hyksos were part of a larger group of peoples who spoke Semitic languages and originally lived in the Arabian peninsula. Some of these Semitic-speaking peoples had moved into northern Mesopotamia as well as Syria and Palestine. The Hyksos infiltrated Egypt in the seventeenth century B.C.E. and came to dominate much of the country. However, the presence of the Hyksos was not entirely negative for Egypt. They introduced Egypt to Bronze Age technology by teaching the Egyptians how to make bronze for use in new agricultural tools and weapons. More significantly, the Hyksos introduced new aspects of warfare to Egypt, including the horse-drawn war chariot, a heavier sword, and the compound bow. Eventually, a new line of pharaohs—the eighteenth dynasty—made use of the new weapons to throw off Hyksos domination, reunite Egypt, establish the New Kingdom (c. 1567–1085 B.C.E.), and launch the Egyptians along a new militaristic and imperialistic path. During the period of the New Kingdom, Egypt became the most powerful state in the Middle East. The Egyptians occupied Palestine and Syria but permitted the local native princes to continue to rule under Egyptian control. Egyptian armies also moved westward into Libya. The achievements of the empire were made visible in the construction of magnificent new buildings and temples, especially the temple centers at Karnak and Luxor.

The eighteenth dynasty was not without its own troubles, however. Amenhotep IV (c. 1364–1347 B.C.E.) introduced the worship of Aton, god of the sun disk, as the chief god (see the box on p. 21) and pursued his worship with great enthusiasm. Changing his own name to Akhenaton ("It is well with Aton"), the pharaoh closed the temples of other gods and especially endeavored to lessen the power of Amon-Re and his priesthood at Thebes. Akhenaton strove to reduce their influence by replacing Thebes as the capital of Egypt with Akhetaton ("dedicated to Aton"), a new city located near modern Tell el-Amarna, two hundred miles north of Thebes.

Akhenaton's attempt at religious change proved to be a failure. It was too much to ask Egyptians to give up their traditional ways and beliefs, especially since they saw the destruction of the old gods as subversive of the very cosmic order upon which Egypt's survival and continuing prosperity depended. Moreover, the priests at Thebes were unalterably opposed to the changes, which had diminished their influence and power. At the same time, Akhenaton's preoccupation with religion caused him to ignore foreign affairs and led to the loss of both Syria and Palestine. Akhenaton's changes were soon undone after his death by those who influenced his successor, the boy-pharaoh Tutankhamon (1347–1338 B.C.E.). Tutankhamon returned the government to Thebes and restored the old gods. The Aton experiment had failed to take hold, and the eighteenth dynasty itself came to an end in 1333.

The nineteenth dynasty managed to restore Egyptian power one more time. Under Rameses II (c. 1279–1213 B.C.E.), the Egyptians regained control of Palestine but were unable to reestablish the borders of their earlier

AKHENATON'S HYMN TO ATON

Amenhotep IV, more commonly known as Akhenaton, created a religious upheaval in Egypt by introducing the worship of Aton, god of the sun disk, as the sole god. Akhenaton's attitude to Aton is seen in this hymn. Some authorities have noted a similarity in spirit and wording to the 104th Psalm of the Old Testament.

HYMN TO ATON

Your rays suckle every meadow.
When you rise, they live, they grow for you.
You make the seasons in order to rear all that you have
*   made,*
The winter to cool them,
And the heat that they may taste you.
You have made the distant sky in order to rise therein,
In order to see all that you do make.
While you were alone,
Rising in your form as the living Aton,
Appearing, shining, withdrawing or approaching,
You made millions of forms of yourself alone.

Cities, towns, fields, road, and river—
Every eye beholds you over against them,
For you are the Aton of the day over the earth. . . .
The world came into being by your hand,
According as you have made them.
When you have risen they live,
When you set they die.
You are lifetime your own self,
For one lives only through you.
Eyes are fixed on beauty until you set.
All work is laid aside when you set in the west.
But when you rise again,
Everything is made to flourish for the king, . . .
Since you did found the earth
And raise them up for your son,
Who came forth from your body:
*   the King of Upper and Lower Egypt, . . .*
*   Akh-en-Aton, . . . and the Chief Wife of the King . . .*
*   Nefert-iti, living and youthful forever and ever.*

empire. New invasions in the thirteenth century by the "Sea Peoples," as Egyptians called them, destroyed Egyptian power in Palestine and drove the Egyptians back within their old frontiers. The days of Egyptian empire were ended, and the New Kingdom itself expired with the end of the twentieth dynasty in 1085. For the next thousand years, despite periodical revivals of strength, Egypt was dominated by Libyans, Nubians, Persians, and finally Macedonians, after the conquest of Alexander the Great (see Chapter 4). In the first century B.C.E., Egypt became a province in Rome's mighty empire. Egypt continued, however, to influence its conquerors through the richness of its heritage and the awesome magnificence of its physical remains.

Daily Life in Ancient Egypt: Family and Marriage

Ancient Egyptians had a very positive attitude toward daily life on earth and followed the advice of the wisdom literature, which suggested that people marry young and establish a home and family. Monogamy was the general rule, although a husband was allowed to keep additional wives if his first wife was childless. Pharaohs, of course, were entitled to harems. The queen was acknowledged, however, as the Great Wife, with a status higher than that of the other wives. The husband was master in the house, but wives were very much respected and in charge of the household and education of the children. From a book

of wise sayings (which the Egyptians called "instructions") came this advice:

> If you are a man of standing, you should found your household and love your wife at home as is fitting. Fill her belly; clothe her back. Ointment is the prescription for her body. Make her heart glad as long as you live. She is a profitable field for her lord. You should not contend with her at law, and keep her far from gaining control. . . . Let her heart be soothed through what may accrue to you; it means keeping her long in your house.[8]

Women's property and inheritance remained in their hands, even in marriage. Although most careers and public offices were closed to women, some did operate businesses. Peasant women worked long hours in the fields and at numerous domestic tasks. Upper-class women could function as priestesses, and a few queens even became pharaohs in their own right. Most famous was Hatshepsut in the New Kingdom. She initially served as regent for her stepson Thutmosis III but then assumed the throne for herself and remained in power until her death.

Hatshepsut's reign was a prosperous one, as is especially evident in her building activity. She is most famous for the temple dedicated to herself at Deir el Bahri, on the west bank of the Nile at Thebes. As pharaoh, Hatshepsut sent out military expeditions, encouraged mining, fostered agriculture, and sent a trading expedition up the Nile. Because pharaohs were almost always male, Hatshepsut's official statues show her clothed and bearded like a king. She was addressed as "His Majesty." That Hatshepsut was aware of her unusual position is evident from an inscription she had boy for his "sister" (lovers referred to each other as "brother" and "sister"):

> Seven days to yesterday I have not seen the sister, and a
>   sickness has invaded me;
> My body has become heavy,
> And I am forgetful of my own self.
> If the chief physicians come to me,
> My heart is not content with their remedies. . . .
> What will revive me is to say to me: "Here she is!"
> Her name is what will lift me up. . . .
> My health is her coming in from outside:
> When I see her, then I am well.[10]

Marriages could and did end in divorce, which was allowed, apparently with compensation for the wife. Adultery, however, was strictly prohibited, with stiff punishments—especially for women, who could have their noses cut off or be burned at the stake.

NEW CENTERS OF CIVILIZATION

Our story of civilization so far has been dominated by Mesopotamia and Egypt. But significant developments were also taking place on the fringes of these civilizations. Farming had spread into the Balkan peninsula of Europe by 6500 B.C.E., and by 4000 B.C.E., it was well established in southern France, central Europe, and the coastal regions of the Mediterranean. Although migrating farmers from the Middle East may have brought some farming techniques into Europe, historians now believe that the Neolithic peoples of Europe domesticated animals and began to farm largely on their own.

One outstanding feature of late Neolithic Europe was the building of megalithic structures. Megalith is Greek for "large stone." Radiocarbon dating, a technique that allows scientists to determine the ages of objects, shows that the first megalithic structures were built around 4000 B.C.E., more than a thousand years before the great pyramids were built in Egypt. Between 3200 and 1500 B.C.E., standing stones that were placed in circles or lined up in rows were erected throughout the British Isles and northwestern France. Other megalithic constructions have been found as far north as Scandinavia and as far south as the islands of Corsica, Sardinia, and Malta. Some archaeologists have demonstrated that the stone circles were used as observatories to detect not only such simple astronomical phenomena as midwinter and midsummer sunrises, but also such sophisticated phenomena as the major and minor standstills of the moon.

The Impact of the Indo-Europeans

In large part, both the details of construction and the purpose of the megalithic structures of Europe remain a mystery. Also puzzling is the role of the Indo-European

STATUE OF HATSHEPSUT. Wife of Thutmosis II, Hatshepsut served as regent for her stepson Thutmosis III after her husband's death. In 1473 B.C.E., however, she proclaimed herself pharaoh. This red granite statue shows her as a woman, although most official statues portrayed her dressed and bearded like a king.

placed on one of her temples. It read: "Now my heart turns to and fro, in thinking what will the people say, they who shall see my monument in after years, and shall speak of what I have done."

Little is known about marital arrangements and ceremonies, although it does appear that marriages were arranged by parents. The primary concerns were family and property, and clearly the chief purpose of marriage was to produce children, especially sons. From the New Kingdom came this piece of wisdom: "Take to yourself a wife while you are [still] a youth, that she may produce a son for you."[9] Only sons could carry on the family name. Daughters were not slighted, however. Numerous tomb paintings show the close and affectionate relationship parents had with both sons and daughters. Although marriages were arranged, some of the surviving love poems from ancient Egypt suggest that some marriages included an element of romance. Here is the lament of a lovesick

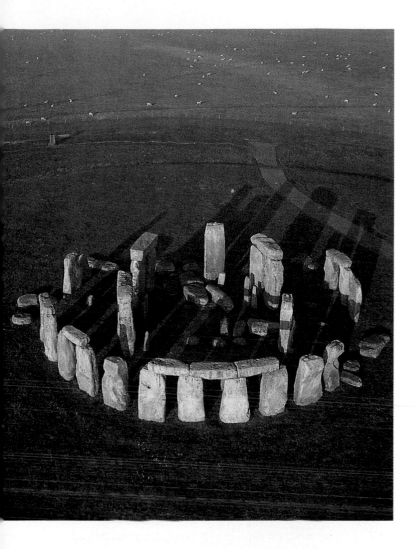

STONEHENGE. By far the most famous megalithic construction, Stonehenge in England, consists of a series of concentric rings of standing stones. Its construction sometime between 2100 and 1900 B.C.E. was no small accomplishment. The eighty bluestones used at Stonehenge weighed four tons each and were transported to the site from their original source, 135 miles away. Like other megalithic structures, Stonehenge indicates a remarkable awareness of astronomy on the part of its builders, as well as an elaborate coordination of workers.

peoples. The term Indo-European refers to people who used a language derived from a single parent tongue. Indo-European languages include Greek, Latin, Persian, Sanskrit, and the Germanic and Slavic languages (see Table 1.2). It has been suggested that the original Indo-European-speaking peoples were based somewhere in the steppe region north of the Black Sea or in southwestern Asia, in modern Iran or Afghanistan. Although there had been earlier migrations, around 2000 B.C.E. the original Indo-European-speaking peoples began major nomadic movements into Europe (including present-day Italy and Greece), India, and western Asia. One group of Indo-Europeans who moved into Asia Minor and Anatolia (modern Turkey) around 1750 B.C.E. coalesced with the native peoples to form the Hittite kingdom, with its capital at Hattusha (Bogazköy in modern Turkey).

Between 1600 and 1200 B.C.E., the Hittites created their own empire in western Asia and even threatened the power of the Egyptians. The Hittites were the first of the Indo-European peoples to make use of iron, enabling them to construct weapons that were stronger and cheaper to make because of the widespread availability of iron ore. But around 1200 B.C.E., new waves of invading Indo-European peoples destroyed the Hittite empire. The destruction of the Hittite kingdom and the weakening of Egypt around 1200 B.C.E. temporarily left no dominant powers in western Asia, allowing a patchwork of petty kingdoms and city-states to emerge, especially in the area of Syria and Palestine. The Phoenicians were one of these peoples.

The Phoenicians

A Semitic-speaking people, the Phoenicians lived in the area of Palestine along the Mediterranean coast on a narrow band of land 120 miles long. Their newfound political independence after the demise of Hittite and Egyptian power helped the Phoenicians expand the trade that was already the foundation of their prosperity. The chief cities

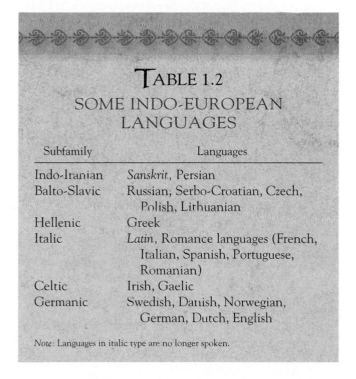

TABLE 1.2
SOME INDO-EUROPEAN LANGUAGES

Subfamily	Languages
Indo-Iranian	*Sanskrit*, Persian
Balto-Slavic	Russian; Serbo-Croatian, Czech, Polish, Lithuanian
Hellenic	Greek
Italic	*Latin*, Romance languages (French, Italian, Spanish, Portuguese, Romanian)
Celtic	Irish, Gaelic
Germanic	Swedish, Danish, Norwegian, German, Dutch, English

Note: Languages in italic type are no longer spoken.

of Phoenicia—Byblos, Tyre, and Sidon—were ports on the eastern Mediterranean, but they also served as distribution centers for the lands to the east in Mesopotamia. The Phoenicians themselves produced a number of goods for foreign markets, including purple dye, glass, wine, and lumber from the famous cedars of Lebanon. In addition, the Phoenicians improved their ships and became great international sea traders. They charted new routes, not only in the Mediterranean, but also in the Atlantic Ocean, where they reached Britain and sailed south along the west coast of Africa. The Phoenicians established a number of colonies in the western Mediterranean, including settlements in southern Spain, Sicily, and Sardinia. Carthage, the Phoenicians' most famous colony, was located on the north coast of Africa.

Culturally, the Phoenicians are best known as transmitters. Instead of using pictographs or signs to represent whole words and syllables (as the Mesopotamians and Egyptians did), the Phoenicians simplified their writing by using twenty-two different signs to represent the sounds of their speech. These twenty-two characters or letters could be used to spell out all the words in the Phoenician language. Although the Phoenicians were not the only people to invent an alphabet, theirs would have special significance because it was eventually passed on to the Greeks. From the Greek alphabet was derived the Roman alphabet that we still use today (see Table 1.3). The Phoenicians achieved much while independent, but they ultimately fell subject to the Assyrians and Persians.

The Hebrews: The "Children of Israel"

To the south of the Phoenicians lived another group of Semitic-speaking people known as the Hebrews. Although they were a minor factor in the politics of the region, their religion—known as Judaism—influenced both Christianity and Islam and flourished as a world religion. The Hebrews had a tradition concerning their origins and history that was eventually written down as part of the Hebrew Bible, known to Christians as the Old Testament. Describing them as a nomadic people, the Hebrews' own tradition states that they were descendants of the patriarch Abraham, who had migrated from Mesopotamia to the land of Palestine, where the Hebrews became identified as the "Children of Israel." Moreover, according to tradition, a drought in Palestine caused many Hebrews to migrate to Egypt, where they lived peacefully until they were enslaved by pharaohs who used them as laborers on their numerous building projects. The Hebrews remained in bondage until Moses led his people out of Egypt in the well-known "exodus," which some historians have argued would have occurred in the first half of the thirteenth century B.C.E. According to the biblical account, the Hebrews then wandered for many years in the desert, until they entered Palestine. Organized into twelve tribes, the Hebrews became embroiled in conflict with the Philistines, a people who

had settled in the coastal area of Palestine but were beginning to move into the inland areas.

Many scholars today doubt that the early books of the Hebrew Bible reflect the true history of the early Israelites. They argue that the early books of the Bible, written centuries after the events described, preserve only what the Israelites came to believe about themselves and that recent archaeological evidence often contradicts the details of the biblical account. Some of these scholars have even argued that the Israelites were not nomadic invaders but indigenous peoples in the Palestinian hill country. What is generally agreed, however, is that between 1200 and 1000 B.C.E., the Israelites emerged as a distinct group of people, possibly organized into tribes or a league of tribes, who established a united kingdom known as Israel.

THE UNITED KINGDOM

The first king of the Israelites was Saul (c. 1020–1000 B.C.E.), who initially achieved some success in the ongoing struggle with the Philistines. But after his death in a disastrous battle with this enemy, a brief period of anarchy ensued, until one of Saul's lieutenants, David (c. 1000–970 B.C.E.), reunited the Israelites, defeated the Philistines, and established control over all of Palestine. Among David's conquests was the city of Jerusalem, which he made into the capital of a united kingdom. David centralized Israel's orga-nization and accelerated the integration of the Israelites into a settled community based on farming and urban life.

David's son Solomon (c. 970–930 B.C.E.) did even more to strengthen royal power. He expanded the political and military establishments and was especially active in extending the trading activities of the Israelites. Solomon is known for his building projects, of which the most famous was the Temple in the city of Jerusalem. The Israelites viewed the Temple as the symbolic center of their religion and hence of the kingdom of Israel itself. The Temple now housed the Ark of the Covenant, the holy chest containing the sacred relics of the Hebrew religion and, symbolically, the throne of the invisible God of Israel. Under Solomon, ancient Israel was at the height of its power, but his efforts to extend royal power throughout his kingdom led to dissatisfaction among some of his subjects.

THE DIVIDED KINGDOM

After Solomon's death, tensions between the northern and southern tribes within Israel led to the establishment of two separate kingdoms—a kingdom of Israel, composed of the ten northern tribes, with its capital eventually at Samaria, and a southern kingdom of Judah, consisting of two tribes, with its capital at Jerusalem. By the end of the ninth century, the independence of the kingdom of Israel was increasingly threatened by the rising power of the Assyrians. In 722 B.C.E., the Assyrians destroyed Samaria,

TABLE 1.3
THE PHOENICIAN, GREEK, AND ROMAN ALPHABETS

PHOENICIAN			GREEK			ROMAN	
Phoenician	Phoenician Name	Modern Symbol	Early Greek	Classical Greek	Greek Name	Early Latin	Classical Latin
𐤀	'aleph	'	Δ	A	alpha	A	A
𐤁	beth	b	B	B	beta		B
𐤂	gimel	g	⅂	Γ	gamma		C
𐤃	daleth	d	Δ	Δ	delta	D	D
𐤄	he	h	E	E	epsilon	E	E
𐤅	waw	w	F		digamma	F	F
							G
𐤆	zayin	z	I	Z	zeta		
𐤇	heth	h	𐤇	H	eta	𐤇	H
𐤈	teth	t	⊗	Θ	theta		
𐤉	yod	y	⟨	I	iota	I	I
𐤊	kaph	k	K	K	kappa	K	K
𐤋	lamed	l	Λ	Λ	lambda		L
𐤌	mem	m	M	M	mu	M	M
𐤍	nun	n	N	N	nu		N
𐤎	samek	s			xi		
𐤏	ayin	'	O	O	omnicron	O	O
𐤐	pe	p	Π	Π	pi		P
𐤑	sade	s	M		saw		
𐤒	qoph	o	Φ		qoppa		Q
𐤓	res	r	P	P	rho		R
𐤔	sin	sh/s	Σ	Σ	sigma	S	S
𐤕	taw	t	X		tau		T
				Y	upsilon	V	V
				X	chi		X
							Y
				Ω	omega		Z

SOURCE: Andrew Robinson, *The Story of Writing* (London, 1995), p. 170.

overran the kingdom of Israel, and deported many Hebrews to other parts of the Assyrian Empire. These dispersed Hebrews (the "ten lost tribes") merged with neighboring peoples and gradually lost their identity.

The southern kingdom of Judah was also forced to pay tribute to Assyria but managed to retain its independence as Assyrian power declined. However, a new enemy appeared on the horizon. The Chaldeans brought the final destruction of Assyria, conquered the kingdom of Judah, and completely destroyed Jerusalem in 586 B.C.E. Many upper-class people from Judah were deported to Babylonia; the memory of their exile is still evoked in the stirring words of Psalm 137:

> By the rivers of Babylon, we sat and wept when we remembered Zion. . . .
> How can we sing the songs of the Lord while in a foreign land?
> If I forget you, O Jerusalem, may my right hand forget its skill.
> May my tongue cling to the roof of my mouth if I do not remember you,
> if I do not consider Jerusalem my highest joy.[11]

But the Babylonian captivity of the people of Judah did not last. A new set of conquerors, the Persians, destroyed the Chaldean kingdom and allowed the people of Judah to return to Jerusalem and rebuild their city and Temple. The revived kingdom of Judah remained under Persian control until the conquests of Alexander the Great in the fourth century B.C.E. The people of Judah survived, eventually becoming known as the Jews and giving their name to Judaism, the religion of Yahweh, the Jewish God.

THE KING OF ISRAEL PAYS TRIBUTE TO THE KING OF ASSYRIA. By the end of the ninth century B.C.E., the kingdom of Israel had been forced to pay tribute to the Assyrian Empire. The Assyrians overran the kingdom in 722 B.C.E. and destroyed the capital city of Samaria. In this scene from a black obelisk, Jehu, king of Israel, is shown paying tribute to the king of Assyria.

THE SPIRITUAL DIMENSIONS OF ISRAEL

The spiritual perspective of the Israelites evolved over a period of time. Early Israelites probably worshiped many gods, including nature spirits dwelling in trees and rocks. For some Israelites, Yahweh was the chief god of Israel, but many, including kings of Israel and Judah, worshiped other gods as well. It was among the Babylonian exiles that Yahweh—the God of Israel—came to be seen as the only God. After the return of these exiles to Judah, their point of view eventually became dominant, which resulted in pure monotheism, or the belief that there is only one God for all peoples, as the major tenet of Judaism.

According to the Jewish conception, there is but one God, whom the Jews called Yahweh. God is the creator of the world and everything in it. Indeed, Yahweh means "he causes to be." To the Jews, the gods of all other peoples were simply idols. The Jewish God ruled the world; he was subject to nothing. All peoples were his servants, whether they knew it or not. This God was also transcendent. He

MAP I.5 Palestine in the First Millennium B.C.E.

- Philistines
- Kingdom of Judah
- Kingdom of Israel
- Phoenicians

CHRONOLOGY

THE ISRAELITES

Israelites	
Saul—First king	c. 1020–1000 B.C.E.
King David	c. 1000–970 B.C.E.
King Solomon	c. 970–930 B.C.E.
Northern kingdom of Israel destroyed by Assyria	722 B.C.E.
Fall of southern kingdom of Judah to Chaldeans; destruction of Jerusalem	586 B.C.E.
Return of exiles to Jerusalem	538 B.C.E.

had created nature but was not in nature. The stars, moon, rivers, wind, and other natural phenomena were not divinities or suffused with divinity, as other peoples of the ancient Near East believed, but God's handiwork. All of God's creations could be admired for their awesome beauty but not worshiped as God.

Nevertheless, this omnipotent creator of the universe was not removed from the life he had created but was a just and good God who expected goodness from his people. If they did not obey his will, they would be punished. But he was also a God of mercy and love: "The Lord is gracious and compassionate, slow to anger and rich in love. The Lord is good to all; he has compassion on all he has made."[12] Despite the powerful dimensions of God as creator and sustainer of the universe, the Jewish message also emphasized that each person could have a personal relationship with this powerful being. As the psalmist sang: "My help comes from the Lord, the Maker of heaven and earth. He will not let your foot slip—he who watches over you will not slumber."[13]

Three aspects of the Jewish religious tradition had special significance: the covenant, the law, and the prophets. The Israelites believed that during the exodus from Egypt, when Moses supposedly led his people out of bondage and into the promised land, a special event occurred that determined the Jewish experience for all time. According to tradition, God entered into a covenant or contract with the tribes of Israel, who believed that Yahweh had spoken to them through Moses (see the box on p. 28). The Israelites promised to obey Yahweh and follow his law. In return, Yahweh promised to take special care of his chosen people, "a peculiar treasure unto me above all people."

This covenant between Yahweh and his chosen people could be fulfilled, however, only through obedience to the law of God. Law became a crucial element of the Jewish world and had a number of different dimensions. In some instances, the law set forth specific requirements, such as payments for offenses. Most important, since the major characteristic of God was his goodness, ethical concerns stood at the center of the law. Sometimes these took the form of specific standards of moral behavior: "You shall not murder. You shall not commit adultery. You shall not steal."[14] But these concerns were also expressed in decrees that regulated the economic, social, and political life of the community since God's laws of morality applied to all areas of life. These laws made no class distinctions and emphasized the protection of the poor, widows, orphans, and slaves.

The prophets were "holy men" who supposedly had special communion with God and felt called upon to serve as his voice to his people. In the ninth century B.C.E., the prophets were particularly vociferous about the tendency of the Israelites to accept other gods, chiefly the fertility and earth gods of other peoples in Palestine. The prophets warned of the terrible retribution that God would exact from the Israelites if they did not keep the covenant to remain faithful to him alone and just in their dealings with one another (see the box on p. 29).

The golden age of prophecy began in the mid-eighth century and continued during the time when the people of Israel and Judah were threatened by Assyrian and Chaldean conquerors. The "men of God" went through the land warning the Israelites that they had failed to keep God's commandments and would be punished for breaking the covenant: "I will punish you for all your iniquities." Amos prophesied the fall of the northern kingdom of Israel to Assyria; twenty years later, Isaiah said the kingdom of Judah too would fall.

Out of the words of the prophets came new concepts that enriched the Jewish tradition, including a notion of universalism and a yearning for social justice. Although their religious practices gave Jews a sense of separateness from other peoples, the prophets transcended this by embracing a concern for all humanity. All nations would someday come to the God of Israel: "all the earth shall worship thee." A universal community of all people under God would someday be established by Israel's efforts. This vision encompassed the elimination of war and the establishment of peace for all the nations of the world. In the words of the prophet Isaiah: "He will judge between the nations and will settle disputes for many people. They will beat their swords into plowshares and their spears into pruning hooks. Nation will not take up sword against nation, nor will they train for war anymore."[15]

The prophets also cried out against social injustice. They condemned the rich for causing the poor to suffer, denounced luxuries as worthless, and threatened Israel with prophecies of dire punishments for these sins. God's command was to live justly, share with one's neighbors, care for the poor and the unfortunate, and act with compassion. When God's command was not followed, the social fabric of the community was threatened. These proclamations

THE COVENANT AND THE LAW:
THE BOOK OF EXODUS

According to the biblical account, it was during the exodus from Egypt that the Israelites supposedly made their covenant with Yahweh. They agreed to obey their God and follow his law. In return, Yahweh promised to take special care of his chosen people. This selection from the book of Exodus describes the making of the covenant and God's commandments to the Hebrews.

EXODUS 19: 1–8

In the third month after the Israelites left Egypt—on the very day—they came to the Desert of Sinai. After they set out from Rephidim, they entered the desert of Sinai, and Israel camped there in the desert in front of the mountain. Then Moses went up to God, and the Lord called to him from the mountain, and said, "This is what you are to say to the house of Jacob and what you are to tell the people of Israel: 'You yourselves have seen what I did to Egypt, and how I carried you on eagles' wings and brought you to myself. Now if you obey me fully and keep my covenant, then out of all nations you will be my treasured possession. Although the whole earth is mine, you will be for me a kingdom of priests and a holy nation.' These are the words you are to speak to the Israelites." So Moses went back and summoned the elders of the people and set before them all the words the Lord had commanded him to speak. The people all responded together, "We will do everything the Lord has said." So Moses brought their answer back to the Lord.

EXODUS 20: 1–3, 7–17

And God spoke all these words, "I am the Lord your God, who brought you out of Egypt, out of the land of slavery. You shall have no other gods before me. . . . You shall not misuse the name of the Lord your God, for the Lord will not hold anyone guiltless who misuses his name. Remember the Sabbath day by keeping it holy. Six days you shall labor and do all your work, but the seventh day is a Sabbath to the Lord your God. On it you shall not do any work, neither you, nor your son or daughter, nor your manservant or maidservant, nor your animals, nor the alien within your gates. For in six days the Lord made the heavens and the earth, the sea, and all that is in them, but he rested on the seventh day. Therefore the Lord blessed the Sabbath day and made it holy. Honor your father and your mother, so that you may live long in the land the Lord your God is giving you. You shall not murder. You shall not commit adultery. You shall not steal. You shall not give false testimony against your neighbor. You shall not covet your neighbor's house. You shall not covet your neighbor's wife, or his manservant or maidservant, his ox or donkey, or anything that belongs to your neighbor."

of Israel's prophets spawned universal ideals of social justice, even if they have never been perfectly realized.

Although the Jewish prophets ultimately developed a sense of universalism, the demands of the Jewish religion (the need to obey their God) eventually encouraged a separation between the Jews and their non-Jewish neighbors. Unlike most other peoples of the Middle East, Jews could not simply be amalgamated into a community by accepting the gods of their conquerors and their neighbors. To remain faithful to the demands of their God, they might even have to refuse loyalty to political leaders.

 THE RISE OF NEW EMPIRES

An independent Israelite state could exist only because there was a power vacuum in western Asia after the destruction of the Hittite kingdom and the weakening of the Egyptian empire. But this condition did not last; new empires soon arose that came to dominate vast stretches of the ancient world.

The Assyrian Empire

The first of these empires was formed in Assyria, located on the upper Tigris River, an area that brought it into both cultural and political contact with Mesopotamia. The Assyrians were a Semitic-speaking people who exploited the use of iron weapons to establish an empire by 700 B.C.E. that included Mesopotamia, parts of the Iranian plateau, sections of Asia Minor, Syria, Palestine, and Egypt down to Thebes. Ashurbanipal (669–626 B.C.E.) was one of the strongest Assyrian rulers, but during his reign it was already becoming apparent that the Assyrian Empire was greatly overextended. Internal strife intensified as powerful Assyrian nobles gained control of vast territories and waged their own private military campaigns. Moreover, subject peoples, such as the Babylonians, greatly resented Assyrian rule and rebelled against it. Soon after Ashurbanipal's reign, the Assyrian Empire began to disintegrate rapidly. The capital city of Nineveh fell to a coalition of Chaldeans and Medes in 612 B.C.E., and in 605 B.C.E., the rest of the empire was finally divided between the coalition powers.

At its height, the Assyrian Empire was ruled by kings whose power was considered absolute. Under their lead-

THE HEBREW PROPHETS:
MICAH, ISAIAH, AND AMOS

The Hebrew prophets warned the Israelites that they must obey God's commandments or face being punished for breaking their covenant with God. These selections from the prophets Micah, Isaiah, and Amos make clear that God's punishment would fall upon the Israelites for their sins. Even the Assyrians, as Isaiah indicated, would be used as God's instrument to punish them.

MICAH 6:9–16

Listen! The Lord is calling to the city—and to fear your name is wisdom—"Heed the rod and the One who appointed it. Am I still to forget, O wicked house, your ill-gotten treasures . . . ? Shall I acquit a man with dishonest scales, with a bag of false weights? Her rich men are violent; her people are liars and their tongues speak deceitfully. Therefore, I have begun to destroy you, to ruin you because of your sins. You will eat but not be satisfied; your stomach will still be empty. You will store up but save nothing, because what you save I will give to the sword. You will plant but not harvest; you will press olives but not use the oil on yourselves, you will crush grapes but not drink the wine. . . . Therefore I will give you over to ruin and your people to derision; you will bear the scorn of the nations."

ISAIAH 10: 1–6

Woe to those who make unjust laws, to those who issue oppressive decrees, to deprive the poor of their rights and withhold justice from the oppressed of my people, making widows their prey and robbing the fatherless. What will you do on the day of reckoning, when disaster comes from afar? To whom will you run for help? Where will you leave your riches? Nothing will remain but to cringe among the captives or fall among the slain. Yet for all this, his anger is not turned away, his hand is still upraised. "Woe to the Assyrian, the rod of my anger, in whose hand is the club of my wrath! I send him against a godless nation, I dispatch him against a people who anger me, to seize loot and snatch plunder, and to trample them down like mud in the streets."

AMOS 3: 1–2

Hear this word the Lord has spoken against you, O people of Israel—against the whole family I brought up out of Egypt: "You only have I chosen of all the families of the earth; therefore I will punish you for all your sins."

---

ership, the Assyrian Empire came to be well organized. By eliminating governorships held by nobles on a hereditary basis and instituting a new hierarchy of local officials directly responsible to the king, the Assyrian kings gained greater control over the resources of the empire. The Assyrians also developed an efficient system of communication to administer their empire more effectively. A network of posting stages was established throughout the empire that used relays of horses (mules or donkeys in mountainous terrain) to carry messages. The system was so effective that a provincial governor anywhere in the empire (except Egypt) could send a question and receive an answer from the king in his palace within a week.

The ability of the Assyrians to conquer and maintain an empire was due to a combination of factors. Over many years of practice, the Assyrians developed effective military leaders and fighters. They were able to enlist and deploy troops numbering in the hundreds of thousands, although most campaigns were not on such a large scale. In 845 B.C.E., an Assyrian army of 120,000 men crossed the Euphrates on a campaign. Size alone was not decisive, however. The Assyrian army was extremely well organized and disciplined. It included a standing army of infantrymen as its core, accompanied by cavalry and horse-drawn war chariots that were used as mobile platforms for shooting arrows. Moreover, the Assyrians had the advantage of having the

first large armies equipped with iron weapons. The Hittites had been the first to develop iron metallurgy, but iron came to be used extensively only after new methods for hardening it became common after 1000 B.C.E.

Another factor in the army's success was its ability to use different kinds of military tactics (see the box on p. 30). The Assyrian army was capable of waging guerrilla warfare in the mountains and set battles on open ground as well as laying siege to cities. The Assyrians were especially renowned for their siege warfare. They would hammer a city's walls with heavy, wheeled siege towers and armored battering rams, while sappers dug tunnels to undermine the walls' foundations and cause them to collapse. The besieging Assyrian armies learned to cut off supplies so effectively that if a city did not fall to them, the inhabitants could be starved into submission.

A final factor in the effectiveness of the Assyrian military machine was its ability to create a climate of terror as an instrument of warfare. The Assyrians became famous for their terror tactics, although some historians believe that their policies were no worse than those of other conquerors. As a matter of regular policy, the Assyrians laid waste the land in which they were fighting, smashing dams, looting and destroying towns, setting crops on fire, and cutting down trees, particularly fruit trees. The Assyrians were especially known for committing atrocities on

THE ASSYRIAN MILITARY MACHINE

The Assyrians achieved a reputation for possessing a mighty military machine. They were able to use a variety of military tactics and were successful whether they were waging guerrilla warfare, fighting set battles, or laying siege to cities. In these three selections, Assyrian kings boast of their military conquests.

KING SENNACHERIB (704–681 B.C.E.)
Describes a Battle with the Elamites in 691

At the command of the god Ashur, the great Lord, I rushed upon the enemy like the approach of a hurricane.... I put them to rout and turned them back. I transfixed the troops of the enemy with javelins and arrows.... I cut their throats like sheep.... My prancing steeds, trained to harness, plunged into their welling blood as into a river; the wheels of my battle chariot were bespattered with blood and filth. I filled the plain with the corpses of their warriors like herbage.... As to the sheikhs of the Chaldeans, panic from my onslaught overwhelmed them like a demon. They abandoned their tents and fled for their lives, crushing the corpses of their troops as they went.... In their terror they passed scalding urine and voided their excrement into their chariots.

KING SENNACHERIB
Describes His Siege of Jerusalem in 701

As to Hezekiah, the Jew, he did not submit to my yoke, I laid siege to 46 of his strong cities, walled forts, and the countless small villages in their vicinity, and conquered them by means of well-stamped earth-ramps, and battering-rams brought thus near to the walls combined with the attack by foot soldiers, using mines, breeches, as well as sapper work. I drove out of them 200,150 people, young and old, male and female, horses, mules, donkeys, camels, big and small cattle beyond counting, and considered them booty. Himself I made a prisoner in Jerusalem, his royal residence, like a bird in a cage. I surrounded him with earthwork in order to molest those who were leaving his city's gate.

KING ASHURBANIPAL (669–626 B.C.E.)
Describes His Treatment of Conquered Babylon

I tore out the tongues of those whose slanderous mouths had uttered blasphemies against my god Ashur and had plotted against me, his god-fearing prince; I defeated them completely. The others, I smashed alive with the very same statues of protective deities with which they had smashed my own grandfather Sennacherib—now finally as a belated burial sacrifice for his soul. I fed their corpses, cut into small pieces, to dogs, pigs, ... vultures, the birds of the sky, and also to the fish of the ocean. After I had performed this and thus made quiet again the hearts of the great gods, my lords, I removed the corpses of those whom the pestilence had felled, whose leftovers after the dogs and pigs had fed on them were obstructing the streets, filling the places of Babylon, and of those who had lost their lives through the terrible famine.

---

their captives. King Ashurnasirpal recorded this account of his treatment of prisoners:

> 3000 of their combat troops I felled with weapons.... Many of the captives taken from them I burned in a fire. Many I took alive; from some of these I cut off their hands to the wrist, from others I cut off their noses, ears and fingers; I put out the eyes of many of the soldiers.... I burned their young men and women to death.

After conquering another city, the same king wrote: "I fixed up a pile of corpses in front of the city's gate. I flayed the nobles, as many as had rebelled, and spread their skins out on the piles.... I flayed many within my land and spread their skins out on the walls."[16] It should be noted that this policy of extreme cruelty to prisoners was not used against all enemies but was primarily reserved for those who were already part of the empire and then rebelled against Assyrian rule.

ASSYRIAN SOCIETY AND CULTURE

Unlike the Hebrews, the Assyrians were not fearful of mixing with other peoples. In fact, Assyrian deportation policies created a polyglot society in which ethnic differences were not very important. What gave identity to the Assyrians themselves was their language, although even that was akin to the language of their southern neighbors in Babylonia, who also spoke a Semitic language. Religion was also a cohesive force. Assyria was literally "the land of Ashur," a reference to its chief god. The king, as the human representative of the god Ashur, provided a final unifying focus.

Agriculture formed the principal basis of Assyrian life. Assyria was a land of farming villages with relatively few significant cities, especially in comparison to Mesopotamia. Unlike Mesopotamia, where farming required the minute organization of large numbers of people to control irrigation, Assyrian farms received sufficient moisture from regular rainfall.

Trade was second to agriculture in economic importance. For internal trade, metals—such as gold, silver, copper, and bronze—were used as a medium of exchange. Various agricultural products also served as a form of payment or exchange. Because of their geographical location, the Assyrians served as intermediaries and participated in an international trade in which they imported timber, wine, and precious metals and stones while exporting textiles produced in palaces, temples, and private workshops.

The culture of the Assyrian Empire was essentially hybrid in nature. The Assyrians assimilated much of Mesopotamian civilization and saw themselves as guardians of Sumerian and Babylonian culture. Ashurbanipal, for example, established a large library at Nineveh that included the available works of Mesopotamian history. Assyrian kings also tried to maintain old traditions when they rebuilt damaged temples by constructing the new buildings on the original foundations, not in new locations. Assyrian religion reflected this assimilation of other cultures as well. Although the Assyrians had their own national god (Ashur) as their chief deity, virtually all of their remaining gods and goddesses were Mesopotamian.

Among the best-known objects of Assyrian art are the relief sculptures found in the royal palaces in three of the Assyrian capital cities, Nimrud, Nineveh, and Khorsabad. These reliefs, which were begun in the ninth century and reached their high point in the reign of Ashurbanipal in the seventh century, depicted two different kinds of subject matter: ritual or ceremonial scenes revolving around the person of the king and scenes of hunting and war. The latter show realistic action scenes of the king and his warriors engaged in battle or hunting animals, especially lions. These pictures depict a strongly masculine world where discipline, brute force, and toughness are the enduring values—indeed, the very values of the Assyrian military monarchy.

The Persian Empire

The Chaldeans, a Semitic-speaking people, had gained ascendancy in Babylonia by the seventh century and came to form the chief resistance to Assyrian control of Mesopotamia. After the collapse of the Assyrian Empire, the Chaldeans, under their king Nebuchadnezzar II (605–562 B.C.E.), restored Babylonia to its position as the leading state in western Asia. Nebuchadnezzar rebuilt Babylon as the center of his empire, giving it a reputation

as one of the great cities of the ancient world. But the splendor of Chaldean Babylonia proved to be short-lived when Babylon fell to the Persians in 539 B.C.E.

The Persians were an Indo-European-speaking people who lived in southwestern Iran and fell subject to the ethnically related Medes. Primarily nomadic, the Persians were organized into tribes or clans led by petty kings assisted by a group of warriors who formed a class of nobles. At the beginning of the seventh century, the Achaemenid dynasty, based in Persis, in southern Iran, managed to unify the Persians. One of the dynasty's members, Cyrus (559–530 B.C.E.), created a powerful Persian state that rearranged the political map of western Asia. In 550 B.C.E., he extended Persian control over the Medes, making Media the first Persian satrapy or province. Three years later, Cyrus defeated the prosperous Lydian kingdom in western Asia Minor, and Lydia became another Persian satrapy. Cyrus's forces then went on to conquer the Greek city-states that had been established on the Ionian coast. Cyrus then turned eastward, subduing the eastern part of the Iranian plateau, Sogdia, and even western India. His eastern frontiers secured, Cyrus entered Mesopotamia in 539 and captured Babylon. His treatment of Babylonia showed remarkable restraint and wisdom. Babylonia was made into a Persian province under a Persian satrap, but many government officials were kept in their positions. Cyrus took the title "King of All, Great King, Mighty King, King of Babylon, King of the Land of Sumer and Akkad, King of the Four Rims (of the Earth), the Son of Cambyses the Great King, King of Anshan"[17] and insisted that he stood in the ancient, unbroken line of Babylonian kings. By appealing to the vanity of the Babylonians, he won their loyalty. Cyrus also issued an edict permitting the Hebrews, who had been brought to Babylon in the sixth century B.C.E., to return to Jerusalem with their sacred temple objects and to rebuild their Temple as well.

To his contemporaries, Cyrus the Great was deserving of his epithet. The Greek historian Herodotus recounted that the Persians viewed him as a "father," a ruler who was "gentle, and procured them all manner of goods."[18] Certainly, Cyrus must have been an unusual ruler for his time,

✿ KING ASHURBANIPAL'S LION HUNT. This relief, sculptured on alabaster as a decoration for the northern palace in Nineveh, depicts King Ashurbanipal engaged in a lion hunt. The relief sculpture, one of the best-known forms of Assyrian art, ironically reached its high point under Ashurbanipal at the same time that the Assyrian Empire began to disintegrate.

a man who demonstrated considerable wisdom and compassion in the conquest and organization of his empire. Cyrus attempted—successfully—to obtain the favor of the priesthoods in his conquered lands by restoring temples and permitting a wide degree of religious toleration. He won approval by using not only Persians, but also native peoples as government officials in their own states. Unlike the Assyrian rulers of an earlier empire, he had a reputation for mercy. Medes, Babylonians, and Hebrews all accepted him as their legitimate ruler. Indeed, the Hebrews regarded him as the anointed one of God: "I am the Lord who says of Cyrus, 'He is my shepherd and will accomplish all that I please'; he will say of Jerusalem, 'Let it be rebuilt'; and of the Temple, 'Let its foundations be laid.' This is what the Lord says to his anointed, to Cyrus, whose right hand I take hold of to subdue nations before him."[19] Cyrus had a genuine respect for ancient civilizations—in building his palaces, he made use of Assyrian, Babylonian, Egyptian, and Lydian practices. Indeed, Cyrus had a sense that he was creating a "world empire" that included peoples who had ancient and venerable traditions and institutions.

Cyrus's successors extended the territory of the Persian Empire. His son Cambyses (530–522 B.C.E.) undertook a successful invasion of Egypt and made it into a satrapy with Memphis as its capital. Darius (521–486 B.C.E.) added a new Persian province in western India that extended to the Indus River and moved into Europe proper, conquering Thrace and making the Macedonian king a vassal. A revolt of the Ionian Greek cities in 499 B.C.E. resulted in temporary freedom for these communities in western Asia Minor. Aid from the Greek mainland, most notably from Athens, encouraged the Ionians to invade Lydia and burn Sardis, center of the Lydian satrap. This event led to Darius's involvement with the mainland Greeks. After reestablishing control of the Ionian Greek cities, Darius undertook an invasion of the Greek mainland, which culminated in the famous Athenian victory in the Battle of Marathon, in 490 B.C.E. (see Chapter 4).

GOVERNING THE EMPIRE

By the reign of Darius, the Persians had created the largest empire the world had yet seen. It not only included all the old centers of power in Egypt and western Asia, but also extended into Thrace and Asia Minor in the west and into India in the east. For administrative purposes, the empire

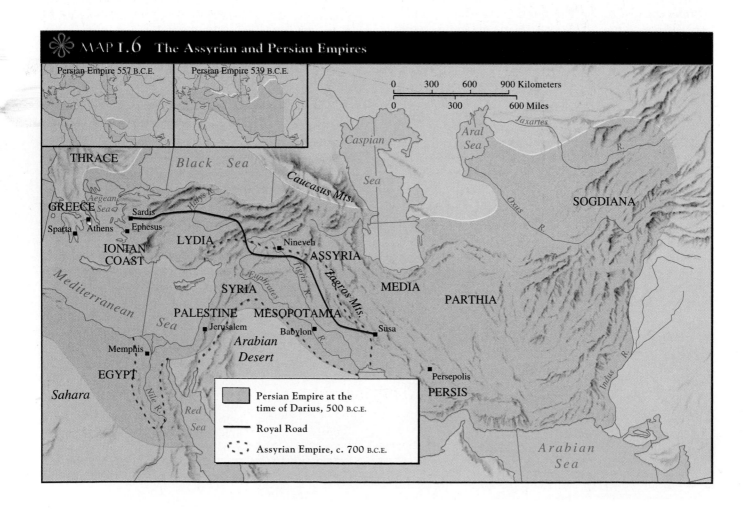

MAP 1.6   The Assyrian and Persian Empires

CHRONOLOGY

THE EMPIRES

The Assyrians	
Height of power	700 B.C.E.
Ashurbanipal	669–626 B.C.E.
Fall of Nineveh	612 B.C.E.
Assyrian Empire destroyed	605 B.C.E.
The Persians	
Unification under Achaemenid dynasty	600s B.C.E.
Persian control over Medes	550 B.C.E.
Conquests of Cyrus the Great	559–530 B.C.E.
Cambyses and conquest of Egypt	530–522 B.C.E.
Reign of Darius	521–486 B.C.E.

had been divided into approximately twenty provinces called satrapies. Each province was ruled by a governor or satrap, literally a "protector of the kingdom." Although Darius had not introduced the system of satrapies, he did see that it was organized more rationally. He created a sensible system for calculating the tribute that each satrapy owed to the central government and gave satraps specific civil and military duties. They collected tributes, were responsible for justice and security, raised military levies for the royal army, and normally commanded the military forces within their satrapies. In terms of real power, the satraps were miniature kings with courts imitative of the Great King's.

From the time of Darius on, satraps were men of Persian descent. The major satrapies were given to princes of the royal family, and their position became essentially hereditary. The minor satrapies were placed in the hands of Persian nobles. Their offices, too, tended to pass from father to son. The hereditary nature of the governors' offices made it necessary to provide some checks to their power. Consequently, royal officials at the satrapal courts acted as spies for the Great King.

An efficient system of communication was crucial to sustaining the Persian Empire. Well-maintained roads facilitated the rapid transit of military and government personnel. One in particular, the so-called Royal Road, stretched from Sardis, the center of Lydia in Asia Minor, to Susa, the chief capital of the Persian Empire. Like the Assyrians, the Persians established staging posts equipped with fresh horses for the king's messengers.

In this vast administrative system, the Persian king occupied an exalted position. Although not considered to be a god in the manner of an Egyptian pharaoh, he was nevertheless the elect one or regent of the Persian god Ahuramazda (see the next section). All subjects were the king's servants, and he was the source of all justice, possessing the power of life and death over everyone. Persian kings were largely secluded and not easily accessible. They resided in a series of splendid palaces. Darius in particular was a palace builder on a grand scale. His description of the construction of a palace in the chief Persian capital of Susa demonstrated what a truly international empire Persia was:

> This is the . . . palace which at Susa I built. From afar its ornamentation was brought. . . . The cedar timber was brought from a mountain named Lebanon; the Assyrians brought it to Babylon, and from Babylon the Carians and Ionians brought it to Susa. Teakwood was brought from Gandara and from Carmania. The gold which was used here was brought from Sardis and from Bactria. The stone—lapis lazuli and carnelian—was brought from Sogdiana. . . . The silver and copper were brought from Egypt. The ornamentation with which the wall was adorned was brought from Ionia. The ivory was brought from Ethiopia, from India, and from Arachosia. The stone pillars were brought from . . . Elam. The artisans who dressed the stone were Ionians and Sardians. The goldsmiths who wrought the gold were Medes and Egyptians. . . . Those who worked the baked brick (with figures) were Babylonians. The men who adorned the wall were Medes and Egyptians. At Susa here a splendid work was ordered; very splendid did it turn out.[20]

But Darius was unhappy with Susa. He did not really consider it his homeland, and it was oppressively hot in the summer months. He built another residence at Persepolis, a new capital located to the east of the old one and at a higher elevation.

The policies of Darius also tended to widen the gap between the king and his subjects. As the Great King himself said of all his subjects: "What was said to them by me, night and day it was done."[21] Over a period of time, the Great Kings in their greed came to hoard immense quantities of gold and silver in the various treasuries located in the capital cities. Both their hoarding of wealth and their later overtaxation of their subjects are considered crucial factors in the ultimate weakening of the Persian Empire.

In its heyday, however, the empire stood supreme, and much of its power depended on the military. By the time of Darius, the Persian monarchs had created a standing army of professional soldiers. This army was truly international in character, composed of contingents from the various peoples who made up the empire. At its core was a cavalry force of 10,000 and an elite infantry force of 10,000 Medes and Persians known as the Immortals because they were never allowed to fall below 10,000 in number. When one was killed, he was immediately replaced. The Persians made effective use of their cavalry, especially for operating behind enemy lines and breaking up lines of communication.

PERSIAN RELIGION

Of all the Persians' cultural contributions, the most original was their religion. The popular religion of the Iranians before the advent of Zoroastrianism in the sixth century focused on the worship of the powers of nature, such as the sun, moon, fire, and winds. Mithras was an especially popular god of light and war who came to be viewed as a sun god. The people worshiped and sacrificed to these powers of nature with the aid of priests, known as Magi.

Zoroaster was a semilegendary figure who, according to Persian tradition, was born in 660 B.C.E. After a period of wandering and solitude, he experienced revelations that caused him to be revered as a prophet of the "true religion." It is difficult to know what Zoroaster's original teachings were since the sacred book of Zoroastrianism, the Zend Avesta, was not written down until the third century C.E. Scholars believe, however, that the earliest section of the Zend Avesta, known as the Yasna, consisting of seventeen hymns or gathas, contains the actual writings of Zoroaster. This enables us to piece together his message.

✤ **ARCHERS OF THE PERSIAN GUARD.** One of the main pillars supporting the Persian Empire was the military. This frieze, composed of enamel brick, depicts members of the famous infantry force known as the Immortals, so called because their number was never allowed to drop below 10,000. Those killed would be replaced immediately. They carry the standard lance and bow and arrow of the infantry.

Zoroaster did not introduce a new god but taught that Ahuramazda, who had long been one of the Iranians' deities, was the only god and that his religion was the only perfect one. Ahuramazda (the "Wise Lord") was the supreme deity who brought all things into being:

This I ask of You, O Ahuramazda; answer me well:
Who at the Creation was the first father of Justice?—
Who assigned their path to the sun and the stars?—
Who decreed the waxing and waning of the moon, if it was
*   not You?— . . .*
Who has fixed the earth below, and the heaven above with its
*   clouds that it might not be moved?—*
Who has appointed the waters and the green things upon the
*   earth?—*
Who has harnessed to the wind and the clouds their
*   steeds?— . . .*
Thus do I strive to recognize in You, O Wise One,
Together with the Holy Spirit, the Creator of all things.[22]

According to Zoroaster, Ahuramazda also possessed abstract qualities or states that all humans should aspire to, such as Good Thought, Right, and Piety. Although Ahuramazda was supreme, he was not unopposed. Right is opposed by the Lie, Truth by Falsehood, Life by Death. At the beginning of the world, the good spirit of Ahuramazda was opposed by the evil spirit (in later Zoroastrianism, the evil spirit is identified with Ahriman). Although it appears that Zoroaster saw it as simply natural that where there is good, there will be evil, later followers had a tendency to make these abstractions concrete and overemphasize the reality of an evil spirit. Humans also played a role in this cosmic struggle between good and evil. Ahuramazda, the creator, gave all humans free will and the power to choose between right and wrong. The good person chooses the right way of Ahuramazda. Zoroaster taught that there would be an end to the struggle between good and evil. Ahuramazda would eventually triumph, and at the last judgment at the end of the world, the final separation of good and evil would occur. Zoroaster also provided for individual judgment. Each soul faced a final evaluation of its actions. If a person had performed good deeds, he or she would achieve paradise, the "House of Song" or the "Kingdom of Good Thought"; if evil deeds, then the soul would be thrown into an abyss, the "House of Worst Thought," where it would experience future ages of darkness, torment, and misery.

The spread of Zoroastrianism was due to its acceptance by the Great Kings of Persia. The inscriptions of Darius make clear that he believed Ahuramazda was the only god. Although Darius himself may have been a monotheist, as the kings and Magi, or priests of Persia, propagated Zoroaster's teachings on Ahuramazda, dramatic changes occurred. Zoroastrianism lost its monotheistic emphasis, and the old nature worship resurfaced. Hence, Persian religion returned to polytheism, with Ahuramazda becoming only the chief of a number of gods of light. Mithras, the sun god, became a helper of Ahuramazda and later, in Roman times, the source of another religion. Persian kings were also very tolerant of other religions, and gods and goddesses of those religions tended to make their way into the Persian pantheon. Moreover, as frequently happens to the ideas of founders of religions, Zoroaster's teachings acquired concrete forms that he had never originally intended. The struggle between good and evil was taken beyond the abstractions of Zoroaster into a strong ethical dualism. The spirit of evil became an actual being, who had to be warded off by the use of spells and incantations. Descriptions of the last judgment came to be filled with minute physical details. Some historians believe that Zoroastrianism, with its emphasis on good and evil, a final judgment, and individual judgment of souls, had an impact on Christianity, a religion that eventually surpassed it in significance.

 # CONCLUSION

The peoples of Mesopotamia and Egypt, like the peoples of India and China, built the first civilizations. They developed cities and struggled with the problems of organized states. They developed writing to keep records and created literature. They constructed monumental architecture to please their gods, symbolize their power, and preserve their culture for all time. They developed new political, military, social, and religious structures to deal with the basic problems of human existence and organization. These first literate civilizations left detailed records that allow us to view how they grappled with three of the fundamental problems that humans have pondered: the nature of human relationships, the nature

of the universe, and the role of divine forces in that cosmos. Although other peoples would provide different answers from those of the Mesopotamians and Egyptians, they posed the questions, gave answers, and wrote them down. Human memory begins with the creation of civilizations.

By the middle of the second millennium B.C.E., much of the creative impulse of the Mesopotamian and Egyptian civilizations was beginning to wane. Around 1200 B.C.E., the decline of the Hittites and Egyptians had created a power vacuum that allowed a number of small states to emerge and flourish temporarily. All of them were eventually overshadowed by the rise of the great empires of the Assyrians and Persians. The Assyrian Empire had been the first to unite almost all of the ancient Middle East. Even larger, however, was the empire of the Great Kings of Persia. Although it owed much to the administrative organization created by the Assyrians, the Persian Empire had its own peculiar strengths. Persian rule was tolerant as well as efficient. Conquered peoples were allowed to keep their own religions, customs, and methods of doing business. The many years of peace that the Persian Empire brought to the Middle East facilitated trade and the general well-being of its peoples. It is no wonder that many peoples expressed their gratitude for being subjects of the Great Kings of Persia. Among these peoples were the Hebrews, who created no empire but nevertheless left an important spiritual legacy. The evolution of Hebrew monotheism created in Judaism one of the world's greatest religions; moreover, Judaism influenced the development of both Christianity and Islam.

The Persians had also extended their empire to the Indus River, which brought them into contact with another river valley civilization that had developed independently of the civilizations in the Middle East and Egypt. It is to India that we must now turn.

3000 B.C.E.	2500 B.C.E.	2000 B.C.E.	1500 B.C.E.	1000 B.C.E.	500 B.C.E.

Emergence of Sumerian city-states

Babylonian kingdom

The Hebrews — Height of Persian power

Emergence of Egyptian civilization — Egypt—Old Kingdom — Egypt—Middle Kingdom — Egypt—New Kingdom

Great Pyramid — Code of Hammurabi — Age of prophets in Israel — Zoroastrianism

CHAPTER NOTES

1. Quoted in Amélie Kuhrt, *The Ancient Near East, c. 3000–330 B.C.* (London, 1995), Vol. 1, p. 68.
2. Quoted in Thorkild Jacobsen, "Mesopotamia," in Henri Frankfort et al., Before Philosophy (Baltimore, 1949), p. 139.
3. James B. Pritchard, Ancient Near Eastern Texts, 3d ed. (Princeton, N.J., 1969), p. 372.
4. Quoted in Milton Covensky, The Ancient Near Eastern Tradition (New York, 1966), p. 51.
5. Quoted in B. G. Trigger, B. J. Kemp, D. O'Connor, and A. B. Lloyd, Ancient Egypt: A Social History (Cambridge, 1983), p. 74.
6. Pritchard, Ancient Near Eastern Texts, p. 34.
7. Ibid., p. 36.
8. Ibid., p. 413.
9. Ibid., p. 420.
10. Quoted in John A. Wilson, The Culture of Ancient Egypt (Chicago, 1956), p. 264.
11. Psalms 137: 1, 4–6.
12. Psalms 145: 8–9.
13. Psalms 121: 2–3.
14. Exodus 20: 13–15.
15. Isaiah 2: 4.
16. Quoted in H. W. F. Saggs, The Might That Was Assyria (London, 1984), pp. 261–62.
17. Quoted in J. M. Cook, The Persian Empire (New York, 1983), p. 32.
18. Herodotus, The Persian Wars, trans. George Rawlinson (New York, 1942), p. 257.
19. Isaiah, 44: 28; 45: 1.
20. Quoted in A. T. Olmstead, History of the Persian Empire (Chicago, 1948), p. 168.
21. Quoted in Cook, The Persian Empire, p. 76.
22. Yasna 44: 3–4, 7, as quoted in A. C. Bouquet, Sacred Books of the World (Harmondsworth, 1954), pp. 111–12.

SUGGESTED READINGS

For a beautifully illustrated introduction to the ancient world, see *Past Worlds: The Times Atlas of Archaeology* (Maplewood, N.J., 1988), written by an international group of scholars. The following works are of considerable value in examining the prehistory of humankind: R. Leakey, *The Making of Mankind* (London, 1981); P. Mellars and C. Stringer, *The Human Revolution* (Edinburgh, 1989); and D. O. Henry, *From Foraging to Agriculture* (Philadelphia, 1989).

A fascinating introduction to the world of ancient Near Eastern studies can be found in W. D. Jones, *Venus and Sothis: How the Ancient Near East Was Rediscovered* (Chicago, 1982). A very competent general survey primarily of the political history of Mesopotamia and Egypt is W. W. Hallo and W. K. Simpson, *The Ancient Near East: A History* (New York, 1971). Also valuable are A. B. Knapp, *The History and Culture of Ancient Western Asia and Egypt* (Chicago, 1987); and W. von Soden, *The Ancient Orient: An Introduction to the Study of the Ancient Near East* (Grand Rapids, Mich., 1994). For a detailed survey, see A. Kuhrt, *The Ancient Near East, c. 3000–330 B.C.*, 2 vols. (London, 1996). H. W. F. Saggs, *Babylonians* (Norman, Okla., 1995) provides an overview of the people of ancient Mesopotamia. On the economic and social history of the ancient Near East, see D. C. Snell, *Life in the Ancient Near East* (New Haven, Conn., 1997). The fundamental collection of translated documents from the ancient Near East is J. B. Pritchard, *Ancient Near Eastern Texts*, 3d ed. with Supplement (Princeton, N.J., 1969).

General works on ancient Mesopotamia include J. N. Postgate, *Early Mesopotamia: Society and Economy at the Dawn of History* (London, 1992); A. L. Oppenheim, *Ancient Mesopotamia*, 2d ed. (Chicago, 1977); and S. Lloyd, *The Archaeology of Mesopotamia*, rev. ed. (London, 1984). A beautifully illustrated survey can be found in M. Roaf, *Cultural Atlas of Mesopotamia and the Ancient Near East* (New York, 1996). The world of the Sumerians has been well described in S. N. Kramer, *The Sumerians* (Chicago, 1963) and *History Begins at Sumer* (New York, 1959). See also the recent summary of the historical and archaeological evidence by H. Crawford, *Sumer and the Sumerians* (Cambridge, 1991). The fundamental work on the spiritual perspective of ancient Mesopotamia is T. Jacobsen, *The Treasures of Darkness: A History of Mesopotamian Religion* (New Haven, Conn., 1976).

For a good introduction to ancient Egypt, see the beautifully illustrated works by J. Baines and J. Málek, *The Cultural Atlas of the World: Ancient Egypt* (Alexandria, Va., 1991); and D. P. Silverman, ed., *Ancient Egypt* (New York, 1997). Other general surveys include N. Grant, *The Egyptians* (New York, 1996); and N. Grimal, *A History of Ancient Egypt*, trans. Ian Shaw (Oxford, 1992). Egyptian religion is covered in S. Morenz, *Egyptian Religion* (London, 1973). The importance of the afterlife in Egyptian civilization is examined in A. Spencer, *Death in Ancient Egypt* (Harmondsworth, 1982). On culture in general, see J. A. Wilson, *The Culture of Ancient Egypt* (Chicago, 1956). The leading authority on the pyramids is I. E. S. Edwards, *The Pyramids of Egypt*, rev. ed. (Harmondsworth, 1976). Daily life in ancient Egypt can be examined in E. Strouhal, *Life of the Ancient Egyptians* (Norman, Okla., 1992). An important new study on women is G. Robins, *Women in Ancient Egypt* (Cambridge, Mass., 1993).

On the Sea Peoples, see the standard work by N. Sanders, *The Sea Peoples: Warriors of the Ancient Mediterranean* (London, 1978). A good introductory survey on the Hittites can be found in O. R. Gurney, *The Hittites*, 2d ed. (Harmondsworth, 1981).

For a good account of Phoenician domestic history and overseas expansion, see D. Harden, *The Phoenicians*, rev. ed. (Harmondsworth, 1980). See also M. E. Aubet, *The Phoenicians and the West: Politics, Colonies and Trade* (Cambridge, 1993). There is an enormous literature on ancient Israel. Two good studies on the archaeological aspects are Y. Aharoni, *The Archaeology of the Land of Israel* (Philadelphia, 1982); and A. Ben-Tor, ed., *The Archaeology of Ancient Israel* (New Haven, 1992). For historical narratives, see especially J. Bright, *A History of Israel*, 3d ed. (Philadelphia, 1981), a fundamental study; the survey by M. Grant, *The History of Ancient Israel* (New York, 1984); and H. Shanks, *Ancient Israel: A Short History from Abraham to the Roman Destruction of the Temple* (Englewood Cliffs, N.J., 1988). For general studies on the religion of the Hebrews, see R. Albertz, *A History of Israelite Religion in the Old Testament Period* (Louisville, Ky., 1994); and W. J. Doorly, *The Religion of Israel* (New York, 1997).

A recent detailed account of Assyrian political, economic, social, military, and cultural history is H. W. F. Saggs, *The Might That Was Assyria* (London, 1984). On one aspect of Assyrian culture, see R. D. Barnett, *Assyrian Sculpture* (Toronto, 1975). The Chaldean empire can be examined in H. W. F. Saggs, *Babylonians* (Norman, Okla., 1995).

The classic work on the Persian Empire is A. T. Olmstead, *History of the Persian Empire* (Chicago, 1948), but a recent work by J. M. Cook, *The Persian Empire* (New York, 1983), provides new material and fresh interpretations on the Persians. Also of value is J. Curtis, *Ancient Persia* (Cambridge, Mass., 1990). On the history of Zoroastrianism, see especially R. C. Zaehner, *The Dawn and Twilight of Zoroastrianism* (London, 1961). Also helpful is M. Boyce, *Zoroastrians: Their Religious Beliefs and Practices* (London, 1979).

INFOTRAC COLLEGE EDITION

For additional reading, go to InfoTrac College Edition, your online research library at http://web1.infotrac-college.com

Enter the search term "Neolithic" using Keywords.

Enter the search term "Mesopotamia" using Keywords.

Enter the search terms "Sumer or Sumerian" using Keywords.

Enter the search term "antiquities" using the Subject Guide.

Enter the search terms "Egypt history" using the Subject Guide.

CHAPTER

2

ANCIENT
INDIA

CHAPTER OUTLINE

- BACKGROUND TO THE EMERGENCE OF CIVILIZATION IN INDIA
- HARAPPAN CIVILIZATION: A FASCINATING ENIGMA
- THE ARRIVAL OF THE ARYANS
- ESCAPING THE WHEEL OF LIFE: THE RELIGIOUS WORLD OF ANCIENT INDIA
- THE RULE OF THE FISHES: INDIA AFTER THE MAURYAS
- THE EXUBERANT WORLD OF INDIAN CULTURE
- CONCLUSION

FOCUS QUESTIONS

- What were the chief features of Harappan civilization, and in what ways was it similar to the civilizations that arose in Egypt and Mesopotamia?
- What effects did the Aryans have on Indian civilization?
- What roles did the caste system and the family play in Indian society?
- What are the main tenets of Hinduism and Buddhism, and how did each religion influence Indian civilization?
- Why was India unable to maintain a unified empire in the first millennium B.C.E., and how was the Mauryan Empire temporarily able to overcome the tendencies toward disunity?

Arjuna was despondent as he prepared for battle. In the opposing army were many of his friends and colleagues, some of whom he had known since childhood. In despair he turned for advice to Krishna, his chariot driver, who, unknown to Arjuna, was in actuality an incarnation of the Indian deity Vishnu. "Do not despair of your duty," Krishna advised his friend.

To be born is certain death,
  to the dead, birth is certain.
It is not right that you should sorrow
  for what cannot be avoided. . . .

If you do not fight this just battle
  you will fail in your own law
and in your honor,
  and you will incur sin.

Krishna's advice to Arjuna is contained in the Bhagavadgita, one of India's most sacred classical writings, and reflects one of the key tenets in Indian philosophy—the belief in reincarnation, or rebirth of the soul. It also points up the importance of doing one's duty without regard for the consequences. Arjuna was a warrior, and according to Aryan tribal tradition, he was obliged to follow the code of his class. "There is more joy in doing one's own duty badly," advised Krishna, "than in doing another man's duty well."

In advising Arjuna to fulfill his obligation as a warrior, the author of the Bhagavadgita, writing around the second century B.C.E. about a battle that took place almost a thousand years earlier, was by implication urging all readers to adhere to their own responsibility as members of one of India's major classes. Henceforth, this hierarchical vision of a society divided into groups, each with clearly distinct roles, would become a defining characteristic of Indian history.

The Bhagavadgita is part of a larger work that deals with the early history of the Aryan peoples who entered India from beyond the mountains north of the Khyber Pass between 1500 and 1000 B.C.E. When the Aryans arrived, India had already had a thriving civilization for almost two thousand years. The Indus valley civilization, although not as well known today as the civilizations of Mesopotamia and Egypt, was just as old; and its political, social, and cultural achievements were equally impressive. That civilization, known to historians by the names of its two major cities, Harappa and Mohenjo-Daro, emerged in the late fourth millennium B.C.E, flourished for over one thousand years, and then came to an abrupt end about 1500 B.C.E. It was soon replaced by a new society dominated by the Aryan peoples. The new civilization that emerged represented a rich mixture of the two cultures—Harappan and Aryan—and evolved over the next three thousand years into what we know today as India.

Thus, India was and still is a land of diversity. This diversity is evident in its languages and cultures as well as in its physical characteristics. India possesses a bewildering array of languages, few of which are mutually intelligible. It has a deserved reputation, along with the Middle East, as a cradle of religion. Two of the world's major religions, Hinduism and Buddhism, originated in India; and a number of others, including Sikhism and Islam (the latter of which entered the South Asian subcontinent in the ninth or tenth century C.E.), continue to flourish there.

Although today this beautiful mosaic of peoples and cultures has been broken up into a number of separate independent states, the region still possesses a coherent history that, despite its internal diversity, is recognizably Indian. It is to the origins and early development of that culture that we now turn. ❁

BACKGROUND TO THE EMERGENCE OF CIVILIZATION IN INDIA

In its size and diversity, India seems more like a continent than a single country. That diversity begins with the geographical environment. The Indian subcontinent, shaped like a spade hanging from the southern ridge of Asia, is composed of a number of core regions. In the far north are the Himalayan and Karakoram mountain ranges, home to the highest mountains in the world. Directly to the south of the Himalayas and the Karakoram range is the rich valley of the Ganges, India's "holy river" and one of the core regions of Indian culture. To the west is the Indus River valley. Today the latter is a relatively arid plateau that forms the backbone of the modern state of Pakistan, but in ancient times it enjoyed a more balanced climate and served as the cradle of Indian civilization.

South of India's two major river valleys lies the Deccan, a region of hills and an upland plateau that extends from the Ganges valley to the southern tip of the Indian subcontinent. The interior of the plateau is relatively hilly and dry, but the eastern and western coasts are occupied by lush plains, which are historically among the most densely populated regions of India. Off the southeastern coast is the island known today as Sri Lanka. Although Sri Lanka is now a separate country quite distinct politically and culturally from India, the island's history is intimately linked with that of its larger neighbor.

In this vast region live a rich mixture of peoples: Dravidians, probably descended from the Indus River culture that flourished at the dawn of Indian civilization, over four thousand years ago; Aryans, descended from the pastoral peoples who flooded southward from Central Asia in the second millennium B.C.E; and hill peoples, who may have lived in the region prior to the rise of organized societies and thus may have been the earliest inhabitants of all.

HARAPPAN CIVILIZATION: A FASCINATING ENIGMA

In the 1920s, archaeologists discovered the existence of agricultural settlements dating back well over six thousand years in the lower reaches of the Indus River valley in modern Pakistan. Those small mudbrick villages eventually gave rise to the sophisticated human communities that historians call Harappan civilization. Although today the area is relatively arid, during the third and fourth millennia B.C.E, it evidently received much more abundant rainfall, and the valleys of the Indus River and its tributaries supported a thriving civilization that extended a distance of several hundred miles, from the Himalayas to the

MAP 2.1 Ancient Harappan Civilization

coast of the Indian Ocean. More than seventy sites have been unearthed since the area was first discovered in the 1850s, but the main sites are at the two major cities, Harappa, in the Punjab, and Mohenjo-Daro, nearly four hundred miles to the south near the mouth of the Indus River.

The origin of the Harappans is still debated, but some scholars have suggested on the basis of ethnographic and linguistic analysis that the language and physical characteristics of the Harappans were similar to those of the Dravidian peoples who live in the Deccan Plateau today. If that is so, Harappa is not simply a dead civilization, whose culture and peoples have disappeared into the sands of history, but a part of the living culture of the Indian subcontinent.

Political and Social Structures

In several respects, Harappan civilization closely resembled the cultures of Mesopotamia and the Nile valley. Like them, it probably began in tiny farming villages scattered throughout the river valley, some dating back to as early as 6500 or 7000 B.C.E. These villages thrived and grew until eventually they could support a privileged ruling elite living in walled cities of considerable magnitude and affluence. The center of power was the city of Harappa, which was surrounded by a brick wall over forty feet thick at its base and more than three and one-half miles in circumference. The city was laid out on an essentially rectangular grid, with some streets as wide as thirty feet. Most buildings were constructed of kiln-dried mudbricks and were square in shape, reflecting the grid pattern. At its height, the city may have had as many as 35,000 inhabitants.

Both Harappa and Mohenjo-Daro were divided into large walled neighborhoods, with narrow lanes separating the rows of houses. Houses varied in size, with some as high as three stories, but all followed the same general plan based on a square courtyard surrounded by rooms. Bathrooms featured an advanced drainage system, which carried wastewater out to drains located under the streets and thence to sewage pits beyond the city walls. But the cities also had the equivalent of the modern slum. At Harappa, tiny dwellings for workers have been found near metal furnaces and the open areas used for pounding grain.

Unfortunately, Harappan writing has not yet been deciphered, so historians know relatively little about the organization of the Harappan state. However, recent archaeological evidence suggests that, unlike its contemporaries in Egypt and Sumer, Harappa was not a centralized monarchy with a theocratic base, but a collection of over 1,500 towns and cities loosely connected by ties of trade and alliance. There was no royal precinct or imposing burial monuments, and there are few surviving stone or terra-cotta images that might represent kings, priests, or military commanders. What was once thought to represent a royal residence at Mohenjo-Daro is now considered to be

MAP **2.2**   The City of Mohenjo-Daro

Priestly residence?

Bath

Stair

Tower

Assembly hall

Fortifications

a Buddhist stupa built at the site centuries later. There are clear signs, however, that religious belief had advanced beyond the stage of spirit worship to belief in a single god or goddess of fertility. Presumably, priests at court prayed to this deity to maintain the fertility of the soil and guarantee the annual harvest. At Mohenjo-Daro archaeologists have found an oblong bathing pool, surrounded by a cloister, that was apparently used for purification ceremonies like the tank in a modern Hindu temple.

As in Mesopotamia and Egypt, the Harappan economy was based primarily on agriculture. Wheat, barley, and peas were apparently the primary crops. The presence of cotton seeds at various sites suggests that the Harappan peoples may have been the first to master the cultivation of this useful crop and possibly introduced it to other societies in the region. But Harappa also developed an extensive trading network that extended to Sumer and other civilizations to the west. Textiles and foodstuffs were apparently imported from Sumer in exchange for metals such as copper, lumber, precious stones, and various types of luxury goods. Much of this trade was conducted by ship via the Persian Gulf, although some undoubtedly went by land.

Harappan Culture

Archaeological remains indicate that the Indus valley peoples possessed a culture as sophisticated as that of the Sumerians to the west. Although Harappan architecture was purely functional and shows little artistic sensitivity, the aesthetic quality of some of the pottery and sculpture is superb. Harappan painted pottery, wheel-turned and kiln-fired, rivals equivalent work produced elsewhere. Sculpture, however, represents the Harappans' highest artistic achievement. Some artifacts possess a wonderful vitality of expression. Fired clay seals show a deft touch in

THE CITY OF THE DEAD.

Mohenjo-Daro was one of the two major cities of the ancient Indus River civilization. In addition to rows on rows of residential housing, it had a ceremonial center, with a royal palace and a sacred bath that was probably used by the priests as a means of achieving ritual purity. The bath is shown in the center of the photograph here, with the remnants of a Buddhist stupa, constructed centuries later, on the right.

✿ HARAPPAN SEALS.   The Harappan peoples, like their contemporaries in Mesopotamia, developed a writing system to record their spoken language. Unfortunately, it has not yet been deciphered. Most extant examples of Harappan writing are found on fired clay seals depicting human figures and animals. These seals have been found in houses and were probably used to identify the owners of goods for sale. Other seals may have been used as amulets or have had other religious significance. Several depict religious figures or ritualistic scenes of sacrifice.

carving animals such as elephants, tigers, rhinoceros, and antelope, and figures made of copper or terra-cotta show a lively sensitivity and a sense of grace and movement that is almost modern.

Unfortunately, the only surviving examples of Harappan writing are the pictographic symbols inscribed on the clay seals. The script contained more than four hundred characters, but most are too stylized to be identified by their shape, and scholars have thus far been unable to decipher them. There are no apparent links with Mesopotamian scripts. Until the script is deciphered, much about the Harappan civilization must remain, as one historian termed it, a fascinating enigma.

✿ THE ARRIVAL OF THE ARYANS

One of the great mysteries of Harappan civilization is how it came to an end. Archaeologists working at Mohenjo-Daro have discovered signs of first a gradual decay and then a sudden destruction of the city and its inhabitants, sometime around 1500 B.C.E. Many of the surviving skeletons have been found in postures of running or hiding, reminiscent of the ruins of the Roman city of Pompeii, destroyed by the eruption of Mount Vesuvius in 79 C.E.

These tantalizing signs of flight before a sudden catastrophe have led some scholars to surmise that the city of Mohenjo-Daro (the name was applied by archaeologists and means "city of the dead") and perhaps the remnants of Harappan civilization were destroyed by the Aryans, nomadic peoples from the north, who arrived in the subcontinent around the middle of the second millennium

B.C.E. Although the Aryans were almost certainly not as sophisticated culturally as the Harappans, like many nomadic peoples, they excelled at the art of war. As in Mesopotamia and the Nile valley, most contacts between pastoral and agricultural peoples proved to be unstable and ended in armed conflict. Nevertheless, it is doubtful that the Aryan invaders were directly responsible for the final destruction of Mohenjo-Daro. More likely, Harappan civilization had already fallen on hard times, perhaps as a result of climatic change in the Indus valley. Archaeologists have found clear signs of social decay, including evidence of trash in the streets, neglect of public services, and overcrowding in urban neighborhoods. Mohenjo-Daro itself may have been destroyed by an epidemic or by natural phenomena such as floods, an earthquake, or a shift in the course of the Indus River. If that was the case, the Aryans conquered a people whose moment of greatness had already passed.

The Early Aryans

Historians know relatively little about the origins and culture of the Aryans before they entered India, although they were part of the extensive group of Indo-European-speaking peoples who inhabited vast areas in what is now Siberia and the steppes of Central Asia. Whereas other Indo-European-speaking peoples moved westward and eventually settled in Europe, the Aryans moved south across the Hindu Kush into the plains of northern India. Between 1500 and 1000 B.C.E., they gradually advanced eastward from the Indus valley, across the fertile plain of the Ganges, and later southward into the Deccan Plateau until they had eventually extended their political mastery over the entire subcontinent and its Dravidian inhabitants. Nevertheless, the Dravidians survived to remain a prominent element in traditional Indian civilization and play a key role in the creation of modern Indian society.

After they settled in India, the Aryans gradually adapted to the geographical realities of their new homeland and abandoned the pastoral life for agricultural pursuits. They were assisted by the introduction of iron, which probably came from the Middle East, where it had first been introduced by the Hittites (see Chapter 1) about 1500 B.C.E. The invention of the iron plow, along with the development of irrigation, allowed the Aryans and their indigenous subjects to clear the dense jungle growth along the Ganges River and transform the Ganges valley into one of the richest agricultural regions in all of South Asia. The Aryans also developed their first writing system and were thus able to transcribe the legends that previously had been passed down from generation to generation by memory. Most of what is known about the early Aryans is based on oral traditions passed on in the Rigveda, an ancient work that was written down after the Aryans arrived in India (the Rigveda is one of several Vedas, or collections of sacred instructions and rituals).

As in other Indo-European societies, each of the various groups of Aryans were led by a tribal chieftain, called a *raja* ("prince"). The chief was assisted by a council of elders composed of other leading members of the tribe, and like them, he was normally a member of the warrior class, called the *kshatriya*. The chief derived his power from his ability to protect his tribe from rival groups, an ability that was crucial in the warring kingdoms and shifting tribal alliances that were typical of early Aryan society. Though the *rajas* claimed to be representatives of the gods, they were not gods themselves.

As Aryan society grew in size and complexity, the chieftains began to be transformed into kings, usually called *maharajas* ("great princes"). Nevertheless, the tradition that the ruler did not possess absolute authority remained strong. Like all human beings, the ruler was required to follow the *dharma*, a set of laws that set behavioral standards for all individuals and classes in Indian society (see the box on p. 44).

While warring groups squabbled for precedence in India, powerful new empires were rising to the west. First came the Persian Empire of Cyrus and Darius. Then came the Greeks. After two centuries of sporadic rivalry and warfare, the Greeks achieved a brief period of regional dominance in the late fourth century B.C.E. with the rise of Macedonia under Alexander the Great. Alexander had heard of the riches of India, and in 330 B.C.E., after conquering Persia, he launched an invasion of the east (see Chapter 4). In 326 his armies arrived in the plains of northwestern India. They departed almost as suddenly as they had come, leaving in their wake Greek administrators and a veneer of cultural influence that would affect the area for generations to come.

The Mauryan Empire

The Alexandrian conquest was only a brief interlude in the history of the Indian subcontinent, but it played a formative role, for on the heels of Alexander's departure came the rise of the first dynasty to control much of the region. The founder of the new state, who took the royal title Chandragupta Maurya (324–301 B.C.E.), drove out the Greek occupation forces after the departure of Alexander and solidified his control over the northern Indian plain. He established the capital of his new Mauryan Empire at Pataliputra (modern Patna) in the Ganges valley (see the map on p. 54). Little is known of his origins, although some sources say he had originally fought on the side of the invading Greek forces but then angered Alexander with his outspoken advice. Other sources say he may have been the illegitimate son of an Indian king, whom he overthrew to form his own dynasty.

Little, too, is known of Chandragupta Maurya's empire. Most accounts of his reign rely on a work (no longer existing) by Megasthenes, a Greek ambassador to the Mauryan court at Pataliputra in about 302 B.C.E. Chandragupta

Maurya was apparently advised by a brilliant court official named Kautilya, whose name has been attached to a treatise on politics called the *Arthasastra*. The work actually dates from a later time, but it may well reflect Kautilya's ideas.

Although the author of the *Arthasastra* follows Aryan tradition in stating that the happiness of the king lies in the happiness of his subjects, the treatise also asserts that when the sacred law of the *dharma* and practical politics collide, the latter must take precedence:

> Whenever there is disagreement between history and sacred law or between evidence and sacred law, then the matter should be settled in accordance with sacred law. But whenever sacred law is in conflict with rational law, then reason shall be held authoritative.[1]

The *Arthasastra* also emphasizes ends rather than means, achieved results rather than the methods employed. For this reason, it has often been compared to the famous political treatise of the Italian Renaissance, Machiavelli's *The Prince,* written over a thousand years later.

✿ NAKED DANCER.   Relatively little remains to indicate the creative talents of the Harappan peoples. This five-inch bronze figure of a young dancer in repose is one of the few surviving metal sculptures from Mohenjo-Daro. The detail and grace of her stance reflect the skill of the artist who molded her four thousand years ago.

THE DUTIES OF A KING

Kautilya, India's earliest known political philosopher, was an adviser to the Mauryan rulers. The Arthasastra, though written down at a later date, very likely reflects his ideas. This passage sets forth some of the necessary characteristics of a king, including efficiency, diligence, energy, compassion, and concern for the security and welfare of the state.

THE ARTHASASTRA

Only if a king is himself energetically active do his officers follow him energetically. If he is sluggish, they too remain sluggish. And, besides, they eat up his works. He is thereby easily overpowered by his enemies. Therefore, he should ever dedicate himself energetically to activity. . . .

A king should attend to all urgent business; he should not put it off. For what has been thus put off becomes either difficult or altogether impossible to accomplish.

The vow of the king is energetic activity; his sacrifice is constituted of the discharge of his own administrative duties; his sacrificial fee [to the officiating priests] is his impartiality of attitude toward all; his sacrificial consecration is his anointment as king.

In the happiness of the subjects lies the happiness of the king; in their welfare, his own welfare. The welfare of the king does not lie in the fulfillment of what is dear to him; whatever is dear to the subjects constitutes his welfare.

Therefore, ever energetic, a king should act up to the precepts of the science of material gain. Energetic activity is the source of material gain; its opposite, of downfall.

In the absence of energetic activity, the loss of what has already been obtained and of what still remains to be obtained is certain. The fruit of one's works is achieved through energetic activity—one obtains abundance of material prosperity.

At least as described in the *Arthasastra*, Chandragupta Maurya's government was highly centralized and even despotic: "It is power and power alone which, only when exercised by the king with impartiality, and in proportion to guilt, over his son or his enemy, maintains both this world and the next."[2] The king possessed a large army and a secret police responsible to his orders (according to the Greek ambassador Megasthenes, Chandragupta Maurya was chronically fearful of assassination, a not unrealistic concern for someone who had allegedly come to power by violence). Reportedly, all food was tasted in his presence, and he made a practice of never sleeping twice in the same bed in his sumptuous palace. To guard against corruption, a board of censors was empowered to investigate cases of possible malfeasance and incompetence within the bureaucracy.

The ruler's authority beyond the confines of the capital may often have been limited, however. The empire was divided into provinces that were ruled by governors. At first, most of these governors were appointed by and reported to the ruler, but later the position became hereditary. The provinces themselves were divided into districts, each under a chief magistrate appointed by the governor. At the base of the government pyramid was the village, where the vast majority of the Indian people lived. The village was governed by a council of elders; membership in the council was normally hereditary and was shared by the wealthiest families in the village.

Caste and Class: Social Structures in Ancient India

When the Aryans arrived in India, they already possessed a strong class system based on a ruling warrior class. They apparently held the indigenous peoples in some contempt and assigned them to a lower position in society. The result was a set of social institutions and class divisions that have persisted with only minor changes down to the present day.

THE CASTE SYSTEM

At the base of the social system that emerged from the clash of cultures was the concept of the superiority of the invading peoples over their conquered subjects. In a sense, it became an issue of color, because the Aryan invaders, a primarily light-skinned people, were contemptuous of their subjects, who were dark. Light skin came to imply high status, whereas dark skin suggested the opposite.

The concept of color, however, was only the physical manifestation of a division that took place in Indian society on the basis of economic functions. Indian classes (called *varna*, literally, "color," and commonly known as "castes" in English) did not simply reflect an informal division of labor. Instead, they were a set of rigid social classifications that determined not only one's occupation, but also one's status in society and one's hope for ultimate salvation (see Escaping the Wheel of Life later in this chapter). There were five major castes in Indian society in ancient times. At the top were two castes, collectively viewed as the aristocracy, which clearly represented the ruling elites in Aryan society prior to their arrival in India: the priests and the warriors.

The priestly caste, known as the *brahmins*, was usually considered to be at the top of the social scale. Descended from a class of seers who had advised the ruler on religious matters in Aryan tribal society (*brahmin* meant "one possessed of *Brahman*," a term for the supreme god in the Hindu religion), they were eventually transformed into an official class after their religious role declined in importance. The Greek ambassador Megasthenes described this caste as follows:

> From the time of their conception in the womb they are under the care and guardianship of learned men who go to the mother and . . . give her prudent hints and counsels, and the women who listen to them most willingly are thought to be the most fortunate in their offspring. After their birth the children are in the care of one person after another, and as they advance in years their masters are men of superior accomplishments. The philosophers reside in a grove in front of the city within a moderate-sized enclosure. They live in a simple style and lie on pallets of straw and [deer] skins. They abstain from animal food and sexual pleasures, and occupy their time in listening to serious discourse and in imparting knowledge to willing ears.[3]

The second caste was the *kshatriya,* or the warriors. Although often listed below the *brahmins* in social status, many *kshatriyas* were probably descended from the ruling warrior class in Aryan society prior to the conquest of India and thus may have originally ranked socially above the *brahmins,* although they were ranked lower in religious terms. Like the *brahmins,* the *kshatriyas* were originally identified with a single occupation—that of fighting—but as the character of Aryan society changed, they often switched to other forms of employment. At the same time, new conquering families from other castes were sometimes tacitly accepted into the ranks of the warriors.

The third-ranked caste in Indian society was the *vaisya* (literally, "commoner"). The *vaisyas* were usually viewed in economic terms as the merchant caste. Some historians have speculated that the *vaisyas* were originally guardians of the tribal herds, but that after settling in India many moved into commercial pursuits. The Greek observer Megasthenes noted that members of this caste "alone are permitted to hunt and keep cattle and to sell beasts of burden or to let them out on hire. In return for clearing the land of wild beasts and birds which infest sown fields, they receive an allowance of corn from the king. They lead a wandering life and dwell in tents."[4] Although this caste was ranked below the first two in social status, it shared with them the privilege of being considered "twice-born," a term referring to a ceremony at puberty whereby young males were initiated into adulthood and introduced into Indian society. After the ceremony, male members of the top three castes were allowed to wear the "sacred thread" for the remainder of their lives.

Below the three "twice-born" castes were the *sudras,* who represented the great bulk of the Indian population. The *sudras* were not considered fully Aryan, and the term probably originally referred to the conquered Dravidian population. Most *sudras* were peasants or artisans or worked at other forms of manual labor. They had only limited rights in society (see the box on p. 46).

At the lowest level of Indian society, and in fact not even considered a legitimate part of the caste system itself, were the untouchables (also known as outcastes, or *pari-*

ahs). The untouchables probably originated as a slave class consisting of prisoners of war, criminals, tribal minorities, and other groups considered outside Indian society. Even after slavery was outlawed, the untouchables were given menial and degrading tasks that other Indians would not accept, such as collecting trash, handling dead bodies, or serving as butchers or tanners (i.e., handling dead meat). According to the estimate of one historian, they may have comprised somewhat more than 5 percent of the total population of India in antiquity.

The life of the untouchables was extremely demeaning. They were not considered human, and their very presence was considered polluting to members of the other *varna.* No Indian would touch or eat food handled or prepared by an untouchable. Untouchables lived in special ghettos and were required to tap two sticks together to announce their presence when they traveled outside their quarters, so that others could avoid them.

Technically, the caste divisions were absolute. Individuals supposedly were born, lived, and died in the same caste. In practice, some upward or downward mobility probably took place in early times, and as time went on, there was undoubtedly some flexibility in economic functions. But throughout most of Indian history caste taboos remained strict. Members were generally not permitted to marry outside their caste (although, in practice, men were occasionally allowed to marry below their caste, but not above it). At first, attitudes toward the handling of food were relatively loose, but eventually that taboo grew stronger, and social mores dictated that sharing meals and marrying outside one's caste were unacceptable.

The people of ancient India did not belong to a particular caste as individuals, but as part of a larger kin group commonly referred to as the *jati,* a system of large extended families that originated in ancient India and still exists in somewhat changed form today. Although the origins of the *jati* system are unknown, the *jati* eventually became identified with a specific caste living in a specific area and carrying out a specific function in society. Each caste was divided into thousands of separate *jatis,* each with its own separate economic function.

Caste was thus the basic social organization into which traditional Indian society was divided. Each *jati* was itself composed of hundreds if not thousands of individual nuclear families and was governed by its own council of elders. Membership in this ruling council was usually hereditary and was based on the wealth or social status of particular families within the community.

In theory, each *jati* was assigned a particular form of economic activity. Obviously, though, not all families in a given caste could take part in the same vocation, and as time went on, members of a single *jati* commonly engaged in several different lines of work. Sometimes an entire *jati* would have to move its location in order to continue a particular form of activity. In other cases, a *jati* would adopt an entirely new occupation in order to remain in a certain

SOCIAL CLASSES IN ANCIENT INDIA

The Law of Manu is a set of behavioral norms allegedly prescribed by India's mythical founding ruler Manu. The treatise was probably written in the first or second century B.C.E. The following excerpt describes the various social classes in India and their prescribed duties.

THE LAW OF MANU

For the sake of the preservation of this entire creation, the Exceedingly Resplendent One [the Creator of the Universe] assigned separate duties to the classes which had sprung from his mouth, arms, thighs, and feet.

Teaching, studying, performing sacrificial rites, so too making others perform sacrificial rites, and giving away and receiving gifts—these he assigned to the [brahmins].

Protection of the people, giving away of wealth, performance of sacrificial rites, study, and nonattachment to sensual pleasures—these are, in short, the duties of a kshatriya.

Tending of cattle, giving away of wealth, performance of sacrificial rites, study, trade and commerce, usury, and agriculture—these are the occupations of a vaisya.

The Lord has prescribed only one occupation [karma] for a sudra, namely, service without malice of even these other three classes.

Of created beings, those which are animate are the best; of the animate, those which subsist by means of their intellect; of the intelligent, men are the best; and of men, the [brahmins] are traditionally declared to be the best.

The code of conduct—prescribed by scriptures and ordained by sacred tradition—constitutes the highest dharma; hence a twice-born person, conscious of his own Self [seeking spiritual salvation], should be always scrupulous in respect of it.

---

area. Such changes in habitat or occupation introduced the possibility of movement up or down the social scale. In this way, an entire *jati* could sometimes engage in upward mobility, even though it was not possible for individuals, who were tied to their caste identity for life, to do so.

The caste system may sound highly constricting, but there were persuasive social and economic reasons why it survived for so many centuries. In the first place, it provided an identity for individuals in a highly hierarchical society. Although an individual might rank lower on the social scale than members of other castes, it was always possible to find others ranked at a lower level. Caste was also a means for new groups, such as mountain tribal people, to achieve a recognizable place in the broader community. Perhaps equally important, caste was a primitive form of welfare system. Each *jati* was obliged to provide for any of its members who were poor or destitute. Caste also provided an element of stability in a society that, all too often, was in a state of political anarchy.

DAILY LIFE IN ANCIENT INDIA

Beyond these rigid social stratifications was the Indian family. Not only was life centered around the family, but the family, not the individual, was the most basic unit in society. The ideal was an extended family, with three generations living under the same roof. It was essentially patriarchal, except along the Malabar coast, near the southwestern tip of the subcontinent, where a matriarchal form of social organization prevailed down to modern times. In the rest of India, the oldest male traditionally possessed legal authority over the entire family unit.

The family was linked together in a religious sense by a series of commemorative rites to ancestral members. This ritual originated in the Vedic era and consisted of family ceremonies to honor the departed and to link the living and the dead. The male family head was responsible for leading the ritual. At his death, his eldest son had the duty of conducting the funeral rites.

The importance of the father and the son in family ritual underlined the importance of males in Indian society. Male superiority was expressed in a variety of ways. Women could not serve as priests (although, in practice, some were accepted as seers), nor were they normally permitted to study the Vedas. In general, males had a monopoly on education, since the primary goal of learning to read was to carry on family rituals. In high-class families, young men, after having been initiated into the sacred thread, began Vedic studies with a *guru* (teacher). Some then went on to higher studies in one of the major cities. The goal of such an education might be either professional or religious. Such young men were not supposed to marry until after twelve years of study.

In general, only males could inherit property, except in a few cases where there were no sons. According to law, a woman was always considered a minor. Divorce was prohibited, although it sometimes took place. According to the *Arthasastra*, a wife who had been deserted by her husband could seek a divorce. Polygamy was fairly rare and apparently occurred mainly among the higher classes, but husbands were permitted to take a second wife if the first was barren. Producing children was an important aspect of marriage, both because they provided security for their parents in old age and because they were a physical proof of male potency. Child marriage was common for young girls, whether because of the desire for children or because daughters represented an economic liability to their parents. But perhaps the most graphic symbol of women's subjection to men was the ritual of *sati* (often written *suttee*), which required the wife to throw herself on her dead husband's funeral pyre. The Greek visitor Megasthenes reported "that he had heard from some persons of wives burning themselves along with their deceased husbands and doing so gladly; and that those women who refused to burn themselves were held in disgrace." All in all, it was undoubtedly a difficult existence. According to the *Law of Manu*, an early treatise on social organization and behavior in ancient India, probably written in the first or second century B.C.E., women were subordinated to men, first to their father, then to their husband, and finally to their sons:

> She should do nothing independently
>   even in her own house.
> In childhood subject to her father,
>   in youth to her husband,
> and when her husband is dead to her sons,
>   she should never enjoy independence. . . .
>
> She should always be cheerful,
>   and skillful in her domestic duties,
> with her household vessels well cleansed,
>   and her hand tight on the purse strings. . . .
>
> In season and out of season
>   her lord, who wed her with sacred rites,
> ever gives happiness to his wife,
>   both here and in the other world.
>
> Though he be uncouth and prone to pleasure,
>   though he have no good points at all,
> the virtuous wife should ever
>   worship her lord as a god.[5]

At the root of female subordination to the male was the practical fact that, as in most agricultural societies, men did most of the work in the fields. Females were viewed as having little utility outside the home and indeed were considered an economic burden, since parents were obliged to provide a dowry to acquire a husband for a daughter. Female children also appeared to offer little advantage in maintaining the family unit, since they joined the families of their husbands after the wedding ceremony.

Despite all of these indications of female subjection to the male, there are numerous signs that in some ways, women often played an influential role in Indian society, and the Hindu code of behavior stressed that they should be treated with respect (see the box on p. 48). Indians appeared to be fascinated by female sexuality, and tradition held that women often used their sexual powers to achieve domination over men. The author of the Mahabharata, a vast epic of early Indian society, complained that "the fire has never too many logs, the ocean never too many rivers, death never too many living souls, and fair-eyed woman never too many men." Despite the legal and social constraints, women often played an important role within the family unit, and many were admired and honored for their

talents. It is probably significant that paintings and sculpture from ancient and medieval India frequently show women in a role equal to that of men, and the tradition of the henpecked husband is as prevalent in India as in many Western societies (see the box on p. 49).

Homosexuality was not unknown in India. It was condemned in the law books, however, and generally ignored by literature, which devoted its attention entirely to erotic heterosexuality. The *Kamasutra*, a textbook on sexual practices and techniques dating from the second century C.E. or slightly thereafter, mentions homosexuality briefly and with no apparent enthusiasm.

The Economy

The Aryan conquest did not drastically change the economic character of Indian society. Not only did most Aryans take up farming, but it is likely that agriculture expanded rapidly under Aryan rule with the invention of the iron plow and the spread of northern Indian culture into the Deccan Plateau. One consequence of this process was to shift the focus of Indian culture from the Indus valley further eastward to the Ganges River valley, which even today is one of the most densely populated regions on earth. The flatter areas in the Deccan Plateau and in the coastal plains were also turned into cropland.

For most Indian farmers, life was harsh indeed. Among the most fortunate were those who owned their own land, although they were, of course, required to pay taxes to the state. Many others were sharecroppers or landless laborers. They were subject to the vicissitudes of the market and often paid exorbitant rents to their landlord. Concentration of land in large holdings was limited by the tradition of dividing property among all the sons, but large estates worked by hired laborers or rented out to sharecroppers were not uncommon, particularly in areas where local *rajas* derived much of their wealth from their property.

Another problem for Indian farmers was the unpredictability of the climate. India is in the monsoon zone. The monsoon is a seasonal wind pattern in southern Asia that blows from the southwest during the summer months and from the northeast during the winter. The southwest monsoon is commonly marked by heavy rains. When the rains were late, thousands starved, particularly in the drier areas, which were especially dependent on rainfall. Strong governments attempted to deal with such problems by building state-operated granaries and maintaining the irrigation works, but strong governments were rare and famine was probably all too common. The staple crops in the north were wheat, barley, and millet, with wet rice common in the fertile river valleys. In the south, grain and vegetables were supplemented by various tropical products, cotton, and spices such as pepper, ginger, cinnamon, and saffron.

By no means were all Indians farmers. As time passed, India became one of the most advanced trading and manufacturing civilizations in the ancient world. After the rise

THE POSITION OF WOMEN IN ANCIENT INDIA

The ambivalence toward women in ancient India is apparent in this passage from the Law of Manu, which states that men should respect women. At the same time, it also makes clear that women's place is in the home. Legal and religious texts delineated the prescribed conduct of women from birth to death, with precise formulae for healing, safe birth, how to love a man, even the ritual for celebrating a baby's first tooth.

THE LAW OF MANU

Women must be honored and adorned by their father, brothers, husbands, and brothers-in-law who desire great good fortune.

Where women, verily, are honored, there the gods rejoice; where, however, they are not honored, there all sacred rites prove fruitless.

Where the female relations live in grief—that family soon perishes completely; where, however, they do not suffer from any grievance—that family always prospers. . . .

Her father protects her in childhood, her husband protects her in youth, her sons protect her in old age—a woman does not deserve independence.

The father who does not give away his daughter in marriage at the proper time is censurable; censurable is the husband who does not approach his wife in due season; and after the husband is dead, the son, verily, is censurable, who does not protect his mother.

Even against the slightest provocations should women be particularly guarded; for unguarded they would bring grief to both the families.

Regarding this as the highest dharma of all four classes, husbands, though weak, must strive to protect their wives.

His own offspring, character, family, self, and dharma does one protect when he protects his wife scrupulously. . . .

The husband should engage his wife in the collection and expenditure of his wealth, in cleanliness, in dharma, in cooking food for the family, and in looking after the necessities of the household. . . .

Women destined to bear children, enjoying great good fortune, deserving of worship, the resplendent lights of homes on the one hand and divinities of good luck who reside in the houses on the other—between these there is no difference whatsoever.

---

of the Mauryas, India's role in regional trade began to expand, and the subcontinent became a major transit point in a vast commercial network that extended from the rim of the Pacific to the Middle East and the Mediterranean Sea. This regional trade went both by sea and by camel caravan. Maritime trade across the Indian Ocean may have begun as early as the fifth century B.C.E. It extended eastward as far as Southeast Asia and China and southward as far as the straits between Africa and the island of Madagascar. Westward went spices, perfumes, jewels, textiles, precious stones and ivory, and wild animals. In return, India received gold, tin, lead, and wine.

India's expanding role as a manufacturing and commercial hub of the ancient world was undoubtedly a spur to the growth of the state. Under Chandragupta Maurya, the central government became actively involved in commercial and manufacturing activities. It owned mines and vast crown lands and undoubtedly earned massive profits from its role in regional commerce. Separate government departments were established for trade, agriculture, mining, and the manufacture of weapons, and the movement of private goods was vigorously taxed. Nevertheless, a significant private sector also flourished; it was dominated by great caste guilds, which monopolized key sectors of the economy. A money economy probably came into operation during the second century B.C.E., when copper and gold coins were introduced from the Middle East. This in turn led to the development of banking. But village trade continued to be conducted by means of cowry shells (a highly polished shell used as a medium of exchange throughout much of Africa and Asia) or barter throughout the ancient period.

ESCAPING THE WHEEL OF LIFE: THE RELIGIOUS WORLD OF ANCIENT INDIA

Like Indian politics and society, Indian religion is a blend of Aryan and Dravidian culture. The clash and subsequent intermingling of those two civilizations gave rise to an extraordinarily complex set of religious beliefs and practices, filled with diversity and contrast. Out of this cultural mix came two of the world's great religions, Buddhism and Hinduism, and several smaller ones, including Jainism and Sikhism.

Hinduism

Evidence about the earliest religious beliefs of the Aryan peoples comes primarily from sacred texts such as the Vedas, a set of four collections of hymns and religious ceremonies transmitted by memory through the centuries by Aryan priests. Many of these religious ideas were probably common to all of the Indo-European peoples before their separation into different groups at least four thousand years

THE HENPECKED MONK

Women were often portrayed in traditional Indian literature as seductresses, luring innocent males from following their higher spiritual nature. This passage is from the Sutrakrtanga, one of the sacred books of the Jain religion. While the object of concern is technically not that familiar figure of ridicule, the henpecked husband, the passage indicates the concern that many men in ancient India felt when exposed to the wiles of their female contemporaries.

THE SUTRAKRTANGA

A celibate monk shouldn't fall in love,
and though he hankers after pleasure he should hold
himself in check,
for these are the pleasures
which some monks enjoy.

If a monk breaks his vows,
and falls for a woman,
she upbraids him and raises her foot to him,
and kicks him on the head.

"Monk, if you won't live with me
as husband and wife,
I'll pull out my hair and become a nun,
for you shall not live without me!"

But when she has him in her clutches
it's all housework and errands!

"Fetch a knife to cut this gourd!"
"Get me some fresh fruit!"

"We want wood to boil the greens,
and for a fire in the evening!"
"Now paint my feet!"
"Come and massage my back!". . .

"Bring me the chair with the twine seat,
and my wooden-soled slippers to go out walking!"
So pregnant women boss their husbands,
just as though they were household slaves.

When a child is born, the reward of their labors,
she makes the father hold the baby.
And sometimes the fathers of sons
stagger under their burdens like camels.

They get up at night, as though they were nurses,
to lull the howling child to sleep,
and, though they are shamefaced about it,
scrub dirty garments, just like washermen. . . .

So, monks, resist the wiles of women;
avoid their friendship and company.
The little pleasure you get from them
will only lead you into trouble!

---

ago. Early Aryan beliefs were based on the common concept of a pantheon of gods and goddesses representing great forces of nature similar to the immortals of Greek mythology. The Aryan ancestor of the Greek father-god Zeus, for example, may have been the deity known in early Aryan tradition as Dyaus (see Chapter 4).

The parent god Dyaus was a somewhat distant figure, however, who was eventually overshadowed by other, more functional gods possessing more familiar human traits. For a while, the primary Aryan god was the great warrior god Indra. Indra summoned the Aryan tribal peoples to war and was represented in nature by thunder. Later, Indra declined in importance and was replaced by Varuna, lord of justice, who eventually evolved into the modern deity Vishnu. Other gods and goddesses represented various forces of nature or the needs of human beings, such as fire, fertility, wealth, and so forth.

The concept of sacrifice was a key element in Aryan religious belief in Vedic times. As in many other ancient cultures, the practice may have begun as human sacrifice, but later animals were used as substitutes, although human sacrifice was practiced in some isolated communities down to modern times. The priestly class, or *brahmins*, played a key role in these ceremonies.

Another element of Aryan religious belief in ancient times was the ideal of asceticism. By the sixth century B.C.E., self-sacrifice or even self-mutilation had begun to replace sacrifice as a means of placating or communicating with the gods. Apparently, the original motive for asceticism was to achieve magical powers, but later, in the Upanishads (a set of commentaries on the Vedas compiled in the sixth century B.C.E.), it was seen as a means of spiritual meditation that would enable the practitioner to reach beyond material reality to a world of truth and bliss beyond earthly joy and sorrow:

Those who practice penance and faith in the forest, the tranquil ones, the knowers of truth, living the life of wandering mendicancy—they depart, freed from passion, through the door of the sun, to where dwells, verily . . . the imperishable Soul.[6]

It is possible that another motive was to permit those with strong religious convictions to communicate directly with metaphysical reality without having to rely on the priestly class at court.

Asceticism, of course, has been practiced in other religions, including Christianity and Islam, but it seems particularly identified with Hinduism, the religion that

✿ **FEMALE EARTH SPIRIT.**   This 2,200-year-old earth spirit, a sandstone gatepost from the Buddhist stupa at Bharhut, illustrates how earlier Indian representations of the fertility goddess were incorporated into Buddhist art. Women were revered as powerful fertility symbols and considered dangerous when menstruating or after having given birth. Voluptuous and idealized, these earth spirits could allegedly cause a tree to blossom if they merely touched a branch with their arm or wrapped a leg around its trunk. Graceful and sensuous, this female spirit seems to be breathing and moving out of the stone.

emerged from early Indian religious tradition. Eventually, asceticism evolved into the modern practice of body training that we know as *yoga* (union), which is accepted today as a meaningful element of Hindu religious practice.

Eventually, as Indians began to speculate about the nature of the cosmic order, they came to believe in the existence of a single monistic force in the universe, a form of ultimate reality called *Brahman*. Today the early form of Hinduism is sometimes called Brahmanism. In the Upanishads, the concept began to emerge as an important element of Indian religious belief. It was the duty of the individual self—called the *Atman*—to achieve an understanding of this ultimate reality so that after death the self would merge in spiritual form with *Brahman*. Sometimes *Brahman* was described in more concrete terms as a creator god—eventually known as Vishnu—but more often in terms of a shadowy ultimate reality. According to one of the Upanishads,

> In the beginning, my dear, this world was just being, one only, without a second. Some people, no doubt, say: "In the beginning, verily, this world was just nonbeing, one only, without a second; from that nonbeing, being was produced." But how, indeed, my dear, could it be so? said he. How could being be produced from nonbeing?
>
> On the contrary, my dear, in the beginning this world was being alone, one only, without a second. Being thought to itself: "May I be many, may I procreate." It produced fire. That fire thought to itself: "May I be many, may I procreate." It produced water. Therefore, whenever a person grieves or perspires, then it is from fire [heat] alone that water is produced. That water thought to itself: "May I be many; may I procreate." It produced food. Therefore, whenever it rains, then there is abundant food; it is from water alone that food for eating is produced. . . . That divinity (Being) thought to itself: "Well, having entered into these three divinities [fire, water, and food] by means of this living self, let me develop names and forms.[7]

REINCARNATION   輪回說

Another new concept also probably began to appear around the time the Upanishads were written—the idea of reincarnation. This is the idea that the individual soul is reborn in a different form after death and progresses through several existences on the wheel of life until it reaches its final destination in a union with the Great World Soul, known as *Brahman*. Because life is harsh, this final release is the objective of all living souls.

A key element in this process is the idea of *karma*—that one's rebirth in a next life is determined by one's *karma* (actions) in this life. Hinduism places all living species on a vast scale of existence, including the four classes and the untouchables in human society. The current status of an individual soul, then, is not simply a cosmic accident, but the inevitable result of actions that that soul has committed in a past existence.

At the top of the scale are the *brahmins* (the priestly caste), who by definition are closest to ultimate release from the law of reincarnation. The *brahmins* are followed in descending order by the other castes in human society and the world of the beasts. Within the animal kingdom, an especially high position is reserved for the cow, which even today is revered by Hindus as a sacred beast. Some have speculated that the unique role played by the cow in Hinduism derives from the value of cattle in Aryan pastoral society. But others have pointed out that cattle were a source of both money and food and suggest that the cow's sacred position may have descended from the concept of the sacred bull in Dravidian culture.

The concept of *karma* is governed by the *dharma*, or the Law. A law regulating human behavior, the *dharma* imposes different requirements on different individuals depending on their status in society. Those high on the social scale, such as *brahmins* and *kshatriyas*, are held to a more strict form of behavior than are *sudras*. The *brahmin*, for example, is expected to abstain from eating meat, because that would entail the killing of another living being, thus interrupting its *karma*.

How the concept of reincarnation originated is not known, although it was apparently not unusual for early peoples to believe that the individual soul would be reborn in a different form in a later life. In any case, in India the concept may have had practical causes as well as consequences. In the first place, it tended to provide religious sanction for the rigid class divisions that had begun to emerge in Indian society after the Aryan conquest, and it provided moral and political justification for the privileges of those on the higher end of the scale.

At the same time, the concept of reincarnation provided certain compensations for those lower on the ladder of life. For example, it gave hope to the poor that if they behaved properly in this life, they might improve their condition in the next. It also provided a means for unassimilated groups such as tribal peoples to find a place in Indian society while at the same time permitting them to maintain their distinctive way of life.

The ultimate goal of achieving "good" *karma*, as we have seen, was to escape the cycle of existence. To the sophisticated, the nature of that release was a spiritual union of the individual soul with the Great World Soul, *Brahman*, described in the Upanishads as a form of dreamless sleep, free from earthly desires. Such a concept, however, was undoubtedly too ethereal for the average Indian, who needed a more concrete form of heavenly salvation, a place of beauty and bliss after a life of disease and privation.

It was probably for this reason that the Hindu religion—in some ways so otherworldly and ascetic—came to be peopled with a multitude of very human gods and goddesses. It has been estimated that the Hindu pantheon contains more than 33,000 deities. Only a small number are primary ones, however, notably the so-called trinity of gods: Brahman the Creator, Vishnu the Preserver, and Siva (originally the Vedic god Rudra) the Destroyer. Although Brahman (sometimes in his concrete form called Brahma) is considered to be the highest god, Vishnu and Siva take

DANCING SIVA. The Hindu deity Siva is often presented in the form of a bronze statue, performing his cosmic dance in which he simultaneously creates and destroys the universe. While his upper right hand creates the cosmos, his upper left hand reduces it in flames, and the lower two hands offer eternal blessing. Siva's dancing statues present to his followers the visual message of his power and compassion.

precedence in the devotional exercises of many Hindus, who can be roughly divided into Vishnuites and Saivites. In addition to the trinity of gods, all of whom have wives with readily identifiable roles and personalities, there are countless minor deities, each again with his or her own specific function, such as bringing good fortune, arranging a good marriage, or guaranteeing a son in childbirth.

The rich variety and earthy character of many Hindu deities are repugnant to many Christians and Muslims, to whom God is an all-seeing and transcendent deity. Many Hindus, however, regard the multitude of gods as simply different manifestations of one ultimate reality. The various deities also provide a useful means for ordinary Indians to personify their religious feelings. Even though some individuals among the early Aryans attempted to communicate with the gods through sacrifice or asceticism, most Indians undoubtedly sought to satisfy their own individual religious needs through devotion, which they expressed through ritual ceremonies and offerings at a Hindu temple. Such offerings were not only a way to seek salvation, but also a means of satisfying all the aspirations of daily life.

Over the centuries, then, Hinduism changed radically from its origins in Aryan tribal society and became a religion of the vast majority of the Indian people. Concern with a transcendental union between the individual soul and the Great World Soul contrasted with practical desires for material wealth and happiness; ascetic self-denial contrasted with an earthy emphasis on the pleasures and values of sexual union between marriage partners. All of these became aspects of Hinduism, the religion of 70 percent of the Indian people.

Buddhism: The Middle Path

In the sixth century B.C.E, a new doctrine appeared in northern India that soon began to rival Hinduism's popularity throughout the subcontinent. This new doctrine was called Buddhism. The historical founder of Buddhism, Siddhartha Gautama, was a native of a small principality in the foothills of the Himalaya Mountains in what is today southern Nepal. He was born in the mid-sixth century B.C.E, the son of a ruling *kshatriya* family. According to tradition, the young Siddhartha was raised in affluent surroundings and trained, like many other members of his class, in the martial arts. On reaching maturity, he married and began to raise a family. However, at the age of twenty-nine he suddenly discovered the pain of illness, the sorrow of death, and the degradation caused by old age in the lives of ordinary people and exclaimed: "Would that sickness, age, and death might be forever bound!" From that time on, he decided to dedicate his life to determining the cause and seeking the cure for human suffering.

To find the answers to these questions, Siddhartha abandoned his home and family and traveled widely. At first he tried to follow the model of the ascetics, but he eventually decided that self-mortification did not lead to a greater understanding of life and abandoned the practice. Then one day after a lengthy period of meditation under a tree, he finally achieved enlightenment as to the meaning of life and spent the remainder of his life preaching it. His conclusions, as embodied in his teachings, became the philosophy (or, as some would have it, the religion) of Buddhism. According to legend, the Devil (the Indian term is *Mara*) attempted desperately to tempt him with political power and the company of beautiful girls. But Siddhartha Gautama resisted:

> Pleasure is brief as a flash of lightning
> Or like an autumn shower, only for a moment.
> Why should I then covet the pleasures you speak of?
> I see your bodies are full of all impurity:
> Birth and death, sickness and age are yours.
> I seek the highest prize, hard to attain by men—
> The true and constant wisdom of the wise.[8]

How much the modern doctrine of Buddhism resembles the original teachings of Siddhartha Gautama is open to debate, since much time has elapsed since his death and original texts relating his ideas are lacking. Nor is it certain that Siddhartha Gautama even intended to found a new religion or doctrine. In some respects, his ideas could be viewed as a reformist form of Hinduism, much as Martin Luther saw Protestantism as a reformation of Christianity. Siddhartha accepted much of the belief system of Hinduism, if not all of its practices. For example, he accepted the concept of reincarnation and the role of *karma* as a means of influencing the movement of individual souls up and down in the scale of life. He followed Hinduism in praising nonviolence and borrowed the idea of living a life of simplicity and chastity from the ascetics. Moreover, his vision of metaphysical reality—commonly known as Nirvana—is closer to the Hindu concept of *Brahman* than it is to the Christian concept of heavenly salvation. Nirvana, which involves an extinction of selfhood and a final reunion with the Great World Soul, is sometimes likened to a dreamless sleep or to a kind of "blowing out" (as of a candle). Buddhists occasionally remark that someone who asks for a description does not understand the concept.

At the same time, the new doctrine differed from existing Hindu practices in a number of key ways. In the first place, Siddhartha denied the existence of an individual soul. To him, the Hindu concept of *Atman*—the individual soul—meant that the soul was subject to rebirth and thus did not achieve a complete liberation from the cares of this world. In fact, Siddhartha denied the ultimate reality of the material world in its entirety and taught that humans' physical surroundings are an illusion to be transcended. Siddhartha's idea of achieving Nirvana was based on his conviction that the pain, poverty, and sorrow that afflict human beings are caused essentially by their attachment to the things of this world. Once worldly cares are abandoned, pain and sorrow can be forgotten. With this knowledge comes *bodhi*, or wisdom (thus, the term Buddhism and the familiar name of Gautama Buddha, or Gautama the Wise, for Siddhartha Gautama).

Achieving this understanding is a key step on the road to Nirvana, which, as in Hinduism, is a form of release from the wheel of life. According to tradition, Siddhartha transmitted this message in a sermon to his disciples in a deer park at Sarnath, not far from the modern city of Benares (also known as Varanasi). Like so many messages, it is deceptively simple and is enclosed in four noble truths: life is suffering; suffering is caused by desire; the way to end suffering is to end desire; and the way to end desire is to avoid the extremes of a life of vulgar materialism and a life of self-torture and to follow the "Middle Path." This Middle Path, which is also known as the Eightfold Way, calls for right knowledge, right purpose, right speech, right conduct, right occupation, right effort, right awareness, and right meditation (see the box on p. 53).

HOW TO ACHIEVE ENLIGHTENMENT

One of the most famous passages in Buddhist literature is the sermon at Sarnath, which Siddhartha Gautama delivered to his followers in a deer park outside the holy city of Varanasi (Benares), in the Ganges River valley. Here he set forth the key ideas that would define Buddhist beliefs for centuries to come.

THE SERMON AT BENARES

Thus have I heard: at one time the Lord dwelt at Benares at Isipatana in the Deer Park. There the Lord addressed the five monks:—

"These two extremes, monks, are not to be practiced by one who has gone forth from the world. What are the two? That conjoined with the passions and luxury, low, vulgar, common, ignoble, and useless; and that conjoined with self-torture, painful, ignoble, and useless. Avoiding these two extremes the Tathagata has gained the enlightenment of the Middle Path, which produces insight and knowledge and tends to calm, to higher knowledge, enlightenment, Nirvana.

"And what, monks, is the Middle Path, of which the Tathagata has gained enlightenment, which produces insight and knowledge, and tends to calm, to higher knowledge, enlightenment, Nirvana? This is the noble Eightfold Way: namely, right view, right intention, right speech, right action, right livelihood, right effort, right mindfulness, right concentration. This, monks, is the Middle Path, of which the Tathagata has gained enlightenment, which produces insight and knowledge, and tends to calm, to higher knowledge, enlightenment, Nirvana.

1. "Now this, monks, is the noble truth of pain: birth is painful, old age is painful, sickness is painful, death is painful, sorrow, lamentation, dejection, and despair are painful. Contact with unpleasant things is painful, not getting what one wishes is painful. In short the five groups of graspings are painful.
2. Now this, monks, is the noble truth of the cause of pain: the craving, which tends to rebirth, combined with pleasure and lust, finding pleasure here and there; namely, the craving for passion, the craving for existence, the craving for nonexistence.
3. Now this, monks, is the noble truth of the cessation of pain, the cessation without a remainder of craving, the abandonment, forsaking, release, nonattachment.
4. Now this, monks, is the noble truth of the way that leads to the cessation of pain: this is the noble Eightfold Way; namely, right view, right intention, right speech, right action, right livelihood, right effort, right mindfulness, right concentration.

"And when, monks, in these four noble truths my due knowledge and insight with its three sections and twelve divisions was well purified, then monks . . . I had attained the highest complete enlightenment. This I recognized. Knowledge arose in me, insight arose that the release of my mind is unshakable; this is my last existence; now there is no rebirth."

Buddhism also differed from Hinduism in its relative egalitarianism. Although Siddhartha accepted the idea of reincarnation (and thereby the idea that human beings differ as a result of *karma* accumulated in a previous existence), he rejected the Hindu division of humanity into rigidly defined castes based on previous reincarnations and taught that all human beings could aspire to Nirvana as a result of their behavior in this life—a message that likely helped Buddhism win support among people at the lower end of the social scale.

In addition, Buddhism was much simpler than Hinduism. Siddhartha rejected the panoply of gods that had become identified with Hinduism and forbade his followers to worship his person or his image after his death. In fact, many Buddhists view Buddhism as a philosophy rather than a religion.

After Siddhartha Gautama's death in 480 B.C.E., dedicated disciples carried his message the length and breadth of India. Buddhist monasteries were established throughout the subcontinent, and temples and stupas (stone towers housing relics of the Buddha) sprang up throughout the countryside.

Women were permitted to join the monastic order but only in an inferior position. As Siddhartha had explained, "Women are soon angered . . . women are full of passion . . . women are stupid . . . That is the reason . . . why women have no place in public assemblies . . . and do not earn their living by any profession." Still, the position of women tended to be better in Buddhist societies than it was elsewhere in ancient India (see the box on p. 54).

During the next centuries, Buddhism began to compete actively with Hindu beliefs, as well as with another new faith known as Jainism. Jainism was founded by Mahavira, a contemporary of Siddhartha Gautama. Resembling Buddhism in its rejection of the reality of the material world, Jainism was more extreme in practice. Where Siddhartha Gautama called for the "middle way" between passion and luxury and pain and self-torture, Mahavira preached a doctrine of extreme simplicity to his followers, who kept no possessions and relied on begging for a living. Some even

THE VOICES OF SILENCE

ost of what is known about the lives of women in ancient India comes from the Vedas, or from other texts written by men. Classical Sanskrit was the exclusive property of upper-caste males for use in religious and court functions. There are a few examples of women's writings, however, that date from this period. In the first poem quoted below, a Buddhist nun living in the sixth century B.C.E. reflects on her sense of spiritual salvation and physical release from the drudgery of daily life. The remaining two poems were produced several hundred years later in southern India by anonymous female authors at a time when strict Hindu traditions had not yet been established in the area. Poetry and song were an essential part of daily life, as women sang while working in the fields, drawing water at the well, or reflecting on the hardships of their daily lives. The second poem quoted below breathes the sensuous joy of sex, while the third expresses the simultaneous grief and pride of a mother as she sends her only son off to war.

"A WOMAN WELL SET FREE! HOW FREE I AM"

A woman well set free! How free I am,
How wonderfully free, from kitchen drudgery.
Free from the harsh grip of hunger,
And from empty cooking pots,
Free too of that unscrupulous man,
The weaver of sunshades.
Calm now, and serene I am,
All lust and hatred purged.
To the shade of the spreading trees I go
And contemplate my happiness.

Translated by Uma Chakravarti and Kumkum Roy

"WHAT SHE SAID TO HER GIRLFRIEND"

What she said to her girlfriend:
On beaches washed by seas
older than the earth,
in the groves filled with bird-cries,
on the banks shaded by a punnai
clustered with flowers,
        when we made love
my eyes saw him
and my ears heard him;

my arms grow beautiful
in the coupling
and grow lean
as they come away.
        What shall I make of this?

Translated by A. K. Ramanujan

"HER PURPOSE IS FRIGHTENING, HER SPIRIT CRUEL"

Her purpose is frightening, her spirit cruel.
That she comes from an ancient house is fitting, surely.
In the battle the day before yesterday,
her father attacked an elephant and died there on the field.
In the battle yesterday,
her husband faced a row of troops and fell.
And today,
she hears the battle drum,
and, eager beyond reason, gives him a spear in his hand,
wraps a white garment around him,
smears his dry tuft with oil,
and, having nothing but her one son,
"Go!" she says, sending him to battle.

Translated by George L. Hart III

---

rejected clothing and wandered through the world naked. Perhaps because of its insistence on a life of poverty, Jainism failed to attract enough adherents to become a major doctrine and never received official support. According to tradition, however, Chandragupta Maurya accepted Mahavira's doctrine after abdicating the throne and fasted to death in a Jain monastery.

ASOKA, A BUDDHIST MONARCH

Buddhism received an important boost when Asoka, the grandson of Chandragupta Maurya, converted to Buddhism sometime in the third century B.C.E. Asoka

(269–232 B.C.E) is generally considered to be the greatest ruler in the history of India. Reportedly, Asoka began his reign conquering, pillaging, and killing, but after his conversion to Buddhism, he began to regret his bloodthirsty past and attempted to rule benevolently.

Asoka directed that banyan trees and shelters be placed along the road to provide shade and rest for weary travelers. He sent Buddhist missionaries throughout India and ordered the erection of stone pillars with official edicts and Buddhist inscriptions to instruct people in the proper way. According to tradition, his son converted the island of Sri Lanka to Buddhism, and the peoples there accepted a tributary relationship with the Mauryan Empire.

THE RULE OF THE FISHES: INDIA AFTER THE MAURYAS

After Asoka's death in 232 B.C.E., the Mauryan Empire began to decline. In 183 B.C.E., the last Mauryan ruler was overthrown by one of his military commanders, and India slipped back into disunity. A number of new kingdoms, some of them perhaps influenced by the memory of the Alexandrian conquests, arose along the fringes of the subcontinent in Bactria, known today as Afghanistan. In the first century C.E., Indo-European-speaking peoples fleeing from the nomadic Xiongnu warriors in Central Asia seized power in the area and proclaimed the new Kushan Kingdom (see Chapter 3). For the next two centuries, the Kushanas extended their political sway over northern India as far as the central Ganges valley, while other kingdoms scuffled for predominance elsewhere on the subcontinent. India would not see unity again for another five hundred years.

Several reasons for India's failure to maintain a unified empire have been proposed. Some historians suggest that a decline in regional trade during the first millennium C.E. may have contributed to the growth of small land-based kingdoms, which drew their primary income from agriculture. The tenacity of the Aryan tradition with its emphasis on tribal rivalries may also have contributed. Although the Mauryan rulers tried to impose a more centralized organization, clan loyalties once again came to the fore after the collapse of the Mauryan dynasty. Furthermore, the behavior of the ruling class was characterized by what Indians call the "rule of the fishes," which glorified warfare as the natural activity of the king and the aristocracy. The *Arthasastra*, which set forth a model of a centralized Indian state, assumed that war was the "sport of kings."

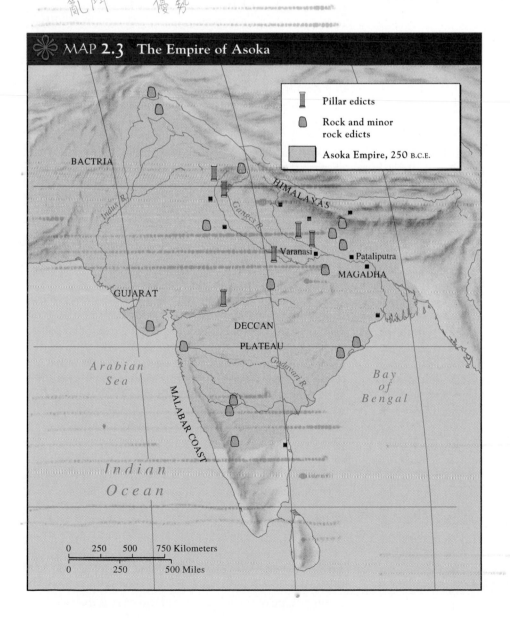

MAP 2.3   The Empire of Asoka

Pillar edicts

Rock and minor rock edicts

Asoka Empire, 250 B.C.E.

BACTRIA

HIMALAYAS

Indus R.

Ganges R.

Varanasi

Pataliputra

MAGADHA

GUJARAT

DECCAN

PLATEAU

Arabian
Sea

Godavari R.

Bay
of
Bengal

MALABAR COAST

Indian
Ocean

0   250   500   750 Kilometers

0   250   500 Miles

CHRONOLOGY

ANCIENT INDIA

Harappan civilization	c. 3000–1500 B.C.E.
Arrival of the Aryans	c. 1500 B.C.E.
Life of Gautama Buddha	c. 560–480 B.C.E.
Invasion of India by Alexander the Great	326 B.C.E.
Mauryan dynasty founded	324 B.C.E.
Reign of Chandragupta Maurya	324–301 B.C.E.
Reign of Asoka	269–232 B.C.E.
Collapse of Mauryan dynasty	183 B.C.E.
Rise of Kushan Kingdom	c. first century C.E.

THE EXUBERANT WORLD OF INDIAN CULTURE

Few cultures in the world are as rich and varied as that of India. Most societies excel in some forms of artistic and literary achievement and not in others, but India has produced great works in almost all fields of cultural endeavor—art and sculpture, science, architecture, literature, and music.

Literature

The earliest known Indian literature consists of the four Vedas, which were passed down orally from generation to generation until they were finally written down after the Aryan conquest of India. The Rigveda dates from the second millennium B.C.E. and consists of over a thousand hymns that were used at religious ceremonies. The other three Vedas were written considerably later and contain instructions for performing ritual sacrifices and other ceremonies. The Brahmanas and the Upanishads served as commentaries on the Vedas.

The language of the Vedas was Sanskrit, one of the Indo-European family of languages. After the Aryan conquest of India, Sanskrit gradually declined as a spoken language and was replaced in northern India by a simpler tongue known as Prakrit. Nevertheless, Sanskrit continued to be used as the language of the bureaucracy and literary expression for many centuries after that and, like Latin in medieval Europe, served as a common language of communication (*lingua franca*) between various regions of India. In the south, a variety of Dravidian languages continued to be spoken.

As early as the fifth century B.C.E., Indian grammarians had already codified Sanskrit in order to preserve the authenticity of the Vedas for the spiritual edification of future generations. A famous grammar written by the scholar Panini in the fourth century B.C.E. set forth four thousand grammatical rules prescribing the correct usage of the spoken and written language. This achievement is particularly impressive in that Europe did not have a science of linguistics until the nineteenth century, when it was developed partly as a result of the discovery of the works of Panini and later Indian linguists.

After the development of a writing system some time in the first millennium B.C.E., India's holy literature was probably inscribed on palm leaves stitched together into a book somewhat similar to the bamboo strips used during the same period in China. Also written for the first time were India's great historical epics, the Mahabharata and the Ramayana. Both of these epics may have originally been recited at religious ceremonies, but they are essentially historical writings that recount the martial exploits of great Aryan rulers and warriors.

The Mahabharata, consisting of more than 90,000 stanzas, was probably written about 100 B.C.E. and describes in great detail a war between cousins for control of the kingdom about 1000 B.C.E. Interwoven in the narrative are many fantastic legends of the Hindu gods. Above all, the Mahabharata is a tale of moral confrontations and an elucidation of the ethical precepts of the *dharma*. The most famous section of the book is the so-called Bhagavadgita, a sermon by the legendary Indian figure Krishna on the eve of a major battle. In this sermon, mentioned at the beginning of this chapter, Krishna sets forth one of the key ethical maxims of Indian society: in taking action, one must be indifferent to success or failure and consider only the moral rightness of the act itself (see the box on p. 58).

The Ramayana, written at about the same time, is much shorter than the Mahabharata. It is an account of a semi-legendary ruler named Rama who, as the result of a palace intrigue, is banished from the kingdom and forced to live as a hermit in the forest. Later, he fights the demon-king of Sri Lanka (Ceylon), who has kidnapped his beloved wife, Sita. Like the Mahabharata, the Ramayana is strongly imbued with religious and moral significance. Rama himself is portrayed as the ideal Aryan hero, a perfect ruler and an ideal son, while Sita projects the supreme duty of female chastity and wifely loyalty to her husband. The Ramayana is a story of the triumph of good over evil, duty over self-indulgence, and generosity over selfishness. It combines filial and erotic love, conflicts of human passion, character analysis, and poetic descriptions of nature.

The Ramayana also has all the ingredients of an enthralling adventure: giants, wondrous flying chariots, invincible arrows and swords, and magic potions and mantras. One of the real heroes of the story is the monkey-

ASOKA'S PILLAR. Stone pillars like this polished sandstone column, which is thirty-two feet high, were erected during the reign of Emperor Asoka in the third century B.C.E. Commemorating events in the life of the Buddha announcing official edicts, or marking routes to the holy sites, they were placed on major trunk roads throughout the Indian subcontinent. The massive size of these pillars, some of which weighed up to fifty tons, underscores the engineering skills of the peoples of ancient India.

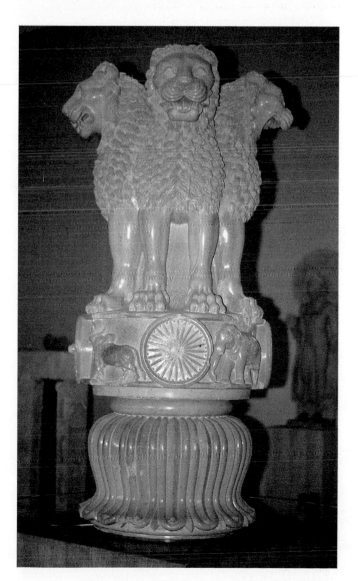

king Hanuman, who flies from India to Sri Lanka to set the great battle in motion. Although the theme is a serious one, there are many humorous moments, such as Hanuman's nocturnal visit to King Ravana's palace (see the box on p. 60). It is no wonder that the Ramayana became a popular favorite among Indians of all age groups and the source of folktales and dramas that have been recited in Indian villages up to the present day.

Architecture and Sculpture

After literature, the greatest achievements of early Indian civilization were in architecture and sculpture. Some of the earliest examples of Indian architecture stem from the time of Emperor Asoka, when Buddhism became the religion of the state. Until the time of the Mauryas, Aryan buildings had been constructed of wood. With the rise of the empire, stone began to be used, as artisans arrived in India seeking employment after the destruction of the Persian Empire by Alexander. Many of these stone carvers accepted the patronage of Emperor Asoka, who used them to spread Buddhist ideas throughout the subcontinent.

THE LIONS OF SARNATH. Their beauty and Buddhist symbolism make the Lions of Sarnath the most famous of the capitals topping Asoka's pillars. Sarnath, located just north of the city of Varanasi, was the holy site where Siddhartha Gautama first preached, and these roaring lions echo the proclamation of Buddhist teachings to the four corners of the world. The wheel not only represents Buddha's law but also proclaims Asoka's imperial legitimacy as the enlightened Indian ruler.

BITS OF WISDOM FROM ANCIENT INDIA

The Mahabharata, the great epic of the early Aryan peoples, includes both moral exhortations for the ruling class and bits of simple wisdom that still touch us today. In this passage, a voice personifying the dharma, or code of behavior, tests the hero's worthiness to become king by posing riddles about the meaning of life. The questions are eternal ones that still have relevance in our own time. The use of riddles as a means of testing mental skills was common to many early societies, including ancient Greece and China.

THE MAHABHARATA

"What is swifter than the wind?"
"The mind is swifter than the wind."
"What is more numerous than the blades of grass in a meadow?"
"Our thoughts number more than that."
"What is the best of all things that are praised?"
"Skill."

"What is the most valuable possession?"
"Knowledge."
"What is not thought of until it departs?"
"Health."
"What is the best happiness?"
"Contentment."
"What covers all the world?"
"Darkness."
"What keeps a thing from discovering itself?"
"That is also darkness."
"What enemy cannot be overcome?"
"That is anger."
"What is honesty?"
"That is to look and to see every living creature as yourself, bearing your own will to live, and your own fear of death."
"How may peace be false?"
"When it is tyranny."

There were three main types of religious structure: the pillar, the stupa, and the rock chamber. During Asoka's reign, many stone columns were erected alongside roads to commemorate the events in the Buddha's life and mark pilgrim routes to holy places. Weighing up to fifty tons each and rising as high as thirty feet, these polished sandstone pillars were topped with a carved capital, usually depicting lions uttering the Buddha's message. Ten remain standing today.

A stupa was originally meant to house a relic of the Buddha, such as a lock of his hair or a branch of the famous Bodhi tree, and was constructed in the form of a burial mound (the pyramids in Egypt also derived from burial mounds). Eventually, the stupa became a place for devo-

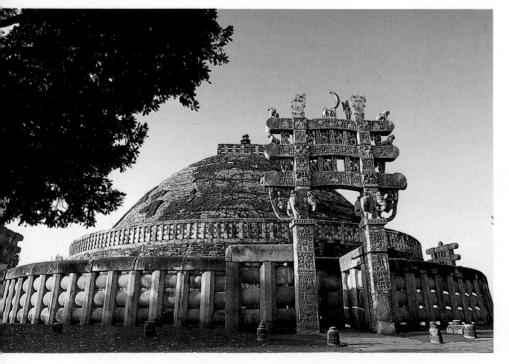

✿ SANCHI GATE AND STUPA.
First constructed during the reign of Emperor Asoka, in the third century B.C.E., the stupa at Sanchi was enlarged over time, eventually becoming the greatest Buddhist monument in the entire Indian subcontinent. Originally intended to house a relic of the Buddha, the stupa became a holy place for devotion and a familiar form of Buddhist architecture. Sanchi's four elaborately carved stone gates, each over forty feet high, display exciting statues of Buddhist symbolism, including both animals and human figures.

🏵 **A BUDDHIST PRAYER HALL.**   Carved out of solid rock cliffs during the Mauryan dynasty, these rock chambers served as small meditation halls for traveling Buddhist monks. By the first century C.E., they had evolved into elaborate temples, the greatest being this example at Karli. Measuring over 120 feet in length and 45 feet high, with pillars, an altar, and a vault, it is reminiscent of the Roman basilica in the West.

tion and the most familiar form of Buddhist architecture. It rose to considerable heights and was surmounted with a spire, possibly representing the stages of existence en route to Nirvana. According to legend, Asoka ordered the construction of 84,000 stupas throughout India to promote the Buddha's message. A few survive today, including the famous stupa at Sanchi, begun under Asoka and completed two centuries later.

The final form of early Indian architecture is the rock chamber carved out of a cliff on the side of a mountain. Asoka began the construction of these chambers to provide rooms to house monks or wandering ascetics and to serve as halls for religious ceremonies. The chambers were rectangular in form, with pillars, an altar, and a vault, reminiscent of the Roman basilica in the West. The three most famous chambers of this period are at Bhaja, Karli, and Ajanta; the latter contains twenty-nine rooms.

All three forms of architecture were embellished with decorations. Consisting of detailed reliefs and free-standing statues of deities, other human figures, and animals, these decorations are permeated with a sense of nature and the vitality of life. Many reflect an amalgamation of popular and sacred themes, of Buddhist, Vedic, and pre-Aryan religious motifs, such as male and female earth spirits. Until the second century C.E., Siddhartha Gautama was represented only through symbols, such as the wheel of life, the Bodhi tree, and the footprint, perhaps because artists felt that it was impossible to render a visual impression of the Buddha in the state of Nirvana. After the spread of Mahayana Buddhism in the second century, when the Buddha was portrayed as a god, his image began to appear in stone.

By this time, India had established its own unique religious art. The art is permeated by sensuousness and exuberance and is often overtly sexual. These scenes are meant to express otherworldly delights, not the pleasures of this world. The sensuous paradise that adorned the religious art of ancient India represented salvation and fulfillment for the ordinary Indian.

Science

Our knowledge of Indian science is limited by the paucity of written sources, but it is evident that ancient Indians had amassed an impressive amount of scientific knowledge in a number of areas. Especially notable was their work in astronomy, where they charted the movements of the heavenly bodies and recognized the spherical nature of the planet at an early date. Their ideas of physics were similar to those of the Greeks; matter was divided into the five elements of earth, air, fire, water, and ether. Many of their technological achievements are impressive, notably the quality of their textiles and the massive stone pillars erected during the reign of Asoka. The pillars weighed up to fifty tons each and were transported many miles to their final destination.

THE MONKEY-KING IN SRI LANKA

In the famous classic the Ramayana, Rama is assisted in his effort to free his wife from Ravana, the king of Sri Lanka, by the monkey-king Hanuman. In this passage, Hanuman unexpectedly intrudes into the royal harem.

THE RAMAYANA

That was the entrance to Ravana's bedroom. Hanuman ducked under the left corner of the draw-curtain and stood just inside with his back to the wall, looking out at a huge floor lit by flaming lamps of gold and covered with sleeping women so tumbled together that Hanuman could not tell where one lady left off and the next began.

There was hardly space to step anywhere. Those were the countless wives of the Demon King asleep in disarray, lying all over each other, women beautiful and bright as flashes of lightning now locked fast in Sleep's embrace. Hanuman thought, "When even the form of a heavenly star is less than enough, virtue's divine reward for a good life must be to receive such fair shapes and lovely limbs as these!"

Once arriving in that room of women, it would be harder for any man to remember who he was or where he stood or why, than to fly across the sea in the first place. And though Hanuman was not a man, still when he looked at each one he thought no other woman could be fairer, and when he saw the next sleeper she was in turn the best and most beautiful as he looked at her. Truly, among those magnificent women the rays of the one's beauty showed off the charms of another; they slept deeply after an evening of drinking and dancing and playing music. Their fragrant hair was loosened and their bracelets scattered; their beauty marks of sandal paste were smudged and their colored robes unclasped and their waist-chains ran loosely straying to the side; their hazy garlands were disbanded and their pearls had gone and their earrings were lost.

Even the bedroom lamps looked openly out at all those women while they had the chance, as Ravana slept. Hanuman picked his way among the love-skilled Queens of Lanka who were draped over the floor and looked at their faces. They smiled or frowned or sighed in their sleep; their pillows were others' arms and legs and laps; they pulled each other's robes and wrapped themselves in them. With their eyes lashed shut in sleep they were desirable as closed flowers; when they touched each other they smiled and drew closer, believing they pressed Ravana with their breasts. Even asleep the dancers moved enticingly; the girl musicians slept embracing drums and hugging lutes like their long-absent lovers.

The golden lamps on the walls watched over them unblinking, and in their light the gold and jewels of those Queens made a river of lights and colors and shimmering waves of gold and silver. Their pearl necklaces were white water-birds asleep between their breasts, rising and falling; their strings of turquoise were families of blue teal and their hips were the waves and the riverbanks; their faces of golden or white or deep blue skin were the lotuses; when they stirred sleepily, the small bells sewn on their silken clothes were the ripples moving with little sounds; and the bruises and scratches of love on their tender breasts were signs of where the lion and tiger had come to drink.

 CONCLUSION

While the peoples of North Africa and the Middle East were actively building the first civilizations, a similar process was getting under way in the Indus River valley. Much has been learned about the nature of the Indus valley civilization in recent years, but without written records there are inherent limits to our understanding. How did the Harappan people deal with those fundamental human problems that were mentioned at the close of the previous chapter? The answers remain tantalizingly elusive.

As often happened elsewhere, however, the collapse of Harappan civilization did not lead to the total disappearance of its culture. The new society that eventually emerged throughout the subcontinent after the coming of the Aryans was clearly the product of an amalgam of two highly distinctive cultures, Aryan and Dravidian, each of which made a significant contribution to the politics, the social institutions, and the creative impulse of ancient Indian civilization.

With the rise of the Mauryan dynasty in the fourth century B.C.E., the distinctive features of a great civilization begin to be clearly visible. It was extensive in its scope, embracing the entire Indian subcontinent and eventually, in the form of Buddhism and Hinduism, spreading to China and Southeast Asia. But the underlying ethnic, linguistic, and cultural diversity of the Indian people posed a constant challenge to the unity of the state. After the collapse of the Mauryas, the subcontinent would not come under a single authority again for several hundred years.

In the meantime, another great experiment was taking place far to the northeast, across the Himalaya Mountains. Like many other civilizations of antiquity, the first Chinese state was concentrated on a major river system. And like them, too, its political and cultural achievements eventually spread far beyond their original habitat. In the next chapter, we turn to the civilization of ancient China.

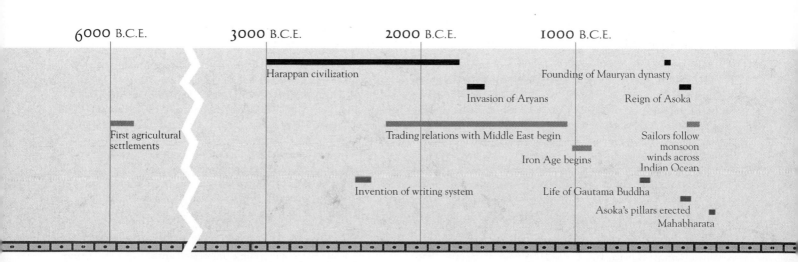

THE IDEAL BUDDHIST COUPLE.   Although originally the Aryans, a pastoral people, espoused a patriarchal religion peopled with male deities preoccupied with conquest and war, after their arrival in India they gradually incorporated female fertility spirits inherited from the local agrarian societies into their pantheon. This stylized couple, who welcome the faithful to the Buddhist rock temple at Karli, symbolize the essence of human life, at harmony with both the temporal and spiritual worlds. This sculpture dates from the first century C.E.

6000 B.C.E.   **3000** B.C.E.   **2000** B.C.E.   **1000** B.C.E.

Harappan civilization

Founding of Mauryan dynasty

Invasion of Aryans

Reign of Asoka

First agricultural settlements

Trading relations with Middle East begin

Sailors follow monsoon winds across Indian Ocean

Iron Age begins

Invention of writing system

Life of Gautama Buddha

Asoka's pillars erected

Mahabharata

CHAPTER NOTES

1. Quoted in Richard Lannoy, *The Speaking Tree: A Study of Indian Culture and Society* (London, 1971), p. 318.
2. The quotation is from ibid., p. 319. Note also that the *Law of Manu* says that "punishment alone governs all created beings. . . . The whole world is kept in order by punishment, for a guiltless man is hard to find."
3. Strabo's *Geography*, Book 15, quoted in Michael Edwardes, *A History of India: From the Earliest Times to the Present Day* (London, 1961), p. 55.
4. Ibid., p. 54.
5. From the *Law of Manu*, quoted in A. L. Basham, *The Wonder That Was India* (London, 1961), pp. 180–81.
6. *Mundaka Upanishad*, 1:2, quoted in William Theodore de Bary, et al., eds., *Sources of Indian Tradition* (New York, 1966), pp. 28–29.
7. *Chandogya Upanishad*, 6:1–3, 12–14 and *passim*, in ibid., pp. 33–35.
8. Quoted in Ananda K. Coomaraswamy, *Buddha and the Gospel of Buddhism* (New York, 1964), p. 34.

SUGGESTED READINGS

For easy reference to the history and archaeology of India, see the colorful and schematic *Past Worlds: The Times Atlas of Archaeology* (Maplewood, N.J., 1988). Several standard histories of India are available today, all of which provide a good overview of the ancient period. One of the most readable and reliable is S. Wolpert, *New History of India*, 3d ed. (New York, 1989). V. A. Smith's edition of *The Oxford History of India*, 4th ed. (Oxford, 1981), although somewhat out of date, contains a wealth of information on various aspects of early Indian history. For a discussion of the Mauryan period directed to the lay reader, see M. Edwardes, *A History of India* (London, 1961). Also of note is H. H. Dodwell, ed., *The Cambridge History of India*, 6 vols. (Cambridge, 1922–1953).

By far the most informative and readable narrative on the history of India in premodern times is still A. L. Basham, *The Wonder That Was India* (London, 1961), which contains informative sections on prehistory, economy, language, art and literature, society, and everyday life. Also useful is A. L. Basham, ed., *A Cultural History of India* (Oxford, 1975). For a stimulating analysis of Indian culture and society in general, consult R. Lannoy, *The Speaking Tree* (London, 1971). R. Thapar, *Interpreting Early India* (Delhi, 1992), provides a view by an Indian historian.

Because of the relatively recent nature of archaeological exploration in South Asia, evidence for the Harappan period is not as voluminous as for areas such as Mesopotamia and the Nile valley. Some of the best work has been written by scholars who actually worked at the sites. For a recent account, see J. M. Kenoyer, *Ancient Cities of the Indus Valley Civilization* (Karachi, Pakistan, 1998). A somewhat more extensive study is A. and B. Allchin, *The Birth of Indian Civilization, India and Pakistan before 500 B.C.* (Harmondsworth, 1968). For a detailed and well-illustrated analysis, see G. L. Possehlt, ed., *Harappan Civilization: A Contemporary Perspective* (Warminster, 1982). Commercial relations between Harappa and its neighbors are treated in S. Ratnagar, *Encounters: The Westerly Trade of the Harappan Civilization* (Oxford, 1981). See also *The Cultural Heritage of India*, vol. 1, *The Early Phase* (Calcutta, 1958) and J. Marshall's classic *Mohenjo-Daro and the Indus Civilization*, 3 vols. (London, 1931).

On the Mauryan period, see D. D. Kosambi, *The Culture and Civilization of Ancient India* (London, 1965) and R. Thapar, *Asoka and the Decline of the Mauryas* (Oxford, 1961).

There are a number of good books on the introduction of Buddhism into Indian society. Buddha's ideals are presented in A. K. Coomaraswamy, *Buddha and the Gospel of Buddhism* (London, 1916; revised, New York, 1964) and E. Conze, *Buddhism: Its Essence and Development* (Oxford, 1951). Also see H. Nakamura and M. B. Dasgupta, *Indian Buddhism: A Survey with Bibliographical Notes* (New Delhi, 1987). H. Akira, *A History of Indian Buddhism: From Sakyamuni to Early Mahayana* (Hawaii, 1990) provides a detailed analysis of early activities by Siddhartha Gautama and his followers. The intimate relationship between Buddhism and commerce is discussed in Liu Hsin-ju, *Ancient India and Ancient China: Trades and Religious Exchanges* (Oxford, 1988).

Hinduism, its origins and development, is the subject of S. Radhakrishnan, *The Hindu View of Life* (Oxford, 1926) and B. Walker, *Hindu World*, 2 vols. (London, 1969). For a more general treatment, see S. N. Dasgupta, *A History of Indian Philosophy*, 5 vols. (Cambridge, 1922–1955) and S. Radhakrishnan, *Indian Philosophy*, revised ed., 2 vols. (London, 1958).

There are a number of excellent surveys of Indian art, including the comprehensive S. L. Huntington, *The Art of Ancient India: Buddhist, Hindu, Jain* (New York, 1985) and the concise *Indian Art* (London, 1976) by R. Craven. See also V. Dehejia's *Devi: The Great Goddess* (Washington, D.C., 1999) and *Indian Art* (London, 1997).

Few general surveys of Indian literature exist, perhaps because of the magnitude and diversity of India's literature. A good textbook for college students is E. C. Dimock, *The Literatures of India: An Introduction* (Chicago, 1974), which traces Indian literary achievement from the epics to the modern Hindi film.

Many editions of Sanskrit literature are available in English translation. Many are available in the multivolume *Harvard Oriental Series*. For a one-volume annotated anthology of selections from the Indian classics, consult S. N. Hay, ed., *Sources of Indian Tradition*, 2 vols. (New York, 1988), or J. B. Alphonso-Karkala, *An*

Anthology of Indian Literature, 2d revised ed. (New Delhi, 1987), put out by the Indian Council for Cultural Relations.

The Mahabharata and Ramayana have been rewritten for 2,500 years. Fortunately, the vibrant versions, retold by William Buck and condensed to 400 pages each, reproduce the spirit of the originals and enthrall today's imagination. See W. Buck, *Mahabharata* (Berkeley, 1973) and *Ramayana* (Berkeley, 1976). For the role played by women writers in ancient India, see S. Tharu and K. Lalita, eds., *Women Writing in India: 600 B.C. to the Present,* vol. 1 (New York, 1991).

INFOTRAC COLLEGE EDITION

For additional reading, go to InfoTrac College Edition, your online research library at http://web1.infotrac-college.com

Enter the search term "Vedas" using Keywords.

Enter the search term "Hinduism" using the Subject Guide.

Enter the search term "Buddhism" using the Subject Guide.

Enter the search terms "India history" using Keywords.

Enter the search terms "Upanishad or Rigveda or Mahabharata" using Keywords.

CHAPTER

3

CHINA IN ANTIQUITY

CHAPTER OUTLINE
- THE LAND AND PEOPLE OF CHINA
- THE DAWN OF CHINESE CIVILIZATION: THE SHANG DYNASTY
- THE ZHOU DYNASTY
- THE RISE OF THE CHINESE EMPIRE: THE QIN AND THE HAN
- DAILY LIFE IN ANCIENT CHINA
- THE WORLD OF CULTURE
- CONCLUSION

FOCUS QUESTIONS
- How did geography influence the civilization that arose in China?
- What concepts of kingship and political and governmental institutions characterized each of the major dynasties of early China—the Shang, the Zhou, the Qin, and the Han?
- What were the major tenets of Confucianism, Legalism, and Daoism, and what role did each play in Chinese civilization?
- What were the key aspects of social and economic life in early China?
- What role did nomadic peoples play in early Chinese history?

The Master said: "If the government seeks to rule by decree, and to maintain order by the use of punishment, the people will seek to evade punishment and have no sense of shame. But if government leads by virtue and governs through the rules of propriety, the people will feel shame and seek to correct their mistakes."

That statement is from the *Analects*, a collection of remarks by the Chinese philosopher Confucius that were gathered together by his disciples and published after his death in the fifth century B.C.E. Confucius lived at a time when Chinese society was in a state of growing disarray. The political principles that had governed society since the founding of the Zhou dynasty six centuries earlier were widely ignored, and squabbling principalities scuffled for primacy as the power of the Zhou court steadily declined. The common people groaned under the weight of an oppressive manorial system that left them at the mercy of their feudal lords.

In the midst of this confusion, Confucius traveled the length of the kingdom observing events and seeking employment as a political counselor. In the process he attracted a number of disciples, to whom he proposed a set of ideas that in later years served as the guiding principles for the Chinese empire. Some of his ideas are strikingly modern in their thrust. Among them is the revolutionary proposition that government depends on the will of the people.

The civilization that produced Confucius had originated more than fifteen hundred years earlier along the two great river systems of East Asia, the Yellow and the Yangtze. This vibrant new civilization, which we know today as ancient China, expanded gradually over its neighboring areas. By the third century B.C.E., it had emerged as a great empire, as well as the dominant cultural and political force in the entire region.

Like Sumer, Harappa, and Egypt, the civilization of ancient China began as a collection of autonomous villages cultivating food crops along a major river system. Improvements in agricultural techniques led to a food surplus and the growth of an urban civilization characterized by more complex political and social institutions, as well as new forms of artistic and intellectual creativity.

Like its counterparts elsewhere, ancient China faced the challenge posed by the appearance of pastoral peoples on its borders. Unlike Harappa, Sumer, and Egypt, however, ancient China was able to avoid destruction at the hands of the invaders, and many of its institutions and cultural values survived intact down to the beginning of the twentieth century. For that reason, Chinese civilization is sometimes described as the oldest continuous civilization on earth. ✿

THE LAND AND PEOPLE OF CHINA

According to Chinese legend, Chinese society was founded by a series of rulers who brought the first rudiments of civilization to the region nearly five thousand years ago. The first was Fu Xi (Fu Hsi), the ox-tamer, who "knotted cords for hunting and fishing," domesticated animals, and introduced the beginnings of family life. The second was Shen Nong (Shen Nung), the divine farmer, who "bent wood for plows and hewed wood for plowshares." He taught the people the techniques of agriculture. Last came Huang Di (Huang Ti), the Yellow Emperor, who "strung a piece of wood for the bow, and whittled little sticks of wood for the arrows." Legend credits Huang Di with creating the Chinese system of writing, as well as with inventing the bow and arrow.[1] Modern historians, of course, do not accept the literal accuracy of such legends but view them instead as part of the process whereby early peoples attempt to make sense of the world and their role in it. Nevertheless, such re-creations of a mythical past often contain an element of truth. Although there is no clear evidence that the "three sovereigns" actually existed, their achievements do symbolize some of the defining characteristics of Chinese civilization: the interaction between nomadic and agricultural peoples, the importance of the family as the basic unit of Chinese life, and the development of a unique system of writing.

Human communities have existed in China for several hundred thousand years. Sometime around the eighth millennium B.C.E., the early peoples living along the riverbanks of northern China began to master the cultivation of crops. A number of these early agricultural settlements were in the neighborhood of the Yellow River, where they gave birth to two Neolithic societies known to archaeologists as the Yangshao and the Longshan cultures (sometimes identified in terms of their pottery as the painted and black pottery cultures). Similar agricultural settlements have been found in the Yangtze valley in central China and along the coast to the south. These settlements were based on the cultivation of rice rather than dry crops such as millet, barley, and wheat, but these settlements are as old as those in the north. Thus, agriculture, and perhaps other elements of early civilization, may have developed spontaneously in several areas of China rather than radiating outward from one central nuclear region.

At first, these simple Neolithic settlements were hardly more than villages, but as the inhabitants mastered the rudiments of agriculture, the little communities gradually gave rise to more sophisticated and complex societies. In a pattern that we have already seen elsewhere, civilization gradually spread from these nuclear settlements in the valleys of the Yellow and Yangtze rivers to other lowland areas of eastern and central China. The two great river valleys, then, can be considered the core regions in the development of Chinese civilization.

Although these densely cultivated valleys were among the great food-producing areas of the ancient world, China is not just a land of fertile fields. In fact, only 12 percent of the total land area is arable, compared with 23 percent in the United States. Much of the remainder consists of mountains and deserts that ring the country on its northern and western frontiers.

This often arid and forbidding landscape is a dominant feature of Chinese life and has played a significant role in Chinese history. The geographical barriers served to isolate the Chinese people from advanced agrarian societies in other parts of Asia. The frontier regions in the Gobi Desert, Central Asia, and the Tibetan plateau were sparsely inhabited by peoples of Mongolian, Indo-European, or Turkish extraction. Most were pastoral societies, and as was the case in the other river valley civilizations, their contacts with the Chinese were often characterized by mutual distrust and conflict. Although fewer in number than the Chinese, many of these peoples possessed impressive skills in war and were sometimes aggressive in seeking wealth or territory in the settled regions south of the Gobi Desert. Over the next two thousand years, the northern frontier became one of the great fault lines of conflict in Asia, as Chinese armies attempted to protect precious farmlands from marauding peoples from beyond the frontier. When China was unified and blessed with capable rulers, it could usually keep the nomadic intruders at bay and even bring them under a loose form of Chinese administration. But in times of internal weakness, China was vulnerable to attack from the north, and on several occasions, nomadic peoples succeeded in overthrowing native Chinese rulers and setting up their own dynastic regimes.

From other directions, China normally had little to fear. To the east lay the China Sea, a lair for pirates and the source of powerful typhoons that occasionally ravaged the Chinese coast, but otherwise rarely a source of concern. South of the Yangtze River was a hilly region inhabited by a mixture of peoples of varied language and ethnic stock who lived by farming, fishing, or food gathering. They were gradually absorbed in the inexorable expansion of Chinese civilization.

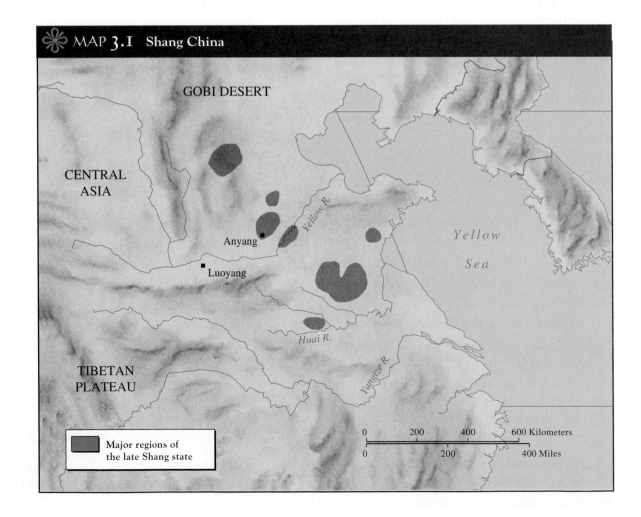

�ள MAP **3.1** **Shang China**

GOBI DESERT

CENTRAL ASIA

Anyang

Luoyang

Yellow R.

Yellow Sea

Huai R.

Yangtze R.

TIBETAN PLATEAU

Major regions of the late Shang state

| 0 | 200 | 400 | 600 Kilometers |

| 0 | | 200 | 400 Miles |

A TREATISE ON THE YELLOW RIVER AND ITS CANALS

Sima Qian (Szu-ma Ch'ien) was a famous historian of the Han dynasty who lived during the second and first centuries B.C.E. In his most famous work, entitled Historical Records, he describes the public works projects undertaken during the Xia dynasty to convert the dangerous waters of the Yellow River to human use. Although the identification of irrigation with Yu may be apocryphal, China later became one of the foremost hydraulic societies in the ancient world.

SIMA QIAN, *HISTORICAL RECORDS*

The documents on the Hsia dynasty tell us that Emperor Yu spent thirteen years controlling and bringing an end to the floods, and during that period, though he passed by the very gate of his own house, he did not take the time to enter. On land he traveled in a cart and on water in a boat; he rode a sledge to cross the mud and wore cleated shoes in climbing the mountains. In this way he marked out the nine provinces, led the rivers along the bases of the mountains, decided what tribute was appropriate for each region in accordance with the quality of its soil, opened up the nine roads, built embankments around the nine marshes, and made a survey of the nine mountains.

Of all the rivers, the Yellow River caused the greatest damage to China by overflowing its banks and inundating the land, and therefore he turned all his attention to controlling it. Thus he led the Yellow River in a course from Chi-shih past Lung-men and south to the northern side of Mount Hua; from there eastward along the foot of Ti-chu Mountain, past the Meng Ford and the confluence of the Lo River to Ta-p'ei. At this point Emperor Yu decided that, since the river was descending from high ground and the flow of the water was rapid and fierce, it would be difficult to guide it over level ground without danger of frequent disastrous breakthroughs. He therefore divided the flow into two channels, leading it along the higher ground to the north, past the Chiang River and so to Ta-lu. There he spread it out to form the Nine Rivers, brought it together again to make the Backward-Flowing River [i.e., tidal river], and thence led it into the Gulf of Pohai. When he had thus opened up the rivers of the nine provinces and fixed the outlets of the nine marshes, peace and order were brought to the lands of the Hsia, and his achievements continued to benefit the Three Dynasties which followed.

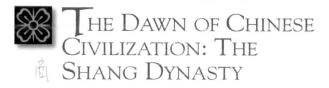

THE DAWN OF CHINESE CIVILIZATION: THE SHANG DYNASTY

Historians of China have traditionally dated the beginning of Chinese civilization to the founding of the Xia (Hsia) dynasty more than four thousand years ago. Although the precise date for the rise of the Xia is in dispute, legend maintains that the founder was a ruler named Yu, who is also credited with introducing irrigation and draining the floodwaters that periodically threatened to inundate the northern China plain (see the box above). The Xia dynasty, in turn, was replaced by a second dynasty, the Shang, around the sixteenth century B.C.E. The Shang capital at Anyang, just north of the Yellow River in north-central China, has been excavated by archaeologists. Among the finds were thousands of so-called oracle bones, ox and chicken bones or turtle shells that were used by Shang rulers for divination and to communicate with the gods. The inscriptions on these oracle bones are the earliest known form of Chinese writing and provide much of our information about the beginnings of civilization in China. They describe a culture gradually emerging from the Neolithic to the early Bronze Age.

Political Organization

China under the Shang dynasty was a predominantly agricultural society ruled by an aristocratic class whose major occupation was war. One ancient chronicler complained that "the big affairs of state consist of sacrifice and soldiery."[2] Combat was carried on by means of two-horse chariots. The appearance of chariots in China in the mid second millennium B.C.E. coincides roughly with similar developments elsewhere, leading some historians to suggest that the Shang ruling class may originally have invaded China from elsewhere in Asia. But items found in Shang burial mounds are similar to Longshan pottery, implying that the Shang ruling elites were linear descendants of the indigenous Neolithic peoples in the area. If that was the case, the Shang may have acquired their knowledge of horse-drawn chariots through contact with the peoples of neighboring regions.

Some recent support for that assumption has come from evidence unearthed in the sandy wastes of Xinjiang, China's far-northwestern province. There archaeologists have discovered corpses dating back as early as the second millennium B.C.E. with physical characteristics that are clearly European. They are also clothed in textiles similar to those worn at the time in Europe, suggesting that they may have been members of an Indo-European migration

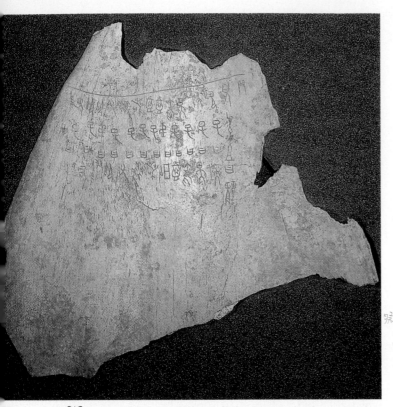

✿ **SHELL AND BONE WRITING.** The earliest known form of writing in China dates back to the early Shang dynasty and was inscribed on shells or animal bones. Questions for the gods were scratched on bones, which cracked after being exposed to fire. The cracks were then interpreted by sorcerers. The questions often expressed practical concerns: Will it rain? Will the king be victorious in battle? Will he recover from his illness? Originally composed of pictographs and ideographs 4,000 years ago, Chinese writing has evolved into an elaborate system of stylized symbols still in use today.

from areas much further to the west. If that is the case, it is not improbable that they were familiar with advances in chariot making that occurred a few hundred years earlier in southern Russia and Kazakstan. By about 2000 B.C.E. spoked wheels were being deposited at grave sites in Ukraine and also in the Gobi Desert, just north of the great bend of the Yellow River. It is thus not unlikely that the new technology became available to the founders of the Shang dynasty and may have aided their rise to power in northern China.

The Shang king ruled with the assistance of a central bureaucracy in the capital city. His realm was divided into a number of territories governed by aristocratic chieftains, but the king appointed these chieftains and could apparently depose them at will. He was also responsible for the defense of the realm and controlled large armies that often fought on the fringes of the kingdom. The transcendent importance of the ruler was graphically displayed in the ritual sacrifices undertaken at his death, when hundreds of his retainers were buried with him in the royal tomb.

As the inscriptions on the oracle bones make clear, the Chinese ruling elite believed in the existence of supernatural forces and thought that they could communicate with those forces to obtain divine intervention on matters of this world. In fact, the purpose of the oracle bones was to communicate with the gods (see the illustration at left). This evidence also suggests that the king was already being viewed as an intermediary between Heaven and earth. In fact, an early Chinese character for king (王) consists of three horizontal lines connected by a single vertical line; the middle horizontal line represents the king's place between human society and the divine forces in nature.

The early Chinese also had a clear sense of life in the hereafter. Though some of the human sacrifices discovered in the royal tombs were presumably intended to propitiate the gods, others were meant to accompany the king or members of his family on the journey to the next world. From this conviction would come the concept of the veneration of ancestors (commonly known in the West as "ancestor worship") and the practice, which continues to the present day in many Chinese communities, of burning replicas of physical objects to accompany the departed on their journey to the next world.

Social Structures

In the Neolithic period, the farm village was apparently the basic social unit of China, at least in the core region of the Yellow River valley. Villages were organized by clans rather than by nuclear family units, and all residents probably took the common clan name of the entire village. In some cases, a village may have included more than one clan. At Banpo (Pan P'o), an archaeological site near modern Xian that dates back at least eight thousand years, the houses in the village are separated by a ditch, which some scholars think may have served as a divider between two clans. The individual dwellings at Banpo housed nuclear families, but a larger building in the village was apparently used as a clan meeting hall. The tribal origins of Chinese society may help to explain the continued importance of the joint family in traditional China, as well as the relatively small number of family names in Chinese society. Even today there are only about four hundred commonly used family names in a society of more than one billion people.

By Shang times, the classes were becoming increasingly differentiated. It is likely that some poorer peasants did not own their farms but were obliged to work the land of the chieftain and other elite families in the village (see the box on p. 69). The aristocrats not only made war and served as officials (indeed, the first Chinese character for official originally meant warrior), but they were also the primary landowners. In addition to the aristocratic elite and the peasants, there were also a small number of merchants and artisans, as well as slaves, probably consisting primarily of criminals or prisoners taken in battle.

LIFE IN THE FIELDS

The following passage is from the Book of Songs, a famous classic that was written sometime during the early Zhou dynasty. This excerpt describes the calendar of peasant life on an estate in ancient China and indicates the various types of service that peasants provided for their lord.

THE BOOK OF SONGS

In the seventh month the Fire Star passes the meridian;
In the ninth month clothes are given out.
In the days of [our] first month, the wind blows cold;
In the days of [our] second, the air is cold.
Without coats, without garments of hair,
How could we get to the end of the year?
In the days of [our] third month we take our plows in hand;
In the days of [our] fourth we make our way to the fields.
Along with wives and children,
We eat in those south-lying acres.
The surveyor of the fields comes and is glad.

In the seventh month the Fire Star passes the meridian;
In the ninth month clothes are given out.
With the spring days the warmth begins,
And the oriole utters its song.
The young women take their deep baskets
And go along the small paths,
Looking for the tender [leaves of the] mulberry trees
As the spring days lengthen out,
They gather in crowds the white southern wood.
The girl's heart is wounded with sadness,
For she will soon be going with one of the young lords.

. . .

In the eighth month spinning is begun;
We make dark fabrics and yellow,
"With our red dye so bright,
We make robes for our young lords."

In the ninth month we prepare the stockyard,
And in the tenth we bring in the harvest.
The millets, the early and the late,
Together with paddy and hemp, beans and wheat.

. . .

Now we go up to work in the manor.
"In the day you gather the thatch-reeds;
In the evening twist them into rope;
Go quickly on to the roofs;
Soon you are to sow the grain."

In the days of [our] second month we cut the ice with
    tingling blows;
In the days of [our] third month [it is] stored in the
    icehouse.
In the days of [our] fourth month, very early,
A lamb with scallions is offered in sacrifice.
In the ninth month are shrewd frosts;
In the tenth month the stockyard is cleared.
With twin pitchers we hold the feast,
Killed for it is a young lamb.
Up we go into the lord's hall,
Raise the cup of buffalo horn;
"Long life for our lord; may he live forever and ever!"

The Shang are perhaps best known for their mastery of the art of bronze casting. Utensils, weapons, and ritual objects made of bronze have been found in royal tombs in urban centers throughout the area known to be under Shang influence (see Metalwork and Sculpture later in this chapter). It is also clear that the Shang had achieved a fairly sophisticated writing system; the oracle bones provide concrete evidence of the existence of a system of ideographs and pictographs that is the direct precursor of the written language used in China today.

THE ZHOU DYNASTY

In the eleventh century B.C.E., the Shang dynasty was overthrown by an aggressive young state located somewhat to the west of Anyang, the Shang capital, and near the great bend of the Yellow River as it begins to flow directly eastward to the sea. The new dynasty, which called itself the Zhou (Chou), survived for about eight hundred years and was thus the longest-lived dynasty in the history of China. According to tradition, the last of the Shang rulers was a tyrant who oppressed the people (Chinese sources assert that he was a degenerate who built "ponds of wine" and ordered the composing of lustful music that "ruined the morale of the nation"), leading the ruler of the principality of Zhou to revolt and establish a new dynasty.[3]

The Zhou located their capital in their home territory, near the present-day city of Xian. Later they established a second capital city at modern Luoyang, farther to the east, to administer new territories captured from the Shang. This established a pattern of eastern and western capitals that would endure off and on in China for nearly two thousand years.

�֎ **SHANG AND ZHOU BRONZES.**   From the eighteenth to the twelfth centuries B.C.E., the most significant artistic contribution of the Shang dynasty was its bronze ritual vessels. Used initially as food containers in ceremonial rites for ancestral devotion by the emperors, these magnificent objects were the product of an advanced technology unmatched by any contemporary civilization. The Zhou dynasty continued the tradition, as illustrated here by the ninth-century bell with four tigers. Note the stylized face of a dragon. This mysterious animal-mask design, known as a Taotie, is characteristic of both Shang and Zhou bronze objects. Sought by museums everywhere, these bronzes are considered one of the art wonders of the world.

Political Structures

The Zhou dynasty (1045–221 B.C.E.) adopted the political system of its predecessors with some changes. The Shang practice of dividing the kingdom into a number of territories governed by officials appointed by the king was continued under the Zhou. At the apex of the government hierarchy was the Zhou king, who was served by a bureaucracy of growing size and complexity. It now included several ministries responsible for rites, education, law, and public works. Beyond the capital, the Zhou kingdom was divided into a number of principalities, governed by members of the hereditary aristocracy, who were appointed by the king and were at least theoretically subordinated to his authority.

But the Zhou kings also introduced some innovations. According to the *Rites of Zhou*, one of the oldest surviving documents on statecraft, the Zhou dynasty ruled China because it possessed the "mandate of Heaven." According to this concept, Heaven (viewed as an impersonal law of nature rather than as an anthropomorphic deity) maintained order in the universe through the Zhou king, who thus ruled as a representative of Heaven, but not as a divine being. The king, who was selected to rule because of his talent and virtue, was then responsible for governing the people with compassion and efficiency. It was his duty to propitiate the gods in order to protect the people from natural calamities or a bad harvest. But if the king failed to rule effectively, theoretically at least he could be overthrown and replaced by a new ruler. As noted earlier, this idea was used to justify the Zhou conquest of the Shang. Eventually, the concept of the heavenly mandate would become a cardinal principle of Chinese statecraft.[4] Each founder of a new dynasty would routinely assert that he had earned the mandate of Heaven, and who could disprove it except by overthrowing the king? As a pragmatic Chinese proverb put it: "He who wins is the king; he who loses is the rebel."

By the sixth century B.C.E., the Zhou dynasty began to decline. As the power of the central government disintegrated, bitter internal rivalries arose among the various principalities, where the governing officials had succeeded in making their positions hereditary at the expense of the king. As the power of these officials grew, they began to regulate the local economy and seek reliable sources of revenue for their expanding armies, such as a uniform tax system and government monopolies on key commodities such as salt and iron.

Economy and Society

During the Zhou dynasty, the essential characteristics of Chinese economic and social institutions began to take shape. The Zhou continued the pattern of land ownership that had existed under the Shang: the peasants worked on lands owned by their lord but also had land of their own that they cultivated for their own use. The practice was called the "well field system," since the Chinese character for well (井) resembles a simplified picture of the division of the farmland into nine separate segments. Each peasant family tilled an outer plot for its own use and then joined with other families to work the inner one for the hereditary lord (see the box on p. 69). How widely this system was used is unclear, but it represented an ideal described by Confucian scholars of a later day. As the following poem indicates, life for the average farmer was a difficult one. The "big rat" is probably a reference to the high taxes imposed on the peasants by the government or lord.

Big rat, big rat
Do not eat my millet!
Three years I have served you,
But you will not care for me.

ENVIRONMENTAL CONCERNS IN ANCIENT CHINA

Even in antiquity, China possessed a large population that often stretched the limits of the productive potential of the land. In the following excerpt, the late Zhou philosopher Mencius appeals to his sovereign to adopt policies that will conserve precious resources and foster the well-being of his subjects. Clearly, Mencius was concerned that environmental needs were being neglected. Unfortunately, his advice has not always been followed, as environmental degradation remains a problem in China today. The destruction of the forests, for example, has deprived China of much of its wood resources, and the present government has launched an extensive program to plant trees.

THE BOOK OF MENCIUS

If you do not interfere with the busy season in the fields, then there will be more grain than the people can eat; if you do not allow nets with too fine a mesh to be used in large ponds, then there will be more fish and turtles than they can eat; if hatchets and axes are permitted in the forests on the hills only in the proper seasons, then there will be more timber than they can use. When the people have more grain, more fish and turtles than they can eat, and more timber than they can use, then in the support of their parents when alive and in the mourning of them when dead, they will be able to have no regrets over anything left undone. This is the first step along the Kingly way.

If the mulberry is planted in every homestead of five mu of land, then those who are fifty can wear silk; if chickens, pigs, and dogs do not miss their breeding season, then those who are seventy can eat meat; if each lot of a hundred mu is not deprived of labor during the busy seasons, then families with several mouths to feed will not go hungry. Exercise due care over the education provided by the village schools, and discipline the people by teaching them the duties proper to sons and younger brothers, and those whose heads have turned gray will not be carrying loads on the roads. When those who are seventy wear silk and eat meat and the masses are neither cold nor hungry, it is impossible for their prince not to be a true King.

Now when food meant for human beings is so plentiful as to be thrown to dogs and pigs, you fail to realize that it is time for garnering, and when men drop dead from starvation by the wayside, you fail to realize that it is time for distribution. When people die, you simply say, "It is none of my doing. It is the fault of the harvest." In what way is that different from killing a man by running him through, while saying all the time, "It is none of my doing. It is the fault of the weapon." Stop putting the blame on the harvest and the people of the whole Empire will come to you.

I am going to leave you
And go to that happy land;
Happy land, happy land,
Where I will find my place.[5]

Trade and manufacturing were carried out by merchants and artisans, who lived in walled towns under the direct control of the local lord. Merchants did not operate independently but were considered the property of the local lord and on occasion could even be bought and sold like chattels. A class of slaves performed a variety of menial tasks and perhaps worked on local irrigation projects. Most of them were probably prisoners of war captured during conflicts with the neighboring principalities. Scholars do not know how extensive slavery was in ancient times, but slaves probably did not comprise a large proportion of the total population.

The period of the later Zhou, from the sixth to the third century B.C.E., was an era of significant economic growth and technological innovation, especially in agriculture. During that time, large-scale water control projects were undertaken to regulate the flow of rivers and distribute water evenly to the fields, as well as to construct canals to facilitate the transport of goods from one region to another (see the box on p. 67). Perhaps the most impressive technological achievement of the period was the construction of the massive water control project on the Min River, a tributary of the Yangtze. This system of canals and spillways, which was put into operation by the state of Qin a few years prior to the end of the Zhou dynasty, diverted excess water from the river into the local irrigation network and watered an area populated by as many as five million people. The system is still in use today, over two thousand years later.

Food production was also stimulated by a number of advances in farm technology. By the mid-sixth century B.C.E., the introduction of iron had led to the development of iron plowshares, which permitted deep plowing for the first time. Other innovations dating from the later Zhou were the use of natural fertilizer, the collar harness, and the technique of leaving land fallow to preserve or replenish nutrients in the soil (see the box above).

The advances in agriculture, which enabled the population of China to rise as high as 20 million people during the late Zhou era, were also undoubtedly a major factor in the growth of commerce and manufacturing. During the later Zhou, economic wealth began to replace noble birth as the prime source of power and influence. Utensils made of iron became more common, and trade developed in a variety of useful commodities, such as cloth, salt, and various manufactured goods.

One of the most important items of trade in ancient China was silk. There is evidence of silkworm raising as early as the Neolithic period. Remains of silk material have been found on Shang bronzes, and a large number of fragments have been recovered in tombs dating from the mid-Zhou era. Silk cloth was used not only for clothing and quilts, but also to wrap the body of the dead prior to burial. Fragments have been found throughout Central Asia and as far away as Athens, suggesting that the famous "Silk Road" was in operation as early as the fifth century B.C.E. (for a discussion of the Silk Road, see Chapter 10).

With the development of trade and manufacturing, China began to move toward a money economy. The first form of money may have been seashells (the Chinese character for goods or property contains the ideographic symbol for "shell"), but by the Zhou dynasty pieces of iron shaped like a knife or round coins with a hole in the middle so they could be carried in strings of a thousand were being used. Most ordinary Chinese, however, simply used a system of barter. Even taxes and rents, as well as the salaries of government officials, were normally paid in grain.

The Hundred Schools of Ancient Philosophy

In China, as in other great river valley societies, the birth of civilization was accompanied by the emergence of an organized effort to comprehend the nature of the cosmos and the role of human beings within it. Speculation over such questions began in the very early stages of civilization and culminated at the end of the Zhou era in the "hundred schools" of ancient philosophy, a wide-ranging debate over the nature of human beings, society, and the universe.

The first hint of religious belief in ancient China comes from relics found in royal tombs of Neolithic times. By then, the Chinese had already developed a religious sense beyond the primitive belief in the existence of spirits in nature. The Shang had already begun to believe in the existence of one transcendent god, known as Shang Di, who presided over all the forces of nature. As time went on, the Chinese concept of religion began to evolve from a vaguely anthropomorphic god to a somewhat more impersonal symbol of universal order known as Heaven (Tian, or T'ien). There was also much speculation among Chinese intellectuals about the nature of the cosmic order. One of the earliest ideas was that the universe was divided into two primary forces of good and evil, light and dark, male and female, called the yang and the yin, represented symbolically by the sun (yang) and the moon (yin). According to this theory, life was a dynamic process of interaction between the forces of yang and yin. Early Chinese could

attempt only to understand the process and perhaps to have some minimal effect on its operation. They could not hope to reverse it. It is sometimes asserted that this belief has contributed to the heavy element of fatalism in Chinese popular wisdom. The Chinese have traditionally believed that bad times will be followed by good times, and vice versa.

The belief that there was some mysterious "law of nature" that could be interpreted by human beings led to various attempts to predict the future, such as the Shang oracle bones and other methods of divination. Philosophers invented various ways to interpret the will of nature, while shamans, playing a role similar to the brahmins in India, were employed at court to assist the emperor in his policy deliberations until at least the fifth century C.E. One of the most famous manuals used for this purpose was the Yi Jing (I Ching), known in English as the Book of Changes.

CONFUCIANISM

Such efforts to divine the mysterious purposes of Heaven notwithstanding, Chinese thinking about metaphysical reality also contained a strain of pragmatism, which is readily apparent in the ideas of the great philosopher Confucius. Confucius (the Latin form of his honorific title Kung Fuci, or K'ung Fu-tzu, meaning Master Kung) was born in the state of Lu (in the modern province of Shandong) in 551 B.C.E. After reaching maturity, he apparently hoped to find employment as a political adviser in one of the principalities into which China was divided at that time, but he had little success in finding a patron. Nevertheless, he made an indelible mark on history as an independent (and somewhat disgruntled) political and social philosopher.

In conversations with his disciples contained in the Analects, Confucius often adopted a detached and almost skeptical view of Heaven. "You are unable to serve man," he commented on one occasion, "how then can you hope to serve the spirits? While you do not know life, how can you know about death?" In many instances, he appeared to advise his followers to revere the deities and the ancestral spirits but to keep them at a distance. Confucius believed it was useless to speculate too much about metaphysical questions. Better by far to assume that there was a rational order to the universe and then concentrate one's attention on ordering the affairs of this world.[6]

Confucius's interest in philosophy, then, was essentially political and ethical. The universe was constructed in such a way that if human beings could act harmoniously in accordance with its purposes, their own affairs would prosper. Much of his concern was with human behavior. The key to proper behavior was to behave in accordance with the Dao (Way). Confucius assumed that all human beings had their own Dao, depending on their individual role in life, and it was their duty to follow it. Even the ruler had

THE WAY OF THE GREAT LEARNING

Unfortunately, *few texts exist today that were written by Confucius himself. Most were written or edited by his disciples. The following text, entitled* The Great Learning, *was probably written two centuries after Confucius's death, but it illustrates his view that good government begins with the cultivation of individual morality and proper human relationships at the basic level. This conviction that "to bring peace to the world, cultivate your own person" continued to win general approval down to modern times.*

THE GREAT LEARNING

The Way of the Great Learning consists in clearly exemplifying illustrious virtue, in loving the people, and in resting in the highest good.

Only when one knows where one is to rest can one have a fixed purpose. Only with a fixed purpose can one achieve calmness of mind. Only with calmness of mind can one attain serene repose. Only in serene repose can one carry on careful deliberation. Only through careful deliberation can one have achievement. Things have their roots and branches; affairs have their beginning and end. He who knows what comes first and what comes last comes himself near the Way.

The ancients who wished clearly to exemplify illustrious virtue throughout the world would first set up good govern-ment in their states. Wishing to govern well their states, they would first regulate their families. Wishing to regulate their families, they would first cultivate their persons. Wishing to cultivate their persons, they would first rectify their minds. Wishing to rectify their minds, they would first seek sincerity in their thoughts. Wishing for sincerity in their thoughts, they would first extend their knowledge. The extension of knowledge lay in the investigation of things. For only when things are investigated is knowledge extended; only when knowledge is extended are thoughts sincere; only when thoughts are sincere are minds rectified; only when minds are rectified are our persons cultivated; only when our persons are cultivated are our families regulated; only when families are regulated are states well governed; and only when states are well governed is there peace in the world.

From the emperor down to the common people, all, without exception, must consider cultivation of the individual character as the root. If the root is in disorder, it is impossible for the branches to be in order. To treat the important as unimportant and to treat the unimportant as important—this should never be. This is called knowing the root; this is called the perfection of knowledge.

---

his own *Dao*, and he ignored it at his peril, for to do so could mean the loss of the mandate of Heaven. The idea of the *Dao* is reminiscent of the concept of *dharma* in ancient India and played a similar role in governing the affairs of society.

Two elements in the Confucian interpretation of the *Dao* are particularly worthy of mention. The first is the concept of duty. It was the responsibility of all individuals to subordinate their own interests and aspirations to the broader need of the family and the community. Confucius assumed that if each individual worked hard to fulfill his or her assigned destiny, the affairs of society as a whole would surely prosper as well. In this respect, it was important for the ruler to set a good example. If he followed his "kingly way," the beneficial effects would radiate throughout society (see the box above).

The second key element is the idea of humanity, sometimes translated as "human heartedness." This concept involves a sense of compassion and empathy for others. It is similar in some ways to Christian concepts, but with a subtle twist. Where Christian teachings call on human beings to "behave toward others as you would have them behave toward you," the Confucian maxim is put in a different way: "Do not do unto others what you would not wish done to yourself." To many Chinese, this attitude symbolizes an element of tolerance in the Chinese character that has not always been practiced in other societies.[7]

Confucius may have considered himself a failure because he never attained the position he wanted, but many of his contemporaries found his ideas appealing, and in the generations after his death, his message spread widely throughout China. Confucius was an outspoken critic of his times and lamented the disappearance of what he regarded as the Golden Age of the early Zhou.

In fact, however, Confucius was not just another disgruntled Chinese conservative mourning the passing of the good old days, but a revolutionary thinker, many of whose key ideas looked forward rather than backward. Perhaps his most striking political idea was that the government should be open to all men of superior quality, and not limited to those of noble birth. As one of his disciples reports in the *Analects:* "The Master said, by nature, men are nearly alike; by practice, they get to be wide apart."[8] Confucius undoubtedly had himself in mind as one of those "superior" men, but the rapacity of the hereditary lords must have added strength to his convictions.

The concept of rule by merit was, of course, not an unfamiliar idea in the China of his day; the *Rites of Zhou* had clearly stated that the king himself deserved to rule because of his talent and virtue, rather than as the result of noble birth. In practice, however, aristocratic privilege must often have opened the doors to political influence, and many of Confucius's contemporaries must have regarded his appeal for government by talent as both exciting and dangerous. Confucius did not explicitly question the right of the hereditary aristocracy to play a leading role in the political process, nor did his ideas have much effect in his lifetime. Still, they introduced a new concept that was later implemented in the form of a bureaucracy selected through a civil service examination (see the section on Confucianism and the State later in this chapter).

Confucius's ideas, passed on to later generations through the *Analects* as well as through other writings allegedly written by Confucius, had a strong impact on Chinese political thinkers of the late Zhou period, a time when the existing system was in disarray and open to serious question. But as with most great thinkers, Confucius's ideas were sufficiently ambiguous to be interpreted in very contradictory ways. Some, like the philosopher Mencius (370–290 B.C.E.), stressed the humanistic side of Confucian ideas, arguing that human beings were by nature good and thus could be taught their civic responsibilities by example. He also stressed that the ruler had a duty to govern with compassion:

> It was because Chieh and Chou lost the people that they lost the empire, and it was because they lost the hearts of the people that they lost the people. Here is the way to win the empire: win the people and you win the empire. Here is the way to win the people: win their hearts and you win the people. Here is the way to win their hearts: give them and share with them what they like, and do not do to them what they do not like. The people turn to a human ruler as water flows downward or beasts take to wilderness.[9]

Here is a prescription for political behavior that could win wide support in our own day. Other thinkers, however, rejected Mencius's rosy view of human nature and argued for a different approach.

LEGALISM

One school of thought that became quite popular during the "hundred schools" era in ancient China was the philosophy of Legalism. Taking issue with the view of Mencius and other disciples of Confucius that human nature was essentially good, the Legalists argued that human beings were by nature evil and would follow the correct path only if coerced by harsh laws and stiff punishments. These thinkers were referred to as the "School of Law," because they rejected the Confucian view that government by "superior men" could solve society's problems and argued instead for a system of impersonal laws.

The Legalists disagreed with the Confucian belief that the universe has a moral core. They therefore believed that only firm action by the state could bring about social order. Fear of harsh punishment, more than the promise of material reward, could best motivate the common people to serve the interests of the ruler. Because human nature was essentially corrupt, officials could not be trusted to carry out their duties in a fair and evenhanded manner, and only a strong ruler could create an orderly society. All human actions should be subordinated to the effort to create a strong and prosperous state subject to his will.

DAOISM

One of the most popular alternatives to Confucianism was the philosophy of Daoism (frequently spelled Taoism). According to Chinese tradition, the Daoist school was founded by a contemporary of Confucius popularly known as Lao Tzu (Lao Zi), or the Old Master. Many modern scholars, however, are skeptical that Lao Tzu actually existed.

Obtaining a clear understanding of the original concepts of Daoism is difficult because its primary document, a short treatise known as the *Dao De Jing* (sometimes translated as *The Way of the Tao*), is an enigmatic book whose interpretation has baffled scholars for centuries. The opening line, for example, explains less what the *Dao* is than what it is not: "The Tao [Way] that can be told of is not the eternal Tao. The name that can be named is not the eternal name."[10]

Nevertheless, the basic concepts of Daoism are not especially difficult to understand. Like Confucianism, Daoism does not anguish over the underlying meaning of the cosmos. Rather, it attempts to set forth proper forms of behavior for human beings here on earth. In most other respects, however, Daoism presents a view of life and its ultimate meaning that is almost diametrically opposed to that of Confucianism. Where Confucian doctrine asserts that it is the duty of human beings to work hard to improve life here on earth, Daoists contend that the true way to interpret the will of Heaven is not action, but inaction (*wu wei*). The best way to act in harmony with the universal order is to act spontaneously and let nature take its course (see the box on p. 75).

Such a message could be very appealing to those who were uncomfortable with the somewhat rigid flavor of the Confucian work ethic and preferred a more individualistic approach. This image would eventually find graphic expression in Chinese landscape painting, which in its classical form would depict naturalistic scenes of mountains, water, and clouds and underscore the fragility and smallness of individual human beings.

Daoism achieved considerable popularity in the waning years of the Zhou dynasty. It was especially popular among intellectuals, who may have found it appealing as

THE DAOIST ANSWER TO CONFUCIANISM

The Dao De Jing (The Way of the Dao) *is the great classic of philosophical Daoism (Taoism). Traditionally attributed to the legendary Chinese philosopher Lao Tzu (Old Master), it was probably written sometime during the era of Confucius. This opening passage illustrates two of the key ideas that characterize Daoist belief: it is impossible to define the nature of the universe, and "inaction" (not Confucian "action") is the key to ordering the affairs of human beings.*

THE WAY OF THE DAO

The Tao that can be told of is not the eternal Tao;
The name that can be named is not the eternal name.
The Nameless is the origin of Heaven and Earth;
The Named is the mother of all things.

Therefore let there always be nonbeing, so we may see their
*　subtlety.*
And let there always be being, so we may see their
*　outcome.*
The two are the same,
But after they are produced, they have different names.
They both may be called deep and profound.

Deeper and more profound,
The door of all subtleties!
When the people of the world all know beauty as beauty,
There arises the recognition of ugliness.
When they all know the good as good,
There arises the recognition of evil.
Therefore:
Being and nonbeing produce each other;
Difficult and easy complete each other;
Long and short contrast each other;
High and low distinguish each other;
Sound and voice harmonize each other;
Front and behind accompany each other.

Therefore the sage manages affairs without action
And spreads doctrines without words.
All things arise, and he does not turn away from them.
He produces them but does not take possession of them.
He acts but does not rely on his own ability.
He accomplishes his task but does not claim credit for it.
It is precisely because he does not claim credit that his
*　accomplishment remains with him.*

an escapist antidote in a world characterized by growing disorder.

POPULAR BELIEFS

Daoism also played a second role as a somewhat loose framework for popular spiritualistic and animistic beliefs among the common people. Popular Daoism was less a philosophy than a religion; it comprised a variety of rituals and forms of behavior that were regarded as a means of achieving heavenly salvation or even a state of immortality on earth. Daoist sorcerers practiced various types of mind- or body-training exercises in the hope of achieving power, sexual prowess, and long life. It was primarily this form of Daoism that survived into a later age.

The philosophical forms of Confucianism and Daoism did not provide much meaning to the mass of the population, for whom philosophical debate over the ultimate meaning of life was not as important as the daily struggle for survival. For most Chinese, Heaven was not a vague impersonal law of nature, as it was for many Confucian and Daoist intellectuals, but a terrain peopled with innumerable gods and spirits of nature, both good and evil, who existed in trees, mountains, and streams as well as in heavenly bodies. As human beings mastered the techniques of farming, they called on divine intervention to guarantee a good harvest. Other gods were responsible for the safety of fishers, transportation workers, or prospective mothers.

Another aspect of popular religion was the belief that the spirits of deceased human beings lived in the atmosphere for a time before ascending to Heaven or descending to Hell. During that period, surviving family members had to care for the spirits through proper ritual, or they would become evil spirits and haunt the survivors.

Thus, in ancient China, human beings were offered a variety of interpretations of the nature of the universe. Confucianism satisfied the need for a rational doctrine of nation building and social organization at a time when the existing political and social structure was beginning to disintegrate. Philosophical Daoism provided an alternative to Confucianism and a framework for a set of diverse animistic beliefs at the popular level. But neither could satisfy the deeper emotional needs that sometimes inspire the human spirit. Neither could effectively provide solace in a time of sorrow or the hope of a better life in the hereafter. Something else would be needed to fill the gap.

THE RISE OF THE CHINESE EMPIRE: THE QIN AND THE HAN

During the last two centuries of the Zhou dynasty (the fourth and third centuries B.C.E.), the authority of the king became increasingly nominal, and several of the small

名我上的

THE ART OF WAR

With the possible exception of the nineteenth-century German military strategist Karl von Clausewitz, there is probably no more famous or respected writer on the art of war than the ancient Chinese thinker Sun Tzu. Yet surprisingly little is known about him. Recently discovered evidence suggests that he lived sometime in the fifth century B.C.E., during the chronic conflict of the Period of Warring States, and that he was an early member of an illustrious family of military strategists who advised Zhou rulers for more than two hundred years. But despite the mystery surrounding his life, there is no doubt of his influence on later generations of military planners. Among his most avid followers in our century have been the revolutionary leaders Mao Zedong and Ho Chi Minh, as well as the Japanese military strategists who planned the attacks on Port Arthur and Pearl Harbor.

The following brief excerpt from his classic The Art of War provides a glimmer into the nature of his advice, still so timely today.

SELECTIONS FROM SUN TZU

Sun Tzu said:

"In general, the method for employing the military is this: . . . Attaining one hundred victories in one hundred battles is not the pinnacle of excellence. Subjugating the enemy's army without fighting is the true pinnacle of excellence. . . .

"Thus the highest realization of warfare is to attack the enemy's plans; next is to attack their alliances; next to attack their army; and the lowest is to attack their fortified cities.

"This tactic of attacking fortified cities is adopted only when unavoidable. Preparing large movable protective shields, armored assault wagons, and other equipment and devices will require three months. Building earthworks will require another three months to complete. If the general cannot overcome his impatience but instead launches an assault wherein his men swarm over the walls like ants, he will kill one-third of his officers and troops, and the city will still not be taken. This is the disaster that results from attacking [fortified cities].

"Thus one who excels at employing the military subjugates other people's armies without engaging in battle, captures other people's fortified cities without attacking them, and destroys others people's states without prolonged fighting. He must fight under Heaven with the paramount aim of 'preservation.' . . .

"In general, the strategy of employing the military is this: If your strength is ten times theirs, surround them; if five, then attack them; if double, then divide your forces. If you are equal in strength to the enemy, you can engage him. If fewer, you can circumvent him. If outmatched, you can avoid him. . . .

"Thus there are five factors from which victory can be known:

"One who knows when he can fight, and when he cannot fight, will be victorious.

"One who recognizes how to employ large and small numbers will be victorious.

"One whose upper and lower ranks have the same desires will be victorious.

"One who, fully prepared, awaits the unprepared will be victorious.

"One whose general is capable and not interfered with by the ruler will be victorious.

"These five are the Way (Tao) to know victory. . . .

"Thus it is said that one who knows the enemy and knows himself will not be endangered in a hundred engagements. One who does not know the enemy but knows himself will sometimes be victorious, sometimes meet with defeat. One who knows neither the enemy nor himself will invariably be defeated in every engagement."

---

principalities into which the Zhou kingdom had been divided began to evolve into powerful states that presented a potential challenge to the Zhou ruler himself. Chief among these were Qu (Ch'u) in the central Yangtze valley, Wu in the Yangtze delta, and Yue (Yueh) along the southeastern coast. At first, their mutual rivalries were in check, but by the late fifth century B.C.E., competition intensified into civil war, giving birth to the "Period of the Warring States" (see the box above). Powerful principalities vied with each other for preeminence and largely ignored the now purely titular authority of the Zhou court. New forms of warfare also emerged with the invention of iron weapons and the introduction of the foot soldier. Cavalry, too, made its first appearance, armed with the powerful crossbow.

Eventually, the relatively young state of Qin, located in the original homeland of the Zhou, became a key player in these conflicts. Benefiting from a strong defensive position in the mountains to the west of the great bend of the Yellow River, as well as from their control of the rich Sichuan plains, the Qin gradually subdued their main rivals through conquest or diplomatic maneuvering. In 221 B.C.E., the Qin ruler declared the establishment of a new dynasty, the first truly unified government in Chinese history.

The Qin Dynasty (221–206 B.C.E.)

One of the primary reasons for the triumph of the Qin was probably the character of the Qin ruler, known to history as Qin Shi Huangdi (Ch'in Shih Huang Ti), or the

First Emperor of Qin. A man of forceful personality and immense ambition, Qin Shi Huangdi had ascended to the throne of Qin in 246 B.C.E. at the age of thirteen. Described by the famous Han dynasty historian Sima Qian as having "the chest of a bird of prey, the voice of a jackal, and the heart of a tiger," the new king of Qin found the Legalist views of his adviser Li Su (Li Ssu) only too appealing. In 221 B.C.E., Qin Shi Huangdi defeated the last of Qin's rivals and founded a new dynasty with himself as emperor.

The Qin dynasty transformed Chinese politics. Philosophical doctrines that had proliferated during the late Zhou period were prohibited, and Legalism was adopted as the official ideology. Those who opposed the policies of the new regime were punished and sometimes executed, while books presenting ideas contrary to the official orthodoxy were publicly put to the torch, perhaps the first example of book burning in history (see the box on p. 79).

MAP 3.2   China During the Period of the Warring States

Area covered by main map:

YEN
JIN
QI
Luoyang
QIN
Xianyang
WEI
LU
ZHENG
SONG
QU
WU
YUE
Yellow Sea
Yellow R.
Yangtze R.

0   250   500   750 Kilometers
0   250   500 Miles

▓ Surviving Zhou royal domain

Legalistic theory gave birth to a number of fundamental administrative and political developments, some of which would survive the Qin and serve as a model for future dynasties. In the first place, unlike the Zhou the Qin was a highly centralized state. The central bureaucracy was divided into three primary ministries: a civil authority, a military authority, and a censorate, whose inspectors surveyed the efficiency of officials throughout the system. This would later become standard administrative procedure for future Chinese dynasties.

Below the central government were two levels of administration: provinces and counties. Unlike the Zhou system, officials at these levels did not inherit their positions but were appointed by the court and were subject to dismissal at the emperor's whim. Apparently, some form of merit system was used, although there is no evidence that selection was based on performance in an examination. The civil servants may have been chosen on the recommendation of other government officials. A penal code provided for harsh punishments for all wrongdoers. Officials were watched by the censors, who reported directly to the throne. Those guilty of malfeasance in office were executed.

Qin Shi Huangdi, who had a passion for centralization, unified the system of weights and measures, standardized the monetary system and the written forms of Chinese characters, and ordered the construction of a system of roads extending throughout the entire empire. He also attempted to eliminate the remaining powers of the landed aristocrats and divided their estates among the peasants, who were now taxed directly by the state. He thus eliminated potential rivals and secured tax revenues for the central government. Members of the aristocratic clans were required to live in the capital city at Xianyang (Hsienyang), just north of modern Xian, so that the court could monitor their activities. Such a system may not have been advantageous to the peasants in all respects, however, since the central government could now collect taxes more effectively and mobilize the peasants for military service and for various public works projects.

The Qin dynasty was equally unsympathetic to the merchants, whom it viewed as parasites. Private commercial activities were severely restricted and heavily taxed; and many of the more vital forms of commerce and manufacturing, such as mining, wine making, and the distribution of salt, were placed under a government monopoly.

Qin Shi Huangdi was equally aggressive in foreign affairs. His armies continued the gradual advance to the south that had taken place during the final years of the Zhou dynasty, extending the border of China to the edge of the Red River in modern Vietnam. To supply the Qin armies operating in the area, a canal was dug that provided

QIN SHI HUANGDI. Qin Shi Huangdi, the First Emperor of Qin, who reigned from 221 to 210 B.C.E., was one of the most influential figures in the history of China. Although considered ruthless by many historians, he created the first unified Chinese state, ordered the construction of a system of roads throughout the country, standardized the Chinese currency and written language, and brought together the scattered defensive battlements into what we now know as the Great Wall.

direct inland navigation from the Yangtze River in central China to what is now the modern city of Guangzhou (Canton) in the south.

BEYOND THE FRONTIER: THE NOMADIC PEOPLES AND THE GREAT WALL OF CHINA

The main area of concern for the Qin emperor, however, was in the north, where a nomadic people, known to the Chinese as the Xiongnu (Hsiung-nu) and possibly related to the Huns (see Chapter 5), had become increasingly active in the area of the Gobi Desert. The area north of the Yellow River had been sparsely inhabited since prehistoric times. At that time, the climate of North China was somewhat milder and moister than it is today, and parts of the region were heavily forested. The local population probably lived by hunting and fishing, practicing limited forms of agriculture, or herding animals such as cattle or sheep.

As the climate gradually became drier, such peoples were forced to rely increasingly on animal husbandry as a means of livelihood. Their response was to master the art of riding on horseback and adopt the nomadic life. Organized loosely into tribes consisting of a number of kinship groups, they ranged far and wide in search of pasture for their herds of cattle, goats, or sheep. As they moved seasonally from one pasture to another, they often traveled several hundred miles carrying their goods and their circular felt tents, called *yurts*.

But the new way of life presented its own challenges. Increased food production led to a growing population, which in times of drought outstripped the available resources. Rival tribes then competed for the best pastures. After they mastered the art of fighting on horseback sometime during the middle of the first millennium B.C.E., territorial warfare became commonplace throughout the entire frontier region from the Pacific Ocean to Central Asia.

By the end of the Zhou dynasty in the third century B.C.E., the nomadic Xiongnu posed a serious threat to the security of China's northern frontier, and a number of Chinese principalities in the area began to build walls and fortifications to keep them out. But warriors on horseback possessed significant advantages over the infantry of the Chinese.

Qin Shi Huangdi's answer to the problem was to strengthen the walls to keep the marauders out. In Sima Qian's words:

> [The] First Emperor of the Ch'in dispatched Meng T'ien to lead a force of a hundred thousand men north to attack the barbarians. He seized control of all the lands south of the Yellow River and established border defenses along the river, constructing forty-four walled district cities overlooking the river and manning them with convict laborers transported to the border for garrison duty. Thus he utilized the natural mountain barriers to establish the border defenses, scooping out the valleys and constructing ramparts and building installations at other points where they were needed. The whole line of defenses stretched over ten thousand *li* [a *li* is one-third of a mile] from Lin-t'ao to Liao-tung and even extended across the Yellow River and through Yang-shan and Pei-chia.[11]

Today, of course, we know Qin Shi Huangdi's project as the Great Wall, which extends nearly four thousand miles from the sandy wastes of Central Asia to the sea. It is constructed of massive granite blocks and is wide enough on top to provide a roadway for horse-drawn chariots. Although the wall that appears in most photographs today was built 1,500 years after the Qin, during the Ming dynasty, some of the walls built by the Qin remain stand-

MEMORANDUM ON THE BURNING OF BOOKS

Li Su, the author of the following passage, was a chief minister of the First Emperor of Qin. An exponent of Legalism, Li Su hoped to eliminate all rival theories on government. His recommendation to the emperor on the subject was recorded by the Han dynasty historian Sima Qian. The emperor approved the proposal and ordered all books contrary to the spirit of Legalist ideology to be destroyed on pain of death. Fortunately, some texts were preserved by being hidden, or even memorized by their owners, and were thus available to later generations. For centuries afterward, the First Emperor of Qin and his minister were singled out for criticism because of their intolerance and their effort to control the very minds of their subjects. Totalitarianism, it seems, is not exclusively a modern concept.

SIMA QIAN, HISTORICAL RECORDS

In earlier times the empire disintegrated and fell into disorder, and no one was capable of unifying it. Thereupon the various feudal lords rose to power. In their discourses they all praised the past in order to disparage the present and embellished empty words to confuse the truth. Everyone cherished his own favorite school of learning and criticized what had been instituted by the authorities. But at present Your Majesty possesses a unified empire, has regulated the distinctions of black and white, and has firmly established for yourself a position of sole supremacy. And yet these independent schools, joining with each other, criticize the codes of laws and instructions. Hearing of the promulgation of a decree, they criticize it, each from the standpoint of his own school. At home they disapprove of it in their hearts; going out they criticize it in the thoroughfare. They seek a reputation by discrediting their sovereign; they appear superior by expressing contrary views, and they lead the lowly multitude in the spreading of slander. If such license is not prohibited, the sovereign power will decline above and partisan factions will form below. It would be well to prohibit this.

Your servant suggests that all books in the imperial archives, save the memoirs of Ch'in, be burned. All persons in the empire, except members of the Academy of Learned Scholars, in possession of the *Book of Odes*, the *Book of History*, and discourses of the hundred philosophers should take them to the local governors and have them indiscriminately burned. Those who dare to talk to each other about the *Book of Odes* and the *Book of History* should be executed and their bodies exposed in the marketplace. Anyone referring to the past to criticize the present should, together with all members of his family, be put to death. Officials who fail to report cases that have come under their attention are equally guilty. After thirty days from the time of issuing the decree, those who have not destroyed their books are to be branded and sent to build the Great Wall. Books not to be destroyed will be those on medicine and pharmacy, divination by the tortoise and milfoil, and agriculture and arboriculture. People wishing to pursue learning should take the officials as their teachers.

---

ing. Their construction was a massive project that required the efforts of thousands of laborers, many of whom met their deaths there and, according to legend, are now buried within the wall.

THE FALL OF THE QIN

The Legalist system put in place by the First Emperor of Qin was designed to achieve maximum efficiency as well as total security for the state. It did neither. Qin Shi Huangdi was apparently aware of the dangers of factions within the imperial family and established a class of eunuchs (males whose testicles have been removed) who served as personal attendants for himself and female members of the royal family. The original idea may have been to restrict the influence of male courtiers, and the eunuch system later became a standard feature of the Chinese imperial system. But as confidential advisers to the royal family, eunuchs were clearly in a position of influence. The rivalry between the "inner" imperial court and the "outer" court of bureaucratic officials led to tensions that persisted until the end of the imperial system.

By ruthlessly gathering control over the empire into his own hands, Qin Shi Huangdi had hoped to establish a rule that, in the words of Sima Qian, "would be enjoyed by his sons for ten thousand generations." In fact, his centralizing zeal alienated many key groups. Landed aristocrats and Confucian intellectuals, as well as the common people, groaned under the censorship of thought and speech, harsh taxes, and forced labor projects. "He killed men," recounted the historian, "as though he thought he could never finish, he punished men as though he were afraid he would never get around to them all, and the whole world revolted against him."[12] Shortly after the emperor died in 210 B.C.E., the dynasty quickly descended into factional rivalry, and four years later it was overthrown.

The disappearance of the Qin brought an end to an experiment in absolute rule that later Chinese historians would view as a betrayal of humanistic Confucian principles. But in another sense, the Qin system was a response—though somewhat extreme—to the problems of administering a large and increasingly complex society. Although later rulers would denounce Legalism and enthrone Confucianism as the new state orthodoxy, in practice they would make use of a number of the key tenets of Legalism to administer the empire and control the behavior of their subjects.

The Glorious Han Dynasty (202 B.C.E.–221 C.E.)

The fall of the Qin was followed by a brief period of civil strife as aspiring successors competed for hegemony. Out of this strife emerged one of the greatest and most durable dynasties in Chinese history—the Han. The Han dynasty would later become so closely identified with the advance of Chinese civilization that even today the Chinese sometimes refer to themselves as "people of Han" and to their language as the "language of Han."

The founder of the Han dynasty was Liu Bang (Liu Pang), a commoner of peasant origin who would be known

THE GREAT WALL. The section of the Great Wall that is often visited by tourists today is not the work of the First Emperor of Qin but was built at the order of a Ming ruler many centuries later. The original walls were often composed of loose stone, dirt, or piled rubble and posed little obstacle to invading nomads from the north. The section illustrated here is located north of the city of Dunhuang in Central Asia.

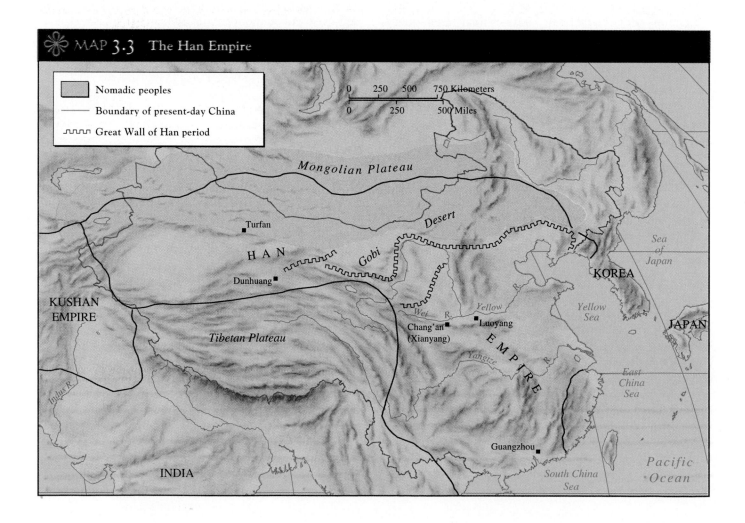

MAP **3.3**   The Han Empire

Nomadic peoples
Boundary of present-day China
Great Wall of Han period

0   250   500   750 Kilometers
0   250   500 Miles

Mongolian Plateau

Turfan

Gobi Desert

HAN

Dunhuang

KUSHAN EMPIRE

Tibetan Plateau

Indus R.

INDIA

KOREA

Sea of Japan

Yellow Sea

JAPAN

Wei R.   Yellow

Chang'an (Xianyang)   Luoyang

EMPIRE

Yangtze

East China Sea

Guangzhou

South China Sea

Pacific Ocean

historically by his title of Han Gaozu (Han Kao Tsu, or Exalted Emperor of Han). Under his strong rule and that of his successors, the new dynasty quickly moved to consolidate its control over the empire and promote the welfare of its subjects. Efficient and benevolent, at least by the standards of the time, Gaozu maintained the centralized political institutions of the Qin but abandoned their harsh Legalistic approach to law enforcement. Han rulers also reversed the effort by the First Emperor of Qin to enforce a single ideology and discovered in Confucian principles a useful foundation for the creation of a new state philosophy. Under the Han, Confucianism began to take on the character of an official ideology.

CONFUCIANISM AND THE STATE

The integration of Confucian doctrine with Legalist practice, creating a system generally known as State Confucianism, did not take long to accomplish. Although the founding Han ruler declared his intention to discard the harsh methods adopted by the Qin, he and his successors found it convenient to retain many of the institutions introduced by the First Emperor of Qin. For example, they borrowed the tripartite division of the central government into civilian and military authorities and a censorate. The government was headed by a Grand Council including representatives from all three segments of government. The Han also retained the system of local government, dividing the empire into provinces and districts.

Finally, and perhaps most important, the Han continued the Qin system of selecting government officials on the basis of merit rather than birth. Shortly after founding the new dynasty, Emperor Gaozu decreed that local officials would be asked to recommend promising candidates for public service. Thirty years later, in 165 B.C.E., the first known civil service examination was administered to candidates for positions in the bureaucracy. Shortly after that, an academy was established to train candidates. Nevertheless, the first candidates were almost all from aristocratic or other wealthy families, and the Han bureaucracy itself was still dominated by the traditional hereditary elite. Still, the principle of selecting officials on the basis of talent had been established and would eventually become standard practice.

Under the Han dynasty, the population increased rapidly—by some estimates rising from about 20 million to over 60 million at the height of the dynasty—creating a growing need for a large and efficient bureaucracy to maintain the state in proper working order. Unfortunately, the Han were unable to resolve all of the problems left over from the past. Factionalism at court remained a serious problem and undermined the efficiency of the central government. Equally important, despite their efforts, the Han rulers were never able to restrain the great aristocratic

CHRONOLOGY

ANCIENT CHINA

Xia (Hsia) dynasty	?–1570? B.C.E
Shang dynasty	1570?–1045? B.C.E
Zhou (Chou) dynasty	1045?–221 B.C.E
Life of Confucius	551–479 B.C.E
Period of the Warring States	403–221 B.C.E
Life of Mencius	370–290 B.C.E
Qin (Ch'in) dynasty	221–206 B.C.E
Life of the First Emperor of Qin	259–210 B.C.E
Formation of Han dynasty	202 B.C.E
Wang Mang interregnum	9–23 C.E.
Collapse of Han dynasty	221 C.E.

families, who continued to play a dominant role in political and economic affairs. The failure to curb the power of the wealthy clans eventually became a major factor in the final collapse of the dynasty.

SOCIETY AND ECONOMY IN THE HAN EMPIRE

Han rulers also retained some of the economic and social policies of their predecessors. In particular, they saw that a free peasantry paying taxes directly to the state would both limit the wealth and power of the great noble families and increase the state's revenues. The Han had difficulty preventing the recurrence of the economic inequities that had characterized the last years of the Zhou, however. The land taxes were relatively light, but the peasants also faced a number of other exactions, including military service and forced labor of up to one month annually. Although the use of iron tools brought new lands under the plow and food production increased steadily, the trebling of the population under the Han eventually reduced the average size of the individual farm plot to about one acre per capita, barely enough for survival. As time went on, many poor peasants were forced to sell their land and become tenant farmers, paying rents ranging up to half of the annual harvest. Thus, land once again came to be concentrated in the hands of the powerful landed clans, which often owned thousands of acres worked by tenants and mustered their own military forces to bully free farmers into becoming tenants.

Although such economic problems contributed to the eventual downfall of the dynasty, in general the Han era was one of unparalleled productivity and prosperity. The

OUTPOST OF EMPIRE. Located at the junction of two rivers passing through the sandy wastes of the Turfan Depression, in modern Xinjiang Province, the town of Jiaohe was one of the first outposts established by the Han Dynasty as it expanded westward into Central Asia in the first century C.E. Previously inhabited by the Indo-European-speaking Tocharian peoples, eventually Jiaohe would become a prominent stopping point on the Silk Road before being overrun by the Mongols in the thirteenth century. The town was located on top of the plateau to the left. On the right side of the photograph are storage bins used today to dry grapes.

MAP 3.4 Trade Routes of the Ancient World

Breakdown of Traded Goods		
Region	Imports	Exports
North India		
South India		
China		
Arabia		
East Africa		

Traded goods:

- tortoiseshell
- ivory
- spices
- incense
- slaves
- precious stones
- wine
- metal
- cloth and clothing
- glassware
- coinage
- weapons
- timber
- silks

period was marked by a major expansion of trade, both domestic and foreign. This was not necessarily due to official encouragement. In fact, the Han were as suspicious of private merchants as their predecessors had been and levied stiff taxes on trade in an effort to limit commercial activities. Merchants were also subject to severe social constraints. They were disqualified from seeking office, restricted in their place of residence, and viewed in general as parasites providing little true value to Chinese society.

The state itself directed much trade and manufacturing; it manufactured weapons, for example, and operated shipyards, granaries, and mines. The government also moved cautiously into foreign trade, mostly with neighboring areas in Central and Southeast Asia, although trade relations were established with countries as far away as India and the Mediterranean. Some of this long-distance trade was carried by sea through southern ports like Quangzhou, but more was transported by overland caravans on the Silk Road (see Chapter 10) and other routes that led westward into Central Asia. Some of the trade was organized in the form of tribute missions, with neighboring countries providing local specialties like tropical products and precious stones in return for Chinese silks, glazed pottery (an early form of porcelain), and various manufactured products. China often gave more than it received to ensure that neighboring monarchs would accept China's benevolent protection and not harbor its enemies.

New technology contributed to the economic prosperity of the Han era. Significant progress was achieved in such areas as textile manufacturing, water mills, and iron casting; the latter led to the invention of steel a few centuries later. Paper was invented under the Han, while the invention of the rudder and fore-and-aft rigging permitted ships to sail into the wind for the first time. Thus equipped, Chinese merchant ships carrying heavy cargoes could sail throughout the islands of Southeast Asia and into the Indian Ocean.

Finally, the Han emperors continued the process of territorial expansion and consolidation that had begun under the Zhou and the Qin. Han rulers, notably Han Wudi (Han Wu Ti, or Martial Emperor of Han), successfully completed the assimilation into the empire of the regions south of the Yangtze River, including the Red River delta in what is today northern Vietnam. Han armies also marched westward as far as the Caspian Sea, pacifying nomadic tribal peoples and extending China's boundary far into Central Asia. The Han continued to have problems with the Xiongnu beyond the Great Wall to the north. Nomadic raids on Chinese territory continued intermittently to the end of the dynasty, once reaching almost to the gates of the capital city, now located at Chang'an (Ch'ang An, or Eternal Peace), on the site of modern Xian.

JADE BURIAL SUIT.   During the Han dynasty, members of the imperial family were buried in jade body suits such as this one, which dates from the second century B.C.E. It is composed of jade squares that were sewn together with gold thread. Extremely expensive to produce, they were eventually banned by the court as too extravagant.

THE DECLINE AND FALL OF THE HAN

In 9 C.E., the reformist official Wang Mang, who was troubled by the plight of the peasants, seized power from the Han court and declared the foundation of a new Xin (New) dynasty. In the years prior to his seizure of power, the empire had begun to fall into decay. As frivolous or depraved rulers amused themselves with the pleasures of court life, the power and influence of the central government began to wane, and the great noble families filled the vacuum, amassing vast landed estates and transforming free farmers into tenants. Wang Mang tried to confiscate the great estates, restore the ancient well field system, and abolish slavery. In so doing, however, he alienated powerful interests, who conspired to overthrow him. In 23 C.E., beset by administrative chaos and a collapse of the frontier defenses, Wang Mang was killed in a coup d'etat.

For a time, strong leadership revived some of the glory of the early Han. The court did attempt to reduce land taxes and carry out land resettlement programs. The growing popularity of nutritious crops like rice, wheat, and soybeans, along with the introduction of new crops such as alfalfa and grapes, helped to boost food production. But the monopoly of land and power by the great landed families continued. Weak rulers were isolated within their imperial chambers and dominated by eunuchs and other powerful figures at court. Official corruption and the concentration of land in the hands of the wealthy led to widespread peasant unrest. The population of the empire, which had been estimated at about 60 million in China's first census in the year 2 C.E., had shrunk to less than 20 million two hundred years later. In the early third century C.E., the dynasty was finally brought to an end when power was seized by Cao Cao (Ts'ao Ts'ao), a general well known to millions of later Chinese as one of the main characters in the famous Chinese epic *The Romance of the Three Kingdoms*. But Cao Cao was unable to consolidate his power, and China entered a period of almost constant anarchy and internal division, compounded by invasions of northern tribal peoples. The next great dynasty did not arise until the beginning of the seventh century, four hundred years later.

✿ FLOODED RICE FIELDS.   Rice is a very labor-intensive crop, which requires many workers to plant the seedlings and organize the distribution of water. Initially, the fields are flooded to facilitate the rooting of the rice seedlings and to add nutrients to the soil. Fish breeding in the flooded fields help keep mosquitoes and other insects in check. As the plants mature, the fields are drained, and the plants complete their four-month growing cycle in dry soil.

DAILY LIFE IN ANCIENT CHINA

Few social institutions have been as closely identified with China as the family. As in most agricultural civilizations, the family served as the basic economic and social unit in society. In traditional China, however, it took on an almost sacred quality as a microcosm of the entire social order.

In Neolithic times, the farm village, organized around the clan, was the basic social unit in China, at least in the core region of the Yellow River valley. Even then, however, the smaller family unit was becoming more important, at least among the nobility, who attached considerable significance to the ritual veneration of their immediate ancestors.

During the Zhou dynasty, the family took on increasing importance, in part because of the need for cooperation in agriculture. The cultivation of rice, which had become the primary crop along the Yangtze River and in the provinces to the south, is highly labor-intensive. The seedlings must be planted in several inches of water in a nursery bed and then transferred individually to the paddy beds, which must be irrigated constantly. During the harvest, the stalks must be cut and the kernels carefully separated from the stalks and husks. As a result, children—and the labor they supplied—were considered essential to the survival of the family, not only during their youthful years but also later, when sons were expected to provide for their parents. Loyalty to family members came to be considered even more important than loyalty to the broader community or the state. Confucius commented that it is the mark of a civilized society that a son should protect his father even if the latter has committed a crime against the community.

At the crux of the concept of family was the idea of filial piety, which called on all members of the family to subordinate their needs and desires to the patriarchal head of the family. More broadly, it created a hierarchical system in which every family member had his or her place. All Chinese learned the "five relationships" that were the key to a proper social order. The son was subordinate to the father, the wife to her husband, the younger brother to the older brother, and all were subject to their king. The final relationship was the proper one between friend and friend. Only if all members of the family and the community as a whole behaved in a properly filial manner would society function effectively.

A stable family system based on obedient and hardworking members can serve as a bulwark for an efficient government, but putting loyalty to the family and the clan over loyalty to the state can also present a threat to a centralizing monarch. For that reason, the Qin dynasty attempted to destroy the clan system in China and assert the primacy of the state. Legalists even imposed heavy taxes on any family with more than two adult sons in order to break down the family concept. The Qin reportedly also originated the practice of organizing several family units into larger groups of five and ten families that would exercise mutual control and surveillance. Later dynasties continued the practice under the name of the *Bao-jia* (*Pao-chia*) system.

But the efforts of the Qin to eradicate or at least reduce the importance of the family system ran against tradition and the dynamics of the Chinese economy, and under the Han the family revived and increased in importance. Under the Han, with official encouragement, the family system began to take on the character that it would possess until our own day. The family was not only the basic economic unit; it was also the basic social unit for education, religious observances, and training in ethical principles.

We know much more about the lifestyle of the elites than that of the common people in ancient China. The first houses were probably constructed of wooden planks, but later Chinese mastered the art of building in tile and brick. By the first millennium B.C.E., most public buildings and the houses of the wealthy were probably constructed in this manner. By Han times, most Chinese probably lived in simple houses of mud, wooden planks, or brick with thatch or occasionally tile roofs. But in some areas, especially the loess (pronounced "less," a type of soil common in North China) regions of North China, cave dwelling remained common down to modern times. The most famous cave dweller of modern times was Mao Zedong, who lived in a cave in Yan'an during his long struggle against Chiang Kai-shek.

Chinese houses usually had little furniture; most people squatted or sat with their legs spread out on the packed mud floor. Chairs were apparently not introduced until the sixth or seventh centuries C.E. Clothing was simple, consisting of cotton trousers and shirts in the summer and wool or burlap in the winter.

The staple foods were millet in the north and rice in the south. Other common foods were wheat, barley, mustard greens, and bamboo shoots. In early times, such foods were often consumed in the form of porridge, but by the Zhou dynasty, stir-frying in a wok was becoming common. Where possible, the Chinese family would vary its diet of grain foods with vegetables, fruit (including pears, peaches, apricots, and plums), and fish or meat; but for most, such additions to the daily plate of rice, millet, or soybeans were a rare luxury.

Alcohol in the form of ale was drunk at least by the higher classes and by the early Zhou era had already begun to inspire official concern. According to the *Book of History*, "King Wen admonished . . . the young nobles . . . that they should not ordinarily use spirits; and throughout all the states he required that they should be drunk only on occasion of sacrifices, and that then virtue should preside so that there might be no drunkenness."[13]

Most Chinese, then as now, lived in the countryside. But as time went on, cities began to play a larger role in Chinese society. The first towns were little more than forts for the local aristocracy; they were small in size and limited in population. By the Zhou era, however, larger towns, usually located on the major trade routes, began to combine administrative and economic functions, serving as regional markets or manufacturing centers. Such cities were usually surrounded by a wall and a moat, and a raised platform might be built within the walls to provide a place for ritual ceremonies and housing for the ruler's family.

By the Han, the major city in China was Chang'an, the imperial capital. The city covered a total area of nearly forty square kilometers and was enclosed by a twelve-foot earthen wall surrounded by a moat. Twelve gates provided entry into the city, and eight major avenues ran east-west or north-south. Each avenue was forty-five meters wide; a center strip in each avenue was reserved for the emperor, whose palace and gardens occupied nearly half the southern and central part of the city.

The Humble Estate: Women in Ancient China

Female subservience was a key element in the social system of ancient China. As in many traditional societies, the male was considered of transcendent importance because of his role as food procurer or, in the case of farming communities, food producer. In ancient China, men worked in the fields and women raised children and served in the home. The Chinese written language graphically demonstrates how ancient Chinese society regarded the sexes. The character for man (**男**) combines the symbols for strength and a rice field, whereas the character for woman (**女**) represents a person in a posture of deference and respect. The character for peace (**安**) is a woman under a roof. A wife is symbolized by a woman with a broom.

Confucian thought, while not denigrating the importance of women as mothers and homemakers, accepted the dual roles of men and women in Chinese society. Men governed society. They carried on family ritual through the veneration of ancestors. They were the warriors, scholars, and ministers. Their dominant role was firmly enshrined in the legal system. Men were permitted to have more than one wife and to divorce a spouse who did not produce a male child. Women were denied the right to own property, and there was no dowry system in ancient China that would have provided the wife with a degree of financial security from her husband and his family. As the third-century C.E. woman poet Fu Xuan lamented:

> How sad it is to be a woman
> Nothing on earth is held so cheap.
> No one is glad when a girl is born.
> By her the family sets no store.
> No one cries when she leaves her home
> Sudden as clouds when the rain stops.[14]

Not surprisingly, women were taught to accept their secondary role in life. Ban Zhao, a prominent female historian of the Han dynasty, whose own career was an exception to the rule, described that role as follows:

> To be humble, yielding, respectful and reverential; to put herself after others . . . these qualities are those exemplifying woman's low and humble estate. To retire late and rise early; not to shirk exertion from dawn to dark . . . this is called being diligent. To behave properly and decorously in serving her husband; to be serene and self-possessed, shunning jests and

laughter . . . this is called being worthy of continuing the husband's lineage. If a woman possess the above-mentioned three qualities, then her reputation shall be excellent.[15]

Some women did become a force in politics, especially at court, where wives of the ruler or other female members of the royal family were often influential in palace intrigues. Such activities were frowned on, however, as the following passage from the *Book of Songs* attests:

> A clever man builds a city,
> A clever woman lays one low;
> With all her qualifications, that clever woman
> Is but an ill-omened bird.
> A woman with a long tongue
> Is a flight of steps leading to calamity;
> For disorder does not come from heaven,
> But is brought about by women.
> Among those who cannot be trained or taught
> Are women and eunuchs.[16]

✤ **HAN POTTERY HOUSE.** During the Han dynasty, the Chinese people thought that even in heaven one could still be surrounded by one's earthly possessions, such as family, servants, and house. Since such material goods could not accompany one directly into the afterworld, pottery models such as the one shown here were made and then placed in tombs with the dead.

THE WORLD OF CULTURE

Modern knowledge about artistic achievements in ancient civilizations is limited because often little has survived the ravages of time. Fortunately, many ancient civilizations, such as Egypt and Mesopotamia, were located in relatively arid areas where many artifacts were preserved, even over thousands of years. In more humid regions, such as China and Southeast Asia, the cultural residue left by the civilizations of antiquity has been adversely affected by climate.

As a result, relatively little remains of the cultural achievements of the prehistoric Chinese aside from Neolithic pottery and the relics found at the site of the Shang dynasty capital at Anyang. In recent years, a rich trove from the time of the Qin Empire has been unearthed near the tomb of Qin Shi Huangdi near Xian in central China and at Han tombs nearby. But little remains of the literature of ancient China and almost none of the painting, architecture, and music.

Metalwork and Sculpture

Discoveries at archaeological sites indicate that ancient China was a society rich in cultural achievement. The pottery found at Neolithic sites such as Banpo, Longshan, and Yangshao exhibits a freshness and vitality of form and design, while the ornaments, such as rings and beads, show a strong aesthetic sense.

The pace of Chinese cultural development began to quicken during the Shang dynasty, which ruled in northern China from the eighteenth to the twelfth century B.C.E. At that time, objects cast in bronze, which are among the most extraordinary and admired creations of Chinese art, began to appear. A variety of bronze vessels were produced for use in preparing and serving food and drink in the ancestral rites. Later vessels were used for decoration or for dining at court.

Shang bronzes, with their highly sophisticated and intricate relief work, are technically unequaled and are considered one of the highest cultural achievements of antiquity. Many Shang bronzes were decorated with a *taotie* (t'ao-t'ieh) mask with two large globular eyes, nostrils, fangs, and sometimes claws and horns. It is normally presented as the silhouette of two dragons face to face, so that each forms half the mask. Although fierce in appearance, the *taotie* represented a guardian force against evil spirits.

The method of casting used was one reason for the extraordinary quality of Shang bronze work. Bronze workers in most ancient civilizations used the lost-wax method, where a model was first made in wax. After a clay mold had been formed around it, the model was heated so that the wax would disappear, and the empty space was filled with molten metal. In China, clay molds composed of several sections were tightly fit together prior to the introduction of the liquid bronze. This technique, which had evolved from ceramic techniques used during the Neolithic period, enabled the artisans to apply the design directly to the mold and thus contributed to the clarity of line and rich surface decoration of the Shang bronzes.

Bronze casting became a large-scale business, and more than ten thousand vessels of an incredible variety of form and design survive today. The art of bronze working continued into the Zhou and the Han dynasties, but the quality and originality declined. The Shang bronzes remain the pinnacle of creative art in ancient China.

One reason for the decline of bronze casting in China was the rise in popularity of iron. Iron making developed in China around the ninth or eighth century B.C.E., much later than in the Middle East, where it had been mastered almost a millennium earlier. Once familiar with the process, however, the Chinese quickly moved to the forefront. Iron workers in Europe and the Middle East, lacking the technology to achieve the high temperatures necessary to melt iron ore for casting, were forced to work with wrought iron, a cumbersome and expensive process. By the fourth century B.C.E., the Chinese had invented the technique of the blast furnace, powered by a person operating a bellows. They were therefore able to manufacture cast-iron ritual vessels and agricultural tools centuries before an equivalent technology appeared in the West.

Another reason for the deterioration of the bronze-casting tradition was the development of lacquerware and ceramics. Lacquer, obtained from a resinous substance

A BRONZE HORSE. This horse from a second-century C.E. Han tomb is a beautiful example of Chinese bronze sculpture. Caught in a pose of suspended animation, it suggests the divine power that the Chinese of this time attributed to horses.

deposited on trees by the *lac* insect, had been produced since Neolithic times, and by the Han it had become a popular method of applying a hard coating to objects made of wood or fabric. Pottery, too, had existed since early times, but technological advances during the Han led to the production of a high-quality form of pottery covered with a brown or gray-green glaze, the latter known popularly as celadon. During the Han, both lacquerware and pottery replaced bronze in popularity and value.

In 1974, in a remarkable discovery, farmers digging a well about thirty-five miles east of Xian unearthed a number of terra-cotta figures in an underground pit about one mile east of the burial mound of the First Emperor of Qin. Chinese archaeologists sent to work at the site discovered a vast terra-cotta army that they believed was a re-creation of Qin Shi Huangdi's imperial guard, which was to accompany the emperor on his journey to the next world.

One of the astounding features of the terra-cotta army is its size. The army is enclosed in four pits that were originally encased in a wooden framework, which has since disintegrated. More than a thousand figures have already been unearthed in the first pit, along with horses, wooden chariots, and seven thousand bronze weapons. Archaeologists estimate that there are more than six thousand figures in that pit alone.

Equally impressive is the quality of the work. Slightly larger than life-size, the figures were molded of finely textured clay, then fired and painted. The detail on the uniforms is realistic and sophisticated, but the most striking feature is the individuality of the facial features of the soldiers. Apparently, ten different head shapes were used and were then modeled further by hand to reflect the variety of ethnic groups and personality types in the army.

The discovery of the terra-cotta army also shows that the Chinese had come a long way from the human sacrifices that had taken place at the death of Shang sovereigns more than a thousand years earlier. But the project must have been ruinously expensive and is additional evidence of the burden the Qin ruler imposed on his subjects. One historian has estimated that one-third of the national income in Qin and Han times may have been spent on preparations for the ruler's afterlife. The emperor's mausoleum has not yet been unearthed, but it is enclosed in a mound seventy-six meters in height and is surrounded by a rectangular wall six kilometers in circumference. According to the Han historian Sima Qian, the ceiling is a replica of the heavens, while the floor contains a relief model of the entire Qin kingdom, with rivers flowing in mercury. According to tradition, traps were set within the mausoleum to prevent intruders, and the workers putting in the final touches were buried alive in the tomb with its secrets.

Qin Shi Huangdi's ambitious effort to provide for his immortality became a pattern for his successors during the Han dynasty, although apparently on a somewhat more modest scale. In 1990, Chinese workers discovered a similar underground army for a Han emperor of the second century B.C.E. Like the imperial guard of the First Qin Emperor, the underground soldiers were buried in parallel pits and possessed their own weapons and individual facial features. But they were smaller—only one-third the height of the average human adult—and were armed with wooden weapons and were dressed in silk clothing, now decayed. A burial pit nearby indicates that as many as ten thousand workers, probably slaves or prisoners, died in the process of building the emperor's mausoleum, which took an estimated ten years to construct.

Language and Literature

Precisely when writing developed in China cannot be determined, but certainly by Shang times, as the oracle bones demonstrate, the Chinese had developed a simple but functional script. Like many other languages of antiquity, it was primarily ideographic and pictographic in form. Symbols, usually called "characters," were created to represent an idea or to form a picture of the object to be represented. For example, the Chinese characters for mountain (山), the sun (日), and the moon (月) were meant to represent the objects themselves. Other characters, such as "big" (大) (a man with his arms outstretched), represent an idea. The word "east" (東) symbolizes the sun coming up behind the trees.

Each character, of course, would be given a sound by the speaker when pronounced. In other cultures, this process led to the abandonment of the system of ideographs and the adoption of a written language based on phonetic symbols. The Chinese language, however, has never entirely abandoned its original ideographical format, although the phonetic element has developed into a significant part of the individual character. In that sense, the Chinese written language is virtually unique in the world today.

One reason the language retained its ideographic quality may have been the aesthetic quality of the written characters. By the time of the Han dynasty, if not earlier, the written language came to be seen as an art form as well as a means of communication, and calligraphy

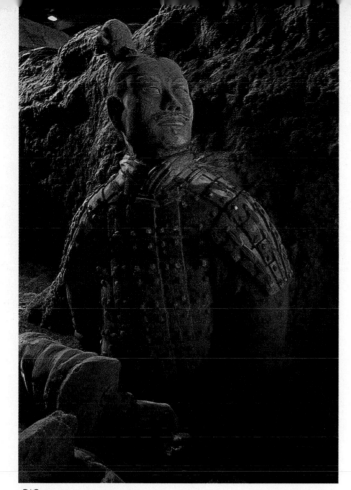

TOMB SOLDIER (QIN SHI HUANGDI'S TOMB). This is one of the 6,000 soldiers guarding the underground palace complex of Emperor Qin Shi Huangdi's tomb. Incredibly, each soldier has individualized facial features and expressions. Originally, they carried real weapons, and their uniforms were painted in brilliant colors. They are a most majestic and foreboding sight.

transmission of Chinese culture to all Chinese from the Great Wall to the southern border and even beyond. The written language, however, was not identical with the spoken. Written Chinese evolved a totally separate vocabulary and grammatical structure from the spoken tongues. As a result, those who used it required special training.

The earliest extant form of Chinese literature dates from the Zhou dynasty. It was written on silk or strips of bamboo and consisted primarily of historical records such as the *Rites of Zhou*, philosophical treatises such as the *Analects* and *The Way of the Dao*, and poetry, as recorded in the *Book of Songs* and the *Song of the South* (see the box on p. 90). In later years, when Confucian principles had been elevated to a state ideology, the key works identified with the Confucian School were integrated into a set of so-called Confucian Classics. These works became required reading for generations of Chinese schoolchildren and introduced them to the forms of behavior that would be required of them as adults.

Under the Han dynasty, although poetry and philosophical essays continued to be popular, historical writing became the primary form of literary creativity. Historians such as Sima Qian and Ban Gu (the dynasty's official historian and the older brother of the female historian Ban Zhao) wrote works that became models for later dynastic histories. These historical works combined political and social history with biographies of key figures. Like so much literary work in China, their primary purpose was moral and political—to explain the underlying reasons for the rise and fall of individual human beings and dynasties.

became one of the most prized forms of painting in China.

More importantly, if the written language had developed in the direction of a phonetic alphabet, it could no longer have served as the written system for all the peoples of an expanding civilization. Although the vast majority spoke a tongue derived from a parent Sinitic language (a system distinguished by its tonal nature, a characteristic that gives Chinese its lilting quality even today), the languages spoken in various regions of the country differed from each other in pronunciation and to a lesser degree in vocabulary and syntax; for the most part, they were (and are today) mutually unintelligible.

The Chinese answer to this problem was to give all the spoken languages the same writing system. Although any character might be pronounced differently in different regions of China, that character would be written the same way (after the standardization undertaken under the Qin) no matter where it was written. This system of written characters could be read by educated Chinese from one end of the country to the other. It became the language of the bureaucracy and the vehicle for the

Music

From early times in China, music was viewed not just as an aesthetic pleasure, but as a means of achieving political order and refining the human character. In fact, music may have originated as a means of accompanying sacred ritual at the royal court. According to the *Historical Records*, a history written during the Han dynasty: "When our sage-kings of the past instituted rites and music, their objective was far from making people indulge in the . . . amusements of singing and dancing. . . . Music is produced to purify the heart, and rites introduced to rectify the behavior."[17] Eventually, however, music began to be appreciated for its own sake as well as for singing and dancing, especially among the common people.

A wide variety of musical instruments were used, including flutes, various stringed instruments, bells and chimes, drums, and gourds. Bells cast in bronze were first used as musical instruments in the Shang period; they were hung in rows and then struck with a wooden mallet. The finest were produced during the mid-Zhou era and are

The Book of Songs is an anthology of about three hundred poems written during the early Zhou dynasty. According to tradition, they were selected by Confucius from a much larger collection. In later years, many were given political interpretations. The poem reprinted here, however, expresses a very human cry of love spurned.

THE BOOK OF SONGS: THE ODES

You seemed a guileless youth enough,
Offering for silk your woven stuff;
But silk was not required by you;
I was the silk you had in view.
With you I crossed the ford, and while
We wandered on for many a mile
I said, "I do not wish delay,
But friends must fix our wedding-day. . . .
Oh, do not let my words give pain,
But with the autumn come again."

And then I used to watch and wait
To see you passing through the gate;
And sometimes, when I watched in vain,
My tears would flow like falling rain;
But when I saw my darling boy,
I laughed and cried aloud for joy.
The fortune-tellers, you declared,
Had all pronounced us duly paired;
"Then bring a carriage," I replied,
"And I'll away to be your bride."

The mulberry tree upon the ground,
Now sheds its yellow leaves around.

Three years have slipped away from me
Since first I shared your poverty;
And now again, alas the day!
Back through the ford I take my way.

My heart is still unchanged, but you
Have uttered words now proved untrue;
And you have left me to deplore
A love that can be mine no more.

For three long years I was your wife,
And led in truth a toilsome life;
Early to rise and late to bed,
Each day alike passed o'er my head.
I honestly fulfilled my part,
And you—well, you have broke my heart.
The truth my brothers will not know,
So all the more their gibes will flow.
I grieve in silence and repine
That such a wretched fate is mine.

Ah, hand in hand to face old age!—
Instead, I turn a bitter page.
O for the riverbanks of yore;
O for the much-loved marshy shore;
The hours of girlhood, with my hair
Ungathered, as we lingered there.
The words we spoke, that seemed so true,
I little thought that I should rue;
I little thought the vows we swore
Would some day bind us two no more.

considered to be among the best examples of early bronze work in China.

By the late Zhou era, bells had begun to give way as the instrument of choice to strings and wind instruments, while the purpose of music shifted from ceremony to entertainment. This led conservative critics to rail against the onset of an age of debauchery.

Ancient historians stressed the relationship between music and court life, but it is highly probable that music, singing, and dancing were equally popular among the common people. The *Book of History*, purporting to describe conditions in the late third millennium B.C.E., suggests that ballads emanating from the popular culture were welcomed at court. Nevertheless, court music and popular music differed in several respects. Among other things, popular music was more likely to be motivated by the desire for pleasure than for the purpose of law and order and moral uplift. Those differences continued to be reflected in the evolution of music in China down to modern times.

 CONCLUSION

Of the great classical civilizations discussed in Part I of this book, China was the last to come into full flower. By the time the Shang began to emerge as an organized state, the societies in Mesopotamia and the Nile valley had already reached an advanced level of civilization.

Unfortunately, not enough is known about the early stages of these civilizations to allow us to determine why some developed earlier than others, but one likely reason for China's late arrival was that it was virtually isolated from other emerging centers of culture elsewhere in the world and thus was compelled to develop essentially on its own. Only at the end of the first millennium B.C.E. did the Han dynasty come into regular contact with other civilizations in South Asia, the Middle East, and the Mediterranean.

Once embarked on its own path toward the creation of a complex society, however, China achieved results that were in all respects the equal of its counterparts elsewhere. During the glory years of the Han dynasty, China extended the boundaries of its empire far into the sands of Central Asia and southward along the coast of the South China Sea into what is now Vietnam. The doctrine of State Confucianism provided an effective ideology for the state, and Chinese culture appeared unrivaled. In many respects, its scientific and technological achievements were unsurpassed.

無以的，卓越的   無敵的

One reason for China's striking success undoubtedly was that, unlike its contemporary civilizations, it long was able to fend off the danger from nomadic peoples (along the northern frontier). By the end of the second century B.C.E., however, the Xiongnu were looming ominously, and tribal warriors began to nip at the borders of the empire. While the dynasty was strong, the problem was manageable, but when internal difficulties began to corrode the unity of the state, China became increasingly vulnerable to the threat from the north and entered its own time of troubles.

During the glory years of the Han, another great civilization was beginning to take form on the northern shores of the Mediterranean Sea. Unlike China and the other ancient societies discussed thus far, this new civilization in Europe was based as much on trade as on agriculture. Yet the political and cultural achievements of ancient Greece were the equal of any of the great human experiments that had preceded it and soon began to exert a significant impact on the rest of the ancient world.

CHAPTER NOTES

1. *Book of Changes,* quoted in Chang Chi-yun, *Chinese History of Fifty Centuries,* vol. 1, *Ancient Times* (Taipei, 1962), pp. 15, 31, and 65.
2. Ibid., p. 381.
3. Quoted in E. N. Anderson, *The Food of China* (New Haven, Conn., 1988), p. 21.
4. According to Chinese tradition, the *Rites of Zhou* was written by the duke of Zhou himself near the time of the found-ing of the Zhou dynasty. However, modern historians believe that it was written much later, perhaps as late as the fourth century B.C.E.
5. From *The Book of Songs,* quoted in Sebastian de Grazia, ed., *Masters of Chinese Political Thought: From the Beginnings to the Han Dynasty* (New York, 1973), pp. 40–41.
6. *Confucian Analects* (Lun Yu), ed. James Legge (Taipei, 1963), 11:11 and 6:20.

7. Ibid., 15:23.

8. Ibid., 17:2.

9. *Book of Mencius (Meng Zi)*, 4 A:9, quoted in William Theodore de Bary et al., eds., *Sources of Chinese Tradition*, (New York, 1960), p. 107.

10. Quoted in de Bary, *Sources of Chinese Tradition*, p. 53.

11. Burton Watson, *Records of the Grand Historian of China* (New York, 1961), vol. 2, pp. 155, 160.

12. Ibid., pp. 32, 53.

13. Clae Waltham, *Shu Ching: Book of History* (Chicago, 1971), p. 154.

14. Arthur Waley, ed., *Chinese Poems* (London, 1983), p. xx.

15. Lloyd E. Eastman, *Family, Fields, and Ancestors: Constancy and Change in China's Social and Economic History, 1550–1949* (New York, 1988), p. 19.

16. Quoted in Herbert A. Giles, *A History of Chinese Literature* (New York, 1923), p. 19.

17. Chang Chi-yun, *Chinese History of Fifty Centuries*, p. 183.

 # SUGGESTED READINGS

There are several general histories of China that provide a useful overview of the period of antiquity. Perhaps the best known is the classic *East Asia: Tradition and Transformation* (Boston, 1973), by J. K. Fairbank, E. O. Reischauer, and A. M. Craig. Also of use are C. Schirokauer, *A Brief History of Chinese and Japanese Civilizations*, 2d ed. (San Diego, 1989); and M. Elvin, *The Pattern of the Chinese Past* (Stanford, Calif., 1973), which presents a provocative interpretation of key issues in Chinese history. Political and social maps of China can be found in A. Herrmann, *An Historical Atlas of China* (Chicago, 1966).

The period of the Neolithic era and the Shang dynasty has received increasing attention in recent years. For an impressively documented and annotated overview, see Kwang-chih Chang, *Shang Civilization* (New Haven, Conn., 1980) and *Studies in Shang Archaeology* (New Haven, Conn., 1982). D. Keightley, *The Origins of Chinese Civilization* (Berkeley, 1983) presents a number of interesting articles on selected aspects of the period. An older but still interesting work is H. Maspero, *China in Antiquity* (Amherst, Mass., 1988), a translation of his *La Chine Antique*.

The Zhou and Qin dynasties have also received considerable attention. The former is exhaustively analyzed in Cho-yun Hsu and J. M. Linduff, *Western Zhou Civilization* (New Haven, Conn., 1988) and Li Xueqin, *Eastern Zhou and Qin Civilizations* (New Haven, Conn., 1985). The latter is a translation of an original work by a mainland Chinese scholar and is especially interesting for its treatment of the development of the silk industry and the money economy in ancient China. Also of interest is the study of Qin Shi Huangdi by A. Cotterell, *The First Emperor of China* (New York, 1981). On bronze casting, see E. L. Shaughnessy, *Sources of Eastern Zhou History* (Berkeley, 1991). Also of value for its treatment of the formation of social classes is Cho-yun Hsu, *Ancient China in Transition* (Stanford, Calif., 1965).

There are a number of useful books on the Han dynasty. Zhongshu Wang, *Han Civilization* (New Haven, Conn., 1982) presents new evidence from the mainland on recent excavations from Han tombs and the old imperial capital of Chang'an. M. Loewe, *Everyday Life in Early Imperial China during the Han Period, 202 BC–220 AD* (London, 1968) contains useful material on religious beliefs and the development of social classes during the Han. Also, see the lavishly illustrated *The Han Civilization of China* (Oxford, 1982) by M. P. Serstevens. For a firsthand view, see B. Watson, *Records of the Grand*

Historian of China (New York, 1961), a translation of key passages from Sima Qian's history of the period. For the historian's life, consult *Ssu-ma Ch'ien: Grand Historian of China* (New York, 1958).

The philosophy of ancient China has attracted considerable attention from Western scholars. Some standard works include A. Waley, *Three Ways of Thought in Ancient China* (New York, 1939); H. G. Creel, *Chinese Thought: From Confucius to Mao Tse-Tung* (Chicago, 1953); Feng Yu-lan, *A Short History of Chinese Philosophy* (New York, 1960); and F. Mote, *Intellectual Foundations of China*, 2d ed. (New York, 1989). On Confucius, see Liu Wu-chi, *A Short History of Confucian Philosophy* (Middlesex, 1955); and H. G. Creel, *Confucius: The Man and the Myth* (London, 1951). The latter is a sympathetic treatment that emphasizes the humanistic side of Confucian philosophy. S. de Grazia, ed., *Masters of Chinese Political Thought: From the Beginnings to the Han Dynasty* (New York, 1973) includes passages from the ancient philosophers that deal with the political realm.

For works on general culture and science, consult the illustrated work by R. Temple, *The Genius of China: 3000 Years of Science, Discovery, and Invention* (New York, 1986); and J. Needham, *Science in Traditional China: A Comparative Perspective* (Boston, 1981). See also E. N. Anderson, *The Food of China* (New Haven, Conn., 1988).

The most comprehensive collection of original writings is W. T. de Bary and Irene Bloom, *Sources of Chinese Tradition*, 2d ed. (New York, 1999), which includes excerpts from most of the ancient texts. The complete translations of the Confucian Classics are in J. Legge, *The Chinese Classics*, 5 vols. (Hong Kong, 1960), with critical and exegetical notes. For a modernized edition of the *Book of History*, see C. Waltham, *Shu Ching: Book of History* (Chicago, 1971). For an annotated version of Lao Tzu, see Wing-Tsit Chan, *The Way of Lao Tzu* (Indianapolis, 1963).

For an introduction to classical Chinese literature, consult the three standard anthologies: Liu Wu-Chi, *An Introduction to Chinese Literature* (New York, 1961); V. H. Mair, ed., *The Columbia Anthology of Traditional Chinese Literature* (New York, 1994); and S. Owen, ed., *An Anthology of Chinese Literature: Beginnings to 1911* (New York, 1996). For a comprehensive introduction to Chinese art, consult M. Sullivan, *The Arts of China*, 4th ed. (Berkeley, 1999), with good illustrations in color. Also, see M. Tregear, *Chinese Art*, revised (London, 1997) and, by the same author, *Art Treasures in China* (New York, 1994).

INFOTRAC COLLEGE EDITION

For additional reading, go to InfoTrac College Edition, your online research library at
http://web1.infotrac-college.com

Enter the search terms "Confucius or Confucian" using Keywords.

Enter the search terms "Taoism or Daoism" using the Subject Guide.

Enter the search terms "Han dynasty" using Keywords.

Enter the search terms "China history" using Keywords.

CHAPTER

4

THE CIVILIZATION OF THE GREEKS

CHAPTER OUTLINE

- EARLY GREECE
- THE GREEKS IN A DARK AGE (c. 1100–c. 750 B.C.E.)
- THE WORLD OF THE GREEK CITY-STATES (c. 750–c. 500 B.C.E.)
- THE HIGH POINT OF GREEK CIVILIZATION: CLASSICAL GREECE
- THE RISE OF MACEDONIA AND THE CONQUESTS OF ALEXANDER
- THE WORLD OF THE HELLENISTIC KINGDOMS
- CULTURE IN THE HELLENISTIC WORLD
- CONCLUSION

FOCUS QUESTIONS

- What was the *polis*, or city-state, and how did the city-states of Athens and Sparta differ?
- What effects did the Persian Wars and the Great Peloponnesian War have on Greek civilization?
- How was Alexander the Great able to amass his empire, and what was his legacy?
- How did the political, economic, and social institutions of the Hellenistic world differ from those of Classical Greece?
- In what ways did the schools of philosophy and major religions of the Hellenistic period differ from those of the classical period, and what do those differences suggest about society in the two periods?

During the era of civil war in China known as the "Period of the Warring States," a civil war also erupted on the northern shores of the Mediterranean Sea. In 431 B.C.E., two very different Greek city-states—Athens and Sparta—fought for domination of the Greek world. The people of Athens felt secure behind their walls and in the first winter of the war held a public funeral to honor those who had died in battle. On the day of the ceremony, the citizens of Athens joined in a procession, with the relatives of the dead wailing for their loved ones. As was the custom in Athens, one leading citizen was asked to address the crowd, and on this day it was Pericles who spoke to the people. He talked about the greatness of Athens and reminded the Athenians of the strength of their political system: "Our constitution," he said, "is called a democracy because power is in the hands not of a minority but of the whole people. When it is a question of settling private disputes, everyone is equal before the law. . . . Just as our political life is free and open, so is our day-to-day life in our relations with each other. . . . Here each individual is interested not only in his own affairs but in the affairs of the state as well."

In this famous funeral oration, Pericles gave voice to the ideals of democracy and the importance of the individual, ideals that were quite different from those of ancient China, in which the individual was subordinated to a larger order based on obedience to an exalted emperor. The Greeks asked some basic questions about human life: What is the nature of the universe? What is the purpose of human existence? What is our relationship to divine forces? What constitutes a community? What constitutes a state? What is true education? What are the true sources of law? What is truth itself and how do we realize it? The Greeks not only gave answers to these questions; they proceeded to create a system of logical, analytical thought in order to examine them. Their answers and their system of rational thought laid the intellectual foundation for Western civilization's understanding of the human condition.

The story of ancient Greek civilization is a remarkable one that begins with the first arrival of the Greeks around 1900 B.C.E. By the eighth century B.C.E., the characteristic institution of ancient Greek life, the *polis* or city-state, had emerged. Greek civilization flourished and reached its height in the classical era of the fifth century B.C.E., which has come to be closely identified with the achievements of Athenian democracy. But the inability of the Greek city-states to end their fratricidal warfare eventually left them vulnerable to the Macedonian king Philip II and helped to bring an end to the Greek world of independent city-states.

Although the Greek city-states were never the same after their defeat by the Macedonian monarch, this defeat did not bring an end to the influence of the Greeks. Philip's son Alexander led the Macedonians and Greeks on a spectacular conquest of the Persian Empire and opened the door to the spread of Greek culture throughout the Middle East. We use the term *Hellenistic* to designate this new period of Greek history. ❀

 # EARLY GREECE

Geography played an important role in the evolution of Greek history. Compared to the landmasses of Mesopotamia and Egypt, Greece occupied a small area. It was a mountainous peninsula that encompassed only 45,000 square miles of territory, about the size of the state of Louisiana. The mountains and the sea played especially significant roles in the development of Greek history. Much of Greece consists of small plains and river valleys surrounded by mountain ranges 8,000–10,000 feet high. The mountainous terrain had the effect of isolating Greeks from one another. Consequently, Greek communities tended to follow their own separate paths and develop their own way of life. Over a period of time, these communities became so fiercely attached to their independence that they were unwilling to join into larger units of organization and only too willing to fight one another to gain advantage. No doubt the small size of these independent Greek communities fostered participation in political affairs and unique cultural expressions, but the rivalry among these communities also led to the internecine warfare that ultimately devastated Greek society.

The sea also influenced the evolution of Greek society. Greece had a long seacoast, dotted by bays and inlets that provided numerous harbors. The Greeks also inhabited a number of islands to the west, south, and particularly the east of the Greek mainland. It is no accident that the Greeks became seafarers who sailed out into the Aegean and the Mediterranean Seas first to make contact with the outside world and later to establish colonies that would spread Greek civilization throughout the Mediterranean world.

Greek topography helped to determine the major territories into which Greece was ultimately divided. South of the Gulf of Corinth was the Peloponnesus, virtually an island as seen on a map. Consisting mostly of hills, mountains, and small valleys, the Peloponnesus was the location of Sparta, as well as the site of Olympia, where the famous athletic games were held. Northeast of the Peloponnesus was the Attic peninsula (or Attica), the home of Athens, hemmed in by mountains to the north and west and surrounded by the sea to the south and east. Northwest of Attica was Boeotia in central Greece, with its chief city of Thebes. To the north of Boeotia was Thessaly, which contained the largest plains and became a great producer of grain and horses. To the north of Thessaly lay Macedonia, which was not of much importance in Greek history until 338 B.C.E., when the Macedonian king Philip II conquered the Greeks.

Minoan Crete

The earliest civilization in the Aegean region emerged on Crete. By 2800 B.C.E., a Bronze Age civilization that used metals, especially bronze, in the construction of weapons had been established on the large island of Crete, southeast of the Greek mainland. The civilization of Minoan Crete was first discovered by the English archaeologist Arthur Evans, who named it Minoan after Minos, the legendary king of Crete. Evans's excavations on Crete at the beginning of the twentieth century led to the discovery of an enormous palace complex at Knossus near modern Heracleion. The remains revealed a rich and prosperous culture with Knossus as the probable center of a far-ranging "sea empire," probably largely commercial in nature. Because Evans found few military fortifications for the defense of Knossus itself, he assumed that Minoan Crete had a strong navy. We do know from archaeological remains that the people of Minoan Crete were accustomed to sea travel and had made contact with the more

advanced civilization of Egypt. Egyptian products have been found in Crete and Cretan products in Egypt. Minoan Cretans also made contact and exerted influence on the Greek-speaking inhabitants of the Greek mainland.

The Minoan civilization reached its height between 2000 and 1450 B.C.E. The palace at Knossus, the royal seat of the kings, demonstrates the obvious prosperity and power of this civilization. It was an elaborate structure built around a central courtyard and included numerous private living rooms for the royal family and workshops for making decorated vases, small sculptures such as ivory figurines, and jewelry. Even bathrooms, with elaborate drains, formed part of the complex. The rooms were decorated with frescoes in bright colors showing sporting events and naturalistic scenes that have led some to assume that the Cretans had a great love of nature. Storerooms in the palace held enormous jars of oil, wine, and grain, presumably paid as taxes in kind to the king. A large bureaucracy that kept detailed records of the payments apparently assisted the kings.

The centers of Minoan civilization on Crete suffered a sudden and catastrophic collapse around 1450 B.C.E. The cause of this destruction has been vigorously debated. Some historians believe that a tsunami triggered by a powerful volcanic eruption on the island of Thera was responsible for the devastation. Most historians, however, maintain

THE MINOAN SPORT OF BULL LEAPING.   Minoan bull games were held on festival days in the great palaces on the island of Crete. As seen in this fresco from the east wing of the palace at Knossus, women and men acrobats (the man in red) somersaulted over the back of the bull. Another person waited behind the bull to catch the leapers.

that the destruction was the result of invasion and pillage by mainland Greeks known as the Mycenaeans.

The Mycenaean Greeks

The term *Mycenaean* is derived from Mycenae, a remarkable fortified site first excavated by the amateur German archaeologist Heinrich Schliemann. Mycenae was one center in a Mycenaean Greek civilization that flourished between 1600 and 1100 B.C.E. The Mycenaean Greeks were part of the Indo-European family of peoples (see Chapter 1), who spread from their original location into southern and western Europe, India, and Iran. One group entered the territory of Greece from the north around 1900 B.C.E. and, over a period of time, managed to gain control of the Greek mainland and develop a civilization.

Mycenaean civilization, which reached its high point between 1400 and 1200 B.C.E., consisted of a number of powerful monarchies based in fortified palace complexes, which were built on hills and surrounded by gigantic stone walls, such as those found at Mycenae, Tiryns, Pylos, Thebes, and Orchomenos. These various centers of power probably formed a loose confederacy of independent states, with Mycenae the strongest. Next in importance to the kings in these states were the army commanders, the priests, and the bureaucrats, who kept careful records. The free citizenry included peasants, soldiers, and artisans, with the lowest rung of the social ladder consisting of serfs and slaves.

The Mycenaeans were, above all, a warrior people who prided themselves on their heroic deeds in battle. Archaeological evidence indicates that the Mycenaean monarchies also developed an extensive commercial network. Mycenaean pottery has been found throughout the Mediterranean basin, in Syria and Egypt to the east and Sicily and southern Italy to the west. But some scholars also believe that the Mycenaeans, led by Mycenae itself, spread outward militarily, conquering Crete and making it part of the Mycenaean world. The most famous of all their supposed military adventures has come down to us in the epic poetry of Homer (see Homer later in this chapter). Did the Mycenaean Greeks, led by Agamemnon, king of Mycenae, sack the city of Troy on the northwestern coast of Asia Minor around 1250 B.C.E.? Since the excavations of Heinrich Schliemann, begun in 1870, scholars have debated this question. Many do believe in the basic authenticity of the Homeric legend, even if the details have become shrouded in mystery.

By the late thirteenth century, Mycenaean Greece was showing signs of serious trouble. Modern scholars have proposed a number of theories to explain the collapse of Mycenaean civilization. According to the Greeks' own legend, their mainland was invaded from the north by another Greek-speaking people who were less civilized than the Mycenaeans. Called the Dorians, these invaders supposedly destroyed the old centers of Mycenaean power

and ultimately established themselves in the Peloponnesus. But there is little archaeological evidence to support the idea of massive Dorian invasions. Other historians argue that internal conflict among the Mycenaean kings and major earthquakes were more important factors in the Mycenaean decline. What is certain is that by 1100 B.C.E., Mycenaean civilization had collapsed.

THE GREEKS IN A DARK AGE (C. 1100–C. 750 B.C.E.)

After the collapse of Mycenaean civilization, Greece entered a difficult era of declining population and falling food production. Moreover, we have few records to help us reconstruct what happened in this period. Because of the difficult conditions and our lack of knowledge about the period, historians refer to it as a Dark Age. Not until 850 B.C.E. did farming revive. At the same time, some new developments were forming the basis for a revived Greece.

During the Dark Age, large numbers of Greeks left the mainland and migrated across the Aegean Sea to various islands, and especially to the southwestern shore of Asia Minor, a strip of territory that came to be called Ionia. Based on their dialect, the Greeks who resided there were called Ionians. Two other major groups of Greeks settled in established parts of Greece. The Aeolian Greeks who were located in northern and central Greece colonized the large island of Lesbos and the adjacent territory of the mainland. The Dorians established themselves in southwestern Greece, especially in the Peloponnesus, as well as on some of the south Aegean islands, including Crete.

Other important activities occurred in this Dark Age as well. There was a revival of some trade and some economic activity besides agriculture. Iron replaced bronze in the construction of weapons, making them affordable for more people. And at some point in the eighth century B.C.E., the Greeks adopted the Phoenician alphabet to give themselves a new system of writing. Near the very end of this so-called Dark Age appeared the work of Homer, who has come to be viewed as one of the truly great poets of all time.

Homer

The origins of the *Iliad* and the *Odyssey*, the first great epics of early Greece, are to be found in the oral tradition of reciting poems recounting the deeds of heroes of the Mycenaean age. It is generally assumed that early in the eighth century B.C.E., Homer made use of these oral traditions to compose the *Iliad*, his epic of the Trojan War. The war was caused by an act of Paris, a prince of Troy. By kidnapping Helen, wife of the king of the Greek state of Sparta, he outraged all the Greeks. Under the leadership of the Spartan king's brother, Agamemnon of Mycenae,

⚜ **THE SLAYING OF HECTOR.** This scene from a late-fifth-century B.C.E. Athenian vase depicts the final battle between Achilles and the Trojan hero Hector. Achilles is shown lunging forward with his spear to deliver the final, deadly blow to the Trojan prince, a scene taken from Homer's *Iliad*. The *Iliad* is Homer's masterpiece and was important to later Greeks as a means of teaching the aristocratic values of courage and honor.

the Greeks attacked Troy. Ten years later, the Greeks finally won and sacked the city.

But the *Iliad* is not so much the story of the war itself as it is the tale of the Greek hero Achilles and how the "wrath of Achilles" led to disaster. As is true of all great literature, the *Iliad* abounds in universal lessons. Underlying them all is the clear message, as one commentator has observed, that "men will still come and go like the generations of leaves in the forest; that he will still be weak, and the gods strong and incalculable; that the quality of a man matters more than his achievement; that violence and recklessness will still lead to disaster, and that this will fall on the innocent as well as on the guilty." [1]

Although the *Odyssey* has long been considered Homer's other masterpiece, some scholars believe that it was composed later than the *Iliad* and was probably not the work of Homer. The *Odyssey* is an epic romance that recounts the journeys of one of the Greek heroes, Odysseus, after the fall of Troy and his ultimate return to his wife. But there is a larger vision here as well: the testing of the heroic stature of Odysseus until, by both cunning and patience, he prevails. In the course of this testing, the underlying moral message is "that virtue is a better policy than vice." [2]

Although the *Iliad* and the *Odyssey* supposedly deal with the heroes of the Mycenaean age of the thirteenth century B.C.E., many scholars believe that they really describe the social conditions of the Dark Age. According to the Homeric view, Greece was a society based on agriculture in which a landed warrior-aristocracy controlled much wealth and exercised considerable power. There is no doubt that Homer's society was divided along class lines with the warrior-aristocrats as the dominant group. Homer's world reflects the values of aristocratic heroes.

This, of course, explains the importance of Homer to later generations of Greeks. Homer did not so much

record history: he made it. The Greeks regarded the *Iliad* and the *Odyssey* as authentic history and as the works of one poet, Homer. These masterpieces gave the Greeks an ideal past with a legendary age of heroes and came to be used as standard texts for the education of generations of Greek males. As one Athenian stated, "My father was anxious to see me develop into a good man . . . and as a means to this end he compelled me to memorize all of Homer." [3] The values Homer inculcated were essentially the aristocratic values of courage and honor (see the box on p. 99). It was important to strive for the excellence befitting a hero, which the Greeks called *arete*. In the warrior-aristocratic world of Homer, *arete* is won in struggle or contest. In his willingness to fight, the hero protects his family and friends, preserves and expands his own honor and that of his family, and earns his reputation. In the Homeric world, aristocratic women, too, were expected to pursue excellence. Penelope, for example, the wife of Odysseus, the hero of the *Odyssey*, remains faithful to her husband and displays great courage and in-telligence in preserving their household during her husband's long absence. Upon his return, Odysseus praises her for her excellence: "Madame, there is not a man in the wide world who could find fault with you. For your fame has reached heaven itself, like that of some perfect king, ruling a populous and mighty state with the fear of god in his heart, and upholding the right." [4]

To a later generation of Greeks, these heroic values formed the core of aristocratic virtue, a fact that explains the tremendous popularity of Homer as an educational tool. Homer gave to the Greeks a single universally accepted model of heroism, honor, and nobility. But in time, as a new world of city-states emerged in Greece, new values of cooperation and community also transformed what the Greeks learned from Homer.

HOMER'S IDEAL OF EXCELLENCE

The Iliad and the Odyssey, which the Greeks believed were both written by Homer, were used as basic texts for the education of Greeks for hundreds of years during antiquity. This passage from the Iliad, describing the encounter between Hector, prince of Troy, and his wife Andromache, illustrates the Greek ideal of gaining honor through combat. At the end of the passage, Homer also reveals what became the Greek attitude toward women: they are supposed to spin and weave and take care of their households and children.

HOMER, ILIAD

Hector looked at his son and smiled, but said nothing. Andromache, bursting into tears, went up to him and put her hand in his. "Hector," she said, "you are possessed. This bravery of yours will be your end. You do not think of your little boy or your unhappy wife, whom you will make a widow soon. Some day the Achaeans [Greeks] are bound to kill you in a massed attack. And when I lose you I might as well be dead. . . . I have no father, no mother, now. . . . I had seven brothers too at home. In one day all of them went down to Hades' House. The great Achilles of the swift feet killed them all. . . .

"So you, Hector, are father and mother and brother to me, as well as my beloved husband. Have pity on me now; stay here on the tower; and do not make your boy an orphan and your wife a widow. . . ."

"All that, my dear," said the great Hector of the glittering helmet, "is surely my concern. But if I hid myself like a coward and refused to fight, I could never face the Trojans and the Trojan ladies in their trailing gowns. Besides, it would go against the grain, for I have trained myself always, like a good soldier, to take my place in the front line and win glory for my father and myself. . . ."

As he finished, glorious Hector held out his arms to take his boy. But the child shrank back with a cry to the bosom of his girdled nurse, alarmed by his father's appearance. He was frightened by the bronze of the helmet and the horsehair plume that he saw nodding grimly down at him. His father and his lady mother had to laugh. But noble Hector quickly took his helmet off and put the dazzling thing on the ground. Then he kissed his son, dandled him in his arms, and prayed to Zeus and the other gods: "Zeus, and you other gods, grant that this boy of mine may be, like me, preeminent in Troy; as strong and brave as I; a mighty king of Ilium. May people say, when he comes back from battle, 'Here is a better man than his father.' Let him bring home the bloodstained armor of the enemy he has killed, and make his mother happy."

Hector handed the boy to his wife, who took him to her fragrant breast. She was smiling through her tears, and when her husband saw this he was moved. He stroked her with his hand and said, "My dear, I beg you not to be too much distressed. No one is going to send me down to Hades before my proper time. But Fate is a thing that no man born of woman, coward or hero, can escape. Go home now, and attend to your own work, the loom and the spindle, and see that the maidservants get on with theirs. War is men's business; and this war is the business of every man in Ilium, myself above all."

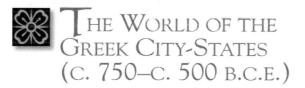

THE WORLD OF THE GREEK CITY-STATES (C. 750–C. 500 B.C.E.)

In the eighth century B.C.E., Greek civilization burst forth with new energies. Two major developments stand out in this era: the evolution of the *polis* as the central institution in Greek life and the Greeks' colonization of the Mediterranean and Black Seas.

The *Polis*

By the eighth century B.C.E., the Greek *polis* (plural, *poleis*) had emerged as a truly unique and fundamental institution in Greek society. In the most basic sense, a *polis* could be defined as a small but autonomous political unit in which all major political, social, and religious activities were carried out at one central location.

In a physical sense, the *polis* encompassed a town or city or even a village and its surrounding countryside. But the town or city or village served as the focus or central point where the citizens of the *polis* could assemble for political, social, and religious activities. In some *poleis*, this central meeting point was a hill, like the Acropolis at Athens, which could serve as a place of refuge during an attack and later in some sites came to be the religious center on which temples and public monuments were erected. Below the acropolis would be an *agora*, an open space that served both as a place where citizens could assemble and as a market. Citizens resided in town and country alike, but the town remained the center of political activity.

Poleis could vary greatly in size, from a few square miles to a few hundred square miles. The larger ones were the product of consolidation. The territory of Attica, for example, had once had twelve *poleis* but eventually became a single *polis* (Athens) through a process of amalgamation. Athens grew to have a population of more than 300,000 by the fifth century B.C.E., with an adult male citizen body of about 43,000. Most *poleis* were considerably smaller than Athens, however.

Although our word *politics* is derived from the Greek term *polis*, the *polis* itself was much more than just a political institution. It was, above all, a community of citizens in which all political, economic, social, cultural, and religious activities were focused. As a community, the *polis* consisted of citizens with political rights (adult males), citizens with no political rights (women and children), and noncitizens (slaves and resident aliens). All citizens of a *polis* possessed fundamental rights, but these rights were coupled with responsibilities. The Greek philosopher Aristotle argued that the citizen did not just belong to himself: "we must rather regard every citizen as belonging to the state." However, the loyalty that citizens had to their city-states also had a negative side. City-states distrusted one

another, and the division of Greece into fiercely patriotic independent units helped bring about its ruin.

The development of the *polis* was paralleled by the emergence of a new military system. Greek fighting had previously been dominated by aristocratic cavalrymen, who reveled in individual duels with enemy soldiers. But by the end of the eighth century and beginning of the seventh century B.C.E., the hoplite infantry formation—the phalanx—came into being. Hoplites were heavily armed infantrymen, who wore bronze or leather helmets, breastplates, and greaves (shin guards). Each carried a round shield, a short sword, and a thrusting spear about nine feet long. Hoplites advanced into battle as a unit, forming a phalanx (a rectangular formation) in tight order, usually eight ranks deep. As long as the hoplites kept their order, were not outflanked, and did not break, they either secured victory or, at the very least, suffered no harm. The phalanx was easily routed, however, if it broke its order. The safety of the phalanx depended, above all, on the soli-

✿ **THE HOPLITE FORCES.**   The Greek hoplites were infantrymen equipped with large round shields and long thrusting spears. In battle they advanced in tight phalanx formation and were dangerous opponents as long as this formation remained unbroken. This vase painting of the seventh century B.C.E. shows two groups of hoplite warriors engaged in battle. The piper on the left is leading another line of soldiers preparing to enter the fray.

darity and discipline of its members. As one seventh-century B.C.E. poet noted, a good hoplite was "a short man firmly placed upon his legs, with a courageous heart, not to be uprooted from the spot where he plants his legs."[5]

The hoplite force had political as well as military repercussions. The aristocratic cavalry was now outdated. Since each hoplite provided his own armor, men of property, both aristocrats and small farmers, made up the new phalanx. Those who could become hoplites and fight for the state could also challenge aristocratic control.

Colonization and the Rise of Tyrants

Between 750 and 550 B.C.E., the Greek people left their homeland in large numbers to settle in distant lands. Poverty and land hunger created by the growing gulf between rich and poor, overpopulation, and the development of trade were all factors that led to the establishment of colonies. Each colony was founded as a *polis* and

was usually independent of the mother *polis* (hence the word *metropolis*) that had established it. Invariably, the colony saw itself as an independent entity whose links to the mother city were not political but were based on sharing common social, economic, and especially religious practices.

In the western Mediterranean, new Greek settlements were established along the coastline of southern Italy, southern France, eastern Spain, and northern Africa west of Egypt. To the north, the Greeks set up colonies in Thrace, where they sought good agricultural lands to grow grains. Greeks also settled along the shores of the Black Sea and secured the approaches to it with cities on the Hellespont and Bosphorus, most notably Byzantium, site of the later Constantinople (Istanbul). By establishing these settlements, the Greeks spread their culture throughout the Mediterranean basin. Colonization also led to increased trade and industry. The Greeks sent their pottery, wine, and olive oil to the colonies; in return, they received grains and

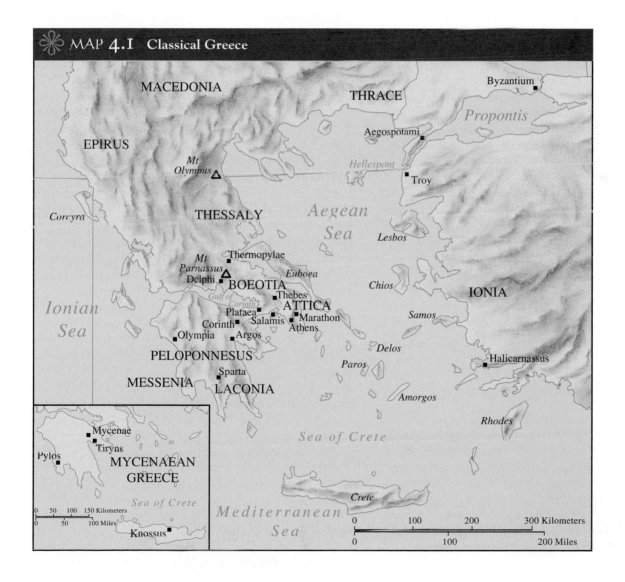

MAP 4.1 Classical Greece

metals from the west and fish, timber, wheat, metals, and slaves from the Black Sea region. In many *poleis*, the expansion of trade and industry created a new group of rich men who desired political privileges commensurate with their wealth but found such privileges impossible to gain because of the power of the ruling aristocrats.

The aspirations of the newly rising industrial and commercial groups opened the door to the rise of tyrants in the seventh and sixth centuries B.C.E. They were not necessarily oppressive or wicked as our word *tyrant* connotes. Greek tyrants were rulers who came to power in an unconstitutional way; a tyrant was not subject to the law. Many tyrants were actually aristocrats who opposed the control of the ruling aristocratic faction in their cities. The support for the tyrants, however, came from the new rich who made their money in trade and industry as well as from poor peasants who were becoming increasingly indebted to landholding aristocrats. Both groups were opposed to the domination of political power by aristocratic oligarchies.

Tyrants usually achieved power by a local coup d'etat and maintained it by using mercenary soldiers. Once in power, they promoted public works projects, such as the construction of new marketplaces, temples, and walls, that not only glorified the city but also enhanced their own popularity. Tyrants also favored the interests of merchants and traders. Despite these achievements, however, tyranny was largely extinguished by the end of the sixth century B.C.E. Its very nature as a system outside the law seemed contradictory to the ideal of law in a Greek community. Although tyranny did not last, it played a significant role in the evolution of Greek history by ending the rule of narrow aristocratic oligarchies. Once the tyrants were eliminated, the door was opened to the participation of new and more people in governing the affairs of the community. Although this trend culminated in the development of democracy in some communities, in other states expanded oligarchies of one kind or another managed to remain in power. Greek states exhibited considerable variety in their governmental structures; this can perhaps best be seen by examining the two most famous and most powerful Greek city-states, Sparta and Athens.

Sparta

Located in the southwestern Peloponnesus, in an area known as Laconia, the Spartans had originally occupied four small villages that eventually became unified into a single *polis*. This unification made Sparta a strong community in Laconia and enabled the Spartans to conquer the Laconians and subject them to serfdom. Known as Helots (the name is derived from a Greek word for "capture"), these conquered Laconians were bound to the land and forced to work on farms and as household servants for the Spartans.

When the land in Laconia proved unable to maintain the growing number of Spartan citizens, the Spartans looked for land nearby and, beginning around 730 B.C.E., undertook the conquest of neighboring Messenia despite its larger size and population. Messenia possessed a large, fertile plain ideal for growing grain. After its conquest, which was not completed until the seventh century B.C.E., the Messenians were reduced to serfdom and made to work for the Spartans. To ensure control over their conquered Laconian and Messenian Helots, the Spartans made a conscious decision to create a military state.

Sometime between 800 and 600 B.C.E., the Spartans instituted a series of reforms that are associated with the name of the lawgiver Lycurgus (see the box on p. 103). Although historians are not sure that Lycurgus ever existed, there is no doubt about the result of the reforms that were made: Sparta was transformed into a perpetual military camp.

The lives of Spartans were now rigidly organized and tightly controlled (thus, our word *spartan*, meaning "highly self-disciplined"). At birth each child was examined by state officials who decided whether he or she was fit to live. Those judged unfit were exposed to die. Boys were taken from their mothers at the age of seven and put under control of the state. They lived in quasi-military barracks, where they were subjected to harsh discipline to make them tough and given an education that stressed military training and obedience to authority. At twenty, Spartan males were enrolled in the army for regular military service. Although allowed to marry, they continued to live in the barracks and ate all their meals in public dining halls with their fellow soldiers. Meals were simple; the famous Spartan black broth consisted of a piece of pork boiled in blood, salt, and vinegar, causing a visitor who ate in a public mess to remark that he now understood why Spartans were not afraid to die. At thirty, Spartan males were recognized as mature and allowed to vote in the assembly and live at home, but they remained in military service until the age of sixty.

While their husbands remained in military barracks until age thirty, Spartan women lived at home. Because of this separation, Spartan women had greater freedom of movement and greater power in the household than was common for women elsewhere in Greece. Spartan women were encouraged to exercise and remain fit to bear and raise healthy children. Like the men, Spartan women engaged in athletic exercises in the nude. At solemn feasts, the young women marched naked in processions, and in the presence of the young men, they sang songs about those who had showed special gallantry or cowardice on the battlefield. Many Spartan women upheld the strict Spartan values, expecting their husbands and sons to be brave in war. The story is told that as a Spartan mother was burying her son, an old woman came up to her and said, "You poor woman, what a misfortune." "No," replied the mother, "because I bore him so that

THE LYCURGAN REFORMS

In order to maintain their control over the conquered Messenians, the Spartans instituted the reforms that created their military state. In this account of the supposed lawgiver Lycurgus, the Greek historian Plutarch discusses the effect of these reforms on the treatment and education of boys.

PLUTARCH, LYCURGUS

Lycurgus was of another mind; he would not have masters bought out of the market for his young Spartans, . . . nor was it lawful, indeed, for the father himself to breed up the children after his own fancy; but as soon as they were seven years old they were to be enrolled in certain companies and classes, where they all lived under the same order and discipline, doing their exercises and taking their play together. Of these, he who showed the most conduct and courage was made captain; they had their eyes always upon him, obeyed his orders, and underwent patiently whatsoever punishment he inflicted; so that the whole course of their education was one continued exercise of a ready and perfect obedience. The old men, too, were spectators of their performances, and often raised quarrels and disputes among them, to have a good opportunity of finding out their different characters, and of seeing which would be valiant, which a coward, when they should come to more dangerous encounters. Reading and writing they gave them, just enough to serve their turn; their chief care was to make them good subjects, and to teach them to endure pain and conquer in battle. To this end, as they grew in years, their discipline was proportionately increased; their heads were close-clipped, they were accustomed to go barefoot, and for the most part to play naked.

After they were twelve years old, they were no longer allowed to wear any undergarments; they had one coat to serve them a year; their bodies were hard and dry, with but little acquaintance of baths and unguents; these human indulgences they were allowed only on some few particular days in the year. They lodged together in little bands upon beds made of the rushes which grew by the banks of the river Eurotas, which they were to break off with their hands with a knife; if it were winter, they mingled some thistledown with their rushes, which it was thought had the property of giving warmth. By the time they were come to this age there was not any of the more hopeful boys who had not a lover to bear him company. The old men, too, had an eye upon them, coming often to the grounds to hear and see them contend either in wit or strength with one another, and this as seriously . . . as if they were their fathers, their tutors, or their magistrates; so that there scarcely was any time or place without someone present to put them in mind of their duty, and punish them if they had neglected it.

[Spartan boys were also encouraged to steal their food.] They stole, too, all other meat they could lay their hands on, looking out and watching all opportunities, when people were asleep or more careless than usual. If they were caught, they were not only punished with whipping, but hunger, too, being reduced to their ordinary allowance, which was but very slender, and so contrived on purpose, that they might set about to help themselves, and be forced to exercise their energy and address. This was the principal design of their hard fare.

he might die for Sparta and that is what has happened, as I wished."[6]

The so-called Lycurgan reforms also reorganized the Spartan government, creating an oligarchy. Two kings from different families were primarily responsible for military affairs and served as the leaders of the Spartan army on its campaigns. Moreover, the kings served as the supreme priests within the state religion and had some role in foreign policy.

The two kings shared power with a body called the *gerousia*, a council of elders. It consisted of twenty-eight citizens over the age of sixty, who were elected for life, and the two kings. The primary task of the *gerousia* was to prepare proposals that would be presented to the *apella*, an assembly of all male citizens. The assembly did not debate but only voted on the proposals put before it by the *gerousia*; rarely did the assembly reject these proposals. The assembly also elected the *gerousia* and another body known as the *ephors*, a group of five men who were responsible for

supervising the education of youth and the conduct of all citizens.

To make their new military state secure, the Spartans deliberately turned their backs on the outside world. Foreigners, who might bring in new ideas, were discouraged from visiting Sparta. Furthermore, except for military reasons, Spartans were not allowed to travel abroad, where they might pick up new ideas that might be dangerous to the stability of the state. Likewise, Spartan citizens were discouraged from studying philosophy, literature, or the arts—subjects that might encourage new thoughts. The art of war was the Spartan ideal, and all other arts were frowned upon.

In the sixth century, Sparta used its military might and the fear it inspired to gain greater control of the Peloponnesus by organizing an alliance of almost all the Peloponnesian states. Sparta's strength enabled it to dominate this Peloponnesian League and determine its policies. By 500 B.C.E., the Spartans had organized a powerful military state that maintained order and stability in the Peloponnesus. Raised from early childhood to believe that total loyalty to the Spartan state was the basic reason for existence, the Spartans viewed their strength as justification for their militaristic ideals and regimented society.

Athens

By 700 B.C.E., Athens had established a unified *polis* on the peninsula of Attica. Although early Athens had been ruled by a monarchy, by the seventh century B.C.E., it had fallen under the control of its aristocrats. They possessed the best land and controlled political and religious life by means of a council of nobles, assisted by a board of nine officials called archons. Although there was an assembly of full citizens, it possessed few powers.

Near the end of the seventh century B.C.E., Athens was experiencing political and social discontent stemming from the development of rival factions within the aristocracy and serious economic problems. Increasing numbers of Athenian farmers found themselves sold into slavery when they were unable to repay the loans they had borrowed from their aristocratic neighbors, pledging themselves as collateral. Repeatedly, revolutionary cries for cancellation of debts and a redistribution of land were heard.

The ruling Athenian aristocrats responded to this crisis by choosing Solon, a reform-minded aristocrat, as sole archon in 594 B.C.E. and giving him full power to make changes. Solon's reforms dealt with both the economic and political problems. He canceled all current land debts, outlawed new loans based on humans as collateral, and freed people who had fallen into slavery for debts. He refused, however, to carry out the redistribution of the land and hence failed to deal with the basic cause of the economic crisis. This failure, however, was overshadowed by the commercial and industrial prosperity that Athens began to experience in the following decades.

Like his economic reforms, Solon's political measures were also a compromise. Though by no means eliminating the power of the aristocracy, they opened the door to the participation of new people, especially the nonaristocratic wealthy, in the government. But Solon's reforms, though popular, did not truly solve Athens's problems. Aristocratic factions continued to vie for power, and the poorer peasants resented Solon's failure to institute land redistribution. Internal strife finally led to the very institution Solon had hoped to avoid—tyranny. Pisistratus, an aristocrat, seized power in 560 B.C.E. Pursuing a foreign policy that aided Athenian trade, Pisistratus remained popular with the mercantile and industrial classes. But the Athenians rebelled against his son and ended the tyranny in 510 B.C.E. Although the aristocrats attempted to reestablish an aristocratic oligarchy, Cleisthenes, another aristocratic reformer, opposed this plan and, with the backing of the Athenian people, gained the upper hand in 508 B.C.E.

Cleisthenes created a new council of 500, chosen by lot by the ten tribes in which all citizens had been enrolled. The new council of 500 was responsible for the administration of both foreign and financial affairs and prepared the business that would be handled by the assembly. This assembly of all male citizens had final authority in the passing of laws after free and open debate; thus, Cleisthenes' reforms had reinforced the central role of the assembly of citizens in the Athenian political system.

The reforms of Cleisthenes created the foundations for Athenian democracy. More changes would come in the fifth century, when the Athenians themselves would begin to use the word *democracy* to describe their system (our word *democracy* comes from the Greek words *demos* [people] and *kratia* [power]). By 500 B.C.E., Athens was more united than it had been and was on the verge of playing a more important role in Greek affairs.

THE HIGH POINT OF GREEK CIVILIZATION: CLASSICAL GREECE

Classical Greece is the name given to the period of Greek history from around 500 B.C.E. to the conquest of Greece by the Macedonian king Philip II in 338 B.C.E. It was a period of brilliant achievement, much of it associated with the flowering of democracy in Athens under the leadership of Pericles. Many of the lasting contributions of the Greeks occurred during this period. The age began with a mighty confrontation between the Greek states and the mammoth Persian Empire.

The Challenge of Persia

As Greek civilization grew and expanded throughout the Mediterranean, it was inevitable that it would come into contact with the Persian Empire to the east. The Ionian Greek cities in western Asia Minor had already fallen subject to the Persian Empire by the mid-sixth century B.C.E. An unsuccessful revolt by the Ionian cities in 499 B.C.E.—assisted by the Athenian navy—led the Persian ruler Darius to seek revenge by attacking the mainland Greeks in 490 B.C.E. The Persians landed an army on the plain of Marathon, only twenty-six miles from Athens. The Athenians and their allies were clearly outnumbered, but led by Miltiades, one of the Athenian leaders who insisted on attacking, the Greek hoplites charged across the plain of Marathon and crushed the Persian forces. Although a minor defeat to the Persians, the Battle of Marathon was of great importance to the Athenians, who had proved that the Persians could be beaten.

Xerxes, the new Persian monarch after the death of Darius in 486 B.C.E., vowed revenge and renewed the inva-

✿ **THE GREEK TRIREME.**   The trireme became the standard warship of ancient Greece. Highly maneuverable, fast, and outfitted with metal prows, Greek triremes were especially effective at ramming enemy ships. The strenuous work of the oarsmen aboard a trireme is shown in the relief dating from the fourth century B.C.E. The photo shows the *Olympias*, a trireme reconstructed by the Greek navy.

sion of Greece. In preparation for the attack, some of the Greek states formed a defensive league under Spartan leadership, while the Athenians pursued a new military policy by developing a navy. By the time of the Persian invasion in 480 B.C.E., the Athenians had produced a fleet of about 200 vessels.

Xerxes led a massive invasion force into Greece: close to 150,000 troops, almost 700 naval ships, and hundreds of supply ships to keep the large army fed. The Greeks decided to fight a delaying action at the pass of Thermopylae along the main road into central Greece, probably to give the Greek fleet of 300 ships the chance to fight the Persian fleet. The Greeks knew that the Persian army was dependent on the fleet for supplies. A Greek force numbering close to 9,000, under the leadership of the Spartan king, Leonidas, and his contingent of 300 Spartans, held off the Persian army for two days. The Spartan troops were especially brave. When told that Persian arrows would darken the sky in battle, one Spartan warrior supposedly responded, "That is good news. We will fight in the shade!" Unfortunately for the Greeks, a traitor told the Persians how to use a mountain path to outflank the Greek force. King Leonidas and the 300 Spartans fought to the last man.

The Athenians, now threatened by the onslaught of the Persian forces, abandoned their city. While the Per-

sians sacked and burned Athens, the Greek fleet remained offshore near the island of Salamis and challenged the Persian navy to fight. Although the Greeks were outnumbered, they managed to outmaneuver the Persian fleet and utterly defeated it. A few months later, early in 479 B.C.E., the Greeks formed the largest Greek army seen up to that time and decisively defeated the Persian army at Plataea, northwest of Attica. The Greeks had won the war and were now free to pursue their own destiny.

The Growth of an Athenian Empire in the Age of Pericles

After the defeat of the Persians, Athens stepped in to provide new leadership against the Persians by forming a confederation called the Delian League. Organized in the winter of 478–477 B.C.E., the Delian League was dominated by the Athenians from the beginning. Its main headquarters was on the island of Delos, but its chief officials, including the treasurers and commanders of the fleet, were Athenian. Under the leadership of the Athenians, the Delian League pursued the attack against the Persian Empire. Virtually all of the Greek states in the Aegean were liberated from Persian control. Arguing that the

CHRONOLOGY

THE PERSIAN WARS

Rebellion of Greek cities in Asia Minor	499–494 B.C.E.
Battle of Marathon	490 B.C.E.
Xerxes invades Greece	480–479 B.C.E.
Battles of Thermopylae and Salamis	480 B.C.E.
Battle of Plataea	479 B.C.E.

Persian threat was now over, some members of the Delian League wished to withdraw. But the Athenians forced them to remain in the league and to pay tribute. In 454 B.C.E., the Athenians moved the treasury of the league from the island of Delos to Athens. By controlling the Delian League, Athens had created an empire.

At home, Athenians favored the new imperial policy, especially after 461 B.C.E., when a political faction, led by a young aristocrat named Pericles, triumphed. Under Pericles, who was a dominant figure in Athenian politics until 429 B.C.E., Athens embarked on a policy of expanding democracy at home and its new empire abroad. This period of Athenian and Greek history, which historians have subsequently labeled the age of Pericles, witnessed the height of Athenian power and the culmination of its brilliance as a civilization.

In the age of Pericles, the Athenians became deeply attached to their democratic system. The will of the people was embodied in the assembly, which consisted of all male citizens over eighteen years of age. In the 440s, that was probably a group of about 43,000. Not all attended, however, and the number present at the meetings, which were held every ten days on a hillside east of the Acropolis, seldom reached 6,000. The assembly passed all laws and made final decisions on war and foreign policy. Pericles expanded the Athenians' involvement in their democracy (see the box on p. 107) by making lower-class citizens eligible for public offices formerly closed to them and introducing state pay for officeholders, including those who served on the large Athenian juries. Poor citizens could now afford to participate in public affairs.

A large body of city magistrates, usually chosen by lot without regard to class, handled routine administrative tasks. The overall directors of policy, a board of ten officials known as generals, were elected by public vote and were usually wealthy aristocrats, even though the people were free to select otherwise. The generals could be reelected, enabling individual leaders to play an important political role. Pericles, for example, was elected to the generalship thirty times between 461 and 429 B.C.E. The Athenians, however, had also devised the practice of ostracism to protect themselves against overly ambitious politicians. Members of the assembly could write on a broken pottery fragment (*ostrakon*) the name of the person they most disliked or considered most harmful to the *polis*. A person who received a majority (if at least 6,000 votes were cast) was exiled for ten years.

Under Pericles, Athens became the leading center of Greek culture. The Persians had destroyed much of the city during the Persian Wars, but Pericles used the treasury money of the Delian League to set in motion a massive rebuilding program. New temples and statues soon made visible the greatness of Athens. Art, architecture, and philosophy flourished, and Pericles broadly boasted that Athens had become the "school of Greece." But the achievements of Athens alarmed the other Greek states, especially Sparta, and soon all Greece was confronted with a new war.

The Great Peloponnesian War and the Decline of the Greek States

During the forty years after the defeat of the Persians, the Greek world came to be divided into two major camps: Sparta and its supporters and the Athenian maritime empire. In his classic *History of the Peloponnesian War*, the great Greek historian Thucydides pointed out that the fundamental, long-range cause of the Peloponnesian War was the fear that the growing Athenian empire aroused in Sparta and its allies. Then, too, Athens and Sparta had created two very different kinds of societies, and neither state was able to tolerate the other's system. A series of disputes finally led to the outbreak of war in 431 B.C.E.

At the beginning of the war, both sides believed they had winning strategies. The Athenians planned to remain behind the protective walls of Athens while the overseas empire and the navy would keep them supplied. Pericles knew perfectly well that the Spartans and their allies could beat the Athenians in pitched battles, which, of course, formed the focus of the Spartan strategy. The Spartans and their allies invaded Attica and ravaged the fields and orchards, hoping that the Athenians would send out their army to fight beyond the walls. But Pericles was convinced that Athens was secure behind its walls and retaliated by sending out naval excursions to ravage the seacoast of the Peloponnesus. In the second year of the war, however, plague devastated the crowded city of Athens and wiped out possibly one-third of the Athenian population. Pericles himself died the following year (429 B.C.E.), a severe loss to Athens. Despite the losses from the plague, the Athenians fought on in a struggle that witnessed numerous instances of futile destruction. War weariness finally led to a truce in 421 B.C.E., but it proved to be short-lived.

ATHENIAN DEMOCRACY: THE FUNERAL ORATION OF PERICLES

I n his History of the Peloponnesian War, *the Greek historian Thucydides presented his reconstruction of the eulogy given by Pericles in the winter of 431–430 B.C.E. to honor the Athenians killed in the first campaigns of the Great Peloponnesian War. It is a magnificent, idealized description of Athenian democracy at its height.*

THUCYDIDES, *HISTORY OF THE PELOPONNESIAN WAR*

Our constitution is called a democracy because power is in the hands not of a minority but of the whole people. When it is a question of settling private disputes, everyone is equal before the law; when it is a question of putting one person before another in positions of public responsibility, what counts is not membership of a particular class, but the actual ability which the man possesses. No one, so long as he has it in him to be of service to the state, is kept in political obscurity because of poverty. And, just as our political life is free and open, so is our day-to-day life in our relations with each other. We do not get into a state with our next-door neighbor if he enjoys himself in his own way, nor do we give him the kind of black looks which, though they do no real harm, still do hurt people's feelings. We are free and tolerant in our private lives; but in public affairs we keep to the law. This is because it commands our deep respect.

We give our obedience to those whom we put in positions of authority, and we obey the laws themselves, especially those which are for the protection of the oppressed, and those unwritten laws which it is an acknowledged shame to break. . . . Here each individual is interested not only in his own affairs but in the affairs of the state as well: even those who are mostly occupied with their own business are extremely well-informed on general politics—this is a peculiarity of ours: we do not say that a man who takes no interest in politics is a man who minds his own business; we say that he has no business here at all. We Athenians, in our own persons, take our decisions on policy or submit them to proper discussions: for we do not think that there is an incompatibility between words and deeds; the worst thing is to rush into action before the consequences have been properly debated. . . . Taking everything together then, I declare that our city is an education to Greece, and I declare that in my opinion each single one of our citizens, in all the manifold aspects of life, is able to show himself the rightful lord and owner of his own person, and do this, moreover, with exceptional grace and exceptional versatility. And to show that this is no empty boasting for the present occasion, but real tangible fact, you have only to consider the power which our city possesses and which has been won by those very qualities which I have mentioned.

The Athenians initiated a second phase of the war in 415 B.C.E., when they decided to invade the island of Sicily, believing that its conquest would give them a strong source of support to carry on a lengthy war. But the "great expedition" of the Athenians suffered a massive defeat outside the city of Syracuse. All of the Athenians were killed or sold into slavery. Despite this disaster, the Athenians refused to give up, but raised new armies and sent out new fleets. The final crushing blow came, however, in 405 B.C.E., when the Athenian fleet was destroyed at Aegospotami on the Hellespont. Athens was besieged and surrendered in 404 B.C.E. Its walls were torn down, the navy disbanded, and the Athenian empire destroyed. The great war was finally over.

The Great Peloponnesian War weakened the major Greek states and certainly destroyed any possibility of cooperation among the Greek states. The next seventy years of Greek history are a sorry tale of efforts by Sparta, Athens, and Thebes, a new Greek power, to dominate Greek affairs. In continuing their petty wars, the Greek states remained oblivious to the growing power of Macedonia to their north and demonstrated convincingly that

the genius of the Greeks did not lie in politics. Culture, however, was quite a different story.

The Culture of Classical Greece

Classical Greece saw a period of remarkable intellectual and cultural growth throughout the Greek world. Historians agree, however, that Periclean Athens was the most important center of classical Greek culture. Indeed, the eighteenth-century French philosopher and writer Voltaire listed the Athens of Pericles as one of four happy ages "when the arts were brought to perfection and which, marking an era of the greatness of the human mind, are an example to posterity."[7]

THE WRITING OF HISTORY

History as we know it, as the systematic analysis of past events, was a Greek creation. Herodotus (c. 484–c. 425 B.C.E.), an Ionian Greek from Asia Minor, was the author of the *History of the Persian Wars*, a work commonly regarded as the first real history in Western civilization.

CHRONOLOGY

THE GREAT PELOPONNESIAN WAR

Invasion of Attica	431 B.C.E.
Athenian invasion of Sicily	415–413 B.C.E.
Battle of Aegospotami	405 B.C.E.
Surrender of Athens	404 B.C.E.

The Greek word *historia* (from which we derive our word *history*) means "research" or "investigation," and it is in the opening line of Herodotus's *History* that we find the first recorded use of the word:

> Here are presented the researches (*historiae*) carried out by Herodotus of Halicarnassus. The purpose is to prevent the traces of human events from being erased by time, and to preserve the fame of the important and remarkable achievements produced by both Greeks and non-Greeks; among the matters covered is, in particular, the cause of the hostilities between Greeks and non-Greeks.[8]

The central theme of Herodotus's work is the conflict between the Greeks and the Persians, which he viewed as a struggle between Greek freedom and oriental despotism. His account demonstrates a remarkable range of interests, including geography, politics, social structures, economics, religion, and even psychology. Herodotus traveled extensively for his information and was dependent for his sources on what we today would call oral history. Although he was a master storyteller and sometimes included considerable fanciful material, Herodotus was also capable of exhibiting a critical attitude toward the materials he used. Regardless of its weaknesses, Herodotus's *History* is an important source of information on the Persians and certainly our chief source for the Persian Wars themselves.

Thucydides (c. 460–c. 400 B.C.E.) was, by far, the better historian; in fact, historians consider him the greatest historian of the ancient world. Thucydides was an Athenian and a participant in the Peloponnesian War. He had been elected a general, but a defeat in battle led the fickle Athenian assembly to send him into exile, which gave him the opportunity to write his *History of the Peloponnesian War*.

Unlike Herodotus, Thucydides was not concerned with underlying divine forces or gods as explanatory causal factors in history. He saw war and politics in purely rational terms, as the activities of human beings. He examined the long-range and immediate causes of the Peloponnesian War in a clear, methodical, objective fashion, placing much emphasis on accuracy and the precision of his facts. As he stated:

> And with regard to my factual reporting of the events of the war I have made it a principle not to write down the first story that came my way, and not even to be guided by my own general impressions; either I was present myself at the events which I have described or else I heard of them from eyewitnesses whose reports I have checked with as much thoroughness as possible.[9]

Thucydides also provided remarkable insight into the human condition. He believed that human nature was a constant. He was not so naive as to believe in an exact repetition of events but felt that political situations recur in similar fashion and that the study of history is therefore of great value in understanding the present.

GREEK DRAMA

Drama as we know it in Western culture was created by the Greeks. Plays were presented in outdoor theaters as part of a religious festival. The form of Greek plays remained rather stable. Three male actors who wore masks acted all the parts. A chorus (also male) spoke the important lines that explained what was going on. Action was very limited, because the emphasis was on the story and its meaning.

The first Greek dramas were tragedies, plays based on the suffering of a hero and usually ending in disaster. Aeschylus (525–456 B.C.E.) is the first tragedian whose plays are known to us. Although he wrote ninety tragedies, only seven have survived. As was customary in Greek tragedy, his plots are simple, and the characters are primarily embodiments of a single passion. The entire drama focuses on a single tragic event and its meaning. At the festival known as the City Dionysia, Greek tragedies were supposed to be presented in a trilogy (a set of three plays) built around a common theme. The only complete trilogy we possess, called the *Oresteia*, was written by Aeschylus. The theme of this trilogy is derived from Homer. Agamemnon, the king of Mycenae, returns a hero from the defeat of Troy. His wife Clytemnestra revenges the sacrificial death of her daughter Iphigenia by murdering Agamemnon, who had been responsible for Iphigenia's death. In the second play of the trilogy, Agamemnon's son Orestes avenges his father by killing his mother. Orestes is now pursued by the avenging furies, who torment him for killing his mother. Evil acts breed evil acts and suffering is one's lot, suggests Aeschylus. But Orestes is put on trial and acquitted by Athena, the patron goddess of Athens. Personal vendetta has been eliminated and law has prevailed. Reason has triumphed over the forces of evil.

Another great Athenian playwright was Sophocles (c. 496–406 B.C.E.), whose most famous play was *Oedipus the King*. In this play, the oracle of Apollo foretells how a man (Oedipus) will kill his own father and marry his mother. Despite all attempts at prevention, the tragic events occur. Although it appears that Oedipus suffered the fate determined by the gods, Oedipus also accepts that he himself as a free man must bear responsibility for his actions: "It was Apollo, friends, Apollo, that brought this bitter bitterness, my sorrows to completion. But the hand that struck me was none but my own."[10]

The third outstanding Athenian tragedian, Euripides (c. 485–406 B.C.E.), moved beyond his predecessors in creating more realistic characters. His plots also became more complex, with a greater interest in real-life situations. Perhaps the greatest of all his plays was *The Bacchae*, which dealt with the introduction of the hysterical rites associated with Dionysus, god of wine. Euripides is often seen as a skeptic, who questioned traditional moral and religious values. Euripides was also critical of the traditional view that war was glorious. He portrayed war as brutal and barbaric and expressed deep compassion for the women and children who suffered from it.

Greek tragedies dealt with universal themes still relevant to our day. They probed such problems as the nature of good and evil, the conflict between spiritual values and the demands of the state or family, the rights of the individual, the nature of divine forces, and the nature of human beings. Over and over again, the tragic lesson was repeated: humans were free and yet could operate only within limitations imposed by the gods. The real task was to cultivate the balance and moderation that led to awareness of one's true position. But the pride in human accomplishment and independence is real. As the chorus chants in Sophocles' *Antigone:* "Is there anything more wonderful on earth, our marvelous planet, than the miracle of man?"[11]

Greek comedy developed later than tragedy. We first see comedies organized at the festival of Dionysus in Athens in 488–487 B.C.E. The plays of Aristophanes (c. 450–c. 385 B.C.E.), who used both grotesque masks and obscene jokes to entertain the Athenian audience, are examples of Old Comedy. But comedy in Athens was also more clearly political than tragedy. It was used to attack or savagely satirize both politicians and intellectuals. In *The Clouds*, for example, Aristophanes characterized the philosopher Socrates as the operator of a thought factory where people could learn deceitful ways of handling other people. Later plays gave up the element of personal attack and featured contemporary issues. Of special importance to Aristophanes was his opposition to the Peloponnesian War. *Lysistrata*, performed in 411 B.C.E., at a time when Athens was in serious danger of losing the war, had a comic but effective message against the war (see the box on p. 110).

THE ARTS: THE CLASSICAL IDEAL

The artistic standards established by the Greeks of the classical period have largely dominated the arts of the Western world. Classical Greek art did not aim at experimentation for experiment's sake, but was concerned with expressing eternally true ideals. Its subject matter was basically the human being, but presented harmoniously as an object of great beauty. The classic style, based on the ideals of reason, moderation, symmetry, balance, and harmony in all things, was meant to civilize the emotions.

In architecture the most important form was the temple dedicated to a god or goddess. Because Greek religious ceremonies were held at altars in the open air, temples were not used to enclose the faithful, as modern churches are. At the center of Greek temples were walled rooms that housed the statues of deities and treasuries in which gifts to the gods and goddesses were safeguarded. These central rooms were surrounded by a screen of columns that made Greek temples open structures rather than closed ones. The columns were originally made of wood but changed to limestone in the seventh century and to marble in the fifth century B.C.E. The most significant formal element in Greek temples was the shape and size of the columns in combination with the features above and below the column. The Doric order, which evolved first in the Dorian Peloponnesus, consisted of thick, fluted columns with simple capitals resting directly on a platform without a base. Above the capitals was a fairly complex entablature. The Greeks considered the Doric order grave, dignified, and masculine. The Ionic style was first developed in western Asia Minor and consisted of slender columns with a more elaborate base and volute or spiral-shaped capitals. The Greeks characterized the Ionic order as slender, elegant, and feminine in principle. Corinthian columns, with their more detailed capitals modeled after acanthus leaves, came later, near the end of the fifth century B.C.E.

Some of the finest examples of Greek classical architecture were built in fifth-century Athens. The most famous building, regarded as the greatest example of the classical Greek temple, was the Parthenon, built between 447 and 432 B.C.E. The master builders Ictinus and Callicrates directed the construction of this temple consecrated to Athena, the patron goddess of Athens. The Parthenon, an expression of Athenian enthusiasm, was also dedicated to the glory of Athens and the Athenians. The Parthenon typifies the principles of classical architecture: the search for calmness, clarity, and freedom from superfluous detail. The individual parts of the temple were constructed in accordance with certain mathematical ratios also found in natural phenomena. The architects' concern with these laws of proportion is paralleled by the attempt of Greek philosophers to understand the general laws underlying nature.

Greek sculpture also developed a classical style that differed significantly from the artificial stiffness of the figures of an earlier period. Statues of the male nude, the favorite subject of Greek sculptors, now exhibited more relaxed

ATHENIAN COMEDY: SEX AS AN ANTIWAR INSTRUMENT

Greek comedy became a regular feature of the dramatic presentations at the festival of Dionysus in Athens beginning in 488–487 B.C.E. Aristophanes used his comedies to present political messages, especially to express his antiwar sentiments. The plot of Lysistrata centers on a sex strike by wives in order to get their husbands to end the Peloponnesian War. In this scene from the play, Lysistrata (whose name means "she who dissolves the armies") has the women swear a special oath. The oath involves a bowl of wine offered as a libation to the gods.

ARISTOPHANES, *LYSISTRATA*

LYSISTRATA: Lampito: all of you women: come, touch the bowl, and repeat after me: I WILL HAVE NOTHING TO DO WITH MY HUSBAND OR MY LOVER

KALONIKE: I will have nothing to do with my husband or my lover

LYSISTRATA: THOUGH HE COME TO ME IN PITIABLE CONDITION

KALONIKE: Though he come to me in pitiable condition (Oh, Lysistrata! This is killing me!)

LYSISTRATA: I WILL STAY IN MY HOUSE UNTOUCHABLE

KALONIKE: I will stay in my house untouchable

LYSISTRATA: IN MY THINNEST SAFFRON SILK

KALONIKE: In my thinnest saffron silk

LYSISTRATA: AND MAKE HIM LONG FOR ME.

KALONIKE: And make him long for me.

LYSISTRATA: I WILL NOT GIVE MYSELF

KALONIKE: I will not give myself

LYSISTRATA: AND IF HE CONSTRAINS ME

KALONIKE: And if he constrains me

LYSISTRATA: I WILL BE AS COLD AS ICE AND NEVER MOVE

KALONIKE: I will be as cold as ice and never move

LYSISTRATA: I WILL NOT LIFT MY SLIPPERS TOWARD THE CEILING

KALONIKE: I will not lift my slippers toward the ceiling

LYSISTRATA: OR CROUCH ON ALL FOURS LIKE THE LIONESS IN THE CARVING

KALONIKE: Or crouch on all fours like the lioness in the carving

LYSISTRATA: AND IF I KEEP THIS OATH LET ME DRINK FROM THIS BOWL

KALONIKE: And if I keep this oath let me drink from this bowl

LYSISTRATA: IF NOT, LET MY OWN BOWL BE FILLED WITH WATER.

KALONIKE: If not, let my own bowl be filled with water.

LYSISTRATA: You have all sworn?

MYRRHINE: We have.

---

attitudes; their faces were self-assured, their bodies flexible and smooth-muscled. Although the figures possessed natural features that made them lifelike, Greek sculptors sought to achieve not realism but a standard of ideal beauty. Polyclitus, a fifth-century sculptor, authored a treatise (now lost) on a canon of proportions that he illustrated in a work known as the *Doryphoros*. His theory maintained that the use of ideal proportions, based on mathematical ratios found in nature, could produce an ideal human form, beautiful in its perfected and refined features. This search for ideal beauty was the dominant feature of the classical standard in sculpture.

THE GREEK LOVE OF WISDOM

Philosophy is a Greek word that originally meant "love of wisdom." Early Greek philosophers were concerned with the development of critical or rational thought about the nature of the universe and the place of divine forces and souls in it. Many Greeks, however, were simply not interested in such speculations. The Sophists were a group of philosophical teachers in the fifth century B.C.E. who rejected such speculation as foolish; they argued that

understanding the universe was beyond the reach of the human mind. It was more important for individuals to improve themselves, so the only worthwhile object of study was human behavior. The Sophists were wandering scholars who sold their services as professional teachers to the young men of Greece, especially those of Athens. The Sophists stressed the importance of rhetoric (the art of persuasive oratory) in winning debates and swaying an audience, a skill that was especially valuable in democratic Athens. The Sophists tended to be skeptics who questioned the traditional values of their societies. To the Sophists, there was no absolute right or wrong. What was right for one individual might be wrong for another. True wisdom consisted of being able to perceive and pursue one's own good. Because of these ideas, many people viewed the Sophists as harmful to society and especially dangerous to the values of young people.

In classical Greece, Athens became the foremost intellectual and artistic center. Its reputation is perhaps strongest of all in philosophy. After all, Socrates, Plato, and Aristotle raised basic questions that have been debated for two thousand years; these are still largely the same philosophical questions we wrestle with today.

Metope   Triglyph

Frieze

Entablature

Architrave

Capital

Shaft

Column

Doric

Frieze

Architrave

Capital

Volute

Shaft

Base

Entablature

Column

Ionic

Frieze

Architrave

Capital

Shaft

Base

Entablature

Column

Corinthian

DORIC, IONIC, AND CORINTHIAN ORDERS.   The illustration depicts the Doric, Ionic, and Corinthian orders of columns. The size and shape of a column constituted one of the most important aspects of Greek temple architecture. The Doric order, with plain capitals and no base, developed first in the Dorian Peloponnesus and was rather simple in comparison to the slender Ionic column, which had an elaborate base and spiral-shaped capitals, and the Corinthian column, which featured leaf-shaped capitals.

Socrates (469–399 B.C.E.) left no writings, but we know about him from his pupils, especially his most famous one, Plato. By occupation, Socrates was a stonemason, but his true love was philosophy. He taught a number of pupils, but not for pay, because he believed that the goal of education was only to improve the individual. He made use of a teaching method that is still known by his name. The "Socratic method" utilizes a question-and-answer technique to lead pupils to see things for themselves by using their own reason. Socrates believed that all real knowledge is within each person; only critical examination was needed to call it forth. This was the real task of philosophy since "the unexamined life is not worth living."

Socrates' questioned authority, and this soon led him into trouble. Athens had had a tradition of free thought and inquiry, but its defeat in the Peloponnesian War had created an environment intolerant of open debate and soul-searching. Socrates was accused and convicted of corrupting the youth of Athens by his teaching. An Athenian jury sentenced him to death.

One of Socrates' disciples was Plato (c. 429–347 B.C.E.), considered by many the greatest philosopher of Western civilization. Unlike his master Socrates, who wrote nothing, Plato wrote a great deal. He was fascinated with the question of reality: How do we know what is real? According to Plato, a higher world of eternal, unchanging Ideas or Forms has always existed. To know these Forms is to know truth. These ideal Forms constitute reality and can

only be apprehended by a trained mind—which, of course, is the goal of philosophy. The objects that we perceive with our senses are simply reflections of the ideal Forms. Hence, they are shadows whereas reality is found in the Forms themselves.

THE PARTHENON.   The arts in classical Greece were designed to express the eternal ideals of reason, moderation, symmetry, balance, and harmony. In architecture, the most important form was the temple, and the classical example of this kind of architecture is the Parthenon, built between 447 and 432 B.C.E. The Parthenon, located on the Acropolis, was dedicated to Athena, the patron goddess of Athens, but it also served as a shining example of the power and wealth of the Athenian empire.

DORYPHOROS. This statue, known as the *Doryphoros*, or spear-carrier, is by the fifth-century B.C.E. sculptor Polyclitus, who believed it illustrated the ideal proportions of the human figure. Classical Greek sculpture moved away from the stiffness of earlier figures but retained the young male nude as the favorite subject matter. The statues became more lifelike, with relaxed poses and flexible, smooth-muscled bodies. The aim of sculpture, however, was not simply realism, but rather the expression of ideal beauty.

Plato's ideas of government were set out in his dialogue entitled *The Republic*. Based on his experience in Athens, Plato had come to distrust the workings of democracy. It was obvious to him that individuals could not attain an ethical life unless they lived in a just and rational state. Plato's search for the just state led him to construct an ideal state in *The Republic* in which the population was divided into three basic groups. At the top was an upper class, a ruling elite, the famous philosopher-kings: "Unless either philosophers become kings in their countries or

those who are now called kings and rulers come to be sufficiently inspired with a genuine desire for wisdom; unless, that is to say, political power and philosophy meet together . . . there can be no rest from troubles . . . for states, nor yet, as I believe, for all mankind."[12] The second group were those who showed courage; they would be the warriors who protected the society. All the rest made up the masses, essentially people driven, not by wisdom or courage, but by desire. They would be the producers of society—the artisans, tradespeople, and farmers. Contrary to common Greek custom, Plato also believed that men and women should have the same education and equal access to all positions.

Plato established a school at Athens known as the Academy. One of his pupils, who studied there for twenty years, was Aristotle (384–322 B.C.E.), who later became a tutor to Alexander the Great. Aristotle did not accept Plato's theory of ideal Forms. Instead he believed that by examining individual objects, we can perceive their form and arrive at universal principles; but that these principles do not exist as a separate higher world of reality beyond material things, but are a part of things themselves. Aristotle's interests, then, lay in analyzing and classifying things based on thorough research and investigation. His interests were wide-ranging, and he wrote treatises on an enormous number of subjects: ethics, logic, politics, poetry, astronomy, geology, biology, and physics.

Like Plato, Aristotle wished for an effective form of government that would rationally direct human affairs. Unlike Plato, he did not seek an ideal state based on the embodiment of an ideal Form of justice, but tried to find the best form of government by a rational examination of existing governments. For his *Politics*, Aristotle examined the constitutions of 158 states and arrived at general categories for organizing governments. He identified three good forms of government: monarchy, aristocracy, and constitutional government. But based on his examination, he warned that monarchy can easily turn into tyranny, aristocracy into oligarchy, and constitutional government into radical democracy or anarchy. He favored constitutional government as the best form for most people.

Aristotle's philosophical and political ideas played an enormous role in the development of Western thought during the Middle Ages (see Chapter 12). So, too, did his ideas on women. Aristotle believed that marriage was meant to provide mutual comfort between man and woman and contributed to the overall happiness of a community: "The community needs both male and female excellences or it can only be half-blessed." Nevertheless, Aristotle maintained that women were biologically inferior to men: "A woman is, as it were, an infertile male. She is female in fact on account of a kind of inadequacy." Therefore, according the Aristotle, women must be subordinated to men, not only in the community but also in marriage: "The association between husband and wife is clearly an aristocracy. The man rules by virtue of merit, and in the sphere that is his by right; but he hands over to his wife such matters as are suitable for her."[13]

Greek Religion

Greek religion was intricately connected to every aspect of daily life; it was both social and practical. Public festivals, which originated from religious practices, served specific functions: boys were prepared to be warriors, girls to be mothers. Since religion was related to every aspect of life, citizens had to have a proper attitude toward the gods. Religion was a civic cult necessary for the well-being of the state. Temples dedicated to a god or goddess were the major buildings in Greek cities.

The poetry of Homer gave an account of the gods that provided Greek religion with a definite structure. Over a period of time, all Greeks came to accept a common Olympian religion. There were twelve chief gods who supposedly lived on Mount Olympus, the highest mountain in Greece. Among the twelve were Zeus, the chief deity and father of the gods; Athena, goddess of wisdom and crafts; Apollo, god of the sun and poetry; Aphrodite, goddess of love; and Poseidon, brother of Zeus and god of the seas and earthquakes.

The twelve Olympian gods were common to all Greeks, who thus shared a basic polytheistic religion. Each *polis* usually singled out one of the twelve Olympians as a guardian deity of the community. Athena was the patron goddess of Athens, for example. But each *polis* also had its own local deities who remained important to the community as a whole, and each family had patron gods as well.

Greek religion did not have a body of doctrine, nor did it focus on morality. It gave little or no hope of life after death for most people. The spirits of most people, regardless of what they had done in life, went to a gloomy underworld ruled by the god Hades. Because the Greeks wanted the gods to look favorably upon their activities, ritual assumed enormous proportions in Greek religion. Prayers were often combined with gifts to the gods based on the principle "I give so that you [the gods] will give [in return]." Ritual also meant sacrifices, whether of animals or agricultural products. Animal victims were burned on an altar in front of a temple or a small altar in front of a home.

Festivals also developed as a way to honor the gods and goddesses. Some of these (the Panhellenic celebrations) came to have international significance and were held at special locations, such as those dedicated to the worship of Zeus at Olympia or to Apollo at Delphi. Numerous events were held in honor of the gods at the great festivals, including athletic competitions to which all Greeks were invited. The first such games were held at the Olympic festival in 776 B.C.E. and were then held every four years thereafter to honor Zeus. Initially, the Olympic contests consisted of footraces and wrestling, but later boxing, javelin throwing, and various other contests were added.

As another practical side of Greek religion, Greeks wanted to know the will of the gods. To do so, they made use of the oracle, a sacred shrine dedicated to a god or goddess who revealed the future. The most famous was the oracle of Apollo at Delphi, located on the side of Mount Parnassus, overlooking the Gulf of Corinth. At Delphi, a priestess listened to questions while in a state of ecstasy that was believed to be induced by Apollo. Her responses were interpreted by the priests and given in verse form to the person asking questions. Representatives of states and individuals traveled to Delphi to consult the oracle of Apollo. States might inquire whether they should undertake a military expedition; individuals might raise such questions as "Heracleidas asks the god whether he will have offspring from the wife he has now." Responses were often enigmatic and at times even politically motivated. Croesus, the king of Lydia in Asia Minor who was known for his incredible wealth, sent messengers to the oracle at Delphi, asking "whether he shall go to war with the Persians." The oracle replied that if Croesus attacked the Persians, he would destroy a mighty empire. Overjoyed to hear these words, Croesus made war on the Persians but was crushed by his enemy. A mighty empire—that of Croesus—was destroyed.

Daily Life in Classical Athens

The Greek city-state was, above all, a male community: only adult male citizens took part in public life. In Athens, this meant the exclusion of women, slaves, and foreign residents, or roughly 85 percent of the total population in Attica. There were probably 150,000 citizens in Athens, of whom about 43,000 were adult males who exercised political power. Resident foreigners, who numbered about 35,000, received the protection of the laws but were also subject to some of the responsibilities of citizens, namely, military service and the funding of festivals. The remaining social group, the slaves, numbered around 100,000.

Slavery was a common institution in the ancient world. Economic needs dictated the desirability of owning at least one slave, although the very poor in Athens did not own any. The really wealthy might own large numbers, but those who did usually employed them in industry. Most often, slaves in Athens performed domestic tasks, such as being cooks and maids, or worked in the fields. Few peasants could afford more than one or two. Other slaves worked as unskilled and skilled laborers. Those slaves who worked in public construction were paid the same as citizens.

The Athenian economy was largely agricultural but highly diversified as well. Agriculture consisted of growing grains, vegetables, and fruit trees for local consumption; raising vines and olive trees for wine and olive oil, which were exportable products; and grazing sheep and goats for wool and milk products. Given the size of the population in Attica and the lack of abundant fertile land,

Athens had to import between 50 and 80 percent of its grain, a staple in the Athenian diet. Trade was thus highly important to the Athenian economy. The building of the port at Piraeus and the Long Walls (a series of defensive walls four and one-half miles long connecting Athens and Piraeus) created the physical conditions that made Athens the leading trade center in the fifth-century Greek world.

Artisans were more important to the Athenian economy than their relatively small numbers might suggest. In particular, Athens was the chief producer of high-quality painted pottery in the fifth century. Other crafts had moved beyond the small workshops into the factory through the use of slave labor. The shield factory of Lysias, for example, employed 120 slaves. Public works projects also provided considerable livelihood for Athenians. The building program of Pericles, financed from the Delian League treasury, made possible the hiring of both skilled and unskilled labor.

✿ WOMEN IN THE LOOM ROOM.   In Athens, women were considered to be citizens and could participate in religious cults and festivals, but they had no rights and were barred from any political activity. Women were thought to belong in the house, caring for the children and the needs of the household. A principal activity of Greek women was the making of clothes. This vase shows two women working on a warp-weighted loom.

The Athenian lifestyle was basically simple. Athenian houses were furnished with necessities bought from artisans, such as beds, couches, tables, chests, pottery, stools, baskets, and cooking utensils. Wives and slaves made clothes and blankets at home. The Athenian diet was rather plain and relied on such basic foods as barley, wheat, millet, lentils, grapes, figs, olives, almonds, bread made at home, vegetables, eggs, fish, cheese, and chicken. Olive oil was widely used, not only for eating, but for lighting lamps and rubbing on the body after washing and exercise. Although country houses kept animals, they were used for reasons other than their flesh: oxen for plowing, sheep for wool, and goats for milk and cheese.

The family was an important institution in ancient Athens. It was composed of husband, wife, and children (a nuclear family), although other dependent relatives and slaves were regarded as part of the family economic unit. The family's primary social function was to produce new citizens. Strict laws of the fifth century had stipulated that a citizen must be the offspring of a legally acknowledged marriage between two Athenian citizens whose parents were also citizens.

Women who were citizens could participate in most religious cults and festivals but were otherwise excluded from public life. They could not own property beyond personal items and always had a male guardian. The function of the Athenian woman as wife was very clear. Her foremost obligation was to bear children, especially male children who would preserve the family line. The marriage formula that Athenians used put it succinctly: "I give this woman for the procreation of legitimate children." Secondly, a wife was to take care of her family and her house, either doing the household work herself or supervising the slaves who did the actual work (see the box on p. 115).

Women were kept under strict control. Since they were married at fourteen or fifteen, they were taught about their responsibilities at an early age. Although many managed to learn to read and play musical instruments, they were often cut off from any formal education. And women were expected to remain at home out of sight unless they attended funerals or festivals. If they left the house, they were to be accompanied. A woman working alone in public was either poverty-stricken or not a citizen.

Male homosexuality was also a prominent feature of Athenian life. The Greek homosexual ideal was a relationship between a mature man and a young male. It is most likely that this was an aristocratic ideal and not one practiced by the common people. While the relationship was frequently physical, the Greeks also viewed it as educational. The older male (the "lover") won the love of his "beloved" by his value as a teacher and by the devotion he demonstrated in training his charge. In a sense, this love relationship was seen as a way of initiating young males into the male world of political and military dominance.

HOUSEHOLD MANAGEMENT AND THE ROLE OF THE ATHENIAN WIFE

In fifth-century Athens, a woman's place was in the home. She had two major responsibilities: the bearing and raising of children and the management of the household. In his dialogue on estate management, Xenophon relates the advice of an Attican gentleman on how to train a wife.

XENOPHON, OECONOMICUS

[Ischomachus addresses his new wife] For it seems to me, dear, that the gods with great discernment have coupled together male and female, as they are called, chiefly in order that they may form a perfect partnership in mutual service. For, in the first place, that the various species of living creatures may not fail, they are joined in wedlock for the production of children. Secondly, offspring to support them in old age is provided by this union, to human beings, at any rate. Thirdly, human beings live not in the open air, like beasts, but obviously need shelter. Nevertheless, those who mean to win stores to fill the covered place, have need of someone to work at the open-air occupations; since plowing, sowing, planting, and grazing are all such open-air employments; and these supply the needful food. . . . For he made the man's body and mind more capable of enduring cold and heat, and journeys and campaigns; and therefore imposed on him the outdoor tasks. To the woman, since he has made her body less capable of such endurance, I take it that God has assigned the indoor tasks. And knowing that he had created in the woman and had imposed on her the nourishment of the infants, he meted out to her a larger portion of affection for newborn babes than to the man. . . . Now since we know, dear, what duties have been assigned to each of us by God, we must endeavor, each of us, to do the duties allotted to us as well as possible. . . .

Your duty will be to remain indoors and send out those servants whose work is outside, and superintend those who are to work indoors, and to receive the incomings, and distribute so much of them as must be spent, and watch over so much as is to be kept in store, and take care that the sum laid by for a year be not spent in a month. And when wool is brought to you, you must see that cloaks are made for those that want them. You must see too that the dry corn is in good condition for making food. One of the duties that fall to you, however, will perhaps seem rather thankless: you will have to see that any servant who is ill is cared for.

The Greeks did not feel that the coexistence of homosexual and heterosexual predilections created any special problems for individuals or their society.

THE RISE OF MACEDONIA AND THE CONQUESTS OF ALEXANDER

While the Greek city-states were continuing to fight each other, to their north a new and ultimately powerful kingdom was emerging in its own right. Its people, the Macedonians, were viewed as barbarians by their southern neighbors, the Greeks. The Macedonians were mostly rural folk, organized in tribes, not city-states, and not until the end of the fifth century B.C.E. did Macedonia emerge as an important kingdom. When Philip II (359–336 B.C.E.) came to the throne, he built an efficient army and turned Macedonia into the chief power of the Greek world. He was soon drawn into the internecine conflicts of the Greeks.

The Greeks had mixed reactions to Philip's growing strength. Some viewed Philip as a savior who would rescue the Greeks from themselves by uniting them. Many Athenians, however, especially the orator Demosthenes, portrayed Philip as ruthless, deceitful, treacherous, and barbaric and called upon the Athenians to undertake a struggle against him. Demosthenes' repeated calls for action, combined with Philip's rapid expansion, finally spurred Athens into action. Allied with a number of other Greek states, Athens fought the Macedonians at the Battle of Chaeronea, near Thebes, in 338 B.C.E. The Macedonian army crushed the Greeks, and Philip was now free to consolidate his control over the Greek peninsula. The Greek states were joined together in an alliance that we call the Corinthian League because they met at Corinth. All members took an oath of loyalty: "I swear by Zeus, Earth, Sun, Poseidon, Athena, Ares, and all the gods and goddesses. I will abide by the peace, and I will not break the agreements with Philip the Macedonian, nor will I take up arms with hostile intent against any one of those who abide by the oaths either by land or by sea."[14] Although Philip allowed the Greek city-states autonomy in domestic affairs, he retained the general direction of their foreign affairs. Many Greeks still objected to being subject to the less civilized master from the north, but Philip insisted that the Greek states end their bitter rivalries and cooperate with him in a war against Persia. Before Philip could undertake his invasion of Asia, however, he was assassinated, leaving the task to his son Alexander.

Alexander the Great

Alexander was only twenty when he became king of Macedonia. The illustrious conqueror was, in many ways, prepared for kingship by his father, who had taken Alexander along on military campaigns and, indeed, had given him control of the cavalry at the important battle of Chaeronea. After his father's assassination, Alexander moved quickly to assert his authority, securing the Macedonian frontiers and smothering a rebellion in Greece. He then turned to his father's dream, the invasion of the Persian Empire.

There is no doubt that Alexander was taking a chance in attacking the Persian Empire, which was still a strong state. Alexander's fleet was inferior to that of the Persians, and his finances were shaky at best. In the spring of 334 B.C.E., Alexander entered Asia Minor with an army of 37,000 men. About half were Macedonians, the rest being Greeks and other allies. The cavalry, which would play an important role as a striking force, numbered about 5,000. Architects, engineers, historians, and scientists accompanied the army, a clear indication of Alexander's grand vision and positive expectations at the beginning of his campaign.

❀ **BUST OF ALEXANDER THE GREAT.** This bust of Alexander the Great is a Roman copy of the head of a statue, possibly by Lysippus. Although he aspired to be another Achilles, the tragic hero of Homer's *Iliad*, Alexander also sought more divine honors. He claimed to be descended from Heracles, a Greek hero worshiped as a god, and as pharaoh of Egypt, he gained recognition as a living deity.

CHRONOLOGY
THE RISE OF MACEDONIA AND THE CONQUESTS OF ALEXANDER

Reign of Philip II	359–336 B.C.E.
Battle of Chaeronea; Philip II conquers Greece	338 B.C.E.
Reign of Alexander the Great	336–323 B.C.E.
Alexander invades Asia; Battle of Granicus River	334 B.C.E.
Battle of Issus	333 B.C.E.
Battle of Gaugamela	331 B.C.E.
Fall of Persepolis, the Persian capital	330 B.C.E.
Alexander enters India	327 B.C.E.
Death of Alexander	323 B.C.E.

His first confrontation with the Persians, at a battle at the Granicus River in 334 B.C.E., almost cost him his life but resulted in a major victory. By the spring of 333 B.C.E., the entire western half of Asia Minor was in Alexander's hands, and the Ionian Greek cities of western Asia Minor had been "liberated" from the Persian oppressor. Meanwhile, the Persian king, Darius III, mobilized his forces to stop Alexander's army. Although the Persian troops outnumbered Alexander's, the Battle of Issus was fought on a narrow field that canceled the advantage of superior numbers and resulted in another Macedonian success. After his victory at Issus in 333 B.C.E., Alexander turned south, and by the winter of 332, Syria, Palestine, and Egypt were under his domination. He took the traditional title of pharaoh of Egypt and founded the first of a series of cities named after him (Alexandria) as the Greek administrative capital of Egypt. It became (and remains today) one of Egypt's and the Mediterranean world's most important cities.

In 331 B.C.E., Alexander renewed his offensive, moved into the territory of the ancient Mesopotamian kingdoms, and fought the decisive battle with the Persians at Gaugamela, not far from Babylon. After his victory, Alexander entered Babylon and then proceeded to the Persian capitals at Susa and Persepolis, where he acquired the Persian treasuries and took possession of vast quantities of gold and silver (see the box on p. 117). By 330, Alexander was again on the march, pursuing Darius. After Darius was killed by one of his own men, Alexander took the title and office of the Great King of the Persians. But he was not content to rest with the spoils of the Persian Empire. Over the next three years, he moved east and northeast, as far as modern Pakistan. By the summer of 327 B.C.E., he had entered India. But two more years of fighting in an exotic and difficult ter-

THE DESTRUCTION OF THE
PERSIAN PALACE AT PERSEPOLIS

After Alexander's decisive victory at Gaugamela, he moved into Persia, where he captured the chief Persian cities. At Persepolis, he burned the Persian grand palace to the ground. The ancient historians Arrian and Diodorus of Sicily gave different explanations for this act: one argues that it was a deliberate act of revenge for the Persian invasion of Greece in the fifth century; the other, that the burning resulted from a wild drinking party. Modern historians do not agree on which version is more plausible. Arrian was a Greek-speaking Roman senator of the second century C.E. *Diodorus of Sicily lived in the first century* B.C.E.

DIODORUS OF SICILY, LIBRARY OF HISTORY

Alexander held games in honor of his victories. He performed costly sacrifices to the gods and entertained his friends bountifully. While they were feasting and the drinking was far advanced, as they began to be drunken a madness took possession of the minds of the intoxicated guests. At this point one of the women present, Thaïs by name and Attic by origin, said that for Alexander it would be the finest of all his feats in Asia if he joined them in a triumphal procession, set fire to the palaces, and permitted women's hands in a minute to extinguish the famed accomplishments of the Persians. This was said to men who were still young and giddy with wine, and so, as would be expected someone shouted out to form the procession and light torches, and urged all to take vengeance for the destruction of the Greek temples. Others took up the cry and said that this was a deed worthy of Alexander alone. When the king had caught fire at their words, all leaped up from their couches and passed the word along to form a victory procession in honor of Dionysus [god of wine and religious ecstasy].

Promptly many torches were gathered. Female musicians were present at the banquet, so the king led them all out for the procession to the sound of voices and flutes and pipes, Thaïs the courtesan leading the whole performance. She was the first, after the king, to hurl her blazing torch into the palace. As the others all did the same, immediately the entire palace area was consumed, so great was the conflagration. It was most remarkable that the impious act of Xerxes, king of the Persians, against the acropolis at Athens should have been repaid in kind after many years by one woman, a citizen of the land which had suffered it, and in sport.

ARRIAN, THE LIFE OF ALEXANDER THE GREAT

Thence he marched to Persepolis with such rapidity that the garrison had no time to plunder the city's treasure before his arrival. He also captured the treasure of Cyrus the First at Pasargadae. . . . He burnt the palace of the Persian kings, though this act was against the advice of Parmenio, who urged him to spare it for various reasons, chiefly because it was hardly wise to destroy what was now his own property, and because the Asians would, in his opinion, be less willing to support him if he seemed bent merely upon passing through their country as a conqueror rather than upon ruling it securely as a king. Alexander's answer was that he wished to punish the Persians for their invasion of Greece; his present act was retribution for the destruction of Athens, the burning of the temples, and all the other crimes they had committed against the Greeks.

rain exhausted his troops, who mutinied and refused to go on. Reluctantly, Alexander turned back, leading his men across the arid lands of southern Iran. Conditions in the desert were appalling; the blazing sun and lack of water led to thousands of deaths before Alexander and his remaining troops reached Babylon. Alexander planned still more campaigns, but in June 323 B.C.E., weakened from wounds, fever, and probably excessive alcohol consumption, he died at the young age of thirty-two.

THE LEGACY OF ALEXANDER

Alexander is one of the most puzzling great figures in history. Historians relying on the same sources give vastly different pictures of him. Some portray him as an ideal-istic visionary and others as a ruthless Machiavellian. How did Alexander the Great view himself? We know that he sought to imitate Achilles, the warrior-hero of Homer's *Iliad*. Alexander kept a copy of the *Iliad*—and a dagger—under his pillow. He also claimed to be descended from Heracles, the Greek hero who came to be worshiped as a god. No doubt, Alexander aspired to divine honors; as pharaoh of Egypt, he became a living god according to Egyptian tradition and at one point even sent instructions to the Greek cities to "vote him a god."

Regardless of his ideals, motives, or views about himself, one fact stands out: Alexander truly created a new age, the Hellenistic era. The word *Hellenistic* is derived from a Greek word meaning "to imitate Greeks." It is an

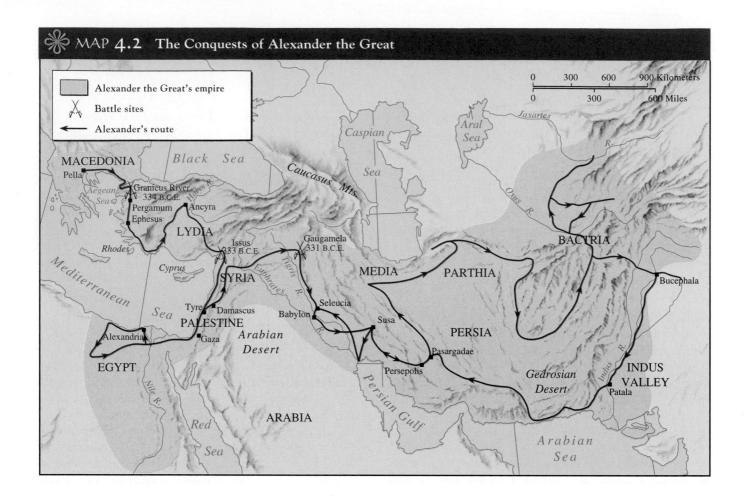

✳ MAP **4.2** **The Conquests of Alexander the Great**

appropriate way, then, to describe an age that saw the extension of the Greek language and ideas to the non-Greek world of the Middle East. Alexander's destruction of the Persian monarchy created opportunities for Greek engineers, intellectuals, merchants, soldiers, and administrators. Those who followed Alexander and his successors participated in a new political unity based on the principle of monarchy. His successors used force to establish military monarchies that dominated the Hellenistic world after his death. Autocratic power became a regular feature of those Hellenistic monarchies and was part of Alexander's political legacy to the Hellenistic world. His vision of empire no doubt inspired the Romans, who were, of course, the real heirs of Alexander's legacy.

But Alexander also left a cultural legacy. As a result of his conquests, Greek language, art, architecture, and literature spread throughout the Middle East. The urban centers of the Hellenistic age, many founded by Alexander and his successors, became springboards for the diffusion of Greek culture. While the Greeks spread their culture in the east, they were also inevitably influenced by eastern ways. Thus, Alexander's legacy created one of the basic characteristics of the Hellenistic world: the clash and fusion of different cultures.

THE WORLD OF THE HELLENISTIC KINGDOMS

The united empire that Alexander created by his conquests disintegrated soon after his death. All too soon, the most important Macedonian generals were engaged in a struggle for power. By 300 B.C.E., any hope of unity was dead, and eventually four Hellenistic kingdoms emerged as the successors to Alexander: Macedonia under the Antigonid dynasty, Syria and the east under the Seleucids, the Attalid kingdom of Pergamum in western Asia Minor, and Egypt under the Ptolemies. All were eventually conquered by the Romans.

The Hellenistic monarchies created a semblance of stability for several centuries, even though Hellenistic kings refused to accept the new status quo and periodically engaged in wars to alter it. At the same time, an underlying strain always existed between the new Greco-Macedonian ruling class and the native populations. Together these factors created a certain degree of tension that was never truly ended until the vibrant Roman state to the west stepped in and imposed a new order.

Although Alexander the Great apparently had planned to fuse Greeks and easterners—he used Persians as admin-

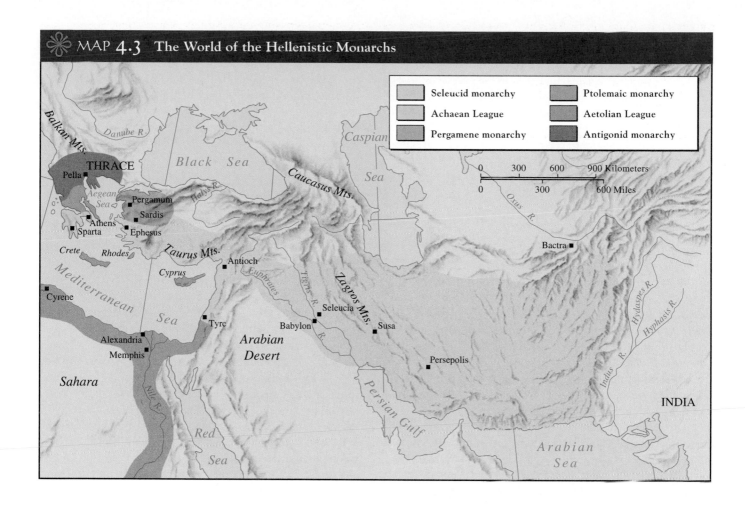

MAP 4.3 The World of the Hellenistic Monarchs

istrators, encouraged his soldiers to marry easterners, and did so himself—Hellenistic monarchs relied primarily on Greeks and Macedonians to form the new ruling class. It has been estimated that in the Seleucid kingdom, for example, only 2.5 percent of the people in authority were non-Greek, and most of them were commanders of local military units. Those who did advance to important administrative posts had learned Greek (all government business was transacted in Greek) and had become hellenized in a cultural sense. The policy of excluding non-Greeks from leadership positions, it should be added, was not due to the incompetence of the natives, but to the determination of the Greek ruling class to maintain its privileged position. It was the Greco-Macedonian ruling class that provided the only unity in the Hellenistic world.

Since the hellenizing process was largely an urban phenomenon, the creation of new Greek cities is an especially important topic. In his conquests, Alexander had founded a series of new cities and military settlements, and Hellenistic kings did likewise. The new population centers varied considerably in size and importance. Military settlements were meant to maintain order and might consist of only a few hundred men strongly dependent on the king. But there were also new independent cities with thousands of inhabitants.

Alexandria in Egypt was the largest city in the Mediterranean region by the first century B.C.E.

Hellenistic rulers encouraged this massive spread of Greek colonists to the Middle East because of their intrinsic value to the new monarchies. Greeks (and Macedonians) provided not only a recruiting ground for the army, but also a pool of civilian administrators and workers who would contribute to economic development. Even architects, engineers, dramatists, and actors were in demand in the new Greek cities. Many Greeks and Macedonians were quick to see the advantages of moving to the new urban centers and gladly sought their fortunes in the Middle East. The Greek cities of the Hellenistic era were the chief agents in the spread of Greek culture in the Middle East—as far, in fact, as modern Afghanistan and India.

Economic and Social Trends

Agriculture was still of primary importance to both the native populations and the new Greek cities of the Hellenistic world. The Greek cities continued their old agrarian patterns. A well-defined citizen body owned land and worked it with the assistance of slaves. But their farms were isolated units in a vast area of land ultimately owned by

A NEW AUTONOMY FOR WOMEN

Upper-class women in Hellenistic society enjoyed noticeable gains, and even in the lives of ordinary women, a new assertiveness came to the fore despite the continuing domination of society by men. The first selection is taken from the letter of a wife to her husband, complaining about his failure to return home. In the second selection, a father complains that his daughter has abandoned him, contrary to an Egyptian law providing that children who have been properly raised should support their parents.

LETTER FROM ISIAS TO HEPHAISTION, 168 B.C.E.

If you are well and other things are going right, it would accord with the prayer that I make continually to the gods. I myself and the child and all the household are in good health and think of you always. When I received your letter from Horos, in which you announce that you are in detention in the Serapeum at Memphis, for the news that you are well I straightway thanked the gods, but about your not coming home, when all the others who had been secluded there have come, I am ill-pleased, because after having piloted myself and your child through such bad times and been driven to every extremity owing to the price of wheat, I thought that now at least, with you at home, I should enjoy some respite, whereas you have not even thought of coming home nor given any regard to our circumstances, remembering how I was in want of everything while you were still here, not to mention this long lapse of time and these critical days, during which you

have sent us nothing. As, moreover, Horos who delivered the letter has brought news of your having been released from detention, I am thoroughly ill-pleased. Notwithstanding, as your mother also is annoyed, for her sake as well as for mine please return to the city, if nothing more pressing holds you back. You will do me a favor by taking care of your bodily health. Farewell.

LETTER FROM KTESIKLES TO KING PTOLEMY, 220 B.C.E.

I am wronged by Dionysios and by Nike my daughter. For though I raised her, my own daughter, and educated her and brought her to maturity, when I was stricken with bodily ill-health and was losing my eyesight, she was not minded to furnish me with any of the necessities of life. When I sought to obtain justice from her in Alexandria, she begged my pardon, and in the eighteenth year she swore me a written royal oath to give me each month twenty drachmas, which she was to earn by her own bodily labor. . . . But now corrupted by Dionysios, who is a comic actor, she does not do for me anything of what was in the written oath, despising my weakness and ill-health. I beg you, therefore, O king, not to allow me to be wronged by my daughter and by Dionysios the actor who corrupted her, but to order Diophanes the strategus [a provincial administrator] to summon them and hear us out; and if I am speaking the truth, let Diophanes deal with her corrupter as seems good to him and compel my daughter Nike to do justice to me. If this is done I shall no longer be wronged but by fleeing to you, O king, I shall obtain justice.

---

the king or assigned to large estate owners and worked by native peasants dwelling in villages. Overall, then, neither agricultural patterns nor methods of production underwent significant changes.

Commerce experienced considerable expansion in the Hellenistic era. Indeed, trading contacts linked much of the Hellenistic world together. The decline in the number of political barriers encouraged more commercial traffic. Although Hellenistic monarchs still fought wars, the conquests of Alexander and the policies of his successors made possible greater trade between east and west. An incredible variety of products were traded: gold and silver from Spain; salt from Asia Minor; timber from Macedonia; ebony, gems, ivory, and spices from India; frankincense (used on altars) from Arabia; slaves from Thrace, Syria, and Asia Minor; fine wines from Syria and western Asia Minor; olive oil from Athens; and numerous exquisite foodstuffs, such as the famous prunes of Damascus. The greatest trade, however, was in the basic staple of life—grain.

One of the more noticeable features of social life in the Hellenistic world was the emergence of new opportunities for women—at least, for upper-class women—especially in the economic area. Documents show increasing numbers of women involved in managing slaves, selling property, and making loans. Even then, legal contracts in which women were involved had to include their official male guardians, although in numerous instances these men no longer played an important function but were only listed to satisfy legal requirements. Only in Sparta were women free to control their own economic affairs. Many Spartan women were noticeably wealthy; females owned 40 percent of Spartan land.

Spartan women, however, were an exception, especially on the Greek mainland. Women in Athens, for example, still remained highly restricted and supervised. Although a few philosophers welcomed female participation in men's affairs, many philosophers rejected equality between men and women and asserted that the traditional roles of wives and mothers were most satisfying for women.

But the opinions of philosophers did not prevent upper-class women from making gains in areas other than the economic sphere (see the box on p. 120). New possibilities for females arose when women in some areas of the Hellenistic world were allowed to pursue education in the traditional fields of literature, music, and even athletics. Education, then, provided new opportunities for women: female poets appeared in the third century, and there are instances of women involved in both scholarly and artistic activities.

The creation of the Hellenistic monarchies, which represented a considerable departure from the world of the city-state, also gave new scope to the role played by the monarchs' wives, the Hellenistic queens. In Macedonia, a pattern of alliances between mothers and sons provided openings for women to take an active role in politics, especially in political intrigue. In Egypt, opportunities for royal women were even greater because the Ptolemaic rulers reverted to an Egyptian custom of kings marrying their own sisters. Of the first eight Ptolemaic rulers, four wed their sisters. Ptolemy II and his sister-wife Arsinoë II were both worshiped as gods in their lifetimes. Arsinoë played an energetic role in government and was involved in the expansion of the Egyptian navy. She was also the first Egyptian queen whose portrait appeared on coins with her husband. Hellenistic queens also showed an intense interest in culture. They wrote poems, collected art, and corresponded with intellectuals.

CULTURE IN THE HELLENISTIC WORLD

Although the Hellenistic kingdoms encompassed vast territories and many diverse peoples, the Greeks provided a sense of unity as a result of the diffusion of Greek culture throughout the Hellenistic world. The Hellenistic era was a period of considerable cultural accomplishment in many areas—literature, art, science, and philosophy. Although these achievements occurred throughout the Hellenistic world, certain centers, especially the great Hellenistic cities of Alexandria and Pergamum, stood out. In both cities, cultural developments were encouraged by the rulers themselves. Rich Hellenistic kings had considerable resources with which to patronize culture.

New Directions in Literature and Art

The Hellenistic age produced an enormous quantity of literature, most of which has not survived. Hellenistic monarchs, who held literary talent in high esteem, subsidized writers on a grand scale. The Ptolemaic rulers of Egypt were particularly lavish. The combination of their largesse and a famous library with over 500,000 scrolls drew a host of scholars and authors to Alexandria, including a circle

of poets. Theocritus (c. 315–250 B.C.E.), originally a native of the island of Sicily, wrote "little poems" or idylls dealing with erotic subjects, lovers' complaints, and, above all, pastoral themes expressing his love of nature and his appreciation of nature's beauties. In writing short poems, Theocritus was following the advice of Greek literary scholars who argued that Homer could never be superseded and urged writers to stick to well-composed, short poems instead.

In the Hellenistic era, Athens remained the theatrical center of the Greek world. While little remained of tragedy, a New Comedy developed, which completely

PORTRAIT OF QUEEN ARSINOË II. Arsinoë II, sister and wife of King Ptolemy II, played an active role in Egyptian political affairs. This statue from around 270–240 B.C.E. shows the queen in the traditional style of a pharaoh.

❀ OLD MARKET WOMAN.   Greek architects and sculptors were highly valued throughout the Hellenistic world, as kings undertook projects to beautify the cities of their kingdoms. Unlike the sculptors of the classical period, Hellenistic sculptors no longer tried to capture ideal beauty in their sculptures but moved toward a more emotional and realistic art. This statue of an old market woman is typical of this new trend in art.

rejected political themes and sought only to entertain and amuse. The Athenian playwright Menander (c. 342–291 B.C.E.) was perhaps the best representative of New Comedy. Plots were simple: typically, a hero falls in love with a not-really-so-bad prostitute, who turns out eventually to be the long-lost daughter of a rich neighbor. The hero marries her and they live happily ever after.

The Hellenistic period saw a great outpouring of historical and biographical literature. The chief historian of the Hellenistic age was Polybius (c. 203–c. 120 B.C.E.), a Greek who lived for some years in Rome. He is regarded by many historians as second only to Thucydides among Greek historians. His major work consisted of forty books narrating the history of the "inhabited Mediterranean world" from 221 to 146 B.C.E. Only the first five books are extant, although long extracts from the rest of the books survive. His history focuses on the growth of Rome from a city-state to a vast empire. It is apparent that Polybius understood the significance of the Romans' achievement. He followed Thucydides in seeking rational motives for

historical events. He also approached his sources critically and used firsthand accounts.

In addition to being patrons of literary talent, the Hellenistic monarchs were eager to spend their money to beautify and adorn the cities within their states. The founding of new cities and the rebuilding of old ones provided numerous opportunities for Greek architects and sculptors. Hellenistic architects laid out their new cities on the rectilinear grid model first used by Hippodamus of Miletus in the fifth century B.C.E. The buildings of the Greek homeland—gymnasia, baths, theaters, and, of course, temples—lined the streets of these cities.

Both Hellenistic kings and rich citizens patronized sculptors. Thousands of statues, many paid for by the people honored, were erected in towns and cities all over the Hellenistic world. Hellenistic sculptors traveled throughout this world, attracted by the material rewards offered by wealthy patrons. As a result, although distinct styles developed in Alexandria, Rhodes, and Pergamum, Hellenistic sculpture was characterized by a considerable degree of uniformity. While maintaining the technical skill of the classical period, Hellenistic sculptors moved away from the idealism of fifth-century classicism to a more emotional and realistic art, seen in numerous statues of old women, drunks, and little children at play.

A Golden Age of Science

The Hellenistic era witnessed a more conscious separation of science from philosophy. In classical Greece, what we would call the physical and life sciences had been divisions of philosophical inquiry. Nevertheless, by the time of Aristotle, the Greeks had already established an important principle of scientific investigation, empirical research or systematic observation as the basis for generalization. In the Hellenistic age, the sciences tended to be studied in their own right. While Athens remained the philosophical center, Alexandria and Pergamum, the two leading cultural centers of the Hellenistic world, played a significant role in the development of Hellenistic science.

By far the most famous scientist of the period, Archimedes (287–212 B.C.E.) of Syracuse, came from the western Mediterranean region. Archimedes was especially important for his work on the geometry of spheres and cylinders, for establishing the value of the mathematical constant pi, and for creating the science of hydrostatics. Archimedes was also a practical inventor. He may have devised the so-called Archimedean screw used to pump water out of mines and to lift irrigation water, as well as a compound pulley for transporting heavy weights. During the Roman siege of his native city of Syracuse, he constructed a number of devices to thwart the attackers. According to Plutarch's account, the Romans became so frightened "that if they did but see a little rope or a

THE STOIC IDEAL OF HARMONY WITH GOD

The Stoic Cleanthes (331–232 B.C.E.) succeeded Zeno as head of this school of philosophy. One historian of Hellenistic civilization has called this work by Cleanthes the greatest religious hymn in Greece. Certainly, it demonstrates that Stoicism, unlike Epicureanism, did have an underlying spiritual foundation. This poem has been compared to the great psalms of the Hebrews.

CLEANTHES, HYMN TO ZEUS

Nothing occurs on the earth apart from you, O God, nor in the heavenly regions nor on the sea, except what bad men do in their folly; but you know how to make the odd even, and to harmonize what is dissonant; to you the alien is akin.
And so you have wrought together into one all things that are good and bad,
So that there arises one eternal logos [rationale] of all things,
Which all bad mortals shun and ignore,
Unhappy wretches, ever seeking the possession of good things
They neither see nor hear the universal law of God,
By obeying which they might enjoy a happy life.

---

piece of wood from the wall, instantly crying out, that there it was again, Archimedes was about to let fly some engine at them, they turned their backs and fled."[15] Archimedes' accomplishments inspired a wealth of semilegendary stories. Supposedly, he discovered specific gravity by observing the water he displaced in his bath and became so excited by his realization that he jumped out of the water and ran home naked, shouting, "Eureka" ("I have found it"). He is said to have emphasized the importance of levers by proclaiming to the king of Syracuse: "Give me a lever and a place to stand and I will move the earth." The king was so impressed that he encouraged Archimedes to lower his sights and build defensive weapons instead.

Philosophy: New Schools of Thought

While Alexandria and Pergamum became the renowned cultural centers of the Hellenistic world, Athens remained the prime center for philosophy. After Alexander the Great, the home of Socrates, Plato, and Aristotle continued to attract the most illustrious philosophers from the Greek world, who chose to establish their schools there. New schools of philosophical thought—the Epicureans and Stoics—reinforced Athens's reputation as a philosophical center.

Epicurus (341–270 B.C.E.), the founder of Epicureanism, established a school in Athens near the end of the fourth century B.C.E. Epicurus believed that human beings were free to follow self-interest as a basic motivating force. Happiness was the goal of life, and the means to achieve it was the pursuit of pleasure, the only true good. But the pursuit of pleasure was not meant in a physical, hedonistic sense (which is what our word *epicurean* has come to mean). Pleasure was not satisfying one's desire in an active, gluttonous fashion, but freedom from emotional turmoil, freedom from worry, the freedom that came from a mind at rest. To achieve this kind of pleasure, one had to free one-self from public activity: "We must release ourselves from the prison of affairs and politics." But this was not a renunciation of all social life, for to Epicurus, a life could only be complete when it was centered on the basic ideal of friendship. Epicurus's own life in Athens was an embodiment of his teachings. He and his friends created their own private community where they could pursue their ideal of true happiness.

Another school of thought was Stoicism, which became the most popular philosophy of the Hellenistic world and later flourished in the Roman Empire as well. It was the product of a teacher named Zeno (335–263 B.C.E.), who came to Athens and began to teach in a public colonnade known as the Painted Portico (the *Stoa Poikile*—hence Stoicism). Like Epicureanism, Stoicism was concerned with how individuals find happiness. But Stoics took a radically different approach to the problem. To them, happiness, the supreme good, could be found only by living in harmony with the will of God, by which people gained inner peace (see the box above). Life's problems could not disturb these people, and they could bear whatever life offered (hence our word *stoic*). Unlike Epicureans, Stoics did not believe in the need to separate oneself from the world and politics. Public service was regarded as noble, and the real Stoic was a good citizen and could even be a good government official. In fact, the Roman emperor Marcus Aurelius was a noted Stoic philosopher.

Epicureanism and especially Stoicism appealed to large numbers of people in the Hellenistic world. Both of these philosophies focused primarily on the problem of human happiness. Their popularity would suggest a fundamental change in the character of the Greek lifestyle. In the classical Greek world, the happiness of individuals and the meaning of life were closely associated with the life of the *polis*: one found fulfillment within the community. In the Hellenistic kingdoms, although the *polis* continued to exist, the sense that one could find satisfaction and fulfillment through life in the *polis* had weakened. Not only

THE CULT OF ISIS.   The cult of Isis was one of the most popular mystery religions in the Hellenistic world. This fresco from Herculaneum in Italy depicts a religious ceremony in front of the temple of Isis. At the top, a priest holds a golden vessel, while below him another priest leads the worshipers with a staff. A third priest fans the flames at the altar.

did individuals seek new philosophies that offered personal happiness, but in the cosmopolitan world of the Hellenistic states, a new openness to thoughts of universality could also emerge. For some people, Stoicism embodied this larger sense of community. The appeal of new philosophies in the Hellenistic era can also be explained by the apparent decline in certain aspects of traditional religion, which we can see by examining the status of Hellenistic religion.

Religion in the Hellenistic World

When the Greeks spread throughout the Hellenistic kingdoms, they took their gods with them. Although the construction of temples may have been less important than in classical times, there were still many demonstrations of a lively religious faith. But over a period of time, there was a noticeable decline in the vitality of the traditional Greek Olympian religion. Much of Greek religion had always revolved around ritual, but the civic cults based on the traditional gods no longer seemed sufficient to satisfy people's emotional needs.

The decline in traditional Greek religion left Greeks receptive to the numerous religious cults of the eastern world. The Greeks were always tolerant of other religious institutions. Hence, in the Hellenistic cities of the Mid-

dle East, the traditional civic cults of their own gods and foreign cults existed side by side. Alexandria had cults of the traditional Greek gods, Egyptian deities, such as Isis and Horus, the Babylonian Astarte, and the Syrian Atargatis. The eastern religions that appealed most to Greeks, however, were the mystery religions. What was the source of their attraction?

The normal forms of religious worship in Hellenistic communities had lost some of their appeal. The practices of traditional, ritualized Greek religion in the civic cults seemed increasingly meaningless. For many people, the search for personal meaning remained unfulfilled, and they sought alternatives. Among educated Greeks, the philosophies of Epicureanism and especially Stoicism offered help. Another source of solace came in the form of mystery religions.

Mystery cults, with their secret initiations and promises of individual salvation, were not new to the Greek world. But the Greeks of the Hellenistic era were also strongly influenced by eastern mystery cults, such as those of Egypt, which offered a distinct advantage over the Greek mystery religions. The latter had usually been connected to specific locations (such as Eleusis), which meant that a would-be initiate had to undertake a pilgrimage in order to participate in the rites. In contrast, the eastern mystery religions were readily available since temples to their gods and goddesses were located throughout the Greek cities of the east. All of the mystery religions were based on the same fundamental premises. Individuals could pursue a path to salvation and achieve eternal life by being initiated into a union with a savior god or goddess who had died and risen again.

The Egyptian cult of Isis was one of the most popular of the mystery religions. The cult of Isis was very ancient but became truly universal in Hellenistic times. Isis was the goddess of women, marriage, and children; as one of her hymns states: "I am she whom women call goddess. I ordained that women should be loved by men: I brought wife and husband together, and invented the marriage contract. I ordained that women should bear children."[16] Isis was also portrayed as the giver of civilization, who had brought laws and letters to all humankind. The cult of Isis offered a precious commodity to its initiates—the promise of eternal life. In many ways, the cult of Isis and the other mystery religions of the Hellenistic era helped to pave the way for the coming and the success of Christianity.

 CONCLUSION

Unlike the great centralized empires of the Persians and the Chinese, ancient Greece consisted of a large number of small, independent city-states, most of which had populations of only a few thousand. Despite the small size of their city-states, these ancient Greeks created a civilization that was the fountainhead of Western culture. Socrates, Plato, and Aristotle established the foundations of Western philosophy. Western literary forms are largely derived from Greek poetry and drama. Greek notions of harmony, proportion, and beauty have remained the touchstones for all subsequent Western art. A rational method of inquiry, so important to modern science, was conceived in ancient Greece. Many political terms are Greek in origin, and so too are concepts of the rights and duties of citizenship, especially as they were conceived in Athens, the first great democracy the world had seen. Especially during their classical period, the Greeks raised and debated the fundamental questions about the purpose of human existence, the structure of human society, and the nature of the universe that have concerned thinkers ever since.

All of these achievements came from a group of small city-states in ancient Greece. And yet there remains an element of tragedy about Greek civilization. For all of their brilliant accomplishments, the Greeks were unable to rise above the divisions and rivalries that caused them to fight each other and undermine their own civilization. Of course, their cultural contributions have outlived their political struggles. And the Hellenistic era, which emerged after the Greek city-states had lost their independence, made possible the spread of Greek ideas to larger areas.

The Hellenistic period was a vibrant one. New cities arose and flourished. New philosophical ideas captured the minds of many. Significant achievements were made in art, literature, and science. Greek culture spread throughout the Middle East and made an impact wherever it was carried. But serious problems remained. Hellenistic kings continued to engage in inconclusive wars. Much of the formal culture was the special preserve of the Greek conquerors, whose attitude of superiority kept them largely separated from the native masses of the Hellenistic kingdoms. Although the Hellenistic world achieved a degree of political stability, by the late third century B.C.E. signs of decline were beginning to multiply. Some of the more farsighted perhaps realized the danger the growing power of Rome presented to the Hellenistic world. The Romans would ultimately inherit Alexander's empire and Greek culture, and we must now turn to them and try to understand what made them such successful conquerors.

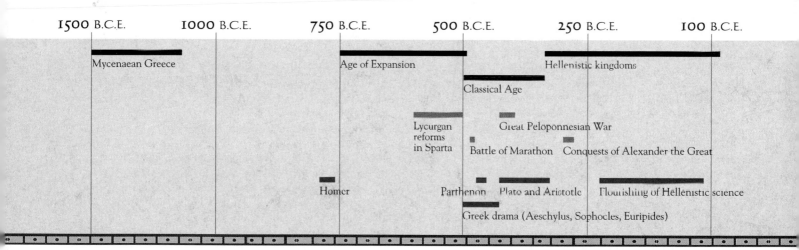

CHAPTER NOTES

1. H. D. F. Kitto, *The Greeks* (Harmondsworth, 1951), p. 64.
2. Homer, *Odyssey*, trans. E. V. Rieu (Harmondsworth, 1946), p. 337.
3. Xenophon, *Symposium*, trans. O. J. Todd (Harmondsworth, 1946), III, 5.
4. Homer, *Odyssey*, trans. E. V. Rieu (Harmondsworth, 1959), pp. 290–91.
5. Quoted in Thomas R. Martin, *Ancient Greece* (New Haven, Conn., 1996), p. 62.
6. These words from Plutarch are quoted in E. Fantham, H. P. Foley, N. B. Kampen, S. B. Pomeroy, and H. A. Shapiro, *Women in the Classical World* (New York, 1994), p. 64.
7. Voltaire, *The Age of Louis XIV*, trans. Martyn Pollack (London, 1926), p. 1.
8. Herodotus, *The Persian Wars*, trans. Robin Waterfield (New York, 1998), p. 3.
9. Thucydides, *The Peloponnesian War*, trans. Rex Warner (Harmondsworth, 1954), p. 24.
10. Sophocles, *Oedipus the King*, trans. David Grene (Chicago, 1959), pp. 68–69.

11. Sophocles, *Antigone,* trans. Don Taylor (London, 1986), p. 146.

12. Plato, *The Republic,* trans. F. M. Cornford (New York, 1945), pp. 178–79.

13. Quotations from Aristotle are in Sue Blundell, *Women in Ancient Greece* (London, 1995), pp. 106, 186.

14. Quoted in Sarah B. Pomeroy, Stanley M. Burstein, Walter Donlan, Jennifer Tolbert Roberts, *Ancient Greece: A Political, Social, and Cultural History* (Oxford, 1999), p. 390.

15. Plutarch, *Life of Marcellus,* trans. John Dryden (New York, n.d.), p. 378.

16. Quoted in W. W. Tarn, *Hellenistic Civilization* (London, 1930), p. 324.

 # SUGGESTED READINGS

A standard one-volume reference work for Greek history is J. B. Bury and R. Meiggs, *A History of Greece to the Death of Alexander the Great,* 4th ed. (New York, 1975). Other good general introductions to Greek history include *The Oxford History of the Classical World,* ed. J. Boardman, J. Griffin, and O. Murray (Oxford, 1986), pp. 19–314; T. R. Martin, *Ancient Greece* (New Haven, Conn., 1996); P. Cartledge, *The Cambridge Illustrated History of Ancient Greece* (Cambridge, 1998); and W. Donlan, S. B. Pomeroy, J. T. Roberts, and S. M. Burstein, *Ancient Greece: A Political, Social, and Cultural History* (New York, 1998). For a general survey of economic and social aspects, see M. M. Austin and P. Vidal-Naquet, *Economic and Social History of Ancient Greece: An Introduction* (Berkeley, 1978).

Early Greek history is examined in O. Murray, *Early Greece,* 2d ed. (Cambridge, Mass., 1993), and J. L. Fitton, *The Discovery of the Greek Bronze Age* (Cambridge, 1995). For a good introduction to Homer and the Homeric problem, see J. Griffin, *Homer* (Oxford, 1980).

A good general work on the Greek age of expansion is A. M. Snodgrass, *Archaic Greece* (London, 1980). Economic and social history of the period is covered in C. Starr, *The Economic and Social Growth of Early Greece, 800–500 B.C.* (Oxford, 1977). On colonization, see J. Boardman, *The Greeks Overseas,* rev. ed. (Baltimore, 1980). On tyranny, see J. F. McGlew, *Tyranny and Political Culture in Ancient Greece* (Ithaca, N.Y., 1993). On Sparta, see W. Forrest, *A History of Sparta, 950–121 B.C.,* 2d ed. (London, 1980). On early Athens, see the still valuable A. Jones, *Athenian Democracy* (London, 1957), and R. Osborne, *Demos* (Oxford, 1985). The Persian Wars are examined in A. Burn, *Persia and the Greeks: The Defense of the West,* rev. ed. (Stanford, Calif., 1984).

A general history of classical Greece can be found in S. Hornblower, *The Greek World, 479–323 B.C.* (London, 1983). Important works on Athens include C. W. Fornara and L. J. Samons II, *Athens from Cleisthenes to Pericles* (Berkeley, 1991); D. Stockton, *The Classical Athenian Democracy* (Oxford, 1990); and D. Kagan, *Pericles of Athens and the Birth of Democracy* (New York, 1991). On the development of the Athenian Empire, see M. F. Mc-Gregor, *The Athenians and Their Empire* (Vancouver, 1987). The best way to examine the Great Peloponnesian War is to read the work of Thucydides, *History of the Peloponnesian War,* trans. R. Warner (Harmondsworth, 1954).

For a comprehensive history of Greek art, see M. Robertson, *A History of Greek Art,* 2 vols. (Cambridge, 1975). A good brief study is J. Boardman, *Greek Art* (London, 1985). On sculpture, see A. Stewart, *Greek Sculpture: An Exploration* (New Haven, Conn., 1990). A basic survey of architecture is H. W. Lawrence, *Greek Architecture,* rev. ed. (Harmondsworth, 1983). On Greek drama, see the general work by J. De Romilly, *A Short History of Greek Literature* (Chicago, 1985). On Greek philosophy, a detailed study is available in W. K. C. Guthrie, *A History of Greek Philosophy,* 6 vols. (Cambridge, 1962–1981). On Greek religion, see J. N. Bremmer, *Greek Religion* (Oxford, 1994).

On the family and women, see S. C. Humphreys, *The Family, Women and Death* (London, 1983); S. B. Pomeroy, *Goddesses, Whores, Wives, and Slaves* (New York, 1975); E. Fantham, H. P. Foley, N. B. Kampen, S. B. Pomeroy, and H. A. Shapiro, *Women in the Classical World* (New York, 1994); and S. Blundell, *Women in Ancient Greece* (Cambridge, Mass., 1995). On homosexuality, see E. Cantarella, *Bisexuality in the Ancient World* (New Haven, Conn., 1992).

The best general survey of the Hellenistic era is F. W. Walbank, *The Hellenistic World* (London, 1981). For a good introduction to the early history of Macedonia, see E. N. Borza, *In the Shadow of Olympus: The Emergence of Macedon* (Princeton, N.J., 1990). Philip of Macedon is covered well in N. Hammond and G. Griffith, *A History of Macedonia,* vol. 2, *550–336 B.C.* (Oxford, 1979). There are considerable differences of opinion on Alexander the Great. The best biographies include R. L. Fox, *Alexander the Great* (London, 1973); J. R. Hamilton, *Alexander the Great* (London, 1973); and P. Green, *Alexander of Macedon* (Berkeley, Calif., 1991).

The various Hellenistic monarchies can be examined in N. G. L. Hammond and F. W. Walbank, *A History of Macedonia,* vol. 3, *336–167 B.C.* (Oxford, 1988); S. Sherwin-White and A. Kuhrt, *From Samarkand to Sardis: A New Approach to the Seleucid Empire* (Berkeley and Los Angeles, 1993); and N. Lewis, *Greeks in Ptolemaic Egypt* (Oxford, 1986). On economic and social trends, see the classic and still indispensable M. I. Rostovtzeff, *Social and Economic History of the Hellenistic World,* 3 vols., 2d ed. (Oxford, 1953). Hellenistic women are examined in two works by S. B. Pomeroy, *Goddesses, Whores, Wives, and Slaves* (New York, 1975), pp. 120–48, and *Women in Hellenistic Egypt* (New York, 1984).

For a general introduction to Hellenistic culture, see J. Onians, *Art and Thought in the Hellenistic Age* (London, 1979). The best general survey of Hellenistic philosophy is A. A. Long, *Hellenistic Philosophy: Stoics, Epicureans, Skeptics,* 2d ed. (London, 1986). A superb work on Hellenistic science is G. E. R. Lloyd, *Greek Science After Aristotle* (London, 1973). On one facet of Hellenistic religion, see R. E. Witt, *Isis in the Graeco-Roman World* (London, 1971). On the entry of Rome into the Hellenistic world, see the basic work by E. S. Gruen, *The Hellenistic World and the Coming of Rome,* 2 vols. (Berkeley, 1984).

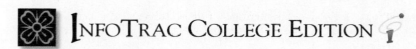

INFOTRAC COLLEGE EDITION

For additional reading, go to InfoTrac College Edition, your online research library at
http://web1.infotrac-college.com

Enter the search terms "Greece history" using Keywords.

Enter the search terms "Peloponnesian War" using Keywords.

Enter the search terms "Greek mythology" using the Subject Guide.

Enter the search terms "Plato or Aristotle or Socrates" using Keywords.

Enter the search terms "Alexander the Great" using Keywords.

CHAPTER

5

THE WORLD OF THE ROMANS

CHAPTER OUTLINE

- THE EMERGENCE OF ROME
- THE ROMAN REPUBLIC
- THE ROMAN CONQUEST OF THE MEDITERRANEAN (264–133 B.C.E.)
- THE DECLINE AND FALL OF THE ROMAN REPUBLIC (133–31 B.C.E.)
- THE AGE OF AUGUSTUS (31 B.C.E.–14 C.E.)
- THE EARLY EMPIRE (14–180)
- CULTURE AND SOCIETY IN THE ROMAN WORLD
- THE TRANSFORMATION OF THE ROMAN WORLD: THE DEVELOPMENT OF CHRISTIANITY
- THE DECLINE AND FALL OF THE ROMAN EMPIRE
- CONCLUSION

FOCUS QUESTIONS

- What policies and institutions help to explain the Romans' success in conquering and then ruling their empire?
- What problems did Rome face during the last century of the Republic, and how were they ultimately resolved?
- What were the chief features of the Roman Empire at its height in the second century C.E., and what happened to bring it near collapse in the next century?
- What characteristics of Christianity enabled it to grow and ultimately to triumph?
- In what ways were the Roman Empire and the Han Chinese Empire similar, and in what ways were they different?

Although the Assyrians, Persians, and Indians under the Mauryan dynasty had created empires, they were neither as large nor as well controlled as the Han Chinese and Roman Empires that flourished at the beginning of the first millennium C.E. These two were the most extensive empires the world had yet seen (the Han Empire, as we saw in Chapter 3, extended from Central Asia to the Pacific Ocean; the Roman Empire encompassed the lands around the Mediterranean as well as parts of the Middle East and western and central Europe). Although there was little contact between them, the Han Empire and the Roman

Empire had some remarkable similarities: their empires lasted for centuries; they had remarkable success in establishing centralized control over their empires; and throughout their empires they maintained their law and political institutions, their technical skills, and their languages. But there were also important differences between the Han and Roman Empires, which will become evident as we examine the world of the Romans in this chapter.

Roman history is basically the remarkable story of how a group of Latin-speaking people who established a small community on a plain called Latium in central Italy went on to conquer all of Italy and then the entire Mediterranean world. Why were the Romans able to do this? Scholars do not really know all the answers, but the Romans had their own explanation. Early Roman history is filled with legendary stories that tell of the heroes who made Rome great. One of the best known is the story of Horatius at the bridge. Threatened by attack from the neighboring Etruscans, Roman farmers abandoned their fields and moved into the city, where they would be protected by the walls. One weak point in the Roman defenses, however, was a wooden bridge over the Tiber River. Horatius was on guard at the bridge when a sudden assault by the Etruscans caused many Roman troops to throw down their weapons and flee. Horatius urged them to make a stand at the bridge behind him while he held the Etruscans back. Astonished at the sight of a single defender, the confused Etruscans threw their spears at Horatius, who caught them on his shield and barred the way. By the time the Etruscans had regrouped and were about to overwhelm the lone defender, the Roman soldiers brought down the bridge. When Horatius heard the bridge crash into the river behind him, he dove fully armed into the water and swam safely to the other side through a hail of arrows. Rome had been saved by the courageous act of a Roman who knew his duty and was determined to carry it out. Courage, duty, determination—these qualities would also serve the

many Romans who believed that it was their divine mission to rule nations and peoples. As one Roman writer proclaimed: "By heaven's will my Rome shall be capital of the world." ✤

THE EMERGENCE OF ROME

Italy is a peninsula extending about 750 miles from north to south. It is not very wide, however, averaging about 120 miles across. The Apennines traverse the peninsula from north to south, forming a ridge down the middle that divides west from east. Nevertheless, Italy has some fairly large fertile plains ideal for farming. Most important were the Po valley in the north, probably the most fertile agricultural area; the plain of Latium, on which Rome was located; and Campania to the south of Latium. To the east of the Italian peninsula is the Adriatic Sea and to the west the Tyrrhenian Sea with the nearby large islands of Corsica and Sardinia. Sicily lies just west of the toe of the boot-shaped Italian peninsula.

Geography had an impact on Roman history. Although the Apennines bisected Italy, they were less rugged than the mountain ranges of Greece and did not divide the peninsula into many small isolated communities. Italy also possessed considerably more productive agricultural land than Greece, enabling it to support a large population. Rome's location was favorable from a geographical point of view. Located eighteen miles inland on the Tiber River, Rome had access to the sea and yet was far enough inland to be safe from pirates. Built on the famous seven hills, it was easily defended. Situated where the Tiber could be readily forded, Rome became a natural crossing point for north-south traffic in western Italy. All in all, Rome had a good central location in Italy from which to expand.

Moreover, the Italian peninsula juts into the Mediterranean, making it an important crossroads between the western and eastern Mediterranean. Once Rome had unified Italy, involvement in Mediterranean affairs was natural. And after the Romans had conquered their Mediterranean empire, governing it was made considerably easier by Italy's central location.

Early Rome

According to Roman legend, Rome was founded by the twin brothers Romulus and Remus in 753 B.C.E., and archaeologists have found that by the eighth century B.C.E. there was a settlement consisting of huts on the tops of Rome's hills. The early Romans, basically a pastoral people, spoke Latin, which, like Greek, belongs to the Indo-European family of languages (see the table in Chapter 1). The Roman historical tradition also maintained that early

ETRUSCAN MARRIED COUPLE. This sculpture, dating from 550 B.C.E., depicts a wealthy Etruscan married couple reclining on a couch. The Etruscans greatly influenced the early development of Rome and had an impact on Roman religion, sporting events, and military institutions.

Rome (753–509 B.C.E.) had been under the control of seven kings and that two of the last three had been Etruscans, a people who were located north of Rome in Etruria. Some historians believe that the king list may have some historical accuracy. What is certain is that Rome did fall under the influence of the Etruscans for about a hundred years during the period of the kings. The Etruscans found Rome a pastoral community but left it a city.

By the beginning of the sixth century B.C.E., under Etruscan influence, Rome began to emerge as an actual city. The Etruscans were responsible for an outstanding building program. They constructed the first roadbed of the chief street through Rome—the Sacred Way—before 575 B.C.E. and oversaw the development of temples, markets, shops, streets, and houses. By 509 B.C.E., the date when the monarchy supposedly was overthrown and a republican form of government established, a new Rome had emerged, essentially a result of the fusion of Etruscan and native Roman elements.

❀ THE ROMAN REPUBLIC

The transition from monarchy to a republican government was not easy. Rome felt threatened by enemies from every direction and, in the process of meeting these threats, embarked on a military course that led to the conquest of the entire Italian peninsula.

The Roman Conquest of Italy

At the beginning of the Republic, Rome was surrounded by enemies, including the Etruscans to the north and the Sabines, Volscians, and Aequi to the east and south. The Latin communities on the plain of Latium posed an even more immediate threat. If we are to believe Livy, one of the chief ancient sources for the history of the early Roman Republic, Rome was engaged in almost continuous warfare with the Volscians, Sabines, Aequi, and others for the next hundred years.

In his account of these years, the historian Livy provided a detailed narrative of Roman efforts. Many of Livy's stories were legendary in character and indeed were modeled after events in Greek history. But Livy, writing in the first century B.C.E., used such stories to teach Romans the moral values and virtues that had made Rome great. These included tenacity, duty, courage, and especially discipline (see the box on p. 131). Indeed, Livy recounted stories of military leaders who executed their own sons for leaving their place in battle, a serious offense, since the success of the hoplite infantry depended on maintaining a precise order. These stories had little basis in fact, but like the story of George Washington and the cherry tree in American history, they provided mythical images to reinforce Roman patriotism.

By 340 B.C.E., Rome had crushed the Latin states in Latium. During the next fifty years, the Romans waged a fierce struggle with the Samnites, a hill people from the central Apennines, some of whom had settled in Campania, south of Rome. Rome was again victorious. The conquest of the Samnites gave Rome considerable control over a large part of Italy and also brought it into direct contact with the Greek communities. The Greeks had arrived on the Italian peninsula in large numbers during the age of Greek colonization (750–550 B.C.E.; see Chapter 4). Initially, the Greeks settled in southern Italy and then crept around the coast and up the peninsula. They also occupied the eastern two-thirds of Sicily. The Greeks had much influence on Rome. They cultivated the olive and the vine, and provided artistic and cultural models through their sculpture, architecture, and literature. Soon after their conquest of the Samnites, the Romans were involved in hostilities with some of these Greek cities and by 267 B.C.E. had completed their conquest of southern Italy. After crushing the remaining Etruscan states to the north in 264 B.C.E., Rome had conquered all of Italy except the extreme north.

To rule Italy, the Romans devised the Roman Confederation. Under this system, Rome allowed some peoples—especially the Latins—to have full Roman citizenship. Most of the remaining communities were made allies. They remained free to run their own local affairs but were required to provide soldiers for Rome. Moreover, the Romans made it clear that loyal allies could improve their status and even have hope of becoming Roman citizens.

CINCINNATUS SAVES ROME:
A ROMAN MORALITY TALE

There is perhaps no better account of how the virtues of duty and simplicity enabled good Roman citizens to prevail during the travails of the fifth century B.C.E. than Livy's account of Cincinnatus. He was chosen dictator, supposedly in 457 B.C.E., to defend Rome against the attacks of the Aequi. The position of dictator was a temporary expedient used only in emergencies; the consuls would resign and a leader with unlimited power would be appointed for a limited period (usually six months). In this account, Cincinnatus did his duty, defeated the Aequi, and returned to his simple farm in just fifteen days.

LIVY, THE EARLY HISTORY OF ROME

The city was thrown into a state of turmoil, and the general alarm was as great as if Rome herself were surrounded. Nautius was sent for, but it was quickly decided that he was not the man to inspire full confidence; the situation evidently called for a dictator, and, with no dissentient voice, Lucius Quinctius Cincinnatus was named for the post.

Now I would solicit the particular attention of those numerous people who imagine that money is everything in this world, and that rank and ability are inseparable from wealth: let them observe that Cincinnatus, the one man in whom Rome reposed all her hope of survival, was at that moment working a little three-acre farm . . . west of the Tiber, just opposite the spot where the shipyards are today. A mission from the city found him at work on his land—digging a ditch, maybe, or plowing. Greetings were exchanged,

and he was asked—with a prayer for divine blessing on himself and his country—to put on his toga and hear the Senate's instructions. This naturally surprised him, and, asking if all were well, he told his wife Racilia to run to their cottage and fetch his toga. The toga was brought, and wiping the grimy sweat from his hands and face he put it on; at once the envoys from the city saluted him, with congratulations, as Dictator, invited him to enter Rome, and informed him of the terrible danger of Municius's army. A state vessel was waiting for him on the river, and on the city bank he was welcomed by his three sons who had come to meet him, then by other kinsmen and friends, and finally by nearly the whole body of senators. Closely attended by all these people and preceded by his lictors he was then escorted to his residence through streets lined with great crowds of common folk who, be it said, were by no means so pleased to see the new Dictator, as they thought his power excessive and dreaded the way in which he was likely to use it.

[Cincinnatus proceeds to raise an army, march out, and defeat the Aequi.]

In Rome the Senate was convened by Quintus Fabius the City Prefect, and a decree was passed inviting Cincinnatus to enter in triumph with his troops. The chariot he rode in was preceded by the enemy commanders and the military standards, and followed by his army loaded with its spoils. . . . Cincinnatus finally resigned after holding office for fifteen days, having originally accepted it for a period of six months.

Thus, the Romans had found a way to give conquered peoples a stake in Rome's success.

The Romans' conquest of Italy can hardly be said to be the result of a direct policy of expansion. Much of it was opportunistic. The Romans did not hesitate to act once they felt their security threatened. And surrounded by potential enemies, Rome in a sense never felt secure. Yet once embarked on a course of expansion, the Romans pursued consistent policies that help to explain their success. The Romans were superb diplomats who excelled at making the correct diplomatic decisions. While firm and even cruel when necessary—rebellions were crushed without mercy—they were also shrewd in extending their citizenship and allowing autonomy in domestic affairs. In addition, the Romans were not only good soldiers, but persistent ones. The loss of an army or a fleet did not cause them to quit, but spurred them on to build new armies and new fleets. Finally, the Romans had a practical sense of strategy. As they conquered, they settled Romans and Latins in new communities outside Latium. By 264 B.C.E., the Romans had established colonies—fortified towns—at all strategic locations. By building roads to these set-

tlements and connecting them, the Romans assured themselves of an impressive military and communications network that enabled them to rule effectively and efficiently. By insisting upon military service from its allies in the Roman confederation, Rome essentially mobilized the entire military might of all Italy for its wars.

The Roman State

In law and politics, as in conquest, the Romans took a practical approach. They did not concern themselves with the construction of an ideal government, but instead fashioned political institutions in response to problems as they arose.

The chief executive officers of the Roman Republic were the consuls and praetors. Two consuls, chosen annually, administered the government and led the Roman army into battle. They possessed *imperium,* or "the right to command." In 366 B.C.E., a new office, that of the praetor, was created. The praetor also possessed *imperium* and could govern Rome when the consuls were away from the city and could also lead armies. The praetor's primary function, however, was the execution of justice. He was in

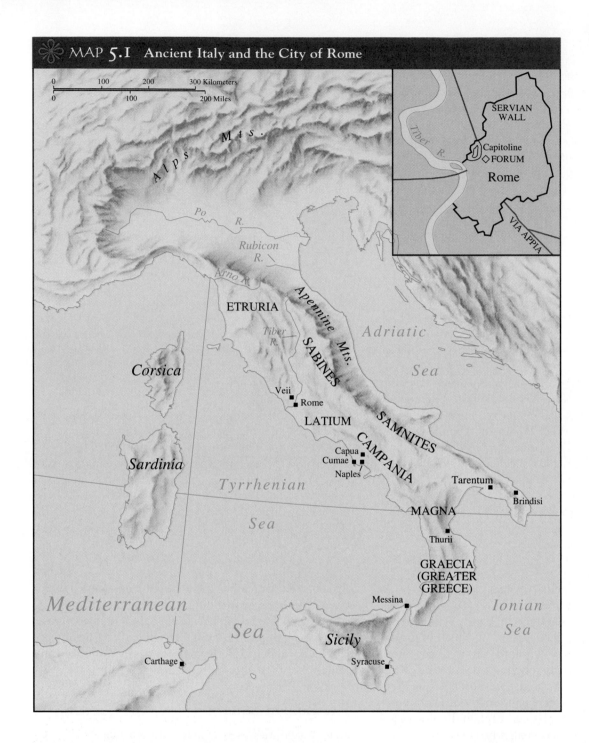

MAP 5.1   Ancient Italy and the City of Rome

charge of the civil law as it applied to Roman citizens. In 242 B.C.E., reflecting Rome's growth, another praetor was added to judge cases in which one or both people were noncitizens. The Roman state also had a number of administrative officials who handled specialized duties, such as the administration of financial affairs and supervision of the public games of Rome.

The Roman senate came to hold an especially important position in the Roman Republic. The senate or council of elders was a select group of about 300 men who served for life. The senate could only advise the magistrates, but this advice of the senate was not taken lightly,

and by the third century B.C.E. had virtually the force of law. No doubt the prestige of the senate's members furthered this development.

The Roman Republic possessed a number of popular assemblies. By far the most important was the centuriate assembly, essentially the Roman army functioning in its political role. Organized by classes based on wealth, it was structured in such a way that the wealthiest citizens always had a majority. The centuriate assembly elected the chief magistrates and passed laws. Another assembly, the council of the plebs, came into being in 471 B.C.E. as a result of the struggle of the orders.

The Roman Republic, then, witnessed the interplay of three major elements. Two consuls and later other elected officials served as magistrates and ran the state. An assembly of adult males (the centuriate assembly), controlled by the wealthiest citizens, elected these officials, while the Senate, a small group of large landowners, advised them. The Roman state, then was an aristocratic republic controlled by a relatively small group of privileged people.

THE STRUGGLE OF THE ORDERS: SOCIAL DIVISIONS IN THE ROMAN REPUBLIC

The most noticeable element in the social organization of early Rome was the division between two groups—the patricians and the plebeians. The patrician class in Rome consisted of those families who were descended from the original senators appointed during the period of the kings. Their initial emergence was probably due to their wealth as great landowners. Thus, patricians constituted an aristocratic governing class. Only they could be consuls, other magistrates, and senators. Through their patronage of large numbers of dependent clients, they controlled the centuriate assembly and many other facets of Roman life. The plebeians constituted the considerably larger group of "independent, unprivileged, poorer and vulnerable men" as well as nonpatrician large landowners, less wealthy landholders, artisans, merchants, and small farmers. Although they were citizens, they did not possess the same rights as the patricians. Both patricians and plebeians could vote, but only the patricians could be elected to governmental offices. Both had the right to make legal contracts and marriages, but intermarriage between patricians and plebeians was forbidden. At the beginning of the fifth century B.C.E., the plebeians began a struggle to seek both political and social equality with the patricians.

The struggle between the patricians and plebeians dragged on for hundreds of years but led to success for the plebeians. A popular assembly for plebeians only, called the council of the plebs, was created in 471 B.C.E., while new officials, known as tribunes of the plebs, were given the power to protect plebeians. A new law allowed marriages between patricians and plebeians, and in the fourth century B.C.E., plebeians were permitted to become consuls. Finally, in 287 B.C.E., the council of the plebs received the right to pass laws for all Romans.

The struggle between the orders, then, had a significant impact on the development of the Roman constitution. Plebeians could now hold the highest offices of state, they could intermarry with the patricians, and they could pass laws binding on the entire Roman community. Theoretically, by 287 B.C.E., all Roman citizens were equal under the law, and all could strive for political office. But in reality, as a result of the right of intermarriage, a select number of patrician and plebeian families formed a new senatorial aristocracy that came to dominate the political offices. The Roman Republic had not become a democracy.

THE ROMAN CONQUEST OF THE MEDITERRANEAN (264–133 B.C.E.)

After their conquest of the Italian peninsula, the Romans found themselves face-to-face with a formidable Mediterranean power—Carthage. Founded around 800 B.C.E. by Phoenicians from Tyre, Carthage in North Africa was located in a favorable position for commanding Mediterranean trade routes and had become an important commercial center. It had become politically and militarily strong as well. By the third century B.C.E., the Carthaginian empire included the coast of northern Africa, southern Spain, Sardinia, Corsica, and western Sicily. With its monopoly of western Mediterranean trade, Carthage

A ROMAN LEGIONARY. The Roman legionaries, with their legendary courage and tenacity, made possible the creation of the Roman Empire. This picture shows a bronze figure of a Roman legionary in full dress at the time of the height of the empire in the second century C.E. The soldier's cuirass is constructed of overlapping metal bands.

was the largest and richest state in the area. The presence of Carthaginians in Sicily made the Romans apprehensive about Carthaginian encroachment on the Italian coast. In 264 B.C.E., mutual suspicions drove the two powers into a lengthy struggle for control of the western Mediterranean.

The Punic Wars

The First Punic War (the Latin word for Phoenician was *punicus*) began in 264 B.C.E. when the Romans decided to intervene in a struggle between two Sicilian cities and sent an army to Sicily. The Carthaginians, who considered Sicily within their own sphere of influence, considered this just cause for war. In going to war, both sides determined on the conquest of Sicily. The Romans—a land power—realized that they could not win the war without a navy and promptly developed a substantial naval fleet. After a long struggle in which both sides lost battles in North Africa and Sicily, a Roman fleet defeated the Carthaginian navy off Sicily, and the war quickly came to an end. In 241 B.C.E., Carthage gave up all rights to Sicily and had to pay an indemnity to Rome. Sicily became the first Roman province.

Carthage vowed revenge and added new lands in Spain to compensate for the loss of Sicily. When the Romans encouraged one of Carthage's Spanish allies to revolt against Carthage, Hannibal, the greatest of the Carthaginian generals, struck back, beginning the Second Punic War (218–201 B.C.E.).

This time the Carthaginian strategy aimed at bringing the war home to the Romans and defeating them in their own backyard. Hannibal crossed the Alps with an army of 30,000–40,000 men and 6,000 horses and elephants and inflicted a series of defeats on the Romans. At Cannae in 216 B.C.E., the Romans lost an army of almost 40,000 men. Rome seemed on the brink of disaster but refused to give up, raised yet another army, and gradually recovered. Although Hannibal remained free to roam in Italy, he had neither the men nor the equipment to lay siege to the major cities, including Rome itself. The Romans began to reconquer some of the Italian cities that had rebelled against Roman rule after Hannibal's successes. More important, the Romans pursued a strategy aimed at undermining the Carthaginian empire in Spain. By 206 B.C.E., the Romans had pushed the Carthaginians out of Spain.

The Romans then took the war directly to Carthage, forcing the Carthaginians to recall Hannibal from Italy. At the Battle of Zama in 202 B.C.E., the Romans decisively defeated Hannibal's forces, and the war was over. By the

MAP 5.2 Roman Conquests in the Mediterranean

THE DESTRUCTION OF CARTHAGE

The Romans used a technical breach of Carthage's peace treaty with Rome to undertake a third and final war with Carthage (149–146 B.C.E.). Although Carthage posed no real threat to Rome's security, the Romans still remembered the traumatic experiences of the Second Punic War, when Hannibal had ravaged much of their homeland. The hard-liners gained the upper hand in the senate and called for the complete destruction of Carthage. The city was razed, the survivors sold into slavery, and the land turned into a province. In this passage, the historian Appian of Alexandria describes the final destruction of Carthage by the Romans under the command of Scipio Aemilianus.

APPIAN, ROMAN HISTORY

Then came new scenes of horror. The fire spread and carried everything down, and the soldiers did not wait to destroy the buildings little by little, but pulled them all down together. So the crashing grew louder, and many fell with the stones into the midst dead. Others were seen still living, especially old men, women, and young children who had hidden in the inmost nooks of the houses, some of them wounded, some more or less burned, and uttering horrible cries. Still others, thrust out and falling from such a height with the stones, timbers, and fire, were torn asunder into all kinds of horrible shapes, crushed and mangled. Nor was this the end of their miseries, for the street cleaners, who were removing the rubbish with axes, mattocks, and boat hooks, and making the roads passable, tossed with these instruments the dead and the living together into holes in the ground, sweeping them along like sticks and stones or turning them over with their iron tools, and man was used for filling up a ditch. Some were thrown in head foremost, while their legs, sticking out of the ground, writhed a long time. Others fell with their feet downward and their heads above ground. Horses ran over them, crushing their faces and skulls, not purposely on the part of the riders, but in their headlong haste. Nor did the street cleaners either do these things on purpose; but the press of war, the glory of approaching victory, the rush of the soldiery, the confused noise of heralds and trumpeters all round, the tribunes and centurions changing guard and marching the cohorts hither and thither—all together made everybody frantic and heedless of the spectacle before their eyes.

Six days and nights were consumed in this kind of turmoil, the soldiers being changed so that they might not be worn out with toil, slaughter, want of sleep, and these horrid sights. . . .

Scipio, beholding this city, which had flourished 700 years from its foundation and had ruled over so many lands, islands, and seas, as rich in arms and fleets, elephants, and money as the mightiest empires, but far surpassing them in hardihood and high spirit . . . now come to its end in total destruction—Scipio, beholding this spectacle, is said to have shed tears and publicly lamented the fortune of the enemy. After meditating by himself a long time and reflecting on the inevitable fall of cities, nations, and empires, as well as of individuals, upon the fate of Troy, that once proud city, upon the fate of the Assyrian, the Median, and afterwards of the great Persian empire, and, most recently of all, of the splendid empire of Macedon, either voluntarily or otherwise the words of the poet [Homer, *Iliad*] escaped his lips:

> The day shall come in which our sacred Troy
> And Priam, and the people over whom
> Spear-bearing Priam rules, shall perish all.

Being asked by Polybius in familiar conversation (for Polybius had been his tutor) what he meant by using these words, Polybius says that he did not hesitate frankly to name his own country, for whose fate he feared when he considered the mutability of human affairs. And Polybius wrote this down just as he heard it.

peace treaty signed in 201 B.C.E., Carthage lost Spain, agreed to pay an indemnity, and promised not to go to war without Rome's permission. Spain was made into another Roman province. Rome had become the dominant power in the western Mediterranean.

Fifty years later, the Romans fought their third and final struggle with Carthage. The Carthaginians had technically broken their peace treaty with Rome by going to war against one of Rome's North African allies who had been encroaching on Carthage's home territory. The Romans used this opportunity to carry out the complete destruction of Carthage in 146 B.C.E., a policy advocated by a number of Romans, especially the conservative politician Cato, who ended every speech he made to the senate with the words, "And I think Carthage must be destroyed"

(see the box above). The territory of Carthage became a Roman province called Africa.

The Eastern Mediterranean

During the Punic Wars, Rome had become acutely aware of the Hellenistic states of the eastern Mediterranean when the king of Macedonia made an alliance with Hannibal after the Roman defeat at Cannae. But Rome was preoccupied with the Carthaginians, and it was not until after the defeat of Carthage that Rome became involved in the world of Hellenistic politics as an advocate of the freedom of the Greek states. This support of the Greeks brought the Romans into conflict with both Macedonia and the kingdom of the Seleucids. Roman military appeared on the horizon, involving them in yet more conflicts. Indeed, the Romans liked to portray themselves as declaring war only for defensive reasons or to protect allies. That is only part of the story, however. It is likely, as some historians have recently suggested, that at some point a group of Roman aristocratic leaders emerged who favored expansion both for the glory it offered and for the economic benefits it provided. Certainly, by the second century B.C.E., aristocratic senators perceived new opportunities for lucrative foreign commands, enormous spoils of war, and an abundant supply of slave labor for their growing landed estates. By that same time, the destruction of Corinth and Carthage indicate Roman imperialism had become more arrogant and brutal as well. Rome's foreign success also had enormous repercussions for the internal development of the Roman Republic.

THE DECLINE AND FALL OF THE ROMAN REPUBLIC (133–31 B.C.E.)

By the mid-second century B.C.E., Roman domination of the Mediterranean Sea was well established. Yet the process of creating an empire had weakened and threatened the internal stability of Rome. This led to a series of crises that plagued Rome for the next hundred years.

Growing Inequality and Unrest

By the second century B.C.E., the senate had become the effective governing body of the Roman state. It comprised some 300 men, drawn primarily from the landed aristocracy; they remained senators for life and held the chief magistracies of the Republic. During the wars of the third and second centuries, the senate came to exercise enormous power. It directed the wars and took control of both foreign and domestic policy, including financial affairs.

Moreover, the magistracies and senate were increasingly controlled by a relatively select circle of wealthy and powerful families—both patrician and plebeian—called the *nobiles* ("nobles"). In the hundred years from 233 to 133 B.C.E., 80 percent of the consuls came from twenty-six families; moreover, 50 percent came from only ten families. Hence, the *nobiles* constituted a governing oligarchy that managed, through its landed wealth, system of patronage, and intimidation, to maintain its hold over the magistracies and senate and thus guide the destiny of Rome while running the state in its own interests.

Of course, these aristocrats formed only a tiny minority of the Roman people. The backbone of the Roman state and army had traditionally been the small farmers. But over a period of time many small farmers had found themselves unable to compete with large, wealthy landowners and had lost their lands. By taking over state-

victories and diplomatic negotiations rearranged the territorial boundaries of the Hellenistic kingdoms and brought the Greek states their freedom in 196 B.C.E. For fifty years, Rome tried to be a power broker in the affairs of the Greeks without assuming direct control of their lands. When these efforts failed, the Romans changed their policy.

In 148 B.C.E., Macedonia was made a Roman province, and when some of the Greek states rose in revolt against Rome's restrictive policies, Rome acted decisively. The city of Corinth, leader of the revolt, was destroyed in 146 B.C.E. to teach the Greeks a lesson, and Greece was placed under the control of the Roman governor of Macedonia. Thirteen years later, in 133 B.C.E., the king of Pergamum deeded his kingdom to Rome, giving Rome its first province in Asia. Rome was now master of the Mediterranean Sea.

The Nature of Roman Imperialism

Rome's empire was built in three stages: the conquest of Italy, the conflict with Carthage and expansion into the western Mediterranean, and the involvement with and domination of the Hellenistic kingdoms in the eastern Mediterranean. The Romans did not possess a master plan for the creation of an empire. Much of their expansion was opportunistic; once involved in a situation that threatened their security, the Romans did not hesitate to act. And the more they expanded, the more threats to their security owned land and buying out small peasant owners, these landed aristocrats had developed large estates called *latifundia* that used slave labor. Thus, the rise of *latifundia* contributed to a decline in the number of small farmers. Since the latter group traditionally provided the foundation of the Roman army, the number of men available for military service declined. Moreover, many of these small farmers drifted to the cities, especially Rome, forming a large class of landless poor.

Some aristocrats tried to remedy this growing economic and social crisis. Two brothers, Tiberius and Gaius Gracchus, came to believe that the underlying cause of Rome's problems was the decline of the small farmer. To help the landless poor, they bypassed the senate by having the council of the plebs pass land-reform bills that called for the government to reclaim public land held by large landowners and distribute it to landless Romans. Many senators, themselves large landowners whose estates included large areas of public land, were furious. A group of senators took the law into their own hands and killed Tiberius in 133 B.C.E. Twelve years later, his brother Gaius suffered the same fate. The attempts of the Gracchus brothers to bring reforms had opened the door to more instability and further violence. Changes in the Roman army soon brought even worse problems.

A New Role for the Roman Army

In the closing years of the second century B.C.E., a Roman general named Marius began to recruit his armies in a new way. The Roman army had traditionally been a conscript army of small farmers who were landholders. Marius recruited volunteers from both the urban and rural poor who possessed no property. These volunteers swore an oath of loyalty to the general, not the senate, thus inaugurating a professional-type army that might no longer be subject to the state. Moreover, to recruit these men, a general would promise them land, forcing generals to play politics in order to get legislation passed that would provide the land for their veterans. Marius left a powerful legacy. He had created a new system of military recruitment that placed much power in the hands of the individual generals.

Lucius Cornelius Sulla was the next general to take advantage of the new military system. The senate had given him command of a war in Asia Minor, but when the council of the plebs tried to transfer command of this war to Marius, a civil war broke out. Sulla won and seized Rome itself in 82 B.C.E., conducting a reign of terror to wipe out all opposition. Then Sulla restored power to the hands of the senate and eliminated most of the powers of the popular assemblies. Sulla hoped that he had created a firm foundation for the traditional Republic governed by a powerful senate, but his real legacy was quite different from what he had intended. His example of using an army to seize power would prove most attractive to ambitious men.

The Collapse of the Republic

For the next fifty years, Roman history would be characterized by two important features: the jostling for power by a number of powerful individuals and the civil wars generated by their conflicts. Three powerful individuals came to hold enormous military and political power—Crassus, Pompey, and Julius Caesar. Crassus, who was known as the richest man in Rome, had successfully put down a major slave rebellion. Pompey had returned from a successful military command in Spain in 71 B.C.E. and been hailed as a military hero. Julius Caesar also had a military command in Spain. In 60 B.C.E., Caesar joined with Crassus and Pompey to form a coalition that historians called the First Triumvirate.

The combined wealth and power of these three men was enormous, enabling them to dominate the political scene and achieve their basic aims: Pompey received lands for his veterans and a command in Spain; Crassus was given a command in Syria; and Caesar was granted a special military command in Gaul (modern France). When Crassus was killed in battle in 53 B.C.E., his death left two powerful men with armies in direct competition. During his time in Gaul, Caesar had conquered all of Gaul and gained fame, wealth, and military experience as well as an army of seasoned veterans who were loyal to him. When leading senators fastened on Pompey as the least harmful to their cause and voted for Caesar to lay down his command and return as a private citizen to Rome, Caesar refused. He chose to keep his army and moved into Italy by illegally crossing the Rubicon, the river that formed the southern boundary of his province. ("Crossing the Rubicon" is a phrase used today to mean doing something after which there is no turning back.) Caesar marched on Rome, thus guaranteeing a civil war between his forces and those of Pompey and his allies. The defeat of Pompey's forces left Caesar in complete control of the Roman government.

Caesar was officially made dictator in 47 B.C.E., and in 44 B.C.E. he was made dictator for life. Realizing the need for reforms, he gave land to the poor and increased the size of the senate to 900 members. By filling it with many of his supporters and increasing the membership, he effectively weakened the power of the senate. He granted citizenship to a number of people in the provinces who had helped him. He also reformed the calendar by introducing the Egyptian solar year of 365 days (with later changes in 1582, it became the basis of our own calendar). Caesar planned much more in the way of building projects and military adventures in the east, but in 44 B.C.E., a group of leading senators assassinated him (see the box on p. 139).

Within a few years after Caesar's death, two men had divided the Roman world between them—Octavian, Caesar's heir and grandnephew, taking the west and Antony, Caesar's ally and assistant, the east. But the empire of the Romans, large as it was, was still too small for two

CHRONOLOGY

THE DECLINE AND FALL OF THE REPUBLIC

Reforms of Tiberius Gracchus	133 B.C.E.
Reforms of Gaius Gracchus	123–121 B.C.E.
Marius: Consecutive consulships	104–100 B.C.E.
Sulla as dictator	82–79 B.C.E.
First Triumvirate (Caesar, Pompey, Crassus)	60 B.C.E.
Caesar as dictator	47–44 B.C.E.
Octavian defeats Antony at Actium	31 B.C.E.

CAESAR. Conqueror of Gaul and member of the First Triumvirate, Julius Caesar is perhaps the best-known figure of the late Republic. Caesar became dictator of Rome in 47 B.C.E. and, after his victories in the civil war, was made dictator for life. Some members of the senate who resented his power assassinated him in 44 B.C.E. Pictured is a marble copy of the bust of Caesar.

masters, and Octavian and Antony eventually came into conflict. Antony allied himself with the Egyptian queen Cleopatra VII, with whom, like Caesar before him, he fell deeply in love. Octavian began a propaganda campaign, accusing Antony of catering to Cleopatra and giving away Roman territory to this "whore of the east." Finally, at the Battle of Actium in Greece in 31 B.C.E., Octavian's forces smashed the army and navy of Antony and Cleopatra. Both fled to Egypt, where, according to the account of the Roman historian Florus, they committed suicide a year later:

> Antony was the first to commit suicide, by the sword. Cleopatra threw herself at Octavian's feet, and tried her best to attract his gaze: in vain, for his self-control was impervious to her beauty. It was not her life she was after, for that had already been granted, but a portion of her kingdom. When she realized this was hopeless and that she had been earmarked to feature in Octavian's triumph in Rome, she took advantage of her guard's carelessness to get herself into the mausoleum, as the royal tomb is called. Once there, she put on the royal robes which she was accustomed to wear, and lay down in a richly perfumed coffin beside her Antony. Then she applied poisonous snakes to her veins and slipped into death as though into a sleep.[1]

Octavian, at the age of thirty-two, stood supreme over the Roman world. The civil wars were ended. And so was the Republic.

THE AGE OF AUGUSTUS (31 B.C.E.–14 C.E.)

In 27 B.C.E., Octavian proclaimed the "restoration of the Republic." He understood that only traditional republican forms would satisfy the senatorial aristocracy. At the same time, Octavian was aware that the Republic could not be fully restored. Although he gave some power to the senate, in fact, Octavian became the first Roman emperor. In 27 B.C.E., the senate awarded him the title of Augustus— "the revered one"—a fitting title in view of his power, previously reserved for gods. Augustus proved to be highly popular. No doubt, people were glad the civil wars had ended. At the same time, his continuing control of the army was the chief source of Augustus's power. The senate gave Augustus the title of *imperator*, or commander-in-chief. *Imperator* is Latin for our word *emperor*.

Augustus maintained a standing army of twenty-eight legions or about 150,000 men (a legion was a military unit of about 5,000 troops). Only Roman citizens could be legionaries, while subject peoples could serve as auxiliary forces, which numbered around 130,000 under Augustus. Augustus was also responsible for setting up a praetorian guard of roughly 9,000 men who had the important task of guarding the person of the emperor. Eventually, the praetorian guard would play a weighty role in making and deposing emperors.

THE ASSASSINATION OF JULIUS CAESAR

When it quickly became apparent that Julius Caesar had no intention of restoring the Republic as they conceived it, about sixty senators, many of them his friends or pardoned enemies, formed a conspiracy to assassinate the dictator. It was led by Gaius Cassius and Marcus Brutus, who naively imagined that this act would restore the traditional Republic. The conspirators set the Ides of March (March 15), 44 B.C.E. as the date for the assassination. Caesar was in the midst of preparations for a campaign in the eastern part of the empire. Although informed that there was a plot against his life, he chose to disregard the warning. This account of Caesar's death is taken from his biography by the Greek writer Plutarch.

PLUTARCH, *LIFE OF CAESAR*

Fate, however, is to all appearance more unavoidable than unexpected. For many strange prodigies and apparitions are said to have been observed shortly before this event. . . . One finds it also related by many that a soothsayer bade him [Caesar] prepare for some great danger on the Ides of March. When this day was come, Caesar, as he went to the senate, met this soothsayer, and said to him by way of raillery, "The Ides of March are come," who answered him calmly, "Yes, they are come, but they are not past. . . ."

All these things might happen by chance. But the place which was destined for the scene of this murder, in which the senate met that day, was the same in which Pompey's statue stood, and was one of the edifices which Pompey had raised and dedicated with his theater to the use of the public, plainly showing that there was something of a supernatural influence which guided the action and ordered it to that particular place. Cassius, just before the act, is said to have looked toward Pompey's statue, and silently implored his assistance. . . . When Caesar entered, the senate stood up to show their respect to him, and of Brutus's confederates, some came about his chair and stood behind it, others met him, pretending to add their petitions to those of Tillius Cimber, in behalf of his brother, who was in exile; and they followed him with their joint applications till he came to his seat. When he was sat down, he refused to comply with their requests, and upon their urging him further began to reproach them severely for their importunities, when Tillius, laying hold of his robe with both his hands, pulled it down from his neck, which was the signal for the assault. Casca gave him the first cut in the neck, which was not mortal nor dangerous, as coming from one who at the beginning of such a bold action was probably very much disturbed; Caesar immediately turned about, and laid his hand upon the dagger and kept hold of it. And both of them at the same time cried out, he that received the blow, in Latin, "Vile Casca, what does this mean?" and he that gave it, in Greek to his brother, "Brother, help!" Upon this first onset, those who were not privy to the design were astonished, and their horror and amazement at what they saw were so great that they dared not fly nor assist Caesar, nor so much as speak a word. But those who came prepared for the business enclosed him on every side, with their naked daggers in their hands. Which way soever he turned he met with blows, and saw their swords leveled at his face and eyes, and was encompassed like a wild beast in the toils on every side. For it had been agreed they should each of them make a thrust at him, and flesh themselves with his blood: for which reason Brutus also gave him one stab in the groin. Some say that he fought and resisted all the rest, shifting his body to avoid the blows, and calling out for help, but that when he saw Brutus's sword drawn, he covered his face with his robe and submitted, letting himself fall, whether it were by chance or that he was pushed in that direction by his murderers, at the foot of the pedestal on which Pompey's statue stood, and which was thus wetted with his blood. So that Pompey himself seemed to have presided, as it were, over the revenge done upon his adversary, who lay here at his feet, and breathed out his soul through his multitude of wounds, for they say he received three-and-twenty. And the conspirators themselves were many of them wounded by each other, whilst they all leveled their blows at the same person.

While claiming to have restored the Republic, Augustus inaugurated a new system for governing the provinces. Under the Republic, the senate had appointed the governors of the provinces. Now, certain provinces were given to the emperor, who assigned deputies known as legates to govern them. The senate continued to name the governors of the remaining provinces, but the authority of Augustus enabled him to overrule the senatorial governors and establish a uniform imperial policy.

Augustus also stabilized the frontiers of the Roman Empire. He conquered the central and maritime Alps and then expanded Roman control of the Balkan peninsula up to the Danube River. His attempt to conquer Germany failed when three Roman legions were massacred in 9 C.E. by a coalition of German tribes. His defeats in Germany taught Augustus that Rome's power was not unlimited and also devastated him; for months he would beat his head on a door, shouting "Varus [the defeated Roman general in Germany], give me back my legions!"

Augustan Society

Roman society in the Early Empire was characterized by a system of social stratification, inherited from the Republic, in which Roman citizens were divided into three basic classes: the senatorial, equestrian, and lower classes.

AUGUSTUS.   Octavian, Caesar's adopted son, emerged victorious from the civil conflict that rocked the Republic after Caesar's assassination. Augustus operated through a number of legal formalities to ensure that control of the Roman state rested firmly in his hands. This marble statue from Prima Porta depicts the *princeps* Augustus.

Although each class had its own functions and opportunities, the system was not completely rigid. There were possibilities for mobility from one group to another.

Augustus had accepted the senatorial order as a ruling class for the empire. Senators filled the chief magistracies of the Roman government, held the most important military posts, and governed the provinces. One needed to possess property worth 1,000,000 sesterces (an unskilled laborer in Rome received 3 sesterces a day; a Roman legionary, 900 sesterces a year in pay) to belong to the senatorial order. The equestrian order was

expanded under Augustus and given a share of power in the new imperial state. The equestrian order was open to all Roman citizens of good standing who possessed property valued at 400,000 sesterces. They, too, could now hold military and governmental offices, but the positions open to them were less important than those of the senatorial order.

Those citizens not of the senatorial or equestrian orders belonged to the lower classes, who obviously constituted the overwhelming majority of the free citizens. The diminution of the power of the Roman assemblies ended whatever political power they may have possessed earlier in the Republic. Many of these people were provided with free grain and public spectacles to keep them from creating disturbances. Nevertheless, by gaining wealth and serving as lower officers in the Roman legions, it was sometimes possible for them to advance to the equestrian order.

The Augustan Age was a lengthy one. Augustus died in 14 C.E. after dominating the Roman world for forty-five years. He had created a new order while placating those who yearned for the old by restoring and maintaining traditional values, a fitting combination for a leader whose favorite maxim was "make haste slowly." By the time of his death, his new order was so well established that few agitated for an alternative. Indeed, as the Roman historian Tacitus pointed out, "Actium had been won before the younger men were born. Even most of the older generation had come into a world of civil wars. Practically no one had ever seen truly Republican government. . . . Political equality was a thing of the past; all eyes watched for imperial commands."[2] The Republic was now only a memory and, given its last century of warfare, an unpleasant one at that. The new order was here to stay.

THE EARLY EMPIRE (14–180)

There was no serious opposition to Augustus's choice of his stepson Tiberius as his successor. By his actions, Augustus established the Julio-Claudian dynasty; the next four successors of Augustus were related either to his own family or that of his wife, Livia.

Several major tendencies emerged during the reigns of the Julio-Claudians (14–68 C.E.). In general, more and more of the responsibilities that Augustus had given to the senate tended to be taken over by the emperors, who also instituted an imperial bureaucracy, staffed by talented freedmen, to run the government on a daily basis. As the Julio-Claudian successors of Augustus acted more openly as real rulers rather than as "first citizens of the state," the opportunity for arbitrary and corrupt acts also increased. Nero (54–68) freely eliminated people he wanted out of the way, including his own mother, whom he had murdered. Without troops, the senators proved unable to oppose these excesses. However, Nero's extravagances did provoke a revolt of the Roman legions. Abandoned by his guards, Nero chose to commit suicide by stabbing himself in the throat after uttering his final words, "What an artist the world is losing in me." A new civil war erupted in 69, known as the year of the four emperors. The significance of the year 69 was summed up precisely by Tacitus when he stated that "a well-hidden secret of the principate had been revealed: it was possible, it seemed, for an emperor to be chosen outside Rome."[3]

The Five "Good Emperors" (96–180)

At the beginning of the second century, however, a series of five so-called good emperors created a period of peace and prosperity that lasted for almost a hundred years. These rulers treated the ruling classes with respect, cooperated with the senate, ended arbitrary executions, maintained peace throughout the empire, and supported domestic policies generally beneficial to the empire. Though absolute monarchs, they were known for their tolerance and diplomacy. By adopting capable men as their successors, the first four good emperors reduced the chances of succession problems.

Under the five good emperors, the powers of the emperor continued to be extended at the expense of the senate. Increasingly, imperial officials appointed and directed by the emperor took over the running of the government. The good emperors also extended the scope of imperial administration to include areas previously untouched by the imperial government. Trajan (98–117) implemented the establishment of an alimentary program that provided state funds to assist poor parents in raising and educating their children.

The good emperors were widely praised by their subjects for their extensive building programs. Trajan and Hadrian (117–138) were especially active in constructing public works—aqueducts, bridges, roads, and harbor facilities—throughout the provinces and in Rome. Trajan built a new forum in Rome to provide a setting for his celebrated

MAP 5.3   The Roman Empire from 14 to 117

Roman Empire at the end of Augustus's reign, 14 C.E.

Roman Empire at the end of Trajan's reign, 117 C.E.

0   300   600   900 Kilometers

0   300   600 Miles

victory column. Hadrian's Pantheon, a temple of "all the gods," is one of the grandest ancient buildings surviving in Rome.

The Roman Empire at Its Height: Frontiers and the Provinces

Although Trajan broke with Augustus's policy of defensive imperialism by extending Roman rule into Dacia (modern Romania), Mesopotamia, and the Sinai peninsula, his conquests represent the high-water mark of Roman expansion. His successors recognized that the empire was overextended and pursued a policy of retrenchment. Hadrian withdrew Roman forces from much of Mesopotamia. Although he retained Dacia and Arabia, he went on the defensive in his frontier policy by reinforcing the fortifications along a line connecting the Rhine and Danube Rivers and building a defensive wall eighty miles long across northern Britain to keep the Scots out of Roman Britain. By the end of the second century, the vulnerability of the empire had become apparent. Frontiers were stabilized, and the Roman forces were established in permanent bases behind the frontiers. But when one frontier was attacked, troops had to be drawn from other frontiers, leaving them vulnerable to attack. The empire lacked a real strategic reserve, and in the next century its weakness would be ever more apparent.

At its height in the second century, the Roman Empire was one of the greatest states the world had seen. It covered about three and a half million square miles and had a population, like that of Han China, that has been estimated at more than 50 million. While the emperors and the imperial administration provided a degree of unity, considerable leeway was given to local customs, and the privileges of Roman citizenship were extended to many people throughout the empire. In 212, the emperor Caracalla completed the process by giving Roman citizenship to every free inhabitant of the empire. Latin was the language of the western part of the empire, while Greek was used in the east. Although Roman culture spread to all parts of the empire, there were limits to romanization since local languages persisted and many of the empire's residents spoke neither Latin nor Greek.

The administration and cultural life of the Roman Empire depended greatly upon cities and towns. A provincial governor's staff was not large, so local city officials were expected to act as Roman agents in carrying out many government functions, especially those related to taxes. Most towns and cities were not large by modern standards. The largest was Rome, but there were also some large cities in the east: Alexandria in Egypt numbered over 300,000 inhabitants, Ephesus in Asia Minor had 200,000, and Antioch in Syria had around 150,000. In the west, cities were usually small, with only a few thousand inhabitants. Cities were important in the spread of Roman culture, law,

and the Latin language. They were also uniform in physical appearance, with similar temples, markets, amphitheaters, and other public buildings.

Magistrates and town councillors chosen from the ranks of the wealthy upper classes directed municipal administration. These municipal offices were unsalaried but were nevertheless desired by wealthy citizens because they received prestige and power at the local level as well as Roman citizenship. Roman municipal policy effectively tied the upper classes to Roman rule and ensured that these classes would retain control over the rest of the population.

The process of romanization in the provinces was reflected in significant changes in the governing classes of the empire. In the course of the first century, there was a noticeable decline in the number of senators from Italian families. By the end of the second century, Italian senators made up less than 50 percent of the total. Increasingly, the Roman senate was being recruited from wealthy provincial equestrian families. The provinces also provided many of the legionaries for the Roman army and, beginning with Trajan, supplied many of the emperors.

Prosperity in the Early Empire

The Early Empire was a period of considerable prosperity. Internal peace resulted in unprecedented levels of trade. Merchants from all over the empire came to the chief Italian ports of Puteoli on the Bay of Naples and Ostia at the mouth of the Tiber. Trade extended beyond the Roman boundaries and included even silk goods from China. But the patterns of trade were somewhat unbalanced. The importation of large quantities of grain to feed the populace of Rome and an incredible quantity of luxury items for the wealthy upper classes in the west led to a steady drainage of gold and silver coins from Italy and the west to the eastern part of the empire.

Increased trade helped to stimulate manufacturing. The cities of the east still produced the items made in Hellenistic times. The first two centuries of the empire also witnessed the high point of industrial development in Italy. Some industries became concentrated in certain areas, such as bronze work in Capua and pottery in Arretium in Etruria. Other industries, such as brick making, were pursued in rural areas as by-products of large landed estates. Much industrial production remained small in scale and was done by individual artisans, usually freedmen or slaves. In the course of the first century, Italian centers of industry began to experience increasing competition from the provinces.

Despite the extensive trade and commerce, agriculture remained the chief occupation of most people and the underlying basis of Roman prosperity. While the large landed estates called *latifundia* still dominated agriculture,

Trade was an important ingredient in the prosperity of the Early Empire. This tomb painting from Ostia, the port of Rome at the mouth of the Tiber, shows workers loading grain onto the *Isis Giminiana*, a small merchant ship, for shipment upriver to Rome. The captain of the ship stands by the rudder. Next to him is Abascantus, the ship's owner.

especially in southern and central Italy, small peasant farms persisted, particularly in Etruria and the Po valley. Although large estates concentrating on sheep and cattle raising used slaves, the lands of some *latifundia* were worked by free tenant farmers who paid rent in labor, produce, or sometimes cash.

In considering the prosperity of the Roman world, it is important to remember the enormous gulf between rich and poor. The development of towns and cities, so important to the creation of any civilization, is based in large degree upon the agricultural surpluses of the countryside. In ancient times, the margin of surplus produced by each farmer was relatively small. Therefore, the upper classes and urban populations had to be supported by the labor of a large number of agricultural producers who never found it easy to produce much more than they needed for themselves. In lean years, when there were no surpluses, the townspeople often took what they wanted, leaving little for the peasants.

❀ CULTURE AND SOCIETY IN THE ROMAN WORLD

One of the most noticeable characteristics of Roman culture and society is the impact of the Greeks. Greek ambassadors, merchants, and artists traveled to Rome and spread Greek thought and practices. After their conquest of the Hellenistic kingdoms, Roman military commanders shipped Greek manuscripts and artworks back to Rome. Multitudes of educated Greek slaves labored in Roman households. Rich Romans hired Greek tutors and sent their sons to Athens to study. As the Roman poet Horace said, "captive Greece took captive her rude conqueror." Greek thought captivated Roman minds, and the Romans became willing transmitters of Greek culture—not, however, without some resistance from Romans who had nothing but contempt for Greek politics and feared that Greek notions would put an end to the old Roman values. Even those who favored Greek culture blamed the Greeks for Rome's new vices, including luxury and homosexual practices.

Roman Literature

The Latin literature that first emerged in the third century B.C.E. was strongly influenced by Greek models, and it was not until the last century of the Republic that the Romans began to produce a new poetry in which Latin poets were able to use various Greek forms to express their own feelings about people, social and political life, and love. The finest example of this can be seen in the work of Catullus (c. 87–54 B.C.E.), the "best lyric poet" Rome produced and one of the greatest in world literature.

Catullus became a master at adapting and refining Greek forms of poetry to express his emotions. He wrote a variety of poems on, among other things, political figures, social customs, the use of language, the death of his brother, and the travails of love. Catullus became infatuated with Clodia, the promiscuous sister of a tribune and wife of a provincial governor, and addressed a number of poems to her (he called her Lesbia), describing his passionate love and hatred for her (Clodia had many other lovers besides Catullus):

> You used to say that you wished to know only Catullus,
>   Lesbia, and wouldn't take even Jove before me!
> I didn't regard you just as my mistress then: I cherished you
>   as a father does his sons or his daughters' husbands.
> Now that I know you, I burn for you even more fiercely,
>   though I regard you as almost utterly worthless.
> How can that be, you ask? It's because such cruelty forces
>   lust to assume the shrunken place of affection.[4]

The ability of Catullus to express in simple fashion his intense feelings and curiosity about himself and his world had a noticeable impact on later Latin poets.

The development of Roman prose was greatly aided by the practice of oratory. Romans had great respect for oratory because the ability to persuade people in public debate meant success in politics. Oratory was brought to perfection in a literary fashion by Cicero (106–43 B.C.E.), the best exemplar of the literary and intellectual interests of the senatorial elite of the late Republic and, indeed, the greatest prose writer of that period. For Cicero, oratory was not simply skillful speaking. An orator was a statesman,

ROMAN THEATER: REHEARSAL OF A GREEK PLAY.
This mosaic found at Pompeii shows Roman actors preparing to
present a Greek play. The seated figure is the chorus master, who
observes two actors dancing to the music of a pipe.

a man who achieved his highest goal by pursuing an active
life in public affairs.

The high point of Latin literature was reached in the age
of Augustus. The literary accomplishments of the Augustan age were such that the period has been called the golden
age of Latin literature. The most distinguished poet of the
Augustan age was Virgil (70–19 B.C.E.). The son of a small
landholder in northern Italy, he welcomed the rule of
Augustus and wrote his greatest work in his honor. Virgil's
masterpiece was *The Aeneid*, an epic poem clearly meant to
rival the work of Homer. The connection between Troy and
Rome is made in the poem when Aeneas, a hero of Troy,
survives the destruction of Troy and eventually settles in
Latium; hence, Roman civilization is linked to Greek history. The character of Aeneas is portrayed as the ideal
Roman—his virtues are duty, piety, and faithfulness. Virgil's
overall purpose was to show that Aeneas had fulfilled his
mission to establish the Romans in Italy and thereby start
Rome on its divine mission to rule the world.

> *Let others fashion from bronze more lifelike, breathing*
>   *images—*
> *For so they shall—and evoke living faces from marble;*
> *Others excel as orators, others track with their instruments*
> *The planets circling in heaven and predict when stars will*
>   *appear.*
> *But, Romans, never forget that government is your medium!*
> *Be this your art:—to practice men in the habit of peace,*
> *Generosity to the conquered, and firmness against aggressors.*[5]

As Virgil expressed it, ruling was Rome's gift.

Another prominent Augustan poet was Horace (65–8
B.C.E.), a friend of Virgil. He was a very sophisticated writer
whose overriding concern was to point out to his contemporaries the "follies and vices of his age." In his *Satires*,
a medley of poems on a variety of subjects, Horace is
revealed as a detached observer of human weaknesses. He

directed his attacks against movements, not living people,
and took on such subjects as sexual immorality, greed, and
job dissatisfaction ("How does it happen, Maecenas, that
no man alone is content with his lot?"[6]). Horace mostly
laughs at the weaknesses of humankind and calls for forbearance: "Supposing my friend has got liquored and wetted my couch, . . . is he for such a lapse to be deemed less
dear as a friend, or because when hungry he snatched up
before me a chicken from my side of the dish?"[7]

Ovid (43 B.C.E.–18 C.E.) was the last of the great poets
of the golden age. He belonged to a youthful, privileged
social group in Rome that liked to ridicule old Roman values. In keeping with the spirit of this group, Ovid wrote
a series of frivolous love poems known as the *Amores*.
Intended to entertain and shock, they achieved their goal.
Another of Ovid's works was *The Art of Love*. This was
essentially a takeoff on didactic poems. Whereas authors
of earlier didactic poems had written guides to farming,
hunting, or some such subject, Ovid's work was a handbook on the seduction of women (see the box on p. 145).

The most famous Latin prose work of the golden age
was written by the historian Livy (59 B.C.E.–17 C.E.). Livy's
masterpiece was the *History of Rome*, which covered the
period from the foundation of the city to 9 B.C.E. Only
35 of the original 142 books have survived, although we
do possess brief summaries of the whole work from other
authors. Livy perceived history in terms of moral lessons.
He stated in the preface that

> The study of history is the best medicine for a sick mind;
> for in history you have a record of the infinite variety of
> human experience plainly set out for all to see; and in that
> record you can find for yourself and your country both examples and warnings: fine things to take as models, base things,
> rotten through and through, to avoid.[8]

For Livy, human character was the determining factor in
history.

Livy's history celebrated Rome's greatness. He included
scene upon scene that not only revealed the character of
the chief figures but also demonstrated the virtues that had
made Rome great. Of course, he had serious weaknesses as
a historian. He was not always concerned about the factual accuracy of his myriad stories and was not overly critical of his sources. But he did tell a good story, and his work
became the standard history of Rome for a long time.

In the history of Latin literature, the century and a half
after Augustus is often labeled the "silver age" to indicate that the literary efforts of the period, while good, were
not equal to the high standards of the Augustan "golden
age." The popularity of rhetorical training encouraged the
use of clever and ornate literary expressions at the expense
of original and meaningful content. A good example of
this trend can be found in the works of Seneca.

Educated in Rome, Seneca (c. 4 B.C.E.–65 C.E.) became
strongly attached to the philosophy of Stoicism. In letters
written to a young friend, he expressed the basic tenets

OVID AND THE ART OF LOVE

Ovid has been called the last great poet of the Augustan golden age of literature. One of his most famous works was The Art of Love, *a guidebook on the seduction of women. Unfortunately for Ovid, the work appeared at a time when Augustus was anxious to improve the morals of the Roman upper class. Augustus considered the poem offensive, and Ovid soon found himself in exile.*

OVID, *THE ART OF LOVE*

Now I'll teach you how to captivate and hold the woman of your choice. This is the most important part of all my lessons. Lovers of every land, lend an attentive ear to my discourse; let goodwill warm your hearts, for I am going to fulfill the promises I made you.

First of all, be quite sure that there isn't a woman who cannot be won, and make up your mind that you will win her. Only you must prepare the ground. Sooner would the birds cease their song in the springtime, or the grasshopper be silent in the summer . . . than a woman resist the tender wooing of a youthful lover. . . .

Now the first thing you have to do is to get on good terms with the fair one's maid. She can make things easy for you. Find out whether she is fully in her mistress's confidence, and if she knows all about her secret dissipations. Leave no stone unturned to win her over. Once you have her on your side, the rest is easy. . . .

In the first place, it's best to send her a letter, just to pave the way. In it you should tell her how you dote on her; pay her pretty compliments and say all the nice things lovers always say. . . . Even the gods are moved by the voice of entreaty. And promise, promise, promise. Promises will cost you nothing. Everyone's a millionaire where promises are concerned. . . .

If she refuses your letter and sends it back unread, don't give up; hope for the best and try again. . . .

Don't let your hair stick up in tufts on your head; see that your hair and your beard are decently trimmed. See also that your nails are clean and nicely filed; don't have any hair growing out of your nostrils; take care that your breath is sweet, and don't go about reeking like a billy goat. All other toilet refinements leave to the women or to perverts. . . .

When you find yourself at a feast where the wine is flowing freely, and where a woman shares the same couch with you, pray to that god whose mysteries are celebrated during the night, that the wine may not overcloud your brain. 'Tis then you may easily hold converse with your mistress in hidden words whereof she will easily divine the meaning. . . .

By subtle flatteries you may be able to steal into her heart, even as the river insensibly overflows the banks which fringe it. Never cease to sing the praises of her face, her hair, her taper fingers and her dainty foot. . . .

Tears, too, are a mighty useful resource in the matter of love. They would melt a diamond. Make a point, therefore, of letting your mistress see your face all wet with tears. Howbeit, if you can't manage to squeeze out any tears—and they won't always flow just when you want them to—put your finger in your eyes.

---

of Stoicism: living according to nature, accepting events dispassionately as part of the divine plan, and a universal love for all humanity. Thus, "the first thing philosophy promises us is the feeling of fellowship, of belonging to mankind and being members of a community. . . . Philosophy calls for simple living, not for doing penance, and the simple way of life need not be a crude one."[9] Viewed in retrospect, Seneca displays some glaring inconsistencies. While preaching the virtues of simplicity, he amassed a fortune and was ruthless at times in protecting it. His letters show humanity, benevolence, and fortitude, but his sentiments are often undermined by an attempt to be clever with words.

The greatest historian of the silver age was Tacitus (c. 56–120). His main works included the *Annals* and *Histories*, which presented a narrative account of Roman history from the reign of Tiberius through the assassination of Domitian (14–96). Tacitus believed that history had a moral purpose: "It seems to me a historian's foremost duty is to ensure that merit is recorded, and to confront evil deeds and words with the fear of posterity's denunciations."[10]

As a member of the senatorial class, Tacitus was disgusted with the abuses of power perpetrated by the emperors and determined that the "evil deeds" of wicked men would not be forgotten. His work *Germania* is especially important as a source of information about the early Germans. But it too is colored by Tacitus's attempt to show the Germans as noble savages in comparison to the decadent Romans.

Art

The Romans were also dependent on the Greeks for artistic inspiration. During the third and second centuries B.C.E., they adopted many features of the Hellenistic style of art. The Romans developed a taste for Greek statues, which they placed not only in public buildings, but in their private houses. Once demand outstripped the supply of original works, reproductions of Greek statues became fashionable. The Romans' own portrait sculpture was characterized by an intense realism that included even unpleasant physical details. Wall paintings and frescoes in the houses of the rich realistically depicted

INTERIOR OF THE COLOSSEUM OF ROME. The Colosseum was a large amphitheater constructed under the emperor Vespasian and his son Titus. The amphitheaters in which the gladiatorial contests were held varied in size throughout the empire. The Roman emperors understood that gladiatorial shows and other forms of entertainment helped to divert the poor and destitute from any political unrest.

landscapes, portraits, and scenes from mythological stories.

The Romans excelled in architecture, a highly practical art. Although they continued to utilize Greek styles and made use of colonnades, rectangular structures, and post and lintel construction, the Romans were also innovative. They made considerable use of curvilinear forms: the arch, vault, and dome. The Romans were also the first people in antiquity to use concrete on a massive scale. By combining concrete and curvilinear forms, they were able to construct massive buildings—public baths, such as those of Caracalla, and amphitheaters, the most famous of which was the Colosseum in Rome, capable of seating 50,000 spectators. These large buildings were made possible by Roman engineering skills. These same skills were put to use in constructing roads (the Romans built a network of 50,000 miles of roads throughout their empire), aqueducts (in Rome, almost a dozen aqueducts kept a population of one million supplied with water), and bridges.

Roman Law

One of Rome's chief gifts to the Mediterranean world of its day and to later generations was its system of law. The Twelve Tables of 450 B.C.E. was Rome's first code of laws, but it was a product of a simple farming society and proved inadequate for later Roman needs. Nevertheless, from the Twelve Tables the Romans developed a system of civil law that applied only to Roman citizens. As Rome expanded, Romans became involved in problems between Romans and non-Romans as well as between two non-Romans. The Romans found that although some of their rules of

civil law could be used in these cases, special rules were often needed. These rules gave rise to a body of law known as the law of nations, defined by the Romans as "that part of the law which we apply both to ourselves and to foreigners." Under the influence of Stoicism (see Chapter 4), the Romans came to identify their law of nations with natural law, or universal law based on reason. This enabled them to establish standards of justice that applied to all people.

These standards of justice included principles that we would immediately recognize. A person was regarded as innocent until proven otherwise. People accused of wrongdoing were allowed to defend themselves before a judge. A judge, in turn, was expected to weigh evidence carefully before arriving at a decision. These principles lived on long after the fall of the Roman Empire.

The Roman Family

At the heart of the Roman social structure stood the family, headed by the *paterfamilias*—the dominant male. The household also included the wife, sons with their wives and children, unmarried daughters, and slaves. A family was virtually a small state within the state, and the power of the *paterfamilias* was parallel to that of the state magistrates over the citizens. Like the Greeks, Roman males believed that the weakness of the female sex necessitated male guardians (see the box on p. 147). The *paterfamilias* exercised that authority; upon his death, sons or nearest male relatives assumed the role of guardians. By the late Republic, however, although the rights of male guardians remained legally in effect, upper-class women found numerous ways to circumvent the power of their guardians.

Fathers arranged the marriages of their daughters, although there are instances of mothers and daughters having influence on the choice. In the Republic, women married "with legal control" passing from father to husband. By the mid-first century B.C.E., the dominant practice had changed to "without legal control," which meant that married daughters officially remained within the father's legal power. Since the fathers of most married women were dead, not being in the "legal control" of a husband entailed independent property rights that forceful women could translate into considerable power within the household and outside it. Traditionally, Roman marriages were intended to be for life, but divorce was introduced in the third century B.C.E. and became relatively easy to obtain since either party could initiate it and no one needed to prove the breakdown of the marriage. Divorce became especially prevalent in the first century B.C.E.—a period of political turmoil—when marriages were used to cement political alliances.

Some parents in upper-class families provided education for their daughters. Some girls had private tutors and others may have gone to primary schools. But, at the

CATO THE ELDER ON WOMEN

During the Second Punic War, the Romans enacted the Oppian Law, which limited the amount of gold women could possess and restricted their dress and use of carriages. In 195 B.C.E., an attempt to repeal the law was made, and women demonstrated in the streets on behalf of this effort. According to the Roman historian Livy, the conservative Roman official Cato the Elder spoke against repeal and against the women favoring it. Although the words are probably not Cato's own, they do reflect a traditional male Roman attitude toward women.

LIVY, *THE HISTORY OF ROME*

"If each of us, citizens, had determined to assert his rights and dignity as a husband with respect to his own spouse, we should have less trouble with the sex as a whole; as it is, our liberty, destroyed at home by female violence, even here in the Forum is crushed and trodden underfoot, and because we have not kept them individually under control, we dread them collectively. . . . But from no class is there not the greatest danger if you permit them meetings and gatherings and secret consultations. . . .

"Our ancestors permitted no women to conduct even personal business without a guardian to intervene in her behalf; they wished them to be under the control of fathers, brothers, husbands; we (Heaven help us!) allow them now even to interfere in public affairs, yes, and to visit the Forum and our informal and formal sessions. What else are they doing now on the streets and at the corners except urging the bill of the tribunes and voting for the repeal of the law? Give loose rein to their uncontrollable nature and to this untamed creature and expect that they will themselves set bounds to their license; unless you act, this is the least of the things enjoined upon women by custom or law and to which they submit with a feeling of injustice. It is complete liberty or, rather, if we wish to speak the truth, complete license that they desire.

"If they win in this, what will they not attempt? Review all the laws with which your forefathers restrained their license and made them subject to their husbands; even with all these bonds you can scarcely control them. What of this? If you suffer them to seize these bonds one by one and wrench themselves free and finally to be placed on a parity with their husbands, do you think that you will be able to endure them? The moment they begin to be your equals, they will be your superiors. . . .

"Now they publicly address other women's husbands, and, what is more serious, they beg for a law and votes, and from sundry men they get what they ask. In matters affecting yourself, your property, your children, you, Sir, can be importuned; once the law has ceased to set a limit to your wife's expenditures you will never set it yourself. Do not think, citizens, that the situation which existed before the law was passed will ever return."

age when boys were entering secondary schools, girls were pushed into marriage. The legal minimum age for marriage was twelve, although fourteen was a more common age in practice. Although some Roman doctors warned that pregnancy could be dangerous for young girls, early marriages persisted due to the desire to benefit from the dowries as soon as possible and the reality of early mortality. A good example is Tullia, Cicero's beloved daughter. She was married at sixteen, widowed at twenty-two, remarried one year later, divorced at twenty-eight, remarried at twenty-nine, and divorced at thirty-three. She died at thirty-four, not unusual for females in Roman society.

By the second century C.E., significant changes were occurring in the Roman family. The foundations of the authority of the *paterfamilias* over his family, which had already begun to weaken in the late Republic, were further undermined. The *paterfamilias* no longer had absolute authority over his children; he could no longer sell them into slavery or have them put to death. Moreover, the husband's absolute authority over his wife also disappeared, a trend that had begun in the late Republic. In the Early Empire, the idea of male guardianship continued to weaken significantly, and by the late second century,

✿ **A ROMAN LADY.** Roman women, especially those of the upper class, developed comparatively more freedom than women in classical Athens despite the persistent male belief that women required guardianship. This mural decoration was found in the remains of a villa destroyed by the eruption of Mount Vesuvius

THE ROMAN FEAR OF SLAVES

The lowest stratum of the Roman population consisted of slaves. They were used extensively in households, at the court, as artisans in industrial enterprises, as business managers, and in numerous other ways. Although some historians have argued that slaves were treated more humanely during the Early Empire, these selections by the Roman historian Tacitus and the Roman statesman Pliny indicate that slaves still rebelled against their masters because of mistreatment. Many masters continued to live in fear of their slaves as witnessed by the saying, "As many enemies as you have slaves."

TACITUS, *THE ANNALS OF IMPERIAL ROME*

Soon afterwards the City Prefect, Lucius Pedanius Secundus, was murdered by one of his slaves [61 C.E.]. Either Pedanius had refused to free the murderer after agreeing to a price, or the slave, in a homosexual infatuation, found competition from his master intolerable. After the murder, ancient custom required that every slave residing under the same roof must be executed. But a crowd gathered, eager to save so many innocent lives; and rioting began. The senate-house was besieged. Inside, there was feeling against excessive severity, but the majority opposed any change. Among the latter was Gaius Cassius Longinus, who when his turn came spoke as follows. . . .

"An ex-consul has been deliberately murdered by a slave in his own home. None of his fellow-slaves prevented or betrayed the murderer, though the senatorial decree threatening the whole household with execution still stands. Exempt them from the penalty if you like. But then, if the City Prefect was not important enough to be immune; who will be? Who will have enough slaves to protect him if Pedanius's four hundred were too few? Who can rely on his household's help if even fear for their own lives does not make them shield us?"

[The sentence of death was carried out.]

PLINY THE YOUNGER TO ACILIUS

This horrible affair demands more publicity than a letter—Larcius Macedo, a senator and ex-praetor, has fallen a victim to his own slaves. Admittedly he was a cruel and overbearing master, too ready to forget that his father had been a slave, or perhaps too keenly conscious of it. He was taking a bath in his house at Formiae when suddenly he found himself surrounded; one slave seized him by the throat while the others struck his face and hit him in the chest and stomach and—shocking to say—in his private parts. When they thought he was dead they threw him onto the hot pavement, to make sure he was not still alive. Whether unconscious or feigning to be so, he lay there motionless, thus making them believe that he was quite dead. Only then was he carried out, as if he had fainted with the heat, and received by his slaves who had remained faithful, while his concubines ran up, screaming frantically. Roused by their cries and revived by the cooler air he opened his eyes and made some movement to show that he was alive, it being now safe to do so. The guilty slaves fled, but most of them have been arrested and a search is being made for the others. Macedo was brought back to life with difficulty, but only for a few days; at least he died with the satisfaction of having revenged himself, for he lived to see the same punishment meted out as for murder. There you see the dangers, outrages, and insults to which we are exposed. No master can feel safe because he is kind and considerate; for it is their brutality, not their reasoning capacity, which leads slaves to murder masters.

---

though guardianships had not been abolished, they had become a formality.

Upper-class Roman women in the Early Empire had considerable freedom and independence. They had acquired the right to own, inherit, and dispose of property. Wives were not segregated from males in the home but were appreciated as enjoyable company and were at the center of household social life. Upper-class women could attend the races, the theater, and events in the amphitheater, although in the latter two places they were forced to sit in separate female sections. Moreover, ladies of rank were still accompanied by maids and companions when they went out. Some women operated businesses, such as shipping firms. Women could not participate in politics, but the Early Empire saw a number of important women who influenced politics through their husbands, including Livia, the wife of Augustus, Agrippina, the mother of Nero, and Plotina, the wife of Trajan.

Slaves and Their Masters

Although slavery was a common institution throughout the ancient world, no people possessed more slaves or relied so much on slave labor as the Romans eventually did. Before the third century B.C.E., a small Roman farmer might possess one or two slaves who would help farm his few acres and perform domestic chores. These slaves would most likely be from Italy and be regarded as part of the family household. Only the very rich would have large numbers of slaves.

The Roman conquest of the Mediterranean brought a drastic change in the use of slaves. Large numbers of foreign slaves were brought back to Italy. During the Republic, Rome's wars were the chief source of slaves, followed by piracy; the children of slaves also became slaves. While some Roman generals brought back slaves to be sold to benefit the public treasury, ambitious generals of the first century, such as Pompey and Caesar, made personal fortunes by treating slaves captured by their armies as their own private property.

The Romans used slaves in many ways. The rich, of course, owned the most and the best. In the late Republic, it became a badge of prestige to be attended by many slaves. Greeks were in much demand as household slaves, where they served as tutors, musicians, doctors, and artists. Many slaves of all nationalities were used as menial household workers, such as cooks, valets, waiters, cleaners, and gardeners. Roman businessmen would employ slaves as shop assistants or artisans. Slaves were also used as farm laborers; in fact, huge gangs of slaves worked the large landed estates under pitiful conditions. Cato the Elder argued that it was cheaper to work slaves to death and then replace them than to treat them favorably. In addition, the roads, aqueducts, and public buildings were constructed by contractors using slave labor. The total number of slaves is difficult to judge—estimates range from two to four free men to every slave.

It is also difficult to generalize about the treatment of Roman slaves. There are numerous instances of humane treatment by masters and situations where slaves even protected their owners from danger out of gratitude and esteem. But there are also examples of slaves murdering their owners, causing some Romans to live in unspoken fear of their slaves (see the box on p. 148). Slaves were also subject to severe punishments, torture, abuse, and hard labor that drove some to run away or even revolt against their owners. The Romans had stringent laws against aiding a runaway slave. The murder of a master by a slave might mean the execution of all the other household slaves. Near the end of the second century B.C.E., large-scale slave revolts occurred in Sicily, where enormous gangs of slaves were subjected to horrible working conditions on large landed estates. Slaves were branded, beaten, fed inadequately, worked in chains, and housed at night in underground prisons. It took three years (from 135 to 132 B.C.E.) to crush a revolt of 70,000 slaves, and the great revolt on Sicily (104–101 B.C.E.) involved most of the island and took a Roman army of 17,000 men to suppress it. The most famous revolt on the Italian peninsula occurred in 73 B.C.E. Led by a Thracian gladiator named Spartacus, the revolt broke out in southern Italy and involved 70,000 slaves. Spartacus managed to defeat several Roman armies before he was finally trapped and killed in southern

Italy in 71 B.C.E. Six thousand of his followers were crucified, the traditional form of execution for slaves.

Imperial Rome

At the center of the colossal Roman Empire was the ancient city of Rome. Truly a capital city, Rome had the largest population of any city in the empire. It is estimated that its population was close to one million by the time of Augustus. Only Chang'an, the imperial capital of the Han Chinese Empire, had a comparable population during this time. For anyone with ambitions, Rome was the place to be. A magnet to many people, Rome was extremely cosmopolitan. Nationalities from all over the empire resided there, with entire sections inhabited by specific groups, such as Greeks and Syrians.

Rome was, no doubt, an overcrowded and noisy city. Because of the congestion, cart and wagon traffic was banned from the streets during the day. The noise from the resulting vehicular movement at night often made sleep difficult. Evening pedestrian travel was dangerous. Although Augustus had organized a police force, lone travelers might be assaulted, robbed, or soaked by filth thrown out of the upper-story windows of Rome's massive apartment buildings.

An enormous gulf existed between rich and poor in the city of Rome. While the rich had comfortable villas, the poor lived in apartment blocks called *insulae*, which might be six stories high. Constructed of concrete, they were often poorly built and not infrequently collapsed. The use

MAP 5.4 Imperial Rome

THE PUBLIC BATHS OF THE ROMAN EMPIRE

T*he public baths in Rome and other cities played an important role in urban life. Introduced to Rome in the second century B.C.E. as a result of Greek influence, the number of public baths grew at a rapid pace in the Early Empire as the emperors contributed funds for their construction. The public baths were especially noisy near the end of the afternoon when Romans stopped in after work to use the baths before dinner. The following description is by Lucian, a traveling lecturer who lived in the second century and wrote satirical dialogues in Greek. This selection is taken from* Hippias, or the Bath.

LUCIAN, *HIPPIAS, OR THE BATH*

The building suits the magnitude of the site, accords well with the accepted idea of such an establishment, and shows regard for the principles of lighting. The entrance is high, with a flight of broad steps of which the tread is greater than the pitch, to make them easy to ascend. On entering, one is received into a public hall of good size, with ample accommodations for servants and attendants. On the left are the lounging rooms, also of just the right sort for a bath, attractive, brightly lighted retreats. Then, besides them, a hall, larger than need be for the purposes of a bath, but necessary for the reception of richer persons. Next, capacious locker rooms to undress in, on each side, with a very high and brilliantly lighted hall between them, in which are three swimming pools of cold water; it is finished in Laconian marble, and has two statues of white marble in the ancient style. . . .

On leaving this hall, you come into another which is slightly warmed instead of meeting you at once with fierce heat; it is oblong, and has an apse on each side. Next to it, on the right, is a very bright hall, nicely fitted up for massage. . . . Then near this is another hall, the most beautiful in the world, in which one can stand or sit with comfort, linger without danger, and stroll about with profit. It also is refulgent with Phrygian marble clear to the roof. Next comes the hot corridor, faced with Numidian marble. The hall beyond it is very beautiful, full of abundant light and aglow with color like that of purple hangings. It contains three hot tubs.

When you have bathed, you need not go back through the same rooms, but can go directly to the cold room through a slightly warmed chamber. Everywhere there is copious illumination and full indoor daylight. . . . Why should I go on to tell you of the exercising floor and of the cloak rooms? . . . Moreover, it is beautiful with all other marks of thoughtfulness—with two toilets, many exits, and two devices for telling time, a water clock that makes a bellowing sound and a sundial.

---

of wooden beams in the floors and movable stoves, torches, candles, and lamps within the rooms for heat and light made the danger of fire a constant companion. Once started, fires were extremely difficult to put out. The famous conflagration of 64 C.E., which Nero was unjustly accused of starting, devastated a good part of the city. Besides the hazards of collapse and fire, living conditions were also poor. High rents forced entire families into one room. The absence of plumbing, central heating, and open fireplaces made life so uncomfortable that poorer Romans spent most of their time outdoors in the streets.

Fortunately for these people, Rome boasted public buildings unequaled anywhere in the empire. Its temples, fora, markets, baths, theaters, triumphal arches, governmental buildings, and amphitheaters gave parts of the city an appearance of grandeur and magnificence (see the box above).

Though the center of a great empire, Rome was also a great parasite. Beginning with Augustus, the emperors accepted responsibility for providing food for the urban populace, with about 200,000 people receiving free grain. Even with the free grain, conditions were grim for the poor. Early in the second century C.E., a Roman doctor claimed that rickets was common among children in the city.

In addition to food, entertainment was provided on a grand scale for the inhabitants of Rome. The poet Juvenal said of the Roman masses: "But nowadays, with no vote to sell, their motto is 'Couldn't care less.' Time was when their plebiscite elected generals, heads of state, commanders of legions: but now they've pulled in their horns, there's only two things that concern them: Bread and Circuses."[11] Public spectacles were provided by the emperor and other state officials as part of the great festivals—most of them religious in origin—celebrated by the state. Over one hundred days a year were given over to these public holidays. The festivals included three major types of entertainment. At the Circus Maximus, horse and chariot races attracted hundreds of thousands, while dramatic and other performances were held in theaters. But the most famous of all the public spectacles were the gladiatorial shows.

The Gladiatorial Shows

The gladiatorial shows were an integral part of Roman society. They took place in amphitheaters, with the first permanent one having been constructed at Rome in 29 B.C.E. Perhaps the most famous was the Flavian amphitheater, called the Colosseum, constructed at Rome to seat

50,000 spectators. Amphitheaters were not limited to the city of Rome but were constructed throughout the empire. They varied greatly in size, with capacities ranging from a few thousand to tens of thousands. Considerable resources and ingenuity went into building them, especially in the arrangements for moving wild beasts efficiently into the arena. In most cities and towns, amphitheaters came to be the biggest buildings, rivaled only by the circuses for races and the public baths. Where a society invests its money gives an idea of its priorities. Since the amphitheater was the primary location for the gladiatorial games, it is fair to say that public slaughter was an important part of Roman culture.

Gladiatorial games were held from dawn to dusk. Contests to the death between trained fighters formed the central focus of these games. Most gladiators were slaves or condemned criminals, although some free men lured by the hope of popularity and patronage by wealthy fans participated voluntarily. They were trained for combat in special gladiatorial schools.

Gladiatorial games included other forms of entertainment as well. Criminals of all ages and both sexes were sent into the arena without weapons to face certain death from wild animals who would tear them to pieces. Numerous kinds of animal contests were also staged: wild beasts against each other, such as bears against buffalo; staged hunts with men shooting safely from behind iron bars; and gladiators in the arena with bulls, tigers, and lions. Reportedly, five thousand beasts were killed in one day of games when the Emperor Titus inaugurated the Colosseum in 80 C.E. Enormous resources were invested in the capture and shipment of wild animals for slaughter, while whole species were hunted to extinction in parts of the empire.

These bloodthirsty spectacles were highly popular with the Roman people. The Roman historian Tacitus said, "Few indeed are to be found who talk of any other subjects in their homes, and whenever we enter a classroom, what else is the conversation of the youths."[12] But the gladiatorial games served a purpose beyond mere entertainment. To the Romans, the gladiatorial games, as well as the other forms of public entertainment, fulfilled both a political and a social need. Certainly, the games served to divert the idle masses from any political unrest. It was said of the Emperor Trajan that he understood that although the distribution of grain and money satisfied the individual, spectacles were necessary for the "contentment of the masses."

THE GLADIATORIAL GAMES. Although some gladiators were free men enticed by the possibility of rewards, most were condemned criminals, slaves, or prisoners of war who were trained in special schools. A great gladiator could win his freedom through the games. This mosaic, from the fourth century C.E., depicts different aspects of gladiatorial fighting and clearly shows the bloody nature of the gladiatorial games.

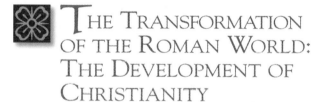

THE TRANSFORMATION OF THE ROMAN WORLD: THE DEVELOPMENT OF CHRISTIANITY

The rise of Christianity marks a fundamental break with the dominant values of the Greco-Roman world. Christian views of God, human beings, and the world were quite different from those of the Greeks and Romans. Nevertheless, Christianity also had much in common with its contemporary religions. Consequently, to understand the rise of Christianity, we must first examine both the religious environment of the Roman world and the Jewish background from which Christianity emerged.

The Religious World of the Romans

Augustus had taken a number of steps to revive the Roman state religion, which had declined during the turmoil of the late Republic. The official state religion focused on the worship of a pantheon of Greco-Roman gods and goddesses, including Juno, the patron goddess of women, Minerva, the goddess of artisans, Mars, the god of war, and Jupiter Optimus Maximus (best and greatest), who became the patron deity of Rome and assumed a central place in the religious life of the city. The Romans believed that observance of proper ritual by state priests brought the Romans into a proper relationship with the gods and guaranteed security, peace, and prosperity. No doubt, the Roman success in creating an empire was a visible confirmation of divine favor. As Cicero, the first-century politician and writer, claimed: "We have overcome all the nations of the world, because we have realized that the world is directed and governed by the gods."[13]

The polytheistic Romans were extremely tolerant of other religions. The Romans allowed the worship of native gods and goddesses throughout their provinces and even adopted some of the local gods. In addition, the imperial cult of Roma and Augustus was developed to bolster support for the emperors. After Augustus, any dead emperors deified by the Roman senate were added to the official imperial cult.

In addition to the formal, official religion, the Romans had cults of household and countryside spirits whose worship appealed especially to the common people. Here, too, proper ritual was important, and it was the responsibility of the *paterfamilias* as head of the family to ensure proper fulfillment of religious obligations. Although these cults gave the Romans a more immediate sense of spiritual contact than they found in the official religion, these cults, too, failed to satisfy many people.

The desire for a more emotional spiritual experience led many people to the mystery religions of the Hellenistic east, which flooded into the western Roman world during the Early Empire. The mystery religions offered secret teachings that supposedly brought special benefits. They promised their followers advantages unavailable through Roman religion: an entry into a higher world of reality and the promise of a future life superior to the present one. They also featured elaborate rituals with deep emotional appeal. By participating in their ceremonies and performing their rites, an adherent could achieve communion with spiritual beings and undergo purification that opened the door to life after death.

The Jewish Background

In Hellenistic times, the Jewish people had been granted considerable independence by their Seleucid rulers (see Chapter 4). Roman involvement with the Jews began in 63 B.C.E., and by 6 C.E., Judaea (which embraced the lands of the old Hebrew kingdom of Judah) had been made a province and placed under the direction of a Roman procurator. But unrest continued, augmented by divisions among the Jews themselves. The Sadducees favored cooperation with the Romans. The Pharisees, although they wanted Judaea to be free from Roman control, did not advocate violent means to achieve this goal. The Essenes, as revealed in the Dead Sea Scrolls, a collection of documents first discovered in 1947, constituted a Jewish sect that lived in a religious community near the Dead Sea. They, like most other Jews, awaited a Messiah who would save Israel from oppression, usher in the kingdom of God, and establish a true paradise on earth. A fourth group, the

Zealots, were militant extremists who advocated the violent overthrow of Roman rule. A Jewish revolt in 66 C.E. was crushed by the Romans four years later. The Jewish Temple in Jerusalem was destroyed, and Roman power once more stood supreme in Judaea.

The Rise of Christianity

It was in the midst of the confusion and conflict in Judaea that Jesus of Nazareth (c. 6 B.C.E.–29 C.E.) began his public preaching. Jesus—a Palestinian Jew—grew up in Galilee, an important center of the militant Zealots. Jesus' message was basically simple. He reassured his fellow Jews that he did not plan to undermine their traditional religion: "Do not think that I have come to abolish the Law or the Prophets; I have not come to abolish them but to fulfill them."[14] According to Jesus, what was important was not strict adherence to the letter of the law and attention to rules and prohibitions, but the transformation of the inner person: "So in everything, do to others what you would have them do to you, for this sums up the Law and the Prophets."[15] God's command was simple—to love God and one another: "Love the Lord your God with all your heart and with all your soul and with all your mind and with all your strength. The second is this: Love your neighbor as yourself."[16] In the Sermon on the Mount (see the box on p. 153), Jesus presented the ethical concepts—humility, charity, and brotherly love—that would form the basis for the value system of medieval Western civilization.

Although some people welcomed Jesus as the Messiah who would save Israel from oppression and establish God's kingdom on earth, Jesus spoke of a heavenly kingdom, not an earthly one: "My kingdom is not of this world."[17] Consequently, he disappointed the radicals. On the other hand, conservative religious leaders believed Jesus was undermining respect for traditional Jewish religion. To the Roman authorities of Palestine and their local allies, the Nazarene was a potential revolutionary who might transform Jewish expectations of a messianic kingdom into a revolt against Rome. Therefore, Jesus found himself denounced on many sides and was given over to the Roman authorities. The procurator Pontius Pilate ordered his crucifixion. But that did not solve the problem. A few loyal followers of Jesus spread the story that Jesus had overcome death, had been resurrected, and had then ascended into heaven. The belief in Jesus' resurrection became an important tenet of Christian doctrine. Jesus was now hailed as the "anointed one" (*Christos* in Greek) or the Messiah who would return and usher in the kingdom of God on earth.

Christianity began, then, as a religious movement within Judaism and was viewed that way by Roman authorities for many decades. Although tradition holds that one of Jesus' disciples, Peter, founded the Christian church at Rome, the most important figure in early Christianity after Jesus was Paul of Tarsus (c. 5–c. 67). Paul

CHRISTIAN IDEALS: THE SERMON ON THE MOUNT

*C*hristianity was simply one of many religions competing for attention in the Roman Empire during the first and second centuries. The rise of Christianity marked a fundamental break with the value system of the upper-class elites who dominated the world of classical antiquity. As these excerpts from the Sermon on the Mount in the Gospel of Saint Matthew illustrate, Christians emphasized humility, charity, brotherly love, and a belief in the inner being and a spiritual kingdom superior to this material world. These values and principles were not those of classical Greco-Roman civilization as exemplified in the words and deeds of its leaders.

THE GOSPEL ACCORDING TO SAINT MATTHEW

Now when he saw the crowds, he went up on a mountainside and sat down. His disciples came to him, and he began to teach them, saying:

> Blessed are the poor in spirit: for theirs is the kingdom of heaven.
>
> Blessed are those who mourn: for they will be comforted.
>
> Blessed are the meek: for they will inherit the earth.
>
> Blessed are those who hunger and thirst for righteousness: for they will be filled.
>
> Blessed are the merciful: for they will be shown mercy.
>
> Blessed are the pure in heart: for they will see God.
>
> Blessed are the peacemakers: for they will be called sons of God.
>
> Blessed are those who are persecuted because of righteousness: for theirs is the kingdom of heaven. . . .

You have heard that it was said, "Eye for eye, and tooth for tooth." But I tell you, Do not resist an evil person. If someone strikes you on the right cheek, turn to him the other also. . . .

You have heard that it was said, "Love your neighbor, and hate your enemy." But I tell you, Love your enemies and pray for those who persecute you. . . .

Do not store up for yourselves treasures on earth, where moth and rust destroy, and where thieves break in and steal. But store up for yourselves treasures in heaven, where moth and rust do not destroy, and where thieves do not break in and steal. For where your treasure is, there your heart will be also. . . .

No one can serve two masters. Either he will hate the one and love the other, or he will be devoted to the one and despise the other. You cannot serve both God and Money.

Therefore I tell you, do not worry about your life, what you will eat or drink; or about your body, what you will wear. Is not life more important than food, and the body more important than clothes? Look at the birds of the air; they do not sow or reap or store away in barns, and yet your heavenly Father feeds them. Are you not much more valuable than they? . . . So do not worry, saying, What shall we eat? or What shall we drink? or What shall we wear? For the pagans run after all these things, and your heavenly Father knows that you need them. But seek first his kingdom and his righteousness, and all these things will be given to you as well.

---

reached out to non-Jews and transformed Christianity from a Jewish sect into a world religion.

Called the "second founder of Christianity," Paul was a Jewish Roman citizen who had been strongly influenced by Hellenistic Greek culture. He believed that the message of Jesus should be preached not only to Jews but to Gentiles (non-Jews) as well. Paul was responsible for founding Christian communities throughout Asia Minor and along the shores of the Aegean.

Paul provided a universal foundation for the spread of Jesus' ideas. He taught that Jesus was, in effect, a savior-god, the son of God, who had come to earth to save all humans, who were basically sinners as a result of Adam's original sin of disobedience against God. By his death, Jesus had atoned for the sins of all humans and made possible a new beginning for all men and women, with the potential for individual salvation. By accepting Jesus as their savior, they too could be saved.

At first, Christianity spread slowly. Although it was disseminated mostly by the preaching of convinced Christians, written materials also appeared. Among them were a series of letters or epistles written by Paul outlining Christian beliefs for different Christian communities. Some of Jesus' disciples may also have preserved some of the sayings of the master in writing and would have passed on personal memories that became the basis of the written gospels—the "good news" concerning Jesus— which were written down between 50 and 150 and which attempted to give a record of Jesus' life and teachings and formed the core of the New Testament. Although Jerusalem was the first center of Christianity, its destruction by the Romans in 70 C.E. dispersed the Christians and left individual Christian churches with considerable independence. By 100, Christian churches had been established in most of the major cities of the east and in some places in the western part of the empire. Many early Christians came from the ranks of Hellenized Jews and the Greek-speaking populations of the east. But in the second and third centuries, an increasing number of followers came from Latin-speaking people. A Latin translation of the Greek New Testament that appeared soon after 200 aided this process.

✿ **JESUS AND HIS APOSTLES.** Pictured is a fourth-century C.E. fresco from a Roman catacomb depicting Jesus and his apostles. Catacombs were underground cemeteries where early Christians buried their dead. Christian tradition holds that in times of imperial repression, Christians withdrew to the catacombs to pray and even hide.

Although some of the fundamental values of Christianity differed markedly from those of the Greco-Roman world, the Romans initially did not pay much attention to the Christians, whom they regarded at first as simply another sect of Judaism. The structure of the Roman Empire itself aided the growth of Christianity. Christian missionaries, including some of Jesus' original twelve disciples or apostles, used Roman roads to travel throughout the empire spreading their "good news."

As time passed, however, the Roman attitude toward Christianity began to change. The Romans were tolerant of other religions except when they threatened public order or public morals. Many Romans came to view Christians as harmful to the order of the Roman state. Since Christians held their meetings in secret and seemed to be connected to Christian groups in other areas, the government could view them as potentially dangerous to the state.

Some Romans felt that Christians were overly exclusive and hence harmful to the community and public order. The refusal of Christians to recognize other gods meant that they abstained from public festivals that honored these divinities. Finally, Christians refused to participate in the worship of the state gods and imperial cult. Since the Romans regarded these as important to the state, the Christians' refusal undermined the security of the state and hence constituted an act of treason, punishable by death. But to the Christians, who believed that there was only one real god, the worship of state gods and the emperors was idolatry and would endanger their own salvation.

Nevertheless, Roman persecution of Christians in the first and second centuries was only sporadic and local, never systematic. Persecution began during the reign of Nero. After the fire that destroyed much of Rome, the emperor used the Christians as scapegoats, accusing them of arson and hatred of the human race and subjecting them to cruel deaths in Rome. In the second century, Christians were largely ignored as harmless. By the end of the reigns of the five good emperors, Christians still represented a small minority, but one of considerable strength.

The Triumph of Christianity

The Romans' sporadic persecution of Christians in the first and second centuries had done nothing to stop the growth of Christianity. It had, in fact, served to strengthen Christianity as an institution in the second and third centuries by causing it to shed the loose structure of the first century and move toward a more centralized organization of its various church communities. Crucial to this change was the emerging role of the bishops, who began to assume more control over church communities. The Christian church was creating a well-defined hierarchical structure in which the bishops and clergy were salaried officers separate from the laity, or regular church members.

Christianity grew slowly in the first century, took root in the second, and by the third had spread widely. Why was Christianity able to attract so many followers? Certainly, the Christian message had much to offer the Roman world. The promise of salvation, made possible by Jesus' death and resurrection, made a resounding impact on a world full of suffering and injustice. Christianity seemed to imbue life with a meaning and purpose beyond the simple material things of everyday reality. Secondly, Christianity was not entirely unfamiliar. It could be viewed as simply another eastern mystery religion, offering immortality as the result of the sacrificial death of a savior-god. At the same time, it offered advantages that the other mystery religions lacked. Jesus had been a human figure, not a mythological one. Moreover, Christianity had universal appeal. Unlike some mystery religions, it was not restricted to men, nor did it require a painful or expensive initiation rite, as other mystery religions did. Initiation was accomplished simply by baptism—a purification by water—through which one entered into a personal relationship with Jesus. In addition, Christianity gave new meaning to life and offered what the Roman state religions could not—a personal relationship with God and connection to higher worlds.

Finally, Christianity fulfilled the human need to belong. Christians formed communities bound to one another in which people could express their love by helping each other and offering assistance to the poor, sick, widows, and orphans. Christianity satisfied the need to belong in a way that the huge, impersonal, and remote Roman Empire could never do.

Christianity proved attractive to all classes. The promise of eternal life was for all—rich, poor, aristocrats, slaves, men, and women. As Paul stated in his Epistle to the Colossians: "And [you] have put on the new self, which is being renewed in knowledge in the image of its Creator. Here there is no Greek nor Jew, circumcised or uncircumcised, barbarian, Scythian, slave or free, but Christ is all, and is in all."[18] Although it did not call for revolution or social upheaval, Christianity emphasized a sense of spiritual equality for all people.

Many women, in fact, found that Christianity offered them new roles and new forms of companionship with other women. Christian women fostered the new religion in their homes and preached their convictions to other people in their towns and villages. Many also died for their faith, and their deaths gave rise to a literature known as the Apocryphal Gospels, in which women were honored for creating new role models as virgins and widows dedicated to their faith, who defied fathers and their traditional gender roles to pursue their new lives.

As the Christian church became more organized, some emperors in the third century responded with more systematic persecutions, but their schemes failed to work. The last great persecution was at the beginning of the fourth century, but by that time Christianity had become too strong to be eradicated by force.

In the fourth century, Christianity prospered as never before after the Emperor Constantine (306–337) became the first Christian emperor. Although he was not baptized until the end of his life, in 313 Constantine issued the famous Edict of Milan, officially tolerating the existence of Christianity. Under Theodosius "the Great" (378–395), it was made the official religion of the Roman Empire. Christianity had triumphed.

THE DECLINE AND FALL OF THE ROMAN EMPIRE

In the course of the third century, the Roman Empire came near to collapse. Military monarchy under the Severan rulers (193–235), which restored order after a series of civil wars, was followed by military anarchy. For a period of almost fifty years, from 235 to 284, the Roman Empire was mired in the chaos of continual civil war. The imperial throne was occupied by anyone who had the military strength to seize it. In these almost fifty years, there were twenty-two emperors, only two of whom did not meet a violent death. At the same time, the empire was beset by a series of invasions, no doubt exacerbated by the civil wars. In the east, the Sassanid Persians made inroads into Roman territory. Germanic tribes also poured into the empire. The Goths overran the Balkans and moved into Greece and Asia Minor. The Franks advanced into Gaul and Spain. Not until the reign of Aurelian (270–275) were most of the boundaries restored.

Invasions, civil wars, and plague came close to causing an economic collapse of the Roman Empire in the third century. The population declined drastically, possibly by as much as one-third. There was a noticeable decline in trade and small industry. The labor shortage created by the plague affected both military recruiting and the economy. Farm production deteriorated significantly. Fields were ravaged by Germanic tribes, but even more often by the defending Roman armies. Provincial governors seemed powerless to stop these depredations, and some even joined in the extortion. The monetary system began to show signs of collapse as a result of debased coinage and the beginnings of serious inflation.

Armies were needed more than ever, but financial strains made it difficult to pay and enlist the necessary soldiers. Whereas in the second century the Roman army had been recruited among the inhabitants of frontier provinces, by the mid-third century, the state had to rely on hiring Germans to fight under Roman commanders. These soldiers had no understanding of Roman traditions and no real attachment to either the empire or the emperors.

The Reforms of Diocletian and Constantine

At the end of the third and beginning of the fourth centuries, the Roman Empire gained a new lease on life through the efforts of two strong emperors, Diocletian and Constantine, who restored order and stability. The Roman Empire was virtually transformed into a new state: the so-called Late Empire, which included a new governmental structure, a rigid economic and social system, and a new state religion—Christianity.

Believing that the empire had grown too large for a single ruler, Diocletian (284–305) divided it into four administrative units. Despite the appearance of four-man rule, however, Diocletian's military seniority enabled him to claim a higher status and hold the ultimate authority. Constantine (306–337) continued and even expanded the autocratic policies of Diocletian. Both rulers greatly strengthened and enlarged the administrative bureaucracies of the Roman Empire. Henceforth, civil and military bureaucracies were sharply separated. Each contained a hierarchy of officials who exercised control at the various levels. The emperor presided over both hierarchies of officials and served as the only link between them. New titles of nobility—such as *illustres* ("illustrious ones") and *illustrissimi* ("the most illustrious ones")—were instituted to dignify the holders of positions in the civil and military bureaucracies.

Additional military reforms were also inaugurated. The army was enlarged to 500,000 men, including German units. Mobile units were established that could be quickly moved to support frontier troops where the borders were threatened.

Constantine's biggest project was the construction of a new capital city in the east on the site of the Greek city of Byzantium on the shores of the Bosporus. Eventually renamed Constantinople (modern Istanbul), it was developed for defensive reasons: it had an excellent strategic location. Calling it his "New Rome," Constantine endowed the city with a forum, large palaces, and a vast amphitheater.

The political and military reforms of Diocletian and Constantine greatly enlarged two institutions—the army and civil service—that drained most of the public funds. Though more revenues were needed to pay for the army and bureaucracy, the population was not growing, so the tax base could not be expanded. Diocletian and Constantine devised new economic and social policies to deal with these financial burdens, but like their political policies, these measures were all based on coercion and loss of individual freedom. To fight inflation, Diocletian resorted to issuing a price edict in 301 that established maximum wages and prices for the entire empire, but despite severe penalties, it was unenforceable and failed to work.

Coercion also came to form the underlying basis for numerous occupations in the Late Roman Empire. In order to ensure the tax base and keep the empire going despite the shortage of labor, the emperors issued edicts that forced people to remain in their designated vocations. Hence, basic jobs, such as bakers and shippers, became hereditary. Free tenant farmers continued to decline and soon found themselves bound to the land by large landowners who

MAP 5.5   Divisions of the Restored Roman Empire

Prefecture of Gaul
Prefecture of Italy
Prefecture of Illyricum
Prefecture of the East

Line of division between East and West

took advantage of depressed agricultural conditions to enlarge their landed estates.

In general, the economic and social policies of Diocletian and Constantine were based on an unprecedented degree of control and coercion. Though temporarily successful, such authoritarian policies in the long run stifled the very vitality the Late Empire needed to revive its sagging fortunes.

The Fall of the Western Roman Empire

The restored empire of Diocletian and Constantine limped along for more than a century. After Constantine, the empire continued to divide into western and eastern parts. The west came under increasing pressure from the invading Germanic tribes. The major breakthrough into the Roman Empire came in the second half of the fourth century. Ferocious warriors from Asia, known as Huns (who may have been related to the Xiongnu, the invaders of the Han Chinese Empire), moved into eastern Europe and put pressure on the Germanic Visigoths, who in turn moved south and west, crossed the Danube into Roman territory, and settled down as Roman allies. But the Visigoths soon revolted, and the Roman attempt to stop them at Adrianople in 378 led to a crushing defeat.

Increasing numbers of Germans now crossed the frontiers. In 410, the Visigoths sacked Rome. Vandals poured into southern Spain and Africa, Visigoths into Spain and Gaul. The Vandals crossed into Italy from North Africa and sacked Rome in 455. Twenty-one years later, the western emperor Romulus Augustulus (475–476) was deposed, and a series of Germanic kingdoms replaced the Roman Empire in the west while an Eastern Roman Empire continued with its center at Constantinople.

The end of the Roman Empire has given rise to numerous theories that attempt to provide a single, all-encompassing reason for the "decline and fall of the Roman Empire." These include the following: Christianity's emphasis on a spiritual kingdom undermined Roman military virtues and patriotism; traditional Roman values declined as non-Italians gained prominence in the empire; lead poisoning through leaden water pipes and cups caused a mental decline; plague decimated the population; Rome failed to advance technologically because of slavery; and Rome was unable to achieve a workable political system. There may be an element of truth in each of these theories, but each of them has also been challenged. History is an intricate web of relationships, causes, and effects. No single explanation will ever suffice to explain historical events. One thing is clear. Weakened by a shortage of manpower, the Roman army in the west was simply not able to fend off the hordes of people invading Italy and Gaul. In contrast, the Eastern Roman Empire, which would survive for another thousand years, remained largely free from invasion.

CHRONOLOGY

THE LATE EMPIRE—CHIEF RULERS AND EVENTS

Military monarchy (Severan dynasty)	193–235
Military anarchy	235–284
Diocletian	284–305
Constantine	306–337
Edict of Milan	313
Theodosius "the Great"	378–395
Visigoths sack Rome	410
Vandals sack Rome	455
Romulus Augustulus is deposed	476

 CONCLUSION

Between 509 and 264 B.C.E., the Latin-speaking community of Rome expanded and brought about the union of almost all of Italy under its control. Even more dramatically, between 264 and 133 B.C.E., Rome expanded to the west and east and became master of the Mediterranean Sea and its surrounding territories, creating one of the largest empires in antiquity. Rome's republican institutions proved inadequate for the task of ruling an empire, however, and after a series of bloody civil wars, Octavian created a new order that would rule the empire in an orderly fashion. His successors established a Roman imperial state.

Like the Han Chinese Empire, however, the Roman Empire was eventually faced with serious problems. Both empires suffered from overexpansion, and both fortified their long borders with walls, forts, and military garrisons to guard against invasions of nomadic peoples. Both empires were eventually overcome by these peoples: the Han dynasty was weakened by the incursions of the Xiongnu, and the western Roman Empire eventually collapsed in the face of invasions by the Germanic peoples. Nevertheless, a significant difference between these two contemporary empires remained. Although the Han dynasty collapsed, the Chinese imperial tradition as well as the class structure and set of values that sustained it continued, and the Chinese Empire, under new dynasties, continued well into the twentieth century as a single political entity.

The Roman Empire, on the other hand, collapsed and lived on only as an idea, although Roman achievements were bequeathed to the future. The Romance languages of today (French, Italian, Spanish, Portuguese, and Romanian) are based on Latin. Western practices of impartial justice and trial by jury owe much to Roman law. As great builders, the Romans left monuments to their skills throughout Europe, some of which, such as aqueducts and roads, are still in use today. Aspects of Roman administrative practices survived in the Western world for centuries. The Romans also preserved the intellectual heritage of the Greco-Roman world of antiquity. Nevertheless, while many aspects of the Roman world would continue, the heirs of Rome created new civilizations—European, Islamic, and Byzantine—that would carry on yet another stage in the development of human society.

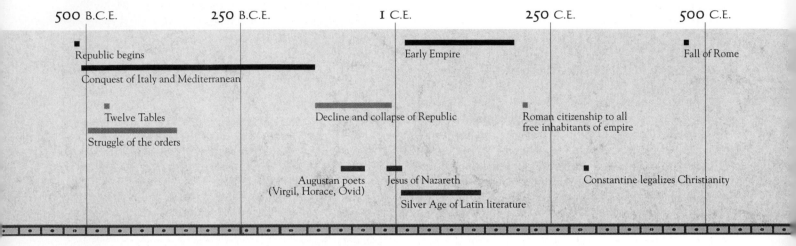

CHAPTER NOTES

1. Florus, *Epitome of Roman History*, trans. E. S. Forster (Cambridge, Mass., 1961), IV, ii, 149–51.
2. Tacitus, *The Annals of Imperial Rome*, trans. Michael Grant (Harmondsworth, 1956), p. 31.
3. Tacitus, *The Histories*, trans. Kenneth Wellesley (Harmondsworth, 1964), p. 23.
4. *The Poems of Catullus*, trans. Charles Martin (Baltimore, 1990), p. 109.
5. Virgil, *The Aeneid*, trans. C. Day Lewis (Garden City, N.Y., 1952), p. 154.
6. Horace, *Satires*, in *The Complete Works of Horace*, trans. Lord Dunsany and Michael Oakley (London, 1961), 1.1, p. 139.
7. Ibid., 1.3, p. 151.
8. Livy, *The Early History of Rome*, trans. Aubrey de Selincourt (Harmondsworth, 1960), p. 18.
9. Seneca, *Letters from a Stoic*, trans. Robin Campbell (Harmondsworth, 1969), Letter 5.
10. Tacitus, *The Annals of Imperial Rome*, p. 147.
11. Juvenal, *The Sixteen Satires*, trans. Peter Green (Harmondsworth, 1967), Satire 10, p. 207.
12. Tacitus, *A Dialogue on Oratory*, in *The Complete Works of Tacitus*, trans. Alfred Church and William Brodribb (New York, 1942), 29, p. 758.
13. Quoted in Chester Starr, *Past and Future in Ancient History* (Lanham, Md., 1987), pp. 38–39.
14. Matthew 5: 17.
15. Matthew 7: 12.
16. Mark 12: 30–31.
17. John 18: 36.
18. Colossians 3: 10–11.

SUGGESTED READINGS

For a general account of Roman history, see J. Boardman, J. Griffin, and O. Murray, eds., *The Oxford History of the Roman World* (Oxford, 1991). A brief but excellent guide to recent trends in scholarship can be found in C. Starr, *Past and Future in Ancient History* (Lanham, Md., 1987), pp. 33–57. A standard one-volume reference on the Roman Republic is M. Cary and H. H. Scullard, *A History of Rome Down to the Reign of Constantine*, 3d ed. (New York, 1975).

Good surveys of the Roman Republic include M. H. Crawford, *The Roman Republic*, 2d ed. (Cambridge, Mass., 1993); H. H. Scullard, *History of the Roman World, 753–146 B.C.*, 4th ed. (London, 1978); M. Le Glay, J.-L. Voisin, and Y. Le Bohec, *A History of Rome*, trans. A. Nevill (Oxford, 1996); and A. Kamm, *The Romans* (London, 1995). For a beautifully illustrated survey, see J. F. Drinkwater and A. Drummond, *The World of the Romans* (New

York, 1993). The history of early Rome is well covered in T. J. Cornell, *The Beginnings of Rome: Italy and Rome from the Bronze Age to the Punic Wars (c. 1000–264 B.C.)* (London, 1995).

Aspects of the Roman political structure can be studied in R. E. Mitchell, *Patricians and Plebeians: The Origin of the Roman State* (Ithaca, N.Y., 1990). Changes in Rome's economic life can be examined in A. H. M. Jones, *The Roman Economy* (Oxford, 1974). On the Roman social structure, see G. Alfoeldy, *The Social History of Rome* (London, 1985).

Accounts of Rome's expansion in the Mediterranean world are provided by J.-M. David, *The Roman Conquest of Italy,* trans. A. Nevill (Oxford, 1996), and R. M. Errington, *The Dawn of Empire: Rome's Rise to World Power* (Ithaca, N.Y., 1971). Especially important works on Roman expansion and imperialism include W. V. Harris, *War and Imperialism in Republican Rome* (Oxford, 1979), and E. Badian, *Roman Imperialism in the Late Republic* (Oxford, 1968).

An excellent account of basic problems in the late Republic can be found in M. Beard and M. H. Crawford, *Rome in the Late Republic* (London, 1984). The classic work on the fall of the Republic is R. Syme, *The Roman Revolution* (Oxford, 1960). Also valuable is D. Shotter, *The Fall of the Roman Republic* (London, 1994).

Good surveys of the Early Roman Empire include P. Garnsey and R. Saller, *The Roman Empire: Economy, Society and Culture* (London, 1987); C. Wells, *The Roman Empire,* 2d ed. (London, 1992); and J. Wacher, *The Roman Empire* (London, 1987). A fundamental work on Roman government and the role of the emperor is F. Millar, *The Emperor in the Roman World* (London, 1977).

The Roman army is examined in G. Webster, *The Roman Imperial Army of the First and Second Centuries* A.D., 2d ed. (London, 1979), and J. B. Campbell, *The Emperor and the Roman Army* (Oxford, 1984). On the provinces and Roman foreign policy, see E. N. Luttwak, *The Grand Strategy of the Roman Empire from the First Century* A.D. *to the Third* (Baltimore, 1976), and B. Isaac, *The Limits of Empire: The Roman Empire in the East* (Oxford, 1990).

A good survey of Roman literature can be found in R. M. Ogilvie, *Roman Literature and Society* (Harmondsworth, 1980). On Roman art and architecture, see R. Ling, *Roman Painting* (New York, 1991); D. E. Kleiner, *Roman Sculpture* (New Haven, Conn., 1992); and M. Wheeler, *Roman Art and Architecture* (London, 1964). General studies of daily life in Rome include F. Dupont, *Daily Life in Ancient Rome* (Oxford, 1994), and J. P. V. D. Balsdon, *Life and Leisure in Ancient Rome* (London, 1969). On the city of Rome, see O. F. Robinson, *Ancient Rome: City Planning and Administration* (New York, 1992). On the Roman family, see S. Dixon, *The Roman Family* (Baltimore, 1992). Roman women are examined in S. Pomeroy, *Goddesses, Whores, Wives, and Slaves: Women in Classical Antiquity* (New York, 1976), pp. 149–226, and R. Baumann, *Women and Politics in Ancient Rome* (New York, 1995). On slavery, see K. R. Bradley, *Slavery and Rebellion in the Roman World* (Bloomington, Ind., 1989). On the gladiators, see T. Wiedemann, *Emperors and Gladiators* (New York, 1992).

For a general introduction to early Christianity, see J. Court and K. Court, *The New Testament World* (Cambridge, 1990). Useful works on early Christianity include W. A. Meeks, *The First Urban Christians* (New Haven, Conn., 1983); W. H. C. Frend, *The Rise of Christianity* (Philadelphia, 1984); and R. MacMullen, *Christianizing the Roman Empire* (New Haven, Conn., 1984). On Christian women, see D. M. Scholer, ed., *Women in Early Christianity* (New York, 1993), and R. Kraemer, *Her Share of the Blessings: Women's Religion Among the Pagans, Jews and Christians in the Graeco-Roman World* (Oxford, 1995).

The classic work on the "decline and fall" of the Roman Empire is Edward Gibbon, *Decline and Fall of the Roman Empire,* J. B. Bury edition (London, 1909–14). An excellent survey is P. Brown, *The World of Late Antiquity* (London, 1971). Also valuable are A. Cameron, *The Later Roman Empire* (Cambridge, Mass., 1993), and R. MacMullen, *Corruption and the Decline of Rome* (New Haven, Conn., 1988). On the fourth century, see T. D. Barnes, *The New Empire of Diocletian and Constantine* (Cambridge, Mass., 1982), and M. Grant, *Constantine the Great: The Man and His Times* (New York, 1993). Recent studies analyzing the aristocratic circles, the barbarian invasions, and the military problem include E. A. Thompson, *Romans and Barbarians* (Madison, Wis., 1982), and A. Ferrill, *The Fall of the Roman Empire: The Military Explanation* (London, 1986).

INFOTRAC COLLEGE EDITION

For additional reading, go to InfoTrac College Edition, your online research library at http://web1.infotrac-college.com

Enter the search terms "Rome history" using Keywords.

Enter the search terms "Roman republic" using Keywords.

Enter the search terms "Julius and Caesar" using Keywords.

Enter the search terms "Roman empire" using Keywords.

Enter the search terms "Roman law" using the Subject Guide.

REFLECTION

THE FIRST CIVILIZATIONS AND THE RISE OF EMPIRES

In Part I of this book, we have focused our attention on the emergence of the first civilizations during the ancient era. As we have seen, each civilization developed somewhat independently of the others, and we have therefore treated them as distinct entities, each with its own pattern of development. But clearly, these civilizations encountered a number of similar experiences, and contacts between the civilizations and with other nearby peoples sometimes played a significant role in their development. Let us now retrace our steps and evaluate the process in a comparative perspective. How and why did these first civilizations arise? What role did cross-cultural contacts play in their development? What was the nature of the relationship between these permanent settlements and nonagricultural peoples living elsewhere in the world, and how did each influence the other? Finally, what brought about the demise of these early civilizations, and what legacy did they leave for their successors in the region?

How and why the first civilizations arose has long been a matter of debate. In his classic work entitled *The Study of History*, historian Arnold Toynbee explained the origins of social change through the concept of challenge and response. Challenges, posed either by the environment or by actions taken by other peoples, compel human beings to make efforts that sometimes result in technological innovations that help to overcome the challenge. The world historian William McNeill carries the idea further, suggesting that encounters with other societies, especially stronger ones, are the primary factor provoking innovation and thus "the principal drive wheel of historic change."

Such theories are undoubtedly helpful to historians as general explanations for the process of social change, but we need to be more specific if we wish to find an explanation for the rise of the first civilizations. Why did some societies transform themselves into civilizations, while others did not? What factors determined how they responded? The evidence from the examples discussed here suggests that an important stimulus behind the rise of all of these early civilizations was the development of settled agriculture, which unleashed a series of changes in the organization of human communities that culminated in the rise of large ancient empires.

The exact time and place that crops were first cultivated successfully is uncertain. Many prehistorians believe that farming may have emerged independently in several different areas of the world when small human communities, driven by increasing population and a decline in available food resources, began to plant seeds in the ground in an effort to guarantee their survival. The first farmers, who may have lived as long as 10,000 years ago, undoubtedly used simple techniques and still relied primarily on other forms of food production, such as hunting, foraging, or pastoralism. The real breakthrough took place when farmers began to cultivate crops along the flood plains of river systems. The advantage was that crops grown in such areas were not as dependent on rainfall and therefore produced a more reliable harvest. An additional benefit was that the sediment carried by the river waters deposited nutrients in the soil, thus enabling the farmer to cultivate a single plot of ground for many years without moving to a new location. Thus, the first truly sedentary (that is, nonmigratory) societies were born. As time went on, such communities gradually learned how to direct the flow of water to enhance the productive capacity of the land, while the introduction of the iron plow eventually led to the cultivation of heavy soils not previously susceptible to agriculture.

The spread of this river valley agriculture in various parts of Asia and Africa was the decisive factor in the rise of the first civilizations. The increase in food production in these regions led to a significant growth in population, while efforts to control the flow of water to maximize the irrigation of cultivated areas and to protect the local inhabitants from hostile forces outside the community provoked the first steps toward cooperative activities on a large scale. The need to oversee the entire process brought about the emergence of an elite that was eventually transformed into a government.

As we have seen, the first clear steps in the rise of the first civilizations took place in the fourth and third millennia B.C.E. in Mesopotamia, northern Africa, India, and China. How the first governments took shape in these areas is not certain, but anthropologists studying the evolution of human communities in various parts of the world have discovered that one common stage in the process is the emergence of what are called "big men" within a single village or a collection of villages. By means of their military prowess, dominant personalities, or political acumen, these people gradually emerge as the leaders of that community. In time, the "big men" begin to assume formal symbols of authority and to pass on that authority to others within their own family. As the communities continue to grow in size and material wealth, the "big men" assume hereditary status, and their allies and family members are transformed into a hereditary monarchy.

The appearance of these sedentary societies has a major impact on the social organizations, religious beliefs, and way of life of the peoples living within their boundaries. With the increase in population and the development of centralized authority came the emergence of cities. While some of these urban centers were identified with a particular economic function, such as proximity to gold or iron deposits or a strategic location on a major trade route, others served primarily as administrative centers or the site of temples for the official cult or other ritual observances. Within these cities, new forms of livelihood appeared to satisfy the growing need for social services and consumer goods. Some people became artisans or merchants, while others became warriors, scholars, or priests. In some cases, the physical divisions within the first cities reflected the strict hierarchical character of the society as a whole, with a royal palace surrounded by an imposing wall and separate from the remainder of the urban population. In other instances, as in the Indus River Valley, the cities lacked a royal precinct and the ostentatious palaces that marked their contemporaries elsewhere. While the layout of many ancient cities followed the natural contours of the land or were built on ancient transportation routes, others, such as was the case in China and India, were sometimes laid out on a grid pattern that was almost modern in its composition.

The quality of housing in the new cities varied according to location and the status of the owner. In general,

RULERS AND GODS

All of the world's earliest civilizations believed that there was a close relationship between rulers and gods. In Egypt, pharaohs were considered gods whose role was to maintain the order and harmony of the universe in their own kingdom. In the words of an Egyptian hymn, "What is the king of Upper and Lower Egypt? He is a god by whose dealings one lives, the father and mother of all men, alone by himself, without an equal." In Mesopotamia, India, and China, rulers were thought to rule with divine assistance. Kings were often seen as rulers who derived their power from the gods and who were the agents or representatives of the gods. As one person said in a petition to his king, "You in your judgment, you are the son of Anu [god of the sky in ancient Mesopotamia]; your commands, like the word of a god, cannot be reversed; your words, like rain pouring down from heaven, are without number."

In ancient India, rulers claimed to be representatives of the gods because they were descended from Manu, the first man who had been made a king by Brahman, the chief god. Many Romans certainly believed that their success in creating an empire was a visible sign of divine favor. As the Roman statesman Cicero stated, "We have overcome all the nations of the world, because we have realized that the world is directed and governed by the gods."

Their supposed connection to the gods also caused rulers to seek divine aid in the affairs of the world. This led to the art of divination, or an organized method to discover the intentions of the gods. In Mesopotamian and Roman society, one form of divination involved the examination of the livers of sacrificed animals; features seen in the livers were interpreted to foretell events to come. Another form of divination for Mesopotamian and Roman rulers was based on a careful observation of natural phenomena; the flights of birds or the movements of planetary bodies in the skies, for example, could also be interpreted to determine the will of the gods. The Chinese used oracle bones to receive advice from supernatural forces that were beyond the power of human beings. Questions to the gods were scratched on turtle shells or animal bones, which were then exposed to fire. Shamans then interpreted the meaning of the resulting cracks on the surface of the shells or bones as messages from supernatural forces. The Greeks divined the will of the gods by use of the oracle, a sacred shrine dedicated to a god or goddess who revealed the future in response to a question.

Underlying all of these divinatory practices was a belief in a supernatural universe, that is, a world in which divine forces were in charge and in which humans were dependent for their own well-being on those divine forces. It was not until the Scientific Revolution of the modern world that many people began to believe in a natural world that was not governed by spiritual forces.

VISHNU. Brahma the Creator, Siva the Destroyer, and Vishnu the Preserver are the three chief Hindu gods of India. Vishnu is known as the Preserver because he mediates between Brahma and Siva and is thus responsible for maintaining the stability of the universe.

THE USE OF METALS

Sometime around 6000 B.C.E., people in western Asia discovered the use of metals. They soon realized the advantage in using metal rather than stone to make both tools and weapons. Metal could be shaped more exactly, allowing artisans to make more refined tools and weapons with sharp edges and more precise shapes. Copper, silver, and gold, which were commonly found in their elemental form, were the first metals to be used. These were relatively soft and could be more easily pounded into different shapes. But an important step was taken when people discovered that a rock that contained metal could be heated to liquefy the metal (a process called smelting). The liquid metal could then be poured into molds of clay or stone to make precisely shaped tools and weapons.

Copper was the first metal to be used in making tools. The first known copper smelting furnace, dated to 3800 B.C.E., was found in the Sinai. At about the same time, however, artisans in Southeast Asia discovered that tin could be added to copper to make bronze. By 3000 B.C.E., artisans in West Asia were also making bronze. Bronze has a lower melting point that makes it easier to cast, but it is also a harder metal than copper and corrodes less. By 1400 B.C.E., the Chinese were making bronze decorative objects as well as battle-axes and helmets. The widespread use of bronze has led historians to speak of a Bronze Age from around 3000 to 1200 B.C.E., although this is a somewhat misleading term, since many people continued to use stone tools and weapons even after bronze became available.

But there were limitations in the use of bronze. Tin was not as available as copper, which made bronze tools and weapons expensive. After 1200 B.C.E., bronze was increasingly replaced by iron, which was probably first used around 1500 B.C.E. in western Asia, where the Hittites made use of it to develop new weapons. Between 1500 and 600 B.C.E., iron making spread across Europe, North Africa, and Asia. Bronze continued to be used, but mostly for jewelry and other domestic purposes. Iron was used to make tools and weapons with sharper edges. Because wrought-iron weapons were cheaper than bronze ones, larger numbers of warriors could be armed, and wars could be fought on a larger scale.

Iron was handled differently than bronze: it was heated until it could be beaten into a desired shape. Each hammering produced increased strength for the metal. This wrought iron, as it was called, was typical of iron manufacturing in the West until the late Middle Ages. In China, however, the use of heat-resistant clay in the walls of their blast furnaces raised temperatures to 1,537 degrees Celsius, enabling artisans already in the fourth century B.C.E. to liquefy iron so that it too could be cast in a mold. Europeans would not develop such blast furnaces until the fifteenth century C.E.

BRONZE AXE HEAD. This axe head was made around 2000 B.C.E. by pouring liquid metal into an axe-shaped mold of clay or stone. Artisans would then polish the surface of the axe to produce a sharp cutting edge.

however, the urban population probably lived better than their less affluent contemporaries in the countryside. Many houses had plumbing facilities, sophisticated heating systems, and a variety of utensils and luxury articles made of wood, glass, metal, or ceramics. The expansion of trade permitted many urban residents to partake of a varied diet and clothing to fit the changing seasons.

Although the emergence of the first civilizations led to the appearance of major cities, the vast majority of the population were undoubtedly peasants or slaves working on the lands of the wealthy. In general, rural peoples were less affected by the change than were their urban counterparts. Most continued to live in simple mud-and-thatch huts and lacked the amenities that were increasingly available to the more affluent residents inside the city walls. Peasants in most societies still faced severe legal restrictions on their freedom of action and move-

ment, and slavery was still commonly practiced in virtually all ancient societies.

Within these civilizations, the nature of social organization and relationship also began to change. As the concept of private property spread, people were less likely to live in large kinship groups, and the concept of the nuclear family became increasingly prevalent. Gender roles increasingly came to be differentiated, with men working in the fields or at various specialized occupations and women remaining in the home. Wives were less likely to be viewed as partners and more often as under the control of their husbands.

With the increase in the availability of food, people were now living longer. At the same time, increasingly crowded conditions in the emerging cities led to a higher incidence of disease. Some reached epidemic proportions and wiped out a high percentage of the population. As the danger of illness increased, families began having larger numbers of children to protect themselves in their old age. As a result of these countervailing trends, it is estimated that the overall population of the world may have increased by about four times between the rise of the Sumerian population in about 3500 B.C.E. and the end of the second millennium B.C.E.

These new civilizations were also the scene of significant religious and cultural developments. All of them gave birth to new religions as a means of explaining the functioning of the forces of nature. In place of a belief in a multitude of deities representing the forces of nature, new religious systems based on the existence of a single transcendent god who presided over a rational universal order began to appear. The approval of gods was deemed critical to a community's chances of success, and a professional class of priests emerged to govern relations with the divine world. Temples were built as places for worship or sacrifice, and painting and sculpture were invented as ritualistic means of portraying the deities or other forces in the natural world.

Writing was an important development in the evolution of these new civilizations. In China and Egypt, priests used writing to communicate with the gods. In Mesopotamia and the Indus River civilization, merchants relied on writing to maintain their accounts. Eventually all of these civilizations used writing as a primary means of communication as well as of creative expression.

The development of writing undoubtedly provided a major impetus to the emergence of sophisticated philosophical ideas concerning the relationship between the individual and society and the nature of the universe. Many historians have remarked on the possible significance of the fact that many of the major religious and philosophical systems of the ancient world emerged within a relatively limited period of two or three centuries in the middle of the first millennium B.C.E. By the end of the era, competition among the advocates of such systems had already become intense and sometimes led to conflict.

At first, the authority of these new civilizations was probably restricted to the area immediately adjacent to the river valleys where they had originated, and they had relatively little contact with peoples in the surrounding regions. But there is growing evidence that a pattern of regional trade had begun to develop in the Middle East, and probably in southern and eastern Asia as well, at a very early date. As the population increased, the volume of trade undoubtedly rose with it, and the new civilizations began to move outward to acquire new lands and access to needed resources. As they expanded, they began to encounter peoples along the periphery of their growing empires.

Not much evidence has survived to chronicle the nature of these first encounters, but it is likely that the results varied widely according to time and place. In some cases, the growing civilizations found it relatively easy to absorb isolated communities of agricultural or food-gathering peoples whom they encountered. Such was the case in southern China and in the southern part of the South Asian peninsula. But in other instances, notably among the nomadic or seminomadic peoples in Central and Northeast Asia, the problem was more complicated and often resulted in bitter and extended conflict.

To the sedentary societies, the peoples living along the frontier appeared hostile and warlike, motivated solely by desire for plunder and lacking in the basic attributes of civilization. Over the centuries, historians generally accepted that assessment. For many recent observers, however, the issue is not that clear-cut. For one thing, many pastoral societies, far from being primitive in character and isolated from the emerging centers of civilization, were as advanced in their own way as were the river valley societies that had sprung up in Eurasia and North Africa. While not possessing the supposed accoutrements of civilization such as a writing system, a complex bureaucracy, and clearly defined economic roles, such "frontier societies" were as well adapted to their own environmental circumstances as were their sedentary counterparts. Often people living on the periphery of civilizations were residing in areas of marginal economic utility and were forced to seek their livelihood through a mixture of farming, hunting, and animal husbandry. Agriculture may have been practiced in parts of Central Asia by the seventh millennium B.C.E., but when the climate throughout the region grew increasingly dry about 5,000 years ago, many of these communities were forced to adapt to changing circumstances by migrating to new areas, or by the domestication of animals, such as the horse. Some, like the Hyksos, the Israelites, and the Indo-European peoples, began to live by a combination of farming and herding. Others, like the Scythians and the Xiongnu, took up the purely nomadic life. Because of their wandering existence, such communities had not generally adopted the concept of statehood and operated as a fluid mixture of semiautonomous tribes, each under its own chieftain.

Contacts between these nomadic or seminomadic peoples and settled civilizations probably developed gradually over an extended period of time. Often the relationship, at least at the outset, was mutually beneficial, as each needed goods produced by the other. Nomadic peoples in Central Asia also served as an important conduit for goods and ideas between sedentary civilizations transporting goods over long distances as early as 3000 B.C.E. At first, the trade was carried by donkeys, but later the camel became the preferred means of transportation. Overland trade throughout Southwest Asia was already well established by the third and second millennia B.C.E. As we have seen, the silk route between China and the Mediterranean became an important avenue of long-distance commerce during the first millennium B.C.E.

Eventually, for reasons that are not always clear, the relationship between the settled peoples and the nomadic peoples became increasingly characterized by conflict. In some cases, the expanding sedentary empires attempted to drive the nomadic peoples off their land or to deprive them of access to trade with settled populations. In other cases, the increasing desiccation of the land may have deprived such peripheral peoples of their livelihood and forced them into desperate measures to find new means of survival. Sometimes the conflict may simply have been a consequence of the increasing aggressiveness of the nomadic peoples, as better techniques of warfare, such as the ability to fight on horseback, gave them new advantages over their rivals. Taking advantage of their military superiority, nomadic peoples often raided settled areas, terrorized the inhabitants, and pillaged their belongings.

Where conflict occurred, the governments of the sedentary civilizations used a variety of techniques to resolve the problem, including negotiations, conquest, or alliance with other pastoral peoples to isolate their primary tormentors. We have seen all of these techniques at work in China, where the Qin and the Han tried a combination of the carrot and the stick to pacify the frontier and bring these unruly peoples under control. The Romans did not hesitate to ally with one Germanic tribe to ward off another.

As it turned out, few of these techniques had any lasting effect. The relationship along the frontier was inherently unstable and in the end was disastrous for the settled empires, all of whom were eventually destroyed or seriously weakened as the result of invasion from beyond the frontier. The first to experience such a fate was the Harappan civilization in the Indus River valley, which may have been brought down at least in part as a result of the intrusion by Indo-European Aryan peoples along the northern frontier. Several hundred years later, the peoples of Mesopotamia fell at the hands of the Assyrians, who were in turn conquered by the Indo-European-speaking Persians. The empire of the pharaohs was conquered by the Hyksos, while the Roman Empire was brought to its knees as the result of constant pressure from the Germanic tribes to the north. Although the empire of the Han was not overthrown by the Xiongnu, pressure along the northern frontier contributed to the weakening of the dynasty, and after its collapse in the early third century B.C.E., the entire northern part of the country was overrun by peoples from beyond the Great Wall.

The nomadic peoples along the frontier understandably sparked fear among peoples in settled areas of the ancient world, but in broad historical terms, these nomadic peoples played an important role in the development of the first civilizations and the later evolution of humankind. Not only were they the crucial link in the growing trade relationship between the Mediterranean, the Middle East, and far-off China, but they were also the means of introducing new technology to sedentary societies. The Assyrians probably introduced the knowledge of iron to the settled peoples of Mesopotamia, while the Hyksos played a similar role for Egypt. Acquaintance with prolific new crops such as wheat and rice may have passed from one society to another by caravan. The pastoral peoples were the first to domesticate the horse and the camel, both destined ultimately to become a useful form of transportation for settled societies, and probably introduced the chariot to several sedentary civilizations throughout the Eurasian supercontinent. Although their unruly behavior undoubtedly posed a serious threat to settled societies, the nomadic peoples were a vital factor in the creation of the first global civilization in the Old World.

The increasing evidence that nomadic peoples outside the bounds of settled civilization played an important role in spreading technological advances throughout the inhabited world has brought about a significant change in the way historians view the classical empires. Until recently, national pride tended to reinforce the view that each of these civilizations evolved essentially on its own. In the last few years, however, there is a growing recognition that "cultural diffusion," as these exchanges of technology and ideas are labeled, played a major role in the emergence of the classical civilizations.

6000 B.C.E.	5000 B.C.E.	4000 B.C.E.	3000 B.C.E.

Middle East

Sumerian civilization

Agriculture and Neolithic towns

India

Harappan civilization

First agricultural settlements

China

First settled agriculture

Egypt and the Mediterranean

Flowering of Egyptian civilization

Agriculture in the Nile Valley

At the same time, it is also increasingly evident that these early civilizations were brought to their knees not just by nomadic invasions, but by their own weaknesses, which made them increasingly vulnerable to attacks along the frontier. In the Roman Empire, bloated bureaucracies as well as excessive taxation to support them, an inability to achieve a workable political system, evident in frequent military struggles over succession to the throne, the decline of Roman military virtues and a reliance on noncitizen mercenaries, and population decline in part caused by plague all played a role in undermining Rome's ability to protect itself. In China, growing internal strains within the Han society more than depredations along the frontier caused the collapse of the Han empire.

Another possible factor in the decline and collapse of the first civilizations was the role of the environment. Although proof is still lacking, much evidence suggests that ecological changes caused severe difficulties for peoples in the ancient world. Floods or drought may have brought an end to the Harappan empire, while the infestation of salt water may have leached the nutrients from the soils of the Fertile Crescent. Imperial Rome may have suffered food shortages as a result of the desiccation of the wheat fields of northern Africa, while the flooding of mines in Spain may have brought about a shortage of silver and the debased coinage of the empire.

The fall of the ancient empires, of course, did not mark the end of civilization. Although the immediate consequences of the fall of Rome and the Han dynasty were a precipitous drop in world trade and a general decline of prosperity throughout the known world, new societies eventually rose on the ashes of the ancient empires. Although many were different in key respects from those they replaced, they still carried the legacy of their predecessors. In the meantime, the forces that had been unleashed in the civilizations of antiquity sent out strands of influence that were laying the basis for new societies elsewhere in the world: south of the Sahara in western and eastern Africa, where

new societies were beginning to take shape; beyond the Alps in central Europe, where the Germanic peoples were in the process of forming a new society; in southeastern Asia, where the influence of India and China was beginning to help shape new societies among the trading and agricultural societies in the region; and across the Sea of Japan in the Japanese islands, where native rulers would import Chinese ideas to form a new civilization uniquely their own. In the meantime, new civilizations were on the verge of creation in the New World, across the oceans in the continents of North and South America. Isolated from contact with the Old World since their migration across the Bering Strait at the end of the Ice Age, the peoples of America were beginning to form civilizations of their own. It is to this new stage of human development, marked by a broadening of global contacts, that we will turn in Part II of this book.

 ## SUGGESTED READINGS

For a beautifully illustrated introduction to the ancient world, see *Past Worlds: The Times Atlas of Archaeology* (Maplewood, N.J., 1988), written by an international group of scholars. A global view of important turning points in world history can be found in M. K. Matossian, *Shaping World History: Breakthroughs in Ecology, Technology, Science, and Politics* (Armonk, N.Y., 1997). For a general introduction to prehistory, see B. M. Fagan, *People of the Earth: An Introduction to World Prehistory*, 8th ed. (New York, 1995), and C. Gamble, *Timewalkers: The Prehistory of Global Colonization* (Cambridge, Mass., 1994). On the importance of the shift to agriculture, see A. W. Johnson and T. Earle, *The Evolution of Human Societies: From Foraging Group to Agrarian State* (Stanford, 1987), and R. S. McNeish, *Origins of Agriculture and Settled Life* (Norman, Okla., 1992). A global perspective on the emergence of civilization can be found in G. Burenhult, *Old World Civilizations: The Rise of Cities and States* (New York, 1994). On the use of metals, see R. Raymond, *Out of the Fiery Furnace: The Impact of Metals on the History of Mankind* (University Park, Pa., 1986).

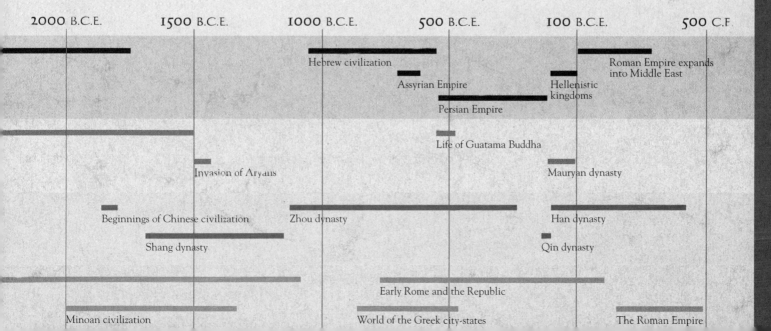

| 2000 B.C.E. | 1500 B.C.E. | 1000 B.C.E. | 500 B.C.E. | 100 B.C.E. | 500 C.E. |

Hebrew civilization

Assyrian Empire

Hellenistic kingdoms

Persian Empire

Roman Empire expands into Middle East

Life of Guatama Buddha

Invasion of Aryans

Mauryan dynasty

Beginnings of Chinese civilization

Zhou dynasty

Han dynasty

Shang dynasty

Qin dynasty

Early Rome and the Republic

Minoan civilization

World of the Greek city-states

The Roman Empire

By the beginning of the first millennium C.E., the great states of the ancient world were mostly in a state of decline; some were even at the point of collapse. On the ruins of these ancient empires, new patterns of civilization began to take shape between 400 and 1500 C.E. In some cases, these new societies were built on the political and cultural foundations of their predecessors. The Tang dynasty in China and the Guptas in India both looked back to the ancient period to provide an ideological model for their own time. The Byzantine Empire carried on parts of the classical Greek tradition while also adopting the powerful creed of Christianity from the Roman Empire. In other cases, new states incorporated some elements of the former classical civilizations while embarking on markedly different directions, as in the new European civilization of the Middle Ages and the Arabic states in the Middle East.

In the meantime, complex societies were also beginning to appear in a number of other parts of the world—in Japan, in Southeast Asia, in sub-Saharan Africa, and across the Atlantic in the Americas. Except for the latter, which was developing in isolation, all of these civilizations were influenced to a greater or lesser degree by older or more powerful empires in the region, and all were increasingly linked by commercial and cultural contacts into the first "global civilization." At the same time, each was able to combine borrowed ideas with indigenous characteristics.

Like their classical predecessors, most of these new states obtained much of their wealth from agriculture. India, China, and medieval Europe were all predominantly agricultural societies. But what is most striking about the period is the growing importance of trade as a factor in national and global development. It was during the first millennium C.E. that the great trade routes of the traditional world—the Silk Road from China to the Middle East and then on to the Mediterranean, the caravan trade route across the Sahara, and the commercial network that stretched across the Indian Ocean—all reached their maturity.

The expansion of regional and global trade also led to the spread of ideas. It was commerce that brought Buddhism to China and Southeast Asia and Islam to sub-Saharan Africa and the Indonesian archipelago. At first the impact was felt primarily in the cities, but eventually it began to spread to the countryside. Kings and princes became converts to the new faiths and provided funds and other forms of patronage for their support.

The spread of religious and cultural ideas sometimes led to conflict. The popularity of Buddhism led eventually to its suppression in China. Tensions between the Islamic and Christian worlds were particularly strong and culminated in the Crusades and the Christian reconquest of Spain and Portugal. But often the assimilation of new religions and cultural ideas took place through a peaceful process, as with the spread of Islam into various areas of sub-Saharan and East Africa. Christianity, aided by the zeal of its missionary monks, was an active agent in converting new peoples in central and eastern Europe and transforming their cultures.

CHAPTER

6

THE NEW WORLD

CHAPTER OUTLINE

- THE FIRST AMERICANS
- EARLY CIVILIZATIONS IN CENTRAL AMERICA
- THE FIRST CIVILIZATIONS IN SOUTH AMERICA
- STATELESS SOCIETIES IN THE NEW WORLD
- CONCLUSION

FOCUS QUESTIONS

- Who were the first Americans, and when and how did they arrive?
- What were the main characteristics of the civilizations of the Maya, the Aztecs, and the Inca?
- What role did religion play in the civilizations of the New World?
- In what ways were the civilizations of the New World similar to the early civilizations of the Old World, and in what ways were they different?
- What were the main characteristics of the stateless societies in the Americas, and how did they differ from the civilizations that arose in Central America and the Andes?

In August 1519, five hundred Spanish soldiers of fortune left their anchorage near the modern city of Veracruz and began the long trek from the coast across the dusty plateau of Mexico to the capital of the Aztecs. At their head was Hernán Cortés, a Spanish conquistador who had just burned their ship to ensure that his followers would not launch a mutiny and sail back to Europe. In Tenochtitlán, the Aztec capital located in what is now Mexico City, Emperor Moctezuma received the news of the foreigners' presence and awaited their arrival with anticipation. According to Aztec legend, one of their ancestors, the godlike Quetzalcoatl, had left the area hundreds of years earlier, vowing to return one day to reclaim his heritage. Could this stranger with his band of men be Quetzalcoatl or his representative? When Cortés and his forces, now accompanied by a crowd of people they had encountered en route, reached the vicinity of Moctezuma's capital, the two men met face to face. With this encounter, the last barrier between the Old World and the previously unknown civilizations in the Western Hemisphere had been bridged, and a new era dawned.

The Aztecs were only the latest in a series of sophisticated societies that had sprung up at various locations in North and South America since human beings first crossed the Bering Strait several millennia earlier. Most of these early peoples, today often referred to as Amerindians, lived by hunting and fishing or by food gathering. But by the second and first millennia B.C.E., the first organized societies began to take root in Central and South America. One key area of development was on the plateau of central Mexico. Another was in the lowland regions along the Gulf of Mexico and extending into modern Guatemala. A third was in the central Andes Mountains, adjacent to the Pacific coast of South America. Others were just beginning to emerge in the river valleys and great plains of North America.

For the next two millennia, these societies developed in apparently total isolation from their counterparts elsewhere in the world. This lack of contact with other human beings deprived them of access to technological and cultural developments taking place in Africa, Asia, and Europe. They did not know of the wheel, for example, and their written languages were rudimentary compared to equivalents in complex civilizations in other parts of the globe. But in other respects, their cultural achievements were the equal of those realized elsewhere. When the first European explorers arrived in the New World at the turn of the sixteenth century, they described much that they observed in glowing terms.

Unfortunately for their own needs, one technological development that the peoples of America lacked was the knowledge of firearms. In a few short years, tiny bands of Spanish conquistadors were able to conquer the magnificent civilizations that we know today as the Aztecs, the Maya, and the Inca and turn them into ruins. Still, enough archaeological evidence remains to enable us to appreciate their impressive achievements. ☸

THE FIRST AMERICANS

When the first human beings arrived in the New World has long been a matter of dispute. In the first centuries following the voyages of Christopher Columbus, speculation centered on the possibility that the first settlers to reach the American continents had crossed the Atlantic Ocean. Were they the lost tribes of Israel? Were they Phoenician seafarers from Carthage? Or were they refugees from the legendary lost continent of Atlantis? In all cases, the assumption was that they were relatively recent arrivals.

By the mid-nineteenth century, under the influence of the new Darwinist concept of evolution, a new theory developed. It proposed that the peopling of America had taken place much earlier as a result of the migration of small communities across the Bering Strait. Recent evidence, including numerous physical similarities between some early Americans and contemporary peoples living in northeastern Asia, has confirmed this hypothesis. The debate on when the migrations began continues, however. Archaeologist Louis Leakey, one of the pioneers in the search for the origins of humankind in Africa, suggested that the first hominids may have arrived in America as long as 100,000 years ago. Others estimate that the first Americans were members of *Homo sapiens sapiens* who crossed from Asia by foot between 10,000 and 15,000 years ago in pursuit of herds of bison and caribou that moved into the area in search of grazing land at the end of the Ice Age. Recently obtained genetic evidence, however, suggests the possibility of an earlier date, perhaps as early as 29,000 years ago. Other recent discoveries indicate that some early settlers may have originally come from Africa, rather than from eastern Asia. Clearly, the question has not yet been definitively answered.

In any case, it is now generally accepted that human beings were living in the New World at least 15,000 years ago. They gradually spread throughout the North American continent and had penetrated almost to the southern tip of South America by about 10,000 B.C.E. These first Americans were hunters and food gatherers, who lived in small nomadic communities close to the source of their food supply. Although it is not known when agriculture was first practiced, beans and squash seeds have been found at sites that date back at least 8,000 years. The cultivation of maize, and perhaps other crops as well, appears to have been under way as early as 5000 B.C.E. in the

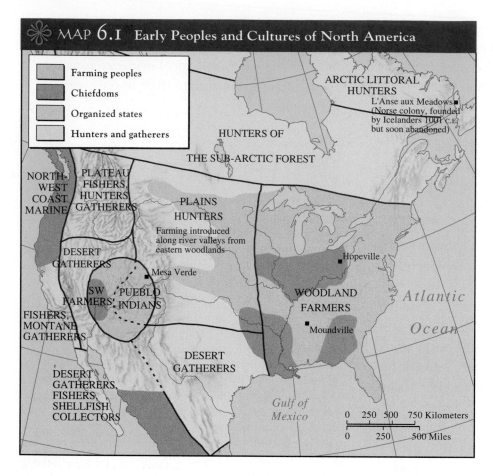

MAP 6.1   Early Peoples and Cultures of North America

Farming peoples

Chiefdoms

Organized states

Hunters and gatherers

ARCTIC LITTORAL HUNTERS

L'Anse aux Meadows (Norse colony, founded by Icelanders 1001 C.E. but soon abandoned)

HUNTERS OF THE SUB-ARCTIC FOREST

NORTH-WEST COAST MARINE

PLATEAU FISHERS, HUNTERS GATHERERS

PLAINS HUNTERS

Farming introduced along river valleys from eastern woodlands

Mesa Verde

DESERT GATHERERS

SW FARMERS

PUEBLO INDIANS

Hopeville

WOODLAND FARMERS

Atlantic Ocean

FISHERS, MONTANE GATHERERS

Moundville

DESERT GATHERERS, FISHERS, SHELLFISH COLLECTORS

DESERT GATHERERS

Gulf of Mexico

0   250   500   750 Kilometers

0   250   500 Miles

glyphs later in this chapter) and may be the ancestor of the first true writing systems in the New World.

Olmec society apparently consisted of several classes, including a class of skilled artisans who produced a series of massive stone heads, some of which are more than ten feet high. The Olmec peoples supported themselves primarily by cultivating crops, such as corn and beans, but also engaged in fishing and hunting. The Olmec apparently played a ceremonial game on a stone ball court, a ritual that would later be widely practiced throughout the region (see The Mysterious Maya later in this chapter).

Eventually, Olmec civilization began to decline and apparently collapsed around the fourth century B.C.E. During its heyday, however, it extended from Mexico City to El Salvador and perhaps to the shores of the Pacific Ocean.

In the meantime, parallel developments were occurring at Monte Alban, on a hillside overlooking the modern city of Oaxaca, in central Mexico. Around the middle of the first millennium B.C.E., the Zapotec peoples created an extensive civilization that flourished for several hundred years in the highlands. Like the Olmec sites, Monte Alban contains a number of temples and pyramids, but they are located in much more awesome surroundings on a massive stone terrace atop a 1,200-foot-high mountain overlooking the Oaxaca valley. The majority of the population, estimated at about 20,000, dwelled on terraces cut into the sides of the mountain.

Tehuacan valley in the southern portion of the central plateau of Mexico. A similar process may have been underway in the lowland regions near the modern city of Veracruz and in the Yucatán peninsula further to the east. There, in the region that archaeologists call Mesoamerica, the first civilizations in the New World began to appear.

EARLY CIVILIZATIONS IN CENTRAL AMERICA

The first signs of civilization in Mesoamerica appeared in the first millennium B.C.E., with the emergence of what is called Olmec culture in the hot and swampy lowlands along the coast of the Gulf of Mexico south of Veracruz. Olmec civilization was characterized by intensive agriculture along the muddy riverbanks in the area and by the carving of stone ornaments, tools, and monuments at sites such as San Lorenzo and La Venta. The site at La Venta includes a ceremonial precinct with a thirty-foot-high earthen pyramid, the largest of its date in all Mesoamerica. The Olmec peoples organized a widespread trading network, carried on religious rituals, and devised an as yet undeciphered system of hieroglyphics that is similar in some respects to later Mayan writing (see Mayan Hiero-

Teotihuacán: America's First Metropolis

The first major metropolis in Mesoamerica was the city of Teotihuacán, capital of an early kingdom about thirty miles northeast of Mexico City that arose sometime around the third century B.C.E. and flourished for nearly a millennium until it collapsed under mysterious circumstances about 800 C.E. Along the main thoroughfare were temples and palaces, all dominated by a massive Pyramid of the Sun, under which archaeologists have discovered the remains of sacrificial victims, probably put to death during the dedication of the structure. In the vicinity are the remains of a large market, where goods from distant regions as well as agricultural produce grown by farmers in the vicinity were exchanged. The products traded included cacao, rubber, feathers, and various types of vegetables and meat. Pulque, a liquor extracted from the agave plant, was used in religious ceremonies. An obsidian mine nearby may explain the location of the city; obsidian is a volcanic glass that was prized in Mesoamerica for use in tools, mirrors, and the blades of sacrificial knives.

Most of the city consisted of one-story stucco apartment compounds; some were as large as 35,000 square feet, sufficient to house more than a hundred people. Each apartment was divided into several rooms, while the compounds were covered by flat roofs made of wooden beams, poles,

and stucco. The compounds were separated by wide streets laid out on a rectangular grid and were entered through narrow alleys.

Living within the fertile Valley of Mexico, an upland plateau surrounded by magnificent snowcapped mountains, the inhabitants of Teotihuacán probably obtained the bulk of their wealth from agriculture. At that time, the valley floor was filled with swampy lakes containing the water runoff from the surrounding mountains. The combination of fertile soil and adequate water combined to make the valley one of the richest farming areas in Mesoamerica.

Sometime during the eighth century, for unknown reasons the wealth and power of the city began to decline, and eventually its ruling class departed, with the priests carrying stone images of local deities on their backs. The next two centuries were a time of troubles throughout the region, as feuding principalities fought over limited farmland. The problem was compounded in later centuries when peoples from surrounding areas, attracted by the rich farmlands, migrated into the Valley of Mexico and began to compete for territory with small city-states already established there. As the local population expanded, farmers began to engage in more intensive agriculture. They drained the lakes to build *chinampas,* swampy islands crisscrossed by canals that provided water for their crops and easy transportation to local markets for their excess produce.

The Mysterious Maya

Far to the east of the Valley of Mexico, another major civilization had taken form in the Yucatán peninsula. This was the civilization of the Maya, which was older and equally as sophisticated as the society at Teotihuacán.

Like the Aztecs and the inhabitants of Teotihuacán, the Maya trace their origins to the parent Olmec civilization in the lowlands along the Gulf of Mexico. It is not known when human beings first inhabited the Yucatán peninsula, but peoples contemporaneous with the Olmecs were already cultivating such crops as corn,

MAP 6.2 Early Peoples and Cultures of Central and Latin America

SAVANNAH FARMERS

Atlantic Ocean

NORTH ANDEAN CHIEFDOMS

FARMING TRIBES

(manioc cultivators) of the Amazon Rain Forest

Amazon R.

Moche

Chavin de Huantar

CENTRAL ANDEAN CIVILIZATION

About 500 C.E. farming introduced from Amazon Basin into Brazilian forest and savannah

SAVANNAH FARMERS

Immigration of Tupi-Guaraní tribes

Pacific Ocean

HUNTERS OF THE CHACO SAVANNAH

- Farming peoples
- Chiefdoms
- Organized states
- Hunters and gatherers

GRASSLAND STEPPE HUNTERS

MARITIME HUNTERS, SHELLFISH COLLECTORS

| 0 | 500 | 1000 | 1500 Kilometers |
| 0 | | 500 | 1000 Miles |

Teotihuacán · Chichen Itza

La Venta · Tikal

Monte Alban

Caribbean Sea

MAIZE AND MANIOC CULTIVATORS OF CARIBBEAN LOWLANDS

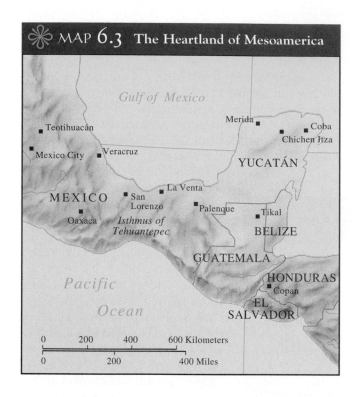

MAP 6.3   The Heartland of Mesoamerica

early civilizations in the region. Cacao trees were the source of chocolate, which was used as a beverage by the upper classes, while cocoa beans, the fruit of the cacao tree, were used as currency in markets throughout the region.

As the population in the area increased, the inhabitants began to migrate into the central Yucatán peninsula to the north. The overcrowding forced farmers in the lowland areas to shift from slash-and-burn cultivation to swamp agriculture of the type practiced in the lake region of the Valley of Mexico. By the middle of the first millennium C.E., the entire area was honeycombed with a patchwork of small city-states competing with each other for land and resources. The most important of such city-states were probably Tikal and Copan, but it is doubtful that any was sufficiently powerful to dominate the entire area. The largest urban centers such as Tikal may have had 100,000 inhabitants at their height.

The power of the rulers of the city-states was certainly impressive. One of the monarchs at Copan—known to scholars as "18 rabbit" from the hieroglyphs composing his name—ordered the construction of a grand palace requiring more than 30,000 person-days of labor. Around the ruler was a class of aristocrats whose wealth was probably based on the ownership of land farmed by their poorer relatives. Eventually, many of the aristocrats became priests or scribes at the royal court or adopted honored professions as sculptors or painters. As the society's wealth grew, so did the need for artisans and traders, who began to form a small middle class.

The majority of the population on the peninsula, however (estimated at roughly three million at the height of Mayan power), were farmers. They lived on their *chinampa* plots or on terraced hills in the highlands. Houses

yams, and manioc in the area during the first millennium B.C.E. As the population increased, an early civilization began to emerge along the Pacific coast directly to the south of the peninsula and in the highlands of modern Guatemala. Contacts were already established with the Olmec to the west.

Since the area was a source for cacao trees and obsidian, the inhabitants soon developed relations with other

THE PYRAMID OF THE SUN, TEOTIHUACÁN.   The first major metropolis in Central America was Teotihuacán, which was inhabited by as many as 150,000 people during its zenith sometime after 400 C.E. Covering an area of at least eight square miles, in size and sophistication it rivaled its contemporary, the city of Rome. The ceremonial center of Teotihuacán, which contained more than five thousand structures, was laid out in a north-south and an east-west axis; it was dominated by the Pyramid of the Sun, rising in four tiers to a height of over two hundred feet.

THE CREATION OF THE WORLD: A MAYAN VIEW

Popul Vuh, a sacred work of the ancient Maya, is an account of Mayan history and religious beliefs. No written version in the original Mayan script is extant, but shortly after the Spanish conquest, it was written down in Quiche (the spoken language of the Maya), using the Latin script, apparently from memory. This version was later translated into Spanish. The following excerpt from the opening lines of Popul Vuh recounts the Mayan myth of the creation.

POPUL VUH: THE SACRED BOOK OF THE MAYA

This is the account of how all was in suspense, all calm, in silence; all motionless, still, and the expanse of the sky was empty.

This is the first account, the first narrative. There was neither man, nor animal, birds, fishes, crabs, trees, stones, caves, ravines, grasses, nor forests; there was only the sky.

The surface of the earth had not appeared. There was only the calm sea and the great expanse of the sky.

There was nothing brought together, nothing which could make a noise, nor anything which might move, or tremble, or could make noise in the sky.

There was nothing standing; only the calm water, the placid sea, alone and tranquil. Nothing existed.

There was only immobility and silence in the darkness, in the night. Only the Creator, the Maker, Tepeu, Gucumatz, the Forefathers, were in the water surrounded with light. They were hidden under green and blue feathers, and were therefore called Gucumatz. By nature they were great sages and great thinkers. In this manner the sky existed and also the Heart of Heaven, which is the name of God and thus He is called.

Then came the word. Tepeu and Gucumatz came together in the darkness, in the night, and Tepeu and Gucumatz talked together. They talked then, discussing and deliberating; they agreed, they united their words and their thoughts.

Then while they meditated, it became clear to them that when dawn would break, man must appear. Then they planned the creation, and the growth of the trees and the thickets and the birth of life and the creation of man. Thus it was arranged in the darkness and in the night by the Heart of Heaven who is called Huracan.

The first is called Caculha Huracan. The second is Chipi-Caculha. The third is Raxa-Caculha. And these three are the Heart of Heaven.

So it was that they made perfect the work, when they did it after thinking and meditating upon it.

---

were built of adobe and thatch and probably resembled the houses of the majority of the population in the area today. There was a fairly clear-cut division of labor along gender lines. The men were responsible for fighting and hunting, and the women for homemaking and the preparation of cornmeal, the staple food of much of the population.

Some noble women seem to have played important roles in both political and religious life. In the seventh century C.E., for example, Pacal became king of Palenque, one of the most powerful of the Mayan city-states, through the royal line of his mother and grandmother, thereby breaking the patrilineal descent twice. His mother ruled Palenque for three years and was the power behind the throne for her son's first twenty-five years of rule. Pacal legitimized his kingship by transforming his mother into a divine representation of the "first mother" goddess.

Mayan religion was polytheistic. Although the names were different, Mayan gods shared many of the characteristics of deities of nearby cultures. The supreme god was named Itzamna (Lizard House). Deities were ranked in order of importance, and some, like the jaguar god of night, were evil rather than good. Some scholars believe that many of the nature deities may have been viewed as manifestations of one supreme godhead (see the box above). As at Teotihuacán, human sacrifice (normally by decapitation) was practiced to propitiate the heavenly forces. Scenes from paintings and rock carvings depict a society preoccupied with war and the seizure of captives for sacrifice.

Physically, the Mayan cities were built around a ceremonial core dominated by a central pyramid surmounted by a shrine to the gods. Nearby were other temples, palaces, and a sacred ball court. The ball court was a rectangular space surrounded by vertical walls with metal rings through which the contestants attempted to drive a hard rubber ball. Although the rules of the game are only imperfectly understood, it apparently had religious significance, and the vanquished players were sacrificed in ceremonies held after the close of the game. Similar courts have been found at sites throughout Mesoamerica.

MAYAN HIEROGLYPHS

In some ways, Mayan culture was more advanced than the later Aztec civilization in the Valley of Mexico. In particular, the Mayan writing system was much more sophisticated than the relatively primitive system used by the

A SAMPLE OF MAYAN WRITING

The Maya were the only Mesoamerican people to devise a complete written language. Like the Sumerian and Egyptian scripts, the Mayan system was composed of a mixture of ideographs and phonetic symbols, which were written in double columns to be read from left to right and top to bottom. The language was rudimentary in many ways. It had few adjectives or adverbs, and the numbering system comprised only three symbols: a shell for zero, a dot for one, and a bar for five.

During the classical era from 300 to 900 C.E., the Maya used the script to record dynastic statistics with deliberate precision, listing the date of the ruler's birth, his accession to power, and his marriage and death, while highlighting victories in battle, the capture of prisoners, and ritual ceremonies. The symbols were carved on stone panels, stelae, and funerary urns or were painted with a brush on folding screen books made of bark paper; only four of these books from the late period remain extant today.

A sample of Mayan hieroglyphs is shown below.

"birth of . . ."   "death of . . ."   warfare

bloodletting rite   "accession of . . ."   *chucah* "he captured . . ."   "captor of . . ."

Aztecs (see the box above). Unfortunately, when the Spanish conquered the remains of Mayan civilization, they made no attempt to decipher the language with the assistance of natives familiar with the script. The Spanish Bishop Diego de Landa, otherwise an astute and sympathetic observer of Mayan culture, remarked: "We found a large number of books in these characters and, as they contained nothing in which there were not to be seen superstition and lies of the devil, we burned them all, which they regretted to an amazing degree, and which caused them much affliction."[1]

The Mayan hieroglyphs remained undeciphered until scholars discovered that many passages contained symbols that recorded dates in the Mayan calendar. This cal-

PREPARING FOR SACRIFICE.
This copy of a wall painting from the 800 C.E. Mayan temple at Bonampak shows a ruler accepting a human sacrifice, which was offered to appease the anger of the deities. The Maya went on raids for victims and then sacrificed them in elaborate rites with ornate costumes and dancing. Here nobles wearing the pelts and the headdress of jaguars, the symbol of power and rank, preside over the ceremonial preparation of the victim.

� **A BALL COURT.** Throughout Mesoamerica a dangerous game was played on ball courts such as this one. A large ball of solid rubber was propelled from the hip at such tremendous speed that players had to wear extensive padding. More than an athletic contest, the game had religious significance. The court is thought to have represented the cosmos and the ball the sun, and the losers were sacrificed to the gods in postgame ceremonies.

endar, which measures time back to a particular date in August 3114 B.C.E., required a sophisticated understanding of astronomical events and mathematics to compile. Starting with these known symbols as a foundation, modern scholars have gradually deciphered the script. Like the scripts of the Sumerians and ancient Egyptians, the Mayan hieroglyphs were both ideographic and phonetic in nature and, in fact, were becoming more phonetic as time passed.

One of the most important repositories of Mayan hieroglyphs is at Palenque, an archaeological site deep in the jungles in the neck of the Mexican peninsula, considerably to the west of the Yucatán. In a chamber located under the Temple of Inscriptions, archaeologists discovered a royal tomb and a massive limestone slab covered with hieroglyphs. By deciphering the message on the slab, archaeologists for the first time identified a historical figure in Mayan history. He was a ruler named Pacal, known from his glyph as "the shield"; Pacal ordered the construction of the Temple of Inscriptions in the midseventh century, and it was his body that was buried in the tomb.

As befits their intense interest in the passage of time, the Maya also had a sophisticated knowledge of astronomy and kept voluminous records of the movements of the heavenly bodies. There were practical reasons for their concern. The arrival of the planet Venus in the evening sky, for example, was a traditional time to prepare for war. The Temple of Inscriptions was oriented so that an

✱ **THE TEMPLE OF THE INSCRIPTIONS.** King Pacal and his eldest son helped to create the "golden age" of Mayan civilization with their innovative architecture and the detailed carvings of glyphs on the many limestone monuments at Palenque. Pacal was apparently obsessed with the need to legitimize his royal status, since his claim to the throne descended not from his father's line, but from that of his mother and grandmother. The Temple of the Inscriptions was built at Pacal's order in 675 C.E. to serve as his mausoleum after his death. His body was placed at the foot of a staircase leading down into the crypt. Adorning the many carved walls of the temple are additional glyphs that attempt to portray his mother as the "first mother" goddess of Palenque and thus confirm his own divine provenance as her offspring. The Temple is considered to be one of the most important monuments in Mesoamerica.

observer could stand on the platform at the spring equinox and watch the setting of the sun.

THE MYSTERY OF MAYAN DECLINE

Sometime in the eighth or ninth century, the classical Mayan civilization in the central Yucatán peninsula began to decline. At Copan, for example, it ended abruptly in 822 C.E., when work on various stone sculptures ordered by the ruler suddenly ceased. The end of Palenque, a rival state to the west, soon followed. Whether the decline was caused by overuse of the land, invasion, internal revolt, or a natural disaster such as a volcanic eruption is a question that has puzzled archaeologists for decades. Recent evidence supports the theory that overcultivation of the land due to a growing population gradually reduced crop yields. Another theory is that a long drought, which lasted for almost two centuries in the ninth and tenth centuries C.E., may have played a major role. Certainly, the period was characterized by an increase in internecine war among the states and the rise of powerful nobles.

Whatever the case, cities like Tikal and Palenque were abandoned to the jungles, though newer urban centers in the northern part of the peninsula, like Uxmal and Chichen Itza, survived and continued to prosper. According to local history, this latter area was taken over by peoples known as the Toltecs, led by a man known as Kukulcan ("feathered serpent"), who migrated to the peninsula from Tula in central Mexico sometime in the tenth century. Some scholars believe this flight was associated with the legend of the departure of Quetzalcoatl, the feathered serpent who promised that he would someday return to reclaim his homeland.

The Toltecs apparently controlled the upper peninsula from their capital at Chichen Itza for several centuries, and then they too declined. When the Spaniards arrived, the area was divided into a number of small principalities, and the cities such as Uxmal and Chichen Itza had been abandoned.

The Aztecs

Among the groups moving into the Valley of Mexico after the fall of Teotihuacán were the Mexica (pronounced Mesheeca). No one knows their origins, although folk legend held that their original homeland was an island in a lake called Aztlan. From that legendary homeland comes the name *Aztec*, by which they are known to the modern world. Sometime during the early twelfth century, the Aztecs left their original habitat and, carrying an image of their patron deity Huitzilopochtli, began a lengthy migration that climaxed with their arrival in the Valley of Mexico sometime late in the century.

Less sophisticated than many of their neighbors, the Aztecs at first were forced to seek alliances with stronger city-states. They were excellent warriors, however, and (like Sparta in ancient Greece and the state of Qin in Zhou dynasty China) had become the leading city-state in the lake region by the early fifteenth century. Establishing their capital at Tenochtitlán, on an island in the middle of Lake Texcoco, they set out to bring the entire region under their domination.

For the remainder of the fifteenth century, the Aztecs consolidated their control over much of what is modern Mexico, from the Atlantic to the Pacific Ocean and as far south as the Guatemalan border. The new kingdom was not a centralized state but a collection of semiautonomous territories. To provide a unifying focus for the kingdom, the Aztecs promoted their patron god Huitzilopochtli as the guiding deity of the entire population, which now numbered several million.

POLITICS AND SOCIETY

Like all great empires in ancient times, the Aztec state was authoritarian in nature. Power was vested in the monarch, whose authority had both a divine and a secular character. The Aztec ruler claimed descent from the gods and served as an intermediary between the material and the metaphysical worlds. Unlike many of his counterparts in the Old World, however, the monarch did not obtain his position by a rigid law of succession. On the death of the ruler, his successor was selected from within the royal family by a small group of senior officials, who were also members of the family and were therefore eligible for the position. Once placed on the throne, the Aztec ruler was advised by a small council of lords, headed by a prime minister who served as the chief executive of the government, and a bureaucracy. Beyond the capital, the power of the central government was limited. Rulers of territories subject to the Aztecs were allowed considerable autonomy in return for paying tribute, in the form of goods or captives, to the central government. The most important government officials in the provinces were the tax collectors, who collected the tribute. They used the threat of military action against those who failed to carry out their tribute obligations and therefore understandably were not popular with the taxpayers. According to Bernal Díaz, a Spaniard who accompanied Hernán Cortés on his expedition to Tenochtitlán in 1519,

> All these towns complained about Montezuma [Moctezuma, the Aztec ruler at the time of the Cortés expedition] and his tax collectors, speaking in private so that the Mexican ambassadors should not hear them, however. They said these officials robbed them of all they possessed, and that if their wives and daughters were pretty they would violate them in front of their fathers and husbands and carry them away. They also said that the Mexicans [that is, the representatives from the capital] made the men work like slaves, compelling them to carry pine trunks and stone and firewood and maize overland and in canoes, and to perform other tasks, such as planting maize fields, and that they took away the people's lands as well for the service of their idols.[2]

Positions in the government bureaucracy were the exclusive privilege of the hereditary nobility, all of whom traced their lineage to the founding family of the Aztec clan. Male children in noble families were sent to temple schools, where they were exposed to a harsh regimen consisting of manual labor, military training, and the memorization of information about Aztec society and religion. On reaching adulthood, they would select a career in the military service, the government bureaucracy, or the priesthood. As a reward for their services, senior officials received large estates from the government, and they alone had the right to hire communal labor.

The remainder of the population consisted of commoners, indentured workers, and slaves. Most indentured workers were landless laborers who contracted to work on the nobles' estates, while slaves served in the households of the wealthy. Slavery was not an inherited status, and the children of slaves were considered to be free citizens. Commoners might sell themselves into slavery when in debt and then later purchase their freedom.

The vast majority of the population were commoners. All commoners were members of large kinship groups called *calpullis*. Each *calpulli*, often consisting of as many as a thousand members, was headed by an elected chief, who ran its day-to-day affairs and served as an intermediary with the central government. Each *calpulli* was responsible for providing taxes (usually in the form of goods) and conscript labor to the state.

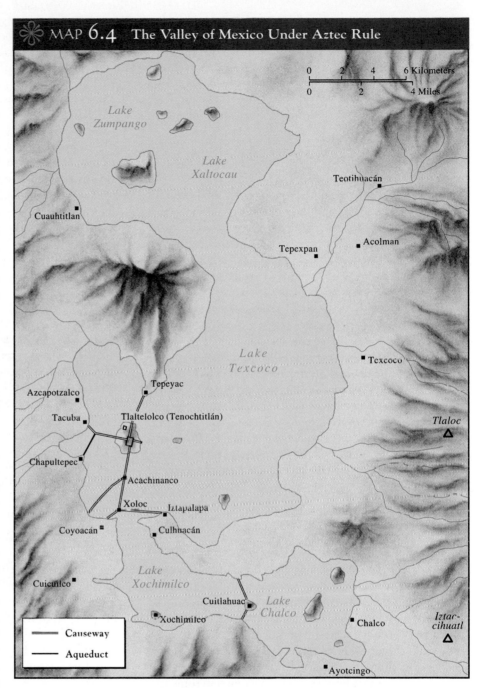

MAP 6.4 The Valley of Mexico Under Aztec Rule

Each *calpulli* maintained its own temples and schools and administered the land held by the community. Farmland within the *calpulli* was held in common and could not be sold, although it could be inherited within the family. Within the cities, each *calpulli* occupied a separate neighborhood, where its members often performed a particular function, such as metalworking, stonecutting, weaving, carpentry, or commerce. Apparently, a large proportion of the population engaged in some form of trade, at least in the densely populated Valley of Mexico, where an estimated half of the people lived in an urban environment. Many farmers brought their goods to the mar-

kets via the canals and sold them directly to retailers (see the box on p. 178).

The *calpulli* compounds themselves were divided into smaller family units. Individual families lived in small flat-roofed dwellings containing one or two rooms. Each house was separate from its neighbors and had direct access to the surrounding streets and canals. The houses of farmers living on the *chinampas* were set on raised dirt platforms built above the surrounding fields to prevent flooding.

Gender roles within the family were rigidly stratified. Male children were trained for war and were expected to

MARKETS AND MERCHANDISE IN AZTEC MEXICO

One of our most valuable descriptions of Aztec civilization is The Conquest of New Spain, written by Bernal Díaz, a Spaniard who accompanied Hernán Cortés on his expedition to Mexico in 1519. In the following passage, Díaz describes the great market at Tenochtitlán.

BERNAL DÍAZ, THE CONQUEST OF NEW SPAIN

Let us begin with the dealers in gold, silver, and precious stones, feathers, cloaks, and embroidered goods, and male and female slaves who are also sold there. They bring as many slaves to be sold in that market as the Portuguese bring Negroes from Guinea. Some are brought there attached to long poles by means of collars round their necks to prevent them from escaping, but others are left loose. Next there were those who sold coarser cloth, and cotton goods and fabrics made of twisted thread, and there were chocolate merchants with their chocolate. In this way you could see every kind of merchandise to be found anywhere in New Spain, laid out in the same way as goods are laid out in my own district of Medina del Campo, a center for fairs, where each line of stalls has its own particular sort. So it was in this great market. There were those who sold sisal cloth and ropes and the sandals they wear on their feet, which are made from the same plant. All these were kept in one part of the market, in the place assigned to them, and in another part were skins of tigers and lions, otters, jackals, and deer, badgers, mountain cats, and other wild animals, some tanned and some untanned, and other classes of merchandise.

There were sellers of kidney beans and sage and other vegetables and herbs in another place, and in yet another they were selling fowls, and birds with great dewlaps, also rabbits, hares, deer, young ducks, little dogs, and other such creatures. Then there were the fruiterers; and the women who sold cooked food, flour and honey cake, and tripe, had their part of the market. Then came pottery of all kinds, from big water jars to little jugs, displayed in its own place, also honey, honey paste, and other sweets like nougat. Elsewhere they sold timber too, boards, cradles, beams, blocks, and benches, all in a quarter of their own.

Then there were the sellers of pitch pine for torches, and other things of that kind, and I must also mention, with all apologies, that they sold many canoe loads of human excrement, which they kept in the creeks near the market. This was for the manufacture of salt and the curing of skins, which they say cannot be done without it. I know that many gentlemen will laugh at this, but I assure them it is true. I may add that on all the roads they have shelters made of reeds or straw or grass so that they can retire when they wish to do so, and purge their bowels unseen by passersby, and also in order that their excrement shall not be lost.

serve in the army on reaching adulthood. Women were expected to work in the home, weave textiles, and raise children, although like their brothers they were permitted to enter the priesthood. According to Bernal Díaz, a female deity presided over the rites of marriage. As in most traditional societies, chastity and obedience were desirable female characteristics. Although women in Aztec society enjoyed more legal rights than women in some traditional Old World civilizations, they were still not equal to men. Women were permitted to own and inherit property and to enter into contracts. Marriage was usually monogamous, although noble families sometimes practiced polygyny (the state or practice of having more than one wife at a time). Wedding partners were normally selected from within the lineage group but not the immediate family. As in most societies at the time, parents usually selected their child's spouse, often for purposes of political or social advancement.

Classes in Aztec society were rigidly stratified. Commoners were not permitted to enter the nobility, although some occasionally rose to senior positions in the army or the priesthood as the result of exemplary service. As in medieval Europe, such occupations often provided a route of upward mobility for ambitious commoners. A woman of noble standing would sometimes marry a commoner, because the children of such a union would inherit her higher status, while she could be expected to be treated better by her husband's family, who would be proud of the marriage relationship.

LAND OF THE FEATHERED SERPENT: AZTEC RELIGION AND CULTURE

The Aztecs, like their contemporaries throughout Mesoamerica, lived in an environment populated by a multitude of gods. Scholars have identified more than a hundred deities in the Aztec pantheon; some of them were nature spirits, like the rain god Tlaloc, and some were patron deities, like the symbol of the Aztecs themselves, Huitzilopochtli. A supreme deity, called Ometeotl, represented the all-powerful and omnipresent forces of the heavens, but he was rather remote, and

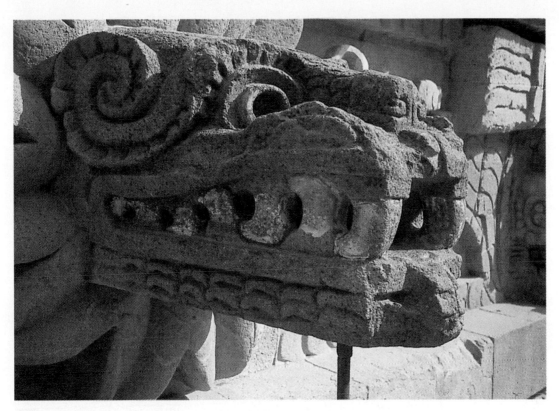

QUETZALCOATL. Quetzalcoatl was one of the favorite deities of the Central American peoples. His visage of a plumed serpent, as shown here, was prominent in the royal capital of Teotihuacán. According to legend, Quetzalcoatl, the leader of the Toltecs, was tricked into drunkenness and humiliated by a rival god. In disgrace he left his homeland but promised to return. In 1519, the Aztec monarch Moctezuma welcomed Hernán Cortés, the leader of the Spanish expedition, believing he was a representative of Quetzalcoatl.

other gods, notably the feathered serpent Quetzalcoatl, had a more direct impact on the lives of the people. Representing the forces of creation, virtue, and learning and culture, Quetzalcoatl bears a distinct similarity to Siva in Hindu belief. According to Aztec tradition, this godlike being had left his homeland in the Valley of Mexico in the tenth century, promising to return in triumph (see The Mystery of Mayan Decline earlier in this chapter).

Aztec cosmology was based on a belief in the existence of two worlds, the material and the divine. The earth was the material world and took the form of a flat disc surrounded by water on all sides. The divine world, which consisted of both heaven and hell, was the abode of the gods. Human beings could aspire to a form of heavenly salvation but first had to pass through a transitional stage, somewhat like Christian purgatory, before reaching their final destination, where the soul was finally freed from the body. To prepare for the final day of judgment, as well as to help them engage in proper behavior through life, all citizens underwent religious training at temple schools during adolescence and took part in various rituals throughout

their lives. The most devout were encouraged to study for the priesthood. Once accepted, they served at temples ranging from local branches at the *calpulli* level to the highest shrines in the ceremonial precinct at Tenochtitlán.

Aztec religion contained a distinct element of fatalism that was inherent in their creation myth, which described an unceasing struggle between the forces of good and evil throughout the universe. This struggle led to the creation and destruction of four worlds, or suns. The world was now living in the time of the fifth sun. But that world, too, was destined to end with the destruction of this earth and all that is within it:

> Even jade is shattered,
> Even gold is crushed,
> Even quetzal plumes are torn . . .
> One does not live forever on this earth:
> We endure only for an instant![3]

In an effort to postpone the day of reckoning, the Aztecs practiced human sacrifice. The Aztecs believed

AZTEC RELIGION THROUGH SPANISH EYES

*A*lthough early Spanish visitors were impressed with many aspects of Aztec culture, they were revolted by its religious beliefs and practices. The following passage from Father Diego Duran's History of the Indies of New Spain *describes the ritual of human sacrifice that was a central part of Aztec religion. The Aztecs believed that only the gift of human hearts would appease their god Huitzilopochtli and prevent him from bringing disaster to their civilization.*

DIEGO DURAN, *HISTORY OF THE INDIES OF NEW SPAIN*

When the day of the feast arrived, [Moctezuma] and Tlacaelel blackened their bodies with soot and applied it in such a way that it caught the light. . . . They placed crowns of fine feathers, adorned with gold and precious stones, upon their heads, and on each arm they wore a sheath of gold reaching from the elbow to the shoulder. On their feet were richly worked jaguar skin sandals, inlaid with gold and gems. . . .

The king and Tlacaelel now appeared before the assembly and went to stand upon the stone which was the likeness and image of the sun. The five priests of sacrifice followed them. They were to hold down the feet, hands, and heads of the victims, and they were painted all over with red ocher, even their loincloths and tunics. Upon their heads they wore paper crowns surmounted by little shields which hung to the middle of their foreheads, also painted in ocher. On the top of their heads they wore long stiff feathers which had been tied to their hair and which stood straight up. On their feet were very common, worthless sandals. . . .

The five priests entered and claimed the prisoner who stood first in the line at the skull rack. Each prisoner they took to the place where the king stood and, when they had forced him to stand upon the stone which was the figure and likeness of the sun, they threw him upon his back. One took him by the right arm, another by the left, one by his left foot, another by his right, while the fifth priest tied his neck with a cord and held him down so that he could not move.

The king lifted the knife on high and made a gash in his breast. Having opened it he extracted the heart and raised it high with his hand as an offering to the sun. When the heart had cooled he tossed it into the circular depression, taking some of the blood in his hand and sprinkling it in the direction of the sun. In this way the sacrificers killed four, one by one; then Tlacaelel came and killed another four in his turn. And so, four by four, the prisoners were slain, till every last man that had been brought from the Mixteca had perished.

that by appeasing the sun god Huitzilopochtli with sacrifices, they could delay the final destruction of their world. Victims were prepared for the ceremony through elaborate rituals and then brought to the holy shrine, where their hearts were ripped out of their chests and presented to the gods as a holy offering. It was an honor to be chosen for sacrifice, and captives in particular were often used as sacrificial victims, since they represented valor, the trait the Aztecs prized most. One of the few descriptions we have of the ceremonies comes from the pen of Father Diego Duran, a Dominican friar who lived in Mexico during the mid-sixteenth century and left a description of the civilization of the Aztecs (see the box above).

Like the art of the Olmecs, most Aztec architecture, art, and sculpture had religious significance. At the center of the capital city of Tenochtitlán was the sacred precinct, dominated by the massive pyramid dedicated to Huitzilopochtli and the rain god Tlaloc. According to Bernal Díaz, at its base the pyramid was equal to the plots of six large European town houses and tapered from there to the top, which was surmounted by a platform containing shrines to the gods and an altar for performing human sacrifices (see the box on p. 181). The entire pyramid was covered with brightly colored paintings and sculptures.

Although little Aztec painting survives, it was evidently of high quality. Bernal Díaz compared the best work with that of Michelangelo. Artisans worked with stone and with soft metals such as gold and silver, which they cast with the lost-wax technique. They did not have the knowledge of making implements in bronze or iron, however. Stoneworking consisted primarily of representations of the gods and bas-reliefs depicting religious ceremonies. Among the most famous is the massive disc called the Stone of the Sun, carved for use at the central pyramid at Tenochtitlán.

The Aztecs had devised a form of writing based on hieroglyphs that represented an object or a concept. The symbols had no phonetic significance and did not constitute a writing system as such but could give the sense of a message and were probably used by civilian or religious officials as notes or memoranda for their orations. Although many of the notes simply recorded dates in the complex calendar that had evolved since Olmec times, others provide insight into the daily lives of the Aztec peoples. A trained class of scribes carefully painted the notes

A DESCRIPTION OF TENOCHTITLÁN

The Aztec capital of Tenochtitlán was built on an island in the Lake of Mexico. After the Spanish conquest, the lake was drained, and the area became the foundation of the modern capital of Mexico, Mexico City. Here Díaz describes the city as he viewed it from the top of the Temple of the Sun. The Spaniards razed the temple and built a cathedral in its place.

BERNAL DÍAZ, *THE CONQUEST OF NEW SPAIN*

When we arrived near the great temple and before we had climbed a single step, the great Moctezuma sent six *papas* [priests] and two chieftains down from the top, where he was making his sacrifices, to escort our Captain; and as he climbed the steps, of which there were one hundred and fourteen, they tried to take him by the arms to help him up in the same way as they helped Moctezuma, thinking he might be tired, but he would not let them near him.

The top of the *cue* [pyramid] formed an open square on which stood something like a platform, and it was here that the great stones stood on which they placed the poor Indians for sacrifice. Here also was a massive image like a dragon, and other hideous figures, and a great deal of blood that had been spilled that day. Emerging in the company of two *papas* from the shrine which housed his accursed images, Moctezuma made a deep bow to us all and said: "My lord Malinche, you must be tired after climbing this great *cue* of ours." And Cortés replied that none of us was ever exhausted by anything. Then Moctezuma took him by the hand, and told him to look at his great city and all the other cities standing in the water, and the many others on the land round the lake; and he said that if Cortés had not had a good view of the great marketplace he could see it better from where he now was. So we stood there looking, because that huge accursed *cue* stood so high that it dominated everything. We saw the three causeways that led into Mexico: the causeway of Iztapalapa by which we had entered four days before, and that of Tacuba along which we were afterwards to flee on the night of our great defeat, when the new prince Cuitlahuac drove us out of the city (as I shall tell in due course), and that of Tepeaqualla. We saw the freshwater which came from Chapultepec to supply the city, and the bridges that were constructed at intervals on the causeways so that the water could flow in and out from one part of the lake to another. We saw a great number of canoes, some coming with provisions and others returning with cargo and merchandise; and we saw too that one could not pass from one house to another of that great city and the other cities that were built on the water except over wooden drawbridges or by canoe. We saw *cues* and shrines in these cities that looked like gleaming white towers and castles: a marvelous sight. All the houses had flat roofs, and on the causeways were other small towers and shrines built like fortresses.

Having examined and considered all that we had seen, we turned back to the great market and the swarm of people buying and selling. The mere murmur of their voices talking was loud enough to be heard more than three miles away. Some of our soldiers who had been in many parts of the world, in Constantinople, in Rome, and all over Italy, said that they had never seen a market so well laid out, so large, so orderly, and so full of people.

THE STONE OF THE FIFTH SUN. This basaltic disc, which weighs twenty-six tons, recorded the Aztec view of the cosmos. It portrays the perpetual struggle between forces of good and evil in the universe; in the center is an intimidating image of the sun god clutching human hearts with his talons. Having previously traversed the creation and destruction of four worlds, the Aztecs believed they were living in the world of the fifth and final sun—hence this stone carving that was found in the central pyramid at Tenochtitlán.

MOCTEZUMA'S GREETING TO HERNÁN CORTÉS

As his small party arrived in the Aztec capital of Tenochtitlán, Cortés was greeted by King Moctezuma, who was under the impression that Cortés was the representative of Quetzalcoatl, the Aztec deity who had departed centuries earlier with a promise that he would one day return. In this letter to Queen Isabella of Spain, Cortés describes the welcoming ceremony and King Moctezuma's opening address. As Moctezuma would soon discover, he had been deceived as to his visitor's identity and intentions.

HERNÁN CORTÉS, *LETTER FROM MEXICO*

Close to the city there is a wooden bridge ten paces wide across a breach in the causeway to allow the water to flow, as it rises and falls. . . .

After we had crossed this bridge, Moctezuma came to greet us and with him some two hundred lords, all barefoot and dressed in a different costume, but also very rich in their way and more so than the others. They came in two columns, pressed very close to the walls of the street, which is very wide and beautiful and so straight that you can see from one end to the other. It is two-thirds of a league long and has on both sides very good and big houses, both dwellings and temples.

[After an exchange of gifts, Moctezuma then] addressed me in the following way:

"For a long time we have known from the writings of our ancestors that neither I, nor any of those who dwell in this land, are natives of it, but foreigners who came from very distant parts; and likewise we know that a chieftain, of whom they were all vassals, brought our people to this region. And he returned to his native land and after many years came again, by which time all those who had remained were married to native women and had built vil-lages and raised children. And when he wished to lead them away again they would not go nor even admit him as their chief; and so he departed. And we have always held that those who descended from him would come and con-quer this land and take us as their vassals. So because of the place from which you claim to come, namely, from where the sun rises, and the things you tell us of the great lord or king who sent you here, we believe and are certain that he is our natural lord, especially as you say that he has known of us for some time. So be assured that we shall obey you and hold you as our lord in place of that great sovereign of whom you speak; . . . I know full well of all that has happened to you from Puntunchan to here, and I also know how those of Cempoal and Tascalteca have told you much evil of me; believe only what you see with your eyes, for those are my enemies, and some were my vassals, and have rebelled against me at your coming and said those things to gain favor with you. I also know that they have told you the walls of my houses are made of gold, and that the floor mats in my rooms and other things in my house-hold are likewise of gold, and that I was, and claimed to be, a god; and many other things besides. The houses as you see are of stone and lime and clay."

Then he raised his clothes and showed me his body, say-ing, as he grasped his arms and trunk with his hands, "See that I am of flesh and blood like you and all other men, and I am mortal and substantial. See how they have lied to you? It is true that I have some pieces of gold left to me by my ancestors; anything I might have shall be given to you whenever you ask. Now I shall go to other houses where I live, but here you shall be provided with all that you and your people require, and you shall receive no hurt, for you are in your own land and your own house."

on paper made from the inner bark of fig trees. Unfortu-nately, many of these notes were destroyed by the Spaniards as part of their effort to eradicate all aspects of Aztec religion and culture.

THE DESTRUCTION OF AZTEC CIVILIZATION

For a century, the Aztec kingdom dominated much of central Mexico from the Atlantic to the Pacific coast, and its influence penetrated as far south as present-day Guatemala. Most local officials had accepted the sovereignty of the king in Tenochtitlán, but in Tlaxcallan to the east, the authorities were restive under Aztec rule.

In 1519, a Spanish expedition under the command of Hernán Cortés landed at Veracruz, on the Gulf of Mex-ico (see Chapter 14). Marching to Tenochtitlán at the head of a small contingent of troops, Cortés received a friendly welcome from the Aztec monarch Moctezuma Xocoyotzin (often called Montezuma), who initially believed his visitor was a representative of Quetzalcoatl, the godlike "feathered serpent" who had departed from his homeland centuries before (see the box above). But tensions soon erupted between the Spaniards and the Aztecs, provoked in part by demands by Cortés that the Aztecs denounce their native beliefs and accept Christianity. When the Spanish took Moctezuma hos-tage and began to destroy Aztec religious shrines, the local population revolted and drove the invaders from the city. Receiving assistance from the state of Tlax-callan, Cortés managed to fight his way back into the city. Meanwhile the Aztecs were beginning to suffer the first effects of the diseases brought by the Europeans, which would eventually wipe out the majority of the local population. In a battle that to many Aztecs must have seemed to symbolize the dying of the legendary fifth sun, the Aztecs were finally vanquished. Within months, their magnificent city and its temples, believed by the conquerors to be the work of Satan, had been destroyed.

THE FIRST CIVILIZATIONS IN SOUTH AMERICA

South America is a vast continent, characterized by extremes in climate and geography. The north is dominated by the vast Amazon River, which flows through dense tropical jungles carrying a larger flow of water than any other river system in the world. Further to the south, the jungles are replaced by prairies and steppes stretching westward to the Andes Mountains, which extend the entire length of the continent, from the Isthmus of Panama to the Strait of Magellan far to the south. Along the Pacific coast, on the western slopes of the mountains, are some of the driest desert regions in the world.

South America has been inhabited by human beings for at least 12,000 years. Wall paintings recently discovered at the "cavern of the painted rock" in the Amazon region suggest that Stone Age peoples were living in the area at least 11,000 years ago. Evidence of human settlement dating back to 9500 B.C.E. has been found on the Tierra del Fuego, at the southern tip of the continent. Early peoples were hunters and food gatherers, but there are indications that irrigated farming was practiced in the northern fringe of the Andes Mountains as early as 2000 B.C.E. Other farming communities of similar age have been discovered in the Amazon River valley and on the western slopes of the Andes Mountains, where evidence of terraced agriculture dates back about four thousand years.

By the sixth millennium B.C.E., more complex societies had emerged in the central Andes Mountains, in the region of modern Peru, Bolivia, and Ecuador. Archaeologists have discovered the remains of ceremonial precincts, complete with temples, ancestral tombs, and pyramids, similar to those of Mesoamerica. This early Andes civilization reached its height during the first millennium B.C.E. with the emergence of the Chavin style, named for a site near the modern city of Chavin de Huantar, in the central mountains of modern Peru. The ceremonial precinct at the Chavin site contained an impressive stone temple complete with interior galleries, a stone-block ceiling, and a system of underground canals that probably channeled water into

the temple complex for ritualistic purposes. The structure was surrounded by stone figures depicting various deities and two pyramids, possibly dedicated to the sun and the moon.

Early in the first millennium C.E., another advanced civilization appeared, at Moche, in northern Peru, in the valley of the Moche River, which flows from the foothills of the Andes Mountains into the Pacific Ocean. Artifacts found at Moche, especially the metalwork and stone and ceramic figures, exhibit a high quality of artisanship. They were imitated at river valley sites throughout the surrounding area, which suggests that the authority of the Moche rulers may have extended as far as four hundred miles along the coast. The artifacts also indicate that the people at Moche, like those in Central America, were preoccupied with warfare. Paintings and pottery as well as other artifacts in stone, metal, and ceramics frequently portray warriors, prisoners, and sacrificial victims. The Moche were also fascinated by the heavens, and much of their art consisted of celestial symbols and astronomical constellations.

The Moche River valley is extremely arid, receiving less than an inch of rain annually. The peoples in the area compensated by building a sophisticated irrigation

MAP 6.5 The Inca Empire About 1500 C.E.

system to carry water from the river to the parched fields. At its zenith, Moche culture was spectacular. By the eighth century C.E., however, the civilization was in a state of collapse, the irrigation canals had been abandoned, and the remaining population suffered from severe malnutrition.

What had happened to bring Moche culture to this untimely end? Archaeologists speculate that environmental changes, perhaps brought on by changes in the water temperature known as El Niño, led to major flooding of coastal regions and the advance of sand dunes into the irrigated fields.

Three hundred years later, a new power, the kingdom of Chimor, with its capital at Chanchan, at the mouth of the Moche River, emerged in the area. Built almost entirely of adobe, Chanchan housed an estimated 30,000 residents in an area of over twelve square miles and included a number of palace compounds surrounded by walls nearly thirty feet high. One compound contained an intricate labyrinth that wound its way progressively inward until it ended in a central chamber, probably occupied by the ruler. Like the Moche before them, the people of Chimor relied on irrigation to funnel the water from the river into their fields. An elaborate system of canals brought the water through hundreds of miles of hilly terrain to the fields near the coast. Nevertheless, by the fifteenth century, Chimor, too, had disappeared, a victim of floods and a series of earthquakes that destroyed the intricate irrigation system that had been the basis of its survival.

The Inca

The Chimor kingdom was eventually succeeded in the late fifteenth century by an invading force from the mountains far to the south. In the late fourteenth century, the Incas were only a small community in the area of Cuzco, a city located at an altitude of 10,000 feet in the mountains of southern Peru. In the 1440s, however, under the leadership of their powerful ruler Pachakuti (sometimes called Pachacutec, or "he who transforms the world"), the Inca peoples launched a campaign of con-

CHRONOLOGY
EARLY AMERICA

Arrival of human beings in America	At least 15,000 years ago
First organized societies in the Andes	c. 6000 B.C.E.
Agriculture first practiced	c. 5000 B.C.E.
Rise of Olmec culture	First millennium B.C.E.
Origins of Mayan civilization	First millennium C.E.
Teotihuacán civilization	c. 300 B.C.E.–800 C.E.
Moche civilization	c. 150 C.E.–800 C.E.
Decline of the Maya	c. ninth century
Civilization of Chimor	c. 1100–1450
Migration of Mexica to Valley of Mexico	Late twelfth century
Kingdom of the Aztecs	Fifteenth century
Inca take over central Andes	Fifteenth century
Arrival of Hernán Cortés in Mexico	1519
Pizarro's conquest of the Inca	1532

✿ **FANTASTIC CREATURE POT.**   Thanks to the elaborate pottery of the Moche valley artists, we have an impressive visual record of the daily lives of the Peruvian peoples living in the sixth to ninth centuries C.E. Many of these colorful pots show scenes from everyday activities, such as hunting, fishing, weaving, cooking, and playing musical instruments. Others display religious ceremonies and sacrifice rituals. As illustrated in the fanged face of this fantastic creature, most probably a jaguar, these potters often blended the natural with the supernatural, which expressed the Moche worldview.

quest that eventually brought the entire region under their authority. Under Pachakuti and his immediate successors, Topa Inca and Huayna Inca (the word *Inca* means "ruler"), the boundaries of the kingdom were extended as far as Ecuador, central Chile, and the edge of the Amazon basin.

THE WORLD OF THE FOUR QUARTERS: INCA POLITICS AND SOCIETY

Pachakuti created a highly centralized state. With a stunning concern for mathematical precision, he divided his empire, called Tahuantinsuyu or "the world of the four quarters," into provinces and districts. Each province contained about 10,000 residents (at least in theory) and was ruled by a governor related to the royal family. Excess inhabitants were transferred to other locations. The capital of Cuzco was divided into four quarters, or residential areas, and the social status and economic functions of the residents of each quarter were rigidly defined.

The state was built on forced labor. Often entire communities of workers were moved from one part of the country to another to open virgin lands or engage in massive construction projects. Under Pachakuti the capital of Cuzco was transformed from a city of mud and thatch into an imposing metropolis of stone. The walls built of close-fitting stones without the use of mortar were a wonder to early European visitors. The most impressive structure in the city was a temple dedicated to the sun. According to a Spanish observer, "all four walls of the temple were covered from top to bottom with plates and slabs of gold."[4] Equally impressive are the ruins of the abandoned city of Machu Picchu, built on a lofty hilltop far above the Urubamba River.

Another major construction project was a system of 24,800 miles of highways and roads that extended from the border of modern Colombia to a point south of modern Santiago, Chile. Two major roadways extended in a north-south direction, one through the Andes Mountains and the other along the coast, with connecting routes between them. Rest houses and storage depots were placed along the roads. Suspension bridges made of braided fiber and fastened to stone abutments on opposite banks were built over ravines and waterways. Use of the highways was restricted to official and military purposes. Trained runners carried messages rapidly from one way station to another, enabling information to travel up to 140 miles in a single day.

In rural areas, the population lived mainly by farming. In the mountains, the most common form was terraced agriculture, watered by irrigation systems that carried precise amounts of water into the fields, which were planted with maize, potatoes, and other crops. The plots were tilled by collective labor regulated by the state. Like other aspects of Inca society, marriage was strictly regulated, and men and women were required to select a marriage partner from within the immediate tribal group. For women, there was one escape from a life of domestic servitude. Fortunate maidens were selected to serve as "chosen virgins" in temples throughout the country (see the box on p. 186). Noblewomen were eligible to compete for service in the Temple of the Sun at Cuzco, while commoners might hope to serve in temples in the provincial capitals. Punishment for breaking the vow of chastity was harsh, and few evidently took the risk.

MACHU PICCHU. Situated in the Andes in modern Peru, Machu Picchu reflects the glory of Inca civilization. To farm such rugged terrain, the Incas constructed terraces and stone aqueducts. To span vast ravines, they built suspension bridges made of braided fiber and fastened them to stone abutments on the opposite banks. The most revered of the many temples and stone altars at Machu Picchu was the thronelike "hitching post of the sun" at the left, so called because of its close proximity to the sun god.

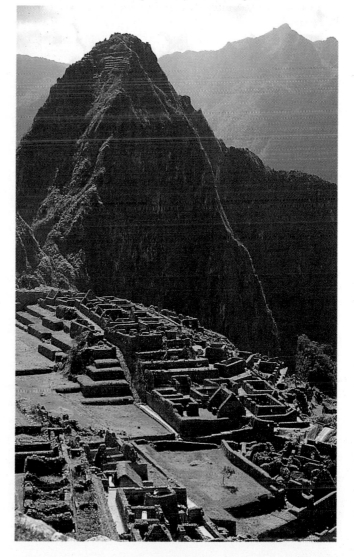

VIRGINS WITH RED CHEEKS

A letter from a Peruvian chief to King Philip III of Spain written four hundred years ago gives us a firsthand account of the nature of traditional Incan society. The purpose of author Huaman Poma was both to justify the history and culture of the Incan peoples and to record their sufferings under Spanish domination. In his letter, Poma describes Incan daily life from birth to death, in minute detail. He explains the different tasks assigned to men and women, beginning with their early education. Whereas boys were taught to watch the flocks and trap animals, girls were taught to dye, spin and weave cloth, as well as to perform other domestic chores. Most interesting, perhaps, was the emphasis that the Inca placed on virginity, as is witnessed in the document below. The Incan tradition of temple virgins is reminiscent of similar practices in ancient Rome, where young girls from noble families were chosen as priestesses to tend the sacred fire in the Temple of Vesta for thirty years. If one lost her virginity, she was condemned to be buried alive in an underground chamber.

HUAMAN POMA, *LETTER TO A KING*

During the time of the Incas certain women, who were called *accla* or "the chosen," were destined for lifelong virginity. Mostly they were confined in houses and they belonged to one of two main categories, namely sacred virgins and common virgins.

The so-called "virgins with red cheeks" entered upon their duties at the age of twenty and were dedicated to the service of the Sun, the Moon, and the Day-Star. In their whole life they were never allowed to speak to a man.

The virgins of the Inca's own shrine of Huanacauri were known for their beauty as well as their chastity. The other principal shrines had similar girls in attendance. At the less important shrines there were the older virgins who occupied themselves with spinning and weaving the silklike clothes worn by their idols. There was a still lower class of virgins, over forty years of age and no longer very beautiful, who performed unimportant religious duties and worked in the fields or as ordinary seamstresses.

Daughters of noble families who had grown into old maids were adept at making girdles, headbands, string bags, and similar articles in the intervals of their pious observances.

Girls who had musical talent were selected to sing or play the flute and drum at Court, weddings and other ceremonies, and all the innumerable festivals of the Inca year.

There was yet another class of *accla* or "chosen," only some of whom kept their virginity and others not. These were the Inca's beautiful attendants and concubines, who were drawn from noble families and lived in his palaces. They made clothing for him out of material finer than taffeta or silk. They also prepared a maize spirit of extraordinary richness, which was matured for an entire month, and they cooked delicious dishes for the Inca. They also lay with him, but never with any other man.

INCA CULTURE

Like many other civilizations in pre-Columbian Latin America, the Inca state was built on war. Soldiers for the 200,000-man Inca army, the largest and best armed in the region, were raised by universal male conscription. Military units were moved rapidly along the highway system and were housed in the rest houses located along the roadside. Since the Inca had no wheeled vehicles, supplies were carried on the backs of llamas. Once an area was placed under Incan authority, the local inhabitants were instructed in the Quechua language, which became the *lingua franca* of the state, and were introduced to the state religion. The Inca had no writing system but kept records using a system of knotted strings called *quipu* (see the box on p. 187).

As in the case of the Aztecs and the Maya, the lack of a fully developed writing system did not prevent the Inca from realizing a high level of cultural achievement. Most

❀ THE QUIPU. Not having a writing system, the Inca tallied the various data of their kingdom on strands of knotted yarn. Highly skilled and esteemed, official secretaries recorded population census data, crop and household inventories, government inspector reports, crime investigations, taxes, legal decisions and contracts, and all the official statistics of the realm by an intricate system of tying knots on a circular grouping of strings of yarn. One Peruvian chronicler boasted 400 years ago that these dextrous officials recorded their facts "with such skill that the knots in their cords had the clarity of written letters."[5]

AN INCAN AIDE-MÉMOIRE

The Inca did not possess a written script. To record events and other aspects of their lives that they wished to remember, they used an ingenious system of knotted strings, called quipu.

This description of the process comes from the Royal Commentaries of the Incas, an account of Inca civilization and history written by Garcilaso de la Vega. Garcilaso, who was of mixed Inca and Spanish blood, was born shortly before the Spanish conquest of the Incan capital of Cuzco.

GARCILASO DE LA VEGA, ROYAL COMMENTARIES OF THE INCAS

These men recorded on their knots all the tribute brought annually to the Inca, specifying everything by kind, species, and quality. They recorded the number of men who went to the wars, how many died in them, and how many were born and died every year, month by month. In short they may be said to have recorded on their knots everything that could be counted, even mentioning battles and fights, all the embassies that had come to visit the Inca, and all the speeches and arguments the king had uttered. But the purpose of the embassies or the contents of the speeches, or any other descriptive matter could not be recorded on the knots, consisting as it did of continuous spoken or written prose, which cannot be expressed by means of knots, since these can give only numbers and not words. To supply this want they used signs that indicated historical events or facts or the existence of any embassy, speech, or discussion in time of peace or war. Such speeches were preserved by the *quipucamayus* by memory in a summarized form of a few words: they were committed to memory and taught by tradition to their successors and descendants from father to son. This was especially practiced in the villages or provinces where the event in question had occurred: there naturally such traditions were preserved better than elsewhere, because the natives would treasure them. Another method too was used for keeping alive in the memory of the people their deeds and the embassies they sent to the Inca and the replies he gave them. The *amautas* who were their philosophers and sages took the trouble to turn them into stories, no longer than fables, suitable for telling to children, young people, and the rustics of the countryside: they were thus passed from hand to hand and age to age, and preserved in the memories of all. Their stories were also recounted in the form of fables of an allegorical nature, some of which we have mentioned, while others will be referred to later. Similarly the *harauicus*, who were their poets, wrote short, compressed poems, embracing a history, or an embassy, or the king's reply. In short, everything that could not be recorded on the knots was included in these poems, which were sung at their triumphs and on the occasion of their greater festivals, and recited to the young Incas when they were armed knights. Thus they remembered their history.

of what survives was recorded by the Spanish and consists of entertainment for the elites. The Inca had a highly developed tradition of court theater, including both tragic and comic works. There was also some poetry, composed in blank verse and often accompanied by music played on reed instruments.

THE CONQUEST OF THE INCA

The Inca empire was still in existence when the first Spanish expeditions arrived in the central Andes. The leader of the Spanish invaders, Francisco Pizarro, was accompanied by only a few hundred companions, but like Hernán Cortés he possessed steel weapons, gunpowder, and horses, none of which were familiar to his hosts. In the meantime, internal factionalism, combined with the onset of contagious diseases spread unknowingly by the Europeans, had weakened the ruling elite, and the empire fell rapidly to the Spanish forces in 1532. The last Inca ruler was tried by the Spaniards and executed. Pre-Columbian South America's greatest age was over.

STATELESS SOCIETIES IN THE NEW WORLD

Beyond Central America and the high ridges of the Andes Mountains, on the Great Plains of North America, along the Amazon River in South America, and on the islands of the Caribbean Sea, other communities of Amerindians were also beginning to master the art of agriculture and to build organized societies.

Although human beings had occupied much of the continent of North America during the early phase of human settlement in the New World, the switch to farming as a means of survival did not occur until the third millennium B.C.E. at the earliest, and not until much later in most areas of the continent. Until that time, most Amerindian communities lived by hunting, fishing, or foraging. As the supply of large animals began to diminish, they turned to smaller game and to fishing and foraging for wild plants, fruits, and nuts.

It was probably during the third millennium B.C.E. that peoples in selected parts of North America began to cultivate indigenous plants for food in a systematic way. As wild game and food became scarce, some communities began to place more emphasis on cultivating crops. This shift first occurred in the Mississippi River valley from Ohio, Indiana, and Illinois down to the Gulf of Mexico. Among the most commonly cultivated crops were maize, squash, beans, and various types of grasses.

As the population in the area increased, people began to congregate in villages, and sedentary communities began to develop in the alluvial lowlands, where the soil could be cultivated for many years at a time because of the nutrients deposited by the river water. Village councils were established to adjudicate disputes, and in a few cases several villages banded together under the authority of a local chieftain. Urban centers began to appear, some of them inhabited by as many as 10,000 people or more. At the same time, regional trade increased. The people of the Hopewell culture in Ohio ranged from the shores of Lake Superior to the Appalachian Mountains and the Gulf of Mexico in search of metals, shells, obsidian, and manufactured items to support their economic needs and religious beliefs.

At the site of Cahokia, near the modern city of East St. Louis, Illinois, archaeologists found a burial mound more than ninety-eight feet high with a base larger than that of the Great Pyramid in Egypt. A hundred smaller mounds were also found in the vicinity. The town itself, which covered almost 300 acres and was surrounded by a wooden stockade, was apparently the administrative capital of much of the surrounding territory until its decline in the thirteenth century C.E. Cahokia carried on extensive trade with other communities throughout the region, and there are some signs of regular contacts with the civilizations in Mesoamerica, such as the presence of ball courts in the Central American style. But wars were not uncommon, leading the Iroquois, who inhabited much of the modern states of Pennsylvania and New York as well as parts of southern Canada, to create a tribal alliance called the League of Iroquois.

West of the Mississippi River basin, most Amerindian peoples lived by hunting or food gathering. During the first millennium C.E., knowledge of agriculture gradually spread up the rivers to the Great Plains, and farming was practiced as far west as southwestern Colorado, where the Anasazi peoples (Navajo for "alien ancient ones") established an extensive agricultural community in an area extending from northern New Mexico and Arizona to southwestern Colorado and parts of southern Utah. Although they apparently never discovered the wheel or used beasts of burden, the Anasazi created a system of roads that facilitated an extensive exchange of technology, products, and ideas throughout the region. By the ninth century, they had mastered the art of irrigation, which allowed them to expand their productive efforts to squash and beans, and had established an important

urban center at Chaco Canyon, in southern New Mexico, where they built a walled city with dozens of three-story adobe houses with timbered roofs. Community religious functions were carried out in two large circular chambers called kivas. Clothing was made from hides or cotton cloth. At its height, Pueblo Bonito contained several hundred compounds housing several thousand residents. Another urban community was eventually established along a cliff face at Mesa Verde, in southwestern Colorado.

Sometime during the late twelfth and thirteenth centuries, however, these settlements were suddenly abandoned, as the inhabitants migrated southward. Their descendants, the Zuni and the Hopi, now occupy pueblos in central Arizona and New Mexico. For years, archaeologists surmised that a severe drought was the root cause of the migration, but in recent years new evidence has raised doubts that decreasing rainfall, by itself, was a sufficient explanation. An increase in internecine warfare, perhaps brought about by climatic changes, may also have played a role in the decision to relocate. Some archaeologists point to evidence that cannibalism was practiced at Pueblo Bonito and suggest that migrants from the south may have arrived in the area, provoking bitter rivalries within Anasazi society. In any event, with increasing aridity and the importation of the horse by the Spanish in the sixteenth century (a native version of the horse had died out thousands of years earlier), hunting revived, and mounted nomads like the Apache and the Navajo came to dominate much of the Southwest.

East of the Andes Mountains in South America, other Amerindian societies were beginning to make the transition to agriculture. Perhaps the most prominent were the Arawak, a people living along the Orinoco River in modern Venezuela. Having begun to cultivate manioc (a tuber used today in the manufacture of tapioca) along the banks of the river, they gradually migrated down to the coast and then proceeded to move eastward along the northern coast of the continent. Some occupied the islands of the Caribbean Sea. In their new island habitat, they lived by a mixture of fishing, hunting, and cultivating maize, beans, manioc, and squash, as well as other crops such as peanuts, peppers, and pineapples. As the population increased, a pattern of political organization above the village level appeared, along with recognizable social classes headed by a chieftain whose authority included control over the economy. The Arawak practiced human sacrifice, and some urban centers contained ball courts, suggesting the possibility of contacts with Mesoamerica.

In most such societies, where clear-cut class stratifications had not as yet taken place, the roles of men and women were considered to be of equal status. Men were responsible for hunting, warfare, and dealing with out-

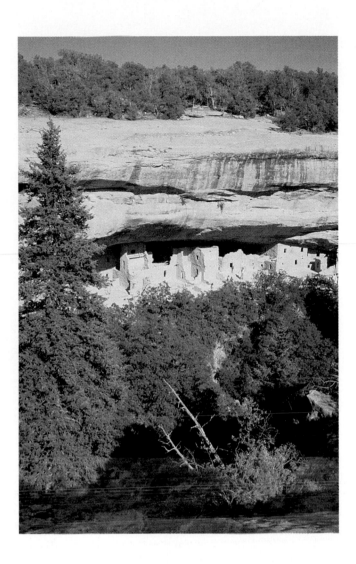

Mesa Verde is one of the best-developed sites of the Anasazi peoples in southwestern North America. At one time they were farmers who tilled the soil atop the mesas, but eventually they were forced to build their settlements in more protected locations. At Cliff Palace, shown here, adobe houses were hidden on the perpendicular face of the mesa. Access was achieved only by a perilous descent via indented finger- and toeholds on the rock face.

siders, while women were accountable for the crops, the distribution of food, maintaining the household, and bearing and raising the children. Their roles were complementary and were often viewed as a divine division of labor. In such cases, Indian women in the stateless societies of North America held a position of greater respect than their counterparts in the river valley civilizations of the Old World.

❀ CONCLUSION

The first human beings did not arrive in the New World until quite late in the prehistorical period. For the next several millennia, their descendants were forced to respond to the challenges of the environment in total isolation from other parts of the world. Nevertheless, around 5000 B.C.E., farming settlements began to appear in river valleys and upland areas in both Central and South America. Not long afterward—at least in historical time—organized communities located along the coast of the Gulf of Mexico and the western slopes of the central Andes Mountains embarked on the long march toward civilization.

What is perhaps most striking about these developments is how closely the process in the New World paralleled that in the Old. Although the civilizations in Central and South America were less advanced in terms of technology (the lack of iron and the wheel, for example, and the absence of a sophisticated writing system), in many other respects the states in Central America and the Andes were the equal of those that we will discuss in later chapters. One need only point to the awed comments of early Spanish visitors, who said that the cities of the Aztecs were the equal of Seville and the other great metropolitan centers of Spain.

What was most repugnant to those early European visitors were the religious beliefs and practices of the civilizations that they encountered. They were repelled, of course, by the worship of strange idols, but even more by the human sacrifices on a massive scale. Before rushing to judgment, however, we should remember that similar practices had been carried out in many societies of the Old World, including the ancient civilizations of Egypt, India, and China. The Spaniards were perhaps most surprised to discover that civilizations that in other respects had achieved such a high degree of culture also practiced human sacrifice.

In recent years, some scholars have speculated that the peoples in the Americas were more peaceful than their counterparts in the Old World. The bulk of the evidence, however, suggests that the Amerindian peoples were every bit as addicted to warfare as were those of the ancient empires of Africa and Asia. Yet in both hemispheres it appears that the first civilizations formed by the human species were brought to an end as much by environmental changes as by war. In the next chapter, we shall return to the Old World, where new civilizations were in the process of replacing the ancient empires.

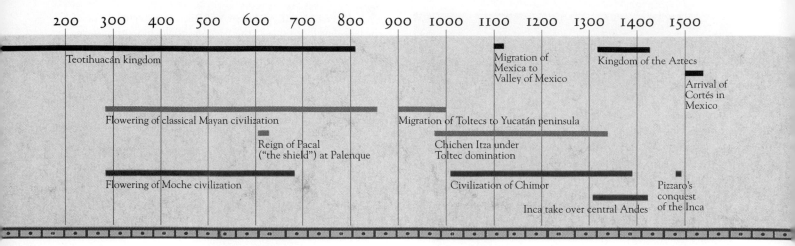

CHAPTER NOTES

1. Quoted in Sylvanus Morley and George W. Brainerd, *The Ancient Maya* (Stanford, Calif., 1983), p. 513.
2. Bernal Díaz, *The Conquest of New Spain* (Harmondsworth, 1975), p. 210.
3. Michael Coe, Dean Snow, and Elizabeth Benson, *Atlas of Ancient America* (New York, 1988), p. 149.
4. Garcilaso de la Vega, El Inca, *Royal Commentaries of the Incas and General History of Peru*, Part I, trans. Harold V. Livermore (Austin, Tex., 1966), p. 180.
5. Quote from Huaman Poma, *Letter to a King* (New York, 1978), p. 101.

SUGGESTED READINGS

For a profusely illustrated and informative overview of the early civilizations of the Americas, see M. Coe, D. Snow, and E. Benson, *Atlas of Ancient America* (New York, 1988). The first arrival of human beings in the New World is discussed in J. D. Jennings, ed., *Ancient Native Americans* (San Francisco, 1978), and B. Fagan, *The Great Journey: The Peopling of Ancient America* (London, 1987).

For an early classical work on Mayan civilization, see S. G. Morley and G. W. Brainerd, *The Ancient Maya* (Stanford, Calif., 1983). N. Hammond, *Ancient Maya Civilization* (New Brunswick, N.J., 1982) provides a general survey for the nonspecialist. See also M. D. Coe, *The Maya* (London, 1993). For a richly illustrated general survey, see G. E. Stuart and G. S. Stuart, *The Mysterious Maya* (Washington, D.C., 1977).

For a recent overview of Aztec civilization in Mexico, see B. Fagan, *The Aztecs* (New York, 1984). S. D. Gillespie, *The Aztec Kings: The Construction of Rulership in Mexican History* (Tucson, 1989) is an imaginative effort to uncover the symbolic meaning in Aztec traditions. On the Olmecs and the Zapotecs, see E. P. Benson, *The Olmec and Their Neighbors* (Washington, D.C., 1981); M. D. Coe and R. A. Diehl, *In the Land of the Olmec* (Austin, Tex., 1980); and R. E. Blanton, *Monte Alban: Settlement Patterns at the Ancient Zapotec Capital* (New York, 1978).

Much of our information about the lives of the peoples of ancient Central America comes from Spanish writers who visited or lived in the area during the sixteenth and seventeenth centuries. For the original Spanish conquest of Mexico, see H. Cortés, *Letters from Mexico* (New Haven, Conn., 1986), and B. Díaz, *The Conquest of New Spain* (Harmondsworth, 1975). See also Fray D. Duran, *The Aztecs: The History of the Indies of New Spain* (New York, 1964).

On the Inca and their predecessors, see R. W. Keatinge, ed., *Peruvian Prehistory: An Overview of Pre-Inca and Inca Society* (Cambridge, 1988); G. Bankes, *Peru Before Pizarro* (Oxford, 1977); and E. P. Lanning, *Peru Before the Incas* (Englewood Cliffs, N.J., 1967). The arrival of the Spanish is chronicled in C. Howard, *Pizarro and the Conquest of Peru* (New York, 1967). For an extended account of Inca civilization, see G. de la Vega, El Inca, *Royal Commentaries of the Incas and General History of Peru* (Austin, Tex., 1966).

On the art and culture of the ancient Americas, see E. Pasztory, *Aztec Art* (New York, 1983); E. Henning and J. Raney, *Monuments of the Inca* (Boston, 1982); and L. Schele and M. E. Miller, *The Blood of Kings: A New Interpretation of Maya Art* (Austin, Tex., 1986). Writing systems are discussed in D. H. Kelley, *Deciphering the Maya Script* (Austin, Tex., 1976), and J. E. S. Thompson, *Maya Hieroglyphic Writing: An Introduction* (Norman, Okla., 1971).

For recent studies on social issues, see Linda Schele and David Freidel, *A Forest of Kings: The Untold Story of the Ancient Maya* (New York, 1990); Rudolph van Zantwijk, *The Aztec Arrangement: The Social History of Pre-Spanish Mexico* (Norman, Okla., 1985); and Nancy Shoemaker, *Negotiators of Change: Historical Perspectives on Native American Women* (New York, 1995).

INFOTRAC COLLEGE EDITION

For additional reading, go to InfoTrac College Edition, your online research library at http://web1.infotrac-college.com

Enter the search terms "Inca or Incan" using Keywords.

Enter the search term "Aztec" using Keywords.

Enter the search terms "Maya or Mayan" using Keywords.

Enter the search terms "Machu Picchu" using Keywords.

Enter the search terms "Latin America history" using Keywords.

CHAPTER

7

THE WORLD
OF ISLAM

CHAPTER OUTLINE
• THE RISE OF ISLAM
• THE TEACHINGS OF MUHAMMAD
• THE ARAB EMPIRE AND ITS SUCCESSORS
• ISLAMIC CIVILIZATION
• CONCLUSION

FOCUS QUESTIONS
• What are the main tenets of Islam, and how does it compare with Judaism and Christianity?
• Why did the Arabs undergo such a rapid expansion in the seventh and eighth centuries, and why were they so successful in amassing an empire?
• What were the basic political structures of the Arab empire under the Umayyads and the Abbasids?
• How did the Seljuk Turks, the Crusades, and the Mongols affect Islamic civilization?
• What were the main features of Islamic society and culture?

In the year 570, in the Arabian city of Mecca, there was born a child named Muhammad whose life changed the course of world history. The son of a merchant, Muhammad grew to maturity in a time of transition. Old empires that had once ruled the entire Middle East were only a distant memory. The region was now divided into many separate states, and the people adhered to many different faiths.

Within a few decades of Muhammad's death, the Middle East was united once again. The initial triumph was primarily political and military. Arab armies marched westward across North Africa and eastward into Mesopotamia and Persia, imposing their authority and creating a new empire that stretched from the Iberian peninsula to the Indus valley. But Arab rule also brought with it a new religion and a new culture—that of Islam.

Islamic beliefs and culture exerted a powerful influence in all areas occupied by Arab armies. Initially, Arab beliefs and customs, as reflected through the prism of Muhammad's teachings, transformed the societies and cultures of the peoples living within the new empire. But eventually the distinctive political and cultural forces that had long characterized the region began to reassert themselves. Factional struggles led to the decline and then the destruction of the Arab empire. Invading forces from Central Asia established their control over the great mercantile cities of the region, while Christian crusaders attacked the empire from the west. New states formed in Spain, North Africa, and Persia and began to put their own stamp on the cultures of the region. Like the empires that had preceded it, the Arab empire, with its capital at Baghdad, became a thing of the past.

Still, the Arab conquest left a powerful legacy that survived the decline of Arab political power. The ideological and emotional appeal of Islam remained strong throughout the Middle East and even extended into areas not occupied by Arab armies, such as the Indian subcontinent, Southeast Asia, and sub-Saharan Africa. At the same time, the political unification of the entire region, although temporary, provided an environment conducive to the revival and expansion of long-distance trade and the exchange of culture and ideas that had taken place before the collapse of the classical empires at the beginning of the first millennium C.E. Although the vision of regional political and cultural unity that had inspired Muhammad and his followers was never realized, Islam remained a powerful force that provided a measure of religious and cultural unity for the region. ✺

THE RISE OF ISLAM

The Arabs were a Semitic-speaking people of southwestern Asia with a long history. They were mentioned in Greek sources of the fifth century B.C.E. and even earlier in the Old Testament. The Greek historian Herodotus had applied the name *Arab* to the entire peninsula, calling it Arabia. In 106 B.C.E., the Romans extended their authority to the Arabian peninsula, transforming it into a province of their growing empire.

During Roman times, the region was inhabited primarily by the Bedouin Arabs, nomadic peoples who came originally from the northern part of the peninsula. Bedouin society was organized on a tribal basis. The ruling member of the tribe was called the *sheikh* and was selected from one of the leading families by a council of elders called the *majlis*. The *sheikh* ruled the tribe with the consent of the council. Each tribe was autonomous but felt a general sense of allegiance to the larger unity of all the clans in the region. In early times, the Bedouins had supported themselves primarily by sheepherding or by raiding passing caravans, but after the domestication of the camel during the first millennium B.C.E., the Bedouins began to participate in the caravan trade themselves and became major carriers of goods between the Persian Gulf and the Mediterranean Sea.

The Arabs of pre-Islamic times were polytheistic, with a supreme god known as Allah presiding over a community of spirits. It was a communal faith, involving all members of the tribe, and had no priesthood. The supreme deity was symbolized by a sacred stone. Each tribe possessed its own stone, but all worshiped a massive black meteorite, which was located in a central shrine called the *Ka'aba* in the commercial city of Mecca.

✺ **THE KA'ABA IN MECCA.** The Ka'aba, a massive black meteorite in the Arabian city of Mecca, is the sacred stone of the Islamic faith. Wherever Muslims pray, they are instructed to face Mecca; each thus becomes a spoke of the Ka'aba, the holy center of the wheel of Islam. If they are able to do so, all Muslims are encouraged to visit the Ka'aba at least once in their lifetime. Called the *hajj*, this pilgrimage to Mecca represents the ultimate in spiritual fulfillment.

In the fifth and sixth centuries C.E., the economic importance of the Arabian peninsula began to increase. As a result of the political disorder in Mesopotamia—a consequence of the constant wars between the Byzantine and Persian Empires—and in Egypt, the trade routes that ran directly across the peninsula or down the Red Sea became increasingly risky, and a third route, which passed from the Mediterranean through Mecca to Yemen and then by ship across the Indian Ocean, became more popular. The communities in that part of the peninsula benefited from the change. As a consequence, relations between the Bedouins of the desert and the increasingly wealthy merchants of the towns began to become strained.

Into this intense world stepped Muhammad (also known as Mohammed), a man whose spiritual visions unified the Arab world with a speed no one would have suspected possible. Born in Mecca to a merchant family and orphaned at the age of six, Muhammad (570–632) grew up to become a caravan manager and eventually married a rich widow, Khadija, who was also his employer. For several years he lived in Mecca as a mer-

chant but was apparently troubled by the growing gap between the Bedouin values of honesty and generosity (he himself was a member of the local Hashemite clan of the Quraishi tribe) and the acquisitive behavior of the affluent commercial elites in the city. Deeply concerned, he began to visit the nearby hills to meditate in isolation.

On one of these occasions, he experienced visions and heard a voice that he was convinced was inspired by Allah. According to tradition, the message was conveyed by the angel Gabriel, who commanded Muhammad to preach the revelations that he would be given.

Muhammad was acquainted with Jewish and Christian beliefs and came to believe that while Allah had already revealed himself in part through Moses and Jesus—and thus through the Hebraic and Christian traditions—the final revelations were now being given to him. Out of his revelations, which were eventually dictated to scribes, came the Koran or Qur'an, the holy scriptures of Islam (meaning "submission to the will of Allah"). The Koran contained the guidelines by which followers of Allah, known as Muslims (i.e., those who practice Islam), were to live. Like the Christians and the Jews, Muslims (also known as Moslems) were a "People of the Book."

After returning home, Muhammad set out to comply with Gabriel's command by preaching to the residents of Mecca about his revelations. At first, many were convinced that he was mad or a charlatan. Others were undoubtedly concerned that his vigorous attacks on traditional beliefs and the corrupt society around him could severely shake the social and political order. After three years of proselytizing, he had only thirty followers.

Discouraged by the systematic persecution of his followers, which was undertaken with a brutality reminiscent of the cruelties suffered by early Christians, as well as the failure of the Meccans to accept his message, in 622 Muhammad and some of his closest supporters (mostly from his own Hashemite clan) left the city and retreated north to the rival city of Yathrib, later renamed Medina, or "city of the Prophet." That flight, known in history as the Hegira (*Hijrah*), marks the first date of the official calendar of Islam. At Medina Muhammad failed in his original purpose—to convert the Jewish community in Medina to his beliefs. But he was successful in win-

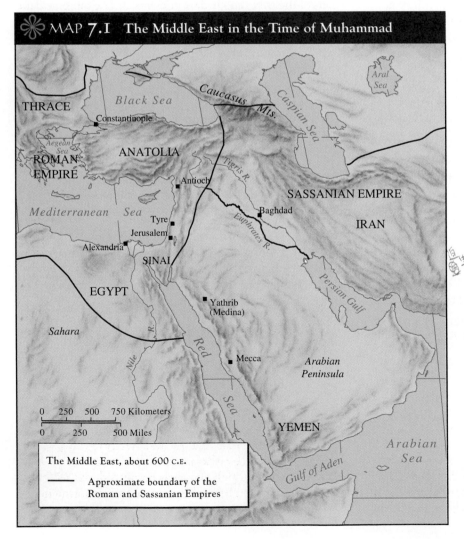

✻ MAP **7.1** The Middle East in the Time of Muhammad

THRACE
Black Sea
Caucasus Mts.
Constantinople
Aral Sea
Caspian Sea
Aegean Sea
ROMAN EMPIRE
ANATOLIA
Tigris R.
Antioch
SASSANIAN EMPIRE
Baghdad
Mediterranean Sea
Tyre
Euphrates R.
IRAN
Jerusalem
Alexandria
SINAI
EGYPT
Persian Gulf
Sahara
Nile R.
Yathrib (Medina)
Red Sea
Mecca
Arabian Peninsula
YEMEN
Arabian Sea
Gulf of Aden

0 250 500 750 Kilometers
0 250 500 Miles

The Middle East, about 600 C.E.

——— Approximate boundary of the Roman and Sassanian Empires

اردادازفام رجل يم وضع والاساس على باس عن سارس وجعل عليهما السلم وعبار الهم اطوما وصلوانى باس رجاه وسم وكان باساس سمس سمهء
دردان لفض من بلك الدانه جااا فلم يزل عالى فيدالان لللاخلى فيدال جميع مكه ترابال فطه قاله سرال جملهءه للبحر لعود الجمر وبزول عن مى الاساب الساس

MUHAMMAD AND THE SACRED STONE.
In pre-Islamic times, the Arabs were polytheistic, with a supreme deity symbolized by a sacred stone. Although each tribe possessed its own stone, all worshiped the black meteorite stone at a shrine in Mecca called the Ka'aba. In 630 Muhammad proclaimed the Ka'aba to be the sacred shrine of Islam. In this fourteenth-century miniature, we see Muhammad restoring the black stone to its rightful place in the wall of the Ka'aba.

ning support from many residents of the city as well as from Bedouins in the surrounding countryside. From this mixture, he formed the first Muslim community (the *umma*). Returning to his birthplace at the head of a considerable military force, Muhammad conquered Mecca and converted the townspeople to the new faith. In 630 he made a symbolic visit to the Ka'aba, where he declared it a sacred shrine of Islam and ordered the destruction of the idols of the traditional faith. Two years later, Muhammad died, just as Islam was beginning to spread throughout the peninsula.

THE TEACHINGS OF MUHAMMAD

Like Christianity and Judaism, Islam is monotheistic. Allah is the all-powerful being who created the universe and everything in it. Islam is also concerned with salvation and offers the hope of an afterlife. Those who hope to achieve it must subject themselves to the will of Allah. Unlike Christianity, Islam makes no claim to the divinity of its founder. Muhammad, like Jesus, Moses, and other figures of the Old Testament, was a prophet, but he was also a man like other men. Because human beings rejected his earlier messengers, Allah sent his final revelation through Muhammad.

At the heart of Islam is the Koran (meaning "recitation"), with its basic message that there is no God but Allah and Muhammad is his Prophet (see the box on p. 196). Consisting of 114 *suras* (chapters) that were drawn together into an integrated whole by a committee established after Muhammad's death, the Koran is not only the sacred book of Islam, but an ethical guidebook and a code of law and political theory combined.

Islam was a direct and simple faith, emphasizing the need to obey the will of Allah. This meant following a basic ethical code that consisted of what are popularly termed the "five pillars" of Islam: belief in Allah and Muhammad as his Prophet; standard prayer five times a day and public prayer on Friday at midday to worship Allah; observation of the holy month of Ramadan including fasting from dawn to sunset; making a pilgrimage, if possible, to Mecca in one's lifetime (see the box on p. 197); and giving alms (called the *zakat*) to the poor and unfortunate. The faithful who observed the law were guaranteed a place in an eternal paradise with the sensuous delights so obviously lacking in the midst of the Arabian desert.

Islam was not just a set of religious beliefs, but a way of life as well. After the death of Muhammad, Muslim scholars, known as the *ulama*, drew up a law code, called the *Shari'ah*, to provide believers with a set of prescriptions to regulate their daily lives. Much of the *Shari'ah* was drawn from the Koran or from the *Hadith*, a collection of the sayings of the Prophet that was used to supplement the revelations contained in the holy scriptures.

Believers were subject to strict behavioral requirements. In addition to the "five pillars," Muslims were forbidden to gamble, to eat pork, to drink alcoholic beverages, and to engage in dishonest behavior. Sexual mores were also strict. Contacts between unmarried men and women were discouraged, and ideally marriages were to be arranged by the parents. In accordance with Bedouin custom, polygyny was permitted, but Muhammad attempted to limit the practice by restricting males to four wives.

THE KORAN AND THE SPREAD
OF THE MUSLIM FAITH

The Koran is the sacred book of Islam, holding a place comparable to that of the Bible in Christianity. In this selection from Chapter 47, it is apparent that Islam encourages the spreading of the faith, known to Muslims as Jihad. A garden of paradise quite unlike the arid desert homeland of the Arab warriors awaited all believers who died for Allah.

THE KORAN: CHAPTER 47, "MUHAMMAD, REVEALED AT MEDINA"

Allah will bring to nothing the deeds of those who disbelieve and debar others from His path. As for the faithful who do good works and believe in what is revealed to Muhammad—which is the truth from their Lord—He will forgive them their sins and ennoble their state.

This, because the unbelievers follow falsehood, while the faithful follow the truth from their Lord. Thus Allah coins their sayings for mankind.

When you meet the unbelievers in the battlefield strike off their heads and, when you have laid them low, bind your captives firmly. Then grant them their freedom or take ransom from them, until War shall lay down her armour.

Thus shall you so. Had Allah willed, He could Himself have punished them; but He has ordained it thus that He might test you, the one by the other.

As for those who are slain in the cause of Allah, He will not allow their works to perish. He will vouchsafe them guidance and ennoble their state; He will admit them to the Paradise He has made known to them.

Believers, if you help Allah, Allah will help you and make you strong. But the unbelievers shall be consigned to perdition. He will bring their deeds to nothing. Because they have opposed His revelations, He will frustrate their works.

Have they never journeyed through the land and seen what was the end of those who have gone before them? Allah destroyed them utterly. A similar fate awaits the unbelievers, because Allah is the protector of the faithful; because the unbelievers have no protector.

Allah will admit those who embrace the true faith and do good works to gardens watered by running streams. The unbelievers take their fill of pleasure and eat as the beasts eat: but Hell shall be their home. . . .

This is the Paradise which the righteous have been promised. There shall flow in it rivers of unpolluted water, and rivers of milk forever fresh; rivers of delectable wine and rivers of clearest honey. They shall eat therein of every fruit and receive forgiveness from their Lord. Is this like the lot of those who shall abide in Hell forever and drink scalding water which will tear their bowels? . . .

Know that there is no god but Allah. Implore Him to forgive your sins and to forgive the true believers, men and women. Allah knows your busy haunts and resting places.

� **THE QUIET SPIRIT OF A MOSQUE.**
For Muslims, the mosque is a revered oasis for worship, reflection, and the reading of the Koran. The practicing Muslim is required to pray to Allah five times a day. While women normally pray at home, men are expected to visit a mosque. If a mosque is not available, they may pray wherever they are at the time of the muezzin's call. At that time, each Muslim stops whatever he is doing and kneels down, facing Mecca, on his portable prayer rug. Above all, the mosque is a place for quiet devotion, a refuge from the bustle of daily life. The artwork in a mosque should reflect motifs from the Koran. In this illustration, two of the faithful pray in a mosque under iron lamps on plush layers of carpets decorated with Koranic symbols.

A PILGRIMAGE TO MECCA

The pilgrimage to Mecca, one of the "five pillars of Islam," is the duty of every Muslim. Ibn Jubayr, a twelfth-century Spanish Muslim, left a description of his trip in his journal. The work is famous for its vivid and abundant detail. In this almost lyrical passage, Ibn Jubayr tells of reaching his final destination, the Ka'aba at Mecca, containing the Black Stone. The Qarmata were an extremist religious sect in ninth- and tenth-century Mesopotamia.

IBN JUBAYR, TRAVELS

The blessed Black Stone is encased in the corner [of the Ka'aba] facing east. The depth to which it penetrates it is not known, but it is said to extend two cubits into the wall. Its breadth is two-thirds of a span, its length one span and a finger joint. It has four pieces, joined together, and it is said that it was the Qarmata—may God curse them—who broke it. Its edges have been braced with a sheet of silver whose white shines brightly against the black sheen and polished brilliance of the Stone, presenting the observer a striking spectacle which will hold his gaze. The Stone, when kissed, has a softness and moistness which so enchants the mouth that he who puts his lips to it would wish them never to be removed. This is one of the special favors of Divine Providence, and it is enough that the Prophet—may God bless and preserve him—declare it to be a covenant of God on earth. May God profit us by the kissing and touching of it. By His favor may all who yearn fervently for it be brought to it. In the sound piece of the stone, to the right of him who presents himself to kiss it, is a small white spot that shines and appears like a mole on the blessed surface. Concerning this white mole, there is a tradition that he who looks upon it clears his vision, and when kissing it one should direct one's lips as closely as one can to the place of the mole.

THE ARAB EMPIRE AND ITS SUCCESSORS

The death of Muhammad presented his followers with a dilemma. Although Muhammad had not claimed divine qualities, Muslims saw no separation between political and religious authority. Submission to the will of Allah meant submission to his Prophet Muhammad. According to the Koran, "Whoso obeyeth the messenger obeyeth Allah."[1] Muhammad's charismatic authority and political skills had been at the heart of his success. But he never named a successor, and although he had several daughters, he left no sons. In a male-oriented society, who would lead the community of the faithful?

Shortly after Muhammad's death, a number of his closest followers selected Abu Bakr, a wealthy merchant from Medina who was Muhammad's father-in-law and one of his first supporters, as caliph (khalifa, literally "successor"). The caliph was the temporal leader of the Islamic community and was also considered, in general terms, to be a religious leader, or imam. Under Abu Bakr's prudent leadership, the movement succeeded in suppressing factional tendencies among some of the Bedouin tribes in the peninsula and began to direct its attention to wider fields. Muhammad had used the Arabic tribal custom of the razzia or raid in the struggle against his enemies. Now his successors turned to the same custom to expand the authority of the movement (see the box on p. 196). The Koran called this activity "striving in the way of the Lord," or jihad. Although sometimes translated as "holy war," the jihad grew out of the Arabic tradition of tribal raids, which were permitted as a way to channel the warlike energies of the Bedouin tribes.

Once the Arabs had become unified under Muhammad's successor, they began to conduct a jihad on a larger scale, directing outward against neighboring peoples the energy they had formerly directed against each other. The Byzantine and the Persian Empires were the first to feel the strength of the newly united Arabs, now aroused to a peak of zeal by their common faith. At Yarmuk in 636, the Muslims defeated the Byzantine army. Four years later, they took possession of the Byzantine province of Syria. To the east, the Arabs defeated a Persian force in 637 and then went on to conquer the entire empire of the Sassanids by 650. In the meantime, Egypt and other areas of North Africa were also brought under Arab authority (see Chapter 8).

What explains this rapid expansion of the Arabs after the rise of Islam in the early seventh century? Historians have proposed various explanations ranging from a prolonged drought on the Arabian peninsula to the desire of Islam's leaders to channel the energies of their new converts. Another hypothesis is that the expansion was deliberately planned by the ruling elites in Mecca to extend their trade routes and bring surplus-producing regions under their control. Whatever the case, Islam's ability to unify the Bedouin peoples certainly played a role. Although the Arab triumph was made substantially easier by the ongoing conflict between the Byzantine and Persian Empires, which had weakened both powers, the strength of the Bedouin armies should not be overlooked. Led by a series of brilliant generals, the Arabs put together a large, highly motivated army, whose valor was enhanced by the belief that Muslim warriors who died in battle were guaranteed a place in paradise.

Once the armies had prevailed, Arab administration of the conquered areas was relatively tolerant. Sometimes, due to a shortage of trained Arab administrators, government was left to local officials. Conversion to Islam was voluntary in accordance with the maxim in the Koran that "there shall be no compulsion in religion."[2] Those who chose not to convert were required only to submit to Muslim rule and pay a head tax in return for exemption from military service, which was required of all Muslim males. Under such conditions, the local populations often welcomed Arab rule as preferable to Byzantine rule or that of the Sassanid dynasty in Persia. Furthermore, the simple and direct character of the new religion, as well as its egalitarian qualities (all people were viewed as equal in the eyes of Allah), were undoubtedly attractive to peoples throughout the region.

Succession Problems and the Rise of the Umayyads

The main challenge to the growing empire came from within. Some of Muhammad's followers had not agreed with the selection of Abu Bakr as the first caliph and promoted the candidacy of Muhammad Ali, Muhammad's cousin and son-in-law, as an alternative. Ali's claim was ignored by other leaders, however, and after Abu Bakr's death, the office was passed to Umar, another of Muhammad's followers. In 656, Umar's successor Uthman was assassinated, and Ali was finally selected for the position. But Ali's rivals were convinced that he had been implicated in the death of his predecessor, and a factional struggle broke out within the Muslim leadership. In 661 Ali himself was assassinated, and Mu'awiyah, the governor of Syria and one of Ali's chief rivals, replaced him in office. Mu'awiyah thereupon made the caliphate hereditary in his own family, called the Umayyads, who were a branch of the Quraishi clan. The new caliphate, with its capital at Damascus, remained in power for nearly a century.

The factional struggle within Islam did not bring an end to Arab expansion. At the beginning of the eighth century, new attacks were launched at both the western and the eastern end of the Mediterranean world. Arab armies advanced across North Africa and conquered the Berbers, a primarily pastoral people living along the Mediterranean coast and in the mountains in the interior. Then, around 710 Arab forces, supplemented by Berber allies under their commander Tariq, crossed the Strait of Gibraltar and occupied southern Spain. The Visigothic kingdom, already weakened by internecine warfare, quickly collapsed, and by 725 most of the Iberian peninsula had become a Muslim state with its center in Andalusia. Seven years later, an Arab force, making a foray into southern France, was defeated by the army of Charles Martel between Tours and Poitiers. Some historians think that internal exhaustion would have forced the invaders to retreat even without their defeat at the hands of the Franks. In any event, the Battle of Tours (or Poitiers) would be the high-water mark of Arab expansion in Europe.

In the meantime, in 717 another Muslim force had launched an attack on Constantinople with the hope of destroying the Byzantine Empire. But the Byzantines' use of Greek fire, an incendiary mixture of unknown composition, destroyed the Muslim fleet, thus saving the empire and indirectly Christian Europe, since the fall of Constantinople would have opened the door to an Arab invasion of eastern Europe. The Byzantine Empire and Islam now established an uneasy frontier in southern Asia Minor.

Arab power also extended to the east, consolidating Islamic rule in Mesopotamia and Persia and northward into Central Asia. But factional disputes continued to plague the empire. Many Muslims of non-Arab extraction resented the favoritism shown by local administrators to Arabs. In some cases, resentment led to revolt, as in Iraq, where Ali's second son, Hussein, disputed the legitimacy of the Umayyads and incited his supporters—to be known in the future as Shi'ites (from the Arabic phrase shi'at Ali, or "partisans of Ali")—to rise up against Umayyad rule in 680. Hussein's forces were defeated, but a schism between Shi'ite and Sunnite (usually translated as "orthodox") Muslims had been created that continues to the present.

Umayyad rule, always (in historian Arthur Goldschmidt's words) "more political than pious," created resentment, not only in Mesopotamia, but also in North Africa, where Berber resistance continued, especially in the mountainous areas south of the coastal plains. The Umayyads contributed to their own demise by their decadent behavior. One caliph allegedly swam in a pool of wine and then imbibed enough of the contents to lower the wine level significantly. Finally, in 750 a revolt led by Abu al-Abbas, a descendant of Muhammad's uncle, led to the overthrow of the Umayyads and the establishment of the Abbasid dynasty (750–1258) in what is now Iraq.

The Abbasids

The Abbasid caliphs brought political, economic, and cultural change to the world of Islam. While stressing religious orthodoxy, they tried to break down the distinctions between Arab and non-Arab Muslims. All Muslims were now allowed to hold both civil and military offices. This change helped to open Islamic culture to the influences of the occupied civilizations. Many Arabs now began to intermarry with the peoples they had conquered. In many parts of the Islamic world, notably North Africa and the eastern Mediterranean, most Muslim converts began to consider themselves Arabs. In 762, the Abbasids built a new capital city at Baghdad, on the Tigris River far to the east of the Umayyad capital at Damascus. The new capital was strategically positioned to take advantage of river traffic to the Persian Gulf and also lay astride the caravan route from the Mediterranean to Central Asia. The move eastward allowed Persian influence to come to the fore, encouraging a new cultural orientation. Under the Abbasids, judges, merchants, and government officials, rather than warriors, were viewed as the ideal citizens.

The new Abbasid caliphate experienced a period of splendid rule well into the ninth century. Best known of the caliphs of the time was Harun al-Rashid (786–809), or Harun "the upright," whose reign is often described as the golden age of the Abbasid caliphate. His son al-Ma'mun (813–833) was a patron of learning who founded an astronomical observatory and established a foundation for undertaking translations of classical Greek works. This was also a period of growing economic prosperity. The Arabs had conquered many of the richest provinces of the Roman Empire and now controlled the routes to the east. Baghdad became the center of an enormous commercial market that extended into Europe, Central Asia, and Africa, greatly adding to the wealth of the Islamic world and promoting an exchange of culture, ideas, and technology from one end of the known world to the other. Paper was introduced from China and eventually passed on to North Africa and Europe. Crops from India and Southeast Asia such as rice, sugar, sorghum, and cotton moved toward the west, while glass, wine, and indigo dye were introduced into China.

Under the Abbasids, the caliphs became more regal. More kings than spiritual leaders, described by such august phrases as the "caliph of God," they ruled by autocratic means hardly distinguishable from the kings and emperors in neighboring civilizations. A thirteenth-century Chinese author, who compiled a world geography based on accounts by Chinese travelers, left the following description of one of the later caliphs:

> The king wears a turban of silk brocade and foreign cotton stuff (buckram). On each new moon and full moon he puts on an eight-sided flat-topped headdress of pure gold, set with the most precious jewels in the world. His robe is of silk brocade and is bound around him with a jade girdle. On his feet he wears golden shoes. . . . The king's throne is set with pearls and precious stones, and the steps of the throne are covered with pure gold.[3]

As the caliph took on more of the trappings of a hereditary autocrat, the bureaucracy assisting him in administering the growing empire grew more complex as well. The caliph was advised by a council (called a *diwan*) headed by a prime minister, known as a *vizier* (*wazir*). The caliph did not attend meetings of the *diwan* in the normal manner, but sat behind a screen and then communicated his divine will to the *vizier*. Some historians have ascribed the change in the caliphate to Persian influence,

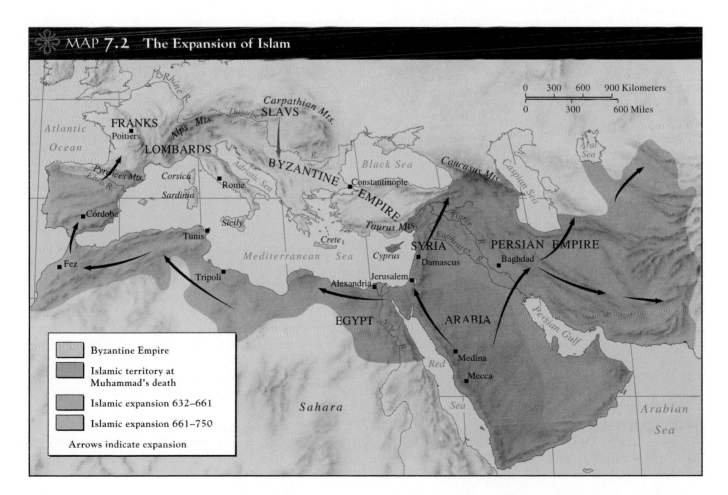

MAP **7.2** The Expansion of Islam

Byzantine Empire

Islamic territory at Muhammad's death

Islamic expansion 632–661

Islamic expansion 661–750

Arrows indicate expansion

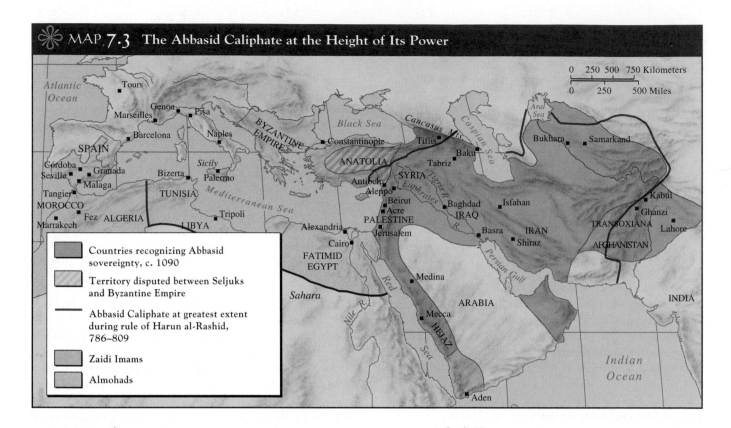

MAP 7.3   The Abbasid Caliphate at the Height of Its Power

which permeated the empire after the capital was moved to Baghdad. Persian influence was indeed strong (the mother of the caliph al-Ma'mun, for example, was a Persian), but more likely, the increase in pomp and circumstance was a natural consequence of the growing power and prosperity of the empire.

However, an element of instability lurked below the aura of prosperity. Disputes over the succession to the caliphate were common. At Harun's death, the rivalry between his two sons Amin and al-Ma'mun led to civil war and the destruction of Baghdad. As described by the tenth-century Muslim historian al-Mas'udi,

> Mansions were destroyed, most remarkable monuments obliterated; prices soared. . . . Brother turned his sword against brother, son against father, as some fought for Amin, others for Ma'mun. Houses and palaces fueled the flames; property was put to the sack.[4]

Vast wealth also contributed to financial corruption. By awarding important positions to court favorites, the Abbasid caliphs began to undermine the foundations of their own power and eventually became mere figureheads. Under Harun al-Rashid, members of his Hashemite clan received large pensions from the state treasury, and his wife Zubaida reportedly spent vast sums while shopping on a pilgrimage to Mecca. One powerful family, the Barmakids, amassed vast wealth and power until Harun al-Rashid eliminated the entire clan in a fit of jealousy (see the box on p. 201).

The life of luxury enjoyed by the caliph and other political and economic elites in Baghdad seemingly undermined the stern fiber of Arab society as well as the strict moral code of Islam. Strictures against sexual promiscuity were widely ignored, and caliphs were rumored to maintain thousands of concubines in their harems. Divorce was common, homosexuality was widely practiced, and alcohol was consumed in public despite Islamic law's prohibition against imbibing spirits.

The process of disintegration was accelerated by changes that were taking place within the armed forces and the bureaucracy of the empire. Given the shortage of qualified Arabs for key positions in the army and the administration, the caliphate began to recruit officials from among the non-Arab peoples in the empire, such as Persians and Turks from Central Asia. These people gradually became a dominant force in the army and administration. Eventually, provincial rulers began to break away from central control and establish their own independent dynasties. Spain had already established its own caliphate when a prince of the Umayyad dynasty had escaped execution and fled there in 750. Morocco became independent, and in 973 a new Shi'ite dynasty under the Fatimids was established in Egypt with its capital at Cairo. With increasing disarray in the empire, the Islamic world was held together only by the common commitment to the Koran and the use of Arabic as the prevailing means of communication.

The Seljuk Turks

In the eleventh century, the Abbasid caliphate faced an even more serious threat in the form of the Seljuk Turks.

THE MURDER OF JA'FAR AL-BARMAKI

The historian al-Mas'udi is our best source for inside information about the reign of the caliph Harun al-Rashid. In this excerpt, Harun begins to suspect his favorite courtier, the handsome Ja'far of the powerful Barmakid family, of breaking his word. The story illustrates the intense jealousies and personal rivalries that affected court life in the Abbasid era. Some historians suspect that Harun's love for Ja'far was sexual.

AL-MAS'UDI, *THE MEADOWS OF GOLD:* *THE FALL OF THE BARMAKIDS*

'Yahya, the son of Khalid ibn Barmak, his two sons Ja'far and Fadl, and other members of this family were at the height of their power, which was without limit, and unassailable in their high offices. The days of their rule, it is said, were like a perpetual wedding feast, filled with unending happiness and joy. It was during this time that Harun al-Rashid said to Ja'far:

"Ja'far, there is no one in the world dearer or closer to me than yourself and no one whose conversation is sweeter or more desirable than yours. Now my sister Abbasa holds in my heart a place not inferior to that which I have given you. I have considered the feelings that each of you inspire in me and I have realized that I cannot easily dispense either with you or with my sister.... I know of only one way to procure myself this double pleasure and to enjoy henceforth the sweetness of both your companies.... I wish to have you marry Abbasa and to give you the right, by this marriage, to pass your evenings with her, to see her, to be near her, whenever I am with you both. But your privileges will end there."

[Ja'far accepted these conditions, and after the marriage took place, considered himself bound by his word and did not assert his conjugal rights. Abbasa, however, was secretly fond of Ja'far and determined to win his love.

When her advances were spurned, she enlisted the help of Ja'far's mother in a secret plot to have a child by her husband. One day Ja'far's mother went to her son and said:]

"My child, I have been told of a young slave girl who ... is lettered and learned, gracious and charming, her beauty is beyond compare.... I resolved to buy her for you and the matter is almost settled with her owner."

[Ja'far was delighted, and ... his mother agreed that on a given night she would present him with the pretty slave. Then she told Abbasa of her plan. When the time came, she dressed as a slave girl and went to the house of Ja'far's mother.] That night Ja'far, his head still turning from wine, left the Caliph's palace to come to the tryst.... Abbasa, on going in to her husband, found a man sufficiently drunk not to know her face or figure. Once the marriage had been consummated and her husband's lust satisfied, Abbasa asked:

"What do you think of the ruses of the daughters of kings?"

"Whom do you mean?" he asked, convinced that he was talking to some Byzantine slave girl.

"Of myself!" she answered. "I, your mistress, Abbasa, daughter of Mahdi!"

Ja'far rose in horror, his drunkenness suddenly gone, and returned to his senses. At once he went to his mother and said to her:

"You have sold me cheap and placed me on the edge of an abyss. See what the outcome of my predicament will be!"

[Abbasa became pregnant, and in due course gave birth to a son, whom she later sent to Mecca in the care of two servants to keep Harun al-Rashid from learning of his identity. But the caliph's wife Zubaida found out about the affair and informed her husband. In revenge, Harun ordered his courtier Ja'far to be assassinated. Then, out of remorse, he executed the assassin.]

The Seljuk Turks were a nomadic people from Central Asia who had converted to Islam and flourished as military mercenaries for the Abbasid caliphate, where they were known for their ability as mounted archers. Moving gradually into Iran and Armenia as the Abbasids weakened, the Seljuk Turks grew in number until by the eleventh century they were able to occupy the eastern provinces of the Abbasid empire. In 1055, a Turkish leader captured Baghdad and assumed command of the empire with the title of sultan (the term means "holder of power"). While the Abbasid caliph remained the chief representative of Sunni religious authority, the real military and political power of the state was in the hands of the Seljuk Turks. The latter did not establish their headquarters in Baghdad, which now entered a period of decline.

By the last quarter of the eleventh century, the Seljuks were exerting military pressure on Egypt and the Byzantine Empire. In 1071, when the Byzantines foolishly challenged the Turks, their army was routed at Manzikert, near Lake Van in eastern Turkey, and the victors took over most of the Anatolian peninsula. In dire straits, the Byzantine Empire turned to the west for help, setting in motion the papal pleas that led to the crusades.

In Europe, and undoubtedly within the Muslim world itself, the arrival of the Turks was regarded as a disaster. The Turks were viewed as barbarians who destroyed civilizations and oppressed populations. In fact, in many respects Turkish rule in the Middle East was probably beneficial. Converted to Islam, the Turkish rulers temporarily brought an end to the fraternal squabbles between Sunni and Shi'ite Muslims, while supporting the Sunnites. They put their energies into revitalizing Islamic law and institutions and provided much-needed political stability to the empire, which helped to restore its former

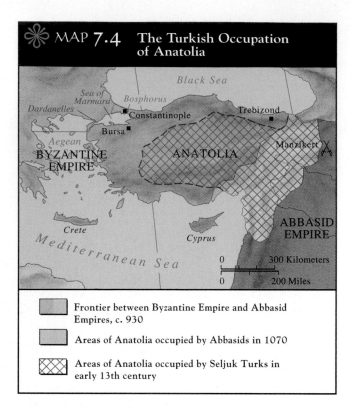

MAP 7.4 The Turkish Occupation of Anatolia

Frontier between Byzantine Empire and Abbasid Empires, c. 930

Areas of Anatolia occupied by Abbasids in 1070

Areas of Anatolia occupied by Seljuk Turks in early 13th century

prosperity. In one respect, however, their policies may have been detrimental to the later development of Islam. Adopting a narrow interpretation of the Koran and the *Shari'ah*, they encouraged a rigid approach to sacred doctrine that would make it more difficult for the faithful to respond effectively to social changes taking place within Islamic society.

The Crusades

Just before the end of the eleventh century, the Byzantine emperor Alexius I desperately called for assistance from other Christian states in Europe to protect his empire against the invading Seljuk Turks. As part of his appeal, he said that the Muslims were desecrating Christian shrines in the Holy Land and also molesting Christian pilgrims en route to the shrines. In actuality, the Muslims had never threatened the shrines or cut off Christian access to them. But tension between Christendom and the world of Islam was on the rise, and the Byzantine emperor's appeal received a ready response in Europe. Beginning in 1096 and continuing into the thirteenth century, a series of crusades brought the Holy Land and adjacent areas on the Mediterranean coast from Antioch to the Sinai peninsula under Christian rule (see Chapter 12).

At first, Muslim rulers in the area were taken aback by the invading crusaders, whose armored cavalry presented a new challenge to local warriors, and their response was ineffectual. The Seljuk Turks by that time were preoccupied with events taking place further to the east and took no action themselves. But in 1169, Sunni Muslims under the leadership of Saladin (Salah al-Din), vizier to the last Fatimid caliph, brought an end to the Fatimid dynasty. Proclaiming himself sultan, Saladin succeeded in establishing his control over both Egypt and Syria, thereby confronting the Christian states in the area with united Muslim power on two fronts. In 1187 Saladin's army invaded the kingdom of Jerusalem and destroyed the Christian forces concentrated there. Further operations reduced Christian occupation in the area to a handful of fortresses along the northern coast. Unlike the Christians, however, Saladin did not permit a massacre of the civilian population and even tolerated the continuation of Christian religious services in conquered territories.

The Christians returned for another try a few years after the fall of Jerusalem, but the campaign succeeded only in securing some of the coastal cities. Although the Christians would retain a toehold on the coast for much of the thirteenth century (Acre, their last stronghold, fell to the Muslims in 1291), they were no longer a significant force in Middle Eastern affairs. In retrospect, the crusades had only minimal importance in the history of the Middle East and may even have served to unite the forces of Islam against the foreign invaders (see the box on p. 203). Far more important in their impact

THE CRUSADES IN MUSLIM EYES

Usamah, an early-twelfth-century Muslim warrior and gentleman, had close associations with the crusaders. When he was ninety years old, he wrote his memoirs including many entertaining observations on the crusaders, or "Franks" as he called them. Here Usamah is astounded at the Franks' rudeness to Muslims and at their assumption of cultural superiority.

USAMAH, BOOK OF REFLECTIONS

1. Everyone who is a fresh emigrant from the Frankish lands is ruder in character than those who have become acclimatized and have held long association with the Moslems. Here is an illustration of their rude character.

   Whenever I visited Jerusalem I always entered the Aqsa Mosque, beside which stood a small mosque which the Franks had converted into a church. When I used to enter the Aqsa Mosque, which was occupied by the Templars [an order of crusading knights], who were my friends, the Templars would evacuate the little adjoining mosque so that I might pray in it. One day I entered this mosque, repeated the first formula, "Allah is great," and stood up in the act of praying, upon which one of the Franks rushed on me, got hold of me, and turned my face eastward, saying, "This is the way thou shouldst pray!" A group of Templars hastened to him, seized him, and repelled him from me. I resumed my prayer. The same man, while the others were otherwise busy, rushed once more on me and turned my face eastward, saying,

   "This is the way thou shouldst pray!" The Templars again came in to him and expelled him. They apologized to me, saying, "This is a stranger who has only recently arrived from the land of the Franks, and he has never before seen anyone praying except eastward." Thereupon I said to myself, "I have had enough prayer." So I went out, and have ever been surprised at the conduct of this devil of a man, at the change in the color of his face, his trembling, and his sentiment at the sight of one praying toward the *qiblah*.

2. In the army of King Fulk, son of Fulk, was a Frankish reverend knight who had just arrived from their land in order to make the holy pilgrimage and then return home. He was of my intimate fellowship and kept such constant company with me that he began to call me "my brother." Between us were mutual bonds of amity and friendship. When he resolved to return by sea to his homeland, he said to me:

   "My brother, I am leaving for my country and I want thee to send with me thy son (my son, who was then fourteen years old, was at that time in my company) to our country, where he can see the knights and learn wisdom and chivalry. When he returns, he will be like a wise man."

   Thus there fell upon my ears words which would never come out of the head of a sensible man; for even if my son were to be taken captive, his captivity could not bring him a worse misfortune than carrying him into the lands of the Franks.

---

were the Mongols, a pastoral people who swept out of the Gobi Desert in the early thirteenth century to seize control over much of the known world (see Chapter 12). Beginning with the advances of Genghis Khan in northern China, Mongol armies later spread across Central Asia, and in 1258, under the leadership of Hulegu, brother of the more famous Khubilai Khan, they seized Persia and Mesopotamia, bringing an end to the caliphate at Baghdad.

The Mongols

Unlike the Seljuk Turks, the Mongols were not Muslims, and they found it difficult to adapt to the settled conditions that they found in the major cities in the Middle East. Their treatment of the local population in conquered territories was brutal (according to one historian, after conquering a city, they wiped out not only entire families but also their household pets) and destructive to the economy. Cities were razed to the ground, and dams and other irri-

gation works were destroyed, reducing prosperous agricultural societies to the point of mass starvation. The Mongols advanced as far as the Red Sea, but their attempt to seize Egypt failed, in part because of the effective resistance posed by the Mamluks (a Turkish military class originally composed of slaves; sometimes written as Mamelukes), who had recently overthrown the administration set up by Saladin and seized power for themselves.

Eventually, the Mongol rulers in the Middle East began to take on the coloration of the peoples that they had conquered. Mongol elites converted to Islam, Persian influence became predominant at court, and the cities began to be rebuilt. By the fourteenth century, the Mongol empire began to split into separate kingdoms and then to disintegrate. In the meantime, however, the old Islamic empire originally established by the Arabs in the seventh and eighth centuries had come to an end. The new center of Islamic civilization was in Cairo, now about to promote a renaissance in Muslim culture under the sponsorship of the Mamluks.

To the north, another new force began to appear on the horizon with the rise of the Ottoman Turks on the Anatolian peninsula. In 1453, Sultan Mehmet II seized Constantinople and brought an end to the decrepit Byzantine Empire. Then the Ottomans began to turn their attention to the rest of the Middle East (see Chapter 16).

ISLAMIC CIVILIZATION

To be a Muslim is not simply to worship Allah but also to live according to his law as revealed in the Koran, which is viewed as fundamental and immutable doctrine, not to be revised by human beings.

As Allah has decreed, so must human beings behave. Therefore, Islamic doctrine must be consulted to determine questions of politics, economic behavior, civil and criminal law, and social ethics. In Islamic society there is no rigid demarcation between church and state, between the sacred and the secular.

A TANGIER SPICE MARKET.   For centuries, the spices of the East have passed through southwestern Asia and North Africa on their way to Europe. Some came by caravan across the Arabian peninsula, while others were carried on ships across the Indian Ocean and up the Red Sea to the Mediterranean. Even today, the markets of the region boast a colorful and pungent display of spices, such as the one shown here in a shop in Tangier, on the coast of Morocco.

The Wealth of Araby: Trade and Cities in the Middle East

As we have noted, overall this era was probably one of the most prosperous periods in the history of the Middle East. Trade in particular flourished, not only within the Islamic world, but also with China (now in a period of efflorescence during the era of the Tang and the Song dynasties—see Chapter 10), with the Byzantine Empire, and with the trading societies in Southeast Asia (see Chapter 9). Trade goods were carried both by ship and by the "fleets of the desert," the camel caravans that traversed the arid land from Morocco in the far west to the countries beyond the Caspian Sea. From the Sahara came gold and slaves; from China, silk and porcelain; from East Africa, gold, ivory, and rhinoceros horn; and from the lands of South Asia, sandalwood, cotton, wheat, sugar, and spices. Within the empire, Egypt contributed grain; Iraq, linens, dates, and precious stones; Spain, leather goods, olives, and wine; and western India, various textile goods. The exchange of goods was facilitated by the development of banking and the use of currency and letters of credit.

Under these conditions, urban areas flourished. While the Abbasids were in power, Baghdad was probably the greatest city in the empire, but after the rise of the Fatimids in Egypt, the focus of trade shifted to Cairo, described by the traveler Leo Africanus as "one of the greatest and most famous cities in all the whole world, filled with stately and admirable palaces and colleges, and most sumptuous temples."[5] Other great commercial cities included Basra at the head of the Persian Gulf, Aden at the southern tip of the Arabian peninsula, Damascus in modern Syria, and Marrakech in Morocco. Within the cities the inhabitants were generally segregated by religion, with Jews and Christians living in separate neighborhoods. But all were equally subject to the most common threats to urban life—fire, flood, and disease.

The most impressive urban buildings were usually the palace for the caliph or the local governor and the great mosque. Houses were often constructed of stone or brick around a timber frame. The larger houses were often built around an interior courtyard, where the residents could retreat from the dust, noise, and heat of the city streets. Sometimes domestic animals such as goats or sheep would be stabled there. The houses of the wealthy were often multistoried, with balconies and windows covered with latticework to provide privacy for those inside. The poor in both urban and rural areas lived in simpler houses composed of clay or unfired bricks. The Bedouins lived in tents that could be dismantled and moved according to their needs.

Eating habits varied in accordance with economic standing and religious preference. Muslims did not eat pork, but those who could afford it often served other meats such as mutton, lamb, poultry, or fish. Fruit, spices, and vari-

A CONSUMER'S GUIDE TO THE IDEAL SLAVE

Slavery was widely practiced in the Middle East under the Abbasid caliphate. In this excerpt from a much longer passage, Kai Ka'us, an eleventh-century Persian, instructs his son on what to look for when buying a slave. Clearly, different slaves would serve different purposes, and the ideal qualities would vary according to the individual case. What is striking is that the slaves were evaluated not as human beings but as pieces of merchandise.

A FATHER'S INSTRUCTIONS TO HIS SON

Now let me describe to the best of my ability what is essential in the purchasing of slaves, both white and black, and what their good and bad points are, so that they may be known to you. Understand then that there are three essentials in the buying of slaves; first is the recognition of their good and bad qualities, whether external or internal, by means of physiognomy; second is the awareness of diseases, whether latent or apparent, by their symptoms; third is the knowledge of the various classes and the defects and merits of each.

With regard to the first requirement, that of physiognomy, it consists of close observation when buying slaves. . . . Whoever it may be that inspects the slave must first look at the face, which is always open to view, whereas the body can only be seen as occasion offers. Then look at eyes and eyebrows, followed by nose, lips and teeth, and lastly at the hair. The reason for this is that God placed the beauty of human beings in eyes and eyebrows, delicacy in the nose, sweetness in the lips and teeth, and freshness in the skin. . . .

The learned say that one must know the indications and signs by which to buy the slaves suited for particular duties. The slave that you buy for your private service and conviviality should be of middle proportions, neither tall nor short, fat nor lean, pale nor florid, thickset nor slender, curly-haired nor with hair overstraight. When you see a slave soft-fleshed, fine-skinned, with regular bones and wine-colored hair, black eyelashes, dark eyes, . . . slender waisted, round-chinned, red-lipped, with white regular teeth, and all his members such as I have described, such a slave will be decorative and companionable, loyal, of delicate character, and dignified.

The mark of the slave suited for arms bearing is that his hair is thick, his body tall and erect, his build powerful, his flesh hard, his bones thick, his skin coarse and his limbs straight, the joints being firm. . . . Shoulders must be broad, the chest deep, the neck thick, and the head round; also for preference he should be bald. . . . Any slave who possesses these qualities will be a champion in single combat, brave and successful.

The mark of the slave suited for employment in the women's apartments is that he should be dark-skinned and sour-visaged and have withered limbs, scanty hair, a shrill voice, little [slender] feet, thick lips, a flat nose, stubby fingers, a bowed figure, and a thin neck. A slave with these qualities will be suitable for service in the women's quarters. He must not have a white skin nor a fair complexion. . . . His eyes, further, should not be languorous or moist; a man having such qualities is either overfond of women or prone to act as a go-between.

ous sweets were delicacies. The poor were generally forced to survive on boiled millet or peas with an occasional lump of meat or fat. Bread—white or whole meal—could be found on tables throughout the region except in the deserts, where boiled grain was the staple food.

Islamic Society

In some ways, Arab society was probably one of the most egalitarian of its time. Both the principles of Islam, which held that all were equal in the eyes of Allah, and the importance of trade to the prosperity of the state probably contributed to this egalitarianism. Although there was a fairly well defined upper class, consisting of the ruling families, senior officials, tribal elites, and the wealthiest merchants, there was no hereditary nobility as in many contemporary societies, and the merchants enjoyed a degree of respect that they did not receive in Europe, China, or India.

Though the Arab empire was more urbanized than most other societies at the time, the bulk of the population continued to live in the countryside and supported themselves by farming or herding animals. During the early stages, most of the farmland was owned by independent peasants, but later some concentration of land in the hands of wealthy owners began to take place. In river valleys like the Tigris and Euphrates and the Nile, the majority of the farmers probably continued to be independent peasants.

Not all benefited from the high degree of social mobility in the Islamic world, however. Slavery was widespread (see the box above). Since a Muslim could not be enslaved, the supply came from sub-Saharan Africa or from non-Islamic populations elsewhere in Asia. Most were employed in the army (which was sometimes a road to power, as in the case of the Mamluks) or as domestic servants, where they were sometimes permitted to purchase their freedom. The slaves who worked the large estates

DRAW THEIR VEILS OVER THEIR BOSOMS

In the early Islamic era, many upper-class women greeted men on the street, entertained their husband's friends at home, went on pilgrimages to Mecca, and even accompanied their husbands to battle. Such women were obviously neither veiled nor secluded. Eventually, however, Muhammad specified that his own wives, who (according to the Koran) were "not like any other women," should be modestly attired and should be addressed by men from behind a curtain. Over the centuries, Muslim theologians, fearful that female sexuality could threaten the established order, interpreted Muhammad's "modest attire" and his reference to curtains to mean segregated seclusion and body concealment for all Muslim women. In fact, one strict scholar in fourteenth-century Cairo went so far as to prescribe that ideally a women should be allowed to leave her home only three times in her life: when entering her husband's home after marriage, after the death of parents, and after her own death.

In traditional Islamic societies, veiling and seclusion were more prevalent among urban women than among their rural counterparts. The latter, who worked in the fields and rarely saw people outside their extended family, were less restricted. In this excerpt from the Koran, women are instructed to "guard their modesty" and "draw veils over their bosoms." Nowhere in the Koran, however, does it stipulate that women should be sequestered or covered from head to toe.

THE KORAN: CHAPTER 24

And say to the believing women
That they should lower
Their gaze and guard
Their modesty: that they
Should not display their
Beauty and ornaments except
What [must ordinarily] appear
Thereof: that they should
Draw their veils over
Their bosoms and not display
Their beauty except
To their husbands, their fathers,
Their husbands' fathers, their sons,
Their husbands' sons,
Their brothers or their brothers' sons,
Or their sisters' sons,
Or their women, or the slaves
Whom their right hands
Possess, or male servants
Free of physical needs,
Or small children who
Have no sense of the shame
Of sex; and that they
Should not strike their feet
In order to draw attention
To their hidden ornaments.

---

probably experienced the worst living conditions and rose in revolt on several occasions.

The Islamic principle of human equality also fell short in the treatment of women. Although the Koran instructed men to treat women with respect, and women did have the right to own and inherit property, in general the male was dominant in Muslim society. Polygyny was permitted, and the right of divorce was in practice restricted to the husband, although some schools of legal thought permitted women to stipulate that their husband could have only one wife or to seek a separation in certain specific circumstances. Adultery and homosexuality were stringently forbidden (although such prohibitions were frequently ignored in practice), and Islamic custom required that women be cloistered in their homes (thus the tradition of the harem) and prohibited from social contacts with males outside their own family. The custom of requiring women to cover virtually all parts of their body when appearing in public was common in urban areas and continues to be practiced in many Islamic societies today. It should be noted, however, that these customs owed more to traditional Arab practice than to Koranic law (see the box above), and that the position of women under Islam was probably better than it had been in former times, when they were often treated like slaves.

The Culture of Islam

From the beginning of their empire, Muslim Arabs had demonstrated a willingness to absorb the culture of their conquered peoples. The Arabs were truly heirs to many elements of the remaining Greco-Roman culture of the Roman Empire. Just as readily, they assimilated Byzantine and Persian culture. In the eighth and ninth centuries, numerous Greek, Syrian, and Persian scientific and philosophical works were translated into Arabic. As the chief language in the southern Mediterranean and the Middle East, Arabic became a truly international language. Later, Persian and Turkish also came to be important in administration and culture.

The spread of Islam led to the emergence of a new culture throughout the entire Arab empire. This was true in all fields of endeavor, from literature to art and architecture. But pre-Islamic traditions were not extinguished and they fre-

LOVE FOR A CAMEL

Early Arabic poetry focused on simple pleasures, such as wine, women, song, and the faithful camel. This excerpt is from a longer work by the sixth-century Arab poet Tarafah. Tarafah was one of a group of seven poets called the "suspended ones." Their poems, having won a prize in an annual competition, were suspended on a wall for all to read.

THE ODE OF TARAFAH

Ah, but when grief assails me, straightway I ride it off
    mounted on my swift, lean-flanked camel, night and day
    racing, . . .
Her long neck is very erect when she lifts it up, calling to
    mind the rudder of a Tigris-bound vessel. Her skull is
    most like an anvil, the junction of its two halves meeting
    together as it might be on the edge of a file.
Her cheek is smooth as Syrian parchment, her split lip
    a tanned hide of Yemen, its slit not bent crooked;
    her eyes are a pair of mirrors, sheltering in the caves of
    her brow-bones, the rock of a pool's hollow, . . .

I am at her with the whip, and my she-camel quickens pace
    what time the mirage of the burning stone-tract shimmers;
    elegantly she steps, as a slave-girl at a party will sway,
    showing her master skirts of a trailing white gown.
I am not one that skulks fearfully among the hilltops, but
    when the folk seek my succor I gladly give it; if you look
    for me in the circle of the folk you'll find me there, and if
    you hunt me in the taverns there you'll catch me.
Come to me when you will, I'll pour you a flowing cup, and
    if you don't need it, well, do without and good luck to
    you!
Whenever the tribe is assembled you'll come upon me at the
    summit of the noble House, the oft-frequented; my boon-
    companions are white as stars, and a singing-wench
    comes to us in her striped gown or her saffron robe, wide
    the opening of her collar, delicate her skin to my compan-
    ions' fingers, tender her nakedness.
When we say, "Let's hear from you," she advances to us
    chanting fluently, her glance languid, in effortless song.

---

quently combined with Muslim motifs to produce creative works of a high degree of imagination and originality.

PHILOSOPHY AND SCIENCE

During the centuries following the rise of the Arab empire, it was the Islamic world that was most responsible for preserving and spreading the scientific and philosophical achievements of ancient civilizations. At a time when ancient Greek philosophy was largely unknown in Europe, key works by Aristotle, Plato, and other Greek philosophers were translated into Arabic and stored in a "House of Wisdom" in Baghdad, where they were read and studied by Muslim scholars. Through the writings of the Spanish Muslim philosopher Ibn Rushd (known in the West as Averroës), the contents of many of these works eventually became known in Europe and influenced Christian thought. Texts on mathematics and linguistics were brought from India. The process was undoubtedly stimulated by the introduction of paper manufacturing from China in the eighth century. By the end of the century, the first paper factories had been established in Baghdad, and booksellers and libraries soon followed. The first paper mill in Europe appeared in the Pyrenees Mountains in Spain in the twelfth century.

Although Islamic scholars are justly praised for preserving much of classical knowledge for the West, they also made considerable advances of their own. Nowhere is this more evident than in mathematics and the natural sciences. Islamic scholars adopted and passed on the numerical system of India, including the use of the zero, and a ninth-century Iranian mathematician created the mathematical discipline of algebra (al-jebr). In astronomy, Muslims set up an observatory at Baghdad to study the position of the stars. They were aware that the earth was round and in the ninth century produced a world map based on the tradition of the Greco-Roman astronomer Ptolemy.

Muslim scholars also made many new discoveries in optics and chemistry and, with the assistance of texts on anatomy by the ancient Greek physician Galen (c. 180–200 C.E.), developed medicine as a distinctive field of scientific inquiry. Especially well known was Ibn Sina (980–1037). Known as Avicenna in the West, he compiled a medical encyclopedia that, among other things, emphasized the contagious nature of certain diseases and showed how they could be spread by contaminated water supplies. After its translation into Latin, Avicenna's work became a basic medical textbook for medieval European university students.

ISLAMIC LITERATURE

Islam brought major changes to the culture of the Middle East, not least to literature. Muslims regarded the Koran as their greatest literary work, but pre-Islamic traditions continued to influence writers throughout the region.

An established tradition of Arabic poetry already existed prior to Muhammad. It extolled Bedouin tribal life, courage in battle, hunting, sports, and respect for the animals of the desert, especially the camel (see the box above). Because the Arabic language did not possess a written script until the fourth century C.E., poetry was

BE THANKFUL FOR SMALL FAVORS

T he Rose Garden, *an entertaining collection of moral anecdotes and maxims, was written in the thirteenth century by Sadi, considered by many to be Persia's greatest author. Here, in his usual mixture of prose and poetry, Sadi advises his readers to be content with what they have.*

SADI, THE ROSE GARDEN: STORY 7

A padshah was in the same boat with a Persian slave who had never before been at sea and experienced the inconvenience of a vessel. He began to cry and to tremble to such a degree that he could not be pacified by kindness, so that at last the king became displeased as the matter could not be remedied. In that boat there happened to be a philosopher, who said: "With thy permission I shall quiet him." The padshah replied: "It will be a great favor." The philosopher ordered the slave to be thrown into the water so that he swallowed some of it, whereon he was caught and pulled by his hair to the boat, to the stern of which he clung with both his hands. Then he sat down in a corner and became quiet. This appeared strange to the king who knew not what wisdom there was in the proceeding and asked for it. The philosopher replied: "Before he had tasted the calamity of being drowned, he knew not the safety of the boat; thus also a man does not appreciate the value of immunity from a misfortune until it has befallen him."

O thou full man, barley-bread pleases thee not.
She is my sweetheart who appears ugly to thee.
To the houris of paradise purgatory seems hell.
Ask the denizens of hell. To them purgatory is paradise.
There is a difference between him whose friend is in his arms
And him whose eyes of expectation are upon the door.

---

originally passed on by memory. Later, in the eighth and ninth centuries, it was compiled in anthologies. 詩選集

Pre-Muslim Persia also boasted a long literary tradition, most of it oral and written down in later centuries in the Arabic alphabet. The Persian poetic tradition remained strong under Islam. Rabe'a of Qozdar, Persia's first known woman poet, lived in the second half of the tenth century. Describing the suffering love brings, she wrote: "Beset with impatience I did not know/That the more one seeks to pull away, the tighter becomes the rope."[6]

To Western observers, the most famous works of Middle Eastern literature are undoubtedly the *Rubaiyat* of Omar Khayyam and *The Tales from 1001 Nights* (also called *The Arabian Nights*). Paradoxically, these two works are not as popular with Middle Eastern readers. Both, in fact, were freely translated into Western languages for nineteenth-century European readers, who found themes of wine, women, and hedonistic pleasure more acceptable when set in a quaint foreign disguise.

Unfortunately, very little is known of the life or the poetry of the twelfth-century poet Omar Khayyam. Skeptical, reserved, and slightly contemptuous of his peers, he combined poetry with scientific works on mathematics and astronomy and a revision of the calendar that was more accurate than the Gregorian version devised in Europe hundreds of years later. Omar Khayyam did not write down his poems, but composed them orally over wine with friends at a neighborhood tavern. They were recorded later by friends or scribes. Many poems attributed to him were actually written long after his death. Among them is the well-known couplet translated into English in the nineteenth century: "Here with a loaf of bread beneath the bough, a flask of wine, a book of verse, and thou."

Omar Khayyam's poetry is simple and down to earth. Key themes are the impermanence of life, the impossibility of knowing God, and disbelief in an afterlife. Ironically, recent translations of his work appeal to modern attitudes of skepticism and minimalist simplicity that may make him even more popular in the West:

In youth I studied for a little while;
Later I boasted of my mastery.
Yet this was all the lesson that I learned:
We come from dust, and with the wind are gone.

Of all the travelers on this endless road
No one returns to tell us where it leads,
There's little in this world but greed and need;
Leave nothing here, for you will not return. . . .

Since no one can be certain of tomorrow,
It's better not to fill the heart with care.
Drink wine by moonlight, darling, for the moon
Will shine long after this, and find us not.[7]

Like Omar Khayyam's verse, *The Arabian Nights* was loosely translated into European languages and adapted to Western tastes. A composite of folktales, fables, and romances of Indian and indigenous origin, the stories interweave the natural with the supernatural. The earliest stories were told orally and were later transcribed, with many later additions, in Arabic and Persian versions. The famous story of Aladdin and the Magic Lamp, for example, was an eighteenth-century addition. Nevertheless, *The Arabian Nights* has entertained readers for centuries, allowing them to enter a land of wish fulfillment through extraordinary plots, sensuality, comic and tragic situations, and a cast of unforgettable characters.

Sadi (1210–1292), considered the Persian Shakespeare, remains to this day the favorite author in Iran. His *Rose Garden* is a collection of entertaining stories written in prose sprinkled with verse (see the box above). He is also

THE PASSIONS OF A SUFI MYSTIC

Sufism was an unorthodox form of Islam that flourished in many parts of the Muslim world. It preached the importance of a highly personal relationship between Allah and the individual believer. Sufi orders began to assume considerable influence by the thirteenth century, perhaps because of the disintegration of the Abbasid empire and the heightened instability throughout the Islamic world. Sufi missionaries played a major role in efforts to spread Islam to India and Central Asia. In this poem, the thirteenth-century Persian poet Rumi describes the mystical relationship achieved by means of passionate music and dance.

RUMI, CALL TO THE DANCE

Come!
But don't join us without music.
We have a celebration here.
Rise and beat the drums.

We are Mansur who said "I am God!"

We are in ecstasy—
Drunk, but not from wine made of grapes.

Whatever your thoughts are about us,
We are far, far from them.

This is the night of the same
When we whirl to ecstasy.

There is light now,
There is light, there is light.

This is true love,
Which means farewell to the mind.
There is farewell today, farewell.

Tonight each flaming heart is a friend of music.
Longing for your lips,
My heart pours out of my mouth.

Hush!
You are made of feeling and thought and passion;
The rest is nothing but flesh and bone.
We are the soul of the world,
Not heavy or sagging like the body.
We are the spirit's treasure,
Not bound to this earth, to time or space.

How can they talk to us of prayer rugs and piety?
We are the hunter and the hunted,
Autumn and spring,
Night and day,
Visible and hidden.
Love is our mother.
We were born of Love.

---

renowned for his sonnetlike love poems, which set a model for generations to come. Sadi was a master of the pithy maxim:

A cat is a lion in catching mice
But a mouse in combat with a tiger.

He has found eternal happiness who lived a good life,
Because, after his end, good repute will keep his name alive.

When thou fightest with anyone, consider
Whether thou wilt have to flee from him or he from thee.[8]

Such maxims are typical of the Middle East, where the proverb, a one-line witty observation on the vagaries of life, has long been popular. Proverbs are not only a distinctive feature of Middle Eastern verse, especially Persian, but are also a part of daily life—a scholar recently recovered over four thousand in one Lebanese village! The following are some typical examples:

Trust in God, but tie up your camel. (Persian)
The world has not promised anything to anybody. (Moroccan)
An old cat will not learn how to dance. (Moroccan)
Lower your voice and strengthen your argument. (Lebanese)
He who has money can eat sherbet in Hell. (Lebanese)

What is brought by the wind will be carried away by the wind. (Persian)
You can't pick up two melons with one hand. (Persian)

Some Arabic and Persian literature reflected the deep spiritual and ethical concerns of the Koran. Many writers, however, carried Islamic thought in novel directions. The thirteenth-century poet Rumi, for example, embraced Sufism, a form of religious belief that called for a mystical relationship between Allah and human beings (the term *Sufism* stems from the Arabic word for wool, referring to the rough wool garments that its adherents wore). Converted to Sufism by a wandering dervish (dervishes, from the word for "poor" in Persian, sought to achieve a mystical union with Allah through violent dancing and chanting in an ecstatic trance), Rumi abandoned orthodox Islam to embrace God directly through ecstatic love. Realizing that love transcends intellect, he sought to reach God through a trance attained by the whirling dance of the dervish, set to mesmerizing music. As he twirled, the poet extemporized some of the most passionate lyrical verse ever conceived. His faith and art remain an important force in Islamic society today (see the box above).

The Islamic world also made a major contribution to historical writing, another discipline that was stimulated by the introduction of paper manufacturing. The first great

Islamic historian was al-Mas'udi. Born in Baghdad in 896, he wrote about both the Muslim and the non-Muslim world, traveling widely in the process. His *Meadows of Gold* is the source of much of our knowledge about the golden age of the Abbasid caliphate. Translations of his work reveal a wide-ranging mind and a keen intellect, combined with a human touch that practitioners of the art in our century might find reason to emulate (see the box on p. 201). Equaling al-Mas'udi in talent and reputation was the fourteenth-century historian Ibn Khaldun. Combining scholarship with government service, Ibn Khaldun was one of the first historians to attempt a philosophy of history.

ISLAMIC ART AND ARCHITECTURE

The art of Islam is a blend of Arab, Turkish, and Persian traditions. Although local influences can be discerned in Egypt, Anatolia, Spain, and other areas and the Mongols introduced an East Asian accent in the thirteenth century, for a long time Islamic art remained remarkably coherent over a wide area. First and foremost, the Arabs, with their new religion and their writing system, served as a unifying force. Fascinated by the mathematics and

astronomy they inherited from the Romans or the Babylonians, they developed a sense of rhythm and abstraction that found expression in their use of repetitive geometric ornamentation. The Turks brought abstraction in figurative and nonfigurative designs, and the Persians added their lyrical poetical mysticism. Much Islamic painting, for example, consists of illustrations of Persian texts.

The ultimate expression of Islamic art is to be found in the magnificent architectural monuments beginning in the late seventh century. The first great example is the Dome of the Rock, which was built in 691 to proclaim the spiritual and political legitimacy of the new religion to the ancient world. Set in the sacred heart of Jerusalem on Muhammad's holy rock and touching both the Western Wall of the Jews and the oldest Christian church, the Dome of the Rock remains one of the most revered Islamic monuments. Constructed on Byzantine lines with an octagonal shape and marble columns and ornamentation, the interior reflects Persian motifs with mosaics of precious stones. Although rebuilt several times and incorporating influences from both East and West, this first monument to Islam represents the birth of a new art.

At first, desert Arabs, whether nomads or conquering armies, prayed in an open court, shaded along the *kibla*

❀ **THE TEMPLE MOUNT AT JERUSALEM.** The Temple Mount is one of the most sacred sites in the city of Jerusalem. Originally it was the site of a temple built during the reign of Solomon, king of the Jews, about 1000 B.C.E. The Western Wall of the temple is shown in the foreground. Beyond the Wall is the Dome of the Rock complex, built on the place from which Muslims believe that Muhammad ascended to heaven.

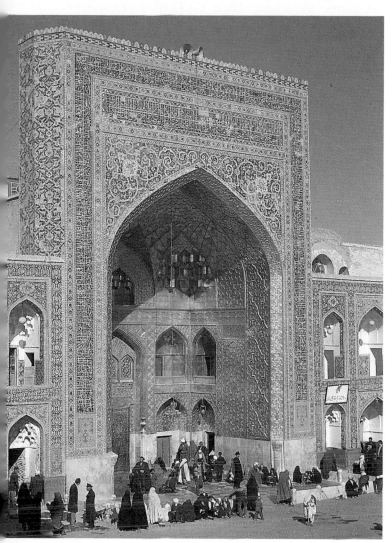

AN ENTRANCE PORTAL.   This entrance gate to an Iranian mosque displays the variety and delicacy of the geometrical decorations that often accompanied Islamic architecture. The brilliant blue-and-white mosaic tile shown here eventually evolved into polychromy by the fifteenth century. Note the veiled women in the foreground.

THE MOSQUE AT CÓRDOBA.   Perhaps the most impressive of all Islamic religious structures is the Mosque of Córdoba, in southern Spain, which was built between the eighth and tenth centuries. Shown here is the interior of the mosque, showing some of the columns that give the entire structure such an effect of mass as well as lightness.

(the wall facing the holy city of Mecca) by a thatched roof supported by rows of palm trunks. There was also a ditch where the faithful could wash off the dust of the desert prior to prayer. As Islam became better established, enormous mosques were constructed, but they were still modeled on the open court, which would be surrounded on all four sides with pillars supporting a wooden roof over the prayer area facing the *kibla* wall. The largest mosque ever built, the Great Mosque of Samarra (848–852), covered ten acres and contained 464 pillars in aisles surrounding the court. Set in the *kibla* wall was a niche, or *mihrab,* containing a decorated panel pointing to Mecca and representing Allah. Remains of the massive thirty-foot-high outer wall still stand, but the most famous section of the Samarra mosque was its ninety-foot-tall minaret, the tower

accompanying a mosque from which the *muezzin* calls the faithful to prayer five times a day.

No discussion of mosques would be complete without mentioning the famous ninth-century mosque at Córdoba in southern Spain, which is still in remarkable condition. Its 514 columns supporting double horseshoe arches transform this architectural wonder into a unique forest of trees pointing upward, contributing to a light and airy effect. The unparalleled sumptuousness and elegance make the Córdoba mosque one of the wonders of world art, let alone Islamic art.

Since the Muslim religion combines spiritual and political power in one, palaces also reflected the glory of Islam. Beginning in the eighth century with the spectacular castles of Syria, the rulers constructed large domiciles reminiscent of Roman design, with protective walls,

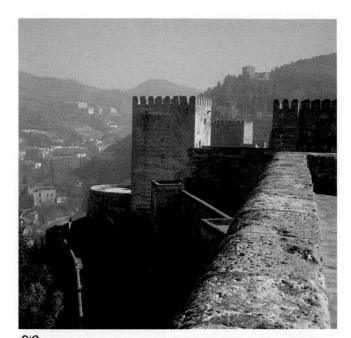

THE ALHAMBRA IN GRANADA. Islamic civilization reached its zenith with the fourteenth-century fairy-tale castle of Alhambra in southern Spain. Perched on a hill high above the city of Granada and framed by snowcapped mountains, the Alhambra is widely considered the most perfect expression of Islamic art. Renowned for its lacelike plaster decorations and imaginative use of reflecting pools and fountains, the Alhambra stands as an exquisite gem of Islam.

gates, and baths. Constructed of brick, they unfortunately no longer exist. With a central courtyard surrounded by two-story arcades and massive gate-towers, they resembled a fortress as much as a palace. Characteristic of such "desert palaces" was the gallery over the entrance gate, with holes through which boiling oil could be poured down on the heads of attacking forces. This architectural feature was exported by the crusaders and was later incorporated repeatedly into medieval European castles.

The ultimate in Islamic palaces, however, is the fourteenth-century Alhambra in Spain. The extensive succession of courtyards, rooms, gardens, and fountains created a fairy-tale castle perched high above the city of Granada. Every inch of surface is decorated in intricate floral and semiabstract patterns; much of the decoration is done in carved plasterwork so fine that it resembles lace. The Lion Court in the center of the harem is world renowned for its lion fountain and surrounding arcade with elegant columns and carvings.

One of the most significant contributions of Islamic art is the knotted woolen rug. Originating in the pre-Muslim era, rugs were initially used to insulate stone palaces against the cold as well as to warm the shepherd's tent. Eventually they were applied to religious purposes, since every practicing Muslim is required to pray five times a day on clean ground. Small rugs served as prayer mats for individual use, while larger and more elaborate ones were given by rulers as rewards for political favors. Bedouins in the Arabian desert covered their sandy floors with rugs to create a cozy environment in their tents.

THE KORAN AS SCULPTURED DESIGN. Muslim sculptors and artists, reflecting the official view that any visual representation of the prophet Muhammad was blasphemous, turned to geometric patterns, as well as to flowers and animals, as a means of fulfilling their creative urge. The predominant motif, however, was the reproduction of Koranic verse in the Arabic script. Calligraphy, which was almost as important in the Middle East as it was in traditional China, used the Arabic script to decorate all of the Islamic arts, from painting to pottery, to tile and iron work, and to wall decorations such as this carved plaster panel in a courtyard of the Alhambra palace in Spain. Since a recitation from the Koran was an important component of the daily devotional activities for all practicing Muslims, elaborate scriptural panels such as this one perfectly blended the spiritual and the artistic realms.

In villages throughout the Middle East, the art of rug weaving has been passed down from mother to daughter over the centuries. Small girls as young as four years old took part in the process by helping to spin and prepare the wool shorn from the family sheep. By the age of six, girls would begin their first rug, and before adolescence their slender fingers would be producing fine carpets. Skilled artisanship represented an extra enticement to prospective bridegrooms, while rugs often became an important part of a woman's dowry to her future husband. After the wedding, the wife would continue to make rugs for home use, as well as for sale to augment the family income. Eventually, rugs began to be manufactured in workshops by professional artisans, who reproduced the designs from detailed painted diagrams.

Most decorations on the rugs, as well as on all forms of Islamic art, consisted of Arabic script and natural plant and figurative motifs. Repeated continuously in naturalistic or semiabstract geometrical patterns called arabesques, these decorations completely covered the surface and left no area undecorated. This dense decor was also evident in brick, mosaic, and stucco ornamentation and culminated in the magnificent tile work of later centuries.

No representation of the Prophet Muhammad ever adorned a mosque, in painting or in any other art form. Although no passage of the Koran forbids representational painting, the *Hadith*, an early collection of the Prophet's sayings, warned against any attempt to imitate God through artistic creation or idolatry. From the time of the Dome of the Rock, no figurative representations appear in Islamic religious art.

Human beings and animals could still be represented in secular art, but relatively little survives from the early centuries aside from a very few wall paintings from the royal palaces. Although the Persians used calligraphy and art to decorate their books, the Arabs had no pictorial tradition of their own and only began to develop the art of book illustration in the late twelfth century to illustrate translations of Greek scientific works.

In the thirteenth century, a Mongol dynasty established at Tabriz, west of the Caspian Sea, offered the Middle East its first direct contact with the art of East Asia. Mongol painting, done in the Chinese manner with a full brush and expressing animated movement and intensity (see Chapter 10), freed Islamic painters from traditional confines and enabled them to experiment with new techniques.

Chinese art also influenced Islamic art with its sense of space. A new sense of perspective pervaded Islamic painting, leading to some of the great paintings of the Herat School under the fifteenth-century autocrat Tamerlane. Artists working in the Herat style often depicted mounted warriors battling on a richly detailed background of trees and birds. These paintings served as the classical model for later Islamic painting, which culminated in the glorious artistic tradition of sixteenth-century Iran, Turkey, and India (see Chapter 16).

 A MIDDLE EAST CARPET BAZAAR.   Treasured by museums and wealthy patrons throughout the world, handwoven Middle Eastern carpets are both colorful and durable and reflect the grandeur of Islamic civilization. The best carpets, made of wool, silk, or cotton, are extremely time-consuming to manufacture. Some have as many as 650 knots per square inch, requiring a considerable amount of time to complete and thus raising the cost of the finished product. A small five-foot-square carpet, for example, could take a single weaver more than a year to complete. Today, among the best carpets are those manufactured in Turkey. Shown here is a rug market in Istanbul.

CONCLUSION

From ancient times, the Middle East has been the site of great empires. In the seventh century, a new force blossomed in the Arabian peninsula and spread rapidly throughout the Middle East. In the eyes of some European writers during the Middle Ages, the Arab empire was a malevolent force that posed a serious threat to the security of Christianity. Indian rajas undoubtedly also felt threatened. The image is not entirely inaccurate, for within half a century after the death of the Prophet, Arab armies overran Christian states in North Africa and the Iberian peninsula, while Turkish Muslims moved eastward onto the fringes of the Indian subcontinent.

But although the teachings of Muhammad brought war and conquest to much of the known world, they also brought hope to millions and a sense of political and economic stability to peoples throughout the region. For many, the arrival of Islam was a welcome event. Islam brought a code of law and a written language to societies that had previously not possessed them. Finally, by creating a revitalized trade network stretching from West Africa to East Asia, it established a vehicle for the exchange of technology and ideas that brought untold wealth to thousands and a better life to millions.

Like other empires in the region, the Arab empire did not last. It fell victim to a combination of internal and external pressures, and by the end of the thirteenth century, it was no more than a memory. But it left a powerful legacy in Islam, which remains one of the great religions of the world. In succeeding centuries, Islam began to penetrate into new areas beyond the fringes of the Sahara and across the Indian Ocean into the islands of the Indonesian archipelago. The next chapters will explore this development.

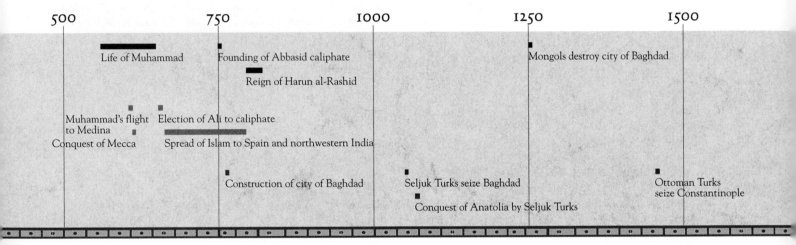

CHAPTER NOTES

1. Mohammed Marmaduke Pickthall, trans., *The Meaning of the Glorious Koran* (New York, 1953), p. 89.
2. Quoted in Thomas W. Lippman, *Understanding Islam: An Introduction to the Moslem World* (New York, 1982), p. 118.
3. Friedrich Hirth and W. W. Rockhill, trans., *Chau Ju-kua: His Work on the Chinese and Arab Trade in the Twelfth and Thirteenth Centuries, Entitled Chu-fan-chi* (New York, 1966), p. 115.
4. Mas'udi, *The Meadows of Gold: The Abbasids*, ed. Paul Lunde and Caroline Stone (London, 1989), p. 151.
5. Leo Africanus, *The History and Description of Africa and of the Notable Things Therein Contained* (New York, n.d.), pp. 820–21.
6. Ehsan Yarshater, ed., *Persian Literature* (Albany, N.Y., 1988), pp. 125–26.
7. Ibid., pp. 154–59.
8. E. Rehatsek, trans., *The Gulistan or Rose Garden of Sa'di* (New York, 1964), pp. 65, 67, 71.

SUGGESTED READINGS

Standard works on the Arab empire and the rise of Islam include B. Lewis, *The Arabs in History* (New York, 1961), and T. Lippman, *Understanding Islam: An Introduction to the Moslem World* (New York, 1982). More up-to-date is G. E. Perry, *The Middle East: Fourteen Islamic Centuries*, 2d ed. (Englewood Cliffs, N.J., 1992). A more detailed treatment can be found in P. M. Holt et al., eds., *The Cambridge History of Islam*, two vols. (Cambridge, 1970), and J. L. Esposito, ed. *The Oxford History of Islam* (New York, 1999). For a popularized history, see A. Nutting, *The Arabs: A Narrative History from Mohammed to the Present* (New York, 1964). For an overview with rich illustrations, see *People and Places of the Past* (National Geographic Society, 1983). For anthropological background, see

D. Bates and A. Rassam, *Peoples and Cultures of the Middle East* (Englewood Cliffs, N.J., 1983). On women, see S. Botman et al., *Women in the Middle East* (London, 1987), and N. Keddie et al., eds., *Women in Middle Eastern History: Shifting Boundaries in Sex and Gender* (New Haven, Conn., 1991).

On Islam, see F. Denny, *An Introduction to Islam* (New York, 1985), and J. Esposito, *Islam: the Straight Path* (New York, 1988). Among the various translations of the Koran, two of the best for the introductory student are N. J. Dawood, trans., *The Koran* (Harmondsworth, 1990), and M. M. Pickthall, trans., *The Meaning of the Glorious Koran* (New York, 1953). See also R. W. Bulliet, *Conversion to Islam in the Medieval Period: An Essay in Quantitative History* (Cambridge, 1979).

Specialized works on various historical periods are numerous. For a view of the crusades from an Arab perspective, see A. Maalouf, *The Crusades Through Arab Eyes* (London, 1984). On the Mamluks, see R. Irwin, *The Middle East in the Middle Ages: The Early Mamluk Sultanate, 1250–1382* (Carbondale, Ill., 1986).

On the economy, see E. Ashtor, *A Social and Economic History of the Near East in the Middle Ages* (Berkeley, 1976); K. N. Chaudhuri, *Asia Before Europe: Economy and Civilization of the Indian Ocean from the Rise of Islam to 1750* (Cambridge, 1990); and C. Issawi, *The Middle East Economy: Decline and Recovery* (Princeton, N.J., 1995). On the crucial role of the camel in Middle Eastern society, see the interesting study by R. W. Bulliet, *The Camel and the Wheel* (Cambridge, 1975). On the role of women during this period, see F. Hussain, *Muslim Women* (New York, 1984).

For the best introduction to Islamic literature, consult J. Kritzeck, ed., *Anthology of Islamic Literature* (New York, 1964), with its concise commentaries and introduction. An excellent introduction to Persian literature can be found in E. Yarshater, *Persian Literature* (Albany, N.Y., 1988). Of particular interest are the chapters on Omar Khayyam, by L. P. Elwell-Sutton, and on Rumi, by T. S. Halman. A stimulating analysis of Persian poetry is found in A. Schimmel, *A Two-Colored Brocade: The Imagery of Persian Poetry* (Chapel Hill, N.C., 1992). For the student, H. Haddawy, trans., *The Arabian Nights* (New York, 1990) is the best version. It presents 271 "nights" in a clear and colorful style.

For the best introduction to Islamic art, consult the concise yet comprehensive work by D. T. Rice, *Islamic Art*, rev. ed. (London, 1975). Also see J. Bloom and S. Blair, *Islamic Arts* (London, 1997). For carpets, a beautifully illustrated source is E. Sakhai's *The Story of Carpets* (London, 1991).

INFOTRAC COLLEGE EDITION

For additional reading, go to InfoTrac College Edition, your online research library at http://web1.infotrac-college.com

Enter the search term "Islam" using the Subject Guide.

Enter the search terms "caliph or caliphate" using Keywords.

Enter the search term "Koran" using Keywords.

Enter the search term "Crusades" using Keywords.

Enter the search terms "Sufi or Sufism or Rumi" using Keywords.

EARLY CIVILIZATIONS IN AFRICA

FOCUS QUESTIONS

• What were the main developments in African history before the coming of Islam, and what contacts did early African civilizations and societies have with civilizations outside Africa?
• What effects did the coming of Islam and the Arabs have on African religion, society, political structures, trade, and culture?
• What were the main characteristics of the West African states of Ghana and Mali?
• What roles did lineage groups, women, and slavery play in African society?
• What are some of the characteristics of African sculpture and carvings, music, and architecture, and what purpose did these forms of creative expression serve in African society?

In 1871, the German explorer Karl Mauch began to search southern Africa's central plateau for the colossal stone ruins of a legendary lost civilization. In late August, he found what he had been looking for. According to his diary: "Presently I stood before it and beheld a wall of a height of about 20 feet of granite bricks. Very close by there was a place where a kind of footpath led over rubble into the interior. Following this path I stumbled over masses of rubble and parts of walls and dense thickets. I stopped in front of a towerlike structure. Altogether it rose to a height of about 30 feet." Mauch was convinced that "a civilized nation must once have lived here." Like many other nineteenth-century Europeans, however, Mauch was equally convinced that the Africans who had lived there could never have built such splendid structures like the ones he had found at Great Zimbabwe. To Mauch and other archaeologists, Great Zimbabwe must have been the work of "a northern race closely akin to the Phoenician and Egyptian." It was not until the twentieth century that Europeans could overcome their prejudices and finally admit that Africans south of Egypt had also developed advanced civilizations with spectacular achievements.

The continent of Africa has played a central role in the long evolution of humankind. It was in Africa that the first hominids appeared more than three million years ago. It was probably in Africa that the immediate ancestors of modern human beings—*Homo sapiens*—emerged for the first time. Both the cultivation of crops and the domestication of animals may have occurred first in Africa. Certainly, one of the first states appeared in Africa, in the Nile valley in the northeastern corner of the continent, in the form of the kingdom of the pharaohs. Recent evidence suggests that Egyptian civilization was significantly influenced by cultural developments taking place to the south, in Nubia in modern Sudan.

After the decline of the Egyptian empire during the first millennium B.C.E., the focus of social change began to shift from the lower Nile valley to other areas of the continent: to West Africa, where a series of major trading states began to take part in the caravan trade with the Mediterranean through the vast wastes of the Sahara; to the region of the upper Nile River, where the states of Kush and Axum dominated trade for several centuries; and to the eastern coast from the Horn of Africa to the straits between the continent and the island of Madagascar, where African peoples began to play an active role in the commercial traffic in the Indian Ocean. In the meantime, a gradual movement of agricultural peoples brought Iron Age farming to the central portion of the continent, leading eventually to the creation of several states in the Zaire River basin and the plateau region south of the Zambezi River. When European sea-

farers began to round the Cape of Good Hope at the end of the fifteenth century C.E., Western historians would herald their voyages as the beginning of an Age of Discovery. That label was a misnomer, however, for the peoples of Africa had played a significant role in the changing human experience since ancient times. ✿

 # THE LAND

After Asia, Africa is the largest of the continents. It stretches nearly five thousand miles from the Cape of Good Hope in the south to the Mediterranean in the north and extends a similar distance from Cape Verde on the west coast to the Horn of Africa on the Indian Ocean. Africa is as diverse as it is vast. The northern fringe, on the coast washed by the Mediterranean Sea, is mountainous through much of its length. South of the mountains lies the greatest desert on earth, the Sahara, which stretches from the Atlantic to the Indian Ocean. To the east is the Nile River, heart of the ancient Egyptian civilization. Beyond that lies the Red Sea, separating Africa from Asia.

The Sahara acts as a great divide separating the northern coast from the rest of the continent. Africa south of the Sahara is itself divided among a number of major regions. In the west is the so-called hump of Africa, which juts like a massive shoulder into the Atlantic Ocean. Here the Sahara gradually gives way to grasslands in the interior and then to tropical jungles along the coast. This region, which is dominated by the Niger River, is rich in natural resources and was the home of many ancient civilizations.

Far to the east bordering the Indian Ocean is a very different terrain of snowcapped mountains, upland plateaus, and lakes. Much of this region is grassland populated by wild beasts, which have given it the modern designation of Safari Country. Here, in the East African Rift valley in the lake district of modern Kenya, early hominids began their long trek to civilization several million years ago.

Further to the south lies the Congo basin, with its jungles watered by the mighty Zaire (formerly Congo) River. The jungles of equatorial Africa then fade gradually into the hills, plateaus, and deserts of the south. This rich land contains some of the most valuable mineral resources known today.

THE EMERGENCE OF CIVILIZATION

It is not certain when agriculture was first practiced on the continent of Africa. Until recently, historians assumed that crops were first cultivated in the lower Nile valley (the northern part near the Mediterranean) about seven or eight thousand years ago, when wheat and barley were introduced, possibly from the Middle East. Eventually, as Chapter 1 explained, this area gave rise to the civilization of ancient Egypt.

Kush

Recent evidence suggests that this hypothesis may need some revision. South of Egypt, near the junction of the White and the Blue Nile, is an area known historically as Nubia. Some archaeologists suggest that agriculture may have appeared first in Nubia rather than in the lower Nile valley. Stone Age farmers from Nubia may have begun to cultivate local crops such as sorghum and millet along the banks of the upper Nile (the southern part near the river's source) as early as the eleventh millennium B.C.E.

Recent archaeological finds also imply that the first true African kingdom may have been located in Nubia rather than in Egypt. A drawing on an incense burner dated at about 3100 B.C.E. or earlier depicts a seated ruler with the falcon motif later adopted by the pharaohs of Egypt. Some scholars suggest that the Nubian concept of kingship may have spread to the north, past the cataracts along the Nile, where it eventually gave birth to the better known civilization of Egypt.

Whatever the truth of such conjectures, it is clear that contacts between the upper and lower Nile had been established by the late third millennium B.C.E., when Egyptian merchants traveled to Nubia to obtain ivory, ebony, frankincense, and leopard skins. A few centuries later Nubia had become an Egyptian tributary. At the end of the second millennium B.C.E., Nubia profited from the disintegration of the Egyptian New Kingdom to become the independent state of Kush. Egyptian influence continued, however, as Kushite culture borrowed extensively from Egypt, including religious beliefs, the practice of interring kings in pyramids, and hieroglyphics.

Although its economy was probably founded primarily on agriculture and animal husbandry, Kush developed into a major trading state that endured for hundreds of years. Its commercial activities were stimulated by the discovery of iron ore in a floodplain near the river at Meroë. Strategically located at the point where a land route across the desert to the north intersected the Nile River, Meroë eventually became the capital of the state. In addition to iron products, Kush supplied goods from Central and East Africa, notably ivory, gold, ebony, and slaves, to the Roman Empire, as well as to Arabia and India. At first goods were transported by donkey caravans to the point where the river north was navigable. By the last centuries of the first millennium B.C.E., however, the donkeys were being replaced by camels, newly introduced from the Arabian peninsula.

Little is known about Kushite society, but it seems likely that it was predominantly urban. At first foreign trade was probably a monopoly of the state, but the extensive luxury goods in the numerous private tombs in the vicinity indicate that at one time material prosperity was relatively widespread. This suggests that commercial activities were being conducted by a substantial merchant class.

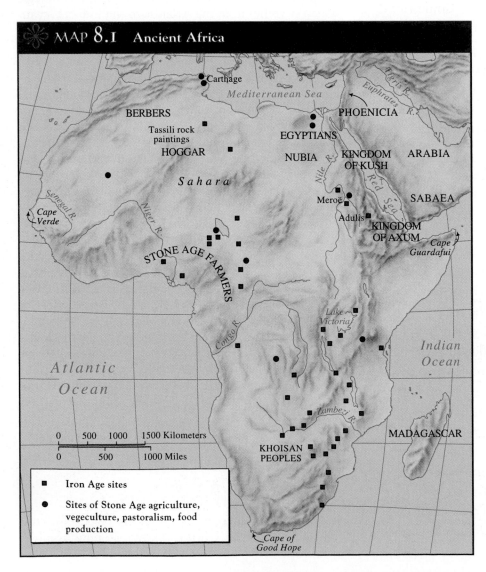

MAP 8.1 Ancient Africa

Axum, Son of Saba

In the first millennium C.E., Kush declined and was eventually conquered by Axum, a new power located in the highlands of modern Ethiopia. Axum had been founded during the first millennium B.C.E. as a colony of the kingdom of Saba (popularly known as Sheba) across the Red Sea on the southern tip of the Arabian peninsula. During antiquity, Saba was a major trading state, serving as a transit point for goods carried from South Asia into the lands surrounding the Mediterranean. Biblical sources credited the "queen of Sheba" with vast wealth and resources. In fact, much of that wealth had originated much further to the east and passed through Saba en route to the countries adjacent to the Mediterranean.

When Saba declined, perhaps because of the desiccation of the Arabian Desert, Axum broke away and survived for centuries as an independent state. Like Saba, Axum owed much of its prosperity to its location on the commercial trade route between India and the Mediterranean, and Greek ships from the Ptolemaic kingdom in Egypt stopped regularly at the port of Adulis on the Red Sea.

Axum exported ivory, frankincense, myrrh, and slaves, while its primary imports were textiles, metal goods, wine, and olive oil. For a time, Axum competed for control of the ivory trade with the neighboring state of Kush, and hunters from Axum armed with imported iron weapons scoured the entire region for elephants. Probably as a result of this competition, in the fourth century C.E., the Axumite ruler, claiming he had been provoked, launched an invasion of Kush and conquered it (see the box on p. 220).

Perhaps the most distinctive feature of Axumite civilization was its religion. Originally, the rulers of Axum (who claimed descent from King Solomon through the visit of the queen of Sheba to Israel in biblical times) followed the religion of their predecessors in Saba. But in the fourth century C.E., Axumite rulers adopted Christianity from the Egyptians. This commitment to the Egyptian form of Christianity (often called Coptic, from the local language of the day) was retained even after the collapse of Axum and the expansion of Islam through the area in later centuries. Later, Axum (now renamed Ethiopia) would be identified by Europeans as the "hermit kingdom" and the home of Prester John, a legendary Christian king of East Africa.

THE PYRAMIDS AT MEROË.   The kingdom of Kush borrowed much of its culture from the Egyptian empire to the north, while placing its own imprint on all imports. Kushite rulers, for example, modeled their political institutions after those of the pharaohs, but governmental authority was somewhat more decentralized, and monarchical power was apparently limited by the influence of priests and the local aristocracy. The pyramids at Meroë, on the banks of the Nile River, are another example. Younger, smaller, unpointed at the top, and more standardized in size and shape than their famous counterparts at Giza, they remain a dramatic reminder of the glory of ancient Kush.

THE CONQUEST OF KUSH

One of the few written descriptions of life along the Nile River in ancient times comes from this inscription, which was included in the Periplus, a Greek account probably written in the first century C.E. Here an Axumite king describes his campaign against Meroë, Axum's neighbor to the west in the upper Nile valley.

AN AXUMITE KING PROCLAIMS HIS VICTORY

With the help of the Lord of Heaven, who in heaven and earth conquers all, Ezana son of Ella Amica, a member of [the group] Halen, king of Axum and of Hemer [Himyar] and of Raydan and of Sab'a and of Salhen and of Tsyamo and of Bega and of Kasu, king of kings . . . never conquered by an enemy . . . by the power of the Lord of the Earth and fought at the Takazi, by the Ford of Kemalke . . . I burnt their towns, those with stone houses and those with straw huts, and [my troops] pillaged their corn and bronze and iron and copper; they destroyed the effigies in their houses [temples], and also their stores of corn and cotton, and threw them into the river Seda. . . . And I reached the Kasu, whom I fought and made captive at the confluence of the rivers Seda and Takazi; and the next day I sent my troops . . . on a campaign up the Seda to the towns of stone and of straw; the names of the towns of stone are Alwa and Daro. . . . Then I sent troops . . . down the Seda to the four straw villages of the Noba and the king. The stone towns of the Kasu which the Noba took [were] Tabito, Pertoti; and they [my troops] went as far as the Red Noba.

❀ **THE STELE AT AXUM.** Axum was a prosperous trading state by the third century C.E., selling ivory, glass crystal, brass, copper, and frankincense and myrrh. The latter were resins, used in burials and as medicines by the peoples of Egypt and the eastern Roman Empire. In the fourth century, the Axumite rulers erected stelae, or slender columns, to mark the location of the royal tombs. Shown here is the tallest of the still-standing Axum stelae, in present-day Ethiopia. Note the differences between these pillars and those constructed in India during the reign of Emperor Asoka.

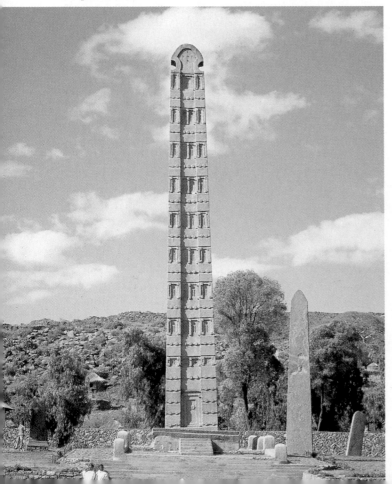

The Sahara and Its Environs

Kush and Axum were part of the ancient trading network originally established by the Egyptians and were affected in various ways by the cross-cultural contacts that took place throughout that region. Elsewhere in Africa, somewhat different patterns prevailed; they varied from area to area depending on the geography and climate.

At one time, when the world's climate was much colder than it is today, Central Africa may have been one of the few areas that was habitable for the first hominids. Later, from 8000 to 4000 B.C.E., a warm, humid climate prevailed in the Sahara, creating lakes and ponds, as well as vast grasslands (known as savannahs) replete with game. Rock paintings found in what are today some of the most uninhabitable parts of the region are a clear indication that the environment was much different several thousand years ago.

By 7000 B.C.E., the peoples of the Sahara were herding animals—first sheep and goats and later cattle. During the sixth and fifth millennia B.C.E., the climate became more arid, however, and the desertification of the Sahara began. From the rock paintings, which for the most part date from the fourth and third millennia B.C.E., we know that by that time the herds were being supplemented by fishing and limited cultivation of crops such as millet, sorghum, and a drought-resistant form of dry rice. After 3000 B.C.E., as the desiccation of the Sahara proceeded and the lakes dried up, farming began to spread into the savannahs on the southern fringes of the desert and eventually into the tropical forest areas to the south, where crops were no longer limited to drought-resistant cereals but could include tropical fruits and tubers.

Historians do not know when goods first began to be exchanged across the Sahara in a north-south direction, but certainly during the first millennium B.C.E. the commercial center of Carthage on the Mediterranean had become a focal point of the trans-Saharan trade. The Berbers, a pastoral people of North Africa, served as intermediaries, carrying food products and manufactured goods from Carthage across the desert and exchanging them for salt, gold and copper, skins, various agricultural products, and perhaps slaves.

This trade initiated a process of cultural exchange that would exert a significant impact on the peoples of tropical Africa. Among other things it may have spread the knowledge of ironworking south of the desert. Although historians once believed that ironworking knowledge reached sub-Saharan Africa from Meroë in the upper Nile valley in the first centuries C.E., recent finds suggest that the peoples along the Niger River were smelting iron as early as the middle of the first millennium B.C.E. Some scholars believe that the technique developed independently there, but others believe that it was introduced by the Berbers, who had learned it from the Carthaginians.

Whatever the case, the Nok culture in northern Nigeria eventually became one of the most active ironworking societies in Africa. Excavations have unearthed numerous terra-cotta and iron figures, as well as stone and iron farm implements, dating back as far as 500 B.C.E. The remains of smelting furnaces confirm that the iron was produced locally.

Early in the first millennium C.E., the introduction of the camel provided a major stimulus to the trans-Saharan trade. With its ability to store considerable amounts of food and water in its hump, the camel was far better equipped to handle the arduous conditions of the desert than the oxen, which had been used previously. The camel caravans of the Berbers became known as the "fleets of the desert."

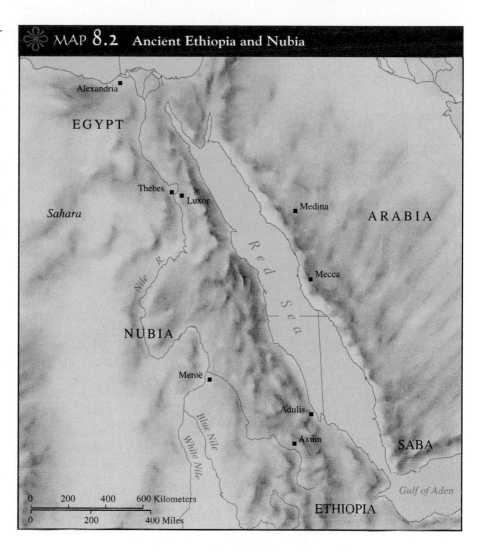

MAP 8.2   Ancient Ethiopia and Nubia

East Africa

South of Axum, along the shores of the Indian Ocean and in the inland plateau that stretches from the mountains of Ethiopia through the lake district of Central Africa, lived a mixture of peoples, some living by hunting and food gathering and others following pastoral pursuits.

Beginning in the first millennium B.C.E., new peoples began to migrate into East Africa from the west. Farming peoples speaking dialects of the Bantu family of languages began to move from the region of the Niger River into East Africa and the Zaire River basin. They were probably responsible for introducing the widespread cultivation of crops and knowledge of ironworking to much of East Africa, although there are signs of some limited iron smelting in the area before their arrival.

The Bantu settled in rural communities based on subsistence farming. The primary crops were millet and sorghum, along with yams, melons, and beans. The land was often tilled with both iron and stone tools, and the former were usually manufactured in a local smelter. Some people kept domestic animals such as cattle, sheep, goats, or chickens or supplemented their diets by hunting and food gathering. Because the population was still small and an ample supply of cultivable land was available, most settlements were relatively small; each village formed a self-sufficient political and economic entity.

As early as the era of the New Kingdom in the second millennium B.C.E., Egyptian ships had plied the waters off the East African coast in search of gold, ivory, palm oil, and perhaps slaves. By the first century C.E., the region was an established part of a trading network that included the Mediterranean and the Red Seas. In that century, a Greek seafarer from Alexandria wrote an

CHRONOLOGY

EARLY AFRICA

Origins of agriculture in Africa	c. 7000 B.C.E.
Desiccation of the Sahara	Begins c. 5000 B.C.E.
Kingship appears in the Nile valley	c. 3100 B.C.E.
Kingdom of Kush in Nubia	c. 500 B.C.E.
Iron Age begins	c. sixth century B.C.E.
Beginnings of trans-Sahara trade	c. first millennium B.C.E.
Rise of Axum	First century C.E.
Conquest of Kush by Axum	Fourth century C.E.
Arrival of Bantus in East Africa	Early centuries C.E.
Arrival of Malays on island of Madagascar	Second century C.E.
Origins of Ghana	Fifth century C.E.
Arab takeover of lower Nile valley	641 C.E.
Development of Swahili culture	c. first millennium C.E.
Spread of Islam across North Africa	Seventh century C.E.
Spread of Islam in Horn of Africa	Ninth century C.E.
Decline of Ghana	Twelfth century C.E.
Establishment of Zagwe dynasty in Ethiopia	c. 1150
Rise of Mali	c. 1250
Kingdom of Zimbabwe	c. 1300–c. 1450
Portuguese ships explore West African coast	Mid-fifteenth century

account of his travels down the coast from Cape Guardafui at the tip of the Horn of Africa to the Strait of Madagascar thousands of miles to the south. Called the *Periplus*, this work provides generally accurate descriptions of the peoples and settlements along the African coast and the trade goods they supplied.

According to the *Periplus*, the port of Rhapta (possibly modern Dar es Salaam) was a commercial metropolis, exporting ivory, rhinoceros horn, and tortoiseshell and importing glass, wine, grain, and metal goods such as weapons and tools. The identity of the peoples taking part in this trade is not clear, but it seems likely that the area was already inhabited by a mixture of local peoples and immigrants from the Arabian peninsula. According to the *Periplus*, the area around Rhapta was under the control of an Arabian kingdom. Out of this mixture would eventually emerge an African-Arabian "Swahili" culture (see East Africa: The Land of Zanj later in this chapter) that continues to exist in coastal areas today. Beyond Rhapta was "unexplored ocean." Some contemporary observers believed that the Indian and Atlantic Oceans were connected. Others were convinced that the Indian Ocean was an enclosed sea and that the continent of Africa could not be circumnavigated (see the box on p. 223).

Trade across the Indian Ocean and down the coast of East Africa, facilitated by the monsoon winds, would gradually become one of the most lucrative sources of commercial profit in the ancient and medieval worlds. Although the origins of the trade remain shrouded in mystery, traders eventually came by sea from as far away as the mainland of Southeast Asia. Early in the first millennium C.E., Malay peoples bringing cinnamon to the Middle East began to cross the Indian Ocean directly and landed on the southeastern coast of Africa. Eventually, a Malay settlement was established on the island of Madagascar, where the population is still of mixed Malay-African origin. Historians suspect that Malay immigrants were responsible for introducing such Southeast Asian foods as the banana and the yam to the African peoples. With its high yield and ability to grow in uncultivated rain forest, the banana often became the preferred crop of the Bantu peoples.

Southern Africa

South of the East African plateau and the Congo basin is a vast land of hills, grasslands, and arid desert stretching almost to the Cape of Good Hope at the tip of the continent. As Bantu-speaking farmers spread southward during the final centuries of the first millennium B.C.E., they began to encounter Stone Age peoples in the area who still lived primarily by hunting and foraging. These peoples, many of whom apparently belonged to the Khoisan family of languages (Khoisan languages are distinguished by their numerous "clicking" sounds), were lighter in skin color and generally shorter than the Bantu speakers who were beginning to arrive from the north.

Available evidence suggests that early relations between these two peoples were relatively harmonious. Intermarriage between members of the two groups was apparently not unusual, and many of the Khoisan-speaking peoples were gradually absorbed into what became a dominantly Bantu-speaking pastoral and agricultural society that spread throughout much of southern Africa during the first millennium C.E.

BEYOND THE PILLARS OF HERCULES

The first suggestion that seafarers could pass from the Atlantic to the Indian Ocean around the southern tip of Africa came from the Greek historian Herodotus. In the following passage from his History of the Persian Wars, *Herodotus describes a voyage by Phoenician sailors that was recounted to him during his visit to Egypt. The reference to the position of the sun reflects a phenomenon that could only have occurred if the Phoenicians were sailing south of the equator.*

HERODOTUS, HISTORY OF THE PERSIAN WARS

Africa proves to be completely surrounded by water except for as much of it as borders on Asia. Of all men of whom we have any knowledge, the Egyptian king Necho was the first to establish this fact. After he had ceased from trying to dig the canal that extends from the Nile to the Arabian Gulf, he dispatched some Phoenicians in ships with orders to sail back into our northern sea by passing through the Pillars of Hercules and so to return to Egypt.

Accordingly these Phoenicians set out and from the Red Sea sailed into the southern ocean. Whenever autumn came, they went ashore wherever in Africa they chanced to be on their voyage, to sow grain in the earth and await the harvest. On reaping the new grain they put again to sea. In this wise, after two years had elapsed, they rounded the Pillars of Hercules and in the third year reached Egypt.

Now, they told a tale that I personally do not believe (though others may, if they choose), how they had the sun on their right hand as they sailed along the African coast.

THE COMING OF ISLAM

As we saw in the previous chapter, the rise of Islam during the first half of the seventh century C.E. had ramifications far beyond the Arabian peninsula. Arab armies swept across North Africa, incorporating it into the Arab empire and isolating the Christian state of Axum to the south. Although East Africa and West Africa south of the Sahara were not conquered by the Arab forces, Islam eventually penetrated these areas as well.

African Religious Beliefs Before Islam

When Islam arrived, most African societies already had well-developed systems of religious beliefs. Like other aspects of African life, early African religious beliefs varied from place to place, but certain characteristics appear to have been shared by most African societies. One of these common features was a belief in a single creator god. The supreme god of the Bantu, for example, was a pantheistic force from whom all things came. Sometimes, the creator god was accompanied by a whole pantheon of lesser deities. The Ashanti people of Ghana in West Africa believed in a supreme being called Nyame, whose sons were lesser gods. Each son served a different purpose: one was the rainmaker, another the compassionate, and a third was responsible for the sunshine. This heavenly hierarchy paralleled earthly arrangements: worship of Nyame was the exclusive preserve of the king through his priests; lesser officials and the common people worshiped Nyame's sons, who might intercede with their father on behalf of ordinary Africans.

Many African religions also shared a belief in a form of afterlife. Human existence was believed to consist of two stages: the first stage was life on earth (*sasa*); the second stage was eternal existence (*zamani*), during which the soul floated in the atmosphere through eternity. Belief in an afterlife was closely connected to the importance of ancestors and the lineage, or clan, in African society. Each lineage group could trace itself back to a founding ancestor or group of ancestors. These ancestral souls would not be extinguished as long as the lineage group continued to perform rituals in their name. The rituals could also benefit the lineage group on earth, for the ancestral souls, being closer to the gods, had the power to influence, for good or evil, the lives of their descendants.

Such beliefs were challenged but not always replaced by the arrival of Islam. In some ways, the tenets of Islam were in conflict with traditional African beliefs and customs. Although the concept of a single transcendent deity presented no problems in many African societies, Islam's rejection of spirit worship and a priestly class ran counter to the beliefs of many Africans and was often ignored in practice. Similarly, as various Muslim travelers observed, Islam's insistence on the separation of the sexes contrasted with the relatively informal relationships that prevailed in many African societies and was probably slow to take root. In the long run, imported ideas were synthesized with native beliefs to create a unique brand of Africanized Islam.

The Arabs in North Africa

In 641, Arab forces advanced into Egypt, seized the delta of the Nile River, and brought two centuries of Byzantine rule to an end. To guard against attacks from the Byzantine fleet, the Arabs eventually built a new capital at Cairo, inland from the previous Byzantine capital of

Alexandria, and began to consolidate their control over the entire region.

The Arab conquerors were probably welcomed by many, if not the majority, of the local inhabitants. Although Egypt had been a thriving commercial center under the Byzantines, the average Egyptian had not shared in this prosperity. Tax rates were generally high, and Christians were subjected to periodic persecution by the Byzantines, who viewed the local Coptic faith and other sects in the area as heresies. Although the new rulers continued to obtain much of their revenue from taxing the local farming population, tax rates were generally lower than they had been under the corrupt Byzantine government, and conversion to Islam brought exemption from taxation. During the next generations, many Egyptians converted to the Muslim faith, but Islam did not move into the upper Nile valley until several hundred years later. As Islam spread southward, it was adopted by many lowland peoples, but it had less success in the mountains of Ethiopia, where Coptic Christianity continued to win adherents (see the next section).

In the meantime, Arab rule was gradually being extended westward along the Mediterranean coast. When the Romans conquered Carthage in 146 B.C.E., they had called their new province Africa, thus introducing a name that would eventually be applied to the entire continent. After the fall of the Roman Empire, much of the area had reverted to the control of local Berber chieftains, but the Byzantines captured Carthage in the mid-sixth century C.E. In 690, the city was seized by the Arabs, who then began to extend their control over the entire area, which they called Al Maghrib (the west).

At first, the local Berber peoples resisted their new conquerors. The Berbers were tough fighters, and for several generations, Arab rule was limited to the towns and lowland coastal areas. But Arab persistence eventually paid off, and by the early eighth century, the entire North African coast as far west as the Strait of Gibraltar was under Arab rule. The Arabs were now poised to cross the strait and expand into southern Europe and to push south beyond the fringes of the Sahara.

The Kingdom of Ethiopia: A Christian Island in a Muslim Sea

By the end of the sixth century C.E., the kingdom of Axum, long a dominant force in the trade network through the Red Sea, was in a state of decline. Both overexploitation of farmland and a shift in trade routes away from the Red Sea to the Arabian peninsula and Persian Gulf contributed to this decline. By the beginning of the ninth century, the capital had been moved further into the mountainous interior, and Axum was gradually transformed from a maritime power into an isolated agricultural society.

The rise of Islam on the Arabian peninsula hastened this process, as the Arab world increasingly began to serve as the focus of the regional trade passing through the area.

By the eighth century, a number of Muslim trading states had been established on the African coast of the Red Sea, a development that contributed to the transformation of Axum into a landlocked society with primarily agricultural interests. At first relations between Christian Axum and its Muslim neighbors were relatively peaceful, as the larger and more powerful Axumite kingdom attempted with some success to compel the coastal Islamic states to accept a tributary relationship. Axum's role in the local commercial network temporarily revived, and the area became a prime source for ivory, resins like frankincense and myrrh, and slaves. Slaves came primarily from the south, where Axum had been attempting to subjugate restive tribal peoples living in the Amharic plateau beyond its southern border.

Beginning in the twelfth century, however, relations between Axum and its neighbors deteriorated, as the Muslim states along the coast began to move inland to gain control over the growing trade in slaves and ivory. Axum responded with force and at first had some success in reasserting its hegemony over the area. But in the early fourteenth century, the Muslim state of Adal, located at the juncture of the Indian Ocean and the Red Sea, launched a new attack on the Christian kingdom.

Axum also underwent significant internal change during this period. The Zagwe dynasty, which seized control of the country in the mid-twelfth century, centralized the government and extended the Christian faith throughout the kingdom, now known as Ethiopia. Military commanders or civilian officials who had personal or kinship ties with the royal court established vast landed estates to maintain security and facilitate the collection of taxes from the local population. In the meantime, Christian missionaries established monasteries and churches to propagate the faith in outlying areas. Close relations were reestablished with leaders of the Coptic church in Egypt and with Christian officials in the Holy Land. This process was continued by the Solomonids, who succeeded the Zagwe dynasty in 1270. But by the early fifteenth century, the state had become more deeply involved in an expanding conflict with Muslim Adal to the east, a conflict that lasted for over a century and gradually took on the characteristics of a holy war.

East Africa: The Land of Zanj

The rise of Islam also had a lasting impact on the coast of East Africa, which the Greeks had called Azania and the Arabs called Zanj. During the seventh and eighth centuries, peoples from the Arabian peninsula and the Persian Gulf began to settle at ports along the coast and on the small islands offshore. Then, according to legend, in the middle of the tenth century, a Persian from Shiraz, a city in southern Iran, sailed to the area with his six sons. As his small fleet stopped along the coast, each son disembarked on one of the coastal islands and founded a small community; these settlements later grew into the commercial centers of Mombasa, Pemba, Zanzibar (literally, "the coast of Zanj"), and Kilwa.

Although the legend underestimates the degree to which the area had already become a major participant in local commerce as well as the role of the local inhabitants in the process, it does reflect the importance of Arab and Persian immigrants in the formation of a string of trading ports stretching from Mogadishu (today the capital of Somalia) in the north to Kilwa (south of present-day Dar es Salaam) in the south. Kilwa became especially important as it was near the southern limit for a ship hoping to complete the round-trip journey in a single season. Goods such as ivory, gold, and rhinoceros horn were exported across the Indian Ocean to countries as far away as China, while imports included iron goods, glassware, Indian textiles, and Chinese porcelain. Merchants in these cities often amassed considerable profit, as evidenced by their lavish stone palaces, some of which still stand in the modern cities of Mombasa and Zanzibar. Though now in ruins, Kilwa was one of the most magnificent cities of its day. The fourteenth-century Arab traveler Ibn Battuta described it as "amongst the most beautiful of cities and most elegantly built. All of it is of wood, and the ceilings of its houses are of *al-dis* [reeds]."[1]

Most of the coastal states were self-governing, although sometimes several towns were grouped together under a single dominant authority. Government revenue came primarily from taxes imposed on commerce. Some trade went on between these coastal city-states and the peoples of the interior, who provided gold and iron, ivory, and various agricultural goods and animal products in return for textiles, manufactured articles, and weapons (see the box on p. 226). Relations apparently varied, and the coastal merchants sometimes resorted to force to obtain goods from the inland peoples. A Portuguese visitor recounted that "the men thereof [of Mombasa] are oft-times at war and but seldom at peace with those of the mainland, and they carry on trade with them, bringing thence great store of honey, wax, and ivory."[2]

By the twelfth and thirteenth centuries, a mixed African-Arabian culture, eventually known as Swahili (from the Arabic *sahel* meaning "coast"; thus, "peoples of the coast"), began to emerge throughout the coastal area. Intermarriage between the immigrants and the local population was common, although a distinct Arab community, made up primarily of merchants, persisted in many areas. The members of the ruling class were often of mixed heritage but usually traced their genealogy to Arab or Persian ancestors. By this time, too, many members of the ruling class had converted to Islam. Middle Eastern urban architectural styles and other aspects of Arab culture were implanted within a society still predominantly African. Arabic words and phrases were combined with Bantu grammatical structures to form a mixed language, also known as Swahili; it is the national language of the countries of Kenya and Tanzania today.

The States of West Africa

During the eighth century, merchants from the Maghrib began to carry Muslim beliefs to the savannah areas south of the Sahara. At first, conversion took place on an individual basis rather than through official encouragement. The first rulers to convert to Islam were the royal

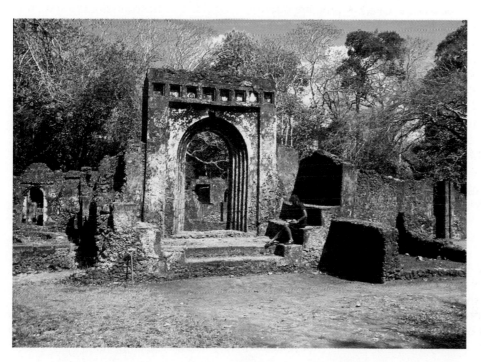

☙ A LOST CITY IN AFRICA.
Gedi was founded in the early fourteenth century and abandoned three hundred years later. Its romantic ruins suggest the grandeur of the Swahili civilization that once flourished along the eastern coast of Africa. Located sixty miles north of Mombasa, in present-day Kenya, Gedi once contained several thousand residents but was eventually abandoned after it was attacked by nomadic peoples from the north. Today the ruins of the town, surrounded by a nine-foot wall, seem dwarfed by towering baobab trees populated only by chattering monkeys. Shown here is the entrance to the palace, which probably served as the residence of the chief official in the town. Neighboring houses, constructed of coral stone, contain sumptuous rooms, with separate women's quarters and enclosed lavatories with urinal channels and double-sink washing benches.

THE COAST OF ZANJ

From early times, the people living on the coast of East Africa took an active part in trade along the coast and across the Indian Ocean. The process began with the arrival of Arab traders early in the first millennium C.E. According to local legends, Arab merchants often married the daughters of the local chieftains and then received title to coastal territories as part of their wife's dowry. This description of the area was written by the Arab traveler al-Mas'udi, who visited the "land of Zanj" in 916.

AL-MAS'UDI IN EAST AFRICA

The land of Zanj produces wild leopard skins. The people wear them as clothes, or export them to Muslim countries. They are the largest leopard skins and the most beautiful for making saddles. . . . They also export tortoise shell for making combs, for which ivory is likewise used. . . . The Zanj are settled in that area, which stretches as far as Sofala, which is the furthest limit of the land and the end of the voyages made from Oman and Siraf on the sea of Zanj. . . . The Zanj use the ox as a beast of burden, for they have no horses, mules or camels in their land. . . . There are many wild elephants in this land but no tame ones.

The Zanj do not use them for war or anything else, but only hunt and kill them for their ivory. It is from this country that come tusks weighing fifty pounds and more. They usually go to Oman, and from there are sent to China and India. This is the chief trade route. . . .

The Zanj have an elegant language and men who preach in it. One of their holy men will often gather a crowd and exhort his hearers to please God in their lives and to be obedient to him. He explains the punishments that follow upon disobedience, and reminds them of their ancestors and kings of old. These people have no religious law: their kings rule by custom and by political expediency.

The Zanj eat bananas, which are as common among them as they are in India; but their staple food is millet and a plant called kalari which is pulled out of the earth like truffles. They also eat honey and meat. They have many islands where the coconut grows: its nuts are used as fruit by all the Zanj peoples. One of these islands, which is one or two days' sail from the coast, has a Muslim population and a royal family. This is the island of Kanbulu [thought to be modern Pemba].

---

family of Gao at the end of the tenth century. By the end of the fifteenth century, much of the population in the grasslands south of the Sahara had accepted Islam.

The expansion of Islam into West Africa had a major impact on the political system. By introducing Arabic as the first written language in the region and Muslim law codes and administrative practices from the Middle East, Islam provided local rulers with the tools to increase their authority and the efficiency of their governments. Moreover, as Islam gradually spread throughout the region, a common religion united previously diverse peoples into a more coherent community.

When Islam arrived in the grasslands south of the Sahara, the region was beginning to undergo significant political and social change. A number of major trading states were in the process of creation, and they eventually transformed the Sahara into one of the leading avenues of world trade, crisscrossed by caravan routes leading to destinations as far away as the Atlantic Ocean, the Mediterranean, and the Red Sea.

GHANA

The first of these great commercial states was Ghana, which emerged in the fifth century C.E. in the upper Niger valley, a grassland region between the Sahara and the tropical forests along the West African coast (the modern state of Ghana, which takes its name from the trading society under discussion here, is located in the forest region to

the south). The majority of the people in the area were Iron Age farmers living in villages under the authority of a local chieftain. Gradually, these local communities were united to form the kingdom of Ghana.

Although the people of the region had traditionally lived from agriculture, a primary reason for Ghana's growing importance was gold. The heartland of the state was located near one of the richest gold-producing areas in all of Africa. Ghanaian merchants transported the gold to Morocco, whence it was distributed throughout the known world. This trade began in ancient times, as the Greek historian Herodotus relates:

> The Carthaginians also tell us that they trade with a race of men who live in a part of Libya beyond the Pillars of Heracles [the Strait of Gibraltar]. On reaching this country, they unload their goods, arrange them tidily along the beach, and then, returning to their boats, raise a smoke. Seeing the smoke, the natives come down to the beach, place on the ground a certain quantity of gold in exchange for the goods, and go off again to a distance. The Carthaginians then come ashore and take a look at the gold; and if they think it represents a fair price for their wares, they collect it and go away; if, on the other hand, it seems too little, they go back aboard and wait, and the natives come and add to the gold until they are satisfied. There is perfect honesty on both sides; the Carthaginians never touch the gold until it equals in value what they have offered for sale, and the natives never touch the goods until the gold has been taken away.[3]

THE GREAT GATE AT MARRAKECH.
The Moroccan city of Marrakech, founded in the ninth century C.E., was a major northern terminus of the trans-Saharan trade and one of the chief commercial centers in premodern Africa. Widely praised by such famous travelers as Ibn Battuta, the city was an architectural marvel in that all its major public buildings were constructed in red sandstone. Shown here is the Great Gate to the city, through which camel caravans passed en route to and from the vast desert. In the Berber language, Marrakech means "pass without making a noise," a reference to the need for caravan traders to be aware of the danger of thieves in the vicinity.

Later, Ghana became known to Arab-speaking peoples in North Africa as "the land of gold." Actually, the name was misleading, for the gold did not come from Ghana, but from a neighboring people, who sold it to merchants from Ghana.

Eventually, other exports from Ghana found their way to the bazaars of the Mediterranean coast and beyond—ivory, ostrich feathers, hides, leather goods, and ultimately slaves. The origins of the slave trade in the area probably go back to the first millennium B.C.E., when Berber tribesmen seized African villagers in the regions south of the Sahara and sold them for profit to buyers in Europe and the Middle East. In return, Ghana imported metal goods (especially weapons), textiles, horses, and salt.

Much of the trade across the desert was still conducted by the nomadic Berbers, but Ghanaian merchants played an active role as intermediaries, trading tropical products such as bananas, kola nuts, and palm oil from the forest states of Guinea along the Atlantic coast to the south. By the eighth and ninth centuries, much of this trade was conducted by Muslim merchants, who purchased the goods from local traders (using iron and copper cash or cowrie shells from Southeast Asia as the primary means of exchange) and then sold them to Berbers, who carried them across the desert. The merchants who carried on this trade often became quite wealthy and lived in splendor in cities like Saleh, the capital of Ghana. So did the king, of course, who taxed the merchants as well as the farmers and the producers.

Like other West African kings, the king of Ghana ruled by divine right and was assisted by a hereditary aristocracy composed of the leading members of the prominent clans, who also served as district chiefs responsible for main-

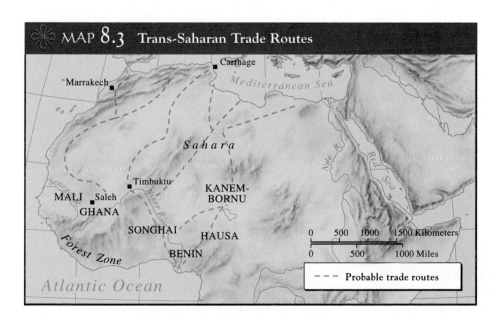

MAP **8.3** **Trans-Saharan Trade Routes**

Carthage

Marrakech

Mediterranean Sea

Sahara

Niger R.

Red Sea

Senegal

Timbuktu

MALI Saleh

GHANA

SONGHAI HAUSA

KANEM-BORNU

Niger R.

BENIN

Forest Zone

Atlantic Ocean

| 0 | 500 | 1000 | 1500 Kilometers |
| 0 | | 500 | 1000 Miles |

- - - Probable trade routes

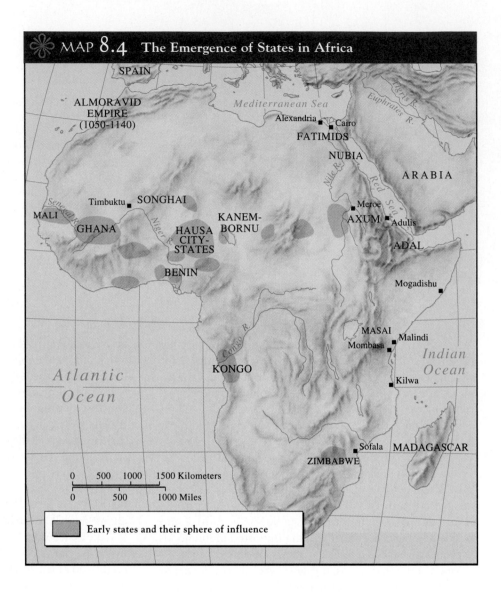

MAP 8.4   The Emergence of States in Africa

taining law and order and collecting taxes. The king was responsible for maintaining the security of his kingdom, serving as an intermediary with local deities, and functioning as the chief law officer to adjudicate disputes. The kings of Ghana did not convert to Islam themselves, although they welcomed Muslim merchants and apparently did not discourage their subjects from adopting the new faith (see the box on p. 229).

MALI

The state of Ghana flourished for several hundred years, but by the twelfth century, weakened by ruinous wars with Berber tribesmen, it had begun to decline, and it collapsed at the end of the century. In its place rose a number of new trading societies, including large territorial states like Mali and Songhai in the west, Kanem-Bornu in the east, and small commercial city-states like the Hausa states, located in what is today northern Nigeria.

The greatest of the states that emerged after the destruction of Ghana was Mali. Extending from the Atlantic coast inland as far as the famous trading metropolis of Timbuktu and Gao, a modern city on the Niger River, Mali built its wealth and power on the gold trade. But the heartland of Mali was situated considerably to the south of the old state of Ghana in the savannah region, where sufficient moisture enabled farmers to grow such crops as sorghum, millet, and even rice. The farmers lived in villages ruled by a local chieftain (called a *mansa*), who served as both religious and administrative leader and was responsible for forwarding tax revenues from the village to higher levels of government.

The primary wealth of the country was accumulated in the cities. Here lived the merchants, who were primarily of local origin, although many were now practicing Muslims. Commercial activities were taxed, but apparently were so lucrative that both the merchants and the kings prospered. One of the most powerful kings of Mali, known as Mansa Musa (1312–1337), was so wealthy that when

A DESCRIPTION OF A GHANAIAN CAPITAL

After its first appearance in West Africa in the decades following the death of the Prophet, Islam competed with native African religions for followers. Eventually, several local rulers converted to the Muslim faith. This passage by the Arab geographer al-Bakri shows how both religions flourished side by side in the state of Ghana during the eleventh century.

AL-BAKRI'S DESCRIPTION OF GHANA

The king's residence comprises a palace and conical huts, the whole surrounded by a fence like a wall. Around the royal town are huts and groves of thorn trees where live the magicians who control their religious rites. These groves, where they keep their idols and bury their kings, are protected by guards who permit no one to enter or find out what goes on in them.

None of those who belong to the imperial religion may wear tailored garments except the king himself and the heir-presumptive, his sister's son. The rest of the people wear wrappers of cotton, silk or brocade according to their means. Most of the men shave their beards and the women their heads. The king adorns himself with female ornaments around the neck and arms. On his head he wears gold-embroidered caps covered with turbans of finest cotton. He gives audience to the people for the redressing of grievances in a hut around which are placed 10 horses covered in golden cloth. Behind him stand 10 slaves carrying shields and swords mounted with gold. On his right are the sons of vassal kings, their heads plaited with gold and wearing costly garments. On the ground around him are seated his ministers, whilst the governor of the city sits before him. On guard at the door are dogs of fine pedigree, wearing collars adorned with gold and silver. The royal audience is announced by the beating of a drum, called daba, made out of a long piece of hollowed-out wood. When the people have gathered, his coreligionists draw near upon their knees sprinkling dust upon their heads as a sign of respect, whilst the Muslims clap hands as their form of greeting.

he embarked on a pilgrimage to Mecca in the early fourteenth century, his spending splurge in Egypt depressed the price of gold there for a dozen years.

Mansa Musa's primary contribution to his people was probably not economic prosperity, but the Muslim faith. Early rulers of Mali apparently adhered to traditional African faiths, assuming the role of *mansa* for their subjects, but later rulers converted to Islam. Mansa Musa strongly encouraged the building of mosques and the study of the Koran in his kingdom and imported scholars and books to introduce his subjects to the message of Allah. One visitor from Europe, writing in the late fifteenth century, reported that in Timbuktu "are a great store of doctors, judges, priests, and other learned men, that are bountifully maintained at the king's cost and charges. And hither are brought divers manuscripts of written books out of Barbary [North Africa] which are sold for more money than any other merchandise."[4]

❀ **MANSA MUSA.** Mansa Musa (1312–1337), king of the West African state of Mali, was one of the richest and most powerful rulers of his day. During his famous pilgrimage to Mecca, he arrived in Cairo with a hundred camels laden with gold and gave away so much gold that its value depreciated there for several years. His fame spread to Europe as well, evidenced by this Spanish map of 1375, which depicts Mansa Musa seated on his throne in Mali, holding an impressive gold nugget.

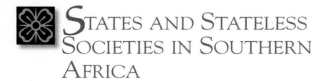

THE CITY OF TIMBUKTU. The city of Timbuktu sat astride one of the major trade routes that passed through the Sahara between the kingdoms of West Africa and the Mediterranean Sea. Caravans transported food and various manufactured articles southward in exchange for salt, gold, copper, skins, agricultural goods, and slaves. Salt was at such a high premium in Timbuktu that a young Moroccan wrote in 1513 that one camel's load, brought 500 miles by caravan, sold for 80 gold ducats, while a horse sold for only 40 ducats. Timbuktu became a prosperous city as well as a great center of Islamic scholarship. By 1550, it had three universities connected to its principal mosques and 180 Koranic schools.

STATES AND STATELESS SOCIETIES IN SOUTHERN AFRICA

In the southern half of the African continent, from the great basin of the Zaire River to the Cape of Good Hope, states formed somewhat more slowly than in the north. Until the eleventh century C.E., most of the peoples in this region lived in what are sometimes called "stateless societies," characterized by autonomous villages organized by clans and ruled by a local chieftain or clan head. Beginning in the eleventh century, in some parts of southern Africa, these independent villages gradually began to consolidate. Out of these groupings came the first states.

One area where this process occurred was the Zaire River valley, where the combination of fertile land and nearby deposits of copper and iron enabled the inhabitants to enjoy an agricultural surplus and engage in regional commerce. Two new states in particular underwent this transition. Sometime during the fourteenth century, the kingdom of Luba was founded in the center of the continent, in a rich agricultural and fishing area near the shores of Lake Kisale. Luba had a relatively centralized government, in which the king appointed provincial governors, who were responsible for collecting tribute from the village chiefs. At about the same time, the kingdom of Kongo was formed just south of the mouth of the Zaire River on the Atlantic coast.

These new states were primarily agricultural, although both had a thriving manufacturing sector and took an active part in the growing exchange of goods throughout the region. As time passed, both began to expand southward to absorb the mixed farming and pastoral peoples in the area of modern Angola. In the drier grassland area to the south, other small communities continued to sup-

port themselves by herding, hunting, or food gathering. We know little about these peoples, however, since they possessed no writing system and had few visitors. A Portuguese sailor who encountered them in the late sixteenth century left the following description:

> These people are herdsmen and cultivators. . . . Their main crop is millet, which they grind between two stones or in wooden mortars to make flour. . . . Their wealth consists mainly in their huge number of dehorned cows. . . . They live together in small villages, in houses made of reed mats, which do not keep out the rain.[5]

Zimbabwe

Further to the east, the situation was somewhat different. In the grassland regions immediately to the south of the Zambezi River, a mixed economy involving farming, cattle herding, and commercial pursuits had begun to develop during the early centuries of the first millennium C.E. Characteristically, villages in this area were constructed inside walled enclosures to protect the animals at night. The most famous of these communities was Zimbabwe, located on the plateau of the same name between the Zambezi and Limpopo Rivers. From the twelfth to the middle of the fifteenth century, Zimbabwe was the most powerful and prosperous state in the region and played a major role in the gold trade with the Swahili trading communities on the eastern coast.

The ruins of Zimbabwe's capital, known as Great Zimbabwe (the term *Zimbabwe* means "sacred house" in the Bantu language), provide a vivid illustration of the kingdom's power and influence. Strategically situated between substantial gold reserves to the west and a small river leading to the coast, Great Zimbabwe was well placed to benefit from the expansion of trade between the coast and the interior. The town sits on a hill overlooking the river and is surrounded by stone walls, which enclosed an area large enough to hold over 10,000 residents. The houses of the wealthy were built of cement on stone foundations, while those of the common people were of dried mud with thatched roofs. In the valley below is the royal palace surrounded by a stone wall thirty feet high. Artifacts found at the site include household implements and ornaments made of gold and copper, as well as jewelry and even porcelain imported from China.

Most of the royal wealth probably came from two sources: the ownership of cattle and the king's ability to levy heavy taxes on the gold that passed through the kingdom en route to the coast. By the middle of the fifteenth century, however, the city was apparently abandoned, possibly because of environmental damage caused by overgrazing. With the decline of Zimbabwe, the focus of economic power began to shift northward to the valley of the Zambezi River.

South of the Limpopo River, pastoralism and hunting continued to be the primary means of livelihood. As we saw earlier, some of these peoples had been absorbed by the Iron Age farming communities that spread southward from Central Africa during the first millennium C.E. Others remained independent in isolated villages or small kingdoms, although they often carried on active trade with the growing states to their north.

One such people were the San, called Bushmen by later Europeans. A hunting and foraging people who spoke a Khoisan language, the San lived in small family communities of twenty to twenty-five members throughout southern Africa from Namibia in the west to the Drakensberg Mountains near the southeastern coast. Scholars have learned about the early life of the San by interviewing their modern descendants and by studying rock paintings found in caves throughout the area. These multicolored paintings, which predate the coming of the Europeans, were drawn with a brush made of small feathers fastened to a reed. They depict various aspects of the San's lifestyle, including their hunting techniques and religious rituals.

When the Europeans arrived in the area, they regarded the San as troublesome pests who raided their cattle. One nineteenth-century European missionary dismissed the San contemptuously, saying: "He has no religion, no laws, no government, no recognized authority, no patrimony, no fixed abode."[6] Over time, as the Europeans constantly encroached on their hunting grounds, the San found it virtually impossible to maintain their way of life. Only a few survive today, most of them in the Kalahari Desert in Botswana.

AFRICAN SOCIETY

Drawing generalizations about social organization, cultural development, and daily life in traditional Africa is difficult because of the diversity of the continent and the absence of written languages in much of the area. Historians must therefore rely on accounts of the occasional vis-

itor, such as al-Mas'udi and the famous fourteenth-century chronicler Ibn Battuta. Such travelers, however, tended to come into contact mostly with the wealthy and the powerful, leaving us to speculate about what life was like for ordinary Africans during this early period.

Urban Life

African towns often began as fortified walled villages and gradually evolved into larger communities serving several purposes. Here, of course, were the center of government and the teeming markets filled with goods from distant regions. Here also were artisans skilled in metal- or woodworking, pottery making, and other crafts. Unlike the rural areas, where

GREAT ZIMBABWE.   Situated on an important trade route and a center for cattle and agriculture, Great Zimbabwe was originally settled by pastoral peoples during the first millennium B.C.E. Later it became the capital of a prosperous state. Its thirty-foot walls were the first in Africa to be constructed without the use of mortar. The section of the walled palace shown here indicate why Great Zimbabwe is generally regarded as the most impressive archaeological site in southern Africa.

a village was usually composed of a single lineage group or clan, the towns drew their residents from several clans, although individual clans usually lived in their own compounds and were governed by their own clan heads.

In the states of West Africa, the focal point of the major towns was the royal precinct. The relationship between the ruler and the merchant class differed from the situation in most Asian societies, where the royal family and the aristocracy were largely isolated from the remainder of the population. In Africa, the chasm between the king and the common people was not so great. Often the ruler would hold an audience to allow people to voice their complaints or to welcome visitors from foreign countries.

This is not to say that the king was not elevated above all others in status. In wealthier states, the walls of the audience chamber would be covered with sheets of beaten silver and gold, and the king would be surrounded by hundreds of armed soldiers and some of his trusted advisers. Nevertheless, the symbiotic relationship between the ruler and merchant class served to reduce the gap between the king and his subjects. The relationship was mutually beneficial, since the merchants received honors and favors from the palace, while the king's coffers were filled with taxes paid by the merchants. Certainly, it was to the benefit of the king to maintain law and order in his domain so that the merchants could ply their trade. As Ibn Battuta observed, among the good qualities of the peoples of West Africa was the prevalence of peace in the region. "The traveler is not afraid in it," he remarked, "nor is he who lives there in fear of the thief or of the robber by violence."[7]

Village Life

The vast majority of Africans lived in small rural villages. Their identities were established by their membership in a nuclear family and a lineage group. At the basic level was the nuclear family composed of parents and preadult children; sometimes it included an elderly grandparent and other family dependents as well. They lived in small round huts constructed of packed mud and topped with a conical thatch roof. In most African societies, these nuclear family units would in turn be combined into larger kinship communities known as households or lineage groups.

The lineage group was similar in many respects to the clan in China or the caste system in India in that it was normally based on kinship ties, although sometimes outsiders such as friends or other dependents may have been admitted to membership. Throughout the precolonial era, lineages served, in the words of one historian, as the "basic building blocks" of African society. The authority of the leading members of the lineage group was substantial. As in China, the elders had considerable power over the economic functions of the other people in the group, which provided mutual support for all members.

A village would usually be composed of a single lineage group, although some communities may have consisted of several unrelated families. At the head of the village was the familiar "big man," who was often assisted by a council of representatives of the various households in the community. Often the "big man" was believed to possess supernatural powers, and as the village grew in size and power, he might eventually be transformed into a local chieftain or monarch.

The Role of Women

Although generalizations are risky, women were usually subordinate to men in Africa, as in most early societies. In some cases, they were valued for the work they could do or for their role in increasing the size of the lineage group. Polygyny was not uncommon, particularly in Muslim societies. Women often worked in the fields while the men of the village tended the cattle or went on hunting expeditions. In some communities, the women specialized in commercial activities. In one area in southern Africa, young girls were sent into the mines to extract gold because of their smaller physiques.

But there were some key differences between the role of women in Africa and elsewhere. In many African societies, lineage was matrilinear rather than patrilinear. In the words of Ibn Battuta, "a man does not pass on inheritance except to the sons of his sister to the exclusion of his own sons." He said he had never encountered this custom before except among the unbelievers of the Malabar coast in India. Women were often permitted to inherit property, and the husband was often expected to move into his wife's house.

Relations between the sexes were also sometimes more relaxed than in China or India, with none of the taboos characteristic of those societies. Again, in the words of Ibn Battuta, himself a Muslim:

> With regard to their women, they are not modest in the presence of men, they do not veil themselves in spite of their perseverance in the prayers. . . . The women there have friends and companions amongst men outside the prohibited degrees of marriage [i.e., other than brothers, fathers, etc.]. Likewise for the men, there are companions from amongst women outside the prohibited degrees. One of them would enter his house to find his wife with her companion and would not disapprove of that conduct.

When Ibn Battuta asked an African acquaintance about these customs, the latter responded: "Women's companionship with men in our country is honorable and takes place in a good way: there is no suspicion about it. They are not like the women in your country." Ibn Battuta noted his astonishment at such a "thoughtless" answer and did not accept further invitations to visit his friend's house.[8]

Such informal attitudes toward the relationship between the sexes were not found everywhere in Africa and were probably curtailed as many Africans converted to Islam (see the box on p. 233). But it is a testimony to

WOMEN AND ISLAM IN NORTH AFRICA

*I*n Muslim societies in North Africa, as elsewhere, women were required to cover their bodies to avoid giving temptations to men, but Islam's puritanical insistence on the separation of the sexes contrasted with the relatively informal relationships that prevailed in many African societies. In this excerpt from The History and Description of Africa, Leo Africanus describes the customs along the Mediterranean coast of Africa. A resident of Spain of Muslim parentage who was captured by Christian corsairs in 1518 and later served under Pope Leo X, Leo Africanus undertook many visits to Africa.

LEO AFRICANUS, *THE HISTORY AND DESCRIPTION OF AFRICA*

Their women (according to the guise of that country) go very gorgeously attired: they wear linen gowns dyed black, with exceeding wide sleeves, over which sometimes they cast a mantle of the same color or of blue, the corners of which mantle are very artificially fastened about their shoulders with a fine silver clasp. Likewise they have rings hanging at their ears, which for the most part are made of silver; they wear many rings also upon their fingers. Moreover they usually wear about their thighs and ankles certain scarfs and rings, after the fashion of the Africans. They cover their faces with certain masks having only two holes for the eyes to peep out at. If any man chance to meet with them, they presently hide their faces, passing by him with silence, except it be some of their allies or kinsfolks; for unto them they always discover their faces, neither is there any use of the said mask so long as they be in presence. These Arabians when they travel any journey (as they oftentimes do) they set their women upon certain saddles made handsomely of wicker for the same purpose, and fastened to their camel backs, neither be they anything too wide, but fit only for a woman to sit in. When they go to the wars each man carries his wife with him, to the end that she may cheer up her good man, and give him encouragement. Their damsels which are unmarried do usually paint their faces, breasts, arms, hands, and fingers with a kind of counterfeit color: which is accounted a most decent custom among them.

---

the tenacity of traditional customs that the relatively puritanical views about the role of women in society brought by Muslims from the Middle East made little impression even among Muslim families in West Africa.

Slavery

African slavery is often associated with the period after 1500. Indeed, the slave trade did reach enormous proportions in the seventeenth and eighteenth centuries, when European slave ships transported millions of unfortunate victims abroad to Europe or the Americas (see Chapter 14).

Slavery did not originate with the coming of the Europeans, however. It had been practiced in Africa since ancient times and probably originated with prisoners of war who were forced into perpetual servitude. Slavery was common in ancient Egypt and became especially prevalent during the New Kingdom, when slaving expeditions brought back thousands of captives from the upper Nile to be used in labor gangs, for tribute, and even as human sacrifices.

Slavery persisted during the early period of state building, in the first and early second millennia C.E. Berber tribes may have regularly raided agricultural communities south of the Sahara for captives who were transported northward and eventually sold throughout the Mediterranean. Some were enrolled as soldiers, while others, often women, were used as domestic servants in the homes of the well-to-do. The use of captives for forced labor or for sale was apparently also common in African societies further to the south and along the eastern coast.

Certainly, life was difficult for the average slave. The least fortunate were probably those who worked on plantations owned by the royal family or other wealthy landowners. Those pressed into service as soldiers were sometimes more fortunate, since in Muslim societies in the Middle East, they might at some point win their freedom. Many slaves were employed in the royal household or as domestic servants in private homes. In general, they probably had the most tolerable existence. Although they normally were not permitted to purchase their freedom, their living conditions were often decent and sometimes were practically indistinguishable from those of the free individuals in the household. In some societies in North Africa, slaves reportedly made up as much as 75 percent of the entire population. Elsewhere, the percentage was much lower, in some cases less than 10 percent.

 AFRICAN CULTURE

In early Africa, as in much of the rest of the world at the time, creative expression, whether in the form of painting, literature, or music, was above all a means of serving religion. Though to the uninitiated a wooden mask or the bronze and iron statuary of southern Nigeria is simply a work of art, to the artist it was often a means of expressing religious convictions. Some African historians reject the use of the term *art* to describe such artifacts because they were produced for religious rather than aesthetic purposes.

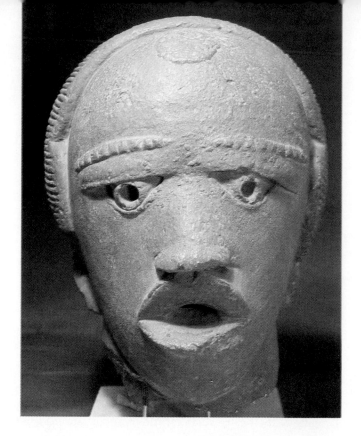

✿ **NOK POTTERY HEAD.**   The Nok peoples of the Niger River are the oldest known culture in West Africa to have created sculpture. This is a typical terra-cotta head from the Nok culture, dating from 500 B.C.E. to 200 C.E. Discovered accidentally in the twentieth century by tin miners, these heads exhibit perforated eyes set in triangles or circles, stylized eyebrows, open thick lips, broad noses with wide perforated nostrils, and large ears. Although the function of these statues is not known for certain, they likely were connected with religious rituals or ancestor devotion.

Painting and Sculpture

The earliest extant art forms in Africa are rock paintings. The most famous examples are in the Tassili Mountains in the central Sahara, where the earliest paintings may date back as far as c. 5000 B.C.E., though the majority are a millennium or so younger. Some of the later paintings depict the two-horse chariots used to transport goods prior to the introduction of the camel. Rock paintings are also found elsewhere in the continent, including the Nile valley and in eastern and southern Africa. Those of the San peoples of southern Africa are especially interesting for their illustrations of ritual ceremonies in which village shamans induce rain, propitiate the spirits, or cure illnesses.

More familiar, perhaps, are African wood carvings and sculpture. Wood-carvers throughout the continent produced remarkable masks (actually headpieces) and statuary. The carvings often represent gods, spirits, or ancestral figures and were believed to embody the spiritual powers of the subject in symbolic form. Terra-cotta and metal figurines served a similar purpose. For example, the impressive figures found near the city of Nok in northern Nigeria are believed to have had religious significance. Dating from the first millennium B.C.E., they include human figures and heads in terra-cotta, as well as in iron and stone.

In the thirteenth and fourteenth centuries C.E., metalworkers at Ife in what is now southern Nigeria produced handsome bronze and iron statues using the lost-wax method, in which melted wax is replaced in a mold by molten metal. The Ife sculptures, in turn, may have influenced artists in Benin, in West Africa, who produced equally impressive works in bronze during the same period. The Benin sculptures include bronze heads, relief plaques depicting life at court, ornaments, and figures of various types of animals.

Westerners once regarded African wood carvings and metal sculpture as a form of "primitive art," but the label is not appropriate. The metal sculpture of Benin, for example, is highly sophisticated, and some of the best works are considered masterpieces. Such artistic works were often created by artisans in the employ of the royal court.

Music

Like sculpture and wood carving, African music and dance often served a religious function. With their characteristic heavy rhythmic beat, dances were a means of communicating with the spirits, and the frenzied movements that are often identified with African dance were intended to represent the spirits acting through humans.

African music during the traditional period varied to some degree from one society to another. A wide variety of instruments were used, including drums and other percussion instruments, xylophones, bells, horns and flutes, and stringed instruments like the fiddle, harp, and zither. Still, the music throughout the continent had sufficient common characteristics to justify a few generalizations. In the first place, a strong rhythmic pattern was an important feature of most African music, although the desired effect was achieved through a wide variety of means, including gourds, pots, bells, sticks beaten together, and hand clapping as well as drums.

Another important feature of African music was the integration of voice and instrument into a total musical experience. Musical instruments and the human voice were often woven together to tell a story, and instruments, such as the famous "talking drum," were often used to represent the voice. Choral music and individual voices were frequently used in a pattern of repetition and variation, sometimes known as the "call and response" technique. Through this technique, the audience participated in the music by uttering a single phrase over and over as a choral response to the changing call sung by the soloist. Sometimes instrumental music achieved a similar result.

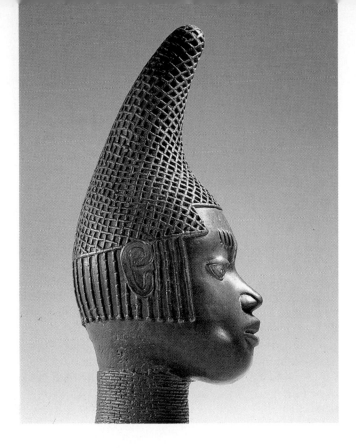

Much music was produced in the context of social rituals, such as weddings and funerals, religious ceremonies, and official inaugurations. It could also serve an educational purpose by passing on to the young people information about the history and social traditions of the community. In the absence of written languages in sub-Saharan Africa (except for the Arabic script, used in Muslim societies in East and West Africa), music served as the primary means of transmitting folk legends and religious traditions from generation to generation. Storytelling, which was usually undertaken by a priestly class or a specialized class of storytellers, served a similar function.

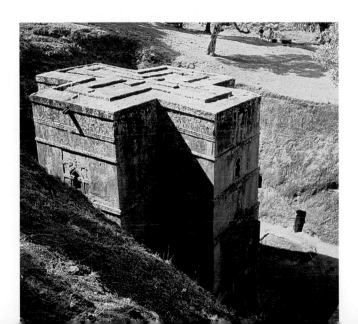

❀ **AFRICAN METALWORK, BENIN.**   By 1500 the West African state of Benin had expanded into an extensive and powerful empire with a highly developed official court art, especially in metalwork. Rulers were commemorated with bronze, brass, and copper sculpture, such as the stunning head of a queen mother shown here. These pieces were intended as ancestral memorial portraits and were placed on the altar of the deceased ruler by his successor. The queen mother, who claimed a revered position in Benin culture, would have ordered several such artistic renderings. The delicate attention to detail and the graceful sense of movement of this head attest to the technical excellence and sophistication of Benin bronze casting.

Architecture

No aspect of African artistic creativity is more varied than architecture. From the pyramids along the Nile to the ruins of Great Zimbabwe south of the Zambezi River, from the Moorish palaces at Zanzibar to the turreted mud mosques of West Africa, African architecture shows a striking diversity of approach and technique that is unmatched in other areas of creative endeavor.

The earliest surviving architectural form found in Africa, of course, is the pyramid (see Chapter 1). The Kushite kingdom at Meroë apparently adopted the pyramidal form from Egypt during the last centuries of the first millennium B.C.E. Although used for the same purpose as their earlier counterparts at Giza, the pyramids at Meroë were distinctive in style; they were much smaller and were topped with a flat platform rather than rising to a point. Remains of temples with massive carved pillars at Meroë also reflect Egyptian influence.

Further to the south, the kingdom of Axum was developing its own architectural traditions. Most distinctive were the carved stone pillars, known as stelae, that were used to mark the tombs of dead kings. Some stood as high as a hundred feet. The advent of Christianity eventually had an impact on Axumite architecture. During the Zagwe dynasty in the twelfth and thirteenth centuries C.E., churches carved out of solid rock were constructed throughout the country. Stylistically, they combined indigenous techniques inherited from the pre-Christian period with elements borrowed from Christian churches in the Holy Land.

❀ **A COPTIC CHURCH IN ETHIOPIA.**   In 1200 C.E., Christian monks in Ethiopia began to construct a remarkable series of eleven churches carved out of solid volcanic rock. After a forty-foot trench was formed by removing the bedrock, the central block of stone was hewed into the shape of a Greek cross; then it was hollowed out and decorated. These churches, which are still in use today, testify to the fervor of Ethiopian Christianity.

A CHINESE VIEW OF AFRICA

This passage from Chau Ju-kua's thirteenth-century treatise on geography describes various aspects of life along the eastern coast of Africa in what is now Somalia, including the urban architecture. The author was an inspector of foreign trade in the city of Quanzhou (sometimes called Zayton) on the southern coast of China. His account was compiled from reports of seafarers. Note the varied uses that the local people make of a whale carcass.

CHAU JU-KUA ON EAST AFRICA

The inhabitants of the Chung-li country [the Somali coast] go bareheaded and barefooted; they wrap themselves in cotton stuffs, but they dare not wear jackets, for the wearing of jackets and turbans is a privilege reserved to the ministers and the king's courtiers. The king lives in a brick house covered with glazed tiles, but the people live in huts made of palm leaves and covered with grass-thatched roofs. Their daily food consists of baked flour cakes, sheep's and camel's milk. There are great numbers of cattle, sheep, and camels....

There are many sorcerers among them who are able to change themselves into birds, beasts, or aquatic animals, and by these means keep the ignorant people in a state of terror. If some of them in trading with some foreign ship have a quarrel, the sorcerers pronounce a charm over the ship so that it can neither go forward nor backward, and they only release the ship when it has settled the dispute. The government has formally forbidden this practice.

When one of the inhabitants dies, and they are about to bury him in his coffin, his kinsfolk from near and far come to condole. Each person, flourishing a sword in his hand, goes in and asks the mourners the cause of the person's death. If he was killed by the hand of man, each one says, we will revenge him on the murderer with these swords. Should the mourners reply that he was not killed by any one, but that he came to his end by the will of Heaven, they throw away their swords and break into violent wailing.

Every year there are driven on the coast a great many dead fish measuring two hundred feet in length and twenty feet through the body. The people do not eat the flesh of these fish, but they cut out their brains, marrow, and eyes, from which they get oil. They mix this oil with lime to caulk their boats, and use it also in lamps. The poor people use the ribs of these fish to make rafters, the backbones for door leaves, and they cut off vertebrae to make mortars with.

In West Africa, buildings constructed in stone were apparently a rarity until the emergence of states during the first millennium C.E. At that time, the royal palace, as well as other buildings of civic importance, were often built of stone or cement, while the houses of the majority of the population continued to be constructed of dried mud. On his visit to the state of Guinea on the West African coast, the sixteenth-century traveler Leo Africanus noted that the houses of the ruler and other elites were built of chalk with roofs of straw. Even then, however, well into the state-building period, mosques were often built of mud.

Along the east coast, the architecture of the elite tended to reflect Middle Eastern styles. In the coastal towns and islands from Mogadishu to Kilwa, the houses of the wealthy were built of stone and reflected Moorish influence. As elsewhere, the common people lived in huts of mud, thatch, or palm leaves (see the box above). Mosques were built of stone.

The most famous stone buildings in sub-Saharan Africa are those at Great Zimbabwe. Constructed of carefully cut stones that were set in place without mortar, the great wall and the public buildings at Great Zimbabwe are an impressive monument to the architectural creativity of the peoples of the region.

Literature

Literature in the sense of written works did not exist in sub-Saharan Africa during the early traditional period, except in regions where Islam had brought the Arabic script from the Middle East. But African societies compensated for the absence of a written language with a rich tradition of oral lore. The bard, or professional storyteller, was an ancient African institution by which history was transmitted orally from generation to generation. In many

❀ THE MOSQUE AT JENNE, MALI. With the opening of the gold fields south of Mali, in present-day Ghana, Jenne became an important trading center for gold. Shown here is its distinctive fourteenth-century mosque made of unbaked clay without reinforcements. The projecting timbers offer easy access for repairing the mud exterior, as was regularly required.

A WEST AFRICAN ORAL TRADITION

I n this passage from the West African Epic of Son-Jara, Son-Jara's sister, Sugulun Kulunkan, offers to seduce his enemy Sumamuru in order to obtain the Manden secret, or magic spell, needed to control the Kingdom of Mali. Sumamuru divulges his all-powerful secret and is rebuked by his mother; both son and mother then disown one another with the trenchant symbols of the slashed breast and cut cloth. After each line of the verse, the bard's assistant would shout the endorsement "true," perhaps the distant origin of today's African American practice of approving each line of religious oratory with "Amen."

THE EPIC OF SON-JARA

Son-Jara's flesh-and-blood sister, Sugulun Kulunkan,
She said, "O Magan Son-Jara,
"One person cannot fight this war.
"Let me go seek Sumamuru.
"Were I then to reach him,
"To you I will deliver him,
"So that the folk of the Manden be yours,
"And all the Mandenland you shield."
Sugulun Kulunkan arose,
And went up to the gates of Sumamuru's fortress:

. . .

"Come open the gates, Susu Mountain Sumamuru!
"Come make me your bed companion!"
Sumamuru came to the gates:
"What manner of person are you?"
"It is I Sugulun Kulunkan!"
"Well, now, Sugulun Kulunkan,
"If you have come to trap me,
"To turn me over to some person,
"Know that none can ever vanquish me.

"I have found the Manden secret,
"And made the Manden sacrifice,
"And in five score millet stalks placed it,
"And buried them here in the earth.
"'Tis I who found the Manden secret,
"And made the Manden sacrifice,
"And in a red piebald bull did place it,
"And buried it here in the earth.
"Know that none can vanquish me.
"'Tis I who found the Manden secret
"And made a sacrifice to it,
"And in a pure white cock did place it.
"Were you to kill it,
"And uproot some barren groundnut plants,
"And strip them of their leaves,
"And spread them round the fortress,
"And uproot more barren peanut plants,
"And fling them into the fortress,
"Only then can I be vanquished."
His mother sprang forward at that:
"Heh! Susu Mountain Sumamuru!
"Never tell all to a woman,
"To a one-night woman!
"The woman is not safe, Sumamuru."
Sumamuru sprang towards his mother,
And came and seized his mother,
And slashed off her breast with a knife, magasi!
She went and got the old menstrual cloth.
"Ah! Sumamuru!" she swore.
"If your birth was ever a fact,
"I have cut your old menstrual cloth!"

West African societies, bards were highly esteemed and served as counselors to kings as well as protectors of local tradition. Bards were revered for their oratory and singing skills, phenomenal memory, and astute interpretation of history. As one African scholar wrote, the death of a bard was equivalent to the burning of a library.

Bards served several necessary functions in society. They were chroniclers of history, preservers of social customs and proper conduct, and entertainers who possessed a monopoly over the playing of several musical instruments, which accompanied their narratives. Because of their unique position above normal society, bards often played the role of mediator between hostile families or clans in a community. They were also credited with possessing occult powers and could read divinations and give blessings and curses. Traditionally, bards also served as advisers to the king, sometimes inciting him to action (such as going to battle) through the passion of their poetry. When captured by the enemy, bards were often treated with respect and released or compelled to serve the victor with their art.

One of the most famous West African epics is *Son-Jara* (also known as *Sunjata* or *Sundiata*). Passed down orally by bards for more than seven hundred years, it relates the heroic exploits of Son-Jara, the founder and ruler (1230–1255) of Mali's empire. Although Mansa Musa is famous throughout the world because of his flamboyant pilgrimage to Mecca in the fourteenth century, Son-Jara is more celebrated in West Africa because of the dynamic and unbroken oral traditions of the West African peoples (see the box above).

In addition to the bards, women too were appreciated for their storytelling talents, as well as for their role as purveyors of the moral values and religious beliefs of African societies. In societies that lacked a written tradition, women represented the societal glue that held the community together. Through the recitation of fables, proverbs, poems, and songs, mothers conditioned the communal bonding and moral fiber of succeeding generations in a way that was rarely encountered in the patriarchal societies of Europe, eastern and southern Asia, and the Middle East. Such activities were not only vital aspects of education in traditional Africa; they also offered a welcome respite from the drudgery of everyday life as well as a spark to develop the imagination and artistic awareness of the young. Renowned for its many proverbs, Africa also offers the following: "A good story is like a garden carried in the pocket."

 CONCLUSION

Thanks to the dedicated work of a generation of archaeologists, anthropologists, and historians, we now have a much better understanding of the evolution of human societies in Africa than we did a few decades ago. Intensive efforts by archaeologists have demonstrated beyond reasonable doubt that the first hominids lived there. Recent evidence suggests that farming may have been practiced in Africa more than 12,000 years ago, while the concept of kingship may have originated not in Sumer or in Egypt, but in the upper Nile valley as long ago as the fourth millennium B.C.E.

Less is known about more recent African history, partly because of the paucity of written records. Still, historians have established that the first civilizations had begun to take shape in sub-Saharan Africa by the first millennium C.E., while the continent as a whole was an active participant in emerging regional and global trade with the Mediterranean world and across the Indian Ocean.

Thus, the peoples of Africa were not as isolated from the main currents of human history as was once assumed. Although the state-building process in sub-Saharan Africa was still in its early stages compared with the ancient civilizations of India, China, and Mesopotamia, in many respects these new states were as impressive and sophisticated as their counterparts elsewhere in the world.

In the fifteenth century, a new factor was added to the equation. Urged on by the tireless efforts of Prince Henry the Navigator, Portuguese fleets began to probe southward along the coast of West Africa. At first their sponsors were in search of gold and slaves, but at the end of the century, Vasco da Gama's voyage around the Cape of Good Hope signaled Portugal's determination to dominate the commerce of the Indian Ocean in the future. The new situation posed a challenge to the peoples of Africa, whose nascent states and technology would be severely tested by the rapacious demands of the Europeans (see Chapter 14).

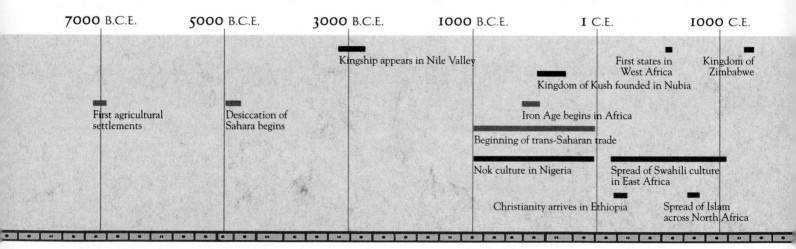

| 7000 B.C.E. | 5000 B.C.E. | 3000 B.C.E. | 1000 B.C.E. | 1 C.E. | 1000 C.E. |

Kingship appears in Nile Valley

First states in West Africa

Kingdom of Zimbabwe

Kingdom of Kush founded in Nubia

First agricultural settlements

Desiccation of Sahara begins

Iron Age begins in Africa

Beginning of trans-Saharan trade

Nok culture in Nigeria

Spread of Swahili culture in East Africa

Christianity arrives in Ethiopia

Spread of Islam across North Africa

 CHAPTER NOTES

1. Said Hamdun and Noel King, eds., *Ibn Battuta in Africa* (London, 1975), p. 19.
2. *The Book of Duarte Barbosa* (Nedeln, Liechtenstein, 1967), p. 28.
3. Herodotus, *The Histories*, trans. Aubrey de Sélincourt (Baltimore, 1964), p. 307.
4. Margaret Shinnie, *Ancient African Kingdoms* (London, 1965), p. 60.
5. C. R. Boxer, ed., *The Tragic History of the Sea, 1589–1622* (Cambridge, 1959), pp. 121–22, quoted in Kevin Shillington, *History of Africa* (New York, 1989), p. 155.
6. Quoted in Brian Fagan, *New Treasures of the Past: Fresh Finds That Deepen Our Understanding of the Archaeology of Man* (Leicester, 1987), p. 154.
7. Hamdun and King, *Ibn Battuta in Africa*, p. 47.
8. Ibid., pp. 28–30.

SUGGESTED READINGS

In few areas of world history is scholarship advancing as rapidly as in African history. New information is constantly forcing archaeologists and historians to revise their assumptions about the early history of the continent. Standard texts therefore quickly become out-of-date as their conclusions are supplanted by new evidence.

Still, there are several worthwhile general surveys that provide a useful overview of the early period of African history. The dean of African historians, and certainly one of the most readable, is B. Davidson. For a sympathetic portrayal of the African people, see his *African History* (New York, 1968) and *Lost Cities in Africa*, rev. ed. (Boston, 1970). Other respected accounts are R. Oliver and J. D. Fage, *A Short History of Africa* (Middlesex, 1986); J. M. Harris, *Africans and Their History* (New York, 1972); and V. B. Khapoya, *The African Experience: An Introduction* (Englewood Cliffs, N.J., 1994). A more detailed interpretation, by four respected historians, is P. Curtin et al., *African History* (Boston, 1978). For a readable treatment embodying recent scholarly evidence, see K. Shillington, *History of Africa* (New York, 1989). R. O. Collins, ed., *Problems in African History: The Precolonial Centuries* (New York, 1993) provides a useful collection of scholarly articles on key issues in precolonial Africa.

Specialized studies are beginning to appear with frequency on many areas of the continent. For a popular account of recent archaeological finds, see B. Fagan, *New Treasures of the Past: Fresh Finds That Deepen Our Understanding of the Archaeology of Man* (Leicester, 1987). For a more detailed treatment of the early period, see the early volumes in *The Cambridge History of Africa* (Cambridge, 1976–1986). See also R. Oliver, ed., *The Dawn of African History* (New York, 1968), and R. Oliver and B. Fagan, *Africa in the Iron Age* (Cambridge, 1975). J. D. Clarke and S. A. Brandt, eds., *From Hunters to Farmers* (Berkeley, Calif., 1984), takes an economic approach. Also see D. A. Welsby, *The Kingdom of Kush: The Napataean Meroitic Empire* (London, British Museum Press, 1996), and J. Middleton, *Swahili: An African Mercantile Civilization* (New Haven, 1992). For a fascinating account of trans-Saharan trade, see E. W. Bovill, *The Golden Trade of the Moors: West African Kingdoms in the Fourteenth Century*, 2d ed. (Princeton, N.J., 1995). On the cultural background, see R. Olaniyan, ed., *African History and Culture* (Lagos, 1982), and J. Vansina, *Paths in the Rainforest: Toward a History of Political Tradition in Equatorial Africa* (Madison, Wis., 1990). Although there exist many editions of *The Epic of Son-Jara*, based on recitations of different bards, the most conclusive edition is by F.-D. Sisòkò, translated and thoroughly annotated by J. W. Johnson (Bloomington, Ind., 1992).

On East Africa, see D. Nurse and T. Spear, *The Swahili: Reconstituting the History and Language of an African Society, 800–1500* (Philadelphia, 1985). The maritime story is recounted with documents in G. S. P. Freeman-Grenville, *The East African Coast: Select Documents from the First to the Earlier Nineteenth Century* (Oxford, 1962). For the larger picture, see K. N. Chaudhuri, *Trade and Civilization in the Indian Ocean: An Economic History from the Rise of Islam to 1750* (Cambridge, 1985). On the early history of Ethiopia, see the classic work by S. H. Sellassie, *Ancient and Medieval Ethiopian History* (1972), and J. D. Fage and R. Oliver, eds., *The Cambridge History of Africa*, vol. 4 (Cambridge, 1977–1985).

For useful general surveys of southern Africa, see N. Parsons, *A New History of Southern Africa* (New York, 1983), and K. Shillington, *A History of Southern Africa* (Essex, 1987), a profusely illustrated account. For an excellent introduction to the art of precolonial Africa, consult O. Egonwa, *African Art* (Benin City, Nigeria, 1994), and the beautifully illustrated T. Phillips, ed., *Africa: The Art of a Continent* (Munich, 1995).

 INFOTRAC COLLEGE EDITION

For additional reading, go to InfoTrac College Edition, your online research library at
http://web1.infotrac-college.com

Enter the search term "Africa" using the Subject Guide.

Enter the search terms "slave trade" using Keywords.

Enter the search term "Bantu" using Keywords.

Enter the search terms "Africa history" using Keywords.

9

THE EXPANSION OF CIVILIZATION IN SOUTHERN ASIA

CHAPTER OUTLINE
- INDIA FROM THE MAURYAS TO THE MUGHALS
- THE GOLDEN REGION: EARLY SOUTHEAST ASIA
- CONCLUSION

FOCUS QUESTIONS
- How did Buddhism change in the centuries after Siddhartha Gautama's death, and why did it ultimately decline in popularity in India?
- What impact did Muslim rule have on Indian society?
- What are some of the most important cultural achievements of Indian civilization in the era between the Mauryas and the Mughals?
- What were the main characteristics of Southeast Asian social and economic life, culture, and religion before 1500 C.E.?
- How did Indian civilization influence the civilizations that arose in Southeast Asia?

As the traveler wandered through the length and breadth of the land, he carefully recorded his impressions of the people, from the king down to his most insignificant subject. Their dress, he remarked, was quite different from that of his own country. People wore loose-fitting clothing gathered at the armpits. Most garments were white and were fashioned of cotton, wool, or silk. The robes of the women fell to the ground and completely covered their shoulders. In some areas, the common people wore garments made of leaves or bark or even went naked.

The visitor was especially impressed with the people's personal cleanliness. All wash themselves before eating, he said, and when they completed their meal, they cleaned their teeth with a willow stick and washed their hands and mouths. After relieving themselves, they washed their bodies and used perfume of sandalwood or turmeric.

The visitor was Xuan Zang (Hsuan Tsang), a Buddhist monk from China who traveled to India in the seventh century C.E. to search for holy scriptures to take back to his own country for translation into Chinese. Because little of the literature of the Indian people from that period survives, Xuan Zang's observations are a valuable resource for our knowledge of the daily lives of the people and show us that the *dhoti* and the *sari*, common forms of Indian dress today, have a long history on the subcontinent.⌖

INDIA FROM THE MAURYAS TO THE MUGHALS

The India Xuan Zang visited was no longer the unified land it had been under the Mauryan dynasty. The overthrow of the Mauryas in the early second century B.C.E. had been followed by several hundred years of disunity, when the subcontinent was divided into a number of separate kingdoms and principalities. The dominant force in the north was the Kushan state, established by Indo-European-speaking peoples who had been driven out of Central Asia by the Xiongnu. The Kushans penetrated into the mountains north of the Indus River, where they eventually formed a kingdom with its capital at Bactria, not far from modern Kabul. Over the next two centuries, the Kushans expanded their supremacy along the Indus River and into the central Ganges valley. Then the dynasty began to weaken, and it collapsed sometime in the third century C.E. After the disintegration of the Kushan state, northern India remained divided until the rise of the Gupta dynasty in the early fourth century. The Guptas revived the ancient tradition of the Mauryas for nearly two hundred years, until they too were overthrown in about 500 C.E.

Meanwhile, to the south, a number of kingdoms arose among the Dravidian peoples of the Deccan Plateau, which had been only partly under Mauryan rule. The most famous of these kingdoms was Cola (sometimes spelled "Chola") on the southeastern coast. Cola developed into a major trading power and sent merchant fleets eastward across the Bay of Bengal, where they introduced Indian culture as well as Indian goods to the peoples of Southeast Asia. In the fourth century C.E., Cola was overthrown by the Pallavas, who ruled from their capital at Kanchipuram (known today as Kanchi), just southwest of modern Madras, for the next four hundred years.

Beginning in the eleventh century, much of northern India fell under the rule of Turkic-speaking peoples who penetrated into the subcontinent from the northwest. Eventually, Turkic dynasties were set up in many areas and introduced the peoples of India to Islamic religion and civilization. These dynasties were able to survive attacks by the forces of Tamerlane (Timur the Lame), but by the end of the fifteenth century, they were coming under severe pressure from the Mughals, a powerful new force from the mountains.

The Kushan Kingdom: Linchpin of the Silk Road

The Kushan kingdom, with its power base beyond the Khyber Pass in modern Afghanistan, became the dominant political force in northern India in the centuries immediately after the fall of the Mauryas. Sitting astride the main trade routes across the northern half of the subcontinent, the Kushans thrived on the commerce that passed through the area. The bulk of that trade was between the Roman Empire and China and was transported along the route known as the Silk Road, one segment of which passed through the mountains northwest of India (see Chapter 10). From there, goods were shipped to Rome through the Persian Gulf or the Red Sea.

Trade between India and Europe had begun even before the rise of the Roman Empire, but it expanded rapidly in the first century C.E., when sailors mastered the pattern of the monsoon winds in the Indian Ocean (from the southwest in the summer and the northeast in the winter). Commerce between the Mediterranean and the Indian Ocean, as described in the *Periplus*, a first-century C.E. account by a Greek participant, was extensive and often profitable, and it resulted in the establishment of several small Roman settlements along the Indian coast. Rome imported ivory, indigo, textiles, precious stones, and pepper from India and silk from China. The Romans sometimes paid cash for these goods but also exported silver, wine, perfume, slaves, and glass and cloth from Egypt. Overall, Rome appears to have imported much more than it sold to the Far East, leading Emperor Tiberius to grumble that "the ladies and their baubles are transferring our money to foreigners."

The emergence of the Kushan kingdom as a major commercial power was due not only to its role as an intermediary in the Rome-China trade, but also to the rising popularity of Buddhism. Sometime during the second century C.E. (the precise dates of his reign are unknown), Kanishka, the greatest of the Kushan monarchs, began to patronize Buddhism. Under Kanishka and his successors, an intimate and mutually beneficial relationship was established between Buddhist monasteries and the local merchant community in thriving urban centers like Taxila and

THE GOOD LIFE IN MEDIEVAL INDIA

Much of what we know about life in medieval India comes from the accounts of Chinese missionaries who visited the subcontinent in search of documents recording the teachings of the Buddha. Here the Buddhist monk Fa Xian, who spent several years there in the fifth century C.E., reports on conditions in the kingdom of Mathura (Mo-tu-lo), a vassal state in western India that was part of the Gupta Empire. Although he could not have been pleased that the Gupta monarchs had adopted the Hindu faith, he found that the people were contented and prosperous except for the outcastes, whom he called Chandalas.

FA XIAN, THE TRAVELS OF FA XIAN

Going southeast from this somewhat less than 80 *joyanas*, we passed very many temples one after another, with some myriad of priests in them. Having passed these places, we arrived at a certain country. This country is called Mo-tu-lo. Once more we followed the Pu-na river. On the sides of the river, both right and left, are twenty *sangharamas*, with perhaps 3,000 priests. The law of Buddha is progressing and flourishing. Beyond the deserts are the countries of western India. The kings of these countries are all firm believers in the law of Buddha. They remove their caps of state when they make offerings to the priests. The members of the royal household and the chief ministers personally direct the food giving; when the distribution of food is over, they spread a carpet on the ground opposite the chief seat (the president's seat) and sit down before it. They dare not sit on couches in the presence of the priests. The rules relating to the almsgiving of kings have been handed down from the time of Buddha till now. Southward from this is the so-called middle country (Madhyadesa). The climate of this country is warm and equable, without frost or snow. The people are very well off, without poll tax or official restrictions. Only those who till the royal lands return a portion of profit of the land. If they desire to go, they go; if they like to stop, they stop. The kings govern without corporal punishment; criminals are fined, according to circumstances, lightly or heavily. Even in cases of repeated rebellion they only cut off the right hand. The king's personal attendants, who guard him on the right and left, have fixed salaries. Throughout the country the people kill no living thing nor drink wine, nor do they eat garlic or onions, with the exception of Chandalas only. The Chandalas are named "evil men" and dwell apart from others; if they enter a town or market, they sound a piece of wood in order to separate themselves; then men, knowing who they are, avoid coming in contact with them. In this country they do not keep swine nor fowls, and do not deal in cattle; they have no shambles or wine shops in their marketplaces. In selling they use cowrie shells. The Chandalas only hunt and sell flesh.

Varanasi. Merchants were eager to build stupas and donate money to monasteries in return for social prestige and the implied promise of a better life in this world or the hereafter.

For their part, the wealthy monasteries ceased to be simple communities where monks could find a refuge from the material cares of the world; instead they became major consumers of luxury goods provided by their affluent patrons. Monasteries and their inhabitants became increasingly involved in the economic life of society, and Buddhist architecture began to be richly decorated with precious stones and glass purchased from local merchants or imported from abroad. The process was highly reminiscent of the changes that occurred in the church in medieval Europe.

The Gupta Dynasty

The Kushan kingdom came to an end under uncertain conditions sometime in the third century C.E. In 320, a new state was established in the central Ganges valley by a local raja named Chandragupta (no relation to Chandragupta Maurya, the founder of the Mauryan dynasty). Chandragupta located his capital at Pataliputra, the site of the now decaying palace of the Mauryas. Under his successor Samudragupta, the territory under Gupta rule was extended into surrounding areas, and eventually the new kingdom became the dominant political force throughout northern India. It also established a loose suzerainty over the Dravidian state of Pallava to the south, thus becoming the greatest state in the subcontinent since the decline of the Mauryan Empire. Under a succession of powerful, efficient, and highly cultured monarchs, notably Samudragupta and Chandragupta II, India enjoyed a new "classical age" of civilization.

The Gupta era was a time of prosperity and thriving commerce with China, Southeast Asia, and the Mediterranean. Great cities, notable for their temples and Buddhist monasteries as well as for their economic prosperity, rose along the main trade routes throughout the subcontinent. The religious trade also prospered, as pilgrims from across India and as far away as China came to visit the major religious centers (see the box above).

As in the Mauryan Empire, much of the trade in the Gupta Empire was managed or regulated by the government. The Guptas owned mines and vast crown lands and earned massive profits from their commercial dealings. But there was also a large private sector, dominated by great caste guilds that monopolized key sectors of the economy. A money economy had probably been in operation since the second century B.C.E., when copper and gold coins had been introduced from the Middle East. This in turn led to the development of banking. Nevertheless, there are indications that the circulation of coins was limited. The Chinese missionary Xuan Zang, who visited India early in the seventh century, remarked that most commercial transactions were conducted by barter.[1]

But the good fortunes of the Guptas proved to be relatively short-lived. Beginning in the late fifth century C.E., incursions by nomadic warriors from the northwest gradually reduced the power of the empire. Soon northern India was once more divided into myriad small kingdoms engaged in seemingly constant conflict.

Buddhism at Bay

The Chinese pilgrims who traveled to India during the Gupta era found a Buddhism that had changed in a number of ways in the centuries since the time of Siddhartha Gautama. They also found a doctrine that was beginning to decline in popularity in the face of a resurgent Hinduism.

The transformation in Buddhism had come about in part because the earliest written sources were transcribed two centuries after Siddhartha's death and in part because his message was reinterpreted as it became part of the everyday life of the people. Abstract concepts of a Nirvana that cannot be described began to be replaced, at least in the popular mind, with more concrete visions of heavenly salvation, and Siddhartha was increasingly regarded as a divinity rather than as a sage. The Buddha's teachings that all four classes were equal gave way to the familiar Hindu conviction that some people, by reason of previous reincarnations, were closer to Nirvana than others.

These developments led to a split in the movement. Purists emphasized what they insisted were the original teachings of the Buddha (describing themselves as the school of Theravada, or "the teachings of the elders"). Followers of Theravada considered Buddhism a way of life, not a salvationist creed. Theravada stressed the importance of strict adherence to personal behavior and the quest for understanding as a means of release from the wheel of life.

In the meantime, another interpretation of Buddhist doctrine was emerging in the northwest. Here Buddhist believers, perhaps hoping to compete with other salvationist faiths circulating in the region, began to promote the view that Nirvana could be achieved through devotion and not just through painstaking attention to one's behavior. According to advocates of this school, eventually to be known as Mahayana ("greater vehicle"), Theravada teachings were too demanding or strict for ordinary people to follow and therefore favored the wealthy, who were more apt to have the time and resources to spend weeks or months away from their everyday occupations. Mahayana Buddhists referred to their rivals as Hinayana, or "lesser vehicle," because in Theravada fewer would reach enlightenment. Mahayana thus attempted to provide hope for the masses in their efforts to reach Nirvana, but to the followers of Theravada, it did so at the expense of an insistence on proper behavior.

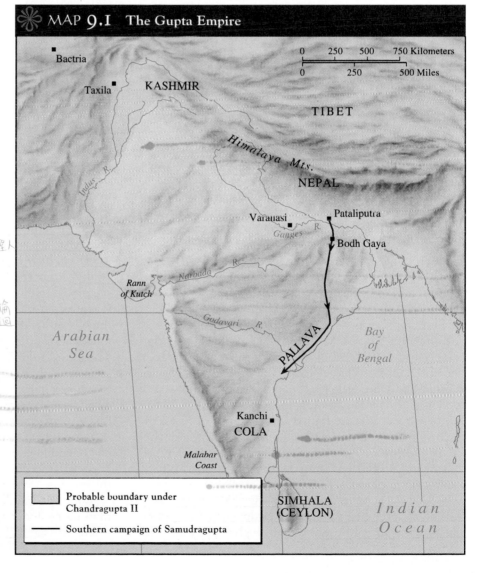

MAP 9.1   The Gupta Empire

0   250   500   750 Kilometers
0   250   500 Miles

Bactria

Taxila
KASHMIR

TIBET

Himalaya Mts.

NEPAL

Indus R.

Varanasi
Ganges
Pataliputra
Bodh Gaya

Rann of Kutch

Narbada R.

Godavari R.

PALLAVA

Arabian Sea

Bay of Bengal

Kanchi
COLA

Malabar Coast

☐ Probable boundary under Chandragupta II

— Southern campaign of Samudragupta

SIMHALA (CEYLON)

Indian Ocean

MAMALLAPURAM OCEAN TEMPLE. The eighth-century remnants of one of the earliest freestanding Hindu temples grace the shore at Mamallapuram, south of Madras. It stands as a visual confirmation of the rising influence of the Hindu faith in southern India during the era of the Colas and the Pallavas. The temple was constructed of granite blocks and was originally covered with ornate carvings, but centuries of wind and sea have softened its surfaces. It would be difficult to conceive of a more romantic temple than this, especially at dawn with the sun and the ocean intensifying its mystery.

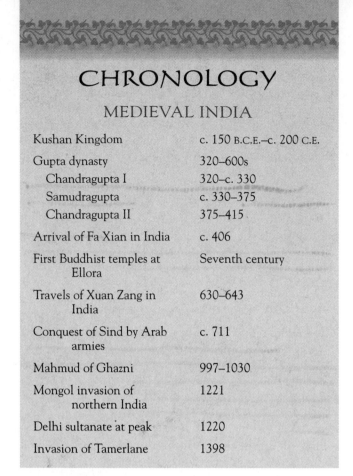

CHRONOLOGY
MEDIEVAL INDIA

Kushan Kingdom	c. 150 B.C.E.–c. 200 C.E.
Gupta dynasty	320–600s
Chandragupta I	320–c. 330
Samudragupta	c. 330–375
Chandragupta II	375–415
Arrival of Fa Xian in India	c. 406
First Buddhist temples at Ellora	Seventh century
Travels of Xuan Zang in India	630–643
Conquest of Sind by Arab armies	c. 711
Mahmud of Ghazni	997–1030
Mongol invasion of northern India	1221
Delhi sultanate at peak	1220
Invasion of Tamerlane	1398

To advocates of the Mahayana school, salvation could also come from the intercession of a bodhisattva ("he who possesses the essence of Buddhahood"). According to Mahayana beliefs, some individuals who had achieved bodhi and were thus eligible to enter the state of Nirvana after death chose instead, because of their great compassion, to remain on earth in spirit form to help all human beings achieve release from the life cycle. Followers of Theravada, who believed the concept of bodhisattva applied only to Siddhartha Gautama himself, denounced such ideas as "the teaching of demons." But to their proponents, such ideas extended the hope of salvation to the masses. Mahayana Buddhists revered the saintly individuals who, according to tradition, had become bodhisattvas at death, and erected temples in their honor, where the local population could pray and render offerings. The most famous bodhisattva was Avalokitesvara, a mythic figure whose name in Sanskrit means "Lord of Compassion." Perhaps because of the identification of Avalokitesvara with the concept of mercy, in China he was gradually transformed into a female figure known as Guan Yin (Kuan Yin).

A final distinguishing characteristic of Mahayana Buddhism was its reinterpretation of Buddhism as a religion rather than as a philosophy. Although Mahayana had philosophical aspects, its adherents increasingly regarded the Buddha as a divine figure, and an elaborate Buddhist cosmology developed. Nirvana was not a form of extinction, but a true heaven with many rest stations along the way for the faithful.

Under Kushan rule, Mahayana achieved considerable popularity in northern India and for a while even made inroads in such Theravada strongholds as the island of Sri Lanka. But in the end, neither Mahayana nor Theravada was able to retain its popularity in Indian society. By the seventh century C.E., Theravada had declined rapidly on the subcontinent, although it retained its foothold in Sri Lanka and across the Bay of Bengal in Southeast Asia, where it remained an influential force to modern times. Mahayana prospered in the northwest for centuries, but eventually it was supplanted by a revived Hinduism and later by a new arrival, Islam. But Mahayana too would find better fortunes abroad, as it was carried over the Silk Road or by sea to China and then to Korea and Japan (see Chapters 10 and 11). In all three countries, Buddhism has coexisted with Confucian doctrine and indigenous beliefs to the present.

Why was Buddhism unable to retain its popularity in its native India, although it became a major force elsewhere in Asia? Some have speculated that in denying the

THE EDUCATION OF A BRAHMIN

Although the seventh-century Chinese traveler Xuan Zang was a Buddhist, he faithfully recorded his impressions of the Hindu religion in his memoirs. Here he describes the education of a brahmin, *the highest class in Indian society.*

XUAN ZANG, RECORDS OF WESTERN COUNTRIES

The Brahmans study the four *Veda Sastras*. The first is called *Shau* [longevity]; it relates to the preservation of life and the regulation of the natural condition. The second is called *Sse* [sacrifice]; it relates to the [rules of] sacrifice and prayer. The third is called *Ping* [peace or regulation]; it relates to decorum, casting of lots, military affairs, and army regulations. The fourth is called *Shue* [secret mysteries]; it relates to various branches of science, incantations, medicine.

The teachers [of these works] must themselves have closely studied the deep and secret principles they contain, and penetrated to their remotest meaning. They then explain their general sense, and guide their pupils in understanding the words that are difficult. They urge them on and skillfully conduct them. They add luster to their poor knowledge, and stimulate the desponding. If they find that their pupils are satisfied with their acquirements, and so

wish to escape to attend to their worldly duties, then they use means to keep them in their power. When they have finished their education, and have attained thirty years of age, then their character is formed and their knowledge ripe. When they have secured an occupation they first of all thank their master for his attention. There are some, deeply versed in antiquity, who devote themselves to elegant studies, and live apart from the world, and retain the simplicity of their character. These rise above mundane presents, and are as insensible to renown as to the contempt of the world. Their name having spread afar, the rulers appreciate them highly, but are unable to draw them to the court. The chief of the country honors them on account of their [mental] gifts, and the people exalt their fame and render them universal homage. . . . They search for wisdom, relying on their own resources. Although they are possessed of large wealth, yet they will wander here and there to seek their subsistence. There are others who, whilst attaching value to letters, will yet without shame consume their fortunes in wandering about for pleasure, neglecting their duties. They squander their substance in costly food and clothing. Having no virtuous principle, and no desire to study, they are brought to disgrace, and their infamy is widely circulated.

---

existence of the soul, Buddhism ran counter to traditional Hindu belief. Perhaps, too, one of Buddhism's strengths was also a weakness. In rejecting the class divisions that defined the Indian way of life, Buddhism appealed to those very groups who lacked an accepted place in Hindu society, such as the untouchables. But at the same time, it represented a threat to those with a higher status. Moreover, by emphasizing the responsibility of each person to seek an individual path to Nirvana, Buddhism undermined the strong social bonds of the Indian caste system.

Perhaps a final factor in the decline of Buddhism was the revival of Hinduism. In its early development, Hinduism had been highly elitist. Not only was observance of court ritual a monopoly of the *brahmin* class (see the box above), but the major route to individual salvation, asceticism, was hardly realistic for the average Indian. However, in the centuries after the fall of the Mauryas, a growing emphasis on devotion (*bhakti*) as a means of religious observance brought the possibility of improving one's *karma* by means of ritual acts within the reach of Indians of all classes. It seems likely that Hindu devotionalism rose precisely to combat the inroads of Buddhism and reduce the latter's appeal among the Indian population. The Chinese Buddhist missionary Fa Xian,

who visited India in the mid-Gupta era, reported that mutual hostility between the Buddhists and the *brahmins* was quite strong:

> Leaving the southern gate of the capital city, on the east side of the road is a place where Buddha once dwelt. Whilst here he bit (a piece from) the willow stick and fixed it in the earth; immediately it grew up seven feet high, neither more or less. The unbelievers and Brahmans, filled with jealousy, cut it down and scattered the leaves far and wide, but yet it always sprung up again in the same place as before.[2]

For a while, Buddhism was probably able to stave off the Hindu challenge by its own salvationist creed of Mahayana, which also emphasized the role of devotion, but the days of Buddhism as a dominant faith in the subcontinent were numbered.

Islam on the March

While India was still suffering from the disarray left by the collapse of the Gupta Empire, a new and dynamic force in the form of Islam was arising in the Arabian peninsula to the west. As we have seen, during the seventh and eighth centuries, Arab armies carried the new faith westward to the Iberian peninsula and eastward across the arid

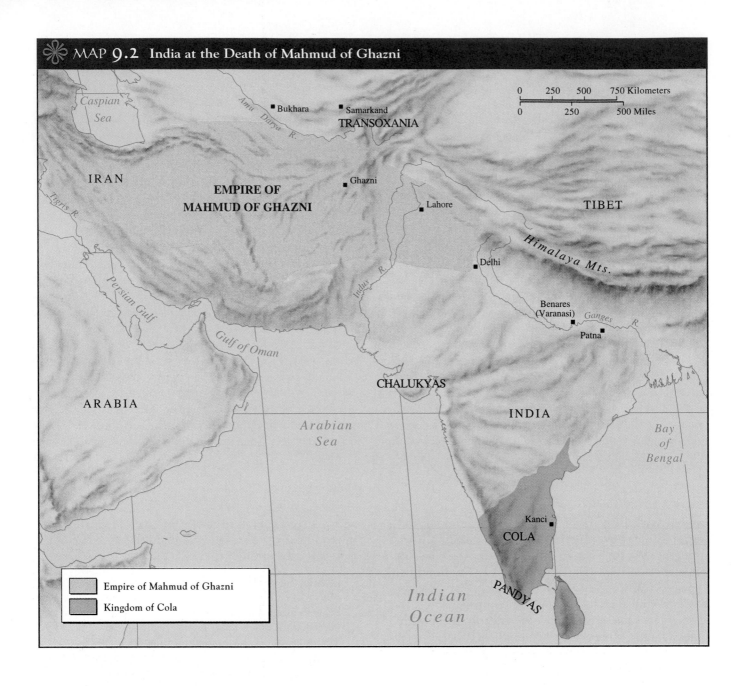

MAP **9.2** India at the Death of Mahmud of Ghazni

wastelands of Persia and into the rugged mountains of the Hindu Kush. Islam first reached India through the Arabs in the eighth century, but a second onslaught in the tenth and eleventh centuries by Turkic-speaking converts had a more lasting effect.

Although Arab merchants had been active along the Indian coasts for centuries, Arab armies did not reach India until the early eighth century. When Indian pirates attacked Arab shipping near the delta of the Indus River, the Muslim ruler in Iraq demanded an apology from the ruler of Sind, a Hindu state in the Indus valley. When the latter refused, Muslim forces conquered lower Sind in 711 and then moved northward into the Punjab, bringing Arab rule into the frontier regions of the subcontinent for the first time.

For the next three centuries, Islam made no further advances into India. But a second phase began at the end of the tenth century with the rise of the state of Ghazni, located in the area of the old Kushan kingdom in present-day Afghanistan. The new kingdom was founded in 962, when Turkic-speaking slaves seized power from the Samanids, a Persian dynasty. When the founder of the new state died in 997, his son, Mahmud of Ghazni (997–1030), succeeded him. Brilliant and ambitious, Mahmud used his patrimony as a base of operations for sporadic forays against neighboring Hindu kingdoms to the southeast. Before his death in 1030, he was able to extend his rule throughout the upper Indus valley and as far south as the Indian Ocean. In wealth and cultural brilliance, his court at Ghazni rivaled that of the Abbasid dynasty in neighboring Baghdad. But his achievements had a dark side. Describing Mahmud's conquests in northwestern India, the contemporary historian al-Biruni wrote:

> Mahmud utterly ruined the prosperity of the country, and performed wonderful exploits by which the Hindus became like atoms scattered in all directions, and like a tale of old in the mouth of the people. Their scattered remains cherish, of course, the most inveterate aversion towards all Muslims. This is the reason, too, why Hindu sciences have retired far away from those parts of the country conquered by us, and have fled to places which our hand cannot yet reach, to Kashmir, Benares, and other places.[3]

Resistance against the advances of Mahmud and his successors into northern India was led by the Rajputs, aristocratic Hindu clans who were probably descended from tribal groups that had penetrated into northwestern India from Central Asia in earlier centuries. The Rajputs possessed a strong military tradition and fought bravely, but their military tactics, based on infantry supported by elephants, were no match for the fearsome cavalry of the invaders, whose ability to strike with lightning speed contrasted sharply with the slow-footed forces of their adversaries. Moreover, the incessant squabbling among the Rajput leaders put them at a disadvantage against the single-minded intensity and religious fervor of Mahmud's armies. Although the power of Ghazni declined after his death, a successor state in the area resumed the advance in the late twelfth century, and by 1200 Muslim power, in the form of a new Delhi sultanate, had been extended over the entire plain of northern India.

South of the Ganges River valley, Muslim influence spread more slowly and in fact had little immediate impact. Muslim armies launched occasional forays into the Deccan Plateau, but at first they had little success, even though the area was divided among a number of warring kingdoms, including the Colas along the eastern coast and the Pandyas far to the south.

One reason the Delhi sultanate failed to take advantage of the disarray of its rivals was the threat posed by the Mongols on the northwestern frontier (see Chapter 10). Mongol armies unleashed by the great tribal warrior Genghis Khan occupied Baghdad and destroyed the Abbasid caliphate in the 1250s, while other forces occupied the Punjab around Lahore, from which they threatened Delhi on several occasions. For the next half-century, the attention of the sultanate was fo-

cused on the Mongols. That threat finally declined in the early fourteenth century with the gradual breakup of the Mongol Empire, and a new Islamic state emerged in the form of a new Tughluq dynasty (1320–1413), which extended its power into the Deccan Plateau. In praise of his sovereign, the Tughluq monarch Ala-ud-din, the poet Amir Khusrau exclaimed:

> Happy be Hindustan, with its splendor of religion,
> Where Islamic law enjoys perfect honor and dignity;
> In learning Delhi now rivals Bukhara;
> Islam has been made manifest by the rulers.
> From Ghazni to the very shore of the ocean
> You see Islam in its glory.[4]

Such happiness was not destined to endure, however. During the latter half of the fourteenth century, the Tughluq dynasty gradually fell into decline. In 1398, a new military force crossed the Indus River from the northwest, raided the capital of Delhi, and then withdrew. According to some contemporary historians, as many as 100,000 Hindu prisoners were massacred before the gates of the city. Such was India's first encounter with Tamerlane.

Tamerlane (b. 1330s), also known as Timur-i-lang (Timur the Lame), was the ruler of a Mongol khanate based in Samarkand to the north of the Pamir Mountains. His kingdom had been founded on the ruins of the Mongol Empire, which had begun to disintegrate as a result of succession struggles in the thirteenth century.

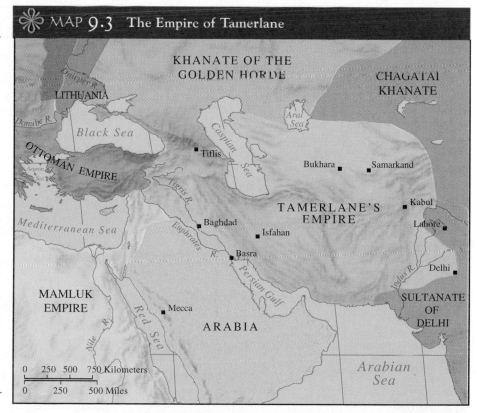

MAP 9.3 The Empire of Tamerlane

Tamerlane, the son of a local aristocrat, seized power in Samarkand in 1369 and immediately launched a program of conquest. During the 1380s, he brought the entire region east of the Caspian Sea under his authority and then conquered Baghdad and occupied Mesopotamia. After his brief foray into northern India, he turned to the west and raided the Anatolian peninsula. Defeating the army of the Ottoman Turks, he advanced almost as far as the Bosporus before withdrawing. "The last of the great nomadic conquerors," as one recent historian described him, died in 1405 in the midst of a final military campaign.

The passing of Tamerlane removed a major menace from the diverse states of the Indian subcontinent. But the respite from external challenge was not a long one. By the end of the fifteenth century, two new challenges had appeared from beyond the horizon: the Mughals, a newly emerging nomadic power beyond the Khyber Pass in the north, and the Portuguese traders, who arrived by sea from the eastern coast of Africa in search of gold and spices. Both, in their different ways, would exert a major impact on the later course of Indian civilization.

ISLAM AND INDIAN SOCIETY

Like their counterparts in other areas that came under Islamic rule, many Muslim rulers in India were quite tolerant of other faiths and used peaceful means, if any, to encourage nonbelievers to convert to Islam. Even the more enlightened, however, could be fierce when their religious zeal was aroused. One ruler, on being informed that a Hindu fair had been held near Delhi, ordered the promoters of the event to be put to death. Hindu temples were razed, and mosques were erected in their place. Eventually, however, most Muslim rulers realized that not all Hindus could be converted and recognized the necessity of accepting what to them was an alien and repugnant

❁ **SAMARKAND, GEM OF AN EMPIRE.**   The city of Samarkand has a long history. First settled during the first millennium B.C.E. as a caravan stop on the Silk Road, it was later occupied by Alexander the Great, the Abbasids, and the Mongols, before becoming the capital of Tamerlane's expanding empire. Tamerlane expended great sums in creating a city worthy of his own imperial ambitions. Shown here is the great square, known as the Registan. Site of a mosque, a library, and a Muslim university, all built in the exuberant Persian style, Samarkand was the jumping-off point for trade with China far to the east.

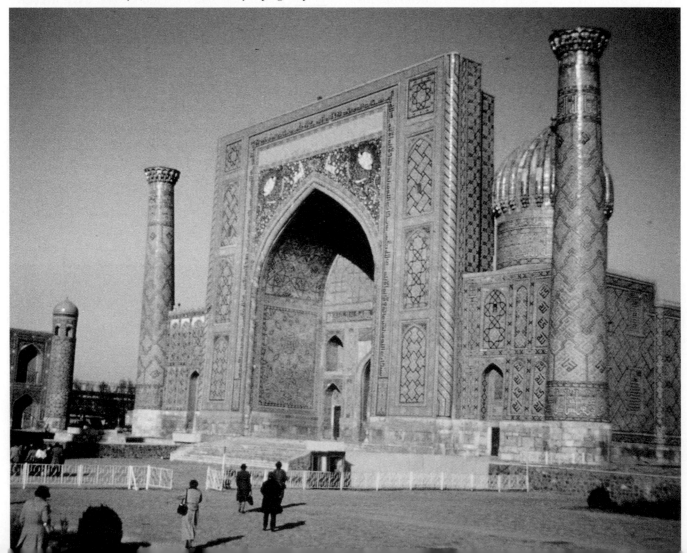

THE ISLAMIC CONQUEST OF INDIA

One consequence of the Muslim conquest of northern India was the imposition of many Islamic customs on Hindu society. In this excerpt, the fourteenth-century Muslim historian Zia-ud-din Barani describes the attempt of one Muslim ruler, Ala-ud-din, to forbid the use of alcohol and gambling, two practices expressly forbidden in Muslim society. Ala-ud-din had seized power in Delhi from a rival in 1294.

A MUSLIM RULER SUPPRESSES HINDU PRACTICES

Thirdly, he forbade wine, beer, and intoxicating drugs to be used or sold; dicing, too, was prohibited. Vintners and beer sellers were turned out of the city, and the heavy taxes which had been levied from them were abolished. All the china and glass vessels of the Sultan's banqueting room were broken and thrown outside the gate of Badaun, where they formed a mound. Jars and casks of wine were emptied out there till they made mire as if it were the season of the rains. The Sultan himself entirely gave up wine parties. Self-respecting people at once followed his example; but the ne'er-do-wells went on making wine and spirits and hid the leather bottles in loads of hay or firewood and by various such tricks smuggled it into the city. Inspectors and gatekeepers and spies diligently sought to seize the contraband and the smugglers; and when seized the wine was given to the elephants, and the importers and sellers and drinkers flogged and given short terms of imprisonment. So many were they, however, that holes had to be dug for their incarceration outside the great thoroughfare of the Badaun gate, and many of the wine bibbers died from the rigor of their confinement and others were taken out half-dead and were long in recovering their health. The terror of these holes deterred many from drinking. Those who could not give it up had to journey ten or twelve leagues to get a drink, for at half that distance, four or five leagues from Delhi, wine could not be publicly sold or drunk. The prevention of drinking proving very difficult, the Sultan enacted that people might distill and drink privately in their own homes, if drinking parties were not held and the liquor not sold. After the prohibition of drinking, conspiracies diminished.

religion. While Hindu religious practices were generally tolerated, non-Muslims were compelled to pay a tax to the state. Some Hindus likely converted to Islam to avoid paying the tax, but were then expected to make the traditional charitable contribution required of Muslims in all Islamic societies.

Over time, millions of Hindus did turn to the Muslim faith. Some were individuals or groups in the employ of the Muslim ruling class, such as government officials, artisans, or merchants catering to the needs of the court. But many others were probably peasants from the *sudra* class or even untouchables who found in the egalitarian message of Islam a way of removing the stigma of low-class status in the Hindu social hierarchy.

Seldom have two major religions been so strikingly different. Where Hinduism tolerated a belief in the existence of several deities (although admittedly they were all considered by some to be manifestations of one supreme god), Islam was uncompromisingly monotheistic. Where Hinduism was hierarchical, Islam was egalitarian. Where Hinduism featured a priestly class to serve as an intermediary with the ultimate force of the universe, Islam permitted no one to come between believers and their god. Such differences contributed to the mutual hostility that developed between the adherents of the two faiths in the Indian subcontinent, but more mundane issues, such as the Muslim habit of eating beef and the idolatry and sexual frankness in Hindu art, were probably a greater source of antagonism at the popular level (see the box above).

In other cases, the two peoples borrowed from each other. Some Muslim rulers found the Indian idea of divine kingship appealing. In their turn, Hindu rajas learned by bitter experience the superiority of cavalry mounted on horses instead of elephants, the primary assault weapon in early India. Some upper-class Hindu males were attracted to the Muslim tradition of *purdah* and began to keep their women in seclusion (termed locally "behind the curtain") from everyday society. Hindu sources claimed that one reason for adopting the custom was to protect Hindu women from the roving eyes of foreigners. But it is likely that many Indian families adopted the practice for reasons of prestige or because they were convinced that *purdah* was a practical means of protecting female virtue. Adult Indian women had already begun to cover their heads with a scarf during the Gupta era.

All in all, Muslim rule probably did not have a significant impact on the lives of most Indian women. *Purdah* was practiced more commonly among high castes than among the lower castes. Though it was probably of little consolation, sexual relations in poor and low-caste families were relatively egalitarian, as men and women worked together on press gangs or in the fields. Muslim customs apparently had little effect on the Hindu tradition of *sati* (see the box on p. 250). In fact, in many respects Muslim women had more rights than their Hindu counterparts. They had more property rights than Hindu women and were legally permitted to divorce under certain conditions and to remarry after the death of their husband. The

THE PRACTICE OF *SATI*

One of the most distinctive aspects of medieval Indian society was the Hindu custom of sati, whereby a widow was immolated on the funeral pyre of her husband during his cremation. In so doing, she was not only honoring her dead husband, but also declaring her allegiance to deeply-held community beliefs in the sanctity of the marriage vow. Here the Portuguese adventurer Duarte Barbosa describes such a practice in the southern state of Narsyngua.

DUARTE BARBOSA, ON SATI

In this kingdom of Narsyngua . . . the women are bound by very ancient custom, when their husbands die, to burn themselves alive with their corpses, which are also burnt. This they do to honor the husband. If such a woman is poor and of low estate, when her husband dies she goes with him to the burning ground, "where there is a great pit" in which a pile of wood burns. When the husband's body has been laid therein and begins to burn she throws herself of her own free will into the midst of the said fire, where both their bodies are reduced to ashes. But if she is a woman of high rank, rich, and with distinguished kindred, whether she be a young maid or an old woman, when her husband dies she accompanies the aforesaid corpse of her husband to the aforesaid burning ground, bewailing him; and there they dig a round pit, very wide and deep, which they fill with wood . . . and, when they have kindled it, they lay the man's body therein, and it is burnt while she weeps greatly. Wishing to do all honor to her husband she then causes all his kindred and her own to be called together, that they may come to feast and honor her thereby. . . . Thereafter she attires herself very richly with all the jewels she possesses, and then distributes to her sons, relatives, and friends all the property that remains. Thus arrayed she mounts on a horse . . . that she may be the better seen of all the people. Mounted on this horse they lead her through the whole city with great rejoicings, until they come back to the very spot where the husband has been burnt, where, they cast a great quantity of wood into the pit itself and on its edge they make a great fire. When it has burnt up somewhat they erect a wooden scaffold with four or five steps where they take her up just as she is. When she is on the top she turns herself round thereon three times, worshipping towards the direction of sunrise, and, this done, she calls her sons, kindred, and friends, and to each she gives a jewel, whereof she has many with her, and in the same way every piece of her clothing until nothing is left except a small piece of cloth with which she is clothed from the waist down. Then she tells the men who are with her on the scaffold to consider what they owe to their wives who, being free to act, yet burn themselves alive for the love of them, and the women she tells to see how much they owe to their husbands, to such a degree as to go with them even to death. Then . . . they place in her hands a pitcher full of oil, and she puts it on her head, and with it she again turns round thrice on the scaffold and again worships towards the rising sun. Then she casts the pitcher of oil into the fire and throws herself after it with as much goodwill as if she were throwing herself on a little cotton, from which she could receive no hurt. The kinsfolk all take part at once and cast into the fire many pitchers of oil and butter which they hold ready for this purpose, and much wood on this, and therewith bursts out such a flame that no more can be seen.

primary role for Indian women in general, however, was to produce children. Sons were preferred over daughters, not only because they alone could conduct ancestral rights, but also because a daughter was a financial liability. Not only did she require a costly dowry in marriage, but after the wedding she would eventually transfer her labor assets to her husband's family. Still, women shared with men a position in the Indian religious pantheon. The cult of the mother-goddess, which had originated in the Harappan era, revived during the Gupta era stronger than ever. The Hindu female deity, known as Devi, was celebrated by both men and women as the source of cosmic power, bestower of wishes, and symbol of fertility.

Overall, the Muslims continued to view themselves as foreign conquerors and generally maintained a strict separation between the Muslim ruling class and the mass of the Hindu population. Although a few Hindus rose to important positions in the local bureaucracy, in general high posts in the central government and the provinces were reserved for Muslims. Only with the founding of the Mughal dynasty was a serious effort undertaken to reconcile the differences.

One result of this effort was the religion of the Sikhs. Founded by the guru Nanak in the early sixteenth century in the Punjab, Sikhism attempted to integrate the best of the two faiths in a single religion. Sikhism (the term means "disciple") originated in the devotionalist movement in Hinduism, which taught that God was the single true reality. All else is illusion. But Nanak rejected the Hindu tradition of asceticism and mortification of the flesh and, like Muhammad, taught his disciples to participate in the world. Sikhism achieved considerable popularity in northwestern India, where Islam and Hinduism confronted each other directly, and eventually evolved into a militant faith that fiercely protected its adherents against its two larger rivals. In the end, Sikhism did not

UNTOUCHABLES IN SOUTH INDIA

Some of the best descriptions of Indian society in the late medieval era came from European merchants and missionaries. The following passage was written by the Portuguese traveler Duarte Barbosa and describes an untouchable caste on the southwestern coast of India in the early sixteenth century. The Nayres mentioned in this excerpt were a higher caste in the region.

DUARTE BARBOSA, FROM THE LAND OF MALABAR

And there is yet another caste of Heathen lower than these whom they call Poleas, who among all the rest are held to be accursed and excommunicate; they dwell in the fields and open campaigns [plots] in secret lurking places, whither folk of good caste never go save by mischance, and live in huts very strait and mean. They are tillers of rice with buffaloes and oxen. They never speak to the Nayres save from afar off, shouting so that they may hear them, and when they go along the roads they utter loud cries, that they may be let past, and whosoever hears them leaves the road, and stands in the wood till they have passed by; and if anyone, whether man or woman, touches them his kinsfolk slay him forthwith, and in vengeance therefore they slay Poleas until they weary without suffering any punishment. In certain months of the year they do their utmost to touch some Nayre woman by night as secretly as they can, and this only for the sake of doing evil. They go by in order to get into the houses of the Nayres to touch women, and during these months the women guard themselves carefully, and if they touch any woman, even though none have seen it, and there may be no witnesses, yet she declares it at once, crying out, and she will stay no longer in her house that her caste may not be destroyed; in general she flees to the house of some other low caste folk, and hides herself, that her kinsfolk may not slay her; and that thence she may help herself and be sold to foreigners, which is ofttimes done. And the manner of touching is this, even though no words are exchanged, they throw something at her, a stone or a stick, and if it touches her she is touched and ruined. These people are also great sorcerers and thieves; they are a very evil race.

---

reconcile Hinduism and Islam but provided an alternative to both.

One complication for both Muslims and Hindus as they tried to come to terms with the existence of a mixed society was the problem of caste. Could non-Hindus form castes, and if so, how were these castes related to the Hindu castes? Where did the Turkic-speaking elites who made up the ruling class in many of the Islamic states fit into the equation?

The problem was resolved in a pragmatic manner that probably followed an earlier tradition of assimilating non-Hindu tribal groups into the system. Members of the Turkic ruling groups formed social groups that were roughly equivalent to the Hindu *brahmin* or *kshatriya* caste. During the Delhi sultanate in the north, members of the local Rajput nobility who converted to Islam were occasionally permitted to join such caste groupings. Ordinary Indians who converted to Islam also formed Muslim castes, although at a lower level on the social scale. Many who did so were probably artisans who converted en masse to obtain the privileges that conversion could bring.

In most of India, then, Muslim rule did not substantially disrupt the caste system. One perceptive European visitor in the early sixteenth century reported that in Malabar, along the southwestern coast, there were separate castes for fishing, pottery making, weaving, carpentry and metalworking, salt mining, sorcery, and labor on the plantations. There were separate castes for doing the laundry, one for the elite and the other for the common people (see the box above).

Economy and Daily Life

India's landed and commercial elites lived in the cities, often in conditions of considerable opulence. The rulers, of course, possessed the most wealth. One maharaja of a relatively small state in southern India, for example, had over 100,000 soldiers in his pay along with 900 elephants and 20,000 horses. Another maintained a thousand high-caste women to serve as sweepers of his palace. Each carried a broom and a brass basin containing a mixture of cow dung and water, and followed him from one house to another, plastering the path where he was to tread. Most urban dwellers, of course, did not live in such style. Xuan Zang, the Chinese Buddhist missionary who visited India in the early seventh century, left us a description of ordinary homes in urban areas:

> Their houses are surrounded by low walls, and form the suburbs. The earth being soft and muddy, the walls of the towns are mostly built of brick or tiles. The towers on the walls are constructed of wood or bamboo; the houses have balconies and belvederes, which are made of wood, with a coating of lime or mortar, and covered with tiles. The different buildings have the same form as those in China; rushes, or dry branches, or tiles, or boards are used for covering them. The walls are covered with lime and mud, mixed with cow's dung for purity. At different seasons they scatter flowers about. Such are some of their different customs.[5]

The majority of India's population (estimated at slightly more than 100 million in the first millennium C.E.), however, lived on the land. Most were peasants who tilled all plots of land with a wooden plow pulled by oxen and paid a percentage of the harvest to their landlord. The landlord, in turn, forwarded part of the payment to the local ruler. In effect, the landlord functioned as a tax collector for the king, who retained ultimate ownership of all farmland in his domain. At best, most peasants lived at the subsistence level. At worst, they were forced into debt and fell victim to moneylenders who charged exorbitant rates of interest.

In the north and in the upland regions of the Deccan Plateau, the primary grain crops were wheat and barley. In the Ganges valley and the southern coastal plains, the main crop was rice. Vegetables were grown everywhere, and southern India produced many spices, fruits, sugarcane, and cotton. The cotton plant apparently originated in the Indus River valley and spread from there. Although some cotton was cultivated in Spain and North Africa by the eighth and ninth centuries, India remained the primary producer of cotton goods. Spices such as cinnamon, pepper, ginger, sandalwood, cardamom, and cumin were also major export products.

Agriculture, of course, was not the only source of wealth in India. Since ancient times, the subcontinent had served as a major entrepôt for trade between the Middle East and the Pacific basin, as well as the source of other goods shipped throughout the known world. Although civil strife and piracy, heavy taxation of the business community by local rulers to finance their fratricidal wars, and increased customs duties between principalities may have contributed to a decline in internal trade, the level of foreign trade remained high, particularly in the Dravidian kingdoms in the south and along the northwestern coast, which were located along the traditional trade routes to the Middle East and the Mediterranean Sea. Much of this foreign trade was carried on by wealthy Hindu castes with close ties to the royal courts. But there were other participants as well, including such non-Hindu minorities as the Muslims, the Parsis, and the Jain community. The Parsis, expatriates from Persia who practiced the Zoroastrian religion, dominated banking and the textile industry in the cities bordering the Rann of Kutch. Later they would become a dominant economic force in the modern city of Bombay. The Jains became prominent in trade and manufacturing even though their faith emphasized simplicity and the rejection of materialism.

According to early European travelers, merchants often lived quite well. One Portuguese observer described the "Moorish" population in Bengal as follows:

> They have girdles of cloth, and over them silk scarves; they carry in their girdles daggers garnished with silver and gold, according to the rank of the person who carries them; on their fingers many rings set with rich jewels, and cotton turbans on their heads. They are luxurious, eat well and spend freely, and have many other extravagances as well. They bathe often in great tanks which they have in their houses. Everyone has three or four wives or as many as he can maintain. They keep them carefully shut up, and treat them very well, giving them great store of gold, silver and apparel of fine silk.[6]

Outside these relatively small, specialized trading communities, most manufacturing and commerce were in the hands of petty traders and artisans, who generally were limited to local markets. This failure to build on the promise of antiquity has led some historians to ask why India failed to produce an expansion of commerce and growth of cities

❀ ROCK PAINTINGS AT SIGIRIYA, SRI LANKA. Closely linked to Indian art and culture are these surviving paintings at the sixth-century rock fortress at Sigiriya, on the island of Sri Lanka. Portraits of serving girls from the king's harem were painted high up along the cliff wall. Many were destroyed by Buddhist monks when they reclaimed the area after the king's sudden death. Thankfully, a few of these graceful, languid maidens were left unharmed to captivate viewers over the centuries.

ROCK TEMPLE AT ELLORA. An estimated 3 million cubic feet of stone were excavated out of solid rock to build the massive eighth-century Kailasantha Rock Temple at Ellora. Renowned for its elaborate sculptures dedicated to the legends of the Hindu deities, Ellora is one of India's greatest architectural sites.

similar to the developments that began in Europe during the High Middle Ages or even in China during the Song dynasty (see Chapter 10). Some have pointed to the traditionally low status of artisans and merchants in Indian society, symbolized by the comment in the *Arthasastra* that merchants were "thieves that are not called by the name of thief."[7] Yet commercial activities were frowned upon in many areas in Europe throughout the Middle Ages, a fact that did not prevent the emergence of capitalist societies throughout much of the West.

Another factor may have been the monopoly on foreign trade held by the government in many areas of India. More important, perhaps, was the impact of the caste system, which reduced the ability of entrepreneurs to expand their activities and have dealings with other members of the commercial and manufacturing community. Successful artisans, for example, normally could not set up as merchants to market their products, nor could merchants compete for buyers outside their normal area of operations. The complex interlocking relationships among the various castes in a given region were a powerful factor inhibiting the development of a thriving commercial sector in medieval India.

The Wonder of Indian Culture

The era between the Mauryas and the Mughals in India was a period of cultural evolution, as Indian writers and artists built on the literary and artistic achievements of their predecessors. This is not to say, however, that Indian culture rested on its ancient laurels. To the contrary, it was an era of tremendous innovation in all fields of creative endeavor.

ART AND ARCHITECTURE

At the end of antiquity, the primary forms of religious architecture were the Buddhist cave temples and monasteries. The next millennium witnessed the evolution of religious architecture from underground cavity to monumental structure.

The twenty-eight caves of Ajanta in the Deccan Plateau are one of India's greatest artistic achievements. They are as impressive for their sculpture and painting as for their architecture. Except for a few examples from the second century B.C.E., most of the caves were carved out of solid rock over an incredibly short period of eighteen years, from 460 to 478 C.E. In contrast to the early unadorned temple halls, these temples were exuberantly decorated with ornate pillars, friezes, beamed ceilings, and statues of the Buddha and bodhisattvas. Several caves served as monasteries, which by then had been transformed from simple holes in the wall to large complexes with living apartments, halls, and shrines to the Buddha.

All of the inner surfaces of the caves, including the ceilings, sculptures, walls, door frames, and pillars, were painted in vivid colors. Perhaps best known are the wall paintings, which illustrate the various lives and incarnations of the Buddha. These paintings are in an admirable state of preservation, making it possible to reconstruct the customs, dress, house interiors, and physical characteristics of the peoples of fifth-century India.

Near Ajanta are the equally famous rock temples at Ellora. These temples, carved out of a mountain of solid rock, were originally built by Buddhists during the eighth century C.E. Later, they were taken over by Hindus and at one time were used by followers of Jainism. Though the complex consists of several temples, the most famous is the Hindu temple of Kailasantha, dedicated to Siva. The floor of the temple is similar in size to the Parthenon in Greece, but the building is three stories high and required the excavation of an estimated three million cubic feet of stone. Unlike earlier temples, which were constructed in the form of caves, the Kailasantha temple was open to the sky (although many of the freestanding shrines are covered with roofs), and the walls are festooned with some of India's finest sculptures. The overall impression is one of wonder and massive grandeur.

Among the most impressive rock carvings in southern India are the cave temples at Mamallapuram (also known as Mahabalipuram), south of the modern city of Madras. The sculpture, called the Descent of the Ganges River, depicts the role played by Siva in intercepting the heavenly waters of the Ganges and allowing them to fall gently on the earth. Mamallapuram also boasts an eighth-century shore temple, which is considered to be one of the earliest surviving freestanding structures in the subcontinent.

From the eighth century until the time of the Mughals, Indian architects built a multitude of magnificent Hindu

✿ **DESCENT OF THE GANGES RIVER.** One of India's most outstanding sculptures is found at Mamallapuram, an eighth-century site on the eastern coast south of Madras. This open relief, known as the Descent of the Ganges River, is about twenty feet high and eighty feet long. It portrays Siva's effort to deflect the waters of the heavenly River Ganges on his head to spare the earth from destruction. Although it presents a rich panorama of gods, animals, and men, the gentle elephant in particular delights one and all.

temples, now constructed exclusively above ground. Each temple consisted of a central shrine surmounted by a sizable tower, a hall for worshipers, a vestibule, and a porch, all set in a rectangular courtyard that might also contain other minor shrines. Temples became progressively more ornate until the eleventh century, when the sculpture began to dominate the structure itself. The towers became higher and the temple complexes more intricate, some becoming virtual walled compounds set one within the other and resembling a town in themselves.

Among the best examples of temple art are those in the eastern state of Orissa. The Sun Temple at Konarak, standing at the edge of the sea and covered with intricate carvings, is generally considered the masterpiece of its genre. Although now in ruins, the Sun Temple still boasts some of India's most memorable sculptures. Especially renowned are the twelve pairs of carved wheels; each is ten feet high and represents one of the twelve signs of the zodiac.

The greatest example of medieval Hindu temple art, however, is probably Khajuraho. Of the original eighty temples, dating from the tenth century, twenty remain standing today. All of the towers are buttressed at various levels on the sides, giving the whole a sense of unity and creating a vertical movement similar to Mount Kailasa in the Himalayas, sacred to Hindus. Everywhere the viewer is entertained by voluptuous temple dancers bringing life to the massive structures. One is removing a thorn from her foot, another is applying eye makeup, and yet another is wringing out her hair.

In the Deccan Plateau, a different style prevailed. The southern temple style was marked by massive oblong stone towers, some as much as two hundred feet high. The towers were often covered with a profusion of sculpted figures and were visible for miles. The walls surrounding the temple complex were also surmounted with impressive gate towers, known as *gopuras*.

LITERATURE

During this period, Indian authors produced a prodigious number of written works, both religious and secular. Indian religious poetry was written in both Sanskrit and the languages of southern India. As Hinduism was transformed from a contemplative to a more devotional religion, its poetry became more ardent and erotic and prompted a sense of divine ecstasy. Much of the religious verse extolled the lives and heroic acts of Siva, Vishnu, Rama, and Krishna by repeating the same themes over and over, which is also a characteristic of Indian art. In the eighth century, a tradition of poet-saints inspired by intense mystical devotion to a deity emerged in southern India. Many were women who sought to escape the drudgery of domestic toil through an imagined sexual union with the god-lover. Such was the case for the twelfth-century mystic whose poem here expresses her sensuous joy in the physical-mystical union with her god:

> It was like a stream
> running into the dry bed
> of a lake,
> like rain pouring on plants
> parched to sticks.
> It was like this world's pleasure
> and the way to the other,
> both walking towards me.
> Seeing the feet of the master,
> O lord white as jasmine
> I was made worthwhile.[8]

The great secular literature of traditional India was also written in Sanskrit in the form of poetry, drama, and prose. Some of the best medieval Indian poetry is found in single-stanza poems, which create an entire emotional scene in just four lines. Witness this poem by the poet Amaru:

> We'll see what comes of it, I thought,
>   and I hardened my heart against her.
> What, won't the villain speak to me? she
>   thought, flying into a rage.
> And there we stood, sedulously refusing to look one
>   another in the face,
> Until at last I managed an unconvincing laugh,
>   and her tears robbed me of my resolution.[9]

One of India's most famous authors was Kalidasa, who lived during the Gupta dynasty. Although little is known of him, including his dates, he probably wrote for the court of Chandragupta II (375–415 C.E.). Even today Kalidasa's hundred-verse poem, *The Cloud Messenger*, remains one of the most popular Sanskrit poems (see the box on p. 256).

In addition to being a poet, Kalidasa was also a great dramatist. He wrote three plays, all dramatic romances that blend the erotic with the heroic and the comic. *Shakuntala*, perhaps the best-known play in all Indian literature, tells the story of a king who, while out hunting, falls in love with the maiden Shakuntala. He asks her to marry him and offers her a ring of betrothal but is suddenly recalled to his kingdom on urgent business. Shakuntala, who is pregnant, goes to him, but the king has been cursed by a hermit and no longer recognizes her. With the help of the gods, the king eventually does recall their love and is reunited with Shakuntala and their son.

Each of Kalidasa's plays is propelled by the magic powers of a goddess, and each ends in affirmation and unity. Another interesting aspect of Kalidasa's plays is that they combine several languages as well as poetry and prose. The language and form of the characters' speeches correspond to their position in the social hierarchy. Thus, the king speaks in Sanskrit poetry, while the other characters in the play use prose in three different vernaculars of everyday life.

Kalidasa was one of the greatest Indian dramatists, but he was by no means the only one. Sanskrit plays typically contained one to ten acts. They were performed in theaters in the palaces or in court temples by troupes of actors of both sexes who were trained and supported by the royal family. The plots were usually taken from Indian legends of gods and kings. No scenery or props were used, but costumes and makeup were elaborate. The theaters had to be small because much of the drama was conveyed through intricate gestures and dance conventions. There were many different positions for various parts of the body, including one hundred for the hands alone.

Like poetry, prose developed in India from the Vedic period. The use of prose was well established by the sixth and seventh centuries C.E. This is truly astonishing considering that the novel did not appear until the tenth century in Japan and until the seventeenth century in Europe.

One of the greatest masters of Sanskrit prose was Dandin, who lived during the seventh century. In *The Ten Princes*, he created a fantastic and exciting world that fuses history and fiction. His keen powers of observation, details of low life, and humor give his writing considerable vitality.

MUSIC

Another area of Indian creativity that developed during this era was music. Ancient Indian music had come from the chanting of the Vedic hymns and thus inevitably had a strong metaphysical and spiritual flavor. The actual physical vibrations of music (*nada*) were considered to be

SCULPTURAL DECORATIONS AT KHAJURAHO. This Hindu temple, one of the greatest in India, is literally covered with the statues of temple dancers, who bring life to its massive architecture. Frozen in stone, they mesmerize the viewer. Many represent the ideal couple or divine lovers, who symbolize the union of the worshipers with the deity, thus blending physical and spiritual beauty.

related to the spiritual world. An off-key or sloppy rendition of a sacred text could upset the harmony and balance of the entire universe.

In form, Indian classical music is based on a scale, called a *raga*. There are dozens, if not hundreds, of separate scales, which are grouped into separate categories depending on the time of day during which they are to be performed. The performers use a stringed instrument called a *sitar* and various types of wind instruments and drums. The performers select a basic *raga* and then are free to improvise the melodic structure and rhythm. A good performer never performs a particular *raga* the same way twice. As with jazz music in the West, the audience is concerned not so much with faithful reproduction, but with the performer's creativity.

AN INDIAN LOVE POEM

Kalidasa, who lived during the Gupta period, was India's greatest dramatist and poet. This is a brief excerpt from The Cloud Messenger, one of the most popular and beautiful poems in the Sanskrit language. It describes the anguish of a young Indian who has been sent into exile and misses his wife. In the poem he watches clouds drifting northward and describes to them the route to his home in the Himalaya Mountains.

KALIDASA, THE CLOUD MESSENGER

Stay for a while over the thickets, haunted by the girls of the
   hill-folk, then press on with faster pace, having shed your
   load of water,
and you'll see the Narmada river, scattered in torrents, by
   the rugged rocks at the foot of the Vindhyas,
looking like the plastered pattern of stripes on the flank of an
   elephant.

Note by the banks the flowers of the nipa trees, greenish
   brown, with their stamens half developed,
and the plantains, displaying their new buds.
Smell the most fragrant earth of the burnt-out woodlands,
   and as you release your raindrops the deer will show you
   the way.

. . . where the wind from the Sipra river prolongs the shrill
   melodious cry of the cranes,

fragrant at early dawn from the scent of the opening lotus,
   and, like a lover, with flattering requests,
dispels the morning languor of women, and refreshes their
   limbs.

Your body will grow fat with the smoke of incense from open
   windows where women dress their hair.
You will be greeted by palace peacocks, dancing to welcome
   you, their friend.
If your heart is weary from travel you may pass the night
   above mansions fragrant with flowers,
whose pavements are marked with red dye from the feet of
   lovely women.

. . . where yaksas dwell with lovely women in white mansions, whose crystal terraces reflect the stars like flowers.
They drink the wine of love distilled from magic trees,
   while drums beat softly, deeper than your thunder.

I see your body in the sinuous creeper, your gaze in the
   startled eyes of deer,
your cheek in the moon, your hair in the plumage of
   peacocks,
and in the tiny ripples of the river I see your sidelong glances,
but alas, my dearest, nowhere do I find your whole
   likeness!

THE GOLDEN REGION: EARLY SOUTHEAST ASIA

Between China and India lies the region that today is called Southeast Asia. It has two major components: a mainland region extending southward from the Chinese border down to the tip of the Malay peninsula and an extensive archipelago, most of which is part of present-day Indonesia and the Philippines. Travel between the islands and regions to the west, north, and east was not difficult, so Southeast Asia has historically served as a vast land bridge for the movement of peoples between China, the Indian subcontinent, and the more than 25,000 islands of the South Pacific.

Mainland Southeast Asia consists of several north-south mountain ranges, separated by river valleys that run in a southerly or southeasterly direction. During the first millennium C.E., two groups of migrants—the Thai from southwestern China and the Burmans from the Tibetan highlands—came down these valleys in search of new homelands, as earlier peoples had done before them. Once

in Southeast Asia, most of these migrants settled in the fertile deltas of the rivers—the Irrawaddy and the Salween in Burma, the Chao Phraya in Thailand, and the Red River and the Mekong in Vietnam—or in lowland areas in the islands to the south.

Although the river valleys facilitated north-south travel on the Southeast Asian mainland, movement between east and west was relatively difficult. The mountains are densely forested and often infested with malaria-carrying mosquitoes. Consequently, the lowland peoples in the river valleys were often isolated from each other and had only limited contacts with the upland peoples in the mountains. These geographical barriers may help explain why Southeast Asia is one of the few regions in Asia that was never unified under a single government.

Given Southeast Asia's location between China and India, it is not surprising that both civilizations influenced developments in the region. In 111 B.C.E. Vietnam was conquered by the Han dynasty and remained under Chinese control for more than a millennium; it will be discussed in Chapter 11. The Indian states never exerted much political control over Southeast Asia, but their influ-

THE KINGDOM OF ANGKOR

Angkor (known to the Chinese as Chon-la) was the greatest kingdom of its time in Southeast Asia. This passage, probably written in the thirteenth century by the Chinese port official Chau Ju-kua, includes a brief description of the capital city, Angkor Thom, which is still one of the great archaeological sites of the region. Angkor was already in decline when Chau Ju-kua described the kingdom, and the capital was abandoned soon afterward, in 1432.

CHAU JU-KUA, RECORDS OF FOREIGN NATIONS

The officials and the common people dwell in houses with sides of bamboo matting and thatched with reeds. Only the king resides in a palace of hewn stone. It has a granite lotus pond of extraordinary beauty with golden bridges, some three hundred odd feet long. The palace buildings are solidly built and richly ornamented. The throne on which the king sits is made of gharu wood and the seven precious substances; the dais is jewelled, with supports of veined wood [ebony?]; the screen [behind the throne] is of ivory.

When all the ministers of state have audience, they first make three full prostrations at the foot of the throne; they then kneel and remain thus, with hands crossed on their breasts, in a circle round the king, and discuss the affairs of state. When they have finished, they make another prostration and retire. . . .

[The people] are devout Buddhists. There are serving [in the temples] some three hundred foreign women; they dance and offer food to the Buddha. They are called *a-nan* or slave dancing girls.

As to their customs, lewdness is not considered criminal; theft is punished by cutting off a hand and a foot and by branding on the chest.

The incantations of the Buddhist and Taoist priests [of this country] have magical powers. Among the former those who wear yellow robes may marry, while those who dress in red lead ascetic lives in temples. The Taoists clothe themselves with leaves; they have a deity called P'o-to-li which they worship with great devotion.

[The people of this country] hold the right hand to be clean, the left unclean, so when they wish to mix their rice with any kind of meat broth, they use the right hand to do so and also to eat with.

The soil is rich and loamy; the fields have no bounds. Each one takes as much as he can cultivate. Rice and cereals are cheap; for every tael of lead one can buy two bushels of rice.

The native products comprise elephants' tusks, the *chan* and *su* [varieties of gharu wood], good yellow wax, kingfisher's feathers, . . . resin, foreign oils, ginger peel, gold-colored incense, . . . raw silk and cotton fabrics.

The foreign traders offer in exchange for these gold, silver, porcelainware, sugar, preserves, and vinegar.

---

ence was pervasive nevertheless. By the first centuries C.E., Indian merchants were sailing to Southeast Asia; they were soon followed by Buddhist and Hindu missionaries. Indian influence can be seen in many aspects of Southeast Asian culture—from political institutions to religion, architecture, language, and literature.

Paddy Fields and Spices: The States of Southeast Asia

The traditional states of Southeast Asia can be generally divided between agricultural societies and trading societies. The distinction between farming and trade was a product of the environment. The agricultural societies—notably, Vietnam, Angkor in what is now Cambodia, and the Burman state of Pagan—were situated in rich river deltas that were conducive to the development of a wet rice economy. Although all produced some goods for regional markets, none was tempted to turn to commerce as the prime source of national income. In fact, none was situated astride the main trade routes that crisscrossed the region.

The kingdom of Angkor, which took shape in the ninth century, was the most powerful state to emerge in mainland Southeast Asia before the sixteenth century (see the box above). The remains of its capital city Angkor Thom give a sense of the magnificence of Angkor civilization. The city formed a square two miles on each side. Its massive stone walls were several feet thick and were surrounded by a moat. Four main gates led into the city, which at its height had a substantial population. By the fourteenth century, however, Angkor had begun to decline, and in 1432 Angkor Thom was destroyed by the Thai, who had migrated into the region from southwestern China in the thirteenth century.

The islands of the Indonesian archipelago gave rise to two of the region's most notable trading societies—Srivijaya and Majapahit. Both were based in large part on spices. As the wealth of the Arab empire in the Middle East and then of western Europe increased, so did the demand for the products of East Asia. Merchant fleets from India and the Arabian peninsula sailed to the Indonesian islands to buy cloves, pepper, nutmeg, cinnamon, precious woods, and other exotic products coveted by the

CHRONOLOGY

EARLY SOUTHEAST ASIA

Chinese conquest of Vietnam	111 B.C.E.
Arrival of Burman peoples	c. seventh century
Formation of Srivijaya	c. 670
Construction of Borobudur	c. eighth century
Creation of Angkor kingdom	c. ninth century
Thai migrations into Southeast Asia	c. thirteenth century
Rise of Majapahit empire	1292
Fall of Angkor kingdom	1432

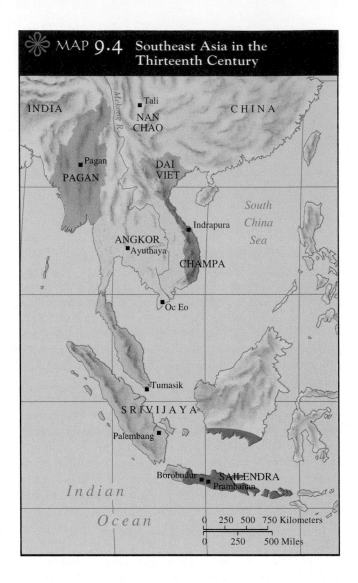

MAP 9.4 Southeast Asia in the Thirteenth Century

wealthy. In the eighth century, Srivijaya, located along the eastern coast of Sumatra, became a powerful commercial state that dominated the trade route passing through the Strait of Malacca, at that time the most convenient route from East Asia into the Indian Ocean. The rulers of Srivijaya had helped to bring the route to prominence by controlling the pirates who had previously plagued shipping in the strait. Another inducement was Srivijaya's capital at Palembang, a deepwater port where sailors could wait out the change in the monsoon season before making their return voyage. In 1025, however, Cola, one of the Dravidian kingdoms of southern India and a commercial rival of Srivijaya, inflicted a devastating defeat on the island kingdom. Although Srivijaya survived, it was unable to regain its former dominance, in part because the main trade route had shifted to the east, through the Strait of Sunda and directly out into the Indian Ocean. In the late thirteenth century, this shift in trade patterns led to the founding of a new kingdom of Majapahit on the island of Java. In the mid-fourteenth century, Majapahit succeeded in uniting most of the archipelago and perhaps even part of the Southeast Asian mainland under its rule.

Indian influence was evident in all of these societies to various degrees. Based on models from the Dravidian kingdoms of southern India, Southeast Asian kings were believed to possess special godlike qualities that set them apart from ordinary people. In some societies such as Angkor, the most prominent royal advisers constituted a *brahmin* class on the Indian model. In Pagan and Angkor, some division of the population into separate classes based on occupation and ethnic background seems to have occurred, although these divisions do not seem to have developed the rigidity of Indian castes.

India also supplied Southeast Asians with a writing system. The societies of the region had no written scripts for their spoken languages before the arrival of the Indian merchants and missionaries. Indian phonetic symbols were borrowed and used to re-cord the spoken language. Initially, Southeast Asian literature was written in the Indian Sanskrit but eventually came to be written in the local languages. Southeast Asian authors borrowed popular Indian themes, such as stories from the Buddhist scriptures and tales from the Ramayana.

A popular form of entertainment among the common people, the *wayang kulit*, or shadow play, may have come originally from India or possibly China, but it became a distinctive art form in Java and other islands of the Indonesian archipelago. In a shadow play, flat leather puppets were manipulated behind an illuminated screen while the narrator recited tales from the Indian classics. The plays were often ac-companied by gamelan, a type of music performed by an orchestra composed primarily of percus-

ANGKOR WAT. The Khmer rulers of Angkor constructed a number of remarkable temples and palaces. Devised as either Hindu or Buddhist shrines, the temples also reflected the power and sanctity of the king. This twelfth-century temple known as Angkor Wat is renowned both for its spectacular architecture and for the thousands of fine bas-reliefs relating Hindu legends and Khmer history. Most memorable are the heavenly dancing maidens and the royal processions with elephants and soldiers.

sion instruments such as gongs and drums that apparently originated in Java.

Daily Life

Because of the diversity of ethnic backgrounds, religions, and cultures, making generalizations about daily life in Southeast Asia during the early historical period is difficult. Nevertheless, it appears that Southeast Asian societies did not always apply the social distinctions that were sometimes imported from India. For example, although the local population, as elsewhere, was divided according to a variety of economic functions, the dividing lines between classes were not as rigid and imbued with religious significance as they were in the Indian subcontinent.

Still, traditional societies in Southeast Asia had some clearly hierarchical characteristics. At the top of the social ladder were the hereditary aristocrats, who monopolized both political power and economic wealth and enjoyed a borrowed aura of charisma by virtue of their proximity to the ruler. Most aristocrats lived in the major cities, which were the main source of power, wealth, and foreign influence. Beyond the major cities lived the mass of the population, composed of farmers, fishers, artisans, and merchants. In most Southeast Asian societies, the vast majority were probably rice farmers, living at a bare level of subsistence and paying heavy rents or taxes to a landlord or a local ruler.

The average Southeast Asian peasant was not actively engaged in commerce except as a consumer of various necessities. But accounts by foreign visitors indicate that in the Malay world some were involved in growing or mining products for export, such as tropical food products, precious woods, tin, and precious gems. Most of the regional trade was carried on by local merchants, who purchased products from local growers and then transported them to the major port cities. During the early state-building era, roads were few and relatively primitive, so most of the

trade was transported by small boats down rivers to the major ports along the coast. There the goods were loaded onto larger ships for delivery outside the region. Growers of export goods in areas near the coast were thus indirectly involved in the regional trade network but received few economic benefits from the relationship.

As we might expect from an area of such ethnic and cultural diversity, social structures differed significantly from country to country. In the Indianized states on the mainland, the tradition of a hereditary tribal aristocracy was probably accentuated by the Hindu practice of dividing the population into separate classes, called *varna* in imitation of the Indian model. In Angkor and Pagan, for example, the divisions were based on occupation or ethnic background. Some people were considered free subjects of the king, although there may have been legal restrictions against changing occupations. Others, however, may have been indentured to an employer. Each community was under a chieftain, who in turn was subordinated to a higher official responsible for passing on the tax revenues of each group to the central government.

In the kingdoms in the Malay peninsula and the Indonesian archipelago, social relations were generally less formal. Most of the people in the region, whether farmers, fishers, or artisans, lived in small *kampongs* (the Malay word for "village") in wooden houses built on stilts to avoid flooding during the monsoon season. Some of the farmers were probably sharecroppers who paid a part of their harvest to a landlord, who was often a member of the aristocracy. But in other areas the tradition of free farming was strong. In some cases, some of the poorer land belonged to the village as a collective unit and was assigned for use by the neediest families.

The women of Southeast Asia during this era have been described as the most fortunate in the world. Although most women worked side by side with men in the fields, as in Africa they often played an active role

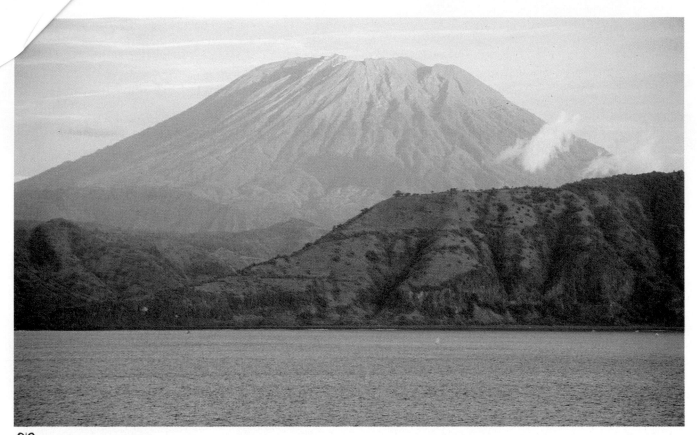

✿ MOUNT AGUNG IN BALI. In Southeast Asia as in many other cultures, mountains are considered to be the abode of the gods. This was notably the case on the island of Bali, where beautiful Mount Agung is still viewed by Hindus as the local equivalent of sacred Mt. Meru in India. In Balinese cosmology, the sea is the home of evil spirits, while humans occupy the profane world in between. An active volcano, Mount Agung erupted in 1964, killing thousands of islanders in a cloud of volcanic ash.

in trading activities. This not only led to a higher literacy rate among women than among their male counterparts, but it also allowed them more financial independence than their counterparts in China and India, a fact that was noticed by the Chinese traveler Zhou Daguan at the end of the thirteenth century: "In Cambodia it is the women who take charge of trade. For this reason a Chinese arriving in the country loses no time in getting himself a mate, for he will find her commercial instincts a great asset."[10]

Although, as elsewhere, warfare was normally part of the male domain, women sometimes played a role as bodyguards as well. According to the Zhou Daguan, women were used to protect the royal family in Angkor, as well as in kingdoms located on the islands of Java and Sumatra. While there is no evidence that such female units ever engaged in battle, they did give rise to wondrous tales of amazon warriors in the writings of foreign travelers such as the fourteenth-century Muslim adventurer Ibn Battuta.

One reason for the enhanced status of women in traditional Southeast Asia is that the nuclear family was more common than the joint family system prevalent in China and the Indian subcontinent. Throughout the region, wealth in marriage was passed from the male to the female, in contrast to the dowry system applied in China and India. In most societies, virginity was usually not a valued commodity in brokering a marriage, and divorce proceedings could be initiated by either party. Still, most marriages were monogamous, and marital fidelity was taken seriously.

The relative availability of cultivable land in the region may help explain the absence of joint families. Joint families under patriarchal leadership tend to be found in areas where land is scarce and individual families must work together to conserve resources and maximize income. With the exception of a few crowded river valleys, few areas in Southeast Asia had a high population density per acre of cultivable land. Throughout most of the area, water was plentiful, and the land was relatively fertile. In parts of Indonesia, it was possible to survive by living off the produce of wild fruit trees—bananas, coconuts, mangoes, and a variety of other tropical fruits.

World of the Spirits: Religious Belief

Indian religions also had a profound effect on Southeast Asia. Traditional religious beliefs in the region took the familiar form of spirit worship and animism that we have seen in other cultures. Southeast Asians believed that spirits dwelled in the mountains, rivers, streams, and other sacred places in their environment. Mountains were probably particularly sacred, since they were considered to be the abode of ancestral spirits, the place to which the souls of all the departed would retire after death.

When Hindu and Buddhist ideas began to penetrate the area early in the first millennium C.E., they exerted a strong appeal among local elites. Not only did the new doctrines offer a more convincing explanation of the nature of the cosmos, but they also provided local rulers with a means of enhancing their prestige and power and conferred an aura of legitimacy on their relations with their subjects. In the Javanese kingdoms and in Angkor, Hindu gods like Vishnu and Siva provided a new and more sophisticated veneer for existing beliefs in nature deities and ancestral spirits. In Angkor, the king's duties included performing sacred rituals on the mountain in the capital city; in time the ritual became a state cult uniting Hindu gods with local nature deities and ancestral spirits in a complex pantheon.

This state cult, financed by the royal court, eventually led to the construction of temples throughout the country. Many of these temples housed thousands of priests and retainers and amassed great wealth, including vast estates farmed by local peasants. It has been estimated that there were as many as 300,000 priests in Angkor at the height of its power. This vast wealth, which was often exempt from taxes, may be one explanation for the gradual decline of Angkor in the thirteenth and fourteenth centuries.

Initially, the spread of Hindu and Buddhist doctrines was essentially an elite phenomenon. Although the common people participated in the state cult and helped construct the temples, they did not give up their traditional beliefs in local deities and ancestral spirits. A major transformation began in the eleventh century, however, when Theravada Buddhism began to penetrate the kingdom of Pagan in mainland Southeast Asia from the island of Sri Lanka. From Pagan, it spread rapidly to other areas in Southeast Asia and eventually became the religion of the masses throughout the mainland west of the Annamite Mountains.

Theravada's appeal to the peoples of Southeast Asia is reminiscent of the original attraction of Buddhist thought centuries earlier on the Indian subcontinent. By teaching that individuals could seek *Nirvana* through their own actions rather than through the intercession of the ruler or a priest, Theravada was more accessible to the masses than were the state cults promoted by the rulers. During the next centuries, Theravada gradually undermined the influence of state-supported religions and became the dominant faith in several mainland societies, including Burma, Thailand, Laos, and Cambodia. In the process, however, it was gradually appropriated by local rulers, who portrayed themselves as "immanent Buddhas," higher than ordinary mortals on the scale of human existence.

Theravada did not penetrate far into the Malay peninsula or the Indonesian island chain, perhaps because it

THE BAYON AT ANGKOR. Whereas Angkor Wat was dedicated to Hindu mythology, the Bayon Temple was a Buddhist structure. In addition to its extraordinary bas-reliefs, which illuminate the everyday life of thirteenth-century Cambodia, the Bayon is known for its huge heads of the Bodhisattva of Mercy. These 172 giant heads, looking in all four cardinal directions for souls to save, are reputedly modeled after the monarch Jayavarman, whose conversion from Hinduism to Buddhism as an adult contributed to the mixture of architectural styles in the temple. The faces are mesmerizing with their haunting smiles, reflecting the mystery of enlightenment.

...ered Southeast Asia through Burma further to the ...orth. But the Malay world found its own popular alternative to state religions when Islam began to enter the area in the thirteenth and fourteenth centuries. Because Islam's expansion into Southeast Asia took place for the most part after 1500, its emergence as a major force in the region will be discussed in a later chapter.

Not surprisingly, Indian influence extended to the Buddhist and Hindu temples of Southeast Asia. Temple architecture reflecting Gupta or southern Indian styles began to appear in Southeast Asia during the first centuries C.E. Most famous is the Buddhist temple at Borobudur, in central Java. Begun in the late eighth century at the behest of a king of Sailendra (an agricultural kingdom based in eastern Java), Borobudur is a massive stupa with nine terraces. Sculpted on the sides of each terrace are bas-reliefs depicting the nine stages in the life of Siddhartha Gautama, from childhood to his final release from the chain of human existence. Surmounted by hollow bell-like towers containing representations of the Buddha and capped by a single stupa, the entire structure dominates the landscape for miles around.

Second only to Borobudur in technical excellence and even more massive in size are the ruins of the old capital city of Angkor Thom. The temple of Angkor Wat is the most famous and arguably the most beautiful of all the existing structures at Angkor Thom. Built on the model of the legendary Mount Meru (the home of the gods in Hindu tradition), it combines Indian architectural techniques with native inspiration in a structure of impressive delicacy and grace.

With its over six hundred years of existence, Angkor Thom serves as a bridge between the Hindu and Buddhist architectural styles. The last of its great temples, known as the Bayon, followed the earlier Hindu model but was topped with sculpted towers containing four-sided representations of a bodhisattva, searching, it is said, for souls to save. Shortly after the Bayon was built, Theravada Buddhist societies in Burma and Thailand began to create a new Buddhist architecture based on the concept of a massive stupa surmounted by a spire. Most famous, perhaps, is the Shwedagon Pagoda in Rangoon, Burma, which is covered with gold leaf contributed by devout Buddhists from around the country.

 THE TEMPLE OF BOROBUDUR. The colossal pyramid temple at Borobudur, on the island of Java, is one of the greatest Buddhist monuments. Constructed in the eighth century, it depicts the path to spiritual enlightenment in stone. The reliefs along the lowest walls depict the world of desire, while the higher levels represent the world of the spirit, culminating at the summit with the empty and closed stupa, signifying the state of Nirvana. Shortly after it was built, Borobudur was abandoned, as a new ruler switched his allegiance to Hinduism and ordered the erection of the Hindu temple of Prambanan nearby. Buried for a thousand years under volcanic ash and jungle, Borobudur was rediscovered in the nineteenth century and recently restored to its former splendor.

FOLLOWERS OF THE BUDDHA AT BOROBUDUR.   Although the primary purpose of the stone carvings on the walls of the temple at Borobudur was to transmit the life of the Buddha, to modern viewers they are an important source of information about life in early Southeast Asia. Intricate bas-relief sculptures decorating the lower levels of the temple reveal the customs and costumes of eighth-century Java. Here followers of Siddhartha Gautama seek enlightenment under the Bodhi tree.

CONCLUSION

During the more than 1,500 years from the fall of the Mauryas to the rise of the Mughals, Indian civilization faced a number of severe challenges. One challenge was primarily external in nature and took the form of a continuous threat from beyond the mountains in the northwest. A second was generated by internal causes and stemmed from the tradition of factionalism and internal rivalry that had marked relations within the aristocracy since the Aryan invasion in the second millennium B.C.E. (see Chapter 2). Despite the abortive efforts of the Guptas, that tradition continued almost without interruption down to the founding of the Mughal Empire in the sixteenth century.

The third challenge was primarily cultural and appeared in the religious divisions between Hindus and Buddhists, and later between Hindus and Muslims, that took place throughout much of this period. It is a measure of the

strength and resilience of Hindu tradition that it was able to surmount the challenge of Buddhism and by the late first millennium C.E. had managed to reassert its dominant position in Indian society. But that triumph was short-lived. One result of the foreign conquest of northern India was the introduction of Islam into the region. As we shall see later, the new religion was about to become a serious rival to traditional beliefs among the Indian people.

During the same period that Indian civilization faced these challenges at home, it was having a profound impact on the emerging states of Southeast Asia. Situated at the crossroads between two oceans and two great civilizations, Southeast Asia has long served as a bridge linking peoples and cultures, and as complex societies began to develop in the area, it is not surprising that they were strongly influenced by the older civilizations of neighboring China and India. At the same time, the Southeast Asian peoples put their own unique stamp on the ideas that they adopted and eventually rejected those that were inappropriate to local conditions.

The result was a region characterized by an almost unparalleled cultural richness and diversity, reflecting influences from as far away as the Middle East, yet preserving indigenous elements that were deeply rooted in the local culture. Unfortunately, that very diversity posed potential problems for the peoples of Southeast Asia as they faced a new challenge from beyond the horizon. We shall deal with that challenge when we return to the region in a later chapter. In the meantime, we must turn our attention to the other major civilization that spread its shadow over the societies of southern Asia—that of China.

Timeline: 100 B.C.E. — 100 C.E. — 300 C.E. — 500 C.E. — 700 C.E. — 900 C.E. — 1100 C.E. — 1300 C.E.

Kushan kingdom; Gupta dynasty; Reign of Mahmud of Ghazni; Invasion of Tamerlane; Chinese conquest of Vietnam; Rise of Srivijaya; Beginning of Indian influence on Southeast Asia; Islamic traders arrive in Southeast Asia; Fa Xian arrives in India; Temple of Borobudur; Building of Angkor Wat; Decline of Buddhism in India

CHAPTER NOTES

1. Hiuen Tsiang, *Si-Yu-Ki: Buddhist Records of the Western World*, trans. Samuel Beal (London, n.d.), pp. 89–90.
2. Fo-Kwo-Ki (Travels of Fa Xian), in ibid., Chapter 20, xliii.
3. E. C. Sachau, *Alberoni's India* (London, 1914), 1:22, quoted in S. M. Ikram, *Muslim Civilization in India* (New York, 1964), pp. 31–32.
4. Ibid., p. 68.
5. Hieun Tsiang, *Si-Yu-Ki*, pp. 73–74.
6. Duarte Barbosa, *The Book of Duarte Barbosa* (Nedeln, Lichtenstein, 1967), pp. 147–48.
7. Quoted in Richard Lannoy, *The Speaking Tree: A Study of Indian Culture and Society* (London, 1971), p. 232.
8. S. Tharu and K. Lalita, *Women Writing in India*, vol. I (New York, 1991), p. 77.
9. Cited in A. L. Basham, *The Wonder That Was India* (London, 1954), p. 426.
10. S. Hughes and B. Hughes, *Women in World History*, vol. I (Armonk, N.Y., 1995), p. 217.

SUGGESTED READINGS

The period from the decline of the Mauryas to the rise of the Mughals in India is not especially rich in terms of materials in English. Still, a number of the standard texts on Indian history contain useful sections on the period. Particularly good are A. L. Basham, *The Wonder That Was India* (London, 1954), and S. Wolpert, *New History of India* (New York, 1989).

A number of studies of Indian society and culture deal with this period. See, for example, R. Lannoy, *The Speaking Tree* (Oxford, 1971) for a sophisticated interpretation of Indian culture during the medieval period. On Buddhism, see H. Nakamura, *Indian Buddhism: A Survey with Bibliographical Notes* (Delhi, 1987), and H. Akira, *A History of Indian Buddhism from Sakyamuni to Early Mahayana* (Hawaii, 1990). For an interesting treatment of the Buddhist influence on commercial activities that is reminiscent of the role of Christianity in Europe, see L. Xinru, *Ancient India and Ancient China: Trade and Religious Changes A.D. 1–600* (Delhi, 1988).

For a discussion of women's issues, see S. Hughes and B. Hughes, *Women in World History*, vol. I (Armonk, N.Y., 1995); S. Tharu and K. Lalita, *Women Writing in India*, vol. I (New York, 1991); and V. Dehejia, *Devi: The Great Goddess* (Washington, D.C., 1999).

The most up-to-date treatment of the Indian economy and, in particular, the regional trade throughout the Indian Ocean is K. N. Chaudhuri, *Trade and Civilization in the Indian Ocean: An Economic History from the Rise of Islam to 1750* (Cambridge, 1985), a groundbreaking comparative study. See also his more recent and massive *Asia Before Europe: Economy and Civilization of the Indian Ocean from the Rise of Islam to 1750* (Cambridge, 1990), which owes a considerable debt to F. Braudel's classical work on the Mediterranean Sea.

The Islamic period in Indian history is treated in S. M. Ikram, *Muslim Civilization in India* (New York, 1964), and C. E. Bosworth, *The Later Ghaznavids: Splendour and Decay* (New York, 1977). On the career of Tamerlane, see B. F. Manz, *The Rise and Rule of Tamerlane* (Cambridge, 1989).

For Indian art during the medieval period, see S. Huntington, *The Art of Ancient India: Buddhist, Hindu and Jain* (New York, 1985), and V. Dehejia, *Indian Art* (London, 1997).

For a brief introduction to Indian literature, see A. L. Basham, *A Cultural History of India* (Oxford, 1975). See also E. C. Dimock, *The Literature of India: An Introduction* (Chicago, 1974), and A. K. Warder, *Indian Kavya Literature*, 5 vols. (Delhi, 1972–1988). For Kalidasa, consult B. S. Miller, ed., *Theater of Memory: The Plays of Kalidasa* (New York, 1984).

The early history of Southeast Asia is not as well documented as that of China or India. Except for Vietnam, where histories written in Chinese appeared shortly after the Chinese conquest, written materials on societies in the region are relatively sparse. Historians have therefore been compelled to rely on stone inscriptions and the accounts of travelers and historians from other countries. Still, a number of us   m are now dated in the light of recent information but still provide a useful overview. The most detailed is D. G. E. Hall, *A History of South-east Asia* (New York, 1966). See also J. F. Cady, *Southeast Asia: Its Historical Development* (New York, 1964). For a more recent account, see D. R. SarDesai, *Southeast Asia: Past and Present* (Boulder, Colo., 1989). For a useful survey of the ethnographic background, see R. Provencher, *Mainland Southeast Asia: An Anthropological Perspective* (Pacific Palisades, Calif., 1975). R. Burling, *Hill Farms and Padi Fields: Life in Mainland Southeast Asia* (Englewood Cliffs, N.J., 1965) provides a short discussion of the dynamic forces that have shaped the mainland societies in the region. See also P. Wheatley, *The Golden Khersonese: Studies in the Historical Geography of the Malay Peninsula Before* A.D. *1500* (Kuala Lumpur, 1961).

Working with limited resources, modern scholars are bringing out some fascinating interpretations of the early history of the region. An extensive analysis of the "Indianized" states of mainland Southeast Asia is available in G. Coedes, *The Making of Southeast Asia* (Berkeley, Calif., 1966). More recently, some scholars have tended to emphasize the role of indigenous forces in the evolution of the region. See, for example, O. W. Wolters, *Early Indonesian Commerce: A Study of the Origins of Sri Vijaya* (Ithaca, N.Y., 1967), and *The Fall of Srivijaya in Malay History* (Ithaca, N.Y., 1970).

The role of commerce has recently been highlighted as a key aspect in the development of the region. For two fascinating accounts, see K. R. Hall, *Maritime Trade and State Development in Early Southeast Asia* (Honolulu, 1985), and A. Reid, *Southeast Asia in the Era of Commerce, 1450–1680: The Lands Below the Winds* (New Haven, Conn., 1989). The latter is also quite useful on the role of women.

The nature of kingship has attracted attention from scholars in recent years. K. R. Hall and J. K. Whitmore, eds., *Explorations in Early Southeast Asian History: The Origins of Southeast Asian Statecraft* (Ann Arbor, Mich., 1976), and L. Gesick, ed., *Centers, Symbols, and Hierarchies: Essays on the Classical States of Southeast Asia* (New Haven, Conn., 1983) provide interesting essays on the subject. See also L. Castles and A. Reid, eds., *Pre-Colonial State Systems in Southeast Asia* (Kuala Lumpur, 1975).

INFOTRAC COLLEGE EDITION

For additional reading, go to InfoTrac College Edition, your online research library at http://web1.infotrac-college.com

Enter the search terms "India history" using Keywords.

Enter the search term "Hinduism" using the Subject Guide.

Enter the search term "Buddhism" using the Subject Guide.

Enter the search term "Tamerlane" using Keywords.

CHAPTER
10

O n his first visit to the city, the traveler was mightily impressed. Its streets were so straight and wide that he could see through the city from one end to the other. Along the wide boulevards were beautiful palaces and inns in great profusion. The city was laid out in squares "like a chessboard," and within each square were spacious courts and gardens. Truly, said the visitor, this must be one of the largest and wealthiest cities on earth—a city so splendid that "it is impossible to give a description that should do it justice."[1]

The visitor was Marco Polo, and the city was Khanbaliq (later known as Beijing), capital of the Yuan dynasty (1279–1368) and one of the great commercial centers of the Chinese Empire. Marco Polo was an Italian merchant who had traveled to China in the late thirteenth century and then served as an official at the court of Khubilai Khan. His diary, published after his return to Italy almost twenty years later, astonished readers with tales of this magnificent but unknown civilization far to the east.

When Marco Polo arrived, China was ruled by the Mongols, a nomadic people from Central Asia who had overthrown the Song (Sung) dynasty and assumed control of the Chinese Empire. The Yuan dynasty, as the Mongol rulers were called, was only one of a succession of dynasties to rule China after the collapse of the Han dynasty in the third century C.E. The end of the Han had led to a period of internal division and civil war that lasted nearly four hundred years and was aggravated by the threat posed by nomadic peoples from the north. This time of troubles ended in the early seventh century C.E., however, when the dynamic Tang dynasty led China to some of its finest achievements.

To this point, Chinese history appeared to be following a pattern similar to that of India. There, as we have seen, the passing of the Mauryan dynasty in the second century B.C.E. unleashed a period of internal division that lasted for several hundred years. Although the Guptas were able to revive the magnificence of India's first golden age, their glorious era soon flickered and died, and it was not until the rise of the Mughal Empire in the early sixteenth century that unity returned to the subcontinent.

But China did not recapitulate the Indian experience. The Tang dynasty collapsed in 907, but after a brief interregnum, China was reunified under the Song, who ruled most of China for nearly three hundred years. The Song in turn were overthrown by the Mongols in the late thirteenth century, and they in turn gave way to a powerful new native dynasty, the Ming, in 1368. Dynasty followed dynasty, with periods of extraordinary cultural achievement alternating with periods of internal disorder, but in general Chinese society continued to build on the political and cultural foundations of the Zhou and the Han.

Chinese historians, viewing this vast process as it evolved over time, began to hypothesize that Chinese history was cyclical in nature, driven by the dynamic interplay of the forces of good and evil, *yang* and *yin*, growth and decay. Beyond the forces of conflict and change lay the essential continuity of Chinese history, based on the timeless principles established by Confucius and other thinkers during the Zhou dynasty in antiquity. If India often appeared to be a politically and culturally diverse entity, only sporadically knit together by ambitious rulers, China, at least in the eyes of its historians, was a coherent civilization struggling to relive the glories of its ancient golden age while contending against the divisive forces of *yin* and *yang* operating throughout the cosmos. In actuality, this picture of a succession of dynasties each seeking to replicate the glories of China's golden age under the early Zhou dynasty disguises the reality that under the surface Chinese society was undergoing significant changes and bore scant resemblance to the kingdom that had been founded by the house of Zhou more than twenty centuries earlier. ❀

CHINA AFTER THE HAN

After the collapse of the Han dynasty at the beginning of the third century C.E., China fell into an extended period of division and civil war. Taking advantage of the absence of organized government in China, nomadic forces from the Gobi Desert penetrated south of the Great Wall and established their own rule over northern China. In the Yangtze valley and further to the south, native Chinese rule was maintained, but constant civil war and instability led later historians to refer to the period as the "era of the six dynasties." 六朝時代

The decline and fall of the Han Empire had a marked effect on the Chinese psyche. The Confucian principles that emphasized hard work, the subordination of the individual to community interests, and belief in the essentially rational order of the universe came under severe challenge, and many Chinese began to turn to more messianic creeds that emphasized the supernatural or the promise of earthly or heavenly salvation. Intellectuals began to reject the stuffy moralism and complacency of State Confucianism and sought emotional satisfaction in hedonistic pursuits or philosophical Daoism (see the box on p. 269).

Eccentric behavior and a preference for philosophical Daoism became a common response to a corrupt age. A group of writers known as the "seven sages of the bamboo forest" exemplified the period. Among the best known

🏵 **THE BUDDHIST PILGRIM XUAN ZANG.** Although the first recorded Buddhist pilgrimage from China across Central Asia to India was that of Fa Xian in 399 C.E., the seventh century was the golden age of these religious pilgrimages. The most famous was that of Xuan Zang, whose sixteen-year journey was recorded by a disciple: "Alone and abandoned he traversed the sandy waste . . . following the heaps of bones and horse-dung." Here Xuan Zang holds a fly whisk in his left hand to drive away demons, while in his right he brandishes the khakkhara, a symbol of the Buddhist monk. With sacred texts on his back and a hat against the desert sun, Xuan Zang proceeds on his pilgrimage protected by the image of the Lord Buddha.

was the poet Liu Ling, whose odd behavior is described in this oft-quoted passage:

> Liu Ling was an inveterate drinker and indulged himself to the full. Sometimes he stripped off his clothes and sat in his room stark naked. Some men saw him and rebuked him. Liu Ling said, "Heaven and earth are my dwelling, and my house is my trousers. Why are you all coming into my trousers?"[2]

But neither popular beliefs in the supernatural nor philosophical Daoism could satisfy deeper emotional needs or provide solace in time of sorrow or the hope of a better life in the hereafter. Instead, Buddhism filled that gap.

Buddhism was brought to China in the first or second century C.E., probably by missionaries and merchants traveling over the Silk Road. The concept of rebirth was probably unfamiliar to most Chinese, and the intellectual hairsplitting that often accompanied discussion of Buddha's message in India was somewhat too esoteric for the Chinese taste. Still, in the difficult years surrounding the decline of the Han dynasty, Buddhist ideas, especially those of the Mahayana school, began to find adherents among intellectuals and ordinary people alike. As Buddhism increased in popularity, it was frequently attacked by supporters of Confucianism and Daoism for its foreign origins. Some even claimed that Gautama Buddha had been a disciple of Lao Tzu. But such sniping did not halt the progress of Buddhism, and eventually the new faith was assimilated into Chinese culture, assisted by the efforts of such tireless advocates as the missionaries Fa Xian and Xuan Zang and the support of ruling elites in both northern and southern China (see The Rise and Decline of Buddhism and Daoism later in this chapter).

🏵 CHINA REUNIFIED: THE SUI, THE TANG, AND THE SONG

After nearly four centuries of internal division, China was unified once again in 581 when Yang Jian (Yang Chien), a member of a respected aristocratic family in northern China, founded a new dynasty, known as the Sui (581–618 C.E.). Yang Jian (who is also known by his reign title of Sui Wendi, or Sui Wen Ti) established his capital at the historic metropolis of Chang'an and began to extend his authority throughout the heartland of China.

Like his predecessors, the new emperor sought to create a unifying ideology for the state to enhance its efficiency. But where Liu Bang, the founder of the Han dynasty, had adopted Confucianism as the official doctrine to hold the empire together, Yang Jian turned to Daoism and Buddhism. He founded monasteries for both doctrines in the capital and appointed Buddhist monks to key positions as political advisers.

A DAOIST CRITIQUE OF CONFUCIANISM

This document is a biting Daoist attack on the type of pompous and hypocritical Confucian "gentleman" who feigned high moral principles while secretly engaging in corrupt and licentious behavior. It was written during the chaotic period following the collapse of the Han dynasty, in the third century C.E.

THE BIOGRAPHY OF A GREAT MAN

What the world calls a gentleman [chun-tzu] is someone who is solely concerned with moral law [fa], and cultivates exclusively the rules of propriety [li]. His hand holds the emblem of jade [authority]; his foot follows the straight line of the rule. He likes to think that his actions set a permanent example; he likes to think that his words are everlasting models. In his youth, he has a reputation in the villages of his locality; in his later years, he is well known in the neighboring districts. Upward, he aspires to the dignity of the Three Dukes; downward, he does not disdain the post of governor of the nine provinces.

Have you ever seen the lice that inhabit a pair of trousers? They jump into the depths of the seams, hiding themselves in the cotton wadding, and believe they have a pleasant place to live. Walking, they do not risk going beyond the edge of the seam; moving, they are careful not to emerge from the trouser leg; and they think they have kept to the rules of etiquette. But when the trousers are ironed, the flames invade the hills, the fire spreads, the villages are set on fire and the towns burned down; then the lice that inhabit the trousers cannot escape.

What difference is there between the gentleman who lives within a narrow world and the lice that inhabit trouser legs?

Yang Jian was a builder as well as a conqueror, ordering the construction of a new canal from the capital to the confluence of the Wei and the Yellow Rivers nearly one hundred miles to the east. His son, the emperor Sui Yangdi (Sui Yang Ti), continued the process, and the 1,400-mile-long Grand Canal, linking the two great rivers of China, the Yellow and the Yangtze, was completed during his reign. The new canal facilitated the shipment of grain and other commodities from the rice-rich southern provinces to the densely populated north. The canal also served other purposes, such as speeding communications between the two regions and permitting the rapid dispatch of troops to troubled provinces. Sui Yangdi also used the canal as an imperial highway for inspecting his empire. One imperial procession from the capital to the central Yangtze region was described as follows:

> The emperor caused to be built dragon boats, . . . red battle cruisers, multi-decked transports, lesser vessels of bamboo slats. Boatmen hired from all the waterways . . . pulled the vessels by ropes of green silk on the imperial progress to Chiang-tu [Yangzhou]. The Emperor rode in the dragon boat, and civil and military officials of the fifth grade and above rode in the multi-decked transports; those of the ninth grade and above were given the vessels of yellow bamboo. The boats followed one another poop to prow for more than 200 leagues [about 65 miles]. The prefectures and counties through which they passed were ordered to prepare to offer provisions. Those who made bountiful arrangements were given an additional office or title; those who fell short were given punishments up to the death penalty.[3]

Despite such efforts to project the majesty of the imperial personage, the Sui dynasty came to an end immediately after Sui Yangdi's death. The Sui emperor was a tyrannical ruler, and his expensive military campaigns aroused widespread unrest. After his return from a failed campaign against Korea in 618, the emperor was murdered in his palace. One of his generals, Li Yuan, took advantage of the instability that ensued and declared the foundation of a new dynasty, known as the Tang (T'ang). Building on the successes of its predecessor, the Tang lasted for three hundred years, until 907.

Li Yuan ruled for a brief period and then was elbowed aside by his son, Li Shimin (Li Shih-min), who assumed the reign title Tang Taizong (T'ang T'ai-tsung). Under his vigorous leadership, the Tang launched a program of internal renewal and external expansion that would make it one of the greatest dynasties in the long history of China. Under the Tang, the northwest was pacified and given the name of Xinjiang, or "new region." A long conflict with Tibet led for the first time to the extension of Chinese control over the vast and desolate plateau north of the Himalaya Mountains. The southern provinces below the Yangtze were fully assimilated into the Chinese Empire, and the imperial court established commercial and diplomatic relations with the states of Southeast Asia. With reason, China now claimed to be the foremost power in East Asia, and the emperor demanded fealty and tribute from all his fellow rulers beyond the frontier. Korea accepted tribute status and attempted to adopt the Chinese model, and the Japanese dispatched official missions to China to learn more about its customs and institutions (see Chapter 11).

Finally, the Tang dynasty witnessed a flowering of Chinese culture. Many modern observers feel that the era represents the apogee of Chinese creativity in poetry and sculpture. One reason for this explosion of culture was the influence of Buddhism, which affected art, literature, and philosophy, as well as religion and politics. Monasteries

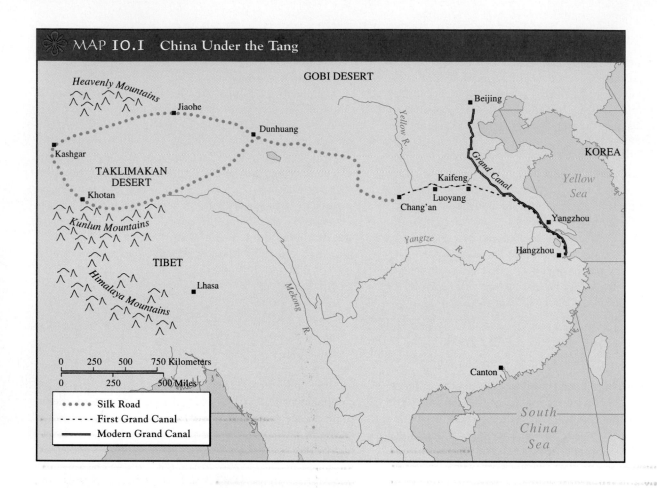

MAP IO.I   China Under the Tang

GOBI DESERT

Heavenly Mountains

Jiaohe

Dunhuang

Beijing

Yellow R.

KOREA

Kashgar

TAKLIMAKAN
DESERT

Kaifeng

Grand Canal

Luoyang

Chang'an

Yellow
Sea

Khotan

Kunlun Mountains

Yangzhou

TIBET

Yangtze R.

Hangzhou

Himalaya Mountains

Lhasa

Mekong R.

| 0 | 250 | 500 | 750 Kilometers |
| 0 | 250 | | 500 Miles |

••••• Silk Road
----- First Grand Canal
——— Modern Grand Canal

Canton

*South
China
Sea*

**MAP IO.2   Chang'an Under the Sui
and the Tang**

Forbidden Park

Palace
City

Imperial
City

Outer City

| 0 | 2 | 4 | 6 Kilometers |
| 0 | 2 | | 4 Miles |

sprang up throughout China, and (as under the Sui) Buddhist monks served as advisers at the Tang imperial court. The city of Chang'an, now restored to the glory it had known as the capital of the Han dynasty, once again became the seat of the empire. It was possibly the greatest city in the world of its time, with an estimated population of nearly two million. The city was filled with temples and palaces, and its markets teemed with goods from all over the known world (see the box on p. 271).

But the Tang, like the Han, sowed the seeds of their own destruction. Tang rulers could not prevent the rise of internal forces that would ultimately weaken the dynasty and bring it to an end. Two ubiquitous problems were court intrigues and official corruption. Xuanzong (Hsuan Tsung, who reigned from 712 to 756), one of the great Tang emperors and a renowned patron of the arts, was dominated in later life by one of his favorite concubines, the beautiful Yang Guifei (Yang Kuei-fei). One of her protégés launched a rebellion in 755 and briefly seized power in the capital of Chang'an. The revolt was eventually suppressed, and Yang Guifei, who is viewed as one of the great villains of Chinese history, was put to death. But the Tang never fully recovered from the catastrophe. The loss of power by the central government led to increased influence by great landed families inside China and chronic instability along

THE GOOD LIFE IN THE HIGH TANG

A t the height of the Tang dynasty, China was at the apex of its power and magnificence. Here the Tang poet Du Fu describes a gala festival in the capital of Chang'an (Ch'ang-an) attended by the favored elite. The author's distaste for the spectacle of arrogance and waste is expressed in muted sarcasm.

DU FU, A POEM

Third day of the third month
The very air seems new
In Ch'ang-an along the water
Many beautiful girls . . .
Firm, plump contours,
Flesh and bone proportioned.
Dresses of gauze brocade
Mirror the end of spring
Peacocks crimped in thread of gold
Unicorns in silver. . . .
Some are kin to the imperial favorite
Among them the Lady of Kuo and the Lady of Ch'in [Qin].
Camel-humps of purple meat
Brought in shining pans

The white meat of raw fish
Served on crystal platters
Don't tempt the sated palate.
All that is cut with fancy and
Prepared with care—left untouched.
Eunuchs, reins a-flying
Disturb no dust
Bring the "eight chef d'oeuvres"
From the palace kitchens.
Music of strings and pipes . . .
Accompanying the feasting
Moving the many guests
All of rank and importance.
Last comes a horseman
See him haughtily
Dismount near the screen
And step on the flowery carpet. . . .
The chancellor is so powerful
His mere touch will scorch
Watch you don't come near
Lest you displease him.

the northern and western frontiers, where local military commanders ruled virtually without central government interference. It was an eerie repetition of the final decades of the Han.

The end finally came in the early tenth century, when border troubles with northern nomadic peoples increased, leading to the final collapse of the dynasty in 907. The Tang had followed the classic strategy of "using a barbarian to oppose a barbarian" by allying with a new nomadic people called the Uighurs (a Turkic-speaking people whose descendants continue to live throughout Central Asia) against their old rivals. But yet another nomadic people called the Kirghiz defeated the Uighurs and then turned on the Tang government in its moment of weakness and overthrew it.

For two generations, China slipped once again into chaos. This time, the period of foreign invasion and division was much shorter. In 960 a new dynasty, known as the Song (960–1279), rose to power. From the start, however, the Song (Sung) rulers encountered more problems than their predecessors. Although the founding emperor Song Taizu (Sung T'ai-tsu) was able to co-opt many of the powerful military commanders whose rivalry had brought the Tang dynasty to an end, he was unable to reconquer the northwestern part of the country from the nomadic Khitan peoples. The emperor therefore established his capital further to the east, at Kaifeng, where the Grand Canal

intersected the Yellow River. Later, when pressures from the nomads in the north increased, the court was forced to move the capital even further south, to Hangzhou (Hangchow), on the coast just south of the Yangtze River delta; the emperors who ruled from Hangzhou are known as the southern Song. The Song also lost control over Tibet. Despite its political and military weaknesses, the dynasty nevertheless ruled during a period of economic expansion, prosperity, and cultural achievement and is therefore considered among the more successful Chinese dynasties.

Yet the Song dynasty was never able to surmount the external challenge from the north, and that failure eventually brought about the end of the dynasty. During its final decades, the Song rulers were forced to pay tribute to the Jurchen peoples from Manchuria. In the early thirteenth century, the Song, ignoring precedent and the fate of the Tang, formed an alliance with the Mongols, a new and obscure nomadic people from the Gobi Desert. As under the Tang, the decision proved to be a disaster. Within a few years, the Mongols had become a much more serious threat to China than the Jurchen. After defeating the Jurchen, the Mongols turned their attention to the Song, advancing on Song territory from both the north and the west. By this time, the Song empire had been weakened by internal factionalism and a loss of tax revenue to wealthy families. After a series of river battles and sieges marked by the use of catapults and gunpowder, the Song were defeated, and the conquerors announced the creation of a new Yuan (Mongol) dynasty. Ironically, the Mongols had first learned about gunpowder from the Chinese (see Explosion in Central Asia: The Mongol Empire later in this chapter).

Political Structures: The Triumph of Confucianism

During the nearly seven hundred years from the Sui to the end of the Song, a mature political system based on principles originally established during the Qin and Han dynasties gradually emerged in China. After the Tang dynasty's brief flirtation with Buddhism, State Confucianism became the ideological cement that held the system together. The development of this system took several centuries, and it did not reach its height until the period of the Song dynasty.

EQUAL OPPORTUNITY IN CHINA: THE CIVIL SERVICE EXAMINATION

At the apex of the government hierarchy was a Grand Council, assisted by a secretariat and a chancellery; it included representatives from all three authorities—civil, military, and censorate. Under the Grand Council was a

❀ **THE GRAND CANAL.** Built over centuries, the Grand Canal is one of the wonders of China and a crucial conduit for carrying goods between northern and southern China. After the Song dynasty, when the region south of the Yangtze River became the heartland of the empire, the canal was used to carry rice and other agricultural products to the food-starved northern provinces. Many of the towns and cities located along the canal became famous for their wealth and cultural achievements. Among the most renowned was Suzhou, a center for silk manufacture, which is sometimes described as the "Venice of China" because of its many canals. Shown here is a classical example of a humpback bridge, crossing an arm of the canal in downtown Suzhou.

CHRONOLOGY
MEDIEVAL CHINA

Arrival of Buddhism in China	c. first century C.E.
Fall of the Han dynasty	220 C.E.
Sui dynasty	581–618
Tang dynasty	618–907
Li Bo and Du Fu	700s
Emperor Xuanzong	712–756
Song dynasty	960–1279
Wang Anshi	1021–1086
Southern Song dynasty	1127–1279
Mongol conquest of China	1279
Reign of Khubilai Khan	1260–1294
Fall of the Yuan dynasty	1368
Ming dynasty	1369–1644

Department of State Affairs composed of six ministries responsible for justice, military affairs, personnel, public works, revenue, and rites (ritual). This department was in effect the equivalent of a modern cabinet.

The Tang dynasty revived the practice of selecting bureaucrats through civil service examinations but was unable to curb the influence of the great aristocratic clans. The Song were more successful at limiting aristocratic control over the bureaucracy, in part because the power of the nobility had been irreparably weakened during the final years of the Tang dynasty and did not recover during the interregnum that followed its collapse.

One way of strengthening the power of the central administration was to make the civil service examination system into the primary route to an official career. To reduce the power of the noble families, relatives of individuals serving in the imperial court, as well as eunuchs, were prohibited from taking the examinations. But if the Song rulers' objective was to make the bureaucracy more subservient to the court, they may have been disappointed. The rising professionalism of the bureaucracy provided it with an esprit de corps and an influence that sometimes enabled it to resist the whims of individual emperors.

Under the Song, the examination system attained the form that it would retain in later centuries. In general, three levels of examinations were administered. The first was a qualifying examination given annually at the provincial capital. Candidates who succeeded in this first stage were considered qualified but normally were not given positions in the bureaucracy except at the local level. Many stopped at this level and accepted positions as village teachers to train other candidates. Candidates who wished to go on could take a second examination given at the provincial capital every three years. Successful candidates could apply for an official position. Some went on to take the final examination, which was given in the imperial capital, including a session at the imperial palace, once every three years. Those who passed were eligible for high positions in the central bureaucracy or for appointments as district magistrates.

During the early Tang the examinations included questions on Buddhist and Daoist as well as Confucian texts, but by Song times examinations were based entirely on the Confucian classics. Candidates were expected to memorize passages and to be able to define the moral lessons they contained. The system guaranteed that successful candidates—and therefore officials—would have received a full dose of Confucian political and social ethics. Whether they followed those ethics, of course, was another matter. Many students complained about the rigors of memorization and the irrelevance of the process. Others brought crib notes into the examination hall (one enterprising candidate concealed an entire Confucian text in the lining of his cloak). One famous Tang scholar complained that if Mencius and other Confucian worthies had lived in his own day, they would have refused to sit for the examinations.

The Song authorities ignored such criticisms, but they did open the system to more people by allowing all males except criminals or members of certain restricted occupations to take the examinations. To provide potential candidates with schooling, training academies were set up at the provincial and district level. Without such academies, only individuals fortunate enough to receive training in the classics in family-run schools would have had the expertise to pass the examinations. Such policies represented a considerable improvement over earlier times, when most candidates came from the ranks of the elite. According to one historian, more than half of the successful candidates during the mid-Song period came from families that had not previously had a successful candidate for at least three generations. In time, the majority of candidates came from the landed gentry, nonaristocratic landowners who controlled much of the wealth in the countryside. Because the gentry prized education and became the primary upholders of the Confucian tradition, they were often called the scholar-gentry.

But certain aspects of the system still prevented it from truly providing equal opportunity to all. In the first place, only males were eligible. Then again, the Song did not attempt to establish a system of universal elementary education. In practice, only those who had been given a basic education in the classics at home were able to enter the state-run academies and compete for a position in the bureaucracy. The poor had little chance.

Despite such weaknesses, the civil service examination system was an impressive achievement for its day and probably provided a more efficient government and more opportunity for upward mobility than were found in any other civilization of its time. Most Western governments, for example, only began to recruit officials on the basis of merit in the nineteenth century. Furthermore, by regulating the content of the examinations, the system helped provide China with a cultural uniformity lacking in empires elsewhere in Asia.

Nor could the system guarantee an honest, efficient bureaucracy. Official arrogance, bureaucratic infighting, corruption, and legalistic interpretations of government regulations were as prevalent in medieval China as in bureaucracies the world over. Another problem was that officials were expected to use their positions to help their relatives. As we observed earlier, even Confucius held that filial duty transcends loyalty to the community. What is nepotism in Western eyes was simply proper behavior in China. Chinese rulers attempted to circumvent this problem by assigning officials outside their home region, but this policy met with only limited success.

The court also attempted to curb official misbehavior through the censorate. These specially trained officials were assigned to investigate possible cases of official wrongdoing and report directly to the court. The censorate was supposed to be independent of outside pressures to ensure that its members would feel free to report wrongdoing wherever it occurred. In practice, censors who displeased high court officials were often removed or even subjected to more serious forms of punishment, which reduced the effectiveness of the system.

LOCAL GOVERNMENT

The Song dynasty maintained the local government institutions that it had inherited from its predecessors. At the base of the government pyramid was the district (or county), governed by a magistrate. The magistrate, assisted by his staff, was responsible for maintaining law and order and collecting taxes within his jurisdiction. A district could exceed 100,000 people. Below the district was the basic unit of Chinese government, the village. Because villages were so numerous in China, the central government did not appoint an official at that level and allowed the villages to administer themselves. Village government was normally in the hands of a village council of elders, usually assisted by a village chief. The council, usually made up of the heads of influential families in the village, maintained the local irrigation and transportation network, adjudicated local disputes, organized and maintained a militia, and assisted in collecting taxes and delivering them to the district magistrate.

As a rule, most Chinese had little involvement with government matters. When they had to deal with the government, they almost always turned to their village officials. Although the district magistrate was empowered to settle local civil disputes, most villagers preferred to resolve the problem among themselves. It was expected that the magistrate and his staff would supplement their income by charging for such services, a practice that reduced the costs of the central government but also provided an opportunity for bribes, a problem that plagued the Chinese bureaucracy down to modern times.

Economy and Society

During the long period between the Sui and the Song, the Chinese economy, like the government, grew considerably in size and complexity. China was still an agricultural society, but major changes were taking place within the economy and the social structure. The urban sector of the economy was becoming increasingly important, new social classes were beginning to appear, and the economic focus of the empire was beginning to shift from the Yellow River valley in the north to the Yangtze River valley in the center—a process that was encouraged both by the expansion of cultivation in the Yangtze delta and by the control exerted over the north by nomadic peoples during the Song.

The economic revival began shortly after the rise of the Tang. During the long period of internal division, land had become concentrated in the hands of aristocratic families, while most peasants were reduced to serfdom or slavery. The early Tang tried to reduce the power of the landed nobility and maximize tax revenue by adopting the ancient "equal field" system, in which land was allocated to farmers for life in return for an annual tax payment and three weeks of conscript labor.

At first the new system was vigorously enforced and led to increased rural prosperity and government revenue. But eventually the rich and the politically influential learned to manipulate the system for their own benefit and accumulated huge tracts of land. The growing population, caused by a rise in food production and the extended period of social stability, also put steady pressure on the system. Finally, the government abandoned the effort to equalize landholdings and returned the land to private hands, while attempting to prevent inequalities through the tax system. The failure to resolve the land problem contributed to the decline and fall of the Tang dynasty in the early tenth century.

The Song tried to resolve the land problem by returning to the successful programs of the early Tang and reducing the power of the wealthy landed aristocrats. During the late eleventh century, the reformist official Wang Anshi (Wang An-shih) attempted to limit the size of landholdings through progressive land taxes and provided cheap credit to poor peasants to help them avoid bankruptcy. His reforms met with some success, but other developments probably contributed more to the general agricultural prosperity under the Song. These included the opening of new lands in the Yangtze River valley, improve-

ments in irrigation techniques such as the chain pump (a circular chain of square pallets on a treadmill that enabled farmers to lift considerable amounts of water or mud to a higher level), and the introduction of a new strain of quick-growing rice from Southeast Asia, which permitted farmers in warmer regions to plant and harvest two crops each year.

Major changes also took place in the Chinese urban economy, which witnessed a significant increase in trade and manufacturing. This process began under the Tang dynasty, but it was not entirely a product of deliberate state policy. In fact, early Tang rulers shared some of the traditional prejudice against commercial activities that had been prevalent under the Han and enacted a number of regulations that restricted trade. As under the Han, the state maintained monopolies over key commodities such as salt.

Despite the restrictive policies of the state, the urban sector grew steadily larger and more complex, helped by several new technological developments. During the Tang, the Chinese mastered the art of manufacturing steel by mixing cast iron and wrought iron. The blast furnace was heated to a high temperature by burning coal, which had been used as a fuel in China from about the fourth century C.E. The resulting product was used in the manufacture of swords, sickles, and even suits of armor. By the eleventh century, more than 35,000 tons of steel were being produced annually. The introduction of cotton offered new opportunities in textile manufacturing. Gunpowder was invented by the Chinese during the Tang dynasty and used primarily for explosives and a primitive form of flamethrower; it reached the West via the Arabs in the twelfth century.

OCEAN TRADE AND THE SILK ROAD

By the late Tang and the Song, the nature of trade was also changing. In the past, most long-distance trade had been undertaken by state monopoly. By the time of the Song, private commerce was being actively encouraged, and many merchants engaged in shipping as well as in wholesale and retail trade. Guilds began to appear, along with a new money economy. Paper currency began to be used in the eighth and ninth centuries. Credit (at first called "flying money") also made its first appearance during the Tang. With the increased circulation of paper money, banking began to develop, as merchants found that strings of copper coins were too cumbersome for their increasingly complex operations. Unfortunately, early issues of paper currency were not backed by metal coinage and led to price inflation. Equally useful, if more prosaic, was the invention of the abacus, an early form of calculator that simplified the calculations needed for commercial transactions.

Long-distance trade, both overland and by sea, expanded under the Tang and the Song. Trade with countries and peoples to the west had been carried on for centuries (see Chapter 3), but it had declined dramatically between the fourth and the sixth century C.E. as a result of the collapse of the Han and the Roman Empire. It began to revive with the rise of the Tang and the simultaneous unification of much of the Middle East under the Arabs. During the Tang era, the Silk Road revived and then reached its zenith. Much of the trade was carried by the Turkic-speaking Uighurs. During the Tang, Uighur caravans of two-humped Bactrian camels (a hardy variety native to Iran and regions to the northeast) carried goods back and forth between China and the countries of South Asia and the Middle East.

In actuality, the Silk Road was composed of a number of separate routes. The first to be used, probably because of the jade found in the mountains south of Khotan, ran along the southern rim of the Taklimakan Desert via Kashgar and thence through the Pamir Mountains into Bactria. The first Buddhist missionaries traveled this route from India to China. Eventually, however, this area began to dry up, and traders were forced to seek other routes. From a climatic standpoint, the best route for the Silk Road was to the north of the Tian Shan (Heavenly Mountains), where moisture-laden northwesterly winds created pastures where animals could graze. But the area was frequently infested by bandits who preyed on unwary travelers. Most caravans therefore followed the southern route, which passed along the northern fringes of the Taklimakan Desert to Kashgar and down into northwestern India. Travelers avoided the direct route through the desert (in the Uighur language, the name means "go in, and you won't come out") and trudged from oasis to oasis along the southern slopes of the Tian Shan. The oases were created by the water runoff from winter snows in the mountains, which then dried up in the searing heat of the desert.

The Silk Road was so hazardous that shipping goods by sea became increasingly popular. China had long been engaged in sea trade with other countries in the region, but most of the commerce was originally in the hands of Korean, Japanese, or Southeast Asian merchants. Chinese maritime trade, however, was stimulated by the invention of the compass and technical improvements in shipbuilding such as the widespread use of the sternpost rudder and the lug sail (which enabled ships to sail close to the wind). If Marco Polo's observations can be believed, by the thirteenth century Chinese junks had multiple sails and weighed up to two thousand tons, much larger than contemporary ships in the West. The Chinese governor of Canton in the early twelfth century remarked:

> According to the government regulations concerning seagoing ships, the larger ones can carry several hundred men, and the smaller ones may have more than a hundred men on board. . . . The ship's pilots are acquainted with the configuration of the coasts; at night they steer by the stars, and in the daytime by the Sun. In dark weather they look at the south-pointing needle. They also use a line a hundred feet long with a hook at the end, which they let down to take samples of mud from the seabottom; by its appearance and smell they can determine their whereabouts.[4]

A wide variety of goods passed through Chinese ports. The Chinese exported tea, silk, and porcelain to the countries beyond the South China Sea, receiving exotic woods, precious stones, and various tropical goods in exchange. Seaports on the southern China coast exported sweet oranges, lemons, and peaches in return for grapes, walnuts, and pomegranates. Along the Silk Road to China came raw hides, furs, and horses. Chinese aristocrats, their appetite for material consumption stimulated by the affluence of Chinese society during much of the Tang and the Song periods, were fascinated by the exotic goods and the flora and the fauna of the desert and the tropical lands of the South Seas. The city of Chang'an became the eastern terminus of the Silk Road and perhaps the wealthiest city in the world during the Tang era. The major port of exit in southern China was Canton, where an estimated 100,000 merchants lived. Their activities were controlled by an imperial commissioner sent from the capital.

Some of this trade was a product of the tribute system, which the Chinese rulers used as an element of their foreign policy. The Chinese viewed the outside world as they viewed their own society—in a hierarchical manner.

✿ **A TANG HORSE.** During the Tang dynasty, trade between China, India, and the Middle East along the famous Silk Road increased rapidly and introduced new Central Asian motifs to Chinese culture. Ceramic representations of the sturdy Central Asian horse and the two-humped Bactrian camel were often produced as decorative objects in the homes of the wealthy, or as tomb figures. Preserved for us today, these ceramic studies of horses and camels, as well as of officials, court ladies, and servants, painted in brilliant gold, green, and blue lead glazes, are among the more impressive examples of Tang cultural achievement.

THE HEAVENLY MOUNTAINS. Of the three possible routes over the Silk Road between China and Central Asia, the most satisfactory, from an ecological point of view, was along the northern slopes of the Heavenly Mountains, where moist northwesterly winds and runoff from the snowy peaks of the mountains provided lush grasses for the camels to feed on and water for parched and weary merchants. Unfortunately, this region, shown above, also harbored nomadic peoples who preyed on merchant caravans for their livelihood.

Rulers of smaller countries along the periphery were viewed as "younger brothers" of the Chinese emperor and owed fealty to him. Foreign rulers who accepted the relationship were required to pay tribute and to promise not to harbor enemies of the Chinese Empire. But the foreign rulers also benefited from the relationship. Not only did it confer legitimacy upon them, but they often received magnificent gifts from their "elder brother" as a reward for good behavior. Merchants from their countries also gained access to the vast Chinese market.

DAILY LIFE IN TRADITIONAL CHINA

These political and economic changes affected Chinese society during the Tang and Song era. For one thing, it became much more complex. Whereas previously China had been almost exclusively rural, with a small urban class of merchants, artisans, and workers almost entirely dependent on the state, the cities had now grown into an important, if statistically still insignificant, part of the population. Urban life, too, had changed. Cities were no longer primarily administrative centers dominated by officials and their families, but now included a much broader mix of officials, merchants, artisans, touts, and entertainers.

In the countryside, equally significant changes were taking place, as the relatively rigid demarcation between the landed aristocracy and the mass of the rural population gave way to a more complex mixture of landed gentry, free peasants, sharecroppers, and landless laborers. Perhaps the most significant development was the rise of the landed gentry as the most influential force in Chinese society. The gentry class controlled much of the wealth in the rural areas and produced the majority of the candidates for the bureaucracy.

By virtue of their possession of land and specialized knowledge of the Confucian classics, the gentry had replaced the aristocracy as the political and economic elite of Chinese society. Unlike the aristocracy, however, the gentry did not form an exclusive class separated by the accident of birth from the remainder of the population. Upward and downward mobility between the scholar-gentry class and the remainder of the population was not uncommon and may have been a key factor in the stability and longevity of the system. A position in the bureaucracy opened the doors to wealth and prestige for the individual and his family, but it was no guarantee of success, and the fortunes of individual families might experience a rapid rise and fall. The soaring ambitions and arrogance of China's landed gentry are vividly described in the following wish list set in poetry by a young bridegroom of the Tang dynasty:

> *Chinese slaves to take charge of treasury and barn,*
> *Foreign slaves to take care of my cattle and sheep.*
> *Strong-legged slaves to run by saddle and stirrup when I ride,*
> *Powerful slaves to till the fields with might and main,*
> *Handsome slaves to play the harp and hand the wine;*
> *Slim-waisted slaves to sing me songs, and dance;*
> *Dwarfs to hold the candle by my dining-couch.*[5]

For affluent Chinese in this era, life offered many more pleasures than had been available to their ancestors. There were new forms of entertainment, such as playing cards and chess (brought from India, although an early form had been invented in China during the Zhou dynasty); new forms of transportation, such as the paddle-wheel boat and horseback riding (made possible by the introduction of the stirrup); better means of communication (block printing was first invented in the eighth century C.E.); and new tastes for the palate introduced from lands beyond the frontier. Tea had been introduced from the Burmese fron-

tier by monks as early as the Han dynasty, and brandy and other concentrated spirits produced by the distillation of alcohol were invented in the seventh century.

The vast majority of the Chinese people still lived off the land in villages ranging in size from a few dozen residents to several thousand. The life of the peasants was bounded by their village. Although many communities were connected to the outside world by roads or rivers, the average Chinese rarely left the confines of their native village except for an occasional visit to a nearby market town. This isolation was psychological as well as physical, for most Chinese identified with their immediate environment and had difficulty envisioning themselves living beyond the bamboo hedges or mud walls that marked the limit of their horizon.

An even more basic unit than the village in the lives of most Chinese, of course, was the family. The ideal was the joint family—with at least three generations under one roof. Because of the heavy labor requirements of rice farming, the tradition of the joint family was especially prevalent in the south. When a son married, he was expected to bring his new wife back to live in his parents' home (see

SPRING FESTIVAL ON THE RIVER.   Besides being an artistic masterpiece, this Chinese scroll, known as *Spring Festival on the River,* is one of the most remarkable social documents of early twelfth-century China. Nearly thirty-three feet in length, it records with encyclopedic detail various aspects of Chinese society, from the imperial court down to the lowliest peasants, as they prepare for the spring festival. The viewer is expected to unfold the scroll slowly from right to left and linger on each segment as the scroll follows the path along the Yellow River to the Song capital of Kaifeng, then the most sophisticated city in the world.

THE SAINTLY MISS WU

The idea that a wife should sacrifice her wants to the needs of her husband and family was deeply embedded in traditional Chinese society. Widows in particular had few rights, and their remarriage was strongly condemned. In this account from a story by Hung Mai, a twelfth-century writer, the widowed Miss Wu wins the respect of the entire community by faithfully serving her mother-in-law.

HUNG MAI, A SONG FAMILY SAGA

Miss Wu served her mother-in-law very filially. Her mother-in-law had an eye ailment and felt sorry for her daughter-in-law's solitary and poverty-stricken situation, so suggested that they call in a son-in-law for her and thereby get an adoptive heir. Miss Wu announced in tears, "A woman does not serve two husbands. I will support you. Don't talk this way." Her mother-in-law, seeing that she was determined, did not press her. Miss Wu did spinning, washing, sewing, cooking, and cleaning for her neighbors, earning perhaps a hundred cash a day, all of which she gave to her mother-in-law to cover the cost of firewood and food. If she was given any meat, she would wrap it up to take home. . . .

Once when her mother-in-law was cooking rice, a neighbor called to her, and to avoid overcooking the rice she dumped it into a pan. Owing to her bad eyes, however, she mistakenly put it in the dirty chamber pot. When Miss Wu returned and saw it, she did not say a word. She went to a neighbor to borrow some cooked rice for her mother-in-law and took the dirty rice and washed it to eat herself.

One day in the daytime neighbors saw [Miss Wu] ascending into the sky amid colored clouds. Startled, they told her mother-in-law, who said, "Don't be foolish. She just came back from pounding rice for someone, and is lying down on the bed. Go and look." They went to the room and peeked in and saw her sound asleep. Amazed, they left.

When Miss Wu woke up, her mother-in-law told her what happened, and she said, "I just dreamed of two young boys in blue clothes holding documents and riding on the clouds. They grabbed my clothes and said the Emperor of Heaven had summoned me. They took me to the gate of heaven and I was brought in to see the emperor, who was seated beside a balustrade. He said 'Although you are just a lowly ignorant village woman, you are able to serve your old mother-in-law sincerely and work hard. You really deserve respect.' He gave me a cup of aromatic wine and a string of cash, saying, 'I will supply you. From now on you will not need to work for others.' I bowed to thank him and came back, accompanied by the two boys. Then I woke up."

There was in fact a thousand cash on the bed, and the room was filled with a fragrance. They then realized that the neighbors' vision had been a spirit journey. From this point on even more people asked her to work for them, and she never refused. But the money that had been given to her she kept for her mother-in-law's use. Whatever they used promptly reappeared, so the thousand cash was never exhausted. The mother-in-law also regained her sight in both eyes.

---

the box above). Often the parents added a new wing to the house for the new family. If a woman married, she went to live with her husband; women who did not marry remained in the home where they grew up.

Chinese village architecture reflected these traditions. Most family dwellings were simple, consisting of one or at most two rooms. They were usually constructed of dried mud, stone, or brick, depending on available materials and the prosperity of the family. Roofs were of thatch or tile, and the floors were usually of packed dirt. Large houses were often built in a square around an inner courtyard, thus guaranteeing privacy from the outside world.

Within the family unit, the eldest male theoretically ruled as an autocrat. He was responsible for presiding over ancestral rites at an altar, usually in the main room of the house. He had traditional legal rights over his wife, and if she did not provide him with a male heir, he was permitted to take a second wife. She, on the other hand, had no recourse to divorce. As the old saying went, "Marry a chicken, follow the chicken; marry a dog, follow the dog." Wealthy Chinese might keep concubines, who lived in a separate room in the house and sometimes competed with the legal wife for precedence.

In accordance with Confucian tradition, children were expected, above all, to obey their parents, who not only determined their children's careers but normally selected their marriage partners. Filial piety was viewed as an absolute moral good, above virtually all other moral obligations. Even today duty to one's parents is considered important in traditional Chinese families, and the tombstones of deceased Chinese are often decorated with tile paintings depicting the filial acts that they performed during their lifetime.

The tradition of male superiority continued from ancient times into the medieval era, especially under the southern Song when it was reinforced by Neo-Confucianism. Female children were considered to be less desirable than males, because they could not undertake heavy work in the fields or carry on the family traditions. Poor families often sold their daughters to wealthy villagers to serve as concubines, and female infanticide was not uncommon in times of famine to ensure there would be food for the remainder of the family. Concubines had few legal rights, and female domestic servants even fewer.

During the Song era, two new practices emerged that changed the equation for women seeking to obtain a successful marriage contract. First, a new form of dowry appeared. Whereas previously the prospective husband offered the bride's family a bride price, now the reverse became the norm, with the bride's parents paying the groom's family a dowry. With the prosperity that characterized Chinese society during much of the Song era, affluent parents sought to buy a satisfactory husband for their daughter, preferably one with a higher social standing and good prospects for an official career.

A second source of marital bait during the Song period was the promise of a bride with tiny bound feet. The process of foot binding, carried out on girls aged five to thirteen, was excruciatingly painful, since it bent and compressed the foot to half its normal size by imprisoning it in restrictive bandages. But the procedure was often performed by ambitious mothers intent on assuring their daughters the best possible prospects for marriage. The zealous mother also wanted her daughter to possess a competitive edge in dealing with the other wives and concubines of her future husband. Bound feet represented submissiveness and self-discipline, two required attributes for the ideal Confucian wife.

Throughout northern China, foot binding became a common practice for women of all social classes. It was less common in southern China, where the cultivation of wet rice could not be carried out with bandaged feet; there it tended to be limited to the scholar-gentry class. Still, most Chinese women with bound feet contributed to the labor force to supplement the family income. Although foot binding was eventually prohibited, the practice lasted into the twentieth century, particularly in rural villages.

As in most traditional societies, there were exceptions to the low status of women in Chinese society. Women had substantial property rights and retained control over their dowries even after divorce or the death of the husband. Wives were frequently an influential force within the home, often handling the accounts and taking primary responsibility for raising the children. Some were active in politics. The outstanding example was Wu Zhao (625?–706?), popularly known as Empress Wu. Selected by Emperor Tang Taizong as a concubine, after his death she rose to a position of supreme power at court. At first she was content to rule through her sons, but in 690 she declared herself empress of China. To bolster her claim of legitimacy, she cited a Buddhist sutra to the effect that a woman would rule the world seven hundred years after the death of Gautama Buddha. For her presumption, she has been vilified by later Chinese historians, but she was actually a quite capable ruler. She was responsible for giving meaning to the civil service examination system and

was the first to select graduates of the examinations for the highest positions in government. During her last years, she reportedly fell under the influence of courtiers and was deposed in 705, at the age of eighty.

EXPLOSION IN CENTRAL ASIA: THE MONGOL EMPIRE

The Mongols, who succeeded the Song as the rulers of China in the late thirteenth century, rose to power in Asia with stunning rapidity. When Genghis Khan (also known as Chinggis Khan), the founder of Mongol greatness, was born, the Mongols were a relatively obscure pastoral people in the region of modern Outer Mongolia. Like most of the nomadic peoples in the region, they were organized loosely into clans and tribes and even lacked a common name for themselves. Rivalry among the various tribes over pasture, livestock, and booty was intense and increased at the end of the twelfth century as a result of a growing population and the consequent overgrazing of pastures.

This challenge was met by the great Mongol chieftain Genghis Khan. Born sometime during the 1160s, Genghis Khan (his original name was Temuchin, or Temujin) was the son of one of the more impoverished nobles of his tribe. When Temuchin was still a child, his father was murdered by a rival, and the young boy was temporarily forced to seek refuge in the wilderness. Nevertheless, through his prowess and the power of his personality he gradually unified the Mongol tribes. In 1206 he was elected Genghis Khan (universal ruler) at a massive tribal meeting. From that time on, he devoted himself to military pursuits. Mongol nomads were now forced to pay taxes and were subject to military conscription. "Man's highest joy," Genghis Khan reportedly remarked, "is in victory: to conquer one's enemies, to pursue them, to deprive them of their possessions, to make their beloved weep, to ride on their horses, and to embrace their wives and daughters."[6]

The army that Genghis Khan unleashed on the world was not exceptionally large—totaling less than 130,000 in 1227, at a time when the total Mongol population numbered between one and two million. But their mastery of military tactics set the Mongols apart from their rivals. Their tireless flying columns of mounted warriors surrounded their enemies and harassed them like cattle, luring them into pursuit, then ambushing them with flank attacks. John Plano Carpini, a contemporary Franciscan friar, described their tactics:

> As soon as they discover the enemy they charge and each one unleashes three or four arrows. If they see that they can't break him, they retreat in order to entice the enemy to pursue, thus luring him into an ambush prepared in advance. . . . Their military stratagems are numerous. At the moment of

A LETTER TO THE POPE

In 1243 Pope Innocent IV dispatched the Franciscan friar John Plano Carpini to the Mongol headquarters at Karakorum to appeal to the great khan to cease his attacks on Christians. After a considerable wait, Carpini was given the following reply, which could not have pleased the pope. The letter was discovered recently in the Vatican archives.

A LETTER FROM KUYUK KHAN TO POPE INNOCENT IV

By the power of the Eternal Heaven, We are the all-embracing Khan of all the Great Nations. It is our command:

This is a decree, sent to the great Pope that he may know and pay heed.

After holding counsel with the monarchs under your suzerainty, you have sent us an offer of subordination, which we have accepted from the hands of your envoy.

If you should act up to your word, then you, the great Pope, should come in person with the monarchs to pay us homage and we should thereupon instruct you concerning the commands of the Yasak.

Furthermore, you have said it would be well for us to become Christians. You write to me in person about this matter, and have addressed to me a request. This, your request, we cannot understand.

Furthermore, you have written me these words: "You have attacked all the territories of the Magyars and other Christians, at which I am astonished. Tell me, what was their crime?" These, your words, we likewise cannot understand. Jenghiz Khan and Ogatai Khakan revealed the commands of Heaven. But those whom you name would not believe the commands of Heaven. Those of whom you speak showed themselves highly presumptuous and slew our envoys. Therefore, in accordance with the commands of the Eternal Heaven the inhabitants of the aforesaid countries have been slain and annihilated. If not by the command of Heaven, how can anyone slay or conquer out of his own strength?

And when you say: "I am a Christian. I pray to God. I arraign and despise others," how do you know who is pleasing to God and to whom He allots His grace? How can you know it, that you speak such words?

Thanks to the power of the Eternal Heaven, all lands have been given to us from sunrise to sunset. How could anyone act other than in accordance with the commands of Heaven? Now your own upright heart must tell you: "We will become subject to you, and will place our powers at your disposal." You in person, at the head of the monarchs, all of you, without exception, must come to tender us service and pay us homage, then only will we recognize your submission. But if you do not obey the commands of Heaven, and run counter to our orders, we shall know that you are our foe.

That is what we have to tell you. If you fail to act in accordance therewith, how can we foresee what will happen to you? Heaven alone knows.

---

an enemy cavalry attack, they place prisoners and foreign auxiliaries in the forefront of their own position, while positioning the bulk of their own troops on the right and left wings to envelop the adversary, thus giving the enemy the impression that they are more numerous than in reality. If the adversary defends himself well, they open their ranks to let him pass through in flight, after which they launch in pursuit and kill as many as possible.[7]

In the years after the election of Temuchin as universal ruler, the Mongols defeated tribal groups to their west and then turned their attention to the seminomadic non-Chinese kingdoms in northern China. There they discovered that their adversaries were armed with a weapon called a fire-lance, an early form of flamethrower. Gunpowder had been invented in China during the late Tang period, and by the early thirteenth century a type of fire-lance had been developed that could spew out a combination of flame and projectiles that could travel as far as thirty or forty yards and inflict considerable damage on the enemy. By the end of the thirteenth century, the fire-lance had evolved into the much more effective handgun and cannon. These inventions came too late to save China from the Mongols, however, and were transmitted to Europe by the early fourteenth century by foreigners employed by the Mongol rulers of China.

While some Mongol armies were engaged in the conquest of northern China, others traveled farther afield and advanced as far as central Europe (see the box above). Only the death of the Great Khan may have prevented an all-out Mongol attack on western Europe. In 1231 they attacked Persia and then defeated the Abbasids at Baghdad in 1258 (see Chapter 7). Mongol forces attacked the Song from the west in the 1260s and finally defeated the remnants of the Song navy in 1279.

By then, the Mongol Empire was quite different from what it had been under its founder. Prior to the conquests of Genghis Khan, the Mongols had been purely nomadic. They spent their winters in the southern plains, where they found suitable pastures for their cattle, and traveled north in the summer to wooded areas where the water was sufficient. They lived in round tents covered with felt (called yurts) that were easily transported. For food, the Mongols depended on milk and meat from their herds and game from hunting.

To administer the new empire, Genghis Khan set up a capital city at Karakorum, in present-day Outer Mongolia, but prohibited his fellow Mongols from practicing sedentary occupations or living in cities. But under his successors, Mongol aristocrats began to enter administrative positions, while commoners took up sedentary occupations as farmers or merchants. As one khan remarked, quoting his Chinese adviser, "Although you inherited the Chinese Empire on horseback, you cannot rule it from that position."[8]

The territorial nature of the empire also changed. Following tribal custom, at the death of the ruling khan, the territory was distributed among his heirs. Genghis Khan's empire was thus divided into several separate khanates, each under the autonomous rule of one of his sons by his principal wife. One of his sons was awarded the khanate of Chaghadai in Central Asia with its capital at Samarkand; another ruled Persia from the conquered city of Baghdad; a third took charge of the khanate of Kipchak (commonly known as the Golden Horde). But it was one of his grandsons, named Khubilai Khan (1260–1294), who completed the conquest of the Song and established a new Chinese

dynasty, called the Yuan (from a phrase in the *Book of Changes* referring to the "original creative force" of the universe). Khubilai moved the capital of China northward to Khanbaliq (the city of the Khan), which was located on a major trunk route from the Great Wall to the plains of northern China. Later the city would be known by the Chinese name Beijing, or Peking (Northern Capital).

Mongol Rule in China

At first China's new rulers exhibited impressive vitality. After a failed attempt to administer their conquest as they had ruled their own tribal society (some advisers reportedly even suggested that the plowed fields be transformed into pasture), Mongol rulers adapted to the Chinese political system and made use of local talents in the bureaucracy, although the highest positions were usually reserved for Mongols. The tripartite division of the administration into civilian, military, and censorate was retained, as were the six ministries. Eventually, even the civil service system was revived, as was the state cult of Confucius, although Khubilai Khan himself was a Buddhist. Some

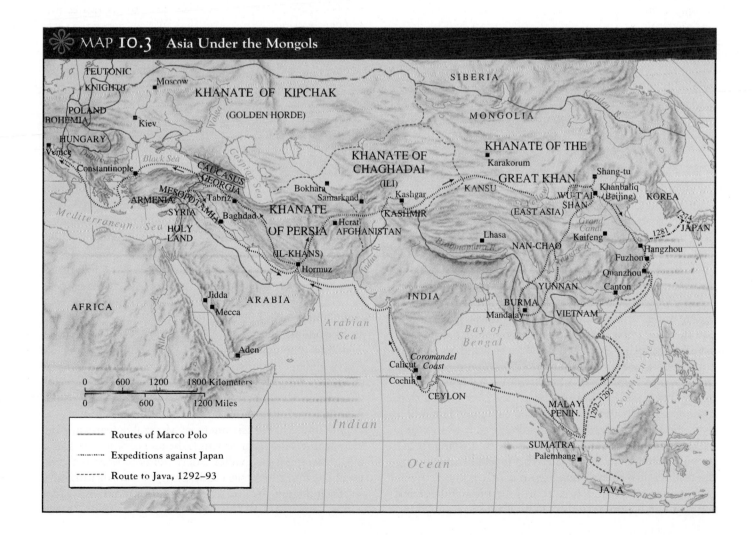

MAP 10.3   Asia Under the Mongols

Routes of Marco Polo

Expeditions against Japan

Route to Java, 1292–93

HOW KHUBILAI KHAN CHOOSES HIS CONSORTS

All Chinese emperors had a number of concubines in addition to their formal wives. Although this practice helped ensure that there would be one or more potential heirs to the throne, it also often led to disputes over the succession. In this passage, the Italian adventurer Marco Polo describes how the great Mongol ruler Khubilai Khan selected members of his harem. Since all of the official wives had large numbers of courtiers in their entourage, rivalry within the imperial court was not uncommon. Although some historians doubt that Marco Polo was ever in China, his account is generally viewed as a reliable description of thirteenth-century China.

MARCO POLO, *THE TRAVELS OF MARCO POLO*

The personal appearance of the great Khan, lord of lords, whose name is Kublai, is such as I shall now tell you. He is of a good stature, neither tall nor short, but of a middle height. He has a becoming amount of flesh, and is very shapely in all his limbs. His complexion is white and red, the eyes black and fine, the nose well formed and well set on. He has four wives, whom he retains permanently as his legitimate consorts. . . .

When the emperor desires the society of one of these four consorts, he will sometimes send for the lady to his apartment and sometimes visit her at her own. He has also a great number of concubines, and I will tell you how he obtains them.

You must know that there is a tribe of Tartars called Kungurat, who are noted for their beauty. The great Khan sends his commissioners to the province to select four or five hundred, or whatever number may be ordered, of the most beautiful young women, according to the scale of beauty enjoined upon them. . . . The commissioners on arriving assemble all the girls of the province, in the presence of appraisers appointed for the purpose. These carefully survey the points of each girl in succession, as for example her hair, her complexion, eyebrows, mouth, lips, and the proportion of all her limbs. . . . And whatever standard the great Khan may have fixed for those that are to be brought to him, . . . the commissioners select the required number from those who have attained that standard, and bring them to him. And when they reach his presence he has them appraised anew by other parties, and has a selection made of thirty or forty of those, who then get the highest valuation. Now every year a hundred of the most beautiful maidens of this tribe are sent to the great Khan, who commits them to the charge of certain elderly ladies dwelling in his palace. And these old ladies make the girls sleep with them, in order to ascertain if they have sweet breath and do not snore, and are sound in all their limbs. Then such of them as are of approved beauty, and are good and sound in all respects, are appointed to attend on the emperor by turns. Thus six of these damsels take their turn for three days and nights, and wait on him when he is in his chamber and when he is in his bed, to serve him in any way, and to be entirely at his orders. At the end of the three days and nights they are relieved by another six. And so throughout the year, there are reliefs of maidens by six and six, changing every three days and nights.

---

leading Mongols followed their ruler in converting to Buddhism, but most commoners retained their traditional religion. In general, the Mongols remained apart as a separate class with their own laws.

The Mongols' greatest achievement may have been the prosperity they fostered. At home, they continued the relatively tolerant economic policies of the southern Song, and by bringing the entire Eurasian landmass under a single rule, they encouraged long-distance trade, particularly along the Silk Road, now dominated by Muslim merchants from Central Asia. To promote trade, the Grand Canal was extended from the Yellow River to the capital. Adjacent to the canal, a paved highway was constructed that extended all the way from the Song capital of Hangzhou to its Mongol counterpart at Khanbaliq.

The capital was a magnificent city. According to the Italian merchant Marco Polo, who resided there during the reign of Khubilai Khan (see the box above), it was twenty-four miles in diameter and surrounded by thick walls of earth penetrated by twelve massive gates. He described the old Song capital of Hangzhou as a noble city where "so many pleasures may be found that one fancies himself to be in Paradise."

But the Yuan eventually fell victim to the same fate that had afflicted other powerful dynasties in China. Excessive spending on foreign campaigns, inadequate tax revenues, factionalism and corruption at court and in the bureaucracy, and growing internal instability, brought about in part by a famine in central China in the 1340s, all contributed to the dynasty's demise. Khubilai Khan's successors lacked his administrative genius, and by the middle of the fourteenth century, the Yuan dynasty in China, like the Mongol khanates elsewhere in Central Asia, had begun to decline rapidly.

The immediate instrument of Mongol defeat was Zhu Yuanzhang (Chu Yuan-chang), the son of a poor peasant in the lower Yangtze valley. After losing most of his family in the famine of the 1340s, Zhu became an itinerant monk and then the leader of a band of bandits. In the 1360s, unrest spread throughout the country, and after

BUDDHIST SHRINE STATUE. The oasis settlement of Jiaohe, located at the confluence of two rivers on a plateau in Chinese Central Asia, had been a stopping point on the Silk Road since the first millennium B.C.E. During the Tang dynasty, when Buddhist merchants carried goods and ideas eastward from India to the Chinese capital at Chang'an, the town's inhabitants were primarily Buddhist. Shown here are the remnants of a Buddhist shrine, with an image of the Buddha set in a niche along the central wall of the building. Like all other structures in the town, the shrine was constructed of sun-dried brick. Eventually the community was occupied by Uighurs, who brought the Muslim faith. Jiaohe was abandoned after the Mongols swept through the area in the thirteenth century, but later a new settlement arose in the nearby Turfan depression, the lowest point in China.

defeating a number of rivals, Zhu Yuanzhang put an end to the disintegrating Yuan regime and declared the foundation of a new Ming (Bright) dynasty (1369–1644).

IN SEARCH OF THE WAY

By the time of the Sui and the Tang dynasties, Buddhism and Daoism had emerged as major rivals of Confucianism as the ruling ideology of the state. But in the eighth and ninth centuries, during the last half of the Tang dynasty, Confucianism revived and once again became dominant at court, a position it would retain to the end of the dynastic period in the early twentieth century. Buddhist and Daoist beliefs, however, remained popular at the local level.

The Rise and Decline of Buddhism and Daoism

As noted earlier, Buddhism arrived in China with merchants from India and found its first adherents among the merchant community and intellectuals intrigued by the new ideas. During the chaotic centuries following the collapse of the Han dynasty, Buddhism and Daoism appealed to those who were searching for more emotional and spiritual satisfaction than Confucianism could provide. Both faiths reached beyond the common people and found support among the ruling classes as well. There was even a small Christian church in the capital of Chang'an, introduced to China by Syrian merchants in the sixth century C.E.

As Buddhism attracted more followers, it began to take on Chinese characteristics and divided into a number of separate sects. Some, like the Chan (Zen in Japanese) sect, called for mind training and a strict regimen as a means of seeking enlightenment, a technique that reflected Daoist ideas and appealed to many intellectuals (see the box on p. 284). Others, like the Pure Land sect, stressed the role of devotion, an approach that was more appealing to ordinary Chinese, who lacked the time and inclination for strict monastic discipline. Still others were mystical sects, like Tantrism, which emphasized the importance of magical symbols and ritual in seeking a preferred way to enlightenment. Some Buddhist sects, like their Daoist counterparts, had political overtones. The White Lotus sect, founded in 1133, often adopted the form of a rebel movement, seeking political reform or the overthrow of a dynasty and forecasting a new era when a "savior Buddha" would come to earth to herald the advent of a new age. Most believers, however, assimilated Buddhism into their daily lives, where it joined Confucian ideology and spirit worship as an element in the highly eclectic and tolerant Chinese worldview.

The burgeoning popularity of Buddhism continued into the early years of the Tang dynasty. Early Tang rulers lent their support to the Buddhist monasteries that had been established throughout the country. Buddhist scriptures were regularly included in the civil service examinations, and Buddhist and Daoist advisers replaced shamans and Confucian scholar-officials as advisers at court. But ultimately, Buddhism and Daoism lost favor at court and were increasingly subjected to official persecution. Part of the reason was xenophobia. Envious Daoists and Confucianists made a point of criticizing the foreign origins of Buddhist doctrines, which one prominent Confucian scholar characterized as nothing but "silly relics." To deflect such criticism, Buddhists attempted to make the doctrine more Chinese, equating the Indian concept of *dharma* (law) with the Chinese concept of *Dao* (the Way). Emperor Tang Taizong ordered the Buddhist monk Xuan Zang to translate Lao Zi's classic *The Way of the Dao* into Sanskrit, reportedly to show visitors from India that China had its own equivalent to the Buddhist scriptures. But another reason for this change of heart may have been financial. The great Buddhist monasteries had accumulated thousands of acres of land and serfs that were exempt from

THE WAY OF THE GREAT BUDDHA

According to Buddhists, it is impossible to describe the state of nirvana, which is sometimes depicted as an extinction of self. Yet Buddhist scholars found it difficult to avoid trying to interpret the term for their followers. The following passage by the Chinese monk Shen-Hui, one of the leading exponents of Chan Buddhism, dates from the eighth century and attempts to describe the means by which an individual may hope to seek enlightenment. There are clear similarities with philosophical Daoism.

SHEN-HUI, ELUCIDATING THE DOCTRINE

"Absence of thought" is the doctrine.
"Absence of action" is the foundation.
True Emptiness is the substance.
And all wonderful things and beings are the function.
True Thusness is without thought; it cannot be known through conception and thought.
The True State is noncreated—can it be seen in matter and mind?
There is no thought except that of True Thusness.
There is no creation except that of the True State.
Abiding without abiding, forever abiding in Nirvana.
Acting without acting, immediately crossing to the Other Shore.
Thusness does not move, but its motion and functions are inexhaustible.

In every instant of thought, there is no seeking; the seeking itself is no thought.
Perfect wisdom is not achieved, and yet the Five Eyes all become pure and the Three Bodies are understood.
Great Enlightenment has no knowledge, and yet the Six Supernatural Powers of the Buddha are utilized and the Four Wisdoms of the Buddha are made great.
Thus we know that calmness is at the same time no calmness, wisdom at the same time no wisdom, and action at the same time no action.
The nature is equivalent to the void and the substance is identical with the Realm of Law.
In this way, the Six Perfections are completed.
None of the ways to arrive at Nirvana is wanting.
Thus we know that the ego and the dharmas are empty in reality and being and nonbeing are both obliterated.
The mind is originally without activity; the Way is always without thought.
No thought, no reflection, no seeking, no attainment;
No this, no that, no coming, no going.
With such reality one understands the True Insight [into previous and future mortal conditions and present mortal suffering].
With such a mind one penetrates the Eight Emancipations [through the eight stages of mental concentration].
By merits one accomplishes the Ten Powers of the Buddha.

---

paying taxes to the state. Such wealth contributed to the corruption of the monks and other Buddhist officials, and this corruption in turn aroused popular resentment and official disapproval. As the state attempted to eliminate the great landholdings of the aristocracy, the large monasteries also attracted its attention. During the later Tang, countless temples and monasteries were destroyed, and over 100,000 monks were compelled to leave the monasteries and return to secular life.

Yet there were probably deeper political and ideological reasons for the growing antagonism between Buddhism and the state. By preaching the illusory nature of the material world, Buddhism was denying the very essence of Confucian teachings—the necessity for filial piety and hard work. By encouraging young Chinese to abandon their rice fields and seek refuge and wisdom in the monasteries, Buddhism was undermining the foundation stones of Chinese society—the family unit and the work ethic. In the last analysis, Buddhism was incompatible with the activist element in Chinese society, an orientation that was most effectively expressed by State Confucianism (see the box on p. 285). In the competition with Confucianism for support by the state, Buddhism, like Daoism, was almost certain to lose, at least in the more this-worldly, secure, and prosperous milieu of late Tang and Song China. The two doctrines continued to win converts at the local level, but official support ceased. In the meantime, Buddhism was under attack in Central Asia as well. In the eighth century, the Uighur kingdom adopted Manichaeanism, an offshoot of the ancient Zoroastrian religion with some influence from Christianity. Manichaeanism spread rapidly throughout the area and may have been a reason for the European belief that a Christian king (the legendary Prester John) ruled somewhere in Asia. By the tenth century, Islam was beginning to move east along the Silk Road, posing a severe threat to both Manichaean and Buddhist centers in the area.

Neo-Confucianism: The Investigation of Things

Into the vacuum left by the decline of Buddhism and Daoism stepped a revived Confucianism. But it was a Confucianism that had been significantly altered by its competition with Buddhist and Daoist teachings. Challenged by Buddhist and Daoist ideas about the nature of the universe, Confucian thinkers began to flesh out the spare metaphysical structure of classical Confucian doctrine

A CONFUCIAN WEDDING CEREMONY

During the twelfth century, the philosopher Zhu Xi attempted to reinvigorate Confucian teachings in a contemporary setting that would be more accessible in its appeal to a broad audience. His goal was militantly Confucian, to combat both popular Buddhist doctrines and the superstitious practices of the common people. With his new moral code, Zhu Xi hoped to point Chinese society back on the Confucian track, with its emphasis on proper behavior. He therefore set forth the proper rituals required to carry out the special days that marked the lives of all Chinese: entry into adolescence, marriage, and funeral and ancestral rites. In the excerpt below he prescribes the proper protocol for the Confucian wedding ceremony.

4. WELCOMING IN PERSON

On the day before the wedding, the bride's family sends people to lay out the dowry furnishings in the groom's chamber. At dawn the groom's family sets places in the chamber. Meanwhile, the bride's family sets up places outside. As the sun goes down, the groom puts on full attire. After the presiding man makes a report at the offering hall, he pledges the groom and orders him to go to fetch the bride. The groom goes out and mounts his horse. When he gets to the bride's home he waits at his place. The presiding man of the bride's family makes a report at the offering hall, after which he pledges the bride and instructs her.

Then he goes out to greet the groom. When the groom enters, he presents a goose. The duenna takes the girl out to climb into the conveyance. The groom mounts his horse and leads the way for the bridal vehicle. When they arrive at his house he leads the bride in and they take their seats. After the eating and drinking are done, the groom leaves the chamber. On reentering, he takes off his clothes and the candles are removed.

5. THE BRIDE IS PRESENTED TO HER PARENTS-IN-LAW

The next day, having risen at dawn, the bride meets her parents-in-law, who entertain her. Then the bride is presented to the elders. If she is the wife of the eldest son, she serves food to her parents-in-law. Then the parents-in-law feast the bride.

6. PRESENTATION AT THE FAMILY SHRINE

On the third day the presiding man takes the bride to be presented at the offering hall.

7. THE GROOM IS PRESENTED TO THE WIFE'S PARENTS

The day after that the groom goes to see his wife's parents. Afterward he is presented to his wife's relatives. The bride's family entertains the groom, as in ordinary etiquette.

---

with a set of sophisticated theories about the nature of the cosmos and humans' place in it. Although the origins of this effort can be traced to the early Tang period, it reached fruition during the intellectually prolific Song dynasty, when it became the dominant ideology of the state.

The fundamental purpose of Neo-Confucianism, as the new doctrine was called, was to unite the metaphysical speculations of Buddhism and Daoism with the pragmatic Confucian approach to society. In response to Buddhism and Daoism, Neo-Confucianism maintained that the world is real, not illusory, and that fulfillment comes from participation, not withdrawal.

The primary contributor to this intellectual effort was the philosopher Zhu Xi (Chu Hsi). Raised during the southern Song era, Zhu Xi accepted the division of the world into a material world and a transcendent world (called by Neo-Confucianists the Supreme Ultimate, or *Tai Ji*). The latter was roughly equivalent to the *Dao*, or Way, in classical Confucian philosophy. To Zhu Xi, this Supreme Ultimate was a set of abstract principles governed by the law of *yin-yang* and the five elements.

Human beings served as a link between the two halves of this bifurcated universe. Although human beings live in the material world, each individual has an identity that is linked with the Supreme Ultimate, and the goal of individual action is to transcend the material world in a Buddhist sense to achieve an essential identity with the Supreme Ultimate. According to Zhu Xi and his followers, the means of transcending the material world is self-cultivation, which is achieved by the "investigation of things."

During the remainder of the Song dynasty and into the early years of the Ming, Zhu Xi's ideas became the central core of Confucian ideology and a favorite source of questions for the civil service examinations. But during the mid-Ming era, his ideas came under attack from a Confucian scholar named Wang Yangming. Wang and his supporters disagreed with Zhu Xi's focus on learning through an investigation of the outside world and asserted that the correct way to transcend the material world was through an understanding of self. According to this "School of Mind," the mind and the universe were a single unit. Knowledge was thus intuitive rather than empirical and was obtained through internal self-searching rather than through an investigation of the outside world. Wang Yangming's ideas attracted many followers during the Ming dynasty, and the school briefly rivaled that of Zhu Xi in popularity among Confucian scholars. Nevertheless, it never won official acceptance, probably because it was too much like Buddhism in denying the importance of a life of participation and social action.

Neo-Confucianism remained the state doctrine until the end of the dynastic system in the twentieth century. Some historians have asked whether the doctrine can help to explain why China failed to experience scientific and industrial revolutions of the sort that occurred in the West. In particular, it has been suggested that Neo-Confucianism tended to encourage an emphasis on the elucidation of moral principles rather than the expansion of scientific knowledge. Though the Chinese excelled in practical technology, inventing gunpowder, the compass, printing and paper, and cast iron, among other things, they had less interest in scientific theory. Their relative backwardness in mathematics is a good example. Chinese scholars had no knowledge of the principles of geometry and lagged behind other advanced civilizations in astronomy, physics, and optics. Until the Mongol era, they had no knowledge of Arabic numerals and lacked the concept of zero. Even after that time, they continued to use a cumbersome numbering system based on Chinese characters.

Furthermore, in China intellectual affairs continued to be dominated by the scholar-gentry, the chief upholders of Neo-Confucianism, who not only had little interest in the natural sciences or economic change, but legitimately viewed them as a threat to their own dominant status within Chinese society. The commercial middle-class, who lacked social status and an independent position in society, had little say in intellectual matters. In contrast, in the West an urban middle-class emerged that was a source not only of wealth, but also of social prestige, political power, and intellectual ideas. The impetus for the intellectual revolution in the West came from the members of the commercial bourgeoisie, who were interested in the conquest of nature and the development of technology. In China, however, the scholar-gentry continued to focus on the sources of human behavior and a correct understanding of the relationship between humankind and the universe. The result was an intellectual environment that valued continuity over change and tradition over innovation.

THE APOGEE OF CHINESE CULTURE

The period between the Tang and the Ming dynasties was in many ways the great age of achievement in Chinese literature and art. Enriched by Buddhist and Daoist images and themes, Chinese poetry and painting reached the pinnacle of their creativity. Porcelain emerged as the highest form of Chinese ceramics, and sculpture flourished under the influence of styles imported from India and Central Asia.

Literature

The development of Chinese literature was stimulated by two technological innovations: the invention of paper during the Han dynasty and the invention of woodblock printing during the Tang. At first, paper was used for clothing, wrapping material, toilet paper, and even for armor, but by the first century B.C.E. it was being used for writing as well.

In the seventh century C.E., the Chinese developed the technique of carving an entire page of text into a wooden block, inking it, and then pressing it onto a sheet of paper. Ordinarily, a text was printed on a long sheet of paper like a scroll. Then the paper was folded and stitched together to form a book. The earliest printed book known today is a Buddhist text published in 868 C.E.; it is more than sixteen feet long. Although the Chinese eventually developed movable type as well, block printing continued to be used until relatively modern times because of the large number of characters needed to produce a lengthy text.

MAKING PAPER.   One of China's most important contributions to the world was the invention of paper during the Han dynasty. Although the first known use of paper for writing dates back to the first century B.C.E., paper was also used for clothing, wrapping materials, military armor, and toilet paper. It was even suggested to a prince in 93 B.C.E. that he use a paper handkerchief. Pounded fibers of hemp and linen were placed on a flat meshed surface and soaked in a large vat. After it dried, the residue was peeled away as a sheet of paper, seen piled at the right in this eighteenth-century painting.

TWO TANG POETS

Li Bo was one of the great poets of the Tang dynasty. The first selection is probably the best-known poem in China and has been memorized by schoolchildren for centuries. The second poem, entitled "Drinking Alone in Moonlight," reflects the poet's carefree attitude toward life.

Du Fu, Li Bo's prime competitor as the greatest poet of the Tang dynasty, was often the more reflective of the two. In the final piece here, the poet has returned to his home in the capital after a rebellion against the dynasty has left the city in ruins.

LI BO, QUIET NIGHT THOUGHTS

Beside my bed the bright moonbeams bound
Almost as if there were frost on the ground.
Raising up, I gaze at the Mountain moon;
Lying back, I think of my old hometown.

LI BO, DRINKING ALONE IN MOONLIGHT

Among the flowers, with a jug of wine,
I drink all alone—no one to share.
Raising my cup, I welcome the moon.
And my shadow joins us, making a threesome.
Alas! the moon won't take part in the drinking,
And my shadow just does whatever I do.
But I'm friends for a while with the moon and my shadow,
And we caper in revels well suited to spring.
As I sing the moon seems to sway back and forth;
As I dance my shadow goes flopping about.
As long as I'm sober we'll enjoy one another,
And when I get drunk, we'll go our own ways:
Forever committed to carefree play,
We'll all meet again in the Milky Way!

DU FU, SPRING PROSPECT

The capital is taken. The hills and streams are left,
And with spring in the city the grass and trees grown dense.
Mourning the times, the flowers trickle their tears;
Saddened with parting, the birds make my heart flutter.
The army beacons have flamed for three months;
A letter from home would be worth ten thousand in gold.
My white hairs I have anxiously scratched ever shorter;
But such disarray! Even hairpins will do no good!

Even with printing, books remained too expensive for most Chinese, but they did help to popularize all forms of literary writing among the educated elite.

During the post-Han era, historical writing and essays continued to be favorite forms of literary activity. Each dynasty produced an official dynastic history of its predecessor to elucidate sober maxims about the qualities of good and evil in human nature, and local gazetteers added to the general knowledge about the various regions. Encyclopedias brought together in a single location information and documents about all aspects of Chinese life.

But it was in poetry, above all, that Chinese of the Tang to the Ming dynasties most effectively expressed their literary talents. Chinese poems celebrated the beauty of nature, the changes of the seasons, the joys of friendship and drink, sadness at the brevity of life, and old age and parting. Given the frequency of imperial banishment and the requirement that officials serve away from their home district, it is little wonder that separation was an important theme. Love poems existed, but were neither as intense as Western verse nor as sensual as Indian poetry.

The nature of the Chinese language imposed certain characteristics on Chinese poetry, the first being compactness. The most popular forms were four-line and eight-line poems, with five or seven words in each line. Because Chinese grammar does not rely on case or gender and makes no distinction between verb tenses, five-character Chinese poems were not only brief but often cryptic and ambiguous. As an illustration, compare the following poem by Du Fu in Chinese with its English translation:

Moonlit Night	月夜
The moon tonight in Fu-chou	今夜鄜州月
She watches alone from her chamber,	閨中只獨看
While faraway I think lovingly on daughters and sons,	遙憐小兒女
Who do not yet know how to remember Ch'ang-an.	未解憶長安
In scented fog, her cloudlike hairdo moist,	香霧雲鬢濕
In its clear beams, her jade-white arms are cold.	清輝玉臂寒
When shall we lean in the empty window,	何時倚虛幌
Moonlit together, its light drying traces of tears.[9]	雙照淚痕乾

Two Tang poets, Li Bo (Li Po, sometimes known as Li Bai or Li Taibo) and Du Fu (Tu Fu), symbolized the genius of the era as well as the two most popular styles. Li Bo was a free spirit. His writing often centered on nature and shifted easily between moods of revelry and melancholy. Two of his best-known poems are "Resolution on Waking with a Hangover on a Spring Morning" and "Drinking Alone in Moonlight." (see the box above).

Where Li Bo was a carefree Daoist, Du Fu was a sober Confucian. His poems often dealt with historical issues or ethical themes, befitting a scholar-official living during the chaotic times of the late Tang era. Many of his works reflect a concern with social injustice and the plight of the unfortunate rarely to be found in the writings of his contemporaries (see the box on p. 287). Neither the poetry nor the prose of the great writers of the Tang and Song dynasties was written for, or penetrated to, the bulk of the Chinese population. The millions of Chinese peasants and artisans living in rural villages and market towns acquired their knowledge of Chinese history, Confucian moralisms, and even Buddhist scripture from stories, plays, and songs passed down by storytellers, wandering minstrels, and itinerant monks in a rich oral tradition.

By the Song dynasty, China had 60 million people, one million in Hangzhou alone. With the growth of cities came an increased demand for popular entertainment. Although the Tang dynasty had imposed a curfew on urban residents, the Song did not. The city gates and bridges were closed at dark, but food stalls and entertainment continued through the night. On fairgrounds throughout the year, one could find comedians, musicians, boxers, fencers, wrestlers, acrobats, puppets and marionettes, shadow plays, and especially storytellers. Many of these arts had come from India centuries before and now became the favorite forms of amusement of the Chinese people.

During the Yuan dynasty, new forms of literary creativity including popular theater and the novel began to appear. The two most famous novels were the *Romance of the Three Kingdoms* and *Tale of the Marshes*. The former had been told orally for centuries, appearing in written form during the Song as a scriptbook for storytellers. It was first printed in 1321 but was not published for mass consumption until 1522. Each new edition was altered in some way, making the final edition a composite effort of generations of the Chinese imagination. The plot recounts the power struggle that took place among competing groups after the fall of the Han dynasty. Packed with court intrigues, descriptions of peasant life, and gripping battles, the *Romance of the Three Kingdoms* stands as a magnificent epic, China's counterpart to the Mahabharata.

Tale of the Marshes is an often violent tale of bandit heroes, who at the end of the northern Song banded together to oppose government taxes and official oppression. They rob from those in power to share with the poor. *Tale of the Marshes* is the first prose fiction that describes the daily ordeal of ordinary Chinese people in their own language. Unlike the picaresque novel in the West, *Tale of the Marshes* does not limit itself to the exploits of one hero, offering instead 108 different story lines. This multitude of plots is a natural outgrowth of the tradition of the professional storyteller, who attempts to keep the audience's attention by recounting as many adventures as the market will bear. The frightening description of a tiger's attack on one of the bandits is typical of the author's exciting style (see the box on p. 289).

Art

Although painting flourished in China under the Han and reached a level of artistic excellence under the Tang, little remains from those periods. The painting of the Song and the Yuan, however, is considered the apogee of painting in traditional China.

Like literature, Chinese painting found part of its inspiration in Buddhist and Daoist sources. Some of the best surviving examples of the Tang period are the Buddhist

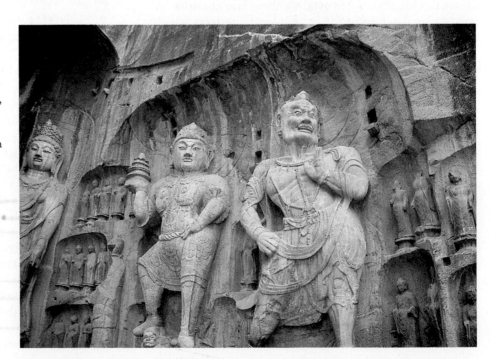

LONGMEN CAVES BUDDHIST SCULPTURE. The Silk Road, which stretched through Central Asia from the Middle East to China, was an avenue for ideas as well as trade. Over the centuries, Christian, Buddhist, and Muslim teachings came to China across the sandy wastes of the Taklimakan Basin. In the seventh century, the Tang emperor Gaozong commissioned this massive temple carving as part of the large complex of cave art devoted to Buddha at Longmen in central China. Bold and grandiose in their construction, these statues reflect the glory that was the Tang dynasty.

A BATTLE TO THE DEATH

Tale of the Marshes *is one of China's earliest novels. It is a swashbuckling tale of epic proportions that recounts the life of a group of bandits living on the margin of Chinese society. In its realistic description, this account of a battle with a tiger is stunningly modern.*

TALE OF THE MARSHES

Seeing it thus, Wu Sung cried "Ah-ya," then rolled down from the green rock. Cudgel in hand, he slipped away alongside the rock. The big beast was both hungry and thirsty. Barely touching the ground with its paws, it sprang upward with its whole body and then swooped down from midair. Wu Sung was so startled that the wine he had drunk turned into cold sweat. In a moment Wu Sung saw the tiger was about to pounce on him and he quickly dodged behind the beast's back. It was most difficult for the beast to find anyone from that position, so planting its front paws on the ground and raising its legs at the waist, it lifted itself up. Wu Sung again dodged and slid to one side. When the tiger saw that it had failed this time, it gave out a big roar like a thunderbolt from the mid sky, shaking the mountain ridge. Then it made a scissors-cut, its iron cudgel–like tail standing upside down, but Wu Sung again slipped aside. Ordinarily, the big beast seized its prey either with one swoop, one lift, or one scissors-cut. Failing to grab him by these three means, it lost half of its spirited temper. After a second failure with a scissors-cut, it roared once more and moved around in another circle. When Wu Sung saw the beast turn back, he lifted his cudgel with both hands and brought it down from midair with one swift and mighty blow. There was a loud sound and a tree fell, its twigs and leaves streaming down all over his face. Opening his eyes, he gazed fixedly. In his excitement, he had missed the big beast but struck instead an old withered tree. The cudgel had broken in two, and one half of it he now held in his hand.

Its temper now thoroughly aroused, the big beast bellowed and again turned round with a forward thrust. Wu Sung made another leap, retreating ten steps. The creature had barely managed to place its forepaws in front of Wu Sung when, throwing away his broken cudgel, he clutched the tiger's mottled neck with a cracking sound and pushing it down, held it tightly. The animal attempted to struggle, but Wu Sung grabbed it with all his might and never relaxed his grip for a moment. With his foot he kicked the beast over its face and eyes. The tiger started roaring again and dug up with its paws two heaps of yellow mud beneath its body, forming an earthen pit. Wu Sung pressed the beast's mouth straight down the yellow mud pit. It became helpless and impotent. With his left hand grasping tightly the beast's mottled neck, Wu Sung freed his right hand and lifting up his fist—the size of an iron hammer—kept pommeling it with all his strength. After it had been struck fifty to seventy times, fresh blood began to gush out from its eyes, mouth, nose, and ears. Wu Sung, using all his superhuman strength and inborn prowess, in a short while pounded the tiger into a heap as it lay there like an embroidered cloth bag.

---

wall paintings in the caves at Dunhuang, in Central Asia. These paintings were commissioned by Buddhist merchants who stopped at Dunhuang and, while awaiting permission to enter China, wished to give thanks for surviving the rigors of the Silk Road. The entrances to the caves were filled with stones after the tenth century, when Muslim zealots began to destroy Buddhist images throughout Central Asia, and have only recently been uncovered. Like the few surviving Tang scroll paintings, these wall paintings display a love of color and refinement that are reminiscent of styles in India and Iran.

Daoism ultimately had a greater influence than Buddhism on Chinese painting. From early times, Chinese artists removed themselves to the mountains to write and paint and find the *Dao*, or Way, in nature. In the fifth century, one Chinese painter, who was too old to travel, began to paint mountain scenes from memory and announced that depicting nature could function as a substitute for contemplating nature itself. Painting, he said, could be the means of realizing the *Dao*. This explains in part the emphasis on nature in traditional Chinese painting. The word *landscape* in Chinese means "mountain-water," and the Daoist search for balance between earth and water, hard and soft, *yang* and *yin*, is at play in the tradition of Chinese painting. To enhance the effect, poems were added to the paintings, underscoring the fusion of poetry and painting in Chinese art. Many artists were proficient in both media, the poem inspiring the painting and vice versa.

To represent the totality of nature, Chinese artists attempted to reveal the quintessential forms of the landscape. Rather than depicting the actual realistic shape of a specific mountain, they tried to portray the idea of "mountain." Empty spaces were left in the paintings because in the Daoist vision, one cannot know the whole truth. Daoist influence was also evident in the tendency to portray human beings as insignificant in the midst of nature. In contrast to the focus on the human body and personality in Western art, Chinese art presented people as tiny figures fishing in a small boat, meditating on a cliff, or wandering up a hillside trail, coexisting with but not dominating nature.

The Chinese displayed their paintings on long scrolls of silk or paper that were attached to a wooden cylindrical bar at the bottom. Varying in length from three to twenty feet, the paintings were unfolded slowly, so that the eye could enjoy each segment, one after the other, beginning at the bottom with water or a village and moving upward into the hills to the mountain peaks and the sky.

By the tenth century, Chinese painters began to eliminate color from their paintings, preferring the challenge of capturing the distilled essence of the landscape in washes of black ink on white silk. Borrowing from calligraphy, now a sophisticated and revered art, they emphasized the brush stroke and created black-and-white landscapes characterized by a gravity of mood and dominated by overpowering mountains.

Other artists turned toward more expressionist and experimental painting. These so-called literati artists were scholars and administrators, highly educated and adept in music, poetry, and painting. Being scholars first and artists second, however, they believed that the purpose of painting was not representation but expression. No longer did painters wish to evoke the feeling of wandering in nature. Instead they tried to reveal to the viewer their own mind and feelings. Like many Western painters in the nineteenth and twentieth centuries, many of these artists were misunderstood by the public and painted only for themselves and one another. They even developed a style of pointillism. Witness the incredibly "modern" painting of the Tang poet Li Bo, created by the thirteenth-century artist Liang Kai. With just a few bold black strokes, he managed to convey the whole man, standing calmly but poised, with inner intensity.

Second only to painting in creativity was the field of ceramics, notably, the manufacture of porcelain. Made of fine clay baked at unusually high temperatures in a kiln, porcelain was first produced during the period after the fall of the Han and became popular during the Tang era. During the Song, porcelain came into its own. Most renowned perhaps are the celadons, in a delicate gray-green, but Song artists also excelled in other colors and techniques. As in painting, Song delicacy and grace contrasted with the bold and often crude styles popular under the Tang. The translucent character of Chinese porcelain represented the final product of a technique that did not reach Europe until the eighteenth century. During the Yuan and the Ming, new styles appeared. Most notable is the cobalt blue and white porcelain usually identified with the Ming dynasty, which actually originated during the Yuan. The Ming also produced a multicolored porcelain—often in green, yellow, and red—covered with exotic designs.

✿ A MOUNTAIN SCENE. As a means of reproducing the totality of nature, Chinese artists often attempted to visualize physical reality. In this famous eleventh-century painting by Fan K'uan, the mountain seems to take on an existence all its own, independent of the interpretation of the artist. Daoist influence is evident here in that human beings play an insignificant role in the grand scheme of nature. The two tiny figures driving mules, a bridge, and a half-hidden temple are eclipsed by the mountain.

✿ CONCLUSION

Traditionally, Chinese historians believed that Chinese history tended to be cyclical in nature. The pattern of history was marked by the rise and fall of great dynasties, interspersed with periods of internal division and foreign invasion. Underlying the waxing and waning of dynasties was the essential continuity of Chinese civilization.

This view of the dynamic forces of Chinese history was long accepted as valid by historians in China and in the West and led many to assert that Chinese history was unique and could not be placed within a European or universal framework. Whereas Western history was linear, leading steadily away from the past, China's always returned to its moorings and was rooted in the values and institutions of antiquity.

In recent years, however, this traditional view of a changeless China has come under increasing challenge from historians who see patterns of change that made the China of 1400 a very different place from the country that had existed at the rise of the Tang dynasty in the seventh century C.E. To such scholars, China had passed through its own version of the "middle ages" and was on the verge of beginning a linear evolution into a posttraditional society.

As we have seen, China at the beginning of the Ming had advanced in many ways since the end of the great Han dynasty over a thousand years earlier. The industrial and commercial sector had grown considerably in size, complexity, and technological capacity, while in the countryside the concentration of political and economic power in the hands of the aristocracy had been replaced by a more stable and equitable mixture of landed gentry, freehold farmers, and sharecroppers. In addition, Chinese society had achieved a level of stability and social tranquillity that not only surpassed conditions during the final years of the Han, but was the envy of observers from other lands, near and far. The civil service provided an avenue of upward mobility that was virtually unknown elsewhere in the world, while the state tolerated a diversity of beliefs that responded to the emotional needs and preferences of the Chinese people. In many respects, China's achievements were unsurpassed throughout the world and marked a major advance beyond the world of antiquity.

Yet there were also some key similarities between the China of the Ming and the China of late antiquity. Ming China was still a predominantly agrarian society, with wealth based primarily on the ownership of land. Commercial activities flourished but remained under a high level of government regulation and by no means represented a major proportion of the national income. China also remained a relatively centralized empire based on an official ideology that stressed the virtue of hard work, social conformity, and hierarchy. In foreign affairs, the long frontier struggle with the nomadic peoples along the northern and western frontiers continued unabated.

Thus, the significant change that China experienced during its medieval era can probably be best described as change within continuity, an evolutionary working out of trends that had first become visible during the Han

dynasty or even earlier. The result was a civilization that was the envy of its neighbors and of the world. It also influenced other states in the region, including Japan, Korea, and Vietnam. It is to these societies along the Chinese rimlands that we now turn.

🌸 **LI BO CHANTING A POEM.**   Li Bo, one of the most celebrated Tang poets, wrote about the changing seasons, the joys of friendship and drink, and his sadness at the brevity of life, old age, and parting. The legend of his death undoubtedly added to his reputation. Reportedly, he drowned while reaching out in a drunken stupor to embrace the reflection of the moon in the water. Here he is portrayed by the thirteenth-century painter Liang Kai, who gave up a promising career as an official to retreat to a Buddhist monastery near Hangzhou.

CHAPTER NOTES

1. The Travels of Marco Polo (New York, n.d.), p. 119.
2. Quoted in Arthur F. Wright, Buddhism in Chinese History (Stanford, Calif., 1959), p. 30.
3. Quoted in Arthur F. Wright, The Sui Dynasty (New York, 1978), p. 180.
4. Chu-yu, P'ing chow Table Talks, quoted in Robert Temple, The Genius of China: 3,000 Years of Science, Discovery, and Invention (New York, 1986), p. 150.
5. Quoted in Edward H. Schafer, The Golden Peaches of Samerkand: A Study of T'ang Exotics (Berkeley, Calif., 1963), p. 43.
6. Quoted in John K. Fairbank, Edwin O. Reischauer, and Albert M. Craig, East Asia: Tradition and Transformation (Boston, 1973), p. 164.
7. John Plano Carpini, quoted in Rene Grousset, L'Empire des Steppes (Paris, 1939), p. 285.
8. A. M. Khazanov, Nomads and the Outside World (Cambridge, 1983), p. 241.
9. Steve Owen, The Great Age of Chinese Poetry: The High T'ang (New Haven, Conn., 1981), p. 200.

SUGGESTED READINGS

A number of general histories of China provide a good overview of this period. See, for example, C. O. Hucker, *China's Imperial Past: An Introduction to Chinese History and Culture* (Stanford, Calif., 1975), and C. Schirokauer, *A Brief History of Chinese and Japanese Civilizations*, rev. ed. (San Diego, Calif., 1989). For an interpretative treatment, see M. Elvin, *The Pattern of the Chinese Past* (Stanford, Calif., 1973). A global perspective is presented in S. A. M. Adshead, *China in World History* (New York, 1988).

A vast body of material is available on almost all periods of early Chinese history. For the post-Han period, see A. E. Dien, ed., *State and Society in Early Medieval China* (Stanford, Calif., 1990); E. Balazs, *Chinese Civilization and Bureaucracy: Variations on a Theme* (New Haven, Conn., 1964); and D. Twitchett and M. Loewe, *Cambridge History of China*, vol. 3, *Medieval China* (Cambridge, 1986).

For a readable treatment of the brief but tempestuous Sui dynasty, see A. F. Wright, *The Sui Dynasty* (New York, 1978). For a popularized treatment of one of China's most controversial female figures, see C. P. Fitzgerald, *The Empress Wu* (London, 1968).

The Song dynasty has been studied in considerable detail by Chinese historians. For a new and exciting interpretation, see

J. T. C. Liu, *China Turning Inward: Intellectual Changes in the Early Twelfth Century* (Cambridge, Mass., 1988). Song problems with the northern frontier are chronicled in Tao Jing-shen, *Two Sons of Heaven: Studies in Sung-Liao Relations* (Tucson, Ariz., 1988).

There are a number of recent studies on the Mongol period in Chinese history. See, for example, W. A. Langlois, *China Under Mongol Rule* (Princeton, N.J., 1981), and J. W. Dardess, *Conquerors and Confucians: Aspects of Political Change in Late Yuan China* (New York, 1973). M. Rossabi, *Khubilai Khan: His Life and Times* (Berkeley, Calif., 1988) is a recent biography of the dynasty's greatest emperor, while M. Rossabi, ed., *China Among Equals: The Middle Kingdom and Its Neighbors* (Berkeley, Calif., 1983) deals with foreign affairs. For the rise of the Mongols, see M. Prawdin, *The Mongol Empire: Its Rise and Legacy* (New York, 1966). A more analytic account of the dynamics of nomadic society is A. M. Khazanov, *Nomads and the Outside World* (Cambridge, 1983). For a provocative new interpretation of Chinese relations with nomadic peoples, see T. J. Barfield, *The Perilous Frontier: Nomadic Empires and China* (Cambridge, 1989).

For an introduction to women's issues during this period, consult P. B. Ebrey, *The Inner Quarters: Marriage and the Lives of Chinese Women in the Sung Period* (Berkeley Calif., 1993); *Chu Hsi's Family Rituals* (Princeton, N.J., 1991); and "Women, Marriage, and the Family in Chinese History," in P. S. Ropp, *Heritage of China: Contemporary Perspectives on Chinese Civilization* (Berkeley, Calif., 1990). For an overview of Chinese foot binding, see C. F. Blake, "Foot-Binding in Neo-Confucian China and the Appropriation of Female Labor," *Signs* 19 (Spring, 1994).

On Central Asia, two popular accounts are J. Myrdal, *The Silk Road* (New York, 1979), and N. Marty, *The Silk Road* (Methuen, Mass., 1987). A more interpretive approach is found in S. A. M. Adshead, *Central Asia in World History* (New York, 1993).

The period from the fall of the Han to the early Ming was an important period in Chinese intellectual history. For developments in Confucianism, see Fung Yu-lan, *A Short History of Chinese Philosophy*, ed. D. Bodde (New York, 1948), and Carsun Chang, *The Development of Neo-Confucian Thought*, 2 vols. (New Haven, Conn., 1963). For a more scholarly study, see W. T. de Bary, *Self and Society in Ming Thought* (New York, 1970). A classic survey of the role of Buddhism

in Chinese society is A. F. Wright, *Buddhism in Chinese History* (Stanford, Calif., 1959). See also E. O. Reischauer, *Ennin's Diary: The Record of a Pilgrimage to China in Search of the Law* (New York, 1955).

The classic work on Chinese literature is Liu Wu-Chi, *An Introduction to Chinese Literature* (Bloomington, Ind., 1966). Also consult the more recent and scholarly S. Owen, *An Anthology of Chinese Literature: Beginnings to 1911* (New York, 1996), and V. Mair, *The Columbia Anthology of Traditional Chinese Literature* (New York, 1994). For poetry see Liu Wu-Chi and I. Yucheng Lo, *Sunflower Splendor: Three Thousand Years of Chinese Poetry* (Bloomington, Ind., 1975), and S. Owen, *The Great Age of Chinese Poetry: The High T'ang* (New Haven, Conn., 1981), the latter presenting poems in both Chinese and English.

For a comprehensive introduction to Chinese art, see the classic M. Sullivan, *The Arts of China*, 4th ed. (Berkeley, Calif., 1999); M. Tregear, *Chinese Art*, rev ed. (London, 1997); and C. Clunas, *Art in China* (Oxford, 1997). The standard introduction to Chinese painting can be found in J. Cahill, *Chinese Painting* (New York, 1985), and Yang Xin, J. Cahill, et al., *Three Thousand Years of Chinese Painting* (New Haven, Conn., 1997).

INFOTRAC COLLEGE EDITION

For additional reading, go to InfoTrac College Edition, your online research library at http://web1.infotrac-college.com

Enter the search terms "Tang Dynasty or Song Dynasty" using Keywords.

Enter the search terms "China history" using Keywords.

Enter the search terms "China and Buddhism" using Keywords.

Enter the search term "Mongol" using Keywords.

Enter the search terms "Taoism or Daoism" using the Subject Guide.

CHAPTER

II

THE EAST ASIAN RIMLANDS: EARLY JAPAN, KOREA, AND VIETNAM

CHAPTER OUTLINE
- JAPAN: LAND OF THE RISING SUN
- KOREA
- VIETNAM: THE SMALLER DRAGON
- CONCLUSION

FOCUS QUESTIONS
- How did Chinese civilization influence the civilizations that arose in Japan, Korea, and Vietnam?
- What centralizing and decentralizing forces were at work in Japan before 1500, and how did they influence the political and governmental structures that arose?
- What were the main characteristics of economic and social life in early Japan?
- What were the most important cultural achievements of early Japan, and how do they illustrate the Japanese ability to blend indigenous and imported elements?
- What were the main developments in Korean and Vietnamese history before 1500?

These people, the exasperated official complained, are like birds and beasts. "They wear their hair tied up and go barefoot, while for clothing they simply cut a hole in a piece of cloth for their head or they fasten their garments on the left side [in barbarian style]." Their women are untrustworthy "and promiscuously wander about." In some areas, "men and women go naked without shame" and are little better than bugs.[1]

The speaker was Xue Tong, a Chinese administrator stationed in northern Vietnam at the end of the Han dynasty. His comments vividly reflected the frustration of Chinese bureaucrats faced with what they regarded as the uncivilized behavior of the untutored peoples living along the frontiers of the Chinese Empire. To Xue Tong and other upright Confucian officials like him, it was hopeless to try to civilize these people.

Such comments should not surprise us. During ancient times, China was the most technologically advanced society in East Asia. To the north and west were nomadic pastoral peoples whose military exploits were often impressive but whose political and cultural attainments were still limited, at least by comparison with the great river valley civilizations of the day. In inland areas south of the Yangtze River were scattered clumps of rice farmers and hill peoples, most of whom had not yet entered the era of state building and certainly had little knowledge of the niceties of Confucian ethics.

But Xue Tong and officials like him were being a little too hasty in their judgments. Along the fringes of Chinese civilization were a number of other agricultural societies that were beginning to follow a pattern of development similar to that of China, although somewhat later in time. One of these was in the islands of Japan, where an organized agricultural society was beginning to take shape just about the time Xue Tong was complaining about the barbarian peoples in the south. These developments may have been hastened by events on the Korean peninsula, where an advanced Neolithic society had begun to develop a few centuries earlier. Even in the Red River valley, where Xue Tong viewed the local inhabitants with such disdain, a relatively advanced civilization had been in existence for several hundred years before the area was conquered by the Han dynasty in the second century B.C.E.

All of these early agricultural societies were eventually influenced to some degree by their great neighbor China. Vietnam remained under Chinese rule for a thousand years. Korea retained its separate existence but was for long a tributary state of China and in many ways followed the cultural example of its larger patron. Only Japan retained both its political independence and its cultural uniqueness. Yet even the Japanese were strongly influenced by the glittering culture of their powerful neighbor, and today many Japanese institutions and customs still bear the imprint of several centuries of borrowing from the Middle Kingdom. In this chapter, we will take a closer look at these emerging societies along the Chinese rimlands and consider how their cultural achievements reflected or contrasted with those of the Chinese Empire. ❀

JAPAN: LAND OF THE RISING SUN

The geographical environment helps to explain some of the historical differences between Chinese and Japanese society. Whereas China is a continental civilization, Japan is an island country. It consists of four main islands: Hokkaido in the north, the main island of Honshu in the center, and the two smaller islands of Kyushu and Shikoku in the southwest. Its total land area is about 146,000 square miles (378,000 square kilometers), about the size of the state of Montana. Japan's main islands are at approximately the same latitude as the eastern seaboard of the United States.

Like the eastern United States, Japan is blessed with a temperate climate. It is slightly warmer on the east coast, which is washed by the Pacific Current that sweeps up from the south. The east coast also has a number of natural harbors that provide protection from the winds and high waves of the Pacific Ocean. As a consequence, in recent times the majority of the Japanese people have tended to live along the east coast, especially in the flat plains surrounding the cities of Tokyo, Osaka, and Kyoto. In these favorable environmental conditions, Japanese farmers have been able to harvest two crops of rice annually since early times.

By no means, however, is Japan an agricultural paradise. Like China, much of the country is mountainous, with only about 20 percent of the total land area susceptible to cultivation. These mountains are volcanic in origin, since the Japanese islands are located at the juncture of the Asian and Pacific tectonic plates. This location is both an advantage and a disadvantage. Volcanic soils are extremely fertile, which helps to explain the exceptionally high productivity of Japanese farmers. At the same time, the area is prone to earthquakes, such as the famous earthquake of 1923, which destroyed almost the entire city of Tokyo.

The fact that Japan is an island country has had a significant impact on Japanese history. As we have seen, the continental character of Chinese civilization, with its constant threat of invasion from the north, had a number of consequences for Chinese history. One effect was to make the Chinese more sensitive to the preservation of their culture from destruction at the hands of non-Chinese

THE EASTERN EXPEDITION OF EMPEROR JIMMU

Japanese myths maintained that the Japanese nation could be traced to the sun goddess Amaterasu, who was the ancestor of the founder of the Japanese imperial family, the Emperor Jimmu. This passage from the Nihon Shoki (The Chronicles of Japan) describes the campaign in which the "devine warrior" Jimmu occupied the central plains of Japan, symbolizing the founding of the Japanese nation. Legend dates this migration to about 660 B.C.E., but modern historians believe that it took place much later (perhaps as late as the fourth century C.E.) and that the account of the "divine warrior" may represent an effort by Japanese chroniclers to find a local equivalent to the Sage Kings of prehistoric China.

THE CHRONICLES OF JAPAN

Emperor Jimmu was forty-five years of age when he addressed the assemblage of his brothers and children: "Long ago, this central land of the Reed Plains was bequeathed to our imperial ancestors by the heavenly deities, Takamimusubi-no-Kami and Amaterasu Omikami. . . . However, the remote regions still do not enjoy the benefit of our imperial rule, with each town having its own master and each village its own chief. Each of them sets up his own boundaries and contends for supremacy against other masters and chiefs."

"I have heard from an old deity knowledgeable in the affairs of the land and sea that in the east there is a beautiful land encircled by blue mountains. This must be the land from which our great task of spreading our benevolent rule can begin, for it is indeed the center of the universe. . . . Let us go there, and make it our capital. . . ."

In the winter of that year . . . the Emperor personally led imperial princes and a naval force to embark on his eastern expedition. . . .

When Nagasunehiko heard of the expedition, he said: "The children of the heavenly deities are coming to rob me of my country." He immediately mobilized his troops and intercepted Jimmu's troops at the hill of Kusaka and engaged in a battle. . . . The imperial forces were unable to advance. Concerned with the reversal, the Emperor formulated a new divine plan and said to himself: "I am the descendant of the Sun Goddess, and it is against the way of heaven to face the sun in attacking my enemy. Therefore our forces must retreat to make a show of weakness. After making sacrifice to the deities of heaven and earth, we shall march with the sun on our backs. We shall trample down our enemies with the might of the sun. In this way, without staining our swords with blood, our enemies can be conquered." . . . So, he ordered the troops to retreat to the port of Kusaka and regroup there. . . .

[After withdrawing to Kusaka, the imperial forces sailed southward, landed at a port in the present-day Kita peninsula, and again advanced north toward Yamato.]

The precipitous mountains provided such effective barriers that the imperial forces were not able to advance into the interior, and there was no path they could tread. Then one night Amaterasu Omikami appeared to the Emperor in a dream: "I will send you the Yatagarasu, let it guide you through the land." The following day, indeed, the Yatagarasu appeared flying down from the great expanse of the sky. The Emperor said: "The coming of this bird signifies the fulfillment of my auspicious dream. How wonderful it is! Our imperial ancestor, Amaterasu Omikami, desires to help us in the founding of our empire."

---

invaders. Proud of their own considerable cultural achievements and their dominant position throughout the region, the Chinese have traditionally been reluctant to dilute the purity of their culture with foreign innovations. Culture more than race is a determinant of the Chinese sense of identity.

By contrast, the island character of Japan probably had the effect of strengthening the Japanese sense of ethnic and cultural distinctiveness. Although the Japanese view of themselves as the most ethnically homogeneous people in East Asia may not be entirely accurate (the modern Japanese probably represent a mix of peoples, much as do their neighbors on the continent), their sense of racial and cultural homogeneity has enabled them to import ideas from abroad without worrying that the borrowings will destroy the uniqueness of their own culture.

A Gift from the Gods: Prehistoric Japan

According to an ancient legend recorded in historical chronicles written in the eighth century C.E., the islands of Japan were formed as a result of the marriage of the god Izanagi and the goddess Izanami. After giving birth to Japan, Izanami gave birth to a sun goddess whose name was Amaterasu. A descendant of Amaterasu later descended to earth and became the founder of the Japanese nation. This Japanese creation myth is reminiscent of similar beliefs in other ancient societies, which often saw themselves as the product of a union of deities. What is interesting about the Japanese version is that it has survived into modern times as an explanation for the uniqueness of the Japanese people and the divinity of the Japanese emperor, who is still believed by some Japanese to be a direct descendant of the sun goddess Amaterasu (see the box above).

Modern scholars have a more prosaic explanation for the origins of Japanese civilization. According to archaeological evidence, the Japanese islands have been occupied by human beings for at least 100,000 years. The earliest known Neolithic inhabitants, known as the Jomon people from the so-called cord pattern of their pottery, lived in the islands as much as 10,000 years ago. They lived

✿ **SIXTH-CENTURY WAREHOUSE.**   During the sixth century C.E. an organized society was just beginning to form in the central valley around the modern cities of Kyoto and Osaka. Shown here is a twentieth-century model of a warehouse, located in downtown Osaka. On this site, one of Japan's early rulers ordered the construction of sixteen such structures to hold grain and perhaps other foodstuffs. Each warehouse measured nine by ten meters and was supported by several massive wooden posts.

by hunting, fishing, and food gathering and probably had not mastered the techniques of agriculture.

Agriculture probably first appeared in Japan sometime during the first millennium B.C.E., although some archaeologists believe that the Jomon people had already learned how to cultivate some food crops considerably earlier than that. About 400 B.C.E. rice cultivation was introduced, probably by immigrants from the mainland by way of the Korean peninsula. Until recently, historians believed that these immigrants drove out the existing inhabitants of the area and gave rise to the emerging Yayoi culture (from the site near Tokyo where pottery from the period was found). It is now thought, however, that Yayoi culture was a product of a mixture between the Jomon people and the new arrivals, enriched by imports such as wet-rice agriculture, which had been brought by the immigrants from the mainland. In any event, it seems clear that the Yayoi peoples were the ancestors of the vast majority of present-day Japanese.

At first the Yayoi lived primarily on the southern island of Kyushu, but eventually they moved northward onto the main island of Honshu, conquering, assimilating, or driving out the previous inhabitants of the area, some of whose descendants, known as the Ainu, still live in the northern islands. Finally, in the first centuries C.E., the Yayoi settled in the Yamato plain in the vicinity of the modern cities of Osaka and Kyoto. Japanese legend recounts the story of a "divine warrior" (in Japanese, Jimmu) who led his people eastward from the island of Kyushu to establish a kingdom in the Yamato plain (see the box on p. 296).

In central Honshu, the Yayoi set up a tribal society based on a number of clans, called *uji*. Each *uji* was ruled by a

hereditary chieftain, who provided protection to the local population in return for a proportion of the annual harvest. The population itself was divided between a small aristocratic class and the majority of the population, composed of rice farmers, artisans, and other household servants of the aristocrats. Yayoi society was highly decentralized, although eventually the chieftain of the dominant clan in the Yamato region, who claimed to be descended from the sun goddess Amaterasu, achieved a kind of titular primacy. There is no evidence, however, of a central ruler equivalent in power to the Chinese rulers of the Shang and the Zhou eras.

The Rise of the Japanese State

Although the Japanese had been aware of China for centuries, they paid relatively little attention to their more advanced neighbor until the early seventh century. Then the rise of the centralized and expansionistic Tang dynasty presented a new challenge. The Tang began to meddle in the affairs of the Korean peninsula, conquering the southwestern coast and arousing anxiety in Japan. Yamato rulers attempted to deal with the potential threat posed by the Chinese in two ways. First, they sought alliances with the remaining Korean states. Second, they attempted to centralize their authority so that they could mount a more effective resistance in the event of a Chinese invasion. The key figure in this effort was Shotoku Taishi (572–622), a leading aristocrat in one of the dominant clans in the Yamato region. Prince Shotoku sent missions

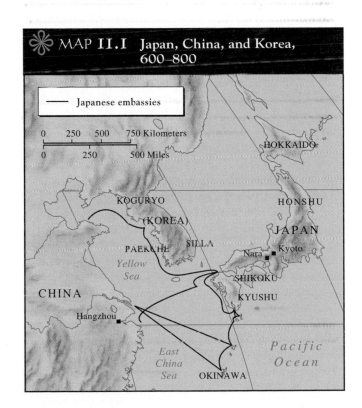

✿ MAP **11.1**   Japan, China, and Korea, 600–800

THE SEVENTEEN-ARTICLE CONSTITUTION

The following excerpt from the Nihon Shoki (The Chronicles of Japan) is a passage from the seventeen-article constitution promulgated in 604 C.E. Although the opening section reflects Chinese influence in its emphasis on social harmony, there is also a strong focus on obedience and hierarchy. The constitution was put into practice during the reign of the famous Prince Shotoku.

THE CHRONICLES OF JAPAN

Summer, 4th month, 3rd day [12th year of Empress Suiko, 604 C.E.]. The Crown Prince personally drafted and promulgated a constitution consisting of seventeen articles, which are as follows:

I. Harmony is to be cherished, and opposition for opposition's sake must be avoided as a matter of principle. Men are often influenced by partisan feelings, except a few sagacious ones. Hence there are some who disobey their lords and fathers, or who dispute with their neighboring villages. If those above are harmonious and those below are cordial, their discussion will be guided by a spirit of conciliation, and reason shall naturally prevail. There will be nothing that cannot be accomplished.

II. With all our heart, revere the three treasures. The three treasures, consisting of Buddha, the Doctrine, and the Monastic Order, are the final refuge of the four generated beings, and are the supreme objects of worship in all countries. Can any man in any age ever fail to respect these teachings? Few men are utterly devoid of goodness, and men can be taught to follow the teachings. Unless they take refuge in the three treasures, there is no way of rectifying their misdeeds.

III. When an imperial command is given, obey it with reverence. The sovereign is likened to heaven, and his subjects are likened to earth. With heaven providing the cover and earth supporting it, the four seasons proceed in orderly fashion, giving sustenance to all that which is in nature. If earth attempts to overtake the functions of heaven, it destroys everything. . . . If there is no reverence shown to the imperial command, ruin will automatically result. . . .

VII. Every man must be given his clearly delineated responsibility. If a wise man is entrusted with office, the sound of praise arises. If a wicked man holds office, disturbances become frequent. . . . In all things, great or small, find the right man, and the country will be well governed. . . . In this manner, the state will be lasting and its sacerdotal functions will be free from danger.

---

to the Tang capital of Chang'an to learn about the political institutions already in use in the relatively centralized Tang kingdom.

EMULATING THE CHINESE MODEL

Shotoku Taishi then launched a series of reforms to create a new system based roughly on the Chinese model. In the so-called seventeen-article constitution, he called for the creation of a centralized government under a supreme ruler and a merit system for selecting and ranking public officials (see the box above). His objective was to limit the powers of the hereditary nobility and enhance the prestige and authority of the Yamato ruler, now emerging as a divine figure and the symbol of the Japanese nation.

After Shotoku Taishi's death in 622, his successors continued to introduce reforms based on the Chinese model to make the government more efficient. In a series of so-called Taika ("great change") reforms that began in the mid-seventh century, a Grand Council of State was established, which presided over a cabinet of eight ministries. To the traditional six ministries of Tang China were added ministers representing the central secretariat and the imperial household. The territory of Japan was divided into administrative districts on the Chinese pattern. The rural village, composed ideally of fifty households, was the basic unit of government. The village chief was responsible for "the maintenance of the household registers, the assigning of the sowing of crops and the cultivation of mulberry trees, the prevention of offenses, and the requisitioning of taxes and forced labor." A law code was introduced, and a new tax system was established; now all farmland technically belonged to the state, so taxes were paid directly to the central government rather than through the local nobility, as had previously been the case.

As a result of their new acquaintance with China, the Japanese also developed a strong interest in Buddhism. Some of the first Japanese to travel to China during this period were Buddhist pilgrims hoping to learn more about the exciting new doctrine and bring back scriptures. Buddhism became quite popular among the aristocrats, who endowed wealthy monasteries that became active in Japanese politics. At first the new faith did not penetrate to the masses, but eventually popular sects such as the Pure Land Sect, an import from China, won many adherents among the common people.

CHRONOLOGY

THE FORMATION OF THE JAPANESE STATE

Shotoku Taishi	572–622
Era of Taika reforms	Mid-seventh century
Nara period	710–784
Heian (Kyoto) period	794–1185
Murasaki Shikibu	978–1016?
Minamoto Yoritomo	1142–1199
Kamakura shogunate	1185–1333
Mongol invasions	Late thirteenth century
Ashikaga period	1333–1600
Onin War	1462–1477

THE NARA AND HEIAN PERIODS

At first the effort to build a new state modeled roughly after the Tang state was successful. After Shotoku Taishi's death in 622, political influence fell into the hands of the powerful Fujiwara clan, which managed to marry into the ruling family and continue the reforms Shotoku had begun. In 710, a new capital, laid out on a grid similar to the great Tang city of Chang'an, was established at Nara, on the eastern edge of the Yamato plain. The Yamato ruler began to use the title "son of Heaven" in the Chinese fashion. In deference to the allegedly divine character of the ruling family, the mandate remained in perpetuity in the imperial house rather than being bestowed on an individual who was selected by Heaven because of his talent and virtue, as was the case in China.

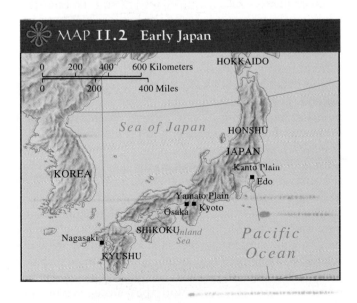

MAP 11.2 Early Japan

Had these reforms succeeded, Japan might have followed the Chinese pattern and developed a centralized bureaucratic government. But as time passed, the central government proved unable to curb the power of the aristocracy. Unlike in Tang China, the civil service examinations in Japan were not open to all but were restricted to individuals of noble birth. Leading officials were awarded large tracts of land, and they and other powerful families were able to keep the taxes from the lands for themselves. Increasingly starved for revenue, the central government steadily lost power and influence.

In 794, the emperor moved the capital to his family's original power base at nearby Heian, on the site of present-day Kyoto. The new capital was laid out in the now familiar Chang'an checkerboard pattern, but on a larger scale than at Nara. Now increasingly self-confident, the rulers ceased to emulate the Tang and sent no more missions to Chang'an. At Heian, the emperor—as the royal line descended from the sun goddess was now styled—continued to rule in name, but actual power was in the hands of the Fujiwara clan, which had managed through intermarriage to link its fortunes closely with the imperial family. A senior member of the clan began to serve as regent (in practice, the chief executive of the government) for the emperor.

In fact, what was happening was a return to the decentralization that had existed prior to Shotoku Taishi. The central government's attempts to impose taxes directly on the rice lands failed, and rural areas came under the control of powerful families whose wealth was based on the ownership of tax-exempt farmland (called *shoen*). To avoid paying taxes, peasants would often surrender their lands to a local aristocrat, who then would allow the peasants to cultivate the lands in return for the payment of rent. To obtain protection from government officials, these local aristocrats in turn might grant title of their lands to a more powerful aristocrat with influence at court. In return, these individuals would receive inheritable rights to a portion of the income from the estate.

With the decline of central power at Heian, local aristocrats tended to take justice into their own hands and increasingly used military force to protect their interests. A new class of military retainers called the samurai emerged whose purpose was to protect the security and property of their patron. They frequently drew their leaders from disappointed aristocratic office seekers, who thus began to occupy a prestigious position in local society, where they often served an administrative as well as a military function. The samurai lived a life of simplicity and self-sacrifice and were expected to maintain an intense and unquestioning loyalty to their lord. Bonds of loyalty were also quite strong among members of the samurai class, and homosexuality was common. Like the knights of medieval Europe, the samurai fought on horseback (although a samurai carried a sword and a bow and arrows

JAPAN'S WARRIOR CLASS

The samurai was the Japanese equivalent of the medieval European knight. Like the knight, he was expected to adhere to a strict moral code. Although this passage comes from a document dating only to the seventeenth century, it shows the importance of hierarchy and duty in a society influenced by the doctrine of Confucius. Note the similarity with Krishna's discourse on the duties of an Indian warrior in Chapter 2.

THE WAY OF THE SAMURAI

The master once said: . . . Generation after generation men have taken their livelihood from tilling the soil, or devised and manufactured tools, or produced profit from mutual trade, so that peoples' needs were satisfied. Thus the occupations of farmer, artisan, and merchant necessarily grew up as complementary to one another. However, the samurai eats food without growing it, uses utensils without manufacturing them, and profits without buying or selling. . . . The samurai is one who does not cultivate, does not manufacture, and does not engage in trade, but it cannot be that he has no function at all as a samurai. . . .

If one deeply fixes his attention on what I have said and examines closely one's own function, it will become clear what the business of the samurai is. The business of the samurai consists in reflecting on his own station in life, in discharging loyal service to his master if he has one, in deepening his fidelity in associations with friends, and, with due consideration of his own position, in devoting himself to duty above all. . . . The samurai dispenses with the business of the farmer, artisan, and merchant and confines himself to practicing this Way; should there be someone in the three classes of the common people who transgresses against these moral principles, the samurai summarily punishes him and thus upholds proper moral principles in the land. . . . Outwardly he stands in physical readiness for any call to service, and inwardly he strives to fulfill the Way of the lord and subject, friend and friend, father and son, older and younger brother, and husband and wife. Within his heart he keeps to the ways of peace, but without he keeps his weapons ready for use. The three classes of the common people make him their teacher and respect him. By following his teachings, they are enabled to understand what is fundamental and what is secondary.

Herein lies the Way of the samurai, the means by which he earns his clothing, food, and shelter; and by which his heart is put at ease, and he is enabled to pay back at length his obligation to his lord and the kindness of his parents. Were there no such duty, it would be as though one were to steal the kindness of one's parents, greedily devour the income of one's master, and make one's whole life a career of robbery and brigandage. This would be very grievous.

---

rather than lance and shield) and were supposed to live by a strict warrior code, known in Japan as *Bushido*, or "way of the warrior" (see the box above). As time went on, they became a major force and almost a pseudo-government in much of the Japanese countryside.

THE KAMAKURA SHOGUNATE AND AFTER

By the end of the twelfth century, as rivalries among noble families led to almost constant civil war, once again centralizing forces asserted themselves. This time the instrument was a powerful noble from a warrior clan named Minamoto Yoritomo (1142–1199), who defeated several rivals and set up his power base on the Kamakura peninsula, south of the modern city of Tokyo. To strengthen the state, he created a more centralized government (the *bakufu*, or "tent government") under a powerful military leader, known as the shogun (general). The shogun attempted to increase the powers of the central government while reducing rival aristocratic clans to vassal status. This "shogunate system," in which the emperor was the titular authority while the shogun exercised actual power, served as the political system in Japan until the last half of the nineteenth century.

At first the system worked effectively, and it was fortunate that it did, because during the next century Japan faced the most serious challenge it had confronted yet. The Mongols, who had destroyed the Song dynasty in China, were now attempting to assert their hegemony throughout all of Asia (see Chapter 10). In 1266 Emperor Khubilai Khan demanded tribute from Japan. When the Japanese refused, he invaded with an army of over 30,000 troops. Bad weather and difficult conditions forced a retreat, but the Mongols tried again in 1281. An army nearly 150,000 strong landed on the northern coast of Kyushu. The Japanese were able to contain them for two months, until virtually the entire Mongol fleet was destroyed by a massive typhoon—a "divine wind" (*kamikaze*). Japan would not face a foreign invader again until American forces landed on the Japanese islands in the summer of 1945.

The resistance to the Mongols had put a heavy strain on the system, however, and in 1333 the Kamakura shogunate was overthrown by a coalition of powerful clans. A new shogun, supplied by the Ashikaga family, arose in Kyoto and attempted to continue the shogunate system. But the Ashikaga were unable to restore the centralized power of their predecessors. With the central government

SAMURAI. During the Kamakura period, painters began to depict the adventures of the new warrior class. Here is an imposing mounted samurai warrior, the Japanese equivalent of the medieval knight in fief-holding Europe. Like his European counterpart, the samurai was supposed to live by a strict moral code and was expected to maintain an unquestioning loyalty to his liege lord. Above all, a samurai's life was one of simplicity and self-sacrifice.

reduced to a shell, the power of the local landed aristocracy increased to an unprecedented degree. Heads of great noble families, now called daimyo (great names), controlled vast landed estates that owed no taxes to the government or to the court in Kyoto. As clan rivalries continued, the daimyo relied increasingly on the samurai for protection, and political power came into the hands of a loose coalition of noble families.

By the end of the fifteenth century, Japan was again close to anarchy. A disastrous civil conflict known as the Onin War (1467–1477) led to the virtual destruction of the capital city of Kyoto and the disintegration of the shogunate. With the disappearance of any central author-

ity, powerful aristocrats in rural areas now seized total control over large territories and ruled as independent great lords. Territorial rivalries and claims of precedence led to almost constant warfare in this period of "warring states," as it is called (in obvious parallel with a similar era during the Zhou dynasty in China). The trend back toward central authority did not begin until the last quarter of the sixteenth century.

Economic and Social Structures

From the time the Yayoi culture was first established on the Japanese islands, Japan was a predominantly agrarian society. Although Japan lacked the spacious valleys and

THE BURNING OF THE PALACE. The Kamakura era is represented in this thirteenth-century action-packed scene from the *Scroll of the Heiji Period*, which depicts the burning of a retired emperor's palace in the middle of the night. Servants and ladies of the court flee in vain from the massive flames. Confusion and violence reign. The determined faces of the warriors only add to the ferocity of the attack.

deltas of the river valley societies, its inhabitants were able to take advantage of their limited amount of tillable land and plentiful rainfall to create a society based on the cultivation of wet rice.

As in China, commerce was slow to develop in Japan. During ancient times, each *uji* had a local artisan class, composed of weavers, carpenters, and ironworkers, but trade was essentially local and was regulated by the local clan leaders. With the rise of the Yamato state, a money economy gradually began to develop, although most trade was still conducted through barter until the twelfth century, when metal coins introduced from China became more popular.

Trade and manufacturing began to develop more rapidly during the Kamakura period, with the appearance of trimonthly markets in the larger towns and the emergence of such industries as paper, iron casting, and porcelain. Foreign trade, mainly with Korea and China, began during the eleventh century. Japan exported raw materials, paintings, swords, and other manufactured items in return for silk, porcelain, books, and copper cash. Some Japanese traders were so aggressive in pressing their interests that authorities in China and Korea attempted to limit the number of Japanese commercial missions that could visit each year. Such restrictions were often ignored, however, and encouraged some Japanese traders to turn to piracy.

Significantly, manufacturing and commerce developed rapidly during the more decentralized period of the Ashikaga shogunate and the era of the "warring states," perhaps because of the rapid growth in the wealth and autonomy of local daimyo families. Market towns, now operating on a full money economy, began to appear, and local manufacturers formed guilds to protect their mutual interests. Sometimes local peasants would sell products made in their homes, such as clothing made of silk or hemp, household items, or food products, at the markets. In general, however, trade and manufacturing remained under the control of the local daimyo, who would often provide tax breaks to local guilds in return for other benefits. Although Japan remained a primarily agricultural society, it was on the verge of a major advance in manufacturing.

DAILY LIFE

One of the first descriptions of the life of the Japanese people comes from a Chinese dynastic history from the third century C.E. It describes lords and peasants living in an agricultural society that was based on the cultivation of wet rice. Laws had been enacted to punish offenders, local trade was conducted in markets, and government granaries stored the grain that was paid as taxes (see the box on p. 303).

❀ **SCENE OF URBAN LIFE.**   Although traditional Japan was largely an agricultural society, trade and manufacturing began to develop during the Kamakura period, sparked by the rapid growth of local daimyo families and market towns. Intraregional trade was transported by horse-drawn carts or by boats on rivers or along the coast. Portrayed here is a detail from a thirteenth-century scroll depicting the bustle and general confusion of the city of Edo (now Tokyo).

LIFE IN THE LAND OF WA

Some of the earliest descriptions of Japan come from Chinese sources. The following passage from the History of the Wei Dynasty was written in the late third century C.E. The term Wa is a derogatory word meaning "dwarf" and was frequently used in China to refer to the Japanese people. The author of this passage, while remarking on the strange habits of the Japanese, writes without condescension.

HISTORY OF THE WEI DYNASTY

The people of Wa make their abode in the mountainous islands located in the middle of the ocean to the southeast of the Taifang prefecture. . . .

All men, old or young, are covered by tattoos. Japanese fishers revel in diving to catch fish and shell-fish. Tattoos are said to drive away large fish and water predators. They are considered an ornament. . . . Men allow their hair to cover both of their ears and wear head-bands. They wear loincloths wrapped around their bodies and seldom use stitches. Women gather their hair at the ends and tie it in a knot and then pin it to the top of their heads. They make their clothes in one piece, and cut an opening in the center for their heads. They plant wet-field rice, China-grass [a type of nettle], and mulberry trees. They raise cocoons and reel the silk off the cocoons. They produce clothing made of China-grass, of coarse silk, and of cotton. In their land, there are no cows, horses, tigers, leopards, sheep, or swan. They fight with halberds, shields, and wooden bows. . . . Their arrows are made of bamboo, and iron and bone points make up the arrowhead.

People . . . live long, some reaching one hundred years of age, and others to eighty or ninety years. Normally men of high echelon have four or five wives, and the plebeians may have two or three. When the law is violated, the light offender loses his wife and children by confiscation, and the grave offender has his household and kin exterminated. There are class distinctions within the nobility and the base, and some are vassals of others. There are mansions and granaries erected for the purpose of collecting taxes. . . .

When plebeians meet the high-echelon men on the road, they withdraw to the grassy area (side of the road) hesitantly. When they speak or are spoken to, they either crouch or kneel with both hands on the ground to show their respect. When responding they say "aye," which corresponds to our affirmative "yes."

Life for the common people probably changed very little over the next several hundred years. Most were peasants, who worked on land owned by their lord or, in some cases, by the state or by Buddhist monasteries. By no means, however, were all peasants equal either economically or socially. Although in ancient times all land was owned by the state and peasants working the land were taxed at an equal rate depending on the nature of the crop, after the Yamato era variations began to develop. At the top were local officials who were often well-to-do peasants. They were responsible for organizing collective labor services and collecting tax grain from the peasants and in turn were exempt from such obligations themselves.

The mass of the peasants were under the authority of these local officials. In general, peasants were free to dispose of their harvest as they saw fit after paying their tax quota, but in practical terms their freedom was limited. Those who were unable to pay the tax sank to the level of genin, or landless laborers, who could be bought and sold by their proprietors like slaves along with the land on which they worked. Some fled to escape such a fate and attempted to survive by clearing plots of land in the mountains or by becoming bandits.

In addition to the genin, the bottom of the social scale was occupied by the eta, a class of hereditary slaves who were responsible for what were considered degrading occupations, such as curing leather and burying the dead. The origins of the eta are not entirely clear, but they probably were descendants of prisoners of war, criminals, or mountain dwellers who were not related to the dominant Yamato peoples. As we shall see, the eta are still a distinctive part of Japanese society, and although their full legal rights are guaranteed under the current constitution, discrimination against them is not uncommon.

Daily life for ordinary people in early Japan resembled that of their counterparts throughout much of Asia. The vast majority lived in small villages, several of which normally made up a single shoen. Housing was simple. Most lived in small two-room houses of timber, mud, or thatch, with dirt floors covered by straw or woven mats (the origin, perhaps, of the well-known tatami, or woven-mat floor, of more modern times). Their diet consisted of rice (if some was left after the payment of the grain tax), wild grasses, millet, roots, and some fish and birds. Life must have been difficult at best; as one eighth-century poet lamented:

> Here I lie on straw
> Spread on bare earth,
> With my parents at my pillow,
> My wife and children at my feet,
> All huddled in grief and tears.
> No fire sends up smoke
> At the cooking place,
> And in the cauldron
> A spider spins its web.[2]

Evidence about the relations between men and women in early Japan presents a mixed picture. The Chinese dynastic history reports that "in their meetings and daily living, there is no distinction between . . . men and women." It notes that a woman "adept in the ways of shamanism" had briefly ruled Japan in the third century C.E. But it also remarks that polygyny was common, with nobles normally having four to five wives, and commoners two or three.[3] An eighth-century law code guaranteed the inheritance rights of women, and wives abandoned by their husbands were permitted to obtain a divorce and remarry. A husband could divorce his wife if she did not produce a male child, committed adultery, disobeyed her parents-in-law, talked too much, engaged in theft, was jealous, or had a serious illness.[4]

When Buddhism was introduced, women were initially relegated to a subordinate position in the new faith. Although they were permitted to take up monastic life—many widows entered a monastery at the death of their husbands—they were not permitted to visit Buddhist holy places, nor were they even (in the accepted wisdom) equal with men in the afterlife. One Buddhist commentary from the late thirteenth century said that a woman could not attain enlightenment because "her sin is grievous, and so she is not allowed to enter the lofty palace of the great Brahma, nor to look upon the clouds which hover over his ministers and people."[5] Other Buddhist scholars were more egalitarian: "Learning the Law of Buddha and achieving release from illusion have nothing to do with whether one happens to be a man or a woman."[6] Such views ultimately prevailed, and women were eventually allowed to participate fully in Buddhist activities in medieval Japan.

Although women did not possess the full legal and social rights of their male counterparts, they played an active role at various levels of Japanese society. Aristocratic women were prominent at court, and some, such as the author Lady Murasaki, became renowned for their artistic or literary talents. Though few commoners could aspire to such prominence, women often appear in the scroll paintings of the period along with men, doing the spring planting, threshing and hulling the rice, and acting as carriers, peddlers, salespersons, and entertainers.

In Search of the Pure Land: Religion in Early Japan

In Japan, as elsewhere, religious belief began with the worship of nature spirits. Early Japanese worshiped spirits, called *kami*, who resided in trees, rivers and streams, and mountains. They also believed in ancestral spirits present in the atmosphere. In Japan, these beliefs eventually evolved into a kind of state religion called Shinto (the Sacred Way or the Way of the Gods) that is still practiced today. Shinto still serves as an ideological and emotional force that knits the Japanese into a single people and nation.

Shinto does not have a complex metaphysical superstructure or an elaborate moral code. It does require certain ritual acts, usually undertaken at a shrine, and a process of purification, which may have originated in primitive concerns about death, childbirth, illness, and menstruation. This traditional concern about physical purity may help to explain the strong Japanese concern for personal cleanliness and the practice of denying women entrance to the holy places.

Another feature of Shinto is its stress on the beauty of nature and the importance of nature itself in Japanese life. Shinto shrines are usually located in places of exceptional beauty and are often dedicated to a nearby physical feature. As time passed, such primitive beliefs contributed to the characteristic Japanese love of nature. In this sense, early Shinto beliefs have been incorporated into the lives of all Japanese.

In time, Shinto evolved into a state doctrine that was linked with belief in the divinity of the emperor and the sacredness of the Japanese nation. A national shrine was established at Ise, north of the early capital of Nara, where the emperor annually paid tribute to the sun goddess. But although Shinto had evolved well beyond its primitive origins, like its counterparts elsewhere it could not satisfy all the religious and emotional needs of the Japanese people. For those needs, the Japanese turned to Buddhism.

As we have seen, Buddhism was introduced into Japan from China during the sixth century C.E. and had begun to spread beyond the court to the general population by the eighth century. As in China, most Japanese saw no contradiction between worshiping both the Buddha and their local nature gods, many of whom were considered to be later manifestations of the Buddha. Most of the Buddhist sects that had achieved popularity in China were established in Japan, and many of them attracted powerful patrons at court. Great monasteries were established that competed in wealth and influence with the noble families that had traditionally ruled the country.

Perhaps the two most influential Buddhist sects were the Pure Land (Jodo) sect and Zen (in Chinese, Chan or Ch'an). The Pure Land sect, which taught that devotion alone could lead to enlightenment and release, was very popular among the common people, for whom monastic life was one of the few routes to upward mobility. Among the aristocracy, the most influential school was Zen, which exerted a significant impact on Japanese life and culture during the era of the warring states. In its emphasis on austerity, self-discipline, and communion with nature, Zen complemented many traditional beliefs in Japanese society and became an important component of the samurai warrior's code.

In Zen teachings, there were various ways to achieve enlightenment (*satori* in Japanese). Some stressed that it could be achieved suddenly. One monk, for example, reportedly achieved *satori* by listening to the sound of a bamboo striking against roof tiles, another by carefully watching the opening of peach blossoms in the spring. But other practitioners, sometimes called adepts, said that enlightenment could come only through studying the scriptures and arduous self-discipline (known as *zazen*, or "seated Zen"). Seated Zen involved a lengthy process of meditation that cleansed the mind of extraneous thoughts so that it could concentrate on the essential.

Sources of Traditional Japanese Culture

Nowhere is the Japanese genius for blending indigenous and imported elements into an effective whole better demonstrated than in culture. In such widely diverse fields as art, architecture, sculpture, and literature, the Japanese from early times showed an impressive capacity to borrow selectively from abroad without destroying essential native elements.

Growing contact with China during the period of the rise of the Yamato state stimulated Japanese artists. Missions sent to China and Korea during the seventh and eighth centuries returned with examples of Tang literature, sculpture, and painting, all of which influenced the Japanese.

LITERATURE

Borrowing from Chinese models was somewhat complicated for Japanese authors, however. The early Japanese had no writing system for recording their own spoken language and initially adopted the Chinese written language for writing. But resourceful Japanese soon began to adapt the Chinese written characters so that they could be used for recording the Japanese language. In some cases, Chinese characters were given Japanese pronunciations. But Chinese characters ordinarily could not be used to record Japanese words, which normally contain more than one syllable. Sometimes the Japanese simply used Chinese characters as phonetic symbols that were combined to form Japanese words. Later they simplified the characters into phonetic symbols that were used alongside Chinese characters. This hybrid system continues to be used today.

At first, many educated Japanese preferred to write in Chinese, and a court literature—consisting of essays, poetry, and official histories—appeared in the classical Chinese language. But the native Japanese spoken language never totally disappeared among the educated classes and eventually became the instrument of a unique literature. With the lessening of Chinese political and cultural influence in the tenth century, Japanese verse resurfaced. Between the tenth and the fifteenth centuries, twenty imperial anthologies of poetry were compiled. Initially, they were written primarily by courtiers, but with the fall of the Heian court and the rise of the warrior and merchant classes, all literate segments of society began to produce poetry.

Japanese poetry is unique. It expresses its themes in a simple form, a characteristic stemming from traditional Japanese aesthetics, Zen religion, and the language itself. The aim of the Japanese poet was to create a mood, perhaps the melancholic effect of gently falling cherry blossoms or leaves. With a few specific references, the poet suggested a whole world, just as Zen Buddhism sought enlightenment from a sudden perception. Poets often alluded to earlier poems by repeating their images with small changes, a technique that was viewed not as plagiarism, but as an elaboration on the meaning of the earlier poem. The following poems in English translation illustrate this technique; the first poem is by Fujiwara no Michimune; the second is by Lady Sagami.

> *The under leaves*
> *In the autumn wind*
> *Must have become cold:*
> *In the moor of little lespedezas*
> *The quail are crying.*

> *The under leaves of the lespedeza*
> *When the dew is gathering*
> *Must be cold:*
> *In the autumn moor*
> *The young deer are crying.*[7]

By the fourteenth century, the technique of the "linked verse" had become the most popular form of Japanese poetry. Known as haiku, it is composed of seventeen syllables divided into lines of five, seven, and five syllables. The poems usually focused on images from nature and the mutability of life. Often the poetry was written by several individuals alternately composing verses and linking them together into long sequences of hundreds and even thousands of lines (see the box on p. 306).

Poetry served a unique function at the Heian court, where it was the initial means of communication between lovers. By custom, aristocratic women were isolated from all contact with men outside their immediate family and spent their days hidden behind screens. Some amused themselves by writing poetry. When courtship began, poetic exchanges were the only means a woman had to attract her prospective lover, who would be enticed solely by her poetic art.

During the Heian period, male courtiers wrote in Chinese, believing that Chinese civilization was superior and worthy of emulation. Like the Chinese, they viewed prose fiction as "vulgar gossip." Consequently, from the ninth to the twelfth century, Japanese women were the most prolific writers of prose fiction in Japanese. Excluded from school, they learned to read and write at home and wrote diaries, stories, and novels to pass the time. Some of the most talented women were invited to court as authors in residence.

From this tradition of female prose appeared one of the world's truly great novels, *The Tale of Genji*, written by the

A SAMPLE OF LINKED VERSE

One of the distinctive features of medieval Japanese literature was the technique of "linked verse." In a manner similar to haiku poetry today, such poems, known as renga, were written by groups of individuals who would join together to compose the poem, verse by verse. The following example, by three famous poets named Sogi, Shohaku, and Socho, is one of the most famous of the period.

THE THREE POETS AT MINASE

Snow clinging to slope,   Sogi
　On mist-enshrouded mountains
　　At eveningtime.
In the distance flows   Shohaku
　Through plum-scented villages.

Willows cluster   Socho
　In the river breeze
　　As spring appears.
The sound of a boat being poled   Sogi
　In the clearness at dawn
Still the moon lingers   Shohaku
As fog o'er-spreads
　The night.
A frost-covered meadow;   Socho
　Autumn has drawn to a close.
Against the wishes   Sogi
　Of droning insects
　　The grasses wither.

diarist and court author Murasaki Shikibu around the year 1000. The novel traces the life and loves of the courtier Genji as he strives to remain in favor with those in power while at the same time pursuing his cult of love and beauty (see the box on p. 307). The essential element in the story line, however, is the artistic refinement and sensitivity of the characters. The most important aspect of their lives is the style with which they write letters and poetry, sing songs, dance, or play the flute or the zither.

After the refined and gentle sadness of the era of Genji, Japanese fiction entered the increasingly pessimistic world of the warring states of Kamakura (1185–1333). Typically, the novels of this period focus on a solitary figure, who is aloof from the refinements of the court and faces battle and possibly death. Understandably, a new genre, that of the heroic war tale, developed out of the new warrior class. Such works described the military exploits of warriors, coupled with an overwhelming sense of sadness and loneliness.

During this period, the famous classical Japanese drama known as Nō also originated. Nō developed out of a variety of entertainment forms, such as dancing and juggling, that were part of the native tradition or had been imported from China and other regions of Asia. The plots were normally based on stories from Japanese history or legend. Eventually, Nō evolved into a highly stylized drama in which the performers wore masks and danced to the accompaniment of instrumental music. Like much of Japanese culture, Nō was restrained, graceful, and refined.

ART AND ARCHITECTURE

In art and architecture, as in literature, the Japanese pursued their interest in beauty, simplicity, and nature. To some degree, Japanese artists and architects were influenced by Chinese forms. As they became familiar with Chinese architecture, Japanese rulers and aristocrats tried to emulate the splendor of Tang civilization and began constructing their palaces and temples in Chinese style.

During the Heian period (794–1185), the search for beauty was reflected in various art forms, such as narrative hand scrolls, screens, sliding door panels, fans, and lacquer decoration. As in the case of literature, nature themes dominated, such as seashore scenes, a spring rain, moon and mist, or flowering wisteria and cherry blossoms. All were intended to evoke an emotional response on the part of the viewer. Japanese painting suggested the frail beauty of nature by presenting it on a smaller scale. The majestic mountain in a Chinese painting became a more intimate Japanese landscape with rolling hills and a rice field. Faces were rarely shown, and human drama was indicated by a woman lying prostrate or hiding her face in her sleeve. Tension was shown by two people talking at a great distance or with their backs to one another.

During the Kamakura period (1185–1333), the hand scroll with its physical realism and action-packed paintings of the new warrior class achieved great popularity. Reflecting these chaotic times, the art of portraiture flourished, and a scroll would include a full gallery of warriors and holy men in starkly realistic detail, including such unflattering features as stubble, worry lines on a forehead, and crooked teeth. Japanese sculptors also produced naturalistic wooden statues of generals, nobles, and saints. By far the most distinctive, however, were the fierce heavenly "guardian kings," who still intimidate the viewer today. In contrast to the refined atmosphere of the Fujiwara court, the Kamakura era was a warrior's world.

THE SEDUCTION OF THE AKASHI LADY

The Tale of Genji, *Japan's most famous novel, is a panoramic portrayal of court life in tenth-century Japan. In this excerpt, the courtier Genji has just seduced a lady at court and now feels misgivings at having betrayed his child bride. A koto is a Japanese string instrument similar to a zither.*

THE TALE OF GENJI

A curtain string brushed against a koto, to tell him that she had been passing a quiet evening at her music.

"And will you not play for me on the koto of which I have heard so much?"

"*Would there were someone with whom I might share my thoughts*
And so dispel some part of these sad dreams."
"*You speak to one for whom the night has no end.*
How can she tell the dreaming from the waking?"

The almost inaudible whisper reminded him strongly of the Rokujo lady.

This lady had not been prepared for an incursion and could not cope with it. She fled to an inner room. How she could have contrived to bar it he could not tell, but it was very firmly barred indeed. Though he did not exactly force his way through, it is not to be imagined that he left matters as they were. Delicate, slender—she was almost too beautiful. Pleasure was mingled with pity at the thought that he was imposing himself upon her. She was even more pleasing than reports from afar had had her. The autumn night, usually so long, was over in a trice. Not wishing to be seen, he hurried out, leaving affectionate assurances behind.

Genji called in secret from time to time. The two houses being some distance apart, he feared being seen by fishers, who were known to relish a good rumor, and sometimes several days would elapse between his visits. . . .

Genji dreaded having Murasaki [his bride] learn of the affair. He still loved her more than anyone, and he did not want her to make even joking reference to it. She was a quiet, docile lady, but she had more than once been unhappy with him. Why, for the sake of brief pleasure, had he caused her pain? He wished it were all his to do over again. The sight of the Akashi lady only brought new longing for the other lady.

He got off a more earnest and affectionate letter than usual, at the end of which he said: "I am in anguish at the thought that, because of foolish occurrences for which I have been responsible but have had little heart, I might appear in a guise distasteful to you. There has been a strange, fleeting encounter. That I should volunteer this story will make you see, I hope, how little I wish to have secrets from you. Let the gods be my judges.

"*It was but the fisherman's brush with the salty sea pine.*
Followed by a tide of tears of longing."

Her reply was gentle and unreproachful, and at the end of it she said: "That you should have deigned to tell me a dreamlike story which you could not keep to yourself calls to mind numbers of earlier instances.

"*Naive of me, perhaps; yet we did make our vows.*
And now see the waves that wash the Mountain of Waiting!"

It was the one note of reproach in a quiet, undemanding letter. He found it hard to put down, and for some nights he stayed away from the house in the hills.

Zen Buddhism, an import from China in the thirteenth century, also influenced Japanese aesthetics. With its emphasis on immediate enlightenment without recourse to intellectual analysis and elaborate ritual, Zen reinforced the Japanese predilection for simplicity and self-discipline. During this era, Zen philosophy found expression in the Japanese garden, the tea ceremony, the art of flower arranging, pottery and ceramics, and miniature plant display (the famous *bonsai*, literally "pot scenery").

Landscape served as an important means of expression in both Japanese art and architecture. Japanese gardens were initially modeled on Chinese examples. Early court texts during the Heian period emphasized the importance of including a stream or pond when creating a garden. The landscape surrounding the fourteenth-century Golden Pavilion in Kyoto displays a harmony of garden, water, and architecture that makes it one of the treasures of the world. Because of the shortage of water in the city, later gardens concentrated on rock composition, using white pebbles to represent water.

Like the Japanese garden, the tea ceremony represents the fusion of Zen and aesthetics. Developed in the fifteenth century, it was practiced in a simple room devoid of external ornament except for a *tatami* floor, sliding doors, and an alcove with a writing desk and asymmetrical shelves. The participants could therefore focus completely on the activity of pouring and drinking tea. "Tea and Zen have the same flavor," goes the Japanese saying. Considered the ultimate symbol of spiritual

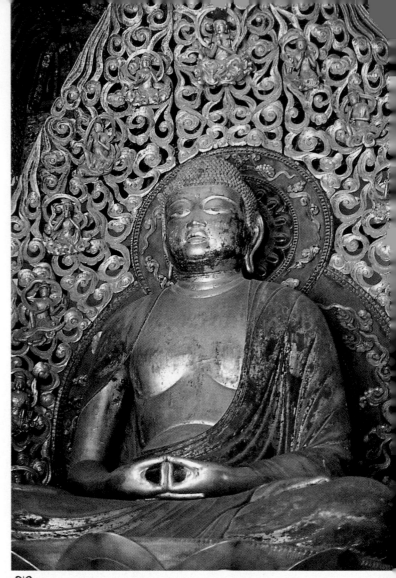

❀ GUARDIAN KINGS. Larger than life and intimidating in its presence, this thirteenth-century wooden statue departs from the refined atmosphere of the Heian court and pulsates with the masculine energy of the Kamakura period. Placed strategically at the entrance to Buddhist shrines, guardian kings such as this one protected the temple and the faithful.

❀ A SEATED BUDDHA. Buddhist statuary originated in India and China, and evolved as a popular art form in Japan from the seventh century on. Characteristic of these statues are the *mudras,* or hand and body positions by which the Buddha communicated with his followers. Here, his connected fingers indicate meditation. Whereas earlier Japanese sculptors worked in bronze, the depletion of metal reserves eventually necessitated the use of wood. This remarkable eleventh-century gilded wood carving, over ten feet in height, is composed of fifty-three pieces of cypress and exudes a feeling of stability and calm, expressing the Buddha's deep spirituality.

deliverance, the tea ceremony had great aesthetic value and moral significance in traditional times as well as today.

Japan and the Chinese Model

Few societies in Asia have historically been as isolated as Japan. Cut off from the mainland by 120 miles of frequently turbulent ocean, the Japanese had only minimal contact with the outside world during most of their early development.

Whether this isolation was ultimately beneficial to Japanese society cannot be determined. The lack of knowl-edge of developments taking place elsewhere probably delayed the process of change in Japan. On the other hand, the Japanese were spared the destructive invasions that afflicted other ancient civilizations. Certainly, once the Japanese became acquainted with Chinese culture at the height of the Tang era, they were quick to take advantage of the opportunity. In the space of a few decades, the young state adopted many aspects of Chinese society and culture and thereby introduced major changes into Japanese life.

Nevertheless, Japanese political institutions failed to follow all aspects of the Chinese pattern. Despite Prince Shotoku's effort to make effective use of the imperial traditions of Tang China, the decentralizing forces inside

308 PART II • NEW PATTERNS OF CIVILIZATION

THE GOLDEN PAVILION IN KYOTO. The landscape surrounding the Golden Pavilion displays a harmony of garden, water, and architecture that makes it one of the treasures of the world. Constructed in the fourteenth century as a retreat for the shoguns to withdraw from their administrative chores, the pavilion is named for the gold foil that covered its exterior. Completely destroyed by an arsonist in 1950 as a protest against the commercialism of modern Buddhism, it was rebuilt and reopened in 1987.

Japanese society remained dominant throughout the period under discussion in this chapter. Adoption of the Confucian civil service examination did not lead to a breakdown of Japanese social divisions; instead, the examination was administered in a manner that preserved and strengthened them. Although Buddhist and Daoist doctrines made a significant contribution to Japanese religious practices, Shinto beliefs continued to play a major role in shaping the Japanese worldview.

Why Japan did not follow the Chinese road to centralized authority has been the subject of some debate among historians. Some argue that the answer lies in differing cultural traditions, while others suggest that Chinese institutions and values were introduced too rapidly to be assimilated effectively by Japanese society. One factor may have been the absence of a foreign threat (except for the Mongols) in Japan. A recent view holds that diseases (such as smallpox and measles) imported inadvertently from China led to a marked decline in the population of the islands, reducing the food output and

preventing the population from coalescing in more compact urban centers.

In any event, Japan was not the only society in Asia to assimilate ideas from abroad while at the same time preserving customs and institutions inherited from the past. Across the Sea of Japan to the west and several thousand miles to the south, other Asian peoples were embarked on a similar journey. We now turn to their experience.

KOREA

No society in East Asia was more strongly influenced by the Chinese model than was that of Korea. Slightly larger than the state of Minnesota, the Korean peninsula was probably first settled by Altaic-speaking fishing and hunting peoples from neighboring Manchuria during the Neolithic Age. Because the area is relatively mountainous (only about one-fifth of the peninsula is adaptable to cultivation), farming was apparently not practiced until about 2000 B.C.E. The other aspect of Korea's geography that has profoundly affected its history is its proximity to both China and Japan.

In 109 B.C.E., the northern part of the peninsula came under direct Chinese rule. During the next several generations, the area was ruled by the Han dynasty, which divided the territory into provinces and introduced Chinese institutions. With the decline of the Han in the third century C.E., power gradually shifted to local tribal leaders, who drove out the Chinese administrators but continued to absorb Chinese cultural influence. Eventually, three separate kingdoms emerged on the peninsula: Koguryo in the north, Paekche in the southwest, and Silla in the southeast. The Japanese, who had recently established their own state on the Yamato plain, maintained a small colony on the southern coast.

The Three Kingdoms

From the fourth to the seventh centuries, the three kingdoms were bitter rivals for influence and territory on the peninsula. At the same time, all began to absorb Chinese political and cultural institutions. Chinese influence was most notable in Koguryo, where Buddhism was introduced in the late fourth century C.E., and the first Confucian academy on the peninsula was established in the capital at Pyongyang. All three kingdoms also appear to have accepted a tributary relationship with one or another of the squabbling states that emerged in China after the fall of the Han. The kingdom of Silla, less exposed than its two rivals to Chinese influence, was at first the weakest of the three, but eventually its greater internal cohesion—perhaps a consequence of the tenacity of its tribal traditions—enabled it to become the dominant power on

RYOANJI TEMPLE GARDEN IN KYOTO. As the result of a water shortage in the fifteenth century, Japanese landscape designers began to make increasing use of rocks and pebbles to represent water. In the Ryoanji Temple in the hills west of Kyoto, seventeen rocks surrounded by wavy raked pebbles are arranged in five groups to suggest mountains emerging from the sea. Here we experience the quintessential Japanese aesthetic expression of allusion, simplicity, restraint, and tranquillity.

the peninsula. Then the rulers of Silla forced the Chinese to withdraw from all but the area adjacent to the Yalu River. To pacify the haughty Chinese, Silla accepted tributary status under the Tang dynasty. The remaining Japanese colonies in the south were eliminated.

With the country unified for the first time, the rulers of Silla attempted to use Chinese political institutions and ideology to forge a centralized state. Buddhism, now rising in popularity, became the state religion, and Korean monks followed the paths of their Japanese counterparts on journeys to the Middle Kingdom. Chinese architecture and art became dominant in the capital at Kyongju and other urban centers, and the written Chinese language became the official means of communication at court. But powerful aristocratic families, long dominant in the southeastern part of the peninsula, were still influential at court. They were able to prevent the adoption of the Tang civil service examination system and resisted the distribution of manorial lands to the poor. The failure to adopt the Chinese model was fatal. Squabbling among noble families steadily increased, and after the assassination of the king of Silla in 780, the country sank into civil war.

Unification

In the early tenth century, a new dynasty called Koryo (the root of the modern word for Korea) arose in the north. The new kingdom adopted Chinese political insti-

tutions in an effort to strengthen its power and unify its territory. The civil service examination system was introduced in 958, but as in Japan, the bureaucracy continued to be dominated by influential aristocratic families.

The Koryo dynasty remained in power for four hundred years, protected from invasion by the absence of a strong dynasty in neighboring China. Under the Koryo, industry and commerce slowly began to develop, but as in China, agriculture was the prime source of wealth. In theory, all land was the property of the king, but in actuality noble families controlled their holdings. The lands were worked by peasants who were subject to burdens similar to those of European serfs. At the bottom of society was a class of "base people" (*chonmin*), composed of slaves, artisans, and other specialized workers.

KOREAN ROYAL CROWN. The Silla dynasty was renowned for the high quality of its gold, jewelry, crowns, and sword sheaths. Shown here is a jewel-inlaid royal crown of the fifth century C.E. that was excavated from a royal tomb in eastern Korea. Although much Silla artwork reflects Chinese influence, royal crowns located in Silla tombs often contain antler-like motifs, reflecting the animistic traditions of Korea's pre-Chinese past. The comma-shaped jewels symbolize the King's Heaven-sanctioned authority on earth.

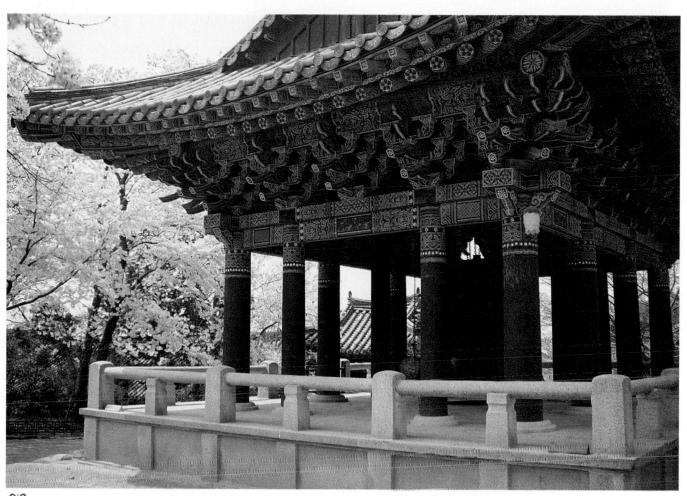

PULGUKSA BELL TOWER. Among the greatest architectural achievements on the Korean peninsula is the Pulguksa (Monastery of the Land of Buddha), built near the ancient capital of Silla in the eighth century C.E. Shown here is the Bell Tower, located in the midst of beautiful parklands on the monastery grounds. Young Korean couples often come to this monastery after their weddings to be photographed in the stunning surroundings.

From a cultural point of view, the Koryo era was one of high achievement. Buddhist monasteries, run by sects introduced from China like the Pure Land and Zen (Chan), controlled vast territories, while their monks served as royal advisers at court. At first Buddhist themes dominated in Korean art and sculpture, and the entire Tripitaka (the "three baskets" of the Buddhist canon) was printed by wooden blocks (see the box on p. 312). Eventually, however, with the appearance of landscape painting and porcelain, Confucian themes began to predominate.

Under the Mongols

Like its predecessor in Silla, the kingdom of Koryo was unable to overcome the power of the nobility and the absence of a reliable tax base. In the thirteenth century, the Mongols seized the northern part of the country and assimilated it into the Yuan empire. The weakened kingdom of Koryo became a tributary of the great khan in Khanbaliq (see Chapter 10).

The era of Mongol rule was one of profound suffering for the Korean people, especially the thousands of peasants and artisans who were compelled to perform corvée labor to help build the ships in preparation for Khubilai Khan's invasion of Japan. On the positive side, the Mongols introduced many new ideas and technology from China and further afield. The Koryo dynasty had managed to survive, but only by accepting Mongol authority, and when the power of the Mongols declined, the kingdom declined with it. With the rise to power of the Ming in China, Koryo collapsed, and power was seized by the military commander Yi Song-gye, who declared the founding of the new Yi dynasty in 1392. Once again, the Korean people were in charge of their own destiny.

THE FLOWER GARDEN SCRIPTURE

By the eighth century, Buddhism had come to Korea from China, and like their counterparts in Christian Europe, Korean monks could accumulate merit toward salvation by copying the scriptures. In this passage, the eighth-century Master Yongi of Hwangyong monastery has volunteered to copy a scripture as a way of expressing gratitude for the love of his parents and assisting others in following the Buddhist eight-fold path to wisdom. Note the careful attention to ritual as the process is brought to realization. This scripture, which was discovered in 1979, consisted of two scrolls of thirty white papers joined together, with characters in black ink. Each scroll was fourteen meters long.

AN EIGHTH-CENTURY BUDDHIST SCRIPTURE

The scripture is made as follows: First scented water is sprinkled around the roots of a paperbark mulberry tree to quicken its growth; the bark is then peeled and pounded to make paper with a clean surface. The copyists, the artisans who make the centerpiece of the scroll, and the painters who draw the images of buddhas and bodhisattvas all receive the bodhisattva ordination and observe abstinence. After relieving themselves, sleeping, eating, or drinking, they take a bath in scented water before returning to the work. Copyists are adorned with new pure garments, loose

trousers, a coarse crown, and a deva crown. Two azure-clad boys sprinkle water on their heads and . . . azure-clad boys and musicians perform music. The processions to the copying site are headed by one who sprinkles scented water on their path, another who scatters flowers, a dharma master who carries a censer, and another dharma master who chants Buddhist verses. Each of the copyists carries incense and flowers and invokes the name of the Buddha as he progresses.

Upon reaching the site, all take refuge in the Three Jewels (the Buddha, the Dharma, and the Order), make three bows, and offer the *Flower Garland Scripture* and others to buddhas and bodhisattvas. Then they sit down and copy the scripture, make the centerpiece of the scroll, and paint the buddhas and bodhisattvas. Thus, azure-clad boys and musicians cleanse everything before a piece of relic is placed in the center.

Now I make a vow that the copied scripture will not break till the end of the future—even when a major chilicosm is destroyed by the three calamities, this scripture shall be intact as the void. If all living beings rely on this scripture, they shall witness the Buddha, listen to his dharma, worship the relic, aspire to enlightenment without backsliding, cultivate the vows of the Universally Worthy Bodhisattva, and achieve Buddhahood.

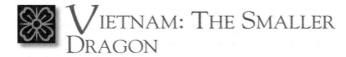 VIETNAM: THE SMALLER DRAGON

While the Korean people were attempting to establish their own identity in the shadow of the powerful Chinese empire, the peoples of Vietnam, on China's southern frontier, were trying to do the same. The Vietnamese began to practice irrigated agriculture in the flooded regions of the Red River delta at an early date and entered the Bronze Age sometime during the second millennium B.C.E. By about 200 B.C.E., a young state had begun to form in the area but immediately encountered the expanding power of the Qin empire (see Chapter 3). The Vietnamese were not easy to subdue, however (see the box on p. 313), and the collapse of the Qin dynasty temporarily enabled them to preserve their independence. Nevertheless, a century later, they were absorbed into the Han empire.

At first, the Han were satisfied to rule the delta as an autonomous region under the administration of the local landed aristocracy. But Chinese taxes were oppressive, and in 39 C.E. a revolt led by the Trung Sisters (widows of local nobles who had been executed by the Chinese) briefly brought Han rule to an end. The Chi-

nese soon suppressed the rebellion, however, and began to rule the area directly through officials dispatched from China. In time, however, these foreign officials began to intermarry with the local nobility and form a Sino-Vietnamese ruling class who, though trained in Chinese culture, began to identify with the cause of Vietnamese autonomy.

For nearly a thousand years, the Vietnamese were exposed to the art, architecture, literature, philosophy, and even the written language of China, as the Chinese attempted to integrate the area culturally as well as politically and administratively into their empire. To all intents and purposes, the Red River delta, then known to the Chinese as the "pacified South" (Annam), became a part of China.

The Rise of Great Viet

Despite the Chinese efforts to assimilate Vietnam, the Vietnamese sense of ethnic and cultural identity proved inextinguishable, and in the tenth century the Vietnamese took advantage of the collapse of the Tang dynasty in China to overthrow Chinese rule.

The new Vietnamese state, which called itself Dai Viet (Great Viet), became a dynamic new force on the South-

THE CHINESE CONQUEST OF VIETNAM

In the third century B.C.E., the armies of the Chinese state of Qin [Ch'in] invaded the Red River delta to launch an attack on the small Vietnamese state located there. As this passage by a Chinese historian shows, the Vietnamese were not easy to conquer, and the new state soon declared its independence from the Qin. It was a lesson that was too often forgotten by would-be conquerors in later centuries.

THE HUAI NAN TZU

Ch'in Shih Huang Ti was interested in the rhinoceros horn, the elephant tusks, the kingfisher plumes, and the pearls of the land of Yueh [Viet]; he therefore sent Commissioner T'u Sui at the head of five hundred thousand men divided into five armies. . . . For three years the sword and the crossbow were in constant readiness. Superintendent Lu was sent; there was no means of assuring the transport of supplies, so he employed soldiers to dig a canal for sending grain, thereby making it possible to wage war on

the people of Yueh. The lord of Western Ou, I Hsu Sung, was killed; consequently, the Yueh people entered the wilderness and lived there with the animals; none consented to be a slave of Ch'in; choosing from among themselves men of valor, they made them their leaders and attacked the Ch'in by night, inflicting on them a great defeat and killing Commissioner T'u Sui; the dead and wounded were many. After this, the emperor deported convicts to hold the garrisons against the Yueh people.

The Yueh people fled into the depths of the mountains and forests, and it was not possible to fight them. The soldiers were kept in garrisons to watch over abandoned territories. This went on for a long time, and the soldiers grew weary. Then the Yueh came out and attacked; the Ch'in soldiers suffered a great defeat. Subsequently, convicts were sent to hold the garrisons against the Yueh.

---

east Asian mainland. As the population of the Red River delta expanded, Dai Viet soon came into conflict with Champa, its neighbor to the south. Located along the central coast of modern Vietnam, Champa was a trading society based on Indian cultural traditions. Over the next several centuries, the two states fought on numerous occasions, until by the end of the fifteenth century Dai Viet had conquered Champa. The Vietnamese then resumed their march southward, establishing agricultural settlements in the newly conquered territory. By the seventeenth century, the Vietnamese had reached the Gulf of Siam.

The Vietnamese faced an even more serious challenge from the north. The Song dynasty in China, beset with its own problems on the northern frontier, eventually accepted the Dai Viet ruler's offer of tribute status, but later dynasties attempted to reintegrate the Red River delta into the Chinese empire. The first effort was made in the late thirteenth century by the Mongols, who attempted on two occasions to conquer the Vietnamese. After a series of bloody battles, during which the Vietnamese displayed an impressive capacity for guerrilla warfare, the invaders were driven out. A little over a century later, the Ming dynasty tried again, and for twenty years Vietnam was once more under Chinese rule. In 1428, the Vietnamese evicted the Chinese again, but the experience had contributed to the strong sense of Vietnamese identity.

THE CHINESE LEGACY

Despite their stubborn resistance to Chinese rule, after the restoration of independence in the tenth century, Vietnamese rulers quickly discovered the convenience of the

Confucian model in administering a river valley society and therefore attempted to follow Chinese practice in forming their own state. The ruler styled himself an emperor like his counterpart to the north (although he prudently termed himself a king in his direct dealings with the Chinese court), adopted Chinese court rituals, claimed the Mandate of Heaven, and arrogated to himself the same authority and privileges in his dealings with his subjects. But unlike a Chinese emperor, who had no particular symbolic role as defender of the Chinese people or Chinese culture, a Vietnamese monarch was viewed, above all, as the symbol and defender of Vietnamese independence.

Like their Chinese counterparts, Vietnamese rulers fought to preserve their authority from the challenges of powerful aristocratic families and turned to the Chinese bureaucratic model, including civil service examinations, as a means of doing so. Under the pressure of strong monarchs, the concept of merit eventually took hold, and the power of the landed aristocracy was weakened if not entirely broken. The Vietnamese adopted much of the Chinese administrative structure, including the six ministries, the censorate, and the various levels of provincial and local administration.

Another aspect of the Chinese legacy was the spread of Buddhist, Daoist, and Confucian ideas, which supplemented the Viets' traditional belief in nature spirits. Buddhist precepts became popular among the local population, who integrated the new faith into their existing belief system by founding Buddhist temples dedicated to the local village deity in the hope of guaranteeing an abundant harvest. Upper-class Vietnamese educated in the Confucian classics tended to follow the

Chinese conquest of Korea and Vietnam	First century B.C.E.
Trung Sisters' Revolt	39 C.E.
Foundation of Champa	192
Era of Three Kingdoms in Korea	Fourth–seventh centuries C.E.
Restoration of Vietnamese independence	939
Mongol invasion of Korea and Vietnam	1257–1285
Foundation of Yi dynasty in Korea	1392
Vietnamese conquest of Champa	1471

❀ **THE TEMPLE OF LITERATURE, HANOI.** When the Vietnamese regained their independence from China in the tenth century C.E., they retained Chinese institutions that they deemed beneficial. A prime example was the establishment of the Temple of Literature, Vietnam's first university, in 1076. Here the sons of mandarins were educated in the Confucian classics in preparation for an official career. Beginning in the fifteenth century, those receiving doctorates had stelae erected to identify their achievements. Shown here is the central hall of the temple, where advanced students took the metropolitan examinations for the doctorate.

more agnostic Confucian doctrine, but some joined Buddhist monasteries. Daoism also flourished at all levels of society and, as in China, provided a structure for animistic beliefs and practices that still predominated at the village level.

During the early period of independence, Vietnamese culture also borrowed liberally from its larger neighbor. Educated Vietnamese tried their hand at Chinese poetry, wrote dynastic histories in the Chinese style, and followed Chinese models in sculpture, architecture, and porcelain. Many of the notable buildings of the medieval period, such as the Temple of Literature and the famous One-Pillar Pagoda in Hanoi, are classic examples of Chinese architecture.

But there were signs that Vietnamese creativity would eventually transcend the bounds of Chinese cultural norms. Although most classical writing was undertaken in literary Chinese, the only form of literary expression deemed suitable by Confucian conservatives, an adaptation of Chinese written characters, called *Chu Nom* (southern characters), was devised to provide a written system for spoken Vietnamese. In use by the early ninth century, it eventually began to be used for the composition of essays and poetry in the Vietnamese language. Such pioneering efforts would lead in later centuries to the emergence of a vigorous national literature totally independent of Chinese forms.

Society and Family Life

Vietnamese social institutions and customs were also strongly influenced by those of China. As in China, the introduction of a Confucian system and the adoption of

THE ONE-PILLAR PAGODA, HANOI. This eleventh-century pagoda was built at the order of a Vietnamese monarch who had dreamed that the Buddhist goddess of mercy, while seated on a lotus, had promised him a son. Shortly after the dream, the emperor fathered a son. In gratitude he constructed this distinctive pagoda on one pillar, resembling a lotus blossom, the Buddhist symbol of purity, rising out of the mud.

civil service examinations undermined the role of the old landed aristocrats and led eventually to their replacement by the scholar-gentry class. Also as in China, the examinations were open to most males, regardless of family background, which opened the door to a degree of social mobility unknown in most of the Indianized states elsewhere in the region. Candidates for the bureaucracy read many of the same Confucian classics and absorbed the same ethical principles as their counterparts in China. At the same time, they were also exposed to the classic works of Vietnamese history, which strengthened their sense that Vietnam was a distinct culture similar to, but separate from, that of China.

The vast majority of the Vietnamese people, however, were peasants. Most were small landholders or sharecroppers, who rented their plots from wealthier farmers, but large estates were rare due to the systematic efforts of the central government to prevent the rise of a powerful local landed elite.

Family life in Vietnam was similar in many respects to that in China. The Confucian concept of family took hold during the period of Chinese rule, along with the related concepts of filial piety and gender inequality. Perhaps the most striking difference between family traditions in China and Vietnam was that Vietnamese women possessed more rights both in practice and by law. Since ancient times wives had been permitted to own property and initiate divorce proceedings. One consequence of Chinese rule was a growing emphasis on male dominance, but the tradition of women's rights was never totally extinguished and was legally recognized in a law code promulgated in 1460.

Moreover, Vietnam had a strong historical tradition associating heroic women with the defense of the homeland. The Trung Sisters were the first but by no means the only example. In the following passage, a Vietnamese historian of the eighteenth century recounts their story:

> The imperial court was far away; local officials were greedy and oppressive. At that time the country of one hundred sons was the country of the women of Lord To. The ladies [the Trung Sisters] used the female arts against their irrec-

oncilable foe; skirts and hairpins sang of patriotic righteousness, uttered a solemn oath at the inner door of the ladies' quarters, expelled the governor, and seized the capital. . . . Were they not grand heroines? . . . Our two ladies brought forward an army of all the people, and, establishing a royal court that settled affairs in the territories of the sixty-five strongholds, shook their skirts over the Hundred Yueh [the Vietnamese people].[8]

CONCLUSION

There are some tantalizing similarities among the three countries we have examined in this chapter. All borrowed liberally from the Chinese model. At the same time, all adapted Chinese institutions and values to the conditions prevailing in their own societies. Though all expressed admiration and respect for China's achievement, all sought to keep Chinese power at a distance.

As an island nation, Japan was the most successful of the three in protecting its political sovereignty and its cultural identity. Both Korea and Vietnam were compelled on various occasions to defend their independence by force of arms. That experience may have shaped their strong sense of national distinctiveness, which we shall discuss further in a later chapter.

The appeal of Chinese institutions can undoubtedly be explained by the fact that Japan, Korea, and Vietnam were all agrarian societies, much like their larger neighbor. But it is undoubtedly significant that the aspect of Chinese political culture that was least amenable to adoption abroad was the civil service examination system. The Confucian concept of meritocracy ran directly counter to the strong aristocratic tradition that flourished in all three societies during their early stage of development. Even when the system was adopted, it was put to quite different uses. Only in Vietnam did the concept of merit eventually triumph over that of birth, as strong rulers of Dai Viet attempted to initiate the Chinese model as a means of creating a centralized system of government.

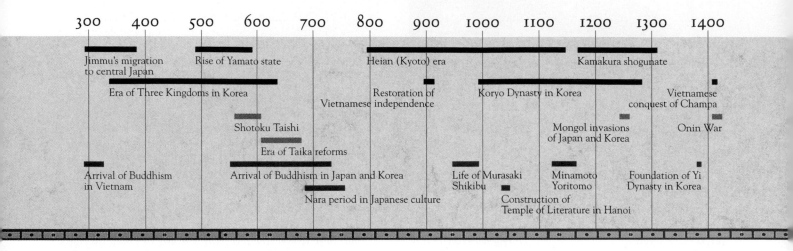

300   400   500   600   700   800   900   1000   1100   1200   1300   1400

Jimmu's migration to central Japan

Rise of Yamato state

Heian (Kyoto) era

Kamakura shogunate

Era of Three Kingdoms in Korea

Restoration of Vietnamese independence

Koryo Dynasty in Korea

Vietnamese conquest of Champa

Shotoku Taishi

Mongol invasions of Japan and Korea

Onin War

Era of Taika reforms

Arrival of Buddhism in Vietnam

Arrival of Buddhism in Japan and Korea

Life of Murasaki Shikibu

Minamoto Yoritomo

Foundation of Yi Dynasty in Korea

Nara period in Japanese culture

Construction of Temple of Literature in Hanoi

CHAPTER NOTES

1. Keith W. Taylor, *The Birth of Vietnam* (Berkeley, Calif., 1983), p. 75.
2. Quoted in David John Lu, *Sources of Japanese History*, vol. 1 (New York, 1974), p. 7.
3. From "The History of Wei," quoted in ibid., p. 10.
4. From "The Law of Households," quoted in ibid., p. 32.
5. From "On the Salvation of Women," quoted in ibid., p. 127.

6. Quoted in Barbara Ruch, "The other side of culture in medieval Japan," in Kozo Yamamura, ed., *The Cambridge History of Japan*, vol. 3, *Medieval Japan* (Cambridge, 1990), p. 506.
7. From Donald Keene, *Anthology of Japanese Literature* (New York, 1955), p. 24.
8. Quoted in Taylor, *The Birth of Vietnam*, pp. 336–37.

SUGGESTED READINGS

Some of the standard treatments of the rise of Japanese civilization appear in textbooks dealing with the early history of East Asia. Two of the best are J. K. Fairbank, E. O. Reischauer, and A. M. Craig, *East Asia: Tradition and Transformation* (Boston, 1973), and C. Schirokauer, *A Brief History of Chinese and Japanese Civilizations* (San Diego, Calif., 1989). A number of historical works deal specifically with early Japan. G. Sansom, *A History of Japan to 1334* (Stanford, Calif., 1958) is now somewhat out of date but is still informative and very well written. For the latest scholarship on the early period, see the first three volumes of *The Cambridge History of Japan*, ed. J. W. Hall, M. B. Jansen, M. Kanai, and D. Twitchett (Cambridge, 1988).

The best available collections of documents on the early history of Japan are D. J. Lu, ed., *Sources of Japanese History*, vol. 1 (New York, 1974), and Ryusaku Tsunoda et al., eds., *Sources of Japanese Tradition*, vol. 1 (New York, 1958). For some stunning illustrations with a brief text, see *Peoples and Places of the Past: The National Geographic Illustrated Cultural Atlas of the Ancient World* (Rockville, Md., 1983).

For specialized books on the early historical period, see R. J. Pearson, ed., *Windows on the Japanese Past: Studies in Archaeology and Prehistory* (Ann Arbor, Mich., 1986). J. W. Hall, *Government and Local Power in Japan, 500–1700* (Princeton, 1966) provides a detailed analysis of the development of Japanese political institutions. The relationship between disease and state building is analyzed in W. W. Farris, *Population, Disease, and Land in Early Japan, 645–900* (Cam-

bridge, 1985). The Kamakura period is covered in J. P. Mass, ed., *Court and Bakufu in Japan: Essays in Kamakura History* (New Haven, 1982). See also H. P. Varley, *The Onin War* (New York, 1977). For Japanese Buddhism, see W. T. de Bary, ed., *The Buddhist Tradition in India, China, and Japan* (New York, 1972).

A concise and provocative introduction to women's issues during this period in Japan, as well as in other parts of the world, can be found in S. S. Hughes and B. Hughes, *Women in World History* (Armonk, N.Y., 1995). For a tenth-century account of daily life for women at the Japanese court, see I. Morris, trans. and ed., *The Pillow Book of Sei Shonagon* (New York, 1991). For the changes that took place from matrilocal and matrilineal marriages to a patriarchal society, consult H. Tonomura, "Black Hair and Red Trousers: Gendering the Flesh in Medieval Japan," in *American Historical Review* 99 (1994).

The best introduction to Japanese literature for college students is still the concise and insightful D. Keene, *Japanese Literature: An Introduction for Western Readers* (London, 1953). The most comprehensive anthology is D. Keene, *Anthology of Japanese Literature* (New York, 1955), while the best history of Japanese literature, also by D. Keene, is *Seeds in the Heart: Japanese Literature from Earlier Times to the Late Sixteenth Century* (New York, 1993).

For the text of *The Tale of Genji*, see A. Waley's translation (New York, 1935) and a more recent one by E. Seidensticker (Tokyo, 1977). The best translation for college students is the latter's abridged Vintage Classics edition of 1990, which captures the spirit of the original in 360 pages. Of the many works on the novel, a most accessible and stimulating presentation is I. Morris, *The World of the Shining Prince: Court Life in Ancient Japan* (New York, 1964).

For the most comprehensive and accessible introduction to Japanese art, consult P. Mason, *History of Japanese Art* (New York, 1993). Also see the concise J. Stanley-Baker, *Japanese Art* (London, 1984). For a stimulating text with magnificent illustrations, see D. and V. Elisseeff, *Art of Japan* (New York, 1985). See also J. E. Kidder, Jr., *The Art of Japan* (London, 1985) for an insightful text accompanied by beautiful photographs.

For an informative and readable history of Korea that emphasizes the early period, see W. E. Henthorn, *A History of Korea* (New York, 1971). P. H. Lee, ed., *Sourcebook of Korean Civilization*, vol. 1 (New York, 1993) is a rich collection of documents dating from the period prior to the sixteenth century.

Vietnam often receives little attention in general studies of Southeast Asia because it was part of the Chinese empire for much of the traditional period. For a detailed investigation of the origins of Vietnamese civilization, see K. W. Taylor, *The Birth of Vietnam* (Berkeley, Calif., 1983). T. Hodgkin, *Vietnam: The Revolutionary Path* (New York, 1981) provides an overall survey of Vietnamese history to modern times. See also J. Buttinger, *The Smaller Dragon: A Political History of Vietnam* (New York, 1966).

INFOTRAC COLLEGE EDITION

For additional reading, go to InfoTrac College Edition, your online research library at http://web1.infotrac-college.com

Enter the search terms "Asia history" using Keywords.

Enter the search terms "Japan history" using Keywords.

Enter the search term "Shinto" using Keywords.

Enter the search terms "Korea history" using Keywords.

Enter the search terms "Zen Buddhism" using Keywords.

CHAPTER 12

THE MAKING OF EUROPE AND THE WORLD OF THE BYZANTINE EMPIRE, 500–1300

CHAPTER OUTLINE

- THE TRANSFORMATION OF THE ROMAN WORLD
- THE WORLD OF LORDS AND VASSALS
- THE GROWTH OF EUROPEAN KINGDOMS
- THE WORLD OF THE PEASANTS
- THE NEW WORLD OF TRADE AND CITIES
- CHRISTIANITY AND MEDIEVAL CIVILIZATION
- THE CULTURAL WORLD OF THE HIGH MIDDLE AGES
- THE BYZANTINE EMPIRE AND THE CRUSADES
- CONCLUSION

FOCUS QUESTIONS

- What contributions did the Romans, the Christian church, and the Germanic peoples make to the new civilization that emerged in Europe after the collapse of the Western Roman Empire?
- What roles did aristocrats and peasants play in medieval European civilization, and how did their lifestyles differ?
- What were the main aspects of the economic, intellectual, cultural, and spiritual revivals that took place in Europe during the High Middle Ages?
- What were the main characteristics of the Byzantine Empire, and how did it differ from the kingdoms that emerged in western Europe?
- What were the main reasons for the Crusades, and what did they accomplish?

In 800, Charlemagne, the king of the Franks, journeyed to Rome to help Pope Leo III, head of the Catholic church, who was barely clinging to power in the face of rebellious Romans. On Christmas Day, Charlemagne and his family, attended by Romans, Franks, and even visitors from the Byzantine Empire, crowded into St. Peter's Basilica to hear mass. Quite unexpectedly, according to a Frankish writer, "as the king rose from praying before the tomb of the blessed apostle Peter, Pope Leo placed a golden crown on his head." In keeping with ancient tradition, the people in the church shouted, "Long life and victory to Charles Augustus, crowned by God the great and peace-loving Emperor of the

Romans." Seemingly, the Roman Empire in the West had been reborn, and Charles had become the first Roman emperor since 476. But this "Roman emperor" was actually a German king, and he had been crowned by the head of the western Christian church. In truth, the coronation of Charlemagne was a sign not of the rebirth of the Roman Empire, but of the emergence of a new European civilization that came into being in western Europe after the collapse of the Western Roman Empire.

This new civilization—European civilization—was formed by the coming together of three major elements: the legacy of the Romans, the Christian church, and the Germanic peoples who moved in and settled the Western Roman Empire. The Germans were another prominent example of the almost constant migration of nomadic peoples during this period. By 800, the contours of a new European civilization were beginning to emerge in western Europe. Increasingly, Europe would become the focus and center of Western civilization. European civilization developed during a period that historians call the Middle Ages, or the medieval period, which lasted from about 500 to 1500. To the historians who first used the title, the Middle Ages were a middle period between the ancient and modern worlds.

At the same time that medieval European civilization was emerging in the west, the eastern part of the old Roman Empire, increasingly Greek in culture, continued to survive as the Byzantine Empire. While serving as a buffer between Europe and the peoples to the east, the Byzantine or Eastern Roman Empire also preserved the intellectual and legal accomplishments of the Greeks and Romans. ❀

THE TRANSFORMATION OF THE ROMAN WORLD

The Germanic peoples were an important component of the new European civilization. Already by the third century C.E., they had begun to move into the lands of the Roman Empire. As imperial authority vanished in the fifth century, a number of German kings set up new states. By 500, the Western Roman Empire had been replaced politically by a series of states ruled by German kings.

The New Germanic Kingdoms

The fusion of Romans and Germans took different forms in the various Germanic kingdoms. Both the kingdom of the Ostrogoths in Italy and the kingdom of the Visigoths in Spain maintained the Roman structure of government for the larger native populations, while a Germanic warrior caste came to dominate. Over a period of time, Germans and natives began to fuse. In Britain, however, when the Roman armies abandoned Britain at the beginning of the fifth century, the Angles and Saxons, Germanic tribes from Denmark and northern Germany, moved in and settled there. Eventually, these peoples succeeded in carving out small kingdoms throughout the island.

THE KINGDOM OF THE FRANKS

Only one of the German states on the European continent proved long-lasting—the kingdom of the Franks. The establishment of a Frankish kingdom was the work of Clovis (c. 482–511), a member of the Merovingian dynasty who became a Catholic Christian around 500. He was not the first German king to convert to Christianity, but the others had joined the Arian sect of Christianity, a group who believed that Jesus had been human and thus not truly God. The Christian church in Rome, which had become known as the Roman Catholic church, regarded the Arians as heretics, or people who believed in teachings different from the official church doctrine. To Catholics, Jesus was human, but of the "same substance" as God and therefore also truly God. Clovis found that his conversion to Catholic Christianity gained him the support of the Roman Catholic church, which was only too eager to obtain the friendship of a major Germanic ruler who was a Catholic Christian.

By 510, Clovis had established a powerful new Frankish kingdom stretching from the Pyrenees in the west to German lands in the east (modern France and western Germany). After Clovis's death, however, his sons divided his newly created kingdom, as was the Frankish custom. During the sixth and seventh centuries, the once united Frankish kingdom came to be divided into three major areas: Neustria, in northern Gaul; Austrasia, consisting of the ancient Frankish lands on both sides of the Rhine; and the former kingdom of Burgundy.

THE SOCIETY OF THE GERMANIC PEOPLES

As Germans and Romans intermarried and began to create a new society, some of the social customs of the Germanic peoples came to play an important role. The crucial

The conversion of Clovis to Catholic Christianity was an important factor in gaining papal support for his Frankish kingdom. In this illustration from a medieval manuscript, bishops and nobles look on while Clovis is baptized. One of the nobles holds a crown while a dove, symbol of the Holy Spirit, descends from heaven, bringing sacred oil for the ceremony.

social bond among the Germanic peoples was the family, especially the extended family of husbands, wives, children, brothers, sisters, cousins, and grandparents. In addition to working the land together and passing it down to future generations, the extended family also provided protection, which was sorely needed in the violent atmosphere of Merovingian times.

The Frankish family structure was quite simple. Males were dominant and made all the important decisions. A woman obeyed her father until she married and then fell under the legal domination of her husband. For most women in the new Germanic kingdoms, their legal status reflected the material conditions of their lives. Archaeological evidence suggests that most women had life expectancies of only thirty or forty years, while about 10 to 15 percent of women died in their childbearing years, no doubt due to complications associated with childbirth. For most women, life consisted of domestic labor: providing food and clothing for the household, caring for the children, and assisting with numerous farming chores. Of all the labors of women, the most important was childbearing, because it was a crucial element in providing for the maintenance of the family and its properties.

The German conception of family affected the way Germanic law treated crime and punishment. In the Roman system, as in our own, a crime such as murder was considered an offense against society or the state and was handled by a court that heard evidence and arrived at a decision. Germanic law was personal. An injury by one person against another could lead to a blood feud in which the family of the injured party took revenge on the family of the wrongdoer. Feuds could lead to savage acts of revenge, such as hacking off hands or feet, gouging out eyes, or slicing off ears and noses. Because this system could

easily get out of control, an alternative system arose that made use of a fine called *wergeld,* which was paid by a wrongdoer to the family of the person he had injured or killed. *Wergeld,* which means "money for a man," was the value of a person in monetary terms. That value varied considerably according to social status. An offense against a nobleman, for example, cost considerably more than one against a freeperson or a slave.

Germanic law provided two common means of determining guilt: compurgation and the ordeal. Compurgation involved the swearing of an oath by the accused person, backed up by a group of twelve or twenty-five "oath helpers," who would also swear that the accused was telling the truth. The ordeal was based on the idea of divine intervention; divine forces (whether pagan or Christian) would not allow an innocent person to be harmed (see the box on p. 321).

The Role of the Christian Church

By the end of the fourth century, Christianity had become the predominant religion of the Roman Empire. As the official Roman state disintegrated, the Christian church played an increasingly important role in the emergence and growth of the new European civilization.

THE ORGANIZATION OF THE CHURCH

By the fourth century, the Christian church had developed a system of government. The Christian community in each city was headed by a bishop, whose area of jurisdiction was known as a bishopric, or diocese; the bishoprics of each Roman province were joined together under the direction of an archbishop. The bishops of four

GERMANIC CUSTOMARY LAW: THE ORDEAL

*I*n Germanic customary law, the ordeal was used as a means by which accused persons might clear themselves. Although the ordeal took different forms, all involved a physical trial of some sort, such as holding a red-hot iron. It was believed that God would protect the innocent and allow them to come through the ordeal unharmed. This sixth-century account by Gregory of Tours describes an ordeal by hot water.

GREGORY OF TOURS, AN ORDEAL OF HOT WATER (c. 580)

An Arian presbyter disputing with a deacon of our religion made venomous assertions against the Son of God and the Holy Ghost, as is the habit of that sect [the Arians]. But when the deacon had discoursed a long time concerning the reasonableness of our faith and the heretic, blinded by the fog of unbelief, continued to reject the truth, . . . the former said: "Why weary ourselves with long discussions? Let acts approve the truth; let a kettle be heated over the fire and someone's ring be thrown into the boiling water. Let him who shall take it from the heated liquid be approved as a follower of the truth, and afterward let the other party be converted to the knowledge of the truth. And do you also understand, O heretic, that this our party will fulfill the conditions with the aid of the Holy Ghost; you shalt confess that there is no discordance, no dissimilarity in the Holy Trinity." The heretic consented to the proposition and they separated after appointing the next morning for the trial. But the fervor of faith in which the deacon had first made this suggestion began to cool through the instigation of the enemy. Rising with the dawn he bathed his arm in oil and smeared it with ointment. But

nevertheless he made the round of the sacred places and called in prayer on the Lord. . . . About the third hour they met in the marketplace. The people came together to see the show. A fire was lighted, the kettle was placed upon it, and when it grew very hot the ring was thrown into the boiling water. The deacon invited the heretic to take it out of the water first. But he promptly refused, saying, "You who did propose this trial are the one to take it out." The deacon all of a tremble bared his arm. And when the heretic presbyter saw it besmeared with ointment he cried out: "With magic arts you have thought to protect yourself, that you have made use of these salves, but what you have done will not avail." While they were thus quarreling there came up a deacon from Ravenna named Iacinthus and inquired what the trouble was about. When he learned the truth he drew his arm out from under his robe at once and plunged his right hand into the kettle. Now the ring that had been thrown in was a little thing and very light so that it was thrown about by the water as chaff would be blown about by the wind; and searching for it a long time he found it after about an hour. Meanwhile the flame beneath the kettle blazed up mightily so that the greater heat might make it difficult for the ring to be followed by the hand; but the deacon extracted it at length and suffered no harm, protesting rather that at the bottom the kettle was cold while at the top it was just pleasantly warm. When the heretic beheld this he was greatly confused and audaciously thrust his hand into the kettle saying, "My faith will aid me." As soon as his hand had been thrust in all the flesh was boiled off the bones clear up to the elbow. And so the dispute ended.

great cities—Rome, Jerusalem, Alexandria, and Antioch—held positions of special power in church affairs because the churches in these cities all asserted that they had been founded by the original apostles sent out by Jesus. Soon, however, one of them—the bishop of Rome—claimed even more, that he was the leader of the western Christian church. According to church tradition, Jesus had given the keys to the kingdom of heaven to Peter, who was considered the chief apostle and the first bishop of Rome. Subsequent bishops of Rome were considered Peter's successors and came to be known as popes (from the Latin word *papa*, meaning father) of the Catholic church.

Although western Christians came to accept the bishop of Rome as head of the church in the fourth and fifth centuries, there was certainly no unanimity on the extent of the powers the pope possessed as a result of his position. Nevertheless, in the sixth century, a strong pope, Greg-

ory I, known as Gregory the Great, strengthened the power of the papacy and the Roman Catholic church. As pope, Gregory I (590–604) assumed direction of Rome and its surrounding territories, thus giving the papacy a source of political power in a territorial unit that eventually came to be known as the Papal States. Gregory also extended papal authority over the Christian church in the west and was especially active in converting the pagan peoples of Germanic Europe. His primary instrument was the monastic movement.

THE MONKS AND THEIR MISSIONS

A monk (Latin *monachus*, meaning "someone who lives alone") was one who sought to live a life divorced from the world, cut off from ordinary human society, in order to pursue an ideal of godliness, or total dedication to the will of God. At first, Christian monasticism was based on the

MAP 12.1   The New Kingdoms of the Old Western Empire

Political Divisions of Britain
- Angles
- Saxons
- Jutes
- Britons

monastic groups and was crucial to the growth of monasticism in the western Christian world.

Benedict's rule divided each day into a series of activities with primary emphasis on prayer and manual labor. All monks were required to perform physical work of some kind for several hours a day because idleness was "the enemy of the soul." At the very heart of community practice was prayer, the proper "Work of God." While this included private meditation and reading, all monks in the monastery gathered together seven times during the day for common prayer and chanting of psalms. A Benedictine life was a communal one. Monks ate, worked, slept, and worshiped together.

Each Benedictine monastery was strictly ruled by an abbot, or "father" of the monastery, who had complete authority over his fellow monks. Unquestioning obedience to the will of the abbot was expected of each monk. Each Benedictine monastery held lands that enabled it to be a self-sustaining community, isolated from and independent of the world surrounding it. Within the monastery, however, monks were to fulfill their vow of poverty: "Let all things be common to all, as it is written, lest anyone should say that anything is his own."[1] The first monks were men, but women (called nuns) also began to withdraw from the world to dedicate themselves to God.

Monasticism played an indispensable role in early medieval civilization. Monks became the new heroes of Christian civilization, and their dedication to God became the highest ideal of Christian life. They were the social workers of their communities: monks provided schools for the young, hospitality for travelers, and hospitals for the sick. Monks also copied Latin works and passed on the legacy of the ancient world to the new European civilization. Monasteries became centers of learning wherever they were located. Moreover, the monks were important in spreading Christianity to the entire European world. English and Irish monks were particularly enthusiastic missionaries, who undertook the conversion of pagan peoples, especially in Germany.

Women, too, played an important role in the monastic missionary movement and the conversion of the Germanic kingdoms. Many of the abbesses (an abbess was the head

model of the solitary hermit who gives up all civilized society to pursue a spiritual life. Saint Simeon the Stylite, for example, lived for thirty years in a basket atop a pillar more than sixty feet high.

These early monks, however, soon found themselves unable to live in solitude. Their feats of holiness attracted followers on a wide scale, and as the monastic ideal spread, a new form of monasticism based on living together in a community soon became the dominant form. Monastic communities came to be seen as the ideal Christian society that could provide a moral example to the wider society around them.

Saint Benedict (c. 480–c. 543), who founded a monastic house for which he wrote a set of rules, established the basic form of monastic life in the western Christian church. The Benedictine rule came to be used by other

THE ACHIEVEMENTS OF CHARLEMAGNE

Einhard, the biographer of Charlemagne, was born in the valley of the Main River in Germany about 775. Raised and educated in the monastery of Fulda, an important center of learning, he arrived at the court of Charlemagne in 791 or 792. Although he did not achieve high office under Charlemagne, he served as private secretary to Louis the Pious, Charlemagne's son and successor. In this selection, Einhard discusses some of Charlemagne's accomplishments.

EINHARD, *LIFE OF CHARLEMAGNE*

Such are the wars, most skillfully planned and successfully fought, which this most powerful king waged during the forty-seven years of his reign. He so largely increased the Frank kingdom, which was already great and strong when he received it at his father's hands, that more than double its former territory was added to it. . . . He subdued all the wild and barbarous tribes dwelling in Germany between the Rhine and the Vistula, the Ocean and the Danube, all of which speak very much the same language, but differ widely from one another in customs and dress. . . .

He added to the glory of his reign by gaining the good will of several kings and nations; so close, indeed, was the alliance that he contracted with Alfonso, King of Galicia and Asturias, that the latter, when sending letters or ambassadors to Charles, invariably styled himself his man. . . . The Emperors of Constantinople [the Byzantine emperors] sought friendship and alliance with Charles by several embassies; and even when the Greeks [the Byzantines] suspected him of designing to take the empire from them, because of his assumption of the title Emperor, they made a close alliance with him, that he might have no cause of offense. In fact, the power of the Franks was always viewed with a jealous eye, whence the Greek proverb, "Have the Frank for your friend, but not for your neighbor."

This King, who showed himself so great in extending his empire and subduing foreign nations, and was constantly occupied with plans to that end, undertook also very many works calculated to adorn and benefit his kingdom, and brought several of them to completion. Among these, the most deserving of mention are the basilica of the Holy Mother of God at Aix-la-Chapelle [Aachen], built in the most admirable manner, and a bridge over the Rhine River at Mainz, half a mile long, the breadth of the river at this point. . . . Above all, sacred buildings were the object of his care throughout his whole kingdom; and whenever he found them falling to ruin from age, he commanded the priests and fathers who had charge of them to repair them, and made sure by commissioners that his instructions were obeyed. . . . Thus did Charles defend and increase as well as beautify his kingdom. . . .

He cherished with the greatest fervor and devotion the principles of the Christian religion, which had been instilled into him from infancy. Hence it was that he built the beautiful church at Aix-la-Chapelle, which he adorned with gold and silver and lamps, and with rails and doors of solid brass. He had the columns and marbles for this structure brought from Rome and Ravenna, for he could not find such as were suitable elsewhere. He was a constant worshiper at this church as long as his health permitted, going morning and evening, even after nightfall, besides attending mass. . . .

He was very forward in caring for the poor, so much so that he not only made a point of giving in his own country and his own kingdom, but when he discovered that there were Christians living in poverty in Syria, Egypt, and Africa, at Jerusalem, Alexandria, and Carthage, he had compassion on their wants, and used to send money over the seas to them. . . . He sent great and countless gifts to the popes, and throughout his whole reign the wish that he had nearest at heart was to reestablish the ancient authority of the city of Rome under his care and by his influence, and to defend and protect the Church of St. Peter, and to beautify and enrich it out of his own store above all other churches.

---

of a monastery or convent for nuns) belonged to royal houses, especially in Anglo-Saxon England. In the kingdom of Northumbria, for example, Saint Hilda founded the monastery of Whitby in 657. As abbess, she was responsible for giving learning an important role in the life of the monastery. Five future bishops were educated under her direction.

Charlemagne and the World of the Carolingians

During the seventh and eighth centuries, within the Frankish kingdom of western Europe, the mayors of the palace of Neustria and Austrasia had expanded their power at the expense of the Merovingian dynasty. One of these mayors, Pepin, finally took the logical step of deposing the decadent Merovingians and assuming the kingship of the Frankish state for himself and his family. Upon his death in 768, his son came to the throne of the Frankish kingdom.

This new king was the dynamic and powerful ruler known to history as Charles the Great or Charlemagne (from the Latin *Carolus magnus*). Charlemagne was a determined and decisive man, highly intelligent and inquisitive. A fierce warrior, he was also a strong statesman (see the box above). Unable to read and write, he was nevertheless a wise patron of learning. He greatly expanded the territory of the Carolingian Empire during his lengthy rule from 768 to 814.

In the tradition of the Germanic kings, Charlemagne was a determined warrior who undertook fifty-four military campaigns, which took him to many areas of Europe. His most successful campaigns were in Germany, especially against the Saxons located between the Elbe River and the North Sea. At its height, Charlemagne's empire covered much of western and central Europe; not until the time of Napoleon in the nineteenth and Hitler in the twentieth century would an empire its size be seen again in Europe.

Charlemagne continued the efforts of his father in organizing the Carolingian kingdom. To administer the empire, Charlemagne depended on both his household staff and the counts who were his chief representatives in local areas. The counts were members of the nobility that had already existed under the Merovingians. They had come to control government functions in their own lands and thus acted as judges, military leaders, and agents of the king. As an important check on the power of the counts, Charlemagne established the *missi dominici* ("messengers of the lord king"), two men, one lay lord and one church official, who were sent out to local dis-

tricts to ensure that the counts were executing the king's wishes.

CHARLEMAGNE AS EMPEROR

As Charlemagne's power grew, so too did his prestige as the most powerful Christian ruler; one monk even wrote that he ruled the "kingdom of Europe." In 800, Charlemagne acquired a new title—emperor of the Romans. Charlemagne welcomed the new title; after all, as an emperor, he was now on a level of equality with the Byzantine emperor (see The Byzantine Empire and the Crusades later in this chapter). Moreover, the coronation also meant that the papacy now had a defender of great stature.

Charlemagne's coronation as Roman emperor demonstrated the strength, even after three hundred years, of the concept of an enduring Roman Empire. More importantly, it symbolized the fusion of those Roman, Christian, and Germanic elements that constituted the foundation of European civilization. A Germanic king had been crowned emperor of the Romans by the spiritual leader of western Christendom. A new civilization had emerged.

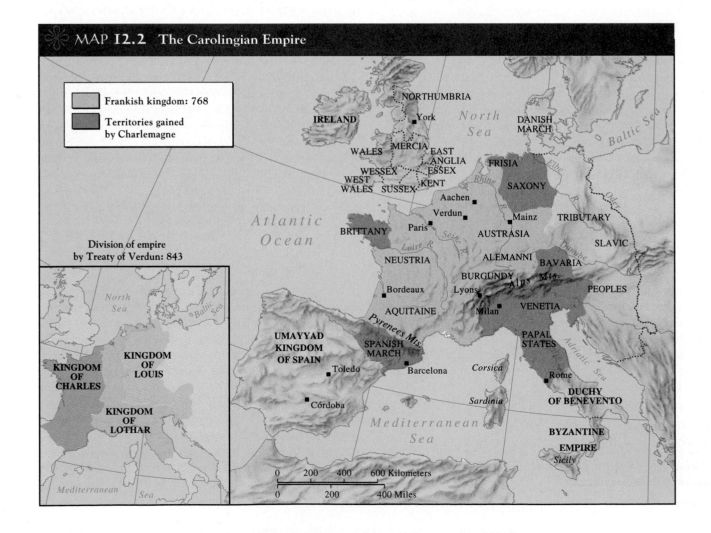

MAP 12.2 The Carolingian Empire

AN INTELLECTUAL RENEWAL

Charlemagne had a strong desire to revive learning in his kingdom, an attitude that stemmed from his own intellectual curiosity as well as the need to provide educated clergy for the church and literate officials for the government. His efforts led to a revival of learning and culture that some historians have labeled a Carolingian Renaissance or "rebirth" of learning.

For the most part, the revival of classical studies and the efforts to preserve Latin culture took place in the monasteries, many of which had been established by Irish and English missionaries in the seventh and eighth centuries. By the ninth century, the "work" required of Benedictine monks was the copying of manuscripts. Monasteries established *scriptoria*, or writing rooms, where monks copied not only the works of early Christianity, such as the Bible, but also the works of Latin classical authors. The copying of manuscripts in Carolingian monastic *scriptoria* was a crucial factor in the preservation of the ancient legacy. About eight thousand manuscripts survive from Carolingian times. Virtually 90 percent of the ancient Roman works that we have today exist because they were copied by Carolingian monks.

THE WORLD OF LORDS AND VASSALS

The Carolingian Empire began to disintegrate soon after Charlemagne's death in 814, and less than thirty years later, in 843, it was divided among his grandsons into three major sections. The division did not lead to peace, however, for the rulers and their heirs engaged in almost incessant struggles—squabbles that allowed powerful aristocrats to acquire even more power in their own local territories at the expense of the rulers. In the meantime, invasions in different parts of the old Carolingian world added to the process of disintegration.

Invasions of the Ninth and Tenth Centuries

In the ninth and tenth centuries, western Europe was beset by several waves of invasions. Muslims raided the southern coast of Europe and sent raiding parties into southern France. The Magyars, a people from western Asia, moved into central Europe at the end of the ninth century and settled on the plains of Hungary; from there they made raids into western Europe. After suffering a crushing defeat at the Battle of Lechfeld in Germany in 955, the Magyars converted to Christianity and settled down to create the kingdom of Hungary.

By far, the most far-reaching attacks of the time came from the Northmen or Norsemen of Scandinavia, also known to us as the Vikings. The Vikings were a Germanic people based in Scandinavia. Their great love of adventure and their search for booty and new avenues of trade may have led them to invade other areas of Europe.

Two features of Viking society help to explain the Vikings' success. First of all, they were warriors. Second, they were superb shipbuilders and sailors. Their ships were the best of the period. Long and narrow with beautifully carved arched prows, the Viking dragon ships carried about fifty men. Their shallow draft enabled the Vikings to sail up European rivers and attack places at some distance

THE CORONATION OF CHARLEMAGNE.
After rebellion in 799 forced Pope Leo III to seek refuge at Charlemagne's court, Charlemagne went to Rome to settle the affair. There, on Christmas Day 800, he was crowned emperor of the Romans by the pope. This manuscript illustration shows Leo III placing a crown on Charlemagne's head.

�✵ **THE VIKINGS ATTACK ENGLAND.** This illustration from an eleventh-century English manuscript depicts a band of armed Vikings invading England. Two ships have already reached the shore, and a few Vikings are shown walking down a long gangplank onto English soil.

inland. In the ninth century, Vikings sacked villages and towns, destroyed churches, and easily defeated small local armies. Viking attacks frightened people and led many a clergyman to plead with them to change their behavior and appease God's anger, as is revealed in this sermon in 1014 by an English archbishop:

> Things have not gone well now for a long time at home or abroad, but there has been devastation and persecution in every district again and again, and the English have been for a long time now completely defeated and too greatly disheartened through God's anger; and the pirates [Vikings] so strong with God's consent that often in battle one puts to flight ten, and sometimes less, sometimes more, all because of our sins. . . . We pay them continually and they humiliate us daily; they ravage and they burn, plunder, and rob and carry on board; and lo, what else is there in all these events except God's anger clear and visible over this people?[2]

Early Viking raids were largely limited to the summer, but by the mid-ninth century, the Norsemen had begun to build settlements and spend the winter in different areas of Europe. By 850, Norsemen from Norway had settled in Ireland, while the Danes occupied northeastern England by 878. Beginning in 911, the ruler of the western Frankish lands gave one band of Vikings land at the mouth of the Seine river in the section of France that came to be known as Normandy. This policy of settling the Vikings and converting them to Christianity was a deliberate one; by their conversion to Christianity, the Vikings were soon made a part of European civilization.

The Development of Fief-holding

The disintegration of all central authority in the Carolingian world and the invasions by Muslims, Magyars, and Vikings led to the emergence of a new type of relationship between free individuals. When governments ceased to be able to defend their subjects, it became important to find some powerful lord who could offer protection in exchange for service. The contract sworn between a lord and his subordinate (known as a vassal) is the basis of a form of social organization that later generations of historians viewed as an organized system of government, which they called feudalism. But feudalism was never a system, and many historians today prefer to avoid using the term.

With the breakdown of royal governments, powerful nobles took control of large areas of land. They needed men to fight for them, so the practice arose of giving grants of land to vassals who in return would fight for their lord. The Frankish army had originally consisted of foot soldiers dressed in coats of mail and armed with swords. But in the eighth century, when larger horses and the stirrup were introduced, a military change began to occur. Earlier, horsemen had been throwers of spears. Now they wore armored coats of mail (the larger horse could carry the weight) and wielded long lances that enabled them to act as battering rams (the stirrups kept them on their horses). For almost five hundred years, warfare in Europe would be dominated by heavily armored cavalry, or knights as they came to be called. The knights came to have the greatest social prestige and formed the backbone of the European aristocracy.

Of course, a horse, armor, and weapons were expensive to purchase and maintain, and learning to wield these instruments skillfully from a horse took much time and practice. Consequently, lords who wanted men to fight for them had to grant each vassal a piece of land that provided for the support of the vassal and his family. In return for the land, the vassal provided his lord with one major service, his fighting skills. Each needed the other. In the society of the Early Middle Ages (the period between 400 and 1000), where there was little trade and wealth was based primarily on land, land became the most important

gift a lord could give to a vassal in return for military service.

The relationship between lord and vassal was made official by a public ceremony. To become a vassal, a man performed an act of homage to his lord, as described in this passage from a medieval treatise on feudal practice:

> The man should put his hands together as a sign of humility, and place them between the two hands of his lord as a token that he vows everything to him and promises faith to him; and the lord should receive him and promise to keep faith with him. Then the man should say: "Sir, I enter your homage and faith and become your man by mouth and hands [i.e., by taking the oath and placing his hands between those of the lord], and I swear and promise to keep faith and loyalty to you against all others, and to guard your rights with all my strength.[3]

Loyalty to one's lord was the chief virtue.

By the ninth century, the land granted to a vassal in return for military service had come to be known as a fief. In time, many vassals who held such grants of land came to exercise rights of jurisdiction or political and legal authority within their fiefs. As the Carolingian world disintegrated politically under the impact of internal dissension and invasions, an increasing number of powerful lords arose. Instead of a single government, many people were now responsible for keeping order.

Fief-holding also became increasingly complicated with the development of subinfeudation. The vassals of a king, who were themselves great lords, might also have vassals, who would owe them military service in return for a grant of land from their estates. Those vassals, in turn, might likewise have vassals, who at this low level would be simple knights with barely enough land to provide their equipment. The lord-vassal relationship, then, bound together both greater and lesser landowners. At all levels, the lord-vassal relationship was always an honorable relationship between free men and did not imply any sense of servitude.

Fief-holding came to be characterized by a set of practices—known as the feudal contract—that determined the relationship between a lord and his vassal. The major obligation of a vassal to his lord was to perform military service, usually about forty days a year. A vassal was also required to appear at his lord's court when summoned to give advice. He might also be asked to sit in judgment in a legal case because the important vassals of a lord were peers and only they could judge each other. Finally, vassals were also responsible for aids, or financial payments to the lord on a number of occasions, including the knighting of the lord's eldest son, the marriage of his eldest daughter, and the ransom of the lord's person in the event he was captured.

In turn, a lord had responsibilities toward his vassal. His major obligation was to protect his vassal, either by defending him militarily or by taking his side in a court of law if necessary. The lord was also responsible for the maintenance of the vassal, usually by granting him a fief.

The Nobility of the Middle Ages

In the High Middle Ages (the period between 1000 and 1300), European society, like that of Japan during the same period, was dominated by men whose chief concern was warfare. Like the Japanese samurai, many nobles loved war. As one nobleman wrote in a poem:

> And well I like to hear the call of "Help" and see the
>   wounded fall,
> Loudly for mercy praying,
> And see the dead, both great and small,
> Pierced by sharp spearheads one and all.[4]

The men of war were the lords and vassals of medieval society.

The lords were the kings, dukes, counts, barons, and viscounts (and even bishops and archbishops), who held extensive lands and considerable political power. They formed an aristocracy or nobility that consisted of people who held real political, economic, and social power. As warriors united by the institution of knighthood, the great lords and ordinary knights came to form a common group, albeit a group with social divisions based on extremes of wealth and landholdings.

Medieval theory maintained that the warlike qualities of the nobility were justified by their role as defenders of society, and the growth of the European nobility in the High Middle Ages was made visible by an increasing number of castles scattered across the landscape. Although castle architecture varied considerably, castles did possess two common features: they were permanent residences for the noble family, its retainers, and servants, and they were defensible fortifications. For defensive purposes, castles were surrounded by open areas and large stone walls. At the heart of the castle was the keep, a large, multistoried building that housed kitchens, stables, storerooms, a great hall for visitors, dining, and administrative business, and numerous rooms for sleeping and living. The growing wealth of the High Middle Ages made it possible for the European nobility to build more elaborate castles, with thicker walls and better furnished and decorated interiors. As castles became more elaborate and securely built, they proved to be more easily defended and harder to seize by force.

THE WAY OF THE WARRIOR

At the age of seven or eight, the sons of the nobility were sent either to a clerical school to pursue a religious career or to another nobleman's castle, where they prepared for the life of a noble. Their chief lessons were military; they learned how to joust, hunt, ride, and handle weapons properly. Occasionally, aristocrats' sons might also learn the basic fundamentals of reading and writing. After his apprenticeship in knighthood, at about the age of twenty-one, a young man formally entered the adult world in a

THE TOURNAMENT. The tournament arose as a socially acceptable alternative to the private warfare that plagued the nobility. This illustration from *The Book of Tourneys*, by King René of Anjou, shows opposing teams behind ropes. At the top center, red-robed judges prepare to signal the men waiting below to cut the cords, at which point the two sides will begin their mock battle. Female supporters of the two sides look on.

ceremony of "knighting." A sponsor girded a sword on the young candidate and struck him on the cheek or neck with an open hand (or later touched him three times on the shoulder with the blade of a sword), possibly signifying the passing of the sponsor's military valor to the new knight.

In the eleventh and twelfth centuries, under the influence of the church, an ideal of civilized behavior called chivalry gradually evolved among the nobility. Chivalry represented a code of ethics that knights were supposed to uphold. In addition to defending the church and the defenseless, knights were expected to treat captives as honored guests instead of putting them in dungeons. Chivalry also implied that knights should fight only for glory, but this account of a group of English knights by a medieval writer reveals another motive for battle: "The whole city was plundered to the last farthing, and then they proceeded to rob all the churches throughout the city, . . . and seizing gold and silver, cloth of all colors, women's ornaments, gold rings, goblets, and precious stones . . . they all

returned to their own lords rich men."[5] Apparently, not all the ideals of chivalry were taken seriously.

After his formal initiation into the world of warriors, a young man returned home to find himself once again subject to his parents' authority. Young men were discouraged from marrying until their fathers died, at which time they could marry and become lords of the castle. Trained to be warriors, but with no adult responsibilities, young knights had little to do but fight. In the twelfth century, tournaments began to appear as an alternative to the socially destructive fighting that the church was increasingly trying to curb. Initially, tournaments consisted of the "melee," in which warriors on horseback fought with blunted weapons in free-for-all combat. By the late twelfth century, the melee was preceded by the joust or individual combat between two knights. Gradually, the joust became the main part of the tournament. Knights saw tournaments as an excellent way to train for war. As one knight explained: "A knight cannot distinguish himself in that

[war] if he has not trained for it in tourneys. He must have seen his blood flow, heard his teeth crack under fist blows, felt his opponent's weight bear down upon him as he lay on the ground and, after being twenty times unhorsed, have risen twenty times to fight."[6]

ARISTOCRATIC WOMEN

Although women could legally hold property, most women remained under the control of men—of their fathers until they married and their husbands after they married. Nevertheless, aristocratic women had many opportunities for playing important roles. Because the lord was often away at war or court, the lady of the castle had to manage the estate. A household could include large numbers of officials and servants, so this was no small responsibility. Maintaining the financial accounts alone took considerable financial knowledge. The lady of the castle was also responsible on a regular basis for overseeing the food supply and maintaining all the other supplies needed for the smooth operation of the household.

Although women were expected to be subservient to their husbands, there were many strong women who advised and sometimes even dominated their husbands. Perhaps the most famous was Eleanor of Aquitaine (c. 1122–1204), heiress to the duchy of Aquitaine in southwestern France. Married to King Louis VII of France (1137–1180), Eleanor accompanied her husband on a crusade, but her alleged affair with her uncle during the crusade led Louis to have their marriage annulled. Eleanor then married Henry, duke of Normandy and count of Anjou, who became King Henry II of England (1154–1189). She took an active role in politics, even assisting her sons in rebelling against Henry in 1173–1174. Imprisoned for her activities, after Henry's death she again assumed an active political life, providing both military and political support for her sons.

THE GROWTH OF EUROPEAN KINGDOMS

The domination of society by the nobility reached its apex in the High Middle Ages. During the same period, however, kings began the process of extending their power in more effective ways. Out of these growing monarchies would eventually come the European states that dominated much of later European and world history.

Kings possessed some sources of power that other lords did not. Usually, kings had greater opportunities to increase their lands through war and marriage alliances and then could use their new acquisitions to reward their followers and bind powerful nobles to them. In the High Middle Ages, kings found new ways to extend their powers. The growth of cities, the revival of commerce, and the emergence of a money economy—all of which we will examine in the next sections—enabled monarchs to hire soldiers and officials and to rely less on their vassals.

England in the High Middle Ages

In 1066, an army of heavily armed knights under William of Normandy landed on the coast of England and soundly defeated King Harold and the Anglo-Saxon foot soldiers at the Battle of Hastings on October 14. William (1066–1087) was crowned king of England at Christmastime in London and then began the process of combining Anglo-Saxon and Norman institutions to create a new England. Many of the Norman knights were given parcels of land that they held as fiefs from the new English king. William made all nobles swear an oath of loyalty to him as sole ruler of England and insisted that all people owed loyalty to the king.

The Norman ruling class spoke French, but as the Norman-French and the Anglo-Saxon nobility intermarried, Anglo-Saxon and French gradually merged to form a new English language. The Normans also took over existing Anglo-Saxon institutions, such as the office of sheriff. William took a census and more fully developed the system of taxation and royal courts begun by the Anglo-Saxon kings of the tenth and eleventh centuries. All in all, William of Normandy created a strong, centralized monarchy.

The Norman conquest of England had other repercussions as well. Because the new king of England was still the duke of Normandy, he was both a king (of England) and at the same time a vassal to a king (of France), but a vassal who was now far more powerful than his lord. This connection with France kept England heavily involved in European affairs throughout the High Middle Ages.

In the twelfth century, the power of the English monarchy was greatly enlarged during the reign of Henry II (1154–1189), the founder of the Plantagenet dynasty. The new king was particularly successful in strengthening the power of the royal courts. Henry expanded the number of criminal cases tried in the king's court and also devised ways of taking property cases from local courts to the royal courts. Henry's goals were clear: expanding the power of the royal courts expanded the king's power and, of course, brought revenues into his coffers. Moreover, because the royal courts were now found throughout England, a body of common law (law that was common to the whole kingdom) began to replace the different law codes that often varied from place to place.

Henry was less successful at imposing royal control over the church and became involved in a famous struggle between church and state in medieval England. Henry claimed the right to punish clergymen in church courts, but Thomas à Becket, archbishop of Canterbury, the highest ranking English cleric, claimed that only church courts could try clerics. Attempts at compromise failed, and

MURDER IN THE CATHEDRAL

*T*he most famous church-state controversy in medieval England arose between Henry II and Thomas à Becket, archbishop of Canterbury, the highest ranking English cleric. This excerpt is from a letter by John of Salisbury, who served as secretary to Theobald, archbishop of Canterbury, and his successor, Thomas à Becket. John was present at the murder of the archbishop in 1170.

JOHN OF SALISBURY TO JOHN OF CANTERBURY, BISHOP OF POITIERS

The martyr [Becket] stood in the cathedral, before Christ's altar, as we have said, ready to suffer; the hour of slaughter was at hand. When he heard that he was sought—heard the knights who had come for him shouting in the throng of clerks and monks "Where is the archbishop?"—he turned to meet them on the steps which he had almost climbed, and said with steady countenance: "Here am I! What do you want?" One of the knight-assassins flung at him in fury: "That you die now! That you should live longer is impossible." No martyr seems ever to have been more steadfast in his agony than he . . . and thus, steadfast in speech as in spirit, he replied: "And I am prepared to die for my God, to preserve justice and my church's liberty. If you seek my head, I forbid you on behalf of God almighty and on pain of anathema to do any hurt to any other man, monk, clerk or layman, of high or low degree. Do not involve them in the punishment, for they have not been involved in the cause: on my head not on theirs be it if

any of them have supported the Church in its troubles. I embrace death readily, so long as peace and liberty for the Church follow from the shedding of my blood. . . ." He spoke, and saw that the assassins had drawn their swords; and bowed his head like one in prayer. His last words were "To God and St. Mary and the saints who protect and defend this church, and to the blessed Denis, I commend myself and the Church's cause." No one could dwell on what followed without deep sorrow and choking tears. A son's affection forbids me to describe each blow the savage assassins struck, spurning all fear of God, forgetful of all fealty and any human feeling. They defiled the cathedral and the holy season [Christmas] with a bishop's blood and with slaughter; but that was not enough. They sliced off the crown of his head, which had been specially dedicated to God by anointing with holy chrism—a fearful thing even to describe; then they used their evil swords, when he was dead, to spill his brain and cruelly scattered it, mixed with blood and bones, over the pavement. . . . Through all the agony the martyr's spirit was unconquered, his steadfastness marvelous to observe; he spoke not a word, uttered no cry, let slip no groan, raised no arm nor garment to protect himself from an assailant, but bent his head, which he had laid bare to their swords with wonderful courage, till all might be fulfilled. Motionless he held it, and when at last he fell his body lay straight; and he moved neither hand nor foot.

---

the angry king publicly expressed the desire to be rid of Becket: "Who will free me of this priest?" he screamed. Four knights took the challenge, went to Canterbury, and murdered the archbishop in the cathedral (see the box above). Faced with public outrage, Henry was forced to allow the right of appeal from English church courts to the papal court.

Many English nobles came to resent the ongoing growth of the king's power and rose in rebellion during the reign of Henry's son, King John (1199–1216). At Runnymeade in 1215, John was forced to put his seal on the Magna Carta (the Great Charter) of feudal liberties. Magna Carta was, above all, a feudal document. Feudal custom had always recognized that the relationship between king and vassals was based on mutual rights and obligations. Magna Carta gave written recognition to that fact and was used in later years to strengthen the idea that the monarch's power was limited, not absolute.

During the reign of Edward I (1272–1307), an institution of great importance in the development of representative government—the English Parliament—

emerged. Originally, the word *parliament* was applied to meetings of the king's Great Council, in which the greater barons and chief prelates of the church met with the king's judges and principal advisers to deal with judicial affairs. But in his need for money, Edward I in 1295 invited two knights from every county and two residents from each town to meet with the Great Council to consent to new taxes. This was the first Parliament.

The English Parliament, then, came to be composed of two knights from every county and two burgesses from every borough, as well as the barons and ecclesiastical lords. Eventually, barons and church lords formed the House of Lords; knights and burgesses, the House of Commons. The Parliaments of Edward I granted taxes, discussed politics, passed laws, and handled judicial business. Although not as yet the important body it would eventually become, the English Parliament had clearly emerged as an institution by the end of the thirteenth century. The law of the realm was beginning to be determined not by the king alone, but by the king in consultation with representatives of various groups that constituted the community.

The Growth of the French Kingdom

In 843, the Carolingian Empire had been divided into three major sections. The west Frankish lands formed the core of the eventual kingdom of France. In 987, after the death of the last Carolingian king, the west Frankish nobles chose Hugh Capet as the new king, thus establishing the Capetian dynasty of French kings. Although they carried the title of kings, the Capetians had little real power. They controlled as the royal domain (the lands of the king) only the lands around Paris known as the Ile-de-France. As kings of France, the Capetians were formally the overlords of the great lords of France, such as the dukes of Normandy, Brittany, Burgundy, and Aquitaine. In reality, however, many of the dukes were considerably more powerful than the Capetian kings. All in all, it would take the Capetian dynasty hundreds of years to create a truly centralized monarchical authority in France.

The reign of King Philip II Augustus (1180–1223) was an important turning point. Philip II waged war against the Plantagenet rulers of England, who also ruled the French territories of Normandy, Maine, Anjou, and Aquitaine, and was successful in gaining control of most of these territories. Through these conquests, Philip II quadrupled the income of the French monarchy and greatly enlarged its power. To administer justice and collect royal revenues in his new territories, Philip appointed new royal officials, thus inaugurating a French royal bureaucracy in the thirteenth century.

Capetian rulers after Philip II continued to add lands to the royal domain. Although Philip had used military force, other kings used both purchase and marriage to achieve the same end. Philip IV the Fair (1285–1314) was especially effective in strengthening the French monarchy. The machinery of government became even more specialized. French kings going back to the early Capetians had possessed a household staff for running their affairs. Over time, however, this household staff was enlarged and divided into three groups to form three major branches of government: a council for advice, a chamber of accounts for finances, and a *parlement* or royal court. By the beginning of the fourteenth century, the

MAP 12.3 Europe in the High Middle Ages

CHRONOLOGY

THE EUROPEAN KINGDOMS

England
Norman Conquest	1066
William the Conqueror	1066–1087
Henry II, founder of Plantagenet dynasty	1154–1189
John	1199–1216
Magna Carta	1215
Edward I	1272–1307
First Parliament	1295

France
Philip II Augustus	1180–1223
Philip IV	1285–1314
First Estates-General	1302

Germany and the Empire
Otto I	936–973
Henry IV	1056–1106
Frederick I Barbarossa	1152–1190
Northern Italian cities defeat Frederick	1176
Frederick II	1212–1250

The Eastern World
Mongol conquest of Russia	1230s
Alexander Nevsky, prince of of Novgorod	c. 1220–1263

Capetians had laid the firm foundations for a royal bureaucracy.

Philip IV also brought a French parliament into being by asking representatives of the three estates—or classes—the clergy (first estate), the nobles (second estate), and the townspeople (third estate) to meet with him. They did so in 1302, inaugurating the Estates-General, the first French parliament, although it had little real power. By the end of the thirteenth century, France was the largest, wealthiest, and best-governed monarchical state in Europe.

The Lands of the Holy Roman Empire

In the tenth century, the powerful dukes of the Saxons became kings of the eastern Frankish kingdom (or Germany, as it came to be called). The best known of the Saxon kings of Germany was Otto I (936–973), who intervened in Italian politics and for his efforts was crowned emperor of the Romans by the pope in 962, reviving a title that had not been used since the time of Charlemagne.

Otto's creation of a new "Roman Empire" in the hands of the eastern Franks (or Germans, as they came to be called) added a tremendous burden to the king of Germany, who now took on the onerous task of ruling Italy as well.

In the eleventh century, German kings created a strong monarchy and a powerful empire by leading armies into Italy. To strengthen their power, they relied on their ability to control the church and select bishops, whom they could then use as royal administrators. But the struggle between church and state during the reign of Henry IV (1056–1106) weakened the king's ability to use church officials in this way (see Reform of the Papacy later in this chapter). The German kings also tried to bolster their power by using their position as emperors to exploit the resources of Italy. But this strategy tended to backfire; many a German king lost armies in Italy in pursuit of a dream of empire, and no German dynasty demonstrates this better than the Hohenstaufens.

The two most famous members of the Hohenstaufen dynasty, Frederick I (1152–1190) and Frederick II (1212–1250), tried to create a new kind of empire. Previous German kings had focused on building a strong German kingdom, but Frederick I planned to get his chief revenues from Italy as the center of a "holy empire," as he called it (hence the name Holy Roman Empire). But his attempt to conquer northern Italy ran into severe problems. The pope opposed him, fearful that the emperor wanted to include Rome and the Papal States as part of his empire. The cities of northern Italy, which had become used to their freedom, were also not willing to be Frederick's subjects. An alliance of these northern Italian cities, with the support of the pope, defeated the emperor's forces in 1176.

The main goal of Frederick II was the establishment of a strong centralized state in Italy dominated by the kingdom in Sicily he had inherited from his mother. Frederick's major task was to gain control of northern Italy. In attempting to conquer Italy, however, he became involved in a deadly struggle with the popes, who feared that a single ruler of northern and southern Italy would mean the end of papal power in central Italy. The northern Italian cities were also unwilling to give up their freedom. Frederick waged a bitter struggle in northern Italy, winning many battles but ultimately losing the war.

The struggle between popes and emperors had dire consequences for the Holy Roman Empire. While they were fighting in Italy, the German emperors left Germany in the hands of powerful German lords who ignored the emperor and created their own independent kingdoms. This ensured that the German monarchy would remain weak and incapable of maintaining a centralized monarchical state; thus, the German Holy Roman emperor had no real power over either Germany or Italy. Unlike France and England, neither Germany nor Italy created a unified national monarchy in the Middle Ages. Both Germany and Italy consisted of many small, independent states, and

both had to wait until the nineteenth century to form united states.

The Slavic Peoples of Central and Eastern Europe

East of the Carolingian Empire lay a spacious plain through which a number of Asiatic nomads, such as the Huns, Bulgars, Avars, and Magyars, had pushed their way westward. Eastern Europe was ravaged by these successive waves of invaders, who found it relatively easy to create large empires that, in turn, were overthrown by the next invaders. Over time, the invaders themselves were largely assimilated with the native Slavic peoples of the area.

The Slavic peoples were originally a single people in central Europe, but they gradually divided into three major groups: the western, southern, and eastern Slavs. The western Slavs eventually formed the Polish and Bohemian kingdoms. German Christian missionaries converted both the Czechs in Bohemia and the Slavs in Poland by the tenth century. The non-Slavic kingdom of Hungary, which emerged after the Magyars settled down after their defeat in 955, was also converted to Christianity by German missionaries. The Poles, Czechs, and Hungarians all accepted Catholic or western Christianity and became closely tied to the Roman Catholic church and its Latin culture.

The southern and eastern Slavic populations largely took a different path because of their proximity to the Byzantine Empire. The Slavic peoples of Moravia were converted to the Orthodox Christianity of the Byzantine Empire by two Byzantine missionary brothers, Cyril and Methodius, who began their activities in 863. They created a Slavonic (Cyrillic) alphabet, translated the Bible into Slavonic, and developed Slavonic church services. Although the southern Slavic peoples accepted Christianity, a split eventually developed between the Croats, who accepted the Roman Catholic church, and the Serbs, who remained loyal to Orthodox Christianity.

Much of the Balkan peninsula was conquered by the Bulgars, who were originally an Asiatic people but were eventually absorbed by the larger native southern Slavic population. Together, they formed a largely Slavic Bulgarian kingdom

that embraced the church services developed earlier by Cyril and Methodius. The acceptance of Eastern Orthodoxy by the southern Slavic peoples, the Serbs and Bulgarians, meant that their cultural life was linked to the Byzantine state.

The eastern Slavic peoples, from whom the modern Russians and Ukrainians are descended, had settled in the territory of present-day Ukraine and European Russia. There, beginning in the late eighth century, they began to encounter Swedish Vikings who moved down the extensive network of rivers into the lands of the eastern Slavs in search of booty and new trade routes (see the box on p. 334). These Vikings built trading settlements and eventually came to dominate the native peoples who called them "the Rus," from which the name Russia is derived.

THE DEVELOPMENT OF RUSSIA

A Viking leader named Oleg (c. 873–913) settled in Kiev at the beginning of the tenth century and created the Rus state known as the principality of Kiev. His successors extended their control over the eastern Slavs and expanded the territory of Kiev until it included all the lands between the Baltic and Black Seas and the Danube and Volga Rivers. By marrying Slavic wives, the Viking ruling class was gradually assimilated into the Slavic population.

The growth of the principality of Kiev attracted religious missionaries, especially from the Byzantine Empire.

MAP 12.4   The World of the Slavs

A MUSLIM'S DESCRIPTION OF THE RUS

Despite the difficulties that travel presented, early medieval civilization did witness some contact among the various cultures. This might occur through trade, diplomacy, or the conquest and migration of peoples. This document is a description of the Swedish Rus, who eventually merged with the native Slavic peoples to form the principality of Kiev, commonly regarded as the first Russian state. It was written by Ibn Fadlan, a Muslim diplomat sent from Baghdad in 921 to a settlement on the Volga River. His comments on the filthiness of the Rus reflect the Muslim preoccupation with cleanliness.

IBN FADLAN, DESCRIPTION OF THE RUS

I saw the Rus folk when they arrived on their trading mission and settled at the river Atul (Volga). Never had I seen people of more perfect physique. They are tall as date palms, and reddish in color. They wear neither coat nor kaftan, but each man carried a cape which covers one half of his body, leaving one hand free. No one is ever parted from his axe, sword, and knife. Their swords are Frankish in design, broad, flat, and fluted. Each man has a number of trees, figures, and the like from the fingernails to the neck. Each woman carried on her bosom a container made of iron, silver, copper, or gold—its size and substance depending on her man's wealth.

They [the Rus] are the filthiest of God's creatures. They do not wash after discharging their natural functions, neither do they wash their hands after meals. They are as lousy as donkeys. They arrive from their distant lands and lay their ships alongside the banks of the Atul, which is a great river, and there they build big houses on its shores. Ten or twenty of them may live together in one house, and each of them has a couch of his own where he sits and diverts himself with the pretty slave girls whom he had brought along for sale. He will make love with one of them while a comrade looks on; sometimes they indulge in a communal orgy, and, if a customer should turn up to buy a girl, the Rus man will not let her go till he has finished with her.

They wash their hands and faces every day in incredibly filthy water. Every morning the girl brings her master a large bowl of water in which he washes his hands and face and hair, then blows his nose into it and spits into it. When he has finished the girl takes the bowl to his neighbor who repeats the performance. Thus the bowl goes the rounds of the entire household. . . .

If one of the Rus folk falls sick they put him in a tent by himself and leave bread and water for him. They do not visit him, however, or speak to him, especially if he is a serf. Should he recover he rejoins the others; if he dies they burn him. But if he happens to be a serf they leave him for the dogs and vultures to devour. If they catch a robber they hang him to a tree until he is torn to shreds by wind and weather.

One Rus ruler, Vladimir (c. 980–1015), married the Byzantine emperor's sister and officially accepted Christianity for himself and his people in 987. From the end of the tenth century, Byzantine Christianity became the model for Russian religious life.

The Kievan Rus state prospered and reached its high point in the first half of the eleventh century. Kievan society was dominated by a noble class of landowners known as the boyars, while Kievan merchants carried on a regular trade with Scandinavia to the north and the Islamic and Byzantine worlds to the south. But civil wars and new invasions by Asiatic nomads caused the principality of Kiev to collapse, and the sack of Kiev by north Russian princes in 1169 brought an end to the first Russian state. That state had remained closely tied to the Byzantine Empire, not to the new Europe. Its Christianity had been Orthodox Christianity, not the Catholicism of Europe. In the thirteenth century, the Mongols conquered Russia and cut it off even more from Europe.

The Mongols had exploded on the scene in the thirteenth century, moving east into China, where they created a new ruling Mongol dynasty, and west into the Middle East and central Europe. Although they conquered Russia, they were not numerous enough to occupy all of its vast lands. Instead, they required the Russian princes to pay tribute to them. One Russian prince soon emerged as more powerful than the others. Alexander Nevsky (c. 1220–1263), prince of Novgorod, defeated a German invading army in northwestern Russia in 1242. His cooperation with the Mongols won him their favor. The khan, leader of the western part of the Mongol empire, rewarded Alexander Nevsky with the title of grand-prince, enabling his descendants to become the princes of Moscow and eventually leaders of all Russia.

 # THE WORLD OF THE PEASANTS

In the Early Middle Ages, Europe had a relatively small population, but in the High Middle Ages, the population increased dramatically. The number of people in Europe almost doubled between 1000 and 1300, rising from 38 million to 74 million. Why this dramatic increase in population? For one thing, conditions in Europe were more settled and peaceful after the invasions of the Early

Middle Ages had stopped. Then, too, agricultural production also expanded dramatically after 1000. Whether this new productivity was a cause or effect of the population increase is uncertain, but without such a significant rise in food supplies, the growth in population could never have been sustained.

The New Agriculture

During the High Middle Ages, Europeans began to farm in new ways. Although an improvement in climate produced better growing conditions, another important factor in increasing the output of food was the expansion of cultivated or arable land, accomplished primarily by clearing forested areas for cultivation. Eager for land, peasants of the eleventh and twelfth centuries cut down trees and drained swamps. By the thirteenth century, the total acreage available for farming in Europe was greater than the amount tilled at any time before or since.

Technological changes also furthered the development of farming. The Middle Ages witnessed an explosion of labor-saving devices, many of which were made from iron, which was mined in different areas of Europe. Iron was in demand to make swords and armor, but it was also used to make scythes, axes, and hoes for use on farms, as well as saws, hammers, and nails for building purposes. Iron was crucial in making the *carruca*, a heavy, wheeled plow with an iron plowshare, which could turn over the heavy clay soil north of the Alps and allow for its drainage.

Because of the *carruca*'s weight, six or eight oxen were needed to pull it, but oxen were slow. Two new inventions for the horse made it possible to plow even faster. A new horse collar, which appeared in the tenth century, distributed the weight around the shoulders and chest, rather than the throat, and could be used to hitch up a series of horses, enabling them to pull the new heavy plow faster and cultivate more land. The use of the horseshoe, an iron shoe nailed to the horse's hooves, made it easier for horses to pull the heavy plow through the rocky and heavy clay soil of northern Europe.

The use of the heavy, wheeled plow also led to the growth of agricultural villages, where people had to work together. Because iron was expensive, a heavy, wheeled plow had to be purchased by the entire community. Likewise an individual family could not afford a team of animals, so villagers shared their beasts. Moreover, the size and weight of the plow made it necessary to plow the land in long strips to minimize the amount of turning that would have to be done.

Besides using horsepower, the High Middle Ages harnessed the power of water and wind to do jobs formerly done by human or animal power. Located along streams, mills powered by water were used to grind grains and produce flour. Where rivers were not available or not easily dammed, Europeans developed windmills to harness the power of the wind. By the end of the twelfth century, they were beginning to dot the European landscape. Like the watermill, the windmill was first used for grinding grains. The watermill and windmill were the most important devices for harnessing power before the invention of the steam engine in the eighteenth century. Their spread had revolutionary consequences in enabling Europeans to produce more food.

The shift from a two-field to a three-field system also contributed to the increase in food production. In the Early Middle Ages, farmers commonly planted one field while allowing another of equal size to lie fallow to regain its fertility. Now estates were divided into three parts. One field was planted in the fall with winter grains, such as rye and wheat, while spring grains, such as oats or barley, and vegetables, such as peas, beans, or lentils, were planted in the second field. The third was allowed to lie fallow. By rotating the fields, only one-third rather than one-half of the land lay fallow at any time. The rotation of crops also kept the soil from being exhausted so quickly, and more crops could now be grown.

The Manorial System

The landholding class of nobles and knights comprised a military elite whose ability to function as warriors depended on having the leisure time to pursue the arts of war. Landed estates, located on the fiefs given to a vassal by his lord and worked by a dependent peasant class, provided the economic sustenance that made this way of life possible. A manor or villa was simply an agricultural estate operated by a lord and worked by peasants. While a large class of free peasants continued to exist, increasing numbers of free peasants became serfs—peasants bound to the land and required to provide labor services, pay rents, and be subject to the lord's jurisdiction. By the ninth century, probably 60 percent of the population of western Europe had become serfs.

Labor services consisted of working the lord's demesne, the land retained by the lord, which might consist of one-third to one-half of the cultivated lands scattered throughout the manor. The rest would be used by the peasants for themselves. Building barns and digging ditches were also part of the labor services. Serfs usually worked about three days a week for their lord.

The serfs paid rents by giving the lord a share of every product they raised. Moreover, serfs paid the lord for the use of the manor's common pasturelands, streams, ponds, and surrounding woodlands. For example, if a serf fished in the pond or stream on a manor, he turned over part of the catch to his lord. Peasants were also obliged to pay a tithe (a tenth of their produce) to their local village church.

Lords possessed a variety of legal rights over their serfs as a result of their unfree status. Serfs were legally bound to the lord's lands and could not leave without his permission. Although free to marry, serfs could not marry anyone outside their manor without the lord's approval. Moreover, lords sometimes exercised public rights or political authority on their lands, which gave them the right to try peasants in their own courts. In fact, the manorial court provided the only law that most peasants knew. Peasants also had to pay the lord for certain services; for example, they might be required to bring their grain to the lord's mill and pay a fee to have it ground into flour.

As the growing towns and cities needed more food, food prices tended to rise in the thirteenth century. This led lords to try to grow more food for profit. One way to do so was to lease their demesne land to their serfs. Labor services were then transformed into money payments or fixed rents, thereby converting many unfree serfs into free peasants. Although many peasants still remained economically dependent on their lords, they were no longer legally tied to the land. Lords, in turn, became collectors of rents, rather than operators of a manor with both political and legal privileges. The political and legal powers formerly exercised by lords were increasingly reclaimed by the monarchical states.

Daily Life of the Peasantry

Peasant activities were largely determined by the seasons of the year. Each season brought a new round of tasks appropriate for the time, although some periods were considerably more hectic than others, especially harvest time in August and September. A new cycle began in October, when the peasants prepared the ground for planting winter crops. In February and March, the land was plowed for spring crops—oats, barley, peas, beans, and lentils. Early summer was a comparatively relaxed time, although there was still weeding and sheepshearing to be done. In every season, the serfs worked not only their own land, but also the lord's demesne. They also tended the small gardens next to their dwellings where they grew the vegetables that made up part of their diet.

The lifestyle of the peasants was quite simple. Their cottages consisted of wood frames covered by sticks with the space between them filled with straw and rubble and then plastered over with clay. Roofs were simply thatched. The houses of poorer peasants consisted of a single room, but

❀ PEASANTS IN THE MANORIAL SYSTEM.
In the manorial system, peasants were required to provide labor services for their lord. This thirteenth-century illustration shows a group of English peasants harvesting grain. Overseeing their work is a bailiff, or manager, who supervised the work of the peasants.

others had at least two rooms—a main room for cooking, eating, and other activities and another room for sleeping. There was little privacy in a medieval peasant household.

Peasant women occupied both an important and a difficult position in manorial society. They were expected to carry and bear their children and at the same time fulfill their obligation to labor in the fields. Their ability to manage the household might determine whether a peasant family would starve or survive in difficult times.

Though simple, a peasant's daily diet was adequate when food was available. The staple of the peasant diet, and the medieval diet in general, was bread. While women made the dough for the bread, the loaves were usually baked in community ovens, which were owned by the lord of the manor. Peasant bread was highly nutritious because it contained not only wheat and rye, but also barley, millet, and oats, giving it a dark appearance and a very heavy, hard texture. Bread was supplemented by numerous vegetables from the household gardens, cheese from cow's or goat's milk, nuts and berries from woodlands, and fruits, such as apples, pears, and cherries. Chickens provided eggs and sometimes meat.

Grains were important not only for bread, but also for making ale. In northern European countries, ale was the most common drink of the poor. If records are accurate, enormous quantities of ale were consumed. A monastery in the twelfth century records a daily allotment to the monks of three gallons a day. Peasants in the field undoubtedly consumed even more. This high consumption of alcohol might help to explain the large number of accidental deaths recorded in medieval court records.

THE NEW WORLD OF TRADE AND CITIES

Medieval Europe was overwhelmingly an agrarian society, with most people living in small villages. In the eleventh and twelfth centuries, however, new elements were introduced that began to transform the economic foundation of European civilization: a revival of trade, the emergence of specialized craftspeople and artisans, and the growth and development of towns. These changes were made possible by the new agricultural practices and subsequent increase in food production, which freed part of the European population from producing their own food. Merchants and craftspeople could now buy their necessities.

The Revival of Trade

The revival of trade was a gradual process. During the chaotic conditions of the Early Middle Ages, large-scale trade had declined in western Europe except for Byzantine

contacts with Italy and the Jewish traders who moved back and forth between the Muslim and Christian worlds. By the end of the tenth century, however, people with both the skills and the products for commercial activity were emerging in Europe. Cities in Italy took the lead in this revival of trade. By the end of the eighth century, for example, Venice had emerged as a town with close trading ties to the Byzantine Empire. It developed a mercantile fleet and by the end of the tenth century had become the chief western trading center for Byzantine and Islamic commerce.

While the northern Italian cities were busy trading in the Mediterranean, the towns of Flanders were doing likewise in northern Europe. Flanders, the area along the coast of present-day Belgium and northern France, was known for its much desired, high-quality woolen cloth. Flanders's location made it an ideal center for the traders of northern Europe. Merchants from England, Scandinavia, France, and Germany converged there to trade their goods for woolen cloth. Flanders prospered in the eleventh and twelfth centuries, and such Flemish towns as Bruges and Ghent became centers for the trade and manufacture of woolen cloth.

By the twelfth century, it was almost inevitable that a regular exchange of goods would develop between Flanders and Italy, the two major centers of northern and southern European trade, respectively. To encourage this trade, the counts of Champagne in northern France instituted an annual series of six fairs in the chief towns of their territory. Northern merchants brought the furs, woolen cloth, tin, hemp, and honey of northern Europe to the fairs of Champagne and exchanged those goods for the cloth and swords of northern Italy and the silks, sugar, and spices of the East.

As trade increased, both gold and silver came to be in demand at fairs and trading markets of all kinds. Slowly, a money economy began to emerge. New trading companies as well as banking firms were set up to manage the exchange and sale of goods. All of these new practices were part of the rise of commercial capitalism, an economic system in which people invested in trade and goods in order to make profits.

The Growth of Cities

The revival of trade led to a revival of cities. Merchants needed places where they could live and build warehouses to store their goods. To meet the needs of merchants, cities were usually located near sources of protection (such as castles) and alongside rivers or roads that provided favorable routes of transportation.

Towns had greatly declined in the Early Middle Ages, especially in Europe north of the Alps. Old Roman cities continued to exist but had dwindled in size and population. With the revival of trade, merchants began to settle in these old cities, followed by craftspeople or artisans, people who on manors or elsewhere had developed skills and now saw an opportunity to ply their trade and make goods that could be sold by the merchants. In the course of the eleventh and twelfth centuries, the old Roman cities came alive with new populations and growth.

Beginning in the late tenth century, many new cities or towns were also founded, particularly in northern Europe. Usually, a group of merchants established a settlement near some fortified stronghold, such as a castle or monastery. The original meaning of the English *borough* or *burgh* and the German *burg* as a fortress or walled enclosure is still evident in the names of many cities, such as Edinburgh and Nuremberg. Castles were particularly favored because they were generally located along major routes of transportation or at the intersection of two trade routes; the lords of the castle also offered protection. If the settlement prospered and expanded, new walls were built to protect it.

Most towns were closely tied to their surrounding territories because they depended on the countryside for their food supplies. In addition, they were often part of the territory belonging to a lord and were subject to his jurisdiction. Although lords wanted to treat towns and townspeople as they would their vassals and serfs, cities had totally different needs and a different perspective. Townspeople needed mobility to trade. Consequently, these townspeople (the merchants and artisans came to be called

⚜ **SHOPS IN A MEDIEVAL TOWN.**   Most urban residents were merchants involved in trade and artisans who manufactured a wide variety of products. Master craftsmen had their workshops in the ground-level rooms of their houses. In this illustration, two well-dressed burghers are touring the shopping district of a French town. Tailors, furriers, a barber, and a grocer (from left to right) are visible at work in their shops.

burghers or bourgeoisie from the word *burgus*, a Latinized version of the German *burg*, meaning a walled enclosure) constituted a revolutionary group who needed their own unique laws to meet their requirements. Since the townspeople were profiting from the growth of trade and the sale of their products, they were willing to pay for the right to make their own laws and govern themselves. In many instances, lords and kings saw that they could also make money and were willing to sell to the townspeople the liberties they were beginning to demand.

By 1100, townspeople were obtaining charters of liberties from their territorial lords that granted them the privileges they wanted, including the right to bequeath goods and sell property, freedom from any military obligation to the lord, written urban law that guaranteed their freedom, and the right to become a free person after residing a year and a day in the town. The last provision made it possible for a runaway serf who could avoid capture to become a free person in a city. Almost all new urban communities gained these elementary liberties, but only some towns obtained the right to govern themselves by choosing their own officials and administering their own courts of law.

Over time, medieval cities developed their own governments for running the affairs of the community. Only males who had been born in the city or had lived there for some time could be citizens. In many cities, these citizens elected members of a city council who served as judges and city officials and passed laws. Elections were carefully rigged to ensure that only members of the wealthiest and most powerful families, who came to be called the patricians, were elected.

City governments kept close watch over the activities of their communities. To care for the welfare of the community, a government might regulate air and water pollution; provide water barrels and delegate responsibility to people in every section of the town to fight fires, which were an ever present danger; construct warehouses to store grain in the event of food shortages; and set the standards for the weights and measures used in local goods and industries.

Urban crime was not a major problem in medieval cities because the relatively small size of the communities made it difficult for criminals to operate openly. But medieval urban governments did hire guards to patrol the streets at night, to break up fights and prevent robberies. People caught committing criminal acts were quickly tried for their offenses. Serious crimes, such as murder, were punished by execution, usually by hanging. Lesser crimes were punished by fines, flogging, or branding.

Medieval cities remained relatively small in comparison to either ancient or modern cities. A large trading city would number about 5,000 inhabitants. By 1200, London was the largest city in England, with 30,000 people. Otherwise, north of the Alps, only a few great urban centers of commerce, such as Bruges and Ghent, had a population

THE MEDIEVAL CITY

Environmental pollution is not new to the twentieth century. Medieval cities and towns had their own problems with filthy living conditions. This excerpt is taken from an order sent by the king of England to the town of Boutham. It demands rectification of the town's pitiful physical conditions. There is little evidence to indicate that the king's order changed the situation dramatically.

THE KING'S COMMAND TO BOUTHAM

To the bailiffs of the abbot of St. Mary's, York, at Boutham. Whereas it is sufficiently evident that the pavement of the said town of Boutham is so very greatly broke up that all and singular passing and going through that town sustain immoderate damages and grievances, and in addition the air is so corrupted and infected by the pigsties situated in the king's highways and in the lanes of that town and by the swine feeding and frequently wandering about in the streets and lanes and by dung and dunghills and many other foul things placed in the streets and lanes, that great repugnance overtakes the king's ministers staying in that town and also others there dwelling and passing through, the advantage of more wholesome air is impeded, the state of men is grievously injured, and other unbearable inconveniences and many other injuries are known to proceed from such corruption, to the nuisance of the king's ministers aforesaid and of others there dwelling and passing through, and to the peril of their lives . . . the king, being unwilling longer to tolerate such great and unbearable defects there, orders the bailiffs to cause the pavement to be suitably repaired within their liberty before All Saints next, and to cause the pigsties, aforesaid streets and lanes to be cleansed from all dung and dunghills, and to cause proclamation to be made throughout their bailiwick forbidding any one, under pain of grievous forfeiture, to cause or permit their swine to feed or wander outside his house in the king's streets or the lanes aforesaid.

---

close to 40,000. Italian cities tended to be larger, with Venice, Florence, Genoa, Milan, and Naples numbering almost 100,000. Even the largest European city, however, seemed small alongside the Byzantine capital of Constantinople or the Arab cities of Damascus, Baghdad, and Cairo. For a long time to come, Europe remained a rural society, but in the long run, the growth of trade and the rise of towns laid the foundations for the eventual transformation of Europe from a rural agricultural society to an urban, industrial one.

DAILY LIFE IN THE MEDIEVAL CITY

Medieval towns were surrounded by stone walls that were expensive to build, so the space within was precious and tightly filled. This gave medieval cities their characteristic appearance of narrow, winding streets with houses crowded against each other and the second and third stories of the dwellings built out over the streets. Because dwellings were constructed mostly of wood before the fourteenth century and candles and wood fires were used for light and heat, the danger of fire was great. Medieval cities burned rapidly once a fire started.

Most of the people who lived in cities were merchants involved in trade and artisans engaged in manufacturing of some kind. Generally, merchants and artisans had their own sections within a city. The merchant area included warehouses, inns, and taverns. Artisan sections were usually divided along craft lines; each craft had its own street where its activity was pursued.

The physical environment of medieval cities was not pleasant. They were often dirty and rife with smells from animal and human waste deposited in backyard privies or on the streets (see the box above). Air pollution was also a fact of life, not only from the ubiquitous wood fires, but also from a cheaper fuel, coal, used industrially by lime burners, brewers, and dyers, as well as poor people who could not afford to purchase wood. Cities were also unable to stop water pollution, especially from the tanning and animal-slaughtering industries. Butchers dumped blood and all remaining waste products from their butchered animals into the river, while tanners unloaded tannic acid, dried blood, fat, hair, and the other waste products of their operations.

Because of the pollution, cities did not use the rivers for drinking water but relied instead on wells. Some cities repaired the aqueducts left over from Roman times and even constructed new ones. Private and public baths also existed in medieval towns. Paris, for example, had thirty-two public baths for men and women. City laws did not allow lepers and people with "bad reputations" to use them, but such measures did not prevent the public baths from being known for permissiveness due to public nudity. One contemporary commented on what occurred in public bathhouses: "Shameful things. Men make a point of staying all night in the public baths and women at the break of day come in and through 'ignorance' find themselves in the men's rooms."[7] Authorities came under increasing pressure to close the baths down, and the great plague of the fourteenth century sealed their fate.

There were considerably more men than women in medieval cities. Women, in addition to supervising the household, purchasing food and preparing meals, raising the children, and managing the family finances, were also often expected to help their husbands in their trades. Some women also developed their own trades to earn extra money. When some master craftspeople died, their widows even carried on their trades. Some women in medieval towns were thus able to lead lives of considerable independence.

Industry in Medieval Cities

The revival of trade enabled cities and towns to become important centers for manufacturing a wide range of goods, such as cloth, metalwork, shoes, and leather goods. A host of crafts were carried on in houses along the narrow streets of the medieval cities. From the twelfth century on, artisans began to organize themselves into guilds, which came to play a leading role in the economic life of the cities.

By the thirteenth century, virtually every group of craftspeople, such as tanners, carpenters, and bakers, had their own guild, while specialized groups of merchants, such as dealers in silk, spices, wool, or banking, had their separate guilds as well. Craft guilds directed almost every aspect of the production process. They established standards for the articles produced, specified the actual methods of production to be used, and even fixed the price at which the finished goods could be sold. Guilds also determined the number of men who could enter a specific trade and the procedure they must follow to do so.

A person who wanted to learn a trade first became an apprentice to a master craftsperson, usually at around the age of ten. Apprentices were not paid but did receive room and board from their masters. After five to seven years of service, in which they learned their craft, apprentices became journeymen (or journeywomen, although most were male), who then worked for wages for other masters. Journeymen aspired to become masters as well. To do so, they were expected to produce a "masterpiece," a finished piece in their craft that allowed the master craftspeople of the guild to judge whether the journeymen were qualified to become masters and join the guild.

CHRISTIANITY AND MEDIEVAL CIVILIZATION

Christianity was an integral part of the fabric of European society and the consciousness of Europe. Papal directives affected the actions of kings and princes alike, while Christian teachings and practices touched the lives of all Europeans.

The Papal Monarchy

Since the fifth century, the popes of the Catholic church had reigned supreme over the affairs of the church. They had also come to exercise control over the territories in central Italy that came to be known as the Papal States; this role kept the popes involved in political matters, often at the expense of their spiritual obligations. At the same time, the church became increasingly entangled in the evolving feudal relationships. High officials of the church, such as bishops and abbots, came to hold their offices as fiefs from nobles. As vassals, they were obliged to carry out the usual duties, including military service. Of course, lords assumed the right to choose their vassals and thus came to appoint bishops and abbots. Because lords often chose their vassals from other noble families for political reasons, these bishops and abbots were often worldly figures who cared little about their spiritual responsibilities.

REFORM OF THE PAPACY

By the eleventh century, church leaders realized the need to free the church from the interference of lords in the appointment of church officials. This issue of lay investiture, or the practice by which secular rulers both chose and invested their nominees to church offices with the symbols of their office, was dramatically taken up by the greatest of the reform popes of the eleventh century, Gregory VII (1073–1085).

Elected pope in 1073, Gregory was convinced that he had been chosen by God to reform the church. In pursuit of those aims, Gregory claimed that he—the pope—was truly God's "vicar on earth" and that the pope's authority extended over all of Christendom, including rulers. Gregory sought nothing less than the elimination of lay investiture. Only in this way could the church regain its freedom, by which Gregory meant the right of the church to appoint clergy and run its own affairs. If rulers did not accept these "divine" commands, then they could be deposed by the pope acting in his capacity as the vicar of Christ.

Gregory VII soon found himself in conflict with the king of Germany over these claims. King Henry IV (1056–1106) of Germany was just as determined as the pope. For many years, German kings had appointed high-ranking clerics, especially bishops, as their vassals in order to use them as administrators. Without them, the king could not hope to maintain his own power vis-à-vis the powerful German nobles. In 1075, Pope Gregory issued a decree forbidding high-ranking clerics from receiving their investiture from lay leaders: "We decree that no one of the clergy shall receive the investiture with a bishopric or abbey or church from the hand of an emperor or king or of any layperson."[8] Henry had no intention of obeying a decree that challenged the very heart of his administration.

The struggle between Henry IV and Gregory VII, which is known as the Investiture Controversy, was one of the great conflicts between church and state in the High Middle Ages. It dragged on until 1122, when a new German king and a new pope reached a compromise called the Concordat of Worms. Under this agreement, a bishop in Germany was first elected by church officials. After election, the nominee paid homage to the king as his feudal lord, who then invested him with the symbols of temporal office. A representative of the pope then invested the new bishop with the symbols of his spiritual office.

THE CHURCH SUPREME

The popes of the twelfth century did not abandon the reform ideals of Pope Gregory VII, but they were less dogmatic and more inclined to consolidate their power and build a strong administrative system. During the papacy of Pope Innocent III (1198–1216), the Catholic church reached the height of its political, intellectual, and secular power. At the beginning of his pontificate, in a letter to a priest, the pope made a clear statement of his views on papal supremacy:

> As God, the creator of the universe, set two great lights in the firmament of heaven, the greater light to rule the day, and the lesser light to rule the night, so He set two great dignities in the firmament of the universal church, . . . the greater to rule the day, that is, souls, and the lesser to rule the night, that is, bodies. These dignities are the papal authority and the royal power. And just as the moon gets her light from the sun, and is inferior to the sun . . . so the royal power gets the splendor of its dignity from the papal authority.[9]

Innocent III's actions were those of a man who believed that he, as pope, was the supreme judge of European affairs. He forced King Philip Augustus of France to take back his wife and queen after Philip had tried to have the marriage annulled. The pope also compelled King John of England to accept the papal choice for the position of archbishop of Canterbury. To achieve his political ends, Innocent did not hesitate to use the spiritual weapons at his command, especially the interdict, which forbade priests to dispense the sacraments of the church in the hope that the people, deprived of the comforts of religion, would exert pressure against their ruler. Pope Innocent's interdict was so effective that it caused Philip to restore his wife to her rightful place as queen of France.

New Religious Orders and New Spiritual Ideals

In the second half of the eleventh century and the first half of the twelfth century, a wave of religious enthusiasm seized Europe, leading to a spectacular growth in the number of monasteries and the emergence of new monastic orders. Most important was the Cistercian order, founded in 1098 by a group of monks dissatisfied with the lack of strict discipline at their own Benedictine monastery. Cistercian monasticism spread rapidly from southern France into the rest of Europe.

✣ A GROUP OF NUNS.   Although still viewed by the medieval church as inferior to men, women were as susceptible to the spiritual fervor of the twelfth century as men, and female monasticism grew accordingly. This miniature shows a group of Flemish nuns listening to the preaching of an abbot, Gilles li Muisis. The nun wearing a white robe at the far left is a novice.

The Cistercians were strict. They ate a simple diet and possessed only a single robe apiece. All decorations were eliminated from their churches and monastic buildings. More time for prayer and manual labor was provided by shortening the number of hours spent at religious services. The Cistercians played a major role in developing a new, activist spiritual model for twelfth-century Europe. A Benedictine monk often spent hours in prayer to honor god. The Cistercian ideal had a different emphasis: "Arise, soldier of Christ, arise! Get up off the ground and return to the battle from which you have fled! Fight more boldly after your flight, and triumph in glory!"[10] These were the words of Saint Bernard of Clairvaux (1090–1153), who more than any other person embodied the new spiritual ideal of Cistercian monasticism (see the box on p. 342).

Women were also active participants in the spiritual movements of the age. The number of women joining religious houses grew perceptibly with the rise of the new orders of the twelfth century. In the High Middle Ages, most nuns were from the ranks of the landed aristocracy. Convents were convenient for families unable or unwilling to find husbands for their daughters and for aristocratic women who did not wish to marry. Female intellectuals found them a haven for their activities. Most of the learned women of the Middle Ages, especially in Germany, were nuns. One of the most distinguished was Hildegard of Bingen (1098–1179), who became abbess of a convent in western Germany.

Hildegard shared in the religious enthusiasm of the twelfth century. Soon after becoming abbess, she began to

A MIRACLE OF SAINT BERNARD

*S*aint Bernard of Clairvaux has been called "the most widely respected holy man of the twelfth century." He was an outstanding preacher, wholly dedicated to the service of God. His reputation reportedly influenced many young men to join the Cistercian order. He also inspired a myriad of stories dealing with his miracles.

A MIRACLE OF ST. BERNARD

A certain monk, departing from his monastery . . . , threw off his habit, and returned to the world at the persuasion of the Devil. And he took a certain parish living; for he was a priest. Because sin is punished with sin, the deserter from his Order lapsed into the vice of lechery. He took a concubine to live with him, as in fact is done by many, and by her he had children.

But as God is merciful and does not wish anyone to perish, it happened that many years after, the blessed abbot [St. Bernard] was passing through the village in which this same monk was living, and went to stay at his house. The renegade monk recognized him, and received him very reverently, and waited on him devoutly . . . but as yet the abbot did not recognize him.

On the morrow, the holy man said Matins and prepared to be off. But as he could not speak to the priest, since he had got up and gone to the church for Matins, he said to the priest's son "Go, give this message to your master." Now the boy had been born dumb. He obeyed the command and feeling in himself the power of him who had given it, he ran to his father and uttered the words of the Holy Father clearly and exactly. His father, on hearing his son's voice for the first time, wept for joy, and made him repeat the same words . . . and he asked what the abbot had done to him. "He did nothing to me," said the boy, "except to say 'Go and say this to your father.'"

At so evident a miracle the priest repented, and hastened after the holy man and fell at his feet saying "My Lord and Father, I was your monk so-and-so, and at such-and-such a time I ran away from your monastery. I ask your Paternity to allow me to return with you to the monastery, for in your coming God has visited my heart." The saint replied unto him, "Wait for me here, and I will come back quickly when I have done my business, and I will take you with me." But the priest, fearing death (which he had not done before), answered, "Lord, I am afraid of dying before then." But the saint replied, "Know this for certain, that if you die in this condition, and in this resolve, you will find yourself a monk before God."

The saint [eventually] returned and heard that the priest had recently died and been buried. He ordered the tomb to be opened. And when they asked him what he wanted to do, he said, "I want to see if he is lying as a monk or a clerk in his tomb." "As a clerk," they said; "we buried him in his secular habit." But when they had dug up the earth, they found that he was not in the clothes in which they had buried him; but he appeared in all points, tonsure and habit, as a monk. And they all praised God.

---

write down an account of the mystical visions she had had for years. "A great flash of light from heaven pierced my brain and . . . in that instant my mind was imbued with the meaning of the sacred books," she wrote in a description typical of the world's mystical literature. Eventually, she produced three books based on her visions. Hildegard gained considerable renown as a mystic and prophet, and popes, emperors, kings, dukes, bishops, abbots, and abbesses eagerly sought her advice.

In the thirteenth century, two new religious orders emerged that had a profound impact on the lives of ordinary people: the Franciscan and Dominican friars. The friars were particularly active in the cities, where, by their example, they strove to provide a more personal religious experience. Like their founder, Saint Francis of Assisi (1182–1226), the Franciscans lived among the people, preaching repentance and aiding the poor. Their calls for a return to the simplicity and poverty of the early church, reinforced by their own example, were especially effective and made them very popular.

Dominicans arose out of the desire of a Spanish priest, Dominic de Guzmán (1170–1221), to defend church teachings from heresy. The spiritual revival of the High Middle Ages had also led to the emergence of heretical movements, which became especially widespread in southern France. Unlike Francis, Dominic was an intellectual, who was appalled by the growth of heresy within the church. He believed that a new religious order of men who lived lives of poverty but were learned and capable of preaching effectively would best be able to attack heresy. The Dominicans became especially well known for their roles as the inquisitors of the papal Inquisition.

The Holy Office, as the papal Inquisition was formally called, was a court that had been established by the church to find and try heretics. Gradually, the Holy Office developed a regular procedure to deal with heretics. If an accused heretic confessed, he or she was forced to perform public penance and was subjected to punishment, such as flogging. The heretic's property was then confiscated and divided between the secular authorities and the church. Beginning in 1252, those who did not confess voluntarily were tortured. Those who refused to confess and were still considered guilty were turned over to the state for execution. So also were relapsed heretics—those who confessed, did penance, and then reverted to heresy again. To the Christians of the thirteenth century, who believed that there was only one path to salvation, heresy was a crime against God and against humanity. In their minds, force should be used to save souls from damnation.

Popular Religion in the High Middle Ages

We have witnessed the actions of popes, bishops, and monks. But what of ordinary clergy and laypeople? What were their religious hopes and fears? What were their spiritual aspirations?

The sacraments of the Catholic church ensured that the church was an integral part of people's lives, from birth to death. There were (and still are) seven sacraments, administered only by the clergy. Sacraments, such as baptism and the eucharist, were viewed as outward symbols of an inward grace and were considered imperative for a Christian's salvation. Therefore, the clergy were seen to have a key role in the attainment of salvation.

Other church practices were also important to ordinary people. Saints were seen as men and women who, through their holiness, had achieved a special position in heaven, enabling them to act as intercessors before the throne of God. The saints' ability to protect poor souls enabled them to take on great importance at the popular level. Jesus' apostles were, of course, recognized throughout Europe as saints, but there were also numerous local saints that were of special significance to a single area. New cults rapidly developed, especially in the intense religious atmosphere of the eleventh and twelfth centuries. The English, for example, introduced Saint Nicholas, the patron saint of children, who is known today as Santa Claus.

In the High Middle Ages, the foremost position among the saints was occupied by the Virgin Mary, the mother of Jesus. Mary was viewed as the most important mediator with her son Jesus, the judge of all sinners. Moreover, from the eleventh century on, a fascination with Mary as Jesus' human mother became more evident. A sign of Mary's importance was the growing number of churches all over Europe that were dedicated to her in the twelfth and thirteenth centuries.

Emphasis on the role of the saints was closely tied to the use of relics, which also increased noticeably in the High Middle Ages. Relics were usually the bones of saints or objects intimately connected to saints that were considered worthy of veneration by the faithful. A twelfth-century English monk began his description of the abbey's relics by saying that "There is kept there a thing more precious than gold, . . . the right arm of St. Oswald. . . . This we have seen with our own eyes and have kissed, and have handled with our own hands. . . . There are kept here also part of his ribs and of the soil on which he fell."[11] The monk went on to list additional relics possessed by the abbey, including two pieces of Jesus' swaddling clothes,

pieces of Jesus' manger, and part of the five loaves of bread with which Jesus fed five thousand people. Because the holiness of the saint was considered to be inherent in his relics, these objects were believed to be capable of healing people or producing other miracles.

THE CULTURAL WORLD OF THE HIGH MIDDLE AGES

The High Middle Ages was a time of extraordinary intellectual and artistic vitality. It witnessed the birth of universities, a quickening of theological thought, a rebirth of interest in ancient culture, new developments in literature, and a building spree that left Europe bedecked with churches and cathedrals.

The Rise of Universities

The university as we know it—with faculty, students, and degrees—was a product of the High Middle Ages. The word *university* is derived from the Latin word *universitas*, meaning a corporation or guild, and referred to either a corporation of teachers or a corporation of students. Medieval universities were educational guilds or corporations that produced educated and trained individuals.

The first European university appeared in Bologna, Italy, where a great teacher named Irnerius (1088–1125), who taught Roman law, attracted students from all over Europe. Most of them were laymen, usually older individuals who served as administrators for kings and princes and were eager to learn more about law so they could apply it in their own jobs. To protect themselves, students at Bologna formed a guild or *universitas*, which was recognized by Emperor Frederick Barbarossa and given a charter in 1158. Although the faculty also organized themselves as a group, the guild of students at Bologna was far more influential. It obtained a promise of freedom for students from local authorities, regulated the price of books and lodging, and determined the curriculum, fees, and standards for their masters. Teachers were fined if they missed a class or began their lectures late.

The first university in northern Europe was the University of Paris. In the second half of the twelfth century, a number of students and masters left Paris and started their own university at Oxford, England. In the Late Middle Ages, kings, popes, and princes competed to found new universities, and by the end of the Middle Ages, Europe had eighty universities, most of them located in England, France, Italy, and Germany.

Students at a medieval university began their studies with the traditional liberal arts curriculum, which consisted of grammar, rhetoric, logic, arithmetic, geometry, music,

✿ A UNIVERSITY CLASSROOM. This illustration shows a university classroom in fourteenth-century Germany. As was customary in medieval classrooms, the master is reading from a text. The students obviously vary considerably in age and in their attentiveness to the lecturer.

and astronomy. Teaching was done through lectures. (The word *lecture* is derived from the Latin and means "to read.") Before the development of the printing press in the fifteenth century, books were prohibitively expensive—few students could afford them—so teachers read from a basic text (such as a collection of law if the subject was law) and then added their explanations. No exams were given after a series of lectures, but when a student applied for a degree, he (women did not attend universities in the Middle Ages) was given a comprehensive oral examination by a committee of teachers. The exam was taken after a four- or six-year period of study. The first degree a student could earn was an A.B., the *artium baccalaureus*, or bachelor of arts; later, he might receive an A.M., *artium magister*, or master of arts. All degrees were licenses to teach, although most students receiving them did not become teachers.

After completing the liberal arts curriculum, a student could go on to study law, medicine, or theology. The latter was the most highly regarded subject of the medieval university. The study of law, medicine, or theology could take a decade or more. A student who passed his final oral examinations was granted a doctor's degree, which officially enabled him to teach his subject. Students who received degrees from medieval universities could pursue other careers besides teaching that would be much more lucrative. A law degree was necessary for those who wished to serve as advisers to kings and princes. The growing administrative bureaucracies of popes and kings also demanded a supply of educated clerks, who could keep records and draw up official documents. Universities provided the teachers, administrators, lawyers, and doctors for medieval society.

The Development of Scholasticism

The importance of Christianity in medieval society made it certain that theology would play a central role in the European intellectual world. Theology, the formal study of religion, was "queen of the sciences" in the new universities.

Beginning in the eleventh century, the effort to apply reason or logical analysis to the church's basic doctrines had a significant impact on the study of theology. The word *scholasticism* refers to the philosophical and theological system of the medieval schools. A primary preoccupation of scholasticism was the attempt to reconcile faith and reason—to demonstrate that what was accepted on faith was in harmony with what could be learned by reason. Scholasticism had its beginnings in the theological world of the eleventh and twelfth centuries but reached its high point in the brilliant synthesis of Thomas Aquinas in the thirteenth century.

The overriding task of scholasticism in the thirteenth century was to harmonize Christian revelation with the work of Aristotle. In the twelfth century, due largely to the work of Muslim and Jewish scholars, western Europe was introduced to a large number of Greek scientific and philosophical works and, above all, to the works of Aristotle. The great influx of Aristotle's works into the West in the High Middle Ages threw many theologians into consternation. Aristotle was so highly regarded that he was called "the philosopher," yet he had arrived at his conclusions by rational thought—not revelation—and some of his doctrines, such as the mortality of the individual soul, contradicted the teachings of the church. The most famous attempt to reconcile Aristotle and the doctrines of Christianity was made by Saint Thomas Aquinas.

Thomas Aquinas (1225–1274) studied theology at Cologne and Paris and taught at both Naples and Paris. It was at the latter that he finished his famous *Summa Theologica* (*A Summa of Theology*—a summa was a compendium of knowledge that attempted to bring together all the received learning of the preceding centuries on a given subject into a single whole). Aquinas's masterpiece was organized according to the dialectical method of the scholastics. Aquinas first posed a question, cited sources that offered opposing opinions on the question, and then resolved them by arriving at his own conclusions. In this fashion, he raised and discussed some six hundred articles.

Aquinas's reputation is based on his masterful attempt to reconcile faith and reason. He took it for granted that there were truths derived by reason and truths derived by faith. He was certain, however, that the two truths could not be in conflict with each other. The natural mind, unaided by faith, could arrive at truths concerning the physical universe. Without the help of God's grace, however, unaided reason alone could not grasp spiritual truths, such as the Trinity or the Incarnation.

Vernacular Literature

Latin was the universal language of medieval civilization. Used in the church and schools, it enabled learned men to communicate anywhere in Europe. But in the twelfth century much new literature was being written in the vernacular (the language used in a particular region, such as Spanish, French, English, or German). A new market for vernacular literature appeared in the twelfth century when educated laypeople at courts and in the cities sought fresh avenues of entertainment.

Perhaps the most popular vernacular literature of the twelfth century was troubadour poetry, which was chiefly the product of nobles and knights. This poetry told of the love of a knight for a lady, who inspires him to become a braver knight and a better poet. A good example is found in the laments of the noble Jaufré Rudel, who cherished a dream lady from afar whom he would always love, but feared he would never meet:

> Most sad, most joyous shall I go away,
> Let me have seen her for a single day,
> My love afar,
> I shall not see her, for her land and mine
> Are sundered, and the ways are hard to find,
> So many ways, and I shall lose my way,
> So wills it God.[12]

Though it originated in southern France, troubadour poetry also spread to northern France, Italy, and Germany.

Romanesque Architecture: "A White Mantle of Churches"

The eleventh and twelfth centuries witnessed an explosion of building, both private and public. The construction of castles and churches absorbed most of the surplus resources of medieval society and at the same time reflected its basic preoccupations, God and warfare. The churches were by far the most conspicuous of the public buildings. As a chronicler of the eleventh century commented,

> As the year 1003 approached, people all over the world, but especially in Italy and France, began to rebuild their churches. Although most of them were well built and in little need of alterations, Christian nations were rivaling each other to have the most beautiful edifices. One might say the world was shaking herself, throwing off her old garments, and robing herself with a white mantle of churches. Then nearly all the cathedrals, the monasteries dedicated to different saints, and even the small village chapels were reconstructed more beautifully by the faithful.[13]

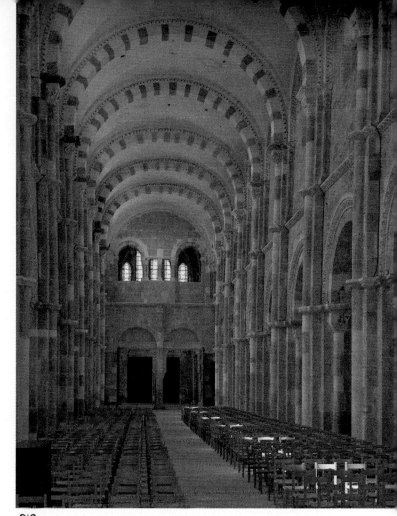

❀ **BARREL VAULTING.** The eleventh and twelfth centuries witnessed an enormous amount of church construction. Utilizing the basilica shape, master builders replaced flat wooden roofs with long, round stone vaults, known as barrel vaults. As this illustration of a Romanesque church in Vienne, France, indicates, the barrel vault limited the size of a church and left little room for windows.

Hundreds of new cathedrals and abbey and pilgrimage churches, as well as thousands of parish churches in rural villages, were built in the eleventh and twelfth centuries. The building spree was a direct reflection of a revived religious culture and the increased wealth of the period produced by agriculture, trade, and the growth of cities.

The cathedrals of the eleventh and twelfth centuries were built in the Romanesque style, a truly international style. The construction of churches required the services of professional master builders, whose employment throughout Europe guaranteed an international uniformity in basic features.

Romanesque churches were normally built in the basilica shape used in the construction of churches in the Late Roman Empire. Basilicas were simply rectangular buildings with flat wooden roofs. While using this basic plan, Romanesque builders made a significant innovation by replacing the flat wooden roof with a long, curved stone vault, called a barrel vault or a cross vault where two barrel vaults intersected. The latter was used when a transept was added to create a church plan in the shape of a cross. Although barrel and cross vaults were difficult to build, they were considered aesthetically more pleasing and technically more proficient than flat roofs and were also less apt to catch fire.

Because stone roofs were extremely heavy, Romanesque churches required massive pillars and walls to hold them up. This left little space for windows, and the churches were correspondingly dark on the inside. Their massive walls and pillars gave Romanesque churches a sense of solidity and almost the impression of a fortress.

The Gothic Cathedral

Begun in the twelfth century and brought to perfection in the thirteenth, the Gothic cathedral remains one of the greatest artistic triumphs of the High Middle Ages. Soaring skyward, almost as if to reach heaven, it was a fitting symbol for medieval people's preoccupation with God.

Two fundamental innovations of the twelfth century made Gothic cathedrals possible. The combination of

THE GOTHIC CATHEDRAL. The Gothic cathedral was one of the great artistic triumphs of the High Middle Ages. Seen here is the cathedral of Notre Dame in Paris. Begun in 1163, it was not completed until the beginning of the fourteenth century.

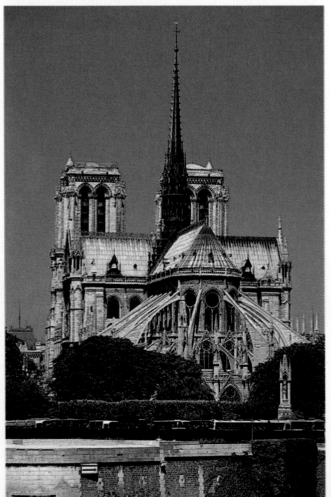

ribbed vaults and pointed arches replaced the barrel vault of Romanesque churches and enabled builders to make Gothic churches higher than their Romanesque counterparts. The use of pointed arches and ribbed vaults created an impression of upward movement, a sense of weightless upward thrust that implied the energy of God. Another technical innovation, the flying buttress, basically a heavy arched pier of stone built onto the outside of the wall, made it possible to distribute the weight of the church's vaulted ceilings outward and down and thus eliminate the heavy walls used in Romanesque churches to hold the weight of the massive barrel vaults. Thus, Gothic cathedrals could be built with thin walls that were filled with magnificent stained-glass windows, which created a play of light inside that varied with the sun at different times of the day. This preoccupation with colored light in Gothic cathedrals was not accidental but was executed by people who believed that natural light was a symbol of the divine light of God.

The first fully Gothic church was the abbey church of Saint-Denis near Paris, inspired by its famous abbot Suger (1122–1151) and built between 1140 and 1150. Although the Gothic style was a product of northern France, by the mid-thirteenth century, French Gothic architecture had spread to England, Spain, Germany— virtually all of Europe. By the mid-thirteenth century, French Gothic architecture was displayed most brilliantly in cathedrals in Paris (Notre Dame), Reims, Amiens, and Chartres.

A Gothic cathedral was the work of an entire community. All classes contributed to its construction. Money was raised from wealthy townspeople, who had profited from the new trade and industries, as well as from kings and nobles. Master masons, who were both architects and engineers, designed the cathedrals. They drew up the plans and supervised the work of construction. Stonemasons and other craftspeople were paid a daily wage and provided the skilled labor to build the cathedrals. A Gothic cathedral symbolized the chief preoccupation of a medieval Christian community, its dedication to a spiritual ideal. As we have observed before, the largest buildings of an era reflect the values of its society. The Gothic cathedral with its towers soaring toward heaven gave witness to an age when a spiritual impulse still underlay most of existence.

THE BYZANTINE EMPIRE AND THE CRUSADES

In the fourth century, a noticeable separation between the western and eastern parts of the Roman Empire began to develop. In the course of the fifth century, the Germanic tribes moved into the western part of the empire and established their states, while the Roman Empire in the east, centered on Constantinople, continued to exist.

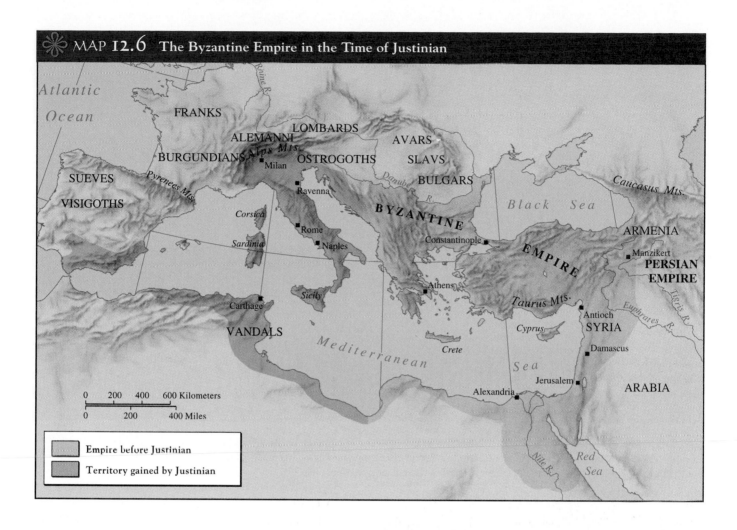

MAP 12.6   The Byzantine Empire in the Time of Justinian

Empire before Justinian

Territory gained by Justinian

The Reign of Justinian (527–565)

When he became emperor of the Eastern Roman Empire, Justinian was determined to reestablish the Roman Empire in the entire Mediterranean world. His army, commanded by Belisarius, probably the best general of the late Roman world, sailed to North Africa and quickly destroyed the Vandals in two major battles. From North Africa Belisarius led his forces onto the Italian peninsula and defeated the Ostrogoths. By 552, Justinian appeared to have achieved his goals. He had restored the Roman Empire in the Mediterranean. His empire included Italy, part of Spain, North Africa, Asia Minor, Palestine, and Syria. But the reconquest of the western empire proved fleeting. Only three years after Justinian's death, the Lombards conquered much of Italy. Although the eastern empire maintained the fiction of Italy as a province, its forces were limited to southern and central Italy, Sicily, and some coastal areas.

Justinian's most important contribution was his codification of Roman law. The eastern empire had inherited a vast quantity of legal materials connected to the development of Roman law, which Justinian wished to simplify. The result was the *Corpus Iuris Civilis* (*The Body of Civil Law*), a codification of Roman law that remained the basis of imperial law in the Eastern Roman Empire until its end in 1453. More importantly, however, because it was written in Latin (it was, in fact, the last product of eastern Roman culture to be written in Latin, which was soon replaced by Greek), it was also eventually used in the west and, in fact, became the basis of the legal systems of all of continental Europe.

From Eastern Roman to Byzantine Empire

Justinian's accomplishments had been spectacular, but he left the Eastern Roman Empire with serious problems: too much territory to protect far from Constantinople, an empty treasury, a decline in population after a plague, and renewed threats to its frontiers. In the first half of the seventh century, the empire was attacked by the Persians to the east and the Slavs to the north. The empire survived, only to face a new series of threats.

The most serious challenge to the Eastern Roman Empire came from the rise of Islam, which unified the Arab tribes and created a powerful new force that swept through the east (see Chapter 8). The defeat of an eastern Roman army at Yarmuk in 636 meant the loss of the

✿ THE EMPEROR JUSTINIAN SURROUNDED BY HIS COURT.   The church of San Vitale at
Ravenna contains some of the finest examples of sixth-century Byzantine mosaics. This mosaic depicts
the Byzantine emperor Justinian and his court dressed in their elaborate court robes.

provinces of Syria and Palestine. Problems arose along the northern frontier as well, especially in the Balkans, where the Bulgars had arrived earlier, in the sixth century. In 679, the Bulgars defeated the eastern Roman forces and took possession of the lower Danube valley, creating a strong Bulgarian kingdom.

By the beginning of the eighth century, the Eastern Roman Empire was greatly diminished in size. Consisting only of the eastern Balkans and Asia Minor, it was no longer an eastern Mediterranean state. The external challenges had important internal repercussions as well. By the eighth century, the Eastern Roman Empire had been transformed into what historians call the Byzantine Empire, a civilization with its own unique character that would last until 1453.

The Byzantine Empire was both a Greek and a Christian state. Increasingly, Latin fell into disuse as Greek became both the common and the official language of the empire. The Byzantine Empire was also a Christian state. The empire was built on a faith in Jesus that was shared in a profound way by almost all of its citizens. An enormous amount of artistic talent was poured into the construction of churches, church ceremonies, and church decoration. Spiritual principles deeply permeated Byzantine art.

The emperor occupied a crucial position in the Byzantine state. Portrayed as chosen by God, the emperor was crowned in sacred ceremonies, and his subjects were expected to prostrate themselves in his presence. His power was considered absolute and was limited in practice only by deposition or assassination. Since the emperor appointed the head of the church (known as the patriarch), he also exercised control over both church and state. The Byzantines believed that God had commanded their state to preserve the true Christian faith. Emperor, clergy, and state officials were all bound together in service to this ideal. It can be said that spiritual values truly held the Byzantine state together.

LIFE IN CONSTANTINOPLE

After riots destroyed much of Constantinople in 532, Emperor Justinian rebuilt the city and gave it the appearance it would keep for almost a thousand years. With a population estimated in the hundreds of thousands, Constantinople was the largest city in Europe during the Middle Ages. But even Constantinople could not compare to the Chinese capital city of Chang'an under the Tang dynasty; it numbered almost two million inhabitants.

Until the twelfth century, Constantinople was Europe's greatest commercial center, the chief marketplace where western and eastern products were exchanged. Highly desired in Europe were the products of the east: silk from China, spices from Southeast Asia and India, jewelry and ivory from India (the latter used by Byzantine craftspeople for church items), wheat and furs from southern Russia, and flax and honey from the Balkans. Many of these eastern goods were then shipped to the Mediterranean area and northern Europe. Some imported raw materials were used in Constantinople for local industries. During Justinian's reign, two Christian monks smuggled silkworms from China to begin a Byzantine silk industry. The state controlled the production of silk cloth, and the workshops themselves were housed in Constantinople's royal palace complex. European demand for silk cloth made it the city's most lucrative product.

Before Justinian's program of rebuilding in the sixth century, Emperor Theodosius II (408–450) in the mid-fifth century had erected an enormous defensive wall to protect the city on its land side. The city was dominated by an immense palace complex, hundreds of churches, and a huge arena known as the Hippodrome. No residential district was particularly fashionable; palaces, tenements, and slums ranged alongside one another. Justinian added many new buildings. His public works projects included roads, bridges, walls, public baths, law courts, and colossal underground reservoirs to hold the city's water supply. He also built hospitals, schools, monasteries, and churches. The latter were his special passion, and in Constantinople alone he built or rebuilt thirty-four of them. His greatest achievement was the famous Hagia Sophia—the Church of the Holy Wisdom—completed in 537. The center of Hagia Sophia consisted of four large piers crowned by an enormous dome, which seemed to be floating in space. In part, this impression was created by ringing the base of the dome with forty-two windows, which allowed an incredible play of light within the cathedral. Light served to remind the worshipers of God. As invisible light illuminates darkness, so too, it was believed, invisible spirit illuminates the world.

The Hippodrome was a huge amphitheater, constructed of brick covered by marble, holding between 40,000 and 60,000 spectators. Although gladiator fights were held there, the main events were the chariot races; twenty-four would usually be presented in one day. The citizens of Constantinople were passionate fans of chariot racing. Successful charioteers were acclaimed as heroes and honored with public statues.

New Heights and New Problems

By 750, the Byzantine Empire consisted only of Asia Minor, some lands in the Balkans, and the southern coast of Italy. But Byzantium recovered and not only endured, but even expanded through the efforts of a new dynasty of Byzantine emperors known as the Macedonians, who ruled from 867 to 1081. This line of emperors managed to beat off the empire's external enemies and switch to the offensive. The empire was expanded to include Bulgaria in the Balkans, the islands of Crete and Cyprus, and Syria. By 1025, the Byzantine Empire was the largest it had been since the beginning of the seventh century.

The Macedonian emperors also fostered a burst of economic prosperity by expanding trade relations with western Europe, especially by selling silks and metalwork. Thanks to this prosperity, the city of Constantinople flourished. Foreign visitors continued to be astounded by its size, wealth, and physical surroundings. To western Europeans, it was the stuff of legends and fables (see the box on p. 350).

Although the Macedonians had restored much of the power of the Byzantine Empire in the tenth and eleventh centuries, their incompetent successors reversed most of the gains as struggles for power between ambitious military leaders and aristocratic families led to political and social disorder in the late eleventh century. The Byzantine Empire had also been troubled by the growing split

INTERIOR VIEW OF HAGIA SOPHIA. Pictured here is the interior of the Church of the Holy Wisdom, constructed under Justinian by Anthemius of Tralles and Isidore of Milan. The pulpits and the great plaques bearing inscriptions from the Koran were introduced when the Turks converted this church into a mosque, in the fifteenth century.

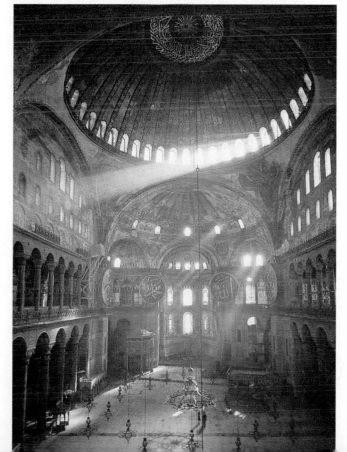

A WESTERN VIEW OF THE BYZANTINE EMPIRE

Bishop Liudprand of Cremona undertook diplomatic missions to Constantinople on behalf of two western kings, Berengar of Italy and Otto I of Germany. This selection is taken from his description of his mission to the Byzantine emperor Constantine VII in 949 as an envoy for Berengar, king of Italy from 950 until his overthrow by Otto I of Germany in 964. Liudprand had mixed feelings about Byzantium: admiration, yet also envy and hostility because of its superior wealth.

LIUDPRAND OF CREMONA, ANTAPODOSIS

Next to the imperial residence at Constantinople there is a palace of remarkable size and beauty which the Greeks call Magnavra . . . the name being equivalent to "Fresh breeze." In order to receive some Spanish envoys, who had recently arrived, as well as myself . . . , Constantine gave orders that this palace should be got ready. . . .

Before the emperor's seat stood a tree, made of bronze gilded over, whose branches were filled with birds, also made of gilded bronze, which uttered different cries, each according to its varying species. The throne itself was so marvelously fashioned that at one moment it seemed a low structure, and at another it rose high into the air. It was of immense size and was guarded by lions, made either of bronze or of wood covered over with gold, who beat the ground with their tails and gave a dreadful roar with open mouth and quivering tongue. Leaning upon the shoulders of two eunuchs I was brought into the emperor's presence. At my approach the lions began to roar and the birds to cry out, each according to its kind; but I was neither terrified nor surprised, for I had previously made enquiry about all these things from people who were well acquainted with them. So after I had three times made obeisance to the emperor with my face upon the ground, I lifted my head, and behold! The man whom just before I had seen sitting on a moderately elevated seat had now changed his raiment and was sitting on the level of the ceiling. How it was done I could not imagine, unless perhaps he was lifted up by some such sort of device as we use for raising the timbers of a wine press. On that occasion he did not address me personally, . . . but by the intermediary of a secretary he enquired about Berengar's doings and asked after his health. I made a fitting reply and then, at a nod from the interpreter, left his presence and retired to my lodging.

It would give me some pleasure also to record here what I did then for Berengar. . . . The Spanish envoys . . . had brought handsome gifts from their masters to the emperor Constantine. I for my part had brought nothing from Berengar except a letter and that was full of lies. I was very greatly disturbed and shamed at this and began to consider anxiously what I had better do. In my doubt and perplexity it finally occurred to me that I might offer the gifts, which on my account I had brought for the emperor, as coming from Berengar, and trick out my humble present with fine words. I therefore presented him with nine excellent cuirasses, seven excellent shields with gilded bosses, two silver gilt cauldrons, some swords, spears, and spits, and what was more precious to the emperor than anything, four carzimasia; that being the Greek name for young eunuchs who have had both their testicles and their penis removed. This operation is performed by traders at Verdun, who take the boys into Spain and make a huge profit.

---

between the Catholic church of the west and the Eastern Orthodox church of the Byzantine Empire. The Eastern Orthodox church was unwilling to accept the pope's claim that he was the sole head of the church. In 1054, Pope Leo IX and Patriarch Michael Cerularius, head of the Byzantine church, formally excommunicated each other, initiating a schism between the two great branches of Christianity that has not been completely healed to this day.

The Byzantine Empire faced threats from abroad as well. The greatest challenge came from the advance of the Seljuk Turks (see Chapter 8) who had moved into Asia Minor—the heartland of the empire and its main source of food and labor. In 1071, a Turkish army disastrously defeated the Byzantine forces under Emperor Romanus IV Diogenes at Manzikert. Lacking the resources to undertake new campaigns against the Turks, the new emperor, Alexius I Comnenus (1081–1118), turned to Europe for military assistance. It was the positive response of Euro-peans to the emperor's request that led to the Crusades. The Byzantine Empire lived to regret it.

The Crusades

The Crusades were based on the idea of a holy war against the infidels or unbelievers. The wrath of Christians was directed against the Muslims, and at the end of the eleventh century, Christian Europe found itself with a glorious opportunity to attack them. The immediate impetus for the Crusades came when the Byzantine emperor Alexius I asked Pope Urban II for help against the Seljuk Turks, who were Muslims. The pope saw a golden opportunity to provide papal leadership for a great cause: to rally the warriors of Europe for the liberation of Jerusalem and the Holy Land from the infidel. At the Council of Clermont in southern France near the end of 1095, Urban II challenged Christians to take up their weapons and join in a holy war to recover the Holy Land. The pope promised remission of sins: "All who die by the way, whether by land or by sea, or in battle against the pagans, shall have immediate remission of sins. This I grant them through the power of God with which I am invested."[14] The enthusiastic crowd cried out in response: "It is the will of God, it is the will of God."

The warriors of western Europe, particularly France, formed the first crusading armies. The knights who made up this first crusading host were motivated by religious fervor, but there were other attractions as well. Some sought adventure and welcomed a legitimate opportunity to pursue their favorite pastime—fighting. Others saw an opportunity to gain territory, riches, and possibly a title. From the perspective of the pope and European monarchs, the Crusades offered the potential of freeing Europe of contentious young nobles who disturbed the peace and wasted lives fighting each other. Then, too, merchants in many Italian cities sought new trading opportunities in Muslim lands.

Three organized crusading bands of noble warriors, most of them French, made their way to the east. The crusading army probably numbered several thousand cavalry and as many as 10,000 infantry. After the capture of Antioch in 1098, much of the crusading host proceeded down the Palestinian coast, evading the well-defended coastal cities, and reached Jerusalem in June 1099. After a five-week

siege, the Holy City was taken amidst a horrible massacre of the inhabitants—men, women, and children.

After further conquest of Palestinian lands, the crusaders ignored the wishes of the Byzantine emperor (who foolishly believed the crusaders were working on his

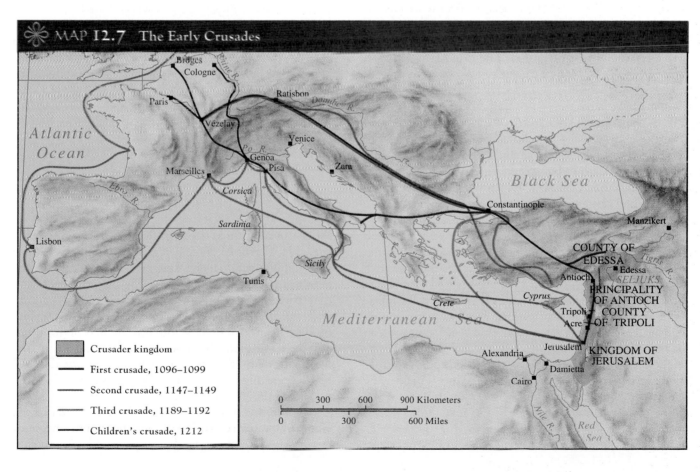

MAP 12.7 The Early Crusades

Crusader kingdom

— First crusade, 1096–1099

— Second crusade, 1147–1149

— Third crusade, 1189–1192

— Children's crusade, 1212

behalf) and organized four Latin crusader states. Because the crusader states were surrounded by Muslims, they grew increasingly dependent on the Italian commercial cities for supplies from Europe. Some Italian cities, such as Genoa, Pisa, and, above all, Venice, grew rich and powerful in the process.

But it was not easy for the crusader states to maintain themselves in the east. Already by the 1120s, the Muslims had begun to strike back. In 1144, Edessa became the first of the four Latin states to be recaptured. Its fall led to renewed calls for another Crusade, especially from the monastic firebrand Saint Bernard of Clairvaux. He exclaimed: "Now, on account of our sins, the enemies of the cross have begun to show their faces. . . . What are you doing, you servants of the cross? Will you throw to the dogs that which is most holy? Will you cast pearls before swine?"[15] Bernard aimed his message at knights and even managed to enlist two powerful rulers, King Louis VII of France (1137–1180) and Emperor Conrad III of Germany (1138–1152). Their Second Crusade, however, proved to be a total failure.

The Third Crusade was a reaction to the fall of the Holy City of Jerusalem in 1187 to the Muslim forces under Saladin. Now all of Christendom was ablaze with calls for a new Crusade. Three major monarchs agreed to lead their forces in person: Emperor Frederick Barbarossa of Germany (1152–1190), Richard I the Lionhearted of England (1189–1199), and Philip II Augustus of France (1180–1223). Some of the crusaders finally arrived in the east by 1189 only to encounter problems. Frederick Barbarossa drowned while swimming in a local river, and his army quickly disintegrated. The English and French arrived by sea and met with success against the coastal cities, where they had the support of their fleets, but when they moved inland, they failed miserably. Eventually, after Philip went home, Richard the Lionhearted negotiated a settlement whereby Saladin agreed to allow Christian pilgrims free access to Jerusalem.

After the death of Saladin in 1193, Pope Innocent III initiated a Fourth Crusade. On its way to the east, the crusading army became involved in a dispute over the succession to the Byzantine throne. The Venetian leaders of the Fourth Crusade saw an opportunity to neutralize their greatest commercial competitor: the Byzantine Empire. Diverted to Constantinople, the crusaders sacked the great capital city of Byzantium in 1204 and created a new Latin Empire of Constantinople. Not until 1261 did a Byzantine army recapture Constantinople. The Byzantine Empire had been saved, but it was no longer a great Mediterranean power. The restored empire now comprised only the city of Constantinople and its surrounding lands as well as some lands in Asia Minor. Though reduced in size, the empire limped along for another 190 years, until its weakened condition finally enabled the Ottoman Turks to conquer it in 1453.

Despite the failures, the crusading ideal was not yet completely lost. In Germany in 1212, a youth known as Nicholas of Cologne announced that God had inspired him to lead a "children's crusade" to the Holy Land. Thousands of young people joined Nicholas and made their way down the Rhine and across the Alps to Italy, where the pope told them to go home. Most tried to do so. At about the same time, a group of about 20,000 French children made their way to Marseilles, where two shipowners agreed to transport them to the Holy Land. Seven ships packed with hymn-singing youths soon left the port. Two of the ships perished in a storm near Sardinia; the other five sailed to North Africa, where the children were sold into slavery. The next Crusades of adult warriors were hardly more successful.

All in all, the Crusades had little impact on the Islamic world; after all, the crusaders failed to accomplish their primary goal of holding the Holy Land for the Christian west. Whether the Crusades had much effect on European civilization is widely debated. Did the Crusades help to stabilize European society by removing large numbers of young warriors who would have fought each other in Europe? Some historians think so and believe that western monarchs established their control more easily as a result. There is no doubt that the Italian seaports, especially Genoa, Pisa, and Venice, benefited economically from the Crusades, but even without the Crusades, Italian merchants would have pursued new trade contacts with the eastern world. The Crusades did have unfortunate side effects that would afflict European society for generations. The first widespread attacks on the Jews occurred during the Crusades. Some Christians argued that to undertake holy wars against infidel Muslims while the "murderers of Christ" ran free at home was unthinkable. The massacre of Jews became a regular feature of medieval European life (see the box on p. 353).

CONCLUSION

After the collapse of the Han dynasty in the third century C.E., China experienced nearly four centuries of internal chaos, until the Tang dynasty in the seventh century C.E. attempted to follow the pattern of the Han dynasty and restore the power of the Chinese empire. The fall of the Roman Empire in the fifth century brought a quite different result as three new civilizations emerged out of the collapse of Roman power in the Mediterranean. A new world of Islam emerged in the east; it occupied large parts of the old Roman Empire, preserved much of Greek culture, and created its own flourishing civilization. The eastern part of the old Roman Empire, increasingly Greek in culture, continued

TREATMENT OF THE JEWS

The development of new religious sensibilities in the High Middle Ages also had a negative side, turning Christians against their supposed enemies. Although the Crusades provide the most obvious example, Christians also turned on the Jews as the "murderers of Christ." As a result, Jews suffered increased persecution. These two documents show different sides of the picture. The first is a chronicler's account of a completely unfounded charge levied against the Jews—that they were guilty of the ritual murder of Christian children to obtain Christian blood for the Passover service. This charge led to the murder of many Jews. The second document, taken from a list of regulations issued by the city of Avignon, France, illustrates the contempt Christian society held for the Jews.

THE JEWS AND THE RITUAL MURDER OF CHRISTIAN CHILDREN

[The eight-year-old boy] Harold, who is buried in the Church of St. Peter the Apostle, at Gloucester . . . is said to have been carried away secretly by Jews, in the opinion of many, on Feb. 21, and by them hidden till March 16. On that night, on the sixth of the preceding feast, the Jews of all England coming together as if to circumcise a certain boy, pretend deceitfully that they are about to celebrate the feast [Passover] appointed by law in such case, and deceiving the citizens of Gloucester with that fraud, they tortured the lad placed before them with immense tortures. It is true no Christian was present, or saw or heard the deed, nor have we found that anything was betrayed by any Jew. But a little while after when the whole convent of monks of Gloucester and almost all the citizens of that city, and innumerable persons coming to the spectacle, saw the wounds of the dead body, scars of fire, the thorns fixed on his head, and liquid wax poured into the eyes and face, and touched it with the diligent examination of their hands, those tortures were believed or guessed to have been inflicted on him in that manner. It was clear that they had made him a glorious martyr to Christ, being slain without sin, and having bound his feet with his own girdle, threw him into the river Severn.

THE REGULATIONS OF AVIGNON, 1243

Likewise, we declare that Jews or whores shall not dare to touch with their hands either bread or fruit put out for sale, and that if they should do this they must buy what they have touched.

---

to survive as the Christian Byzantine Empire. At the same time, a new Christian European civilization was establishing its roots in the West. By the eleventh and twelfth centuries, these three heirs of Rome began their own conflict for control of the lands of the eastern Mediterranean.

The coronation of Charlemagne (who was a descendant of a Germanic tribe converted to Christianity) as Roman emperor in 800 symbolized the fusion of the three chief components of the new European civilization: the German tribes, the Roman legacy, and the Christian church. In the long run, the creation of Charlemagne's empire fostered the idea of a distinct European identity. The lands north of the Alps now became the political center of Europe.

With the disintegration of the Carolingian Empire, new forms of political institutions began to develop in Europe. Power came into the hands of many different lords, who came to constitute a powerful group of nobles that dominated the political, economic, and social life of Europe. But quietly and surely, within this world of castles and private power, kings gradually began to extend their public power. Though they could not know it then, their actions laid the foundations for the European kingdoms that in one form or another have dominated the European political scene ever since.

European civilization began to flourish in the High Middle Ages. The revival of trade, the expansion of towns and cities, and the development of a money economy did not mean the end of a predominantly rural European society, but they did open the door to new ways to make a living and new opportunities for people to expand and enrich their lives. At the same time, the High Middle Ages also gave birth to an intellectual and spiritual revival that transformed European society.

While a new Christian civilization arose in Europe, the Byzantine Empire created its own unique Christian civilization in the eastern Mediterranean. While Europe struggled in the Early Middle Ages, the Byzantine world continued to prosper and flourish. The Crusades to Palestine, however, ostensibly for religious motives, eventually had the result of weakening the Christian power that had initiated the whole process: the Byzantine Empire.

Growth and optimism had characterized the new European civilization of the High Middle Ages, but underneath the calm exterior lay seeds of discontent and change. In the fourteenth and fifteenth centuries, Europe would experience both a real time of troubles and a dramatic revival, while Constantinople and the remnants of the Byzantine Empire would finally fall to the world of Islam.

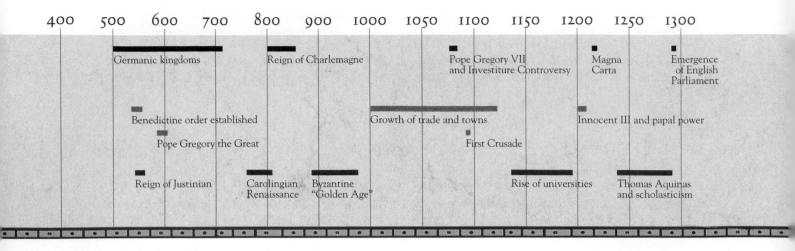

Germanic kingdoms

Reign of Charlemagne

Pope Gregory VII
and Investiture Controversy

Magna
Carta

Emergence
of English
Parliament

Benedictine order established

Growth of trade and towns

Innocent III and papal power

Pope Gregory the Great

First Crusade

Reign of Justinian

Carolingian   Byzantine
Renaissance   "Golden Age"

Rise of universities

Thomas Aquinas
and scholasticism

❈ CHAPTER NOTES

1. Norman F. Cantor, ed., *The Medieval World: 300–1300* (New York, 1963), p. 104.
2. Quoted in Simon Keynes, "The Vikings in England, c. 790–1016," in Peter Sawyer, ed., *The Oxford Illustrated History of the Vikings* (Oxford, 1997), p. 81.
3. Quoted in Oliver Thatcher and Edgar McNeal, eds., *A Source Book for Medieval History* (New York, 1905), p. 363.
4. Quoted in Marvin Perry, Joseph Peden, and Theodore Von Laue, *Sources of the Western Tradition*, vol. 1 (Boston, 1987), p. 218.
5. Quoted in Joseph and Frances Gies, *Life in a Medieval Castle* (New York, 1974), p. 175.
6. Quoted in Robert Delort, *Life in the Middle Ages*, trans. Robert Allen (New York, 1972), p. 218.
7. Quoted in Jean Gimpel, *The Medieval Machine* (Harmondsworth, 1977), p. 92.

8. Ernest F. Henderson, ed., *Select Historical Documents of the Middle Ages* (London, 1892), p. 365.
9. Thatcher and McNeal, *A Source Book for Medieval History*, p. 208.
10. Quoted in R. H. C. Davis, *A History of Medieval Europe from Constantine to Saint Louis*, 2d ed. (London and New York, 1988), p. 252.
11. Quoted in Rosalind Brooke and Christopher Brooke, *Popular Religion in the Middle Ages* (London, 1984), p. 19.
12. Helen Waddell, *The Wandering Scholars* (New York, 1961), p. 222.
13. Quoted in John W. Baldwin, *The Scholastic Culture of the Middle Ages, 1000–1300* (Lexington, Mass., 1971), p. 15.
14. Thatcher and McNeal, *A Source Book for Medieval History*, p. 517.
15. Quoted in Hans E. Mayer, *The Crusades*, trans. John Gillingham (New York, 1972), pp. 99–100.

❈ SUGGESTED READINGS

Good general histories of the entire medieval period can be found in B. Tierney and S. Painter, *Western Europe in the Middle Ages, 300–1475* (New York, 1983); E. Peters, *Europe and the Middle Ages*, 2d ed. (Englewood Cliffs, N.J., 1989); and D. Nicholas, *The Evolution of the Medieval World: Society, Government, and Thought in Europe, 312–1500* (London, 1993). For a good general survey of the social history of the Middle Ages, see C. B. Bouchard, *Life and Society in the West: Antiquity and the Middle Ages* (San Diego, 1988). A brief history of the Early Middle Ages can be found in R. Collin, *Early Medieval Europe, 300–1000* (New York, 1991).

Surveys of Carolingian Europe include P. Riche, *The Carolingians, A Family Who Forged Europe* (Philadelphia, 1993), and R. McKitterick, *The Frankish Kingdoms Under the Carolingians, 751–987* (London, 1983). On Charlemagne, see H. R. Loyn and J. Percival, *The Reign of Charlemagne* (New York, 1976).

Two introductory works on feudalism are J. R. Strayer, *Feudalism* (Princeton, N.J., 1985), and the classic work by M. Bloch, *Feudal Society* (London, 1961). For an important revisionist view, see S. Reynolds, *Fiefs and Vassals* (Oxford, 1994). Works on the function and activities of the nobility in the High Middle Ages include S. Reynolds, *Kingdoms and Communities in Western Europe, 900–1300* (Oxford, 1984); R. W. Barber, *The Knight and Chivalry* (Rochester, N.Y., 1995); and G. Duby, *The Chivalrous Society* (Berkeley, Calif., 1977). G. Duby discusses the theory of medieval social order in *The Three Orders* (Chicago, 1980).

There are numerous works on the various feudal principalities. On England, see F. Barlow, *The Feudal Kingdom of England, 1042–1216*, 3d ed. (New York, 1972). On Germany, see H. Fuhrmann, *Germany in the High Middle Ages, c. 1050–1250* (Cambridge, 1986), an excellent account, and B. Arnold, *Princes* and *Territories in Medieval Germany* (Cambridge, 1991). On France, see J. Dunbabin, *France in the Making, 843–1180* (Oxford, 1985). On Italy, see D. J. Herlihy, *Cities and Society in Medieval Italy* (London, 1980). On eastern Europe, see N. Davies, *God's Playground: A History of Poland*, vol. 1 (Oxford, 1981), and C. J. Halperin, *Russia and the Golden Horde: The Mongol Impact on Medieval Russian History* (Bloomington, Ind., 1987).

On economic conditions in the Middle Ages, see N. J. G. Pounds, *An Economic History of Medieval Europe* (New York, 1974), and R. S. Lopez, *The Commercial Revolution of the Middle Ages, 950–1350* (Englewood Cliffs, N.J., 1971). Urban history is covered in D. Nicholas, *The Growth of the Medieval City: From Late Antiquity to the Early Fourteenth Century* (New York, 1997). A good short introduction to medieval society is C. Brooke, *The Structure of Medieval Society* (London, 1971). On women in general, see L. Bitel, "Women in Early Medieval Northern Europe," in R. Bridenthal, S. M. Stuard, and M. E. Wiesner, *Becoming Visible*, 3d ed. (New York, 1998), and D. Herlihy, *Opera Muliebria: Women and Work in Medieval Europe* (New York, 1990). On peasant life, see R. Fossier, *Peasant Life in the Medieval West* (New York, 1988).

For a general survey of church life, see R. W. Southern, *Western Society and the Church in the Middle Ages*, rev. ed. (New York, 1990). On the papacy in the High Middle Ages, see C. Morris, *The Papal Monarchy* (Oxford, 1989), and I. S. Robinson, *The Papacy* (Cambridge, 1990). The papacy of Innocent III is covered in J. E. Sayers, *Innocent III, Leader of Europe, 1198–1216* (New York, 1994). Good works on monasticism include B. Bolton, *The Medieval Reformation* (London, 1983); C. H. Lawrence, *Medieval Monasticism* (London, 1984), a good general account; and H. Leyser, *Hermits and the New Monasticism* (London, 1984). For a good introduction to popular religion in the eleventh and twelfth centuries, see R. Brooke

and C. N. L. Brooke, *Popular Religion in the Middle Ages* (London, 1984). On the Inquisition, see B. Hamilton, *The Medieval Inquisition* (New York, 1981).

The development of universities is covered in S. Ferruolo, *The Origin of the University* (Stanford, 1985), and the brief, older work by C. H. Haskins, *The Rise of Universities* (Ithaca, N.Y., 1957). Various aspects of the intellectual and literary developments of the High Middle Ages are examined in J. W. Baldwin, *The Scholastic Culture of the Middle Ages, 1000–1300* (Lexington, Mass., 1971); T. O'Meara, *Thomas Aquinas Theologian* (Notre Dame, Ind., 1997); and H. Waddell, *The Wandering Scholars* (New York, 1961). A good introduction to Romanesque style is A. Petzold, *Romanesque Art* (New York, 1995). On the Gothic movement, see M. Camille, *Gothic Art: Glorious Visions* (New York, 1996), and C. Wilson, *The Gothic Cathedral* (London, 1990).

Brief but good introductions to Byzantine history can be found in H. W. Haussig, *A History of Byzantine Civilization* (New York, 1971), and C. Mango, *Byzantium: The Empire of New Rome* (London, 1980). The best single political history is G. Ostrogorsky, *A History of the Byzantine State*, 2d ed. (New Brunswick, N.J., 1968). For a comprehensive survey of the Byzantine Empire, see W. Treadgold, *A History of the Byzantine State and Society* (Stanford, 1997). On Justinian, see J. Moorhead, *Justinian* (London, 1995). The zenith of Byzantine civilization is examined in R. Jenkins, *Byzantium: The Imperial Centuries, 610–1071* (New York, 1969).

Two good general surveys on the crusades are H. E. Mayer, *The Crusades* (London, 1970), and J. Riley-Smith, *The Crusades: A Short History* (New Haven, Conn., 1987). Other works of value are J. Riley-Smith, ed., *The Oxford Illustrated History of the Crusades* (New York, 1995), and R. C. Smail, *Crusading Warfare, 1097–1193*, 2d ed. (New York, 1995).

INFOTRAC COLLEGE EDITION

For additional reading, go to InfoTrac College Edition, your online research library at
http://web1.infotrac-college.com

Enter the search term "Charlemagne" using the Keywords.

Enter the search term "Byzantium" using the Subject Guide.

Enter the search terms "early Christianity" using the Keywords.

Enter the search term "feudalism" and also the search term "feudal" using the Subject Guide.

Enter the search terms "Cities and Towns, Medieval" using the Subject Guide.

CHAPTER

13

CRISIS AND REBIRTH: EUROPE IN THE FOURTEENTH AND FIFTEENTH CENTURIES

CHAPTER OUTLINE

- A TIME OF TROUBLES: BLACK DEATH AND SOCIAL CRISIS
- POLITICAL INSTABILITY AND POLITICAL RENEWAL
- THE DECLINE OF THE CHURCH
- MEANING AND CHARACTERISTICS OF THE ITALIAN RENAISSANCE
- THE MAKING OF RENAISSANCE SOCIETY
- THE INTELLECTUAL RENAISSANCE IN ITALY
- THE ARTISTIC RENAISSANCE
- CONCLUSION

FOCUS QUESTIONS

- What problems did Europe face during the fourteenth century, and what impact did they have on European economic and social life?
- What were the "new monarchies" of the late fifteenth century, and how did their political structures differ from those found in eastern Europe and Italy?
- How and why did the moral prestige of the papacy decline after the thirteenth century?
- What were the main features of the Renaissance, and how did it differ from the Middle Ages?
- What were the chief characteristics of Renaissance art, and how did it differ in Italy and northern Europe?

As a result of their conquests in the thirteenth and fourteenth centuries, the Mongols created a vast empire, stretching from Russia in the west to China in the east. Mongol rule brought stability to the Eurasian trade routes; increased trade brought prosperity but also facilitated the spread of flea-infested rats that brought bubonic plague to both East Asia and Europe. In the mid-fourteenth century, one of the most destructive natural disasters in history erupted—the Black Death. A contemporary observer named Henry Knighton, a canon of Saint Mary-of-the-Meadow Abbey in Leicester, England, was simply overwhelmed by the magnitude of the catastrophe. Knighton began his account of the great plague with these words: "In this year [1348] and in the following one there was a general mortality of people throughout the whole world." Few were left untouched; even in isolated monasteries, the plague struck: "At Montpellier, there remained out of a hundred and forty friars only seven." Knighton was also stunned by the economic and social consequences of the Black Death. Prices dropped: "And the price of everything was cheap, because of the fear of death; there were very few who took any care for their wealth, or for anything else." Laborers became scarce, and their wages increased: "In the following autumn, one could not hire a reaper at a lower wage than eight pence with food, or a mower at less than twelve pence with food. Because of this, much grain rotted in the fields for lack of harvesting." So many people died that some towns were deserted and some villages disappeared altogether: "Many small villages and hamlets were completely deserted; there was not one house left in them, but all those who had lived in them were dead." To some people, the end of the world seemed at hand.

Plague was not the only disaster in the fourteenth century, however. Signs of disintegration were everywhere: famine, economic depression, war, social upheaval, a rise in crime and violence, and a decline in the power of the Catholic church. Periods of disintegration, however, are often fertile grounds for change and new developments. Although the disintegrative patterns of the fourteenth century continued into the fifteenth, at the same time elements of recovery made the fifteenth century a period of significant political, economic, artistic, and intellectual change. The humanists or intellectuals of the age called their period (from the mid-fourteenth to the mid-sixteenth century) an age of rebirth, believing that they had restored arts and letters to new glory after they had been "neglected" or "dead" for centuries. The humanists' view of their age as a rebirth of the classical civilizations of the Greeks and Romans ultimately led historians to use the word *Renaissance* to identify this period.

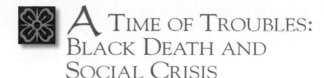

A TIME OF TROUBLES: BLACK DEATH AND SOCIAL CRISIS

At the beginning of the fourteenth century, there were noticeable changes in weather patterns as Europe entered a period that has been called a "little Ice Age." Shortened growing seasons and disastrous weather conditions, including heavy storms and constant rain, led to widespread famine and hunger. The great famine of 1315–1317 in northern Europe began an all-too-familiar pattern, as evident in this scene described by a contemporary chronicler:

> We saw a larger number of both sexes, not only from nearby places but from as much as five leagues away, barefooted and maybe even, except for women, in a completely nude state, together with their priests coming in procession at the Church of the Holy Martyrs, their bones bulging out, devoutly carrying bodies of saints and other relics to be adorned, hoping to get relief.[1]

Some historians have pointed out that famine could have led to chronic malnutrition, which in turn contributed to increased infant mortality, lower birthrates, and higher susceptibility to disease because malnourished people are less able to resist infection. This, they argue, helps to explain the high mortality of the great plague known as the Black Death.

The Black Death

The Black Death of the mid-fourteenth century was the most devastating natural disaster in European history, ravaging Europe's population and causing economic, social, political, and cultural upheaval. Contemporary chroniclers lamented how parents abandoned their children; one related the words: "Oh father, why have you abandoned me? . . . Mother, where have you gone?"[2] People were horrified by an evil force they could not understand and by the subsequent breakdown of all normal human relations.

Bubonic plague, which was the most common and most important form of plague in the diffusion of the Black Death, was spread by black rats infested with fleas who were host to the deadly bacterium *Yersinia pestis*. Symptoms of bubonic plague include high fever, aching joints, swelling of the lymph nodes, and dark blotches caused by bleeding beneath the skin. Bubonic plague was actually the least toxic form of plague but nevertheless killed 50 to 60 percent of its victims. In pneumonic plague, the bacterial infection spread to the lungs, resulting in severe coughing, bloody sputum, and the relatively easy spread of the bacillus from human to human by coughing.

The Black Death was all the more horrible because it was the first major epidemic disease to strike Europe since the seventh century, an absence that helps explain medieval Europe's remarkable population growth. This great plague originated in Asia. After disappearing from Europe and the Middle East in the Middle Ages, bubonic plague continued to haunt areas of southwestern China, especially isolated rural territories. The arrival of Mongol troops in this area in the mid-thirteenth century became the means for the spread of the plague, as flea-infested rats carrying bubonic plague spread with the movement of the Mongols into central and northwestern China and Central Asia. From there, trading caravans brought the plague to Caffa, on the Black Sea, in 1346.

The plague reached Europe in October of 1347 when Genoese merchants brought it from Caffa to the island of Sicily, off the coast of southern Italy. It quickly spread to southern Italy and southern France by the end of 1347. Usually, the diffusion of the Black Death followed commercial trade routes. In 1348, the plague spread through Spain, France, and the Low Countries and into Germany. By the end of that year, it had moved to England, ravaging it in 1349. By the end of 1349, the plague had reached northern Europe and Scandinavia. Eastern Europe and Russia were affected by 1351, although mortality rates were never as high in eastern Europe as they were in western and central Europe.

Overall, mortality figures for the Black Death were incredibly high. Italy was especially hard hit. Its crowded cities suffered losses of 50 to 60 percent. In northern France, farming villages suffered mortality rates of 30 percent, while cities such as Rouen were more severely affected and experienced losses of 30 to 40 percent. In England and Germany, entire villages simply disappeared from history. In Germany, of approximately 170,000 inhabited locations, only 130,000 were left by the end of the fourteenth century.

It has been estimated that the European population declined by 25 to 50 percent between 1347 and 1351. If we accept the recent scholarly assessment of a European population of 75 million in the early fourteenth century, this means a death toll in four years of 19 to 38 million

MAP 13.1   Spread of the Black Death

December 1347
June 1348
December 1348
June 1349
December 1349
June 1350
December 1350
City or area partially or totally spared
Date line

people. And the plague did not end in 1351. There were major outbreaks again in 1361–1362 and 1369 and then regular recurrences during the remainder of the fourteenth and all of the fifteenth century. The European population did not start to recover until the end of the fifteenth century; not until the mid-sixteenth century did Europe begin to regain its thirteenth-century population levels.

The attempt of contemporaries to explain the Black Death and mitigate its harshness led to extreme sorts of behavior. To many, the plague had either been sent by God as a punishment for humans' sins or caused by the evil one, the devil. Some—the flagellants—resorted to extreme measures to gain God's forgiveness. Groups of flagellants, both men and women, wandered from town to town, flogging each other with whips to win the forgiveness of a God who they felt had sent the plague to punish humans for their sinful ways. One contemporary chronicler described their activities:

> The penitents went about, coming first out of Germany. They were men who did public penance and scourged themselves with whips of hard knotted leather with little iron spikes. Some made themselves bleed very badly between the shoulder blades, and some foolish women had cloths ready to catch the blood and smear it on their eyes, saying it was miraculous blood. While they were doing penance, they sang very mournful songs about the nativity and the passion of Our Lord. The object of this penance was to put a stop to the mortality, for in that time . . . at least a third of all the people in the world died.[3]

The flagellants attracted attention and created mass hysteria wherever they went. The Catholic church, however, became alarmed when flagellant groups began to kill Jews and attack the clergy who opposed them. Pope Clement VI condemned the flagellants in October 1349 and urged the public authorities to crush them. By the end of 1350, most of the flagellant movements had been destroyed.

An outbreak of virulent anti-Semitism also accompanied the Black Death. Jews were accused of causing the plague by poisoning town wells. Although Jews were persecuted in Spain, the worst pogroms against this minority were carried out in Germany, where more than sixty major Jewish communities were exterminated by 1351 (see the box on p. 360). Many Jews fled eastward to Russia and especially to Poland, where the king offered them protection. Eastern Europe became home to large Jewish communities.

Economic Dislocation and Social Upheaval

The death of so many people in the fourteenth century also had severe economic consequences. Trade declined, and some industries suffered greatly. Florence's woolen industry, one of the giants, had produced 70,000 to 80,000 pieces of cloth in 1338; in 1378, it was yielding only 24,000 pieces.

Both peasants and noble landlords were also affected. A shortage of workers caused a dramatic rise in the price of labor, while the decline in the number of people lowered the demand for food, resulting in falling prices. Landlords were now paying more for labor at the same time that their rents or income was declining. Concurrently, the decline in the number of peasants after the Black Death made it easier for some to convert their labor services to rent, thus freeing them from serfdom. But there were limits to how much the peasants could advance. They faced the same economic hurdles as the lords, while the latter also attempted to impose wage restrictions and reinstate old forms of labor service. New governmental taxes also hurt. Peasant complaints became widespread and soon gave rise to rural revolts.

In 1358, a peasant revolt known as the *Jacquerie* broke out in northern France. The outburst of peasant anger led to savage confrontations. Castles were burned and nobles murdered (see the box on p. 361). Such atrocities did not go unanswered, however. The *Jacquerie* soon failed

✿ MASS BURIAL OF PLAGUE VICTIMS. The Black Death had spread to northern Europe by the end of 1348. Shown here is a mass burial of victims of the plague in Tournai, located in modern Belgium. As is evident in the illustration, at this stage of the plague, there was still time to make coffins for the victims' burial. Later, as the plague intensified, the dead were thrown into open pits.

A MEDIEVAL HOLOCAUST: THE CREMATION OF THE STRASBOURG JEWS

In their attempt to explain the widespread horrors of the Black Death, medieval Christian communities looked for scapegoats. As at the time of the Crusades, the Jews were accused of poisoning wells and hence spreading the plague. This selection by a contemporary chronicler, written in 1349, gives an account of how Christians in the town of Strasbourg in the Holy Roman Empire dealt with their Jewish community. It is apparent that financial gain was also an important factor in killing the Jews.

JACOB VON KÖNIGSHOFEN, "THE CREMATION OF THE STRASBOURG JEWS"

In the year 1349 there occurred the greatest epidemic that ever happened. Death went from one end of the earth to the other. . . . And from what this epidemic came, all wise teachers and physicians could only say that it was God's will. . . . This epidemic also came to Strasbourg in the summer of the above-mentioned year, and it is estimated that about sixteen thousand people died.

In the matter of this plague the Jews throughout the world were reviled and accused in all lands of having caused it through the poison which they are said to have put into the water and the wells—that is what they were accused of—and for this reason the Jews were burnt all the way from the Mediterranean into Germany. . . .

[The account then goes on to discuss the situation of the Jews in the city of Strasbourg.]

On Saturday . . . they burnt the Jews on a wooden platform in their cemetery. There were about two thousand people of them. Those who wanted to baptize themselves were spared. [Some say that about a thousand accepted baptism.] Many small children were taken out of the fire and baptized against the will of their fathers and mothers. And everything that was owed to the Jews was canceled, and the Jews had to surrender all pledges and notes that they had taken for debts. The council, however, took the cash that the Jews possessed and divided it among the workingmen proportionately. The money was indeed the thing that killed the Jews. If they had been poor and if the feudal lords had not been in debt to them, they would not have been burnt. . . .

Thus were the Jews burnt at Strasbourg, and in the same year in all the cities of the Rhine, whether Free Cities or Imperial Cities or cities belonging to the lords. In some towns they burnt the Jews after a trial; in others, without a trial. In some cities the Jews themselves set fire to their houses and cremated themselves.

It was decided in Strasbourg that no Jew should enter the city for a hundred years, but before twenty years had passed, the council and magistrates agreed that they ought to admit the Jews again into the city for twenty years. And so the Jews came back again to Strasbourg in the year 1368 after the birth of our Lord.

⚜ **PEASANT REBELLION.** The fourteenth century witnessed a number of revolts of the peasantry against noble landowners. Although the revolts were initially successful, they were soon crushed. This illustration shows nobles massacring the rebels in the French *Jacquerie.*

as the privileged classes closed ranks, savagely massacred the rebels, and ended the revolt.

The English Peasants' Revolt of 1381 was the most prominent of all. It was not a revolt caused by desperation but was a product of rising expectations. After the Black Death, the English peasants had enjoyed improved conditions, with greater freedom and higher wages or lower rents. Aristocratic landlords had fought back with legislation to depress wages and an attempt to reimpose old feudal dues. The most immediate cause of the revolt, however, was the monarchy's attempt to raise revenues by imposing a poll tax, or a flat charge on each adult member of the population. Peasants in eastern England, the wealthiest part of the country, refused to pay the tax and expelled the collectors forcibly from their villages.

This action produced a widespread rebellion of both peasants and townspeople led by a well-to-do peasant called Wat Tyler and a preacher named John Ball. The revolt was initially successful as the rebels burned down the manor houses of aristocrats, lawyers, and government officials and murdered several important officials, including the archbishop of Canterbury. After the peasants

A REVOLT OF FRENCH PEASANTS

In 1358, French peasants rose up in a revolt known as the Jacquerie. The relationship between aristocrats and peasants had degenerated as a result of the social upheavals and privations caused by the Black Death and the Hundred Years' War. This excerpt from the chronicle of an aristocrat paints a horrifying picture of the barbarities that occurred during the revolt.

JEAN FROISSART, CHRONICLES

Not long after the King of Navarre had been set free, there were very strange and terrible happenings in several parts of the kingdom of France. . . . They began when some of the men from the country towns came together in the Beauvais region. They had no leaders and at first they numbered scarcely a hundred. One of them got up and said that the nobility of France, knights and squires, were disgracing and betraying the realm, and that it would be a good thing if they were all destroyed. At this they all shouted: "He's right! He's right! Shame on any man who saves the gentry from being wiped out!"

They banded together and went off, without further deliberation and unarmed except for pikes and knives, to the house of a knight who lived nearby. They broke in and killed the knight, with his lady and his children, big and small, and set fire to the house. Next they went to another castle and did much worse; for, having seized the knight and bound him securely to a post, several of them violated his wife and daughter before his eyes. Then they killed the wife, who was pregnant, and the daughter and all the other children, and finally put the knight to death with great cruelty and burned and razed the castle.

They did similar things in a number of castles and big houses, and their ranks swelled until there were a good six thousand of them. Wherever they went their numbers grew, for all the men of the same sort joined them. The knights and squires fled before them with their families. They took their wives and daughters many miles away to put them in safety, leaving their houses open with their possessions inside. And those evil men, who had come together without leaders or arms, pillaged and burned everything and violated and killed all the ladies and girls without mercy, like mad dogs. Their barbarous acts were worse than anything that ever took place between Christians and Saracens. Never did men commit such vile deeds. They were such that no living creature ought to see, or even imagine or think of, and the men who committed the most were admired and had the highest places among them. I could never bring myself to write down the horrible and shameful things which they did to the ladies. But, among other brutal excesses, they killed a knight, put him on a spit, and turned him at the fire and roasted him before the lady and her children. After about a dozen of them had violated the lady, they tried to force her and the children to eat the knight's flesh before putting them cruelly to death.

---

marched on London, the young king Richard II (1377–1399) promised to accept the rebels' demands if they would return to their homes. They accepted the king's word and began to disperse, but the king reneged and with the assistance of the aristocrats brutally crushed the rebels. The poll tax was eliminated, however.

Although the peasant revolts sometimes resulted in short-term gains for the participants, the uprisings were relatively easily crushed and their gains quickly lost. Accustomed to ruling, the established classes easily combined and crushed dissent when faced with social uprising. Nevertheless, the revolts of the fourteenth century had introduced a new element to European life; henceforth social unrest would be a characteristic of European history.

FAMILY LIFE AND GENDER ROLES IN LATE MEDIEVAL CITIES

The effects of plague were also felt in other areas of medieval urban life. The basic unit of the late medieval urban environment was the nuclear family of husband, wife, and children. Especially in wealthier families, there might also be servants, apprentices, and other relatives, including widowed mothers and the husband's illegitimate children.

Before the Black Death, late marriages were common for urban couples. It was not unusual for husbands to be in their late thirties or forties and wives in their early twenties. The expense of setting up a household probably necessitated the delay in marriage. But the situation changed dramatically after the plague, as the survivors found new economic opportunities and were reluctant to postpone living after experiencing so much death. The economic difficulties of the fourteenth century also tended to strengthen the development of gender roles and to set new limits on employment opportunities for women. Based on the authority of Aristotle, Thomas Aquinas and other thirteenth-century scholastic theologians had advanced the belief that according to the natural order, men were active and domineering while women were passive and submissive. As more and more lawyers, doctors, and priests, who had been trained in universities where these notions were taught, entered society, these ideas of the different natures of men and women became widely accepted.

Increasingly, women were expected to forgo any active functions in society and remain subject to direction from males. A fourteenth-century Parisian provost commented on glass cutters that "no master's widow who keeps working at his craft after her husband's death may take on apprentices, for the men of the craft do not believe that a woman can master it well enough to teach a child to master it, for the craft is a very delicate one."[4] Although this statement suggests that some women were in fact running businesses, it also reveals that they were viewed as incapable of undertaking all of men's activities. Based on this view of gender, Europeans created a division of labor roles between men and women that persisted until the Industrial Revolution of the eighteenth and nineteenth centuries.

Economic Recovery

After the severe economic reversals and social upheavals of the second half of the fourteenth century, the European economy gradually recovered during the fifteenth century as manufacturing and trade increased in volume. Before the plague, Italian merchants were already carrying on a flourishing commerce throughout the Mediterranean and had also expanded their lines of trade north along the Atlantic seaboard. The great galleys of the Venetian Flanders Fleet maintained a direct sea route from Venice to England and the Netherlands, where Italian merchants came into contact with the increasingly powerful Hanseatic League of merchants. Hard hit by the plague, the Italians lost their commercial preeminence in the second half of the fourteenth century, while the Hanseatic League continued to prosper.

As early as the thirteenth century, a number of north German coastal towns had formed a commercial and military league known as the Hansa or Hanseatic League to protect themselves from marauding pirates and competition from Scandinavian merchants. By 1500, more than eighty cities belonged to the league, which established settlements and commercial bases in northern Europe and England. For almost two hundred years, the Hansa had a monopoly on northern European trade in timber, fish, grain, metals, honey, and wines. Its southern outlet in Flanders, the city of Bruges, became the economic crossroads of Europe in the fourteenth century because it served as the meeting place between Hanseatic merchants and the Flanders Fleet of Venice. In the fifteenth century, however, Bruges, as its harbor began to silt up, slowly began to decline, paralleling the decline of the Hanseatic League itself as it proved increasingly unable to compete with the developing larger territorial states.

Overall, trade recovered dramatically from the economic contraction of the fourteenth century. The Italians and especially the Venetians continued to maintain a wealthy commercial empire. Not until the sixteenth century, when the overseas discoveries gave new importance to the states facing the Atlantic, did the small Italian city-states begin to suffer from the competitive advantages of the ever growing and more powerful national territorial states.

The economic depression of the fourteenth century also affected patterns of manufacturing. The woolen industries of Flanders and the northern Italian cities had been particularly devastated. By the beginning of the fifteenth century, however, the Florentine woolen industry was experiencing a recovery. At the same time, the Italian cities began to develop and expand luxury industries, especially lace and silk, glassware, and handworked items in metal and precious stones.

Other new industries, especially printing, mining, and metallurgy, began to rival the textile industry in importance in the fifteenth century. New machinery and techniques for digging deeper mines and for separating metals from ore and purifying them were put into operation. When rulers began to transfer their titles to underground mineral rights to financiers as collateral for loans, these entrepreneurs quickly developed large mining operations to produce copper, iron, and silver. Especially valuable were the rich mineral deposits in central Europe, Hungary, the Tyrol, Bohemia, and Saxony. Expanding iron production and new skills in metalworking, in turn, contributed to the development of firearms that were more effective than the crude weapons used in the fourteenth century.

The city of Florence regained its preeminence in banking in the fifteenth century, primarily due to the Medici family. In its best days (in the fifteenth century), the House of Medici was the greatest banking house in Europe, with branches in Venice, Milan, Rome, Avignon, Bruges, London, and Lyons. Moreover, the family had controlling interests in industrial enterprises for wool, silk, and the mining of alum, which was used in dyeing textiles. Despite its great success in the early and middle part of the fifteenth century, the Medici bank declined suddenly at the end of the century due to poor management and a series of bad loans, especially uncollectible loans to rulers. In 1494, when the French expelled the Medici from Florence and confiscated their property, the Medicean financial edifice collapsed.

POLITICAL INSTABILITY AND POLITICAL RENEWAL

Famine, plague, economic turmoil, social upheaval, and violence were not the only problems of the fourteenth century. War and political instability must also be added to the list. Of all the struggles that ensued in the fourteenth century, the Hundred Years' War was the most violent.

CHRONOLOGY

THE HUNDRED YEARS' WAR

Outbreak of hostilities	1337
Battle of Crécy	1346
Henry V renews the war	1415
Battle of Agincourt	1415
French recovery under Joan of Arc	1429–1431
End of the war	1453

The Hundred Years' War

In the thirteenth century, the English king, Henry III, still held one small possession in France known as the duchy of Gascony. As duke of Gascony, the English king pledged loyalty as a vassal to the French king, but when King Philip VI of France (1328–1350) seized Gascony in 1337, the duke of Gascony—King Edward III of England (1327–1377)—declared war on Philip. The attack on Gascony was a convenient excuse; Edward III had already laid claim to the throne of France after the senior branch of the Capetian dynasty had become extinct in 1328.

The Hundred Years' War began in a burst of knightly enthusiasm. Trained to be warriors, knights viewed the clash of battle as the ultimate opportunity to demonstrate their fighting abilities. The Hundred Years' War proved to be an important watershed, however, because peasant foot soldiers, not knights, decided the chief battles of the war. The French army of 1337 with its heavily armed noble cavalry resembled its twelfth- and thirteenth-century forebears. Considering themselves a fighting elite, the noble cavalry looked with contempt upon the foot soldiers and crossbowmen, whom they regarded as social inferiors. The English army, however, had evolved differently and made use of paid foot soldiers. Armed with pikes, many of these foot soldiers had also adopted the longbow, invented by the Welsh. The longbow had greater striking power, longer range, and more rapid speed of fire than the crossbow. Although the English also used heavily armed cavalry, they relied even more on their large numbers of foot soldiers.

Edward III's early campaigns in France were indecisive and achieved little. In 1346, Edward was forced to fight at Crécy, just south of Flanders. The larger French army followed no battle plan but simply attacked the English lines in a disorderly fashion. The arrows of the English archers decimated the French cavalry. As the chronicler Froissart described it, "[with their long-bows] the English continued to shoot into the thickest part of the crowd, wasting none of their arrows. They impaled or wounded horses and riders, who fell to the ground in great distress, unable to get up again without the help of several men."[5] It was a stunning victory for the English.

The Battle of Crécy was not decisive, however. The English simply did not possess the resources to subjugate all of France, and hostilities continued intermittently for another fifty years until a twenty-year truce was negotiated in 1396, seemingly bringing an end to this protracted series of struggles. In 1415, however, the English king, Henry V (1413–1422), renewed the war. At the Battle of Agincourt (1415), the heavily armored French knights attempted to attack across a field turned to mud by heavy rain; the result was a disastrous French defeat and the death of 1,500 French nobles. Henry went on to forge an alliance with the duke of Burgundy, making the English masters of northern France.

The seemingly hopeless French cause fell into the hands of the dauphin Charles, the heir to the throne, who governed the southern two-thirds of France. Charles's cause seemed doomed until a French peasant woman quite unexpectedly saved the timid prince. Born in 1412, the daughter of well-to-do peasants, Joan of Arc was a deeply religious person who experienced visions and came to believe that her favorite saints had commanded her to free France. In February 1429, Joan made her way to the dauphin's court, where her sincerity and simplicity persuaded Charles to allow her to accompany a French army to Orléans. Apparently inspired by the faith of the peasant woman who called herself "the Maid," the French armies found new confidence in themselves and liberated Orléans. Within a few weeks, the entire Loire valley had been freed of the English. Joan had brought the war to a decisive turning point.

But she did not live to see the war concluded. Captured by the Burgundian allies of the English in 1430, Joan was turned over first to the English and then to the Inquisition to face charges of witchcraft (see the box on p. 364). In the fifteenth century, spiritual visions were thought to be inspired either by God or the devil. Joan was condemned to death as a heretic and burned at the stake in 1431. To the end, as the flames rose up around her, she declared "that her voices came from God and had not deceived her." Twenty-five years later, a new ecclesiastical court exonerated her of these charges, and five centuries later, in 1920, she was made a saint of the Roman Catholic church.

Joan of Arc's accomplishments proved decisive. Although the war dragged on for another two decades, defeats of English armies in Normandy and Aquitaine led to French victory by 1453. Important to the French success was the use of the cannon, a new weapon made possible by the invention of gunpowder. The Chinese had

THE TRIAL OF JOAN OF ARC

E eared by the English and Burgundians, Joan of Arc was put on trial on charges of witchcraft and heresy after her capture. She was condemned for heresy and burned at the stake on May 30, 1431. This excerpt is taken from the records of Joan's trial, which presented a dramatic confrontation between the judges, trained in the complexities of legal questioning, and a nineteen-year-old woman who relied only on the "voices" of saints who gave her advice. In this selection, Joan describes what these voices told her to do.

THE TRIAL OF JOAN OF ARC

Afterward, she declared that at the age of thirteen she had a voice from God to help her and guide her. And the first time she was much afraid. And this voice came towards noon, in summer, in her father's garden. . . . She heard the voice on her right, in the direction of the church; and she seldom heard it without a light. This light came from the same side as the voice, and generally there was a great light. . . .

Asked what instruction this voice gave her for the salvation of her soul: she said it taught her to be good and to go to church often. . . . She said that the voice told her to come, and she could no longer stay where she was; and the voice told her again that she should raise the siege of the city of Orléans. She said moreover that the voice told her that she, Joan, should go to Robert de Baudricourt, in the town of Vaucouleurs of which he was captain, and he would provide an escort for her. And the said Joan answered that she was a poor maid, knowing nothing of riding or fighting. She said she went to an uncle of hers, and told him she wanted to stay with him for some time; and she stayed there about eight days. And she told her uncle she must go to the said town of Vaucouleurs, and so her uncle took her.

Then she said that when she reached Vaucouleurs she easily recognized Robert de Baudricourt, although she had never seen him before; and she knew him through her voice, for the voice had told her it was he. . . . The said Robert twice refused to hear her and repulsed her; the third time he listened to her and gave her an escort. And the voice had told her that it would be so.

---

invented gunpowder in the eleventh century and devised a simple cannon by the thirteenth century. The Mongols greatly improved this technology, developing more accurate cannons and cannonballs; both spread to the Middle East by the thirteenth century and to Europe by the fourteenth. The use of gunpowder eventually brought drastic changes to European warfare by making castles, city walls, and armored knights obsolete.

The "New Monarchies"

By the fourteenth century, the feudal order had begun to break down. With money from taxes, kings could now hire professional soldiers, who tended to be more reliable than feudal knights anyway. No longer needed as warriors, some nobles banded together, looking for new opportunities to advance their power and wealth at the expense of their monarchs. Others went to the royal courts, offering to serve the kings.

Fourteenth-century kings had their own problems, however. Many dynasties in Europe were unable to produce male heirs, while the founders of new dynasties had to fight for their positions as groups of nobles, trying to gain advantages for themselves, supported opposing candidates. Rulers found themselves with financial problems as well. Hiring professional soldiers left monarchs always short on cash, adding yet another element of uncertainty and confusion to fourteenth-century politics.

In the second half of the fifteenth century, however, recovery set in as attempts were made to reestablish the centralized power of monarchical governments. To characterize the results, some historians have spoken of the "new monarchies," especially those of France, England, and Spain at the end of the fifteenth century. There were, of course, variations from area to area in the degree to which monarchs were successful in extending their political authority. Unlike in western Europe, in central and eastern Europe, rulers were often weak and unable to impose their authority.

WESTERN EUROPE

The Hundred Years' War left France prostrate. Depopulation, desolate farmlands, ruined commerce, and independent and unruly nobles made it difficult for the kings to assert their authority. But the war had also developed a strong degree of French national feeling toward a common enemy, which the kings could use to reestablish monarchical power. The process of developing a French territorial state was greatly advanced by King Louis XI (1461–1483), known as the Spider because of his wily and devious ways. Louis strengthened the use of the *taille*—an annual direct tax usually on land or property—as a permanent tax imposed by royal authority, giving him a sound, regular source of income. Louis also repressed the French nobility and brought the provinces of Anjou, Maine, Bar, and Provence under royal control. Many historians believe that Louis created a base for the later development of a strong French monarchy.

The Hundred Years' War had also strongly affected the other protagonist in that conflict—the English. The cost

Pictured here in a suit of armor, Joan of Arc is holding aloft a banner that shows Jesus and two angels. This portrait dates from the late fifteenth century; there are no portraits of Joan made from life.

of the war in its final years and the losses in manpower strained the English economy. Moreover, with the end of the war, England experienced even greater domestic turmoil as a civil war erupted and aristocratic factions fought over the monarchy until 1485, when Henry Tudor established a new dynasty.

As the first Tudor king, Henry VII (1485–1509) worked to reduce internal dissension and establish a strong monarchical government. Henry eliminated the private wars of the nobility by abolishing their private armies. The new king was particularly successful in obtaining sufficient income from the traditional financial resources of the English monarch, such as crown lands, judicial fees and fines, and customs duties. By using diplomacy to avoid wars, which are always expensive, the king avoided having to call Parliament on any regular basis to grant him funds. By not overburdening the landed gentry and middle class with taxes, Henry won their favor, and they provided much support for his monarchy. Henry's policies enabled him to leave England with a stable and prosperous government and an enhanced status for the monarchy itself.

Spain, too, experienced the growth of a strong national monarchy by the end of the fifteenth century, a development that might have seemed unlikely at the beginning of the century. During the Middle Ages, several independent Christian kingdoms had emerged in the course of the long reconquest of the Iberian peninsula from the Muslims. Aragon and Castile were the strongest Spanish kingdoms; in the west was the independent monarchy of

Portugal; in the north the small kingdom of Navarre; and in the south the Muslim kingdom of Granada. Few people at the beginning of the fifteenth century could have predicted the national unification of Spain.

A major step in that direction was taken with the marriage of Isabella of Castile (1474–1504) and Ferdinand of Aragon (1479–1516) in 1469. This marriage was a dynastic union of two rulers, not a political union. Both kingdoms maintained their own parliaments (Cortes), courts, laws, coinage, speech, customs, and political organs. Nevertheless, the two rulers worked to strengthen royal control of government, especially in Castile. The royal council, which was supposed to supervise local administration and oversee the implementation of government policies, was stripped of aristocrats and filled primarily with middle-class lawyers. Trained in the principles of Roman law, these officials operated on the belief that the monarchy embodied the power of the state.

The towns were also enlisted in the policy of state building. Medieval town organizations known as *hermandades* ("brotherhoods"), which had been organized to maintain law and order, were revived. Ferdinand and Isabella transformed them into a kind of national militia whose primary goal was to stop the wealthy landed aristocrats from disturbing the peace. The *hermandades* were disbanded by 1498 when the royal administration became strong enough to deal with lawlessness.

Ferdinand and Isabella reorganized the military forces of Spain, seeking to replace the undisciplined feudal levies they had inherited with a more professional royal army. The development of a strong infantry force as the heart of the new Spanish army made it the best in Europe by the sixteenth century, and Spain emerged as an important power in European affairs.

Recognizing the importance of controlling the Catholic church with its vast power and wealth, Ferdinand and Isabella secured from the pope the right to select the most important church officials in Spain, virtually making the clergy an instrument for the extension of royal power. Ferdinand and Isabella also pursued a policy of strict religious uniformity. Spain possessed two large religious minorities, the Jews and Muslims, both of whom had generally been tolerated in medieval Spain. Increased persecution in the fourteenth century, however, led the majority of Spanish Jews to convert to Christianity. But complaints that these Jewish converts were not always faithful to Christianity prompted Ferdinand and Isabella to ask the pope to introduce the Inquisition into Spain in 1478. Under royal control, the Inquisition worked with cruel efficiency

✻ MAP 13.2 Europe in the Fifteenth Century

to guarantee the orthodoxy of the converts but had no authority over practicing Jews. Consequently, in 1492, flush with the success of the conquest of Muslim Granada, Ferdinand and Isabella took the drastic step of expelling all professed Jews from Spain. It is estimated that 150,000 out of possibly 200,000 Jews fled. Muslims, too, were then "encouraged" to convert to Christianity, and in 1502, Isabella issued a decree expelling all professed Muslims from her kingdom. To a very large degree, the "Most Catholic" monarchs had achieved their goal of absolute religious orthodoxy as a basic ingredient of the Spanish state. To be Spanish was to be Catholic, a policy of uniformity enforced by the Inquisition.

CENTRAL EUROPE:
THE HOLY ROMAN EMPIRE

Unlike France, England, and Spain, the Holy Roman Empire failed to develop a strong monarchical authority. The failure of the Hohenstaufens in the thirteenth cen-

tury ended any chance of centralized monarchical authority, and Germany became a land of hundreds of virtually independent states. These varied in size and power and included princely states, such as the duchies of Bavaria and Saxony; free imperial city-states, such as Nuremberg; modest territories of petty imperial knights; and ecclesiastical states in which a high church official, such as a bishop, archbishop, or abbot, served in a dual capacity as an administrative official of the Catholic church and a secular lord over the territories of his ecclesiastical state. Although all of the rulers of these various states had some obligations to the German king and Holy Roman emperor, increasingly they acted independently of the German ruler. After 1438, the position of Holy Roman emperor was in the hands of the Habsburg dynasty. Having gradually acquired a number of possessions along the Danube, known collectively as Austria, the house of Habsburg had become one of the wealthiest landholders in the empire and by the mid-fifteenth century began to play an important role in European affairs. Much of the Habsburg success in the fifteenth century was due not to military prowess, but to a well-executed policy of dynastic marriages. So successful were the Habsburgs in matrimonial arrangements that at the beginning of the sixteenth century, one of their members, Charles, succeeded in inheriting the traditional lands of the Habsburg, Burgundian, and Spanish monarchical lines, making him the leading monarch of his age (see Chapter 15).

EASTERN EUROPE

In eastern Europe, rulers struggled to achieve the centralization of their territorial states but faced serious obstacles to that goal. Although the population was mostly Slavic, there were islands of other ethnic groups who caused untold difficulties. Religious differences also troubled the area, as Roman Catholics, Greek Orthodox Christians, and pagans confronted each other.

Much of Polish history revolved around a bitter struggle between the crown and the landed nobility, until the end of the fifteenth century when the Polish monarchy's preoccupation with problems in Bohemia and Hungary as well as war with the Russians and Turks enabled the aristocrats to reestablish their power. Through their control of the *Sejm*, or national diet, the magnates reduced the peasantry to serfdom by 1511 and established the right to elect their kings. The Polish kings proved unable to establish a strong royal authority.

Since the conversion of Hungary to Roman Catholicism by German missionaries, its history had been closely tied to that of central and western Europe. The church became a large and prosperous institution. Wealthy bishops, along with great territorial lords, became powerful, independent political figures. For a brief while, however, Hungary developed into an important European state, the dominant power in eastern Europe. King Matthias Corvinus (1458–1490) broke the power of the wealthy lords and created a well-organized central administration. After his death, Hungary returned to weak rule, however, and the work of Corvinus was largely undone.

Since the thirteenth century, Russia had been under the domination of the Mongols. Gradually, the princes of Moscow rose to prominence by using their close relationship to the Mongol khans to increase their wealth and expand their possessions. During the reign of the great prince Ivan III (1462–1505), a new Russian state was born. Ivan III annexed other Russian principalities and took advantage of dissension among the Mongols to throw off their yoke by 1480.

The Ottoman Turks and the End of the Byzantine Empire

Eastern Europe was increasingly threatened by the steadily advancing Ottoman Turks. The Byzantine Empire had served as a buffer between the Muslim Middle East and the

Latin West for centuries, but it was severely weakened by the sack of Constantinople in 1204 and its occupation by the west. Although the Paleologus dynasty (1260–1453) had tried to reestablish Byzantine power in the Balkans after the overthrow of the Latin Empire, the threat from the Turks finally doomed the long-lasting empire.

Beginning in northeastern Asia Minor in the thirteenth century, the Ottoman Turks spread rapidly, seizing the lands of the Seljuk Turks and the Byzantine Empire (see Chapter 16). In 1345, they bypassed Constantinople and moved into the Balkans, which they conquered by the end of the century. Finally, in 1453, the great city of Constantinople fell to the Turks after a siege of several months. After consolidating their power, the Turks prepared to exert renewed pressure on the west, both in the Mediterranean and up the Danube valley toward Vienna. By the end of the fifteenth century, they were threatening Hungary, Austria, Bohemia, and Poland.

The Italian States

As we have seen, by the end of the fifteenth century, many European rulers had begun to rebuild their governments by restraining turbulent nobles, curbing violence, and establishing internal order. But like the Holy Roman

Empire, Italy failed to develop a centralized monarchical state. Papal opposition to the Hohenstaufens in the thirteenth century had virtually guaranteed that. Moreover, the kingdom of Naples in the south was dominated by the French house of Anjou (Sicily was ruled by the Spanish house of Aragon), while the papacy remained in shaky control of much of central Italy as rulers of the Papal States. Lack of centralized authority had enabled numerous city-states in northern and central Italy to remain independent of any political authority. Three of them—Milan, Venice, and Florence—managed to become fairly well centralized territorial states.

Milan, located at the crossroads of the main trade routes from Italian coastal cities to the Alpine passes, was one of the richest city-states in Italy. In the fourteenth century, members of the Visconti family established themselves as dukes of Milan and extended their power over all of Lombardy. After the death of the last Visconti ruler of Milan in 1447, Francesco Sforza, one of the leading *condottieri* (a *condottiere* was a leader of a mercenary band) of the time, turned on his Milanese employers, conquered the city, and became its new duke. Both the Visconti and the Sforza rulers worked to create the institutions of a strongly centralized territorial

state. They were especially successful in devising systems of taxation that generated enormous revenues for the government.

The second major northern Italian state was the maritime republic of Venice, which had grown rich from commercial activity throughout the eastern Mediterranean and

CHRONOLOGY
THE ITALIAN STATES

Duchy of Milan	
Visconti establish themselves as rulers of Milan	1322
Sforzas	1450–1494
Florence	
Cosimo de' Medici	1434–1464
Beginning of Italian Wars— French invasion of Italy	1494
Sack of Rome	1527

MAP **13.3**   The Italian States in the Fifteenth Century

P   Printing press
📖   Library
🎨   School of art
Rome   Location of important Renaissance building

✿ **PIERO DELLA FRANCESCA, *DUKE AND DUCHESS OF URBINO*.** Federigo da Montefeltro and his wife, Battista Sforza, ruled the small central Italian principality of Urbino. These profile portraits by Piero della Francesca gave a realistic rendering of the two figures. Visible in the background are the hills and valleys of Urbino.

into northern Europe. Venice remained an extremely stable political entity governed by a small oligarchy of merchant-aristocrats who had become extremely wealthy through their trading activities. Venetian government was respected by contemporaries for its stability. Venice's commercial empire brought in enormous revenues and gave it the status of an international power. At the end of the fourteenth century, Venice embarked upon the conquest of a territorial state in northern Italy to protect its food supply and its overland trade routes.

The republic of Florence dominated the region of Tuscany. In the course of the fourteenth century, a small but wealthy merchant oligarchy took control of the Florentine government, led the Florentines in a series of successful wars against their neighbors, and established Florence as a major territorial state in north-central Italy. In 1434, Cosimo de' Medici (1434–1464) assumed control of the ruling oligarchy. Although the wealthy Medici family maintained republican forms of government for appearance's sake, they ran the government from behind the scenes. Through their lavish patronage and careful courting of political allies, the Medici were successful in dominating the city at a time when Florence was the cultural center of Italy.

A number of independent city-states under the control of powerful ruling families also became brilliant centers of culture in the fifteenth century. Perhaps the most famous was Urbino, ruled by the Montefeltro dynasty. Federigo da Montefeltro, who ruled Urbino from 1444 to 1482, received a classical education. He had also learned the skills of fighting, since the Montefeltro family compensated for the poverty of Urbino by hiring themselves out as *condottieri*. Federigo was not only a good ruler, but a rather unusual *condottiere* by fifteenth-century standards. Although not a brilliant general, he was reliable and honest. At the same time, Duke Federigo was one of the greatest patrons of Renaissance culture. Under his direction, Urbino became a well-known cultural and intellectual center. Though despotic, he was also benevolent. It was said that he could walk safely through the streets of Urbino, unaccompanied by a bodyguard, a feat few Italian rulers dared to emulate.

A noticeable feature of these smaller Italian courts was the important role played by women. The most famous of the Italian ruling women was Isabella d'Este (1474–1539), daughter of the duke of Ferrara, who married Francesco Gonzaga, marquis of Mantua. Their court was another important center of art and learning in the Renaissance. Educated at the brilliant court of Ferrara, Isabella was known for her intelligence and political wisdom. Called the "first lady of the world," she attracted artists and intellectuals to the Mantuan court and was

THE LETTERS OF ISABELLA D'ESTE

Many Italian and European rulers at the beginning of the sixteenth century saw Isabella d'Este as an important political figure. In these excerpts from her letters, Isabella reveals her political skills and her fierce determination. After her husband was taken prisoner by the Venetians in 1509, she refused to accept the condition for his release—namely, that her son Federico would be kept as a hostage by the Venetians or the Holy Roman emperor. She wrote to both the emperor and her husband, refusing to agree to their demands.

LETTER OF ISABELLA D'ESTE TO THE IMPERIAL ENVOY

As to the demand for our dearest first-born son Federico, besides being a cruel and almost inhuman thing for anyone who knows the meaning of a mother's love, there are many reasons which render it difficult and impossible. Although we are quite sure that his person would be well cared for and protected by His Majesty [the Holy Roman emperor], how could we wish him to run the risk of this long and difficult journey, considering the child's tender and delicate age? And you must know what comfort and solace, in his father's present unhappy condition, we find in the presence of this dear son, the hope and joy of all our people and subjects. To deprive us of him, would be to deprive us of life itself, and of all we count good and precious. If you take Federico away you might as well take away our life and state. . . . Once for all, we will suffer any loss rather than part from our son, and this you may take to be our deliberate and unchanging resolution.

LETTER OF ISABELLA D'ESTE TO HER HUSBAND [WHO HAD ORDERED HER TO SEND THE BOY TO VENICE]

If in this matter Your Excellency were to despise me and deprive me of your love and grace, I would rather endure such harsh treatment, I would rather lose our State, than deprive us of our children. I am hoping that in time your own prudence and kindness will make you understand that I have acted more lovingly toward you than you have to yourself.

Have patience! You can be sure that I think continuously of your liberation and when the time comes I will not fail you, as I have not relaxed my efforts. As witness I cite the Pope, the Emperor, the King of France, and all the other reigning heads and potentates of Christendom. Yes, and the infidels as well [she had written to the Turkish sultan for help]. If it were *really* the only means of setting you free, I would not only send Federico but all the other children as well. I will do everything imaginable. Someday I hope I can make you understand. . . .

Pardon me if this letter is badly written and worse composed, but I do not know if I am dead or alive.

> Isabella, who desires the
> best for Your Excellency,
> written with her own hand

[Isabella's husband was not pleased with her response. His angry reaction was: "That whore of a wife is the cause of it all. Send me into battle alone, do what you like with me. I have lost in one blow my state, my honor, and my freedom. If she does not obey, I'll cut her vocal cords."]

---

responsible for amassing one of the finest libraries in all of Italy. Her numerous letters to friends, family, princes, and artists all over Europe disclose her political acumen as well as a good sense of humor (see the box above). Both before and after the death of her husband Francesco, she effectively ruled Mantua and was well known as a clever negotiator.

The growth of powerful monarchical states led to trouble for the Italians and brought an end to the independence of the Italian states. Attracted by the riches of Italy, the French king Charles VIII (1483–1498) led an army of 30,000 men into Italy and occupied the kingdom of Naples. Other Italian states turned for help to the Spanish, who gladly complied. For the next thirty years, the French and Spanish competed to dominate Italy, which was only a pawn for the two great powers, a convenient arena for fighting battles. The terrible sack of Rome in 1527 by the armies of the Spanish king Charles I brought a temporary end to the Italian wars. Thereafter, the Spaniards dominated Italy.

Machiavelli and the New Statecraft

No one gave better expression to the Italians' preoccupation with political power than Niccolò Machiavelli (1469–1527). Although he ably served as a diplomat for Florence, he was eventually forced into exile. Embittered by this and compelled by the great love of his life—politics—he wrote *The Prince*, one of the most influential works on political power in the Western world.

Machiavelli's major concerns in *The Prince* were the acquisition, maintenance, and expansion of political power as the means to restore and maintain order in his time. In the Middle Ages, many political theorists stressed the ethical side of a prince's activity—how a ruler ought to behave based on Christian moral principles. Machiavelli bluntly contradicted this approach:

> But my hope is to write a book that will be useful, at least to those who read it intelligently, and so I thought it sensible to go straight to a discussion of how things are in real life and not waste time with a discussion of an imaginary world . . . for the gap between how people actually behave and how they ought to behave is so great that anyone who ignores everyday reality in order to live up to an ideal will soon discover he had been taught how to destroy himself, not how to preserve himself.[6]

Machiavelli considered his approach far more realistic than that of his medieval forebears.

In Machiavelli's view, a prince's attitude toward power must be based on an understanding of human nature, which he perceived as basically self-centered. He said, "For of men one can, in general, say this: They are ungrateful, fickle, deceptive and deceiving, avoiders of danger, eager to gain." Political activity, therefore, could not be restricted by moral considerations. The prince acts on behalf of the state, and for the sake of the state, he must be willing to let his conscience sleep. As Machiavelli put it:

> You need to understand this: A ruler, and particularly a ruler who is new to power, cannot conform to all those rules that men who are thought good are expected to respect, for he is often obliged, in order to hold on to power, to break his word, to be uncharitable, inhumane, and irreligious. So he must be mentally prepared to act as circumstances and changes in fortune require. As I have said, he should do what is right if he can; but he must be prepared to do wrong if necessary.[7]

In Cesare Borgia, the son of Pope Alexander VI, who used ruthless measures to achieve his goal of carving out a new state in central Italy, Machiavelli found a good example of the new Italian ruler. As he said, "So anyone who decides that the policy to follow when one has newly acquired power is to destroy one's enemies, to secure some allies, to win wars, whether by force or by fraud, to make oneself both loved and feared by one's subjects, . . . cannot hope to find, in the recent past, a better model to imitate than Cesare Borgia."[8] Machiavelli was among the first to abandon morality as the basis for the analysis of political activity.

 # THE DECLINE OF THE CHURCH

The papacy of the Roman Catholic church reached the height of its power in the thirteenth century. Theories of papal supremacy included a doctrine of "fullness of power" as the spiritual head of Christendom and claims to universal temporal authority over all secular rulers. But the growing secular monarchies of Europe presented a challenge to papal claims of temporal supremacy, which led the papacy into a conflict with these territorial states that it was unable to win. Papal defeat, in turn, led to other crises that brought into question and undermined not only the pope's temporal authority over all Christendom, but his spiritual authority as well.

Boniface VIII and the Conflict with the State

The struggle between the papacy and the secular monarchies began during the pontificate of Pope Boniface VIII (1294–1303). One major issue appeared to be at stake between the pope and King Philip IV (1285–1314) of France. Looking for a source of new revenues, Philip asserted the right to tax the clergy of France. Boniface VIII claimed that the clergy of any state could not pay taxes to their secular ruler without the pope's consent. Underlying this issue, however, was a basic conflict between the claims of the papacy to universal authority over both church and state, which necessitated complete control over the clergy, and the claims of the monarchs that all subjects, including the clergy, were under the jurisdiction of the crown and subject to the king's authority on matters of taxation and justice. In short, the fundamental issue was the universal sovereignty of the papacy versus the royal sovereignty of the monarchs.

Boniface VIII asserted his position in a series of papal bulls or letters, the most important of which was *Unam Sanctam*, issued in 1302. It was the strongest statement ever made by a pope on the supremacy of the spiritual authority over the temporal authority (see the box on p. 372). When it became apparent that the pope had decided to act on his principles by excommunicating Philip IV of France, the latter sent a small contingent of French soldiers to capture Boniface and bring him back to France for trial. The pope was captured in Anagni, although Italian nobles from the surrounding countryside soon rescued him. Boniface died shortly thereafter from the shock of this experience, however. Philip's strong-arm tactics had produced a clear victory for the national monarchy over the papacy since no later pope dared renew the extravagant claims of Boniface VIII. To ensure his position and avoid any future papal threat, Philip IV brought enough pressure on the college of cardinals to achieve the election of a Frenchman, Clement V (1305–1314), as pope. Using the excuse of turbulence in the city of Rome, the new pope took up residence in Avignon, on the east bank of the Rhone River. Although Avignon was located in the Holy Roman Empire and was not a French possession, it lay just across the river from the territories of King Philip IV and was French in culture.

BONIFACE VIII'S DEFENSE OF PAPAL SUPREMACY

One of the more remarkable documents of the fourteenth century was the exaggerated statement of papal supremacy issued by Pope Boniface VIII in 1302 in the heat of his conflict with the French king Philip IV. Ironically, this strongest statement ever made of papal supremacy was issued at a time when the rising power of the secular monarchies made it increasingly difficult for the premises to be accepted. Not long after issuing it, Boniface was taken prisoner by the French. Although freed by his fellow Italians, the humiliation of his defeat brought his death a short time later.

POPE BONIFACE VIII, UNAM SANCTAM

We are compelled, our faith urging us, to believe and to hold—and we do firmly believe and simply confess—that there is one holy catholic and apostolic church, outside of which there is neither salvation nor remission of sins. . . . In this church there is one Lord, one faith, and one baptism. . . . Therefore, of this one and only church there is one body and one head . . . Christ, namely, and the vicar of Christ, St. Peter, and the successor of Peter. For the Lord himself said to Peter, feed my sheep. . . .

We are told by the word of the gospel that in this His fold there are two swords—a spiritual, namely, and a temporal. . . .

Both swords, the spiritual and the material, therefore, are in the power of the church; the one, indeed, to be wielded for the church, the other by the church; the one by the hand of the priest, the other by the hand of kings and knights, but at the will and sufferance of the priest. One sword, moreover, ought to be under the other, and the temporal authority to be subjected to the spiritual. . . .

Therefore if the earthly power err it shall be judged by the spiritual power; but if the lesser spiritual power err, by the greater. But if the greatest, it can be judged by God alone, not by man, the apostle bearing witness. A spiritual man judges all things, but he himself is judged by no one. This authority, moreover, even though it is given to man and exercised through man, is not human but rather divine, being given by divine lips to Peter and founded on a rock for him and his successors through Christ himself whom he has confessed; the Lord himself saying to Peter: "Whatsoever thou shalt bind, etc." Whoever, therefore, resists this power thus ordained by God, resists the ordination of God. . . .

Indeed, we declare, announce, and define that it is altogether necessary to salvation for every human creature to be subject to the Roman pontiff.

The Papacy at Avignon (1305–1378)

The residency of the popes in Avignon for almost three-quarters of the fourteenth century led to a decline in papal prestige and a growing antipapal sentiment. The city of Rome was the traditional capital of the church. The pope was the bishop of Rome, and his position was based on being the successor to the apostle Peter, the first bishop of Rome. It was unseemly that the head of the Catholic church should reside in Avignon instead of Rome. In the 1330s, the popes began to construct a stately palace in Avignon, a clear indication that they intended to stay for some time.

Other factors also led to a decline in papal prestige during the Avignonese residency. Many contemporaries believed that the popes at Avignon were captives of the French king. Although questionable, since Avignon did not belong to the French monarchy, it was easy to believe in view of Avignon's proximity to French lands. Moreover, during the seventy-three years of the Avignonese papacy, of the 134 new cardinals created by the popes, 113 of them were French. At the same time, the popes attempted to find new sources of revenue to compensate for their loss of revenue from the Papal States and began to impose new taxes on the clergy. Furthermore, the splendor in which the pope and cardinals were living in Avignon led to a highly vocal criticism of both clergy and papacy. Avignon had become a powerful symbol of abuses within the church, and many people began to call for the pope's return to Rome. One of the most prominent calls came from Catherine of Siena (c. 1347–1380), whose saintly demeanor and claims of visions from God led the city of Florence to send her on a mission to Pope Gregory XI in Avignon. She told the pope: "Because God has given you authority and because you have accepted it, you ought to use your virtue and power; if you do not wish to use it, it might be better for you to resign what you have accepted; it would give more honor to God and health to your soul."[9]

The Great Schism

Catherine of Siena's admonition seemed to be heeded in 1377, when at long last Pope Gregory XI, perceiving the disastrous decline in papal prestige, returned to Rome. He died soon afterward, however, in the spring of 1378. When the college of cardinals met in conclave to elect a new pope, the citizens of Rome, fearful that the French majority would choose another Frenchman who would return the papacy to Avignon, threatened that the cardinals would not leave Rome alive unless a Roman or Italian was elected pope. Wisely, the terrified cardinals duly elected the Italian archbishop of Bari as Pope Urban VI (1378–1389). Five months later, a group of dissenting cardinals—the French ones—declared Urban's election null and void and chose one of their number, a Frenchman, who took the title of Clement VII and promptly returned to Avignon. Since Urban remained in Rome, there were now two popes, initiating what has been called the Great Schism of the church. Europe became divided in its loyalties: France, Spain, Scotland, and southern Italy supported Clement, while England, Germany, Scandinavia, and most of Italy supported Urban. These divisions generally followed political lines. Since the French supported the Avignonese, so did their allies; their enemies, particularly England and its allies, supported the Roman pope. The need for political support caused both popes to subordinate their policies to the policies of these states.

The Great Schism badly damaged the faith of Christian believers. The pope was widely believed to be the true leader of Christendom and, as Boniface VIII had pointed out, held the keys to the kingdom of heaven. Since both lines of popes denounced the other as the Antichrist, such a spectacle could not help but undermine the institution that had become the very foundation of the church. The Great Schism introduced uncertainty into the daily lives of ordinary Christians.

As dissatisfaction with the papacy grew, so also did the calls for a revolutionary approach to solving the church's institutional problems. Final authority in spiritual matters must reside not with the popes, reformers claimed, but with a general church council representing all members. The Great Schism led large numbers of serious churchmen to take up the theory of conciliarism in the belief that only a general council of the church could end the schism and bring reform to the church in its "head and members."

Leadership in convening a council eventually passed to the Holy Roman emperor Sigismund, and as a result of his efforts, an ecumenical church council met at Constance from 1414 to 1418. It had three major objectives: to end the schism, to eradicate heresy, and to reform the church in "head and members." The ending of the schism proved to be the Council of Constance's easiest task. After the competing popes either resigned or were deposed, a new conclave elected a Roman cardinal, a member of a prominent Roman family, as Pope Martin V (1417–1431). The council was much less successful in dealing with the problems of heresy and reform.

The Problems of Heresy and Reform

The crisis in the Catholic church led to renewed calls for reform. A group of Czech reformers led by the chancellor of the university of Prague, John Hus (1374–1415),

CHRONOLOGY

THE DECLINE OF THE CHURCH

Pope Boniface VIII	1294–1303
Unam Sanctam	1302
The papacy at Avignon	1305–1378
Pope Gregory XI returns to Rome	1377
The Great Schism begins	1378
Pope Urban VI	1378–1389
Council of Constance	1414–1418
End of the Great Schism	1417
The Renaissance papacy	
Sixtus IV	1471–1484
Alexander VI	1492–1503
Julius II	1503–1513
Leo X	1513–1521

called for an end to the worldliness and corruption of the clergy and attacked the excessive power of the papacy within the Catholic church. Hus's objections fell on receptive ears because there was already widespread criticism of the Catholic church as one of the largest landowners in Bohemia. Moreover, many clergymen were German, and the native Czechs' strong resentment of the Germans who dominated Bohemia also contributed to Hus's movement.

The Council of Constance attempted to deal with the growing problem of heresy by summoning John Hus to the council. Granted a safe conduct by Emperor Sigismund, Hus went in the hope of receiving a free hearing for his ideas. Instead he was arrested, condemned as a heretic, and burned at the stake in 1415. This action turned the unrest in Bohemia into revolutionary upheaval, and the resulting Hussite wars wracked the Holy Roman Empire until a truce was arranged in 1436.

The reform of the church in "head and members" was even less successful than the attempt to eradicate heresy. The Council of Constance passed two startling reform decrees. One boldly stated that a general council of the church received its authority from God; hence, every Christian, including the pope, was subject to its authority. The other decree provided for the regular holding of general councils in order to maintain an ongoing reform of the church. Decrees alone, however, proved insufficient to reform the church. Councils could issue decrees, but popes had to execute them, and popes would not cooperate with councils that diminished their absolute authority. Beginning already in 1417, successive popes worked

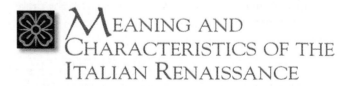 **A RENAISSANCE POPE: SIXTUS IV.** The Renaissance popes allowed secular concerns to overshadow their spiritual duties. They became concerned with territorial expansion, finances, and Renaissance culture. Pope Sixtus IV built the Sistine Chapel and later had it decorated by some of the leading artists of his day. This fresco by Melozzo da Forlì shows the pope on his throne receiving the humanist Platina (kneeling), who was keeper of the Vatican Library.

steadfastly for the next thirty years to defeat the conciliar movement.

By the mid-fifteenth century, the popes had reasserted their supremacy over the Catholic church. No longer, however, did they have any possibility of asserting supremacy over temporal governments as the medieval papacy had. The papal monarchy had been maintained, although it had lost much moral prestige. In the fifteenth and early sixteenth centuries, the Renaissance popes contributed to an even further decline in the moral leadership of the papacy.

The Renaissance Papacy

The phrase *Renaissance papacy* refers to the line of popes from the end of the Great Schism (1417) to the beginnings of the Reformation in the early sixteenth century. The primary concern of the papacy is governing the Catholic church as its spiritual leader. But as heads of the church, popes had temporal preoccupations as well, and the story of the Renaissance papacy is really an account of how the latter came to overshadow the pope's spiritual functions.

The manner in which Renaissance popes pursued their interests in the Papal States and Italian politics, especially their use of intrigue, deceit, and open bloodshed, seemed shocking. Of all the Renaissance popes, Julius II (1503–1513) was most involved in war and politics. The fiery "warrior-pope" personally led armies against his enemies, much to the disgust of pious Christians who viewed the pope as a spiritual leader. As one intellectual wrote at the beginning of the sixteenth century: "How, O bishop standing in the room of the Apostles, dare you teach the people the things that pertain to war?"

To further their territorial aims in the Papal States, the popes needed loyal servants. Because they were not hereditary monarchs, popes could not build dynasties over several generations and came to rely on the practice of nepotism to promote their families' interests. Pope Sixtus IV (1471–1484), for example, made five of his nephews (the word *nepotism* is, in fact, derived from *nepos*, meaning nephew) cardinals and gave them an abundance of church offices to build up their finances. The infamous Borgia pope, Alexander VI (1492–1503), known for his debauchery and sensuality, raised one son, one nephew, and the brother of one mistress to the cardinalate. Alexander scandalized the church by encouraging his son Cesare to carve a territorial state out of the territories of the Papal States in central Italy.

The Renaissance popes were great patrons of Renaissance culture, and their efforts made Rome a cultural leader at the beginning of the sixteenth century. For the warrior-pope Julius II, the patronage of Renaissance culture was mostly a matter of policy as he endeavored to add to the splendor of his pontificate by tearing down the old basilica of Saint Peter and beginning construction of what was to be the greatest building in Christendom, Saint Peter's Basilica. Julius's successor, Leo X (1513–1521), was also a patron of Renaissance culture, not as a matter of policy, but as a deeply involved participant. A member of the Medici family, he was made a cardinal at the age of thirteen and acquired a refined taste in art, manners, and social life among the Florentine elite. He became pope at the age of thirty-seven, supposedly remarking to the Venetian ambassador, "Let us enjoy the papacy, since God has given it to us." Raphael was commissioned to do paintings, and the construction of St. Peter's was accelerated as Rome became the literary and artistic center of the Renaissance.

MEANING AND CHARACTERISTICS OF THE ITALIAN RENAISSANCE

The word *Renaissance* means "rebirth." A number of people who lived in Italy between c. 1350 and c. 1550 believed that they had witnessed a rebirth of antiquity or

Greco-Roman civilization, which marked a new age. To them, the approximately thousand years between the end of the Roman Empire and their own era was a middle period (hence the "Middle Ages"), characterized by darkness because of its lack of classical culture. Historians of the nineteenth century later used similar terminology to describe this period in Italy. The Swiss historian and art critic Jacob Burckhardt created the modern concept of the Renaissance in his celebrated work *The Civilization of the Renaissance in Italy*, published in 1860. He portrayed Italy in the fourteenth and fifteenth centuries as the birthplace of the modern world and saw the revival of antiquity, the "perfecting of the individual," and secularism ("worldliness of the Italians") as its distinguishing features. No doubt, Burckhardt exaggerated the individuality and secularism of the Renaissance and failed to recognize the depths of its religious sentiment. Nevertheless, he established the framework for all modern interpretations of the Renaissance. Although contemporary scholars do not believe that the Renaissance represents a sudden or dramatic cultural break with the Middle Ages (as Burckhardt argued)—there was after all much continuity between the two periods in economic, political, and social life—the Renaissance can still be viewed as a distinct period of European history, which manifested itself first in Italy and then spread to the rest of Europe. What, then, are the characteristics of the Italian Renaissance?

Renaissance Italy was largely the product of an urban society. The city-states became the centers of Italian political, economic, and social life. Within this new urban society, a secular spirit emerged as increasing wealth created new possibilities for the enjoyment of worldly things.

Above all, the Renaissance was an age of recovery from the "calamitous fourteenth century." Italy and Europe began a slow process of recuperation from the effects of the Black Death, political disorder, and economic recession. Recovery was accompanied by rebirth, specifically, a rebirth of classical antiquity. Increasingly aware of their own historical past, Italian intellectuals became intensely interested in the Greco-Roman culture that had informed the ancient Mediterranean world. This revival of classical antiquity affected activities as diverse as politics and art and led to new attempts to see human beings in a new light.

Though not entirely new, a revived emphasis on individual ability became characteristic of the Italian Renaissance. As the fifteenth-century Florentine architect Leon Battista Alberti expressed it, "Men can do all things if they will."[10] A high regard for human dignity and worth and a realization of individual potentiality created a new social ideal of the well-rounded personality or universal person (*l'uomo universale*) who was capable of achievements in many areas of life.

These general features of the Italian Renaissance were not characteristic of all Italians, but were primarily the preserve of the wealthy upper classes who constituted a small

percentage of the total population. The Italian Renaissance was an elitist, not a mass, movement, although indirectly it did have some impact on ordinary people, especially in the cities, where so many of the intellectual and artistic accomplishments of the period were most apparent.

THE MAKING OF RENAISSANCE SOCIETY

The Renaissance inherited a tripartite division of society from the Middle Ages. Society was fundamentally divided into three estates: the clergy, whose preeminence was grounded in the belief that people should be guided to spiritual ends; the nobility, whose privileges rested on the principle that the nobles provided security and justice for society; and the third estate, which consisted of the peasants and inhabitants of the towns and cities. This social order experienced certain adaptations in the Renaissance, which we can see by examining the second and third estates (the clergy will be examined in Chapter 15).

The Social Classes: The Nobility

Throughout much of Europe, the landholding nobles were faced with declining real incomes during the greater part of the fourteenth and fifteenth centuries. But many members of the old nobility survived, while new blood infused their ranks. A reconstruction of the aristocracy was well under way by 1500. As a result of this reconstruction, the nobles, old and new, who constituted between 2 and 3 percent of the population in most countries, managed to dominate society as they had done in the Middle Ages, holding important political posts and serving as advisers to the king.

By 1500, certain ideals came to be expected of the noble or aristocrat. These were best expressed in *The Book of the Courtier*, by the Italian Baldassare Castiglione (1478–1529). First published in 1528, Castiglione's work soon became popular throughout Europe, and it remained a fundamental handbook for European aristocrats well into the twentieth century.

In *The Book of the Courtier*, Castiglione described the three basic attributes of the perfect courtier. First, nobles should possess fundamental native endowments, such as impeccable character, grace, talents, and noble birth. The perfect courtier must also cultivate certain achievements. Primarily, he should participate in military and bodily exercises because the principal profession of a courtier was arms. For a medieval knight, military skill had been the only requirement, but this was not true of the Renaissance courtier, who must seek a classical education and adorn his life with the arts by playing a musical instrument, drawing, and painting. In Castiglione's hands, the Renaissance ideal of the well-developed personality became a social ideal of the aristocracy. Finally, the aristocrat was expected to follow a certain standard of conduct. Nobles were expected to make good impressions; while being modest, they should not hide their accomplishments, but show them off with grace.

But what was the purpose of these courtly standards? Castiglione said:

> Therefore, I think that the aim of the perfect Courtier, which we have not spoken of up to now, is so to win for himself, by means of the accomplishments ascribed to him by these gentlemen, the favor and mind of the prince whom he serves that he may be able to tell him, and always will tell him, the truth about everything he needs to know, without fear or risk of displeasing him; and that when he sees the mind of his prince inclined to a wrong action, he may dare to oppose him . . . so as to dissuade him of every evil intent and bring him to the path of virtue.[11]

The aim of the perfect noble, then, was to serve his prince in an effective and honest way. Nobles would adhere to Castiglione's principles for hundreds of years while they continued to dominate European life socially and politically.

The Social Classes: The Third Estate of Peasants and Townspeople

Traditionally, peasants made up the overwhelming mass of the third estate and indeed continued to constitute as much as 85 to 90 percent of the total European popula-

tion, except in the highly urbanized areas of northern Italy and Flanders. The most noticeable trend produced by the economic crisis of the fourteenth century was the decline of the manorial system and the continuing elimination of serfdom. The contraction of the peasantry after the Black Death simply accelerated the process of converting servile labor dues into rents paid in money. By the end of the fifteenth century, serfdom was declining, especially in western Europe, and more and more peasants were becoming legally free.

The remainder of the third estate centered around the people of the towns and cities, originally the merchants and artisans who formed the so-called middle class. The town or city of the fifteenth century actually possessed a multitude of inhabitants widely separated socially and economically.

At the top of urban society were the patricians, whose wealth from capitalistic enterprises in trade, industry, and banking enabled them to dominate their urban communities economically, socially, and politically. Below them were the petty burghers, the shopkeepers, artisans, guildmasters, and guildsmen, who were largely concerned with providing goods and services for local consumption. Below these two groups were the propertyless workers earning pitiful wages and the unemployed, who lived squalid and miserable lives. These people constituted as much as 30 or 40 percent of the urban population. Everywhere in Europe in the late fourteenth and fifteenth centuries, urban poverty had increased dramatically. One rich merchant of Florence wrote:

> Those that are lazy and indolent in a way that does harm to the city, and who can offer no just reason for their condition, should either be forced to work or expelled from the Commune. The city would thus rid itself of that most harmful part of the poorest class. . . . If the lowest order of society earn enough food to keep them going from day to day, then they have enough.[12]

But even this large group was not at the bottom of the social scale; beneath them stood a significantly large group of slaves, especially in the cities of Italy.

Family and Marriage in Renaissance Italy

The family bond was a source of great security in the dangerous urban world of Renaissance Italy. To maintain the family, careful attention was given to marriages, which were arranged by parents, often to strengthen business or family ties. Details were worked out well in advance, sometimes when children were only two or three, and reinforced by a legally binding marriage contract (see the box on p. 377). The important aspect of the contract was the size of the dowry, a sum of money presented by the wife's family to the husband upon marriage. He would control this money thereafter. The

✤ **WEDDING BANQUET.** Parents arranged marriages in Renaissance Italy to strengthen business or family ties. A legally binding marriage contract was considered a necessary part of the marital arrangements. So, too, was a wedding feast. This painting by Botticelli shows the wedding banquet in Florence that celebrated the marriage of Nastagio degli Onesti and the daughter of Paulo Traversaro.

MARRIAGE NEGOTIATIONS

Marriages were so important in maintaining families in Renaissance Italy that much energy was put into arranging them. Parents made the choices for their children, most often for considerations that had little to do with the modern notion of love. This selection is taken from the letters of a Florentine matron of the illustrious Strozzi family to her son Filippo in Naples. The family's considerations were complicated by the fact that the son was in exile.

ALESSANDRA STROZZI TO HER SON FILIPPO IN NAPLES

[April 20, 1464] Concerning the matter of a wife [for Filippo], it appears to me that if Francesco di Messer Tanagli wishes to give his daughter, that it would be a fine marriage. . . . Now I will speak with Marco [Parenti, Alessandra's son-in-law], to see if there are other prospects that would be better, and if there are none, then we will learn if he wishes to give her [in marriage]. . . . Francesco Tanagli has a good reputation, and he has held office, not the highest, but still he has been in office. You may ask: "Why should he give her to someone in exile?" There are three reasons. First, there aren't many young men of good family who have both virtue and property. Secondly, she has only a small dowry, 1,000 florins, which is the dowry of an artisan [although not a small sum, either—senior officials in the government bureaucracy earned 300 florins a year]. . . . Third, I believe that he will give her away, because he has a large family and he will need help to settle them. . . .

[July 26, 1465] Francesco is a good friend of Marco and he trusts him. On S. Jacopo's day, he spoke to him discreetly and persuasively, saying that for several months he had heard that we were interested in the girl and . . . that when we had made up our minds, she will come to us willingly. [He said that] you were a worthy man, and that his family had always made good marriages, but that he had only a small dowry to give her, and so he would prefer to send her outside of Florence to someone of worth, rather than to give her to someone here, from among those who were available, with little money. . . . We have information that she is affable and competent. She is responsible for a large family (there are twelve children, six boys and six girls), and the mother is always pregnant and isn't very competent. . . .

[August 31, 1465] I have recently received some very favorable information [about the Tanagli girl] from two individuals. . . . They are in agreement that whoever gets her will be content. . . . Concerning her beauty, they told me what I had already seen, that she is attractive and well-proportioned. Her face is long, but I couldn't look directly into her face, since she appeared to be aware that I was examining her . . . and so she turned away from me like the wind. . . . She reads quite well . . . and she can dance and sing. . . .

So yesterday I sent for Marco and told him what I had learned. And we talked about the matter for a while, and decided that he should say something to the father and give him a little hope, but not so much that we couldn't withdraw, and find out from him the amount of the dowry. . . . May God help us to choose what will contribute to our tranquility and to the consolation of us all. . . .

[September 13, 1465] Marco came to me and said that he had met with Francesco Tanagli, who had spoken very coldly, so that I understand that he had changed his mind. [Filippo Strozzi eventually married Fiametta di Donato Adimari in 1466.]

---

dowry could involve large sums of money and was expected of all families.

The father-husband was the center of the Italian family. He gave it his name, was responsible for it in all legal matters, managed all finances (his wife had no share in his wealth), and made the crucial decisions that determined his children's lives. A father's authority over his children was absolute until he died or formally freed his children. In Renaissance Italy, children did not become adults on reaching a certain age; instead adulthood came only when the father went before a judge and formally emancipated them. The age of emancipation varied from early teens to late twenties.

The wife managed the household, a position that gave women a certain degree of autonomy in their daily lives.

Most wives, however, also knew that their primary function was to bear children. Upper-class wives were frequently pregnant; Alessandra Strozzi of Florence, for example, who had been married at the age of sixteen, bore eight children in ten years. Poor women did not conceive at the same rate since they nursed their own babies. Wealthy women gave their infants out to wet nurses, which enabled them to become pregnant more quickly after the birth of a child.

For women in the Renaissance, childbirth was a fearful occasion. Not only was it painful, but it could be deadly; possibly as many as 10 percent of mothers died in childbirth. In his memoirs, the Florence merchant Gregorio Dati recalled that three of his four wives died in childbirth. His third wife, after bearing eleven children in fifteen years, "died in childbirth after lengthy suffering, which she bore with remarkable strength and patience."[13] Nor did the tragedies end with childbirth. Surviving mothers often faced the death of their children as well. In Florence in the fifteenth century, for example, almost 50 percent of the children born to merchant families died before the age of twenty. Given these mortality rates, many upper-class families sought to have as many children as possible in order to ensure a surviving male heir to the family fortune. This concern is evident in the Florentine humanist Leon Battista Alberti's treatise *On the Family*, when one of the characters remarks, "How many families do we see today in decadence and ruin! . . . Of all these families not only the magnificence and greatness but the very men, not only the men but the very names are shrunk away and gone. Their memory . . . is wiped out and obliterated."[14]

THE INTELLECTUAL RENAISSANCE IN ITALY

Individualism and secularism—two characteristics of the Italian Renaissance—were most noticeable in the intellectual and artistic realms. Italian culture had matured by the fourteenth century. During the fifteenth and sixteenth centuries, Italy was the cultural leader of Europe. This new Italian culture was primarily the product of a relatively wealthy, urban lay society. The most important literary movement associated with the Renaissance was humanism.

Italian Renaissance Humanism

Renaissance humanism was an intellectual movement based on the study of the classics, or the literary works of Greece and Rome. Humanists studied the liberal arts—grammar, rhetoric, poetry, moral philosophy or ethics, and history—all based on the study of ancient Greek and Roman authors. These subjects are what we call the humanities.

Petrarch (1304–1374) has often been called the father of Italian Renaissance humanism. He did more than any other individual in the fourteenth century to foster the development of Renaissance humanism. He was the first intellectual to characterize the Middle Ages as a period of darkness, promoting the mistaken belief that medieval culture was ignorant of classical antiquity. Petrarch's interest in the classics led him on a passionate search for forgotten Latin manuscripts and set in motion a ransacking of monastic libraries throughout Europe. In his preoccupation with the classics and their secular content, Petrarch doubted at times whether he was sufficiently attentive to spiritual ideals. His qualms, however, did not prevent him from inaugurating the humanist emphasis on pure classical Latin, making it fashionable for humanists to use Cicero as a model for prose and Virgil for poetry. As Petrarch said, "Christ is my God; Cicero is the prince of the language." Humanists would always have a tendency to emphasize style, often at the expense of content.

In Florence, the humanist movement took a new direction at the beginning of the fifteenth century. Fourteenth-century humanists such as Petrarch had glorified intellectual activity pursued in a life of solitude and had rejected a life of action in the community and family. In the busy civic world of Florence, intellectuals began to take a new view of their role as intellectuals, a trend that intensified when the city's liberty was threatened at the beginning of the fifteenth century by the Milanese tyrant Giangaleazzo Visconti. Cicero, the classical Roman statesman and intellectual, became their model. Leonardo Bruni (1370–1444), a humanist, Florentine patriot, and chancellor of the city, wrote a biography of Cicero entitled *New Cicero*, in which he waxed enthusiastically about the fusion of political action and literary creation in Cicero's life. Cicero's literary and political activities were simply two sides of the same coin, the work of a Roman citizen on behalf of his state. From Bruni's time on, Cicero served as the inspiration for the Renaissance ideal that one must live an active life for one's state, and everything, including riches, must be considered good if it increases one's power of action. An active civic life does not distract from but actually stimulates the highest intellectual energies. An individual only "grows to maturity—both intellectually and morally—through participation" in the life of the state.

Civic humanism emerged in Florence but soon spread to other Italian cities and beyond. It reflected the values of the urban society of the Italian Renaissance. Civic humanism intensified the involvement of humanist intellectuals in government and guaranteed that the rhetorical discipline they praised would be put to the service of the state. It is no accident that humanists served the state as chancellors, councillors, and advisers. Rhetoricians had become diplomats.

Also evident in the humanism of the first half of the fifteenth century was a growing interest in classical Greek civilization. One of the first Italian humanists to gain a thorough knowledge of Greek was Leonardo Bruni, who became an enthusiastic pupil of the Byzantine scholar Manuel Chrysoloras, who taught in Florence from 1396 to 1400. Humanists eagerly perused the works of Plato as well as Greek poets, dramatists, historians, and orators, such as Thucydides, Euripides, and Sophocles, all of whom had been neglected by the scholastics of the High Middle Ages.

Humanism and Philosophy

The second half of the fifteenth century saw a dramatic upsurge of interest in the works of Plato. Cosimo de' Medici, the de facto ruler of Florence, encouraged this development by commissioning a translation of Plato's dialogues by Marsilio Ficino (1433–1499), who dedicated his life to the translation of Plato and the exposition of the Platonic philosophy known as Neoplatonism.

In two major works, Marsilio Ficino undertook the synthesis of Christianity and Platonism into a single system. His Neoplatonism was based on two primary ideas, the Neoplatonic hierarchy of substances and a theory of spiritual love. The former postulated a hierarchy of substances, or great chain of being, from the lowest form of physical matter (plants) to the purest spirit (God), in which humans occupied a central or middle position. They were the link between the material world (through the body) and the spiritual world (through the soul), and their highest duty was to apprehend higher things and ascend toward that union with God that was the true end of human existence. Ficino's theory of spiritual or Platonic love maintained that just as all people are bound together in their common humanity by love, so too are all parts of the universe held together by bonds of sympathetic love.

Renaissance Hermeticism was another product of the Florentine intellectual environment of the late fifteenth century. Upon the request of Cosimo de' Medici, Marsilio Ficino translated into Latin a Greek manuscript entitled *Corpus Hermeticum*. This work contained two kinds of writings. One type stressed the occult sciences with emphasis on astrology, alchemy, and magic. The other focused on theological and philosophical beliefs and speculations. For Renaissance intellectuals, the Hermetic revival offered a new view of humankind. They believed that human beings had been created as divine beings endowed with divine creative power, but had freely chosen to enter the material world (nature). They could recover their divinity, however, through a regenerative experience or purification of the soul. Thus regenerated, they became true sages or magi, as the Renaissance called them, who had knowledge of God and of truth. In regaining their original divinity, they reacquired an intimate knowledge of nature and the ability to employ its powers for beneficial purposes. Serious Renaissance magi believed in humans' ability to control nature and became involved in the practice of magic as a means of organizing and controlling experience.

In Italy, the most prominent magi in the late fifteenth century were Ficino and his friend and pupil Giovanni Pico della Mirandola (1463–1494). Pico produced one of the most famous writings of the Renaissance, the *Oration on the Dignity of Man*. Pico combed diligently through the writings of many philosophers of different backgrounds for the common "nuggets of universal truth" that he believed were all part of God's revelation to humanity. In the *Oration* (see the box on p. 380), Pico offered a ringing statement of unlimited human potential: "To him it is granted to have whatever he chooses, to be whatever he wills."[15] Like Ficino, Pico took an avid interest in Hermetic magic, accepting it as the "science

of the Divine," which "embraces the deepest contemplation of the most secret things, and at last the knowledge of all nature."[16]

Education in the Renaissance

The humanist movement had a profound effect on education. Renaissance humanists believed that human beings could be dramatically changed by education, and as a result, they wrote treatises on education and opened schools based on their ideas. At the core of humanist schools were the "liberal studies." Humanists believed that the "liberal studies" (what we call the liberal arts) were the key to true freedom, enabling individuals to reach their full potential. According to one humanist, "we call those studies liberal which are worthy of a free man; those studies by which we attain and practice virtue and wisdom; that education which calls forth, trains, and develops those highest gifts of body and mind which ennoble men."[17] What, then, were the "liberal studies"? According to the humanists, they included history, moral philosophy, and eloquence (or rhetoric), letters (grammar and logic), poetry, mathematics, astronomy, and music. In short, the purpose of a liberal education—and thus the purpose of the study of the liberal arts—was to produce individuals who followed a path of virtue and wisdom and possessed the rhetorical skills by which they could persuade others to take it. Following the Greek precept of a sound mind in a sound body, humanist educators also stressed physical education. Pupils were taught the skills of javelin throwing, archery, and dancing and encouraged to run, wrestle, hunt, and swim.

The purpose of these humanist schools was to educate an elite, the ruling classes of their communities. Largely absent from such schools were females. The few female students who did attend humanist schools studied the classics and were encouraged to know some history and to ride, dance, sing, play the lute, and appreciate poetry. But they were told not to learn mathematics and rhetoric. Religion and morals were thought to "hold the first place in the education of Christian ladies," helping to prepare them for their roles as mothers and wives.

Humanist educators thought that humanist education was a practical preparation for life. Its aim was not the creation of a great scholar but a complete citizen. As one humanist said, "Not everyone is obliged to excel in philosophy, medicine, or the law, nor are all equally favored by nature; but all are destined to live in society and to practice virtue."[18] Humanist schools provided the model for the basic education of the European ruling classes until the twentieth century.

The Development of Vernacular Literature

The humanist emphasis on classical Latin led to its widespread use in the fifteenth and sixteenth centuries,

PICO DELLA MIRANDOLA AND
THE DIGNITY OF MAN

Giovanni Pico della Mirandola was one of the foremost intellects of the Italian Renaissance. Pico boasted that he had studied all schools of philosophy, which he tried to demonstrate by drawing up nine hundred theses for public disputation at the age of twenty-four. As a preface to his theses, he wrote his famous oration, On the Dignity of Man, in which he proclaimed the unlimited potentiality of human beings.

PICO DELLA MIRANDOLA, ORATION ON THE DIGNITY OF MAN

At last the best of artisans [God] ordained that that creature to whom He had been able to give nothing proper to himself should have joint possession of whatever had been peculiar to each of the different kinds of being. He therefore took man as a creature of indeterminate nature, and assigning him a place in the middle of the world, addressed him thus: "Neither a fixed abode nor a form that is yours alone nor any function peculiar to yourself have we given you, Adam, to the end that according to your longing and according to your judgment you may have and possess what abode, what form, and what functions you yourself shall desire. The nature of all other beings is limited and constrained within the bounds of laws prescribed by Us. You, constrained by no limits, in accordance with your own free will, in whose hand We have placed you, shall ordain yourself the limits of your nature. We have set you at the world's center that you may from there more easily observe whatever is in the world. We have made you neither of heaven nor of earth, neither mortal nor immortal, so that with freedom of choice and with honor, as though the maker and molder of yourself, you may fashion yourself in whatever shape you shall prefer. You shall have the power to degenerate into the lower forms of life, which are brutish. You shall have the power, out of your soul's judgment, to be reborn into the higher forms, which are divine."

O supreme generosity of God the Father, O highest and most marvelous felicity of man! To him it is granted to have whatever he chooses, to be whatever he wills. Beasts as soon as they are born bring with them from their mother's womb all they will ever possess. Spiritual beings, either from the beginning or soon thereafter, become what they are to be forever and ever. On man when he came into life the Father conferred the seeds of all kinds and the germs of every way of life. Whatever seeds each man cultivates will grow to maturity and bear in him their own fruit. If they be vegetative, he will be like a plant. If sensitive, he will become brutish. If rational, he will grow into a heavenly being. If intellectual, he will be an angel and the son of God.

---

especially among scholars, lawyers, and theologians. However, some writers used the vernacular (the language spoken in their own regions, such as Italian, French, or German) to write their works. In the fourteenth and fifteenth centuries, the works of Dante and Christine de Pizan helped make vernacular languages more popular. By the late fifteenth and early sixteenth centuries, vernacular languages became broad enough in scope to create national literary forms that could compete with and eventually replace Latin.

Dante (1265–1321) came from an old Florentine noble family that had fallen on hard times. His masterpiece in the Italian vernacular was *The Divine Comedy*, written between 1313 and 1321. Cast in a typical medieval framework, *The Divine Comedy* is basically the story of the soul's progression to salvation, a fundamental medieval preoccupation. The lengthy poem was divided into three major sections corresponding to the realms of the afterworld: hell, purgatory, and heaven or paradise. In "Inferno," Dante is led on an imaginary journey through hell by his guide, the classical author Virgil (see the box on p. 381). Symbolically, "Inferno" reflects despair, while "Purgatory," the second stage of his journey, reflects hope. In "Paradise," Dante is eventually guided by Saint Bernard, a symbol of mystical contemplation. The saint turns Dante over to the Virgin Mary because grace is necessary to achieve the final step of entering the presence of God, where one beholds "The love that moves the sun and the other stars."[19] Allegorically, "Paradise" reflects perfection or salvation.

One of the extraordinary vernacular writers of the age was Christine de Pizan (c. 1364–1430). Because of her father's position at the court of Charles V of France, she received a good education. When her husband died when she was only twenty-five (they had been married for ten years), she was left with little income and the need to support her three small children and her mother. Christine took the unusual step of becoming a writer in order to earn her living. Her poems were soon in demand, and by 1400 she had achieved financial security.

Christine de Pizan is best known, however, for her French prose works written in defense of women. In *The Book of the City of Ladies*, written in 1404, she de-

DANTE'S VISION OF HELL

The Divine Comedy of Dante Alighieri is regarded as one of the greatest literary works of all time. Many consider it the supreme summary of medieval European thought. It combines allegory with a remarkable amount of contemporary history. Indeed, forty-three of the seventy-nine people consigned to hell in the "Inferno" were Florentines. This excerpt is taken from Canto XVIII of the "Inferno," in which Dante and Virgil visit the eighth circle of hell, which is divided into ten trenches containing those who had committed malicious frauds upon their fellow human beings.

DANTE, "INFERNO," THE DIVINE COMEDY

We had already come to where the walk
crosses the second bank, from which it lifts
another arch, spanning from rock to rock.

Here we heard people whine in the next chasm,
and knock and thump themselves with open palms,
and blubber through their snouts as if in a spasm.

Steaming from that pit, a vapor rose
over the banks, crusting them with a slime
that sickened my eyes and hammered at my nose.

That chasm sinks so deep we could not sight
its bottom anywhere until we climbed
along the rock arch to its greatest height.

Once there, I peered down, and I saw long lines
of people in a river of excrement
that seemed the overflow of the world's latrines.

I saw among the felons of that pit
one wraith who might or might not have been tonsured—
one could not tell, he was so smeared with shit.

He bellowed: "You there, why do you stare at me
more than at all the others in this stew?"
And I to him: "Because if memory

serves me, I knew you when your hair was dry.
You are Alessio Interminelli da Lucca.
That's why I pick you from this filthy fry."

And he then, beating himself on his clown's head:
"Down to this have the flatteries I sold
the living sunk me here among the dead."

And my Guide prompted then: "Lean forward a bit
and look beyond him, there—do you see that one
scratching herself with dungy nails, the strumpet

who fidgets to her feet, then to a crouch?
It is the whore Thäis who told her lover
when he sent to ask her, 'Do you thank me much?'

'Much? Nay, past all believing!' And with this
Let us turn from the sight of this abyss."

---

nounced the many male writers who had argued that women by their very nature were prone to evil, unable to learn, and easily swayed, as a result of which they needed to be controlled by men. With the help of Reason, Righteousness, and Justice, who appear to her in a vision, Christine refutes these antifeminist attacks. Women, she argues, are not evil by nature, and they, too, could learn as well as men if they could attend the same schools: "Should I also tell you whether a woman's nature is clever and quick enough to learn speculative sciences as well as to discover them, and likewise the manual arts. I assure you that women are equally well-suited and skilled to carry them out and to put them to sophisticated use once they have learned them."[20] Much of the book includes a detailed discussion of women from the past and present who have distinguished themselves as leaders, warriors, wives, mothers, and martyrs for their religious faith. She ends by encouraging women to defend themselves against the attacks of men who are unable to understand them.

The Impact of Printing

The period of the Renaissance witnessed the development of printing, one of the most important technological innovations of civilization. The art of printing made an immediate impact on European intellectual life and thought. Printing from hand-carved wooden blocks had been present in the West since the twelfth century and in China even before that. What was new in the fifteenth century in Europe was multiple printing with movable metal type. The development of printing from movable type was a gradual process that culminated sometime between 1445 and 1450; Johannes Gutenberg

Christine de
Pizan is one of the extraordinary vernacular writers of the late
fourteenth and early fifteenth centuries. She is pictured here in
a cover illustration from her book, *The Book of the City of Ladies*.
Reason, Righteousness, and Justice are shown appearing to
Christine in a dream.

sics, medieval grammars, legal handbooks, works on philosophy, and an ever growing number of popular romances.

Printing became one of the largest industries in
Europe, and its effects were soon felt in many areas of
European life. Although some humanists condemned
printing because they believed that it vulgarized learning, the printing of books actually encouraged the development of scholarly research and the desire to attain
knowledge. Moreover, printing facilitated cooperation
among scholars and helped produce standardized and
definitive texts. Printing also stimulated the rise of an
ever expanding lay reading public, a development that
had an enormous impact on European society. Indeed,
the new religious ideas of the Reformation would never
have spread as rapidly as they did in the sixteenth century without the printing press.

THE ARTISTIC RENAISSANCE

Leonardo da Vinci, one of the great Italian Renaissance
artists, once explained: "Hence the painter will produce
pictures of small merit if he takes for his standard the pictures of others, but if he will study from natural objects he
will bear good fruit . . . those who take for their standard
anyone but nature . . . weary themselves in vain."[21]
Renaissance artists considered the imitation of nature to
be their primary goal. Their search for naturalism became
an end in itself: to persuade onlookers of the reality of the
object or event they were portraying. At the same time,
the new artistic standards reflected a new attitude of mind
as well, one in which human beings became the focus of
attention, the "center and measure of all things," as one
artist proclaimed.

The frescoes by Masaccio (1401–1428) in the Brancacci Chapel have long been regarded as the first masterpieces of Early Renaissance art. With his use of
monumental figures, the demonstration of a more realistic relationship between figures and landscape, and the
visual representation of the laws of perspective, a new realistic style of painting was born. Onlookers become aware
of a world of reality that appears to be a continuation of
their own.

This new or Renaissance style was absorbed and modified by other Florentine painters in the fifteenth century. Especially important was the development of an
experimental trend that took two directions. One
emphasized the mathematical side of painting, the working out of the laws of perspective and the organization of
outdoor space and light by geometry and perspective.
The other aspect of the experimental trend involved the
investigation of movement and anatomical structure.

of Mainz played an important role in bringing the
process to completion. Gutenberg's Bible, completed in
1455 or 1456, was the first real book produced from
movable type.

The new printing spread rapidly throughout Europe
in the last half of the fifteenth century. Printing presses
were established throughout the Holy Roman Empire in
the 1460s and within ten years had spread to Italy, France,
the Low Countries, Spain, and eastern Europe. Especially
well known as a printing center was Venice, home by 1500
to almost one hundred printers, who among them had produced almost two million volumes.

By 1500, there were more than a thousand printers in
Europe, who collectively had published almost 40,000
titles (between eight and ten million copies). Probably 50
percent of these books were religious in character—Bibles
and biblical commentaries, books of devotion, and sermons. Next in importance were the Latin and Greek clas-

�֎ **MASACCIO, *TRIBUTE MONEY*.**   With the frescoes of Masaccio, regarded by many as the first great works of Early Renaissance art, a new realistic style of painting was born. *Tribute Money* was one of a series of frescoes that Masaccio painted in the Brancacci Chapel in the church of Santa Maria del Carmine in Florence. In illustrating a story from the Bible, Masaccio used a rational system of perspective to create a realistic relationship between the figures and their background.

Indeed, the realistic portrayal of the human nude became one of the foremost preoccupations of Italian Renaissance art. The fifteenth century, then, was a period of experimentation and technical mastery. By the end of the century, Italian painters had created a new artistic environment. Many artists had mastered the new techniques for a scientific observation of the world around them and were now ready to move into individualistic forms of creative expression. This marked the shift to the High Renaissance.

The High Renaissance was dominated by the work of three artistic giants, Leonardo da Vinci (1452–1519), Raphael (1483–1520), and Michelangelo (1475–1564). Leonardo represents a transitional figure in the shift to High Renaissance principles. He carried on the fifteenth-century experimental tradition by studying everything and even dissecting human bodies in order to better see how nature worked. But Leonardo stressed the need to advance beyond such realism and initiated the High Renaissance's preoccupation with the idealization of nature, or the attempt to generalize from realistic portrayal to an ideal form. Leonardo's *Last Supper* is a brilliant summary of fifteenth-century trends in its organization of space and use

of perspective to depict subjects three-dimensionally in a two-dimensional medium. But it is also more. The figure of Philip is idealized, and there are profound psychological dimensions to the work. The words of Jesus that "one of you shall betray me" are experienced directly as each of the apostles reveals his personality and his relationship to the Savior. In one of his notebooks, Leonardo wrote that the highest and most difficult aim of painting is to depict "the intention of man's soul." Through gestures and movement, Leonardo hoped to reveal a person's inner life.

Raphael blossomed as a painter at an early age; at twenty-five, he was already regarded as one of Italy's best painters. Raphael was acclaimed for his numerous Madonnas, in which he attempted to achieve an ideal of beauty far surpassing human standards. He is well-known for his frescoes in the Vatican Palace; his *School of Athens* reveals a world of balance, harmony, and order—basically, the underlying principles of the art of the classical world of Greece and Rome.

Michelangelo, an accomplished painter, sculptor, and architect, was another giant of the High Renaissance. Fiercely driven by his desire to create, he worked with great passion and energy on a remarkable number of projects. Michelangelo was influenced by Neoplatonism,

✿ **LEONARDO DA VINCI, *THE LAST SUPPER*.**   Leonardo da Vinci was the impetus behind the High Renaissance concern for the idealization of nature, moving from a realistic portrayal of the human figure to an idealized form. Evident in Leonardo's *Last Supper* is his effort to depict a person's character and inner nature through gesture and movement. Unfortunately, Leonardo used an experimental technique in this fresco, which soon led to its physical deterioration.

✿ **RAPHAEL, *SCHOOL OF ATHENS*.** Raphael arrived in Rome in 1508 and began to paint a series of frescoes commissioned by Pope Julius II for the papal apartments at the Vatican. In *School of Athens*, painted about 1510–1511, Raphael created an imaginary gathering of ancient philosophers. In the center stand Plato and Aristotle. At the left is Pythagoras, showing his system of proportions on a slate. At the right is Ptolemy, holding a celestial globe.

MICHELANGELO, *CREATION OF ADAM*.   In 1508, Pope Julius II recalled Michelangelo to Rome and commissioned him to decorate the ceiling of the Sistine Chapel. This colossal project was not completed until 1512. Michelangelo attempted to tell the story of the Fall of Man by depicting nine scenes from the biblical book of Genesis. In this scene, the well-proportioned figure of Adam, meant by Michelangelo to be a reflection of divine beauty, awaits the divine spark.

especially evident in his figures on the ceiling of the Sistine Chapel. These muscular figures reveal an ideal type of human being with perfect proportions. In good Neoplatonic fashion, their beauty is meant to be a reflection of divine beauty; the more beautiful the body, the more God-like the figure.

The Northern Artistic Renaissance

In trying to provide an exact portrayal of their world, the artists of the north (especially the Low Countries) and Italy took different approaches. In Italy, the human form became the primary vehicle of expression as Italian artists sought to master the technical skills that allowed them to portray humans in realistic settings. The large wall spaces of Italian churches had given rise to the art of fresco painting, but in the north, the prevalence of Gothic cathedrals with their stained glass windows resulted in more emphasis on illuminated manuscripts and wooden panel painting for altarpieces. The space available in these works was limited, and great care was required to depict each object, leading northern painters to become masters at rendering details.

The most influential northern school of art in the fifteenth century was centered in Flanders. Jan van Eyck (1380?–1441) was among the first to use oil paint, a medium that enabled the artist to use a varied range of colors and make changes to create fine details. In his *Giovanni Arnolfini and His Bride*, van Eyck's attention to detail is staggering: precise portraits, a glittering chandelier, a mirror reflecting the objects in the room, and the effects of light filtering through the window. Although each detail was rendered as observed, it is evident that van Eyck's comprehension of perspective was still uncertain. His work is truly indicative of northern Renaissance painters, who, in their effort to imitate nature, did so not by mastery of the laws of perspective and proportion, but by empirical observation of visual reality and the accurate portrayal of details. Moreover, northern painters placed great emphasis on the emotional intensity of religious feeling. Michelangelo summarized the difference between northern and Italian Renaissance painting in these words:

> In Flanders, they paint, before all things, to render exactly and deceptively the outward appearance of things. The painters choose, by preference, subjects provoking transports of piety, like the figures of saints or of prophets. But most of the time they paint what are called landscapes with plenty of figures. Though the eye is agreeably impressed, these pictures have neither choice of values nor grandeur. In short, this art is without power and without distinction; it aims at rendering minutely many things at the same time, of which a single one would have sufficed to call forth a man's whole application.[22]

JAN VAN EYCK, GIOVANNI ARNOLFINI AND HIS BRIDE.
Northern painters took great care in depicting each object and
became masters at rendering details. This emphasis on a realistic
portrayal is clearly evident in this oil painting, supposedly a
portrait of Giovanni Arnolfini, an Italian merchant who had
settled in Bruges, and his wife, Giovanna Cenami.

ALBRECHT DÜRER, ADORATION OF THE MAGI.   By
the end of the fifteenth century, northern artists began studying
in Italy and adopting many of the techniques used by Italian
painters. As is evident in this painting, which was the central
panel for an altarpiece done for Frederick the Wise in 1504,
Albrecht Dürer masterfully incorporated the laws of perspective
and the ideals of proportion into his works. At the same time, he
did not abandon the preoccupation with detail typical of
northern artists.

By the end of the fifteenth century, however, artists from
the north began to study in Italy and were visually influenced by what artists were doing there.

One northern artist of this later period who was greatly
affected by the Italians was Albrecht Dürer (1471–1528),
from Nuremberg. Dürer made two trips to Italy and
absorbed most of what the Italians could teach, as is evident in his mastery of the laws of perspective and Renaissance theories of proportion. He wrote detailed treatises
on both subjects. At the same time, as in his famous Adoration of the Magi, Dürer did not reject the use of minute
details characteristic of northern artists. He did try, however, to integrate those details more harmoniously into
his works and, like the Italian artists of the High Renaissance, tried to achieve a standard of ideal beauty by a
careful examination of the human form.

 # CONCLUSION

In the High Middle Ages, European civilization developed
many of its fundamental features. Territorial states, parliaments, capitalist trade and industry, banks, cities, and
vernacular literatures were all products of that fertile
period. During the same time, the Catholic church under
the direction of the papacy reached its apogee. Fourteenth-
century European society, however, was challenged by
an overwhelming number of disintegrative forces. Devastating plague, decline in trade and industry, bank failures, peasant revolts pitting lower classes against the upper
classes, seemingly constant warfare, aristocratic factional
conflict that undermined political stability, the absence of
the popes from Rome, and even the spectacle of two popes
condemning each other as the Antichrist all seemed to
overpower Europeans in this "calamitous century." Not
surprisingly, much of the art of the period depicted the
Four Horsemen of the Apocalypse described in the New

Testament book of Revelation: Death, Famine, Pestilence, and War. No doubt, to some people it appeared that the last days of the world were at hand.

The new European society, however, proved remarkably resilient. Periods of disintegration are usually paralleled by the emergence of new ideas and new practices. The Renaissance was a period of transition that witnessed a continuation of the economic, political, and social trends that had begun in the High Middle Ages. It was also a new age in which intellectuals and artists proclaimed a new vision of humankind and raised fundamental questions about the value and importance of the individual.

Europeans were also engaging in new adventures in the age of the Renaissance. The discovery of new trade routes to the East and the "accidental" discovery of the Americas encouraged Europeans to venture outside the medieval world in which they had been enclosed for virtually a thousand years. For much of that period, Europeans had been unable to match the achievements and splendors of civilizations in the Middle East and China. Europeans had, however, borrowed many of the tools, including gunpowder and firearms, that they would now use to move out into the world and impose their power on much of it. A new era of world history was beginning to dawn, and it is to that story that we must now turn.

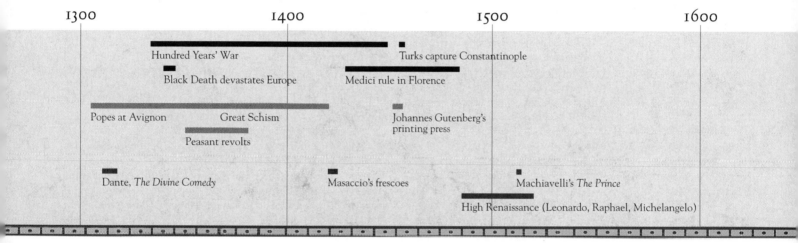

| 1300 | 1400 | 1500 | 1600 |

Hundred Years' War

Turks capture Constantinople

Black Death devastates Europe

Medici rule in Florence

Popes at Avignon   Great Schism

Johannes Gutenberg's printing press

Peasant revolts

Dante, *The Divine Comedy*   Masaccio's frescoes   Machiavelli's *The Prince*

High Renaissance (Leonardo, Raphael, Michelangelo)

❁ CHAPTER NOTES

1. Quoted in H. S. Lucas, "The Great European Famine of 1315, 1316, and 1317," *Speculum* 5 (1930): 359.
2. Quoted in David Herlihy, *The Black Death and the Transformation of the West*, ed. Samuel K. Cohn, Jr. (Cambridge, Mass., 1997), p. 9.
3. Jean Froissart, *Chronicles*, ed. and trans. Geoffrey Brereton (Harmondsworth, 1968), p. 111.
4. Quoted in Susan Stuard, "Dominion of Gender: Women's Fortunes in the High Middle Ages," in Renate Bridenthal, Claudia Koonz, and Susan Stuard, eds., *Becoming Visible: Women in European History*, 2d ed. (Boston, 1987), p. 169.
5. Froissart, *Chronicles*, p. 89.
6. Niccolò Machiavelli, *The Prince*, trans. David Wootton (Indianapolis, 1995), p. 48.
7. Ibid., p. 55.
8. Ibid., p. 27.
9. Quoted in Robert Coogan, *Babylon on the Rhone: A Translation of Letters by Dante, Petrarch, and Catherine of Siena* (Washington, D.C., 1983), p. 115.
10. Quoted in Jacob Burckhardt, *The Civilization of the Renaissance in Italy*, trans. S. G. C. Middlemore (London, 1960), p. 81.
11. Baldassare Castiglione, *The Book of the Courtier*, trans. Charles S. Singleton (Garden City, N.Y., 1959), pp. 288–89.
12. Quoted in De Lamar Jensen, *Renaissance Europe* (Lexington, Mass., 1981), p. 94.
13. Gene Brucker, ed., *Two Memoirs of Renaissance Florence* (New York, 1967), p. 132.
14. Quoted in Margaret L. King, *Women of the Renaissance* (Chicago, 1991), p. 3.
15. Giovanni Pico della Mirandola, *Oration on the Dignity of Man*, in E. Cassirer, P. O. Kristeller, J. H. Randall, Jr., eds., *The Renaissance Philosophy of Man* (Chicago, 1948), p. 225.
16. Ibid., pp. 247–49.
17. W. H. Woodward, *Vittorino da Feltre and Other Humanist Educators* (Cambridge, 1897), p. 102.
18. Quoted in Iris Origo, "The Education of Renaissance Man," in *The Light of the Past* (New York, 1959), p. 136.

19. Dante Alighieri, *The Divine Comedy*, trans. Dorothy Sayers (New York, 1962), "Paradise," Canto XXXIII, line 145.

20. Christine de Pizan, *The Book of the City of Ladies*, trans. E. Jeffrey Richards (New York, 1982), pp. 83–84.

21. Quoted in Elizabeth G. Holt, ed., *A Documentary History of Art* (Garden City, N.Y., 1957), 1:286.

22. Quoted in Johan Huizinga, *The Waning of the Middle Ages* (Garden City, N.Y., 1956), p. 265.

SUGGESTED READINGS

For a general introduction to the fourteenth and fifteenth centuries, see D. P. Waley, *Later Medieval Europe*, 2d ed. (London, 1985), and G. Holmes, *Europe: Hierarchy and Revolt, 1320–1450* (New York, 1975).

On the Black Death, see P. Ziegler, *The Black Death* (New York, 1969), and D. Herlihy, *The Black Death and the Transformation of the West*, ed. S. K. Cohn, Jr. (Cambridge, Mass., 1997). On the peasant and urban revolts of the fourteenth century, see M. Mollat and P. Wolff, *The Popular Revolutions of the Late Middle Ages* (Winchester, Mass., 1973). Brief but basic works on economic matters are H. A. Miskimin, *The Economy of Early Renaissance Europe, 1300–1460* (New York, 1975), and *The Economy of Later Renaissance Europe, 1460–1600* (New York, 1978).

Recent accounts of the Hundred Years' War include A. Curry, *The Hundred Years' War* (New York, 1993), and R. H. Neillands, *The Hundred Years' War* (New York, 1990). On Joan of Arc, see M. Warner, *Joan of Arc: The Image of Female Heroism* (New York, 1981). On the political history of the fourteenth and fifteenth centuries, see B. Guenée, *States and Rulers in Later Medieval Europe*, trans. J. Vale (Oxford, 1985). Works on individual countries and their rulers include P. M. Kendall, *Louis XI: The Universal Spider* (New York, 1971); J. R. Lander, *Crown and Nobility, 1450–1509* (London, 1976); F. R. H. Du Boulay, *Germany in the Later Middle Ages* (London, 1983); and J. N. Hillgarth, *The Spanish Kingdoms, 1250–1516*, vol. 2, *Castilian Hegemony, 1410–1516* (New York, 1978). Some good works on eastern Europe include P. W. Knoll, *The Rise of the Polish Monarchy* (Chicago, 1972), and C. A. Macartney, *Hungary: A Short History* (Edinburgh, 1962). On the fall of Constantinople, see the classic work by S. Runciman, *The Fall of Constantinople, 1453* (Cambridge, 1965).

The best overall study of the Italian states is L. Martines, *Power and Imagination: City-States in Renaissance Italy* (New York, 1979), although D. Hay and J. Law, *Italy in the Age of the Renaissance* (London, 1989) is also a good, up-to-date survey. The best introduction to Renaissance Florence is G. A. Brucker, *Renaissance Florence*, rev. ed. (New York, 1983). On the Medici period, see J. R. Hale, *Florence and the Medici: The Pattern of Control* (London, 1977). A popular biography of Isabella d'Este is G. Marek, *The Bed and the Throne* (New York, 1976). On the *condottieri*, see M. Mallett, *Mercenaries and Their Masters: Warfare in Renaissance Italy* (Totowa, N.J., 1974). Machiavelli's life can be examined in Q. Skinner, *Machiavelli* (Oxford, 1981).

A good general study of the church in the fourteenth century is F. P. Oakley, *The Western Church in the Later Middle Ages* (Ithaca, N.Y., 1980). On the Avignonese papacy, see Y. Renouard, *The Avignon Papacy, 1305–1403* (London, 1970). Aspects of the Renaissance papacy can be examined in E. Lee, *Sixtus IV and Men of Letters* (Rome, 1978); M. Mallet, *The Borgias* (New York, 1969); and P. Partner, *Renaissance Rome, 1500–1559: A Portrait of a Society* (Berkeley, Calif., 1976).

The classic study of the Italian Renaissance is J. Burckhardt, *The Civilization of the Renaissance in Italy* (London, 1960), first published in 1860. General works on the Renaissance in Europe include D. L. Jensen, *Renaissance Europe*, 2d ed. (Lexington, Mass., 1991); P. Burke, *The European Renaissance: Centres and Peripheries* (Oxford, 1998); E. Breisach, *Renaissance Europe, 1300–1517* (New York, 1973); J. Hale, *The Civilization of Europe in the Renaissance* (New York, 1994); and the classic work by M. P. Gilmore, *The World of Humanism, 1453–1517* (New York, 1962). For a good summary of recent literature on the Renaissance, see P. Burke, *The Renaissance* (New York, 1997). For beautifully illustrated introductions to the Renaissance, see G. Holmes, *Renaissance* (New York, 1996), and M. Aston, ed., *The Panorama of the Renaissance* (New York, 1996).

Numerous facets of social life in the Renaissance are examined in J. R. Hale, *Renaissance Europe: The Individual and Society* (London, 1971); B. Pullan, *Rich and Poor in Renaissance Venice* (Cambridge, Mass., 1971); and G. Ruggiero, *The Boundaries of Eros: Sex Crime and Sexuality in Renaissance Venice* (Oxford, 1985). On family and marriage, see D. Herlihy, *The Family in Renaissance Italy* (St. Louis, 1974); the valuable C. Klapisch-Zuber, *Women, Family, and Ritual in Renaissance Italy* (Chicago, 1985); and the well-told story by G. Brucker, *Giovanni and Lusanna: Love and Marriage in Renaissance Florence* (Berkeley, Calif., 1986). Women are examined in M. L. King, *Women of the Renaissance* (Chicago, 1991).

Brief introductions to Renaissance humanism can be found in D. Kelley, *Renaissance Humanism* (Boston, 1991), and C. G. Nauert, Jr., *Humanism and the Culture of Renaissance Europe* (Cambridge, 1995). The fundamental work on fifteenth-century civic humanism is H. Baron, *The Crisis of the Early Italian Renaissance*, 2d ed. (Princeton, N.J., 1966). The impact of printing is exhaustively examined in E. Eisenstein, *The Printing Press as an Agent of Change*, 2 vols. (New York, 1978). The best work on Christine de Pizan is by C. C. Willard, *Christine de Pizan: Her Life and Works* (New York, 1984). Good surveys of Renaissance art include R. Turner, *Renaissance Florence: The Invention of a New Art* (New York, 1997); F. Hartt, *History of Italian Renaissance Art*, 4th ed. (Englewood Cliffs, N.J., 1994); and L. Murray, *The High Renaissance* (New York, 1967). Also of value is B. Cole, *The Renaissance Artist at Work from Pisano to Titian* (London, 1983).

INFOTRAC COLLEGE EDITION

For additional reading, go to InfoTrac College Edition, your online research library at
http://web1.infotrac-college.com

Enter the search terms "Middle Ages" using the Subject Guide.

Enter the search terms "Black Death" using Keywords.

Enter the search terms "Medieval England" using Keywords.

Enter the search term "Renaissance" using the Subject Guide.

Enter the search term "Machiavelli" using Keywords.

REFLECTION

NEW PATTERNS OF CIVILIZATION

In Part II of this book, we examined the period that followed the collapse of the civilizations of antiquity down to the end of the fifteenth century, a date that marks the beginning of the European Age of Exploration and the inauguration of a new stage of world history. During this period of over one thousand years, a number of significant forces were at work in human society. The concept of civilization gradually spread from such heartland regions as the Middle East, the Mediterranean basin, the South Asian subcontinent, and China into new areas of the world—to sub-Saharan Africa, to central and western Europe, to Southeast Asia, and even to the islands of Japan, off the eastern edge of the Eurasian landmass. Across the oceans, unique but advanced civilizations began to take shape in the Americas. In the meantime, the vast migration of peoples continued, leading not only to bitter conflict but also to increased interchange of technology as well as ideas. The end result was the transformation of separate and distinct cultures and civilizations into an increasingly complex and vast world system embracing not only technology and trade, but also ideas and religious beliefs. Although this world system did not by any means extend to all the peoples and societies in the world—the Amerindian civilizations in the New World were almost certainly totally isolated from it, as were peoples living in stateless societies in various parts of Africa and Asia—its network of goods and ideas extended from the Atlantic to the Pacific and created (in a phrase often used today) an interdependent world, in which the economic livelihood, the physical well-being, and even the religious beliefs of one people were linked to the fate of other peoples often living thousands of miles away.

What explains this explosion in human activity? Certainly one answer is the advance in technology. Better technology, in the form of improved irrigation methods, the introduction of new crops, and the increased use of the iron plow, led to a substantial rise in food production, thus creating wealth that could be used for the purchase of other goods. Improved technology also contributed to advances in ship construction and navigational techniques. Other factors were the mastery of monsoon patterns in the Indian Ocean and the domestication of the camel in North Africa and the Middle East. The wealth brought about by increased trade undoubtedly helped to stimulate the demand for new luxury goods and other commodities, many of which could only be imported from foreign countries. During the first millennium C.E., the great trade routes of the traditional world—the Silk Road from China to the Middle East and then on to the Mediterranean, the caravan trade across the Sahara, and the maritime network that stretched across the Indian Ocean—all reached their maturity.

As had been the case during antiquity, the Middle East was the heart of this activity. During the first centuries of the first millennium C.E., trade passing through the region declined as a result of the collapse of the Han dynasty and the Roman Empire, but it began to revive in the sixth century and then spurted forward with the rise of the Tang in China and the gradual revival of societies in the Mediterranean. The Arab Empire, which took shape after the death of Muhammad in the early seventh century, provided the key link in the revived trade routes through the region. Muslim traders—both Arab and Berber—opened contacts with West African societies south of the Sahara, while their ships followed the monsoon winds eastward as far as the Spice Islands in Southeast Asia. Nomads from Central Asia carried goods back and forth along the Silk Road between the Middle East and China. For the next several hundred years, the great cities of the Middle East— Mecca, Damascus, and Baghdad—became among the wealthiest in the known world. The great Chinese city of Chang'an lay at the eastern extremity of the Silk Road as it snaked eastward across Central Asia.

Islam's contributions to the human experience during this period were cultural and technological as well as economic. Muslim philosophers preserved the works of the ancient Greeks for posterity, Muslim scientists and mathematicians made new discoveries about the nature of the universe and the human body, and Arab cartographers and historians mapped the known world and speculated about the fundamental forces in human society. The mosques in Córdoba and Cairo were built with techniques unknown to the architects and engineers of medieval Europe.

But the Middle East was not the only or necessarily even the primary contributor to world trade and civilization during this period. While the Arab Empire became the linchpin of trade between the Mediterranean and eastern and southern Asia, a new center of primary importance in world trade was emerging in East Asia, focused on China. China had been a major participant in regional trade during the Han dynasty, when its silks were already being transported to Rome via Central Asia, but its role had declined after the fall of the Han. Now, with the rise of the great Tang and Song dynasties, China reemerged as a major commercial power in East Asia, trading by sea with Southeast Asia and Japan and by land with the nomadic peoples of Central Asia. In general, overland trade was carried on by non-Chinese peoples in Central Asia, but the Chinese themselves became directly involved in the maritime trade with the countries in the South Seas.

By now, China was not only a regional economic power, but a global one as well. The Silk Road through Turkestan became one of the most important trade routes of the era, and during the Ming dynasty, Chinese fleets briefly sailed across the Indian Ocean as far as the Red Sea and the eastern coast of Africa.

Like the Middle East, China was also a prime source of new technology. From China came paper, printing, and

TRADE AND CIVILIZATION

Traditionally, historians have viewed the great civilizations that arose in the classical era as essentially autonomous entities, each representing the product of its own local environment. In Part I, we sought to qualify that assumption by pointing out that even in antiquity, the great river valley civilizations had already begun to learn from each other. While each civilization was unique and distinctive, they had all been influenced in various ways by developments taking place beyond their frontiers.

Between 500 and 1500, the level of interdependence among human societies began to intensify, as three major trade routes—the Indian Ocean, the Silk Road, and the trans-Saharan caravan route—began to create the framework for a single world trade system. New technology, new crops, and new ideas crossed from one end of the known world to the other. Contacts occurred in the realm of technology as in that of ideas, including inventions such as paper, the compass, and gunpowder; crops such as sugar, cotton, and spices; and great religious systems such as Buddhism, Hinduism, Christianity, and Islam. One interesting aspect of this process was the close relationship between missionary activities and trade. Buddhist merchants first brought the teachings of Siddhartha Gautama to China, and Muslim traders carried the words of the prophet Muhammad to Southeast Asia and sub-Saharan Africa. At the same time, Christian missionaries may have brought the first accurate knowledge of silk manufacturing from China to the Mediterranean.

What were the major causes of the rapid expansion of trade during this period? One key factor was the introduction of new technology in the field of transportation. The development of the compass, improved techniques in mapmaking

✸ ARAB MERCHANTS IN A CARAVAN.
By land or by sea, Arab trade routes extended over half the globe. The world of Islam and the camel, both portrayed in this thirteenth-century miniature, were essential components of Muslim commercial ventures.

and shipbuilding, and greater knowledge of wind patterns all contributed to the expansion of maritime trade far from familiar shores. Caravan trade, once carried by wheeled chariots or on the backs of oxen, now used the camel as the preferred beast of burden through the parched deserts of Africa and the Middle East. With its ability to store considerable amounts of food and water in its hump, the camel was well equipped to handle the arduous conditions of the desert and soon became the standard means by which nomads carried goods from oasis to oasis on the long trek to their eventual destination.

Another factor in the expansion of commerce during this period was the appearance of several multinational empires that created zones of stability and affluence in key areas from North Africa eastward toward the Pacific. Central to the process was the emergence of the empire of the Abbasids in the Middle East, which created, in the words of the historian K. N. Chaudhuri, "an enormously powerful zone of economic consumption" throughout the region. To the east was China, which reached a zenith of prosperity during the Tang and Song dynasties; to the west was Europe, slowly emerging from the collapse of the Roman Empire. In the thirteenth century, the Mongol invasions brought this era to an end but then created a new era of peace and stability that lasted for over a century and fostered long-distance trade throughout the known world.

The global impact of the expansion in international commerce was enormous. Although humans still had only a limited awareness of their fellow creatures (Europeans, after all, still knew almost nothing about Chinese civilization), the stage was set for a more dramatic period of expansion in the near future.

FEUDAL ORDERS AROUND THE WORLD

When we use the word *feudalism*, we usually think of European knights on horseback clad in iron coats and armed with sword and lance. However, between 800 and 1500, a form of social organization that a later generation of historians called feudalism developed in different parts of the world. By the term *feudalism*, these historians meant a decentralized political order in which local lords owed loyalty and provided military service to a king or more powerful lord. In Europe, a feudal order based on lords and vassals arose between 800 and 900 and flourished for the next four hundred years.

In Japan, a feudal order much like that found in Europe developed between 800 and 1500. By the end of the ninth century, powerful nobles in the countryside, while owing a loose loyalty to the Japanese emperor, began to exercise political and legal power in their own extensive lands. In order to protect their property and security, these nobles retained samurai, or warriors who owed loyalty to the nobles and provided military service for them. Like knights in Europe, the samurai followed a warrior code and fought on horseback, clad in iron. However, they carried a sword and bow and arrow rather than a sword and lance.

In some respects, the political relationships among the Indian states beginning in the fifth century took on the character of the feudal system that emerged in Europe in the Middle Ages. Like medieval European lords, local Indian rajas were technically vassals of the king, but unlike in European feudalism, the relationship was not a contractual one. Still, the Indian model became highly complex, with "inner" and "outer" vassals, depending on their physical or political proximity to the king, and "greater" or "lesser" vassals, depending on their power and influence. As in Europe, the vassals themselves often had vassals. The one constant factor was the perennial state of rivalry and civil strife that characterized the vassals' relationships and plagued the lives of ordinary Indians.

In the Valley of Mexico, the Aztecs developed a political system between 1300 and 1500 that bore some similarities to the Japanese, Indian, and European feudal orders. Although the Aztec king was a powerful, authoritarian ruler, the local rulers of lands outside the capital city were allowed considerable freedom. However, they did pay tribute to the king and also provided him with military forces. Unlike the knights and samurai of Europe and Japan, however, Aztec warriors were armed with sharp knives made of stone and spears of wood fitted with razor-sharp blades cut from stone.

❀ A KNIGHT'S EQUIPMENT.

Pictured here is a charging European knight with his equipment. The introduction of the high saddle, stirrups, and larger horses allowed horsemen to wear heavier armor and to wield long lances. Compare the equipment of the European knight to that of the samurai warrior on page 301.

the compass as well as gunpowder. The double-hulled Chinese junks that entered the Indian Ocean during the Ming dynasty were slow and cumbersome but extremely seaworthy and capable of carrying substantial quantities of goods over long distances. Among China's other contributions were porcelain, chess, the mechanical clock, and the iron stirrup. Many such inventions arrived in Europe by way of India or the Middle East, and therefore their Chinese origins were unknown in the West.

Increasing trade on a regional or global basis also led to the exchange of ideas. Buddhism was brought to China by merchants, and Islam first arrived in sub-Saharan Africa and the Indonesian archipelago in the same manner. In their new environments, these religions initially had an impact mainly on other merchant groups and in the cities, but in some cases they gradually gained favor in the countryside. Sometimes this was the result of support from kings or princes, who viewed conversion to the new faith as politically or economically advantageous. Not all religions, of course, succeeded in transplanting themselves. Although a small community of Christians established roots in Central Asia and China, their religion was never able to make the transition to a mass faith.

Merchants were not the only way religious and cultural ideas spread, however. Sometimes migration, conquest, or relatively peaceful processes played a part. The case of the Bantu-speaking peoples in Central Africa is apparently an example of peaceful expansion; while Islam sometimes followed the path of Arab warriors, although they apparently rarely imposed their religion by force on the local population. In some instances, as with the Mongols, the conquerors made no effort to convert others to their own religions. Christian monks, motivated by missionary fervor, converted many of the peoples of central and eastern Europe. Roman Catholic monks brought Latin Christianity to the Germanic and western Slavic peoples, while monks from the Byzantine Empire largely converted the southern and eastern Slavic populations to Eastern Orthodox Christianity.

How precisely did the exchange of ideas and beliefs work during this period? According to Jerry Bentley, author of *Old World Encounters: Cross-Cultural Contacts and Exchanges in Pre-Modern Times,* the process was quite complex and varied considerably, depending on the time and place. When conversion to a different religion did occur, it usually took place over a protracted period of time and was undertaken primarily for practical reasons. Those who attempted to promote conversions often used incentives or various forms of punishment for noncompliance, such as exemption from taxation for Muslims. One way to facilitate conversions was to use the syncretic technique—to relate or identify new beliefs and rituals to familiar ones, as Buddhists did by adopting Daoist concepts in China.

Attempts at conversion did not always work. Sometimes new religions were resisted fiercely, as the Christians in the Balkans and Spain resisted Islam. On the other hand, conversion to Christianity was resisted in the Middle East during the Crusades and in Central Asia during the Mongol era. In general, Islam and Buddhism were the most successful. Islam spread quite quickly and readily throughout the Middle East and Central Asia as well as in much of North Africa, while Buddhism took root in China, Japan, and Southeast Asia.

Why were conversion efforts successful in some areas but not in others? In the case of Islam, successful conversion was often the result of strong state sponsorship, as well as a variety of incentives such as exemption from the poll tax and access to various means of livelihood. Islam also undoubtedly benefited from its egalitarian character and its association with material rewards. This was apparently the case in Africa as well as in much of Central Asia. The success of Buddhism in China and Southeast Asia can be partly ascribed to state support, but also to its salvationist message in societies that did not possess any other form of universal world religion. In general, it seems clear that conversion was easier and much more likely to succeed in societies that did not already possess a world religion. Where such religions already existed, as in India and much of Europe, conversion to Islam was less likely. Followers of Gautama Buddha had the same experience in India.

In any event, as Bentley points out, conversion usually was an extended process, even when it did occur. Although the conversion to Islam in much of the Middle East was relatively rapid, it took much longer among the Berbers. Buddhism took several hundred years to spread beyond the urban community in China and among the Mongol tribal peoples.

Even when conversion did take place, key elements of the core doctrine were often changed to adapt to new circumstances. Buddhism in China took on a strong local character, as did Islam in Southeast Asia, where it was forced to coexist with existing spirit beliefs. The practice of Christianity was much different in the Byzantine Empire than it was in areas controlled by the pope in Rome. In the end, religion took on much of the color of local society.

The same can be said about the transfer of political and social institutions from one society to another. Throughout this period, ruling elites in societies along the periphery of the major empires borrowed liberally from the political and social systems of their more powerful neighbors as a means of strengthening their own power and status. Confucian ideology, Muslim law, and the Indian god-king concept were also useful in hastening the state-building process. Similarly, the influence of patriarchal values emanating from China, India, and the Middle East gradually took root in the small societies in Southeast Asia and sub-Saharan Africa. Still, impact was always limited by local conditions. In Japan, Korea, and Vietnam, Confucian values were significantly altered to fit the local environment, as were Indian values after crossing the Bay of Bengal to the rising states of Southeast Asia. In Africa, Muslim travelers were sometimes scandalized by the degree of freedom possessed by women in states that had already accepted the word of the Koran.

Another characteristic of the period between 500 and 1500 C.E. was the almost constant migration of nomadic and seminomadic peoples. Dynamic forces in the Gobi Desert, Central Asia, the Arabian peninsula, and Central Africa provoked vast numbers of peoples to abandon their homelands and seek their livelihood elsewhere. Sometimes the migration was peaceful, as was apparently the case with the Bantu-speaking peoples in Central Africa. More often than not, however, migration produced violent conflict and sometimes invasion and subjugation. Peoples had been moving since the earliest times, as human communities shifted their habitat in search of grazing lands, herds, or fertile lands for agriculture, and migration continued to be a major factor in this period. As had been the case during antiquity, the most active source of migration was Central Asia. From here, Turkic-speaking peoples spilled over the Hindu Kush into northern India, southwest into Persia, and farther west into the Balkans in southeastern Europe. Later, Central Asia gave birth to an even more fearsome force in the form of the Mongols. Mongol expansion began with the unification of Mongol tribes in the Gobi Desert by Genghis Khan and culminated in the advance of Mongolian armies to the gates of central Europe and the conquest of China in the thirteenth century. Wherever they went, they left a train of enormous destruction and loss of life. Contemporaries recount that entire cities were laid waste, and their populations massacred and irrigation networks destroyed. Inadvertently, the Mongols were also the source of a new wave of epidemics that swept through much of Europe and the Middle East in the fourteenth century. The spread of the plague known at the time as the Black Death—took much of the population of Europe to an early grave.

But there was another side to the era of nomadic expansion. Often, as historian Thomas J. Barfield has noted, the nomadic peoples had a symbiotic relationship with the sedentary societies, propping up governments like the Tang dynasty in China in order to protect their source of income. Once nomadic warriors completed their conquests, they settled down to become administrators. Often the results were constructive. The spread of Islam across the Middle East and North Africa not only introduced millions of people to a dynamic new faith but brought a measure of political stability and economic prosperity to the area that it had not possessed since the fall of the Persian Empire. German migrations and Viking incursions contributed to the creation of dynamic new societies in Europe, while Turkish invasions led to the rise of states in the Anatolian Peninsula and North India.

Even the invasions of the Mongols—the "scourge of God" as Europeans of the thirteenth and fourteenth centuries called them—had constructive as well as destructive consequences. After their initial conquests, for a brief period of three generations, the Mongols provided an avenue for trade throughout the most extensive empire (known as the Pax Mongolica) the world had yet seen. When the pope dispatched envoys to the imperial court in Mongolia in the mid-thirteenth century, it was the first time Europeans had traveled the entire distance by land to East Asia.

What had caused this vast movement of peoples? Probably a number of factors were involved, but perhaps the major ones were ecological—changes in the climate or the exhaustion of the land by population pressure. Exhaustion of the land may have driven the Bantu peoples from their original habitat in the Niger River valley and forced the Aztecs and related Amerindian communities into the Valley of Mexico. Other peoples, such as the Thai and the Burmese, may have been forced to move into Southeast Asia because they in turn had been displaced by new arrivals in their own territories.

The Mongols were the last, and arguably the greatest, of the nomadic peoples who came thundering out of the steppes of Central Asia, pillaging and conquering the territories of their adversaries all the way to the shores of the South Pacific and the plains of eastern Europe. What caused this extraordinary burst of energy, and why were the Mongols so much more successful than their predecessors? Historians are divided. Some have suggested that drought and overpopulation may have depleted the available pasture on the steppes. Others have cited the ambition and genius of Genghis Khan, who was able to arouse a sense of personal loyalty unusual in a society where commitments were ordinarily tribal in nature. Still others point to his reliance on the organizational unit known as the *ordos*, described by the historian S. A. M. Adshead as "a system of restructuring tribes into decimal units whose top level of leadership was organized on bureaucratic lines." Although the *ordos* system had been used by other nomadic peoples before them, the Mongols applied it to create disciplined military units that were especially effective against the mobile tactics of their rivals on the steppes and devastating against the relatively immobile armies of the sedentary states in their path. Once organized, the Mongols used their superior horsemanship and blitzkrieg tactics effectively, while taking advantage of divisions within the enemy ranks and borrowing more advanced military technology. Once in power, however, the Mongols' underlying weaknesses eventually proved fatal. Unlike some of their predecessors, the Mongols had difficulty making the transition from the nomadic life of the steppes to the sedentary life of conquered peoples. Still, although the Mongol era was a relatively brief interlude in the long sweep of human history, it was rich in consequences.

The approximately thousand-year period following the destruction of the ancient empires brought about enormous changes in human society. During the era of Mongol expansion there was widespread death and suffering throughout the known world. At the same time, by the early fifteenth century the world had witnessed a significant expansion in the technological and material capacity of human societies and in the depth of contact among

them. The era of widespread peace brought about as the result of the Mongol conquests also inaugurated what one scholar has described as the "idea of the unified conceptualization of the globe," creating a "basic information circuit" that spread commodities, ideas, and inventions from one end of the Eurasian supercontinent to the other. The way was prepared for a new stage of world history.

 ## SUGGESTED READINGS

The importance of international trade in this period is discussed in P. D. Curtin, *Cross-Cultural Trade in World History* (Cambridge, 1984); Janet L. Abu-Lughod, *Before European Hegemony, the World System A.D. 1250–1350* (New York, 1989); M. Adas, ed., *Islamic and European Expansion: The Forging of a Global Order* (Philadelphia, 1993); and J. D. Tracy, *The Political Economy of Merchant Empires: State Power and World Trade, 1350–1750* (New York, 1991). For an informative study on the exchange of ideas and beliefs, see J. H. Bentley, *Old World Encounters: Cross-Cultural Contacts and Exchanges in Pre-Modern Times* (New York, 1993). The migration of nomadic peoples is examined in S. A. M. Adshead, *Central Asia in World History* (New York, 1993), and T. S. Barfield, *The Perilous Frontier: Nomadic Empires and China* (Cambridge, Mass., 1989).

1000 C.E.	1100 C.E.	1200 C.E.	1300 C.E.	1400 C.E.	1500 C.E.

in northern India

Conquest of Baghdad by the Mongols

Ottoman Turks seize Constantinople

Portuguese ships explore West African coast

Kingdom of Zimbabwe

Spread of Mongols across East Asia

Beginning of Ming dynasty in China

Civilization of Chimor

Kingdom of the Aztecs

Rise of European kingdoms

The Black Death

The Renaissance in Italy

PART III

THE EMERGENCE OF NEW WORLD PATTERNS

(1500–1800)

Beginning in the late fifteenth century, a new force entered the world scene in the form of a revived Europe. The period of history known as the early modern era (1500–1800) was marked in Europe by an explosion of scientific knowledge and the appearance of a new secular ideology that emphasized the power of human beings to dominate nature and improve their material surroundings. After the breakdown of Christian unity in the Reformation era, Europeans engaged in a vigorous period of state building that resulted in the creation of independent monarchies in western and central Europe, which formed the basis for a new European state system.

The rise of early modern Europe had an immediate as well as a long-term impact on the rest of the world. The first stage began with the discovery of the Americas by Christopher Columbus in 1492 and the equally important voyages of Vasco da Gama and Ferdinand Magellan into the Indian and Pacific Oceans. These voyages and those that followed—collectively known as the Age of Discovery or Age of Exploration—not only injected European sea power into new areas of the world, but also vastly extended the maritime trade network, until for the first time it literally encircled the globe. Some historians have labeled this period the beginning of an era of European dominance.

Significant as it was, however, the emergence of Europe as a major player on the world stage was by no means the only important feature of this period. An excessive emphasis on the expanding European civilization tends to overlook the fact that other areas of the world were realizing impressive achievements of their own. Two great new Islamic empires, the Ottomans in Turkey and the Safavids in Persia, arose in the Middle East, while a third—the Mughals—unified the Indian subcontinent for the first time in nearly two thousand years. The religion of Islam was now firmly established in Africa south of the Sahara, and as far east as the Indonesian archipelago.

Another area of the world where the level of achievement was little affected by the European revival was East Asia. Portuguese merchants reached the coast of China in the early sixteenth century and landed on the islands of Japan a generation later. Merchants and missionaries from various European countries were active in both countries by the end of the century. But the ruling authorities in China and Japan, like their counterparts in the mainland states in Southeast Asia, became increasingly wary of the impact of Europeans activities on their own societies, and by the eighteenth century the Western presence in the region had markedly declined.

The first thrust of European expansion, then, significantly changed the shape of the world, but it did not firmly establish European dominance. China remained, in the eyes of many, the most advanced and sophisticated civilization on the face of the earth, and its achievements were imitated by its neighbors and admired by philosophers in far-off Europe. The era of Muslim dominance over the seas had come to an end, but Islam was still a force to be reckoned with. The bulk of Africa remained essentially outside the purview of European influence.

CHAPTER

14

NEW ENCOUNTERS: THE CREATION OF A WORLD MARKET

CHAPTER OUTLINE
- AN AGE OF EXPLORATION AND EXPANSION
- AFRICA IN AN ERA OF TRANSITION
- SOUTHEAST ASIA IN THE ERA OF THE SPICE TRADE
- CONCLUSION

FOCUS QUESTIONS
- Why did Europeans begin to embark on voyages of discovery and expansion at the end of the fifteenth century?
- How did Portugal and Spain acquire their overseas empires, and how did their empires differ?
- How and why did the Europeans expand into Africa, and what were the main consequences of their presence there?
- What were the main features of the African slave trade, and what effects did it have on Africa?
- What were the main characteristics of Southeast Asian civilization, and how was it affected by the coming of Islam and the Europeans?

When a local official asked the Portuguese explorer Vasco da Gama why he had come all the way to India from his homeland in Europe, the latter replied simply, "Christians and spices." Da Gama might have been more accurate if he had reversed the order of his objectives. As it turned out, God was probably much less important than gold and glory to Europeans like himself who participated in the Age of Exploration that was already under way. Still, da Gama's comments at Calicut were an accurate forecast of the future, for his voyage inaugurated an extended period of European expansion into Asia, led by merchant adventurers and missionaries, that lasted for several hundred years and had effects that are still felt today. Eventually, it resulted in a Western takeover of existing trade routes in the Indian Ocean and the establishment of colonies throughout Asia, Africa, and

Latin America. So complete did Western dominance seem that some historians assumed that the peoples of the non-Western world were mere passive recipients in this process, absorbing and assimilating the advanced knowledge of the West and offering nothing in return. Historians writing about the period after 1500 often talked metaphorically about the "impact of the West" and the "response" of non-Western peoples.

That image of impact and response, however, is not an entirely accurate description of what took place between the end of the fifteenth and the end of the eighteenth century. Although European rule was firmly established in Latin America and the island regions of Southeast Asia, traditional governments and institutions elsewhere remained largely intact and, in some areas, notably South Asia and the Middle East, displayed considerable vitality. Moreover, although da Gama and his contemporaries are deservedly famous for their contribution to a new era of maritime commerce that circled the globe, they were not alone in extending the world trade network and transporting goods and ideas from one end of the earth to the other. Islam, too, was on the march, blazing new trails into Southeast Asia and across the Sahara to the civilizations that flourished along the banks of the Niger River. In this chapter we shall turn our attention to the stunning expansion in the scope and volume of commercial and cultural contacts that took place in the generations preceding and following da Gama's historic voyage to India, as well as to the factors that brought about this expansion. ✿

AN AGE OF EXPLORATION AND EXPANSION

The voyage of Vasco da Gama has customarily been seen as a crucial step in the opening of trade routes to the East. In the sense that the voyage was a harbinger of future European participation in the spice trade, this view undoubtedly has merit. In fact, however, as has been pointed out in earlier chapters, the Indian Ocean had been a busy thoroughfare for centuries. The spice trade had been carried on by sea in the region since the days of the legendary Queen of Sheba, and Chinese junks had sailed to the area in search of cloves and nutmeg since the Tang dynasty. Then, during the early fifteenth century, Chinese fleets sailed into the Indian Ocean and all the way to the coast of East Africa in search of trade and alliances (see Chapter 17).

Islam and the Spice Trade

By the fourteenth century, a growing percentage of the spice trade was being transported in Muslim ships sailing from ports in India or the Middle East. Muslims, either Arabs or Indian converts, had taken part in the Indian Ocean trade for centuries, and by the thirteenth century, Islam had established a presence in seaports on the islands of Sumatra and Java and was gradually moving inland. In 1292 the Venetian traveler Marco Polo observed that Muslims were engaging in missionary activity in northern Sumatra: "This kingdom is so much frequented by the Saracen merchants that they have converted the natives to the Law of Mahomet—I mean the townspeople only, for the hill people live for all the world like beasts, and eat human flesh, as well as other kinds of flesh, clean or unclean."[1]

But the major impact of Islam came in the early fifteenth century with the rise of the new sultanate at Malacca, whose founder was a Muslim convert. With its strategic location astride the strait of the same name, Malacca "is a city that was made for commerce; . . . the trade and commerce between the different nations for a thousand leagues on every hand must come to Malacca,"[2] said a sixteenth-century Portuguese visitor. Within a few years, Malacca had surpassed the old Hindu state of Majapahit on the island of Java and become the leading power in the region.

Unfortunately for the Muslim traders who had come to Southeast Asia for the spice trade, others would also covet that trade. Although China's interest in the area would soon come to an end, the arrival of Vasco da Gama's fleet was a sure sign that others would soon follow. Southeast Asia was on the verge of a new era in which outside forces would compete aggressively to exploit the region's vast riches.

A New Player Enters the Game

For almost a millennium, Catholic Europe had been confined to one area. Its one major attempt to expand beyond those frontiers, the Crusades, had largely failed. Of course, Europe had never completely lost contact with the outside world: the goods of Asia and Africa made their way into medieval castles; the works of Muslim philosophers were read in medieval universities; and the Vikings in the

❋ MAP 14.1 European Voyages and Possessions in the Sixteenth and Seventeenth Centuries

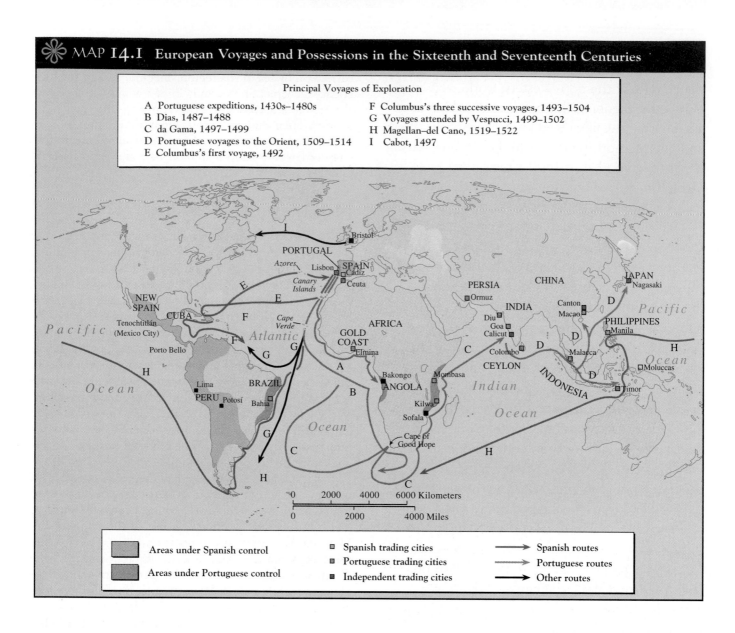

Principal Voyages of Exploration

A Portuguese expeditions, 1430s–1480s
B Dias, 1487–1488
C da Gama, 1497–1499
D Portuguese voyages to the Orient, 1509–1514
E Columbus's first voyage, 1492

F Columbus's three successive voyages, 1493–1504
G Voyages attended by Vespucci, 1499–1502
H Magellan–del Cano, 1519–1522
I Cabot, 1497

Areas under Spanish control
Areas under Portuguese control

□ Spanish trading cities
□ Portuguese trading cities
■ Independent trading cities

→ Spanish routes
→ Portuguese routes
→ Other routes

ninth and tenth centuries had even made their way to the eastern fringes of North America. Nevertheless, Europe's contacts with non-European civilizations remained limited until the end of the fifteenth century, when Europeans embarked on a remarkable series of overseas journeys. What caused European seafarers to undertake such dangerous voyages to the ends of the earth?

Europeans had long been attracted to the east. In the Middle Ages, myths and legends of an exotic land of great riches and magic were widespread. Although Muslim control of Central Asia cut Europe off from the countries further east, the Mongol conquests in the thirteenth century had reopened the doors. The most famous medieval travelers to the East were the Polos of Venice. In 1271, Nicolò and Maffeo, merchants from Venice, accompanied by Nicolò's son Marco, undertook the lengthy journey to the court of the great Mongol ruler Khubilai Khan (see Chapter 10). As one of the great Khan's ambassadors,

Marco traveled to Japan as well and did not return to Italy until 1295. An account of his experiences, the *Travels*, proved to be the most informative of all the descriptions of Asia by medieval European travelers. Others, like the Franciscan friar John Plano Carpini, had preceded the Polos, but in the fourteenth century the conquests of the Ottoman Turks and then the breakup of the Mongol Empire reduced Western traffic to the east. With the closing of the overland routes, a number of people in Europe became interested in the possibility of reaching Asia by sea. Christopher Columbus had a copy of Marco Polo's *Travels* in his possession when he began to envision his epoch-making voyage across the Atlantic Ocean.

An economic motive thus looms large in Renaissance European expansion. The rise of capitalism in Europe was undoubtedly a powerful spur to the process. Merchants, adventurers, and government officials had high hopes of finding precious metals and expanding the areas of trade, especially for the spices of the East. The latter continued to be transported to Europe via Arab intermediaries but were outrageously expensive. Adventurous Europeans did not hesitate to express their desire to share in the wealth. As one Spanish conquistador explained, he and his kind went to the New World to "serve God and His Majesty, to give light to those who were in darkness, and to grow rich, as all men desire to do."[3]

This statement expresses another major reason for the overseas voyages—religious zeal. A crusading mentality was particularly strong in Portugal and Spain, where the Muslims had largely been driven out in the Middle Ages. Contemporaries of Prince Henry the Navigator of Portugal (see the next section) said that he was motivated by "his great desire to make increase in the faith of our Lord Jesus Christ and to bring him all the souls that should be saved." The naval academy established by the prince to promote overseas exploration was subsidized in part by a militantly anti-Muslim Christian brotherhood. Although most scholars believe that the religious motive was secondary to economic considerations, it would be foolish to overlook the genuine desire on the part of both explorers and conquistadors, let alone missionaries, to convert the heathen to Christianity. Hernán Cortés, the conqueror of Mexico, asked his Spanish rulers if it was not their duty to ensure that the native Mexicans "are introduced into

and instructed in the holy Catholic faith."[4] Spiritual and secular affairs were closely intertwined in the sixteenth century. No doubt, grandeur and glory as well as plain intellectual curiosity and a spirit of adventure also played some role in European expansion.

If "God, glory, and gold" were the primary motives, what made the voyages possible? First of all, the expansion of Europe was a state enterprise, tied to the growth of centralized monarchies during the Renaissance. By the second half of the fifteenth century, European monarchies had increased both their authority and their resources and were in a position to turn their energies beyond their borders. That meant the invasion of Italy for France, but for Portugal, a state not strong enough to pursue power in Europe, it meant going abroad. The Spanish scene was more complex, since the Spanish monarchy was strong enough by the sixteenth century to pursue power on both the continent and beyond.

At the same time, by the end of the fifteenth century, European states had a level of knowledge and technology that enabled them to achieve a regular series of voyages beyond Europe. Although the highly schematic and symbolic medieval maps were of little help to sailors, the *portolani*, or detailed charts made by medieval navigators and mathematicians in the thirteenth and fourteenth centuries, were more useful. With details on coastal contours, distances between ports, and compass readings, they proved of great value for voyages in European waters. But because the *portolani* were drawn on a flat scale and took no account of the curvature of the earth, they were of little use for longer overseas voyages. Only when seafarers began to venture beyond the coasts of Europe did they begin to accumulate information about the actual shape of the earth. By the end of the fifteenth century, cartography had developed to the point that Europeans possessed fairly accurate maps of the known world.

In addition, Europeans had developed remarkably seaworthy ships as well as new navigational techniques.

❀ **A SIXTEENTH-CENTURY MAP OF AFRICA.**
Advances in mapmaking also contributed to the European Age of Exploration. Here a section of a world map by the early-sixteenth-century Spanish cartographer Juan de la Cosa shows the continent of Africa. Note the drawing of the legendary Prester John, mentioned in Chapter 8, at the right, and the Portuguese caravels with their lateen sails in the South Atlantic Ocean.

European shipmakers had mastered the use of the stern-post rudder (an import from China) and had learned how to combine the use of lateen sails with a square rig. With these innovations, they could construct ships mobile enough to sail against the wind and engage in naval warfare and also large enough to mount heavy cannon and carry a substantial amount of goods over long distances. Previously, sailors had used a quadrant and their knowledge of the position of the polestar to ascertain their latitude. Below the equator, however, this technique was useless. Only with the assistance of new navigational aids such as the compass and the astrolabe (an astronomical instrument used to measure the altitude of the sun and the stars above the horizon) were they able to explore the high seas with confidence.

A final spur to exploration was the growing knowledge of the wind patterns in the Atlantic Ocean (see Map 14.4, on p. 420). The first European fleets sailing southward along the coast of West Africa had found their efforts to return hindered by the strong winds that blew steadily from the north along the coast. By the late fifteenth century, however, sailors had learned to tack out into the ocean, where they were able to catch westerly winds in the vicinity of the Azores islands that brought them back to the coast of western Europe. Christopher Columbus used this technique in his voyages to the Americas, and others relied on their new knowledge of the winds to round the continent of Africa in search of the Spice Islands.

MALINDI, GATEWAY TO ASIA. The seaport of Malindi, located on the eastern coast of present-day Kenya, was Vasco da Gama's jumping-off point for his historic voyage to India. It was here that he located a navigator willing to guide his fleet eastward across the Indian Ocean. A few years later, the Portuguese erected this monument to mark the spot of his departure. Inspecting the site in this photograph are students from a high school in Mombasa, Kenya's primary port city, about fifty miles to the south. A few yards from this monument is the first church erected by the Portuguese on the eastern coast of Africa.

The Development of a Portuguese Maritime Empire

Portugal took the lead in exploration when it began exploring the coast of Africa under the sponsorship of Prince Henry the Navigator (1394–1460). Prince Henry's motives were a blend of seeking a Christian kingdom as an ally against the Muslims, acquiring new trade opportunities for Portugal, and extending Christianity. In 1419, he founded a school for navigators on the southwestern coast of Portugal. Shortly thereafter, Portuguese fleets began probing southward along the western coast of Africa in search of gold, which had for centuries been carried northward from south of the Atlas Mountains in central Morocco. In 1441, Portuguese ships reached the Senegal River, just north of Cape Verde, and brought home a cargo of black Africans, most of whom were sold as slaves to wealthy buyers elsewhere in Europe. Within a few years, an estimated thousand slaves were shipped annually from the area back to Lisbon. Inadvertently, the Portuguese had found a way to circumvent the traditional trans-Saharan slave route from central Africa to the Mediterranean.

Continuing southward, in 1471 the Portuguese discovered a new source of gold along the southern coast of the hump of West Africa (an area that would henceforth be known to Europeans as the Gold Coast). A few years later, they established contact with the state of Bakongo, near the mouth of the Zaire (Congo) River in Central Africa, and with the inland state of Benin, north of the Gold Coast. To facilitate trade in gold, ivory, and slaves (some of the latter were brought back to Lisbon and others were bartered to local merchants for gold), the Portuguese leased land from local rulers and built stone forts along the coast.

Hearing reports of a route to India around the southern tip of Africa, Portuguese sea captains continued their probing. In 1487, Bartolomeu Dias took advantage of westerly winds in the South Atlantic to round the Cape of Good Hope, but he feared a mutiny from his crew and returned home without continuing onward. Ten years later, a fleet under the command of Vasco da Gama rounded the cape and stopped at several ports controlled by Muslim merchants along the coast of East Africa, including Sofala, Kilwa, and Mombasa. Then, having located a Muslim navigator who was familiar with seafaring in the region, da Gama's fleet crossed the Arabian Sea and arrived off the port of Calicut on the southwestern coast of India, on May 18, 1498. The Portuguese crown had sponsored da Gama's voyage with the clear objective of destroying the Muslim monopoly over the spice trade, a monopoly that had been intensified by the Ottoman conquest of Constantinople in 1453 (see Chapter 16). Calicut was a major entrepôt on the long route from the Spice Islands to the Mediterranean Sea, but the ill-informed Europeans believed it was the source of the spices themselves. They had also heard there was a Chris-

THE PORTUGUESE CONQUEST OF MALACCA

In 1511, a Portuguese fleet led by Afonso de Albuquerque attacked the Muslim sultanate at Malacca, on the west coast of the Malay peninsula. Occupation of the port gave the Portuguese control over the strategic Strait of Malacca and the route to the Spice Islands. In this passage, Albuquerque tells his men the reasons for the attack. Note that he sees control of Malacca as a way to reduce the power of the Muslim world. The relevance of economic wealth to military power continues to underlie conflicts among nations today. The Pacific War in the 1940s, for example, began as a result of a conflict over control of the rich resources of Southeast Asia.

THE COMMENTARIES OF THE GREAT AFONSO DE ALBUQUERQUE, SECOND VICEROY OF INDIA

Although there be many reasons which I could allege in favor of our taking this city and building a fortress therein to maintain possession of it, two only will I mention to you, on this occasion. . . .

The first is the great service which we shall perform to Our Lord in casting the Moors out of this country. . . . If we can only achieve the task before us, it will result in the Moors resigning India altogether to our rule, for the greater part of them—or perhaps all of them—live upon the trade of this country and are become great and rich, and lords of extensive treasures. . . . For when we were committing ourselves to the business of cruising in the Straits (of the Red Sea), where the King of Portugal had often ordered me to go (for it was there that His Highness considered we could cut down the commerce which the Moors of Cairo, of Mecca, and of Judah, carry on with these parts), Our Lord for his service thought right to lead us hither, for when Malacca is taken the places on the Straits must be shut up, and they will never more be able to introduce their spiceries into those places.

And the other reason is the additional service which we shall render to the King D. Manuel in taking this city, because it is the headquarters of all the spiceries and drugs which the Moors carry every year hence to the Straits without our being able to prevent them from so doing; but if we deprive them of this their ancient market there, there does not remain for them a single port, nor a single situation, so commodious in the whole of these parts, where they can carry on their trade in these things. . . . I hold it as very certain that if we take this trade of Malacca away out of their hands, Cairo and Mecca are entirely ruined, and to Venice will no spiceries be conveyed except that which her merchants go and buy in Portugal.

---

tian community in the area, supposedly established by the apostle Thomas in the first century C.E.

On arriving in Calicut, da Gama announced to his surprised hosts that he had arrived in search of "Christians and spices." He did not find the first, but he did find the second. Although he lost two ships en route, da Gama's remaining vessels returned to Europe with their holds filled with ginger and cinnamon, a cargo that earned the investors a profit of several thousand percent.

During the next years, the Portuguese set out to gain control of the spice trade. In 1510, Admiral Afonso de Albuquerque established his headquarters at Goa, on the western coast of India south of present-day Bombay. From there the Portuguese raided Arab shippers, provoking the following comment from an Arab source: "[The Portuguese] took about seven vessels, killing those on board and making some prisoner. This was their first action, may God curse them."[5] In 1511, Albuquerque attacked Malacca itself.

For Albuquerque, control of Malacca would serve two purposes. It could help to destroy the Arab spice trade network by blocking passage through the Strait of Malacca, and it could also provide the Portuguese with a way station en route to the Spice Islands and other points east (see the box above). After a short but bloody battle, the Portuguese seized the city and put the local Arab population to the sword. They then proceeded to erect the normal accoutrements of the day—a fort, a factory (a common term at the time for a warehouse), and a church.

From Malacca, the Portuguese launched expeditions further east, to China and the Moluccas, then known as the Spice Islands. There they signed a treaty with a local sultan for the purchase and export of cloves to the European market. Within a few years, they had managed to seize control of the spice trade from Muslim traders and had garnered substantial profits for the Portuguese monarchy.

Why were the Portuguese so successful? Basically, their success was a matter of guns and seamanship. The first Portuguese fleet to arrive in Indian waters was relatively modest in size. It consisted of three ships and twenty guns, a force sufficient for self-defense and intimidation, but not for serious military operations. Sixteenth-century Portuguese fleets were more heavily armed and were capable of inflicting severe defeats if necessary on local naval and land forces. The Portuguese by no means possessed a monopoly on the use of firearms and explosives, but they used the manueverability of their light ships to maintain their distance while bombarding the enemy with their powerful cannon. Such tactics gave them a military superiority over lightly armed rivals that they were able to exploit until the arrival of other European forces several decades later.

THE CARAVEL SANTA MARIA, IN WHICH COLUMBUS FIRST SAILED ACROSS THE ATLANTIC.

✤ **THE CARAVEL, WORKHORSE OF THE AGE OF EXPLORATION.** Prior to the fifteenth century, most European ships were either small craft with lateen sails used in the Mediterranean or slow, unwieldy square-rigged vessels operating in the North Atlantic. By the sixteenth century, European naval architects began to build ships that combined the maneuverability and speed offered by lateen sails with the carrying capacity and seaworthiness of the square-riggers. For a century, caravels were the feared "sea-raiders" of the oceans. Shown here is a representation of Christopher Columbus's flagship *Santa Maria*, which combined lateen with square sails and took part in the first Spanish voyage across the Atlantic Ocean.

Voyages to the "New World"

While the Portuguese were seeking access to the spice trade of the Indies by sailing eastward through the Indian Ocean, the Spanish attempted to reach the same destination by sailing westward across the Atlantic. Although the Spanish came to overseas discovery and exploration later than the Portuguese, their greater resources enabled them to establish a far grander overseas empire.

An important figure in the history of Spanish exploration was an Italian from Genoa, Christopher Columbus (1451–1506). Knowledgeable Europeans were aware that the world was round but had little understanding of its cir-

cumference or the extent of the continent of Asia. Convinced that the circumference of the earth was smaller than contemporaries believed and that Asia was larger, Columbus felt that Asia could be reached by sailing west instead of east around Africa. After being rejected by the Portuguese, he persuaded Queen Isabella of Spain to finance his exploratory expedition, which reached the Americas in October 1492 and explored the coastline of Cuba and the northern shores of the neighboring island of Hispaniola. Columbus believed that he had reached Asia and in three subsequent voyages (1493, 1498, and 1502) sought in vain to find a route through the outer islands to the Asian mainland. In his four voyages, Columbus reached all the major islands of the Caribbean and Honduras in Central America, which he called the Indies.

Although Columbus clung to his belief until his death, other explorers soon realized that he had discovered a new frontier altogether. State-sponsored explorers joined the race to the New World. A Venetian seafarer, John Cabot, explored the New England coastline of the Americas under a license from King Henry VII of England. The continent of South America was discovered accidentally by the Portuguese sea captain Pedro Cabral in 1500. Amerigo Vespucci, a Florentine, accompanied several voyages and wrote a series of letters describing the geography of the New World. The publication of these letters led to the use of the name "America" (after Amerigo) for the new lands.

The newly discovered territories were called the New World, although they possessed flourishing civilizations populated by millions of people when the Europeans arrived. The Americas were, of course, new to the Europeans, who quickly saw opportunities for conquest and exploitation. The Spanish, in particular, were interested because in 1494 the Treaty of Tordesillas had divided the newly discovered world into separate Portuguese and Spanish spheres of influence. Hereafter the route east around the Cape of Good Hope was to be reserved for the Portuguese, while the route across the Atlantic (except for the eastern hump of South America) was assigned to Spain. The Spanish conquistadors were a hardy lot of mostly upper-class individuals motivated by a typical sixteenth-century blend of glory, greed, and religious crusading zeal. Although sanctioned by the Castilian crown, these groups were financed and outfitted privately, not by the government.

Their superior weapons, organizational skills, and determination brought the conquistadors incredible success. Beginning in 1519 with a small band of men, Hernán Cortés took three years to overthrow the mighty Aztec empire in central Mexico, led by the chieftain Moctezuma (see Chapter 6). Between 1531 and 1550, the Spanish gained control of northern Mexico. Between 1531 and 1536, another expedition led by a hardened and somewhat corrupt soldier, Francisco Pizarro (1470–1541), took control of the Inca empire high in the Peruvian Andes. The

Spanish conquests were undoubtedly facilitated by the previous arrival of European diseases, which had decimated the local population. Although it took another three decades before the western part of Latin America was brought under Spanish control (the Portuguese took over Brazil), already by 1535, the Spanish had created a system of colonial administration that made the New World an extension of the old—at least in European eyes.

THE ADMINISTRATION OF THE SPANISH EMPIRE IN THE NEW WORLD

Spanish policy toward the Indians of the New World was a combination of confusion, misguided paternalism, and cruel exploitation. Confusion arose over the nature of the Indians. Unsure whether these strange creatures were "full men" or not, Spanish doctors of law debated how to fit them into currently existing European legal patterns.

While the conquistadors made decisions based on expediency and their own interests, Queen Isabella declared the Indians (literally, "Indios") to be subjects of Castile and instituted the *encomienda* system, which permitted the conquering Spaniards to collect tribute from the natives and use them as laborers. In return, the holders of an *encomienda* were supposed to protect the Indians and supervise their spiritual and material needs. In practice, this meant that the settlers were free to implement the system as they pleased. Three thousand miles from Spain, Spanish settlers largely ignored their government and brutally used the Indians to pursue their own economic interests. Indians were put to work on sugar plantations and in the lucrative gold and silver mines. Forced labor, starvation, and especially disease took a fearful toll of Indian lives. With little or no natural resistance to European diseases, the Indians of America were ravaged by smallpox, measles, and typhus. These "killers" came

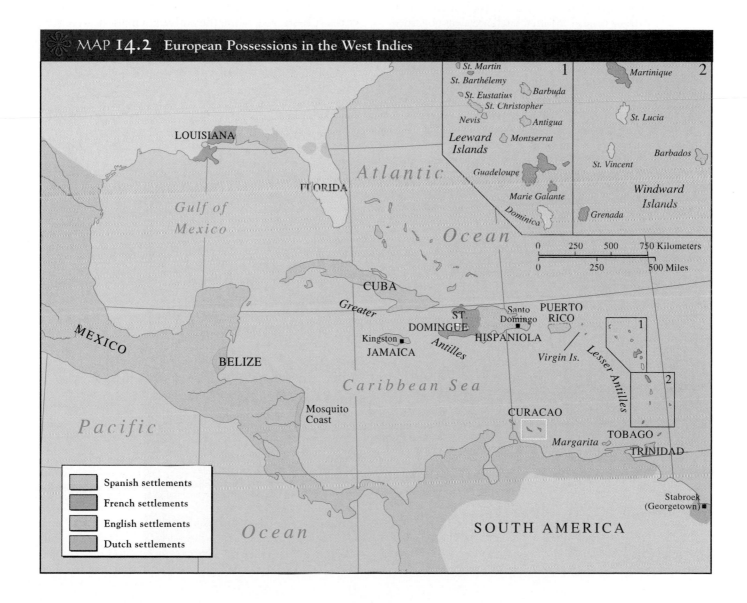

MAP **14.2**   **European Possessions in the West Indies**

with the explorers and the conquistadors. Although scholarly estimates of native populations vary drastically, a reasonable guess is that at least half of the natives died of European diseases. On Hispaniola alone, out of an initial population of 100,000 natives when Columbus arrived in 1493, only 300 Indians survived by 1570. In 1542, largely in response to the publications of Bartolomé de Las Casas, a Dominican monk who championed the Indians (see the box on p. 407), the government abolished the *encomienda* system and provided more protection for the natives.

A board of trade known as the *Casa de Contratación* supervised all economic matters related to the New World, but the chief organ of colonial administration was the Council of the Indies. The council nominated colonial viceroys, oversaw their activities, and kept an eye on ecclesiastical affairs in the colonies. Spanish possessions in the New World were initially divided between New Spain (Mexico, Central America, and the Caribbean islands), with its center in Mexico City, and Peru (western South America), with its capital at Lima. Each area was governed by a viceroy who served as the king's chief civil and military officer and was aided by advisory groups called *audiencias*, which also functioned as supreme judicial bodies.

By papal agreement, the Catholic monarchs of Spain were given extensive rights over ecclesiastical affairs in the New World. They could nominate church officials, build churches, collect fees, and supervise the various religious orders that conducted missionary activities. Catholic monks had remarkable success converting and baptizing hundreds of thousands of Indians in the early years of the conquest. Soon after the missionaries came the establishment of dioceses, parishes, schools, and hospitals—all the trappings of a European society.

The Impact of European Expansion

The arrival of the Europeans had an enormous impact on both the conquerors and the conquered. The native American civilizations, which (as we discussed in Chapter 6) had their own unique qualities and a degree of sophistication rarely appreciated by the conquerors, were virtually destroyed, while the native populations were ravaged by diseases inadvertently introduced by the Euro-

❀ **COLUMBUS LANDS IN THE NEW WORLD.**   In the log that he wrote during his first voyage to the Americas, Christopher Columbus noted that the peoples of the New World were intelligent and friendly, and relations between them and the Spanish were amicable at first. Later, however, the conquistadors began to mistreat the local people. Here is a somewhat imaginative painting of the first encounter from a European perspective.

LAS CASAS AND THE SPANISH TREATMENT OF THE AMERICAN NATIVES

Bartolomé de Las Casas (1474–1566) was a Dominican monk who participated in the conquest of Cuba and received land and Indians in return for his efforts. But in 1514 he underwent a radical transformation that led him to believe that the Indians had been cruelly mistreated by his fellow Spaniards. He spent the remaining years of his life (he lived to the age of ninety-two) fighting for the Indians. This section is taken from his most influential work, Brevísima Relación de la Destrucción de las Indias, known to English readers as The Tears of the Indians. This work was largely responsible for the legend of the Spanish as inherently "cruel and murderous fanatics." Many scholars today feel that Las Casas may have exaggerated his account to shock his contemporaries into action.

BARTOLOMÉ DE LAS CASAS, THE TEARS OF THE INDIANS

There is nothing more detestable or more cruel than the tyranny which the Spaniards use toward the Indians for the getting of pearl. Surely the infernal torments cannot much exceed the anguish that they endure, by reason of that way of cruelty; for they put them under water some four or five ells deep, where they are forced without any liberty of respiration, to gather up the shells wherein the Pearls are; sometimes they come up again with nets full of shells to take breath, but if they stay any while to rest themselves, immediately comes a hangman row'd in a little boat, who as soon as he hath well beaten them, drags them again to their labor. Their food is nothing but filth, and the very same that contains the Pearl, with small portion of that bread which that Country affords; in the first whereof there is little nourishment; and as for the latter, it is made with great difficulty, besides that they have not enough of that neither for sustenance; they lie upon the ground in fetters, lest they should run away; and many times they are drown'd in this labor, and are never seen again till they swim upon the top of the waves; oftentimes they also are devoured by certain sea monsters, that are frequent in those seas. Consider whether this hard usage of the poor creatures be consistent with the precepts which God commands concerning charity to our neighbor, by those that cast them so undeservedly into the dangers of a cruel death, causing them to perish without any remorse or pity, or allowing them the benefit of the Sacraments, or the knowledge of Religion; it being impossible for them to live any time under the water; and this death is so much the more painful, by reason that by the coarctation of the breast, while the lungs strive to do their office, the vital parts are so afflicted that they die vomiting the blood out of their mouths. Their hair also, which is by nature black, is hereby changed and made of the same color with that of the sea Wolves; their bodies are also so besprinkled with the froth of the sea, that they appear rather like monsters than men.

peans. Ancient social and political structures were ripped up and replaced by European institutions, religion, language, and culture (see the box on p. 408).

How does one evaluate the psychological impact of colonization on the colonizers? The relatively easy European success in dominating native peoples undoubtedly reinforced the conviction of Europeans in the inherent superiority of their civilization. The Scientific Revolution of the eighteenth century, to be followed by the era of imperialism a century later, then served to strengthen the Eurocentric perspective that has long pervaded Western civilization in its relationship with the rest of the world.

European expansion also affected the conquerors in the economic arena. Wherever they went in the Americas, Europeans sought gold and silver. One Aztec observer commented that the Spanish conquerors "longed and lusted for gold. Their bodies swelled with greed, and their hunger was ravenous; they hungered like pigs for that gold."[6] Rich silver deposits were found and exploited in Mexico and southern Peru (modern Bolivia). When the mines at Potosí in Peru were opened in 1545, the value of precious metals imported into Europe quadrupled. It has been estimated that between 1503 and 1650, sixteen million kilograms of silver and 185,000 kilograms of gold entered the port of Seville, helping to create a price revolution that affected the Spanish economy.

But gold and silver were only two of the products sent to Europe from the New World. Into Seville flowed sugar, dyes, cotton, vanilla, and hides from livestock raised on the South American pampas. New agricultural products native to the Americas such as potatoes, coffee, corn, manioc, and tobacco were also imported. Because of its trading posts in Asia, Portugal soon challenged the Italian states as the chief entry point of the eastern trade in spices, jewels, silk, carpets, ivory, leather, and perfumes, although the Venetians clung tenaciously to a portion of the spice trade until they lost out to the Dutch in the seventeenth century. Economic historians believe that the increase in the volume and area of European trade and the rise in fluid capital due to this expansion were crucial factors in producing a new era of commercial capitalism that

AN AZTEC'S LAMENT

*I*n a previous chapter, we observed the Spanish conquest of Mexico from the point of view of the invaders. Here we present an Aztec account. Aztec memoirs of the battle were collected by the Spanish a few years after the seizure of Tenochtitlán and were later translated from the original Nahuatl language into Spanish or other European languages. In this passage, an Aztec observer describes the enormous sense of sorrow he felt at the tragedy that had befallen his compatriots. Note that the writer concludes that the defeat was ordained by the "Giver of Life" because of his displeasure with the Aztec people.

FLOWERS AND SONGS OF SORROW

Nothing but flowers and songs of sorrow
are left in Mexico and Tlatelolco,
where once we saw warriors and wise men.

We know it is true
that we must perish,
for we are mortal men.
You, the Giver of Life,
you have ordained it.

We wander here and there
in our desolate poverty.
We are mortal men.
We have seen bloodshed and pain
where once we saw beauty and valor.

We are crushed to the ground;
we lie in ruins.
There is nothing but grief and suffering
in Mexico and Tlatelolco,
where once we saw beauty and valor.

Have you grown weary of your servants?
Are you angry with your servants,
O Giver of Life?

---

represented the first step toward the world economy that has characterized the modern era.

European expansion, which was in part a product of European rivalries, also deepened those rivalries and increased the tensions among European states. Bitter conflicts arose over the cargoes coming from the New World and Asia. Although the Spanish and Portuguese were first in the competition, by the end of the sixteenth century, new competitors were entering the scene and beginning to challenge the dominance of the Iberian powers. The first to arrive were the English and the Dutch.

Why did Europeans risk their lives to explore new lands far from friendly shores? For some, expansion abroad brought hopes for land, riches, and social advancement. One Spaniard commented in 1572 that many "poor young men" left Spain for Mexico, where they might hope to acquire landed estates and call themselves "gentlemen."

Although some wives accompanied their husbands abroad, many ordinary European women found new opportunities for marriage in the New World because of the lack of white women. In the violence-prone world of early Spanish America, a number of women also found themselves rich after their husbands were killed unexpectedly. In one area of Central America, women owned about 25 percent of the landed estates by 1700.

New Rivals Enter the Scene

Portugal's efforts to dominate the trade of the Indian Ocean were never totally successful. The Portuguese lacked both the numbers and the wealth to overcome local resistance and colonize the Asian regions. Moreover, their massive investments in ships and laborers for their empire (hundreds of ships and hundreds of thousands of workers in ship-

HAVANA, SPAIN'S LIFELINE TO THE NEW WORLD. After the conquest of Mexico by Hernán Cortés, trade between Spain and its new possession flourished. Spanish navigators soon discovered that the city of Havana, the capital of present-day Cuba, was an ideal stopping-point for fleets en route to and from the New World, and a city sprang up along the banks of its protected harbor. To protect the population from the ravages of enemy fleets—notably the English—Spanish authorities erected a number of fortifications on both shores of the bay that borders the city. Shown here is the Castle of the Royal Force, erected in 1559 and the first stone castle built in the New World. A previous wooden fort had been set aflame by pirates.

yards and overseas bases) proved very costly. Only half of the ships involved in the India trade survived for a second journey. Disease, shipwreck, and battles took a heavy toll of life. The empire was simply too large and Portugal too small to maintain it, and by the end of the century, the Portuguese were being severely challenged by rivals.

The Spanish had established themselves in Asia in the early 1520s, when Ferdinand Magellan, seeking a western route to the Spice Islands across the Pacific Ocean, had landed on the island of Cebu in the Philippine Islands. Although Magellan and some forty of his crew were killed in a skirmish with the local population, one of the two remaining ships, now under the command of the Spanish navigator Sebastian del Cano, sailed on to Tidor, in the Moluccas, and thence around the world via the Cape of Good Hope. In the words of a contemporary historian, they arrived in Cádiz "with precious cargo and fifteen men surviving out of a fleet of five sail."[7]

As it turned out, the Spanish could not follow up on Magellan's accomplishment, and in 1529 they sold their rights in Tidor to the Portuguese. But Magellan's voyage was not a total loss. In the absence of concerted resistance from the local population, the Spanish managed to consolidate their control over the Philippines, which eventually became a major Spanish base in the carrying trade across the Pacific. Spanish galleons carried silk and other luxury goods to Acapulco in exchange for silver from the mines of Mexico.

The primary threat to the Portuguese toehold in Southeast Asia, however, came from the English and the Dutch both of whom were now strongly influenced by mercantilist theory (see Chapter 15). In 1591, the first English

CHRONOLOGY
SPANISH ACTIVITIES IN THE AMERICAS

Christopher Columbus's first voyage to the Americas	1492
Last voyages of Columbus	1502–1504
Spanish conquest of Mexico	1519–1522
Francisco Pizarro's conquest of the Incas	1531–1536

expedition to the Indies through the Indian Ocean arrived in London with a cargo of pepper. Nine years later, a private joint-stock company, the East India Company, was founded to provide a stable source of capital for future voyages. In 1608, an English fleet landed at Surat, on the northwestern coast of India. Eventually, a commercial treaty was signed, and a permanent English representative was assigned to the Mughal imperial court. Trade with Southeast Asia soon followed.

The Dutch were quick to follow suit. Dutch sailors had managed to obtain Portuguese maps of the Indian coast, and the first Dutch fleet arrived in India in 1595. In 1602, the Dutch East India Company was established under government sponsorship and soon was actively competing with the English and the Portuguese in the region.

The Dutch and the English also began to make inroads on Spanish and Portuguese possessions in the Americas. War and steady pressure from their Dutch and English rivals eroded Portuguese trade in both the west and east, although Portugal continued to profit from its large colonial empire in Brazil. A formal administration system had been instituted in Brazil in 1549, and Portuguese migrants had established massive plantations there to produce sugar for export to the Old World. The Spanish also maintained an enormous South American empire, but Spain's importance as a commercial power declined rapidly in the seventeenth century because of a drop in the output of the silver mines, the poverty of the Spanish monarchy, and the stifling hand of the Spanish aristocracy as well as the pressure of its English rival.

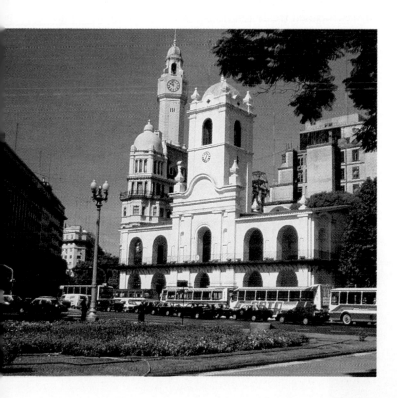

SEAT OF ARGENTINE INDEPENDENCE. The Argentine city of Buenos Aires was founded in 1536 by the Spanish explorer Pedro de Mendoza. In 1580 a town council was erected on the city's main square, the Plaza de Mayo. In 1751 it was replaced with a new building, shown below. It was here that Argentine patriots planned their struggle for independence from Spain in 1810.

The Dutch formed their own Dutch West India Company in 1621 to compete with Spanish and Portuguese interests in the Americas. But although it made some inroads in Portuguese Brazil and the Caribbean, the company's profits were never large enough to compensate for the expenditures. Dutch settlements were also established on the North American continent. The mainland colony of New Netherlands stretched from the mouth of the Hudson River as far north as Albany, New York. Present-day names such as Staten Island, Harlem, and the Catskills remind us that it was the Dutch who initially settled the Hudson River valley.

In the second half of the seventeenth century, however, rivalry and years of warfare with the English and the French (who had also become active in North America) brought the decline of the Dutch commercial empire in the New World. In 1664, the English seized the colony of New Netherlands and renamed it New York, while the Dutch West India Company soon went bankrupt. In 1663, Canada became the property of the French crown and was administered like a French province. But the French failed to provide adequate men or money, allowing their continental wars to take precedence over the conquest of the North American continent. By the early eighteenth century, the French began to cede some of their American possessions to their English rival.

The English meanwhile had proceeded to create a colonial empire in the New World along the Atlantic seaboard of North America. The failure of the Virginia Company made it evident that colonizing American lands was not necessarily conducive to quick profits. But the desire to escape from religious oppression combined with economic interests did make successful colonization possible, as the Massachusetts Bay Company demonstrated. The Massachusetts colony had only 4,000 settlers in its early years, but by 1660 their number had swelled to 40,000. Although the English had established control over most of the east-ern seaboard by the end of the seventeenth century, the North American colonies still remained of minor significance to the English economy.

Africa in an Era of Transition

Although the primary objective of the Portuguese in rounding the Cape of Good Hope was to find a sea route to the Spice Islands, they soon discovered that profits were to be made en route, along the eastern coast of Africa. In the early sixteenth century, a Portuguese fleet commanded by Francisco de Almeida seized a number of East African port cities, including Kilwa, Sofala, and Mombasa, and built forts along the coast in an effort to control the trade in the area. Above all, the Portuguese wanted to monopolize the trade in gold, which was mined by Bantu workers in the hills along the upper Zambezi River and then shipped to Sofala on the coast (see Chapter 8). For centuries, the gold trade had been monopolized by local Shona peoples at Zimbabwe. In the fifteenth century, it had come under the control of a Shona dynasty known as the Mwene Metapa (known to Europeans as Monomotapa). The Mwene Metapa had originally controlled the region south of the Zambezi River and may have been the builders of the impressive city known today as Great Zimbabwe, but sometime in the fifteenth century, they moved northeast-ward to the valley of the Zambezi. Here they encountered the arriving Portuguese, who had begun to move inland to gain access to the lucrative gold trade and had established ports at Tete and Sena on the Zambezi River. The Portuguese opened treaty relations with the Mwene Metapa, and Jesuit priests were eventually posted to the court in 1561. At first the Mwene Metapa found the Europeans useful as an ally against local rivals, but by the end of the

PASSAGE TO THE UNKNOWN. During its historic first voyage around the world in the early sixteenth century, Ferdinand Magellan's fleet passed through this passage near the southern tip of South America. Now known as the Strait of Magellan, this narrow body of water between the mainland and the nearby island of Tierra del Fuego remains to sailors one of the most terrifying in the world, with 100-mile-per-hour winds gusting regularly through this passage between the Pacific and the Atlantic Oceans.

sixteenth century, the Portuguese had transformed the kingdom of the Mwene Metapa into a protectorate and forced the local ruler to grant title to large tracts of land to Portuguese officials and private individuals living in the area. Eventually, those lands would be integrated into the colony of Mozambique. The Portuguese, however, lacked the personnel, the capital, and the expertise to dominate the trade in the area. In the late seventeenth century, a vassal of the Mwene Metapa succeeded in driving the Portuguese from the plateau; his descendants maintained control of the area for the next two hundred years.

North of the Zambezi River, Bantu peoples were coming under pressure not only from the Portuguese, but also from pastoralists migrating southward from the southern Sudan. The latter were frequently aggressive and began to occupy the rift valley and parts of the lake district that had previously been controlled by Bantu farmers. In some cases, the conflict between farmers and pastoralists was fairly clear-cut. In Rwanda and Burundi, immediately west of Lake Victoria, farming Hutu peoples (Bantu speakers) defended their hilltop communities against roving Tutsi pastoralists occupying the surrounding lowlands.

The first Europeans to settle in southern Africa were the Dutch. After an unsuccessful attempt to seize the Portuguese settlement on the island of Mozambique off the East African coast, in 1652 the Dutch set up a way station at the Cape of Good Hope to serve as a base for Dutch fleets en route to the East Indies. At first, the new settlement was meant simply to provide food and other provisions to Dutch ships, but eventually it developed into a permanent colony. Dutch farmers, known as Boers and speaking a Dutch dialect that evolved into Afrikaans, began to settle in the sparsely occupied areas outside the city of Capetown. The temperate climate and the absence of tropical diseases made the territory near the cape almost the only land south of the Sahara that the Europeans had found suitable for habitation.

West Africa had been penetrated from across the Sahara since ancient times, and contact undoubtedly increased after the establishment of Muslim control over the Mediterranean coastal regions. Muslim traders crossed the desert carrying Islamic values, political culture, and legal traditions along with their goods. The early stage of state formation had culminated with the kingdom of Mali, symbolized by the renowned Mansa Musa, whose pilgrimage to Mecca in the fourteenth century had left an indelible impression on observers.

After Mali's decline, it was succeeded in the east by the kingdom of Songhai. Under King Askia Mohammed (1493–1528), the leader of a pro-Islamic faction who had seized power from members of the original founding family, the state increasingly relied on Islamic institutions and ideology to strengthen national unity and centralize authority (see the box on p. 412). Askia Mohammed himself embarked on a pilgrimage to Mecca

and was recognized by the caliph of Cairo as the Muslim ruler of the Niger River valley. On his return from Mecca, he tried to revive Timbuktu as a major center of Islamic learning but had little success in converting his subjects. He did preside over a significant increase in trans-Saharan trade, which provided a steady source of income to Songhai and other kingdoms in the region. Despite the efforts of Askia Mohammed and his successors, centrifugal forces within Songhai eventually led to its breakup after his death.

The period of Songhai's decline was also a time of increased contact with Europeans. The English, the French, and the Dutch all became active in the West African trade in the mid-sixteenth century. The Dutch, in particular, encroached on the Portuguese spheres of influence. During the mid-seventeenth century, the Dutch seized a number of Portuguese forts along the West African coast, while at the same time taking over the bulk of the Portuguese trade across the Indian Ocean.

The Slave Trade

The European exploration of the African coastline had little apparent significance for most peoples living in the interior of the continent, except for a few who engaged in direct or indirect trade with the foreigners. But for peoples living on or near the coast, the impact was often great indeed. As the trade in slaves increased during the

�ⓧ **FORT JESUS AT MOMBASA.**   Mombasa, a port city on the eastern coast of Africa, was a jumping-off point for the Portuguese as they explored the lands bordering on the Indian Ocean. Erected in the early sixteenth century atop a bluff overlooking the harbor, Fort Jesus remained an imposing symbol of European power until 1698, when the Portuguese were expelled by the Arabs. Castles built in this style are situated along the sea routes to the Spice Islands, but the European presence has now departed.

KING OF SONGHAI

T he Epic of Askia Mohammed is an oral history passed
down through generations of West Africans. It relates the
heroic deeds of the famous monarch who led the kingdom
of Songhai to the zenith of its power in the early sixteenth
century. In the epic, the young hero, called Mamar Kassaye,
becomes chieftain by killing his evil uncle Si (Sonni Ali Ber, who
ruled Songhai from 1463 to 1492). Once in power, Mamar consolidated the expanding Songhai kingdom and ruled it until his death
in 1528. He was revered for his piety, his patronage of scholarship
at Timbuktu, and his celebrated pilgrimage to Mecca. The following passage describes his assumption of power and the means
he used to convert his subjects to Islam.

THE EPIC OF ASKIA MOHAMMED

His father gave him a white stallion, really white, really,
   really, really, really, really, really, really white like, like
   percale.
He gave him all the things necessary.
He gave him two lances.
He gave him a saber, which he wore.
He gave him a shield.
He bid him good-bye.

…

The horse gallops swiftly, swiftly, swiftly, swiftly, swiftly,
   swiftly he is approaching.
He comes into view suddenly, leaning forward on his mount.
Until, until, until, until, until, until, until he touches the
   prayer skin of his uncle, then he reins his horse there.

…

As he approaches the prayer skin of his uncle,
He reins his horse.
He unslung his lance, and pierced his uncle with it until the
   lance touched the prayer skin.

Until the spear went all the way to the prayer skin.

…

They took away the body, and Mamar came to sit down on
   the prayer skin of his uncle.
They prayed.
They took away the body to bury it.
That is how Mamar took the chieftaincy.

…

He ruled then, he ruled, he ruled, he ruled, he converted.
Throughout Mamar's reign, what he did was to convert
   people.
Any village that he hears is trying to resist,
That is not going to submit,
He gets up and destroys the village.
If the village accepts, he makes them pray.
If they resist, he conquers the village, he burns the village.
Mamar made them convert, Mamar made them convert,
   Mamar made them convert.
Until, until, until, until, until, until he got up and said he
   would go to Mecca.

…

They build a mosque before his arrival.
When he arrives, he and his people,
He teaches the villagers prayers from the Koran.
He makes them pray.
They—they learn how to pray.
After that, in the morning, he continues on.
Every village that follows his orders, that accepts his wishes,
He conquers them, he moves on.
Every village that refuses his demand,
He conquers it, he burns it, he moves on.
Until the day—Mamar did that until, until, until, until the
   day he arrived at the Red Sea.

---

sixteenth through the eighteenth centuries, thousands,
and then millions, were removed from their homes and
forcibly exported to plantations in the New World.

Traffic in slaves had existed for centuries before the
arrival of Portuguese fleets along African shores. West
African states like the kingdoms of Mali and Songhai routinely used slaves (mostly captured in battles with neighboring rivals) as agricultural laborers. In East Africa and
the upper Nile valley, slavery had been practiced since
ancient times and continued at a fairly steady level during
the fifteenth century, with the major trade routes snaking
across the Sahara and up the Nile River. The primary market for African slaves was the Middle East, where most
were used as domestic servants. Slavery also existed in
many European countries, where a few slaves from Africa
or war captives from the regions north of the Black Sea
were used for domestic purposes or as agricultural workers in the lands adjacent to the Mediterranean.

At first, the Portuguese simply replaced European
slaves with African ones. During the last half of the fifteenth century, about a thousand slaves were taken to
Portugal each year; the vast majority were apparently destined to serve as domestic servants for affluent families
throughout Europe. But the discovery of the New World
in the 1490s and the subsequent planting of sugarcane in
South America and the islands of the Caribbean changed
the situation. Cane sugar was native to Indonesia and had
first been introduced to Europeans from the Middle East
during the Crusades. By the fifteenth century, it was
grown (often by slaves from Africa or the region of the
Black Sea) in modest amounts on Cyprus, Sicily, and
southern regions of the Iberian peninsula. In 1490, the

Portuguese established sugar plantations worked by African laborers at São Tomé, an island in the Bay of Biafra off the central coast of Africa. Demand increased as sugar gradually replaced honey as a sweetener, especially in northern Europe.

But the primary impetus to the sugar industry came from the colonization of the Americas. During the sixteenth century, plantations were established along the eastern coast of Brazil and on several islands in the Caribbean. Because the cultivation of cane sugar is an arduous process demanding both skill and large quantities of labor, the new plantations required more workers than could be provided by the small and inexperienced American Indian population in the New World, many of whom had in any case died of diseases imported from the Old World. Since the climate and soil of much of West Africa were not especially conducive to the cultivation of sugar, African slaves began to be shipped to Brazil and the Caribbean to work on the plantations. The first were sent from Portugal, but in 1518 a Spanish ship carried the first boatload of African slaves directly from Africa to the New World.

During the next two centuries, the trade in slaves increased by massive proportions. An estimated 275,000 enslaved Africans were exported to other countries during the sixteenth century, with 2,000 going annually to the Americas alone. During the next century, the total climbed to over a million and jumped to six million in the eighteenth century, when the trade spread from West and Central Africa to East Africa. Even during the nineteenth century, when Great Britain and a number of other European countries attempted to end the slave trade, nearly two million were exported. It has been estimated that altogether as many as ten million African slaves were transported to the Americas between the early sixteenth and the late nineteenth century. As many as two million were exported to other areas during the same period.

One reason for these astonishing numbers, of course, was the tragically high death rate. Though figures on the number of slaves who died on the journey are almost entirely speculative, a high proportion undoubtedly died on the voyage before arriving at their destination. According to one source, mortality rates among crew

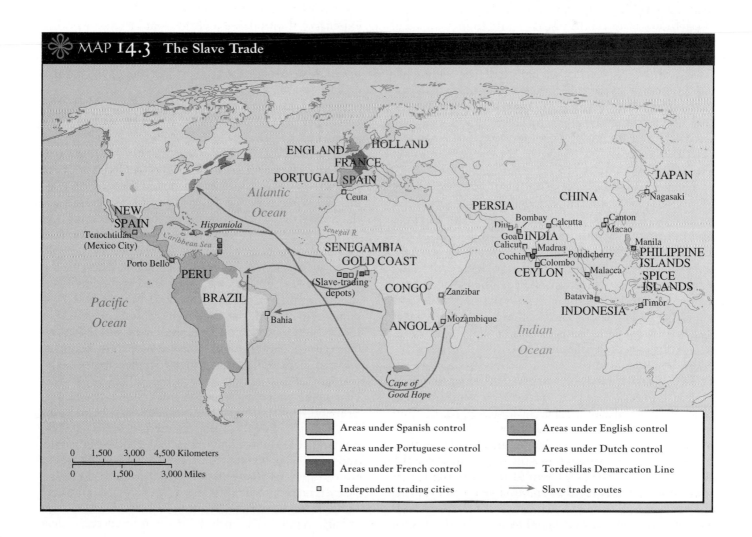

MAP **14.3**   The Slave Trade

Plan of an African Ship's lower Deck, with Negroes, in the proportion of not quite one to a Ton.

Men's room   *Boys' room*   *Women's room*   *Store room*   *Store room*

❀ **A SLAVE SHIP.**   Beginning in the sixteenth century, European traders began to ship native Africans to the Americas to be used as slave labor on the plantations. During the first shipments, up to one-third of the human cargo died of disease. Later merchants became more efficient and reduced losses to about 10 percent. As this sketch shows, the victims were still crammed together in an inhumane manner.

members were as high as one in four. Later, mortality rates among slaves were apparently reduced to an average of about 10 percent per voyage, still a figure of epidemic proportions. Mortality rates for Europeans in the West Indies were ten to twenty times higher on average than in Europe, and a European arriving in the West Indies had a life expectancy of five to ten years (in Africa, where yellow fever was prevalent, the average life expectancy for an arriving European was only about one year). Ironically, African slaves fared somewhat better if they survived the brutal voyage. Death rates for newly arrived Europeans in the West Indies averaged over 125 per 1,000 annually, but the figure for Africans was only about 30 per 1,000.

The reason for these staggering death rates was clearly more than maltreatment, although that was certainly a factor. As we have seen, the transmission of diseases from one continent to another brought high death rates among those lacking immunity. African slaves were somewhat less susceptible to European diseases than the American Indian populations. Indeed, they seem to have possessed a degree of immunity, perhaps because their ancestors had developed antibodies to "white people's diseases" owing to the trans-Saharan trade. The Africans would not have had immunity to native American diseases, however.

The mortality rates, of course, were higher for immigrants than for those born in the New World, who as children gradually developed at least a partial immunity to many of the more fatal diseases. Death rates for native-born slaves tended to be significantly lower than for recent arrivals, which raises the question of why the slave population did not begin to rise after the initial impact of settlement had worn off. The answer appears to be a matter of economics. In the first place, only half as many women were enslaved as men, birthrates for

women living in slavery were low, and infant mortality was high. In the second place, as long as the price of slaves was low, many slave owners in the West Indies apparently believed that purchasing a new slave was less expensive than raising a child from birth to working age at adolescence. After the price of slaves began to rise during the eighteenth century, plantation owners started to devote more efforts to replenishing the supply of workers by natural means.

Slaves were obtained by traditional means. Before the coming of the Europeans in the fifteenth century, most slaves in Africa were prisoners or war captives or had inherited their status. Many served as domestic servants or as wageless workers for the local ruler, and some were permitted to purchase their freedom under certain conditions. When Europeans first began to take part in the slave trade, they would normally purchase slaves from local African merchants at the infamous "slave markets" in exchange for gold, guns, or other European manufactured goods such as textiles or copper or iron utensils (see the box on p. 415). At first, local slave traders obtained their supply from immediately surrounding regions, but as demand increased, they had to move further inland to locate their victims. In a few cases, local rulers became concerned about the impact of the slave trade on the political and social well-being of their societies. In a letter to the king of Portugal in 1526, King Affonso of Congo (Bakongo) complained that "so great, Sire, is the corruption and licentiousness that our country is being completely depopulated."[8] As a general rule, however, local monarchs viewed the slave trade as a source of income, and many launched forays against defenseless villages in search of unsuspecting victims.

Historians once thought that Europeans controlled the terms of the slave trade and were able to obtain victims at bargain prices. Recently, however, it has become clear

A SLAVE MARKET IN AFRICA

Traffic in slaves had been carried on in Africa since the kingdom of the pharaohs in ancient Egypt. But the slave trade increased dramatically after the arrival of European ships off the coast of West Africa. The following passage by a Dutch observer describes a slave market in Africa and the conditions on the ships that carried the slaves to the New World. Note the difference in tone between this account and the far more critical views expressed in Chapter 22.

SLAVERY IN AFRICA: A FIRSTHAND REPORT

Not a few in our country fondly imagine that parents here sell their children, men their wives, and one brother the other. But those who think so deceive themselves, for this never happens on any other account but that of necessity, or some great crime; most of the slaves that are offered to us are prisoners of war, who are sold by the victors as their booty.

When these slaves come to Fida, they are put in prison all together; and when we treat concerning buying them, they are brought out into a large plain. There, by our surgeons, whose province it is, they are thoroughly examined, even to the smallest member, and that naked too, both men and women, without the least distinction or modesty. Those that are approved as good are set on one side; and the lame or faulty are set by as invalids. . . .

The invalids and the maimed being thrown out, . . . the remainder are numbered, and it is entered who delivered them. In the meanwhile, a burning iron, with the arms or name of the companies, lies in the fire, with which ours are marked on the breast. This is done that we may distinguish them from the slaves of the English, French, or others (which are also marked with their mark), and to prevent the Negroes exchanging them for worse, at which they have a good hand.

I doubt not but this trade seems very barbarous to you, but since it is followed by mere necessity, it must go on; but we take all possible care that they are not burned too hard, especially the women, who are more tender than the men.

When we have agreed with the owners of the slaves, they are returned to their prison. There from that time forward they are kept at our charge, costing us two pence a day a slave; which serves to subsist them, like our criminals, on bread and water. To save charges, we send them on board our ships at the very first opportunity, before which their masters strip them of all they have on their backs so that they come aboard stark naked, women as well as men. In this condition they are obliged to continue, if the master of the ship is not so charitable (which he commonly is) as to bestow something on them to cover their nakedness.

You would really wonder to see how these slaves live on board, for though their number sometimes amounts to six or seven hundred, yet by the careful management of our masters of ships, they are so regulated that it seems incredible. And in this particular our nation exceeds all other Europeans, for the French, Portuguese and English slave ships are always foul and stinking; on the contrary, ours are for the most part clean and neat.

The slaves are fed three times a day with indifferent good victuals, and much better than they eat in their own country. Their lodging place is divided into two parts, one of which is appointed for the men, the other for the women, each sex being kept apart. Here they lie as close together as it is possible for them to be crowded.

We are sometimes sufficiently plagued with a parcel of slaves which come from a far inland country who very innocently persuade one another that we buy them only to fatten and afterward eat them as a delicacy. When we are so unhappy as to be pestered with many of this sort, they resolve and agree together (and bring over the rest to their party) to run away from the ship, kill the Europeans, and set the vessel ashore, by which means they design to free themselves from being our food.

I have twice met with this misfortune; and the first time proved very unlucky to me, I not in the least suspecting it, but the uproar was quashed by the master of the ship and myself by causing the abettor to be shot through the head, after which all was quiet.

---

that African intermediaries—whether private merchants, local elites, or trading state monopolies—were very active in the process and were often able to dictate the price, volume, and availability of slaves to European purchasers. The majority of the slaves sold to European buyers were males; females, who were in great demand in Africa and on the trans-Saharan trade, tended to be reserved for those markets. The slave merchants were often paid in various types of imported goods, including East Asian textiles (highly desired for their bright colors and durability), furniture, and other manufactured products. Until the end of

the seventeenth century, the Portuguese preferred gold to slaves and would sometimes pay for the gold by selling slaves to African kingdoms that were short of labor. In fact, not until the beginning of the eighteenth century did slaves surpass gold and ivory as the continent's leading exports.

The effects of the slave trade varied from area to area. It might be assumed that, apart from the tragic effects on the lives of individual victims and their families, the practice would have led to the depopulation of vast areas of the continent. This did occur in some areas, notably in modern Angola, south of the Zaire River basin, and in

CHRONOLOGY

THE PENETRATION OF AFRICA

Life of Prince Henry the Navigator	1394–1460
Portuguese ships reach the Senegal River	1441
Bartolomeo Dias sails around the tip of Africa	1487
First Portuguese sugar plantation at São Tomé	1490
First boatload of slaves to the Americas	1518
Dutch way station established at Cape of Good Hope	1652
Ashanti kingdom established in West Africa	1680
Portuguese expelled from Mombasa	1728

thinly populated areas in East Africa, but it was less true in West Africa. There high birthrates were often able to counterbalance the loss of able-bodied adults, and the introduction of new crops from the New World, such as maize, peanuts, and manioc, led to an increase in food production that made it possible to support a larger population. One of the many cruel ironies of history is that while the institution of slavery was a tragedy for many, it benefited others.

Still, there is no denying the reality that from a moral point of view, the slave trade represented a tragic loss for millions of Africans, not only for the individual victims, but also for their families. One of the more poignant aspects of the trade is that as many as 20 percent of those sold to European slavers were children, a statistic that may be partly explained by the fact that many European countries had enacted regulations that permitted more children than adults to be transported aboard the ships.

Political and Social Structures in a Changing Continent

Of course, the Western economic penetration of Africa had other dislocating effects. As in other parts of the non-Western world, the importation of inexpensive manufactured goods from Europe undermined the foundations of local cottage industry and impoverished countless families. Both the demand for slaves and the introduction of firearms intensified political instability and civil strife. At the same time, the impact of the Europeans should not

be exaggerated. Only in a few isolated areas, such as South Africa and Mozambique, were anything like permanent European settlements established. Elsewhere, at the insistence of African rulers and merchants, European influence generally did not penetrate beyond the coastal regions.

Nevertheless, inland areas were often affected by events taking place elsewhere. In the western Sahara, for example, the diversion of trade routes toward the coast led to the irreparable weakening of the old Songhai trading empire and its eventual conquest by a vigorous new Moroccan dynasty in the late sixteenth century. Morocco had long hoped to expand its influence into the Sahara in order to seize control over the commerce in gold and salt, and in 1590 Moroccan forces defeated Songhai's army at Gao, on the Niger River, and then occupied the great caravan center of Timbuktu. Even after the departure of the invaders, Songhai was beyond recovery, and the next two centuries were marked by civil disorder among tribal groups and intense competition between Muslims in the cities and towns and adherents of traditional African religions in rural areas.

European influence had a more direct impact along the coast of West Africa, especially in the vicinity of European forts and factories such as Dakar and Sierra Leone, but no European colonies were established there before 1800. Most of the numerous African states in the area from Cape Verde to the delta of the Niger River were sufficiently strong to resist Western encroachments, and they often allied with each other to force European purchasers to respect their monopoly on trading operations. Some, like the powerful Ashanti kingdom, established in 1680 on the Gold Coast, profited substantially from the rise in seaborne commerce. Some states, particularly along the so-called Slave Coast, in what is now Dahomey and Togo, or in the densely populated Niger River delta, took an active part in the slave trade. The demands of slavery and the temptations of economic profit, however, also contributed to the increase in conflict among the states in the area.

This was especially true in the region of the Zaire River, where Portuguese activities eventually led to the splintering of the Congo Empire and two centuries of rivalry and internal strife among the successor states in the area. A similar pattern developed in East Africa, where Portuguese activities led to the decline and eventual collapse of the Mwene Metapa. Northward along the coast, in present-day Kenya and Tanzania, African rulers, assisted by Arab forces from Oman and Muscat in the Arabian peninsula, expelled the Portuguese from Mombasa in 1728. Swahili culture now regained some of the dynamism it had possessed before the arrival of Vasco da Gama and his successors. But with much shipping now diverted southward to the route around the Cape of Good Hope, the commerce of the area never completely recovered and was increasingly dependent on the export of slaves and ivory obtained through contacts with African states in the interior.

SOUTHEAST ASIA IN THE ERA OF THE SPICE TRADE

In Southeast Asia, the encounter with the West that began with the arrival of Portuguese fleets in the Indian Ocean at the end of the fifteenth century eventually resulted in the breakdown of traditional societies and the advent of colonial rule. In general, however, the process was a gradual one. By 1700, although the Dutch retained their hold on the islands, Europeans had generally abandoned the Southeast Asian mainland. As we will see in a later chapter, though, the mainland's reprieve was only temporary.

The Arrival of the West

As we have seen, the Spanish soon followed the Portuguese into Southeast Asia. By the seventeenth century, the Dutch, English, and French had begun to join the scramble for rights to the lucrative spice trade.

Within a short time, the Dutch, through the aggressive and well-financed Dutch East India Company (Vereenigde Oost-Indische Compagnie, or VOC, which possessed ten times the capital of the English East India Company), had not only succeeded in elbowing their rivals out of the spice trade but had also begun to consolidate their political and military control over the area. On the island of Java, where they established a fort at Batavia (today's Jakarta) in 1619, the Dutch found that it was necessary to bring the inland regions under their control to protect their position. Rather than establishing a formal colony, however, they tried to rule as much as possible through the local landed aristocracy. On Java and the neighboring island of Sumatra, the VOC established pepper plantations, which soon became the source of massive profits for Dutch merchants in Amsterdam. Elsewhere they attempted to monopolize the clove trade by limiting cultivation of the crop to one island. By the end of the eighteenth century, the Dutch had succeeded in bringing almost the entire Indonesian archipelago under their control.

The arrival of the Europeans had somewhat less impact on mainland Southeast Asia, where cohesive monarchies in Burma, Thailand, and Vietnam resisted foreign encroachment. In addition, the coveted spices did not thrive on the mainland, so the Europeans' efforts there were far less determined than in the islands. In the sixteenth century, the Portuguese established limited trade relations with several mainland states, including the Thai kingdom at Ayuthaya, Burma, Vietnam, and the

CHRONOLOGY

THE SPICE TRADE

Vasco da Gama lands at Calicut in southwestern India	1498
Portuguese seize Malacca	1511
Portuguese ships land in southern China	1514
Magellan's voyage around the world	1519–1522
East India Company established	1600
Vereenigde Oost-Indische Compagnie (VOC) established	1602
English arrive at Surat in northwestern India	1608
Dutch fort established at Batavia	1619
Dutch seize Malacca from the Portuguese	1641
Burmese sack of Ayuthaya	1767
British seize Malacca from the Dutch	1795

remnants of the old Angkor kingdom in Cambodia. By the early seventeenth century, other nations had followed and had begun to compete actively for trade and missionary privileges. As was the case elsewhere, the Europeans soon became involved in local factional disputes as a means of obtaining political and economic advantages. In Burma, the English and the French supported rival groups in the internal struggles of the monarchy until a new dynasty emerged and threw the foreigners out. A similar process took place at Ayuthaya, where the French were forced to evacuate the area in the late seventeenth century.

In Vietnam, the arrival of Western merchants and missionaries coincided with a period of internal conflict among ruling groups in the country. After their arrival in the mid-seventeenth century, the European powers characteristically began to intervene in local politics, with the Portuguese and the Dutch supporting rival factions. By the end of the century, when it became clear that economic opportunities were limited, most European states abandoned their factories (trading stations) in the area. French missionaries attempted to remain, but their efforts were hampered by the local authorities, who viewed the Catholic insistence that converts give their primary loyalty to the pope as a threat to the legal status and prestige of the Vietnamese emperor (see the box on p. 419).

State and Society in Precolonial Southeast Asia

Between 1500 and 1800, Southeast Asia experienced the last flowering of traditional culture before the advent of European colonial rule in the nineteenth century. Although the coming of the Europeans had an immediate and direct impact in some areas, notably the Philippines and parts of the Malay world, in most areas Western influence was still relatively limited. Europeans occasionally dabbled in local politics and modified regional trade patterns, but they generally were not a decisive factor in the evolution of local political or social systems.

Nevertheless, Southeast Asian societies were changing in several subtle ways—in their trade patterns, their means of livelihood, and their religious beliefs. In some ways, these changes accentuated the differences between individual states in the region. Yet beneath these differences was an underlying commonality of life for most people. Despite the diversity of cultures and religious beliefs in the area, in most respects, Southeast Asians were closer to

THE THAI CAPITAL AT AYUTHAYA. The Thai peoples arrived in Southeast Asia in the thirteenth century, after being driven out of southern China by the Mongols. They then destroyed the Angkor Empire and set up their capital at Ayuthaya, which was one of the finest cities in Asia from the fifteenth to the eighteenth century. After a Burmese invasion in 1767, most of Ayuthaya's inhabitants were killed, and all official Thai records were destroyed. Here the remains of some Buddhist stupas, erected in a ceremonial precinct in the center of the city, are a visual confirmation of the influence of Theravada Buddhism on Thai society.

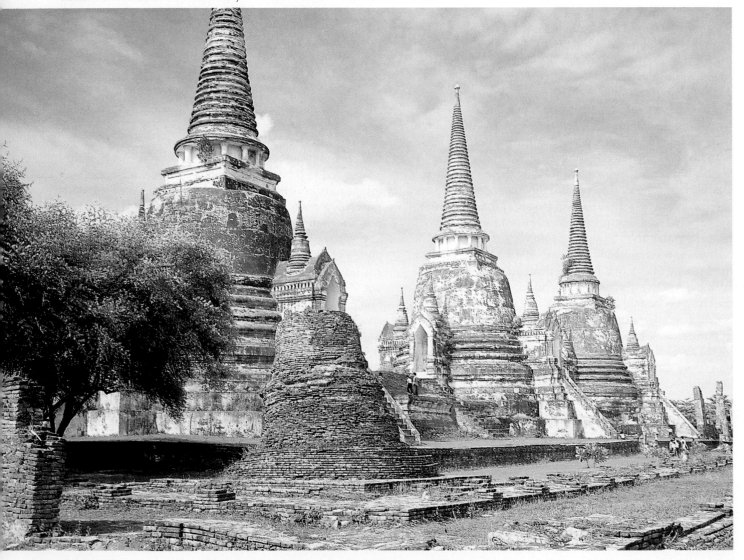

AN EXCHANGE OF ROYAL CORRESPONDENCE

In 1681, King Louis XIV of France wrote a letter to the "king of Tonkin" (the Trinh family head, then acting as viceroy to the Vietnamese ruler) requesting permission for Christian missionaries to proselytize in Vietnam. The latter politely declined the request on the grounds that such activity was prohibited by ancient custom. In fact, Christian missionaries had been active in Vietnam for years, and their intervention in local politics had aroused the anger of the court in Hanoi.

A LETTER TO THE KING OF TONKIN FROM LOUIS XIV

Most high, most excellent, most mighty, and most magnanimous Prince, our very dear and good friend, may it please God to increase your greatness with a happy end!

We hear from our subjects who were in your Realm what protection you accorded them. We appreciate this all the more since we have for you all the esteem that one can have for a prince as illustrious through his military valor as he is commendable for the justice which he exercises in his Realm. We have even been informed that you have not been satisfied to extend this general protection to our subjects but, in particular, that you gave effective proofs of it to Messrs. Deydier and de Bourges. We would have wished that they might have been able to recognize all the favors they received from you by having presents worthy of you offered you; but since the war which we have had for several years, in which all of Europe had banded together against us, prevented our vessels from going to the Indies, at the present time, when we are at peace after having gained many victories and expanded our Realm through the conquest of several important places, we have immediately given orders to the Royal Company to establish itself in your kingdom as soon as possible, and have commanded Messrs. Deydier and de Bourges to remain with you in order to maintain a good relationship between our subjects and yours, also to warn us on occasions that might present themselves when we might be able to give you proofs of our esteem and of our wish to concur with your satisfaction as well as with your best interests.

By way of initial proof, we have given orders to have brought to you some presents which we believe might be agreeable to you. But the one thing in the world which we desire most, both for you and for your Realm, would be to obtain for your subjects who have already embraced the law of the only true God of heaven and earth, the freedom to profess it, since this law is the highest, the noblest, the most sacred, and especially the most suitable to have kings reign absolutely over the people.

We are even quite convinced that, if you knew the truths and the maxims which it teaches, you would give first of all to your subjects the glorious example of embracing it. We wish you this incomparable blessing together with a long and happy reign, and we pray God that it may please Him to augment your greatness with the happiest of endings.

Written at Saint-Germain-en-Laye, the 10th day of January, 1681,

Your very dear and good friend,
Louis

ANSWER FROM THE KING OF TONKIN TO LOUIS XIV

The King of Tonkin sends to the King of France a letter to express to him his best sentiments, saying that he was happy to learn that fidelity is a durable good of man and that justice is the most important of things. Consequently practicing of fidelity and justice cannot but yield good results. Indeed, though France and our Kingdom differ as to mountains, rivers, and boundaries, if fidelity and justice reign among our villages, our conduct will express all of our good feelings and contain precious gifts. Your communication, which comes from a country which is a thousand leagues away, and which proceeds from the heart as a testimony of your sincerity, merits repeated consideration and infinite praise. Politeness toward strangers is nothing unusual in our country. There is not a stranger who is not well received by us. How then could we refuse a man from France, which is the most celebrated among the kingdoms of the world and which for love of us wishes to frequent us and bring us merchandise? These feelings of fidelity and justice are truly worthy to be applauded. As regards your wish that we should cooperate in propagating your religion, we do not dare to permit it, for there is an ancient custom, introduced by edicts, which formally forbids it. Now, edicts are promulgated only to be carried out faithfully; without fidelity nothing is stable. How could we disdain a well-established custom to satisfy a private friendship? . . .

We beg you to understand well that this is our communication concerning our mutual acquaintance. This then is my letter. We send you herewith a modest gift, which we offer you with a glad heart.

This letter was written at the beginning of winter and on a beautiful day.

each other than they were to peoples outside the region. For the most part, the states and peoples of Southeast Asia were still in control of their own destiny.

RELIGION AND KINGSHIP

During the early modern era, both Buddhism and Islam became well established in Southeast Asia, and Christianity began to attract some converts, especially in the Philippines. Buddhism became dominant on the mainland, at least in lowland areas, from Burma to Vietnam. At first, Muslim influence was felt mainly on the Malay peninsula and along the northern coast of Java and Sumatra, where urban merchants encountered their Muslim counterparts from foreign lands on a regular basis. At the same time, traditional religious beliefs continued to survive, especially in the inland villages, where the local populations either ignored the new doctrines or integrated them into their traditional forms of spirit worship. Buddhists in rural Burma and Thailand, for example, might also believe in nature spirits. On Java and Sumatra, where Islam was slow to penetrate into the interior, the result was a division between devout Mus-

lims in the cities and the still essentially animist peasants in the rural villages that persists to this day in Indonesian society.

Both Buddhism and Islam brought other changes in their train—temple education for Buddhists and schools for Islamic scholars and new religious and moral restrictions on human behavior such as refraining from eating pork and drinking wine for Muslims (though some foreign Muslims complained that the latter was not always followed). Because Islam discouraged the traditional tattooing of the body, Muslim converts turned to the technique of decorating textiles called *batik*.

Buddhism and Islam also helped to shape Southeast Asian political institutions. As the political systems began to mature, they evolved into four main types: Buddhist kings, Javanese kings, Islamic sultans, and Vietnamese emperors (for the case of Vietnam, which was strongly influenced by China, see Chapter 11). In each case, institutions and concepts imported from abroad were adapted to local circumstances.

The Buddhist style of kingship took shape between the eleventh and the fifteenth century, as Theravada Buddhism spread throughout the area. It became the pre-

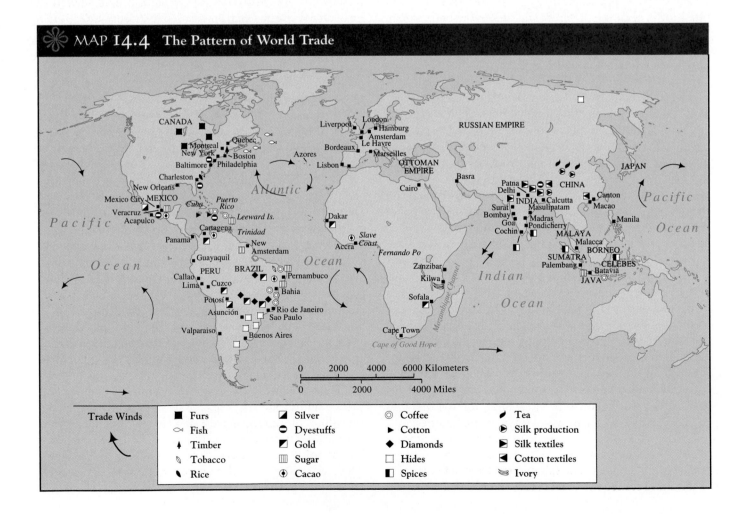

MAP 14.4   The Pattern of World Trade

THE TIMELY END OF SULTAN ZAINAL-'ABIDIN

Acheh, on the northern tip of the island of Sumatra, was one of the first areas in Southeast Asia to be converted to Islam. This passage from the History of Acheh *describes the cruel habits of Sultan Zainal-'Abidin, who ruled in the early seventeenth century. Note the understated way in which the author describes his deposition.*

HISTORY OF ACHEH

Then Sultan Seri'Alam was deposed and Sultan Zainal was installed.

The former had occupied the throne for one year before passing away. He passed away in the year 995 (A.H.) [1617 C.E.]. . . .

After the kingdom of Acheh Dar as-Salam and all its subject territories had been handed over to Sultan Zainal-'Abidin, he would always go out on to the arena and would have rutting elephants as well as ones which were not rutting charge each other, and as a result several people were gored to death by them, and the Bunga Setangkai palace was rammed and then collapsed in ruins together with its annexes. . . . He would order men to beat each other and to duel with staves and shields, and would order Achehnese champion fencers to compete with Indian ones, so that several of the Achehnese and Indian fencers were killed and some were wounded. . . .

If the Sultan were holding audience in a certain place all the chiefs were instructed to sit in homage in the hot sun or in the rain without distinction between the good or the evil. . . .

When the chiefs noticed these habits of the Sultan, and observed that they were growing worse day by day, they said to each other, "What should we do about our lord, for if his oppression of us is like this while he is still young, what will it be like when he is older? According to us, if he continues to be ruler everything will certainly fall in ruins about our ears." Then Sharif al-Muluk Maharaja Lela said, "If that is how it is, it would be best for us to depose our lord the Sultan."

After the chiefs had reached agreement on this matter, one evening the Sultan summoned persons to recite texts in praise of God, and the chiefs were summoned along with them. On that occasion they were reciting texts in the Friday annex. The Sultan was then put on an elephant and was taken to Makota 'Alam. When he arrived at Makota 'Alam . . . [where he was put to death] . . . the Sultan had occupied the throne for two years when he passed away. He passed away in the year 997 (A.H.) [1619 C.E.]. In that same year Sultan 'Ala ad-Din Ri'ayat Shah Marhum Sayyid al-Mukkamil was installed.

---

dominant form of political system in the Buddhist states of mainland Southeast Asia—Burma, Ayuthaya, Laos, and Cambodia. Perhaps the dominant feature of the Buddhist model was the godlike character of the monarch. The king, by virtue of his karma, was considered to be innately superior to other human beings and, in fact, served as a link between human society and the cosmos. Court rituals stressed the sacred character of the monarch, and even the palace was modeled after the symbolic design of the Hindu universe. In its center was an architectural rendering of sacred Mount Meru, the legendary home of the gods.

The Javanese model was a blend of Buddhist and Islamic political traditions. Like their Buddhist counterparts, Javanese monarchs possessed a sacred quality and maintained the balance between the sacred and the material world, but as Islam penetrated the Indonesian islands in the fifteenth and sixteenth centuries, the monarchs began to lose their semidivine quality.

The Islamic model was found mainly on the Malay peninsula and in the small coastal states of the Indonesian archipelago. In this pattern, the head of state was a sultan, who was viewed as a mortal, although he still possessed some magical qualities. The sultan served as a defender of the faith and staffed his bureaucracy mainly with aristo-

crats, but he also frequently relied on the Muslim community of scholars—the *ulama*—and was expected, at least in theory, to rule according to the *Shari'ah* (see the box above).

ECONOMY AND SOCIETY

During the early period of European penetration, the economy of virtually all Southeast Asian societies continued to be based on agriculture, as it had been for thousands of years. Still, by the sixteenth century, commerce was beginning to affect the daily lives of many Southeast Asians, especially in the cities that were beginning to proliferate along the coasts or on navigable rivers. In part, this was because agriculture itself was becoming more commercialized to a limited degree, as cash crops like sugar and spices replaced subsistence farming in rice or other cereals in some areas.

Regional and interregional trade were already expanding before the coming of the Europeans. The central geographical location of Southeast Asia enabled it to become a focal point in an interregional trading network. The spices, of course, were the mainstay of the interregional trade, but Southeast Asia exchanged other products as

✳ **BRINGING LUMBER TO JAVA.**   Long before the Europeans arrived, a brisk trade was taking place throughout the Indonesian islands and the South China Sea. Many of the goods that were transported through the area were carried on sturdy boats—called pinisi—that were manned by the Bugi, a trading people who lived mainly in the eastern islands. This trade continues today, as these cargo ships in the harbor of Jakarta attest. The Bugi were also widely feared as pirates.

well. The region exported tin (mined in Malaya since the tenth century), copper, gold, tropical fruits and other agricultural products, cloth, gems, and luxury goods in exchange for manufactured goods, ceramics including Chinese porcelain, and high-quality textiles such as silk from China. Although Southeast Asia on balance was an importer of manufactured goods, the region produced some high-quality goods of its own. The ceramics of Vietnam and Thailand, though not made with the high-firing techniques used in China, were still of good quality. The Portuguese traveler Duarte Barbosa observed that the Javanese were skilled cabinetmakers, weapons manufacturers, shipbuilders, and locksmiths. The royal courts were both the main producers and the primary consumers of luxury goods, most of which were produced by highly skilled slaves in the employ of the court.

In general, Southeast Asians probably enjoyed a somewhat higher living standard than most of their contemporaries elsewhere in Asia. Although most of the population was poor by modern Western standards, starvation and even widespread hunger were probably fairly rare. Several factors help explain this relative prosperity. In the first place, most of Southeast Asia has been blessed by a salubrious climate. The uniformly high temperatures and the abundant rainfall enable as many as two or even three crops to be grown each year. Second, although the soil in some areas is poor, the alluvial deltas on the mainland are fertile, and the volcanoes of Indonesia periodically spew forth rich volcanic ash that renews the mineral resources of the soil of Sumatra and Java. Finally, with some exceptions, most of Southeast Asia was relatively thinly populated. According to one estimate, the population of the entire region in 1600 was about 20 million, or about 5.5 persons per square kilometer, well below levels elsewhere in Asia. Only in a few areas such as the Red River delta in northern Vietnam was overpopulation a serious problem.

Social institutions tended to be fairly homogeneous throughout Southeast Asia. Compared with China and India, there was little social stratification, and the nuclear family predominated. In general, women fared better in Southeast Asia than anywhere else in Asia. Although they were usually restricted to specialized work, such as making ceramics, weaving, or transplanting the rice seedlings into the main paddy fields, and rarely possessed legal rights equal to those of men, they enjoyed a comparatively high degree of freedom and status in most societies in the region and, as we saw in Chapter 9, were sometimes involved in commerce. Daughters often had the same inheritance rights as sons, and family property was held jointly between husband and wife. Wives were often permitted to divorce their husbands, and monogamy was the rule rather than the exception. In some cases, the family of the groom provided the dowry in marriage, and married couples often went to live in the wife's village.

 # CONCLUSION

At the end of the fifteenth century, Europeans burst upon the world scene. Beginning with the seemingly modest ventures of the Portuguese ships that sailed southward along the West African coast in the mid-fifteenth century, the process accelerated with the epoch-making voyages of Christopher Columbus to the Americas and Vasco da Gama to the Indian Ocean in the 1490s. Soon a number of other European states had entered the scene, and by the end of the eighteenth century, they had created a global trade network dominated by Western ships and Western power.

In less than three hundred years, the European Age of Exploration changed the shape of the world. In some areas, such as the Americas and the Spice Islands, it led to the destruction of indigenous civilizations and the establishment of European colonies. In others, as in Africa, South Asia, and mainland Southeast Asia, it left native regimes intact but had a strong impact on local societies and regional trade patterns.

At the time, many European observers viewed the process in a favorable light. It not only expanded world trade and introduced new crops and discoveries between the Old and the New Worlds (a process sometimes called the "Columbian Exchange" that will be discussed in the Reflection at the end of Part III), but it also introduced "heathen peoples" to the message of Jesus Christ. Some modern historians have been much more critical,

FLEETS OF THE FOREST.   The peoples of Nias, a small island off the western coast of Sumatra, had long been isolated from other societies in the region, until the arrival of Dutch traders in the seventeenth century. Although Christian missionaries converted much of the population to the Christian faith two hundred years later, much of their Stone Age way of life has survived. In this hilltop village located in the center of the island, however, the houses in the background strongly resemble the hulls of the sturdy Dutch galleons that once anchored offshore.

concluding that European activities during the sixteenth and seventeenth centuries had already created a "tributary mode of production" based on European profits from unequal terms of trade that foreshadowed the highly exploitative relationship characteristic of the later colonial period. Some recent scholars have questioned that contention, however, and argue that although Western commercial operations had a significant impact on global trade patterns, they did not —at least before the eighteenth century —freeze out non-European participants. Muslim merchants, for example, were long able to evade European efforts to eliminate them from the spice trade, and the trans-Saharan caravan trade was relatively unaffected by European merchant shipping along the West African coast. In some cases, the European presence may even have encouraged new economic activity, as in the Indian subcontinent (see Chapter 16). If there was an "age of Western dominance," then, it did not take shape before the end of the period under consideration here.

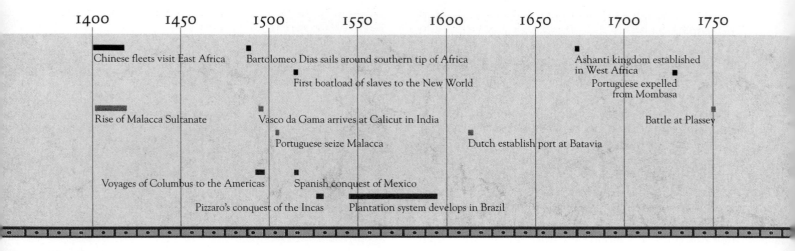

| 1400 | 1450 | 1500 | 1550 | 1600 | 1650 | 1700 | 1750 |

Chinese fleets visit East Africa   Bartolomeo Dias sails around southern tip of Africa   Ashanti kingdom established in West Africa

First boatload of slaves to the New World   Portuguese expelled from Mombasa

Rise of Malacca Sultanate   Vasco da Gama arrives at Calicut in India   Battle at Plassey

Portuguese seize Malacca   Dutch establish port at Batavia

Voyages of Columbus to the Americas   Spanish conquest of Mexico

Pizzaro's conquest of the Incas   Plantation system develops in Brazil

CHAPTER NOTES

1. Harry J. Benda and John A. Larkin, eds., *The World of Southeast Asia: Selected Historical Readings* (New York, 1967), p. 13.
2. J. H. Parry, *The European Reconnaissance: Selected Documents* (New York, 1968), p. 113, quoting from Armando Cortesao, *The Summa Oriental of Tome Pires* (London, 1944), 2:283–87.
3. Quoted in J. H. Parry, *The Age of Reconnaissance: Discovery, Exploration and Settlement, 1450 to 1650* (New York, 1963), p. 33.
4. Quoted in Richard B. Reed, "The Expansion of Europe," in Richard DeMolen, ed., *The Meaning of the Renaissance and Reformation* (Boston, 1974), p. 308.

5. K. N. Chaudhuri, *Trade and Civilization in the Indian Ocean: An Economic History from the Rise of Islam to 1750* (Cambridge, 1985), p. 65.
6. Miguel Leon-Portilla, ed., *The Broken Spears: The Aztec Account of the Conquest of Mexico* (Boston, 1969), p. 51.
7. Quoted in Parry, *The Age of Reconnaissance*, pp. 176–77.
8. Quoted in Basil Davidson, *Africa in History: Themes and Outlines* (London, 1968), p. 137.

SUGGESTED READINGS

Classic works on the period of European expansion include J. H. Parry, *The Age of Reconnaissance: Discovery, Exploration and Settlement, 1450 to 1650* (New York, 1963); B. Penrose, *Travel and Discovery in the Renaissance, 1420–1620* (New York, 1962); and the brief work by J. H. Parry, *The Establishment of European Hegemony, 1415–1715* (New York, 1961). Also, see K. M. Panikkar, *Asia and Western Dominance* (London, 1959), and H. Furber, *Rival Empires of Trade in the Orient, 1600–1800* (Minneapolis, 1976). For a more critical interpretation, see E. Wolf, *Europe and the People Without History* (Berkeley, Calif., 1982), and A. G. Frank, *World Accumulation, 1492–1789* (New York, 1978).

On the technological aspects, see C. M. Cipolla, *Guns, Sails, and Empires: Technological Innovation and the Early Phases of European Expansion, 1400–1700* (New York, 1965); F. Fernandez-Armesto, ed., *The Times Atlas of World Exploration* (New York, 1991); R. C. Smith, *Vanguard of Empire: Ships of Exploration in the Age of Columbus* (Oxford, 1993); and D. Boorstin, *The Discoverers* (New York, 1983). For an overview on the impact of European expansion

in the Indian Ocean, see K. N. Chaudhuri, *Trade and Civilization in the Indian Ocean: An Economic History from the Rise of Islam to 1750* (Cambridge, 1985). For a series of stimulating essays reflecting recent scholarship, see J. D. Tracy, *The Rise of Merchant Empires: Long-Distance Trade in the Early Modern World, 1350–1750* (Cambridge, 1990).

On European expansion in the Americas, see S. E. Morison, *The European Discovery of America: The Southern Voyages*, A.D. 1492–1616 (New York, 1974). On Columbus, see the brief biography by J. S. Collis, *Christopher Columbus* (London, 1976). For a fundamental work on Spanish colonization, see J. H. Parry, *The Spanish Seaborne Empire* (New York, 1966). The standard work on the conquistadors is F. A. Kirkpatrick, *The Spanish Conquistadores* (Cleveland, 1968). See also the richly illustrated H. Innes, *The Conquistadors* (New York, 1969). The human effects of the interaction of New and Old World cultures are examined thoughtfully in A. W. Crosby, *The Columbia Exchange: Biological and Cultural Consequences of 1492* (Westport, Conn., 1972).

On Portuguese expansion, the fundamental work is C. R. Boxer, *The Portuguese Seaborne Empire, 1415–1825* (New York, 1969). For a more recent interpretation, see W. B. Diffie and G. D. Winius, *Foundations of the Portuguese Empire, 1415–1580* (Minneapolis, 1979). On the Dutch, see J. I. Israel, *Dutch Primacy in World Trade, 1585–1740* (Oxford, 1989). The effects of European trade in Southeast Asia are discussed in A. Reid, *Southeast Asia in the Age of Commerce, 1450–1680* (New Haven, Conn., 1989).

On the African slave trade, the standard work is P. Curtin, *The African Slave Trade: A Census* (Madison, Wis., 1969). For more recent treatments, see H. S. Klein, *The Middle Passage: Comparative Studies in the Atlantic Slave Trade* (Princeton, N.J., 1978); P. Lovejoy, *Transformations in Slavery: A History of Slavery in Africa* (1983); and P. Manning, *Slavery and African Life* (1990). Also, see C. Palmer, *Human Cargoes: The British Slave Trade to Spanish America,* *1700–1739* (Urbana, Ill., 1981), and K. F. Kiple, *The Caribbean Slave: A Biological History* (Cambridge, 1984).

For a brief introduction to women's experiences during the Age of Exploration and global trade, see S. Hughes and B. Hughes, *Women in World History,* vol. 2 (Armonk, N.Y., 1997). For a more theoretical discussion of violence and gender in the early modern period, consult R. Trexler, *Sex and Conquest: Gendered Violence, Political Order and the European Conquest of the Americas* (Ithaca, N.Y., 1995). The native American female experience with the European encounter is presented in R. Gutierrez, *When Jesus Came the Corn Mothers Went Away: Marriage, Sexuality and Power in New Mexico, 1500–1846* (Stanford, Calif., 1991), and K. Anderson, *Chain Her by One Foot: The Subjugation of Women in Seventeenth Century New France* (London, 1991).

INFOTRAC COLLEGE EDITION

For additional reading, go to InfoTrac College Edition, your online research library at http://web1.infotrac-college.com

Enter the search terms "Vasco da Gama" using Keywords.

Enter the search terms "Christopher Columbus" using the Subject Guide.

Enter the search term "mercantilism" using the Subject Guide.

Enter the search terms "Africa history" using Keywords.

CHAPTER 15

RELIGIOUS REFORM AND STATE BUILDING IN EUROPE

CHAPTER OUTLINE

- THE PROTESTANT REFORMATION
- THE CATHOLIC REFORMATION
- EUROPE IN CRISIS: WAR, REVOLUTION, AND SOCIAL DISINTEGRATION, 1560–1650
- RESPONSE TO CRISIS: THE PRACTICE OF ABSOLUTISM
- LIMITED MONARCHY: ENGLAND AND THE EMERGENCE OF CONSTITUTIONAL MONARCHY
- THE WORLD OF EUROPEAN CULTURE
- CONCLUSION

FOCUS QUESTIONS

- What were Martin Luther's main disagreements with the Roman Catholic church, and why did the movement he started spread so quickly across Europe?
- What were the main tenets of Lutheranism, Zwinglianism, Calvinism, and Anabaptism, and how did they differ from each other and from Catholicism?
- Why is the period between 1560 and 1650 in Europe called an age of crisis, and how did the turmoil contribute to the artistic and intellectual developments of the period?
- What was absolutism, and what were the main characteristics of the absolute monarchies that emerged in France, Prussia, Austria, and Russia?
- What were the main issues in the struggle between king and Parliament in seventeenth-century England, and how were they resolved?

O n April 18, 1520, a lowly monk stood before the emperor and princes of Germany in the city of Worms. He had been called before this august gathering to answer charges of heresy, charges that could threaten his very life. The monk was confronted with a pile of his books and asked if he wished to defend them all or reject a part. Courageously, Martin Luther defended them all and asked to be shown where any part was in error on the basis of "Scripture and plain reason." The emperor was outraged by Luther's response and made his own position clear the next day: "Not only I, but you of this noble German nation, would be forever disgraced if by our negligence not only heresy but the very suspicion of heresy were to survive. After having heard yesterday the obstinate defense of Luther, I regret that I have so long delayed in proceeding against him and his false teaching. I will have no more to do with him." Luther's appearance at Worms set the stage for a serious challenge to the authority of the Catholic church. It was by no means the first in the church's fifteen-hundred-year history, but its consequences were more far-reaching than anyone at Worms in 1520 could have imagined. The unity of Christendom was shattered by the Protestant Reformation initiated by Martin Luther.

Although the Protestant and Catholic Reformations of the sixteenth century made religion a central focus of people's lives, by the middle of the sixteenth century this renewal of religious passion had been accomplished at a great cost—the breakup of the religious unity of medieval Europe. This religious division (Catholics versus Protestants) was instrumental in beginning a series of wars that dominated much of European history from 1560 to 1650 and, in turn, exacerbated the economic and social crises that were besetting Europe. Wars, revolutions and constitutional crises, economic depression, social disintegration, the witchcraft craze, and demographic crisis all afflicted Europe.

One of the responses to these crises was a search for order and harmony. The most general trend was an extension of monarchical power as a stabilizing force. This development, which historians have called absolutism or absolute monarchy, was most evident in France during the flamboyant reign of Louis XIV. But other states, such as England, responded differently to domestic crisis, and another very different system emerged in which monarchs were limited by the power of their representative assemblies. Whether absolutist or limited monarchies, European states also developed larger military forces and economies to support larger governmental bureaucracies and more wars. In the process, European states gained the resources to move out into the global stage in a dramatic fashion. ❁

THE PROTESTANT REFORMATION

Beginning in the Late Middle Ages, there seemed to be an increasing number of calls for the reform of the Catholic church, whether it be to end the corruption in the clergy or to reduce the excessive power of the papacy. The church had managed to crush these early efforts at reform, but at the beginning of the sixteenth century it came to face an even more menacing reform movement. The Protestant Reformation had its beginnings in a typical medieval question: What must I do to be saved? Martin Luther, a deeply religious man, found an answer that did not fit within the traditional teachings of the late-medieval church. Ultimately he split with that church, destroying the religious unity of western Christendom. That other people were concerned with the same question is evident in the rapid spread of the Reformation.

Prelude to Reformation

Martin Luther's reform movement was not the first in sixteenth-century Europe. During the second half of the fifteenth century, the new classical learning that was part of Italian Renaissance humanism spread to northern Europe and spawned a movement called Christian or Northern Renaissance humanism, whose major goal was the reform of Christendom.

The Christian humanists believed in the ability of human beings to reason and improve themselves. They thought that if people would read the classics, and especially the basic works of Christianity, they would become more pious. This inner piety, or inward religious feeling, would bring about a reform of the church and society. For this reason, Christian humanists supported schools, brought out new editions of the classics, and prepared new editions of the Bible and writings of early Christianity. In the preface to his edition of the Greek New Testament, the famous humanist Erasmus wrote:

> Indeed, I disagree very much with those who are unwilling that Holy Scripture, translated into the vulgar tongue, be read by the uneducated, as if Christ taught such intricate doctrines that they could scarcely be understood by very few theologians, or as if the strength of the Christian religion consisted in men's ignorance of it . . . I would that even the lowliest women read the Gospels and the Pauline Epistles. And I would that they were translated into all languages so that they could be read and understood not only by Scots and Irish but also by Turks and Saracens. . . . Would that, as a result, the farmer sing some portion of them at the plow, the weaver hum some parts of them to the movement of his shuttle, the traveler lighten the weariness of the journey with stories of this kind![1]

This belief in the power of education would remain an important characteristic of European civilization. Like later intellectuals, Christian humanists believed that to change society they must first change the human beings who compose it.

The most influential of all the Christian humanists was Erasmus (1466–1536). After withdrawing from a monastery, he wandered to France, England, Italy, Germany, and Switzerland, conversing everywhere in the classical Latin that might be called his mother tongue. *The Handbook of the Christian Knight*, published in 1503, reflected his preoccupation with religion. He called his conception of religion "the philosophy of Christ," by which he meant that Christianity should be a guiding philosophy for the direction of daily life rather than the system of dogmatic beliefs and practices that the medieval church seemed to stress. In other words, he emphasized inner piety and ethics while de-emphasizing the external forms of religion (such as the sacraments, pilgrimages, fasts, veneration of saints, and relics).

To reform the church, Erasmus wanted to spread the philosophy of Christ, provide education in the works of Christianity, and criticize the abuses in the church. In his work *The Praise of Folly*, written in 1509, Erasmus humorously criticized aspects of his society that he believed were most in need of reform. He was especially harsh on the abuses in the church and singled out the monks for special treatment. Monks, he said, "insist that everything be done in precise detail. . . . Just so many knots must be on each shoe and the shoelace must be of only one color, . . . and they can sleep only the specified number of hours per day." Because of this attention to detail, he continued, "they think that they are superior to all people" and will be rewarded in heaven.

Erasmus's reform program, however, did not achieve its goal. Undoubtedly, his work helped to prepare the way for the Reformation; as contemporaries proclaimed, "Erasmus laid the egg that Luther hatched." Yet Erasmus eventually disapproved of Luther and the Protestant reformers. He had no intention of destroying the unity of the medieval Christian church; instead, his whole program was based on reform within the church.

Church and Religion on the Eve of the Reformation

Corruption in the Catholic church was another factor that encouraged people to want reform. No doubt, the failure of the Renaissance popes to provide spiritual leadership had affected the spiritual life of all Christendom. The preoccupation of the papal court with finances had an especially strong impact on the clergy. So, too, did the economic changes of the fourteenth and fifteenth centuries. The highest positions of the clergy were increasingly held by either nobles or wealthy members of the bourgeoisie. At the same time, to increase their revenues, high church officials (such as bishops, archbishops, and cardinals) took over more than one church office. This practice of plu-

ralism (the holding of many church offices) led, in turn, to the problem of absenteeism. Church officeholders ignored their duties and paid underlings to run their offices who were often little interested in performing their duties. No wonder that so many people complained in the fifteenth century about the ignorance and failure of parish priests.

While the leaders of the church were failing to meet their responsibilities, ordinary people were clamoring for meaningful religious expression and certainty of salvation. As a result, for some the process of salvation became almost mechanical. Collections of relics grew as more and more people sought certainty of salvation through their veneration. Frederick the Wise, elector of Saxony and Luther's prince, had amassed over 5,000 relics to which were attached indulgences that could reduce one's time in purgatory by 1,443 years (an indulgence is a remission of the penalties due to sin). Other people sought certainty of salvation in the popular mystical movement known as the Modern Devotion. The Modern Devotion downplayed religious dogma and stressed the need to follow the teachings of Christ. Thomas à Kempis, author of *The Imitation of Christ*, wrote that "Truly, at the day of judgment we shall not be examined by what we have read, but what we have done; not how well we have spoken, but how religiously we have lived."

What is striking about the revival of religious piety in the fifteenth century—whether expressed through such external forces as the veneration of relics and the buying of indulgences or the mystical path—was its adherence to the orthodox beliefs and practices of the Catholic church. The agitation for certainty of salvation and spiritual peace was done within the framework of the "holy mother Church." But disillusionment grew as the devout experienced the clergy's inability to live up to their expectations. The deepening of religious life, especially in the second half of the fifteenth century, found little echo among the worldly-wise clergy, and it is this divergence that helps to explain the tremendous and immediate impact of Luther's ideas.

Martin Luther and the Reformation in Germany

Martin Luther was born in Germany on November 10, 1483. His father wanted him to become a lawyer, so Luther enrolled at the University of Erfurt. In 1505, after becoming a master in the liberal arts, the young Martin began to study law. But Luther was not content with the study of law and all along had shown religious inclinations. In the summer of 1505, en route back to Erfurt after a brief visit home, he was caught in a ferocious thunderstorm and vowed that if he were spared, he would become a monk. He then entered the monastic order of the Augustinian Hermits in Erfurt. Later, he studied theology at the University of Wittenberg, where he received his doctorate in 1512 and then became a professor in the theological

LUTHER AND THE NINETY-FIVE THESES

To most historians, the publication of Luther's Ninety-Five Theses marks the beginning of the Reformation. To Luther, they were simply a response to what he considered to be the blatant abuses committed by sellers of indulgences. Although written in Latin, the theses were soon translated into German and disseminated widely across Germany. They made an immense impression on Germans already dissatisfied with the ecclesiastical and financial policies of the papacy.

MARTIN LUTHER, SELECTIONS FROM THE NINETY-FIVE THESES

5. The Pope has neither the will nor the power to remit any penalties beyond those he has imposed either at his own discretion or by canon law.

20. Therefore the Pope, by his plenary remission of all penalties, does not mean "all" in the absolute sense, but only those imposed by himself.

21. Hence those preachers of Indulgences are wrong when they say that a man is absolved and saved from every penalty by the Pope's Indulgences.

27. It is mere human talk to preach that the soul flies out [of purgatory] immediately [when] the money clinks in the collection box.

28. It is certainly possible that when the money clinks in the collection box greed and avarice can increase; but the intercession of the Church depends on the will of God alone.

50. Christians should be taught that, if the Pope knew the exactions of the preachers of Indulgences, he would rather have the basilica of St. Peter reduced to ashes than built with the skin, flesh, and bones of his sheep [the indulgences that so distressed Luther were being sold to raise money for the construction of the new St. Peter's Basilica in Rome].

81. This wanton preaching of pardons makes it difficult even for learned men to redeem respect due to the Pope from the slanders or at least the shrewd questionings of the laity.

82. For example: "Why does not the Pope empty purgatory for the sake of most holy love and the supreme need of souls? This would be the most righteous of reasons, if he can redeem innumerable souls for sordid money with which to build a basilica, the most trivial of reasons."

86. Again: "Since the Pope's wealth is larger than that of the crassest Crassi of our time, why does he not build this one basilica of St. Peter with his own money, rather than with that of the faithful poor?"

90. To suppress these most conscientious questionings of the laity by authority only, instead of refuting them by reason, is to expose the Church and the Pope to the ridicule of their enemies, and to make Christian people unhappy.

94. Christians should be exhorted to seek earnestly to follow Christ, their Head, through penalties, deaths, and hells.

95. And let them thus be more confident of entering heaven through many tribulations rather than through a false assurance of peace.

faculty, lecturing on the Bible. Probably sometime between 1513 and 1516, through his study of the Bible, he arrived at an answer to a problem—the assurance of salvation—that had disturbed him since his entry into the monastery.

Catholic doctrine had emphasized that both faith and good works were required of a Christian to achieve personal salvation. In Luther's eyes, human beings, weak and powerless in the sight of an almighty God, could never do enough good works to merit salvation. Through his study of the Bible, Luther rediscovered another way of viewing this problem. To Luther, humans are not saved through their good works, but through faith in the promises of God, made possible by the sacrifice of Christ on the cross. The doctrine of salvation or justification by grace through faith alone became the primary doctrine of the Protestant Reformation. Because Luther had arrived at this doctrine from his study of the Bible, the Bible became for him, as it would be for all other Protestants, the chief guide to religious truth. Justification by faith and the Bible as the sole authority in religious affairs were the twin pillars of the Protestant Reformation.

Luther did not see himself as a rebel, but he was greatly upset by the widespread selling of indulgences. Especially offensive in his eyes was the monk Johann Tetzel, who hawked indulgences with the slogan: "As soon as the coin in the coffer [money box] rings, the soul from purgatory springs." Luther believed that people were simply harming their chances for salvation by buying these pieces of paper. Greatly angered, he issued his Ninety-Five Theses, which were a stunning indictment of the abuses in the sale of indulgences (see the box above). Luther did not intend any break with the church over the issue of indulgences, but he did want the pope to stop their sale. But the Renaissance pope Leo X did not take the issue seriously and is reported to have said that Luther was simply "some drunken German who will amend his ways when he sobers up." Thousands of copies of the Ninety-Five Theses were printed and quickly spread to all parts of Germany.

Under pressure from the church and his followers, Luther began to move toward a more definite break with the Catholic church. He called on the German princes to overthrow the papacy in Germany and establish a

In the 1520s, after Luther's return to Wittenberg, his teachings began to spread rapidly, ending ultimately in a reform movement supported by state authorities. Pamphlets containing picturesque woodcuts were important in the spread of Luther's ideas. In the woodcut shown here, the crucified Jesus attends Luther's service on the left, while on the right the pope is at a table selling indulgences.

reformed German church. He attacked the system of sacraments as the means by which the pope and church had destroyed the real meaning of the Gospel for one thousand years. He kept only two sacraments, baptism and the Lord's Supper, and called for the clergy to marry. Through all these calls for change, Luther expounded more and more on his new doctrine of salvation. It is faith alone, he said, not good works, which justifies and brings salvation through Christ.

Unable to accept Luther's forcefully worded dissent from traditional Catholic teachings, the church excommunicated him in January 1521. He was also summoned to appear before the imperial diet or Reichstag of the Holy Roman Empire, convened by the newly elected emperor Charles V (1519–1556). Expected to recant the heretical doctrines he had espoused, Luther refused and made the famous reply that became the battle cry of the Reformation:

> Since then Your Majesty and your lordships desire a simple reply, I will answer without horns and without teeth. Unless I am convicted by Scripture and plain reason—I do not accept the authority of popes and councils, for they have contradicted each other—my conscience is captive to the Word of God. I cannot and I will not recant anything, for to go against conscience is neither right nor safe. Here I stand; I cannot do otherwise. God help me. Amen.[2]

The young emperor Charles was outraged at Luther's audacity and gave his opinion that "a single friar who goes counter to all Christianity for a thousand years must be wrong." By the Edict of Worms, Martin Luther was made an outlaw within the empire. His works were to be burned and Luther himself captured and delivered to the emperor.

Between 1521 and 1525, Luther's religious movement became a revolution. Luther was able to gain the support of his prince, the elector of Saxony, as well as other German rulers among the three hundred–odd states that made up the Holy Roman Empire. These rulers were instrumental in instituting new state-dominated churches in their territories. The Lutheran churches in Germany (and later in Scandinavia) quickly became territorial or state churches in which the state supervised and disciplined church members. As part of the development of these state-dominated churches, Luther also instituted new religious services to replace the mass. These featured a worship service consisting of a German liturgy that focused on Bible reading, preaching of the word of God, and song. Following his own denunciation of clerical celibacy, Luther married a former nun, Katherina von Bora, in 1525. His union provided a model of married and family life for the new Protestant minister.

A series of crises in the mid-1520s made it apparent, however, that spreading the word of God was not as easy as Luther had originally envisioned, the usual plight of most reformers. Luther experienced dissent within his own ranks in Wittenberg as well as defection from many Christian humanists who feared that Luther's movement threatened the unity of Christendom. The Peasants' War constituted Luther's greatest challenge, however. In June 1524, peasants in Germany rose in revolt against their lords and looked to Luther for support. But Luther, who knew how much his reformation of the church depended on the full support of the German princes and magistrates, supported the rulers. To Luther, God had ordained the state and its rulers and given them the authority to maintain the peace and order necessary for the spread of the Gospel. It was the duty of princes to suppress all revolts. By May 1525, the German princes had ruthlessly suppressed the peasant hordes. By this time, Luther found himself ever more dependent on state authorities for the growth and maintenance of his reformed church.

Politics and Religion in the German Reformation

From its very beginning, the fate of Luther's movement had been closely tied to political affairs. In 1519, Charles I, king of Spain and the grandson of the Emperor Maximilian, had been elected Holy Roman emperor as

�֎ **CHARLES V.** Charles V sought to maintain religious unity throughout his vast empire by keeping all his subjects within the bounds of the Catholic church. Due to his conflict with Francis I as well as difficulties with the Turks, the papacy, and the German princes, Charles was never able to check the spread of Lutheranism. This is a portrait of Charles V by the Venetian painter Titian.

Charles V (1519–1556). Charles V ruled over an immense empire, consisting of Spain and its overseas possessions, the traditional Austrian Habsburg lands, Bohemia, Hungary, the Low Countries, and the kingdom of Naples in southern Italy. Politically, Charles wanted to maintain his dynasty's control over his enormous empire; religiously, he hoped to preserve the unity of his empire in the Catholic faith. Despite his strengths, Charles spent a lifetime in futile pursuit of his goals. Four major problems—the French, the papacy, the Turks, and Germany's internal situation—kept him preoccupied and cost him both his dream and his health. At the same time, these four factors contributed to the survival of Lutheranism by giving the Lutherans time to organize before having to face the concerted onslaught of the Catholic forces.

Between 1521 and 1544, Charles fought a series of wars with his chief rival, the French king Francis I (1515–1547). At the same time, Charles faced opposition from Pope Clement VII (1523–1534), who, guided by political considerations, joined the side of Francis I. The advance of the Ottoman Turks (see Chapter 16) into the eastern part of Charles's empire forced the emperor to divert forces there as well.

Finally, the internal political situation in the Holy Roman Empire was also not in Charles's favor. Germany was a land of several hundred territorial states: princely states, ecclesiastical principalities, and free imperial cities. Although all owed loyalty to the emperor, Germany's development in the Middle Ages had enabled these states to become quite independent of imperial authority. They had no desire to have a strong emperor. By the time Charles V was able to bring military forces to Germany—in 1546—Lutheranism had become well established and the Lutheran princes well organized. Unable to impose his will on Germany, Charles was forced to negotiate a truce. An end to religious warfare in Germany came in 1555 with the Peace of Augsburg, which marks an important turning point in the history of the Reformation. The division of Christianity was formally acknowledged when Lutheranism was granted the same legal rights as Catholicism. Moreover, the peace settlement accepted the right of each German ruler to determine the religion of his subjects.

The Peace of Augsburg was a victory for the German princes. The independence of the numerous German territorial states guaranteed the weakness of the Holy Roman Empire and the continued decentralization of Germany. Charles's hope for a united empire had been completely dashed. At the same time, what had at first been merely feared was now confirmed: the ideal of medieval Christian unity was irretrievably lost. The rapid proliferation of new Protestant groups served to underscore the new reality.

The Spread of the Protestant Reformation

Switzerland was home to two major Reformation movements, Zwinglianism and Calvinism. Ulrich Zwingli (1484–1531) was ordained a priest in 1506 and accepted an appointment as a cathedral priest in the Great Minster of Zürich in 1518. Zwingli's preaching of the Gospel caused such unrest that in 1523 the city council held a public disputation or debate in the town hall. Zwingli's party was accorded the victory, and the council declared that "Mayor, Council and Great Council of Zürich, in order to do away with disturbance and discord, have upon due deliberation and consultation decided and resolved that Master Zwingli should continue as heretofore to proclaim the Gospel and

A REFORMATION DEBATE:
THE MARBURG COLLOQUY

Debates played a crucial role in the Reformation period. They were a primary instrument in introducing the Reformation into innumerable cities as well as a means of resolving differences among like-minded Protestant groups. This selection contains an excerpt from Luther's and Zwingli's vivacious and often brutal debate over the sacrament of the Lord's Supper at Marburg in 1529. The two protagonists failed to reach agreement.

THE MARBURG COLLOQUY, 1529

THE HESSIAN CHANCELLOR FEIGE: My gracious prince and lord [Landgrave Philip of Hesse] has summoned you for the express and urgent purpose of settling the dispute over the sacrament of the Lord's Supper. . . . And let everyone on both sides present his arguments in a spirit of moderation, as becomes such matters. . . . Now then, Doctor Luther, you may proceed.

LUTHER: Noble prince, gracious lord! Undoubtedly the colloquy is well intentioned. . . . Although I have no intention of changing my mind, which is firmly made up, I will nevertheless present the grounds of my belief and show where the others are in error. . . . Your basic contentions are these: In the last analysis you wish to prove that a body cannot be in two places at once, and you produce arguments about the unlimited body which are based on natural reason. I do not question how Christ can be God and man and how the two natures can be joined. For God is more powerful than all our ideas, and we must submit to his word.

Prove that Christ's body is not there where the Scripture says, "This is my body!" Rational proofs I will not listen to. . . . God is beyond all mathematics and the words of God are to be revered and carried out in awe. It is God who commands, "Take, eat, this is my body." I request, therefore, valid scriptural proof to the contrary.

Luther writes on the table in chalk, "This is my body," and covers the words with a velvet cloth.

OECOLAMPADIUS [leader of the reform movement in Basel and a Zwinglian partisan]: The sixth chapter of John clarifies the other scriptural passages. Christ is not speaking there about a local presence. "The flesh is of no avail," he

says [John 6:63]. It is not my intention to employ rational, or geometrical, arguments—neither am I denying the power of God—but as long as I have the complete faith I will speak from that. For Christ is risen; he sits at the right hand of God; and so he cannot be present in the bread. Our view is neither new nor sacrilegious, but is based on faith and Scripture. . . .

ZWINGLI: I insist that the words of the Lord's Supper must be figurative. This is ever apparent, and even required by the article of faith: "taken up into heaven, seated at the right hand of the Father." Otherwise, it would be absurd to look for him in the Lord's Supper at the same time that Christ is telling us that he is in heaven. One and the same body cannot possibly be in different places. . . .

LUTHER: I call upon you as before: your basic contentions are shaky. Give way, and give glory to God!

ZWINGLI: And we call upon you to give glory to God and to quit begging the question! The issue at stake is this: Where is the proof of your position? I am willing to consider your words carefully—no harm meant! You're trying to outwit me. I stand by this passage in the sixth chapter of John, verse 63 and shall not be shaken from it. You'll have to sing another tune.

LUTHER: You're being obnoxious.

ZWINGLI *(excitedly)*: Don't you believe that Christ was attempting in John 6 to help those who did not understand?

LUTHER: You're trying to dominate things! You insist on passing judgment! Leave that to someone else! . . . It is your point that must be proved, not mine. But let us stop this sort of thing. It serves no purpose.

ZWINGLI: It certainly does! It is for you to prove that the passage in John 6 speaks of a physical repast.

LUTHER: You express yourself poorly and make about as much progress as a cane standing in a corner. You're going nowhere.

ZWINGLI: No, no, no! This is the passage that will break your neck!

LUTHER: Don't be so sure of yourself. Necks don't break this way. You're in Hesse, not Switzerland. . . .

---

the pure sacred Scriptures."[3] Over the next two years, evangelical reforms were promulgated in Zürich by a city council strongly influenced by Zwingli. Relics and images were abolished; all paintings and decorations were removed from the churches and replaced by whitewashed walls. The mass was replaced by a new liturgy consisting of Scripture reading, prayer, and sermons. Monasticism, pilgrimages, the veneration of saints, clerical celibacy, and the pope's authority were all abolished as remnants of papal Christianity.

As his movement began to spread to other cities in Switzerland, Zwingli sought an alliance with Martin Luther and the German reformers. Although both the German and the Swiss reformers realized the need for unity to defend against the opposition of the Catholic authorities, they were unable to agree on the interpretation of the Lord's Supper (see the box above). Zwingli believed that the scriptural words "This is my Body, This is my blood" should be taken figuratively, not literally, and refused to accept Luther's insistence on the real presence of the body and blood of Christ "in, with, and under the bread and wine." In October 1531, war erupted between the Swiss Protestant and Catholic states. Zürich's army was routed, and Zwingli was found wounded on the battlefield. His enemies killed him, cut up his body, and burned the pieces, scattering the ashes. The leadership of Swiss Protestantism now passed to John Calvin (1509–1564), the systematic theologian and organizer of the Protestant movement.

John Calvin was educated in his native France, but after his conversion to Protestantism, he was forced to flee France for the safety of Switzerland. In 1536, he published the first edition of the *Institutes of the Christian Religion*, a masterful synthesis of Protestant thought and a work that immediately secured his reputation as one of the new leaders of Protestantism.

On most important doctrines, Calvin stood very close to Luther. He adhered to the doctrine of justification by faith alone to explain how humans achieved salvation. But Calvin also placed much emphasis on the absolute sovereignty of God or the "power, grace, and glory of God." Thus, "God asserts his possession of omnipotence, and claims our acknowledgment of this attribute; not such as is imagined by sophists, vain, idle, and almost asleep, but vigilant, efficacious, operative and engaged in continual action."[4]

One of the ideas derived from his emphasis on the absolute sovereignty of God—predestination—gave a unique cast to Calvin's teachings. This "eternal decree," as Calvin called it, meant that God had predestined some people to be saved (the elect) and others to be damned (the reprobate). According to Calvin, "He has once for all determined, both whom he would admit to salvation, and whom he would condemn to destruction."[5] Although Calvin stressed that there could be no absolute certainty of salvation, his followers did not always make this distinction. The practical psychological effect of predestination was to give later Calvinists an unshakable conviction that they were doing God's work on earth. Thus, Calvinism became a dynamic and activist faith. It is no accident that Calvinism became the militant international form of Protestantism.

In 1536, Calvin began working to reform the city of Geneva. He created a church government that used both clergy and laymen in the service of the church. The Consistory, a special body for enforcing moral discipline, was set up as a court to oversee the moral life and doctrinal purity of Genevans. The Consistory had the right to punish people who deviated from the church's teachings and moral principles. Indeed, citizens in Geneva were punished for such varied "crimes" as dancing, singing obscene songs, drunkenness, swearing, and playing cards.

Calvin's success in Geneva enabled the city to become a vibrant center of Protestantism. John Knox, the Calvinist reformer of Scotland, called Geneva "the most perfect school of Christ on earth." Following Calvin's lead,

missionaries trained in Geneva were sent to all parts of Europe. Calvinism became established in France, the Netherlands, Scotland, and central and eastern Europe. By the mid-sixteenth century, Calvinism had replaced Lutheranism as the militant international form of Protestantism, while Calvin's Geneva stood as the fortress of the Reformation.

While Calvin was forging his militant brand of Protestantism in Switzerland, the English Reformation had been initiated by an act of state. King Henry VIII (1509–1547) had a strong desire to divorce his first wife, Catherine of Aragon, who had failed to produce a male heir. Normally, church authorities might have been willing to grant the king an annulment of his marriage, but Pope Clement VII was dependent on the Holy Roman emperor Charles V, who happened to be the nephew of Queen Catherine.

JOHN CALVIN.   After a conversion experience, John Calvin abandoned his life as a humanist and became a reformer. In 1536, Calvin began working to reform the city of Geneva, where he remained until his death in 1564. This sixteenth-century portrait of Calvin pictures him near the end of his life.

CHRONOLOGY

KEY EVENTS OF THE REFORMATION ERA

Luther's Ninety-Five Theses	1517
Excommunication of Luther	1521
Beginning of Zwingli's reformation in Switzerland	1523
Peasants' War in Germany	1524–1525
Act of Supremacy in England	1534
Pontificate of Paul III	1534–1549
John Calvin's *Institutes of the Christian Religion*	1536
Jesuits recognized as a religious order	1540
Council of Trent	1545–1563
Peace of Augsburg	1555

Impatient with the pope's inaction, Henry sought to obtain an annulment of his marriage in England's own ecclesiastical courts. As archbishop of Canterbury and head of the highest ecclesiastical court in England, Thomas Cranmer held official hearings on the king's case and ruled in May 1533 that the king's marriage to Catherine was "null and absolutely void."

In 1534, upon Henry's request, Parliament moved to finalize the break of the Church of England with Rome. An Act of Supremacy of 1534 declared that the king was "taken, accepted, and reputed the only supreme head on earth of the Church of England," a position that gave him control of doctrine, clerical appointments, and church discipline. Using his new powers, Henry dissolved the monasteries. About four hundred religious houses were closed in 1536, and their land and possessions confiscated by the king. Many were sold to nobles, gentry, and some merchants. The king not only received a great boost to his treasury, but also created a group of supporters who now had a stake in the new Tudor order.

Although Henry VIII had broken with the papacy, little change occurred in matters of doctrine, theology, and ceremony. Some of his supporters, such as Archbishop Thomas Cranmer, wished to have a religious reformation as well as an administrative one, but Henry was unyielding. He died in 1547 and was succeeded by his son, the underage and sickly Edward VI (1547–1553). During Edward's reign, Archbishop Cranmer and others inclined toward Protestant doctrines were able to move the Church of England (or Anglican church) in more of a Protestant direction. New acts of Parliament instituted the right of the clergy to marry and the creation of a revised Protes-

tant liturgy that was elaborated in a new prayer book and liturgical guide known as the Book of Common Prayer. These rapid changes in doctrine and liturgy aroused much opposition and prepared the way for the reaction that occurred when Mary, Henry's first daughter by Catherine of Aragon, came to the throne.

There was no doubt that Mary (1553–1558) was a Catholic who intended to return England to Roman Catholicism. But her restoration of Catholicism aroused much opposition. There was widespread antipathy to Mary's unfortunate marriage to Philip II, the son of Charles V and future king of Spain. Philip was strongly disliked in England, and Mary's foreign policy based on alliance with Spain aroused further hostility. The burning of over three hundred Protestant heretics roused further ire against "bloody Mary." As a result of her policies, Mary managed to achieve the opposite of what she had intended: England was more Protestant by the end of her reign than it had been at the beginning.

Although many reformers were ready to allow the state to play an important, if not dominant, role in church affairs, some people rejected this kind of magisterial reformation and favored a far more radical reform movement. Collectively called the Anabaptists, these radicals actually formed a large variety of different groups, who nevertheless shared some common characteristics. Anabaptism was especially attractive to those peasants, weavers, miners, and artisans who had been adversely affected by the economic changes of the age.

Anabaptists everywhere shared some common ideas. To them, the true Christian church was a voluntary association of believers who had undergone spiritual rebirth and had then been baptized into the church. Anabaptists advocated adult rather than infant baptism. They also took literally a return to the practices and spirit of early Christianity. Adhering to the accounts of early Christian communities in the New Testament, they followed a strict sort of democracy in which all believers were considered equal. Each church chose its own minister, who might be any member of the community because all Christians were considered priests (though women were often excluded). Those chosen as ministers led the services, which were very simple and contained nothing not found in the early church. Anabaptists rejected theological speculation in favor of simple Christian living according to what they believed was the pure word of God. The Lord's Supper was interpreted as a remembrance, a meal of fellowship celebrated in the evening in private houses according to Christ's example. Finally, unlike the Catholics and other Protestants, most Anabaptists believed in the complete separation of church and state. Not only was government to be excluded from the realm of religion, but it was not even supposed to exercise political jurisdiction over real Christians. Anabaptists refused to hold political office or bear arms because many took literally the commandment "Thou shall not kill," although

A PROTESTANT WOMAN

In the initial zeal of the Protestant Reformation, women were frequently allowed to play unusual roles. Catherine Zell of Germany (c. 1497–1562) first preached beside her husband in 1527. After the death of her two children, she devoted the rest of her life to helping her husband and their Anabaptist faith. This selection is taken from one of her letters to a young Lutheran minister who had criticized her activities.

CATHERINE ZELL TO LUDWIG RABUS OF MEMMINGEN

I, Catherine Zell, wife of the late lamented Mathew Zell, who served in Strasbourg, where I was born and reared and still live, wish you peace and enhancement in God's grace. . . .

From my earliest years I turned to the Lord, who taught and guided me, and I have at all times, in accordance with my understanding and His grace, embraced the interests of His church and earnestly sought Jesus. Even in youth this brought me the regard and affection of clergymen and others much concerned with the church, which is why the pious Mathew Zell wanted me as a companion in marriage; and I, in turn, to serve the glory of Christ, gave devotion and help to my husband, both in his ministry and in keeping his house. . . . Ever since I was ten years old I have been a student and a sort of church mother, much given to attending sermons. I have loved and frequented the company of learned men, and I conversed much with them, not about dancing, masquerades, and worldly pleasures but about the kingdom of God. . . .

Consider the poor Anabaptists, who are so furiously and ferociously persecuted. Must the authorities everywhere be incited against them, as the hunter drives his dog against wild animals? Against those who acknowledge Christ the Lord in very much the same way we do and over which we broke with the papacy? Just because they cannot agree with us on lesser things, is this any reason to persecute them and in them Christ, in whom they fervently believe and have often professed in misery, in prison, and under the torments of fire and water?

Governments may punish criminals, but they should not force and govern belief, which is a matter for the heart and conscience not for temporal authorities. . . . When the authorities pursue one, they soon bring forth tears, and towns and villages are emptied.

---

some Anabaptist groups did become quite violent. Their political beliefs as much as their religious beliefs caused the Anabaptists to be regarded as dangerous radicals who threatened the very fabric of sixteenth-century society. Indeed, the chief thing Protestants and Catholics could agree on was the need to persecute Anabaptists.

The Social Impact of the Protestant Reformation

Christianity was such an integral part of European life that it was inevitable that the Reformation would have an impact on the family and popular religious practices.

THE FAMILY

For centuries, Catholicism had praised the family and sanctified its existence by making marriage a sacrament. But the Catholic church's high regard for abstinence from sex as the surest way to holiness made the celibate state of the clergy preferable to marriage. Nevertheless, since not all men could remain chaste, marriage offered the best means to control sexual intercourse and give it a purpose, the procreation of children. To some extent, this attitude persisted among the Protestant reformers; Luther, for example, argued that sex in marriage allowed one to "make use of this sex in order to avoid sin," and Calvin advised that every man should "abstain from marriage only so long as he is fit to observe celibacy." If "his power to tame lust fails him," then he must marry.

But the Reformation did bring some change to the conception of the family. Both Catholic and Protestant clergy preached sermons emphasizing a more positive side to family relationships. The Protestants were especially important in developing this new view of the family. Because Protestantism had eliminated any idea of special holiness for celibacy, abolishing both monasticism and a celibate clergy, the family could be placed at the center of human life, and a new stress on "mutual love between man and wife" could be extolled. But were doctrine and reality the same? For more radical religious groups, at times they were (see the box above). One Anabaptist wrote to his wife before his execution: "My faithful helper, my loyal friend. I praise God that he gave you to me, you who have sustained me in all my trial."[6] But more often reality reflected the traditional roles of husband as the ruler and wife as the obedient servant whose chief duty was to please her husband. Luther stated it clearly:

> The rule remains with the husband, and the wife is compelled to obey him by God's command. He rules the home and the state, wages war, defends his possessions, tills the soil, builds, plants, etc. The woman on the other hand is like a nail driven into the wall . . . so the wife should stay at home and look after the affairs of the household, as one who has been deprived of the ability of administering those affairs that

are outside and that concern the state. She does not go beyond her most personal duties.[7]

Obedience to her husband was not a wife's only role; her other important duty was to bear children. To Calvin and Luther, this function of women was part of the divine plan. God punishes women for the sins of Eve by the burdens of procreation and feeding and nurturing their children. Although Protestantism sanctified this role of woman as mother and wife, viewing it as a holy vocation, it also left few alternatives for women. Because monasticism had been destroyed, that career avenue was no longer available; for most Protestant women, family life was their only destiny. At the same time, by emphasizing the father as "ruler" and hence the center of household religion, Protestantism even removed the woman from her traditional role as controller of religion in the home. Overall, the Protestant Reformation did not noticeably transform women's subordinate place in society.

RELIGIOUS PRACTICES AND POPULAR CULTURE

The attacks of Protestant reformers on the Catholic church led to radical changes in religious practices. The Protestant Reformation abolished or severely curtailed such customary practices as indulgences, the veneration of relics and saints, pilgrimages, monasticism, and clerical celibacy. The elimination of saints put an end to the numerous celebrations of religious holy days and changed a community's sense of time. Thus, in Protestant communities, religious ceremonies and imagery, such as processions and statues, tended to be replaced with individual private prayer, family worship, and collective prayer and worship at the same time each week on Sunday.

In addition to abolishing saints' days and religious carnivals, some Protestant reformers even tried to eliminate customary forms of entertainment. English Puritans (as English Calvinists were called), for example, attempted to ban drinking in taverns, dramatic performances, and dancing. Dutch Calvinists denounced the tradition of giving small presents to children on the feast of Saint Nicholas, near Christmas. Many of these Protestant attacks on popular culture were unsuccessful, however. The importance of taverns in English social life made it impossible to eradicate them, while celebrating at Christmastime persisted in the Dutch Netherlands.

THE CATHOLIC REFORMATION

By the mid-sixteenth century, Lutheranism had become established in Germany and Scandinavia and Calvinism in Switzerland, France, the Netherlands, and eastern Europe. In England, the split from Rome had resulted in the creation of a national church. The situation in Europe did not look particularly favorable to the Roman Catholic church. But even at the beginning of the sixteenth century, constructive, positive forces were at work for reform within the Catholic church, and by the mid-sixteenth century, these forces had given the Catholic church new strength. There were three chief pillars of the Catholic Reformation: the development of the Jesuits, the emergence of a reformed and revived papacy, and the Council of Trent.

The Society of Jesus, known as the Jesuits, was founded by a Spanish nobleman, Ignatius of Loyola (1491–1556). Loyola gathered together a small group of individuals who were recognized as a religious order by a papal bull in 1540.

IGNATIUS LOYOLA. The Jesuits became the most important new religious order of the Catholic Reformation. Shown here in a sixteenth-century painting by an unknown artist is Ignatius Loyola, founder of the Society of Jesus. Loyola is seen kneeling before Pope Paul III, who officially recognized the Jesuits in 1540.

The new order was grounded on the principles of absolute obedience to the papacy, a strict hierarchical order for the society, the use of education to achieve its goals, and a dedication to engage in "conflict for God." Jesuit organization came to resemble the structure of a military command. Executive leadership was put in the hands of a general, who nominated all important positions in the order and was to be revered as its absolute head. Loyola served as the first general of the order until his death in 1556. A special vow of absolute obedience to the pope made the Jesuits an important instrument for papal policy. Jesuit missionaries proved singularly successful in restoring Catholicism to parts of Germany and eastern Europe.

Another prominent Jesuit activity was the propagation of the Catholic faith among non-Christians. Francis Xavier (1506–1552), one of the original members of the Society of Jesus, carried the message of Catholicism to the East, ministering to India and Japan before dying of fever. Although conversion efforts in Japan proved short-lived, Jesuit activity in China, especially that of the Italian Matteo Ricci, was more long lasting.

A reformed papacy was another important factor in the development of the Catholic Reformation. The involvement of the Renaissance papacy in dubious finances and Italian political and military affairs had created numerous sources of corruption. It took the jolt of the Protestant Reformation to bring about serious reform. The pontificate of Pope Paul III (1534–1549) proved to be a turning point. He perceived the need for change and expressed it decisively. Advocates of reform were made cardinals. In 1535, Paul took the audacious step of appointing a Reform Commission to ascertain the church's ills. The commission's report in 1537 blamed the church's problems on the corrupt policies of popes and cardinals. It was also Paul III who formally recognized the Jesuits and initiated the Council of Trent, the third major pillar of the Catholic Reformation.

In March 1545, a group of cardinals, archbishops, bishops, abbots, and theologians met in the city of Trent, on the border between Germany and Italy, and initiated the Council of Trent, which met intermittently from 1545 to 1563 in three major sessions. Moderate Catholic

MAP 15.1 Catholics and Protestants in Europe by 1560

reformers hoped that compromises would be made in formulating doctrinal definitions that would encourage Protestants to return to the church. Conservatives, however, favored an uncompromising restatement of Catholic doctrines in strict opposition to Protestant positions. The latter group won. The final doctrinal decrees of the Council of Trent reaffirmed traditional Catholic teachings in opposition to Protestant beliefs. Scripture and tradition were affirmed as equal authorities in religious matters; only the church could interpret Scripture. Both faith and good works were declared necessary for salvation. The seven sacraments, the Catholic doctrine of transubstantiation, and clerical celibacy were all upheld. Belief in purgatory and in the efficacy of indulgences was strengthened, although hawking of indulgences was prohibited.

After the Council of Trent, the Roman Catholic church possessed a clear body of doctrine and a unified church under the acknowledged supremacy of the popes who had triumphed over bishops and councils. The Roman Catholic church had become one Christian denomination among many, with an organizational framework and doctrinal pattern that would not be significantly altered until Vatican Council II four hundred years later. With a new spirit of confidence, the Catholic church entered a militant phase, as well prepared as the Calvinists to do battle for the Lord. An era of religious warfare was about to unfold.

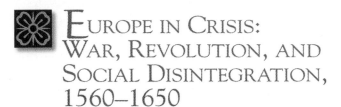

EUROPE IN CRISIS: WAR, REVOLUTION, AND SOCIAL DISINTEGRATION, 1560–1650

Between 1560 and 1650, Europe experienced religious wars, revolutions and constitutional crises, economic and social disintegration, and a witchcraft craze. It was truly an age of crisis.

Politics and the Wars of Religion in the Sixteenth Century

The so-called wars of religion were a product of Reformation ideologies that allowed little room for compromise or toleration of differing opinions. By the middle of the sixteenth century, Calvinism and Catholicism had become highly militant religions dedicated to spreading the word of God as they interpreted it. While their struggle for the minds and hearts of Europeans was at the heart of the religious wars of the sixteenth century, economic, social, and political forces also played an important role in these conflicts. Of the sixteenth-century religious wars, none was more momentous nor shattering than the French civil wars known as the French Wars of Religion.

THE FRENCH WARS OF RELIGION (1562–1598)

Religion was at the heart of the French civil wars of the sixteenth century. The growth of Calvinism had led to persecution by the French kings, but the latter did little to stop the spread of Calvinism. Huguenots (as the French Calvinists were called) came from all layers of society: artisans and shopkeepers hurt by rising prices and a rigid guild system, merchants and lawyers in provincial towns whose local privileges were tenuous, and members of the nobility. Possibly 40 to 50 percent of the French nobility became Huguenots, including the house of Bourbon, which stood next to the Valois in the royal line of succession and ruled the southern French kingdom of Navarre. The conversion of so many nobles made the Huguenots a potentially dangerous political threat to

monarchical power. Although the Calvinists constituted only about 7 percent of the population, they were a dedicated, determined, and well-organized minority.

The Calvinist minority was greatly outnumbered by the Catholic majority. The Valois monarchy was staunchly Catholic, and its control of the Catholic church gave it little incentive to look favorably upon Protestantism. At the same time, an extreme Catholic party—known as the ultra-Catholics—favored strict opposition to the Huguenots. Possessing the loyalty of Paris and large sections of northern and northwestern France, the ultra-Catholics could recruit and pay for large armies and received support abroad from the papacy and Jesuits, who favored their noncompromising Catholic position.

The religious issue was not the only factor that contributed to the French civil wars. Towns and provinces, which had long resisted the growing power of monarchical centralization, were only too willing to join a revolt against the monarchy. This was also true of the nobility, and the fact that so many of them were Calvinists created an important base of opposition to the crown. The French Wars of Religion, then, constituted a major constitutional crisis for France and temporarily halted the development of the French centralized territorial state. The claim of the ruling dynasty to a person's loyalties was temporarily superseded by loyalty to one's religious belief. For thirty years, battles raged in France between Catholic and Calvinist parties, who obviously considered the unity of France less important than religious truth. But there also emerged in France a group of *politiques* who placed politics before religion and believed that no religious truth was worth the ravages of civil war. The *politiques* ultimately prevailed, but not until both sides were exhausted by bloodshed.

Finally, in 1589, Henry of Navarre, the political leader of the Huguenots and a member of the Bourbon dynasty, succeeded to the throne as Henry IV (1589–1610). Realizing, however, that he would never be accepted by Catholic France, Henry took the logical way out and converted to Catholicism. With his coronation in 1594, the wars of religion finally came to an end. The Edict of Nantes in 1598 solved the religious problem by acknowledging Catholicism as the official religion of France while guaranteeing the Huguenots the right to worship and to enjoy all political privileges, including the holding of public offices.

PHILIP II AND THE CAUSE OF MILITANT CATHOLICISM

The greatest advocate of militant Catholicism in the second half of the sixteenth century was King Philip II of Spain (1556–1598), the son and heir of Charles V. Philip's reign ushered in an age of Spanish greatness, both politically and culturally. His first major goal was to consolidate and secure the lands he had inherited from his father. These included Spain, the Netherlands, and possessions in Italy and the New World. To strengthen his control, Philip insisted on a strict conformity to Catholicism and a strong, monarchical authority. Achieving the latter was not easy, because each of the states and territories of his empire had its own structure of government. Even in Spain, there was no really deep sense of nationhood. Philip did manage, however, to expand royal power by making the monarchy less dependent on the landed aristocrats.

The Catholic faith was crucial to both Philip II and the Spanish people. During the Late Middle Ages, Catholic kingdoms in Spain had gradually reconquered most of the land from the Muslims and expelled the Spanish Jews. Driven by this heritage of crusading fervor, it was not difficult for Spain to see itself as a nation of people chosen by God to save Catholic Christianity from the Protestant heretics. Philip II, the "Most Catholic King," became the champion of Catholicism throughout Europe, a role that led to spectacular victories and equally spectacular defeats for the Spanish king. Spain's leadership of a Holy League against Turkish encroachments in the Mediterranean resulted in a stunning victory over the Turkish fleet in the Battle of Lepanto in 1571. But Philip's attempt to crush the revolt in the Netherlands and his tortured policy with the English Queen Elizabeth led to his greatest misfortunes.

One of the richest parts of Philip's empire, the Spanish Netherlands was of great importance to the "Most Catholic King." Philip's attempt to strengthen his control in the Netherlands, which consisted of seventeen provinces (modern Netherlands, Belgium, and Luxembourg), soon led to a revolt. The nobles, who stood to lose the most politically if their jealously guarded privileges and freedoms were weakened, strongly opposed Philip's efforts. Resentment against Philip was also aroused by the collection of taxes when the residents of the Netherlands realized that these revenues were being used for Spanish interests. Finally, religion became a major catalyst for rebellion when Philip attempted to crush Calvinism. Violence erupted in 1566, when Calvinists—especially nobles—began to destroy statues and stained glass windows in Catholic churches. Philip responded by sending 10,000 veteran Spanish and Italian troops to crush the rebellion.

But the revolt became organized, especially in the northern provinces, where the Dutch, under the leadership of William of Nassau, the prince of Orange, offered growing resistance. The struggle dragged on for decades until 1609, when a twelve-year truce ended the war, virtually recognizing the independence of the northern provinces. These seven northern provinces, which began to call themselves the United Provinces of the Netherlands in 1581, became the core of the modern Dutch state. The new state was officially recognized by the Peace of Westphalia in 1648. The seventeenth century has often been called the "golden age" of the Dutch Republic as the United Provinces held center stage as one of Europe's great powers. Like France and England, the United Provinces

was an Atlantic power, underlining the importance of the shift of political and economic power in the seventeenth century from the Mediterranean Sea to the countries on the Atlantic seaboard.

At the beginning of the seventeenth century, Spain possessed the most populous empire in the world, controlling almost all of South America and a number of settlements in Asia and Africa. To most Europeans, Spain still seemed the greatest power of the age, but the reality was quite different. The treasury was empty; Philip II went bankrupt in 1596 from excessive expenditures on war, while his successor did the same in 1607 by spending a fortune on his court. The armed forces were out-of-date, and the government was inefficient. Spain continued to play the role of a great power, but appearances were deceiving.

THE ENGLAND OF ELIZABETH

When Elizabeth Tudor, the younger daughter of Henry VIII, ascended the throne in 1558, the population of England numbered fewer than four million people. During her reign, England rose to prominence as the relatively small island kingdom, became the leader of the Protestant nations of Europe, and laid the foundations for a world empire.

Intelligent, cautious, and self-confident, Elizabeth moved quickly to solve the difficult religious problem she inherited from her half sister, Queen Mary Tudor. Elizabeth's religious policy was based on moderation and compromise. The Catholic laws of Mary's reign were repealed, and a new Act of Supremacy designated Elizabeth "the only supreme governor" of both church and state. The church service used during the reign of Edward VI was revised to make it more acceptable to Catholics. The Church of England under Elizabeth was basically Protestant, but it was a moderate Protestantism that kept most people satisfied in the second half of the sixteenth century.

Caution, moderation, and expediency also dictated Elizabeth's foreign policy. Fearful of other countries' motives, Elizabeth realized that war could be disastrous for her island kingdom and her own rule. While encouraging English piracy and providing clandestine aid to French Huguenots and Dutch Calvinists to weaken France and Spain, she pretended complete aloofness and avoided alliances that would force her into war with any major power. Gradually, however, Elizabeth was drawn into conflict with Spain. After resisting for years the idea of invading England as too impractical, Philip II of Spain was finally persuaded to do so by advisers who assured him that the people of England would rise against their queen when the Spaniards arrived. Moreover, Philip was easily convinced that the revolt in the Netherlands would never be crushed as long as England provided support for it. In any case, a successful invasion of England would mean the overthrow of heresy and the return of England to Catholicism. Accordingly, Philip ordered preparations for an armada to spearhead the invasion of England.

The Spanish Armada proved to be a disaster. The Spanish fleet that finally set sail had neither the ships nor the troops that Philip had planned to send. Battered by a number of encounters with the English, the Spanish fleet sailed back to Spain by a northerly route around Scotland and Ireland, where it was further pounded by storms. Although the English and Spanish would continue their war for another sixteen years, the defeat of the armada guaranteed for the time being that England would remain a Protestant country. Although Spain made up for its losses within a year and a half, the defeat was a psychological blow to the Spaniards.

Economic and Social Crises: The Witchcraft Craze

The period of European history from 1560 to 1650 witnessed severe economic and social crises as well as political upheaval. The inflation-fueled prosperity of the sixteenth century showed signs of slackening by the beginning of the seventeenth century. Economic contraction began to be evident in some parts of Europe by the 1620s. In the 1630s and 1640s, as imports of silver from the Americas declined, economic recession intensified, especially in the Mediterranean area. Italy, the industrial and financial center of Europe in the age of the Renaissance, was now becoming an economic backwater. Spain's economy was also encountering serious problems by the decade of the 1640s.

Population trends of the sixteenth and seventeenth centuries also reveal Europe's worsening conditions. The sixteenth century was a period of expanding population, possibly related to a warmer climate and increased food supplies. It has been estimated that the population of Europe increased from 60 million in 1500 to 85 million by 1600, the first major recovery of the European population since the devastation of the Black Death in the mid-fourteenth century. However, records also indicate a leveling off of the population by 1620 and even a decline by 1650, especially in central and southern Europe. Europe's longtime adversaries—war, famine, and plague—continued to affect population levels. Another "little ice

❀ **THE PERSECUTION OF WITCHES.**   Hysteria over witchcraft affected the daily lives of many Europeans in the sixteenth and seventeenth centuries. This picture by Frans Francken the Young, painted in 1607, shows a number of activities commonly attributed to witches. In the center, several witches are casting spells with their magic books and instruments, while at the top, a witch on a post prepares to fly off on her broomstick.

age" after the middle of the sixteenth century, when average temperatures fell, affected harvests and gave rise to famines. These economic problems created social tensions that manifested themselves in various ways, including the witchcraft craze.

Hysteria over witchcraft affected the lives of many Europeans in the sixteenth and seventeenth centuries. Witchcraft trials were prevalent in England, Scotland, Switzerland, Germany, some parts of France and the Low Countries, and even New England in America.

Witchcraft was not a new phenomenon in the sixteenth and seventeenth centuries. Although its practice had been part of traditional village culture for centuries, the medieval church made witchcraft both sinister and dangerous by connecting witches to the activities of the devil, thereby transforming witchcraft into a heresy that had to be extirpated. By the thirteenth century, after the creation of the Inquisition, people were being accused of a variety of witchcraft practices and, following the biblical injunction "Thou shalt not suffer a witch to live," were turned over to secular authorities for burning at the stake or hanging (in England).

What distinguished witchcraft in the sixteenth and seventeenth centuries from these previous developments was the high level of hysteria at which neighbors accused neighbors of witchcraft, leading to widespread trials of witches. Perhaps more than 100,000 people were prosecuted throughout Europe on charges of witchcraft. As more and more people were brought to trial, the fear of witches as well as the fear of being accused of witchcraft escalated to frightening proportions. Although larger cities were affected first, the trials also spread to smaller towns and rural areas as the hysteria persisted well into the seventeenth century (see the box on p. 442).

Although even city officeholders were not immune to persecution, women of the lower classes were more likely to be accused of witchcraft. Indeed, where lists are given, those mentioned most often are milkmaids, peasant women, and servant girls. In the witchcraft trials of the sixteenth and seventeenth centuries, more than 75 percent of those accused were women, most of them single or widowed and many over fifty years old. Moreover, almost all victims belonged to the lower classes, the poor and propertyless.

The accused witches usually confessed to a number of practices, most often after intense torture. Many said that they had sworn allegiance to the devil and attended sabbats or nocturnal gatherings where they feasted, danced, and even copulated with the devil in sexual orgies. More common, however, were admissions of using evil incantations and special ointments and powders to wreak havoc on neighbors by killing their livestock, injuring their children, or raising storms to destroy their crops.

A number of contributing factors have been suggested to explain why the witchcraft craze became so widespread in the sixteenth and seventeenth centuries. Religious uncertainties clearly played some part. Many witchcraft trials occurred in areas where Protestantism had been recently victorious or in regions, such as southwestern Germany, where Protestant-Catholic controversies still raged. As religious passions became inflamed, accusations of being in league with the devil became common on both sides. Recently, however, historians have emphasized the importance of social conditions, especially the problems of a society in turmoil, in explaining the witchcraft hysteria. At a time when the old communal values that stressed working together for the good of the community were disintegrating, property owners became more fearful of the growing numbers of poor among them and transformed them psychologically into agents of the devil. Old women were particularly susceptible to suspicion. Many of them, no longer the recipients of the local charity found in traditional society, may even have tried to survive by selling herbs, potions, or secret remedies for healing. When problems arose, and there were many in this crisis-laden period, these same women were the most likely scapegoats.

That women should be the chief victims of witchcraft trials was hardly accidental. Nicholas Rémy, a witchcraft judge in France in the 1590s, found it "not unreasonable that this scum of humanity, i.e., witches, should be drawn chiefly from the feminine sex." To another judge, it came as no surprise that witches would confess to sexual experiences with satan: "The devil uses them so, because he knows that women love carnal pleasures, and he means to bind them to his allegiance by such agreeable provocations."[8] Of course, witch hunters were not the only ones to hold such low estimates of women. Most theologians, lawyers, and philosophers in early modern Europe maintained a belief in the natural inferiority of women, making it plausible to them that women would be more susceptible to witchcraft.

By the mid-seventeenth century, the witchcraft hysteria began to subside. The destruction of the religious wars had at least forced people to accept a grudging toleration that allowed religious passions to subside. Moreover, as governments began to stabilize after the period of crisis, fewer magistrates were willing to accept the unsettling and divisive conditions generated by the trials of witches. Finally, by the end of the seventeenth century and the beginning of the eighteenth, more and more people were questioning their old attitudes toward religion altogether and found it especially contrary to reason to believe in a world haunted by evil spirits.

Seventeenth-Century Crises: Revolution and War

Although many Europeans responded to the upheavals of the second half of the sixteenth century with a desire for peace and order, the first fifty years of the seventeenth century continued to be a period of crisis. A series of rebellions and civil wars stemming from the discontent of both nobles and commoners rocked the domestic stability of

A WITCHCRAFT TRIAL IN FRANCE

*P*ersecutions for witchcraft reached their high point in the sixteenth and seventeenth centuries, when tens of thousands of people were brought to trial. In this excerpt from the minutes of a trial in France in 1652, we can see why the accused witch stood little chance of exonerating herself.

THE TRIAL OF SUZANNE GAUDRY

28 May, 1652. . . . Interrogation of Suzanne Gaudry, prisoner at the court of Rieux. . . . During interrogations on May 28 and May 29, the prisoner confessed to a number of activities involving the devil.]

Deliberation of the Court—June 3, 1652

The undersigned advocates of the Court have seen these interrogations and answers. They say that the aforementioned Suzanne Gaudry confesses that she is a witch, that she had given herself to the devil, that she had renounced God, Lent, and baptism, that she has been marked on the shoulder, that she has cohabited with the devil and that she has been to the dances, confessing only to have cast a spell upon and caused to die a beast of Philippe Cornié. . . .

Third Interrogation, June 27

This prisoner being led into the chamber, she was examined to know if things were not as she had said and confessed at the beginning of her imprisonment.

—Answers no, and that what she has said was done so by force.

Pressed to say the truth, that otherwise she would be subjected to torture, having pointed out to her that her aunt was burned for this same subject.

—Answers that she is not a witch. . . .

She was placed in the hands of the officer in charge of torture, throwing herself on her knees, struggling to cry, uttering several exclamations, without being able, nevertheless, to shed a tear. Saying at every moment that she is not a witch.

The Torture

On this same day, being at the place of torture.

This prisoner, before being strapped down, was admonished to maintain herself in her first confessions and to renounce her lover.

—Says that she denies everything she has said, and that she has no lover. Feeling herself being strapped down, says that she is not a witch, while struggling to cry . . . and upon being asked why she confessed to being one, said that she was forced to say it.

Told that she was not forced, that on the contrary she declared herself to be a witch without any threat.

—Says that she confessed it and that she is not a witch, and being a little stretched [on the rack] screams ceaselessly that she is not a witch.

Asked if she did not confess that she had been a witch for twenty-six years.

—Says that she said it, that she retracts it, crying that she is not a witch.

Asked if she did not make Philippe Cornié's horse die, as she confessed.

—Answers no, crying Jesus-Maria, that she is not a witch.

The mark having been probed by the officer, in the presence of Doctor Bouchain, it was adjudged by the aforesaid doctor and officer truly to be the mark of the devil.

Being more tightly stretched upon the torture rack, urged to maintain her confessions.

—Said that it was true that she is a witch and that she would maintain what she had said.

Asked how long she has been in subjugation to the devil.

—Answers that it was twenty years ago that the devil appeared to her, being in her lodgings in the form of a man dressed in a little cowhide and black breeches. . . .

Verdict

July 9, 1652. In the light of the interrogations, answers, and investigations made into the charge against Suzanne Gaudry, . . . seeing by her own confessions that she is said to have made a pact with the devil, received the mark from him, . . . and that following this, she had renounced God, Lent, and baptism and had let herself be known carnally by him, in which she received satisfaction. Also, seeing that she is said to have been a part of nocturnal carols and dances.

For expiation of which the advice of the undersigned is that the office of Rieux can legitimately condemn the aforesaid Suzanne Gaudry to death, tying her to a gallows, and strangling her to death, then burning her body and burying it here in the environs of the woods.

---

many European governments. To strengthen their power, monarchs attempted to extend their authority at the expense of traditional powerful elements who resisted their rulers' efforts. At the same time, to pay for armies to fight their battles, governments increased taxes and created such hardships that common people also rose in opposi-

tion. By far the most famous and wide-ranging struggle was the civil war and rebellion in England, commonly known as the English Revolution (see Limited Monarchy: England and the Emergence of Constitutional Monarchy later in this chapter). A devastating war that affected much of Europe also added to the sense of crisis.

CHRONOLOGY

EUROPE IN CRISIS, 1560–1650: KEY EVENTS

Reign of Philip II	1556–1598
The French Wars of Religion	1562–1598
Outbreak of revolt in the Netherlands	1566
The Spanish Armada	1588
Edict of Nantes	1598
Twelve-year truce (Spain and the Netherlands)	1609
The Thirty Years' War	1618–1648
Peace of Westphalia	1648
Independence of the United Provinces	1648

THE THIRTY YEARS' WAR (1618–1648)

Religion, especially the struggle between a militant Catholicism and a militant Calvinism, certainly played an important role in the outbreak of the Thirty Years' War, often called the "last of the religious wars." As the war progressed, however, it became increasingly clear that secular, dynastic-nationalist considerations were far more important.

The Thirty Years' War began in 1618 in the Germanic lands of the Holy Roman Empire as a struggle between Catholic forces, led by the Habsburg Holy Roman emperors, and Protestant—primarily Calvinist—nobles in Bohemia who rebelled against Habsburg authority. What began as a struggle over religious issues soon became a wider conflict perpetuated by political considerations as both minor and major European powers—Denmark, Sweden, France, and Spain—entered the war. The rivalry between the Bourbon dynasty of France and the Habsburg dynasties of Spain and the Holy Roman Empire for European leadership was an especially important factor. Nevertheless, most of the battles were fought on German soil, with devastating results for the German people.

The war in Germany was officially ended by the Peace of Westphalia in 1648. What were the results of this "basically meaningless conflict," as one historian has called it? The Peace of Westphalia ensured that all German states, including the Calvinist ones, were free to determine their own religion. The major combatants gained new territories, and one of them, France, emerged as the dominant nation in Europe. The more than three hundred states that made up the Holy Roman Empire were virtually recognized as independent, since each received the power to conduct its own foreign policy; this brought an end to the Holy Roman Empire as a political entity and ensured German disunity for another two hundred years. The Peace of Westphalia made it clear that religion and politics were now separate worlds. Political motives became the guiding forces in public affairs as religion was in the process of becoming primarily a matter of personal conviction and individual choice.

Germany suffered the most from the Thirty Years' War. Some areas of the country were completely devastated. Many people in Germany would have agreed with this comment by Otto von Guericke, a councillor in the city of Magdeburg, which was sacked ten times:

> Then there was nothing but beating and burning, plundering, torture, and murder. Most especially was every one of the enemy bent on securing much booty.... In this frenzied rage, the great and splendid city ... was now ... given over to the flames, and thousands of innocent men, women and children, in the midst of a horrible din of heartrending shrieks and cries, were tortured and put to death in so cruel and shameful a manner that no words would suffice to describe.... Thus in a single day this noble and famous city, the pride of the whole country, went up in fire and smoke.[9]

The Thirty Years' War was undoubtedly the most destructive conflict Europeans had yet experienced.

By the end of the Thirty Years' War, it was apparent that a number of important innovations had occurred in European warfare. These military changes included an increased use of firearms and cannons, greater flexibility and mobility in tactics, and better disciplined and trained armies. These innovations necessitated standing armies, based partly on conscription, which grew ever larger and more expensive as the seventeenth century progressed. Such armies could only be maintained by levying heavier taxes, making war an economic burden and an ever more important part of the early modern European state. To some historians, the creation of large bureaucracies to supervise the military resources of the state was the real reason for the rise of royal absolutism in the seventeenth century.

RESPONSE TO CRISIS: THE PRACTICE OF ABSOLUTISM

Many people responded to the crises of the seventeenth century by searching for order and harmony. An increase in monarchical power became an obvious means of achieving stability. The result was what historians have called absolutism or absolute monarchy. Absolute monarchy or absolutism meant that the sovereign power or ultimate authority in the state rested in the hands of a king or queen who claimed to rule by divine right—the idea that rulers received their power from God and were responsible to no one (including parliaments) except God. But what did sovereignty mean? Late-sixteenth-century political theorists believed that sovereign power consisted of the authority to make laws, tax, administer justice, control the state's administrative system, and determine foreign policy. These powers made a ruler sovereign.

The Practice of Absolutism: France Under Louis XIV

France during the reign of Louis XIV (1643–1715) has traditionally been regarded as the best example of the practice of absolute monarchy in the seventeenth century. French culture, language, and manners reached into all levels of European society. French diplomacy and wars overwhelmed the political affairs of western and central Europe. The court of Louis XIV seemed to be imitated everywhere

in Europe. Of course, the stability of Louis's reign was magnified by the instability that had preceded it.

The fifty years of French history before Louis were a period of struggle by royal and ministerial governments to avoid the breakdown of the state. The situation was especially complicated by the fact that in both 1610 and 1643, when Louis XIII and Louis XIV, respectively, succeeded to the throne, they were only boys, leaving the government dependent on royal ministers. Two especially competent ministers played crucial roles in maintaining monarchical authority.

Cardinal Richelieu, Louis XIII's chief minister from 1624 to 1642, initiated policies that eventually strengthened the power of the monarchy. By eliminating the political and military rights of the Huguenots while preserving their religious ones, Richelieu transformed the Huguenots into more reliable subjects. Richelieu acted more cau-

MAP 15.2 Europe in the Seventeenth Century

tiously in "humbling the pride of the great men," the important French nobility. He understood the influential role played by the nobles in the French state. The dangerous ones were those who asserted their territorial independence when they were excluded from participating in the central government. Proceeding slowly but determinedly, Richelieu developed an efficient network of spies to uncover noble plots and then crushed the conspiracies and executed the conspirators.

When Louis XIV succeeded to the throne in 1643 at the age of four, Cardinal Mazarin, the trained successor of Cardinal Richelieu, came to dominate the government. The most important event during Mazarin's rule was the Fronde, a revolt led primarily by nobles who wished to curb the centralized administrative power being built up at the expense of the provincial nobility. The Fronde was crushed by 1652, and with its end, a vast number of French people concluded that the best hope for stability in France lay in the crown. When Mazarin died in 1661, the greatest of the seventeenth-century monarchs, Louis XIV, took over supreme power. The day after Cardinal Mazarin's death, the new king, at the age of twenty-three, expressed his determination to be a real king and the sole ruler of France:

> Up to this moment I have been pleased to entrust the government of my affairs to the late Cardinal. It is now time that I govern them myself. You [secretaries and ministers of state] will assist me with your counsels when I ask for them. I request and order you to seal no orders except by my command, . . . I order you not to sign anything, not even a passport . . . without my command; to render account to me personally each day and to favor no one.[10]

Louis proved willing to pay the price of being a strong ruler.

Although Louis may have believed in the theory of absolute monarchy and consciously fostered the myth of himself as the Sun King, the source of light for all of his people, historians are quick to point out that the realities fell far short of the aspirations. Despite the centralizing efforts of Cardinals Richelieu and Mazarin, France in the seventeenth century still possessed a bewildering system of overlapping authorities. Provinces had their own regional courts, their own local Estates, and their own sets of laws. Members of the high nobility with their huge estates and clients among the lesser nobility still exercised much authority. Both towns and provinces possessed privileges and powers seemingly from time immemorial that they would not easily relinquish.

One of the keys to Louis's power was that he was able to restructure the central policy-making machinery of government because it was part of his own court and household. The royal court located at Versailles was an elaborate structure that served three purposes simultaneously: it was the personal household of the king, the location of central governmental machinery, and the

✿ **LOUIS XIV.** Louis XIV was determined to be the sole ruler of France. Louis eliminated the threat of the high nobility by removing them from the royal council and replacing them with relatively new aristocrats, whom he could dominate. This portrait by Hyacinth Rigaud captures the king's sense of royal dignity and grandeur.

place where powerful subjects came to find favors and offices for themselves and their clients, as well as the main arena where rival aristocratic factions jostled for power. The greatest danger to Louis's personal rule came from the very high nobles and princes of the blood (the royal princes), who considered it their natural function to assert the policy-making role of royal ministers. Louis eliminated this threat by removing them from the royal council, the chief administrative body of the king and overseer of the central machinery of government, and enticing them to his court, where he could keep them preoccupied with court life and out of politics. Instead of the high nobility and royal princes, Louis relied for his ministers on nobles who came from relatively new aristocratic families. His ministers were expected to be subservient; said Louis, "I had no intention of sharing my authority with them."

PALACE OF VERSAILLES. Louis XIV spent untold sums of money in the construction of a new royal residence at Versailles. The enormous palace of Versailles also housed the members of the king's government and served as home for thousands of French nobles. As the largest royal residence in Europe, Versailles impressed foreigners and became a source of envy for other rulers.

Louis's domination of his ministers and secretaries gave him control of the central policy-making machinery of government and thus authority over the traditional areas of monarchical power: the formulation of foreign policy, the making of war and peace, the assertion of the secular power of the crown against any religious authority, and the ability to levy taxes to fulfill these functions. However, Louis had considerably less success with the internal administration of the kingdom. The traditional groups and institutions of French society—the nobles, officials, town councils, guilds, and representative Estates in some provinces—were simply too powerful for the king to have direct control over the lives of his subjects. As a result, the control of the central government over the provinces and the people was carried out largely by carefully bribing the important people to ensure that the king's policies were executed.

The maintenance of religious harmony had long been considered an area of monarchical power. The desire to keep it led Louis to pursue an anti-Protestant policy, aimed at converting the Huguenots to Catholicism. In October 1685, Louis revoked the Edict of Nantes and ordered the destruction of Huguenot churches and the closing of their schools. Although they were forbidden to leave France, an estimated 200,000 Huguenots left for shelter in England, the United Provinces, and the German states.

The cost of building palaces, maintaining his court, and pursuing his wars made finances a crucial issue for Louis XIV. He was most fortunate in having the services of Jean-Baptiste Colbert (1619–1683) as controller-general of finances. Colbert sought to increase the wealth and power of France by general adherence to mercantilism, a name historians use to identify a set of economic principles that dominated economic thought in the seventeenth century. According to the mercantilists, the prosperity of a nation depended on a plentiful supply of bullion, or gold and silver. For this reason, it was desirable to achieve a favorable balance of trade, in which exported goods were of greater value than those imported, promoting an influx of gold and silver payments that would increase the quantity of bullion. To encourage exports, governments should stimulate and protect export industries and trade by granting trade monopolies, encouraging investment in new industries through subsidies, and improving transportation systems by building roads, bridges, and canals. By imposing high tariffs on foreign goods, they could be kept out of the country and prevented from competing with the products of domestic industries. Colonies were also deemed valuable as sources of raw materials and markets for finished goods. As a system of economic principles, mercantilism focused on the role of the state, believing that state intervention in some aspects of the economy was desirable for the sake of the national good.

Colbert was an avid practitioner of mercantilism. To decrease imports and increase exports, he founded new luxury industries and granted special privileges, including tax exemptions, loans, and subsidies to those who established new industries. To improve communications and the transportation of goods internally, he built roads and canals. To decrease imports directly, Colbert raised tariffs on foreign manufactured goods and created a merchant marine to carry French goods.

The increase in royal power that Louis pursued led the king to develop a professional army numbering 100,000 men in peacetime and 400,000 in time of war. Louis made war an almost incessant activity of his reign. To achieve the prestige and military glory befitting a Sun King, and also, to ensure the domination of his Bourbon dynasty over European affairs, Louis waged four wars between 1667 and 1713. His ambitions roused much of Europe to form coalitions aimed at preventing a Bourbon hegemony that would mean the certain destruction of the European balance of power. Although Louis added some territory to France's northeastern frontier and established a member of his own Bourbon dynasty on the throne of Spain, he also left France impoverished and surrounded by enemies.

Absolutism in Central and Eastern Europe

During the seventeenth century, a development of great importance for the modern Western world took place in central and eastern Europe, the appearance of three new powers: Prussia, Austria, and Russia.

The Peace of Westphalia, which officially ended the Thirty Years' War in 1648, left each of the three hundred or more German states comprising the Holy Roman Empire virtually autonomous and sovereign. Properly speaking, there was no German state, but rather over three hundred "Germanies." Of these states, two emerged in the seventeenth and eighteenth centuries as great European powers.

The development of Brandenburg as a state was largely the story of the Hohenzollern dynasty. By the seventeenth century, the dominions of the house of Hohenzollern, now called Brandenburg-Prussia, consisted of three disconnected masses in western, central, and eastern Germany. Frederick William the Great Elector (1640–1688) laid the foundation for the Prussian state. Realizing that Brandenburg-Prussia was a small, open territory with no natural frontiers for defense, Frederick William built a competent and efficient standing army. By 1678, he possessed a force of 40,000 men, making the Prussian army the fourth largest in Europe. To sustain the army and his own power, Frederick William established the General War Commissariat to levy taxes for the army and oversee its growth and training. The Commissariat soon evolved into an agency for civil government as well. Directly responsible to the elector, the new bureaucratic machine became his chief instrument for governing the state. Many of its officials were members of the Prussian landed aristocracy, the Junkers, who also served as officers in the all-important army.

Frederick William the Great Elector established the foundations for the Prussian state. In 1701, his son Frederick officially gained the title of king. Elector Frederick III was transformed into King Frederick I, and Brandenburg-Prussia became simply Prussia. In the eighteenth century, Prussia emerged as a great power on the European stage.

The Austrian Habsburgs had long played a significant role in European politics as Holy Roman emperors. By the end of the Thirty Years' War, the Habsburg hopes of creating an empire in Germany had been dashed. In the seventeenth century, the house of Austria made a difficult transition; the German empire was lost, but a new empire was created in eastern and southeastern Europe.

The nucleus of the new Austrian Empire remained the traditional Austrian hereditary possessions: Lower and Upper Austria, Carinthia, Carniola, Styria, and Tyrol. To these had been added the kingdom of Bohemia and parts of northwestern Hungary. After the defeat of the Turks in 1687 (see Chapter 18), Austria took control of all of Hungary, Transylvania, Croatia, and Slovenia, thus establishing an Austrian Empire in southeastern Europe. By the beginning of the eighteenth century, the house of Austria had acquired a new empire of considerable size.

The Austrian monarchy, however, never became a highly centralized, absolutist state, primarily because it contained so many different national groups. The Austrian Empire remained a collection of territories held together by a personal union. The Habsburg emperor was archduke of Austria, king of Bohemia, and king of Hungary. Each of these areas, however, had its own laws, Estates-General, and political life. There was no common sentiment to tie the regions together; only the ideal of service to the house of Habsburg, whether as military officers or government bureaucrats, provided a common bond that linked the landed aristocracies throughout the empire. Nevertheless, by the beginning of the eighteenth century, Austria was a populous empire in central Europe of great potential military strength.

FROM MUSCOVY TO RUSSIA

A new Russian state had emerged in the fifteenth century under the leadership of the principality of Muscovy and its grand dukes. In the sixteenth century, Ivan IV the Terrible (1533–1584), who was the first ruler to take the title of tsar (the Russian word for *Caesar*), expanded the territories of Russia eastward, after finding westward expansion blocked by the powerful Swedish and Polish states. Ivan also extended the autocracy of the tsar by crushing the power of the Russian nobility known as the boyars. Ivan's dynasty came to an end in 1598 and was followed by a resurgence of aristocratic power in a period of anarchy known as the Time of Troubles. It did not end until the Zemsky Sobor or national assembly chose Michael Romanov as the new tsar, establishing a dynasty that lasted until 1917.

In the seventeenth century, Muscovite society was highly stratified. At the top was the tsar, who claimed to be a divinely ordained autocratic ruler. Russian society was dominated by an upper class of landed aristocrats who, in the course of the seventeenth century, managed to bind their peasants to the land. An abundance of land and a shortage of peasants made serfdom desirable to the landowners, who sustained a highly oppressive system. Townspeople were also controlled. Many merchants were not allowed to move from their cities without government permission or to sell their businesses to anyone outside their class. In the seventeenth century, merchant and peasant revolts as well as a schism in the Russian Orthodox church created very unsettled conditions. In the midst of these political and religious upheavals, seventeenth-century Muscovy was experiencing more frequent contacts with the West while Western ideas also began to penetrate a few Russian circles. At the end of the seventeenth century, Peter the Great noticeably accelerated this westernizing process.

Peter the Great (1689–1725) was an unusual character. A strong, towering man at six feet, nine inches tall, Peter was coarse in his tastes and rude in his behavior. He enjoyed a low kind of humor—belching contests and crude jokes—and vicious punishments including floggings, impalings, and roastings (see the box on p. 449). Peter obtained a firsthand view of the West when he made a trip there in 1697–1698 and returned to Russia with a firm determination to westernize Russia. Perhaps too much has been made of Peter's desire to westernize a "backward country." Peter's policy was largely technical. He admired Western technology and gadgets and wanted to transplant them to Russia. Only this kind of modernization could give him the army and navy he needed to make Russia a great power.

As could be expected, one of his first priorities was the reorganization of the army and the creation of a navy. Employing both Russians and Europeans as officers, he conscripted peasants for twenty-five-year stints of service to build a standing army of 210,000 men. Peter has also been given credit for forming the first Russian navy.

To impose the rule of the central government more effectively throughout the land, Peter divided Russia into eight provinces and later, in 1719, into fifty. Although he hoped to create a "police state," by which he meant a well-ordered community governed in accordance with law, few of his bureaucrats shared his concept of honest service and duty to the state. Peter hoped for a sense of civic duty, but his own forceful personality created an atmosphere of fear that prevented it. He wrote to one administrator: "According to these orders act, act, act. I won't write more, but you will pay with your head if you interpret orders again."[11] Peter wanted his administrators to be slaves and freemen at the same time, and it did not occur to him that the task was impossible.

To satisfy his insatiable need of money for an army and navy that absorbed as much as four-fifths of the state revenue, Peter adopted Western mercantilistic policies to stimulate economic growth. He tried to increase exports and develop new industries while exploiting domestic resources like the iron mines in the Urals. But his military needs were endless, and he came to rely on the old expedient of simply raising taxes, placing additional burdens on hapless peasants, whose position in Peter's Russia grew ever more oppressed.

Peter also sought to gain state control of the Russian Orthodox church. In 1721, he abolished the position of patriarch and created a body called the Holy Synod to make decisions for the church. At its head stood a procurator, a layman who represented the interests of the tsar and assured Peter of effective domination of the church.

Already after his first trip to the West in 1697–1698, Peter had begun to introduce Western customs, practices, and manners into Russia. He ordered the preparation of

PETER THE GREAT. Peter the Great wished to westernize Russia, especially in the realm of technical skills. His foremost goal was the creation of a strong army and navy in order to make Russia a great power. A Dutch artist painted this portrait of the armored tsar during his visit to the West in 1697.

the first Russian book of etiquette to teach Western manners. Among other things, it pointed out that it was not polite to spit on the floor or scratch oneself at dinner. Since westerners did not wear beards or the traditional long-skirted coat, Russian beards had to be shaved and coats shortened, a reform Peter personally enforced at court by shaving off his nobles' beards and cutting their coats at the knees with his own hands. Outside the court, the edicts were enforced by barbers and tailors planted at town gates with orders to cut the beards and cloaks of those who entered or left. One group of Russians benefited greatly from Peter's cultural reforms—women. Having watched women mixing freely with men in Western courts, Peter shattered the seclusion of upper-class Russian women and demanded that they remove the traditional veils that covered their faces. Peter also encouraged gatherings in which both sexes could mix for conversation and dancing, which Peter had learned in the West. The tsar also now insisted that women could marry of their own free will.

The object of Peter's domestic reforms was to make Russia into a great state and military power. His primary goal

PETER THE GREAT DEALS WITH A REBELLION

During his first visit to the West, in 1697–1698, Peter received word that the Streltsy, an elite military unit stationed in Moscow, had revolted against his authority. Peter hurried home and crushed the revolt in a very savage fashion. This selection is taken from an Austrian account of how Peter dealt with the rebels.

PETER AND THE STRELTSY

How sharp was the pain, how great the indignation, to which the tsar's Majesty was mightily moved, when he knew of the rebellion of the Streltsy, betraying openly a mind panting for vengeance! He was still tarrying at Vienna, quite full of the desire of setting out for Italy; but, fervid as was his curiosity of rambling abroad, it was, nevertheless, speedily extinguished on the announcement of the troubles that had broken out in the bowels of his realm. Going immediately to Lefort . . . , he thus indignantly broke out: "Tell me, Francis, how I can reach Moscow by the shortest way, in a brief space, so that I may wreak vengeance on this great perfidy of my people, with punishments worthy of their abominable crime. Not one of them shall escape with impunity. Around my royal city, which, with their impious efforts, they planned to destroy, I will have gibbets and gallows set upon the walls and ramparts, and each and every one of them will I put to a direful death." Nor did he long delay the plan for his justly excited wrath; he took the quick post, as his ambassador suggested,

and in four weeks' time he had got over about three hundred miles without accident, and arrived the 4th of September, 1698 —a monarch for the well disposed, but an avenger for the wicked.

His first anxiety after his arrival was about the rebellion—in what it consisted, what the insurgents meant, who dared to instigate such a crime. And as nobody could answer accurately upon all points, and some pleaded their own ignorance, others the obstinacy of the Streltsy, he began to have suspicions of everybody's loyalty. . . . No day, holy or profane, were the inquisitors idle; every day was deemed fit and lawful for torturing. There were as many scourges as there were accused, and every inquisitor was a butcher. . . . The whole month of October was spent in lacerating the backs of culprits with the knout and with flames; no day were those that were left alive exempt from scourging or scorching; or else they were broken upon the wheel, or driven to the gibbet, or slain with the ax. . . .

To prove to all people how holy and inviolable are those walls of the city which the Streltsy rashly meditated scaling in a sudden assault, beams were run out from all the embrasures in the walls near the gates, in each of which two rebels were hanged. This day beheld about two hundred and fifty die that death. There are few cities fortified with as many palisades as Moscow has given gibbets to her guardian Streltsy.

---

was to "open a window to the west," meaning an ice-free port easily accessible to Europe. This could only be achieved on the Baltic, but at that time the Baltic coast was controlled by Sweden, the most important power in northern Europe. A long and hard-fought war with Sweden, then ruled by Charles XII, a brilliant military leader, enabled Peter to acquire the lands he sought. Already in 1703, in these northern lands on the Baltic, Peter had begun the construction of a new city, St. Petersburg, his window on the west and a symbol that Russia was looking westward to Europe. Built on marshland, St. Petersburg cost the lives of thousands of peasants during its construction. Nevertheless, the city was finished during Peter's lifetime and remained the Russian capital until 1917.

Peter modernized and westernized Russia to the extent that it became a great military power, and by his death in 1725, it was an important member of the European state system. But his policies were also detrimental to Russia. Westernization was a bit of a sham, since Western culture reached only the upper classes, while the real object of the reforms, the creation of a strong military, only added more burdens to the masses of the Russian people. Moreover,

the forceful way in which Peter the Great brought westernization led many Russians to distrust Europe and Western civilization.

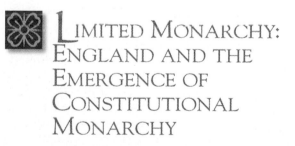

LIMITED MONARCHY: ENGLAND AND THE EMERGENCE OF CONSTITUTIONAL MONARCHY

One of the most prominent examples of resistance to absolute monarchy came in seventeenth-century England where king and Parliament struggled to determine the roles each should play in governing England. But the struggle over this political issue was complicated by a deep and profound religious controversy. With the victory of Parliament, the foundation for constitutional monarchy was laid by the end of the seventeenth century.

Revolution and Civil War

With the death of Queen Elizabeth I in 1603, the Tudor dynasty became extinct, and the Stuart line of rulers was inaugurated with the accession to the throne of Elizabeth's cousin, King James VI of Scotland, who became James I (1603–1625) of England. Although used to royal power as king of Scotland, James understood little about the laws, institutions, and customs of the English. He espoused the divine right of kings, the belief that kings receive their power directly from God and are responsible to no one except God. This viewpoint alienated Parliament, which had grown accustomed under the Tudors to act on the premise that monarch and Parliament together ruled England as a "balanced polity." Then, too, the Puritans—those Protestants within the Anglican church who, inspired by Calvinist theology, wished to eliminate any trace of popery from the Church of England—were alienated by the king's strong defense of the Anglican church. Many of England's lesser landed nobility, the gentry, had become Puritans, and these Puritan gentry not only formed an important and substantial part of the House of Commons, the lower house of Parliament, but also held important positions locally as justices of the peace and sheriffs. It was not wise to alienate them.

The conflict that had begun during the reign of James came to a head during the reign of his son Charles I (1625–1649). Charles believed as strongly in divine-right monarchy as his father had, and from the first stormy session of Parliament, it became apparent that the constitutional issues between this king and Parliament would not be easily resolved. In 1628, Parliament passed a Petition of Right that the king was supposed to accept before being granted any taxes. This petition prohibited taxes without Parliament's consent, arbitrary imprisonment, the quartering of soldiers in private houses, and the declaration of martial law in peacetime. Although he initially accepted it, Charles later reneged on the agreement because of its limitations on royal power.

Religious differences also added to the hostility between Charles I and Parliament. The king's attempt to impose more ritual on the Anglican church struck the Puritans as a return to Catholic "popery." Charles's efforts to force them to conform to his religious policies infuriated the Puritans, thousands of whom went to the "howling wildernesses" of America.

Grievances mounted until England finally slipped into a civil war (1642–1648) that was won by the parliamentary forces. Most important to Parliament's success was the creation of the New Model Army by Oliver Cromwell, the only real military genius of the war. The New Model Army was composed primarily of more extreme Puritans known as the Independents, who, in typical Calvinist fashion, believed they were doing battle for God. As Cromwell wrote in one of his military reports, "Sir, this is none other

EXECUTION OF CHARLES I. When Charles I attempted to arrest radical members of Parliament, a civil war erupted that eventually led to the rise of Oliver Cromwell and the execution of the king. This contemporary painting of the execution of Charles I shows a woman fainting at the bottom while the executioner holds the king's head aloft at the top. At the top left is a portrait of Charles I.

but the hand of God; and to Him alone belongs the glory." We might give some credit to Cromwell as well, because his soldiers were well disciplined and trained in the new military tactics developed in the course of the Thirty Years' War.

Between 1648 and 1660, England faced a trying situation. After the execution of Charles I on January 30, 1649, Parliament abolished the monarchy and the House of Lords and proclaimed England a republic or Commonwealth. But Cromwell and his army, unable to work effectively with Parliament, dispersed it by force and established a military dictatorship. Unable to find a constitutional basis for a working government, Cromwell had resorted to military force to maintain the rule of the Independents, ironically using even more arbitrary policies than those of Charles I.

Oliver Cromwell died in 1658. After floundering for eighteen months, the military establishment decided that arbitrary rule by the army was no longer feasible and reestablished the monarchy in the person of Charles II (1660–1685), the son of Charles I. The restoration of the Stuart monarchy ended England's time of troubles, but it would not be long before England would experience yet another constitutional crisis.

Restoration and a Glorious Revolution

The restoration of the monarchy did not mean that the work of the English Revolution was undone. Parliament kept much of the power it had won; arbitrary courts were still abolished; Parliament's role in government was acknowledged; and the necessity for its consent to taxation was accepted. Yet Charles II continued to push his own ideas, some of which were clearly out of step with many of the English people.

Charles was sympathetic to and perhaps even inclined toward Catholicism. Moreover, Charles's brother James, heir to the throne, did not hide the fact that he was a Catholic. Parliament's suspicions were therefore aroused in 1672 when Charles took the audacious step of issuing a Declaration of Indulgence that suspended the laws that Parliament had passed against Catholics and Puritans after the restoration of the monarchy. Parliament would have none of it and induced the king to suspend the declaration. Propelled by a strong anti-Catholic sentiment, Parliament then passed a Test Act in 1673, specifying that only Anglicans could hold military and civil offices.

The accession of James II (1685–1688) to the crown virtually guaranteed a new constitutional crisis for England. An open and devout Catholic, his attempt to further Catholic interests made religion once more a primary cause of conflict between king and Parliament. In 1687, James issued a Declaration of Indulgence, which suspended all laws excluding Catholics and Puritans from office. Parliamentary outcries against James's policies stopped short

of rebellion because members knew that he was an old man and his successors were his Protestant daughters Mary and Anne, born to his first wife. But on June 10, 1688, a son was born to James's second wife, also a Catholic. Suddenly, the specter of a Catholic hereditary monarchy loomed large. A group of prominent English noblemen invited the Dutch chief executive, William of Orange, husband of James's daughter Mary, to invade England. William and Mary raised an army and invaded England, while James, his wife, and their infant son fled to France. With almost no bloodshed, England had undergone a "Glorious Revolution," not over the issue of whether there would be a monarchy, but rather over who would be the monarch.

THE BILL OF RIGHTS

I n 1688, *the English experienced yet another revolution, a rather bloodless one in which the Stuart king James II was replaced by Mary, James's daughter, and her husband, William of Orange. After William and Mary had assumed power, Parliament passed a Bill of Rights that specified the rights of Parliament and laid the foundation for a constitutional monarchy.*

THE BILL OF RIGHTS

Whereas the said late King James II having abdicated the government, and the throne being thereby vacant, his Highness the prince of Orange (whom it hath pleased Almighty God to make the glorious instrument of delivering this kingdom from popery and arbitrary power) did (by the device of the lords spiritual and temporal, and diverse principal persons of the Commons) cause letters to be written to the lords spiritual and temporal, being Protestants, and other letters to the several counties, cities, universities, boroughs, and Cinque Ports, for the choosing of such persons to represent them, as were of right to be sent to parliament, to meet and sit at Westminster upon the two and twentieth day of January, in this year 1689, in order to such an establishment as that their religion, laws, and liberties might not again be in danger of being subverted; upon which letters elections have been accordingly made.

And thereupon the said lords spiritual and temporal and Commons, pursuant to their respective letters and elections, being now assembled in a full and free representation of this nation, taking into their most serious consideration the best means for attaining the ends aforesaid, do in the first place (as their ancestors in like case have usually done), for the vindication and assertion of their ancient rights and liberties, declare:

1. That the pretended power of suspending laws, or the execution of laws, by regal authority, without consent of parliament is illegal.

2. That the pretended power of dispensing with the laws, or the execution of law by regal authority, as it hath been assumed and exercised of late, is illegal.
3. That the commission for erecting the late court of commissioners for ecclesiastical causes, and all other commissions and courts of like nature, are illegal and pernicious.
4. That levying money for or to the use of the crown by pretense of prerogative, without grant of parliament, for longer time or in other manner than the same is or shall be granted, is illegal.
5. That it is the right of the subjects to petition the king, and all commitments and prosecutions for such petitioning are illegal.
6. That the raising or keeping a standing army within the kingdom in time of peace, unless it be with consent of parliament, is against law.
7. That the subjects which are Protestants may have arms for their defense suitable to their conditions, and as allowed by law.
8. That election of members of parliament ought to be free.
9. That the freedom of speech, and debates or proceedings in parliament, ought not to be impeached or questioned in any court or place out of parliament.
10. That excessive bail ought not to be required, nor excessive fines imposed, nor cruel and unusual punishments inflicted.
11. That jurors ought to be duly impaneled and returned, and jurors which pass upon men in trials for high treason ought to be freeholders.
12. That all grants and promises of fines and forfeitures of particular persons before conviction are illegal and void.
13. And that for redress of all grievances, and for the amending, strengthening, and preserving of the laws, parliament ought to be held frequently.

The events of late 1688 constituted only the initial stage of the Glorious Revolution. In January 1689, Parliament offered the throne to William and Mary, who accepted it along with the provisions of a Bill of Rights (see the box above). The Bill of Rights affirmed Parliament's right to make laws and levy taxes and made it impossible for kings to oppose or do without Parliament by stipulating that standing armies could be raised only with the consent of Parliament. The rights of citizens to petition the sovereign, keep arms, have a jury trial, and not be subject to excessive bail were also confirmed. The Bill of Rights helped to fashion a system of government based on the rule of law and a freely elected Parliament, thus laying the foundation for a constitutional monarchy.

The Bill of Rights did not settle the religious questions that had played such a large role in England's troubles in the seventeenth century. The Toleration Act of 1689 granted Puritan Dissenters the right of free public worship (Catholics were still excluded). Although the Toleration Act did not mean complete religious freedom and equality, it marked a departure in English history because few people would ever again be persecuted for religious reasons.

Many historians have viewed the Glorious Revolution as the end of the seventeenth-century struggle between king and Parliament. By deposing one king and establishing another, Parliament had destroyed the divine-right theory of kingship (William was, after all, king by grace of

Parliament, not God) and confirmed its right to participate in the government. Parliament did not have complete control of the government, but it now had an unquestioned right to participate in affairs of state. Over the next century, it would gradually prove to be the real authority in the English system of constitutional monarchy.

Responses to Revolution

The English revolutions of the seventeenth century prompted very different responses from two English political thinkers—Thomas Hobbes and John Locke. Thomas Hobbes (1588–1679), who lived during the English civil wars, was alarmed by the revolutionary upheavals in his contemporary England. Hobbes's name has since been associated with the state's claim to absolute authority over its subjects, which he elaborated in his major treatise on political thought, *Leviathan*, published in 1651.

Hobbes claimed that in the state of nature, before society was organized, human life was "solitary, poor, nasty, brutish, and short." Humans were guided not by reason and moral ideals, but by animalistic instincts and a ruthless struggle for self-preservation. To save themselves from destroying each other, people contracted to form a commonwealth, which Hobbes called "that great Leviathan (or rather, to speak more reverently, that mortal god) to which we owe our peace and defense." This commonwealth placed its collective power into the hands of a sovereign authority, preferably a single ruler, who served as executor, legislator, and judge. This absolute ruler possessed unlimited power. Subjects may not rebel; if they do, they must be suppressed.

John Locke (1632–1704), who wrote a political work called *Two Treatises of Government*, viewed the exercise of political power quite differently from Hobbes and argued against the absolute rule of one man. Like Hobbes, Locke began with the state of nature before human existence became organized socially. But, unlike Hobbes, Locke believed humans lived then in a state of equality and freedom rather than a state of war. In this state of nature, humans had certain inalienable natural rights—to life, liberty, and property. Like Hobbes, Locke did not believe all was well in the state of nature. People found it difficult to protect these natural rights, so they mutually agreed to establish a government to ensure the protection of their rights. This agreement established mutual obligations: government would protect the people's rights while the people would act reasonably toward government. But if a government broke this agreement—if a monarch, for example, failed to live up to his obligation to protect the natural rights or claimed absolute authority and made laws without the consent of the community—the people might form a new government. For Locke, however, the community of people meant primarily the landholding aris-

tocracy, who were represented in Parliament, not the landless masses. Locke was hardly an advocate of political democracy, but his ideas proved important to both Americans and French in the eighteenth century and were used to support demands for constitutional government, the rule of law, and the protection of rights.

THE WORLD OF EUROPEAN CULTURE

In the sixteenth and seventeenth centuries, European art and literature passed through a number of stylistic stages. These changes were closely linked to the religious, political, and intellectual developments of the period.

Art

The artistic Renaissance came to an end when a new movement called Mannerism emerged in Italy in the decades of the 1520s and 1530s. The age of the Reformation had brought a revival of religious values accompanied by much political turmoil. Especially in Italy, the worldly enthusiasm of the Renaissance gave way to anxiety, uncertainty, suffering, and a yearning for spiritual experience. Mannerism reflected this environment in its deliberate attempt to break down the High Renaissance principles of balance, harmony, and moderation. Italian Mannerist painters deliberately distorted the rules of proportion by portraying elongated figures that conveyed a sense of suffering and a strong emotional atmosphere filled with anxiety and confusion.

Mannerism spread from Italy to other parts of Europe and perhaps reached its apogee in the work of El Greco (1541–1614). Doménikos Theotocópoulos (called "the Greek"—El Greco) was from Crete, but after studying in Venice and Rome, in the 1570s he moved to Spain, where he became a church painter in Toledo. El Greco's elongated and contorted figures, portrayed in unusual shades of yellow and green against an eerie background of turbulent grays, reflect well the artist's desire to create a world of intense emotions.

Mannerism was eventually replaced by a new movement—the Baroque—that dominated the artistic world for another century and a half. The Baroque began in Italy in the last quarter of the sixteenth century and spread to the rest of Europe. Baroque artists sought to harmonize the classical traditions of Renaissance art with the intense religious feelings fostered by the revival of religion in the Reformation. Although Protestants were also influenced, it was the Catholic reform movement that most wholeheartedly adopted the Baroque, as is evident at Catholic courts, especially those of the Habsburgs in Madrid, Prague, Vienna, and Brussels. Eventually, the Baroque style spread to all of Europe and Latin America.

In large part, Baroque art and architecture reflected the search for power that was characteristic of much of the seventeenth century. Baroque churches and palaces featured richly ornamented facades, sweeping staircases, and an overall splendor that were meant to impress people. Kings and princes wanted other kings and princes as well as their subjects to be in awe of their power.

Baroque painting was known for its use of dramatic effects to heighten emotional intensity, especially evident in the works of Peter Paul Rubens (1577–1640), a prolific artist and an important figure in the spread of the Baroque from Italy to other parts of Europe. In his artistic masterpieces, bodies in violent motion, heavily fleshed nudes, a dramatic use of light and shadow, and rich sensuous pigments converge to show intense emotions. The restless forms and constant movement blend together into a dynamic unity.

Perhaps the greatest figure of the Baroque was the Italian architect and sculptor Gian Lorenzo Bernini

❀ EL GRECO, LAOCÖON.   Mannerism reached one of its highest expressions in the work of El Greco. Born in Crete, trained in Venice and Rome, and settling finally in Spain, El Greco worked as a church painter in Toledo. Pictured here is his version of the *Laocöon*, a famous piece of Hellenistic sculpture that had been discovered in Rome in 1506. The elongated, contorted bodies project a world of suffering while the somber background scene of the city of Toledo adds a sense of terror and doom.

🍀 PETER PAUL RUBENS, *THE LANDING OF MARIE DE'
MEDICI AT MARSEILLES.*   Peter Paul Rubens played a key role
in spreading the Baroque style from Italy to other parts of Europe.
In *The Landing of Marie de' Medici at Marseilles*, Rubens made a
dramatic use of light and color, bodies in motion, and luxurious
nudes to heighten the emotional intensity of the scene. This was
one of a cycle of twenty-one paintings dedicated to the queen
mother of France.

🍀 ARTEMISIA GENTILESCHI, *JUDITH BEHEADING
HOLOFERNES.*   Artemisia Gentileschi painted a series of
pictures portraying scenes from the lives of courageous Old
Testament women. In this painting, a determined Judith,
armed with her victim's sword, struggles to saw off the head
of Holofernes. Gentileschi realistically and dramatically
shows the bloody nature of Judith's act.

(1598–1680), who completed Saint Peter's Basilica and
designed the vast colonnade enclosing the piazza in front
of it. Action, exuberance, profusion, and dramatic effects
mark Bernini's work in the interior of Saint Peter's, where
his *Throne of St. Peter* hovers in midair. Above the chair,
rays of heavenly light drive a mass of clouds and angels
toward the spectator.

Less well known than the male artists who dominated
the seventeenth-century art world in Italy but prominent
in her own right was Artemisia Gentileschi (1593–1653).
Born in Rome, she studied painting under her father's
direction. In 1616, she moved to Florence and began a successful career as a painter. At the age of twenty-three,
she became the first woman to be elected to the Florentine Academy of Design. Although she was known inter-
nationally in her day as a portrait painter, her fame now
rests on a series of pictures of heroines from the Old Testament, including Judith, Esther, and Bathsheba. Most

famous is her *Judith Beheading Holofernes*, a dramatic rendering of the biblical scene in which Judith slays the Assyrian general Holofernes in order to save her besieged town
from the Assyrian army.

In the second half of the seventeenth century, France
replaced Italy as the cultural leader of Europe. Rejecting
the Baroque style as overly showy and passionate, the
French remained committed to the classical values of the
High Renaissance. French late classicism, with its emphasis on clarity, simplicity, balance, and harmony of design
was, however, a rather "frigid" version of the High Renaissance style. Its triumph reflected the shift in seventeenth-
century French society from chaos to order. While French
classicism rejected the emotionalism and high drama of
the Baroque, the latter's conception of grandeur was still
evident in the portrayal of noble subjects, especially those
from classical antiquity. The paintings of Nicholas Poussin
(1594–1665) exemplified these principles.

✤ NICHOLAS POUSSIN, *LANDSCAPE WITH THE BURIAL OF PHOCIAN.* France became the new cultural leader of Europe in the second half of the seventeenth century. French classicism upheld the values of High Renaissance style, but in a more static version. In Nicholas Poussin's work, we see the emphasis of French classicism on the use of scenes from classical sources and the creation of a sense of grandeur and noble strength in both human figures and landscape.

A Golden Age of Literature: England and Spain

Periods of crisis often produce great writing, and this period, which was characterized by a golden age of theater, was no exception. In both England and Spain, writing for the stage reached new heights between 1580 and 1640. The golden age of English literature is often called the Elizabethan Era because much of the English cultural flowering of the late sixteenth and early seventeenth centuries occurred during her reign. Elizabethan literature exhibits the exuberance and pride associated with English exploits under Queen Elizabeth (see the box on p. 457). Of all the forms of Elizabethan literature, none expressed the energy and intellectual versatility of the era better than drama. Of all the dramatists, none is more famous than William Shakespeare (1564–1614).

Shakespeare was the son of a prosperous glover from Stratford-upon-Avon. When he appeared in London in 1592, Elizabethans were already addicted to the stage. By 1576, two professional theaters run by actors' companies were in existence. Elizabethan theater became a tremendously successful business. Soon at least four to six theaters were open six afternoons a week in or near London. They ranged from the Globe, which was a circular unroofed structure holding 3,000, to the Blackfriars, which was roofed and held only 500. In the former, an admission charge of one or two pennies enabled even the lower classes to attend, while the higher prices in the latter ensured an audience of the well-to-do. Elizabethan audiences varied greatly, putting pressure on playwrights to write works that pleased nobles, lawyers, merchants, and even vagabonds.

William Shakespeare was a "complete man of the theater." Although best known for writing plays, he was also an actor and shareholder in the chief company of the time, the Lord Chamberlains' Company, which played in theaters as diverse as the Globe and the Blackfriars. Shakespeare has long been recognized as a universal genius. A master of the English language, he was instrumental in transforming a language that was still in a period of transition. His technical proficiency, however, was matched by an incredible insight into human psychology. Whether in his tragedies or comedies, Shakespeare exhibited a remarkable understanding of the human condition.

The theater was one of the most creative forms of expression during Spain's golden century. The first professional theaters established in Seville and Madrid in the 1570s were run by actors' companies as in England. Soon, every large town had a public playhouse, including Mexico City in the New World. Touring companies brought the latest Spanish plays to all parts of the Spanish empire. Beginning in the 1580s, the agenda for playwrights was set by Lope de Vega (1562–1635). Like Shakespeare, he was from a middle-class background. He was an incredibly prolific writer; almost 500 of his 1,500 plays survive. They have been characterized as witty, charming, action-packed, and realistic. Lope de Vega made no apologies for the fact that he wrote his plays to please his audiences. In a treatise on drama written in 1609, he stated that the foremost duty of the playwright was to satisfy public demand. He remarked that if anyone thought he had written his plays for fame, "undeceive him and tell him that I wrote them for money."

WILLIAM SHAKESPEARE: IN PRAISE OF ENGLAND

William Shakespeare is one of the most famous playwrights in the Western world. He was a universal genius, outclassing all others in his psychological insights, depth of characterization, imaginative skills, and versatility. His historical plays reflected the patriotic enthusiasm of the English in the Elizabethan Era, as this excerpt from Richard II illustrates.

WILLIAM SHAKESPEARE, RICHARD II

This royal throne of kings, this sceptered isle,
This earth of majesty, this seat of Mars,
This other Eden, demi-Paradise,
This fortress built by Nature for herself
Against infection and the hand of war,
This happy breed of men, this little world,
This precious stone set in the silver sea,
Which serves it in the office of a wall
Or as a moat defensive to a house
Against the envy of less happier lands—
This blessed plot, this earth, this realm, this England,

This nurse, this teeming womb of royal kings,
Feared by their breed and famous by their birth,
Renowned for their deeds as far from home,
For Christian service and true chivalry,
As is the sepulcher in stubborn Jewry [the Holy Sepulcher in
    Jerusalem]
Of the world's ransom, blessed Mary's Son—
This land of such dear souls, this dear dear land,
Dear for her reputation through the world,
Is now leased out, I die pronouncing it,
Like a tenement or pelting farm.
England, bound in with the triumphant sea,
Whose rocky shore beats back the envious siege
Of watery Neptune, is now bound in with shame,
With inky blots and rotten parchment bonds.
That England, that was wont to conquer others,
Hath made a shameful conquest of itself.
Ah, would the scandal vanish with my life,
How happy then were my ensuing death!

One of the crowning achievements of the golden age of Spanish literature was the work of Miguel de Cervantes (1547–1616), whose *Don Quixote* has been acclaimed as one of the greatest literary works of all time. In the two main figures of his famous work, Cervantes presented the dual nature of the Spanish character. The knight Don Quixote from La Mancha is the visionary who is so involved in his lofty ideals that he is oblivious to the hard realities around him. To him, for example, windmills appear as four-armed giants. In contrast, the knight's fat and earthy squire, Sancho Panza, is the realist who cannot get his master to see the realities in front of him. But after adventures that took them to all parts of Spain, each came to see the value of the other's perspective. We are left with Cervantes's conviction that both visionary dreams and the hard work of reality are necessary to the human condition.

CONCLUSION

In Chapter 14, we observed how the movement of Europeans outside of Europe began to change the shape of world history. But what had made this development possible? After all, the religious division of Europe had led to almost a hundred years of religious warfare complicated by serious political, economic, and social issues—the worst series of wars and civil wars since the collapse of the Western Roman Empire—before Europeans finally admitted that they would have to tolerate different ways to worship God.

At the same time, the concept of a united Christendom, held as an ideal since the Middle Ages, had been irrevocably destroyed by the religious wars, enabling a system of nation-states to emerge in which power politics took on increasing significance. The growth of political thought focusing on the secular origins of state power reflected the changes that were going on in seventeenth-century society. Within those states slowly emerged some of the machinery that made possible a growing centralization of power. In those states called absolutist, strong monarchs with the assistance of their aristocracies took the lead in providing the leadership for greater centralization. In all the major European states, a growing concern for power led to larger armies, stronger economies, and more powerful governments. From a global point of view, the political and economic power of Europeans was beginning to slowly outstrip that of other peoples.

And yet, despite the spread of European states to the rest of the world, where they began to dominate global trade markets, Europeans had not yet achieved their goal of diminishing the power of Islam, a goal that had first begun during the Crusades. In fact, as we shall see in the next chapter, in the midst of European expansion and exploration, three new and powerful Muslim empires were taking shape in the Middle East and South Asia.

| 1500 | 1550 | 1600 | 1650 | 1700 | 1750 |

Martin Luther's Ninety-Five Theses

French Wars of Religion

Reign of Louis XIV

Reign of Peter the Great

Witchcraft trials

English Bill of Rights

Calvin's *Institutes of the Christian Religion*

Work of Gian Lorenzo Bernini

John Locke, *Two Treatises of Government*

Shakespeare's work in London

CHAPTER NOTES

1. Erasmus, *The Paraclesis*, in John Olin, ed., *Christian Humanism and the Reformation: Selected Writings of Erasmus*, 3d ed. (New York, 1987), p. 101.
2. Quoted in Roland Bainton, *Here I Stand: A Life of Martin Luther* (New York, 1950), p. 144.
3. Quoted in De Lamar Jensen, *Reformation Europe* (Lexington, Mass., 1981), p. 83.
4. John Calvin, *Institutes of the Christian Religion*, trans. John Allen (Philadelphia, 1936), 1:220.
5. Ibid., 1:228; 2:181.
6. Quoted in Roland Bainton, *Women of the Reformation in Germany and Italy* (Boston, 1971), p. 154.
7. Quoted in Bonnie S. Anderson and Judith P. Zinsser, *A History of Their Own: Women in Europe from Prehistory to the Present* (New York, 1988), 1:259.
8. Quoted in Joseph Klaits, *Servants of Satan: The Age of the Witch Hunts* (Bloomington, Ind., 1985), p. 68.
9. Quoted in James Harvey Robinson, *Readings in European History* (Boston, 1934), 2:211–12.
10. Quoted in John B. Wolf, *Louis XIV* (New York, 1968), p. 134.
11. Quoted in B. H. Sumner, *Peter the Great and the Emergence of Russia* (New York, 1962), p. 122.

SUGGESTED READINGS

Basic surveys of the Reformation period include H. J. Grimm, *The Reformation Era, 1500–1650*, 2d ed. (New York, 1973); D. L. Jensen, *Reformation Europe*, 2d ed. (Lexington, Mass., 1990); G. R. Elton, *Reformation Europe, 1517–1559* (Cleveland, 1963); C. Lindberg, *The European Reformations* (Cambridge, Mass., 1996); and E. Cameron, *The European Reformation* (New York, 1991). Also see the interesting and useful book by S. Ozment, *Protestants: The Birth of a Revolution* (New York, 1992). The best general biography of Erasmus is still R. Bainton, *Erasmus of Christendom* (New York, 1969), although the shorter works by J. K. Sowards, *Desiderius Erasmus* (Boston, 1975), and J. McConica, *Erasmus* (Oxford, 1991) are also good.

The classic account of Martin Luther's life is R. Bainton, *Here I Stand: A Life of Martin Luther* (New York and Nashville, 1950). More recent works include J. M. Kittelson, *Luther the Reformer: The Story of the Man and His Career* (Minneapolis, Minn., 1986), and H. A. Oberman, *Luther: Man Between God and the Devil* (New York, 1992). The best account of Ulrich Zwingli is G. R. Potter, *Zwingli* (Cambridge, 1976), although W. P. Stephens, *Zwingli* (Oxford, 1994) is an important study of Zwingli's ideas. The most comprehensive

account of the various groups and individuals who are called Anabaptist is G. H. Williams, *The Radical Reformation*, 2d ed. (Kirksville, Mo., 1992). Two worthwhile surveys of the English Reformation are A. G. Dickens, *The English Reformation*, 2d ed. (New York, 1989), and G. R. Elton, *Reform and Reformation: England, 1509–1558* (Cambridge, Mass., 1977). On John Calvin, see A. McGrath, *A Life of John Calvin: A Study in the Shaping of Western Culture* (Cambridge, Mass., 1990), and W. J. Bouwsma, *John Calvin* (New York, 1988).

On the impact of the Reformation on the family, see J. F. Harrington, *Reordering Marriage and Society in Reformation Germany* (New York, 1995). M. E. Wiesner's *Working Women in Renaissance Germany* (New Brunswick, N.J., 1986) covers primarily the sixteenth century. A good introduction to the Catholic Reformation can be found in M. R. O'Connell, *The Counter Reformation, 1559–1610* (New York, 1974).

General works on the sixteenth and seventeenth centuries include C. Wilson, *The Transformation of Europe, 1558–1648* (Berkeley, 1976); D. H. Pennington, *Europe in the Seventeenth Century*, 2d ed. (London and New York, 1989); R. S. Dunn, *The Age of Reli-*

gious Wars, 1559–1715, 2d ed. (New York, 1979); and R. Bonney, The European Dynastic States 1494–1660 (Oxford, 1991).

For good introductions to the French Wars of Religion, see M. P. Holt, The French Wars of Religion, 1562–1629 (New York, 1995), and R. J. Knecht, The French Wars of Religion, 1559–1598, 2d ed. (New York, 1996). The best biographies of Philip II are P. Pierson, Philip II of Spain (London, 1975), and G. Parker, Philip II, 3d ed. (Chicago, 1995). Elizabeth's reign can be examined in C. Haigh, Elizabeth I, 2d ed. (New York, 1998). On the Thirty Years' War, see G. Parker, The Thirty Years War, 2d ed. (London, 1997), and R. G. Asch, The Thirty Years War: The Holy Roman Empire and Europe, 1618–1648 (New York, 1997). A good general work on the period of the English Revolution is M. A. Kishlansky, A Monarchy Transformed (London, 1996). On Oliver Cromwell, see R. Howell, Jr., Cromwell (Boston, 1977), and P. Gaunt, Oliver Cromwell (Cambridge, Mass., 1996).

The story of the witchcraft craze can be examined in two works, J. B. Russell, A History of Witchcraft (London, 1980), and B. P. Levack, The Witch-Hunt in Early Modern Europe (London, 1987).

For brief accounts of seventeenth-century French history, see R. Briggs, Early Modern France, 1560–1715 (Oxford, 1977), and J. B. Collins, The State in Early Modern France (Cambridge, 1995). A solid and very readable biography of Louis XIV is J. B. Wolf, Louis XIV (New York, 1968). For a brief study, see P. R. Campbell, Louis XIV, 1661–1715 (London, 1993). A now classic work on life in Louis XIV's France is W. H. Lewis, The Splendid Century (Garden City,

N.Y., 1953). Well-presented summaries of revisionist views on Louis's monarchical power are R. Mettam, Power and Faction in Louis XIV's France (Oxford, 1988), and W. Beik, Absolutism and Society in Seventeenth-Century France (Cambridge, 1985). On the creation of an Austrian state, see R. J. W. Evans, The Making of the Habsburg Monarchy, 1550–1700 (Oxford, 1979), and C. Ingrao, The Habsburg Monarchy, 1618–1815 (Cambridge, 1994). The older work by F. L. Carsten, The Origins of Prussia (Oxford, 1954), remains an outstanding study of early Prussian history. Works on Peter the Great include M. S. Anderson, Peter the Great, 2d ed. (New York, 1995); L. Hughes, Russia in the Age of Peter the Great (New Haven, Conn., 1998); and the massive popular biography by R. K. Massie, Peter the Great (New York, 1980). On England, see J. P. Kenyon, Stuart England (London, 1978). A more specialized study is W. A. Speck, The Revolution of 1688 (Oxford, 1988).

For a brief, readable guide to Mannerism, see L. Murray, The Late Renaissance and Mannerism (New York, 1967). For a general survey of Baroque culture, see J. S. Held, Seventeenth and Eighteenth Century Art: Baroque Painting, Sculpture, Architecture (New York, 1971). On French classicism, see A. Merot, French Painting in the Seventeenth Century (New Haven, Conn., 1995). On the Spanish golden century of literature, see R. O. Jones, The Golden Age: Prose and Poetry, which is volume 2 of The Literary History of Spain (London, 1971). The literature on Shakespeare is enormous. For a biography, see A. L. Rowse, The Life of Shakespeare (New York, 1963).

INFOTRAC COLLEGE EDITION

For additional reading, go to InfoTrac College Edition, your online research library at http://web1.infotrac-college.com

Enter the search term "Reformation" using the Subject Guide.

Enter the search term "Counter-Reformation" using the Subject Guide.

Enter the search terms "Martin and Luther not King" using Keywords.

Enter the search terms "Thirty Years' War" using Keywords.

Enter the search terms "Louis XIV" using Keywords.

CHAPTER

16

THE MUSLIM EMPIRES

CHAPTER OUTLINE

- THE OTTOMAN EMPIRE
- THE SAFAVIDS
- THE GRANDEUR OF THE MUGHALS
- CONCLUSION

FOCUS QUESTIONS

- Why are the Ottoman, Safavid, and Mughal Empires sometimes called "gunpowder empires," and how accurate is that characterization?
- How did each of the great Muslim empires—Ottoman, Safavid, and Mughal—come into existence, and why did they ultimately decline?
- What were the main characteristics of each of the Muslim empires, and in what ways were they similar?
- What contact did each of the Muslim empires have with Europeans, and how was each empire affected by that contact?
- What role did women play in each of the Muslim empires?

One of the European states' primary objectives in seeking a route to the Spice Islands was to lessen the political and economic power of Islam by reducing the Muslims' strong position in the global trade network. As we saw in Chapter 14, Portuguese fleets, followed by those of the Spanish, the English, and the Dutch, had some success in wresting control over the spice trade from Muslim shippers, although the latter were never totally driven out of the business. By the eighteenth century, the Indian Ocean had ceased to be an Arab preserve and had become, in some respects, a European lake.

Thus, the European dream of controlling global trade markets had become a reality. But in the broader scheme of things, the goal of crippling the power of Islam was not entirely realized, for Europe's success had not been achieved by the collapse of its great Muslim rival. To the contrary, the Muslim world, which appeared to have entered a period of decline with the collapse of the Abbasid caliphate during the era of the Mongols, managed to revive in the shadow of Europe's Age of Exploration, a period that also saw the rise of three great Muslim empires. Known as the Ottomans, the Safavids, and the Mughals, these three powerful Muslim states dominated the Middle East and the South Asia subcontinent and brought stability to a region that had been in turmoil for centuries.

This stability lasted for about two hundred years. By the end of the eighteenth century, much of India and the Middle East had come under severe European pressure and had returned to a state of anarchy, and the Ottoman Empire had entered a period of gradual decline. But that decline was due more to internal factors than to the challenge posed by a resurgent Europe. ✿

THE OTTOMAN EMPIRE

The Ottoman Turks were among the various Turkic-speaking peoples who had spread westward from Central Asia in the ninth to the eleventh centuries C.E. The first to dominate were the Seljuk Turks, who initially attempted to revive the declining Abbasid caliphate in Baghdad. Later they established themselves in the Anatolian peninsula at the expense of the Byzantine Empire. Turks served as warriors or administrators, while the peasants who tilled the farmland were mainly Greek.

In the late thirteenth century, a new group of Turks under the tribal leader Osman (1280–1326) began to

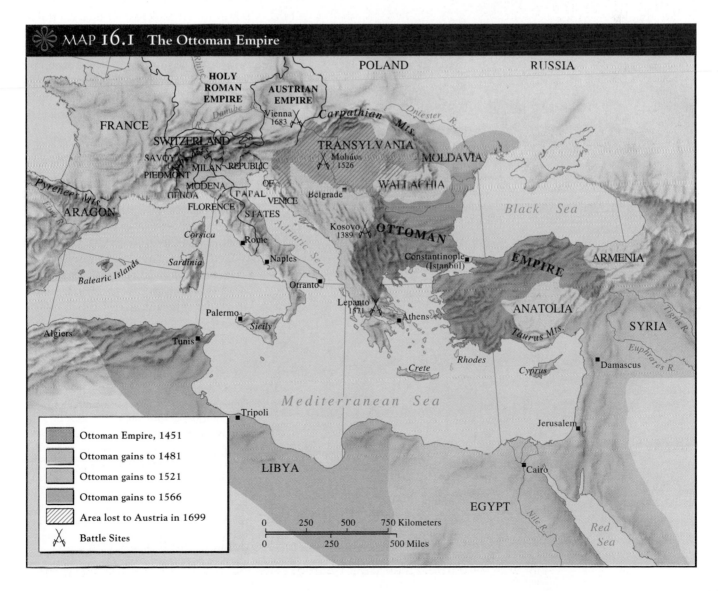

MAP 16.1 The Ottoman Empire

- Ottoman Empire, 1451
- Ottoman gains to 1481
- Ottoman gains to 1521
- Ottoman gains to 1566
- Area lost to Austria in 1699
- ✕ Battle Sites

0   250   500   750 Kilometers
0   250   500 Miles

consolidate their power in the northwestern corner of the Anatolian peninsula. That land had been given to them by the Seljuk rulers as a reward for helping to drive out the Mongols in the late thirteenth century. At first, the Osman Turks were relatively peaceful and engaged in pastoral pursuits, but as the Seljuk empire began to disintegrate in the early fourteenth century, they began to expand and founded the Osmanli (later to be known as Ottoman) dynasty.

A key advantage for the Ottomans was their location in the northwestern corner of the peninsula. From there they were able to expand westward and eventually control the Bosporus and the Dardanelles, between the Mediterranean and the Black Seas. The Byzantine Empire, of course, had controlled the area for centuries, serving as a buffer between the Muslim Middle East and the Latin West. The Byzantines, however, had been severely weakened by the sack of Constantinople in the Fourth Crusade (of 1204) and the Western occupation of much of the empire for the next half century. In 1345, Ottoman forces under their leader Orkhan I (1326–1360) crossed the Bosporus for the first time to support a usurper against the Byzantine emperor in Constantinople. Setting up their first European base at Gallipoli at the Mediterranean entrance to the Dardanelles, Turkish forces expanded gradually into the Balkans and allied with fractious Serbian and Bulgar forces against the Byzantines. In these unstable conditions, the Ottomans gradually established permanent settlements throughout the area, where Turkish beys (provincial governors in the Ottoman Empire; from the Turkish *beg*, "knight") drove out the previous landlords and collected taxes from the local Slavic peasants. The Ottoman leader now began to claim the title of sultan or sovereign of his domain.

In 1360, Orkhan was succeeded by his son Murad I, who consolidated Ottoman power in the Balkans, set up a capital at Edirne (today Adrianople), and gradually reduced the Byzantine emperor to a vassal. Murad did not initially attempt to conquer Constantinople, because his forces were composed mostly of the traditional Turkish cavalry and lacked the ability to breach the strong walls of the city. Instead, he began to build up a strong military administration based on the recruitment of Christians into an elite guard. Called Janissaries (from the Turkish *Yeni Cheri*, "new troops"), they were recruited from the local Christian population in the Balkans and then converted to Islam and trained as foot soldiers or administrators. One of the major advantages of the Janissaries was that they were directly subordinated to the sultanate and therefore owed their loyalty to the person of the sul-

THE TURKISH CONQUEST OF CONSTANTINOPLE. Mehmet II put a stranglehold on the Byzantine capital of Constantinople with a surprise attack by Turkish ships, which were dragged overland and placed in the water behind the enemy's defense lines. In addition, the Turks made use of massive cannons that could launch stone balls weighing up to 1,200 pounds each. The heavy bombardment of the city walls presaged the beginning of a new era of warfare in Europe. Notice the fanciful Gothic interpretation of the city in this contemporary French miniature of the siege of Constantinople.

CHRONOLOGY

THE OTTOMAN EMPIRE

Reign of Osman I	1280–1326
Ottoman Turks first cross the Bosporus	1345
Murad I consolidates Turkish power in the Balkans	1360
Ottomans defeat Serbian Army at Kosovo	1389
Tamerlane defeats Ottoman army at Ankara	1402
Rule of Mehmet II (the Conqueror)	1451–1481
Turkish conquest of Constantinople	1453
Turks defeat Mamluks in Syria and seize Cairo	1516–1517
Reign of Suleyman I (the Magnificent)	1520–1566
Defeat of Hungarians at Battle of Mohács	1526
Defeat of Turks at Vienna	1529
Battle of Lepanto	1571
Sinan era in Ottoman architecture	Sixteenth century

The last Byzantine emperor desperately called for help from the Europeans, but only the Genoese came to his defense. With 80,000 troops ranged against only 7,000 defenders, Mehmet laid siege to Constantinople in 1453. In their attack on the city, the Turks made use of massive cannons with twenty-six-foot barrels that could launch stone balls weighing up to 1,200 pounds each. The Byzantines stretched heavy chains across the Golden Horn the inlet that forms the city's harbor, to prevent a naval attack from the north and prepared to make their final stand behind the thirteen-mile-long wall along the western edge of the city. But Mehmet's forces seized the tip of the peninsula north of the Golden Horn and then dragged their ships overland across the peninsula from the Bosporus and put them into the water behind the chains. Finally, the walls were breached; the Byzantine emperor died in the final battle (see the box on p. 464). Mehmet II, standing before the palace of the emperor, paused to reflect on the passing nature of human glory. But it was not long before he and the Ottomans were again on the march.

Expansion of the Empire

With their new capital at Constantinople, renamed Istanbul, the Ottoman Turks were now a dominant force in the Balkans and the Anatolian peninsula. At the end of the fifteenth century, they began to advance to the east against the Shi'ite kingdom of the Safavids in Persia (see The Safavids later in this chapter), which had been promoting rebellion among the Anatolian tribal population and disrupting Turkish trade through the Middle East. After defeating the Safavids at a major battle in 1514, Emperor Selim I (1512–1520) consolidated Turkish control over Mesopotamia and then turned his attention to the Mamluks in Egypt, who had failed to support the Ottomans in their struggle against the Safavids. The Mamluks were defeated in Syria in 1516; Cairo fell a year later. Now controlling several of the holy cities of Islam, including Jerusalem, Mecca, and Medina, Selim declared himself to be the new caliph, or successor to Muhammad. During the next few years, Turkish armies and fleets advanced westward along the African coast, occupying Tripoli, Tunis, and Algeria and eventually penetrating almost to the Strait of Gibraltar. In their advance, the invaders had taken advantage of the progressive disintegration of the Nasrid dynasty in Morocco, which had been in decline for decades and had lost its last foothold on the European continent when Granada fell to the rising power of Spain in 1492.

The impact of Turkish rule on the peoples of North Africa was relatively light. Like their predecessors, the Turks were Muslims, and they preferred where possible to administer their conquered regions through local rulers. Central government direction was achieved through appointed *pashas* who collected taxes (and then paid a

tan. Other military forces were organized by the beys and were thus loyal to their local tribal leaders.

The Janissary corps also represented a response to changes in warfare. As the knowledge of firearms spread in the late fourteenth century, the Turks began to master the new technology, including siege cannons and muskets. The traditional nomadic cavalry charge was now outmoded and was superseded by infantry forces armed with muskets. Thus, the Janissaries provided a well-armed infantry who served both as an elite guard to protect the palace and as a means of extending Turkish control in the Balkans. With his new forces, Murad defeated the Serbs at the famous Battle of Kosovo in 1389 and ended Serbian hegemony in the area.

Under Murad's successor Bayazid I (1389–1402), the Ottomans advanced northward, annexed Bulgaria, and slaughtered the flower of French cavalry at a major battle on the Danube. A defeat at the hands of the Mongol warrior Tamerlane (see Chapter 9) in 1402 proved to be only a temporary setback. When Mehmet II (1451–1481) succeeded to the throne, he was determined to capture Constantinople. Already in control of the Dardanelles, he ordered the construction of a major fortress on the Bosporus just north of the city, which put the Turks in a position to strangle the Byzantines.

THE FALL OF CONSTANTINOPLE

Few events in the history of the Ottoman Empire are more dramatic than the conquest of Constantinople in 1453. In this excerpt, the conquest is described by Kritovoulos, a Greek who later served in the Ottoman administration. Although the author did not witness the conquest itself, he was apparently well informed about the event and provides us with a vivid description.

KRITOVOULOS, *LIFE OF MEHMED THE CONQUEROR*

So saying, he [the Sultan] led them himself. And they, with a shout on the run and with a fearsome yell, went on ahead of the Sultan, pressing on up to the palisade. After a long and bitter struggle they hurled back the Romans [Byzantines] from there and climbed by force up the palisade. They dashed some of their foe down into the ditch between the great wall and the palisade, which was deep and hard to get out of, and they killed them there. The rest they drove back to the gate.

He had opened this gate in the great wall, so as to go easily over to the palisade. Now there was a great struggle there and great slaughter among those stationed there, for they were attacked by the heavy infantry and not a few others in irregular formation, who had been attracted from many points by the shouting. There the Emperor Constantine [Constantine XIII Paleologus], with all who were with him, fell in gallant combat.

The heavy infantry were already streaming through the little gate into the City, and others had rushed in through the breach in the great wall. Then all the rest of the army, with a rush and a roar, poured in brilliantly and scattered all over the City. And the Sultan stood before the great wall, where the standard also was and the ensigns, and watched the proceedings. The day was already breaking. . . .

The soldiers fell on them [the citizens] with anger and great wrath. For one thing, they were actuated by the hardships of the siege. For another, some foolish people had hurled taunts and curses at them from the battlements all through the siege. Now, in general they killed so as to frighten all the City, and to terrorize and enslave all by the slaughter.

When they had had enough of murder, and the City was reduced to slavery, some of the troops turned to the mansions of the mighty, by bands and companies and divisions, for plunder and spoil. Others went to the robbing of churches, and others dispersed to the simple homes of the common people, stealing, robbing, plundering, killing, insulting, taking and enslaving men, women, and children, old and young, priests, monks—in short, every age and class. . . .

They say that many of the maidens, even at the mere unaccustomed sight and sound of these men, were terror-stricken and came near losing their very lives. And there were also honorable old men who were dragged by their white hair, and some of them beaten unmercifully. And well-born and beautiful young boys were carried off. . . .

After this the Sultan entered the City and looked about to see its great size, its situation, its grandeur and beauty, its teeming population, its loveliness, and the costliness of its churches and public buildings and of the private houses and community houses and those of the officials. . . . When he saw what a large number had been killed, and the ruin of the buildings, and the wholesale ruin and destruction of the City, he was filled with compassion and repented not a little at the destruction and plundering. Tears fell from his eyes as he groaned deeply and passionately: "What a city we have given over to plunder and destruction."

Thus he suffered in spirit. And indeed this was a great blow to us, in this one City, a disaster the like of which had occurred in no one of the great renowned cities of history, whether one speaks of the size of the captured City or of the bitterness and harshness of the deed. And no less did it astound all others than it did those who went through it and suffered, through the unreasonable and unusual character of the event and through the overwhelming and unheard-of horror of it.

As for the great City of Constantine, raised to a great height of glory and dominion and wealth in its own times, overshadowing to an infinite degree all the cities around it, renowned for its glory, wealth, authority, power, and greatness, and all its other qualities, it thus came to its end.

---

fixed percentage as tribute to the central government), maintained law and order, and were directly responsible to Istanbul. The Turks ruled from coastal cities like Algiers, Tripoli, and Tunis and made no attempt to control the interior beyond maintaining the trade routes through the Sahara to the trading centers along the Niger River. Meanwhile local pirates along the Barbary Coast competed with their Christian rivals in raiding the shipping that passed through the Mediterranean.

By the seventeenth century, the links between the imperial court in Istanbul and its appointed representa-tives in the Turkish regencies in North Africa had begun to decline. Some of the *pashas* were dethroned by local elites while others, such as the bey of Tunis, became hereditary rulers. Even Egypt, whose agricultural wealth and control over the route to the Red Sea made it the most important country in the area to the Turks, gradually became autonomous under a new official class of Janissaries. Many of them became wealthy landowners by exploiting their official function to collect tax revenues far in excess of what they had to remit to Istanbul. In the early eighteenth century, the Mamluks returned to power,

A PORTRAIT OF SULEYMAN THE MAGNIFICENT

Suleyman the Magnificent was perhaps the greatest of all Ottoman sultans. Like King Louis XIV of France and Emperor Kangxi of China, he presided over his domain at the peak of its military and cultural achievement. This description of him was written by Ghislain de Busbecq, the Habsburg ambassador to Constantinople. Busbecq observed Suleyman at firsthand and, as this excerpt indicates, was highly impressed by the Turkish ruler.

GHISLAIN DE BUSBECQ, *THE TURKISH LETTERS*

The Sultan was seated on a rather low sofa, no more than a foot from the ground and spread with many costly coverlets and cushions embroidered with exquisite work. Near him were his bow and arrows. His expression, as I have said, is anything but smiling, and has a sternness which, though sad, is full of majesty. On our arrival we were introduced into his presence by his chamberlains, who held our arms—a practice which has always been observed since a Croatian sought an interview and murdered the Sultan Amurath in a revenge for the slaughter of his master, Marcus the Despot of Serbia. After going through the pretense of kissing his hand, we were led to the wall facing him backwards, so as not to turn our backs or any part of them toward him. He then listened to the recital of my message, but, as it did not correspond with his expectations (for the demands of my imperial master [the Habsburg emperor Ferdinand I] were full of dignity and independence, and, therefore, far from acceptable to one who thought that his slightest wishes ought to be obeyed) he assumed an expression of disdain, and merely answered "Giusel, Giusel," that is, "Well, Well." We were then dismissed to our lodging....

You will probably wish me to describe the impression which Suleyman made upon me. He is beginning to feel the weight of years, but his dignity of demeanor and his general physical appearance are worthy of the ruler of so vast an empire. He has always been frugal and temperate, and was so even in his youth, when he might have erred without incurring blame in the eyes of the Turks. Even in his earlier years he did not indulge in wine or in those unnatural vices to which the Turks are often addicted. Even his bitterest critics can find nothing more serious to allege against him than his undue submission to his wife and its result in his somewhat precipitate action in putting Mustapha [his firstborn son, by another wife] to death, which is generally imputed to her employment of love potions and incantations. It is generally agreed that, ever since he promoted her to the rank of his lawful wife, he has possessed no concubines, although there is no law to prevent his doing so. He is a strict guardian of his religion and its ceremonies, being not less desirous of upholding his faith than of extending his dominions. For his age—he has almost reached his sixtieth year—he enjoys quite good health, though his bad complexion may be due to some hidden malady; and indeed it is generally believed that he has an incurable ulcer or gangrene on his leg. This defect of complexion he remedies by painting his face with a coating of red powder, when he wishes departing ambassadors to take with them a strong impression of his good health; for he fancies that it contributes to inspire greater fear in foreign potentates if they think that he is well and strong. I noticed a clear indication of this practice on the present occasion; for his appearance when he received me in the final audience was very different from that which he presented when he gave me an interview on my arrival.

---

although the Turkish government managed to retain some control by means of a viceroy appointed from Istanbul.

TURKISH EXPANSION IN EUROPE

After their conquest of Constantinople in 1453, the Ottoman Turks tried to complete their conquest of the Balkans, where they had been established since the fourteenth century. Although they were successful in taking the Romanian territory of Wallachia in 1476, the resistance of the Hungarians initially kept the Turks from advancing up the Danube valley. From 1480 to 1520, internal problems and the need to consolidate their eastern frontiers kept the Turks from any further attacks on Europe.

Suleyman I the Magnificent (1520–1566), the greatest of the Ottoman sultans (see the box above), however, brought the Turks back to Europe's attention. Advancing up the Danube, the Turks seized Belgrade in 1521 and won a major victory over the Hungarians at the Battle of Mohács on the Danube in 1526. Subsequently, the Turks overran most of Hungary, moved into Austria, and advanced as far as Vienna, where they were finally repulsed in 1529. At the same time, the Turks extended their power into the western Mediterranean and threatened to turn it into a Turkish lake until a large Turkish fleet was destroyed by the Spanish at Lepanto in 1571. Despite the defeat, the Turks continued to hold nominal suzerainty over the southern shores of the Mediterranean.

Although Europeans frequently called for new Christian crusades against the "infidel" Turks, by the beginning of the seventeenth century the Ottoman Empire was being treated like any other European power by European rulers seeking alliances and trade concessions. During the first half of the seventeenth century, the Ottoman Empire was a "sleeping giant." Involved in domestic bloodletting and heavily threatened by a challenge from Persia, the Ottomans were content with the status quo in eastern Europe. But under a new line of grand vezirs in the second half of the seventeenth century, the Ottoman Empire again took the offensive. By mid-1683, the Ottomans had marched through the Hungarian plain and laid siege to Vienna. Repulsed by a mixed army of Austrians, Poles, Bavarians, and Saxons, the Turks retreated and were pushed out of Hungary by a new European coalition. Although they retained the core of their empire, the Ottoman Turks would never again be a threat to Europe. Although the Turkish empire held together for the rest of the seventeenth and the eighteenth centuries, it would be faced with new challenges from the ever growing Austrian Empire in southeastern Europe and the new Russian giant to the north.

The Nature of Turkish Rule

Like other Muslim empires in Persia and India, the Ottoman political system was the result of the evolution of tribal institutions into a sedentary empire. The three states are often called "gunpowder empires" because to a considerable extent they owed their success to their mastery of the technology of firearms. At the apex of the Ottoman system was the sultan, who was the supreme authority in both a political and a military sense. The origins of this system can be traced back to the bey, who was only a tribal leader, a first among equals, who could claim loyalty from his chiefs so long as he could provide booty and grazing lands for his subordinates. Disputes were settled by tribal law, while Muslim laws were secondary. Tribal leaders collected taxes—or booty—from areas under their control and sent one-fifth on to the bey. Both administrative and military power were centralized under the bey, and the capital was wherever the bey and his administration happened to be.

But the rise of empire brought about changes and an adaptation to Byzantine traditions of rule. The status and prestige of the sultan now increased relative to the subordinate tribal leaders, and the position took on the trappings of imperial rule. Court rituals were inherited from the Byzantines and Persians, and a centralized administrative system was adopted that increasingly isolated the sultan in his palace. The position of the sultan was hereditary, with a son, although not necessarily the eldest, always succeeding the father. This practice led to chronic succession struggles upon the death of individual sultans, and the losers were often executed (strangled with a silk bowstring) or later imprisoned. Heirs to the throne were assigned as provincial governors to provide them with experience.

The heart of the sultan's power was in the Topkapi (meaning "cannon gate") Palace in the center of Istanbul. Topkapi was constructed in 1459 by Mehmet II and served as an administrative center as well as the private residence of the sultan and his family. Eventually, it had a staff of 20,000 employees. The private domain of the sultan was called the harem (sacred place). Here he resided with his concubines. Normally, a sultan did not marry but chose several concubines as his favorites; they were accorded this status after they gave birth to sons. When a son became a sultan, his mother became known as the queen mother and served as adviser to the throne. This tradition, initiated by the influential wife of Suleyman the Magnificent, often resulted in considerable authority for the queen mother in the affairs of state.

Members of the harem, like the Janissaries, were often of slave origins and formed an elite element in Ottoman society. Since the enslavement of Muslims was forbidden, slaves were taken among non-Islamic peoples. Some concubines were prisoners selected for the position, while others were purchased or offered to the sultan as a gift. They were then trained and educated like the Janissaries in a system called *devshirme* (collection). The *devshirme* had originated in the practice of requiring local clan leaders to

MEHMET II, CONQUEROR OF CONSTANTINOPLE. Identified with the seizure of Constantinople from the Byzantine Empire in 1453, Mehmet II was one of the most illustrious Ottoman sultans. This Turkish miniature portrays Mehmet II with his handkerchief, a symbol of the supreme power of the Ottoman ruler. He is also smelling a rose, representing his cultural interests, especially as patron of the arts.

provide prisoners to the sultan as part of their tax obligation. Talented males were given special training for eventual placement in military or administrative positions, while their female counterparts were trained for service in the harem, with instruction in reading, the Koran, sewing and embroidery, and musical performance. They were ranked according to their status, and some were permitted to leave the harem to marry officials. If they were later divorced, they were sometimes allowed to return to the harem.

Unique to the Ottoman Empire from the fifteenth century onward was the exclusive use of slaves to reproduce its royal heirs. Contrary to myth, few of the women of the imperial harem were used for sexual purposes, as the majority were relatives of the sultan's extended family, comprised of sisters, daughters, widowed mothers, and in-laws, with their own personal slaves and entourage. Contemporary European observers compared the atmosphere in the Topkapi harem to a Christian nunnery, with its hierarchical organization, enforced chastity, and the rule of silence.

Because of their proximity to the sultan, the women of the harem often wielded so much political power that the era has been called "the sultanate of women." Queen mothers administered the imperial household and engaged in diplomatic relations with other countries, while controlling the marital alliances of their daughters with senior civilian and military officials or members of other royal families in the region. One princess was married seven separate times from the age of two after her previous husbands died either in battle or by execution.

The sultan ruled through an imperial council that met four days a week and was chaired by the chief minister known as the grand vezir (wazir, sometimes known in English as vizier). The sultan often attended behind a screen, whence he could privately indicate his desires to the grand vezir. The latter presided over the imperial bureaucracy. Like the palace guard, the bureaucrats were not an exclusive group, but were chosen at least partly by merit from a palace school for training officials. Most officials were Muslims by birth, but some talented Janissaries became senior members of the bureaucracy, and almost all the later grand vezirs came from the devshirme system.

Local administration during the imperial period was a product of Turkish tribal tradition and was similar in some respects to fief holding in Europe. The empire was divided into provinces and districts governed by officials who, like their tribal predecessors, combined both civil and military functions. They were assisted by bureaucrats trained in the palace school in Istanbul. Senior officials were assigned land in fief by the sultan and were then responsible for collecting taxes and supplying armies to the empire. These lands were then farmed out to the local cavalry elite called the sipahis, who exacted a tax from all peasants in their fiefdoms for their salary. These local officials were not hereditary aristocrats, but sons often inherited their father's landholdings, and the vast majority were descendants of the tribal beys who had served as a tribal elite during the preimperial period.

Religion and Society in the Ottoman World

Like most Turkic-speaking peoples in the Anatolian peninsula and throughout the Middle East, the Ottoman ruling elites were Sunni Muslims. Ottoman sultans had claimed the title of caliph (defender of the faith) since the early sixteenth century and thus theoretically were responsible for guiding the flock and maintaining Islamic law, the Shari'ah. In practice, the sultan assigned these duties to a supreme religious authority, who administered the law and maintained a system of schools for educating Muslims.

Islamic law and customs were applied to all Muslims in the empire. Like their rulers, most Turkic-speaking people were Sunni Muslims, but some communities were attracted to Sufism (see Chapter 7) or other heterodox doctrines. The government tolerated such activities so long as their practitioners remained loyal to the empire, but in the early sixteenth century unrest among these groups—some of whom converted to the Shi'ite version of Islamic doctrine—outraged the conservative ulama and eventually led to the war against the Safavids (see The Safavids later in this chapter).

Non-Muslims—mostly Orthodox Christians (Greeks and Slavs), Jews, and Armenian Christians—formed a significant minority within the empire, which treated them with relative tolerance. Non-Muslims were compelled to pay a head tax (because of their exemption from military service), but they were permitted to practice their religion or convert to Islam, although Muslims were prohibited from adopting another faith. Most of the population in European areas of the empire remained Christian, but in some places, such as the territory now called Bosnia, substantial numbers converted to Islam.

Each religious group within the empire was organized as an administrative unit called a millet (nation or community). Each group, including the Muslims themselves, had its own patriarch or grand rabbi who dealt as an intermediary with the government and administered the community according to its own laws. The leaders of the individual nations were responsible to the sultan and his officials for the behavior of the subjects under their care and collected taxes for transmission to the government. Each nation established its own system of justice, set its own educational policies, and provided welfare for the needy.

Technically, women in the Ottoman Empire were subject to the same restrictions that afflicted their counterparts in other Muslim societies, but their position was ameliorated to some degree by various factors. In the first place, non-Muslims were subject to the laws and customs of their own religions; thus, Orthodox Christian, Jewish, and Armenian Christian women were spared some of the

A TURKISH DISCOURSE ON COFFEE

Coffee was first introduced to Turkey from the Arabian peninsula in the mid-sixteenth century and allegedly came to Europe during the Turkish seige of Vienna in 1527. The following account was written by Katib Chelebi, a seventeenth-century Turkish author who, among other things, compiled an extensive encyclopedia and bibliography. Here, in The Balance of Truth, he describes how coffee entered the empire and the problems it caused for public morality. Chelebi died in Istanbul in 1657, reportedly while drinking a cup of coffee.

KATIB CHELEBI, *THE BALANCE OF TRUTH*

It [coffee] originated in Yemen and has spread, like tobacco, over the world. Certain sheikhs, who lived with their dervishes in the mountains of Yemen, used to crush and eat the berries . . . of a certain tree. Some would roast them and drink their water. Coffee is a cold dry food, suited to the ascetic life and sedative of lust. . . .

It came to Asia Minor by sea, about 1543, and met with a hostile reception, fetwas [decrees] being delivered against it. For they said, Apart from its being roasted, the fact that it is drunk in gatherings, passed from hand to hand, is suggestive of loose living. It is related of Abul-Suud Efendi that he had holes bored in the ships that brought it, plunging their cargoes of coffee into the sea. But these strictures and prohibitions availed nothing. . . . One coffeehouse was opened after another, and men would gather together, with great eagerness and enthusiasm, to drink. Drug addicts in particular, finding it a life-giving thing, which increased their pleasure, were willing to die for a cup.

Storytellers and musicians diverted the people from their employments, and working for one's living fell into disfavor. Moreover the people, from prince to beggar, amused themselves with knifing one another. Toward the end of 1633, the late Ghazi Gultan Murad, becoming aware of the situation, promulgated an edict, out of regard and compassion for the people, to this effect: Coffeehouses throughout the Guarded Domains shall be dismantled and not opened hereafter. Since then, the coffeehouses of the capital have been as desolate as the heart of the ignorant. . . . But in cities and towns outside Istanbul, they are opened just as before. As has been said above, such things do not admit of a perpetual ban.

---

restrictions applied to their Muslim sisters. In the second place, Islamic laws as applied in the Ottoman Empire defined the legal position of women comparatively tolerantly. Women were permitted to own and inherit property, including their dowries. They could not be forced into marriage and in certain cases were permitted to seek a divorce. As we have seen, women often exercised considerable influence in the palace and in a few instances even served as senior officials, such as governors of provinces. The relatively tolerant attitude toward women in Ottoman-held territories has been ascribed by some to Turkish tribal traditions, which took a more egalitarian view of sex roles than did the sedentary societies of the region.

The Ottomans in Decline

The Ottoman Empire reached its zenith under Suleyman the Magnificent, often known as Suleyman Kanuni, or "the lawgiver," who launched the conquest of Hungary. But Suleyman also sowed the seeds of the Ottomans' eventual decline. He executed his two most able sons on suspicion of factionalism and was succeeded by Selim II (the Sot, or "the drunken sultan"), the only surviving son.

By the seventeenth century, signs of internal rot had begun to appear, although the first loss of imperial territory did not occur until 1699, at the Battle of Carlowitz. Apparently, a number of factors were involved. In the first place, the administrative system inherited from the tribal period began to break down. Although the *devshirme* system of training officials continued to function, *devshirme* graduates were now permitted to marry and inherit property and to enroll their sons in the palace corps. Thus, they were gradually transformed from a meritocratic administrative elite into a privileged and often degenerate hereditary caste. Local administrators were corrupted and taxes rose as the central bureaucracy lost its links with rural areas. The imperial treasury was depleted by constant wars, and transport and communications were neglected. In addition, the empire was increasingly beset by economic difficulties, caused by the diversion of trade routes away from the eastern Mediterranean and the price inflation brought about by the influx of cheap American silver.

Another sign of change within the empire was the increasing degree of material affluence and the impact of Western ideas and customs. Sophisticated officials and merchants began to mimic the habits and lifestyles of their European counterparts, dressing in the European fashion, purchasing Western furniture and art objects, and ignoring Muslim strictures against the consumption of alcohol and sexual activities outside marriage. During the sixteenth and early seventeenth centuries, coffee and tobacco were introduced into polite Ottoman society, and cafés for the consumption of both began to appear in the major cities (see the box above). One sultan in the early seventeenth century issued a decree prohibiting the consumption of both coffee and tobacco, arguing (correctly, no doubt) that many cafés were nests of antigovernment intrigue. He even began to wander incognito through the streets of Istanbul at night. Any of his subjects detected in immoral or illegal acts were summarily executed and their bodies left on the streets as an example to others.

There were also signs of a decline in competence within the ruling family. Whereas the first sultans reigned twenty-seven years on average, later ones averaged only thirteen years. The throne now went to the oldest surviving male, while his rivals were kept secluded in a latticed cage and thus had no governmental experience if they succeeded to rule. Later sultans also became less involved in government, and more power flowed to the office of the grand vezir (called the *Sublime Porte*) or to eunuchs and members of the harem. Palace intrigue increased as a result.

Ottoman Art

The Ottoman sultans were enthusiastic patrons of the arts and maintained large ateliers of artisans and artists, primarily at the Topkapi Palace in Istanbul but also in other important cities of the vast empire. The period from Mehmet II in the fifteenth century to the early eighteenth century witnessed the flourishing of pottery, rugs, silk and other textiles, jewelry, arms and armor, and calligraphy. All adorned the palaces of the new rulers, testifying to their opulence and exquisite taste. The artists came from all parts of the realm and beyond. Besides Turks, there were Persians, Greeks, Armenians, Hungarians, and Italians, all vying for the esteem and generous rewards of the sultans and fearing that losing favor might mean losing their heads! In the second half of the sixteenth century, Istanbul alone listed over 150 craft guilds, ample proof of the artistic activity of the era.

By far the greatest contribution of the Ottoman Empire to world art was its architecture, especially the magnificent mosques of the last half of the sixteenth century. Traditionally, prayer halls in mosques were subdivided by numerous pillars that supported small individual domes, creating a private forestlike atmosphere. The Turks, however, modeled their new mosques on the open floor plan of the Byzantine church of Santa Sophia (completed in 537), which had been turned into a mosque by Mehmet II, and began to push the pillars toward the outer wall to create a prayer hall with an uninterrupted central area under one large dome. With this plan, large numbers of believers could worship in unison in accordance with Muslim preference. By the mid-sixteenth century, the greatest of all Ottoman architects, Sinan, began erecting the first of his eighty-one mosques with an uncluttered prayer area. Each was topped by an imposing dome, and often, as at Edirne, the entire building was framed with four towering narrow minarets. By emphasizing its vertical lines, the minarets camouflaged the massive stone bulk of the structure and gave it a feeling of incredible lightness. These four graceful minarets would find new expression sixty years

later in India's white marble Taj Mahal (see Mughal Culture later in this chapter).

The lightness of the exterior was reinforced in the mosque's interior by the soaring height of the dome and the numerous windows. Added to this were delicate plasterwork and tile decoration that transformed the mosque into a monumental oasis of spirituality, opulence, and power. Sinan's masterpieces, such as the Suleymaniye and the Blue Mosque of Istanbul, were always part of a large socioreligious compound that included a library, school, hospital, mausolea, and even bazaars, all of equally magnificent construction.

Earlier, the thirteenth-century Seljuk Turks of Anatolia had created beautiful tile decorations with two-color mosaics. Now Ottoman artists invented a new glazed tile art with painted flowers and geometrical designs in brilliant blue, green, yellow, and their own secret "tomato red." Entire walls, both interior and exterior, were covered with the painted tiles, which adorned palaces as well as mosques. Produced at Iznik (the old Nicaea), the distinctive tiles and pottery were in great demand; the city's ateliers boasted more than three hundred artisans in the late sixteenth century.

The sixteenth century also witnessed the flourishing of textiles and rugs. The Byzantine emperor Justinian had introduced the cultivation of silkworms to the West in the sixth century, and the silk industry resurfaced under the Ottomans. Its capital was at Bursa, where factories produced silks for wall hangings, soft covers, and especially court costumes. Perhaps even more famous than Turkish silk are the rugs. But whereas silks were produced under the patronage of the sultans, rugs were a peasant industry. Each village boasted its own distinctive design and color scheme for the rugs it produced. Common to all the rugs, however, was the use of the knot from the Gordes region—hence the term "Gordian knot."

 # THE SAFAVIDS

After the collapse of the empire of Tamerlane in the early fifteenth century, the area extending from Persia into Central Asia lapsed into anarchy. The Uzbeks, Turkic-speaking peoples from Central Asia, were the chief political and military force in the area. From their capital at Bokhara, they maintained a semblance of control over the highly fluid tribal alignments until the emergence of the Safavid dynasty in Persia at the beginning of the sixteenth century.

The Safavid dynasty was founded by Shah Ismail, the descendant of a sheikh called Safi al-Din (thus the name Safavid), who traced his origins to Ali, the fourth imam of the Muslim faith. In the early fourteenth century, Safi had been the leader of a community of Turkic-speaking tribespeople in Azerbaijan, near the Caspian Sea. Safi's community was only one of many Sufi mystical religious groups throughout the area. In time the doctrine spread among nomadic groups throughout the Middle East and was transformed into the more activist Shi'i heresy. Its adherents were known as "red heads" because of their distinctive red cap with twelve folds, meant to symbolize allegiance to the twelve imams of the Shi'i faith.

In 1501, Ismail's forces seized much of Iran and Iraq, and he called himself the shah of a new Persian state. Baghdad was subdued in 1508 and the Uzbeks in Bokhara shortly thereafter. Ismail (1487–1524) now sent Shi'ite preachers into Anatolia to proselytize and promote rebellion among Turkish tribal peoples in the Ottoman Empire. In retaliation, the Ottoman sultan Selim I advanced against the Safavids in Iran and won a major battle near Tabriz in 1514. But Selim could not maintain control of the area, and Ismail regained Tabriz a few years later.

The Ottomans returned to the attack in the 1580s and forced the new Safavid shah, Abbas I (1587–1629), to sign a punitive peace in which much territory was lost. The capital was subsequently moved from Tabriz in the northwest to Isfahan in the south. Still, it was under Shah Abbas that the Safavids reached the zenith of their glory. He established a system similar to the Janissaries in Turkey to train administrators to replace the traditional warrior elite. He also used the period of peace to strengthen his army, now armed with modern weapons, and in the early seventeenth century he attempted to regain the lost territories. Although he had some initial success, war resumed in the 1620s, and a lasting peace was not achieved until 1638.

Abbas the Great had managed to strengthen the dynasty significantly, and for a time after his death in 1629, it remained stable and vigorous. But succession conflicts plagued the dynasty. Partly as a result, the power of the more militant Shi'ites began to increase at court and in Safavid society at large. The intellectual freedom that had characterized the empire at its height was cur-

THE BLUE MOSQUE, ISTANBUL.   The magnificent mosques built under the patronage of Suleyman the Magnificent are a great legacy of the Ottoman Empire and a fitting supplement to Santa Sophia (Hagia Sophia) Cathedral, built by the Byzantine emperor Justinian in the sixth century C.E. Towering under a central dome, they seem to defy gravity, and, like European Gothic cathedrals, convey to the viewer a sense of weightlessness. The Blue Mosque, so called for the blue tiles in its interior, is one of the most impressive and graceful in Istanbul. A far cry from the seventh-century desert mosques constructed of palm trunks, the Ottoman mosques stand as one of the architectural wonders of the world.

CHRONOLOGY

THE SAFAVIDS

Ismail seizes Iran and Iraq and becomes shah of Persia	1501
Ismail conquers Baghdad and defeats Uzbeks	1508
Reign of Shah Abbas I	1587–1629
Truce achieved between Ottomans and Safavids	1638
Collapse of Safavid empire	1723

削減   正統性

tailed under the pressure of religious orthodoxy, and Iranian women, who had enjoyed considerable freedom and influence during the early empire, were forced to withdraw into seclusion and to the veil. Meanwhile, attempts to suppress the religious beliefs of minorities led to increased popular unrest. In the early eighteenth century, Afghan warriors took advantage of local revolts to seize the capital of Isfahan, forcing the remnants of the Safavid

ruling family to retreat to Azerbaijan, their original homeland. The Ottomans seized territories along the western border. Eventually, order was restored by the military adventurer Nadir Shah Afshar, who launched an extended series of campaigns that restored the country's borders and even occupied the Mughal capital of Delhi (see Twilight of the Mughals later in this chapter). After his death, the Zand dynasty ruled until the end of the eighteenth century.

Safavid Politics and Society

Like the Ottoman Empire, Iran under the Safavids was a mixed society. The Safavids had come to power with the support of nomadic Turkic-speaking tribal groups, and leading elements from those groups retained considerable influence within the empire. But the majority of the population were Iranian; most of them were farmers or townspeople, with attitudes inherited from the relatively sophisticated and urbanized culture of pre-Safavid Iran. Faced with the problem of integrating unruly Turkic-speaking tribal peoples with the sedentary Persian-speaking population of the urban areas, the Safavids used the Shi'ite faith as a unifying force (see the box on p. 472). The shah himself acquired an almost divine

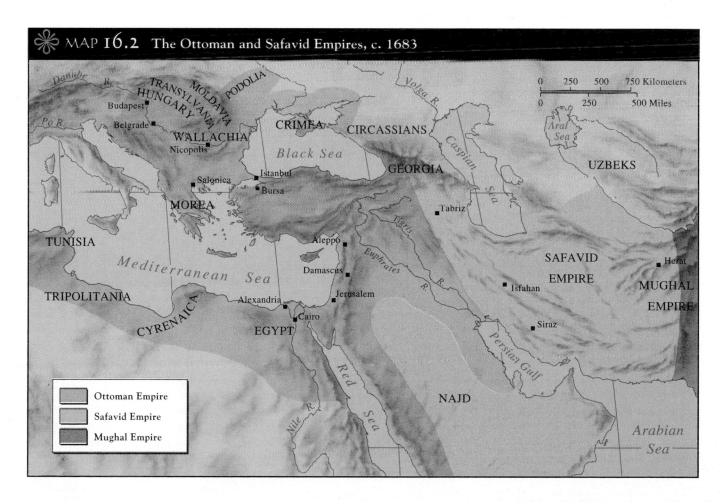

MAP 16.2 The Ottoman and Safavid Empires, c. 1683

- Ottoman Empire
- Safavid Empire
- Mughal Empire

THE RELIGIOUS ZEAL OF SHAH ABBAS THE GREAT

Shah Abbas I, probably the greatest of the Safavid rulers, expanded the borders of his empire into areas of the southern Caucasus inhabited by Christians and other non-Muslim peoples. After Persian control was assured, he instructed that the local population be urged to convert to Islam for their own protection and the glory of God. In this passage, his biographer, the Persian historian Eskander Beg Monshi, recounts the story of that effort.

THE CONVERSION OF A NUMBER OF CHRISTIANS TO ISLAM

This year the Shah decreed that those Armenians and other Christians who had been settled in [the southern Caucasus] and had been given agricultural land there, should be invited to become Muslims. Life in this world is fraught with vicissitudes, and the Shah was concerned lest, in a period when the authority of the central government was weak, these Christians, . . . might be subjected to attack by the neighboring Lor tribes (who are naturally given to causing injury and mischief), and their women and children carried off into captivity. In the areas in which these Christian groups resided, it was the Shah's purpose that the places of worship which they had built should become mosques, and the muezzin's call should be heard in them, so that these Christians might assume the

guise of Muslims, and their future status accordingly be assured. . . .

Some of the Christians, guided by God's grace, embraced Islam voluntarily; others found it difficult to abandon their Christian faith and felt revulsion at the idea. They were encouraged by their monks and priests to remain steadfast in their faith. After a little pressure had been applied to the monks and priests, however, they desisted, and these Christians saw no alternative but to embrace Islam, though they did so with reluctance. The women and children embraced Islam with great enthusiasm, vying with one another in their eagerness to abandon their Christian faith and declare their belief in the unity of God. Some five thousand people embraced Islam. As each group made the Muslim declaration of faith, it received instruction in the Koran and the principles of the religious law of Islam, and all bibles and other Christian devotional material were collected and taken away from the priests.

In the same way, all the Armenian Christians who had been moved to [the area] were also forcibly converted to Islam. . . . Most people embraced Islam with sincerity, but some felt an aversion to making the Muslim profession of faith. True knowledge lies with God! May God reward the Shah for his action with long life and prosperity!

---

quality and claimed to be the spiritual leader of all Islam. Shi'ism was declared the state religion.

Although there was a landed aristocracy, aristocratic power and influence were firmly controlled by strong-minded shahs, who confiscated aristocratic estates when possible and brought them under the control of the crown. Appointment to senior positions in the bureaucracy was by merit rather than birth. To avoid encouraging competition between Turkish and non-Turkish elements, Shah Abbas I hired a number of foreigners from neighboring countries for positions in his government.

The Safavid shahs took a direct interest in the economy and actively engaged in commercial and manufacturing activities, although there was also a large and affluent urban bourgeoisie. Like the Ottoman sultan, one shah regularly traveled the city streets incognito to check on the honesty of his subjects. When he discovered that a baker and butcher were overcharging for their products, he had the baker cooked in his own oven and the butcher roasted on a spit.

At its height, Safavid Iran was a worthy successor of the great Persian empires of the past, although it was probably not as wealthy as its Mughal and Ottoman neighbors to the east and west. Hemmed in by the sea power of the Europeans to the south and by the land power of the

Ottomans to the west, the early Safavids had no navy and were forced to divert overland trade with Europe through southern Russia to avoid an Ottoman blockade. In the early seventeenth century, the situation improved when Iranian forces, in cooperation with the English, seized the island of Hormuz from Portugal and established a new seaport on the southern coast at Bandar Abbas. As a consequence, commercial ties with Europe began to increase.

Safavid Art and Literature

Persia witnessed an extraordinary flowering of the arts during the reign of Shah Abbas I. His new capital of Isfahan was a grandiose planned city with wide visual perspectives and a sense of order almost unique in the region. Shah Abbas ordered his architects to position his palaces, mosques, and bazaars around the Maydan-i-Shah, a massive rectangular polo ground. Much of the original city is still in good condition and remains the gem of modern Iran. The immense mosques are richly decorated with elaborate blue tiles. The palaces are delicate structures with unusual slender wooden columns. These architectural wonders of Isfahan epitomize the grandeur, delicacy, and color that defined the Safavid golden age. To adorn the splendid buildings, Safavid artisans created

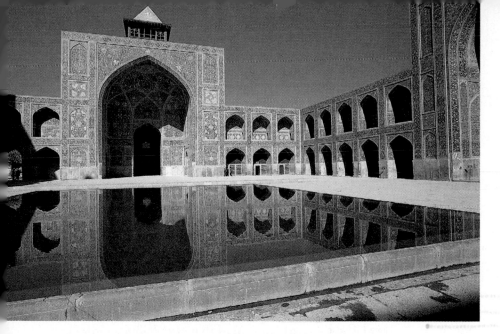

THE ROYAL ACADEMY OF ISFAHAN.
Along with institutions such as libraries and hospitals, theological schools were often included in the mosque compound. One of the most sumptuous was the Royal Academy of Isfahan, built by the shah of Iran in the early eighteenth century. This view shows the large courtyard surrounded by arcades of student rooms, reminiscent of the arrangement of monks' cells in European cloisters.

imaginative metalwork, tile decorations, and original and delicate glass vessels. The ceramics of the period, imitating Chinese prototypes of celadon or blue-and-white Ming design, largely ignored traditional Persian designs.

The greatest area of productivity, however, was in textiles. Silk weaving based on new techniques became a national industry. The silks depicted birds, animals, and flowers in a brilliant mass of color with silver and gold threads. Above all, carpet weaving flourished, stimulated by the great demand for Persian carpets in the West. Still highly prized all over the world, these seventeenth-century carpets reflect the grandeur and artistry of the Safavid dynasty.

The long tradition of Persian painting continued in the Safavid era, but changed from paintings to line drawings and from landscape scenes to portraits, mostly of young ladies, boys, lovers, or dervishes. Although some Persian artists studied in Rome, Safavid art was little influenced by the West. Riza-i-Abassi, the most famous artist of this period, created exquisite works on simple naturalistic subjects, such as an ox plowing, hunters, or lovers. Soft colors, delicacy, and flowing movement were the dominant characteristics of the painting of this era.

TWO LOVERS. Safavid painting continued Persian tradition but shifted from landscapes to portraits, mostly of young ladies, boys, lovers, or dervishes. This delicate painting of a couple embracing was produced in the early seventeenth century by Riza-i-Abassi, the most famous artist of Isfahan. It conveys passion with refined elegance.

THE GRANDEUR OF THE MUGHALS

In retrospect, the period from the sixteenth to the eighteenth century can be viewed both as a high point of traditional culture in India and as the first stage of perhaps its greatest challenge. The era began with the creation of one of the subcontinent's greatest empires—that of the Mughals. Mughal rulers, although foreigners and Muslims like many of their immediate predecessors, nevertheless brought India to a peak of political power and cultural achievement. For the first time since the Mauryan dynasty, the entire subcontinent was united under a single government, with a common culture that inspired admiration and envy throughout the entire region.

The Mughal Empire reached its peak in the sixteenth century under the famed Emperor Akbar and maintained its vitality under a series of strong rulers for another century. Then the dynasty began to weaken, a process that was hastened by the increasingly insistent challenge of the foreigners arriving by sea. The Portuguese, who first arrived in 1498, were little more than an irritant. Two centuries later, however, Europeans began to seize control of regional trade routes and to meddle in the internal politics of the subcontinent. By the end of the eighteenth century, nothing remained of the empire but a shell.

But some historians see the seeds of decay less in the challenge from abroad than in internal weakness—in the very nature of the dynasty itself, which was always more a heterogeneous collection of semiautonomous political forces than a centralized empire in the style of neighboring China. At its height, the dynasty was fully capable of fending off the demands of the Europeans. But after two centuries of expansion and consolidation, it began to lose its vitality, and by the end of the eighteenth century, it had lapsed into a mere shadow of its former self. Into the vacuum left by its final decrepitude stepped the British, who used a combination of firepower and guile to consolidate their power over the subcontinent.

The Mughal Dynasty: A "Gunpowder Empire"?

When the Portuguese fleet led by Vasco da Gama arrived at the port of Calicut in the spring of 1498, the Indian subcontinent was still divided into a number of Hindu and Muslim kingdoms. But it was on the verge of a new era of unity that would be brought about by a foreign dynasty called the Mughals. Like so many recent rulers of northern India, the founders of the Mughal Empire were not natives of India, but came from the mountainous region north of the Ganges River. The founder of the dynasty, known to history as Babur (1483–1530), had an illustrious pedigree. His father was descended from the great Asian conqueror Tamerlane, his mother from the Mongol conqueror Genghis Khan.

Babur had inherited a fragment of Tamerlane's empire in an upland valley of the Syr Darya River. Driven south by the rising power of the Uzbeks and then the Safavid dynasty in Persia, Babur and his warriors seized Kabul in 1504 and, thirteen years later, crossed the Khyber Pass to India.

Following a pattern that we have seen before, Babur began his rise to power by offering to help an ailing dynasty against its opponents. Although his own forces were far smaller than those of his adversaries, he possessed advanced weapons, including artillery, and used them to great effect. His use of mobile cavalry was particularly successful against the massed forces, supplemented by mounted elephants, of his enemy. In 1526, with only 12,000 troops against an enemy force nearly ten times that size, Babur captured Delhi and established his power in the plains of northern India (see the box on p. 475). Over the next several years, he continued his conquests in northern India, until his early death in 1530 at the age of forty-seven.

Babur's success was due in part to his vigor and his charismatic personality, which earned him the undying loyalty of his followers. His son and successor Humayun (1530–1556) was, in the words of one British historian, "intelligent but lazy." Whether or not this is a fair characterization, Humayun clearly lacked the will to consolidate his father's conquests and the personality to inspire personal loyalty among his subjects. In 1540 he was forced to flee to Persia, where he lived in exile for sixteen years. Finally, with the aid of the Safavid shah of Persia, he returned to India and reconquered Delhi in 1555, but died the following year in a household accident, reportedly from injuries suffered from a fall after smoking a pipeful of opium.

Humayun was succeeded by his son Akbar (1556–1605). Born while his father was living in exile, Akbar was only fourteen when he mounted the throne. Illiterate but highly intelligent and industrious, Akbar set out to extend his domain, then limited to Punjab and the upper Ganges River valley. "A monarch," he remarked, "should be ever intent on conquest, otherwise his neighbors rise in arms against him. The army should be exercised in warfare, lest from want of training they become self-indulgent."[1] By the end of his life, he had brought Mughal rule to most of the subcontinent, from the Himalaya Mountains to the Godavari River in central India and from Kashmir to the mouths of the Brahmaputra and the Ganges. In so doing, Akbar had created the greatest Indian empire since the Mauryan dynasty nearly two thousand years before. Some historians believe Akbar's success was due to the use of heavy artillery, which enabled his armies to besiege and subdue the traditional stone fortresses of his rivals. This "gunpowder empire" thesis has been challenged by the historian Douglas Streusand, who argues that the Mughals used the "carrot and the stick" to extend their authority, relying not just on heavy artillery, but also on other forms of siege warfare and

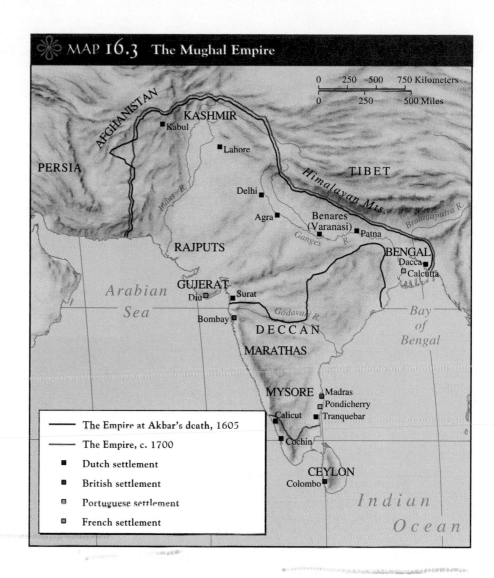

MAP 16.3   The Mughal Empire

The Empire at Akbar's death, 1605
The Empire, c. 1700
■ Dutch settlement
■ British settlement
□ Portuguese settlement
□ French settlement

the offer of negotiations. Whatever the case, the end result was an empire that appeared highly centralized from the outside, but was actually a collection of semiautonomous principalities ruled by provincial elites and linked together by the overarching majesty of the Mughal emperor.

Akbar and Indo-Muslim Civilization

Although Akbar was probably the greatest of the conquering Mughal monarchs, like his famous predecessor Asoka, he is best known for the humane character of his rule. Above all, he accepted the diversity of Indian society and took steps to reconcile his Muslim and Hindu subjects.

Though raised an orthodox Muslim, Akbar had been exposed to other beliefs during his childhood and had little patience with the pedantic views of Muslim scholars at court. As emperor, he displayed a keen interest in other religions, not only tolerating Hindu practices in his own domains, but also welcoming the expression of Christian views by his Jesuit advisers. Akbar put his policy of religious tolerance into practice by taking a Hindu princess as one of his wives, and the success of this marriage may well have had an effect on his religious convictions. He patronized classical Indian arts and architecture and abolished many of the restrictions faced by Hindus in a Muslim-dominated society.

During his later years, Akbar became steadily more hostile to Islam. To the dismay of many Muslims at court, he sponsored a new form of worship called the "Divine Faith" (Din-i-Ilahi), which combined characteristics of several religions with a central belief in the infallibility of all decisions reached by the emperor. Some historians have maintained that Akbar totally abandoned Islam and adopted a Persian model of imperial divinity. But others have pointed out that the emperor was claiming only divine guidance, not divine status, and suggest that the new ideology was designed to cement the loyalty of officials to the person of the monarch. Whatever the case, the new faith aroused deep hostility in Muslim circles and rapidly vanished after his death.

Akbar also extended his innovations to the empire's administration. Although the upper ranks of the govern-

THE MUGHAL CONQUEST OF NORTHERN INDIA

Babur, the founder of the great Mughal dynasty, began his career by allying with one Indian prince against another and then turned on his ally to put himself in power, a tactic that had been used by the Ottomans and the Mongols before him. In this excerpt from his memoirs, Babur describes his triumph over the powerful army of his Indian enemy, the Sultan Ibrâhim.

BABUR, MEMOIRS

They made one or two very poor charges on our right and left divisions. My troops making use of their bows, plied them with arrows, and drove them in upon their center. The troops on the right and the left of their center, being huddled together in one place, such confusion ensued, that the enemy, while totally unable to advance, found also no road by which they could flee. The sun had mounted spear-high when the onset of battle began, and the combat lasted till midday, when the enemy were completely broken and routed, and my friends victorious and exulting. By the grace and mercy of Almighty God, this arduous undertaking was rendered easy for me, and this mighty army, in the space of half a day, laid in the dust. Five or six thousand men were discovered lying slain, in one spot, near Ibrâhim. We reckoned that the number lying slain, in different parts of this field of battle, amounted to fifteen or sixteen thousand men. On reaching Agra, we found, from the accounts of the natives of Hindustân, that forty or fifty thousand men had fallen in this field. After routing the enemy, we continued the pursuit, slaughtering, and making them prisoners. . . .

It was now afternoon prayers when Tahir Taberi, the younger brother of Khalîfeh, having found Ibrâhim lying dead amidst a number of slain, cut off his head, and brought it in. . . .

In consideration of my confidence in Divine aid, the Most High God did not suffer the distress and hardships that I had undergone to be thrown away, but defeated my formidable enemy, and made me the conqueror of the noble country of Hindustân. This success I do not ascribe to my own strength, nor did this good fortune flow from my own efforts, but from the fountain of the favor and mercy of God.

---

ment continued to be dominated by nonnative Muslims, a substantial proportion of lower-ranking officials were Hindus, and a few Hindus were appointed to positions of importance. At first, most officials were paid salaries, but later they were ordinarily assigned sections of agricultural land for their temporary use; they kept a portion of the taxes paid by the local peasants in lieu of a salary. These local officials, known as *zamindars*, were expected to forward the rest of the taxes from the lands under their control to the central government. *Zamindars* often recruited a number of military and civilian retainers and accumulated considerable power in their localities.

The same tolerance that marked Akbar's attitude toward religion and administration extended to the Mughal legal system. While Muslims were subject to the Islamic codes (the *Shari'ah*), Hindu law (the *Dharmashastra*) applied to areas settled by Hindus, who after 1579 were no longer required to pay the hated *jizya*, or poll tax on non-Muslims. Punishments for crime were relatively mild, at least by the standards of the day, and justice was administered in a relatively impartial and efficient manner.

Overall, Akbar's reign was a time of peace and prosperity. Although all Indian peasants were required to pay about one-third of their annual harvest to the state through the *zamindars*, the system was applied fairly, and when drought struck in the 1590s, the taxes were reduced or even suspended altogether. Thanks to a long period of relative peace and political stability, commerce and manufacturing flourished. Foreign trade, in particular, thrived as Indian goods, notably textiles, tropical food products, spices, and precious stones, were exported in exchange for gold and silver. Tariffs on imports were low. Much of the foreign commerce was handled by Arab traders, since the Indians, like their Mughal rulers, did not care for travel by sea. Internal trade, however, was dominated by large merchant castes, who also were active in banking and handicrafts.

Twilight of the Mughals

Akbar died in 1605 and was succeeded by his son Jahangir (1605–1628). During the early years of his reign, Jahangir continued to strengthen central control over the vast empire. Eventually, however, his grip began to weaken (according to his memoirs, he "only wanted a bottle of wine and a piece of meat to make merry"), and the court fell under the influence of one of his wives, the Persian-born Nur Jahan. The empress took advantage of her position to enrich her own family and arranged for her niece Mumtaz Mahal to marry her husband's third son and ultimate successor Shah Jahan. When Shah Jahan succeeded to the throne in 1628, he quickly demonstrated the single-minded quality of his grandfather (albeit in a much more brutal manner), ordering the assassination of all of his rivals in order to secure his position.

During a reign of three decades, Shah Jahan maintained the system established by his predecessors while expanding the boundaries of the empire by successful campaigns in the Deccan Plateau and against Samarkand, north of the Hindu Kush. But Shah Jahan's rule was marred by his failure to deal with the growing domestic problems.

❈ AKBAR RESTRAINS AN ELEPHANT.   Akbar was probably the greatest of the conquering Mughal monarchs. In this contemporary Indian miniature, the young Akbar is seen mounted on a fierce elephant, leading an attack. The pontoon bridge is sinking under the heavy weight, while on the shore, before the towers of the royal palace at the Red Fort of Agra, his chief minister is begging Akbar to cease his reckless behavior.

He had inherited a nearly empty treasury because of Empress Nur Jahan's penchant for luxury and ambitious charity projects. Though the majority of his subjects lived in grinding poverty, Shah Jahan's frequent military campaigns and expensive building projects put a heavy strain on the imperial finances and compelled him to raise taxes. At the same time, the government did little to improve rural conditions. In a country where transport was primitive (it often took three months to travel the 600 miles between Patna, in the middle of the Ganges River valley, and Delhi) and drought conditions frequent, the dynasty made few efforts to increase agricultural efficiency or to improve the roads or the irrigation network. A Dutch merchant in Gujarat described conditions during a famine in the mid-seventeenth century:

> As the famine increased, men abandoned towns and villages and wandered helplessly. It was easy to recognize their condition: eyes sunk deep in head, lips pale and covered with slime, the skin hard, with the bones showing through, the belly nothing but a pouch hanging down empty, knuckles and kneecaps showing prominently. One would cry and howl for hunger, while another lay stretched on the ground dying in misery; wherever you went, you saw nothing but corpses.[2]

In 1648, Shah Jahan moved his capital from Agra to Delhi and built the famous Red Fort in his new capital city (see the box on p. 478). But he is best known for the Taj Mahal in Agra, widely considered to be the most beautiful building in India, if not in the entire world. The story is a romantic one—that the Taj was built by the emperor in memory of his wife Mumtaz Mahal, who had died giving birth to her thirteenth child at the age of thirty-nine. But the story has a less attractive side: the expense of the building, which employed 20,000 masons over twenty years, forced the government to raise agricultural taxes, further impoverishing many Indian peasants.

Succession struggles returned to haunt the dynasty in the mid-1650s when Shah Jahan's illness led to a struggle for power between his sons Dara Shikoh and Aurangzeb. Dara Shikoh was described by his contemporaries as progressive

AN ELEPHANT FIGHT FOR
THE KING'S ENTERTAINMENT

François Bernier was a well-traveled Frenchman who visited India during the mid-seventeenth century. In this excerpt from his account of the visit, he describes a festival held just outside the Red Fort at Delhi for the amusement of the emperor. Bernier's sympathy is obviously with the elephants. The account is indicative of the wealth and majesty of the Mughal Empire at its height.

FRANÇOIS BERNIER, *TRAVELS IN THE MOGUL EMPIRE*

The festivals generally conclude with an amusement unknown in Europe—a combat between two elephants; which takes place in the presence of all the people on the sandy space near the river: the King, the principal ladies of the court, and the *Omrahs* viewing the spectacle from different apartments in the fortress.

A wall of earth is raised three or four feet wide and five or six high. The two ponderous beasts meet one another face to face, on opposite sides of the wall, each having a couple of riders, that the place of the man who sits on the shoulders, for the purpose of guiding the elephant with a large iron hook, may immediately be supplied if he should be thrown down. The riders animate the elephants either by soothing words, or by chiding them as cowards, and urge them on with their heels, until the poor creatures approach the wall and are brought to the attack. The shock is tremendous, and it appears surprising that they ever survive the dreadful wounds and blows inflicted with their teeth, their heads, and their trunks. There are frequent pauses during the fight; it is suspended and renewed; and the mud wall being at length thrown down, the stronger or more courageous elephant passes on and attacks his opponent, and, putting him to flight, pursues and fastens upon

him with so much obstinacy, that the animals can be separated only by means of *cherkys,* or fireworks, which are made to explode between them; for they are naturally timid, and have a particular dread of fire, which is the reason why elephants have been used with so very little advantage in armies since the use of firearms. The boldest come from Ceylon, but none are employed in war which have not been regularly trained, and accustomed for years to the discharge of muskets close to their heads, and the bursting of crackers between their legs.

The fight of these noble creatures is attended with much cruelty. It frequently happens that some of the riders are trodden underfoot, and killed on the spot, the elephant having always cunning enough to feel the importance of dismounting the rider of his adversary, whom he therefore endeavors to strike down with his trunk. So imminent is the danger considered, that on the day of combat the unhappy men take the same formal leave of their wives and children as if condemned to death. They are somewhat consoled by the reflection that if their lives should be preserved, and the King be pleased with their conduct, not only will their pay be augmented, but a sack of *Peyssas* (equal to fifty francs) will be presented to them the moment they alight from the elephant. . . . The mischief with which this amusement is attended does not always terminate with the death of the rider: it often happens that some of the spectators are knocked down and trampled upon by the elephants, or by the crowd; for the rush is terrible when, to avoid the infuriated combatants, men and horses in confusion take to flight. The second time I witnessed this exhibition I owed my safety entirely to the goodness of my horse and the exertions of my two servants.

---

and humane, although possessed of a violent temper and a strong sense of mysticism. But he apparently lacked political acumen and was outmaneuvered by Aurangzeb (1658–1707), who had Dara Shikoh put to death and then imprisoned his father in the fort at Agra.

Aurangzeb is one of the most controversial individuals in the history of India. A man of high principle, he attempted to eliminate many of what he considered to be India's social evils, prohibiting the immolation of widows on their husband's funeral pyre (*sati*), the castration of eunuchs, and the exaction of illegal taxes. With less success, he tried to forbid gambling, drinking, and prostitution. But Aurangzeb, a devout and somewhat doctrinaire Muslim, also adopted a number of measures that reversed the policies of religious tolerance established by his predecessors. The building of new Hindu temples was prohibited and

the Hindu poll tax was restored. Forced conversions to Islam were resumed and non-Muslims were driven from the court. Aurangzeb's heavy-handed religious policies led to considerable domestic unrest and to a revival of Hindu fervor during the last years of his reign. A number of revolts also broke out against imperial authority.

During the eighteenth century, Mughal power was threatened from both within and without. Fueled by the growing power and autonomy of the local gentry and merchants, rebellious groups in provinces throughout the empire, from the Deccan to the Punjab, began to reassert local authority and reduce the power of the Mughal emperor to that of a "tinsel sovereign." Increasingly divided, India was vulnerable to attack from abroad. In 1739, Delhi was sacked by the Persians, who left it in ashes and carried off its splendid Peacock Throne (see The Safavids earlier in this chapter).

CHRONOLOGY

THE MUGHAL ERA

Arrival of Vasco da Gama at Calicut	1498
Babur seizes Delhi	1526
Death of Babur	1530
Humayun recovers throne in Delhi	1555
Death of Humayun and accession of Akbar	1556
First Jesuit Mission to Agra	1580
Death of Akbar and accession of Jahangir	1605
Arrival of English at Surat	1608
Reign of Emperor Shah Jahan	1628–1657
Foundation of English fort at Madras	1639
Aurangzeb succeeds to the throne	1658
Bombay ceded to England	1661
Death of Aurangzeb	1707
French capture Madras	1746
Battle of Plassey	1757

The situation changed at the end of the sixteenth century, when the English and the Dutch entered the scene. Soon both powers were in active competition with Portugal, and with each other, for trading privileges in the region (see the box on p. 480).

Penetration of the new market was not easy. When the first English fleet arrived at Surat (a thriving port along the northwestern coast of India) in 1608, their request for trading privileges was rejected by Emperor Jahangir, at the suggestion of the Portuguese advisers already in residence at the imperial court. Needing lightweight Indian cloth to trade for spices in the East Indies, the English persisted, and in 1616 they were finally permitted to install their own ambassador at the imperial court in Agra. Three years later the first English factory was established at Surat.

During the next several decades, the English presence in India steadily increased while Mughal power gradually waned. By mid-century additional English factories had been established at Fort William (now the great city of Calcutta) on the River Hoogly near the Bay of Bengal and at Madras on the southeastern coast. From there English ships carried Indian-made cotton goods to the East Indies, where they were bartered for spices, which were shipped back to England. Tensions between local

✿ **THE CHINESE NETS AT COCHIN.**   Cochin, one of the port cities visited by Vasco da Gama during his first visit to India in 1498, had long been a major stopover on the trade routes across the Indian Ocean. Nearly a century previously, it had been visited by Chinese fleets en route to Africa. These voyages, to be discussed in the next chapter, left their own legacy, as Indian fishers learned from Chinese sailors how to place large nets in the water of the harbor to catch fish. After the arrival of the Portuguese, much of the local population was converted to Christianity. Shown here are the "Chinese nets" of Cochin, which are still in use. A few yards away is the first Christian church erected in India. An old synagogue, which perhaps dates back to the pre-European era, is located a mile away.

A number of obvious reasons for the virtual collapse of the Mughal Empire can be identified, including the draining of the imperial treasury and the decline in competence of the Mughal rulers. But it should also be noted that even at its height under Akbar, the empire was a loosely knit collection of heterogeneous principalities held together by the authority of the throne, which tried to combine Persian concepts of kingship with the Indian tradition of decentralized power. Decline set in when centrifugal forces gradually began to predominate over centripetal ones.

Ironically, one element in this process was the very success of the system, which led to the rapid expansion of wealth and autonomous power at the local level. As local elites increased their wealth and influence, they became less willing to accept the authority and financial demands from Delhi. The reassertion of Muslim orthodoxy under Aurangzeb and his successors simply exacerbated the problem. This process was hastened by the growing European military and economic presence along the periphery of the empire.

The Impact of Western Power in India

As we have seen, the first to arrive were the Portuguese. Although they established a virtual monopoly over regional trade in the Indian Ocean, they did not aggressively seek to penetrate the interior of the subcontinent.

THE USES OF THE COCONUT

*T*he Portuguese traveler Duarte Barbosa was one of the most astute observers of the lands that he visited as an official of the Portuguese crown in the early sixteenth century. Here, in a section devoted to the lands of Malabar, on the southwestern coast of India, he writes of the many uses that the local population made of the coconut palm. Many peoples of Asia still use the coconut in similar ways in our own day.

DUARTE BARBOSA, *THE BOOK OF DUARTE BARBOSA*

This land, or rather the whole land of Malabar, is covered along the strand with palm trees as high as lofty cypresses, the trunk whereof is extremely clean and smooth, and on the top a crown of branches among which grows a great fruit which they call *cocos*, it is a fruit of which they make great profit, and whereof they load many cargoes yearly. They bear their fruit every year without fail, never either more or less. All the folk of Malabar have these palms, and by their means they are free from any dearth, even though other food be lacking, for they produce ten or twelve things all very needful for the service of man, by which they help and profit themselves greatly, and everything is produced in every month of the year.

In the first place they produce these cocos, a very sweet and grateful fruit when green; from them is drawn milk like that of almonds, and each one when green, has within it a pint of a fresh and pleasant water, better than that from a spring. When they are dry this same water thickens within them into a white fruit as large as an apple which also is very sweet and dainty. The coco itself after being dried is eaten, and from it they get much oil by pressing it, as we do. And from the shell which they have close to the kernel is made charcoal for the goldsmiths, who work with no other kind. And from the outer husk which throws out certain threads, they make all the cord which they use, a great article of trade in many parts. And from the sap of the tree itself they extract a *must*, from which they make wine, or properly speaking a strong water, and that in such abundance that many shops are laden with it, for export. From this same *must* they make very good vinegar, and also a sugar of extreme sweetness which is much sought after in India. From the leaf of the tree they make many things, in accordance with the size of the branch. They thatch the houses with them, for as I have said above, no house is roofed with tiles, save the temples or the palaces; all others are thatched with palm leaves. From the same tree they get timber for their houses and firewood as well, and all this in such abundance that ships take in cargoes thereof for export.

Other palm trees there are of a lower kind whence they get the leaves on which the Heathen write; it serves as paper. There are other very slender palms the trunks of which are of extreme height and smoothness; these bear a fruit as large as walnuts which they call Areca, which they eat with betel. Among them it is held in high esteem. It is very ugly and disagreeable in taste.

---

authorities and the English over the payment of taxes led to a short war in 1686. The English were briefly expelled, but after differences were patched up, Aurangzeb permitted them to return.

English success in India attracted rivals, including the Dutch and the French. The Dutch abandoned their interests to concentrate on the spice trade in the middle of the seventeenth century, but the French were more persistent and established factories of their own. For a brief period, under the ambitious empire builder Joseph François Dupleix, the French competed successfully with the British. But the military genius of Sir Robert Clive, an aggressive British administrator and empire builder who eventually became the chief representative of the East India Company in the subcontinent, and the refusal of the French government to provide financial support for Dupleix's efforts eventually left the French with only their fort at Pondicherry and a handful of small territories on the southeastern coast.

In the meantime, Clive began to consolidate British control in Bengal, where the local ruler had attacked Fort William and imprisoned the local British population in the infamous "Black Hole of Calcutta" (an underground prison for holding the prisoners, many of whom died in captivity). In 1757, a small British force numbering about 3,000 defeated a Mughal-led army over ten times that size in the Battle of Plassey. As part of the spoils of victory, the British East India Company exacted from the now-decrepit Mughal court the authority to collect taxes from extensive lands in the area surrounding Calcutta. Less than ten years later, British forces seized the reigning Mughal emperor in a skirmish at Buxar, and the British began to consolidate their economic and administrative control over Indian territory through the surrogate power of the now powerless Mughal court.

To officials of the East India Company, the expansion of their authority into the interior of the subcontinent probably seemed like a simple commercial decision, a move designed to seek guaranteed revenues to pay for the increasingly expensive military operations in India. To historians, it marks a major step in the gradual transfer of all of the Indian subcontinent to the British East India Company and later, in 1858, to the British crown. The process was more haphazard than deliberate. Under a new governor general, Warren Hastings, the British attempted to consolidate areas under their control and defeat such rivals as the rising Hindu Marathas, who exploited the decline of the Mughals to expand their own empire in Maharashtra.

The company's takeover of vast landholdings, notably in the eastern Indian states of Orissa and Bengal, may have been a windfall for enterprising British officials, but it was a disaster for the Indian economy. In the first place, it resulted in the transfer of capital from the local Indian aristocracy to company officials, most of whom sent their profits back to Britain. Second, it hastened the destruction of once healthy local industries, because British goods such as machine-made textiles were imported duty-free into India to compete against local products. Finally, British expansion hurt the peasants. As the British took over the administration of the land tax, they also applied British law, which allowed the lands of those unable to pay the tax to be confiscated. In the 1770s, a series of massive famines led to the death of an estimated one-third of the population in the areas under company administration. The British government

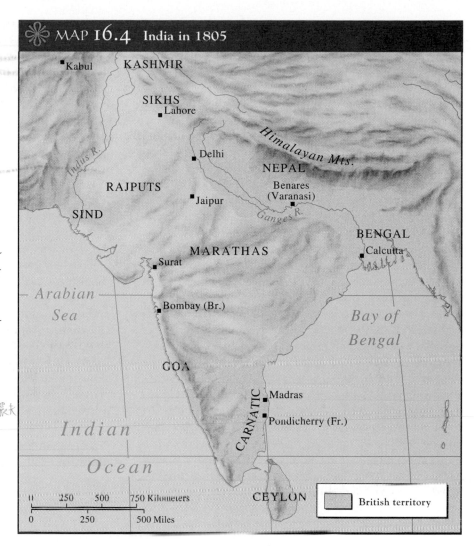

MAP 16.4 India in 1805

Kabul · KASHMIR
SIKHS
Lahore
Himalayan Mts.
Indus R.
Delhi
NEPAL
RAJPUTS
Benares
(Varanasi)
Jaipur
Ganges R.
SIND
BENGAL
Calcutta
MARATHAS
Surat
Arabian
Sea
Bombay (Br.)
Bay of
Bengal
GOA
Indian
Madras
CARNATIC
Pondicherry (Fr.)
Ocean
CEYLON

0   250   500   750 Kilometers
0   250   500 Miles

British territory

attempted to resolve the problem by assigning tax lands to the local revenue collectors (*zamindars*) in the hope of transforming them into English-style rural gentry, but many collectors themselves fell into bankruptcy and sold their lands to absentee bankers while the now landless peasants remained in abject poverty. It was hardly an auspicious beginning to "civilized" British rule.

As a result of such problems, Britain's rise to power in India did not go unchallenged. Astute Indian commanders avoided pitched battles with the well-armed British troops but harassed and ambushed them in the manner of guerrillas in our time. Said Haidar Ali, one of Britain's primary rivals for control in southern India:

> You will in time understand my mode of warfare. Shall I risk my cavalry which cost a thousand rupees each horse, against your cannon ball which cost two pice? No! I will march your troops until their legs swell to the size of their bodies. You shall not have a blade of grass, nor a drop of water. I will hear of you every time your drum beats, but you shall not know where I am once a month. I will give your army battle, but it must be when I please, and not when you choose.[3]

Unfortunately for India, not all its commanders were as astute as Haidar Ali. In the last years of the eighteenth century, when the East India Company's authority came into the capable hands of Lord Cornwallis and his successor, Lord Mornington, the future marquess of Wellesley, the stage was set for the final consolidation of British rule over the subcontinent.

Society and Culture Under the Mughals

The Mughals were the last of the great traditional Indian dynasties. Like so many of their predecessors since the fall of the Guptas nearly a thousand years before, the Mughals were Muslims. But to their credit, the best Mughal rulers did not simply impose Islamic institutions and beliefs on a predominantly Hindu population, but combined Muslim with Hindu and even Persian concepts and cultural values in a unique social and cultural synthesis that still today seems to epitomize the greatness of Indian civilization.

DAILY LIFE

Whether Mughal rule had much effect on the lives of ordinary Indians seems somewhat problematic. The treatment of women is a good example. Women had traditionally played an active role in Mongol tribal society—many actually fought on the battlefield alongside the men—and Babur and his successors often relied on the women in their families for political advice. Women from aristocratic families were often awarded honorific titles, received salaries, and were permitted to own land and engage in business. Women at court sometimes received an education, and Emperor Akbar reportedly established a girls' school at Fatehpur Sikri to provide teachers for his own daughters. Aristocratic women often expressed their creative talents by writing poetry, painting, or playing music. Women of all castes were adept at spinning thread, either for their own use or to sell to weavers to augment the family income. Weaving was carried out in home production units by all the members of the subcaste weaving families. They sold simple cloth to local villages and fine cottons, silks, and wool to the Mughal court. By Akbar's rule, in fact, the textile manufacturing was of such high quality and so well established that India sold cloth to much of the world: Arabia, the coast of East Africa, Egypt, Southeast Asia, and especially Europe.

To a certain degree, these Mughal attitudes toward women may have had an impact on Indian society. Women were allowed to inherit land, and some even possessed *zamindar* rights. Women from mercantile castes sometimes took an active role in business activities. At the same time, however, as Muslims, the Mughals subjected women to certain restrictions under Islamic law. On the whole, these Mughal practices coincided with and even accentuated existing tendencies in Indian society. The Muslim practice of isolating women and preventing them from associating with men outside the home (*purdah*) was adopted by many upper-class Hindus as a means of enhancing their status or protecting their women from unwelcome advances by Muslims in positions of authority. In other ways, Hindu practices continued unabated. The custom of *sati* continued to be practiced despite efforts by the Mughals to abolish it, and child marriage (most women were betrothed before the age of ten) remained common. Women were still instructed to obey their husbands without question and to remain chaste.

For their part, Hindus sometimes attempted to defend themselves and their religious practices against the efforts of some Mughal monarchs to impose the Islamic religion and Islamic mores on the indigenous population. In some cases, despite official prohibitions Hindu men forcibly married Muslim women and then converted them to the native faith, while converts to Islam normally lost all of their inheritance rights within the Indian family. Government orders to destroy Hindu temples were often ignored by local officials, sometimes as the result of bribery or intimidation. Sometimes Indian practices had an influence on the Mughal elites, as many Mughal chieftains married Indian women and adopted Indian forms of dress.

Long-term stability led to increasing commercialization and the spread of wealth to new groups within Indian society. The Mughal era saw the emergence of an affluent landed gentry and a prosperous merchant class. Members of prestigious castes from the pre-Mughal period reaped many of the benefits of the increasing wealth, but some of these changes transcended caste boundaries and led to the emergence of new groups who achieved status and wealth on the basis of economic achievement rather than traditional kinship ties. During the late eighteenth century, this economic prosperity was shaken by the decline of the Mughal Empire

❀ **THE PALACE OF THE WINDS AT JAIPUR.** Built by the maharaja of Jaipur in 1799, this imposing building, part of a palace complex, is today actually only a facade. Behind the intricate pink sandstone window screens, the women of the palace were able to observe city life while at the same time remaining invisible to prying eyes. The palace, like most of the buildings in the city of Jaipur, was constructed of sandstone, a product of the nearby desert of Rajasthan.

and the increasing European presence. But many prominent Indians reacted by establishing commercial relationships with the foreigners. For a time, that relationship often worked to the Indians' benefit. Later, as we shall see, they would have cause to regret the arrangement.

MUGHAL CULTURE

The era of the Mughals was one of synthesis in culture as well as in politics and religion. The Mughals combined Islamic themes with Persian and indigenous motifs to produce a unique style that enriched and embellished Indian art and culture. The Mughal emperors were zealous patrons of the arts and enticed painters, poets, and artisans from as far away as the Mediterranean. Apparently, the generosity of the Mughals made it difficult to refuse a trip to India. It was said that they would reward a poet with his weight in gold.

Undoubtedly, the Mughals' most visible achievement was in architecture. Here they integrated Persian and Indian styles in a new and sometimes breathtakingly beautiful form best symbolized by the Taj Mahal, built by the emperor Shah Jahan in the mid-seventeenth century. Although the human and economic cost of the Taj tarnishes the romantic legend of its construction, there is no denying the beauty of the building. It had evolved from a style that originated several decades earlier with the tomb of Humayun, which was built by his widow in Agra in 1565 during the reign of Akbar.

Humayun's mausoleum had combined Persian and Islamic motifs in a square building finished in red sandstone and topped with a dome. The style was repeated in a number of other buildings erected throughout the empire, but the Taj brought the style to perfection. Working with a model created by his Persian architect, Shah Jahan raised the dome and replaced the red sandstone with brilliant white marble. The entire exterior and interior surface is decorated with cut-stone geometrical patterns, delicate black stone tracery, or intricate inlay of colored precious stones in floral and Koranic arabesques. The technique of creating dazzling floral mosaics of lapis lazuli, malachite, carnelian, turquoise, and mother of pearl may have been introduced by Italian artists at the Mughal court. Shah Jahan had intended to erect a similar building in black marble across the river for his own remains, but the plans were abandoned after he was deposed by his son Aurangzeb. Shah Jahan spent his last years imprisoned in a room in the Red Fort at Agra; from his windows, he could see the beautiful memorial to his beloved wife.

The Taj was by no means the only magnificent building erected during the Mughal era. Akbar, who, in the words of a contemporary, "dresses the work of his mind and heart in the garment of stone and clay," was the first of the great Mughal builders. His first palace at Agra, the Red Fort, was begun in 1565. A few years later, he ordered the construction of a new palace at Fatehpur Sikri, twenty-six miles west of Agra. The new palace was built in honor of a Sufi mystic who had correctly forecast the birth of a son to the emperor. In gratitude, Akbar decided to build a new capital city and palace on the site of the mystic's home in the village of Sikri. Over a period of fifteen years, from 1571 to 1586, a magnificent new city in red sandstone was constructed. Unfortunately, it was soon discovered that water resources in the area were inadequate, and shortly before completion the city was abandoned and now stands almost untouched, although it is a popular destination for tourists and pilgrims.

The other major artistic achievement of the Mughal period was painting. Painting had never been one of the great attainments of Indian culture due in part to a technological difficulty. Paper was not introduced to India from Persia until the latter part of the fourteenth century, so traditionally painting had been done on palm leaves, which had severely hampered artistic creativity. By the fifteenth century, Indian painting had made the transition from palm leaf to paper, and the new medium eventually stimulated a burst of creativity, particularly in the genre of miniatures, or book illustrations.

❀ **THE TAJ MAHAL.** The Taj Mahal was completed in 1653 by Emperor Shah Jahan as a tomb to glorify his beloved wife's memory. Raised on a marble platform above the Jumna River, the Taj is dramatically framed by contrasting twin red sandstone mosques, magnificent gardens, and a long reflecting pool that mirrors and magnifies its beauty. The effect is one of monumental size, near blinding brilliance, and delicate lightness.

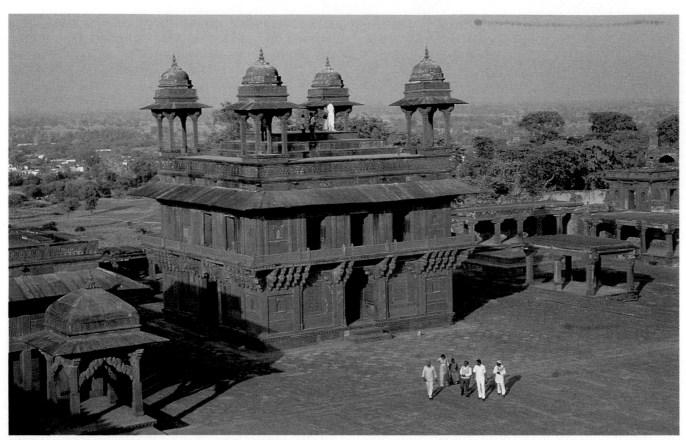

❀ **FATEHPUR SIKRI.** In gratitude to a Sufi mystic who had correctly forecast the birth of his son, Akbar chose the mystic's village of Sikri as the site for his new palace and capital city. Completed at great speed in 1586, the splendid city, which was built of red sandstone and measured two miles long and one mile wide, was soon abandoned because of an inadequate water supply. Its elaborate palaces, mosque, reflecting pools and courtyards, harems, and impressive Gate of Victory all symbolize the elegance and greatness of Akbar's reign.

As in so many other areas of endeavor, painting in Mughal India resulted from the blending of two cultures. While living in exile, Emperor Humayun had learned to admire Persian miniatures. On his return to India in 1555, he invited two Persian masters to live in his palace and introduce the technique to his adopted land. His successor, Akbar, appreciated the new style and popularized it with his patronage. He established a state workshop at Fatehpur Sikri for two hundred artists, mostly Hindus, who worked under the guidance of the Persian masters to create the Mughal school of painting.

The "Akbar style" combined Persian with Indian motifs, such as the use of extended space and the portrayal of physical human action, characteristics not usually seen in Persian art. Akbar also apparently encouraged the imitation of European art forms, including the portrayal of Christian subjects, the use of perspective, lifelike portraits, and the shading of colors in the Renaissance style. The depiction of the human figure in Mughal painting outraged orthodox Muslims at court, but Akbar argued that

the painter, "in sketching anything that has life . . . must come to feel that he cannot bestow individuality upon his work, and is thus forced to think of God, the Giver of Life, and will thus increase in knowledge."[4]

Painting during Akbar's reign followed the trend toward realism and historical narrative that had originated in the Ottoman Empire. For example, Akbar had the illustrated *Book of Akbar* made to record his military exploits and court activities. Many of these paintings of Akbar's life portray him in action in his real world. After his death, his son and grandson continued the patronage of the arts.

The development of Indian literature was held back by the absence of printing, which was not introduced until the end of the Mughal era. Literary works were inscribed by calligraphers, and one historian has estimated that the library of Agra contained more than 24,000 volumes. Poetry, in particular, flourished under the Mughals, who established poet laureates at court. Poems were written in the Persian style and in the Persian language. In fact, Persian became the official language of the court until the sack of Delhi in 1739. At the time, the Indians' anger at their conquerors led them to adopt Urdu as the new language for the court and for poetry. By that time, Indian verse on the Persian model had already lost its original vitality and simplicity and had become more artificial in the manner of court literature everywhere.

Another aspect of the long Mughal reign was a Hindu revival of devotional literature, much of it dedicated to Krishna and Rama. The retelling of the Ramayana in the vernacular, beginning in the southern Tamil languages in the eleventh century and spreading slowly northward, culminated in the sixteenth-century Hindi version by the great poet Tulsidas (1532–1623). His *Ramcaritmanas* presents the devotional story with a deified Rama and Sita. Tulsidas's genius was in combining the conflicting cults of Vishnu and Siva into a unified and overwhelming love for the divine, which he expressed in some of the most moving of all Indian poetry. The *Ramcaritmanas* has eclipsed its 2,000-year-old Sanskrit ancestor in popularity and even became the basis of an Indian television series in the late 1980s.

CONCLUSION

The three empires that we have discussed in this chapter exhibit a number of striking similarities. First of all, they were, of course, Muslim in their religious affiliation, although the Safavids were Shi'ite rather than Sunni in persuasion, a distinction that often led to mutual tensions and conflict. More importantly, perhaps, they were all nomadic in origin, and the political and social institutions that they adopted carried the imprint of their preimperial past. Once they achieved imperial power, however, all three ruling dynasties displayed an impressive capacity to administer a large empire and brought a degree of stability to peoples who had all too often lived in conditions of internal division and war.

Another similarity is that the mastery of the techniques of modern warfare, including the use of firearms, played a central role in all three empires' ability to overcome their rivals and rise to regional hegemony. Some scholars have therefore labeled them "gunpowder empires" in the belief that technical prowess in the art of warfare was a key element in their success. Although that is undoubtedly true, we should not forget that other factors, such as dynamic

leadership, political acumen, and the possession of an ardent following motivated by religious zeal, were equally if not more important in their drive to power and ability to retain it. Weapons by themselves do not an empire make.

The rise of these powerful Muslim states coincided with the opening period of European expansion at the end of the fifteenth and the beginning of the sixteenth century. The military and political talents of these empires helped to protect much of the Muslim world from the resurgent forces of Christianity. To the contrary, the Ottoman Turks carried their empire into the heart of Christian Europe and briefly reached the gates of the great city of Vienna. By the end of the eighteenth century, however, the Safavid dynasty had collapsed, and the powerful Mughal Empire was in a state of virtual collapse. Only the Ottoman Empire was still a functioning enterprise. Yet it too had lost much of its early expansionistic vigor and was showing signs of internal decay.

The reasons for the decline of these empires have inspired considerable debate among historians. One factor was undoubtedly the expansion of European power into the Indian Ocean and the Middle East. But internal causes were probably more important in the long run. All three empires experienced growing factionalism within the ruling elite, incompetence within the palace, and the emergence of divisive forces in the empire at large—factors that have marked the passing of traditional empires since early times. Climatic change (the region was reportedly hotter and drier after the beginning of the seventeenth century) may have been a hidden reason. Paradoxically, one of the greatest strengths of these empires—their mastery of gunpowder—may have simultaneously been a serious weakness in that it allowed them to develop a complacent sense of security. With little incentive to turn their attention to new developments in science and technology, they were increasingly vulnerable to attack by the advanced nations of the West. The weakening of the "gunpowder empires" created a political vacuum into which the dynamic and competitive forces of European capitalism were quick to enter.

The gunpowder empires, however, were not the only states in the Old World that were able to resist the first outward thrust of European expansion. Further to the east, the mature civilizations in China and Japan successfully faced a similar challenge from Western merchants and missionaries. Unlike their counterparts in South Asia and the Middle East, as the nineteenth century dawned, they continued to thrive.

1450   1500   1550   1600   1650   1700   1750

Ottoman Turks capture Constantinople

Turks defeat Mamluks in Syria and seize Cairo

Ottomans evicted from central Europe

Portuguese defeat Turkish fleet in Indian Ocean

Reign of Suleyman I (the Magnificent)

Ismail becomes shah of Persia

Collapse of Safavid empire

Ismail conquers Baghdad from Uzbeks

Reign of Shah Abbas I

Babur seizes Delhi

Reign of Shah Jahan

Death of Aurangzeb

Reign of Akbar

Building of Taj Mahal

CHAPTER NOTES

1. Vincent A. Smith, *The Oxford History of India* (Oxford, 1967), p. 341.
2. Quoted in Michael Edwardes, *A History of India: From the Earliest Times to the Present Day* (London, 1961), p. 188.
3. Quoted in Edwardes, *A History of India*, p. 220.
4. Quoted in Roy C. Craven, *Indian Art: A Concise History* (New York, 1976), p. 205.

SUGGESTED READINGS

The most complete general survey of the Ottoman Empire is S. J. Shaw, *History of the Ottoman Empire and Modern Turkey* (Cambridge, 1976). Volume 2 of the two-volume set deals with the period up to the beginning of the nineteenth century. Shaw is difficult reading but informative on administrative matters. A more readable albeit less definitive account is Lord Kinross, *The Ottoman Centuries: The Rise and Fall of the Ottoman Empire* (New York, 1977), which is larded with human-interest stories. Also of interest is B. Lewis, *Istanbul and the Civilization of the Ottoman Empire* (Norman, Okla., 1963), written by a veteran Arabist.

For a dramatic account of the conquest of Constantinople in 1453, see S. Runciman, *The Fall of Constantinople, 1453* (Cambridge, 1965). The life of Mehmet II is chronicled in F. Babinger, *Mehmed the Conqueror and His Time*, trans. R. Manheim (Princeton, N.J., 1979). On Suleiman the Magnificent, see R. Merriman, *Suleiman the Magnificent, 1520–1566* (Cambridge, 1944). On the Safavids, see R. M. Savory, *Iran Under the Safavids* (Cambridge, 1980), and E. B. Monshi, *History of Shah Abbas the Great*, 2 vols. (Boulder, Colo., 1978).

For a concise introduction to Ottoman art, consult D. T. Rice, *Islamic Art* (London, 1975), and E. J. Grube, *The World of Islam* (New York, 1967). For Ottoman architecture, see G. Michell, ed., *Architecture of the Islamic World* (London, 1978). For an interesting discussion of the minor military arts of the Ottomans, see Z. Zygulski, Jr., *Ottoman Art in the Service of the Empire* (New York, 1992).

For an overview of the Mughal era, see such standard works as S. Wolpert, *New History of India* (New York, 1989), and the more detailed V. A. Smith, *The Oxford History of India* (Oxford, 1967). A

more dramatic account for the general reader is W. Hansen, *The Peacock Throne: The Drama of Mogul India* (New York, 1972).

There are a number of specialized works on various aspects of the period. For a treatment of the Mughal era in the context of Islamic rule in India, see S. M. Ikram, *Muslim Civilization in India* (New York, 1964). The concept of "gunpowder empires" is persuasively analyzed in D. E. Streusand, *The Formation of the Mughal Empire* (Delhi, 1989). Economic issues predominate in much of the recent scholarship. For example, S. Subrahmanyan, *The Political Economy of Commerce: Southern India, 1500–1650* (Cambridge, 1990) focuses on the interaction between internal and external trade in southern India during the early stages of the period. For a persuasive view of the relationship between economic changes and the extension of British rule, see C. A. Bayly, *Indian Society and the Making of the British Empire* (Cambridge, 1988). Finally, K. N. Chaudhuri, *Trade and Civilization in the Indian Ocean: An Economic History from the Rise of Islam to 1750* (Cambridge, 1985) views Indian commerce in the perspective of the regional trade network throughout the Indian Ocean.

Personal accounts of the period are numerous, although most are by European visitors. For some examples, see R. C. Temple, ed., *The Travels of Peter Mundy, in Europe and Asia, 1608–1667* (Cambridge, 1907–1936); J. B. Tavernier, *Travels in India* (London, 1925); T. Roe, *The Embassy of Sir Thomas Roe, 1615–1619* (London, 1926); and F. Bernier, *Travels in the Mogul Empire*, A.D. *1656–1668* (London, 1968). For an inside look, see J. Leyden and W. Erskine, trans., *Memoirs of Zehir-ed-Din Muhammad Babur* (London, 1921). Excerpts from this and other works cited here can be found in M. Edwardes, *A History of India: From the Earliest Times to the Present Day* (London,

1961); J. Kritzeck, *Anthology of Islamic Literature* (New York, 1964); and J. H. Parry, ed., *The European Reconnaissance: Selected Documents* (New York, 1968).

Standard works on Mughal art and culture include A. L. Basham, *A Cultural History of India* (Oxford, 1975); E. C. Dimock, *The Literature of India: An Introduction* (Chicago, 1974); and R. C. Craven, *Indian Art: A Concise History* (New York, 1976).

For treatments of all three Muslim empires in a comparative context, see J. J. Kissling et al., *The Last Great Muslim Empires* (Princeton, N.J., 1996), and M. G. S. Hodgson, *Rethinking World History: Essays on Europe, Islam, and World History* (Cambridge, 1993).

For an introduction to the women of the Ottoman Empire and those of the Mughal Empire, see S. Hughes and B. Hughes, *Women in World History*, vol. 2 (Armonk, N.Y., 1997). For a more detailed presentation of women in the imperial harem, consult L. P. Peirce, "Beyond Harem Walls: Ottoman Royal Women and the Exercise of Power," in *Gendered Domains: Rethinking Public and Private in Women's History*, ed. D. O. Helly and S. M. Reverby (Cornell, 1992), and L. P. Peirce, *The Imperial Harem: Women and Sovereignty in the Ottoman Empire* (Oxford, 1993). The fascinating story of the royal woman who played an important role behind the scenes is found in E. B. Findly, *Nur Jahan: Empress of Mughal India* (Oxford, 1993).

INFOTRAC COLLEGE EDITION

For additional reading, go to InfoTrac College Edition, your online research library at http://web1.infotrac-college.com

Enter the search term "Islam" using the Subject Guide.

Enter the search terms "Ottoman Empire" using Keywords.

Enter the search term "Safavid" using Keywords.

Enter the search term "Mughal" using Keywords.

CHAPTER

17

THE
EAST ASIAN
WORLD

CHAPTER OUTLINE

- CHINA AT ITS APEX
- TOKUGAWA JAPAN
- KOREA: THE HERMIT KINGDOM
- CONCLUSION

FOCUS QUESTIONS

- Why were the Manchus so successful at establishing a foreign dynasty in China, and what were the main characteristics of their rule?
- How did the economy and society of China change during the Ming and Qing eras, and to what degree did these changes seem to be leading toward an industrial revolution on the Western model?
- How did China and Japan respond to the coming of the Europeans, and what impact did the Europeans have on these East Asian civilizations in the sixteenth through eighteenth centuries?
- How did the unification of Japan come about, and how did the Tokugawa rulers maintain that unity?
- How did the economy and society of Japan change during the Tokugawa era, and how did Japanese culture reflect those changes?

In December 1717, the emperor Kangxi returned from a hunting trip north of the Great Wall and began to suffer from dizzy spells. Conscious of his approaching date with mortality—he was now nearly seventy years of age— the emperor called together his sons and leading government officials in the imperial palace and issued the following edict:

> *The rulers of the past all took reverence for Heaven's laws and reverence for their ancestors as the fundamental way in ruling the country. To be sincere in reverence for Heaven and ancestors entails the following: Be kind to men from afar and keep the able ones near, nourish the people, think of the profit of all as being the real profit and the mind of the whole country as being the real mind, be considerate to officials and act as the father to the people, protect the state before danger comes and govern well before there is any disturbance, be always diligent and always careful, and maintain the balance between leniency and strictness, between principle and expediency, so that long-range plans can be made for the country: That's all there is to it.*[1]

As a primer for political leadership, the emperor's edict reflects the genius of Confucian philosophy at its best and has a timeless quality that applies to our age as well as to the Golden Age of the Qing dynasty.

Kangxi reigned during one of the most glorious eras in the long history of China. Under the Ming (1369–1644) and the early Qing (1644–1911) dynasties, the empire expanded its borders to a degree not seen since the Han and the Tang. Chinese culture was the envy of its neighbors and earned the admiration of many European visitors, including Jesuit priests and Enlightenment philosophes.

On the surface, China appeared to be an unchanging society patterned after the Confucian vision of a "Golden Age" in the remote past. This indeed was the image presented by China's rulers, who referred constantly to tradition as a model for imperial institutions and cultural values. In actuality, however, China was changing—and rather rapidly. Although few observers could have been aware of it at the time, Confucian precepts were increasingly irrelevant in a society that was becoming ever more complex.

A similar process was under way in neighboring Japan. A vigorous new shogunate called the Tokugawa rose to power in the early seventeenth century and managed to revitalize the traditional system in a somewhat more centralized form that enabled it to survive for another two hundred fifty years. But major structural changes were taking place in Japanese society, and by the nineteenth century, tensions were growing as the gap between theory and reality widened.

One of the many factors involved in the quickening pace of change in both countries was contact with the West, which began with the arrival of Portuguese ships in Chinese and Japanese ports in the first half of the sixteenth century. The Ming and the Tokugawa initially opened their doors to European trade and missionary activity. Later, however, Chinese and Japanese rulers became concerned at the corrosive effects of Western ideas and practices and attempted to protect their traditional societies from external intrusion. But neither could forever resist the importunities of Western trading nations, nor could they arrest the pace of change taking place within. When the doors to the West were finally reopened in the mid-nineteenth century, both societies were ripe for radical change. ✤

CHINA AT ITS APEX

In 1514, a Portuguese fleet dropped anchor off the coast of China, just south of the Pearl River estuary and present-day Hong Kong. It was the first direct contact between the Chinese Empire and the West since the arrival of Marco Polo two centuries earlier, and it opened an era that would eventually change the face of China and, indeed, all of Asia.

From the Ming to the Qing

The magnificence of China had originally been reported to Europe by the Venetian adventurer Marco Polo, who visited Beijing during the reign of Khubilai Khan, the great Mongol ruler. By the time the Portuguese fleet arrived off the coast of China, of course, the Mongol Empire had long since disappeared. It had gradually weakened after the death of Khubilai Khan and was finally overthrown in 1368 by a massive peasant rebellion under the leadership of Zhu Yuanzhang, who had declared himself the founding emperor of a new Ming (Bright) dynasty and assumed the reign title of Ming Hongwu (Ming Hung Wu, or Ming Martial Emperor). The Ming inaugurated a new era of greatness in Chinese history. Under a series of strong rulers, China extended its rule into Mongolia and Central Asia. The Ming even briefly reconquered Vietnam, which, after a thousand years of Chinese rule, had reclaimed its independence following the collapse of the Tang dynasty in the tenth century. Along the northern frontier, the Emperor Yongle (Yung Lo; 1402–1424) strengthened the Great Wall and pacified the nomadic tribespeople who had troubled China in previous centuries. A tributary relationship was established with the Yi dynasty in Korea.

The internal achievements of the Ming were equally impressive. When they replaced the Mongols in the fourteenth century, the Ming turned to traditional Confucian institutions as a means of ruling their vast empire. These included the six ministries at the apex of the bureaucracy, the use of the civil service examinations to select members of the bureaucracy, and the division of the empire into provinces, districts, and counties. As before, Chinese villages were relatively autonomous, and local councils

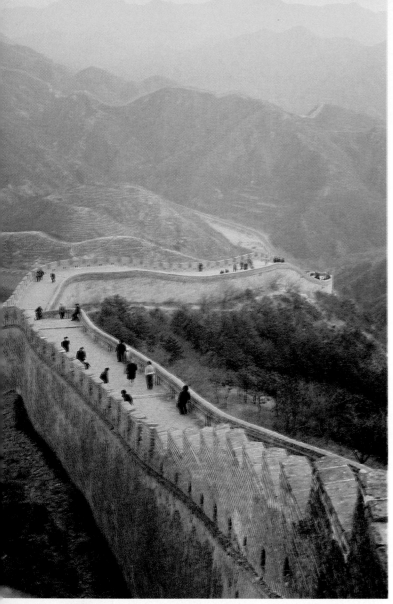

THE GREAT WALL OF CHINA Although the Great Wall is popularly believed to be over 2,000 years old, in actuality the part of the wall that is most frequently visited by tourists was a reconstruction undertaken during the early Ming Dynasty as a means of protection against invasion from the north. Part of that wall, which was built to protect the imperial capital of Beijing, appears here.

of elders continued to be responsible for adjudicating disputes, initiating local construction and irrigation projects, mustering a militia, and assessing and collecting taxes.

The society that was governed by this vast hierarchy of officials was a far cry from the predominantly agrarian society that had been ruled by the Han and the Tang. In the burgeoning cities near the coast and along the rich Yangtze River valley, factories and workshops were vastly increasing the variety and output of their manufactured goods. The population had doubled, and new crops had been introduced, greatly expanding the agricultural economy of the empire.

In 1405, in a splendid display of Chinese maritime might, Yongle sent a fleet of Chinese trading ships under the eunuch admiral Zhenghe (Cheng Ho) through the Strait of Malacca and out into the Indian Ocean; there they traveled as far west as the east coast of Africa, stopping on the way at ports in South Asia. The size of the fleet was impressive: it included nearly 28,000 sailors on sixty-two ships, some of them junks larger by far than any other oceangoing vessels the world had yet seen. China seemed about to become a direct participant in the vast trade network that extended as far west as the Atlantic Ocean, thus culminating the process of opening China to the wider world that had begun with the Tang dynasty.

Why the expeditions were undertaken has been a matter of some debate. Some historians assume that economic profit was the main reason. Others point to Yongle's native curiosity and note that the voyage—and the six others that followed it—returned not only with goods, but also with a plethora of information about the outside world as well as with some items unknown in China (the emperor was especially intrigued by the giraffes and placed them in the imperial zoo, where they were identified by soothsayers with the coming of good government). Others speculate that the emperor was seeking to ascertain the truth of rumors that his immediate predecessor, Emperor Jianwen or Chien Wen (1398–1402), had escaped to Southeast Asia to live in exile.

Whatever the case, the voyages resulted in massive profits for their sponsors, including individuals connected with the admiral Zhenghe at court. This aroused resentment among conservatives within the bureaucracy, some of whom viewed commercial activities with a characteristic measure of Confucian disdain. One commented that an end to the voyages would provide the Chinese people with a respite "so that they can devote themselves to husbandry [agriculture] and schooling."

Shortly after Yongle's death, the voyages were discontinued, never to be revived. An early European visitor reported that "no one sails the sea from north to south; it is prohibited by the king, in order that the country may not become known."[2] The decision had long-term consequences and in the eyes of many modern historians marks a turning inward of the Chinese state, away from commerce and toward a more traditional emphasis on agriculture, away from the exotic lands to the south and toward the heartland of the country in the Yellow River valley.

Ironically, the move toward the Yellow River had been initiated by Yongle himself, when he had decided to move the Ming capital from Nanjing, in central China (where the ships were built and the voyages launched), back to Beijing (where official eyes were firmly focused on the threat from beyond the Great Wall to the north). As a means of reducing that threat, Yongle ordered the resettlement of thousands of families from the rich Yangtze valley. The emperor had presumably not intended to set forces in motion that would divert the country from its growing contacts with the external world. After all, he had been the driving force behind Zhenghe's voyages. But the end result was a shift in the balance of power from central China (where it had been since the southern Song dynasty) back to northern China, where it had originated and would remain for the rest of the Ming era. China would not look outward again for over four centuries.

FIRST CONTACTS WITH THE WEST

Despite the Ming's retreat from active participation in the maritime trade, when the Portuguese arrived in 1514, China was in command of a vast empire that stretched from the steppes of Central Asia to the China Sea, from the Gobi Desert to the tropical rain forests of Southeast Asia. From the lofty perspective of the imperial throne in Beijing, the Europeans could only have seemed like an unusually exotic form of barbarian to be placed within the familiar framework of the tributary system, the hierarchical arrangement in which rulers of all other countries were regarded as "younger brothers" of the Son of Heaven. Indeed, the bellicose and uncultured behavior of the Portuguese so outraged Chinese officials that they expelled the Europeans, but after further negotiations the Portuguese were permitted to occupy the tiny territory of Macao, a foothold they would retain until the end of the twentieth century.

Initially, the arrival of the Europeans did not have much impact on Chinese society. Direct trade between Europe and China was limited, and Portuguese ships became involved in the regional trade network, carrying silk to Japan in return for Japanese silver. Eventually, the Spanish also began to participate, using the Philippines as an anchor in the galleon trade between China and the great silver mines in the Americas.

More influential than trade, perhaps, were the ideas introduced by Christian missionaries. Among the most active and the most effective were highly educated Jesuits, who were familiar with European philosophical and scientific developments. Recognizing the Chinese pride in their own culture, the Jesuits attempted to draw parallels between Christian and Confucian concepts (for example, they identified the Western concept of God with the Chinese character for Heaven) and to show the similarities between Christian morality and Confucian ethics. European inventions such as the clock, the prism, and various astronomical and musical instruments impressed Chinese officials, hitherto deeply imbued with a sense of the superiority of Chinese civilization, and helped Western ideas win acceptance at court. An elderly Chinese scholar expressed his wonder at the miracle of eyeglasses:

> White glass from across the Western Seas
> Is imported through Macao:
> Fashioned into lenses big as coins,
> They encompass the eyes in a double frame.
> I put them on—it suddenly becomes clear;
> I can see the very tips of things!
> And read fine print by the dim-lit window
> Just like in my youth.[3]

For their part, the missionaries were much impressed with many aspects of Chinese civilization, and reports of their experiences heightened European curiosity about this great society on the other side of the world (see the box on p. 492).

THE MING BROUGHT TO EARTH

During the late sixteenth century, however, the Ming began to decline as a series of weak rulers led to an era of corruption, concentration of land ownership, and ultimately peasant rebellions and tribal unrest along the northern frontier. The inflow of vast amounts of foreign

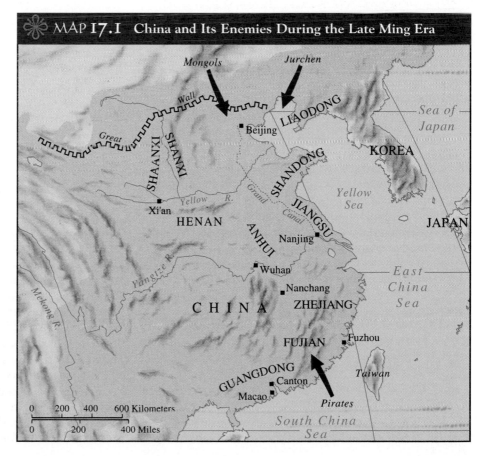

MAP 17.1 China and Its Enemies During the Late Ming Era

THE ART OF PRINTING

Europeans obtained much of their early information about China from the Jesuits who served at the Ming court in the sixteenth and seventeenth centuries. Clerics such as the Italian Matteo Ricci (1552–1610) found much to admire in Chinese civilization. Here Ricci expresses a keen interest in Chinese printing methods, which at that time were well in advance of the techniques used in the West.

MATTEO RICCI, *THE DIARY OF MATTHEW RICCI*

The art of printing was practiced in China at a date somewhat earlier than that assigned to the beginning of printing in Europe, which was about 1405. It is quite certain that the Chinese knew the art of printing at least five centuries ago, and some of them assert that printing was known to their people before the beginning of the Christian era, about 50 B.C. Their method of printing differs widely from that employed in Europe, and our method would be quite impracticable for them because of the exceedingly large number of Chinese characters and symbols. . . .

Their method of making printed books is quite ingenious. The text is written in ink, with a brush made of very fine hair, on a sheet of paper which is inverted and pasted on a wooden tablet. When the paper has become thoroughly dry, its surface is scraped off quickly and with great skill, until nothing but a fine tissue bearing the characters remains on the wooden tablet. Then, with a steel graver, the workman cuts away the surface following the outlines of the characters until these alone stand out in low relief. From such a block a skilled printer can make copies with incredible speed, turning out as many as fifteen hundred copies in a single day. . . . This scheme of engraving wooden blocks is well adapted for the large and complex nature of the Chinese characters, but I do not think it would lend itself very aptly to our European type, which could hardly be engraved upon wood because of its small dimensions.

Their method of printing has one decided advantage, namely, that once these tablets are made, they can be preserved and used for making changes in the text as often as one wishes. Additions and subtractions can also be made as the tablets can be readily patched. . . . We have derived great benefit from this method of Chinese printing, as we employ the domestic help in our homes to strike off copies of the books on religious and scientific subjects which we translate into Chinese from the languages in which they were written originally. In truth, the whole method is so simple that one is tempted to try it for himself after once having watched the process. The simplicity of Chinese printing is what accounts for the exceedingly large numbers of books in circulation here and the ridiculously low prices at which they are sold.

---

silver led to an alarming increase in inflation. Then the arrival of the English and the Dutch disrupted the silver trade; silver imports plummeted, severely straining the Chinese economy by raising the value of the metal relative to that of copper. Crop yields declined due to harsh weather—linked to the "Little Ice Age" of the early seventeenth century—and the resulting scarcity reduced the ability of the government to provide food in times of imminent starvation. High taxes, provoked in part by increased official corruption, led to peasant unrest and worker violence in urban areas. A folk song of the period, addressed to the "Lord of Heaven," complained,

> *Old skymaster,*
> *You're getting on, your ears are deaf, your eyes are gone.*
> *Can't see people, can't hear words.*
> *Glory for those who kill and burn;*
> *For those who fast and read the scriptures,*
> *Starvation.*
> *Fall down, old master sky, how can you be so high?*
> *How can you be so high? Come down to earth.*[4]

As always, internal problems were accompanied by unrest along the northern frontier. Following long precedent, the Ming had attempted to pacify the frontier tribes by forging alliances with them, arranging marriages between them and the local aristocracy, and granting trade privileges. One of the alliances was with the Manchus (also known as the Jurchen), the descendants of peoples who had briefly established a kingdom in northern China during the early thirteenth century. The Manchus, a mixed agricultural and hunting people, lived northeast of the Great Wall in the area known today as Manchuria.

At first the Manchus were satisfied with consolidating their territory and made little effort to extend their rule south of the Great Wall. But during the first decades of the seventeenth century, the problems of the Ming dynasty began to come to a head. A major epidemic devastated the population in many areas of the country. The suffering brought on by the epidemic helped spark a vast peasant revolt led by Li Zicheng (Li Tzu-ch'eng, 1604–1651). Li was a postal worker in central China who had been dismissed from his job as part of a cost-saving measure by the imperial court, now increasingly preoccupied by tribal attacks along the frontier. In the 1630s, Li managed to extend the revolt throughout the country and finally occupied the capital of Beijing in 1644. The last Ming emperor committed suicide by hanging himself from a tree in the palace gardens.

But Li was unable to hold his conquest. The overthrow of the Ming dynasty presented a great temptation to the Manchus. With the assistance of many military commanders who had deserted from the Ming, they conquered Beijing on their own. Li Zicheng's army disintegrated, and the Manchus declared the creation of a new dynasty with the reign title of the Qing (Ch'ing, or Pure). Once again, China was under foreign rule.

The Greatness of the Qing

The accession of the Manchus to power in Beijing was not universally applauded. Their ruthless policies and insensitivity to Chinese customs soon provoked resistance. Some Ming loyalists fled to Southeast Asia, but others continued their resistance to the new rulers from inside the country. To make it easier to identify the rebels, the government ordered all Chinese to adopt Manchu dress and hairstyles. All Chinese males were to shave their foreheads and braid their hair into a queue; those who refused were to be executed. As a popular saying put it, "lose your hair or lose your head."[5]

But the Manchus eventually proved to be more adept at adapting to Chinese conditions than their predecessors, the Mongols. Unlike the latter, who had tried to impose their own methods of ruling, the Manchus adopted the Chinese political system (although, as we shall see, they retained their distinct position within it) and were gradually accepted by most Chinese as the legitimate rulers of the country.

Like all of China's great dynasties, the Qing was blessed with a series of strong early rulers who pacified the country, rectified many of the most obvious social and economic inequities, and restored peace and prosperity. For the Ming dynasty, these strong emperors had been Hongwu and Yongle; under the Qing, they would be Kangxi (K'ang Hsi) and Qianlong (Ch'ien Lung). The two Qing monarchs ruled China for well over a century, from the middle of the seventeenth century to the end of the eighteenth, and were responsible for much of the greatness of Manchu China.

Kangxi (1661–1722) was arguably the greatest ruler in Chinese history. Ascending to the throne at the age of seven, he was blessed with diligence, political astuteness, and a strong character and began to take charge of Qing administration while still in his adolescence. During the six decades of his reign, Kangxi not only stabilized imperial rule by pacifying the restive peoples along the northern and western frontiers, but he also managed to make the dynasty acceptable to the general population. As an active patron of arts and letters, he cultivated the support of scholars through a number of major projects.

During Kangxi's reign, the activities of the Western missionaries, Dominicans and Franciscans as well as Jesuits, reached their height. The emperor was quite tolerant of the Christians, and several Jesuit missionaries became influential at court. Several hundred court officials converted to Christianity, as did an estimated 300,000 ordinary Chinese.

But ultimately the Christian effort was undermined by squabbling among the Western religious orders over the Jesuit policy of accommodating local beliefs and practices in order to facilitate conversion. The Jesuits had acquiesced to the emperor's insistence that traditional Confucian rituals such as ancestor worship were civil ceremonies and thus could be undertaken by Christian converts. Jealous Dominicans and Franciscans complained to the pope, who issued an edict ordering all missionaries and converts to conform to the official orthodoxy set forth in Europe. At first Kangxi attempted to resolve the problem by appealing directly to the Vatican, but the pope was uncompromising. After Kangxi's death, his successor began to suppress Christian activities throughout China.

Kangxi's achievements were carried on by his successors, Yongzheng (Yung Cheng, 1722–1736) and Qianlong (1736–1795). Like Kangxi, Qianlong was known for his diligence, tolerance, and intellectual curiosity, and he too combined vigorous military action against the unruly tribes along the frontier with active efforts to promote economic prosperity, administrative efficiency, and scholarship and artistic excellence. The result was continued growth for the Manchu Empire throughout much of the eighteenth century.

QING POLITICS

Certainly, one reason for the success of the Manchus was their ability to adapt to their new environment. They retained the Ming political system with relatively few changes. They also tried to establish their legitimacy as

A CONFUCIAN SIXTEEN COMMANDMENTS

Although the Qing dynasty was of foreign origin, its rulers found Confucian maxims convenient for maintaining the social order. In 1670, the great emperor Kangxi issued the Sacred Edict to popularize Confucian values among the common people. The edict was read publicly at periodic intervals in every village in the country and set the standard for behavior throughout the empire. Note the similarities and differences with the Japanese decree on p. 509 later in this chapter.

KANGXI'S SACRED EDICT

1. Esteem most highly filial piety and brotherly submission, in order to give due importance to the social relations.
2. Behave with generosity toward your kindred, in order to illustrate harmony and benignity.
3. Cultivate peace and concord in your neighborhoods, in order to prevent quarrels and litigations.
4. Recognize the importance of husbandry and the culture of the mulberry tree, in order to ensure a sufficiency of clothing and food.
5. Show that you prize moderation and economy, in order to prevent the lavish waste of your means.
6. Give weight to colleges and schools, in order to make correct the practice of the scholar.
7. Extirpate strange principles, in order to exalt the correct doctrine.
8. Lecture on the laws, in order to warn the ignorant and obstinate.
9. Elucidate propriety and yielding courtesy, in order to make manners and customs good.
10. Labor diligently at your proper callings, in order to stabilize the will of the people.
11. Instruct sons and younger brothers, in order to prevent them from doing what is wrong.
12. Put a stop to false accusations, in order to preserve the honest and good.
13. Warn against sheltering deserters, in order to avoid being involved in their punishment.
14. Fully remit your taxes, in order to avoid being pressed for payment.
15. Unite in hundreds and tithing, in order to put an end to thefts and robbery.
16. Remove enmity and anger, in order to show the importance due to the person and life.

China's rightful rulers by stressing their devotion to the principles of Confucianism. Emperor Kangxi ostentatiously studied the sacred Confucian classics and issued a "Sacred Edict" that proclaimed to the entire empire the importance of the moral values established by the master (see the box above).

Still, the Manchus, like the Mongols, were ethnically, linguistically, and culturally distinct from their subject population. The Qing attempted to cope with this reality by adopting a two-pronged strategy. On the one hand, the Manchus, representing less than 2 percent of the entire population, were legally defined as distinct from everyone else in China. The Manchu nobles retained their aristocratic privileges, while their economic base was protected by extensive landholdings and revenues provided from the state treasury. Other Manchus were assigned farmland and organized into military units, called banners, which were stationed as separate units in various strategic positions throughout China. These "bannermen" were the primary fighting force of the empire. Ethnic Chinese were prohibited from settling in Manchuria and were still compelled to wear their hair in a queue as a sign of submission to the ruling dynasty.

But while the Qing attempted to protect their distinct identity within an alien society, they also recognized the need to bring ethnic Chinese into the top ranks of imperial administration. Their solution was to create a system, known as dyarchy, in which all important administrative positions were shared equally by Chinese and Manchus. Of the six members of the grand secretariat, three were Manchu and three were Chinese. Each of the six ministries had an equal number of Chinese and Manchu members, and Manchus and Chinese also shared responsibilities at the provincial level. Below the provinces, Chinese were dominant. Although the system did not work perfectly, the Manchus' willingness to share power did win over the allegiance of many Chinese. Meanwhile, the Manchus themselves, despite official efforts to preserve their separate language and culture, were increasingly assimilated into Chinese civilization.

The new rulers also tinkered with the civil service examination system. In an effort to make it more equitable, quotas were established for each major ethnic group and each province to prevent the positions from being monopolized by candidates from certain provinces in central China that had traditionally produced large numbers of officials. In practice, however, the examination system probably became less equitable during the Manchu era, because increasingly positions were assigned to candidates who had purchased their degree rather than competing through the system. Moreover, positions were becoming harder to obtain because their number did not rise fast enough to match the unprecedented increase in population under Qing rule.

CHINA ON THE EVE OF THE WESTERN ONSLAUGHT

In some ways, China was at the height of its power and glory in the mid-eighteenth century. But it was also under Qianlong that the first signs of the internal decay of the Manchu dynasty began to appear. The clues were familiar ones. Qing military campaigns along the frontier were expensive and placed heavy demands on the imperial treasury. As the emperor aged, he became less astute in selecting his subordinates and fell under the influence of corrupt elements at court, including the notorious Manchu official Heshen (Ho Shen). Funds officially destined for military or other official use were increasingly siphoned off to Heshen or his favorites, arousing resentment among military and civilian officials.

Corruption at the center led inevitably to unrest in rural areas, where higher taxes, bureaucratic venality, and rising pressure on the land because of the growing population had produced economic hardship. The heart of the unrest was in central China, where discontented peasants who had recently been settled on infertile land launched a revolt known as the White Lotus Rebellion (1796–1804). The revolt was eventually suppressed but at great expense.

Unfortunately for China, the decline of the Qing dynasty occurred just as China's modest relationship with the West was about to give way to a new era of military confrontation and increased pressure for trade. The first problems came in the north, where Russian traders seeking skins and furs began to penetrate the region between Siberian Russia and Manchuria. Earlier the Ming dynasty had attempted to deal with the Russians by the traditional method of placing them in a tributary relationship and playing them off against other non-Chinese groups in the area. But the tsar refused to play by Chinese rules. His envoys to Beijing ignored the tribute system and refused to perform the kowtow (the ritual of prostration and knocking the head on the ground performed by foreign emissaries before the emperor), the classical symbol of fealty demanded of all foreign ambassadors to the Chinese court.

MAP 17.2   The Qing Empire in the Eighteenth Century

— Boundary of Qing Empire

■ States participating in tributary system

Formal diplomatic relations were finally established in 1689, when the Treaty of Nerchinsk (negotiated with the aid of Jesuit missionaries resident at the Qing court) settled the boundary dispute and provided for regular trade between the two countries. Through such arrangements, the Manchus were able not only to pacify the northern frontier but also to extend their rule over Xinjiang and Tibet to the west and southwest. In the meantime, tributary relations were established with such neighboring countries as Korea, Burma, Vietnam, and Ayuthaya.

Dealing with the foreigners who arrived by sea was more difficult. By the end of the seventeenth century, the English had replaced the Portuguese as the dominant force in European trade. Operating through the East India Company, which served as both a trading unit and the administrator of English territories in Asia, the English established their first trading post at Canton in 1699. Over the next decades, trade with China, notably the export of tea and silk to England, increased rapidly. To limit contact between Chinese and Europeans, the Qing licensed Chinese trading firms at Canton to be the exclusive conduit for trade with the West. Eventually, the Qing confined the Europeans to a small island just outside the city walls and permitted them to reside there only from October through March.

For a while, the British tolerated this system, which brought considerable profit to the East India Company and its shareholders. But by the end of the eighteenth century, the British had begun to demand access to other cities along the Chinese coast and that the country be opened to British manufactured goods. The British government and traders alike were restive at the uneven balance of trade between the two countries, which forced the British to ship vast amounts of silver bullion to China in exchange for its silks, porcelains, and teas. In 1793, a mission under Lord Macartney visited Beijing to press for liberalization of trade restrictions. A compromise was reached on the kowtow (Macartney was permitted to bend on one knee as was the British custom), but Qianlong expressed no interest in British manufactured products (see the box on p. 497). An exasperated Macartney compared the Chinese Empire to "an old, crazy, first-rate man-of-war" that had once awed its neighbors "merely by her bulk and appearance" but was now destined under incompetent leadership to be "dashed to pieces on the shore."[6] With his contemptuous dismissal of the British request, the emperor had inadvertently sowed the seeds for a century of humiliation.

Changing China

During the late Ming and Qing periods, China remained a predominantly agricultural society; nearly 85 percent of the population were farmers. But although most Chinese still lived in rural villages, the economy was undergoing a number of changes that have led some historians to suggest that China, under other circumstances, might have undergone an industrial revolution as in the West. In this view, the arrival of Western imperialism in the nineteenth century not only failed to stimulate economic change but may actually have hindered it.

✿ **EMPEROR QIANLONG MEETS LORD MACARTNEY.** In 1793, Lord Macartney was dispatched to China to press for the liberalization of trade restrictions. Although he offered gifts of Western scientific instruments and texts, the Chinese, who believed their nation had been the cultural center of the world for the last two thousand years, were not impressed. Lord Macartney won little Chinese sympathy for his refusal to kowtow to the emperor. Here the two prepare to meet.

THE TRIBUTE SYSTEM IN ACTION

n 1793, the British emissary Lord Macartney visited the Qing Empire to request the opening of formal diplomatic and trading relations between his country and China. Emperor Qianlong's reply, addressed to King George III of Britain, illustrates how the imperial court in Beijing viewed the world. King George could not have been pleased. The document provides a good example of the complacency with which the Celestial Empire viewed the world beyond its borders.

A DECREE OF EMPEROR QIANLONG

An Imperial Edict to the King of England: You, O King, are so inclined toward our civilization that you have sent a special envoy across the seas to bring to our Court your memorial of congratulations on the occasion of my birthday and to present your native products as an expression of your thoughtfulness. On perusing your memorial, so simply worded and sincerely conceived, I am impressed by your genuine respectfulness and friendliness and greatly pleased.

As to the request made in your memorial, O King, to send one of your nationals to stay at the Celestial Court to take care of your country's trade with China, this is not in harmony with the state system of our dynasty and will definitely not be permitted. Traditionally people of the European nations who wished to render some service under the Celestial Court have been permitted to come to the capital. But after their arrival they are obliged to wear Chinese court costumes, are placed in a certain residence, and are never allowed to return to their own countries. This is the established rule of the Celestial Dynasty with which presumably you, O King, are familiar. Now you, O King, wish to send one of your nationals to live in the capital, but he is not like the Europeans who come to Peking as Chinese employees, live there, and never return home again, nor can he be allowed to go and come and maintain any correspondence. This is indeed a useless undertaking.

Moreover the territory under the control of the Celestial Court is very large and wide. There are well-established regulations governing tributary envoys from the outer states to Peking, giving them provisions (of food and traveling expenses) by our post-houses and limiting their going and coming. There has never been a precedent for letting them do whatever they like. Now if you, O King, wish to have a representative in Peking, his language will be unintelligible and his dress different from the regulations; there is no place to accommodate him. . . .

The Celestial Court has pacified and possessed the territory within the four seas. Its sole aim is to do its utmost to achieve good government and to manage political affairs, attaching no value to strange jewels and precious objects. The various articles presented by you, O King, this time are accepted by my special order to the office in charge of such functions in consideration of the offerings having come from a long distance with sincere good wishes. As a matter of fact, the virtue and prestige of the Celestial Dynasty having spread far and wide, the kings of the myriad nations come by land and sea with all sorts of precious things. Consequently there is nothing we lack, as your principal envoy and others have themselves observed. We have never set much store on strange or ingenious objects, nor do we need any more of your country's manufactures. . . .

THE POPULATION EXPLOSION

In the first place, the center of gravity was continuing to shift steadily from the north to the south. In the early centuries of Chinese civilization, the bulk of the population had been located along the Yellow River. Smaller settlements were located along the Yangtze and in the mountainous regions of the south, but the administrative and economic center of gravity was clearly in the north. By the Song period, however, that emphasis had already begun to shift drastically as a result of climatic changes, deforestation, and continuing pressure from nomads in the Gobi Desert. By the late Ming and early Qing, the economic breadbasket of China, if not the administrative headquarters, was located along the Yangtze River or in the mountains to the south. One concrete indication of this shift occurred during the Ming dynasty, when Emperor Yongle ordered the renovation of the Grand Canal to facilitate the shipment of rice from the Yangtze delta to the food-starved north.

Moreover, the population was beginning to increase rapidly. For centuries, China's population had remained within a range of 50 to 100 million, rising in times of peace and prosperity and falling in periods of foreign invasion and internal anarchy. During the late Ming and the early Qing, however, the population increased from an estimated 70 to 80 million in 1390 to over 300 million at the end of the eighteenth century. There were probably several reasons for this population increase: the relatively long period of peace and stability under the early Qing; the introduction of new crops from the Americas, including peanuts, sweet potatoes, and maize; and the planting of a new species of faster-growing rice from Southeast Asia.

Of course, this population increase meant much greater population pressure on the land, smaller farms, and a razor-thin margin of safety in case of climatic disaster. The imperial court attempted to deal with the problem through a variety of means, most notably by preventing the concentration of land in the hands of wealthy landowners. Nevertheless, by the eighteenth century, almost all the land that could be irrigated was already under cultivation, and the problems of rural hunger and landlessness became increasingly serious.

SEEDS OF INDUSTRIALIZATION

Another change that took place during the early modern period in China was the steady growth of manufacturing and commerce. Taking advantage of the long era of peace and prosperity, merchants and manufacturers began to expand their operations beyond their immediate provinces. Commercial networks began to operate on a regional and sometimes even a national basis, as trade in silk, metal and wood products, porcelain, cotton goods, and cash crops like cotton and tobacco developed rapidly. Foreign trade also expanded, as Chinese merchants set up extensive contacts with countries in Southeast Asia.

Although this rise in industrial and commercial activity resembles the changes occurring in Western Europe, China and western Europe differed in several key ways. In the first place, the bourgeoisie in China were not as independent as their European counterparts. In China, trade and manufacturing remained under the firm control of the state. In addition, political and social prejudices against commercial activity remained strong. Reflecting an ancient preference for agriculture over manufacturing and trade, the state levied heavy taxes on manufacturing and commerce while attempting to keep agricultural taxes low.

One of the consequences of these differences was a growing technological gap between China and Europe. The Chinese reaction to European clock-making techniques provides an example. In the early seventeenth century, the Jesuit Matteo Ricci introduced advanced European clocks driven by weights or springs. The emperor was fascinated and found the clocks more reliable than Chinese methods of keeping time. Over the next decades, European timepieces became a popular novelty at court, but the Chinese expressed little curiosity about the technology involved, provoking one European to remark that playthings like cuckoo clocks "will be received here with much greater interest than scientific instruments or *objets d'art*."[7]

Daily Life in Qing China

Despite the changes in the economy, daily life in China under the Ming and early Qing dynasties continued to follow traditional patterns. As in earlier periods, Chinese society was organized around the family. As in earlier times, the ideal family unit in Qing China was the joint family, in which as many as three or even four generations lived under the same roof. When sons married, they brought their wives to live with them in the family homestead. Prosperous families would add a separate section to the house to accommodate the new family unit.

Unmarried daughters would also remain in the house. Aging parents and grandparents remained under the same roof until they died and were cared for by younger members of the household. This ideal did not always correspond to reality, however, since many families did not possess sufficient land to support a large household. One historian has estimated that only about 40 percent of Chinese families actually lived in joint families.

The family continued to be important in early Qing China for much the same reasons as in earlier times. As a labor-intensive society based primarily on the cultivation of rice, the Chinese needed large families not only to help with the harvest, but also to provide security for the parents when they were too old to work in the fields. Sons were particularly prized, not only because they had strong backs, but also because they would raise their own families under the parental roof. With few opportunities for employment outside the family, sons had little choice but to remain with their parents and help on the land. Within the family, the oldest male was king, and his wishes theoretically had to be obeyed by all family members. These values were reiterated in Emperor Kangxi's Sacred Edict, which listed filial piety and loyalty to the family as its first two maxims (see the box on p. 494).

For many Chinese, the effects of these values were most apparent in the choice of a marriage partner. Marriages were normally arranged for the benefit of the family, often by a go-between, and the groom and bride were usually not consulted. Frequently, they did not meet until the marriage ceremony. Under such conditions, love was clearly a secondary consideration. In fact, it was often viewed as detrimental, since it inevitably distracted the attention of the husband and wife from their primary responsibility to the larger family unit.

Although this emphasis on filial piety might seem to represent a blatant disregard for individual rights, the obligations were not all on the side of the children. The father was expected to provide support for his wife and children and, like the ruler, was supposed to treat those in his care with respect and compassion. All too often, however, the male head of the family was able to exact his privileges without performing his responsibilities in return.

Beyond the joint family was the clan. Sometimes called a lineage, a clan was an extended kinship unit consisting of dozens or even hundreds of joint and nuclear families linked together by a clan council of elders and a variety of other common social and religious functions. The clan served a number of useful purposes. Some clans possessed lands that could be rented out to poorer families, or richer families within the clan might provide land for the poor. Since there was no general state-supported educational system, sons of poor families might be invited to study in a school established in the home of a more prosperous relative. If the young man succeeded in becoming an official, he would be expected to provide favors and prestige for the clan as a whole.

Like joint families, clans were not universal, and millions of Chinese had none. The clans apparently originated in the great landed families of the Tang period and managed to survive despite periodic efforts by the imperial court to weaken and destroy them. In many cases, clan solidarity was weakened by intralineage conflicts or differing levels of status and economic achievement. Nevertheless, in the early modern period, they were still an influential force at the local level and were particularly prevalent in the south.

THE ROLE OF WOMEN

In traditional China, the role of women had always been inferior to that of men. A sixteenth-century Spanish visitor to South China observed that Chinese women were "very secluded and virtuous, and it was a very rare thing for us to see a woman in the cities and large towns, unless it was an old crone." Women were more visible, he said, in rural areas, where they frequently could be seen working in the fields.[8]

The concept of female inferiority had deep roots in Chinese history. This view was embodied in the belief that only a male would carry on sacred family rituals and that only males had the talent to govern others. Only males could aspire to a career in government or scholarship. Within the family system, the wife was clearly subordinated to the husband. Legally, she could not divorce her husband or inherit property. The husband, however, could divorce his wife if she did not produce male heirs, or he could take a second wife as well as a concubine for his pleasure. A widow suffered especially, because she had to either raise her children on a single income or fight off her former husband's greedy relatives, who would coerce her to remarry since, according to the law, they would then inherit all of her previous property and her original dowry.

Female children were less desirable because of their limited physical strength and because their parents would be required to pay a dowry to the parents of their future husband. Female children normally did not receive an education, and in times of scarcity when food was in short supply, daughters might even be put to death.

Though women were clearly inferior to men in theory, this was not always the case in practice. Capable women often compensated for their legal inferiority by playing a strong role within the family. Women were often in charge of educating the children and handled the family budget. Some privileged women also received training in the Confucian classics, although their schooling was generally for a shorter time and less rigorous than that of their male counterparts. A few produced significant works of art and poetry.

All in all, however, life for women in traditional China was undoubtedly difficult. In Chinese novels, women were treated as scullery maids or love objects. They were frequently under the domination of both their husband and their mother-in-law, and in some cases the bullying was so brutal that suicide appeared to be the only way out.

Cultural Developments

During the late Ming and the early Qing dynasties, traditional culture in China reached new heights of achievement. With the rise of a wealthy urban class, the demand for art, porcelain, textiles, and literature was at a premium.

THE RISE OF THE CHINESE NOVEL

During the Ming dynasty, a new form of literature arose that eventually evolved into the modern Chinese novel. Although considered less respectable than poetry and nonfiction prose, these groundbreaking works (often written anonymously or under pseudonyms) were enormously popular, especially among well-to-do urban dwellers.

Written in a colloquial style, the new fiction was characterized by a realism that resulted in vivid portraits of Chinese society. Many of the stories sympathized with society's downtrodden, often helpless maidens, and dealt with such crucial issues as love, money, marriage, and power. Adding to the realism were sexually explicit passages that depicted the private side of Chinese life. Readers delighted in sensuous tales that, no matter how pornographic, always professed a moral lesson; the villains were punished and the virtuous rewarded. During the more puritanical Qing era, a number of the more erotic works were censored or banned and found refuge in Japan, where several have recently been rediscovered by scholars.

Gold Vase Plum, known in English translation as The Golden Lotus, presents a cutting exposé of the decadent aspects of late Ming society. Considered by many the first realistic social novel—preceding its European counterparts by two centuries—The Golden Lotus depicts the depraved life of a wealthy landlord who cruelly manipulates those around him for sex, money, and power. In a rare exception in Chinese fiction, the villain is not punished for his evil ways; justice is served instead by the misfortunes that befall his descendants.

Even today The Dream of the Red Chamber is generally considered to be China's most distinguished popular novel (see the box on p. 500). Published in 1791, 150 years after The Golden Lotus, it tells of the tragic love between two young people caught in the financial and moral disintegration of a powerful Chinese clan. The hero and the heroine, both sensitive and spoiled, represent the inevitable decline of the Chia family and come to an equally inevitable tragic end, she in death and he in an unhappy marriage to another.

THE ART OF USING CHOPSTICKS

This passage from The Dream of the Red Chamber *is characteristic of the historical detail of the novel. It describes a country cousin's visit to the elegant mansion of her city relatives and the comic scene that she provokes by her naïveté. Such writing brings to life the wealth and luxury of the Qing dynasty and shows that Europeans were not the only people who had trouble with chopsticks.*

THE DREAM OF THE RED CHAMBER

As soon as Old Dame Liu was seated, she picked up the chopsticks, which were uncannily heavy and hard to manage. It was because Phoenix and Mandarin Duck had previously plotted to give her a pair of old-fashioned, angular-shaped ivory chopsticks gilded with gold. Looking at them, Old Dame Liu remarked: "These forklike things are even heavier than our iron prongs. How can one hold them up?" Everyone laughed. By this time a woman servant had brought in a tiny food box and, as she stood there, another maid came forward to lift the lid. Inside were two bowls of food. Li Huan took one bowl and placed it on the Matriarch's table as Phoenix picked up a bowl of pigeon eggs to place it on Old Dame Liu's table.

Just as the Matriarch had finished saying, "Please eat," Old Dame Liu rose from her seat and said aloud:

> Old Liu, Old Liu, her appetite as big as a cow!
> She eats like an old sow without lifting her head.

Having said her piece, with her cheeks puffed out she looked straight ahead without uttering another word. At first, all those present were astonished, but upon a moment's reflection, all burst out laughing at the same time. Unable to restrain herself, River Cloud (Matriarch's grandniece) spluttered out a mouthful of tea; Black Jade was choked with laughter and leaning on the table, could only cry and groan, "Ai-ya!" Madame Wang also laughed, then pointed her finger at Phoenix, but could not utter one word. . . . Only Phoenix and Mandarin Duck controlled themselves and kept urging Old Dame Liu to eat.

Old Dame Liu lifted up the chopsticks but they were hardly manageable. Looking at the bowl in front of her, she remarked: "Well, well, even your hens are smarter than ours! They lay such tiny delicate eggs, very dainty indeed. Let me try one!" All the people had just stopped laughing but they burst out again upon hearing these words. The Matriarch laughed so much that tears dropped down; she just couldn't stop them, and Amber (Matriarch's maidservant) had to pound her back to relieve her.

Old Dame Liu was still exclaiming about how tiny and dainty the eggs were when Phoenix said jocularly to her: "They cost an ounce of silver apiece. You had better hurry up and taste one before they get cold." Old Dame Liu then stretched out her chopsticks to seize the eggs with both ends, but how could she pick them up? After having chased them all over the bowl, she finally captured one with no little effort and was about to crane her neck to eat it when lo! it slipped off and fell on the floor. She was going to pick it up herself when a woman servant got it and took it out. Old Dame Liu sighed: "An ounce of silver! How it disappears without even making a noise!"

THE ART OF THE MING AND THE QING

During the Ming and the early Qing, China produced its last outpouring of traditional artistic brilliance. Although most of the creative work was modeled on past examples, the art of this period is impressive for its technical perfection and breathtaking quantity.

In architecture, the most outstanding example is the Imperial City in Beijing. Building on the remnants of the palace of the Yuan dynasty, the third Ming emperor ordered renovations when he returned the capital to Beijing in 1421. Succeeding emperors continued to add to the palace, but the basic design has not changed since the Ming era. Surrounded by six and one-half miles of walls, the immense enclosed compound is divided into a maze of private apartments and offices and an imposing ceremonial quadrangle with a series of stately halls for imperial audiences and banquets. The grandiose scale, richly carved marble, spacious gardens, and graceful upturned roofs also contribute to the splendor of the "Forbidden City."

The decorative arts flourished in this period, especially the intricately carved lacquerware and the boldly shaped and colored cloisonné, a type of enamelwork in which colored areas are attached to a piece by metal bands. Silk production reached its zenith, and the best-quality silks were highly prized in Europe, where chinoiserie, as Chinese art of all kinds was called, was in vogue. Perhaps the most famous of all the achievements of the Ming era was the blue-and-white porcelain, which is still prized by collectors throughout the world. One variety caused a sensation in Holland and led to the manufacture of blue-and-white porcelain at the Dutch porcelain factory at Delft.

During the Qing dynasty, artists produced great quantities of paintings, mostly for home consumption. The wealthy city of Yangzhou on the Grand Canal emerged as an active artistic center. Inside the Forbidden City in Beijing, court painters worked alongside Jesuit artists and experimented with Western techniques. European art, however, did not greatly influence Chinese painting at this

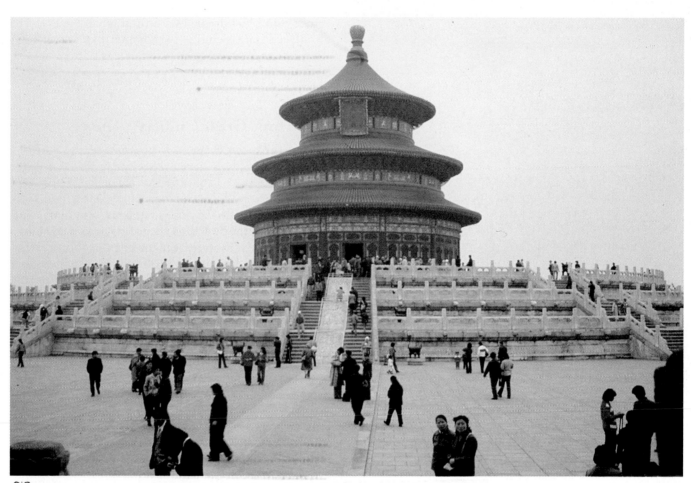

✿ **THE TEMPLE OF HEAVEN.** This temple, located in the capital Beijing, is one of the most important historical structures in China. Built in 1420 at the order of the Ming emperor Yongle, it served as the location for the emperor's annual ceremony appealing to Heaven for a good harvest. Yongle's temple burned to the ground in 1889 but was immediately rebuilt according to the original design.

✿ **THE IMPERIAL CITY IN BEIJING.** During the fifteenth century, the Ming dynasty erected an immense Imperial City on the remnants of the palace of Khubilai Khan in Beijing. Surrounded by six and one-half miles of walls, the enclosed compound is divided into a maze of private apartments and offices; it also includes an imposing ceremonial quadrangle with stately halls for imperial audiences and banquets. Because it was off-limits to commoners, the compound was known as the "Forbidden City."

WORLD-CLASS CHINA WARE. Ming porcelain was noted throughout the world for its delicate blue-and-white floral decorations. The blue coloring was produced with cobalt that had originally been brought from the Middle East along the Silk Road and was known in China as "Mohammadan blue." In the early seventeenth century, the first Ming ware arrived in Holland, where it was called "kraak" because it had been loaded on two Portuguese carracks seized by the Dutch fleet. It took Dutch artisans over a century to learn how to produce a porcelain as fine as the examples brought from China.

time; some dismissed it as mere "craftsmanship." Scholarly painters and the literati totally rejected foreign techniques and became obsessed with traditional Chinese styles. As a result, Qing painting became progressively more repetitive and stale. Ironically, the Qing dynasty thus represents the apogee of traditional Chinese art and the beginning of its decline.

TOKUGAWA JAPAN

At the end of the fifteenth century, the traditional Japanese system was at a point of near anarchy. With the decline in the authority of the Ashikaga shogunate at Kyoto, clan rivalries had exploded into an era of "warring states" similar to the period of the same name in Zhou dynasty China. Even at the local level, power was frequently diffuse. The typical daimyo (great lord) domain had often become little more than a coalition of fief holders held together by a loose allegiance to the manor lord.

Prince Shotoku's dream of a united Japan appeared to be only a distant memory (see Chapter 11). In actuality, Japan was on the verge of an extended era of national unification and peace under the rule of its greatest shogunate—the Tokugawa.

The Three Great Unifiers

The process began in the mid-sixteenth century with the emergence of three very powerful political figures, Oda Nobunaga (1568–1582), Toyotomi Hideyoshi (1582–1598), and Tokugawa Ieyasu (1598–1616). In 1568, Oda Nobunaga, the son of a samurai and a military commander under the Ashikaga shogunate, seized the imperial capital of Kyoto and placed the reigning shogun under his domination. During the next few years, the brutal and ambitious Nobunaga attempted to consolidate his rule throughout the central plains by defeating his rivals and suppressing the power of the Buddhist estates, but he was killed by one of his generals in 1582 before the process was complete. He was succeeded by Toyotomi Hideyoshi, a farmer's son who had worked his way up within the ranks to become a military commander. Originally lacking a family name of his own, he eventually adopted the name Toyotomi ("abundant provider") to embellish his reputation for improving the material standards of his domain. Hideyoshi located his capital at Osaka, where he built a castle to accommodate his headquarters, and gradually extended his power outward to the southern islands of Shikoku and Kyushu. By 1590, he had persuaded most of the daimyo on the Japanese islands to accept his authority and created a national currency. Then he invaded Korea in an abortive effort to export his rule to the Asian mainland.

Despite their efforts, however, neither Nobunaga nor Hideyoshi was able to eliminate the power of the local daimyo. Both were compelled to form alliances with some daimyo in order to destroy other more powerful rivals. At the conclusion of his conquests in 1590, Toyotomi Hideyoshi could claim to be the supreme proprietor of all registered lands in areas under his authority. But he then reassigned those lands as fiefs to the local daimyo, who declared their allegiance to him. The daimyo in turn began to pacify the countryside, carrying out extensive "sword hunts" to disarm the population and attracting samurai to their service. The Japanese tradition of decentralized rule had not been overcome.

After Hideyoshi's death in 1598, Tokugawa Ieyasu, the powerful daimyo of Edo (modern Tokyo), moved to fill the vacuum. Neither Hideyoshi nor Oda Nobunaga had claimed the title of shogun, but Ieyasu named himself shogun in 1603, initiating the most powerful and long-lasting of all Japanese shogunates. The Tokugawa rulers completed the restoration of central authority begun by Nobunaga and Hideyoshi and remained in power until 1868, when a war dismantled the entire system. As a contemporary phrased it, "Oda pounds the national rice cake, Hideyoshi kneads it, and in the end Ieyasu sits down and eats it."[9]

Opening to the West

The unification of Japan took place almost simultaneously with the coming of the Europeans. Portuguese traders sailing in a Chinese junk that may have been blown off course by a typhoon had landed on the islands in 1543. Within a few years, Portuguese ships were stopping at Japanese ports on a regular basis to take part in the regional trade between Japan, China, and Southeast Asia. The first Jesuit missionary, Francis Xavier, arrived in 1549.

Initially, the visitors were welcomed. The curious Japanese (the Japanese were "very desirous of knowledge," said Francis Xavier) were fascinated by tobacco, clocks, spectacles, and other European goods, and local daimyo were interested in purchasing all types of European weapons and armaments (see the box on p. 504). Oda Nobunaga and Toyotomi Hideyoshi found the new firearms helpful in defeating their enemies and unifying the islands. The effect on Japanese military architecture was particularly striking, as local lords began to erect castles on the European model. Many of these castles, such as Hideyoshi's castle at Osaka, still exist today.

The missionaries also had some success. Though confused by misleading translations of sacred concepts in both cultures (Francis Xavier was notoriously poor at learning foreign languages), they converted a number of local daimyo, some of whom may have been motivated in part by the desire for commercial profits. By the end of the sixteenth century, thousands of Japanese in the southernmost islands of Kyushu and Shikoku had become Christians. One converted daimyo ceded the superb natural harbor of the modern city of Nagasaki to the Society of Jesus, which proceeded to use the new settlement for both missionary and trading purposes. But papal claims to the loyalty of all Japanese Christians and the European habit of intervening in local politics soon began to arouse suspicion in official circles. Missionaries added to the problem by deliberately destroying local idols and shrines and turning some temples into Christian schools or churches.

Inevitably, the local authorities reacted. In 1587, Toyotomi Hideyoshi issued an edict prohibiting further Christian activities within his domains. Japan, he declared, was "the land of the Gods" and the destruction of shrines by the foreigners was "something unheard of in previous ages." To "corrupt and stir up the lower classes" to commit such sacrileges, he declared, was "outrageous."[10] Those responsible (the Jesuits) were ordered to leave the country within twenty days. Hideyoshi was careful to distinguish

❀ **THE SIEGE OF OSAKA CASTLE.**   After the death of Toyotomi Hideyoshi in 1598, titular authority in Japan passed on to his infant son Hideyori, whose supporters located their headquarters at Osaka Castle in central Japan. In 1615, the powerful warlord Tokugawa Ieyasu seized the castle as shown here, and scattered Hideyori's supporters. The family's control over Japan lasted nearly 250 years.

A PRESENT FOR LORD TOKITAKA

The Portuguese introduced firearms to Japan in the sixteenth century, and Japanese warriors were quick to explore the possibilities of these new weapons. In this passage, the daimyo of a small island off the southern tip of Japan receives an explanation of how to use the new weapons and is fascinated by the results. Note how Lord Tokitaka attempts to understand the procedures in terms of traditional Daoist beliefs.

THE JAPANESE DISCOVER FIREARMS

"There are two leaders among the traders, the one called Murashusa, and the other Christian Mota. In their hands they carried something two or three feet long, straight on the outside with a passage inside, and made of a heavy substance. The inner passage runs through it although it is closed at the end. At its side there is an aperture which is the passageway for fire. Its shape defies comparison with anything I know. To use it, fill it with powder and small lead pellets. Set up a small . . . target on a bank. Grip the object in your hand, compose your body, and closing one eye, apply fire to the aperture. Then the pellet hits the target squarely. The explosion is like lightning and the report like thunder. Bystanders must cover their ears. . . . This thing with one blow can smash a mountain of silver and a wall of iron. If one sought to do mischief in another man's domain and he was touched by it, he would lose his life instantly. Needless to say this is also true for the deer and stag that ravage the plants in the fields."

Lord Tokitaka saw it and thought it was the wonder of wonders. He did not know its name at first nor the details of its use. Then someone called it "iron-arms," although it was not known whether the Chinese called it so, or whether it was so called only on our island. Thus, one day, Tokitaka spoke to the two alien leaders through an interpreter: "Incapable though I am, I should like to learn about it." Whereupon, the chiefs answered, also through an interpreter: "If you wish to learn about it, we shall teach you its mysteries." Tokitaka then asked, "What is its secret?" The chief replied: "The secret is to put your mind aright and close one eye." Tokitaka said: "The ancient sages have often taught how to set one's mind aright, and I have learned something of it. If the mind is not set aright, there will be no logic for what we say or do. Thus, I understand what you say about setting our minds aright. However, will it not impair our vision for objects at a distance if we close an eye? Why should we close an eye?" To which the chiefs replied: "That is because concentration is important in everything. When one concentrates, a broad vision is not necessary. To close an eye is not to dim one's eyesight but rather to project one's concentration farther. You should know this." Delighted, Tokitaka said: "That corresponds to what Lao Tzu has said, 'Good sight means seeing what is very small.' "

That year the festival day of the Ninth Month fell on the day of the Metal and the Boar. Thus, one fine morning the weapon was filled with powder and lead pellets, a target was set up more than a hundred paces away, and fire was applied to the weapon. At first the people were astonished; then they became frightened. But in the end they all said in unison: "We should like to learn!" Disregarding the high price of the arms, Tokitaka purchased from the aliens two pieces of the firearms for his family treasure. As for the art of grinding, sifting, and mixing of the powder, Tokitaka let his retainer, Shinokawa Shoshiro, learn it. Tokitaka occupied himself, morning and night, and without rest in handling the arms. As a result, he was able to convert the misses of his early experiments into hits—a hundred hits in a hundred attempts.

---

missionary from trading activities, however, and merchants were permitted to continue their operations (see the box on p. 505).

The Jesuits protested the expulsion, and eventually Hideyoshi relented, permitting them to continue proselytizing so long as they were discreet. But he refused to repeal the edicts, and when the aggressive activities of newly arrived Spanish Franciscans aroused his ire, he ordered the execution of nine missionaries and a number of their Japanese converts. When the missionaries continued to interfere in local politics (some even tried to incite the daimyo in the southern islands against the shogunate government in Edo), Tokugawa Ieyasu completed the process by ordering the eviction of all missionaries in 1612. The persecution of Japanese Christians intensified, leading to an abortive revolt by Christian peasants on the island of Kyushu in 1637, which was bloodily suppressed.

At first, Japanese authorities hoped to maintain commercial relations with European countries even while suppressing the Western religion, but eventually they decided to prohibit foreign trade altogether and closed the two major foreign factories on the island of Hirado and at Nagasaki. The sole remaining opening to the West was at Deshima Island in Nagasaki harbor, where a small Dutch community was permitted to engage in limited trade with Japan (the Dutch, unlike the Portuguese and the Spanish, had not allowed missionary activities to interfere with their commercial interests). Dutch ships were permitted to dock at Nagasaki harbor only once a year and, after close inspection, were allowed to remain for two or three months. Conditions on the island of Deshima itself were

TOYOTOMI HIDEYOSHI EXPELS THE MISSIONARIES

When Christian missionaries in sixteenth-century Japan began to interfere in local politics and criticize traditional religious practices, Toyotomi Hideyoshi issued an edict calling for their expulsion. In this letter to the Portuguese viceroy in Asia, Hideyoshi explains his decision. Note his conviction that Buddhists, Confucianists, and followers of Shinto all believe in the same God and his criticism of Christianity for rejecting all other faiths.

TOYOTOMI HIDEYOSHI, LETTER TO THE VICEROY OF THE INDIES

Ours is the land of the Gods, and God is mind. Everything in nature comes into existence because of mind. Without God there can be no spirituality. Without God there can be no way. God rules in times of prosperity as in times of decline. God is positive and negative and unfathomable. Thus, God is the root and source of all existence. This God is spoken of by Buddhism in India, Confucianism in China, and Shinto in Japan. To know Shinto is to know Buddhism as well as Confucianism.

As long as man lives in this world, Humanity will be a basic principle. Were it not for Humanity and Righteousness, the sovereign would not be a sovereign, nor a minister of a state a minister. It is through the practice of Humanity and Righteousness that the foundations of our relationships between sovereign and minister, parent and child, and husband and wife are established. If you are interested in the profound philosophy of God and Buddha, request an explanation and it will be given to you. In your land one doctrine is taught to the exclusion of others, and you are not yet informed of the [Confucian] philosophy of Humanity and Righteousness. Thus there is no respect for God and Buddha and no distinction between sovereign and ministers. Through heresies you intend to destroy the righteous law. Hereafter, do not expound, in ignorance of right and wrong, unreasonable and wanton doctrines. A few years ago the so-called Fathers came to my country seeking to bewitch our men and women, both of the laity and clergy. At that time punishment was administered to them, and it will be repeated if they should return to our domain to propagate their faith. It will not matter what sect or denomination they represent—they shall be destroyed. It will then be too late to repent. If you entertain any desire of establishing amity with this land, the seas have been rid of the pirate menace, and merchants are permitted to come and go. Remember this.

THE PORTUGUESE ARRIVE AT NAGASAKI. Portuguese traders landed in Japan by accident in 1543. In a few years, they arrived regularly, taking part in a regional trade network between Japan, China, and Southeast Asia. In these panels done in black lacquer and gold leaf, we see a late-sixteenth-century Japanese interpretation of the first Portuguese landing at Nagasaki.

quite confining: the Dutch physician Engelbert Kaempfer complained that the Dutch lived in "almost perpetual imprisonment."[11] Nor were the Japanese free to engage in foreign trade. A small amount of commerce took place with China, but Japanese subjects of the shogunate were forbidden to leave the country on penalty of death.

The Tokugawa "Great Peace"

Once in power, the Tokugawa attempted to strengthen the system that had governed Japan for over three hundred years. They followed precedent in ruling through the *bakufu*, composed now of a coalition of daimyo, and a council of elders. But the system was more centralized than it had been previously. Now the shogunate government played a dual role. It set national policy on behalf of the emperor in Kyoto while simultaneously governing the shogun's own domain, which included about one-quarter of the national territory as well as the three great cities of Edo, Kyoto, and Osaka. As before, the state was divided into separate territories, called domains (*han*), which were ruled by a total of about 250 individual daimyo lords. The daimyo were themselves divided into two types: the *fudai* (inside) daimyo, who were mostly small daimyo directly subordinate to the shogunate, and the *tozama* (outside) daimyo, who were larger and more independent lords usually more distant from the center of shogunate power in Edo.

In theory, the daimyo were essentially autonomous, since they were able to support themselves from taxes on their lands (the shogunate received its own revenues from its extensive landholdings). In actuality, the shogunate was able to guarantee daimyo loyalties by compelling daimyo lords to maintain two residences, one in their own domains and the other at Edo, and to leave their families in Edo as hostages for the daimyo's good behavior. Keeping up two residences also placed the Japanese nobility in a difficult economic position. Some were able to defray the high costs by concentrating on cash crops such as sugar, fish, and forestry products, but most were rice producers, and their revenues remained roughly the same throughout the period. The daimyo were also able to protect their economic interests by depriving their samurai retainers of their proprietary rights over the land and transforming them into salaried officials. The fief thus became a stipend, and the personal relationship between the daimyo and his retainers gradually gave way to a bureaucratic authority.

The Tokugawa also tinkered with the social system by limiting the size of the samurai class and reclassifying samurai who supported themselves by tilling the land as commoners. In fact, with the long period of peace brought about by Tokugawa rule, the samurai gradually ceased to be a warrior class and were required to live in the castle towns. As a gesture to their glorious past, samurai were still permitted to wear their two swords, and a rigid separation was maintained between persons of samurai status and the nonaristocratic segment of the population. Jesuit missionary Francis Xavier observed that "on no account would a poverty-stricken gentleman marry with someone outside the gentry, even if he were given great sums to do so."[12]

SEEDS OF CAPITALISM

The long period of peace under the Tokugawa shogunate made possible a dramatic rise in commerce and manufacturing, especially in the growing cities of Edo, Kyoto, and Osaka. By the mid-eighteenth century, Edo, with a population of more than one million, was one of the largest cities in the world. The growth of trade and industry was stimulated by a rising standard of living—driven in part by technological advances in agriculture and an expansion of arable land—and the voracious appetites of the aristocrats for new products. The daimyo's need for income also contributed as many of them began to promote the sale of local goods from their domains, such as textiles, forestry products, sugar, and sake (a Japanese rice wine).

Most of this commercial expansion took place in the major cities and the castle towns, where the merchants and artisans lived along with the samurai, who were clustered in neighborhoods surrounding the daimyo's castle. Banking flourished and paper money became the normal medium of exchange in commercial transactions. Merchants formed guilds not only to control market conditions, but also to facilitate government control and the collection of taxes. Under the benign if somewhat contemptuous supervision of Japan's noble rulers, a Japanese merchant class gradually began to emerge from the shadows to play a significant role in the life of the Japanese nation. Some historians view the Tokugawa era as the first stage in the rise of an indigenous form of capitalism.

Eventually, the increased pace of industrial activity spread beyond the cities into rural areas. As in Great Britain, cotton was a major factor. Cotton had been introduced to China during the Song dynasty and had spread to Korea and Japan shortly thereafter. Traditionally, however, cotton cloth had been too expensive for the common people, who instead wore clothing made of hemp. Imports increased during the sixteenth century, however, when cotton cloth began to be used for uniforms, matchlock fuses, and sails. Eventually, technological advances reduced the cost, and specialized communities for producing cotton cloth began to appear in the countryside and were gradually transformed into towns. By the eighteenth century, cotton had firmly replaced hemp as the clothing of choice for most Japanese.

Not everyone benefited from the economic changes of the seventeenth and eighteenth centuries, however, notably the samurai, who were barred by tradition and prejudice from commercial activities. Although some profited from their transformation into a managerial class on the daimyo domains, most still relied on their revenues from

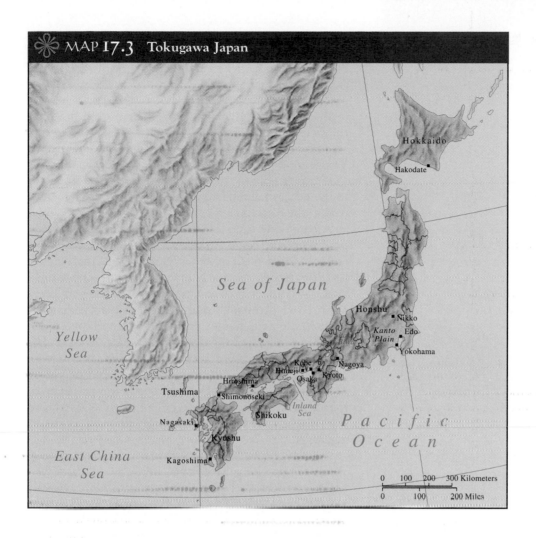

MAP 17.3 Tokugawa Japan

rice lands, which were often insufficient to cover their rising expenses; consequently, they fell heavily into debt. Others were released from servitude to their lord and became "masterless samurai." Occasionally, these unemployed warriors (known as *ronin*, or "wave men") revolted or plotted against the local authorities. In one episode, made famous in song and story as the "Forty-Seven Ronin," the masterless samurai of a local lord who had been forced to commit suicide by a shogunate official later assassinated the official in revenge. Although their act received wide popular acclaim, the *ronin* were later forced to take their own lives.

The effects of economic developments on the rural population during the Tokugawa era are harder to estimate. Some farm families benefited by exploiting the growing demand for cash crops. But not all prospered. Most peasants continued to rely on rice cultivation and were whipsawed between declining profits and rising costs and taxes (as daimyo expenses increased, land taxes often took up to 50 percent of the annual harvest). Many were forced to become tenants or to work as wage laborers on the farms of wealthy neighbors or in village industries. When rural conditions

in some areas became desperate, peasant revolts erupted. According to one estimate, nearly seven thousand disturbances took place during the Tokugawa era. In general, though, the rural unrest during the Tokugawa era was probably motivated less by a decline in the standard of living than by local factors and a new sense of peasant assertiveness. Peasant disturbances became a more or less routine means of protesting against rising taxes and official corruption or of demanding "benevolence" from the manor lord in times of climatic disaster.

Some Japanese historians, influenced by a Marxist view of history, have interpreted such evidence as an indication that the Tokugawa economic system was highly exploitative, with feudal aristocrats oppressing powerless peasants. Recent scholars, however, have tended to adopt a more balanced view, maintaining that agriculture as well as manufacturing and commerce experienced extensive growth. Some point out that although the population doubled in the seventeenth century, a relatively low rate for the time period, so did the amount of cultivable land, while agricultural technology made significant advances.

CHRONOLOGY

JAPAN AND KOREA DURING THE EARLY MODERN ERA

First phonetic alphabet in Korea	Fifteenth century
Portuguese merchants arrive in Japan	1543
Francis Xavier arrives in Japan	1549
Rule of Oda Nobunaga	1568–1582
Seizure of Kyoto	1568
Rule of Toyotomi Hideyoshi	1582–1598
Edict prohibiting Christianity in Japan	1587
Invades Korea	1592
Death of Toyotomi Hideyoshi and withdrawal of army from Korea	1598
Rule of Tokugawa Ieyasu	1598–1616
Creation of Tokugawa shogunate	1603
Dutch granted permission to trade at Nagasaki	1609
Order evicting Christian missionaries	1612
Christian uprising suppressed	1637
Dutch post at Nagasaki transferred to Hirado	1641
Incident of forty-seven *ronin*	1702

The relatively low rate of population growth probably meant that Japanese peasants were spared the kind of land hunger that many of their counterparts in China faced. Recent evidence indicates that the primary reasons for the relatively low rate of population growth were late marriage, abortion, and infanticide. As Honda Toshiaki, a late-eighteenth-century demographer, described:

> Aware that if they have many children they will not have any property to leave them, [husbands and wives] confer and decide that rather than rear children who in later years will have great difficulty in making a decent living, it is better to take precautions before they are born and not add another mouth to feed. If they do have a child, they secretly destroy it, calling the process by the euphemism of "thinning out."[13]

Life in the Village

The changes that took place during the Tokugawa era had a major impact on the lives of ordinary Japanese. In some respects, the result was an increase in the power of the central government at the village level. The shogunate increasingly relied on Confucian maxims advocating obedience and hierarchy to enhance its authority with the general population. Decrees from the *bakufu* instructed the peasants on all aspects of their lives, including their eating habits and their behavior (see the box on p. 509). At the same time, the increased power of the government led to more autonomy from the local daimyo for the peasants. Villages now had more control over their local affairs and were responsible to the central government as much as to the nearby manor lord, although land taxes were still paid to the daimyo.

At the same time, the Tokugawa era saw the emergence of the nuclear family (*ie*) as the basic unit in Japanese society. In previous times, Japanese peasants had few legal rights. Most were too poor to keep their conjugal family unit intact or to pass property on to their children. Many lived at the manorial residence or worked as servants in the households of more affluent villagers. Now, with farm income on the rise, the nuclear family took on the same form as in China, although without the joint family concept. The Japanese system of inheritance was based on primogeniture. Family property was passed on to the eldest son, although younger sons often received land from their parents to set up their own families after marriage.

Another result of the changes under the Tokugawa was that women were somewhat more restricted than they had been previously. The rights of females were especially restricted in the samurai class, where Confucian values were highly influential. Male heads of households had broad authority over property, marriage, and divorce; wives were expected to obey their husbands on pain of death. Males often took concubines or homosexual partners, while females were expected to remain chaste. The male offspring of samurai parents studied the Confucian classics in schools established by the daimyo, while females were reared at home, where only the fortunate might receive a rudimentary training in Chinese characters. Some women, however, became accomplished poets and painters since, in aristocratic circles, female literacy was prized for enhancing the refinement, social graces, and moral virtue of the home. Under the Tokugawa, it was the obligation of the wife in elite families to reflect her husband's rank and status through a strict code of comportment and dress.

Women were similarly at a disadvantage among the common people. Marriages were arranged, and as in China, the new wife moved in with the family of her husband. A wife who did not meet the expectations of her spouse or his family was likely to be divorced. Still, gender relations were more egalitarian than among the nobility. Women were generally valued as childbearers and homemakers, and both sexes worked in the fields. Coeducational schools were established in villages and

FOLLOWING THE STRAIGHT AND NARROW IN TOKUGAWA JAPAN

Like the Qing dynasty in China, the Tokugawa shoguns attempted to keep their subjects in line with decrees that carefully prescribed all kinds of behavior. As this decree, which was circulated in all Japanese villages, shows, the bakufu *sought to be the moral instructor as well as the guardian and protector of the Japanese people. Compare and contrast this decree with Emperor Kangxi's Sacred Edict in the box earlier in this chapter.*

MAXIMS FOR PEASANT BEHAVIOR

1. Young people are forbidden to congregate in great numbers.
2. Entertainments unsuited to peasants, such as playing the samisen or reciting ballad dramas, are forbidden.
3. Staging sumo matches is forbidden for the next five years.
4. The edict on frugality issued by the *han* at the end of last year must be observed.
5. Social relations in the village must be conducted harmoniously.
6. If a person has to leave the village for business or pleasure, that person must return by ten at night.
7. Father and son are forbidden to stay overnight at another person's house. An exception is to be made if it is to nurse a sick person.
8. Corvée [obligatory labor] assigned by the *han* must be performed faithfully.
9. Children who practice filial piety must be rewarded.
10. One must never get drunk and cause trouble for others.
11. Peasants who farm especially diligently must be rewarded.
12. Peasants who neglect farm work and cultivate their paddies and upland fields in a slovenly and careless fashion must be punished.
13. The boundary lines of paddy and upland fields must not be changed arbitrarily.
14. Recognition must be accorded to peasants who contribute greatly to village political affairs.
15. Fights and quarrels are forbidden in the village.
16. The deteriorating customs and morals of the village must be rectified.
17. Peasants who are suffering from poverty must be identified and helped.
18. This village has a proud history compared to other villages, but in recent years bad times have come upon us. Everyone must rise at six in the morning, cut grass, and work hard to revitalize the village.
19. The punishments to be meted out to violators of the village code and gifts to be awarded the deserving are to be decided during the last assembly meeting of the year.

market towns, and about one-quarter of the students were female. Poor families, however, often put infant daughters to death or sold them into prostitution and the "floating world" of entertainment (see The Literature of the New Middle Class later in this chapter). During the late Tokugawa era, peasant women became more outspoken and active in social protests and in some cases played a major role in provoking demonstrations against government exactions or exploitative acts by landlords or merchants.

Such attitudes toward women operated within the context of the increasingly rigid stratification of Japanese society. Deeply conservative in their social policies, the Tokugawa rulers established strict legal distinctions between the four main classes in Japan (warriors, artisans, peasants, and merchants). Intermarriage between classes was forbidden in theory, although sometimes the prohibitions were ignored in practice. Below these classes were Japan's outcasts, the *eta*. Formerly, they were permitted to escape their status, at least in theory. The Tokugawa made their status hereditary and enacted severe discriminatory laws against them, regulating their place of residence, their dress, and even their hairstyles.

Tokugawa Culture

Under the Tokugawa, the tensions between the old society and the emerging new one were starkly reflected in the arena of culture. On the one hand, the classical culture, influenced by Confucian themes, Buddhist quietism, and the samurai warrior tradition, continued to flourish under the patronage of the shogunate. On the other, a vital new set of cultural values began to appear, especially in the cities. This innovative era witnessed the rise of popular literature written by and for the townspeople. With the development of woodblock printing in the early seventeenth century, literature became available to the common people, literacy levels rose, and lending libraries increased the accessibility of the printed word. In contrast to the previous mood of doom and gloom, the new prose was cheerful and even frivolous, its primary aim being to divert and amuse.

THE LITERATURE OF THE NEW MIDDLE CLASS

The best examples of this new urban fiction are the works of Saikaku (1642–1693), considered to be one of Japan's greatest novelists. Saikaku's greatest novel, *Five Women Who Loved Love*, relates the amorous exploits of five women of the merchant class. Based partly on real-life experiences, it broke from the Confucian ethic of wifely fidelity to her husband and portrayed women who were willing to die for love—and all but one eventually did. Despite the tragic circumstances, the tone of the novel is upbeat and sometimes comic, as the author's wry comments prevent the reader from becoming emotionally involved with the heroines' misfortunes. After all, they are experiencing a unique passionate love, and death is but a small price to pay for ecstasy.

❀ **THE FLOATING WORLD OF EDO.**   In eighteenth-century Japan, the self-confidence of the newly affluent bourgeoisie expressed itself in the woodblock print. Many prints portrayed "the floating world," as the pleasure district in Edo was called. Seen here are courtesans, storytellers, jesters, and various other entertainers. Like their counterparts in Europe, city-dwellers in Japan were beginning to create a new popular culture distinct from the elite culture of the nobility.

In addition to heterosexual novels for the merchant class, Saikaku wrote of homosexual liaisons among the samurai.

In the theater, the rise of *kabuki* threatened the long dominance of the *no* play, replacing the somewhat restrained and elegant thematic and stylistic approach of the classical drama with a new emphasis on violence, music, and dramatic gestures. Significantly, the new drama emerged not from the rarefied world of the court but from the new world of entertainment and amusement. Its very commercial success, however, led to difficulties with the government, which periodically attempted to restrict or even suppress it. Early *kabuki* was often performed by prostitutes and depicted the increasingly popular "floating world" of brothels, teahouses, and dance halls that began to proliferate in the growing cities. Shogunate officials feared that such activities could have a corrupting effect on the nation's morals and prohibited women from appearing on the stage; at the same time, they attempted to create a new professional class of male actors to impersonate female characters on stage. The decree had a mixed effect, however, because it encouraged homosexual activities, which had been popular among the samurai and in Buddhist monasteries since medieval times. Yet the use of male actors also promoted a greater emphasis on physical activities such as acrobatics and swordplay and furthered the evolution of *kabuki* into a mature dramatic art.

In contrast to the popular literature of the Tokugawa period, poetry persevered in its more serious tradition. Although linked verse, so popular in the fourteenth and fifteenth centuries, found a more lighthearted expression in the sixteenth century, the most exquisite poetry was produced in the seventeenth century by the greatest of all Japanese poets, Basho (1644–1694). He was concerned with the search for the meaning of existence and the poetic expression of his experience. Basho's genius lies in his sudden juxtaposition of a general or eternal condition with an immediate perception, an electrical spark that instantly reveals a moment of truth. With his love of Daoism and Zen Buddhism, Basho found answers to his quest for the meaning of life in nature, and his poems are grounded in seasonal imagery. The following are among his most famous poems:

> *The ancient pond*
> *A frog leaps in*
> *The sound of the water.*
>
> *On the withered branch*
> *A crow has alighted—*
> *The end of autumn.*

His last poem, dictated to a disciple only three days prior to his death, succinctly expressed his frustration with the unfinished business of life:

> *On a journey, ailing—*
> *my dreams roam about*
> *on a withered moor.*

✿ **A JAPANESE CASTLE.** In imitation of European castle architecture, the Japanese perfected a new type of fortress-palace in the early seventeenth century. Strategically placed high on a hilltop, constructed of heavy stone with tiny windows and fortified by numerous watchtowers and massive walls, these strongholds were impregnable to arrows and catapults. They served as a residence for the local daimyo, while the castle compound also housed his army and contained the seat of the local government. Himeji castle, shown here, is one of the most beautiful in Japan.

Like all great artists, Basho made his poems appear effortless and simple. He speaks directly to everyone, everywhere.

TOKUGAWA ART

Art also reflected the dynamism and changes in Japanese culture under the Tokugawa regime. The shogun's order that all daimyo and their families live every other year in Edo set off a burst of building as provincial rulers competed to erect the most magnificent mansion. Furthermore, the shoguns themselves constructed splendid castles adorned with sumptuous, almost ostentatious decor and furnishings. Lastly, the prosperity of the newly rising merchant class added fuel to the fire. Japanese paintings, architecture, textiles, and ceramics all flourished during this affluent era.

Court painters filled magnificent multipaneled screens with gold foil, which was also used to cover walls and even ceilings. This lavish use of gold foil mirrored the grandeur of the new Japanese rulers but also served a practical purpose: it reflected light in the dark castle rooms, where windows were kept small for defensive purposes. In contrast to the almost gaudy splendors of court painting, however, some Japanese artists of the late sixteenth century returned to the tradition of black ink wash. No longer copying the Chinese, these masterpieces expressed Japanese themes and techniques. In *Pine Forest* by Tohaku, a pair of six-panel screens depicting pine trees, 85 percent of the paper is left blank, suggesting mist and the quiet of an autumn dawn.

Although Japan was isolated from the Western world during much of the Tokugawa era, Japanese art was enriched by ideas from other cultures. Japanese pottery makers borrowed both techniques and designs from Korea to produce handsome ceramics. The passion for "Dutch learning" inspired Japanese to study Western medicine, astronomy, and languages and also led to experimentation with oil painting and Western ideas of perspective and the interplay of light and dark. Some painters depicted the "southern barbarians," with their strange ships and costumes, large noses, and plumed hats. Europeans desired Japanese lacquerware and metalwork, inlaid with ivory and mother-of-pearl, and especially the ceramics, which were now as highly prized as those of the Chinese.

Perhaps the most famous of all Japanese art of the Tokugawa era is the woodblock print. Genre painting, or representations of daily life, began in the sixteenth century and found its new mass-produced form in the eighteenth-century woodblock print. The now literate mercantile class was eager for illustrated texts of the amusing and bawdy tales that had circulated in oral tradition. At first, these prints were done in black and white, but later they included vibrant colors. The self-confidence of the age is dramatically captured in these prints, which represent a collective self-portrait of the late Tokugawa urban classes. Some prints depict entire city blocks filled with people, trades, and festivals, while others show the interiors of houses; thus, they provide us with excellent visual documentation of the times. Others portray the "floating world" of the entertainment quarter, with scenes of carefree revelers enjoying the pleasures of life.

One of the most renowned of the numerous block-print artists was Utamaro (1754–1806), who painted erotic and sardonic women in everyday poses, such as walking down the street, cooking, or drying their bodies after a bath. Hokusai (1760–1849) was famous for *Thirty-Six Views of Mount Fuji*, which created a new and bold interpretation of the Japanese landscape. Finally, Hiroshige (1797–1858) developed the genre of the travelogue print in his *Fifty-Three Stages of the Tokaido Highway*, which presented ordinary scenes of daily life, both in the country and in the cities, all enveloped in a lyrical, quiet mood.

Why did a new popular culture begin to appear in Tokugawa Japan, while traditional values continued to prevail in neighboring China? Certainly, one factor was the rapid growth of the cities as the main point of convergence for all the dynamic forces taking place in Japanese society. But other factors may have been at work as well. Despite the patent efforts of the Tokugawa rulers to promote traditional Confucian values, Confucian doctrine had historically occupied a relatively weak position in Japanese society. In China the scholar-gentry class served as the traditional defenders and propagators of traditional orthodoxy, but the samurai, who were steeped in warrior values and had little exposure to Confucian learning, did not play a similar role in Japan. Tokugawa policies also contributed. Whereas the scholar-gentry class in Qing China continued to reside in the villages, serving as members of the local council or as instructors in local schools, the samurai class in Japan was deliberately isolated by government fiat and class privilege from the remainder of the population. The result was an ideological and cultural vacuum that would eventually be filled by the growing population of merchants and artisans in the major cities.

KOREA: THE HERMIT KINGDOM

While Japan was gradually moving away from its agrarian origins, the Yi dynasty in Korea was attempting to pattern its own society on the Chinese model. The dynasty had been founded by the military commander Yi Song Gye in the late fourteenth century and immediately set out to establish close political and cultural relations with the Ming dynasty. From their new capital at Seoul, located on the Han River in the center of the peninsula, the Yi rulers accepted a tributary relationship with their powerful neighbor and engaged in the wholesale adoption of Chinese institutions and values. As in China, the civil service examinations tested candidates on their knowledge of the Confucian classics, and success was viewed as an essential step toward upward mobility.

There were differences, however. As in Japan, the dynasty continued to restrict entry into the bureaucracy to members of the aristocratic class, known in Korea as the *yangban* (or "two groups," the civilian and military). At the same time, the peasantry remained in virtually serflike conditions, working on government estates or on the manor holdings of the landed elite. A class of slaves (*chonmin*) labored on government plantations or served in certain occupations, such as butchers and entertainers, considered beneath the dignity of other groups in the population.

Eventually, Korean society began to show signs of independence from Chinese orthodoxy. In the fifteenth century, a phonetic alphabet for writing the Korean spoken language (*hangul*) was devised. Although it was initially held in contempt by the elites and used primarily as a teaching device, eventually it became the medium for private correspondence and the publishing of fictional stories for a popular audience. At the same time, changes were taking place in the economy, where rising agricultural production contributed to a population increase and the appearance of a small urban industrial and commercial sector, and in society, where the long domination of the *yangban* class began to weaken. As their numbers increased and their power and influence declined, some *yangban* became merchants or even moved into the ranks of the peasantry, thus further blurring the distinction between the aristocratic class and the common people.

In general, Korean rulers tried to keep the country isolated from the outside world, but they were not always successful. The Japanese invasion under Toyotomi Hideyoshi in the late sixteenth century had a disastrous impact on Korean society. A Manchu force invaded northern Korea in the 1630s and eventually compelled the Yi dynasty to grant allegiance to the new imperial government in Beijing. Korea was relatively untouched by the arrival of European merchants and missionaries, although information about Christianity was brought to the peninsula by Koreans returning from tribute missions to China, and a small Catholic community was established there in the late eighteenth century.

CONCLUSION

When Christopher Columbus sailed from southern Spain in his three ships in August of 1492, he was seeking a route to China and Japan. He did not find it, but others soon

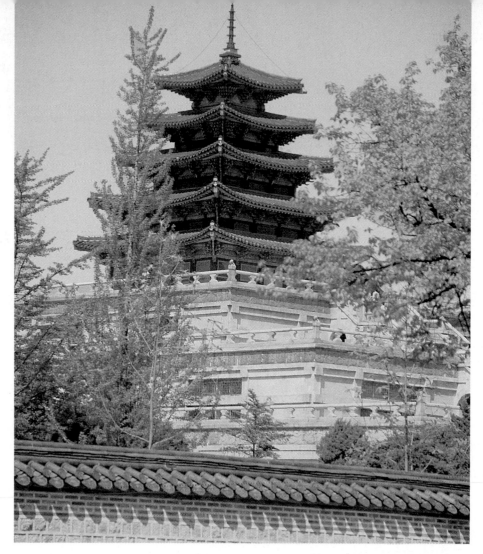

✿ SEOUL PALACE PAGODA.
When the Yi dynasty came into power in
the late fourteenth century, it established
its capital at Seoul on the Han River.
There it constructed a new palace.
Korean public architecture was highly
influenced by the Chinese classical
model, as the multitiered pagoda on the
palace grounds attests.

did. In 1514, Portuguese ships arrived on the coast of southern China. Thirty years later, a small contingent of Portuguese merchants became the first Europeans to set foot on the islands of Japan.

At first the new arrivals were welcomed, if only as curiosities. Eventually, several European nations established trade relations with China and Japan, and Christian missionaries of various religious orders were active in both countries and in Korea as well. But their success was short-lived. Europeans eventually began to appear as a detriment to law and order, and during the seventeenth century, the majority of the foreign merchants and missionaries were evicted from all three countries. From that time until the middle of the nineteenth century, China, Japan, and Korea were relatively little affected by events taking place beyond their borders.

For long, that fact has deluded many observers into the assumption that the societies of East Asia were essentially stagnant, characterized by agrarian institutions and values reminiscent of those of the feudal era in Europe. As we have seen, however, that picture is misleading, for all three countries were changing and by the early nineteenth century were quite different from what they had been three centuries earlier.

Ironically, these changes were especially marked in Tokugawa Japan, an allegedly "closed country," where traditional classes and institutions were under increasing strain, not only from the emergence of a new merchant class, but also from the centralizing tendencies of the powerful Tokugawa shogunate. Some historians have seen strong parallels between Tokugawa Japan and early modern Europe, which gave birth to centralized empires and a strong merchant class during the same period. The image of the monarchy is reflected in a song sung at the shrine of Toyotomi Hideyoshi in Kyoto:

> Who's that
> Holding over four hundred provinces
> In the palm of his hand
> And entertaining at a tea-party?
> It's His Highness
> So mighty, so impressive![14]

By the beginning of the nineteenth century, then, powerful tensions, reflecting a growing gap between ideal and reality, were at work in both Chinese and Japanese society. Under these conditions, both countries were soon forced to face a new challenge from the aggressive power of an industrializing Europe.

1400	1450	1500	1550	1600	1650	1700	1750	1800

Rise of Ming dynasty

Phonetic alphabet for Korean language devised

Manchus seize China

Reign of Qianlong

Reign of Kangxi

White Lotus Rebellion

Rule of Oda Nobunaga

Rule of Tokugawa Ieyasu

European post established in Korea

Rule of Toyotomi Hideyoshi

Christian uprising suppressed

Voyage of Zhenghe

Portuguese arrive in southern China

Portuguese sailors land in Japan

Christian missionaries expelled from Japan

First English trading post at Canton

CHAPTER NOTES

1. From Jonathan D. Spence, *Emperor of China: Self-Portrait of K'ang Hsi* (New York, 1974), pp. 143–44.
2. Quoted in J. H. Parry, ed., *The European Reconnaissance: Selected Documents* (New York, 1968), p. 129.
3. Richard Strassberg, *The World of K'ang Shang-jen: A Man of Letters in Early Ch'ing China* (New York, 1983), p. 275.
4. Quoted in Frederick Wakeman, Jr., *The Great Enterprise* (Berkeley, Calif., 1985), p. 16.
5. Lynn Struve, *The Southern Ming, 1644–1662* (New Haven, Conn., 1984), p. 61.
6. Jonathan D. Spence, *The Search for Modern China* (New York, 1990), p. 123, citing J. L. Cranmer-Byng, *An Embassy to China: Lord MacArtney's Journal, 1793–1794* (London, 1912), p. 340.
7. Daniel J. Boorstin, *The Discoverers: A History of Man's Search to Know His World and Himself* (New York, 1983), p. 63.
8. Parry, *The European Reconnaissance*, citing C. R. Boxer, ed., *South China in the Sixteenth Century* (London, 1953), p. 265.
9. Chie Nakane and Sinzaburo Oishi, eds., *Tokugawa Japan* (Tokyo, 1990), p. 14.
10. Quoted in Jurgis Elisonas, "Christianity and the daimyo," in John Whitney Hall, ed., *The Cambridge History of Japan*, vol. 4 (Cambridge, 1991), p. 360.
11. Engelbert Kaempfer, *The History of Japan: Together with a Description of the Kingdom of Siam, 1690–1692*, vol. 2 (Glasgow, 1906), pp. 173–74.
12. Parry, *The European Reconnaissance*, p. 144.
13. Quoted in Donald Keene, *The Japanese Discovery of Europe, 1720–1830*, rev. ed. (Stanford, Calif., 1969), p. 114.
14. Quoted in Ryusaku Tsunda et al., *Sources of Japanese Tradition* (New York, 1964), p. 313.

SUGGESTED READINGS

For a general overview of this period in East Asian history, see J. K. Fairbank, E. O. Reischauer, and A. Craig, *East Asia: Tradition and Transformation* (Boston, 1973), and C. Shirokauer, *A Brief History of Chinese and Japanese Civilizations*, 2d ed. (San Diego, 1989). A more detailed treatment of specific issues can be found in volumes 8 and 9 of F. W. Mote and D. Twitchett, eds., *The Cambridge History of China* (Cambridge, 1976), and J. W. Hall, ed., *The Cambridge History of Japan*, vol. 4 (Cambridge, 1991).

The best documentary surveys are W. T. de Bary, *Sources of Chinese Tradition* (New York, 1964), and R. Tsunoda, W. T. de Bary, and D. Keene, *Sources of Japanese Tradition* (New York, 1958). Also, see F. Schurmann and O. Schell, *The China Reader*, vol. 1 (New York, 1967). Early documents on European activities can be found in J. H. Parry, *The European Reconnaissance: Selected Documents* (New York, 1968).

On the late Ming, see J. D. Spence, *The Search for Modern China* (New York, 1990), and L. Struve, *The Southern Ming, 1644–1662*

(New Haven, Conn., 1984). On the rise of the Qing, see F. Wakeman, Jr., *The Great Enterprise: The Manchu Reconstruction of Imperial Order in Seventeenth Century China* (Berkeley, Calif., 1985). On Kangxi, see J. D. Spence, *Emperor of China: Self-Portrait of K'ang Hsi* (New York, 1974). Social issues are discussed in S. Naquin and E. Rawski, *Chinese Society in the Eighteenth Century* (New Haven, Conn., 1987). Also, see J. D. Spence and J. Wills, eds., *From Ming to Ch'ing* (New Haven, Conn., 1979). For a very interesting account of Jesuit missionary experiences in China, see L. J. Gallagher, ed. and trans., *China in the Sixteenth Century: The Journals of Matthew Ricci, 1583–1616* (New York, 1953). For brief biographies of Ming-Qing luminaries such as Wang Yangming, Zheng Chenggong, and the Emperor Qianlong, see J. E. Wills, Jr., *Mountains of Fame: Portraits in Chinese History* (Princeton, N.J., 1994).

The best surveys of Chinese literature are Liu Wu-chi, *An Introduction to Chinese Literature* (Bloomington, Ind., 1966); S. Owen, *An Anthology of Chinese Literature: Beginnings to 1911* (New York,

1996); and V. Mair, *The Columbia Anthology of Traditional Chinese Literature* (New York, 1994). For a concise and comprehensive introduction to the Chinese art of this period, see M. Sullivan, *The Arts of China*, 4th ed. (Berkeley, Calif., 1999); C. Clunas, *Art in China* (Oxford, 1997); and M. Tregear, *Chinese Art*, rev. ed. (London, 1997). For the best introduction to the painting of this era, see J. Cahill, *Chinese Painting* (New York, 1977), and Yang Xin et al., *Three Thousand Years of Chinese Paintings* (New Haven, Conn., 1997).

On Japan before the rise of the Tokugawa, see J. W. Hall, et al., eds., *Japan Before Tokugawa: Political Consolidation and Economic Growth* (Princeton, N.J., 1981), and G. Elison and B. L. Smith, eds., *Warlords, Artists, and Commoners: Japan in the Sixteenth Century* (Honolulu, 1981). See also M. E. Berry, *Hideyoshi* (Cambridge, Mass., 1982), the first biography of this fascinating figure in Japanese history. On the first Christian activities, see G. Elison, *Deus Destroyed: The Image of Christianity in Early Modern Japan* (Cambridge, Mass., 1973), and C. R. Boxer, *The Christian Century in Japan, 1549–1650* (Berkeley, Calif., 1951). Buddhism is dealt with in N. McMullin, *Buddhism and the State in Sixteenth Century Japan* (Princeton, N.J., 1984).

On the Tokugawa, see H. Bolitho, *Treasures Among Men: The Fudai Daimyo in Tokugawa Japan* (New Haven, Conn., 1974), and R. B. Toby, *State and Diplomacy in Early Modern Japan: Asia in the Development of the Tokugawa Bakufu* (Princeton, N.J., 1984). See also R. N. Bellah, *Tokugawa Religion: The Values of Pre-Industrial Japan* (New York, 1957). For a provocative interpretation of this period, see J. W. Dower, ed., *The Origins of the Meiji State: Selected Writings of E. H. Norman* (New York, 1975). See also C. I. Mulhern, ed., *Heroic with Grace: Legendary Women of Japan* (Armonk, N.Y., 1991). Three other recent studies are S. Vlastos, *Peasant Protests and Uprisings in Tokugawa Japan* (Berkeley, Calif., 1986); H. Ooms, *Tokugawa Ideology: Early Constructs, 1570–1680* (Princeton, N.J., 1985); and C. Nakane, ed., *Tokugawa Japan: The Social and Economic Antecedents of Modern Japan* (Tokyo, 1990).

For a brief introduction to women in the Ming and Qing dynasties as well as the Tokugawa era, see S. Hughes and B. Hughes, *Women in World History*, vol. 2 (Armonk, N.Y., 1997). To witness Chinese village life in 1670, consult the classic J. Spence, *The Death of Woman Wang* (New York, 1978). For women's literacy in seventeenth-century China, see J. Handlin, "Lu K'un's New Audience: The Influence of Women's Literacy on Sixteenth Century Thought," in *Women in Chinese Society*, eds. M. Wolf and R. Witke (Stanford, Calif., 1975), and D. Ko's, *Teachers of the Inner Chambers: Women and Culture in Seventeenth Century China* (Stanford, Calif., 1994). Most valuable is the collection of articles edited by G. L. Bernstein, *Recreating Japanese Women, 1600–1945* (Berkeley, Calif., 1991). For the role of peasant women in social protests, consult A. Walthall "Devoted Wives/Unruly Women: Invisible Presence in the History of Japanese Social Protest," in *Signs: Journal of Women in Culture and Society*, 1994, vol. 20, no. 1.

Of specific interest to Japanese literature of the Tokugawa era are D. Keene, *World Within Walls: Japanese Literature of the Pre-Modern Era, 1600–1867* (New York, 1976). Of special value for the college student are D. Keene's *Anthology of Japanese Literature* (New York, 1955), *The Pleasures of Japanese Literature* (New York, 1988), and *Japanese Literature: An Introduction for Western Readers* (London, 1953). For an introduction to Basho's life, poems, and criticism, consult the stimulating *Basho and His Interpreters: Selected Hokku with Commentary* (Stanford, Calif., 1991), by M. Ueda.

For the most comprehensive and accessible overview of Japanese art, see P. Mason, *Japanese Art* (New York, 1993). For a concise introduction to Japanese art of the Tokugawa era, see J. Stanley-Baker, *Japanese Art* (London, 1984). For magnificent photographs and stimulating interpretation, consult D. and V. Elisseeff, *Art of Japan* (New York, 1985), and J. E. Kidder, Jr., *The Art of Japan* (London, 1985).

INFOTRAC COLLEGE EDITION

For additional reading, go to InfoTrac College Edition, your online research library at http://web1.infotrac-college.com

Enter the search terms "Ming China" using Keywords.

Enter the search terms "China history" using Keywords.

Enter the search terms "Japan history" using Keywords.

Enter the search term "Tokugawa" using Keywords.

Enter the search term "Qing" using Keywords.

CHAPTER

18

TOWARD A NEW HEAVEN AND A NEW EARTH: AN INTELLECTUAL REVOLUTION IN THE WEST

CHAPTER OUTLINE

- THE SCIENTIFIC REVOLUTION
- THE ENLIGHTENMENT
- CULTURE AND SOCIETY IN AN AGE OF ENLIGHTENMENT
- RELIGION AND THE CHURCHES
- CONCLUSION

FOCUS QUESTIONS

- What did Copernicus, Kepler, Galileo, and Newton contribute to a new vision of the universe, and how did their vision differ from the Ptolemaic conception of the universe?
- Who were the leading figures of the Enlightenment, and what were their main contributions?
- What role did women play in the Scientific Revolution and the Enlightenment?
- How were the ideas of the Scientific Revolution and the Enlightenment disseminated, and what impact did they have on society?
- How did popular culture and popular religion differ from high culture and institutional religion in the eighteenth century?

In 1633, the Italian scientist Galileo was put on trial by the Catholic church for maintaining that the sun was the center of the universe and that the earth moves around the sun. Galileo, who was sixty-eight years old and in ill health, was kept waiting for two months before being tried and found guilty of heresy and disobedience. Completely shattered by the experience, he denounced his errors: "With a sincere heart and unfeigned faith I curse and detest the said errors and heresies contrary to the Holy Church, and I swear that I will nevermore in future say or assert anything that will give rise to a similar suspicion of me." Legend holds that when he left the trial room, Galileo muttered to himself: "And yet it does move!" Galileo was but one of the scientists of the seventeenth century who set the Western world on a new path known as the Scientific Revolution, which brought to Europeans a new way of viewing the universe and their place in it. In time, the Scientific Revolution would add to the European world's growing sense of power as the changes occurring in government, the economy, and military power increasingly enabled Europeans to dominate much of the rest of the world.

The Scientific Revolution affected only a small number of Europe's educated elite. But in the eighteenth century, this changed dramatically as a group of intellectuals known as the philosophes popularized the ideas of the Scientific Revolution and used them to undertake a dramatic reexamination of all aspects of life. The widespread impact of the philosophes' ideas on their society has caused historians ever since to call the eighteenth century in Europe the Age of Enlightenment.

For most of the philosophes, "enlightenment" included the rejection of traditional Christianity. The religious wars and intolerance of the sixteen and seventeenth centuries had created an environment in which intellectuals had become so disgusted with religious fanaticism that they were open to the new ideas of the Scientific Revolution. Whereas the great scientists of the seventeenth century believed that their work exalted God, the intellectuals of the eighteenth century read their conclusions a different way and increasingly turned their backs on their Christian heritage. Consequently, European intellectual life in the eighteenth century was marked by a revolutionary transition to the largely secular, rational, and materialistic perspective that in the nineteenth and twentieth centuries defined the modern Western mentality and dramatically affected much of the rest of the world as well. ❂

THE SCIENTIFIC REVOLUTION

In one sense, the Scientific Revolution was not a revolution. It was not characterized by the explosive change and rapid overthrow of traditional authority that we normally associate with the word *revolution*. The Scientific Revolution did overturn centuries of authority, but only in a gradual and piecemeal fashion.

Background to the Scientific Revolution

To say that the Scientific Revolution brought about a dissolution of the medieval worldview is not to say that the Middle Ages was a period of scientific ignorance. Many educated Europeans took an intense interest in the world around them because it was, after all, "God's handiwork" and therefore an appropriate subject for study. Many "natural philosophers," as medieval scientists were called, placed unquestioning reliance on a few ancient authorities, especially Aristotle and Galen, and preferred refined logical analysis to systematic observations of the natural world. A number of changes and advances in the fifteenth and sixteenth centuries may have played a major role in helping "natural philosophers" abandon their old views and develop new ones.

The Renaissance humanists mastered Greek as well as Latin and made available new works of Galen, Ptolemy, and Archimedes as well as Plato. These writings made it apparent that even the unquestioned authorities of the Middle Ages, Aristotle and Galen, had been contradicted by other thinkers. The desire to discover which school of thought was correct stimulated new scientific work that sometimes led to a complete rejection of the classical authorities.

Renaissance artists have also been credited with having an impact on scientific study. Their desire to imitate nature led them to rely on a close observation of nature. Their accurate renderings of rocks, plants, animals, and human anatomy established new standards for the study of natural phenomena. At the same time, the "scientific" study of the problems of perspective and correct anatomical proportions led to new insights. "No painter," one Renaissance intellectual declared, "can paint well without a thorough knowledge of geometry."[1]

Technical problems, such as calculating the tonnage of ships accurately, also stimulated scientific activity because they required careful observation and precise measurements. Then, too, the invention of new instruments and machines, such as the telescope and microscope, often made fresh scientific discoveries possible. Above all, the printing press played a crucial role in spreading innovative ideas quickly and easily.

Mathematics, which played such a fundamental role in the scientific achievements of the sixteenth and seventeenth centuries, was promoted in the Renaissance by the rediscovery of the works of ancient mathematicians and the influence of Plato, who had emphasized the importance of mathematics in explaining the universe. During the Renaissance, mathematics was not only applauded as the key to navigation, military science, and geography, but was also widely believed to be the key to

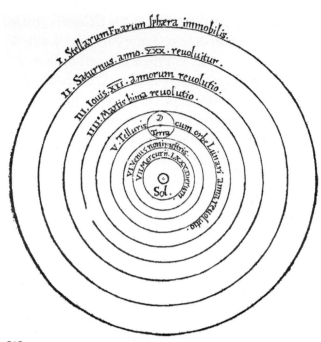

✿ **MEDIEVAL CONCEPTION OF THE UNIVERSE.** As this sixteenth-century illustration shows, the medieval cosmological view placed the earth at the center of the universe, surrounded by a series of concentric spheres. The earth was imperfect and constantly changing, while the heavenly bodies that surrounded it were perfect and incorruptible. Beyond the tenth and final sphere was heaven, where God and all the saved souls were located.

✿ **THE COPERNICAN SYSTEM.** The Copernican system was presented in *On the Revolutions of the Heavenly Spheres*, published shortly before Copernicus's death. As shown in this illustration from the first edition of the book, Copernicus maintained that the sun was the center of the universe while the planets, including the earth, revolved around it. Moreover, the earth rotated daily on its axis.

understanding the nature of things. According to Leonardo da Vinci, God eternally geometrizes, so nature is inherently mathematical. Copernicus, Kepler, Galileo, and Newton were all great mathematicians who believed that the secrets of nature were written in the language of mathematics.

Another possible contributor to the origins of the Scientific Revolution was magic. Renaissance magic was the preserve of an intellectual elite from all of Europe. By the end of the sixteenth century, Hermetic magic had fused with alchemical thought to form a single intellectual framework. According to this tradition, the world was a living embodiment of divinity. Humans, who were also thought to have that spark of divinity within, could use magic, especially mathematical magic, to understand and dominate the world of nature or employ the powers of nature for beneficial purposes. Was it Hermeticism, then, that inaugurated the shift in consciousness that made the Scientific Revolution possible, since the desire to control and dominate the natural world was a crucial motivating force in the Scientific Revolution? Scholars debate the issue, but histories of the Scientific Revolution frequently overlook the fact that the great names we associate with the revolution in cosmology—Copernicus,

Kepler, Galileo, and Newton—all had a serious interest in Hermetic ideas and the fields of astrology and alchemy. The mention of these names also reminds us of one final consideration in the origins of the Scientific Revolution: it largely resulted from the work of a handful of great intellectuals.

Toward a New Heaven: A Revolution in Astronomy

The philosophers of the Middle Ages had used the ideas of Aristotle, Claudius Ptolemy (the greatest astronomer of antiquity, who lived in the second century C.E.), and Christianity to construct the Ptolemaic or geocentric conception of the universe. In this conception, the universe was seen as a series of concentric spheres with a fixed or motionless earth at its center. Composed of material substance, the earth was imperfect and constantly changing. The spheres that surrounded the earth were made of a crystalline, transparent substance and moved in circular orbits around the earth. Circular movement, according to Aristotle, was the most "perfect" kind of motion and hence appropriate for the "perfect" heavenly bodies, which were thought to consist of a nonmaterial, incorruptible "quin-

ON THE REVOLUTIONS OF THE HEAVENLY SPHERES

Nicolaus Copernicus began a revolution in astronomy when he argued that the sun, not the earth, was at the center of the universe. Expecting controversy and scorn, Copernicus hesitated to publish the work in which he put forth his heliocentric theory. He finally relented, however, and managed to see a copy of it just before he died.

NICOLAUS COPERNICUS, ON THE REVOLUTIONS OF THE HEAVENLY SPHERES

For a long time, then, I reflected on this confusion in the astronomical traditions concerning the derivation of the motions of the universe's spheres. I began to be annoyed that the movements of the world machine, created for our sake by the best and most systematic Artisan of all, were not understood with greater certainty by the philosophers, who otherwise examined so precisely the most insignificant trifles of this world. For this reason I undertook the task of rereading the works of all the philosophers which I could obtain to learn whether anyone had ever proposed other motions of the universe's spheres than those expounded by the teachers of astronomy in the schools. And in fact first I found in Cicero that Hicetas supposed the earth to move. Later I also discovered in Plutarch that certain others were of this opinion. I have decided to set his words down here, so that they may be available to everybody.

Some think that the earth remains at rest. But Philolaus the Pythagorean believes that, like the sun and moon, it revolves around the fire in an oblique circle. Heraclides of Pontus and Ecphantus the Pythagorean make the earth move, not in a progressive motion, but like a wheel in a rotation from the west to east about its own center.

Therefore, having obtained the opportunity from these sources, I too began to consider the mobility of the earth. And even though the idea seemed absurd, nevertheless I knew that others before me had been granted the freedom to imagine any circles whatever for the purpose of explaining the heavenly phenomena. Hence I thought that I too would be readily permitted to ascertain whether explanations sounder than those of my predecessors could be found for the revolution of the celestial spheres on the assumption of some motion of the earth.

Having thus assumed the motions which I ascribe to the earth later on in the volume, by long and intense study I finally found that if the motions of the other planets are correlated with the orbiting of the earth, and are computed for the revolution of each planet, not only do their phenomena follow therefrom but also the order and size of all the planets and spheres, and heaven itself is so linked together that in no portion of it can anything be shifted without disrupting the remaining parts and the universe as a whole. . . .

Hence I feel no shame in asserting that this whole region engirdled by the moon, and the center of the earth, traverse this grand circle amid the rest of the planets in an annual revolution around the sun. Near the sun is the center of the universe. Moreover, since the sun remains stationary, whatever appears as a motion of the sun is really due rather to the motion of the earth.

---

tessence." These heavenly bodies, pure orbs of light, were embedded in the moving, concentric spheres and in 1500 numbered ten. Working outward from the earth, the first eight spheres contained the moon, Mercury, Venus, the sun, Mars, Jupiter, Saturn, and the fixed stars. The ninth sphere imparted to the eighth sphere of the fixed stars its daily motion, while the tenth sphere was frequently described as the prime mover that moved itself and imparted motion to the other spheres. Beyond the tenth sphere was the Empyrean Heaven—the location of God and all the saved souls. This Christianized Ptolemaic universe, then, was a finite one. It had a fixed end in harmony with Christian thought and expectations. God and the saved souls were at one end of the universe, while humans were at the center. They had been given power over the earth, but their real purpose was to achieve salvation.

In May 1543, shortly before his death, Nicolaus Copernicus (1473–1543), who had studied mathematics and astronomy first at Cracow in his native Poland and later at the Italian universities of Bologna and Padua, published his famous book *On the Revolutions of the Heavenly Spheres*. Copernicus was a mathematician who felt that Ptolemy's geocentric system was too complicated and failed to accord with the observed motions of the heavenly bodies (see the box above). Copernicus hoped that his heliocentric or sun-centered conception would offer a more accurate explanation.

Copernicus argued that the universe consisted of eight spheres with the sun motionless at the center and the sphere of the fixed stars at rest in the eighth sphere. The planets revolved around the sun in the order of Mercury, Venus, the earth, Mars, Jupiter, and Saturn. The moon, however, revolved around the earth. Moreover, according to Copernicus, what appeared to be the movement of the sun and the fixed stars around the earth was really explained by the daily rotation of the earth on its axis and

THE STARRY MESSENGER

The Italian Galileo Galilei was the first European to use a telescope to make systematic observations of the heavens. His observations, as reported in The Starry Messenger in 1610, stunned European intellectuals by revealing that the celestial bodies were not perfect and immutable, as had been believed, but were apparently composed of material substance similar to the earth. In this selection, Galileo describes how he devised a telescope and what he saw with it.

GALILEO GALILEI, THE STARRY MESSENGER

About ten months ago a report reached my ears that a certain Fleming had constructed a spyglass by means of which visible objects, though very distant from the eye of the observer, were distinctly seen as if nearby. Of this truly remarkable effect several experiences were related, to which some persons gave credence while others denied them. A few days later the report was confirmed to me in a letter from a noble Frenchman at Paris, Jacques Badovere, which caused me to apply myself wholeheartedly to inquire into the means by which I might arrive at the invention of a similar instrument. This I did shortly afterwards, my basis being the theory of refraction. First I prepared a tube of lead, at the ends of which I fitted two glass lenses, both plane on one side while on the other side one was spherically convex and the other concave. Then placing my eye near the concave lens I perceived objects satisfactorily large and near, for they appeared three times closer and nine times larger than when seen with the naked eye alone. Next I constructed another one, more accurate, which represented objects as enlarged more than sixty times. Finally, sparing neither labor nor expense, I succeeded in constructing for myself so excellent an instrument that objects seen by means of it appeared nearly one thousand times larger and over thirty times closer than when regarded with our natural vision.

It would be superfluous to enumerate the number and importance of the advantages of such an instrument at sea as well as on land. But forsaking terrestrial observations, I turned to celestial ones, and first I saw the moon from as near at hand as if it were scarcely two terrestrial radii. After that I observed often with wondering delight both the planets and the fixed stars, and since I saw these latter to be very crowded, I began to seek (and eventually found) a method by which I might measure their distances apart. . . .

Now let us review the observations made during the past two months, once more inviting the attention of all who are eager for true philosophy to the first steps of such important contemplations. Let us speak first of that surface of the moon which faces us. For greater clarity I distinguish two parts of this surface, a lighter and a darker; the lighter part seems to surround and to pervade the whole hemisphere, while the darker part discolors the moon's surface like a kind of cloud, and makes it appear covered with spots. . . . From observation of these spots repeated many times I have been led to the opinion and conviction that the surface of the moon is not smooth, uniform, and precisely spherical as a great number of philosophers believe it (and the other heavenly bodies) to be, but is uneven, rough, and full of cavities and prominences, being not unlike the face of the earth, relieved by chains of mountains and deep valleys.

the journey of the earth around the sun each year. Copernicus, however, was basically conservative. He did not reject Aristotle's principle of the existence of heavenly spheres moving in circular orbits, and his system did not work considerably better than the Ptolemaic system.

The immediate response to Copernicus was muted—no revolution occurred overnight. Nevertheless, although most people were not yet ready to accept his theory, there were growing doubts about the Ptolemaic system. The next step in destroying the geocentric conception and supporting the Copernican system was taken by Johannes Kepler (1571–1630).

Kepler was a brilliant mathematician and astronomer who took a post as imperial mathematician to Emperor Rudolf II. Using the detailed astronomical data compiled by his predecessor, the astronomer Tycho Brahe, Kepler arrived at his laws of planetary motion that confirmed Copernicus's heliocentric theory. In his first law, however, he contradicted Copernicus by showing that the orbits of the planets around the sun were not circular but elliptical in shape with the sun at one focus of the ellipse rather than at the center.

Kepler's work effectively eliminated the idea of uniform circular motion as well as the idea of crystalline spheres revolving in circular orbits. The basic structure of the traditional Ptolemaic system had been destroyed, and people had been freed to think in new terms of the actual paths of planets revolving around the sun in elliptical orbits. By the end of Kepler's life, the Ptolemaic system was rapidly losing ground to the new ideas. Important questions remained unanswered, however. What were the planets made of? And how could motion in the universe be explained? It was an Italian scientist who achieved the next important breakthrough to a new cosmology by answering the first question.

Galileo Galilei (1564–1642) taught mathematics, first at Pisa and later at Padua, one of the most prestigious universities in Europe. Galileo was the first European to make systematic observations of the heavens by means of a telescope, thereby inaugurating a new age in astronomy. He had heard of a Flemish lens grinder who had created a "spyglass" that magnified objects seen at a distance and soon constructed his own after reading about it. Instead of peering at terrestrial objects, Galileo turned his telescope to the skies and made a remarkable series of discoveries: mountains on the moon, four moons revolving around Jupiter, the phases of Venus, and sunspots. Galileo's observations seemed to destroy yet another aspect of the geocentric conception in that the universe seemed to be composed of material substance similar to that of the earth rather than ethereal or perfect and unchanging substance.

Galileo's revelations, published in *The Starry Messenger* in 1610, stunned his contemporaries and probably did more to make Europeans aware of the new picture of the universe than did the mathematical theories of Copernicus and Kepler (see the box on p. 520). But even in the midst of his newfound acclaim, Galileo found himself increasingly suspect by the authorities of the Catholic church. The Roman Inquisition (or Holy Office) of the Catholic church condemned Copernicanism and ordered Galileo to abandon the Copernican thesis. The church attacked the Copernican system because it threatened not only Scripture, but also an entire conception of the universe. The heavens were no longer a spiritual world, but a world of matter. Humans were no longer at the center and God was no longer in a specific place. The new system raised such uncertainties that it seemed prudent simply to condemn it. In 1633, Galileo was found guilty of teaching the condemned Copernican system and was forced to recant his errors. Placed under house arrest on his estate near Florence, he spent the remaining eight years of his life studying mechanics, a field in which he made significant contributions.

The condemnation of Galileo by the Inquisition seriously hampered further scientific work in Italy, which had been at the forefront of scientific innovation. Leadership in science now passed to the northern countries, especially England, France, and the Dutch Netherlands. By the 1630s and 1640s, no reasonable astronomer could overlook that Galileo's discoveries combined with Kepler's mathematical laws had made nonsense of the Ptolemaic-Aristotelian world system and clearly established the reasonableness of the Copernican model. Nevertheless, the problem of explaining motion in the universe and tying together the ideas of Copernicus, Galileo, and Kepler had not yet been solved. This would be the work of an Englishman who has long been considered the greatest genius of the Scientific Revolution.

Born in 1642, the young Isaac Newton showed little brilliance until he attended Cambridge University. In 1669, he accepted a chair of mathematics at the university. During an intense period of creativity from 1684 to 1686, he wrote his major work, *Mathematical Principles of Natural Philosophy*, known simply as the *Principia* by the first word of its

GALILEO'S SKETCH OF THE PHASES OF THE MOON. Galileo Galilei was the first European scientist to use a telescope in making systematic observations of the heavens. Galileo discovered mountains on the moon, sunspots, and the phases of Venus. Shown here are drawings of the moon from Galileo's notes for one of his books.

Latin title. In this work, Newton set out the mathematical proofs demonstrating his universal law of gravitation. Newton's work was the culmination of the theories of Copernicus, Kepler, and Galileo. Although each had undermined some part of the Ptolemaic-Aristotelian cosmology, no one until Newton had pieced together a coherent synthesis for a new cosmology.

In the first book of the *Principia*, Newton defined the basic concepts of mechanics by elaborating the three laws of motion: the law of inertia, that every object continues in a state of rest or uniform motion in a straight line unless deflected by a force; that the rate of change of motion of an object is proportional to the force acting on it; and that to every action there is always an equal and opposite reaction. In Book Three, Newton applied his theories of mechanics to the problems of astronomy by demonstrating that these three laws of motion govern the planetary bodies as well as terrestrial objects. Integral to his whole argument was the use of the universal law of gravitation to explain why the planetary bodies did not go off in straight lines but continued in elliptical orbits about the sun. In mathematical terms, Newton explained that every object in the universe was attracted to every other object by a force called gravity.

The implications of Newton's universal law of gravitation were enormous, although it took another century before they were widely recognized. Newton had demonstrated that one universal law mathematically proved could explain all motion in the universe. The secrets of the natural world could be known by human investigations. At the same time, the Newtonian synthesis created a new cosmology in which the world was seen largely in mechanistic terms. The universe was one huge, regulated, and uniform machine that operated according to natural laws in absolute time, space, and motion. Although Newton believed that God was "everywhere present" and acted as the force that moved all bodies on the basis of the laws he had discovered, later generations dropped his spiritual assumptions. Newton's world-machine, conceived as operating absolutely in space, time, and motion, dominated the modern worldview until the twentieth century, when the Einsteinian revolution based on a concept of relativity superseded the Newtonian mechanistic concept.

The Breakthrough in Medicine

There was also a Scientific Revolution in medicine. Medicine in the Late Middle Ages was dominated by the teachings of the Greek physician Galen, who, like Ptolemy, had lived in the second century C.E. Galen had relied on animal, rather than human, dissection to arrive at a picture of human anatomy that was quite wrong in many instances. Physiology, the study of the functioning of the body, was also dominated by the ideas of Galen, including the belief that there were two separate blood systems: one controlled muscular activities and contained bright red blood moving upward and downward through the arteries; the other governed the digestive functions and contained dark red blood that ebbed and flowed in the veins.

Two major figures are associated with the changes in medicine in the sixteenth and seventeenth centuries: Andreas Vesalius and William Harvey. The new anatomy of the sixteenth century was the work of Andreas Vesalius (1514–1564), who studied medicine at Paris including the works of Galen. Especially important to him was a recently discovered text of Galen, *On Anatomical Procedures*, that led Vesalius to emphasize practical research as the principal avenue for understanding human anatomy. After receiving a doctorate in medicine at the University of Padua in 1536, he accepted a position there as professor of surgery. In 1543, he published his masterpiece, *On the Fabric of the Human Body*.

This book was based on his Paduan lectures, in which he deviated from traditional practice by personally dissecting

a body to illustrate what he was discussing. Vesalius's anatomical treatise presented a careful examination of the individual organs and general structure of the human body. The book would not have been feasible without both the artistic advances of the Renaissance and the technical developments in the art of printing. Together, they made possible the creation of illustrations superior to any hitherto produced.

Vesalius's hands-on approach to teaching anatomy enabled him to overthrow some of Galen's most glaring errors. He did not hesitate, for example, to correct Galen's assertion that the great blood vessels originated at the liver because his own observations made it apparent that they came from the heart. Nevertheless, Vesalius still clung to a number of Galen's erroneous assertions, including the Greek physician's ideas on the ebb and flow of two kinds of blood in the veins and arteries. It was not until William Harvey's work on the circulation of the blood that this Galenic misperception was corrected.

William Harvey (1578–1657) attended Cambridge University and later Padua, where he received a doctorate of medicine in 1602. His reputation rests on his book *On the Motion of the Heart and Blood*, published in 1628. Although questions had been raised in the sixteenth century about Galen's physiological principles, no major break from his system had occurred. Harvey's work, which was based on meticulous observations and experiments, led him to demolish the ancient Greek's work. Harvey demonstrated that the heart and not the liver was the beginning point of the circulation of blood in the body, that the same blood flows in both veins and arteries, and, most importantly, that the blood makes a complete circuit as it passes through the body. Although Galen's ideas had received a severe blow, Harvey's work did not begin to achieve general recognition until the 1660s, when the capillaries, which explained how the body's blood passed from the arteries to the veins, were discovered. Harvey's theory of the circulation of the blood laid the foundation for modern physiology.

Women in the Origins of Modern Science

During the Middle Ages, except for members of religious orders, women who sought a life of learning were severely hampered by the traditional attitude that a woman's proper role was to be a daughter, wife, and mother. But in the late fourteenth and early fifteenth centuries, new opportunities for elite women emerged as enthusiasm for the new secular learning called humanism led Europe's privileged and learned men to encourage women to read and study classical and Christian texts. The ideal of a humanist education for some of the daughters of Europe's elite persisted into the seventeenth century.

In the same fashion as they were drawn to humanism, women were also attracted to the Scientific Revolution. Unlike females educated formally in humanist schools, women attracted to science had to obtain a largely informal education. European nobles had the leisure and resources that gave them easy access to the world of learning. This door was also open to noblewomen, who could participate in the informal scientific networks of their fathers and brothers. One of the most prominent female scientists of the seventeenth century, Margaret Cavendish (1623–1673), came from an aristocratic background. Cavendish was not a popularizer of science for women but a participant in the crucial scientific debates of her time. Despite her achievements, however, she was excluded from membership in the Royal Society (see The Spread of Scientific Knowledge later in this chapter), although she was once allowed to attend a meeting. She wrote a number of works on scientific matters, including *Observations upon Experimental Philosophy* and *Grounds of Natural Philosophy*. In these works she was especially critical of the growing belief that through science humans could master nature: "We have no power at all over natural causes and effects. . . . For man is but a small part, . . . his powers are but particular actions of Nature, and he cannot have a supreme and absolute power."[2]

As an aristocrat, the duchess of Cavendish was a good example of the women in France and England who worked in science. Women interested in science who lived in Germany came from a different background. There the tradition of female participation in crafts enabled some women to become involved in observational science, especially astronomy. Between 1650 and 1710, women constituted 14 percent of all German astronomers.

The most famous of the female astronomers in Germany was Maria Winkelmann (1670–1720). She was educated by her father and uncle and received advanced training in astronomy from a nearby self-taught astronomer. Her opportunity to be a practicing astronomer came when she married Gottfried Kirch, Germany's foremost astronomer. She became his assistant at the astronomical observatory operated in Berlin by the Academy of Science. She made some original contri-

MARGARET CAVENDISH. Shown in this portrait is Margaret Cavendish, the duchess of Newcastle. Her husband, who was thirty years older than she, encouraged her to pursue her literary interests. In addition to scientific works, she wrote plays, an autobiography, and a biography of her husband entitled *The Life of the Thrice Noble, High and Puissant Prince, William Cavendish, Duke, Marquess and Earl of Newcastle*. The autobiography and biography led one male literary critic to call her "a mad, conceited, and ridiculous woman."

butions, including a hitherto undiscovered comet, as her husband related:

> Early in the morning (about 2:00 A.M.) the sky was clear and starry. Some nights before, I had observed a variable star, and my wife (as I slept) wanted to find and see it for herself. In so doing, she found a comet in the sky. At which time she woke me, and I found that it was indeed a comet . . . I was surprised that I had not seen it the night before.[3]

When her husband died in 1710, Winkelmann submitted herself as a candidate for a position as assistant astronomer, for which she was highly qualified. As a woman—with no university degree—she was denied the post by the Berlin Academy, which feared that it would establish a precedent by hiring a woman ("mouths would gape").

Winkelmann's difficulties with the Berlin Academy reflect the obstacles women faced in being accepted in scientific work, which was considered a male preserve.

Although no formal statutes excluded women from membership in the new scientific societies, no woman was invited to join either the Royal Society of England or the French Academy of Sciences until the twentieth century. All of these women scientists were exceptional women because a life devoted to any kind of scholarship was still viewed as at odds with the domestic duties women were expected to perform.

The nature and value of women had been the subject of an ongoing, centuries-long debate. Male opinions in the debate were largely a carryover from medieval times and were not favorable. Women were portrayed as inherently base, prone to vice, easily swayed, and "sexually insatiable." Hence, men needed to control them. Learned women were viewed as having overcome female liabilities to become like men. One man praised a woman scholar by remarking that her writings were so good that you "would hardly believe they were done by a woman at all."

In the seventeenth century, women joined this debate by arguing against the distorted images of women held by men. They argued that women also had rational minds and could grow from education. Further, since most women were pious, chaste, and temperate, there was no need for male authority over them. These female defenders of women emphasized education as the key to women's ability to move into the world. How, then, did the Scientific Revolution affect this debate over the nature of women? Since it was an era of intellectual revolution in which traditional authorities were being overthrown, we might expect significant change in men's views of women. But by and large, instead of becoming an instrument for liberation, science was used to find new support for the old, traditional views about a woman's true place in the scheme of things.

Overall the Scientific Revolution reaffirmed traditional ideas about women's nature. Male scientists used the new science to spread the view that women were inferior by nature, subordinate to men, and suited by nature to play a domestic role as nurturing mothers. The widespread distribution of books ensured the continuation of these ideas. Jean de La Bruyère, the seventeenth-century French moralist, was typical when he remarked that an educated woman was like a gun that was a collector's item, "which one shows to the curious, but which has no use at all, any more than a carousel horse."[4]

Toward a New Earth: Descartes, Rationalism, and a New View of Humankind

The fundamentally new conception of the universe contained in the cosmological revolution of the sixteenth and seventeenth centuries inevitably had an impact on the Western view of humankind. Nowhere is this more evident than in the work of René Descartes (1596–1650). Descartes began by reflecting the doubt and uncertainty that seemed pervasive in the confusion of the seventeenth century and ended with a philosophy that dominated Western thought until the twentieth century.

The starting point for Descartes's new system was doubt. As Descartes explained at the beginning of his most famous work, *Discourse on Method*, written in 1637, he decided to set aside all that he had learned and begin again. One fact seemed to Descartes beyond doubt—his own existence:

> But I immediately became aware that while I was thus disposed to think that all was false, it was absolutely necessary that I who thus thought should be something; and noting that this truth *I think, therefore I am*, was so steadfast and so assured that the suppositions of the skeptics, to whatever extreme they might all be carried, could not avail to shake it, I concluded that I might without scruple accept it as being the first principle of the philosophy I was seeking.[5]

With this emphasis on the mind, Descartes asserted that he would accept only those things that his reason said were true.

From his first postulate, Descartes deduced an additional principle, the separation of mind and matter. Descartes argued that since "the mind cannot be doubted but the body and material world can, the two must be radically different." From this came an absolute dualism between mind and matter, or what has also been called Cartesian dualism. Using mind or human reason, the path to certain knowledge, and its best instrument, mathematics, humans can understand the material world because it is pure mechanism, a machine that is governed by its own physical laws because it was created by God—the great geometrician.

Descartes's separation of mind and matter allowed scientists to view matter as dead or inert, as something that was totally separate from themselves and could be investigated independently by reason. The split between mind and body led Westerners to equate their identity with mind and reason rather than with the whole organism. Descartes has rightly been called the father of modern rationalism (see the box on p. 525). His books were placed on the papal Index of Forbidden Books and condemned by many Protestant theologians. The radical Cartesian split between mind and matter, and between mind and body, had devastating implications not only for traditional religious views of the universe, but for how Westerners viewed themselves; the perspective it provided would not be seriously questioned or challenged until the twentieth century.

Science and Religion in the Seventeenth Century

In Galileo's struggle with the Catholic church, we see the beginning of the conflict between science and religion that has marked the history of modern civilization. For centuries, theology had seemed to be the queen of the sciences. It was natural that the churches would continue to believe that religion was the final measure of everything. The emerging scientists, however, were discovering things about the nat-

THE FATHER OF MODERN RATIONALISM

René Descartes has long been viewed as the founder of modern rationalism and modern philosophy because he believed that human beings could understand the world—itself a mechanical system—by the same rational principles inherent in mathematical thinking. In his Discourse on Method, *he elaborated on his approach to discovering truth.*

RENÉ DESCARTES, *DISCOURSE ON METHOD*

In place of the numerous precepts which have gone to constitute logic, I came to believe that the four following rules would be found sufficient, always provided I took the firm and unswerving resolve never in a single instance to fail in observing them.

The first was to accept nothing as true which I did not evidently know to be such, that is to say, scrupulously to avoid precipitance and prejudice, and in the judgments I passed to include nothing additional to what had presented itself to my mind so clearly and so distinctly that I could have no occasion for doubting it.

The second, to divide each of the difficulties I examined into as many parts as may be required for its adequate solution.

The third, to arrange my thoughts in order, beginning with things the simplest and easiest to know, so that I may then ascend little by little, as it were step by step, to the knowledge of the more complex, and in doing so, to assign an order of thought even to those objects which are not of themselves in any such order of precedence.

And the last, in all cases to make enumerations so complete, and reviews so general, that I should be assured of omitting nothing.

Those long chains of reasonings, each step simple and easy, which geometers are wont to employ in arriving even at the most difficult of their demonstrations, have led me to surmise that all the things we human beings are competent to know are interconnected in the same manner, and that none are so remote as to be beyond our reach or so hidden that we cannot discover them—that is, provided we abstain from accepting as true what is not thus related, i.e., keep always to the order required for their deduction one from another. And I had no great difficulty in determining what the objects are with which I should begin, for that I already knew, namely, that it was with the simplest and easiest. Bearing in mind, too, that of all those who in time past have sought for truth in the sciences, the mathematicians alone have been able to find any demonstrations, that is to say, any reasons which are certain and evident, I had no doubt that it must have been by a procedure of this kind that they had obtained them.

---

ural world that were at odds with the teachings of religious leaders. These "natural philosophers" then tried to draw lines between the knowledge of religion and the knowledge of "natural philosophy" or nature. Many seventeenth-century intellectuals were both religious and scientific and believed that the split between science and religion would have tragic implications. Some believed that this split was largely unnecessary while others felt the need to combine God, humans, and a mechanistic universe into a new philosophical synthesis. Blaise Pascal illustrates how one European intellectual responded to the implications of the cosmological revolution of the seventeenth century.

Blaise Pascal (1623–1662) sought to keep science and religion united. Pascal had a brief but checkered career. He was an accomplished scientist and brilliant mathematician, who was at home with both the practical and the abstract; in the former area, he invented a calculating machine, while in the latter he devised a theory of chance or probability and worked on conic sections. After a profound mystical vision on the night of November 23, 1654, which assured him that God cared for the human soul, he devoted the rest of his life to religious matters. He planned to write an "Apology for the Christian Religion" but died before he could do so. He did leave a set of notes for the larger work, however, which in published form became known as *Pensées* or *The Thoughts*.

In *Pensées*, Pascal tried to convert rationalists to Christianity by appealing to both their reason and their emotions. Humans, he argued, were frail creatures, often deceived by their senses, misled by reason, and battered by their emotions. And yet they were beings whose very nature involved thinking: "Man is but a reed, the weakest in nature; but he is a thinking reed."[6]

Pascal was determined to show that the Christian religion was not contrary to reason: "If we violate the principles of reason, our religion will be absurd, and it will be laughed at." Christianity, he felt, was the only religion that recognized people's true state of being as both vulnerable and great. To a Christian, a human being was both fallen and at the same time God's special creation. But it was not necessary to emphasize one at the expense of the other—to view humans as only rational or only hopeless. Pascal even had an answer for skeptics in his famous wager. God is a reasonable bet; it is worthwhile to assume that God exists. If he does, then we win all; if he does not, we lose nothing.

Despite his own background as a scientist and mathematician, Pascal refused to rely on the scientist's world of order and rationality to attract people to God: "If we submit everything to reason, there will be no mystery and no supernatural element in our religion." In the new cosmology of the seventeenth century, "finite man," Pascal

✿ **DESCARTES WITH QUEEN CHRISTINA OF SWEDEN.** René Descartes was one of the primary figures in the Scientific Revolution. Claiming to use reason as his sole guide to truth, Descartes posited a sharp distinction between mind and matter. He is shown here, standing to the right of Queen Christina of Sweden. The queen had a deep interest in philosophy and invited Descartes to her court.

believed, was lost in the new infinite world, a realization that frightened him: "The eternal silence of those infinite spaces strikes me with terror." The world of nature, then, could never reveal God: "Because they have failed to contemplate these infinities, men have rashly plunged into the examination of nature, as though they bore some proportion to her. . . . Their assumption is as infinite as their object." A Christian could only rely on a God who through Jesus cared for human beings. In the final analysis, after providing reasonable arguments for Christianity, Pascal came to rest on faith. Reason, he believed, could take people only so far: "The heart has its reasons of which the reason knows nothing." As a Christian, faith was the final step: "The heart feels God, not the reason. This is what constitutes faith: God experienced by the heart, not by the reason."[7]

In retrospect, it is obvious that Pascal failed to achieve his goal. Increasingly, the gap between science and traditional religion grew wider as Europe continued along its path of secularization. Of course, traditional religions were not eliminated, nor is there any evidence that churches had yet lost their numbers. That would happen later. Nevertheless, more and more of the intellectual, social, and political elites began to act on the basis of secular rather than religious assumptions.

The Spread of Scientific Knowledge

In the course of the seventeenth century, scientific learning and investigation began to increase dramatically. Major European universities established new chairs of science, especially in medicine. Royal and princely patronage of individual scientists became an international phenomenon. Of particular importance to the work of science were the creation of a scientific method and the emergence of new learned societies that enabled the new scientists to communicate their ideas to each other and to disseminate them to a wider, literate public.

In the course of the Scientific Revolution, attention was paid to the problem of establishing the proper means for examining and understanding the physical realm. This creation of a scientific method was crucial to the evolution of science in the modern world. Curiously enough, it was an Englishman with few scientific credentials who attempted to put forth a new method of acquiring knowledge that made an impact on English scientists in the seventeenth century and other European scientists in the eighteenth century. Francis Bacon (1561–1626), a lawyer and lord chancellor, rejected Copernicus and Kepler and misunderstood Galileo. And yet in his unfinished work *The Great Instauration* (*The Great Restoration*), he called for his contemporaries "to commence a total reconstruction of sciences, arts, and all human knowledge, raised upon the proper foundations." Bacon did not doubt humans' ability to know the natural world but believed that they had proceeded incorrectly: "The entire fabric of human reason which we employ in the inquisition of nature is badly put together and built up, and like some magnificent structure without foundation."

Bacon's new foundation—a correct scientific method—was to be built upon inductive principles. Rather than beginning with assumed first principles from which logical conclusions could be deduced, he urged scientists to proceed from the particular to the general. Carefully organized experiments and systematic, thorough observations would lead to the development of correct generalizations. Bacon was clear about what he believed his method could accomplish. His concern was more for practical than for pure science. He stated that "the true and lawful goal of the sciences is none other than this: that human life be endowed with new discoveries and power." He wanted science to contribute to the "mechanical arts" by creating devices that would benefit industry, agriculture, and trade. Bacon was prophetic when he said that "I am laboring to lay the foundation, not of any sect or doctrine, but of human utility and power." And how would this "human power" be used? To "conquer nature in action."[8] The control and domination of nature became a central proposition of modern science and the technology that accompanied it. Only in the twentieth and twenty-first centuries have some scientists wondered whether this assumption might not be at the heart of our present ecological crisis.

The first of the scientific societies appeared in Italy, but those of England and France were ultimately of more significance. The English Royal Society evolved out of informal gatherings of scientists at London and Oxford in the 1640s, although it did not receive a formal charter from King Charles II until 1662. The French Royal Academy of Sciences also arose out of informal scientific meetings, in Paris during the 1650s. In 1666, Louis XIV formally recognized the group. The French Academy received abundant state support and remained under government control; its members were appointed and paid salaries by the state. In contrast, the Royal Society of England received little government encouragement, and its fellows simply coopted new members.

Early on, both the English and French scientific societies formally emphasized the practical value of scientific research. The Royal Society appointed a committee to investigate technological improvements for industry, while the French Academy collected tools and machines. This concern with the practical benefits of science proved short-lived, however, as both societies came to focus their attention on theoretical work in mechanics and astronomy. The construction of observatories at Paris in 1667 and at Greenwich, England, in 1675 greatly facilitated research in astronomy by both groups. Although both the English and French societies made useful contributions to scientific knowledge in the second half of the seventeenth century, their true significance arose from their example that science should proceed along the lines of a cooperative venture.

The importance of science in the history of modern civilization is usually taken for granted. But how did science become such an integral part of Western culture in the seventeenth and early eighteenth centuries? Recent research has stressed that one cannot simply assert that people perceived that science was a rationally superior system. An important social factor, however, might help to explain the relatively rapid acceptance of the new science.

It has been argued that the literate mercantile and propertied elites of Europe were soon attracted to a new science that offered new ways to exploit resources for profit. Some of the early scientists made it easier for these groups to accept the new ideas when they showed how these ideas could be applied directly to specific industrial and technological needs. Galileo, for example, consciously sought an alliance between science and the material interests of the educated elite when he assured his listeners that the science of mechanics would be quite useful "when it becomes necessary to build bridges or other structures over water, something occurring mainly in affairs of great importance." At the same time, Galileo stressed that science was fit for the "minds of the wise" and not for "the shallow minds of the common people." This made science part of the high culture of Europe's wealthy elites at a time when that culture was being increasingly separated from the popular culture of the lower classes.

 # THE ENLIGHTENMENT

In 1784, the German philosopher Immanuel Kant defined the Enlightenment as "man's leaving his self-caused immaturity." Whereas earlier periods had been handicapped by the inability to "use one's intelligence without the guidance of another," Kant proclaimed as the motto of the Enlightenment: "Dare to Know!: Have the courage to use your own intelligence!" The eighteenth-century Enlightenment was a movement of intellectuals who dared to know. They were greatly impressed with the accomplishments of the Scientific Revolution, and when they used the word *reason*—one of their favorite words—they were advocating the application of the scientific method to the understanding of all life. All institutions and all systems of thought were subject to the rational, scientific way of thinking if people would only free themselves from the shackles of past, worthless traditions, especially religious ones. If Isaac Newton could discover the natural laws regulating the world of nature, then eighteenth-century intellectuals by using reason could find the laws that governed human society. This belief in turn led them to hope that they could make progress toward a better society than the one they had inherited. Reason, natural law, hope, progress—these were common words in the heady atmosphere of the eighteenth century.

The Paths to Enlightenment

The Enlightenment did not arrive full-blown in the eight-eenth century, but was the culmination of four intellectual developments that had begun in the seventeenth century: the popularization of science, skepticism about religion, the growth of travel literature, and the work of Isaac Newton and John Locke.

Although the intellectuals of the eighteenth century were much influenced by the scientific ideas of the seventeenth century, they did not always acquire this knowledge directly from the original sources. After all, Newton's *Principia* was not an easy book to read or comprehend. The spread of scientific ideas to ever widening circles of educated Europeans was accomplished not so much by the scientists themselves as by popularizers. Especially important as a direct link between the Scientific Revolution of the seventeenth century and the intellectuals of the eighteenth was Bernard de Fontenelle (1657–1757).

In his *Plurality of Worlds*, he used the form of an intimate conversation between a lady aristocrat and her lover to present a detailed account of the new mechanistic universe. Scores of the educated elite of Europe learned the new cosmology in this lighthearted fashion.

Although religion had once again become the central focus of people's lives during the Reformation, it was perhaps inevitable that the dogmatic controversies, religious intolerance, and religious warfare engendered by it would open the door to the questioning of religious truths and values. The overthrow of medieval cosmology and the advent of scientific ideas and rational explanations in the seventeenth century likewise affected the belief of educated men and women in the traditional teachings of Christianity. Skepticism about religion and a growing secularization of thought were important factors in the emergence of the Enlightenment.

Skepticism about Christianity as well as about European culture itself was nourished by travel reports. In the course of the seventeenth century, traders, missionaries, physicians, and navigators began to publish an increasing number of travel books that gave accounts of many different cultures. By the end of the seventeenth century, this travel literature had begun to make an impact on the minds of educated Europeans. The discovery of highly developed civilizations with different customs such as the civilization of China forced Europeans to evaluate their own civilization relative to others. What had seemed to be practices grounded in reason now appeared to be matters of custom.

A final source of inspiration for the Enlightenment came primarily from two Englishmen, Isaac Newton and John Locke. Enchanted by the grand design of the Newtonian world-machine, the intellectuals of the Enlightenment were convinced that by following Newton's rules of reasoning they could discover the natural laws that governed politics, economics, justice, religion, and the arts. They regarded the world and everything in it as a giant machine.

John Locke's theory of knowledge made a great impact on eighteenth-century intellectuals. In his *Essay Concerning Human Understanding*, written in 1690, Locke denied Descartes's belief in innate ideas. Instead, argued Locke, every person was born with a *tabula rasa*, a blank mind:

> Let us then suppose the mind to be, as we say, white paper, void of all characters, without any ideas. How comes it to be furnished? Whence comes it by that vast store which the busy and boundless fancy of man has painted on it with an almost endless variety? Whence has it all the materials of reason and knowledge? To this I answer, in one word, from experience. . . . Our observation, employed either about external sensible objects or about the internal operations of our minds perceived and reflected on by ourselves, is that which supplies our understanding with all the materials of thinking.[9]

Our knowledge, then, is derived from our environment, not from heredity; from reason, not from faith. By denying innate ideas, Locke's philosophy implied that people were molded by their environment, by the experiences that they received through their senses from their surrounding world. By changing the environment and subjecting people to proper influences, they could be changed and a new society created. And how should the environment be changed? Newton had already paved the way by showing how reason enabled enlightened people to discover the natural laws to which all institutions should conform. No wonder the philosophes were enamored of Newton and Locke. Taken together, their ideas seemed to offer the hope of a "brave new world" built on reason.

The Philosophes and Their Ideas

The intellectuals of the Enlightenment were known by the French name of *philosophes*, although they were not all French and few were *philosophers* in the strict sense of the term. They were literary people, professors, journalists, statesmen, economists, political scientists, and, above all, social reformers. They came from both the nobility and the middle class, and a few even stemmed from lower-middle-class origins. Although it was a truly international and cosmopolitan movement, the Enlightenment also enhanced the dominant role being played by French culture; Paris was its recognized capital, and most of its leaders were French. The French philosophes, in turn, affected intellectuals elsewhere and created a movement that touched the entire Western world, including the British and Spanish colonies in America.

To the philosophes, the role of philosophy was to change the world, not just discuss it. As one writer said, the philosophe is one who "applies himself to the study of society with the purpose of making his kind better and happier." To the philosophes, rationalism did not mean the creation of a grandiose system of thought to explain all things. Reason was scientific method, and it meant an appeal to facts, to experience, to reasonableness. A spirit of rational criticism was to be applied to everything, including religion and politics. The philosophes aggressively pursued a secular view of life because their focus was not on an afterlife, but on this world and how it could be improved and enjoyed.

Although the philosophes constituted a kind of "family circle" bound together by common intellectual bonds, they often disagreed as well. Spanning almost an entire century, the Enlightenment evolved over time, with each succeeding generation becoming more radical as it built upon the contributions of its predecessors. A few people, however, dominated the landscape completely, and we might best begin our survey of the ideas of the philosophes by looking at the three French giants—Montesquieu, Voltaire, and Diderot.

Charles de Secondat, the baron de Montesquieu (1689–1755), came from the French nobility. His most famous work, *The Spirit of the Laws,* was published in 1748. This treatise was a comparative study of governments in which Montesquieu attempted to apply the scientific method to the social and political arena to ascertain the "natural laws" governing the social relationships of human beings. Montesquieu distinguished three basic kinds of governments: republics, suitable for small states and based on citizen involvement; monarchy, appropriate for middle-sized states and grounded in the ruling class's adherence to law; and despotism, apt for large empires and dependent on fear to inspire obedience. Montesquieu used England as an example of monarchy, and it was his praise and analysis of England's constitution that led to his most far-reaching and lasting contribution to political thought—the importance of checks and balances created by means of a separation of powers. He believed that England's system, with its separate executive, legislature, and judiciary that served to limit and control each other, provided the greatest freedom and security for a state. His work was translated into English two years after publication and was read by American philosophes, who incorporated its principles into the U.S. constitution.

The greatest figure of the Enlightenment was François-Marie Arouet, known simply as Voltaire (1694–1778). Son of a prosperous middle-class family from Paris, Voltaire

VOLTAIRE. François-Marie Arouet, better known as Voltaire, achieved his first success as a playwright. A philosophe, Voltaire was well known for his criticism of traditional religion and his support of religious toleration.

THE ATTACK ON RELIGIOUS INTOLERANCE

Although Voltaire's ideas on religion were in no way original, his lucid prose, biting satire, and clever wit caused his attacks to be widely read and all the more influential. These two selections present different sides of Voltaire's attack on religious intolerance. The first is from his straightforward treatise The Ignorant Philosopher, *while the second is from his only real literary masterpiece, the novel Candide, where he uses humor to make the same fundamental point about religious intolerance.*

VOLTAIRE, *THE IGNORANT PHILOSOPHER*

The contagion of fanaticism then still subsists. . . . The author of the Treatise upon Toleration has not mentioned the shocking executions wherein so many unhappy victims perished in the valleys of Piedmont. He has passed over in silence the massacre of six hundred inhabitants of Valtelina, men, women, and children, who were murdered by the Catholics in the month of September, 1620. I will not say it was with the consent and assistance of the archbishop of Milan, Charles Borome, who was made a saint. Some passionate writers have averred this fact, which I am very far from believing; but I say, there is scarce any city or borough in Europe where blood has not been spilt for religious quarrels; I say, that the human species has been perceptibly diminished because women and girls were massacred as well as men; I say, that Europe would have had a third larger population if there had been no theological disputes. In fine, I say, that so far from forgetting these abominable times, we should frequently take a view of them, to inspire an eternal horror for them; and that it is for our age to make reparation by toleration, for this long collection of crimes, which has taken place through the want of toleration, during sixteen barbarous centuries.

Let it not then be said, that there are no traces left of that shocking fanaticism, of the want of toleration; they are still everywhere to be met with, even in those countries that are esteemed the most humane. The Lutheran and Calvinist preachers, were they masters, would, perhaps, be as little inclined to pity, as obdurate, as insolent as they upbraid their antagonists with being.

VOLTAIRE, *CANDIDE*

At last he [Candide] approached a man who had just been addressing a big audience for a whole hour on the subject of charity. The orator peered at him and said:

"What is your business here? Do you support the Good Old Cause?"

"There is no effect without a cause," replied Candide modestly. "All things are necessarily connected and arranged for the best. It was my fate to be driven from Lady Cunégonde's presence and made to run the gauntlet, and now I have to beg my bread until I can earn it. Things could not have happened otherwise."

"Do you believe that the Pope is Antichrist, my friend?" said the minister.

"I have never heard anyone say so," replied Candide; "but whether he is or he isn't, I want some food."

"You don't deserve to eat," said the other. "Be off with you, you villain, you wretch! Don't come near me again or you'll suffer for it."

The minister's wife looked out of the window at that moment, and seeing a man who was not sure that the Pope was Antichrist, emptied over his head a chamber pot, which shows to what lengths ladies are driven by religious zeal.

---

received a classical education typical of Jesuit schools. Although he studied law, he wished to be a writer and achieved his first success as a playwright. Voltaire was a prolific author and wrote an almost endless stream of pamphlets, novels, plays, letters, philosophical essays, and histories. His writings brought him both fame and wealth.

Voltaire was especially well known for his criticism of traditional religion and his strong attachment to the ideal of religious toleration (see the box above). He lent his prestige and skills as a polemicist to fight cases of intolerance in France. In 1763, he penned his *Treatise on Toleration*, in which he argued that religious toleration had created no problems for England and Holland and reminded governments that "all men are brothers under God." As he grew older, Voltaire's denunciations became ever more strident. "Crush the infamous thing," he thundered repeatedly—the infamous thing being religious fanaticism, intolerance, and superstition.

Throughout his life, Voltaire championed not only religious tolerance, but also deism, a religious outlook shared by most other philosophes. Deism was built upon the Newtonian world-machine, which implied the existence of a mechanic (God) who had created the universe. To Voltaire and most other philosophes, God had no direct involvement in the world he had created and allowed it to run according to its own natural laws. Jesus might be a "good fellow," as Voltaire called him, but he was not divine as Christianity claimed. Deism proved to be a halfway house between belief in religion and disbelief and satisfied most philosophes. Voltaire feared atheism, however, feeling that it posed a threat to social stability among the masses.

DIDEROT QUESTIONS CHRISTIAN SEXUAL STANDARDS

Denis Diderot was one of the bolder thinkers of the Enlightenment. He moved from outspoken criticism of the Christian religion to outright atheism. Although best remembered for the Encyclopedia, he wrote many other works that he considered too advanced and withheld from publication. In his Supplement to the Voyage of Bougainville, he constructed a dialogue between Orou, a Tahitian, who symbolizes the wisdom of a philosophe, and a chaplain who defends Christian sexual mores. The dialogue gave Diderot the opportunity to criticize the practice of sexual chastity and monogamy.

DENIS DIDEROT, SUPPLEMENT TO THE VOYAGE OF BOUGAINVILLE

[Orou:] "You are young and healthy [speaking to the chaplain] and you have just had a good supper. He who sleeps alone, sleeps badly; at night a man needs a woman at his side. Here is my wife and here are my daughters. Choose whichever one pleases you most, but if you would like to do me a favor, you will give your preference to my youngest girl, who has not yet had any children. . . ."

The chaplain replied that his religion, his holy orders, his moral standards, and his sense of decency all prevented him from accepting Orou's invitation.

Orou answered: "I don't know what this thing is that you call religion, but I can only have a low opinion of it because it forbids you to partake of an innocent pleasure to which Nature, the sovereign mistress of us all, invites everybody. It seems to prevent you from bringing one of your fellow creatures into the world, from doing a favor asked of by a father, a mother, and their children, from repaying the kindness of a host, and from enriching a nation by giving it an additional citizen. . . . Look at the distress you have caused to appear on the faces of these four women—they are afraid you have noticed some defect in them that arouses your distaste. . . ."

The Chaplain: "You don't understand—it's not that. They are all four of them equally beautiful. But there is my religion! My holy orders! . . . [God] spoke to our ancestors and gave them laws; he prescribed to them the way in which he wishes to be honored; he ordained that certain actions are good and others he forbade them to do as being evil."

Orou: "I see. And one of these evil actions which he has forbidden is that of a man who goes to bed with a woman or girl. But in that case, why did he make two sexes?"

The Chaplain: "In order that they might come together—but only when certain conditions are satisfied and only after certain initial ceremonies have been performed. By virtue of these ceremonies one man belongs to one woman and only to her; one woman belongs to one man and only to him."

Orou: "For their whole lives?"

The Chaplain: "For their whole lives. . . ."

Orou: "I find these strange precepts contrary to nature, and contrary to reason. . . . Furthermore, your laws seem to me to be contrary to the general order of things. For in truth is there anything so senseless as a precept that forbids us to heed the changing impulses that are inherent in our being, or commands that require a degree of constancy which is not possible, that violate the liberty of both male and female by chaining them perpetually to one another? . . . I don't know what your great workman [God] is, but I am very happy that he never spoke to our forefathers, and I hope that he never speaks to our children, for if he does, he may tell them the same foolishness, and they may be foolish enough to believe it."

Denis Diderot (1713–1784) was the son of a skilled artisan from eastern France. He received a Jesuit education and went on to the University of Paris to fulfill his father's hopes that he would be a lawyer or pursue a career in the church. Diderot did neither. Instead he became a freelance writer so that he could be free to study and read in many subjects and languages.

Diderot wrote numerous essays that reflected typical Enlightened interests. One of his favorite topics was Christianity, which he condemned as fanatical and unreasonable. As he grew older, his literary attacks on Christianity grew more vicious. Of all religions, he averred, Christianity was the worst, "the most absurd and the most atrocious in its dogma" (see the box above). This progression reflected his own transformation from deism to atheism, ending with a basic materialistic conception of life: "This world is only a mass of molecules."

Diderot's most famous contribution to the Enlightenment was the Encyclopedia, or Classified Dictionary of the Sciences, Arts, and Trades, a twenty-eight-volume compendium of knowledge that he edited and referred to as the "great work of his life." Its purpose, according to Diderot, was to "change the general way of thinking." It did precisely that, becoming a major weapon of the philosophes' crusade against the old French society. The contributors attacked religious superstition and advocated toleration as well as a program for social, legal, and political improvements that would lead to a society that was more cosmopolitan, more tolerant, more humane, and more reasonable. In later editions, the price of the Encyclopedia was drastically reduced, dramatically increasing its sales and making it available to doctors, clergy, teachers, lawyers, and even military officers, thus furthering the spread of the ideas of the Enlightenment.

TOWARD A NEW "SCIENCE OF MAN"

The Enlightenment belief that Newton's scientific methods could be used to discover the natural laws underlying all areas of human life led to the emergence in the eighteenth century of what the philosophes called a "science of man" or what we would call the social sciences. In a number of areas, such as economics, philosophes arrived at natural laws that they believed governed human actions. If these "natural laws" seem less than universal to us, it reminds us how much the philosophes were people of their times reacting to the conditions they faced. Nevertheless, their efforts laid the foundations for the modern social sciences.

The Physiocrats and Adam Smith have been viewed as the founders of the modern discipline of economics. The leader of the Physiocrats was François Quesnay (1694–1774), a highly successful French court physician. Quesnay and the Physiocrats claimed they would discover the natural economic laws that governed human society. Their major "natural law" of economics represented a repudiation of mercantilism, specifically, its emphasis on controlling the economy for the benefit of the state. Instead the Physiocrats stressed that the existence of the natural economic forces of supply and demand made it imperative that individuals be left free to pursue their own economic self-interest. All society would ultimately benefit from the actions of these individuals. Consequently, the Physiocrats argued that the state should in no way interrupt the free play of natural economic forces by imposing government regulations on the economy, but should leave it alone, a doctrine that subsequently became known by its French name, *laissez-faire* (to let alone).

The best statement of *laissez-faire* was made in 1776 by a Scottish philosopher, Adam Smith (1723–1790), in his famous work, *Inquiry into the Nature and Causes of the Wealth of Nations*, known simply as *The Wealth of Nations*. Like the Physiocrats, Smith believed that the state should not interfere in economic matters; indeed, he gave to government only three basic functions: it should protect society from invasion (army); defend individuals from injustice and oppression (police); and keep up certain public works, such as roads and canals that private individuals could not afford. Thus, in Smith's view the state should be a kind of "passive policeman" that remains out of the lives of individuals. In emphasizing the economic liberty of the individual, the Physiocrats and Adam Smith laid the foundation for what became known in the nineteenth century as economic liberalism.

THE LATER ENLIGHTENMENT

By the late 1760s, a new generation of philosophes who had grown up with the worldview of the Enlightenment began to move beyond their predecessors' beliefs. The

CHRONOLOGY

WORKS OF THE PHILOSOPHES

Montesquieu, *The Spirit of the Laws*	1748
Diderot, *Encyclopedia*	1751–1765
Rousseau, *The Social Contract* and *Emile*	1762
Voltaire, *Treatise on Toleration*	1763
Smith, *The Wealth of Nations*	1776

most famous of these later philosophes was Jean-Jacques Rousseau (1712–1778). Almost entirely self-educated, he wandered about as a youth holding various jobs in France and Italy. Eventually, he made his way to Paris, where he became a friend of Diderot and was introduced into the circles of the philosophes. He never really liked the social life of the cities, however, and frequently withdrew into long periods of solitude.

Rousseau's political beliefs were presented in two major works. In his *Discourse on the Origins of the Inequality of Mankind*, Rousseau argued that people had adopted laws and governors in order to preserve their private property. In the process, they had become enslaved by government. In his celebrated treatise *The Social Contract*, published in 1762, Rousseau tried to harmonize individual liberty with governmental authority. The social contract was basically an agreement on the part of an entire society to be governed by its general will. If any individual wished to follow his own self-interest, then he should be compelled to abide by the general will. "This means nothing less than that he will be forced to be free," said Rousseau, because the general will represented a community's highest aspirations, that which was best for the entire community. Thus, liberty was achieved by being forced to follow what was best for each individual. To Rousseau, because everybody was responsible for framing the general will, the creation of laws could never be delegated to a parliamentary institution:

> Thus the people's deputies are not and could not be its representatives; they are merely its agents; and they cannot decide anything finally. Any law which the people has not ratified in person is void; it is not law at all. The English people believes itself to be free; it is gravely mistaken; it is free only during the election of Members of Parliament; as soon as the Members are elected, the people is enslaved; it is nothing.[10]

This is an extreme, idealistic statement, but it is the ultimate statement of participatory democracy.

Another influential treatise by Rousseau also appeared in 1762. Entitled *Emile*, it is one of the Enlightenment's most important works on education. Written in the form of a novel, the work was really a general treatise "on the education of the natural man." Rousseau's fundamental concern was that education should foster rather than

MAP 18.1   The Age of Enlightenment in Europe

restrict children's natural instincts. Life's experiences had shown Rousseau the importance of the promptings of the heart, and what he sought was a balance between heart and mind, between sentiment and reason. This emphasis on heart and sentiment made him a precursor of the intellectual movement called Romanticism, which dominated Europe at the beginning of the nineteenth century.

But Rousseau did not necessarily practice what he preached. His own children were sent to foundling homes, where many children died at a young age. Rousseau also viewed women as "naturally" different from men: "to fulfill [a woman's] functions, an appropriate physical constitution is necessary to her . . . she needs a soft sedentary life to suckle her babies. How much care and tenderness does she need to hold her family together." In Rousseau's

Emile, Sophie, who was Emile's intended wife, was educated for her role as wife and mother by learning obedience and the nurturing skills that would enable her to provide loving care for her husband and children. Not everyone in the eighteenth century agreed with Rousseau, however, making ideas of gender an important issue in the Enlightenment.

THE "WOMAN QUESTION" IN THE ENLIGHTENMENT

For centuries, men had dominated the debate about the nature and value of women. In general, many male intellectuals had argued that the base nature of women made them inferior to men and necessitated male domination

THE RIGHTS OF WOMEN

Mary Wollstonecraft responded to an unhappy childhood in a large family by seeking to lead an independent life. Few occupations were available for middle-class women in her day, but she survived by working as a teacher, chaperone, and governess to aristocratic children. All the while, she wrote and developed her ideas on the rights of women. This excerpt was taken from her Vindication of the Rights of Woman, *written in 1792. This work led to her reputation as the foremost British feminist thinker of the eighteenth century.*

MARY WOLLSTONECRAFT, *VINDICATION OF THE RIGHTS OF WOMAN*

It is a melancholy truth—yet such is the blessed effect of civilization—the most respectable women are the most oppressed; and, unless they have understandings far superior to the common run of understandings, taking in both sexes, they must, from being treated like contemptible beings, become contemptible. How many women thus waste life away the prey of discontent, who might have practiced as physicians, regulated a farm, managed a shop, and stood erect, supported by their own industry, instead of hanging their heads surcharged with the dew of sensibility, that consumes the beauty to which it at first gave luster. . . .

Proud of their weakness, however, [women] must always be protected, guarded from care, and all the rough toils that dignify the mind. If this be the fiat of fate, if they will make themselves insignificant and contemptible, sweetly to waste "life away," let them not expect to be valued when their beauty fades, for it is the fate of the fairest flowers to be admired and pulled to pieces by the careless hand that plucked them. In how many ways do I wish, from the purest benevolence, to impress this truth on my sex; yet I fear that they will not listen to a truth that dear-bought experience has brought home to many an agitated bosom, nor willingly resign the privileges of rank and sex for the privileges of humanity, to which those have no claim who do not discharge its duties. . . .

Would men but generously snap our chains, and be content with rational fellowship instead of slavish obedience, they would find us more observant daughters, more affectionate sisters, more faithful wives, and more reasonable mothers—in a word, better citizens. We should then love them with true affection, because we should learn to respect ourselves; and the peace of mind of a worthy man would not be interrupted by the idle vanity of his wife.

---

of women. In the seventeenth and eighteenth centuries, many male thinkers reinforced this view by arguing that it was based on "natural" biological differences between men and women. Like Rousseau, they argued that the female constitution made women mothers. Male writers, in particular, were critical of the attempts of some women in the Enlightenment to write on intellectual issues and insisted that women by nature were intellectually inferior to men. Nevertheless, some Enlightenment thinkers offered more positive views of women. Diderot, for example, maintained that men and women were not all that different, while Voltaire asserted that "women are capable of all that men are" in intellectual affairs.

It was women thinkers, however, who added new perspectives to the "woman question" by making specific suggestions for improving the condition of women. Mary Astell (1666–1731), daughter of a wealthy English coal merchant, argued in 1697 in *A Serious Proposal to the Ladies* that women needed to become better educated. Men, she believed, would resent her proposal, "but they must excuse me, if I be as partial to my own sex as they are to theirs, and think women as capable of learning as men are, and that it becomes them as well."[11]

The strongest statement for the rights of women in the eighteenth century was advanced by the English writer Mary Wollstonecraft (1759–1797), viewed by many as the founder of modern European feminism. In *Vindication of the Rights of Woman*, written in 1792, Wollstonecraft pointed out two contradictions in the views of women held by such Enlightenment thinkers as Rousseau. To argue that women must obey men, she said, was contrary to the beliefs of the same individuals that a system based on the arbitrary power of monarchs over their subjects or slave owners over their slaves was wrong. The subjection of women to men was equally wrong. In addition, she argued that the Enlightenment was based on an ideal of reason innate in all human beings. If women have reason, then they too are entitled to the same rights that men have. Women, Wollstonecraft declared, should have equal rights with men in education and in economic and political life as well (see the box above).

The Social Environment of the Philosophes

Of great importance to the Enlightenment was the spread of its ideas to the literate elite of European society. While the publication and sale of books and treatises were important to this process, equally important was the salon. Salons came into being in the seventeenth century but rose to new heights in the eighteenth. The salons were the elegant drawing rooms of the wealthy class's great urban

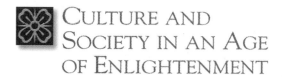

A LONDON COFFEEHOUSE. Coffeehouses first appeared in Venice and Constantinople but quickly spread throughout Europe by the beginning of the eighteenth century. In addition to drinking coffee, patrons of coffeehouses could read magazines and newspapers, exchange ideas, play chess, smoke, and even engage in business transactions. In this scene from a London coffeehouse of 1705, well-attired gentlemen make bids on commodities. Bidding went on until pins, which had been placed in lit candles, fell to the table. Thus, bidding stopped when patrons could "hear a pin drop."

houses where invited philosophes and guests gathered together and engaged in witty, sparkling conversations often centered on the new ideas of the philosophes. In France's rigid hierarchical society, the salons were important in bringing writers and artists together with aristocrats, government officials, and wealthy bourgeoisie.

In Paris, the cultural capital of Europe, women took the lead in bringing together groups of men and women to discuss the new ideas of the philosophes. At her fashionable home in the Rue St.-Honoré, Marie-Thérèse de Geoffrin (1699–1777), wife of a wealthy merchant, held sway over gatherings that became the talk of France and even Europe. Distinguished foreigners, including a future king of Sweden and a future king of Poland, competed to receive invitations. When Madame Geoffrin made a visit to Vienna, she was so well received that she exclaimed, "I am better known here than a couple of yards from my own house." Madame Geoffrin was an amiable but firm hostess who allowed wide-ranging discussions as long as they remained in good taste. When she found that artists and philosophers did not mix particularly well (the artists were high-strung and the philosophers talked too much), she set up separate meetings. Artists were only invited on Mondays; philosophers on Wednesdays. These gatherings were but one of many avenues for the spread of the ideas of the philosophes.

Other means of spreading Enlightenment ideas were also available. Coffeehouses, cafés, reading clubs, and public lending libraries created by the state were gathering places to exchange ideas. Learned societies spread to cities throughout Europe and America. At such gatherings as the Select Society of Edinburgh in Scotland and the American Philosophical Society in Philadelphia, lawyers, doctors, and local officials gathered to discuss Enlightened ideas. Secret societies were also formed. The most famous was the Freemasons, established in London in 1717, France and Italy in 1726, and Prussia in 1744. It was no secret that the Freemasons were sympathetic to the ideas of the philosophes.

CULTURE AND SOCIETY IN AN AGE OF ENLIGHTENMENT

The intellectual adventure fostered by the philosophes was accompanied by both traditional practices and important changes in the eighteenth-century world of culture and daily life.

Innovations in Art, Music, and Literature

Although the Baroque and Neoclassical styles that had dominated the seventeenth century continued into the eighteenth century, by the 1730s, a new style of decoration and architecture known as Rococo had spread all over Europe. Though a French invention and enormously popular in Germany, Rococo became a truly international style.

Unlike the Baroque, which stressed majesty, power, and movement, Rococo emphasized grace and gentle action. Rococo rejected strict geometrical patterns and had a fondness for curves; it liked to follow the wandering lines of natural objects, such as seashells and flowers. It made much use of interlaced designs colored in gold with delicate contours and graceful curves. Highly secular, its lightness and charm spoke of the pursuit of pleasure, happiness, and love.

Some of Rococo's appeal is evident already in the painting of Antoine Watteau (1684–1721), whose lyrical views of aristocratic life—refined, sensual, civilized, with gentlemen and ladies in elegant dress—revealed a world of upper-class pleasure and joy. Underneath that exterior, however, was an element of sadness as the artist revealed the fragility and transitory nature of pleasure, love, and life.

The palace of Versailles had made an enormous impact on Europe. "Keeping up with the Bourbons" became important as the Austrian emperor, the Swedish king, German princes and prince-bishops, Italian princes, and even a Russian tsar built grandiose palaces. While imitating Versailles's size, they drew less upon its French classical

✿ ANTOINE WATTEAU,
THE PILGRIMAGE TO CYTHERA.
Antoine Watteau was one of the most
gifted painters in eighteenth-century
France. His portrayal of aristocratic life
reveals a world of elegance, wealth, and
pleasure. In this painting, Watteau depicts
a group of aristocratic pilgrims about to
depart the island of Cythera, where they
have paid homage to Venus, the goddess
of love.

style than on the seventeenth-century Italian Baroque, as modified by a series of brilliant German and Austrian sculptor-architects. This Baroque-Rococo architectural style of the eighteenth century was conceived of as a total work of art in which building, sculptural figures, and wall and ceiling paintings were blended into a harmonious whole. This style was used in both palaces and ecclesiastical buildings, and often the same architects did both. This is evident in the work of one of the greatest architects of the eighteenth century, Balthasar Neumann (1687–1753).

Neumann's two masterpieces are the pilgrimage church of the Vierzehnheiligen (The Fourteen Saints) in southern Germany and the Bishop's Palace known as the Residenz, the residential palace of the Schönborn prince-bishop of Würzburg. Secular and spiritual become easily interchangeable as lavish and fanciful ornaments, light, bright colors, and an elaborate and rich detail greet visitors in both buildings.

The eighteenth century was one of the greatest in the history of European music. In the first half of the eighteenth century, two composers—Handel and Bach—stand out as musical geniuses. Johann Sebastian Bach (1685–1750) came from a family of musicians. Bach held the post of organist and music director at a number of small German courts before becoming director of church music at the church of St. Thomas in Leipzig in 1723. There Bach composed his Mass in B Minor, his St. Matthew Passion, and the cantatas and motets that have established his reputation as one of the greatest composers of all time. Above all, for Bach music was a means of worshiping God; in his own words, his task in life was to make "well-ordered music in the honor of God."

The other great musical giant of the early eighteenth century, George Frederick Handel (1685–1759) was, like Bach, born in Saxony in Germany and in the same year. Unlike Bach, however, he was profoundly secular in temperament. He began his career by writing operas in the

Italian manner and thereafter remained faithful to the Italian Baroque style. In 1712, he moved to England and remained there the rest of his life. Although he found patrons at the English royal court, Handel wrote music for large public audiences and was not averse to writing huge, unusual-sounding pieces. The orchestra for his *Fireworks Music,* for example, was supposed to be accompanied by 101 cannons. Although he wrote much secular music, ironically the worldly Handel is probably best known for his religious music. He had no problem moving from Italian operas to religious oratorios when they proved to be in greater demand by his English public. An oratorio was an extended musical composition on a religious subject, usually taken from a biblical story. Handel's oratorio known as the *Messiah* has been called "one of those rare works that appeal immediately to everyone, and yet is indisputably a masterpiece of the highest order."[12]

Bach and Handel perfected the Baroque musical style with its monumental and elaborate musical structures. Two geniuses of the second half of the eighteenth century—Haydn and Mozart—were innovators who wrote music called Classical rather than Baroque. Their renown caused the musical center of Europe to shift from Italy to the Austrian Empire.

Franz Joseph Haydn (1732–1809) spent most of his adult life as musical director for the wealthy Hungarian princes, the Esterhazy brothers. Haydn was incredibly prolific, composing 104 symphonies in addition to string quartets, concerti, songs, oratorios, and masses. His visits to England in 1790 and 1794 introduced him to another world, where musicians wrote for public concerts rather than princely patrons. This "liberty," as he called it, induced him to write his two great oratorios *The Creation* and *The Seasons,* both of which were dedicated to the common people.

Wolfgang Amadeus Mozart (1756–1791) was truly a child prodigy: he gave his first harpsichord concert at six and wrote his first opera at twelve. He, too, sought a patron, but his discontent with the overly demanding archbishop of Salzburg forced him to move to Vienna, where his failure to achieve a permanent patron made his life miserable. Nevertheless, he wrote music prolifically and passionately: string quartets, sonatas, symphonies, concerti, and operas. *The Marriage of Figaro*, *The Magic Flute*, and *Don Giovanni* are three of the world's greatest operas. Mozart composed with an ease of melody and a blend of grace, precision, and emotion that arguably no one has ever excelled. Haydn remarked to Mozart's father that "your son is the greatest composer known to me either in person or by reputation."

The eighteenth century was also decisive in the development of the novel. The novel was not a completely new literary genre but grew out of the medieval romances and the picaresque stories of the sixteenth century. The English are credited with establishing the "modern novel as the chief vehicle" for fiction writing. With no established rules, the novel was open to much experimentation. It also proved especially attractive to women readers and women writers.

Henry Fielding (1707–1754) wrote novels about people without scruples who survived by their wits. His best work was *The History of Tom Jones, a Foundling*, a lengthy novel about the numerous adventures of a young scoundrel. Fielding presented scenes of English life from the hovels of London to the country houses of the English aristocracy. In a number of hilarious episodes, he described characters akin to real types in English society. Although he emphasized action rather than inner feeling, Fielding did his own moralizing by attacking the hypocrisy of his age.

High Culture

Historians and cultural anthropologists have grown accustomed to distinguishing between a civilization's high and popular culture. By high culture is usually meant the literary and artistic culture of the educated and wealthy ruling classes; by popular culture is meant the written and unwritten culture of the masses, most of which is passed down orally. By the eighteenth century, European high culture consisted of a learned culture of theologians, scientists, philosophers, intellectuals, poets, and dramatists, for whom Latin remained a truly international language. Their work was supported by a wealthy and literate lay group, the most important of whom were the landed aristocracy and the wealthier upper classes in the cities. European high culture was noticeably cosmopolitan. In addition to Latin, French had become an international language of the cultural elites. This high culture of Europe's elite was institutionally expressed in the salons, universities, and academies.

Especially noticeable in the eighteenth century was the expansion of both publishing and the reading public. A recent study of French publishing, for example, reveals that the number of titles issued annually by French publishers rose from 300 titles in 1750 to about 1,600 in the 1780s. Although many of these titles were still geared

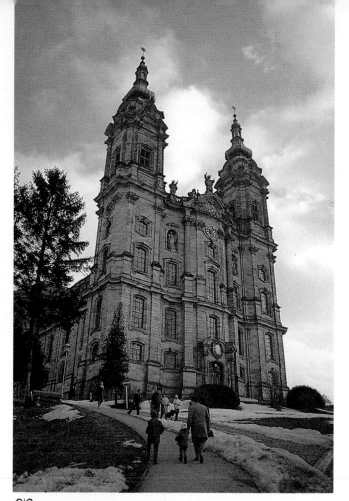

VIERZEHNHEILIGEN, EXTERIOR VIEW. Balthasar Neumann, one of the most prominent architects of the eighteenth century, used the Baroque-Rococo style of architecture to design some of the most beautiful buildings of the century. Pictured here is the exterior of his pilgrimage church of the Vierzehnheiligen (The Fourteen Saints), located in southern Germany.

for small groups of the educated elite, many were also directed to the new reading public of the middle classes, which included women and even urban artisans. The growth of publishing houses made it possible for authors to make money from their works and be less dependent on wealthy patrons.

An important aspect of the growth of publishing and reading in the eighteenth century was the development of magazines for the general public. Great Britain, an important center for the new magazines, saw 25 periodicals published in 1700, 103 in 1760, and 158 in 1780. Along with magazines came daily newspapers. The first was printed in London in 1702, but by 1780, thirty-seven other English towns had their own newspapers. Filled with news and special features, they were relatively cheap and were available free in coffeehouses.

Popular Culture

Popular culture refers to the often unwritten and unofficial culture passed down orally that was fundamental to the lives of most people. The distinguishing characteristic of popular culture is its collective and public nature. Group activity was especially common in the festival, a broad name used to cover a variety of celebrations: family festivals, such as weddings; community festivals in Catholic Europe that celebrated the feast day of the local patron saint; annual festivals, such as Christmas and Easter, which go back to medieval Christianity; and Carnival, the most spectacular form of festival, which was celebrated in the Mediterranean world of Spain, Italy, and France as well as in Germany and Austria. All of these festivals shared common characteristics. While having a spiritual function, they were celebrated in a secular fashion. They were special occasions on which people ate, drank, and celebrated to excess. In traditional societies, festival was a time of play because much of the rest of the year was a time of unrelieved work. As the poet Thomas Gray said of Carnival in Turin in 1739: "This Carnival lasts only from Christmas to Lent; one half of the remaining part of the year is passed in remembering the last, the other in expecting the future Carnival."[13]

"The example par excellence of the festival" was Carnival, which started in January and lasted until the beginning of Lent, traditionally the forty-day period of fasting and purification leading up to Easter. Carnival was a time of great indulgence, just the reverse of Lent, when people were expected to abstain from meat, sex, and most recreations. A heavy consumption of food, especially meat and other delicacies, and heavy drinking were the norm. Carnival was a time of intense sexual activity as well. Songs with double meanings could be sung publicly at this time of year, whereas otherwise they would be considered offensive to the community. A float of Florentine "key-makers," for example, sang this ditty to the ladies: "Our tools are fine, new and useful; We always carry them with us; They are good for anything; If you want to touch them, you can." Finally, Carnival was a time of aggression, a time to release pent-up feelings. Most often this took the form of verbal aggression because people could openly insult other people and were even allowed to criticize their social superiors and authorities. But other acts of violence were also permitted. People pelted each other with apples, eggs, flour, and pigs' bladders filled with water.

The same sense of community evident in festival was also present in the chief gathering places of the common people, the local taverns or cabarets. Taverns functioned as a regular gathering place for neighborhood men to talk, play games, conduct small business matters, and, of course, drink. In some countries, the favorite drinks of the poor, such as gin in England and vodka in Russia, proved devastating as poor people regularly drank themselves into oblivion. Gin was cheap; the classic sign in English taverns, "Drunk for a penny, dead drunk for two pence," was literally true. In England, the consumption of gin rose from two to five million gallons between 1714 and 1733 and only declined when complaints finally led to strict laws to restrict sales in the 1750s.

In the eighteenth century, the separation between elite and poor grew ever wider. In 1500, popular culture was for everyone; a second culture for the elite, it was the only culture for the rest of society. But between 1500 and 1800, the nobility, clergy, and bourgeoisie had abandoned popular culture to the lower classes. This was, of course, a gradual process, and in abandoning the popular festivals, the upper classes were also abandoning the popular worldview as well. The new scientific outlook had brought a new mental world for the upper classes, and they now viewed such things as witchcraft, faith healing, fortune-telling, and prophecy as the beliefs of "such as are of the weakest judgment and reason, as women, children, and ignorant and superstitious persons."

Crime and Punishment

By the eighteenth century, most European states had developed a hierarchy of courts to deal with civil and criminal cases. With the exception of England, they continued to use judicial torture as an important means of obtaining evidence before trial until almost the end of the century. Courts used the rack, thumbscrews, and other instruments to obtain confessions in criminal cases. Seventeenth-century legal reforms, however, led to the gradual demise of judicial torture. It persisted longer in France than in other European states but was finally abolished there in 1780.

Punishments for crimes were often cruel and even spectacular. Public spectacle was a basic part of traditional punishment because it was believed to deter potential offenders in an age when the state's police arm was too weak to assure the capture of criminals. Although nobles were executed by simple beheading, lower-class criminals condemned to death were tortured, broken on the wheel, or drawn and quartered (see the box on page 539). The death penalty was still commonly used in property as well as criminal cases. By 1800, the English listed over two hundred crimes that were subject to the death penalty. In addition to executions, European states resorted to forced labor in mines, forts, and navies. England also sent criminals as indentured servants to colonies in the New World and, after the American Revolution, to Australia.

 # RELIGION AND THE CHURCHES

The music of Bach and the pilgrimage and monastic churches of southern Germany and Austria make us cognizant of a curious fact. While much of the great art and music of the time was religious, the thought of the time was antireligious as life became increasingly secularized and men of reason attacked the established churches. And yet most Europeans were still Christians. Except for gov-

THE PUNISHMENT OF CRIME

Torture and capital punishment remained common features of European judicial systems well into the eighteenth century. Public spectacles were especially gruesome, as this excerpt from the Nocturnal Spectator *of Restif de la Bretonne demonstrates.*

RESTIF DE LA BRETONNE, NOCTURNAL SPECTATOR: THE BROKEN MAN

I went home by way of rue Saint-Antoine and the Place de Grève. Three murderers had been broken on the wheel there, the day before. I had not expected to see any such spectacle, one that I had never dared to witness. But as I crossed the square I caught sight of a poor wretch, pale, half dead, wracked by the pains of the interrogation inflicted on him twenty hours earlier; he was stumbling down from the Hôtel de Ville supported by the executioner and the confessor. These two men, so completely different, inspired an inexpressible emotion in me! I watched the latter embrace a miserable man consumed by fever, filthy as the dungeons he came from, swarming with vermin! And I said to myself, "O Religion, here is your greatest glory!"

I saw a horrible sight, even though the torture had been mitigated. . . . The wretch had revealed his accomplices. He was garroted before he was put to the wheel. A winch set under the scaffold tightened a noose around the victim's neck and he was strangled; for a long while the confessor and the hangman felt his heart to see whether the artery still pulsed, and the hideous blows were dealt only after it beat no longer. . . . I left, with my hair standing on end in horror.

---

ernments, churches remained the most important institutions in people's lives. Even many of those most critical of the churches accepted that society could not function without religious faith.

In the eighteenth century, the established Catholic and Protestant churches were basically conservative institutions that upheld society's hierarchical structure, privileged classes, and traditions. Although churches experienced change because of new state policies, they did not sustain any dramatic internal changes. Whether in Catholic or Protestant countries, the parish church run by priest or pastor remained the center of religious practice. In addition to providing religious services, the parish church kept records of births, deaths, and marriages, provided charity for the poor, supervised whatever primary education there was, and cared for orphans.

Toleration and Religious Minorities

One of the chief battle cries of the philosophes had been a call for religious toleration. Out of political necessity, a certain level of tolerance of different creeds had occurred in the seventeenth century in such places as Germany after the Thirty Years' War and France after the divisive religious wars. But many rulers still found it difficult to accept. Louis XIV had turned back the clock in France at the end of the seventeenth century, insisting on religious uniformity and suppressing the rights of the Huguenots. Devout rulers continued to believe that there was only one path to salvation; it was the true duty of a ruler not to allow subjects to be condemned to hell by being heretics. Catholic minorities in Protestant countries and Protestant minorities in Catholic countries did not enjoy full civil or political rights. Persecution of heretics continued; the last burning of a heretic took place in 1781.

The Jews remained the despised religious minority of Europe. The largest population of Jews (known as the Ashkenazic Jews) lived in eastern Europe. Except in relatively tolerant Poland, Jews were restricted in their movements, forbidden to own land or hold many jobs, forced to pay burdensome special taxes, and also subject to periodic outbursts of popular wrath. The resulting pogroms in which Jewish communities were looted and massacred made Jewish existence precarious and dependent on the favor of their territorial rulers.

Another major group was the Sephardic Jews who had been expelled from Spain in the fifteenth century. Although many had migrated to Turkish lands, some of them had settled in cities—such as Amsterdam, Venice, London, and Frankfurt—where they were relatively free to participate in the banking and commercial activities that Jews had practiced since the Middle Ages. The highly successful ones came to provide valuable services to rulers, especially in central Europe, where they were known as the court Jews. But even these Jews were insecure because their religion set them apart from the Christian majority and served as a catalyst to social resentment.

Some Enlightenment thinkers in the eighteenth century favored a new acceptance of Jews. They argued that Jews and Muslims were all human and deserved the full rights of citizenship despite their religion. Many philosophes denounced persecution of the Jews but made no attempt to hide their hostility and ridiculed Jewish customs. Diderot, for example, said that the Jews had "all the defects peculiar to an ignorant and superstitious nation." Many Christians favored the assimilation of the Jews into the mainstream of society as the basic solution to the "Jewish problem," but only by the conversion of the Jews to Christianity. This, of course, was not acceptable to most Jews.

The Austrian emperor Joseph II (1780–1790) attempted to adopt a new policy toward the Jews, although it too was limited. It freed Jews from nuisance taxes and allowed them more freedom of movement and job opportunities, but they were still restricted from owning land and worshiping in public. At the same time, Joseph II encouraged Jews to learn German and work toward greater assimilation into Austrian society.

Popular Religion in the Eighteenth Century

Despite the rise of skepticism and the intellectuals' belief in deism and natural religion, it would appear that religious devotion remained strong in the eighteenth century. It is difficult to assess precisely the religiosity of Europe's Catholics. The Catholic parish church remained an important center of life for the entire community. How many people went to church regularly cannot be known exactly, but it has been established that 90 to 95 percent of Catholic populations did go to mass on Easter Sunday, one of the church's most special celebrations.

After the initial religious fervor that created Protestantism in the sixteenth century, Protestant churches in the seventeenth century had settled down into well-established patterns controlled by state authorities and served by a well-educated clergy. In time, these churches became bureaucratized and bereft of religious enthusiasm. In Germany and England, where rationalism and deism had become influential and moved some theologians to a more "rational" Christianity, the desire of ordinary Protestant churchgoers for greater depths of religious experience led to new and dynamic religious movements.

One of the most famous movements—Methodism—was the work of John Wesley (1703–1791). An ordained Anglican minister, John Wesley took religion very seriously, experienced a deep spiritual crisis, and underwent a mystical experience: "I felt I did trust in Christ alone for salvation; and an assurance was given me, that He had taken away my sins, even mine, and saved me from the law of sin and death. I felt my heart strangely warmed." To Wesley, "the gift of God's grace" assured him of salvation and led him to become a missionary to the English people, to bring the "glad tidings" of salvation to all people, despite opposition from the Anglican church, which criticized this emotional mysticism or religious enthusiasm as superstitious nonsense. To Wesley, all could be saved by experiencing God and opening the doors to his grace.

In taking the Gospel to the people, Wesley preached to the masses in open fields, appealing especially to the lower classes neglected by the socially elitist Anglican church. He tried, he said, "to lower religion to the level of the lowest people's capacities." Wesley's fiery preaching often provoked highly charged and even violent conversion experiences (see the box on p. 541). Afterward, converts were organized into so-called Methodist soci-

 JOHN WESLEY. In leading a deep spiritual revival in Britain, John Wesley founded a religious movement that came to be known as Methodism. He loved to preach to the masses, and this 1766 portrait by Nathaniel Hope shows him as he might have appeared before a crowd of people.

eties or chapels in which they could aid each other in doing the good works that Wesley considered a component of salvation. A Central Methodist Conference supervised new lay preachers from Methodist circles. Controlled by Wesley, it enabled him to dominate the evangelical movement he had created. Although Wesley sought to keep Methodism within the Anglican church, after his death it became a separate and independent sect. Methodism represents an important revival of Christianity and proved that the need for spiritual experience had not been expunged by the eighteenth-century search for reason.

CONCLUSION

The Scientific Revolution represents a major turning point in modern civilization. In the Scientific Revolution, the Western world overthrew the medieval, Ptolemaic-Aristotelian worldview and arrived at a new conception of the universe: the sun at the center, the planets as material bodies revolving around the sun in elliptical orbits, and an infinite rather than a finite world. With the changes in the conception of "heaven" came changes in the conception of "earth." The work of Bacon and Descartes left Europeans with the separation of mind and matter and the belief that by using only reason they could, in fact, understand and dominate the world of nature. The development of a scientific method furthered the work

THE CONVERSION EXPERIENCE
IN WESLEY'S METHODISM

After his own conversion experience, John Wesley traveled extensively to bring the "glad tidings" of Christ to other people. It has been estimated that he preached over 40,000 sermons, some of them to audiences numbering 20,000 listeners. Wesley gave his message wherever people gathered—in the streets, hospitals, private houses, and even pubs. In this selection from his journal, Wesley describes how emotional and even violent conversion experiences could be.

THE WORKS OF THE REVEREND JOHN WESLEY

Sunday, May 20 [1759], being with Mr. B—ll at Everton, I was much fatigued, and did not rise: but Mr. B. did, and observed several fainting and crying out, while Mr. Berridge was preaching: afterwards at Church, I heard many cry out, especially children, whose agonies were amazing: one of the eldest, a girl of ten or twelve years old, was full in my view, in violent contortions of body, and weeping aloud, I think incessantly, during the whole service. . . . The Church was equally crowded in the afternoon, the windows being filled within and without, and even the outside of the pulpit to the very top; so that Mr. B. seemed almost stifled by their breath; yet feeble and sickly as he is, he was continually strengthened, and his voice, for the most part, distinguishable, in the midst of all the outcries. I believe there were present three times more men than women, a great part of whom came from far; thirty of them having set out at two in the morning, from a place thirteen miles off. The text was, *Having a form of godliness, but denying the power thereof.* When the power of religion began to be spoken of, the presence of God really filled the place: and while poor sinners felt the sentence of death in their souls, what sounds of distress did I hear! The greatest number of them who cried or fell, were men: but some women, and several children, felt the power of the same almighty Spirit, and seemed just sinking into hell. This occasioned a mixture of several sounds; some shrieking, some roaring aloud. The most general was a loud breathing, like that of people half strangled and gasping for life: and indeed almost all the cries were like those of human creatures, dying in bitter anguish. Great numbers wept without any noise: others fell down as death: some sinking in silence; some with extreme noise and violent agitation. I stood on the pew-seat, as did a young man in the opposite pew, an able-bodied, fresh, healthy countryman: but in a moment, while he seemed to think of nothing less, down he dropped with a violence inconceivable. The adjoining pews seemed to shake with his fall: I heard afterwards the stamping of his feet; ready to break the boards, as he lay in strong convulsions, at the bottom of the pew. Among several that were struck down in the next pew, was a girl, who was as violently seized as he. . . . Among the children who felt the arrows of the Almighty, I saw a sturdy boy, about eight years old, who roared above his fellows, and seemed in his agony to struggle with the strength of a grown man. His face was as red as scarlet: and almost all on whom God laid his hand, turned either very red or almost black. . . .

The violent struggling of many in the above-mentioned churches, has broken several pews and benches. Yet it is common for people to remain unaffected there, and afterwards to drop down in their way home. Some have been found lying as dead on the road: others, in Mr. B.'s garden; not being able to walk from the Church to his house, though it is not two hundred yards.

of scientists, while the new scientific societies and learned journals spread their results. Although traditional churches stubbornly resisted the new ideas and a few intellectuals pointed to some inherent flaws, nothing was able to halt the replacement of the traditional ways of thinking by new ways of thinking that created a more fundamental break with the past than that represented by the breakup of Christian unity in the Reformation.

Highly influenced by the new worldview created by the Scientific Revolution, the philosophes of the eighteenth century hoped that they could create a new society by using reason to discover the natural laws that governed it. They believed that education could produce better human beings and a better human society. They attacked traditional religion as the enemy and developed the new "sciences of man" in economics, politics, and education. Together, the Scientific Revolution of the seventeenth century and the Enlightenment of the eighteenth century constituted an intellectual revolution that laid the foundations for a modern worldview based on rationalism and secularism.

An interesting question that arises is why the Scientific Revolution occurred in the West and not in China. In the Middle Ages, China had been the most technologically advanced civilization in the world. After 1500, that distinction passed to the West. Historians are not sure why. Some have compared the sense of order in Chinese society to the competitive spirit existing in Europe. Others have emphasized China's ideological viewpoint that favored living in harmony with nature rather than trying to dominate it. One historian has even suggested that China's civil service system drew the "best and the brightest" into government service rather than other occupations.

Whatever the reasons, this intellectual revolution contributed to the increased confidence of Western civilization as Europeans—with their strong governments, prosperous economies, and strengthened military forces—began to dominate other parts of the world, adding to a growing belief in the superiority of their civilization. And as we shall see in the next chapter, in the midst of intellectual revolution, economic, political, and social transformations of great importance were also taking shape that by the end of the eighteenth century were to lead to both political and industrial revolutions.

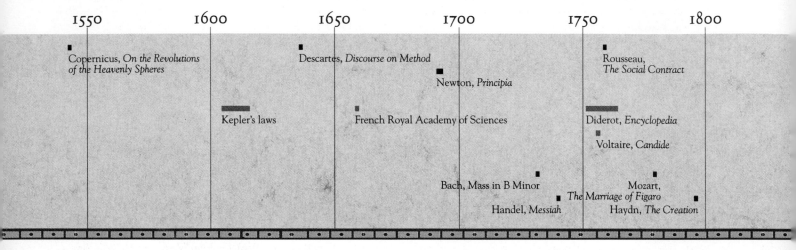

1550   1600   1650   1700   1750   1800

Copernicus, *On the Revolutions of the Heavenly Spheres*

Kepler's laws

Descartes, *Discourse on Method*

Newton, *Principia*

French Royal Academy of Sciences

Bach, Mass in B Minor

Handel, *Messiah*

Rousseau, *The Social Contract*

Diderot, *Encyclopedia*

Voltaire, *Candide*

Mozart, *The Marriage of Figaro*

Haydn, *The Creation*

CHAPTER NOTES

1. Quoted in Alan G. R. Smith, *Science and Society in the Sixteenth and Seventeenth Centuries* (London, 1972), p. 59.
2. Quoted in Londa Schiebinger, *The Mind Has No Sex? Women in the Origins of Modern Science* (Cambridge, Mass., 1989), pp. 52–53.
3. Ibid., p. 85.
4. Quoted in Phyllis Stock, *Better Than Rubies: A History of Women's Education* (New York, 1978), p. 16.
5. René Descartes, *Philosophical Writings*, ed. and trans. Norman K. Smith (New York, 1958), p. 118–19.
6. Blaise Pascal, *Pensées*, trans. J. M. Cohen (Harmondsworth, 1961), p. 100.
7. Ibid., pp. (in order of appearance) 31, 31, 52–53, 164, 165.
8. Francis Bacon, *The Great Instauration*, trans. Jerry Weinberger (Arlington Heights, Ill., 1989), pp. (in order of appearance) 2, 8, 2, 16, 21.
9. John Locke, *An Essay Concerning Human Understanding* (New York, 1964), pp. 89–90.
10. Jean-Jacques Rousseau, *The Social Contract*, trans. Maurice Cranston (Harmondsworth, 1968), p. 141.
11. Mary Astell, *A Serious Proposal to the Ladies*, in Moira Ferguson, ed., *First Feminists: British Women Writers, 1578–1799* (Bloomington, Ind., 1985), p. 190.
12. Kenneth Clark, *Civilisation* (New York, 1969), p. 231.
13. Quoted in Peter Burke, *Popular Culture in Early Modern Europe* (New York, 1978), p. 179.

SUGGESTED READINGS

Four general surveys of the entire Scientific Revolution are A. G. R. Smith, *Science and Society in the Sixteenth and Seventeenth Centuries* (London, 1972); J. R. Jacob, *The Scientific Revolution: Aspirations and Achievements, 1500–1700* (Atlantic Highlands, N. J., 1998); S. Shapin, *The Scientific Revolution* (Chicago, 1996); and J. Henry, *The Scientific Revolution and the Origins of Modern Science* (New York, 1997). Also of much value is A. G. Debus, *Man and Nature in the Renaissance* (Cambridge, 1978), which covers the period from the mid-fifteenth through the mid-seventeenth century. On the relationship of magic to the beginnings of the Scientific Revolution, see the pioneering works by F. Yates, *Giordano Bruno and the Hermetic Tradition* (New York, 1969), and *The Rosicrucian Enlightenment* (London, 1975).

On the important figures of the revolution in astronomy, see E. Rosen, *Copernicus and the Scientific Revolution* (New York, 1984); M. Sharratt, *Galileo: Decisive Innovator* (Oxford, 1994); S. Drake, *Galileo, Pioneer Scientist* (Toronto, 1990); M. Casper, *Johannes Kepler*, trans. C. D. Hellman (London, 1959), the standard biography;

and R. S. Westfall, *The Life of Isaac Newton* (New York, 1993). On Newton's relationship to alchemy, see M. White, *Isaac Newton: The Last Sorcerer* (Reading, Mass., 1997).

The standard biography of Vesalius is C. D. O'Malley, *Andreas Vesalius of Brussels, 1514–1564* (Berkeley, Calif., 1964). Harvey's work is discussed in G. Whitteridge, *William Harvey and the Circulation of the Blood* (London, 1971). The importance of Francis Bacon in the early development of science is underscored in P. Zagorin, *Francis Bacon* (Princeton, N.J., 1998). A good introduction to the work of Descartes can be found in G. Radis-Lewis, *Descartes: A Biography* (Ithaca, N.Y., 1998).

On the subject of women and early modern science, see the comprehensive and highly informative work by L. Schiebinger, *The Mind Has No Sex? Women in the Origins of Modern Science* (Cambridge, Mass., 1989). See also C. Merchant, *The Death of Nature: Women, Ecology, and the Scientific Revolution* (San Francisco, 1980). The social and political context for the triumph of science in the seventeenth and eighteenth centuries is examined in M. Jacobs, *The Cultural Meaning of the Scientific Revolution* (New York, 1988).

Two sound, comprehensive surveys of eighteenth-century Europe are I. Woloch, *Eighteenth-Century Europe* (New York, 1982), and M. S. Anderson, *Europe in the Eighteenth Century* (London, 1987).

Good introductions to the Enlightenment can be found in N. Hampson, *A Cultural History of the Enlightenment* (New York, 1968); U. Im Hof, *The Enlightenment* (Oxford, 1994); D. Goodman, *The Republic of Letters: A Cultural History of the French Enlightenment* (Ithaca, N.Y., 1994); and D. Outram, *The Enlightenment* (Cambridge, 1995). A more detailed synthesis can be found in the two volumes by P. Gay, *The Enlightenment: An Interpretation*, 2 vols. (New York,

1966–1969). For a short, popular survey on the French philosophes, see F. Artz, *The Enlightenment in France* (Kent, Oh., 1968). Studies on the major Enlightenment intellectuals include J. Sklar, *Montesquieu* (Oxford, 1987); H. T. Mason, *Voltaire: A Biography* (Baltimore, 1981); P. N. Furbank, *Diderot: A Critical Biography* (New York, 1992); and M. Cranston, *The Noble Savage: Jean-Jacques Rousseau* (New York, 1991). On women in the eighteenth century, see N. Z. Davis and A. Farge, eds., *A History of Women: Renaissance and Enlightenment Paradoxes* (Cambridge, Mass., 1993); C. Lougee, *Le Paradis des Femmes. Women, Salons, and Social Stratification* (Princeton, N.J., 1976); O. Hufton, *The Prospect Before Her: A History of Women in Western Europe, 1500–1800* (New York, 1998); and B. S. Anderson and J. P. Zinsser, *A History of Their Own*, vol. 2 (New York, 1988).

Two readable general surveys on the arts and literature are M. Levy, *Rococo to Revolution* (London, 1966), and H. Honour, *Neoclassicism* (Harmondsworth, 1968). Different facets of crime and punishment are examined in the important work by M. Foucault, *Discipline and Punish: The Birth of the Prison* (New York, 1977). Important studies on popular culture include P. Burke, *Popular Culture in Early Modern Europe* (New York, 1978), and R. Darnton, *The Great Cat Massacre and Other Episodes in French Cultural History* (New York, 1984).

A good introduction to the religious history of the eighteenth century can be found in G. R. Cragg, *The Church and the Age of Reason, 1648–1789* (London, 1966). On John Wesley, see H. Rack, *Reasonable Enthusiast: John Wesley and the Rise of Methodism* (New York, 1989).

INFOTRAC COLLEGE EDITION

For additional reading, go to InfoTrac College Edition, your online research library at
http://web1.infotrac-college.com

Enter the search terms "Isaac Newton or Copernicus" using Keywords.

Enter the search term "Enlightenment" using the Subject Guide.

Enter the search term "Rousseau" using Keywords.

Enter the search terms "John Locke" using Keywords.

Enter the search terms "scientific revolution" using Keywords.

CHAPTER 19

EUROPE ON THE EVE OF A NEW WORLD ORDER

CHAPTER OUTLINE

- ECONOMIC CHANGES AND THE PERSISTENCE OF A TRADITIONAL SOCIAL ORDER
- CHANGING PATTERNS OF WAR: GLOBAL CONFRONTATION
- COLONIAL EMPIRES AND REVOLUTION
- TOWARD A NEW POLITICAL ORDER
- CONCLUSION

FOCUS QUESTIONS

- What changes occurred in the European economy in the eighteenth century, and to what degree were these changes reflected in social patterns?
- How did Spain and Portugal administer their American colonies, and what were the main characteristics of Latin American society in the eighteenth century?
- What do historians mean by the term *enlightened absolutism*, and to what degree did eighteenth-century Prussia, Austria, and Russia exhibit its characteristics?
- What were the causes, the main events, and the results of the American Revolution and the French Revolution?
- What aspects of the French Revolution did Napoleon preserve, and which did he destroy?

Historians have often portrayed the eighteenth century as the final phase of Europe's old order before the violent upheaval and reordering of society associated with the French Revolution. The old order—still largely agrarian, dominated by kings and landed aristocrats—and grounded in privileges for nobles, clergy, towns, and provinces—seemed to continue a basic pattern that had prevailed in Europe since medieval times. Recent scholarship, however, has tended to undermine the idea of uniformity in the eighteenth century. Just as a new intellectual order based on rationalism and secularism was emerging in Europe from the intellectual revolution of the Scientific Revolution and the Enlightenment, demographic, economic, social, and political patterns were beginning to change in ways that reflect the emergence of a new modern order.

A key factor in the emergence of a new world order was the French Revolution. On the morning of July 14, 1789, a Parisian mob of some eight thousand men and women in search of weapons streamed toward the Bastille, a royal armory filled with arms and ammunition. The Bastille was also a state prison, and although it now held only seven prisoners, in the eyes of these angry Parisians, it was a glaring symbol of the government's despotic policies. It was defended by the Marquis de Launay and a small garrison of 114 men. The attack on the Bastille began in earnest in the early afternoon, and after three hours of fighting, de Launay and the garrison surrendered. Angered by the loss of ninety-eight of their members, the victors beat de Launay to death, cut off his head, and carried it aloft in triumph through the streets of Paris. When King Louis XVI was told the news of the fall of the Bastille by the Duc de La Rochefoucauld-Liancourt, he exclaimed, "Why, this is a revolt." "No, Sire," replied the duke. "It is a revolution."

The French Revolution has been portrayed as a major turning point in European political and social history, as a time when the institutions of the "old regime" were destroyed and a new order was created based on individual rights, representative institutions, and a concept of loyalty to the nation rather than the monarch. The revolutionary upheaval of the era, especially in France, did create new liberal and national political ideals, summarized in the French revolutionary slogan "Liberty, Equality, and Fraternity," that transformed France and then spread to other European countries and the rest of the world. ✿

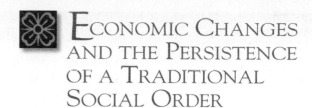

ECONOMIC CHANGES AND THE PERSISTENCE OF A TRADITIONAL SOCIAL ORDER

The eighteenth century witnessed the beginning of economic changes in Europe that ultimately had a strong impact on the rest of the world. Rapid population growth, an agricultural revolution, the beginnings of an industrial revolution, and an increase in worldwide trade characterized the economic patterns of the eighteenth century.

Population, Food, and Industry

Europe's population began to grow around 1750 and continued a slow upward movement. The total European population was probably around 120 million in 1700, expanded to 140 million by 1750, and then grew to 190 million by 1790; thus, the growth rate in the second half of the century was more than double that of the first half. These increases occurred during the same period that several million Europeans were going abroad as colonists. A falling death rate was perhaps the most important cause of population growth. But why did the death rate decline? More plentiful food and better transportation of available food supplies led to some improvement in diet and relief from devastating famines. Also of great significance in lowering death rates was the disappearance of bubonic plague.

Food became more abundant due in part to improvements in agricultural practices and methods in the eighteenth century, especially in Britain, parts of France, and the Low Countries. The increases in food production can be attributed to four interrelated factors: more land under cultivation, increased yields per acre, healthier and more abundant livestock, and an improved climate. Climatologists believe that the "little ice age" of the seventeenth century declined in the eighteenth, especially evident in the moderate summers that provided more ideal growing conditions. Important to the increased yields was the spread of new vegetables, including two important American crops, the potato and maize (Indian corn). Although they were not grown in quantity until after 1700, they had been brought to Europe from America in the sixteenth century and were part of what some historians have called the Columbian exchange—a reciprocal exchange of plants and animals between Europe and America (see Map 19.1). The potato became a staple in Germany, the Low Countries, and especially Ireland, where repression by British landlords forced large numbers of poor peasants to survive on small plots of marginal land. The potato took relatively little effort to produce in large quantities. High in carbohydrates and calories, rich in vitamins A and C, it could be easily stored for winter use.

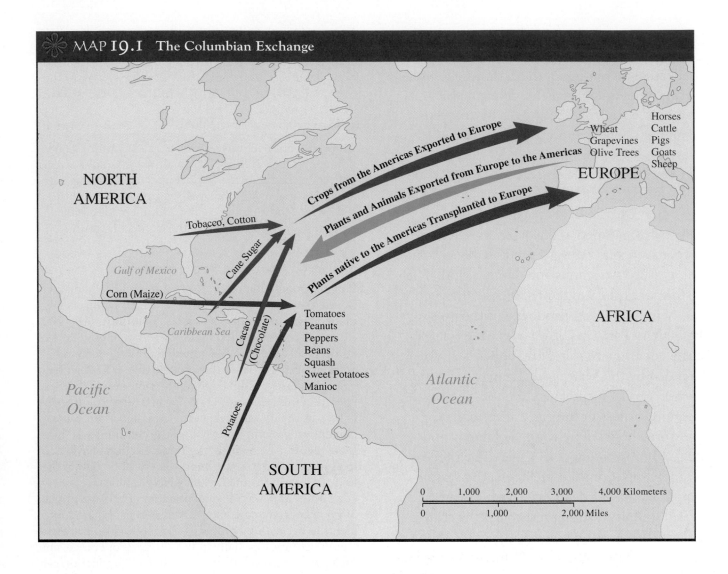

MAP 19.1 The Columbian Exchange

In the eighteenth century, it was primarily the British who adopted the new techniques that have been characterized as an agricultural revolution. This early modernization of British agriculture with its noticeable increase in productivity made possible the feeding of an expanding population about to enter a new world of industrialization and urbanization.

The most important product of European industry in the eighteenth century was textiles, most of which were still produced by traditional methods. In cities that were textile centers, master artisans used timeworn methods to produce finished goods in their guild workshops. But by the eighteenth century, textile production had begun to shift to the countryside in some parts of Europe. Textiles were produced in the countryside by the "putting-out" or "domestic" system in which a merchant-capitalist entrepreneur bought the raw materials, mostly wool and flax, and "put them out" to rural workers who spun the raw material into yarn and then wove it into cloth on simple looms. Capitalist entrepreneurs sold the finished products, made a profit, and used it to manufacture more. This system was also called "cottage industry," because spinners and weavers did their work on spinning wheels and looms in their own cottages. Cottage industry was truly a family enterprise because women and children could spin while men wove on the looms, enabling rural people to earn incomes that supplemented their pitiful wages as agricultural laborers. The cottage system with its traditional methods of manufacturing was established in many rural areas of Europe during the eighteenth century. But in the second half of the century, significant changes in industrial production began to occur that would lead to an industrial revolution (see Chapter 20).

Worldwide Trade

Although bankers and industrialists would come to dominate the nineteenth century economically, in the eighteenth century merchants and traders still reigned supreme. Intra-European trade still dominated total trade figures as wheat, timber, and naval stores from the Baltic, wines from France, wool and fruit from Spain, and silk from Italy were exchanged along with a host of other products. But the eighteenth century witnessed only a slight increase in this trade while overseas trade boomed. This increase in overseas trade has led some historians to speak of the emergence of a truly global economy in the eighteenth century.

To justify the term *global economy*, historians have usually pointed to the patterns of trade that interlocked Europe, Africa, the Far East, and the American continents. One such pattern involved the influx of gold and silver into Spain from its colonial American empire. Much of this gold and silver made its way to Britain, France, and the Netherlands in return for manufactured goods. British, Dutch, and French merchants in turn used their profits to buy tea, spices, silk, and cotton goods from China and India to sell in Europe. Another important source of trading activity came from the plantations of the Western Hemisphere. Plantations, extending from the southern colonies of North America through the West Indies and into Brazil, were worked by African slaves and produced tobacco, cotton, coffee, and sugar, all products in demand by Europeans. A third pattern of trade involved British merchant ships, which carried British manufactured goods to Africa, where they were traded for a cargo of slaves, which were then shipped to Virginia and paid for with tobacco, which in turn was shipped back to Britain, where it was processed and then sold in Germany for cash. Of all the goods traded in the eighteenth century, perhaps the most profitable and certainly the most infamous were African slaves (see Chapter 14).

Overseas trade created enormous prosperity for some European countries. By the beginning of the eighteenth century, Spain, Portugal, and the Dutch Republic, which had earlier monopolized overseas trade, found themselves increasingly overshadowed by France and Britain, which built enormously profitable colonial empires in the course of the eighteenth century. After 1763, however, when France lost the Seven Years' War and much of its overseas empire, Britain emerged as the world's strongest overseas trading nation, and London became the world's greatest port.

Society in the Eighteenth Century

Although dramatic economic changes were taking place in the eighteenth century, European society itself still clung to many of the social patterns established centuries earlier in the Middle Ages. The resulting tensions between

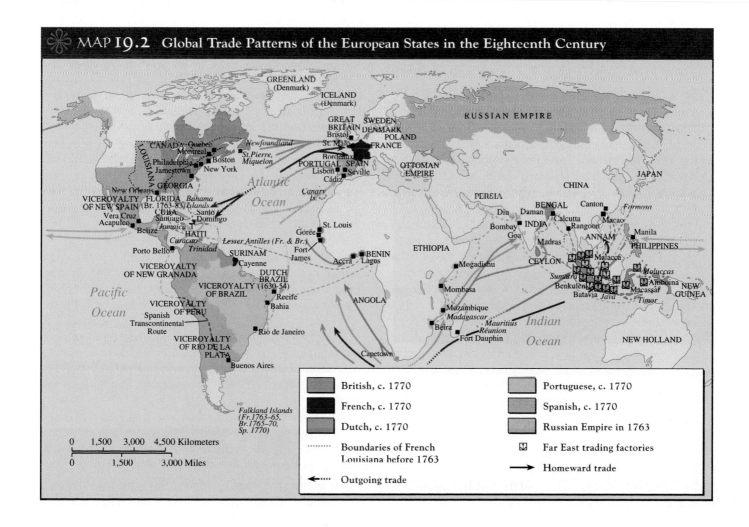

MAP **19.2** Global Trade Patterns of the European States in the Eighteenth Century

THE ARISTOCRATIC WAY OF LIFE.   The eighteenth-century country house in Britain fulfilled the desire of aristocrats for both elegance and greater privacy. The painting above by Richard Wilson shows a typical English country house of the eighteenth century, surrounded by a simple and serene landscape. Thomas Gainsborough's *Conversation in the Park*, shown at right, captures the relaxed life of two aristocrats in the park of their country estate.

the new economic patterns and the old social institutions would contribute to the revolutionary upheavals at the end of the eighteenth century.

Social status in the eighteenth century was still largely determined not by wealth and economic standing but by the division into the traditional "orders" or "estates" determined by heredity. This divinely sanctioned division of society into traditional orders was supported by Christian teaching, which emphasized the need to fulfill the responsibilities of one's estate. Although Enlightenment intellectuals attacked these traditional distinctions, they did not die easily. In the Prussian law code of 1794, marriage between noble males and middle-class females was forbidden without a government dispensation. Even without government regulation, however, different social groups could be easily distinguished everywhere in Europe by the distinctive, traditional clothes they wore.

Nevertheless, some forces of change were at work in this traditional society. The ideas of the Enlightenment made headway as reformers argued that the concept of an unchanging social order based on privilege was hostile to the progress of society. Despite these ideas, however, it would take the revolutionary upheavals at the end of the eighteenth century before the old order would finally begin to disintegrate.

Since society was still mostly rural in the eighteenth century, the peasantry constituted the largest social group, making up as much as 85 percent of Europe's population. There were rather wide differences, however, between peasants from area to area. The most important distinction—at least legally—was between the free peasant and the serf. In Britain, northern Italy, the Low Countries, Spain, most of France, and some areas of western Germany, peasants were largely free. Legally free peasants, however, were not exempt from burdens. Many peasants owned little or no land. And peasants who did own land were not free from compulsory services. Peasants could still owe a variety of dues and fees. Local aristocrats claimed hunting rights on peasant land and had monopolies over the flour mills, community ovens, and wine and oil presses needed by the peasants. Hunting rights, dues, and fees were all deeply resented.

The local villages in which they dwelt remained the centers of peasants' social lives. Villages, especially in western Europe, maintained public order; provided poor relief, a village church, and sometimes a schoolmaster; collected taxes for the central government; maintained roads and bridges; and established common procedures for sowing, plowing, and harvesting crops. But villages were often dominated by richer peasants and proved highly resistant to innovations, such as new crops and agricultural practices.

The nobles, who constituted about 2 or 3 percent of the European population, played a dominating role in society. Being born a noble automatically guaranteed a place at the top of the social order with all of its attendant special privileges and rights. The legal privileges of the nobility included judgment by their peers, immunity from severe punishment, exemption from many forms of taxation, and rights of jurisdiction. Especially in central and eastern Europe, the rights of landlords over their serfs were overwhelming.

Nobles also played important roles in military and government affairs. Since medieval times, landed aristocrats had functioned as military officers. Although monarchs found it impossible to exclude commoners from the ranks of officers, the tradition remained that nobles made the most natural and hence the best officers. Moreover, the eighteenth-century nobility played a significant role in the administrative machinery of state. In some countries, such as Prussia, the entire bureaucracy reflected aristocratic values. Moreover, in most of Europe, the landholding nobility controlled much of the life of their local districts.

Townspeople were still a distinct minority of the total population except in the Dutch Republic, Britain, and parts of Italy. At the end of the eighteenth century, about one-sixth of the French population lived in towns of 2,000 or more. The biggest city in Europe was London, with its 1,000,000 inhabitants, while Paris numbered between 550,000 and 600,000. Altogether, at least twenty European cities in twelve countries had populations over 100,000, including Naples, Lisbon, Moscow, St. Petersburg, Vienna, Amsterdam, Berlin, Rome, and Madrid.

Although urban dwellers were vastly outnumbered by rural inhabitants, towns played an important role in Western culture. The contrasts between a large city with its education, culture, and material consumption and the surrounding, often poverty-stricken countryside were striking, as is evident in this British traveler's account of Russia's St. Petersburg in 1741:

> The country about Petersburg has full as wild and desert a look as any in the Indies; you need not go above 200 paces out of the town to find yourself in a wild wood of firs, and such a low, marshy, boggy country that you would think God when he created the rest of the world for the use of mankind had created this for an inaccessible retreat for all sorts of wild beasts.[1]

Peasants often resented the prosperity of towns and their exploitation of the countryside to serve urban interests. Palermo in Sicily used one-third of the island's food production while paying only one-tenth of the taxes. Towns lived off the countryside not by buying, but by using tithes, rents, and feudal dues to acquire peasant produce.

Many cities in western and even central Europe had a long tradition of patrician oligarchies that continued to control their communities by dominating town and city councils. Despite their domination, patricians constituted only a small minority of the urban population. Just below the patricians stood an upper crust of the middle classes: nonnoble officeholders, financiers and bankers, merchants, wealthy rentiers who lived off their investments, and important professionals, including lawyers. Another large urban group was the petty bourgeoisie or lower middle class

made up of master artisans, shopkeepers, and small traders. Below them were the laborers or working classes. Much urban industry was still done in small guild workshops by masters, journeymen, and apprentices. Urban communities also had a large group of unskilled workers who served as servants, maids, and cooks at pitifully low wages.

Despite an end to the ravages of plague, eighteenth-century cities still experienced high death rates, especially among children, because of unsanitary living conditions, polluted water, and a lack of sewerage facilities. One observer compared the stench of Hamburg to an open sewer that could be smelled for miles around. Overcrowding also exacerbated urban problems as cities continued to grow from an influx of rural immigrants. But cities proved no paradise for them as unskilled workers found few employment opportunities. The result was a serious problem of poverty in the eighteenth century (see the box on p. 550).

CHANGING PATTERNS OF WAR: GLOBAL CONFRONTATION

The philosophes had denounced war as a foolish waste of life and resources in stupid quarrels of no value to humankind. Rulers, however, paid little attention to these comments and continued their costly struggles. By the eighteenth century, the European system of self-governing, individual states was grounded largely in the principle of self-interest. Because international relations were based on considerations of power, the eighteenth-century concept of a "balance of power" was predicated on how to counterbalance the power of one state by another to prevent any one power from dominating the others. This balance of power, however, did not imply a desire for peace. Large armies created to defend a state's security were often used for offensive purposes as well. As Frederick the Great of Prussia remarked: "The fundamental rule of governments is the principle of extending their territories." Nevertheless, the regular use of diplomacy served at times to lead to compromise.

The diplomacy of the eighteenth century still focused primarily on dynastic interests or the desire of ruling families to provide for their dependents and extend their dynastic holdings. But the eighteenth century also saw the emergence of the concept of "reason of state," on the basis of which rulers looked beyond dynastic interests to the long-term future of their states.

International rivalry and the continuing centralization of the European states were closely related. The need for taxes to support large armies and navies created its own imperative for more efficient and effective control of power in the hands of bureaucrats who could collect taxes and organize states for the task of winning

POVERTY IN FRANCE

*P*overty was a highly visible problem in the eighteenth century. Unlike the British, who had a system of public-supported poor relief, the French responded to poverty with ad hoc policies when conditions became acute. This selection is taken from an intendant's report to the controller-general at Paris describing his suggestions for a program to relieve the grain shortages expected for the winter months.

M. DE LA BOURDONNAYE, INTENDANT OF BORDEAUX, TO THE CONTROLLER-GENERAL, SEPTEMBER 30, 1708

Having searched for the means of helping the people of Agen in this cruel situation and having conferred with His Eminence, the Bishop, it seems to us that three things are absolutely necessary if the people are not to starve during the winter.

Most of the inhabitants do not have seed to plant their fields. However, we decided that we would be going too far if we furnished it, because those who have seed would also apply [for more]. Moreover, we are persuaded that all the inhabitants will make strenuous efforts to find some seed, since they have every reason to expect prices to remain high next year. . . .

But this project will come to nothing if the collectors of the taille continue to be as strict in the exercise of their functions as they have been of late and continue to employ troops [to force collection]. Those inhabitants who have seed grain would sell it to be freed from an oppressive garrison, while those who must buy seed, since they had none left from their harvest and have scraped together a little money for this purchase, would prefer to give up that money [for taxes] when put under police constraint. To avoid this, I feel it is absolutely necessary that you order the receivers-general to reduce their operations during this winter, at least with respect to the poor. . . .

We are planning to import wheat for this region from Languedoc and Quercy, and we are confident that there will be enough. But there are two things to be feared: one is the greed of the merchants. When they see that general misery has put them in control of prices, they will raise them to the point where the calamity is almost as great as if there were no provisions at all. The other fear is that the artisans and the lowest classes, when they find themselves at the mercy of the merchants, will cause disorders and riots. As a protective measure, it would seem wise to establish two small storehouses. . . . Ten thousand ecus [30,000 livres] would be sufficient for each. . . .

A third point demanding our attention is the support of beggars among the poor, as well as of those who have no other resources than their wages. Since there will be very little work, these people will soon be reduced to starvation. We should establish public workshops to provide work as was done in 1693 and 1694. I should choose the most useful kind of work, located where there are the greatest number of poor. In this manner, we should rid ourselves of those who do not want to work and assure the others of a moderate subsistence. For these workshops, we would need about 40,000 livres, or altogether 100,000 livres. The receiver-general of the taille of Agen could advance this sum. The 60,000 livres for the storehouses he would get back very soon. I shall await your orders on all of the above.

MARGINAL COMMENTS BY THE CONTROLLER-GENERAL

Operations for the collection of the taille are to be suspended. The two storehouses are to be established; great care must be taken to put them to good use. The interest on the advances will be paid by the king. His Majesty has agreed to the establishment of the public workshops for the able-bodied poor and is willing to spend up to 40,000 livres on them this winter.

---

wars. At the same time, the development of large standing armies ensured that political disputes would periodically be resolved by armed conflict rather than diplomacy.

Between 1715 and 1740, however, it seemed that Europeans preferred peace. But in 1740, a major conflict erupted over the succession to the Austrian throne. After the death of the Habsburg emperor Charles VI (1711–1740), King Frederick II of Prussia (1740–1786) took advantage of the succession of a woman, Maria Theresa (1740–1780), to the throne of Austria by invading Austrian Silesia. The vulnerability of Maria Theresa encouraged France to enter the war against its traditional enemy Austria; in turn, Maria Theresa made an alliance

with the British, who feared French hegemony over continental affairs. All too quickly, the Austrian succession had produced a worldwide conflagration. The war was fought not only in Europe, where Prussia seized Silesia, and France occupied the Austrian Netherlands, but in the East, where France took Madras in India from the British, and in North America, where the British captured the French fortress of Louisbourg at the entrance to the St. Lawrence River. By 1748, all parties were exhausted and agreed to stop. The peace treaty guaranteed the return of all occupied territories to their original owners except for Silesia. Prussia's refusal to return Silesia guaranteed another war, at least between the two hostile central European powers of Prussia and Austria.

The Seven Years' War (1756–1763): A Global War

Maria Theresa refused to accept the loss of Silesia and prepared for its return by rebuilding her army while working diplomatically to separate Prussia from its chief ally, France. In 1756, Austria achieved what was soon labeled a diplomatic revolution. French-Austrian rivalry had been a fact of European diplomacy since the late sixteenth century. But two new rivalries made this old one seem superfluous: Britain and France over colonial empires, and Austria and Prussia over Silesia. France now abandoned Prussia and allied with Austria. Russia, which saw Prussia as a major hindrance to Russian goals in central Europe, joined the new alliance. In turn, Great Britain allied with Prussia. This diplomatic revolution of 1756 now led to another worldwide war.

There were three major areas of conflict: Europe, India, and North America. Europe witnessed the clash of the two major alliances: the British and Prussians against the Austrians, Russians, and French. With his superb army and military prowess, Frederick the Great of Prussia was able for some time to defeat the Austrian, French, and Russian armies. Under attack from three different directions, however, Frederick's forces were gradually worn down and

faced utter defeat until a new Russian tsar, Peter III (1762), withdrew Russian troops from the conflict and from the Prussian lands that the Russians had occupied. His withdrawal guaranteed a stalemate and led the parties to negotiate a peace. The European conflict ended in 1763. All occupied territories were returned, while Austria officially recognized Prussia's permanent control of Silesia.

The Anglo-French struggle in the rest of the world had more decisive results. Known as the Great War for Empire, it was fought in India and North America. The French had returned Madras to Britain after the War of the Austrian Succession, but jockeying for power continued as both the French and the British claimed the support of opposing native Indian princes. The British under Robert Clive (1725–1774) ultimately won out, not because they had better forces but because they were more persistent. By the Treaty of Paris in 1763, the French withdrew and left India to the British (see Chapter 16).

By far, the greatest conflicts of the Seven Years' War took place in North America. Both the French and British colonial empires in the New World consisted of large parts of the West Indies and the North American continent. In the former, the British held Barbados, Jamaica, and Bermuda, while the French possessed Saint Dominique, Martinique, and Guadeloupe. On these tropical islands,

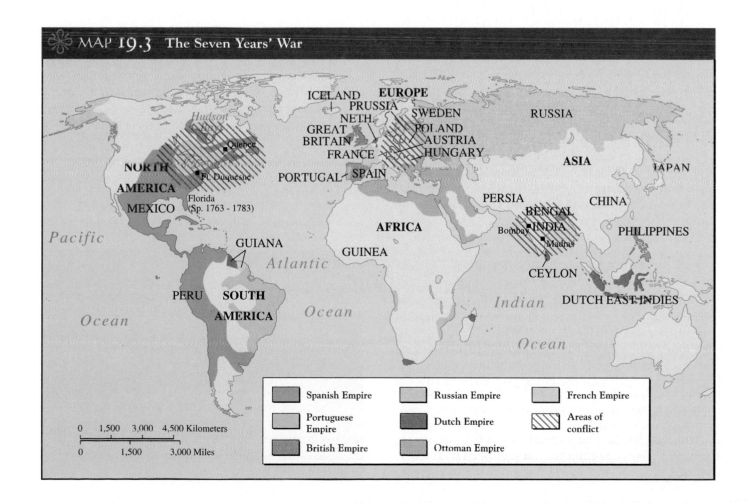

MAP **19.3**   The Seven Years' War

both the British and the French had developed plantation economies, worked by African slaves, which produced tobacco, cotton, coffee, and sugar.

On the North American continent, the French and British colonies were structured in different ways. French North America (Canada and Louisiana) was run autocratically as a vast trading area, valuable for the acquisition of fur, leather, fish, and timber. However, the inability of the French state to get its people to emigrate to these North American possessions left them thinly populated.

British North America had come to consist of thirteen colonies on the eastern coast of the present United States. They were well populated, containing about 1.5 million people by 1750, and were also prosperous. Supposedly run by the British Board of Trade, the Royal Council, and Parliament, these thirteen colonies had legislatures that tended to act independently. Merchants in such port cities as Boston, Philadelphia, New York, and Charleston resented and resisted regulation from the British government.

Both the North American and West Indian colonies of Britain and France were assigned roles in keeping with mercantilist theory. They provided raw materials for the mother country while buying the latter's manufactured goods. Navigation acts regulated what could be taken from and sold to the colonies. Theoretically, the system was supposed to provide a balance of trade favorable to the mother country.

British and French rivalry in North America led to two primary areas of contention. One consisted of the waterways of the Gulf of St. Lawrence, guarded by the fortress of Louisbourg and by forts near the Great Lakes and Lake Champlain that protected French Quebec and French traders. The other was the unsettled Ohio River valley. The French began to move down from the Great Lakes and up from their forts on the Mississippi to establish forts from the Appalachians to the Mississippi River. To British settlers in the thirteen colonies, French activity threatened to cut off this vast area from exploitation by the settlers. The French were able to gain the support of the Indians; as traders and not settlers, they were viewed by the natives with less hostility than the British.

Despite initial French successes, British fortunes were revived by the efforts of William Pitt the Elder, who was convinced that the destruction of the French colonial empire was a necessary prerequisite for the creation of Britain's own colonial empire. Pitt's policy focused on making a minimal effort in Europe while concentrating resources on the colonial war, especially through use of the British navy. Although the French troops outnumbered the British, the ability of the French to use their troops in the New World was contingent upon naval support. The defeat of French fleets in major naval battles in 1759 gave the British an advantage because the French could no longer easily reinforce their garrisons. A series of British victories soon followed. In 1759, British forces under General James Wolfe defeated the French under General Louis-Joseph Montcalm on the Plains of Abraham outside Quebec. Both generals died in the battle. The British went on to seize Montreal, the Great Lakes area, and the Ohio valley. The French were forced to make peace. By the Treaty of Paris, they ceded Canada and the lands east of the Mississippi to Britain. Their ally Spain transferred Spanish Florida to British control; in return, the French gave their Louisiana territory to the Spanish. By 1763, Great Britain had become the world's greatest colonial power.

European Armies and Warfare in the Eighteenth Century

The professional standing army, initiated in the seventeenth century, became a standard feature of eighteenth-century Europe. Especially noticeable was the increase in the size of armies, which paralleled the development of absolutist states. From 1740 to 1780, the French army grew from 190,000 to 300,000 men; the Prussian from 83,000 to 200,000; the Austrian from 108,000 to 282,000; and the Russian from 130,000 to 290,000.

The composition of these armies reflected the hierarchical structure of European society and the great chasm that separated the upper and lower classes. Officers were primarily from the landed aristocracy, which had for centuries regarded military activity as one of its major functions. Middle-class individuals were largely kept out of the higher ranks of the officer corps while being admitted to the middle ranks. Rank-and-file soldiers came mostly from the lower classes of society. Some states, such as Prussia and Russia, conscripted able-bodied peasants. But many

THE DEATH OF WOLFE. The great powers of Europe fought the Seven Years' War in Europe, India, and North America. Despite initial French successes in North America, the British went on to win the war. This painting by Benjamin West presents a heroic rendering of the death of General Wolfe, the British commander who defeated the French forces at the Battle of Quebec.

states realized that this was counterproductive because they could not afford to waste agricultural labor. For that reason, eighteenth-century armies were partially composed of foreign troops, many from Switzerland or the petty German states. Of the great powers, Britain alone had no regular standing army and relied on mercenaries, evident in its use of German troops in America. Most troops in European armies, especially the French and the Austrian, were natives who enlisted voluntarily for six-year terms. Some were not exactly volunteers; often vagabonds and the unemployed were pressed into service. Most, however, came from the lower classes—peasants and also artisans from the cities—who saw the military as an opportunity to escape from hard times or personal problems.

The maritime powers, such as Britain and the Dutch Republic, regarded navies as more important than armies. In the second half of the eighteenth century, the British possessed 174 warships manned by 80,000 sailors. Conditions on these ships were often poor. Diseases such as scurvy and yellow fever were rampant, and crews were frequently gang-pressed into duty.

COLONIAL EMPIRES AND REVOLUTION

As we have seen, the colonial empires in the Western Hemisphere were an integral part of the European economy in the eighteenth century and became entangled in the conflicts of the European states. Despite these close ties with Europe, the colonies of Latin America and British North America were developing along lines that sometimes differed significantly from those of Europe.

The Society of Latin America

In the sixteenth century, Portugal came to dominate Brazil, while Spain established an enormous colonial empire in the New World that included Central America, most of South America, and parts of North America. Within the lands of Central and South America, a new civilization arose that we have come to call Latin America. It was a multiracial society. Iberian (Spanish and Portuguese) settlers who arrived in the Western Hemisphere were small in number compared to the native Indians; many of the newcomers, especially in the early decades of colonization, were males who not only used female natives for their sexual pleasure, but married them as well. Already by 1501, Spanish rulers had authorized intermarriage between Europeans and native American Indians. As a result, a new people—the mestizos—appeared. Europeans also used native Indians to do their work for them. So many Indians succumbed to European diseases (see Chapter 14), however, that another group of people was brought to Latin America—the Africans.

African slaves were first imported to the Western Hemisphere in 1502. Over a period of three centuries, possibly as many as eight million slaves were brought to Spanish and Portuguese America. In Brazil and the Caribbean, where the cultivation of cane sugar by the plantation system demanded much human labor, Africans constituted almost the entire labor force. Because plantation owners preferred males as field hands, two out of every three Africans were male. Although female slaves also worked in the fields, many were used as domestic servants, prostitutes, and mistresses. Over a period of time, Africans were also brought to the cities, where they worked as artisans, servants, small tradesmen, and miners. Although Africans made enormous contributions to the economic life of Spanish America and Portuguese Brazil, they were usually treated with contempt and badly abused. But in many ways—music, dance, folklore, diet, language, religion—African influence remained a permanent part of Latin American culture.

Africans also contributed to Latin America's multiracial character. Mulattoes—the offspring of Africans and whites—joined mestizos and descendants of whites, Africans, and native Indians to produce a unique society in Latin America (see the box on p. 554). Unlike Europe, and unlike British North America, which remained a largely white offshoot of Europe, Latin America developed a multiracial society with less rigid attitudes about race.

THE ECONOMIC FOUNDATIONS

After realizing that the Americas were not Asia, both the Portuguese and the Spanish sought ways to benefit economically from their discoveries. The search for precious metals became a major objective. The Spaniards were especially successful, finding supplies of gold in the Caribbean and New Granada (Colombia) and silver in Mexico and the viceroyalty of Peru. The silver mine of Potosí in Upper Peru (Bolivia) was one of the world's richest. Overall, mines in the viceroyalty of New Spain (largely Mexico) produced half of the precious metals found in the New World. Most of the gold and silver was sent to Europe, and little remained in the New World to benefit those whose labor had produced it.

Although the pursuit of gold and silver offered prospects of fantastic financial rewards, agriculture proved to be a more long-lasting and rewarding source of prosperity for Latin America. Early on, the Spanish had instituted the *encomienda* system, which enabled individual Spaniards to collect tribute from the natives and use them as laborers. Protests from Catholic missionaries, who were appalled at the mistreatment of Indians and the rapid decline in their numbers, forced the Spanish government to change its policy. Beginning in 1542, the monarchy abolished the *encomienda* and replaced it with the *repartimento*, a new system under which landowners were permitted to use Indian laborers only on a temporary basis and only with

CLASS AND CASTE IN COLONIAL LATIN AMERICA

The mixture of white Iberians, African slaves, and native Indians created a multiracial society in Latin America. Gradually, a caste system emerged in which individuals' social status was often determined by their racial background. These excerpts, which are taken from an account by two Spanish travelers, describe this complex class and caste system in the Caribbean port of Cartagena, Colombia, and Lima, Peru.

GEORGE JUAN AND ANTONIO DE ULLOA, VOYAGE TO SOUTH AMERICA

The inhabitants may be divided into different castes or tribes, who derive their origin from a coalition of Whites, Negroes, and Indians. Of each of these we shall treat particularly.

The Whites may be divided into two classes, the Europeans and Creoles, or Whites born in the country. The former are commonly called Peninsulars, but are not numerous; most of them either return into Spain after acquiring a competent fortune, or remove up into inland provinces in order to increase it. Those who are settled at Cartagena, carry on the whole trade of that place, and live in opulence; whilst the other inhabitants are indigent, and reduced to have recourse to mean and hard labor for subsistence. The families of the White Creoles compose the landed interest; some of them have large estates, and are highly respected, because their ancestors came into the country invested with honorable posts, bringing their families with them when they settled here. . . .

Among the other tribes which are derived from an intermarriage of the Whites with the Negroes, the first are the Mulattoes. Next to these the *Tercerones*, produced from a White and a Mulatto. . . . After these follow the *Quarterones*, proceeding from a White and a *Terceron*. The last are the *Quinterones*, who owe their origin to a White and a *Quarteron*. This is the last gradation, there being no visible difference between them and the Whites, either in color or features. . . . Every person is so jealous of the order of their tribe or caste, that if, through inadvertence, you call them by a degree lower than what they actually are, they are highly offended. . . . These castes, from the Mulattoes, . . . are the mechanics of the city; the Whites, whether Creoles or Peninsulars, disdaining such a mean occupation follow nothing below merchandise. . . .

The inhabitants of Lima are composed of whites, or Spaniards, Negroes, Indians, Mestizos, and other castes, proceeding from the mixture of all three.

The Spanish families are very numerous. . . . Among these are reckoned a third or fourth part of the most distinguished nobility of Peru. . . . All these families live in a manner becoming their rank, having estates equal to their generous dispositions, keeping a great number of slaves and other domestics, and those who affect making the greatest figure, have coaches, while others content themselves with chaises, which are here so common, that no family of any substance is without one. . . . The funds to support these expenses, which in other parts would ruin families, are their large estates and plantations, civil and military employments or commerce, which is here accounted no derogation to families of the greatest distinction; but by this commerce is not to be understood the buying and selling by retail or in shops, every one trading proportional to his character and substance. . . .

The Negroes, Mulattoes, and their descendants, form the greater number of the inhabitants; and of these are the greatest part of the mechanics. . . . The third, and last class of inhabitants are the Indians and Mestizos, but these are very small in proportion to the largeness of the city, and the multitudes of the second class. They are employed in agriculture, in making earthen ware, and bringing all kinds of provisions to market, domestic services being performed by Negroes and Mulattoes, either slaves or free, though generally by the former.

---

the permission of the royal officials, who, it was thought, would be more responsible for the welfare of the Indians.

By the seventeenth century, the decline in the number of Indians led to a new system in which the owners of large estates paid wages to their Indian agricultural workers. By making loans to the Indians that the Indians could not repay in their lifetimes because of their low wages, the large landowners created a class of peons—native peasants permanently dependent on the landowners.

This creation of an oppressed class of wage laborers reminds us of another noticeable feature of Latin American agriculture—the dominating role of the large landowners. Both Spanish and Portuguese landowners amassed immense estates, leaving the Indians to work either as peons on the estates or as poor farmers on marginal lands. This system of large landowners and dependent peasants has remained one of the persistent features of Latin American society. Haciendas (as the estates were called in Spanish America) and fazendas (in Portuguese Brazil) could reach enormous sizes. Some haciendas in Mexico, for example, included over a million acres. By the eighteenth century, both Spanish haciendas and Brazilian fazendas were producing primarily for sale abroad.

Trade was another avenue for the economic exploitation of the American colonies. Colonies, according to classic mercantilist theory, were intended to be sources of raw materials. The American colonies were certainly that for both Spain and Portugal, as gold, silver, sugar, tobacco, diamonds, animal hides, and a number of other natural products made their way to Europe. The decline of Spain and Portugal had led these two states to depend even more on resources from their colonies, and they imposed strict mercantilist rules on them to keep others out. Spain, in particular, closely regulated the trade of its American colonies. Only two Spanish ports, Cádiz and Seville, were permitted to trade with the American colonies. Each year two fleets sailed from these ports to Vera Cruz and Portobelo, the only officially recognized ports in Spanish America for the transshipment of Latin American goods in the New World. From these two ports, the products of the immense colonial empire were shipped to Spain.

The British and French, however, proved too powerful to be excluded from this lucrative Latin American market. The British cajoled the Portuguese into allowing them into their Brazilian trade. The French were the first to break into the Spanish Latin American market when the French Bourbons became kings of Spain. The British entered the Spanish American markets in 1713, when Britain was granted the privilege, known as the *asiento*, of transporting 4,500 slaves a year to Spanish Latin America.

In accordance with mercantilist theory, both Spain and Portugal tried to limit the role of their colonies to providing raw materials, while the mother countries supplied their colonists with manufactured goods. Decrees aimed at prohibiting manufacturing in the New World tended to be ignored, however. By the eighteenth century, Latin America was producing cotton cloth, pottery, shoes, and furniture for local markets.

THE STATE AND THE CHURCH IN COLONIAL LATIN AMERICA

Portuguese Brazil and Spanish America were colonial empires that lasted over three hundred years. The difficulties of communication and travel between the New World and Europe made it virtually impossible for the Spanish and Portuguese monarchs to maintain close regulation of their empires. Consequently, colonial officials

MAP 19.4   Latin America in the Eighteenth Century

in Latin America had much autonomy in implementing imperial policies, although the Iberians tried to keep the most important posts of colonial government in the hands of Europeans.

Beginning in the mid-sixteenth century, the Portuguese monarchy began to assert its control over Brazil by establishing the position of governor-general. The governor-general (later called a viceroy) developed a bureaucracy but had at best a loose control over the captains-general, who were responsible for governing the districts into which Brazil was divided. In the course of the eighteenth century, the Portuguese monarchy attempted to strengthen its control over Brazil by weakening the power of the captains-general and municipal governments. By 1800, the king and his viceroy were more powerful in Brazil than they had ever been.

THE MISSION

In 1609, two Jesuit priests embarked on a missionary calling with the Guarani Indians in eastern Paraguay. Eventually, the Jesuits established more than thirty missions in the region. Well organized and zealous, the Jesuits transformed their missions into profitable business activities. This description of a Jesuit mission in Paraguay was written by Félix de Azara, a Spanish soldier and scientist.

FÉLIX DE AZARA, DESCRIPTION AND HISTORY OF PARAGUAY AND RIO DE LA PLATA

Having spoken of the towns founded by the Jesuit fathers, and of the manner in which they were founded, I shall discuss the government which they established in them. . . . In each town resided two priests, a curate and a subcurate, who had certain assigned functions. The subcurate was charged with all the spiritual tasks, and the curate with every kind of temporal responsibility. . . .

The curate allowed no one to work for personal gain; he compelled everyone, without distinction of age or sex, to work for the community, and he himself saw to it that all were equally fed and dressed. For this purpose the curates placed in storehouses all the fruits of agriculture and the products of industry, selling in the Spanish towns their surplus of cotton, cloth, tobacco, vegetables, skins, and wood, transporting them in their own boats down the nearest rivers, and returning with implements and whatever else was required.

From the foregoing one may infer that the curate disposed of the surplus funds of the Indian towns, and that no Indian could aspire to own private property. This deprived them of any incentive to use reason or talent, since the most industrious, able, and worthy person had the same food, clothing, and pleasures as the most wicked, dull, and indolent. It also follows that although this form of government was well designed to enrich the communities it also caused the Indian to work at a languid pace, since the wealth of his community was of no concern to him.

It must be said that although the Jesuit fathers were supreme in all respects, they employed their authority with a mildness and a restraint that command admiration. They supplied everyone with abundant food and clothing. They compelled the men to work only half a day, and did not drive them to produce more. Even their labor was given a festive air, for they went in procession to the fields, to the sound of music . . . and the music did not cease until they had returned in the same way they had set out. They gave them many holidays, dances, and tournaments, dressing the actors and the members of the municipal councils in gold or silver tissue and the most costly European garments, but they permitted the women to act only as spectators.

They likewise forbade the women to sew; this occupation was restricted to the musicians, sacristans, and acolytes. But they made them spin cotton; and the cloth that the Indians wove, after satisfying their own needs, they sold together with the surplus cotton in the Spanish towns, as they did with the tobacco, vegetables, wood, and skins. The curate and his companion, or subcurate, had their own plain dwellings, and they never left them except to take the air in the great enclosed yard of their college. They never walked through the streets of the town or entered the house of any Indian or let themselves be seen by any woman—or indeed, by any man, except for those indispensable few through whom they issued their orders.

To rule his American empire, the king of Spain appointed a viceroy, the first of which was established for New Spain (Mexico) in 1535. Another viceroy was appointed for Peru in 1543. Not until the eighteenth century were two additional viceroyalties—New Granada and La Plata—added. Viceroyalties in turn were subdivided into smaller units administered by presidents and captains-general, who were theoretically subordinate to the viceroys. All of these major government positions were held by Spaniards. For creoles—American-born whites—the chief opportunity to hold a government post was the *cabildo* or city council.

In the eighteenth century, a new monarchical dynasty in Spain—the Bourbons—brought some noticeable changes to Spanish America. New royal officials called intendants were sent out to oversee financial and administrative affairs; they gave the monarchy more direct control of colonial Latin America—especially over finances. The Spanish Bourbon kings also liberalized economic policies by eliminating the old monopolistic trading practices.

From the beginning of their conquest of the New World, Iberian monarchs were determined to Christianize the native peoples. This policy meant that the Catholic church would play an important role in the New World, and one that added considerably to church power. It was also a role that facilitated the goals of the state. Conversion to Christianity meant conversion to European cultural patterns, and from the monarch's point of view, that meant a more stable empire. Church and state were closely interlinked in colonial Latin America.

Catholic missionaries—especially the Dominicans, Franciscans, and Jesuits—fanned out to different parts of the Spanish empire (see the box above). To facilitate their efforts, the missionaries brought Indians together into villages, where the natives could be converted, taught trades, and encouraged to grow crops. A German tourist in the eighteenth century commented, "The road leads through plantations of sugar, indigo, cotton, and coffee. The regularity which we observed in the construction of the villages reminded us that they all owe their origin to monks and missions. The streets are straight and parallel; they cross each other at right angles; and the church is erected in the great square situated in the center."[2] These missions enabled the missionaries to control the lives of the Indians and helped ensure that they would remain docile members of the empire. In such frontier districts as California and Texas, missions also served as military barriers to foreign encroachment.

The mass conversion of the Indians brought the organizational structures of Catholicism to the New World. By 1800, Spanish America possessed ten archbishoprics and thirty-eight bishoprics; Portuguese Brazil had one archbishopric and seven bishoprics. The Catholic church constructed hospitals and orphanages and accepted responsibility for educating native Americans. Monastic schools instructed Indian students in the basic rudiments of reading, writing, and arithmetic. Catholic clergy held most of the professorships at the University of Mexico, founded in 1551, as well as at the other twelve Spanish American universities. The Catholic church also provided outlets for women other than marriage. Nunneries were places of prayer and quiet contemplation, but women in religious orders, many of them of aristocratic background, often lived well and operated outside their establishments by running schools and hospitals. Indeed, one of these nuns, Sor Juana Inés de la Cruz (1651–1695), was one of seventeenth-century Latin America's best-known literary figures. She wrote poetry and prose and urged that women be educated.

The legacies bequeathed to the church by the rich enabled the Catholic church to build the magnificent cathedrals that adorn the cities of Latin America. Even today, their architectural splendor reminds us of the wealth and power that the Catholic church exercised in the Iberian colonial empires of the New World.

British North America

In the eighteenth century, Spanish power in the New World was increasingly challenged by the growing presence of the British. (The United Kingdom of Great Britain had come into existence in 1707 when the governments of England and Scotland were united; the term *British* came into use to refer to both English and Scots.) The eighteenth-century British political system was characterized by a sharing of power between king and Parliament, with Parliament gradually gaining the upper hand. The king chose ministers responsible to himself who set policy and guided Parliament; Parliament had the power to make laws, levy taxes, pass the budget, and indirectly influence the king's ministers. The eighteenth-century British Parliament was dominated by a landed aristocracy that historians usually divide into two groups: an upper aristocracy, or the peers who sat for life in the House of Lords, and the landed gentry, lesser nobles who were elected to the House of Commons. The two groups had much in common; both were landowners with similar economic interests, and they frequently intermarried. The deputies to the House of Commons were chosen from the boroughs and counties but not by popular voting and hardly in any equitable fashion. The number of persons eligible to vote in the boroughs varied wildly and was often quite small, enabling wealthy landed aristocrats to gain support by patronage and bribery. Although deputies from the counties were elected by holders of property worth at least forty shillings a year, members of the leading landed gentry families were elected over and over again.

SOR JUANA INÉS DE LA CRUZ. Nunneries in colonial Latin America gave women—especially upper-class women—some opportunity for intellectual activity. As a woman, Juana Inés de la Cruz was denied admission to the University of Mexico. Consequently, she entered a convent, where she wrote poetry and plays until her superiors forced her to focus on less worldly activities.

In 1714, a new dynasty—the Hanoverians—was established when the last Stuart ruler, Queen Anne (1702–1714), died without an heir. The crown was offered to the Protestant rulers of the German state of Hanover. Since the first Hanoverian king (George I) did not speak English and neither the first nor the second George had much familiarity with the British system, their chief ministers were allowed to handle Parliament. Robert Walpole served as prime minister from 1721 to 1742 and pursued a peaceful foreign policy to avoid new land taxes. But new forces were emerging in eighteenth-century Britain as growing trade and industry led an ever increasing middle class to favor expansion of trade and world empire. The exponents of empire found a spokesman in William Pitt the Elder, who became prime minister in 1757 and furthered imperial ambitions by acquiring Canada and India in the Seven Years' War.

THE AMERICAN REVOLUTION AND THE BIRTH OF A NEW NATION

At the end of the Seven Years' War in 1763, Great Britain had become the world's greatest colonial power. In North America, Britain now controlled Canada and the lands east of the Mississippi. After the war, British policy makers sought to obtain new revenues from the colonies to pay the expenses the British army incurred in defending the colonists. An attempt to levy new taxes by the Stamp Act in 1765 led to riots and the statute's quick repeal. The immediate crisis had ended, but the fundamental cause of the dispute had not been resolved.

In the course of the eighteenth century, significant differences had arisen between the American and British political worlds. Both peoples shared the same property requirement for voting—voters had to possess property that could be rented for at least forty shillings a year—but it resulted in a disparity in the number of voters in the two countries. In Britain fewer than one in five adult males had the right to vote. In the colonies, where a radically different economic structure led to an enormous group of independent farmers, the property requirement allowed over 50 percent of adult males to vote.

The Americans and British also had different ideas of empire. The British viewed their empire as a single entity with Parliament as the supreme authority throughout. Only Parliament could make laws for all the people in the empire, including the American colonists. The Americans, on the other hand, had their own representative assemblies; to them, neither king nor Parliament should interfere in their internal affairs. American colonists believed strongly that no tax could be levied without the consent of an assembly whose members actually represented the people.

THE DECLARATION OF INDEPENDENCE.   John Trumbull's famous painting, *The Signing of the Declaration*, shows members of the committee responsible for the Declaration of Independence (from left to right, John Adams, Roger Sherman, Robert Livingston, Thomas Jefferson, and Benjamin Franklin) standing before John Hancock, president of the Second Continental Congress.

Crisis followed crisis in the 1770s. The colonies' desire to take collective action against what was perceived as Britain's repressive actions led to the First Continental Congress, which met at Philadelphia in September 1774. The more militant members refused to compromise and urged the colonists to "take up arms and organize militias." When a British army attempted to stop rebel mobilization in Massachusetts, fighting erupted at Lexington and Concord between colonists and redcoats (British soldiers) in April 1775.

Despite the outbreak of hostilities, the colonists did not rush headlong into rebellion and war. It was more than a year after Lexington and Concord before the decision was made to declare their independence from the British Empire. On July 4, 1776, the Second Continental Congress approved a Declaration of Independence written by Thomas Jefferson. A stirring political document, the Declaration of Independence affirmed the Enlightenment's natural rights of "life, liberty, and the pursuit of happiness" and declared the colonies to be "free and independent states absolved from all allegiance to the British crown." The war for American independence had formally begun.

The war against Great Britain was a great gamble. Britain was a strong European military power with enormous financial resources; by 1778, Britain had sent 50,000 regular British troops and 30,000 German mercenaries to America. The Second Continental Congress had authorized the formation of a Continental Army under George Washington as commander-in-chief. As a southerner, Washington added balance to an effort that up to now had been led by New Englanders. Nevertheless, compared to the British forces, the Continental Army consisted of undisciplined amateurs whose terms of service were usually very brief. The colonies also had militia units, but they likewise tended to be unreliable. Although 400,000 men served in the Continental Army and the militias during the course of the war, Washington never had more than 20,000 troops available for any single battle.

Of great importance to the colonies' cause was the support they received from foreign countries that were eager to gain revenge for their defeats in earlier wars at the hands of the British. The French were particularly generous in supplying arms and money to the rebels from the beginning of the war. French officers and soldiers also served in Washington's army. The defeat of the British at Saratoga in October 1777 finally led the French to grant diplomatic recognition to the American state. When Spain in 1779 and the Dutch Republic in 1780 entered the war against Great Britain, and Russia formed the League of Armed Neutrality in 1780 to protect neutral shipping from British attacks, the British were faced with war against much of Europe as well as the Americans. Despite having won most of the battles, the British were in danger of losing the war. When the army of General Cornwallis was forced to surrender to a combined American and French army and French fleet under Washington at Yorktown in 1781, the

British decided to call it quits. After extensive negotiations, the Treaty of Paris was signed in 1783. It recognized the independence of the American colonies and surprisingly granted the Americans control of the western territory from the Appalachians to the Mississippi River.

Although the thirteen American colonies agreed to "hang together" to gain their independence from the British, a fear of concentrated power and concern for their own interests caused them to have little enthusiasm for establishing a united nation with a strong central government. The Articles of Confederation, ratified in 1781, did little to provide for a strong central government. A series of economic, political, and international problems soon led to a movement for a different form of national government. In the summer of 1787, fifty-five delegates met in a convention in Philadelphia that was authorized by the Confederation Congress "for the sole and express purpose of revising the Articles of Confederation." The convention's delegates—wealthy, politically experienced, well-educated, and nationalistically inclined—rejected revision and decided to devise a new constitution.

The proposed Constitution created a central government distinct from and superior to the governments of the individual states. The national government was given the power to levy taxes, raise a national army, regulate domestic and foreign trade, and create a national currency. Following Montesquieu's principle of a "separation of powers" to provide a system of "checks and balances," the central or federal government was divided into three branches, each with some power to check the functioning of the others. A president would serve as the chief executive with the power to execute laws, veto the legislature's acts, make judicial and executive appointments, supervise foreign affairs, and direct military forces. Legislative power was vested in the second branch of government, a bicameral legislature composed of a Senate elected by the state legislatures and a House of Representatives elected directly by the people. The federal judiciary, embodied in a Supreme Court and other courts "as deemed necessary" by Congress, provided the third branch of government. With judges nominated by the executive and approved by the legislative branch, the federal judiciary would enforce the Constitution as the "supreme law of the land."

The constitutional convention had stipulated that the new Constitution would have to be ratified by popularly chosen conventions in nine of the thirteen states before it would take effect. After fierce contests, the Federalists, who favored the new Constitution, won, although the margin of victory was quite slim. Important to their success had been a promise to add a Bill of Rights to the Constitution as the new government's first piece of business. Accordingly, in March of 1789, the new Congress enacted the first ten amendments to the Constitution, ever since known as the Bill of Rights. These guaranteed freedom of religion, speech, press, petition, and assembly, as well as the right to bear arms, the right to be protected against unreasonable searches and

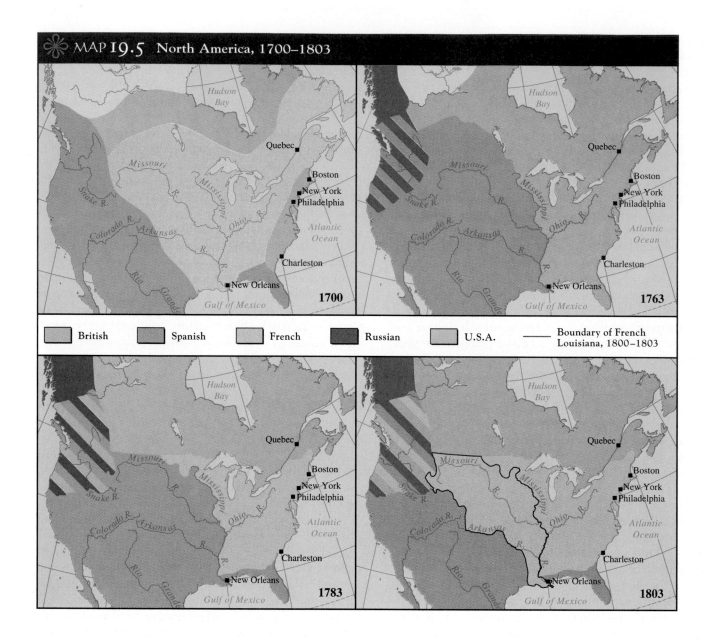

MAP 19.5 North America, 1700–1803

British · Spanish · French · Russian · U.S.A. · —— Boundary of French Louisiana, 1800–1803

arrests, trial by jury, due process of law, and the protection of property rights. Although many of these rights had their origins in English law, others were derived from the natural rights philosophy of the eighteenth-century philosophes and the American experience. Is it any wonder that many European intellectuals saw the American Revolution as the embodiment of the Enlightenment's political dreams?

TOWARD A NEW POLITICAL ORDER

The year 1789 witnessed two far-reaching events, the beginning of a new United States of America and the eruption of the French Revolution. Compared to the American Revolution, the French Revolution was more complex, more violent, and far more radical, with its attempt to reconstruct both a new political order and a new social order. But while the French were trying to create a new kind of state and a new kind of society, the rulers of other European states were attempting to come to terms with the ideas of the Enlightenment. Their failure helped ensure that the lessons of the French Revolution would find willing listeners elsewhere in Europe.

Background: Enlightened Absolutism in the Eighteenth Century

There is no doubt that Enlightenment thought had some impact on the political development of European states in the eighteenth century. Closely related to the Enlightenment idea of natural laws was the belief in natural rights, which were thought to be inalienable privileges that ought not to be withheld from any person. These natural rights included equality before the law, freedom of religious worship, freedom of speech and press, and the right to assemble, hold property, and pursue happiness. The American Declaration of Independence summarized the Enlightenment concept of natural rights in its opening paragraph: "We hold these truths to be self-evident, that all men are created equal; that they are endowed by their creator with certain unalienable rights; that among these are life, liberty and the pursuit of happiness."

But how were these natural rights to be established and preserved? In the opinion of many philosophes, most people needed the direction provided by an enlightened ruler. What, however, made rulers enlightened? They must allow religious toleration, freedom of speech and press, and the rights of private property. They must foster the arts, sciences, and education. Above all, they must not be arbitrary in their rule; they must obey the laws and enforce them fairly for all subjects. Only strong monarchs seemed capable of overcoming vested interests and effecting the reforms society needed. Reforms then should come from above—from the rulers—rather than from the people below. Distrustful of the masses, the philosophes believed that absolute rulers, swayed by enlightened principles, were the best hope of reforming their societies.

The extent to which rulers actually put these principles into practice has been much discussed. Many historians once assumed that a new type of monarchy emerged in the later eighteenth century, which they called "enlightened despotism" or "enlightened absolutism." Monarchs such as Frederick II of Prussia, Catherine the Great of Russia, and Joseph II of Austria supposedly followed the advice of the philosophes and ruled by enlightened principles, creating a path to modern nationhood. Recently, however, scholars have questioned the usefulness of the concept of "enlightened absolutism." We can best determine the extent to which it can be applied by examining the major "enlightened absolutists" of the later eighteenth century.

PRUSSIA: THE ARMY AND THE BUREAUCRACY

Two able Prussian kings in the eighteenth century, Frederick William I and Frederick II, further developed the two major institutions—the army and the bureaucracy—that were the backbone of Prussia. Frederick William I (1713–1740) promoted the evolution of Prussia's highly efficient civil bureaucracy by establishing the General Directory. Its supervision of military, police, economic, and financial affairs made it the chief administrative agent of the central government. Frederick William strove to maintain a highly efficient bureaucracy of civil service workers. It had its own code in which the supreme values were obedience, honor, and service to the king as the highest duty. As Frederick William asserted: "One must serve the king with life and limb, with goods and chattels, with honor and conscience, and surrender everything except salvation. The latter is reserved for God. But everything else must be mine."[3]

Frederick William's other major concern was the army. By the end of his reign, he had doubled its size. Though tenth in geographical size and thirteenth in population in Europe, Prussia had the fourth largest army, after France, Russia, and Austria. The nobility or landed aristocracy known as Junkers, who owned large estates with many serfs, were the officers in the Prussian army. They too had a strong sense of service to the king or state. Prussian nobles believed in duty, obedience, and sacrifice. At the same time, because of its size and reputation as one of the best armies in Europe, the Prussian army was the most important institution in the state.

Frederick the Great (1740–1786) was one of the best educated and most cultured monarchs in the eighteenth century. He was well versed in Enlightenment thought and even invited Voltaire to live at his court for several years. A believer in the king as the "first servant of the state," Frederick the Great became a conscientious ruler who made few innovations in administration. His diligence in overseeing its operation, however, made the Prussian bureaucracy famous for both efficiency and honesty.

For a time, Frederick seemed quite willing to follow the philosophes' recommendations for reform. He established a single code of laws for his territories that eliminated the use of torture except in treason and murder cases. He also granted a limited freedom of speech and press as well as complete religious toleration, no difficult task since he had no strong religious convictions anyway. Although Frederick was well aware of the philosophes' condemnation of serfdom, he was too dependent on the Prussian nobility to interfere with it or with the hierarchical structure of Prussian society. In fact, Frederick II was a social conservative who made Prussian society even more aristocratic than it had been before. Frederick reversed his father's policy of allowing commoners to have power in the civil service and reserved the higher positions in the bureaucracy for members of the nobility. The upper ranks of the bureaucracy came close to constituting a hereditary caste over time.

Like his predecessors, Frederick the Great took a great interest in military affairs and enlarged the Prussian army (to 200,000 men). Unlike his predecessors, he had no objection to using it. As we have seen, Frederick did not hesitate to take advantage of a succession crisis in the Habsburg monarchy to seize the Austrian province of Silesia for Prussia. This act led to Austria's bitter hostility toward Prussia and Frederick's engagement in two major wars, the War of the Austrian Succession and the Seven Years' War. Although the latter war left his country exhausted, Frederick succeeded in keeping Silesia. After the wars, the first partition of Poland with Austria and Russia in 1772 gave

✲ MAP 19.6 Europe in 1763

him the Polish territory between Prussia and Brandenburg, which linked some of the scattered lands of Prussia. By the end of his reign, Prussia was recognized as a great European power.

THE AUSTRIAN EMPIRE OF THE HABSBURGS

The Austrian Empire had become one of the great European states by the beginning of the eighteenth century. The city of Vienna, center of the Habsburg monarchy, was filled with magnificent palaces and churches built in the Baroque style and became the music capital of Europe. And yet Austria—by its very nature as a sprawling empire composed of many different nationalities, languages, religions, and cultures—found it difficult to provide common laws and administrative centralization for its people. Although Empress Maria Theresa (1740–1780) managed to make administrative reforms that helped centralize the Austrian Empire, these reforms were done for practical reasons—to strengthen the power of the Habsburg state—and were accompanied by an enlargement and modernization of the armed forces. Maria Theresa remained staunchly conservative and was

not open to the philosophes' calls for wider reform. But her successor was.

Joseph II (1780–1790) was determined to make changes; at the same time, he carried on his mother's chief goal of enhancing Habsburg power within the monarchy and Europe. Joseph II was an earnest man who believed in the need to sweep away anything standing in the path of reason. As Joseph expressed it: "I have made Philosophy the lawmaker of my empire; her logical applications are going to transform Austria."

Joseph's reform program was far-reaching. He abolished serfdom and tried to give the peasants hereditary rights to their holdings. A new penal code was instituted that abrogated the death penalty and established the principle of equality of all before the law. Joseph produced drastic religious reforms as well, including complete religious toleration and restrictions on the Catholic church. Altogether, Joseph II issued 6,000 decrees and 11,000 laws in his effort to transform Austria.

Joseph's reform program proved overwhelming for Austria, however. He alienated the nobility by freeing the serfs and alienated the church by his attacks on the monastic establishment. Even the serfs were unhappy, unable to

CHRONOLOGY

THE EUROPEAN STATES— ENLIGHTENED ABSOLUTISM IN THE EIGHTEENTH CENTURY

Prussia	
Frederick William I	1713–1740
Frederick II the Great	1740–1786
The Austrian Empire	
Maria Theresa	1740–1780
Joseph II	1780–1790
Russia	
Peter III	1762
Catherine II the Great	1762–1796
Pugachev's rebellion	1773–1775
Charter of the Nobility	1785
Poland	
First partition	1772
Second partition	1793
Third partition	1795

comprehend the drastic changes inherent in Joseph's policies. His attempt to rationalize the administration of the empire by imposing German as the official bureaucratic language alienated the non-German nationalities. As Joseph complained, there were not enough people for the kind of bureaucracy he needed. He realized his failure when he wrote his own epitaph for his gravestone: "Here lies Joseph II who was unfortunate in everything that he undertook." His successors undid many of his reform efforts.

RUSSIA UNDER CATHERINE THE GREAT

In Russia, Peter the Great was followed by a series of six weak successors who were made and unmade by the palace guard. After the last of these weak tsars, Peter III, was murdered by a faction of nobles, his German wife emerged as autocrat of all the Russias. Catherine II the Great (1762–1796) was an intelligent woman who was familiar with the works of the philosophes and seemed to favor enlightened reforms. She invited the French philosophe Diderot to Russia and, when he arrived, urged him to speak frankly "as man to man." He did, outlining a far-reaching program of political and financial reform. But Catherine was skeptical about impractical theories, which, she said, "would have turned everything in my kingdom upside down." She did consider the idea of a new law code that would recognize the principle of the equality of all people in the eyes of the law (see the box on p. 564). But in the end she did nothing, knowing that her success depended on the support of the Russian nobility. In 1785, she gave the nobles a Charter of Nobility that exempted them from taxes.

Catherine's policy of favoring the landed nobility led to even worse conditions for the Russian peasants and a rebellion. Led by an illiterate Cossack, Emelyan Pugachev, the rebellion spread across southern Russia. But the rebellion soon faltered, and Pugachev was captured, tortured, and executed. The rebellion collapsed completely, and Catherine responded by even greater measures against the peasantry. All rural reform was halted, and serfdom was expanded into newer parts of the empire.

Above all, Catherine proved a worthy successor to Peter the Great in her policies of territorial expansion westward (into Poland) and southward (to the Black Sea). Russia spread southward by defeating the Turks and gaining some land and the privilege of protecting Greek Orthodox Christians in the Ottoman Empire. Russian expansion westward occurred at the expense of neighboring Poland. In the three partitions of Poland, Russia gained about 50 percent of Polish territory.

CATHERINE THE GREAT. Autocrat of Russia, Catherine was an intelligent ruler who favored reform. She found it expedient, however, to retain much of the old system in order to keep the support of the landed nobility. This portrait by Dmitry Levitsky shows her in legislative regalia in the Temple of Justice in 1783.

THE PROPOSALS OF CATHERINE II
FOR A NEW LAW CODE

Catherine II the Great of Russia appeared for a while to be an enlightened ruler. In 1767, she convened a legislative commission to prepare a new code of laws for Russia. In her famous Instruction, *she gave the delegates a detailed guide to the principles they should follow. Although the guidelines were obviously culled from the liberal ideas of the philosophes, the commission itself accomplished nothing, and Catherine's* Instruction *was soon forgotten.*

CATHERINE II, PROPOSALS FOR A NEW LAW CODE

13. What is the true End of Monarchy? Not to deprive People of their natural Liberty; but to correct their Actions, in order to attain the supreme good.

33. The Laws ought to be so framed, as to secure the Safety of every Citizen as much as possible.

34. The Equality of the Citizens consists in this; that they should all be subject to the same Laws.

38. A Man ought to form in his own Mind an exact and clear Idea of what Liberty is. Liberty is the Right of doing whatsoever the Laws allow: And if any one Citizen could do what the Law forbid,

there would be no more Liberty; because others would have an equal Power of doing the same.

123. The Usage of Torture is contrary to all the Dictates of Nature and Reason; even Mankind itself cries out against it, and demands loudly the total Abolition of it.

180. That Law, therefore, is highly beneficial to the Community where it is established, which ordains that every Man shall be judged by his Peers and Equals. For when the Fate of a Citizen is in Question, all Prejudices arising from the Difference of Rank or Fortune should be stifled; because they ought to have no Influence between the Judges and the Parties accused.

194. No Man ought to be looked upon as guilty, before he has received his judicial Sentence; nor can the Laws deprive him of their Protection, before it is proved that he has forfeited all Right to it. What Right therefore can Power give to any to inflict Punishment upon a Citizen at a Time, when it is yet dubious, whether he is Innocent or guilty?

ENLIGHTENED ABSOLUTISM REVISITED

Of the three major rulers most closely associated traditionally with enlightened absolutism—Joseph II, Frederick II, and Catherine the Great—only Joseph II sought truly radical changes based on Enlightenment ideas. Both Frederick and Catherine liked to be cast as disciples of the Enlightenment, expressed interest in enlightened reforms, and even attempted some. But the policies of neither seemed seriously affected by Enlightenment thought. Necessities of state and maintenance of the existing system took precedence over reform. Indeed, many historians maintain that Joseph, Frederick, and Catherine were all primarily guided by a concern for the power and well-being of their states and that their policies were not all that different from those of their predecessors. In the final analysis, heightened state power was used to create armies and wage wars to gain more power. Nevertheless, in their desire to build stronger state systems, these rulers did pursue such enlightened measures as legal reform, religious toleration, and the extension of education because these served to create more satisfied subjects and strengthened the state in significant ways.

It would be foolish, however, to overlook the fact that the ability of enlightened rulers to make reforms was also limited by political and social realities. Everywhere in Europe the hereditary aristocracy was still the most powerful class in society. Enlightened reforms were often limited to those administrative and judicial reforms that did not seriously undermine the powerful interests of the European nobility. As the chief beneficiaries of a system based on traditional rights and privileges for their class, they were certainly not willing to support a political ideology that trumpeted the principle of equal rights for all. The first serious challenge to their supremacy would come in the French Revolution, which opened the door to a more modern world of politics.

The French Revolution Begins

Although we associate events like the French Revolution with sudden changes, the causes of such events involve long-range problems as well as immediate, precipitating forces. Hence the causes of the French Revolution must be found in a multifaceted examination of French society and its problems in the late eighteenth century.

BACKGROUND TO THE FRENCH REVOLUTION

The long-range or indirect causes of the French Revolution must first be sought in the condition of French society. Before the Revolution, France was a society grounded in the inequality of rights or the idea of privilege. Its population of 27 million was divided, as it had been since the Middle Ages, into three orders or estates.

The First Estate consisted of the clergy and numbered about 130,000 people, who owned approximately 10 percent of the land. Clergy were exempt from the *taille*, France's chief tax, although the church had agreed to pay a "voluntary" contribution every five years to the state. The clergy were also radically divided: the higher clergy, stemming from aristocratic families, shared the interests of the nobility, while the parish priests were often poor and from the class of commoners.

The Second Estate was the nobility, composed of 120,000 to 350,000 people, who nevertheless owned about 25 to 30 percent of the land. The nobility had continued to play an important and even crucial role in French society in the eighteenth century, holding many of the leading positions in the government, the military, the law courts, and the higher church offices. The French nobility was also divided. The nobility of the robe derived their status from officeholding, which had often opened the doors for commoners to receive noble status. These nobles now dominated the royal law courts and important administrative offices. The nobility of the sword claimed to be descended from the original medieval nobility. The nobles as a whole sought to expand their power at the expense of the monarchy—to defend liberty by resisting the arbitrary actions of the crown, as some nobles asserted—and to maintain their monopolistic control over positions in the military, church, and government. Moreover, the possession of privileges remained a hallmark of the nobility. Common to all nobles were tax exemptions, especially from the *taille*.

The Third Estate, or the commoners of society, constituted the overwhelming majority of the French population. They were divided by vast differences in occupation, level of education, and wealth. The peasants, who alone constituted 75 to 80 percent of the total population, were by far the largest segment of the Third Estate. They owned about 35 to 40 percent of the land, although their landholdings varied from area to area and over half had no or little land on which to survive. Serfdom no longer existed on any large scale in France, but French peasants still had obligations to their local landlords that they deeply resented. These "relics of feudalism," survivals from an earlier age, included the payment of fees for the use of village facilities, such as the flour mill, community oven, and winepress, as well as tithes to the clergy.

Another part of the Third Estate consisted of skilled artisans, shopkeepers, and other wage earners in the cities. Although the eighteenth century had been a period of rapid urban growth, 90 percent of French towns had fewer than 10,000 inhabitants, while only nine cities had more than 50,000. In the eighteenth century, consumer prices rose faster than wages, causing these urban groups to experience a noticeable decline in purchasing power. In Paris, for example, income lagged behind food prices and especially behind a 140 percent rise in rents for working people in skilled and unskilled trades. The economic discontent of this segment of the Third Estate and often simply their struggle to survive led them to play an important role in the Revolution, especially in the city of Paris.

About 8 percent of the population, or 2.3 million people, constituted the bourgeoisie or middle class, who owned about 20 to 25 percent of the land. This group included merchants, industrialists, and bankers, who controlled the resources of trade, manufacturing, and finance and benefited from the economic prosperity after 1730. The bourgeoisie also included professional people—lawyers, holders of public offices, doctors, and writers. Many members of the bourgeoisie sought security and status through the purchase of land. They had their own set of grievances because they were often excluded from the social and political privileges monopolized by the nobles. At the same time, remarkable similarities existed at the upper levels of society between the wealthier bourgeoisie and the nobility. It was still possible for wealthy middle-class individuals to enter the ranks of the nobility by obtaining public offices and entering the nobility of the robe. During the eighteenth century, 6,500 new noble families were created. Moreover, the new and critical ideas of the Enlightenment proved attractive to both aristocrats and bourgeoisie. Members of both groups shared a common world of liberal political thought. Both aristocratic and bourgeois elites, long accustomed to a new socioeconomic reality based on wealth and economic achievement, were increasingly frustrated by a monarchical system resting on privileges and an old and rigid social order based on the concept of estates. The opposition of these elites to the old order ultimately led them to take drastic action against the monarchical regime, although they soon split over the problem of how far to proceed in eliminating traditional privileges. In a real sense, the Revolution had its origins in political grievances.

The inability of the French monarchy to deal with new social realities and problems was exacerbated by specific problems in the 1780s. Although France had enjoyed fifty years of economic expansion, the French economy still experienced periodic crises. Bad harvests in 1787 and 1788 and the beginnings of a manufacturing depression resulted in food shortages, rising prices for food and other necessities, and unemployment in the cities. The number of poor, estimated by some at almost one-third of the population, reached crisis proportions on the eve of the Revolution.

The immediate cause of the French Revolution was the near collapse of government finances. French governmental expenditures continued to grow due to costly wars and royal extravagance. On the verge of a complete financial collapse, the government of Louis XVI (1774–1792) was finally forced to call a meeting of the Estates-General, the French parliamentary body, which had not met since 1614. The Estates-General consisted of representatives from the three orders of French society. In the elections for the Estates-General, the government had ruled that the Third Estate should get double representation (it did, after all, constitute 97 percent of the population). Consequently, while both the First Estate (the clergy) and the Second (the nobility) had about 300 delegates each, the commoners had almost 600 representatives. Two-thirds of the latter were people with legal training, while three-fourths were from towns of over 2,000 inhabitants, giving the Third Estate a particularly strong legal and urban representation. Most members of the Third Estate advocated a regular constitutional government that would abolish the fiscal privileges of the church and nobility as the major way to regenerate France.

FROM ESTATES-GENERAL TO A NATIONAL ASSEMBLY

The Estates-General opened at Versailles on May 5, 1789. It was troubled from the start with the problem of whether voting should be by order or by head (each delegate hav-ing one vote). Traditionally, each order would vote separately; each would have veto power over the other two, thus guaranteeing aristocratic control over reforms. But the Third Estate was opposed to this approach and pushed its demands for voting by head. Since it had double representation, with the assistance of liberal nobles and clerics, it could turn the three estates into a single-chamber legislature that would reform France in its own way. Most delegates still desired to make changes within a framework of respect for the authority of the king; revival or reform did not mean the overthrow of traditional institutions. But when the First Estate declared in favor of voting by order, the Third Estate felt compelled to respond in a significant fashion. On June 17, 1789, the Third Estate voted to constitute itself a "National Assembly" and decided to draw up a constitution. Three days later, on June 20, the deputies of the Third Estate arrived at their meeting place, only to find the doors locked; thereupon they moved to a nearby indoor tennis court and swore (hence, the Tennis Court Oath) that they would continue to meet until they had produced a French constitution. These actions

✿ **STORMING OF THE BASTILLE.**   Louis XVI planned to use force to dissolve the Estates-General, but a number of rural and urban uprisings by the common people prevented this action. The fall of the Bastille, pictured here in an anonymous painting, is perhaps the most famous of the urban risings.

of June 17 and June 20 constitute the first step in the French Revolution because the Third Estate had no legal right to act as the National Assembly. This revolution, largely the work of the lawyers of the Third Estate, was soon in jeopardy, however, as the king sided with the First Estate and threatened to dissolve the Estates-General. Louis XVI now prepared to use force.

The intervention of the common people, however, in a series of urban and rural uprisings in July and August of 1789 saved the Third Estate from the king's attempted counterrevolution. The most famous of the urban risings was the fall of the Bastille. Parisians organized a popular force and on July 14 attacked the Bastille, a royal armory. But the Bastille had also been a state prison, and though it now contained only seven prisoners, its fall quickly became a popular symbol of triumph over despotism. Paris was abandoned to the insurgents, and Louis XVI was soon informed that the royal troops were unreliable. Louis's acceptance of that reality signaled the collapse of royal authority; the king could no longer enforce his will. The fall of the Bastille had saved the National Assembly.

At the same time, independently of what was going on in Paris, popular revolutions broke out in numerous cities. The collapse of royal authority in the cities was paralleled by peasant revolutions in the countryside. Behind the popular uprisings was a growing resentment of the entire landholding system, with its fees and obligations. With the fall of the Bastille and the king's apparent capitulation to the demands of the Third Estate, the peasants decided to take matters into their own hands. From July 19 to August 3, peasant rebellions occurred throughout France. The agrarian revolts served as a backdrop to the Great Fear, a vast panic that spread like wildfire through France between July 20 and August 6. The fear of invasion by foreign troops, aided by a supposed aristocratic plot, encouraged the formation of citizens' militias and permanent committees. The greatest impact of the agrarian revolts and the Great Fear was on the National Assembly meeting in Versailles.

THE DESTRUCTION OF THE OLD REGIME

One of the first acts of the National Assembly was to destroy the relics of feudalism or aristocratic privileges. On the "night of 4 August" 1789, the National Assembly in an astonishing session voted to abolish landlords' feudal rights as well as the fiscal privileges of nobles, clergy, towns, and provinces. On August 26, the assembly provided the ideological foundation for its actions and an educational device for the nation by adopting the Declaration of the Rights of Man and the Citizen (see the box on p. 568). This charter of basic liberties began with a ringing affirmation of "the natural and imprescriptible rights of man" to "liberty, property, security and resistance to oppression." It went on to affirm the destruction of aristocratic privileges by proclaiming an end to exemptions from taxation, freedom and equal rights for all men, and access to public office based on talent. Freedom of speech and press were guaranteed, and arbitrary arrests were outlawed.

The declaration also raised another important issue. Did the ideal of equal rights for all men extend to women? Many deputies insisted that it did, at least in terms of civil liberties, provided that, as one said, "women do not aspire to exercise political rights and functions." Olympe de Gouges, a playwright and pamphleteer, refused to accept this exclusion of women from political rights. Echoing the words of the official declaration, she penned a Declaration of the Rights of Woman and the Female Citizen, in which she insisted that women should have all the same rights as men (see the box on p. 569). The National Assembly ignored her demands.

In the meantime, Louis XVI had remained inactive at Versailles. He did refuse to promulgate the decrees on the abolition of feudalism and the Declaration of Rights, but an unexpected turn of events soon forced the king to change his mind. On October 5, crowds of Parisian women, numbering in the thousands and described by one eyewitness as "detachments of women coming up from every direction, armed with broomsticks, lances, pitchforks, swords, pistols, and muskets," marched to Versailles and forced the king to accept the constitutional decrees. The crowd now insisted that the royal family return to Paris. On October 6, the king complied. As a goodwill gesture, he brought along wagonloads of flour from the palace stores, escorted by women armed with pikes singing, "We are bringing back the baker, the baker's wife, and the baker's boy" (the king, queen, and their son). The king was virtually a prisoner in Paris, and the National Assembly, now meeting in Paris, would also feel the influence of Parisian insurrectionary politics.

Because the Catholic church was viewed as an important pillar of the old order, reforms soon overtook it. Most of the lands of the church were confiscated to pay state debts, and the church was also secularized. In July 1790, a new Civil Constitution of the Clergy was put into effect. Both bishops and priests were to be elected by the people and paid by the state. All clergy were also required to swear an oath of allegiance to the Civil Constitution. Only 54 percent of the French parish clergy took the oath, while the majority of bishops refused. The Catholic church, still an important institution in the life of the French people, now became an enemy of the Revolution.

A NEW CONSTITUTION

By 1791, the National Assembly had finally completed a new constitution that established a limited, constitutional monarchy. There was still a monarch (now called king of the French), but he enjoyed few powers not subject to review by the new Legislative Assembly. The Legislative Assembly, in which sovereign power was vested, was to sit for two years and consist of 745 representatives chosen by

DECLARATION OF THE RIGHTS
OF MAN AND THE CITIZEN

O*ne of the important documents of the French Revolution, the Declaration of the Rights of Man and
the Citizen was adopted in August 1789 by the
National Assembly. The declaration affirmed that
"men are born and remain free and equal in rights," that governments must protect these natural rights, and that political power
is derived from the people.*

DECLARATION OF THE RIGHTS
OF MAN AND THE CITIZEN

The representatives of the French people, organized as a
national assembly, considering that ignorance, neglect, and
scorn of the rights of man are the sole causes of public
misfortunes and of corruption of governments, have
resolved to display in a solemn declaration the natural,
inalienable, and sacred rights of man, so that this declaration, constantly in the presence of all members of society,
will continually remind them of their rights and their
duties. . . . Consequently, the National Assembly recognizes
and declares, in the presence and under the auspices of the
Supreme Being, the following rights of man and citizen:

1. Men are born and remain free and equal in rights;
   social distinctions can be established only for the
   common benefit.
2. The aim of every political association is the
   conservation of the natural and imprescriptible
   rights of man; these rights are liberty, property,
   security, and resistance to oppression.
3. The source of all sovereignty is located in essence
   in the nation; no body, no individual can exercise
   authority which does not emanate from it expressly.
4. Liberty consists in being able to do anything that
   does not harm another person. . . .
6. The law is the expression of the general will; all
   citizens have the right to concur personally or
   through their representatives in its formation; it

must be the same for all, whether it protects or
punishes. All citizens being equal in its eyes are
equally admissible to all honors, positions, and
public employments, according to their capabilities
and without other distinctions than those of their
virtues and talents.

7. No man can be accused, arrested, or detained
   except in cases determined by the law, and
   according to the forms which it has prescribed. . . .
10. No one may be disturbed because of his opinions,
    even religious, provided that their public
    demonstration does not disturb the public order
    established by law.
11. The free communication of thoughts and opinions
    is one of the most precious rights of man: every
    citizen can therefore freely speak, write, and
    print. . . .
12. The guaranteeing of the rights of man and citizen
    necessitates a public force; this force is therefore
    instituted for the advantage of all, and not for the
    private use of those to whom it is entrusted. . . .
14. Citizens have the right to determine for themselves
    or through their representatives the need for
    taxation of the public, to consent to it freely, to
    investigate its use, and to determine its rate, basis,
    collection, and duration.
15. Society has the right to demand an accounting of
    his administration from every public agent.
16. Any society in which guarantees of rights are not
    assured nor the separation of powers determined has
    no constitution.
17. Property being an inviolable and sacred right, no
    one may be deprived of it unless public necessity,
    legally determined, clearly requires such action, and
    then only on condition of a just and prior
    indemnity.

an indirect system of election that preserved power in the
hands of the more affluent members of society. Only active
citizens (those men over the age of twenty-five paying in
taxes the equivalent of three days' unskilled labor) could
vote for electors (those men paying taxes equal in value
to ten days' labor). This relatively small group of 50,000
electors then chose the deputies. To qualify as a deputy,
one had to pay taxes equal in value to fifty-four days' labor.

Thus, by 1791 a revolutionary consensus, largely the
work of the wealthier bourgeoisie, had moved France to
a drastic reordering of the old regime. By mid-1791, however, this consensus faced growing opposition from clerics
opposed to the Civil Constitution of the Clergy, lower

classes hurt by a rise in the cost of living, peasants angry
that some dues still had not been abandoned, and political clubs like the Jacobins that offered more radical solutions to France's problems. In addition, by mid-1791, the
government was still facing several financial difficulties
due to massive tax evasion. Despite all of their problems,
however, the bourgeois politicians in charge remained relatively unified on the basis of their trust in the king. But
Louis XVI disastrously undercut them. Quite upset with
the whole turn of revolutionary events, he sought to flee
France in June 1791 and almost succeeded before being
recognized, captured, and brought back to Paris. In this
unsettled situation, with a discredited and seemingly dis-

DECLARATION OF THE RIGHTS OF WOMAN AND THE FEMALE CITIZEN

*O*lympe de Gouges (a pen name for Marie Gouze) was a butcher's daughter who wrote plays and pamphlets. She argued that the Declaration of the Rights of Man and the Citizen did not apply to women and composed her own Declaration of the Rights of Woman.

DECLARATION OF THE RIGHTS OF WOMAN AND THE FEMALE CITIZEN (1791)

Mothers, daughters, sisters and representatives of the nation demand to be constituted into a national assembly. Believing that ignorance, omission, or scorn for the rights of woman are the only causes of public misfortunes and of the corruption of governments, the women have resolved to set forth in a solemn declaration the natural, inalienable, and sacred rights of woman in order that this declaration, constantly exposed before all the members of the society, will ceaselessly remind them of their rights and duties. . . .

Consequently, the sex that is as superior in beauty as it is in courage during the sufferings of maternity recognizes and declares in the presence and under the auspices of the Supreme Being, the following Rights of Woman and of Female Citizens.

1. Woman is born free and lives equal to man in her rights. Social distinctions can be based only on the common utility.

2. The purpose of any political association is the conservation of the natural and imprescriptible rights of woman and man; these rights are liberty, property, security, and especially resistance to oppression.

3. The principle of all sovereignty rests essentially with the nation, which is nothing but the union of woman and man; no body and no individual can exercise any authority which does not come expressly from it [the nation].

4. Liberty and justice consist of restoring all that belongs to others; thus, the only limits on the exercise of the natural rights of woman are perpetual male tyranny; these limits are to be reformed by the laws of nature and reason. . . .

6. The law must be the expression of the general will; all female and male citizens must contribute either personally or through their representatives to its formation; it must be the same for all: male and female citizens, being equal in the eyes of the law, must be equally admitted to all honors, positions, and public employment according to their capacity and without other distinctions besides those of their virtues and talents.

7. No woman is an exception; she is accused, arrested, and detained in cases determined by law. . . .

10. No one is to be disquieted for his very basic opinions; woman has the right to mount the scaffold; she must equally have the right to mount the rostrum, provided that her demonstrations do not disturb the legally established public order.

11. The free communication of thoughts and opinions is one of the most precious rights of woman, since that liberty assured the recognition of children by their fathers. . . .

12. The guarantee of the rights of woman and the female citizen implies a major benefit; this guarantee must be instituted for the advantage of all, and not for the particular benefit of those to whom it is entrusted. . . .

14. Female and male citizens have the right to verify, either by themselves or through their representatives, the necessity of the public contribution. This can only apply to women if they are granted an equal share, not only of wealth, but also of public administration, and in the determination of the proportion, the base, the collection, and the duration of the tax.

15. The collectivity of women, joined for tax purposes to the aggregate of men, has the right to demand an accounting of his administration from any public agent.

16. No society has a constitution without the guarantee of rights and the separation of powers; the constitution is null if the majority of individuals comprising the nation have not cooperated in drafting it.

17. Property belongs to both sexes whether united or separate; for each it is an inviolable and sacred right; no one can be deprived of it, since it is the true patrimony of nature.

---

loyal monarch, the new Legislative Assembly held its first session in October 1791. France's relations with the rest of Europe soon led to Louis's downfall.

Meanwhile, some other European rulers had become concerned about the French example and feared that revolution would spread to their countries. On August 27, 1791, the monarchs of Austria and Prussia invited other European monarchs to use force to reestablish monarchical authority in France. Insulted by this threat, the Legislative Assembly declared war on Austria on April 20, 1792. The French fared badly in the initial fighting, and loud recriminations were soon heard in Paris. A frantic search for scapegoats began; as one observer noted, "Everywhere you hear the cry that the king is betraying us, the generals are betraying us, that nobody is to be trusted; . . . that Paris will be taken in six weeks by the Austrians . . . we are on a volcano ready to spout flames."[4] Defeats in war coupled with economic shortages in the spring reinvigorated popular groups that had been dormant since the previous summer and led to renewed political demonstrations, especially against the king. Radical Parisian political groups, declaring themselves an insurrectionary commune, organized a mob attack on the royal palace and Legislative Assembly in August 1792, took the king captive, and forced the Legislative Assembly to suspend the monarchy and call for a National Convention, chosen on the basis of universal male suffrage, to decide on the future form of government. The French Revolution was about to enter a more radical stage.

From Radical Revolution to Reaction

In September 1792, the newly elected National Convention began its sessions. Although it was called to draft a new constitution, it also acted as the sovereign ruling body of France. Socially, the composition of the National Convention was similar to that of its predecessors. Dominated by lawyers, professionals, and property owners, two-thirds of its deputies were under the age of forty-five, and almost all had had political experience as a result of the Revolution. Almost all were also intensely distrustful of the king and his activities. It was therefore no surprise that the convention's first major step on September 21 was to abolish the monarchy and establish a republic. At the beginning of 1793, the convention passed a decree condemning Louis XVI to death. On January 21, 1793, the king was executed and the destruction of the old regime was complete. There could be no turning back. But the execution of the king produced new challenges by creating new enemies for the Revolution both at home and abroad while strengthening those who were already its enemies.

Within Paris the local government known as the Commune, which drew a number of its leaders from the work-

ing classes, favored radical change and put constant pressure on the convention, pushing it to ever more radical positions. Moreover, the National Convention itself still did not rule all France. Peasants in western France as well as inhabitants of France's major provincial cities refused to accept its authority. Domestic turmoil was paralleled by a foreign crisis. By the beginning of 1793, after the king had been executed, most of Europe—an informal coalition of Austria, Prussia, Spain, Portugal, Britain, the Dutch Republic, and even Russia—was pitted against France, and by late spring some members of the anti-French coalition were poised for an invasion of France. If it succeeded, both the Revolution and the revolutionaries would be destroyed and the old regime reestablished.

To meet these crises, the convention gave broad powers to an executive committee of twelve known as the Committee of Public Safety, which came to be dominated by Maximilien Robespierre, the leader of the Jacobins. For a twelve-month period, from 1793 to 1794, virtually the same twelve members were reelected and gave the country the leadership it needed to weather the domestic and foreign crises of 1793.

To meet the foreign crisis and save the Republic from its foreign enemies, the Committee of Public Safety decreed a universal mobilization of the nation on August 23, 1793:

> Young men will fight, young men are called to conquer. Married men will forge arms, transport military baggage and guns and will prepare food supplies. Women, who at long last are to take their rightful place in the revolution and follow their true destiny, will forget their futile tasks: their delicate hands will work at making clothes for soldiers; they will make tents and they will extend their tender care to shelters where the defenders of the Patrie will receive the help that their wounds require. Children will make lint of old cloth. It is for them that we are fighting: children, those beings destined to gather all the fruits of the revolution, will raise their pure hands toward the skies. And old men, performing their missions again, as of yore, will be guided to the public squares of the cities, where they will kindle the courage of young warriors and preach the doctrines of hate for kings and the unity of the Republic.[5]

A VICTIM OF THE REIGN OF TERROR

The Reign of Terror created a repressive environment in which even quite innocent people could be accused of crimes against the Republic. As seen in this letter by Anne-Félicité Guinée, wife of a wig maker, merely insulting an official could lead to arrest and imprisonment.

LETTER OF ANNE-FÉLICITÉ GUINÉE

Citizen Anne-Félicité Guinée, twenty-four years old . . . informs you that she was arrested at the Place des Droits de l'Homme, where I had gone to get butter. I point out to you that for a long time I have had to feed the members in my household on bread and cheese and that, tired of complaints from my husband and my boys, I was compelled to go wait in line to get something to eat. For three days I had been going to the same market without being able to get anything, despite the fact that I had waited from 7 or 8 A.M. until 5 or 6 P.M. After the distribution of butter on the twenty-second, . . . a citizen came over to me and said that I was in a very delicate condition. To that I answered, "You can't be delicate and be on your legs for so long. I wouldn't have come if there were any other food." He replied that I needed to drink milk. I answered that I had men in my house who worked and that I couldn't nourish them with milk, that I was convinced that if he, the speaker, was sensitive to the difficulty of obtaining food, he would not vex me so, and that he was an imbecile and wanted to play despot, and no one had that right. Here, on the spot, I was arrested and brought to the guard house. I wanted to explain myself. I was silenced and dragged off to prison . . . About 7 P.M., I was led to the Revolutionary Committee [of the section], where I was called a counterrevolutionary and was told I was asking for the guillotine because I told them I preferred death to being treated ignominiously the way he was treating me. . . . I was asked if I knew whom I had called a despot. I answered, "I didn't know him," and I was told that he was the commander of the post. I said that he was more [a commander] beneath his own roof than anyone, given that he was there to maintain order and not to provoke bad feelings. . . . I was told that I had done three times more than was needed to get the guillotine and that I would be explaining myself before the Revolutionary Tribunal. The next day, I was taken to the Revolutionary Committee, which, without waiting to hear me, had me taken to the Mairie, where I stayed for nine days without a bed or a chair with vermin and with women addicted to all sorts of crimes. . . .

On the ninth day I was transferred to the prison of La Force. . . . In the end I can give you only the very slightest idea of all the horrors that are committed in these terrible prisons. . . . I was thrown together not with women but with monsters who gloried in all their crimes and who gave themselves over to all the most horrible excesses. One day, two of them fought each other with knives. Day and night I lived in mortal fear. The food that was sent in to me was grabbed away immediately. That was my cruel situation for seventeen days. My whole body was swollen from . . . the poor treatment I had endured, . . . [Anne-Félicité Guinée was discharged provisionally after the authorities realized that she was pregnant.]

In less than a year, the French revolutionary government had raised an army of 650,000; by September 1794, it numbered 1,169,000. The Republic's army was the largest ever seen in European history. It now pushed the allies back across the Rhine and even conquered the Austrian Netherlands.

Historians have focused on the French revolutionary army as an important step in the creation of modern nationalism. Previously, wars had been fought between governments or ruling dynasties by relatively small armies of professional soldiers. Although innocent civilians had suffered in those struggles, all parties had considered them noncombatants, with no direct involvement in the conflicts. The new French army, however, was the creation of a "people's" government; its wars were now "people's" wars. The entire nation was to be involved in the war. But when dynastic wars became people's wars, warfare increased in ferocity and restraints disappeared. The wars of the French revolutionary era opened the door to the total war of the modern world.

To meet the domestic crisis, the National Convention and the Committee of Public Safety initiated the "Reign of Terror." Revolutionary courts were instituted to protect the revolutionary Republic from its internal enemies. In the course of nine months, 16,000 people were officially killed under the blade of the guillotine, the latter a revolutionary device for the quick and efficient separation of heads from bodies. But the true number of the Terror's victims was probably closer to 30,000. The bulk of the Terror's executions took place in cities and districts that had been in open rebellion against the authority of the National Convention. The Terror demonstrated no class prejudice. Estimates are that the nobles constituted 8 percent of its victims, the middle classes, 25, the clergy, 6, and the peasant and laboring classes, 60. To Robespierre and the Committee of Public Safety, this bloodletting was only a temporary expedient. Once the war and domestic emergency were over, "the republic of virtue" would follow, and the Declaration of the Rights of Man and the Citizen would be fully established (see the box above).

Military force in the form of revolutionary armies was used to bring recalcitrant cities and districts back under the control of the National Convention. The Committee of Public Safety decided to make an example of Lyons, which was France's second city after Paris and had defied the National Convention during a time when the Republic was in peril. By April 1794, 1,880 citizens of Lyons had been executed. When guillotining proved too slow, cannon fire was used to blow condemned men into open graves. A German observed:

> . . . whole ranges of houses, always the most handsome, burnt. The churches, convents, and all the dwellings of the former patricians were in ruins. When I came to the guillotine, the blood of those who had been executed a few hours beforehand was still running in the street. . . . I said to a group of sansculottes that it would be decent to clear away all this human blood. Why should it be cleared? one of them said to me. It's the blood of aristocrats and rebels. The dogs should lick it up.[6]

Along with the Terror, the Committee of Public Safety took other steps to control France. By spring 1793, they were sending "representatives on mission" as agents of the central government to all parts of the country to implement the laws dealing with the wartime emergency. The committee also attempted to provide some economic controls by establishing price limits on goods declared of first necessity, ranging from food and drink to fuel and clothing. The controls failed to work very well, however, because the government lacked the machinery to enforce them.

The National Convention also pursued a policy of dechristianization. A new calendar was instituted in which years were no longer numbered from the birth of Christ but from September 22, 1792, the first day of the French Republic. The new calendar also eliminated Sundays and church holidays. In Paris, the cathedral of Notre Dame was designated a Temple of Reason; in November 1793, a public ceremony dedicated to the worship of reason was held in the former cathedral in which patriotic maidens clad in white dresses paraded before a temple of reason where the high altar once stood.

By the summer of 1794, the French had been successful on the battlefield against their foreign foes. The military successes meant that there was now less need for the Terror. But the Terror continued because Robespierre, who had become a figure of power and authority, had become obsessed with purifying the body politic of all the corrupt. Many deputies in the National Convention began to fear that they were not safe while he was free to act. Forming an anti-Robespierre coalition in the National Convention, they soon gathered enough votes to condemn him. Robespierre was guillotined on July 28, 1794.

After the death of Robespierre, a reaction set in called the Thermidorean Reaction, named after the month of Thermidor on the new French calendar. The Terror came to a halt. The National Convention reduced the power of the Committee of Public Safety, closed the Jacobin club, and tried to provide better protection for its deputies against the Parisian mobs. Churches were allowed to reopen for public worship. Economic regulation was dropped in favor of *laissez-faire* policies, another clear indication that moderate forces were again gaining control of the Revolution. In addition, a new constitution was framed in August 1795 that reflected this more conservative republicanism or a desire for a stability that did not sacrifice the ideals of 1789. The constitution provided for five directors to act as the executive authority or Directory.

The period of the Revolution under the government of the Directory was an era of stagnation, corruption, and graft, a materialistic reaction to the sufferings and sacrifices that had been demanded in the Reign of Terror. Speculators made fortunes in property by taking advantage of the Republic's severe monetary problems. At the same time, the government of the Directory was faced with political enemies from both the left and the right of the political spectrum. On the right, royalists, who desired the restoration of the monarchy, continued their agitation. On the left, Jacobin hopes of power were revived by continuing economic problems. Battered by the left and right, unable to find a definitive solution to the country's economic problems, and still carrying on the wars left from the Committee of Public Safety, the Directory increasingly relied

✿ **WOMEN PATRIOTS.** Women played a variety of roles in the events of the French Revolution. This picture shows a women's patriotic club discussing the decrees of the National Convention, an indication that some women became highly politicized by the upheavals of the revolution.

NAPOLEON AND PSYCHOLOGICAL WARFARE

I n 1796, at the age of twenty-seven, Napoleon Bonaparte was given command of the French army in Italy, where he won a series of stunning victories. His use of speed, deception, and surprise to overwhelm his opponents is well known. In this selection from a proclamation to his troops in Italy, Napoleon also appears as a master of psychological warfare.

NAPOLEON BONAPARTE, PROCLAMATION TO FRENCH TROOPS IN ITALY (APRIL 26, 1796)

Soldiers:

In a fortnight you have won six victories, taken twenty-one standards [flags of military units], fifty-five pieces of artillery, several strong positions, and conquered the richest part of Piedmont [in northern Italy]; you have captured 15,000 prisoners and killed or wounded more than 10,000 men. . . . You have won battles without cannon, crossed rivers without bridges, made forced marches without shoes, camped without brandy and often without bread. Soldiers of liberty, only republican troops could have endured what you have endured. Soldiers, you have our thanks! The grateful Patrie [nation] will owe its prosperity to you. . . .

The two armies which but recently attacked you with audacity are fleeing before you in terror; the wicked men who laughed at your misery and rejoiced at the thought of the triumphs of your enemies are confounded and trembling.

But, soldiers, as yet you have done nothing compared with what remains to be done. . . . Undoubtedly the greatest obstacles have been overcome; but you still have battles to fight, cities to capture, rivers to cross. Is there one among you whose courage is abating? No. . . . All of you are consumed with a desire to extend the glory of the French people; all of you long to humiliate those arrogant kings who dare to contemplate placing us in fetters; all of you desire to dictate a glorious peace, one which will indemnify the Patrie for the immense sacrifices it has made; all of you wish to be able to say with pride as you return to your villages, "I was with the victorious army of Italy!"

on the military to maintain its power. This led to a coup d'etat in 1799 in which the successful and popular military general Napoleon Bonaparte was able to seize power.

The Age of Napoleon

Napoleon dominated both French and European history from 1799 to 1815. He was born in Corsica in 1769, only a few months after France had annexed the island. The son of a lawyer whose family stemmed from the Florentine nobility, the young Napoleon obtained a royal scholarship to study at a military school in France. When the revolution broke out in 1789, Napoleon was a lieutenant. The French Revolution and the European war that followed broadened his sights and presented him with new opportunities. Napoleon rose quickly through the ranks. In 1794, at the age of only twenty-five, he was promoted to the rank of brigadier general by the Committee of Public Safety. Two years later, he was made commander of the French army in Italy (see the box above), where he won a series of victories and dictated peace to the Austrians in 1797. He returned to France as a conquering hero. After a disastrous expedition to Egypt, Napoleon returned to Paris, where he participated in the coup d'etat that ultimately led to his virtual dictatorship of France. He was only thirty years old at the time.

With the coup d'etat of 1799, a new form of the Republic was proclaimed in which, as first consul, Napoleon directly controlled the entire executive authority of government. He had overwhelming influence over the legislature, appointed members of the administrative bureaucracy, controlled the army, and conducted foreign affairs. In 1802, Napoleon was made consul for life, and in 1804 he returned France to monarchy when he had himself crowned as Emperor Napoleon I. The revolutionary era that had begun with an attempt to limit arbitrary government had ended with a government far more autocratic than the monarchy of the old regime.

One of Napoleon's first domestic moves was to establish peace with the oldest and most implacable enemy of the Revolution, the Catholic church. In 1801, Napoleon arranged a Concordat with the pope that recognized Catholicism as the religion of a majority of the French people. Although the Catholic church was permitted to hold processions again and reopen the seminaries, the pope agreed not to raise the question of the church lands confiscated during the Revolution. As a result of the Concordat, the Catholic church was no longer an enemy of the French government. At the same time, the agreement reassured those who had acquired church lands during the Revolution that they would not be taken away, an assurance that obviously made the new owners supporters of the Napoleonic regime.

Napoleon's most famous domestic achievement was his codification of the laws. Before the Revolution, France did not have a single set of laws, but rather virtually three hundred different legal systems. During the Revolution, efforts were made to prepare a codification of the laws for the entire nation, but it remained for Napoleon to bring the work to completion in the famous Civil Code. This preserved most of the revolutionary gains by recognizing the principle of the equality of all citizens before the law, the

CHRONOLOGY

THE FRENCH REVOLUTION

	1789
Meeting of Estates-General	May 5
Formation of National Assembly	June 17
Tennis Court Oath	June 20
Fall of the Bastille	July 14
Great Fear	Summer
Abolition of feudalism	August 4
Declaration of the Rights of Man and the Citizen	August 26
March to Versailles; king's return to Paris	October 5–6
	1790
Civil Constitution of the Clergy	July 12
	1791
Flight of the king	June 20–21
	1792
France declares war on Austria	April 20
Attack on the royal palace	August 10
Abolition of monarchy	September 21
	1793
Execution of the king	January 21
Levy-in-mass	August 23
	1794
Execution of Robespierre	July 28
	1795
Constitution of 1795 is adopted—the Directory	August 22

right of the individual to choose his profession, religious toleration, and the abolition of serfdom and feudalism. Property rights continued to be carefully protected, while the interests of employers were safeguarded by outlawing trade unions and strikes. The Civil Code clearly reflected the revolutionary aspirations for a uniform legal system, legal equality, and protection of property and individuals.

At the same time, the Civil Code strictly curtailed the rights of some people. During the radical phase of the French Revolution, new laws had made divorce an easy process for both husbands and wives, restricted the rights of fathers over their children (they could no longer have their children put in prison arbitrarily), and allowed all children (including daughters) to inherit property equally. The Civil Code undid most of this legislation. The control of fathers over their families was restored. Divorce was still allowed but was made more difficult for women to obtain. A wife caught in adultery, for example, could be divorced by her husband and even imprisoned. A husband, however, could be accused of adultery only if he moved his mistress into his home. Women were now "less equal than men" in other ways as well. When they married, their property came under the control of their husbands. In lawsuits they were treated as minors, and their testimony was regarded as less reliable than that of men.

Napoleon also worked on rationalizing the bureaucratic structure of France by developing a powerful, centralized administrative machine. Administrative centralization required a bureaucracy of capable officials, and Napoleon worked hard to develop one. Early on, the regime showed its preference for experts and cared little whether that expertise had been acquired in royal or revolutionary bureaucracies. Promotion, whether in civil or military offices, was to be based not on rank or birth but only on demonstrated abilities. This was, of course, what many bourgeoisie had wanted before the Revolution. Napoleon, however, also created a new aristocracy based on merit in the state service. Napoleon created 3,263 nobles between 1808 and 1814; nearly 60 percent were military officers while the remainder came from the upper ranks of the civil service and other state and local officials. Socially, only 22 percent of Napoleon's aristocracy came from the nobility of the old regime; almost 60 percent were bourgeois in origin.

In his domestic policies, then, Napoleon both destroyed and preserved aspects of the Revolution. While equality was preserved in the law code and the opening of careers to talent, the creation of a new aristocracy, the strong protection accorded to property rights, and the use of conscription for the military demonstrate a loss of equality. Liberty had been replaced by an initially benevolent despotism that grew increasingly arbitrary. Napoleon shut down sixty of France's seventy-three newspapers and insisted that all manuscripts be subjected to government scrutiny before they were published. Even the mail was opened by government police. One prominent writer—Germaine de Staël—refused to accept Napoleon's growing despotism. Educated in Enlightenment ideas, Madame de Staël wrote novels and political works that denounced Napoleon's rule as tyrannical. Napoleon banned her books in France and exiled her to the German states, where she continued to write.

NAPOLEON'S EMPIRE AND THE EUROPEAN RESPONSE

When Napoleon became first consul in 1799, France was at war with a second European coalition, consisting of Russia, Great Britain, and Austria. Napoleon realized the need for a pause and achieved a peace treaty in 1802, which left France with new frontiers and a number of client territories

�֎ **THE CORONATION OF NAPOLEON.** In 1804, Napoleon restored monarchy to France when he had himself crowned as emperor. In the coronation scene painted by Jacques-Louis David, Napoleon is shown crowning the empress Josephine while the pope looks on. The painting shows Napoleon's mother seated in the box in the background, even though she was not at the ceremony.

from the North Sea to the Adriatic. But the peace did not last, and in 1803 war was renewed with Britain, which was soon joined by Austria, Russia, and Prussia in the Third Coalition. In a series of battles from 1805 to 1807, Napoleon's Grand Army defeated the continental members of the coalition, giving Napoleon the opportunity to create a new European order. The Grand Empire was composed of three major parts: the French empire, dependent states, and allied states. The French empire, the inner core of the Grand Empire, consisted of an enlarged France extending to the Rhine in the east and including the western half of Italy north of Rome. Dependent states were kingdoms under the rule of Napoleon's relatives; these came to include Spain, Holland, the kingdom of Italy, the Swiss Republic, the Grand Duchy of Warsaw, and the Confederation of the Rhine, the latter a union of all German states except Austria and Prussia. Allied states were those defeated by Napoleon and forced to join his struggle against Britain; they included Prussia, Austria, Russia, and Sweden.

Within his empire, Napoleon sought acceptance everywhere of certain revolutionary principles, including legal equality, religious toleration, and economic freedom. As he explained to his brother Jerome after he had made him king of the new German state of Westphalia:

What the peoples of Germany desire most impatiently is that talented commoners should have the same right to your esteem and to public employments as the nobles, that any trace of serfdom and of an intermediate hierarchy between the sovereign and the lowest class of the people should be completely abolished. The benefits of the Code Napoléon, the publicity of judicial procedure, the creation of juries must be so many distinguishing marks of your monarchy. . . . What nation would wish to return under the arbitrary Prussian government once it had tasted the benefits of a wise and liberal administration? The peoples of Germany, the peoples of France, of Italy, of Spain all desire equality and liberal ideas. I have guided the affairs of Europe for many years now, and I have had occasion to convince myself that the buzzing of the privileged classes is contrary to the general opinion. Be a constitutional king.[7]

In the inner core and dependent states of his Grand Empire, Napoleon tried to destroy the old order. Nobility and clergy everywhere in these states lost their special privileges. He decreed equality of opportunity with offices open to talent, equality before the law, and religious toleration. This spread of French revolutionary principles was an important factor in the development of liberal traditions in these countries.

Like Hitler one hundred and thirty years later, Napoleon hoped that his Grand Empire would last for centuries; like Hitler's empire, it collapsed almost as rapidly as it had been formed. Two major reasons help to explain this: the survival of Great Britain and the force of nationalism. Britain's survival was primarily due to its sea power. As long as Britain ruled the waves, it was almost invulnerable to military attack. Although Napoleon contemplated an invasion of Britain and even collected ships for it, he could not overcome the British navy's decisive defeat of a combined French-Spanish fleet at Trafalgar

in 1805. Napoleon then turned to his Continental System to defeat Britain. Put into effect between 1806 and 1808, it attempted to prevent British goods from reaching the European continent in order to weaken Britain economically and destroy its capacity to wage war. But the Continental System failed. Allied states resented the ever tightening French economic hegemony; some began to cheat and others to resist, thereby opening the door to collaboration with the British. New markets in the Levant and in Latin America also provided compensation for the British. Indeed, by 1809–1810, British overseas exports were at near-record highs.

A second important factor in the defeat of Napoleon was nationalism. This political creed had arisen during the French Revolution in the French people's emphasis on brotherhood (*fraternité*) and solidarity against other peoples. Nationalism involved the unique cultural identity

� MAP **19.7**   Napoleon's Grand Empire

�e French empire	→ Napoleon's route, 1812
▒ Under French control	⚔ Battle site
▓ Allied to France	

CHRONOLOGY

THE AGE OF NAPOLEON, 1799–1815

Napoleon as first consul	1799–1804
Concordat with Catholic church	1801
Emperor Napoleon I	1804–1815
Continental System established	1806
Invasion of Russia	1812
War of liberation	1813–1814
Exile to Elba	1814
Battle of Waterloo; exile to St. Helena	1815
Death of Napoleon	1821

of a people based on common language, religion, and national symbols. The spirit of French nationalism had made possible the mass armies of the revolutionary and Napoleonic eras and had also opened the political process to new people who were not aristocrats. But by extending the principles of the French Revolution beyond France, Napoleon had inadvertently spread nationalism as well. The French aroused nationalism by making themselves hated oppressors, thus arousing the patriotism of others in opposition to French nationalism, and by showing the people of Europe what nationalism was and what a nation in arms could do. It was a lesson not lost on other peoples and rulers. A Spanish uprising against Napoleon's rule, aided by the British, kept a French force of 200,000 pinned down for years.

The beginning of Napoleon's downfall came in 1812 with the invasion of Russia. The latter's defection from the Continental System left Napoleon with little choice. Although aware of the risks in invading such a large country, he also knew that if the Russians were allowed to challenge the Continental System unopposed, others would soon follow suit. In June 1812, he led a Grand Army of over 600,000 men into Russia. Napoleon's hopes for victory depended on quickly meeting and defeating the Russian armies, but the Russian forces refused to give battle and retreated for hundreds of miles, torching their own villages and countryside to prevent Napoleon's army from finding food and forage. When the Russians did stop to fight at Borodino, Napoleon's forces won an indecisive and costly victory. When the remaining forces of the Grand Army arrived in Moscow, they found the city ablaze. Lacking food and supplies, Napoleon abandoned Moscow late in October and made the "Great Retreat" across Russia in terrible winter conditions. Only 40,000 out of the original army managed to arrive back in Poland

in January 1813. This military disaster then led to a war of liberation all over Europe, culminating in Napoleon's defeat in April 1814.

The defeated emperor of the French was allowed to play ruler on the island of Elba, off the coast of Tuscany, while the Bourbon monarchy was restored to France in the person of Louis XVIII, brother of the executed king. But the new king had little support, and Napoleon, bored on the island of Elba, slipped back into France. The troops sent to capture him went over to his side, and Napoleon entered Paris in triumph on March 20, 1815. The powers who had defeated him pledged once more to fight this person they called the "Enemy and Disturber of the Tranquility of the World." Having decided to strike first at his enemies, Napoleon raised yet another army and moved to attack the nearest allied forces, stationed in Belgium. At Waterloo on June 18, Napoleon met a combined British and Prussian army under the Duke of Wellington and suffered a bloody defeat. This time the victorious allies exiled him to St. Helena, a small, forsaken island in the South Atlantic. Only Napoleon's memory would continue to haunt French political life.

 CONCLUSION

Everywhere in Europe at the beginning of the eighteenth century, the old order remained strong. Nobles, clerics, towns, and provinces all had privileges. Everywhere in the eighteenth century, monarchs sought to enlarge their bureaucracies to raise taxes to support the new large standing armies that had originated in the seventeenth century. The existence of these armies guaranteed wars. The existence of five great powers, with two of them (France and Great Britain) in conflict in the East and the Western Hemisphere, initiated a new scale of global conflict; the Seven Years' War could legitimately be viewed as the first world war. Although the wars changed little on the European continent, British victories enabled Great Britain to emerge as the world's greatest naval and colonial power. Everywhere in Europe, increased demands for taxes to support these conflicts led to attacks on the privileged orders and a desire for change not met by the ruling monarchs. At the same time, sustained population growth and dramatic changes in finance, trade, and industry created tensions that undermined the traditional foundations of the old order. The inability of that old order to deal meaningfully with these changes led to a revolutionary outburst at the end of the eighteenth century that marked the beginning of the end for the old order.

The revolutionary era of the late eighteenth century witnessed a dramatic political transformation. Revolutionary upheavals, beginning in North America and continuing in France, produced movements for political liberty and equality. The documents created by these revolutions, the Declaration of Independence and the Declaration of the Rights of Man and the Citizen, embodied the fundamental ideas of the Enlightenment and created a liberal political agenda based on a belief in popular sovereignty—the people are the source of political power—and the principles of liberty and equality. Liberty, frequently limited in practice, meant, in theory, freedom from arbitrary power as well as the freedom to think, write, and worship as one chose. Equality meant equality in rights and the equality of opportunity based on talent rather than birth. In practice, equality remained limited; those who owned property had greater opportunities for voting and officeholding, while there was certainly no equality between men and women.

The French Revolution created a modern revolutionary concept. No one had foreseen or consciously planned the upheaval that began in 1789, but after 1789 "revolutionaries" knew that the proper use of mass uprisings could produce the overthrow of unwanted governments. For these people, the French Revolution became a symbol of hope; for those who feared such changes, it became a symbol of dread. The French Revolution became the classical political and social model for revolution. At the same time, the liberal and national political ideals created by the Revolution dominated the political landscape of the nineteenth and early twentieth centuries. A new era had begun, and the world would never be the same.

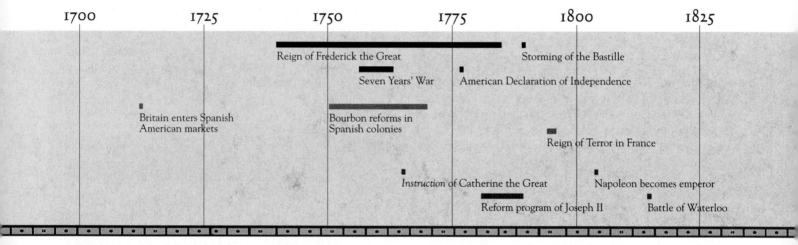

CHAPTER NOTES

1. Igor Vinogradoff, "Russian Missions to London, 1711–1789: Further Extracts from the Cottrell Papers," *Oxford Slavonic Papers*, New Series (1982), 15:76.
2. Quoted in E. Bradford Burns, *Latin America: A Concise Interpretative History*, 4th ed. (Englewood Cliffs, N.J., 1986), p. 62.
3. Quoted in Reinhold A. Dorwart, *The Administrative Reforms of Frederick William I of Prussia* (Cambridge, Mass., 1953), p. 36.
4. Quoted in William Doyle, *The Oxford History of the French Revolution* (Oxford, 1989), p. 184.
5. Quoted in Leo Gershoy, *The Era of the French Revolution* (Princeton, N.J., 1957), p. 157.
6. Quoted in Doyle, *The Oxford History of the French Revolution*, p. 254.
7. Quoted in J. Christopher Herold, ed., *The Mind of Napoleon* (New York, 1955), pp. 74–75.

SUGGESTED READINGS

For a good introduction to the history of eighteenth-century Europe, see the relevant chapters in the general works by Woloch and Anderson listed in Chapter 18. See also G. Treasure, *The Making of Modern Europe, 1648–1780* (London, 1985), and O. Hufton, *Europe: Privilege and Protest, 1730–1789* (London, 1980). A good intro-

duction to European population can be found in M. W. Flinn, *The European Demographic System, 1500–1820* (Brighton, 1981). A different perspective on economic history can be found in F. Braudel's *Capitalism and Material Life, 1400–1800* (New York, 1973). The subject of mercantile empires and worldwide trade is covered in J. H. Parry, *Trade and Dominion: European Overseas Empires in the Eighteenth Century* (London, 1971), and P. K. Liss, *Atlantic Empires: The Network of Trade and Revolution, 1713–1826* (Baltimore, Md., 1983). Eighteenth-century cottage industry and the beginnings of industrialization are examined in the early chapters of D. Landes, *The Unbound Prometheus: Technological Change and Industrial Development in Western Europe from 1750 to the Present* (New York, 1969).

On the European nobility, see J. Dewald, *The European Nobility 1400–1800* (Cambridge, 1996), and H. M. Scott, *The European Nobility in the Seventeenth and Eighteenth Centuries* (London, 1995). On European cities, see J. de Vries, *European Urbanization, 1500–1800* (Cambridge, Mass., 1984). There is no better work on the problem of poverty in the eighteenth century than O. Hufton, *The Poor of Eighteenth-Century France* (Oxford, 1974). The warfare of this period is examined in M. S. Anderson, *War and Society in Europe of the Old Regime, 1615–1789* (New York, 1988).

For a brief survey of Latin America, see E. B. Burns, *Latin America: A Concise Interpretative History*, 4th ed. (Englewood Cliffs, N.J., 1986). More detailed works on colonial Latin American history include S. J. Stein and B. H. Stein, *The Colonial Heritage of Latin America* (New York, 1970), and J. Lockhardt and S. B. Schwartz, *Early Latin America: A History of Colonial Spanish America and Brazil* (New York, 1983). A history of the revolutionary era in America can be found in R. Middlekauff, *The Glorious Cause: The American Revolution: 1763–1789* (New York, 1982), and C. Bonwick, *The American Revolution* (Charlottesville, Va., 1991). The importance of ideology is treated in G. Wood, *The Radicalism of the American Revolution* (New York, 1992). For an interesting comparative study, see the stimulating work by P. Higonnet, *Sister Republics: Origins of the French and American Revolutions* (Cambridge, Mass., 1988).

On enlightened absolutism, see H. M. Scott, ed., *Enlightened Absolutism: Reform and Reformers in Later Eighteenth-Century Europe* (Ann Arbor, Mich., 1990). Good biographies of some of Europe's monarchs include R. Asprey, *Frederick the Great: The Magnificent Enigma* (New York, 1986); I. De Madariaga, *Catherine the Great, A Short History* (New Haven, Conn., 1990); and T. C. W. Blanning, *Joseph II* (New York, 1994).

A well written, up-to-date introduction to the French Revolution can be found in W. Doyle, *The Oxford History of the French Revolution* (Oxford, 1989). For the entire revolutionary and Napoleonic eras, see O. Connelly, *The French Revolution and Napoleonic Era*, 2d ed. (Fort Worth, Tex., 1991), and D. M. G. Sutherland, *France 1789–1815: Revolution and Counter-Revolution* (London, 1985). Two brief works are A. Forrest, *The French Revolution* (Oxford, 1995), and J. M. Roberts, *The French Revolution*, 2d ed. (New York, 1997). A different approach to the French Revolution can be found in E. Kennedy, *A Cultural History of the French Revolution* (New Haven, Conn., 1989).

The origins of the French Revolution are examined in W. Doyle, *Origins of the French Revolution* (Oxford, 1988). On the early years of the Revolution, see T. Tackett, *Becoming a Revolutionary* (Princeton, N.J., 1996), and N. Hampson, *Prelude to Terror* (Oxford, 1988). Important works on the radical stage of the French Revolution include N. Hampson, *The Terror in the French Revolution* (London, 1981); R. R. Palmer, *Twelve Who Ruled* (Princeton, N.J., 1941); and R. Cobb, *The People's Armies* (London, 1987). The importance of the revolutionary wars in the radical stage of the Revolution is underscored in T. C. W. Blanning, *The French Revolutionary Wars, 1787–1802* (New York, 1996). On the Directory, see M. Lyons, *France Under the Directory* (Cambridge, 1975). On the Great Fear, there is the classic work by G. Lefebvre, *The Great Fear of 1789: Rural Panic in Revolutionary France* (London, 1973). On the role of women in revolutionary France, see O. Hufton, *Women and the Limits of Citizenship in the French Revolution* (Toronto, 1992), and J. Landes, *Women and the Public Sphere in the Age of the French Revolution* (Ithaca, N.Y., 1988). The best brief biography of Napoleon is F. Markham, *Napoleon* (New York, 1963). Also valuable are M. Lyons, *Napoleon Bonaparte and the Legacy of the French Revolution* (New York, 1994); G. J. Ellis, *Napoleon* (New York, 1997); and the recent massive biographies by F. J. McLynn, *Napoleon: A Biography* (London, 1997), and A. Schom, *Napoleon Bonaparte* (New York, 1997).

INFOTRAC COLLEGE EDITION

For additional reading, go to InfoTrac College Edition, your online research library at
http://web1.infotrac-college.com

Enter the search terms "American Revolution" using Keywords.

Enter the search terms "French Revolution" using Keywords.

Enter the search term "Napoleon" using Keywords.

Enter the search terms "Napoleonic Wars" using Keywords.

THE EMERGENCE OF NEW WORLD PATTERNS (1500–1800)

Historians often refer to the period from the end of the fifteenth to the end of the eighteenth century as the early modern era. The phrase is not chosen lightly, for it was during these years that several factors were at work that created the conditions of our own time. It was during that era that maritime exploration opened the entire world to trade and colonization. It was then that centralized monarchies—and later nation-states—formed that led to the modern concept of statehood. It was then that an intellectual revolution laid the foundations for a modern worldview based on rationalism and secularism. And it was at the close of that era that technological advances began to lay the basis for the Industrial Revolution.

In a global perspective, perhaps the most noteworthy event of the period was the extension of the maritime trade network throughout the entire populated world. The primary instrument of that expansion, of course, was a resurgent Europe, which exploded onto the world scene with the initial explorations of the Portuguese and the Spanish at the end of the fifteenth century and then gradually came to dominate shipping on international trade routes during the next three centuries. The Chinese had inaugurated the process with their groundbreaking voyages to East Africa in the early fifteenth century but had inexplicably abandoned the effort shortly thereafter.

Some contemporary historians argue that it was this sudden burst of energy from Europe that created the first truly global economic system. According to Immanuel Wallerstein, one of the leading proponents of this theory, the age of exploration led to the creation of a new "world system" characterized by the emergence of global trade networks dominated by the rising force of European capitalism, which now began to scour the periphery of the system for access to markets and cheap raw materials.

Strictly speaking, it is true that only in the sixteenth century did trade patterns first encircle the earth. In the view of other contemporary historians, however, Wallerstein's view must be qualified. Some, for example, point to the Mongol expansion beginning in the thirteenth century, or even to the rise of the Arab empire in the Middle East a few centuries earlier, as signs of the creation of a global communications network enabling goods and ideas to travel from one end of the Eurasian supercontinent to the other.

Others take issue with the assertion that modern capitalism was the exclusive product of Europe during the fifteenth and sixteenth centuries and argue that its roots can be found in earlier centuries and in other environments. China during the Tang and the Song dynasties and the Arab empire under the Abbasid both displayed a vitality in the manufacturing and commercial sectors that compared favorably with that of Europe during the early modern era. Finally, some historians dispute the view of world system theorists that the year 1500 inaugurated an era of European dominance, pointing to the continuing vitality of many traditional Asian civilizations well into the nineteenth century. Only then, with the onset of the Industrial Revolution, would the global hegemony of the West become clearly established.

Whatever the truth of these debates, there are still many reasons for considering the end of the fifteenth century as a crucial date in world history. In the most basic sense, it marked the end of the long isolation of the Western Hemisphere from the rest of the inhabited world. In so doing, it led to the creation of the first truly global network of ideas and commodities, which would introduce plants, ideas, and (unfortunately) many new diseases to all humanity (see the box on p. 581). Second, the period gave birth to a stunning increase in trade and manufacturing that stimulated major economic changes not only in Europe but in other parts of the world as well. The world would never be the same again.

The period from 1500 to 1800, then, was an incubation period for the modern world and the launching pad for an era of Western domination that began in the nineteenth century. To understand why the West emerged as the leading force in the world at that time, it is necessary to understand what factors at work in Europe led to the scientific and industrial revolutions and why such factors were absent in other major civilizations around the globe.

Historians have identified the changes—in the form of improvements in navigation, shipbuilding, and weaponry—that took place in Europe in the early modern era as essential elements in the Age of Exploration. As we have seen, many of these technological advances were based on earlier discoveries that had taken place elsewhere—in China, India, and the Middle East—and had then been brought to Europe on Muslim ships or along the trade routes through Central Asia. Gunpowder, for example, had been invented in China, and eventually its mil-

THE COLUMBIAN EXCHANGE

In the Western world, the discovery of the Americas has traditionally been viewed essentially in a positive sense, as the first step in a process that expanded the global trade network and eventually led to the emergence of economic well-being and political democracy in societies throughout the world. That view has come under sharp attack from some observers, however, who claim that for the peoples of the New World, the primary legacy of the European conquest was not improved living standards but harsh colonial exploitation and the spread of pestilential diseases that decimated the local population. In recent years, the brunt of such criticism has been directed at Christopher Columbus, one of the chief initiators of the discovery and conquest of the Americas. Taking issue with the prevailing image of Columbus as a heroic figure in world history, critics view him as a symbol of Spanish colonial repression and a prime mover in the virtual extinction of the peoples and cultures of the New World.

There is no doubt that the record of the European conquistadors in the Western Hemisphere leaves much to be desired, and certainly the voyages of Columbus were not of universal benefit to his contemporaries or to the generations later to come. But to focus solely on the evils that were committed in the name of exploration and the propagation of Christianity distorts the historical realities of the era. The age of European expansion that began with Prince Henry the Navigator and Christopher Columbus was only the latest in a series of population movements that included the spread of nomadic peoples across Central Asia and the expansion of Islam from the Middle East after the death of the prophet Muhammad. In fact, the migration of peoples in search of survival and a better livelihood has been a central theme in the evolution of the human race since the dawn of prehistory.

More importantly, it seems clear that the consequences of such population movements are too complex to be summed up in moral or ideological simplifications. The European expansion into the Americas, for example, not only brought the destruction of cultures and dangerous new diseases, but also initiated the exchange of plant and animal species that have ultimately been of widespread benefit to peoples living throughout the globe. The introduction of the horse, cow, and various grain crops vastly increased food productivity in the New World. The cultivation of corn, manioc, and the potato have had the same effect in Asia, Africa, and Europe. Whether Christopher Columbus was a hero or a villain is a matter of debate. That he and his contemporaries played a key role in the emergence of the modern world is a matter on which there can be no doubt.

✿ **MASSACRE OF THE INDIANS.**
This sixteenth-century engraving is an imaginative treatment of what was probably an all-too-common occurrence, as the Spanish attempted to enslave the American peoples and convert them to Christianity.

itary uses came to the attention of the Ottomans, the Safavids, and the Mughals, as well as the Russian empire of Peter the Great, all of whom became dependent on the new military hardware. But it was the capacity and the desire of the Europeans to enhance their wealth and power by making practical use of the discoveries of others that was the significant factor in the equation. It was the firearms and artillery of European nations, in fact, that enabled them to dominate international sea lanes and create vast colonial empires in the New World.

But technological innovations by themselves cannot provide the final answer to the question of why at this time in history Europe suddenly became the engine for rapid global change. Another factor, certainly, was the change in the European worldview, the shift from a metaphysical to a materialist perspective and the growing inclination among European intellectuals to question first principles. Whereas in China, for example, the "investigation of things" had been put to the use of analyzing and confirming principles first established by Confucius during the Chinese "Golden Age," in early modern Europe, empirical scientists rejected received religious ideas, developed a new conception of the universe, and sought ways to improve material conditions around them.

But why were European thinkers more interested in practical applications for their discoveries than their counterparts elsewhere? One explanation, certainly, lies in the growing strength of the urban bourgeoisie in many areas of early modern Europe and the deliberate appeal that early scientists made to the literate mercantile elites of Europe when they showed how the new scientific ideas could be applied directly to specific technological needs. As we have seen, thriving commercial and manufacturing communities existed in the countries of East Asia, India, Central and East Africa, and the Middle East and were playing an increasingly important role in the life of their societies. But the European mercantile sector had begun to carve out an independent existence in the autonomous cities of southern and central Europe as early as the eleventh and twelfth centuries and by the eve of the early modern era suffered from few of the political and economic restrictions imposed on their counterparts elsewhere. By the sixteenth century, these affluent sectors of the community were enjoying increasing wealth and prosperity.

A final factor can be attributed to political changes that were beginning to take place in Europe during this period. The breakup of the world of Christendom, a consequence of the religious wars of the sixteenth and seventeenth centuries, helped to give birth to independent and relatively centralized monarchies in many areas of Europe. In the eighteenth century, the process of centralization that had characterized the growth of states since the Middle Ages continued as most European states enlarged their bureaucratic machinery and consolidated their governments in order to collect the revenues and amass the armies they needed to compete militarily with the other European states. In this highly competitive environment—evident in the wars of the century—political leaders desperately sought ways to enhance their wealth and power at the expense of rivals and grasped eagerly at whatever tools were available to guarantee their survival and prosperity. Where necessary and appropriate, they were more than willing to form alliances with the urban bourgeoisie to enhance state power and the prosperity of the people.

At the end of the eighteenth century, profound political upheavals led to additional political change and the emergence of a new political order. In discussing the upheavals of the late eighteenth century, it is appropriate to speak of a liberal movement to extend political rights and power to the bourgeoisie "possessing capital," namely, those besides the aristocracy who were literate and had become wealthy through capitalist enterprises in trade, industry, and finance. The years preceding and accompanying the French Revolution included attempts at reform and revolt in the North American colonies, Britain, the Dutch Republic, some Swiss cities, and the Austrian Netherlands. The success of the revolutionary upheavals in North America and France created a liberal political agenda based on principles of liberty and equality and a new sense of nationhood. The identity of citizens with their nation rather than their monarch created a new and powerful force—nationalism—that would lead to revolutionary movements throughout the world in the nineteenth and twentieth centuries.

Conditions in many areas of Asia and Africa were less conducive to these economic and political developments. In China, a centralized monarchy continued to rely on a prosperous agricultural sector as the economic foundation of the empire. Though Emperor Yongle briefly toyed with the idea of expanding China's commercial contacts with the outside world, his successor, urged on by domestic interests, reversed the process and unilaterally brought China's own Age of Exploration to an end. In Japan, power was centralized under the powerful Tokugawa shogunate, and the era of peace and stability that ensued saw an increase in manufacturing and commercial activity. But Japanese elites, after initially expressing interest in the outside world, abruptly shut the door on European trade and ideas in an effort to protect "the land of the gods" from external contamination.

In India and the Middle East, commerce and manufacturing had played a vital role in the life of societies since the emergence of the Indian Ocean trade network in the first centuries C.E. And while India was still a predominantly agricultural society, commerce was almost literally the life blood of many states in the Middle East, including the powerful Abbasid caliphate that had dominated the entire area during its apogee in the eighth and ninth centuries. But beginning in the eleventh century, the area had suffered through an extended period of political instability, marked by invasions by nomadic peoples from Central Asia. Although the Turks and the Mongols eventually formed their own states in the area and continued to promote trade with countries outside the region, the violence of the period and the local rulers' lack of experience in promoting maritime commerce had a severe depressing effect on urban manufacturing and commerce.

In the meantime, the countries of sub-Saharan Africa had their own problems. A number of trading states had begun to emerge in West Africa and along the eastern coast of the continent in the seventh and eighth centuries C.E., a process that was accelerated by Muslim penetration of the area in later centuries. But except for the eastern fringes, most parts of the continent still lacked the necessary infrastructure in terms of means of transportation, technology, and centralized states to compete aggressively for an active role in the regional trade passing through the area. For the most part, African states were suppliers rather than carriers of goods and remained too isolated from the main trade routes to benefit substantially from the technological and cultural diffusion that was taking place in many other areas of the world.

In the early modern era, then, Europe was best placed to take advantage of the technological innovations that

POPULATION EXPLOSION

Between 1700 and 1800, Europe, China, and to a lesser degree, India and the Ottoman Empire, experienced a dramatic growth in population. In Europe, for example, the population grew from 120 million people to almost 200 million by 1800; China, from less than 200 million to 300 million during the same period.

Four factors were important in causing this population explosion. First, better growing conditions, made possible by an improvement in climate, affected wide areas of the world and enabled people to produce more food. Summers in both China and Europe, for example, were warmer beginning in the early eighteenth century. Second, by the eighteenth century, people had begun to develop immunities to the epidemic diseases that had caused such widespread loss of life between 1500 and 1700. The spread of people by ship after 1500 had led to devastating epidemics. For example, the arrival of Europeans in Mexico led to smallpox, measles, and chicken pox among a native population that had no immunities to European diseases. In 1500, between 11 and 20 million people lived in the area of Mexico; by 1650, only 1.5 million remained. Gradually, however, people developed immunities to these diseases. By 1750, both epidemic diseases and plagues were no longer devastating in Europe, China, India, and the Middle East.

A third factor in population increase came from new food sources. As a result of the Columbian exchange (see the box on p. 581) American food crops—such as corn, potatoes, and sweet potatoes—were brought to other parts of the world, where they became important food sources: corn and potatoes were grown extensively in Africa and Europe, while sweet potatoes spread rapidly in southern China and West Africa. China, too, had imported a new species of rice from Southeast Asia that had a shorter harvest cycle than that of existing varieties. These new foods provided additional sources of nutrition that enabled more people to live for a longer time. At the same time, land development and canal building in the eighteenth century also enabled government authorities to move food supplies to areas threatened with crop failure and famine.

Finally, the use of new weapons based on gunpowder allowed states to control larger territories and ensure a new degree of order. The early rulers of the Qing dynasty, for example, pacified the Chinese empire and ensured a long period of peace and stability. Absolute monarchs achieved similar goals in a number of European states. Less violence led to fewer deaths at the same time that an increase in food supplies and a decrease in death from diseases were occurring, thus making possible in the eighteenth century the beginning of the world population explosion that persists to this day.

FESTIVAL OF THE YAM. The spread of a few major food crops made possible new sources of nutrition to feed more people. The importance of the yam to the Asante people of West Africa is evident in this celebration of a yam festival at harvest time in 1817.

had now become increasingly available throughout the Old World. It possessed the political stability, the capital, and what today might be called the "modernizing elite" that provided the spur to active efforts to take advantage of new conditions for their own benefit. Where other regions were still beset by internal obstacles or had deliberately "turned inward" to seek their destiny, Europe now turned outward to seek a new and dominant position in the world.

European expansion was not fueled solely by economic considerations, however. As had been the case with the rise of Islam in the seventh and eighth centuries, religion played a major role in motivating the European Age of Exploration in the early modern era. Although Christianity was by no means a new religion in the fifteenth century (as Islam had been at the moment of Arab expansion), the world of Christendom was in the midst of a major period of rivalry with the forces of Islam, a rivalry that was severely exacerbated by the conquest of the Byzantine Empire by the Ottoman Turks in the mid-fifteenth century.

Although the claims of Portuguese and Spanish adventurers that their activities were motivated primarily by a desire to bring the word of God to non-Christian peoples undoubtedly included a considerable measure of self-delusion and hypocrisy, there seems no reason to doubt that religious motives played a meaningful part in the European Age of Exploration. A perusal of the diaries of such famous explorers as Columbus, Vasco da Gama, and Francisco Pizarro attests to the sincerity and depth of their Christian beliefs. Religion undoubtedly provided a moral justification for some of the more heinous acts that were committed by Europeans in distant lands.

Religious motives were perhaps less evident in the activities of the non-Catholic powers that entered the competition beginning in the seventeenth century. English and Dutch merchants and officials were more inclined to be motivated purely by the pursuit of economic profit or by the prevailing "beggar thy neighbor" mercantile philosophy of the day. Eventually, however, the idea that trade benefits all participants provided a new moral justification, especially in the last quarter of the eighteenth century, when the free trade philosophy of Adam Smith became accepted wisdom in official and mercantile circles throughout much of Europe. The importance of free trade as a prerequisite for economic prosperity and political democracy became a common tenet of enlightened thinking in the colonial era in the nineteenth century and continues to be influential in our own day.

The fact that the early modern era was the incubation period for two of the most powerful forces that have dominated the nineteenth and twentieth centuries—the Industrial Revolution and the era of global imperialism—and that the explosive power of such forces originated in Europe, should not blind us to the facts that significant changes were taking place in other parts of the world as well and that many of these changes had relatively little to do with the situation in the West (see the box on p. 583). As we have seen, the impact of European expansion on the rest of the world was still limited up to the end of the eighteenth century. While European political authority was firmly established in a few key areas, such as the Spice Islands and Latin America, in most regions of Africa and Asia traditional societies remained relatively intact. And processes at work in these societies were often operating independently of events in Europe and would later give birth to forces that acted to limit or shape the Western impact.

One of these forces was the progressive emergence of centralized states, some of them built on the concept of ethnic unity. In Japan, the Tokugawa shogunate had asserted an unprecedented degree of political and cultural authority over a population traditionally ruled by decentralized forces reminiscent of the feudal era in medieval Europe. In India, a centralized empire had been created for the first time since the fall of the Mauryas

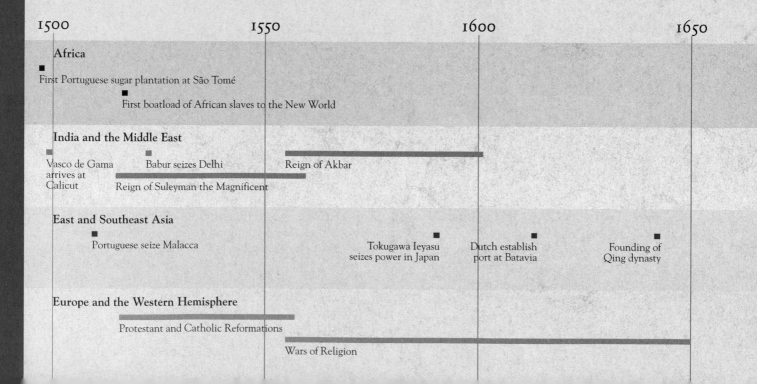

1500   1550   1600   1650

Africa
First Portuguese sugar plantation at São Tomé
First boatload of African slaves to the New World

India and the Middle East
Vasco de Gama arrives at Calicut   Babur seizes Delhi   Reign of Akbar
Reign of Suleyman the Magnificent

East and Southeast Asia
Portuguese seize Malacca   Tokugawa Ieyasu seizes power in Japan   Dutch establish port at Batavia   Founding of Qing dynasty

Europe and the Western Hemisphere
Protestant and Catholic Reformations
Wars of Religion

in the era of antiquity. In mainland Southeast Asia, organized states emerged in Burma, Thailand, and Vietnam that were broadly based on rising ethnic consciousness. This trend was somewhat less apparent in the Middle East, where the Ottoman Empire still laid claim to universal hegemony over the entire eastern Mediterranean and Mesopotamia, and in sub-Saharan Africa, where the forces of state building were still in an embryonic stage. But the concept of statehood was strengthening and laid the basis for the spread of nationalism in the twentieth century.

Within these centralized states, the steady growth of a commercial and manufacturing sector was beginning to create the conditions for a future industrial revolution. A number of Asian societies made technological advances during this period and witnessed the emergence of a more visible and articulate urban bourgeoisie. This process was especially evident in China and Japan, but it also occurred in India, the Middle East, and parts of North Africa. The restraints on industrial growth were political, social, and intellectual, not economic or technological.

For the moment, however, such forces were mere portents for the future, not signs of an imminent industrial revolution. At the beginning of the nineteenth century, the primary fact of life for most Asian and African societies was the expansionist power of an industrializing and ever more aggressive Europe. The power and ambition of the West provided an immediate challenge to the independence and destiny of societies throughout the rest of the world. The nature of that challenge will be the subject of our next section.

SUGGESTED READINGS

On different aspects of the global trade patterns of this era, see A. K. Smith, *Creating a World Economy: Merchant Capital, Capitalism, and World Trade, 1400–1825* (New York, 1991), and P. D. Curtin, *Cross-Cultural Trade in World History* (Cambridge, 1984). Important cultural exchanges of the period are examined in S. B. Schwartz, ed., *Implicit Understandings: Observing, Reporting, and Reflecting on the Encounters Between Europeans and Other Peoples in the Early Modern Era* (New York, 1994), and J. Thornton, *Africa and Africans in the Formation of the Atlantic World, 1400–1680* (Cambridge, 1992). On the Columbian Exchange, see the basic work by A. W. Crosby, *The Columbian Exchange: The Biological and Cultural Consequences of 1492* (Westport, Conn., 1972); N. D. Cook, *Born to Die. Disease and New World Conquest* (Cambridge, 1998); and W. H. McNeil, *The Global Connection: Conquerors, Catastrophes, and Community* (Princeton, N.J., 1992). For a broad perspective on the population explosion beginning in the eighteenth century, see M. Livi-Bacci, *A Concise History of World Population*, trans. C. Ipsen (Cambridge, Mass., 1992).

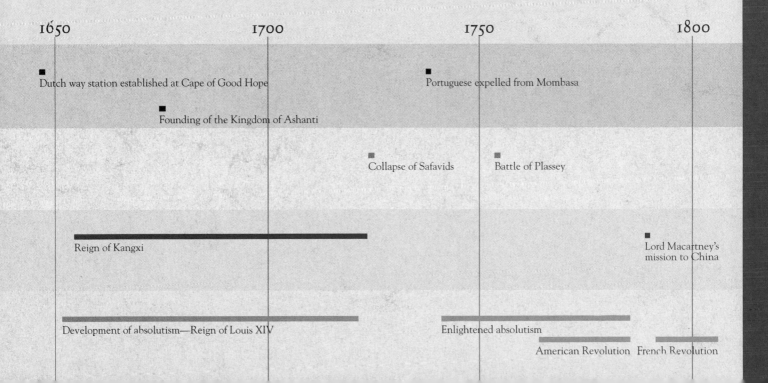

| 1650 | 1700 | 1750 | 1800 |

Dutch way station established at Cape of Good Hope

Portuguese expelled from Mombasa

Founding of the Kingdom of Ashanti

Collapse of Safavids

Battle of Plassey

Reign of Kangxi

Lord Macartney's mission to China

Development of absolutism—Reign of Louis XIV

Enlightened absolutism

American Revolution   French Revolution

GLOSSARY

absolutism a form of government where the sovereign power or ultimate authority rested in the hands of a monarch who claimed to rule by divine right and was therefore responsible only to God.

Agricultural (Neolithic) Revolution the shift from hunting animals and gathering plants for sustenance to producing food by systematic agriculture that occurred gradually between 10,000 and 4000 B.C. (the Neolithic or "New Stone" Age).

agricultural revolution the application of new agricultural techniques that allowed for a large increase in productivity in the eighteenth century.

anarchism a political theory that holds that all governments and existing social institutions are unnecessary and advocates a society based on voluntary cooperation.

ANC the African National Congress. Founded in 1912, it was the beginning of political activity by South African blacks. Banned by politically dominant European whites in 1960, it was not officially "unbanned" until 1990. It is now the official majority party of the South African government.

Anelects the body of writing containing conversations between Confucius and his disciples which preserves his worldly wisdom and pragmatic philosophies.

anti-Semitism hostility toward or discrimination against Jews.

appeasement the policy, followed by the European nations in the 1930s, of accepting Hitler's annexation of Austria and Czechoslovakia in the belief that meeting his demands would assure peace and stability.

Arianism a Christian heresy that taught that Jesus was inferior to God. Though condemned by the Council of Nicaea in 325, Arianism was adopted by many of the Germanic peoples who entered the Roman Empire over the next centuries.

aristocracy a class of hereditary nobility in medieval Europe; a warrior class who shared a distinctive lifestyle based on the institution of knighthood, although there were social divisions within the group based on extremes of wealth.

Arthasastra an early Indian political treatise that sets forth many fundamental aspects of the relationship of rulers and their subjects. It has been compared to Machiavelli's well-known book, *The Prince*, and has provided principles upon which many aspects of social organization have developed in the region.

ASEAN the Association for the Southest Asian Nations formed in 1967 to promote the properity and political stability of its member nations. Currently Brunei, Indonesia, Laos, Malaysia, Myanmar, the Philippines, Singapore, Thailand, and Vietnam are members. Other countries in the region participate as "observer" members.

Ausgleich the "Compromise" of 1867 that created the dual monarchy of Austria-Hungary. Austria and Hungary each had its own capital, constitution, and legislative assembly, but were united under one monarch.

authoritarian state a state that has a dictatorial government and some other trappings of a totalitarian state, but does not demand that the masses be actively involved in the regime's goals as totalitarian states do.

auxiliaries troops enlisted from the subject peoples of the Roman Empire to supplement the regular legions composed of Roman citizens.

balance of power a distribution of power among several states such that no single nation can dominate or interfere with the interests of another.

benefice in the Christian church, a position, such as a bishopric, that consisted of both a sacred office and the right of the holder to the annual revenues from the position.

bicameral legislature a legislature with two houses.

Black Death the outbreak of plague (mostly bubonic) in the mid-fourteenth century that killed from 25 to 50 percent of Europe's population.

Blitzkrieg "lightning war." A war conducted with great speed and force, as in Germany's advance at the beginning of World War II.

Bolsheviks a small faction of the Russian Social Democratic Party who were led by Lenin and dedicated to violent revolution; seized power in Russia in 1917 and were subsequently renamed the Communists.

boyars the Russian nobility.

Brezhnev Doctrine the doctrine, enunciated by Leonid Brezhnev, that the Soviet Union had a right to intervene if socialism was threatened in another socialist state; used to justify the use of Soviet troops in Czechoslovakia in 1968.

caliph the secular leader of the Islamic community.

capital material wealth used or available for use in the production of more wealth.

caste system a system of rigid social hierarchy in which all members of that society are assigned by birth to specific "ranks," and inherit specific roles and privileges.

cartel a combination of independent commercial enterprises that work together to control prices and limit competition.

Cartesian dualism Descartes's principle of the separation of mind and matter (and mind and body) that enabled scientists to view matter as something separate from themselves that could be investigated by reason.

chaebol a South Korean business structure similar to the Japanese keiretsu.

chansons de geste a form of vernacular literature in the High Middle Ages that consisted of heroic epics focusing on the deeds of warriors.

chivalry the ideal of civilized behavior that emerged among the nobility in the eleventh and twelfth centuries under the influence of the church; a code of ethics knights were expected to uphold.

Christian (northern) humanism an intellectual movement in northern Europe in the late fifteenth and early sixteenth centuries that combined the interest in the classics of the Italian Renaissance with an interest in the sources of early Christianity, including the New Testament and the writings of the church fathers.

civic humanism an intellectual movement of the Italian Renaissance that saw Cicero, who was both an intellectual and a statesman, as the ideal and held that humanists should be involved in government and use their rhetorical training in the service of the state.

civil rights the basic rights of citizens including equality before the law, freedom of speech and press, and freedom from arbitrary arrest.

Cold War the ideological conflict between the Soviet Union and the United States after World War II.

collective farms large farms created in the Soviet Union by Stalin by combining many small holdings into one large farm worked by the peasants under government supervision.

collective security the use of an international army raised by an association of nations to deter aggression and keep the peace.

coloni free tenant farmers who worked as sharecroppers on the large estates of the Roman Empire (singular: *colonus*).

common law law common to the entire kingdom of England; imposed by the king's courts beginning in the twelfth century to replace the customary law used in county and feudal courts that varied from place to place.

commune in medieval Europe, an association of townspeople bound together by a sworn oath for the purpose of obtaining basic liberties from the lord of the territory in which the town was located; also, the self-governing town after receiving its liberties.

conciliarism a movement in fourteenth- and fifteenth-century Europe that held that final authority in spiritual matters resided with a general church council, not the pope; emerged in response to the Avignon papacy and the Great Schism and used to justify the summoning of the Council of Constance (1414–1418).

condottieri leaders of bands of mercenary soldiers in Renaissance Italy who sold their services to the highest bidder.

conquistadors "conquerors." Leaders in the Spanish conquests in the Americas, especially Mexico and Peru, in the sixteenth century.

conscription a military draft.

conservatism an ideology based on tradition and social stability that favored the maintenance of established institutions, organized religion, and obedience to authority and resisted change, especially abrupt change.

consuls the chief executive officers of the Roman Republic. Two were chosen annually to administer the government and lead the army in battle.

consumer society a term applied to Western society after World War II as the working classes adopted the consumption patterns of the middle class and installment plans, credit cards, and easy credit made consumer goods such as appliances and automobiles widely available.

Continental System Napoleon's effort to bar British goods from the Continent in the hope of weakening Britain's economy and destroying its capacity to wage war.

cosmopolitanism the quality of being sophisticated and having wide international experience.

cottage industry a system of textile manufacturing in which spinners and weavers worked at home in their cottages using raw materials supplied to them by capitalist entrepreneurs.

cultural relativism the belief that no culture is superior to another because culture is a matter of custom, not reason, and derives its meaning from the group holding it.

cuneiform "wedge-shaped." A system of writing developed by the Sumerians that consisted of wedge-shaped impressions made by a reed stylus on clay tablets.

daimyo prominent Japanese families who provided allegiance to the local shogun in exchange for protection; similar to vassals in Europe.

decolonization the process of becoming free of colonial status and achieving statehood; occurred in most of the world's colonies between 1947 and 1962.

deism belief in God as the creator of the universe who, after setting it in motion, ceased to have any direct involvement in it and allowed it to run according to its own natural laws.

demesne the part of a manor retained under the direct control of the lord and worked by the serfs as part of their labor services.

depression a very severe, protracted economic downturn with high levels of unemployment.

destalinization the policy of denouncing and undoing the most repressive aspects of Stalin's regime; begun by Nikita Khrushchev in 1956.

détente the relaxation of tension between the Soviet Union and the United States that occurred in the 1970s.

dialectic logic, one of the seven liberal arts that made up the medieval curriculum. In Marxist thought, the process by which all change occurs through the clash of antagonistic elements.

Diaspora the scattering of Jews throughout the ancient world after the Babylonian captivity in the sixth century B.C.

dictator in the Roman Republic, an official granted unlimited power to run the state for a short period of time, usually six months, during an emergency.

diocese the area under the jurisdiction of a Christian bishop; based originally on Roman administrative districts.

direct representation a system of choosing delegates to a representative assembly in which citizens vote directly for the delegates who will represent them.

divination the practice of seeking to foretell future events by interpreting divine signs, which could appear in various forms, such as in entrails of animals, in patterns in smoke, or in dreams.

divine-right monarchy   a monarchy based on the belief that monarchs receive their power directly from God and are responsible to no one except God.

domino theory   the belief that if the Communists succeeded in Vietnam, other countries in Southeast and East Asia would also fall (like dominoes) to communism; a justification for the U.S. intervention in Vietnam.

dualism   the belief that the universe is dominated by two opposing forces, one good and the other evil.

dynastic state   a state where the maintenance and expansion of the interests of the ruling family is the primary consideration.

economic imperialism   the process in which banks and corporations from developed nations invest in underdeveloped regions and establish a major presence there in the hope of making high profits; not necessarily the same as colonial expansion in that businesses invest where they can make a profit, which may not be in their own nation's colonies.

empiricism   the practice of relying on observation and experiment.

enclosure movement   in the eighteenth century, the fencing in of the old open fields, combining many small holdings into larger units that could be farmed more efficiently.

encyclical   a letter from the pope to all the bishops of the Roman Catholic church.

enlightened absolutism   an absolute monarchy where the ruler follows the principles of the Enlightenment by introducing reforms for the improvement of society, allowing freedom of speech and the press, permitting religious toleration, expanding education, and ruling in accordance with the laws.

Enlightenment   an eighteenth-century intellectual movement, led by the philosophes, that stressed the application of reason and the scientific method to all aspects of life.

entrepreneur   one who organizes, operates, and assumes the risk in a business venture in the expectation of making a profit.

Epicureanism   a philosophy founded by Epicurus in the fourth century B.C. that taught that happiness (freedom from emotional turmoil) could be achieved through the pursuit of pleasure (intellectual rather than sensual pleasure).

equestrians   a group of extremely wealthy men in the late Roman Republic who were effectively barred from high office, but sought political power commensurate with their wealth; called equestrians because many had gotten their start as cavalry officers (*equites*).

ethnic cleansing   the policy of killing or forcibly removing people of another ethnic group; used by the Serbs against Bosnian Muslims in the 1990s.

eucharist   a Christian sacrament in which consecrated bread and wine are consumed in celebration of Jesus' Last Supper; also called the Lord's Supper or communion.

evolutionary socialism   a socialist doctrine espoused by Eduard Bernstein who argued that socialists should stress cooperation and evolution to attain power by democratic means rather than by conflict and revolution.

fascism   an ideology or movement that exalts the nation above the individual and calls for a centralized government with a dictatorial leader, economic and social regimentation, and forcible suppression of opposition; in particular, the ideology of Mussolini's Fascist regime in Italy.

feminism   the belief in the social, political, and economic equality of the sexes; also, organized activity to advance women's rights.

fief   a landed estate granted to a vassal in exchange for military services.

Final Solution   the physical extermination of the Jewish people by the Nazis during World War II.

folk culture   the traditional arts and crafts, literature, music, and other customs of the people; something that people make, as opposed to modern popular culture, which is something people buy.

free trade   the unrestricted international exchange of goods with low or no tariffs.

general strike   a strike by all or most workers in an economy; espoused by Georges Sorel as the heroic action that could be used to inspire the workers to destroy capitalist society.

gentry   well-to-do English landowners below the level of the nobility; played an important role in the English Civil War of the seventeenth century.

geocentric theory   the idea that the earth is at the center of the universe and that the sun and other celestial objects revolve around the earth.

glasnost   "openness." Mikhail Gorbachev's policy of encouraging Soviet citizens to openly discuss the strengths and weaknesses of the Soviet Union.

good emperors   the five emperors who ruled from 96 to 180 (Nerva, Trajan, Hadrian, Antoninus Pius, and Marcus Aurelius), a period of peace and prosperity for the Roman Empire.

Great Schism   the crisis in the late medieval church when there were first two and then three popes; ended by the Council of Constance (1414–1418).

guest workers   foreign workers working temporarily in European countries.

guild   an association of people with common interests and concerns, especially people working in the same craft. In medieval Europe, guilds came to control much of the production process and to restrict entry into various trades.

gymnasium   in classical Greece, a place for athletics; in the Hellenistic Age, a secondary school with a curriculum centered on music, physical exercise, and literature.

heliocentric theory   the idea that the sun (not the earth) is at the center of the universe.

Hellenistic   literally, "to imitate the Greeks"; the era after the death of Alexander the Great when Greek culture spread into the Near East and blended with the culture of that region.

helots   serfs in ancient Sparta, who were permanently bound to the land that they worked for their Spartan masters.

heresy   the holding of religious doctrines different from the official teachings of the church.

Hermeticism   an intellectual movement beginning in the fifteenth century that taught that divinity is embodied in all aspects of nature; included works on alchemy and magic as well as theology and philosophy. The tradition continued into the seventeenth century and influenced many of the leading figures of the Scientific Revolution.

hetairai   highly sophisticated courtesans in ancient Athens who offered intellectual and musical entertainment as well as sex.

hieroglyphics   a highly pictorial system of writing most often associated with ancient Egypt. Also used (with different "pictographs") by other ancient peoples such as the Mayans.

high culture   the literary and artistic culture of the educated and wealthy ruling classes.

Holocaust   the mass slaughter of European Jews by the Nazis during World War II.

hoplites   heavily armed infantry soldiers used in ancient Greece in a phalanx formation.

Huguenots   French Calvinists.

humanism   an intellectual movement in Renaissance Italy based upon the study of the Greek and Roman classics.

iconoclasm   an eighth-century Byzantine movement against the use of icons (pictures of sacred figures), which was condemned as idolatry.

ideology   a political philosophy such as conservatism or liberalism.

imperium   "the right to command." In the Roman Republic, the chief executive officers (consuls and praetors) possessed the *imperium*; a military commander was an *imperator*. In the Roman Empire, the title *imperator*, or emperor, came to be used for the ruler.

indirect representation   a system of choosing delegates to a representative assembly in which citizens do not choose the delegates directly but instead vote for electors who choose the delegates.

individualism   emphasis on and interest in the unique traits of each person.

indulgence   the remission of part or all of the temporal punishment in purgatory due to sin; granted for charitable contributions and other good deeds. Indulgences became a regular practice of the Christian church in the High Middle Ages, and their abuse was instrumental in sparking Luther's reform movement in the sixteenth century.

infanticide   the practice of killing infants.

inflation   a sustained rise in the price level.

intendants   royal officials in seventeenth-century France who were sent into the provinces to execute the orders of the central government.

intervention, principle of   the idea, after the Congress of Vienna, that the great powers of Europe had the right to send armies into countries experiencing revolution to restore legitimate monarchs to their thrones.

isolationism   a foreign policy in which a nation refrains from making alliances or engaging actively in international affairs.

jihad   "striving in the way of the Lord." In Islam, the practice of conducting raids against neighboring peoples, which was an expansion of the Arab tradition of tribal raids against their persecutors.

joint-stock company   a company or association that raises capital by selling shares to individuals who receive dividends on their investment while a board of directors runs the company.

joint-stock investment bank   a bank created by selling shares of stock to investors. Such banks potentially have access to much more capital than do private banks owned by one or a few individuals.

justification of faith   the primary doctrine of the Protestant Reformation; taught that humans are saved not through good works, but by the grace of God, bestowed freely through the sacrifice of Jesus.

keiretsu   a type of powerful industrial or financial conglomerate that emerged in post-World War II Japan following the abolition of zaibatsu.

laissez-faire   "to let alone." An economic doctrine that holds that an economy is best served when the government does not interfere but allows the economy to self-regulate according to the forces of supply and demand.

latifundia   large landed estates in the Roman Empire (singular: *latifundium*).

lay investiture   the practice in which a layperson chose a bishop and invested him with the symbols of both his temporal office and his spiritual office; led to the Investiture Controversy, which was ended by compromise in the Concordat of Worms in 1122.

Lebensraum   "living space." The doctrine, adopted by Hitler, that a nation's power depends on the amount of land it occupies; thus, a nation must expand to be strong.

legitimacy, principle of   the idea that after the Napoleonic wars peace could best be reestablished in Europe by restoring legitimate monarchs who would preserve traditional institutions; guided Metternich at the Congress of Vienna.

Leninism   Lenin's revision of Marxism that held that Russia need not experience a bourgeois revolution before it could move toward socialism.

liberal arts   the seven areas of study that formed the basis of education in medieval and early modern Europe. Following Boethius and other late Roman authors, they consisted of grammar, rhetoric, and dialectic or logic (the *trivium*) and arithmetic, geometry, astronomy, and music (the *quadrivium*).

liberalism   an ideology based on the belief that people should be as free from restraint as possible. Economic liberalism is the idea that the government should not interfere in the workings of the economy. Political liberalism is the idea that there should be restraints on the exercise of power so that people can enjoy basic civil rights in a constitutional state with a representative assembly.

limited liability   the principle that shareholders in a joint-stock corporation can be held responsible for the corporation's debts only up to the amount they have invested.

limited (constitutional) monarchy   a system of government in which the monarch is limited by a representative assembly and by the duty to rule in accordance with the laws of the land.

mandates   a system established after World War I whereby a nation officially administered a territory (mandate) on behalf of the League of Nations. Thus, France administered Lebanon and Syria as mandates, and Britain administered Iraq and Palestine.

manor   an agricultural estate operated by a lord and worked by peasants who performed labor services and paid various rents and fees to the lord in exchange for protection and sustenance.

Marshall Plan   the European Recovery Program, under which the United States provided financial aid to European countries to help them rebuild after World War II.

Marxism   the political, economic, and social theories of Karl Marx, which included the idea that history is the story of class struggle and that ultimately the proletariat will overthrow the bourgeoisie and establish a dictatorship en route to a classless society.

mass education   a state-run educational system, usually free and compulsory, that aims to ensure that all children in society have at least a basic education.

mass leisure   forms of leisure that appeal to large numbers of people in a society including the working classes; emerged at the end of the nineteenth century to provide workers with amusements after work and on weekends; used during the twentieth century by totalitarian states to control their populations.

mass politics   a political order characterized by mass political parties and universal male and (eventually) female suffrage.

mass society   a society in which the concerns of the majority—the lower classes—play a prominent role; characterized by extension of voting rights, an improved standard of living for the lower classes, and mass education.

materialism   the belief that everything mental, spiritual, or ideal is an outgrowth of physical forces and that truth is found in concrete material existence, not through feeling or intuition.

Meiji Restoration   the period during the late 19th and early 20th century in which fundamental economic and cultural changes occured in Japan, tranforming it from a fuedal and agrarian society to an industrial and technological society.

mercantilism   an economic theory that held that a nation's prosperity depended on its supply of gold and silver and that the total volume of trade is unchangeable; therefore, advocated that the government play an active role in the economy by encouraging exports and discouraging imports, especially through the use of tariffs.

Mesolithic Age   the period from 10,000 to 7000 B.C., characterized by a gradual transition from a food-gathering/hunting economy to a food-producing economy.

metics   resident foreigners in ancient Athens; not permitted full rights of citizenship but did receive the protection of the laws.

militarism   a policy of aggressive military preparedness; in particular, the large armies based on mass conscription and complex, inflexible plans for mobilization that most European nations had before World War I.

ministerial responsibility   a tenet of nineteenth-century liberalism that held that ministers of the monarch should be responsible to the legislative assembly rather than to the monarch.

Modernism   the new artistic and literary styles that emerged in the decades before 1914 as artists rebelled against traditional efforts to portray reality as accurately as possible (leading to Impressionism and Cubism) and writers explored new forms.

monotheistic/monotheism   having only one god; the doctrine or belief that there is only one god.

mutual deterrence   the belief that nuclear war could best be prevented if both the United States and the Soviet Union had sufficient nuclear weapons so that even if one nation launched a preemptive first strike, the other could respond and devastate the attacker.

mystery religions   religions that involve initiation into secret rites that promise intense emotional involvement with spiritual forces and a greater chance of individual immortality.

nationalism   a sense of national consciousness based on awareness of being part of a community—a "nation"—that has common institutions, traditions, language, and customs and that becomes the focus of the individual's primary political loyalty.

nationalities problem   the dilemma faced by the Austro-Hungarian Empire in trying to unite a wide variety of ethnic groups including, among others, Austrians, Hungarians, Poles, Croats, Czechs, Serbs, Slovaks, and Slovenes in an era when nationalism and calls for self-determination were coming to the fore.

nationalization   the process of converting a business or industry from private ownership to government control and ownership.

nation in arms   the people's army raised by universal mobilization to repel the foreign enemies of the French Revolution.

nation-state   a form of political organization in which a relatively homogeneous people inhabits a sovereign state, as opposed to a state containing people of several nationalities.

NATO   the North Atlantic Treaty Organization; a military alliance formed in 1949 in which the signatories (Belgium, Canada, Denmark, France, Great Britain, Iceland, Italy, Luxembourg, the Netherlands, Norway, Portugal, and the United States) agreed to provide mutual assistance if any one of them was attacked; later expanded to include other nations, including former members of the Warsaw Pact—Poland, the Czech Republic and Hungary.

natural laws   a body of laws or specific principles held to be derived from nature and binding upon all human society even in the absence of positive laws.

natural rights   certain inalienable rights to which all people are entitled; include the right to life, liberty, and property, freedom of speech and religion, and equality before the law.

natural selection   Darwin's idea that organisms that are most adaptable to their environment survive and pass on the variations that enabled them to survive, while other, less adaptable organisms become extinct; "survival of the fittest."

Nazi New Order   the Nazis' plan for their conquered territories; included the extermination of Jews and others considered inferior, ruthless exploitation of resources, German colonization in the east, and the use of Poles, Russians, and Ukrainians as slave labor.

negritude   a philosophy shared among African blacks that there exists a distinctive "African personality" that owes nothing to Western values and provides a common sense of purpose and destiny for black Africans.

Neoplatonism   a revival of Platonic philosophy. In the third century A.D., a revival associated with Plotinus; in the Italian Renaissance, a revival associated with Marsilio Ficino who attempted to synthesize Christianity and Platonism.

New Economic Policy   a modified version of the old capitalist system introduced in the Soviet Union by Lenin in 1921 to revive the economy after the ravages of the civil war and war communism.

new imperialism   the revival of imperialism after 1880 in which European nations established colonies throughout much of Asia and Africa.

new monarchies   the governments of France, England, and Spain at the end of the fifteenth century, where the rulers were successful in reestablishing or extending centralized royal authority, suppressing the nobility, controlling the church, and insisting upon the loyalty of all peoples living in their territories.

nobiles   "nobles." The small group of families from both patrician and plebeian origins who produced most of the men who were elected to office in the late Roman Republic.

nominalism   a school of thought in medieval Europe that, following Aristotle, held that only individual objects are real and that universals are only names created by humans.

nuclear family   a family group consisting only of father, mother, and children.

old regime/old order   the political and social system of France in the eighteenth century before the Revolution.

oligarchy   rule by a few.

optimates   "best men." Aristocratic leaders in the late Roman Republic who generally came from senatorial families and wished to retain their oligarchical privileges.

orders/estates   the traditional tripartite division of European society based on heredity and quality rather than wealth or economic standing, first established in the Middle Ages and continuing into the eighteenth century; traditionally consisted of those who pray (the clergy), those who fight (the nobility), and those who work (all the rest).

organic evolution   Darwin's principle that all plants and animals have evolved over a long period of time from earlier and simpler forms of life.

Paleolithic Age   the period of human history when humans used simple stone tools (c. 2,500,000–10,000 B.C.).

pan-Africanism   the concept of African continental unity and solidarity in which the common interests of African countries transcend regional boundries.

pantheism   a doctrine that equates God with the universe and all that is in it.

paterfamilias   the dominant male in a Roman family whose powers over his wife and children were theoretically unlimited, though they were sometimes circumvented in practice.

patriarchal/patriarchy   a society in which the father is supreme in the clan or family; more generally, a society dominated by men.

patriarchal family   a family in which the husband/father dominates his wife and children.

patricians   great landowners who became the ruling class in the Roman Republic.

patronage   the practice of awarding titles and making appointments to government and other positions to gain political support.

Pax Romana   "Roman peace." A term used to refer to the stability and prosperity that Roman rule brought to the Mediterranean world and much of western Europe during the first and second centuries A.D.

Pentateuch   the first five books of the Hebrew Bible (Genesis, Exodus, Leviticus, Numbers, and Deuteronomy).

perestroika   "restructuring." A term applied to Mikhail Gorbachev's economic, political, and social reforms in the Soviet Union.

permissive society   a term applied to Western society after World War II to reflect the new sexual freedom and the emergence of a drug culture.

Petrine supremacy   the doctrine that the bishop of Rome—the pope—as the successor of Saint Peter (traditionally considered the first bishop of Rome) should hold a preeminent position in the church.

phalanx   a rectangular formation of tightly massed infantry soldiers.

philosophes   intellectuals of the eighteenth-century Enlightenment who believed in applying a spirit of rational criticism to all things, including religion and politics, and who focused on improving and enjoying this world, rather than on the afterlife.

plebeians   the class of Roman citizens who included nonpatrician landowners, craftspeople, merchants, and small farmers in the Roman Republic. Their struggle for equal rights with the patricians dominated much of the Republic's history.

pluralism   the practice in which one person holds several church offices simultaneously; a problem of the late medieval church.

pogroms   organized massacres of Jews.

polis   an ancient Greek city-state encompassing both an urban area and its surrounding countryside; a small but autonomous political unit where all major political and social activities were carried out in a central location.

political democracy   a form of government characterized by universal suffrage and mass political parties.

politiques   a group who emerged during the French Wars of Religion in the sixteenth century; placed politics above religion and believed that no religious truth was worth the ravages of civil war.

polytheistic/polytheism   having many gods; belief in or the worship of more than one god.

popular culture   as opposed to high culture, the unofficial, written and unwritten culture of the masses, much of which was passed down orally; centers on public and group activities such as festivals. In the twentieth century, refers to the entertainment, recreation, and pleasures that people purchase as part of mass consumer society.

populares   "favoring the people." Aristocratic leaders in the late Roman Republic who tended to use the people's assemblies in an effort to break the stranglehold of the *nobiles* on political offices.

popular sovereignty   the doctrine that government is created by and subject to the will of the people, who are the source of all political power.

praetorian guard   the military unit that served as the personal bodyguard of the Roman emperors.

predestination   the belief, associated with Calvinism, that God, as a consequence of his foreknowledge of all events, has predetermined those who will be saved (the elect) and those who will be damned.

price revolution   the dramatic rise in prices (inflation) that occurred throughout Europe in the sixteenth and early seventeenth centuries.

primogeniture   an inheritance practice in which the eldest son receives all or the largest share of the parents' estate.

principate   the form of government established by Augustus for the Roman Empire; continued the constitutional forms of the Republic and consisted of the *princeps* ("first citizen") and the senate, although the *princeps* was clearly the dominant partner.

proletariat   the industrial working class. In Marxism, the class who will ultimately overthrow the bourgeoisie.

Puritans   English Protestants inspired by Calvinist theology who wished to remove all traces of Catholicism from the Church of England.

querelles des femmes   "arguments about women." A centuries-old debate about the nature of women that continued during the Scientific Revolution as those who argued for the inferiority of women found additional support in the new anatomy and medicine.

rationalism   a system of thought based on the belief that human reason and experience are the chief sources of knowledge.

realism   in medieval Europe, the school of thought that, following Plato, held that the individual objects we perceive are not real but merely manifestations of universal ideas existing in the mind of God. In the nineteenth century, a school of painting that emphasized the everyday life of ordinary people, depicted with photographic realism.

Realpolitik   "politics of reality." Politics based on practical concerns rather than theory or ethics.

real wages/income/prices   wages/income/prices that have been adjusted for inflation.

reason of state   the principle that a nation should act on the basis of its long-term interests and not merely to further the dynastic interests of its ruling family.

relativity theory   Einstein's theory that holds, among other things, that (1) space and time are not absolute but are relative to the observer and interwoven into a four-dimensional space-time continuum and (2) matter is a form of energy ($E = mc^2$).

relics   the bones of Christian saints or objects intimately associated with saints that were considered worthy of veneration.

Renaissance   the "rebirth" of classical culture that occurred in Italy between c. 1350 and c. 1550; also, the earlier revivals of classical culture that occurred under Charlemagne and in the twelfth century.

rentier   a person who lives on income from property and is not personally involved in its operation.

reparations   payments made by a defeated nation after a war to compensate another nation for damage sustained as a result of the war; required from Germany after World War I.

revisionism   a socialist doctrine that rejected Marx's emphasis on class struggle and revolution and argued instead that workers should work through political parties to bring about gradual change.

revolution   a fundamental change in the political and social organization of a state.

revolutionary socialism   the socialist doctrine espoused by Georges Sorel who held that violent action was the only way to achieve the goals of socialism.

rhetoric   the art of persuasive speaking; in the Middle Ages, one of the seven liberal arts.

sacraments   rites considered imperative for a Christian's salvation. By the thirteenth century consisted of the eucharist or Lord's Supper, baptism, marriage, penance, extreme unction, holy orders, and confirmation of children; Protestant reformers of the sixteenth century generally recognized only two—baptism and communion (the Lord's Supper).

salons   gatherings of philosophes and other notables to discuss the ideas of the Enlightenment; so-called from the elegant drawing rooms (salons) where they met.

samurai   literally "retainer"; similar to European knights. Usually in service to a particular shogun, these warriors lived by a strict code of ethics and duty.

sans-culottes   the common people who did not wear the fine clothes of the upper classes (sans-culottes means "without breeches") and played an important role in the radical phase of the French Revolution.

sati   the Hindu ritual requiring a wife to throw herself upon her deceased husband's funeral pyre.

satrap/satrapy   a governor with both civil and military duties in the ancient Persian Empire, which was divided into satrapies, or provinces, each administered by a satrap.

scholasticism the philosophical and theological system of the medieval schools, which emphasized rigorous analysis of contradictory authorities; often used to try to reconcile faith and reason.

scientific method a method of seeking knowledge through inductive principles; uses experiments and observations to develop generalizations.

Scientific Revolution the transition from the medieval worldview to a largely secular, rational, and materialistic perspective; began in the seventeenth century and was popularized in the eighteenth.

secularization the process of becoming more concerned with material, worldly, temporal things and less with spiritual and religious things.

self-determination the doctrine that the people of a given territory or a particular nationality should have the right to determine their own government and political future.

senate/senators the leading council of the Roman Republic; composed of about 300 men (senators) who served for life and dominated much of the political life of the Republic.

serf a peasant who is bound to the land and obliged to provide labor services and pay various rents and fees to the lord; considered unfree but not a slave because serfs could not be bought and sold.

shogunate system the system of government in Japan in which the emporor exercised only titular authority while the shogun (regional military dictators) exercised actual political power.

skepticism a doubtful or questioning attitude, especially about religion.

Social Darwinism the application of Darwin's principle of organic evolution to the social order; led to the belief that progress comes from the struggle for survival as the fittest advance and the weak decline.

socialism an ideology that calls for collective or government ownership of the means of production and the distribution of goods.

social security/social insurance government programs that provide social welfare measures such as old age pensions and sickness, accident, and disability insurance.

Socratic method a form of teaching that uses a question-and-answer format to enable students to reach conclusions by using their own reasoning.

Sophists wandering scholars and professional teachers in ancient Greece who stressed the importance of rhetoric and tended toward skepticism and relativism.

soviets councils of workers' and soldiers' deputies formed throughout Russia in 1917; played an important role in the Bolshevik Revolution.

sphere of influence a territory or region over which an outside nation exercises political or economic influence.

Stoicism a philosophy founded by Zeno in the fourth century B.C. that taught that happiness could be obtained by accepting one's lot and living in harmony with the will of God, thereby achieving inner peace.

subinfeudation the practice in which a lord's greatest vassals subdivided their fiefs and had vassals of their own, and those vassals, in turn, subdivided their fiefs and so on down to simple knights whose fiefs were too small to subdivide.

suffrage the right to vote.

suffragists those who advocate the extension of the right to vote (suffrage), especially to women.

surplus value in Marxism, the difference between a product's real value and the wages of the worker who produced the product.

syncretism the combining of different forms of belief or practice, as, for example, when two gods are regarded as different forms of the same underlying divine force and are fused together.

tariffs duties (taxes) imposed on imported goods; usually imposed both to raise revenue and to discourage imports and protect domestic industries.

tetrarchy rule by four; the system of government established by Diocletian (284–305) in which the Roman Empire was divided into two parts, each ruled by an "Augustus" assisted by a "Caesar."

theocracy a government ruled by a divine authority.

three-field system in medieval agriculture, the practice of dividing the arable land into three fields so that one could lie fallow while the others were planted in winter grains and spring crops.

tithe a tenth of one's harvest or income; paid by medieval peasants to the village church.

Tongmenghui the political organization—"Revolutionary Alliance"—formed by Sun Yat-sen in 1905 which united various revolutionary factions and ultimately toppled the Manchu dynasty.

Torah the body of law in Hebrew Scripture, contained in the Pentateuch (the first five books of the Hebrew Bible).

totalitarian state a state characterized by government control over all aspects of economic, social, political, cultural, and intellectual life, the subordination of the individual to the state, and insistence that the masses be actively involved in the regime's goals.

total war warfare in which all of a nation's resources, including civilians at home as well as soldiers in the field, are mobilized for the war effort.

trade union an association of workers in the same trade, formed to help members secure better wages, benefits, and working conditions.

transubstantiation a doctrine of the Roman Catholic church that teaches that during the eucharist the substance of the bread and wine is miraculously transformed into the body and blood of Jesus.

trench warfare warfare in which the opposing forces attack and counterattack from a relatively permanent system of trenches protected by barbed wire; characteristic of World War I.

trivium and *quadrivium*   together formed the seven liberal arts that were the basis of medieval and early modern education. Grammar, rhetoric, and dialectic or logic made up the *trivium*; arithmetic, geometry, astronomy, and music made up the *quadrivium*.

Truman Doctrine   the doctrine, enunciated by Harry Truman in 1947, that the United States would provide economic aid to countries that said they were threatened by Communist expansion.

tyrant/tyranny   in an ancient Greek *polis* (or an Italian city-state during the Renaissance), a ruler who came to power in an unconstitutional way and ruled without being subject to the law.

uncertainty principle   a principle in quantum mechanics, posited by Heisenberg, that holds that one cannot determine the path of an electron because the very act of observing the electron would affect its location.

unconditional surrender   complete, unqualified surrender of a belligerent nation.

utopian socialists   intellectuals and theorists in the early nineteenth century who favored equality in social and economic conditions and wished to replace private property and competition with collective ownership and cooperation; deemed impractical and "utopian" by later socialists.

vassal   a person granted a fief, or landed estate, in exchange for providing military services to the lord and fulfilling certain other obligations such as appearing at the lord's court when summoned and making a payment on the knighting of the lord's eldest son.

vernacular   the everyday language of a region, as distinguished from a language used for special purposes. For example, in medieval Paris, French was the vernacular, but Latin was used for academic writing and for classes at the University of Paris.

volkish thought   the belief that German culture is superior and that the German people have a universal mission to save Western civilization from inferior races.

war communism   Lenin's policy of nationalizing industrial and other facilities and requisitioning the peasants' produce during the civil war in Russia.

War Guilt Clause   the clause in the Treaty of Versailles that declared that Germany (and Austria) were responsible for starting World War I and ordered Germany to pay reparations for the damage the Allies had suffered as a result of the war.

Warsaw Pact   a military alliance, formed in 1955, in which Albania, Bulgaria, Czechoslovakia, East Germany, Hungary, Poland, Romania, and the Soviet Union agreed to provide mutual assistance. Dissolved in 1991, some former members joined NATO.

welfare state   a social/political system in which the government assumes the primary responsibility for the social welfare of its citizens by providing such things as social security, unemployment benefits, and health care.

wergeld   "money for a man." In early Germanic law, a person's value in monetary terms, which was paid by a wrongdoer to the family of the person who had been injured or killed.

world-machine   Newton's conception of the universe as one huge, regulated, and uniform machine that operated according to natural laws in absolute time, space, and motion.

zaibatsu   powerful business cartels formed in Japan during the Meiji era and outlawed following World War II.

ziggurat   a massive stepped tower upon which a temple dedicated to the chief god or goddess of a Sumerian city was built.

Zionism   an international movement that called for the establishment of a Jewish state or a refuge for Jews in Palestine.

Zoroastrianism   a religion founded by the Persian Zoroaster in the seventh century B.C.; characterized by worship of a supreme god Ahuramazda who represents the good against the evil spirit, identified as Ahriman.

PRONUNCIATION GUIDE

Abbasid AB-uh-sid *or* a-BA-sid
Adenauer, Konrad AD-n'our-er
Aeschylus ESS-kuh-lus
Afrikaners a-fri-KAH-ners
Agincourt AJ-in-kor
Ahuramazda ah-HOOR-ah-MAHZ-duh
Akhenaton ah-kuh-NAH-tun
Akkadian a-KAY-dee-un
Albigensian al-bi-GEN-see-un
Albuquerque, Afonso de AL-buh-kur-kee, ah-FON-soh d'
Allah AH-luh *or* AL-uh
al-Ma'mun al-MAH-moon
al-Rahman, Abd al-RAH-mun, abd
Amenhotep ah-mun-HOE-tep
Andropov, Yuri an-DROP-ov, YOOR-ee
Antigonid an-TIG-oh-nid
apella a-PELL-uh
Aquinas, Thomas uh-KWIGH-nus
aratrum a-RA-trum
Archimedes are-kuh-MEE-deez
Argonautica ARE-guh-NOT-i-kuh
Aristotle ar-i-STAH-tul
Arsinoë ar-SIN-oh-ee
Arthasastra ar-tuh-SAHS-tra
Ashkenazic ash-kuh-NAH-zic
Ashurnasirpal ah-shoor-NAH-suh-pul
asiento a-SEE-en-toh
assignat as-seen-YAH *or* AS-sig-nat
Assyrians uh-SEER-ee-uns
Attalid AT-a-lid
audiencias ah-DEE-en-CEE-ahs
Augustine AW-gus-STEEN
Auschwitz-Birkenau OUSH-vitz-BUR-kuh-now
Ausgleich OUS-glike
Avicenna av-i-SEN-uh
Avignon ah-veen-YONE
Axum OX-oom
Bach, Johann Sebastian BAHK, yoh-HAHN
  suh-BASS-chen
Barbarossa bar-buh-ROH-suh
Bastille ba-STEEL
Beauvoir, Simone de boh-VWAH, see-MOAN duh
Bebel, August BAY-bul
Beguines bi-GEENS
Belisarius bell-i-SAR-ee-us
benefice BEN-uh-fiss
Bernini, Gian Lorenzo bur-NEE-nee, JAHN
  loh-RENT-soh

Bhagavadgita bog-ah-vahd-GEE-ta
Blitzkrieg BLITZ-kreeg
Boccaccio, Giovanni boh-KAH-chee-oh, joe-VAHN-nee
Boer BOHR
Boleyn, Anne BUH-lin
Bólívar, Simón BOH-luh-VAR, see-MOAN
Bologna buh-LOHN-yuh
Boticelli, Sandro BOT-i-CHELL-ee, SAHN-droh
Boulanger, Georges boo-lahn-ZHAY, ZHORZH
Bracciolini, Poggio braht-choh-LEE-nee, POD-joh
Brahe, Tycho BRAH, TIE-koh
Bramante, Donato brah-MAHN-tee, doe-NAY-toe
Brandt, Willy BRAHNT, VIL-ee
Brétigny bray-tee-NYEE
Brezhnev, Leonid BREZH-nef, lyi-on-YEET
Briand, Aristide bree-AHN, a-ree-STEED
Brunelleschi, Filippo BROO-nuh-LES-kee, fee-LEEP-poe
Brüning, Heinrich BROO-ning, HINE-rik
Bulganin, Nilolai bul-GAN-in, nyik-uh-LYE
Bund deutscher Mädel BUNT DOICHer MAIR-del
Burschenschaften BOOR-shen-shaft-un
Buthelezi, Mangosuthu boo-teh-LAY-zee, man-go-SOO-tu
Calais ka-LAY
caliph/caliphate KAY-lif/KAY-li-FATE
Cambyses kam-BY-seez
Camus, Albert kuh-MOO, al-BEAR
Canaanites KAY-nuh-nites
Cao Cao tsau tsau
Capet/Capetian ka-PAY *or* KAY-put/kuh-PEE-shun
Caraffa, Gian Pietro kah-RAH-fuh, JAHN PYEE-troh
carbonari kar-buh-NAH-ree
Carolingian kar-oh-LIN-jun
carruca ca-ruh-kuh
Carthage/Carthaginian KAR-thij/KAR-thuh-JIN-ee-un
Castlereagh, Viscount KAS-ul-RAY
Catharism KA-tha-ri-zem
Catullus ka-TULL-us
Cavendish, Margaret KAV-un-dish
Cavour, Camillo di ka-VOOR, kah-MIL-oh
Cèzanne, Paul say-ZAN
Chaeronea ker-oh-NEE-uh
Chaldean kal-DEE-un
chanson de geste shahn-SAWN duh ZHEST
Charlemagne SHAR-luh-mane
Chernenko, Konstantin cher-NYEN-koh, kon-stun-TEEN
Chiang Kai-Shek CHANG KIGH-shek
Chrétien de Troyes KRAY-tee-ahn duh TRWAH
Cicero SIS-uh-roh

ciompi   CHOM-pee

Cistercians   si-STIR-shuns

Cixi   TSE-she

Cleisthenes   KLISE-thuh-neez

Clemenceau, Georges   klem-un-SOH, ZHORZH

Clovis   KLOH-vis

colonus   kuh-LOH-nus

Columbanus   kol-um-BAHN-us

comitia centuriata   kuh-MISH-ee-uh sen-TYOO-ree-ah-tuh

concilium plebis   con-CIL-ee-um PLE-bis

Concordat of Worms   kon-KOR-dat of WURMZ *or* VAWRMZ

condottieri   kon-dah-TEE-AIR-ee

consul   KON-sul

conversos   kon-VAIR-sohs

Copernicus, Nicolaus   koh-PURR-nuh-kus, nee-koh-LAH-us

Corinth   KOR-inth

corregidores   kor-REG-uh-DOR-ays

Cortés, Hernán   kor-TEZ, er-NAHN

Courbet, Gustave   koor-BAY, guh-STAWV

Crassus   KRASS-us

Crécy   kray-SEE

Crédit Mobilier   kred-EE mohb-eel-YAY

d'Este, Isabella   ES-tay

d'Holbach, Paul   awl-BAHK

Daimyo   die-AIM-yo

Dao De Jing   dow duh JING

Darius   duh-RYE-us

dauphin   DAW-fin

de Gaulle, Charles   duh GOLL, SHARL

Debussy, Claude   de-BYOO-see, KLODE

Decameron   di-KAM-uh-run

Delacroix, Eugène   del-uh-KWAW, yoo-ZHAHN

Deng Xiaoping   DUNG shee-ow-ping

Descartes, René   day-KART, ruh-NAY

Dias, Bartholomeu   DEE-us, bar-too-loo-MAY

Diaspora   die-AS-pur-uh

Diderot, Denis   DEE-duh-roh, duh-NEE

Diem, Ngo Dinh   dzee-EM, NGOH Den

Diocletian   die-uh-KLEE-shun

Domitian   doh-MISH-un

Dorians   DOR-ee-uns

Douhet, Giulio   doo-EE, JOOL-yoh

Duma   DOO-muh

Dürer, Albrecht   DOO-er, AWL-brekt

ecclesia   eh-KLEE-zee-uh

encomienda   en-koh-mee-EN-dah

Engels, Friedrich   ENG-ulz, FREE-drik

Entente Cordiale   ahn-TAHNT kor-DYALL

Epaminondas   i-PAM-uh-NAHN-dus

ephor   EF-or

Epicurus/Epicureanism   EP-i-KYOOR-us/EP-i-kyoo-REE-uh-ni-zem

Erasmus, Desiderius   i-RAZZ-mus, des-i-DIR-ee-us

eremitical   air-uh-MITT-i-cul

Erhard, Ludwig   AIR-hart

Etruscan   i-TRUSS-kuhn

Euripides   yoo-RIP-i-deez

exchequer   EX-chek-ur

Fa Xian   fa SHIEN

fasces   FASS-eez

Fascio di Combattimento   FASH-ee-oh di com-BATT-ee-men-toh

Fatimid   FAT-i-mid

Ficino, Marsilio   fee-CHEE-noh, mar-SIL-ee-oh

Flaubert, Gustave   floh-BEAR, guh-STAWV

Fleury, Cardinal   floe-REE

Fontainebleau   FAWN-tin-BLOW

Fontenelle, Bernard de   fawnt-NELL, BER-nar duh

Frequens   FREE-kwens

Friedan, Betty   fri-DAN

Frimaire   free-MARE

Fronde   FROND

Führerprinzip   FYOOR-ur-PRIN-tseep

gabelle   gah-BELL

Garibaldi, Giuseppe   gar-uh-BAWL-dee, joo-ZEP-pay

Gaugamela   gaw-guh-MEE-luh

Gentileschi, Artemisia   jen-tul-ESS-kee, are-tee-MISS-ee-uh

gerousia   juh-ROO-see-uh

Gierek, Edward   GYER-ek

Gilgamesh   GILL-guh-mesh

glasnost   GLAZ-nohst

Gleichschaltung   GLIKE-shalt-ung

Gomulka, Wladyslaw   goh-MOOL-kuh, vla-DIS-lawf

gonfaloniere   gon-fa-loh-NEE-ree

Gorbachev, Mikhail   GOR-buh-chof, meek-HALE

grandi   GRAHN-dee

Gropius, Walter   GROH-pee-us, VAHL-ter

Grossdeutsch   gross-DOICH

Habsburg   HAPS-burg

Hadrian   HAY-dree-un

Hagia Sophia   HAG-ee-uh soh-FEE-uh

hajj   HAJ

Hammurabi   ham-uh-RAH-bee

Hannibal   HAN-uh-bul

Harappan   har-RAP-an

Hatshepsut   hat-SHEP-soot

Haussmann, Baron   HOUS-mun

Havel, Vaclav   HAH-vuhl, VAHT-slaf

Haydn, Franz Joseph   HIDE-n, FRAHNTS

hegemon   HEJ-uh-mon

Hellenistic   hell-uh-NIS-tik

helots   HELL-uts

hermandades   er-mahn-DAHDH-ays

Herodotus   hi-ROD-oh-tus

Herzen, Alexander   HER-tsun

Herzl, Theodor   HERT-sul, TAY-oh-dor
Heydrich, Reinhard   HIGH-drik, RINE-hart
hieroglyph   HIGH-ur-oh-glif
Hildegard of Bingen   HILL-duh-gard of BING-en
Hitler Jugend   JOO-gunt
Ho Chi Minh   HOE CHEE MIN
Höch, Hannah   HOKH
Hohenstaufen   HOE-un-SHTAU-fun
Hohenzollern   HOE-un-ZAHL-lurn
hoplites   HOP-lites
Horace   HOR-us
Huguenots   HYOO-guh-nots
Husak, Gustav   HOO-sahk, guh-STAHV
Ibn Sina   ib-en SEE-nuh
Ieyasu, Tokugawa   ee-eye-AY-soo, toe-koo-GAH-wah
Ignatius of Loyola   ig-NAY-shus of loi-OH-luh
Il Duce   eel DOO-chay
imperator   im-puh-RAH-tor
imperium   im-PIER-ee-um
intendant   in-TEN-duhnt
Isis   EYE-sis
Issus   ISS-us
ius gentium   YOOS GEN-tee-um
Jacobin   JAK-uh-bin
Jacquerie   zhah-KREE
Jagiello   yah-GYELL-oh
Jahn, Friedrich Ludwig   YAHN, FREE-drik
Jaruzelski, Wojciech   yahr-uh-ZEL-skee, VOI-chek
Jaurés, Jean   zhaw-RESS, ZHAHN
Jiang Qing   JIANG CHING
jihad   ji-HAHD
Jinnah, Mohammed Ali   JEE-nah, moe-HA-mud a-LEE
Judaea   joo-DEE-uh
Judas Maccabaeus   JOO-dus mak-uh-BEE-us
Junkers   YOONG-kers
Justinian   juh-STIN-ee-un
Juvenal   JOO-vuh-nul
Ka'aba stone   KAH-BAH
Kadar, Janos   KAY-dahr, YAHN-us
Kadinsky, Vasily   kan-DIN-skee, vus-YEEL-yee
Kangxi   KANG-she
Keiretsu business arrangement   kai-RET-su
Kerensky, Alexander   kuh-REN-skee
Keynes, John Maynard   KAYNZ
Khan, Khubilai   KHAN, KOO-bil-eye
Khmer Rouge   ka-MEHR roozh
Khoisan   KOY-SAN
Khrushchev, Nikita   KROOSH-chef, nuh-KEE-tuh
Kleindeutsch   kline-DOICH
Koguryo   ko-GOOR-yo
Kohl, Helmut   KOLE, HELL-mut
koiné   koi-NAY
Kollantai, Alexandra   kawl-un-TIE

kouros   KOO-raws
Kraft durch Freude   CRAFT durch FROI-duh
Kristallnacht   KRIS-tal-NAHCHT
Kshatriya   kuh-SHOT-ria
Kuchuk-Kainarji   koo-CHOOK-kigh-NAR-jee
kulaks   koo-LAKS
kulturkampf   kool-TOOR-kahmf
laissez-faire   les-ay-FAIR
Lamarck, Jean-Baptiste   luh-MAHRK, ZHAHN-buh-TEEST
Lao Tzu   LAUW DZU
latifundia   lat-uh-FUN-dee-uh
Latium   LAY-shee-um
Lebensraum   LAY-benz-roum
Lee Kuan-yew   LEE KWAN YEW
Lespinasse, Julie de   les-peen-AHS
Lévesque, René   luh-VEK, ruh-NAY
Leyster, Judith   LE-ster
Liebenfels, Lanz von   LEE-bun-felz, LAHNZ
Liebknecht   LEEP-knekt
Liszt, Franz   LIST, FRAHNZ
Livy   LIV-ee
Luddites   LUD-ites
Ludendorff, Erich   LOOD-un-dorf
Luftwaffe   LUFT-vaf-uh
Machiavelli, Niccolò   mak-ee-uh-VELL-ee, nee-koh-LOH
Magyars   MAG-yars
Mahabharata   MA-HA-bah-rah-tah
Maistre, Joseph de   MES-truh
Majapahit   mah-ja-PAH-heet
Malleus Maleficarum   mall-EE-us mal-uh-FIK-ar-um
Manetho   MAN-uh-THOH
Mao Zedong   mau zee-DONG
Marie Antoinette   muh-REE an-twuh-NET
Marius   MAR-ee-us
Mazarin   maz-uh-RAN
Mbecki, Thabo   mu-BEK-ee, TYE-bo
Meiji   MAY-jee
Mein Kampf   mine KAHMF
Menander   me-NAN-der
Mendeleyev, Dmitri   men-duh-LAY-ef, di-MEE-tri
Meroë   mer-OH-ee
Mesopotamia   mess-oh-poh-TAME-ee-uh
Metternich, Klemens von   MET-er-nik, KLAY-mens
Michelangelo   my-kell-AN-juh-loh
Mieszko   MYESH-koh
Millet, Jean-François   mi-LAY, ZHAHN-FRAN-swah
missi dominici   MISS-ee doe-MIN-ee-chee
Moche   MO-chay
Moctezuma   mahk-tuh-ZOO-muh
Moldavia   mahl-DAY-vee-uh
Molière, Jean-Baptiste   mole-YAIR, ZHAHN-buh-TEEST

Monet, Claude   moh-NAY, KLODE

Montefeltro, Federigo da   mahn-tuh-FELL-troh, fay-day-REE-goh dah

Montesquieu   MONT-ess-skyoo

Montessori, Maria   mon-ti-SOR-ee

Morisot, Berthe   mor-ee-ZOH, BERT

Muawiyah   moo-AH-wee-yah

Mughal   MOO-gahl

Muhammad   moe-HA-mud

Muslim   MUZ-lum

Mutsuhito   moo-tsoo-HEE-toe

Mycenaean   my-suh-NEE-un

Nagy, Imry   NAHJD, IM-re

Nebuchadnezzar   neb-uh-kad-NWZZ-ar

Nehru, Jawaharlal   NAY-roo, jah-WAH-har-lahl

Nero   NEE-roh

Neumann, Balthasar   NOI-mahn, BAHL-tah-zar

Nevsky, Alexander   NEW-skee

Ngo Dinh Diem   NGOH din dee-EM

Ngugi Wa Thiong'o   en-GU-ji WA THIE-ong-oh

Nietzsche, Friedrich   NEE-chuh, FREE-drik

Nimwegen   NIM-vay-gun

Ninhursaga   nin-HUR-sah-guh

Nkrumah, Kwame   en-KRU-may, KWA-may

Novotny, Antonin   noh-VOT-nee, AN-ton-yeen

Nyerere, Julius   nyay-RARE-ee

Nystadt   nee-STAHD

Octavian   ok-TAY-vee-un

optimates   opp-tuh-MAH-tays

Osiris   oh-SIGH-ris

Ovid   OV-id

Pahlavi dynasty   pah-LAH-vee

Palenque   pah-LENG-kay

Paleologus   pay-lee-OHL-uh-gus

papal curia   PAY-pul KOOR-ee-uh

Parlement   par-luh-MAHN

Pascal, Blaise   pass-KAL, BLEZ

paterfamilias   pay-ter-fuh-MILL-ee-us

Pentateuch   PEN-tuh-tuke

Pepin   PEP-in

perestroika   pair-ess-TROY-kuh

Pergamum   PURR-guh-mum

Pericles   PER-i-kleez

perioeci   per-ee-EE-sie

Pétain, Henri   pay-TAN, AHN-ree

Petrarch   PE-trark

philosophe   fee-luh-ZAWF

Phoenicians   fi-NISH-uns

Picasso, Pablo   pi-KAW-soh

Pisistratus   pi-SIS-truh-tus

Pissaro, Camille   pi-SARR-oh, kah-MEEYL

Pizarro, Francesco   pi-ZARR-oh, frahn-CHASE-koh

Planck, Max   PLAHNK

Plantagenet   plan-TA-juh-net

Plato   PLAY-toe

Poincaré, Raymond   pwan-kah-RAY, re-MOAN

polis   POE-lis

politiques   puh-lee-TEEKS

Polybius   poe-LIB-ee-us

Pompey   POM-pee

pontifex maximus   PON-ti-feks MAK-suh-mus

populares   POP-yoo-lar-ays

populo grasso   POP-uh-loh GRAH-soh

Poussin, Nicholas   poo-SAN, NEE-kaw-lah

Praecepter Germaniae   PREE-sep-ter ger-MAN-ee-eye

praetor   PREE-ter

princeps   PRIN-seps

procurator   PROK-yuh-ray-ter

Ptolemy/Ptolemaic   TOL-uh-mee/TOL-uh-MAY-ik

Punic   PYOO-nik

Pyrrhus/Pyrrhic   PIR-us/PIR-ik

Qin Shi Huangdi   chin SHE hwang-DEE

Qing dynasty   CHING

quaestors   KWES-ters

Quetzelcoatl   ket-SAHL-koh-AHT-ul

Quipu   KEE-poo

Quran   kuh-RAN

Racine, Jean-Baptiste   ra-SEEN, ZHAHN-buh-TEEST

Rameses   RAM-i-seez

Raphael   RAFF-ee-ul

Rasputin   rass-PYOO-tin

Realpolitik   ray-AHL-poe-li-teek

Reichsrat   RIKES-raht

Rembrandt van Rijn   REM-brant vahn RINE

Ricci, Matteo   REECH-ee, mah-TAY-oh

Richelieu   RISH-uh-loo

Rilke, Rainer Maria   RILL-kuh, RYE-ner

risorgimento   ree-SOR-jee-men-toe

Robespierre, Maximilien   ROHBZ-pee-air, mak-SEE-meel-yahn

Rococo   ro-KOH-koh

Rousseau, Jean-Jacques   roo-SOH ZHAHN-ZHAHK

Sacrosancta   sak-roh-SANK-tuh

Sakharov, Andrei   SAH-kuh-rof, ahn-DRAY

Saladin   SAL-uh-din

Sallust   SALL-ust

Samnites   SAM-nites

Sartre, Jean-Paul   SAR-truh, ZHAHN-PAUL

satrap/satrapy   SAY-trap/SAY-truh-pee

Satyricon   SAY-tir-ee-kon

Schleswig-Holstein   SCHLES-vig-HOLE-stine

Schmidt, Helmut   SHMIT, HELL-mut

Schönberg, Arnold   SHURN-burg, ARR-nawlt

Schutzmannschaft   SHOOTS-mun-shaft

Scipio Aemilianus   SI-pee-oh i-mill-ee-AY-nus

Scipio Africanus   SI-pee-oh af-ri-KAY-nus

scriptoria   skrip-TOR-ee-uh
Sejm   SAME
Seleucus/Seleucid   si-LOO-kus/si-LOO-sid
Seljuk Turks   SELL-juke
Seneca   SEN-i-kuh
Sephardic   suh-FAR-dik
Septimius Severus   sep-TIM-ee-us se-VIR-us
Sforza   SFORT-zuh
Shi'ite   SHE-ite
Shotoku Taishi   show-TOE-koo tie-ISH-ee
Siddhartha Gautama   sid-AR-tha guh-TAW-mah
Sieveking, Amalie   SEEVE-king
signoria   seen-YOOR-ee-uh
Socrates   SOK-ruh-teez
Solon   SOH-lun
Solzhenitsyn, Alexander   SOLE-zhuh-NEET-sin
Sophocles   SOF-uh-kleez
Spartacus   SPAR-tuh-kus
Speer, Albert   SHPIER
squadristi   sqah-DREES-tee
Srivijaya   sree-vee-JAH-ya
Stoicism   STOH-i-siz-um
Stravinsky, Igor   struh-VIN-skee, EE-gor
Stresemann, Gustav   SHTRAY-zuh-mahn, GUS-tahf
Suleyman I the Magnificent   soo-lee-MAHN
Sumerian   soo-MER-ee-un
Suttner, Bertha von   ZOOT-ner
Taafe, Edward von   TAH-fuh
Tacitus   TASS-i-tus
taille   TAH-yuh *or* TIE
Tang Taizong   TANG TYE-zawng
Tanzania   tan-zah-NEE-ah
Tenochtitlán   tay-NAWCH-teet-LAHN
Teotihuacán   TAY-oh-tee-WAH-kahn
Tertullian   tur-TULL-yun
Theocritus   thee-OCK-ri-tus
Thermidor   ter-mee-DOR
Thermopylae   thur-MOP-uh-lee
Thucydides   thoo-SID-uh-deez
Thutmosis   thoot-MOH-sus
Tiberius   tie-BIR-ee-us
Tito   TEE-toh
Tlaxcala   tlah-SKAHL-uh
Torah   TOR-uh
Tordesillas   tor-duh-SEE-yus
Trajan   TRAY-jun

Trevithick, Richard   TREV-uh-thik
Tyche   TIE-kee
Uighur   yu-EE-gur
Ulbricht, Walter   UL-brikt, VAHL-ter
Umayyads   oo-MY-ads
Unam Sanctam   OON-ahm SANK-tahm
universitas   yoo-ni-VER-si-tahs
Valois   VAL-wah
van Eyck, Jan   van IKE
van Gogh, Vincent   van GOE
Vega, Lope de   VAY-guh, LOH-pay day
Venetia   vuh-NEE-shee-uh
Vesalius, Andreas   vi-SAY-lee-us, ahn-DRAY-us
Vespucci, Amerigo   ves-POO-chee, ahm-ay-REE-goe
Vierzenheiligen   feer-tsun-HILE-i-gun
Virchow, Rudolf   FEER-koh, roo-DOLF
Virgil   VUR-jul
Volkschulen   FOLK-shool-un
Voltaire   vole-TAIR
von Bora, Katherina   BOR-uh
Walesa, Lech   va-WENZ-uh, LEK
Wallachia   wah-lay-KEE-uh
Watteau, Antoine   wah-TOE, AHN-twahn
Weizsäcker, Richard von   VITS-zek-er, RIK-art
wergeld   wur-GELD
Winkelmann, Maria   VING-kul-mun
Xavier, Francis   ZAY-vee-ur
Xerxes   ZURK-seez
Xhosa   KOH-suh
Xinjiang   shin-JI-ang
Xiongnu (Hsiung-nu)   she-ONG-noo
Yahweh   YAH-wah
Yeats, William Butler   YATES
Yeltsin, Boris   YELT-sun
Yi Song-gye   YEE sohn-GEE
yishuv   YISH-uv
zemstvos   ZEMPST-voh
Zeno   ZEE-noh
Zhang Xueliang   JANG shwee-lee-ONG
Zhou   JOE
Zhu Yuanzhang   jew whan-JANG
ziggurat   ZIG-guh-rat
Zimbabwe   zim-BAH-bway
Zola, Emile   ZOH-luh, ay-MEEL
zollverein   TSOL-fuh-rine
Zoroaster   ZOR-oh-as-ter

PHOTO CREDITS

COVER

The Battle of Badr, © Erich Lessing/Art Resource, NY

PART I OPENING

xxxii Werner Forman Archive, British Library/Art Resource, NY

CHAPTER I

2 © British Museum, London, reproduced by Courtesy of the Trustees of the British Museum 5 Francois Ducasse/Photo Researchers, Inc. 7 Courtesy of the Arthur M. Sackler Gallery, Smithsonian Institution, Washington, DC. 10 © British Museum, London, reproduced by Courtesy of the Trustees of the British Museum 11 Babylonian, *Stele of Hammurabi,* Musée du Louvre, © Photo R.M.N. 14 Musée du Louvre, © Photo R.M.N.—Herve Lewandowski 18 *Pair Statue of King Mycerinus and His Queen;* From Giza, Dynasty IV, 2599–1571 B.C.E. Slate Schist, 54 1/2 in. Harvard MFA Expedition. Courtesy, Museum of Fine Arts, Boston 19 © Will & Deni McIntyre/Photo Researchers, Inc. 22 © Brian Blake/Photo Researchers, Inc. 23 © Adam Woolfitt/Robert Harding Picture Library 26 © British Museum, London, reproduced by Courtesy of the Trustees of the British Museum 31 © British Museum, London, reproduced by Courtesy of the Trustees of the British Museum 34 *Archers of the Persian Guard,* Musée du Louvre, © Photo R.M.N.

CHAPTER 2

38 Robert Harding Picture Library 41 Borromeo/Art Resource, NY 42 Scala/Art Resource, NY 43 © Royal Smeets Offset, Weert 50 Courtesy of the British Library, Oriental and India Office Collection 51 © Royal Smeets Offset, Weert 57 Borromeo/Art Resource, NY 58 **top/bottom** Robert Harding Picture Library 60 **left** Borromeo/Art Resource, NY 60 **right** © Royal Smeets Offset, Weert

CHAPTER 3

64 Courtesy of William J. Duiker 68 Werner Forman Archive, British Library/Art Resource, NY 70 Courtesy of William J. Duiker 78 Robert Harding Picture Library 80 Courtesy of William J. Duiker 82 Courtesy of William J. Duiker 83 Robert Harding Picture Library 84 Courtesy of William J. Duiker 86 © Michael Holford, London 87 Robert Harding Picture Library 88 Robert Harding Picture Library 89 O. Louis Mazzatenta/National Geographic Society Image Collection

CHAPTER 4

95 Leonard von Matt/Photo Researchers, Inc. 96 Robert Harding Picture Library 98 © Michael Holford, London 100 Scala/Art Resource, NY 105 © G. Dagli Orti, PARIS 105 **inset** Courtesy of William M. Murray 111 **bottom** © Michael Holford, London 111 **top** Art Resource, NY 112 Scala/Art Resource, NY 114 The Metropolitan Museum of Art, Fletcher Fund, 1931(31.11.10) 116 *Bust of Alexander,* Musée du Louvre, © Photo R.M.N. 121 The Metropolitan Museum of Art, Fletcher Fund, 1920 (20.2.21) 122 The Metropolitan Museum of Art, Rogers Fund, 1909 (09.39) 124 Leonard von Matt/Photo Researchers, Inc.

CHAPTER 5

128 Leonard von Matt/Photo Researchers, Inc. 130 Art Resource, NY 133 British Museum, Photo © Michael Holford, London 138 Scala/Art Resource, NY 140 Photo Vatican Museums 143 Photo © Eberhard Thiem, Lotos-Film,Kaufbeuren, Germany 144 Leonard von Matt/Photo Researchers, Inc. 146 © Thomas S. England/Photo Researchers, Inc. 147 The Metropolitan Museum of Art/Rogers Fund, 1903 (03.14.5) 151 Scala/Art Resource, NY 154 Scala/Art Resource, NY 161 Fitzwilliam Museum, University of Cambridge 162 © British Museum, London, reproduced by Courtesy of the Trustees of the British Museum 166 Bibliotheque Nationale, Paris 01 Atlas Catalan RcC 2102

PART II OPENING

166 Bibliotheque Nationale, Paris 01 Atlas Catalan RcC 2102

CHAPTER 6

168 Richard A Cooke III/Stone 172 Richard A Cooke III/Stone 174 **top** From *Atlas of Ancient America* by Michael Coe, Dean Snow and Elizabeth Benson/Andromeda Oxford Limited, Oxford, England 174 **bottom** Detail-Mural Room 2, Bonampak, Chiapas, Mexico. © Pres. and fellows of Harvard College, 1988, All rights reserved. Peabody Museum, Harvard, Photography by Hillel Burger 175 **top** Lee Boltin Picture Library 175 **bottom** Courtesy of William J. Duiker 179 Courtesy of William J. Duiker 181 Lee Boltin Picture Library 184 Courtesy of William J. Duiker 185 Robert Harding Picture Library 186 Courtesy of William J. Duiker 189 Courtesy of William J. Duiker

CHAPTER 7

192 Courtesy of William J. Duiker 193 Robert Harding Picture Library 195 E.U.L.M.S. 20, fol.25r, reproduced by permission of the Edinburgh University Library 196 Courtesy of William J. Duiker 204 Courtesy of William J. Duiker 210 Courtesy of William J. Duiker 211 **left** Fred J. Maroon/Photo Researchers, Inc. 211 **right** Scala/Art Resource, NY 212 **top** Courtesy of William J. Duiker 212 **bottom** Courtesy of William J. Duiker 213 Courtesy of William J. Duiker

CHAPTER 8

216 Robert Harding Picture Library 219 Robert Harding Picture Library 220 Werner Forman/Art Resource, NY 225 Courtesy of William J. Duiker 227 Courtesy of William J. Duiker 229 Bibliotheque Nationale, Paris 01 Atlas Catalan RcC 2102 230 10095 i3; drawing by Caillie of Timbuktu; reproduced by permission of the British Library 231 Corbis 234 © Michael Holford, London 235 **bottom** Werner Forman /Art Resource, NY 235 **top** Werner Forman/British Museum/Art Resource, NY 236 Angela Fisher/Robert Estall Photographs

CHAPTER 9

240 Courtesy of William J. Duiker 244 Courtesy of William J. Duiker 248 Courtesy of William J. Duiker 252 S. Fiore/Explorer 253 Courtesy of William J. Duiker 254 Courtesy of William J. Duiker 255 Marcello Berntinetti/Photo Researchers, Inc.

258 Courtesy of Sharon Littlefield   260 Courtesy of William J. Duiker   261 Courtesy of Sharon Littlefield   262 Courtesy of William J. Duiker   263 Courtesy of William J. Duiker

CHAPTER 10

266 Courtesy of William J. Duiker   268 Bibliotheque Nationale, Paris, *Pelliot Chinois* 4518 (39) RcB4296   272 Courtesy of William J. Duiker   275 Courtesy of Yvonne V. Duiker   276 Courtesy of William J. Duiker   277 *Spring Festival on the River*; Detail, The Metropolitan Museum of Art, Fletcher Fund, 1947, The A.W. Bahr Collection, (47.18.1)   283 Courtesy of William J. Duiker   286 Courtesy of the Board of Trustees of the Victoria and Albert Museum   288 Courtesy of William J. Duiker   290 National Palace Museum, Taipei, Taiwan, Republic of China   291 Courtesy of the Tokyo National Museum

CHAPTER 11

294 Courtesy of William J. Duiker   297 Courtesy of William J. Duiker, 301 top © Michael Holford, London   301 bottom Detail— troops fighting as palace burns, scroll w/depictions of the night attack on the Sanjo Palace, from the *Illustrated scrolls of the events of the Heiji Period* second half of the thirteenth c., Unknown, Japanese, Kamakura Period, hand scroll; ink and colors on paper, Fenollosa-Weld Collection, Courtesy of the Museum of Fine Arts, Boston   302 Courtesy of the Tokyo National Museum   308 left Courtesy of the Freer Gallery of Art, Smithsonian Institution, Washington, D.C. #49.21   308 right Robert Harding Picture Library   309 Courtesy of William J. Duiker   310 top Courtesy of Matthew Kroenig   310 bottom Courtesy of the Korean Cultural Service Library   311 Courtesy of William J. Duiker   314 Courtesy of William J. Duiker   315 Courtesy of William J. Duiker

CHAPTER 12

318 Scala/Art Resource, NY   320 Bibliotheque Nationale, Paris, Ms. Nouv. Acq. Fr. 1098   325 The Granger Collection   326 The Pierpont Morgan Library/Art Resource, New York, M.736, f.9v   328 Bibliotheque Nationale, Paris   336 E.T. Archive, London, from the collections of the British Library, Psalter, Calendar, c 1250–1260   338 Bibliotheque Nationale, Paris   341 © Bibliotheque royale Albert ler (Ms IV 119, fol.72 verso)   344 Staatliche Museen, Berlin, Photo © Bildarchiv Preussischer Kulturbesitz, Berlin   345 © G. Dagli Orti   346 © Sylvain Grandadam/Photo Researchers, Inc.   348 Scala/Art Resource, NY   349 © Erich Lessing/Art Resource, NY

CHAPTER 13

356 Photo Vatican Museums   359 © Bibliotheque royale Albert ler, Bruxelles (Ms. 13076–77, f. 12v)   360 Bibliotheque Nationale, Paris   365 Giraudon/Art Resource, NY   369, left Scala/Art Resource, NY   369, right Scala/Art Resource, NY   374 Photo Vatican Museums   376 Private Collection/The Bridgeman Art Library   382 British Library, London, folio 290, Harley ms. 4431   383 Scala/Art Resource, NY   384 top Scala/Art Resource, NY   384 bottom Erich Lessing/Art Resource, NY   385 Photo Vatican Museums   386 left Reproduced by Courtesy of the Trustees; The National Gallery, London   386 right Alinari/Art Resource, NY   391 Bibliotheque Nationale, Paris   Paris Arabe 5847, FOL 138, RcC1230   392 Leiden, University Library, BPL 20, f.60r   396 Collection Musée Guimet, Paris, Photo © Michael Holford, London

PART III OPENING

396 Collection Musée Guimet, Paris, Photo © Michael Holford, London

CHAPTER 14

398 Courtesy of William J. Duiker   401 Jomard, *Les Monuments de la Geographie*: Paris, 1862, Photo courtesy of the New York Public Library, Map Division, Stor, Lenox and Tilden Foundations   402 Courtesy of William J. Duiker   404 North Wind Picture Archives   406 North Wind Picture Archives   408 Courtesy of William J. Duiker   409 Courtesy of William J. Duiker   410 Courtesy of William J. Duiker   411 Courtesy of William J. Duiker   414 Historical Society of Pennsylvania   418 Courtesy of William J. Duiker   422 Courtesy of William J. Duiker   423 Courtesy of William J. Duiker

CHAPTER 15

426 The National Galleries of Scotland, by permission of Earl of Rosebery   430 Staliche Museen Preussicher Kulturbesitz, Kupferstichkabinett, Berlin (West), Photo: Jorg P. Anders   431 Alte Pinakothek, Munich   433 Bibliotheque Publique et Universitaire, Geneva   436 Scala/Art Resource, NY   440 Kunsthishorisches Museum, Vienna   445 Hyacinthe Rigaud, *Louise XIV*, Musée du Louvre, © Photo R.M.N.   446 Giraudon/Art Resource, NY   448 Russian School, *Czar Peter the Great*, Rijksmuseum, Amsterdam   450 The National Galleries of Scotland, by permission of Earl of Rosebery   454 Laocoon, El Greco, National Gallery of Art, Washington, Samuel H. Kress Collection   455 left Peter Paul Reubens, *The Landing of Marie de Medicis at Marseilles*, Musée du Louvre, © Photo R.M.N.   455 right Alinari/Art Resource, NY   456 Nicholas Poussin, *Landscape with the Burial of a Phocian*, Musée du Louvre, © Photo R.M.N.

CHAPTER 16

460 George Holton/Photo Researchers, Inc.   462 MS Fr.9087,f.207, Bibliotheque Nationale, Paris; photo © Sonia Halliday Photographs   467 Courtesy of the Topkapi Sarayi Musezi, Istanbul   470 Giraudon/ Art Resource, NY   473 top George Holton/Photo Researchers, Inc.   473 bottom Reza-ye Abbasi, *Two Lovers*, 1630, The Metropolitan Museum of Art, Francis M. Weld Fund 1950(50.164)   477 Courtesy of the Board of Trustees of the Victoria and Albert Museum   479 Courtesy of William J. Duiker   482 SEF/Art Resource, NY   483 Stone   484 Werner Forman/Art Resource, NY

CHAPTER 17

488 Courtesy of William J. Duiker   490 Courtesy of William J. Duiker   496 © British Museum, London, reproduced by Courtesy of the Trustees of the British Museum   501 bottom Dean Conger/ National Geographic Image Collection   501 top Courtesy of William J. Duiker   502 Werner Forman/Art Resource, NY   503 Courtesy of William J. Duiker   505 Collection Musée Guimet, Paris, Photo © Michael Holford, London   510 Torii Kiyotada, Japanese,act.c.1720–1750, *Naka-no-cho Street of the Yoshiwara*, wood block print, c. 1740, Clarence Buckingham Collection, 1939.2152, Photograph © 1993, The Art Institute of Chicago   511 Courtesy of William J. Duiker   513 Courtesy of William J. Duiker

CHAPTER 18

516 Dumesnil, *Queen Christina of Sweden with Descartes*, Musée du Louvre, © Photo R.M.N.   521 left Courtesy of the Lilly Library, Indiana University, Bloomington, Indiana   521 right Courtesy of

MAP CREDITS

The authors wish to acknowledge their use of the following books as reference in preparing the maps listed here:

MAP 2.2   Geoffrey Barraclough, ed., *Times Atlas of World History*, (Maplewood, N.J.: Hammond Inc., 1978), p. 65.

MAP 3.2   Geoffrey Barraclough, ed., *Times Atlas of World History*, (Maplewood, N.J.: Hammond Inc., 1978), p. 63.

MAP 3.3   Conrad Schirokauer, *A Brief History of Chinese and Japanese Civilizations*, 2d ed. (San Diego: Harcourt Brace Jovanovich, 1989), p. 52.

MAP 3.4   Hammond Past Worlds: *The Times Atlas of Archeology*, (Maplewood, N.J.: Hammond Inc. 1988), pp. 190–191.

MAPS 6.1 & 6.2   Geoffrey Barraclough, ed., *Times Atlas of World History*, (Maplewood, N.J.: Hammond Inc., 1978), p. 47.

MAP 6.4   Michael Coe, Dean Snow and Elizabeth Benson, *Atlas of Ancient America* (New York: Facts on File, 1988), p. 144.

MAP 6.5   Phillipa Fernandez-Arnesto, *Atlas of World Exlporation*, (New York: Harper Collins, 1991), p. 35.

MAP 7.3   Geoffrey Barraclough, ed., *Times Atlas of World History*, (Maplewood, N.J.: Hammond Inc., 1978), pp. 134–135.

MAP 7.4   Geoffrey Barraclough, ed., *Times Atlas of World History*, (Maplewood, N.J.: Hammond Inc., 1978), p. 135.

MAP 8.1   Geoffrey Barraclough, ed., *Times Atlas of World History*, (Maplewood, N.J.: Hammond Inc., 1978), pp. 44–45.

MAP 8.4   Geoffrey Barraclough, ed., *Times Atlas of World History*, (Maplewood, N.J.: Hammond Inc., 1978), pp. 136–137.

MAP 9.1   Michael Edwardes, *A History of India* (London: Thames and Hudson, 1961), p. 79.

MAP 10.1   John K. Fairbank, Edwin O. Reischauer, and Albert M. Craig, *East Asia: Tradition and Transformation* (Boston: Houghton Mifflin, 1973), p. 103.

MAP 10.2   Albert Hermann, *An Historical Atlas of China* (Chicago: Aidine, 1966), p. 13.

MAP 11.1   John K. Fairbank, Edwin O. Reischauer, and Albert M. Craig, *East Asia: Tradition and Transformation* (Boston: Houghton Mifflin, 1973), p. 363.

MAP 14.1   Geoffrey Barraclough, ed., *Times Atlas of World History*, (Maplewood, N. J.: Hammond, Inc. 1978), p. 160.

MAP 16.3   Geoffrey Barraclough, ed., *Times Atlas of World History*, (Maplewood, N. J.: Hammond, Inc. 1978), p. 173.

MAP 17.1   Jonathan Spence, *The Search for Modern China*, (New York: W. W. Norton, 1990), p. 19.

MAP 17.2   Conrad Schirokauer, *A Brief History of Chinese and Japanese Civilizations*, 2d ed., (San Diego: Harcourt Brace Jovanovich, 1989), p. 330.

MAP 17.3   John K. Fairbank, Edwin O. Reischauer, and Albert M. Craig, *East Asia: Tradition and Tranformation*, (Boston: Houghton Mifflin, 1973), pp. 402–403.

MAP 18.1   *Atlas of World History*, (New York: Harper & Row Publishers, 1987), p. 187.

INDEX